Transnational Intellectual Property Law

Transnational Intellectual Property Law

TEXT AND CASES

Robert P. Merges

Wilson Sonsini Goodrich & Rosati Professor of Law and Technology and Co-Director, Berkeley Center for Law and Technology, University of California, Berkeley, USA

Seagull Haiyan Song

Loyola Law School, Los Angeles, USA

Cheltenham, UK • Northampton, MA, USA

© Robert P. Merges and Seagull Haiyan Song 2018

All rights reserved. No part of this publication may be reproduced, stored in a retrieval system or transmitted in any form or by any means, electronic, mechanical or photocopying, recording, or otherwise without the prior permission of the publisher.

Published by
Edward Elgar Publishing Limited
The Lypiatts
15 Lansdown Road
Cheltenham
Glos GL50 2JA
UK

Edward Elgar Publishing, Inc.
William Pratt House
9 Dewey Court
Northampton
Massachusetts 01060
USA

A catalogue record for this book
is available from the British Library

Library of Congress Control Number: 2017959519

ISBN 978 1 78536 824 0 (cased)
ISBN 978 1 78536 826 4 (paperback)
ISBN 978 1 78536 825 7 (eBook)

Typeset by Servis Filmsetting Ltd, Stockport, Cheshire.
Printed by CPI Group (UK) Ltd, Croydon CR0 4YY

Contents in brief

Full contents	vii
Preface	xv
Table of cases	xix

PART I   INTRODUCTION

1	What is "transnational" IP law?	3

PART II   PATENT PROTECTION

2	Introduction to patent law at the transnational level	25
3	Patentable subject matter	42
4	Novelty	75
5	Inventive step/non-obviousness	122
6	Adequate disclosure and enablement	142
7	Claim interpretation and infringement	163
8	Remedies	196
	Patent office invalidity trials: the US PTAB as a case study	240
9	Business aspects of patents	244

PART III   COPYRIGHT PROTECTION

10	Introduction	263
11	Subject matter, originality, authorship	274
12	Rights of the copyright owner	331
13	Limitations and exceptions	417
14	Infringement and remedies	457
15	Digital copyright	473

PART IV   TRADEMARK LAW

16	Introduction to trademark protection	481
17	Acquisition of trademark rights	484
18	Enforcement	584

19 Licensing issues: quality supervision, exclusive territories, termination   658

PART V   TRADE SECRETS

20 Introduction   669
21 What can be protected as a trade secret?   678
22 Reasonable efforts to protect trade secrets   695
23 Misappropriation   702
24 Remedies   729

PART VI   DESIGN PROTECTION

25 Introduction   739
26 Subject matter and originality requirements   745
27 Infringement   776
28 Defenses   783
29 Remedies   790

Index   795

Full contents

Preface	xv
Table of cases	xix

PART I INTRODUCTION

1 What is "transnational" IP law? 3
- 1.1 Introduction 3
  - 1.1.1 Structures of transnational IP law and practice 4
  - 1.1.2 The domestic (national) basis of IP law 6
- 1.2 Patent law treaties: the evolution of the international law of patents 7
  - 1.2.1 Paris, 1883; and the Patent Cooperation Treaty of the 1970s 8
  - 1.2.2 The European Patent Convention and the structure of European IP law 12
  - 1.2.3 Uruguay Round and TRIPs, 1995 13
- 1.3 Transnational legal strategy: a quick overview 17
- 1.4 Other themes of this book 21
  - 1.4.1 Formal law vs. practical enforcement 21
  - 1.4.2 Convergence vs. divergence 22

PART II PATENT PROTECTION

2 Introduction to patent law at the transnational level 25
- Introductory problem 25
- 2.1 Introduction 31
- 2.2 Some basic transnational institutions and practices 34
  - 2.2.1 Introduction to European patent law 35
  - 2.2.2 The basics of Chinese patent law 37
- 2.3 Patent validity determinations 40

3 Patentable subject matter 42
- 3.1 Software and business methods 45
- 3.2 Introduction to patentable subject matter in China 53
  - 3.2.1 Technical solution of Article 2.2 53

		3.2.2	A computer program itself is not a patentable subject matter but invention relating to a computer program can be a patentable subject matter	54
	3.3	Subject matter patentability: Europe		58
	3.4	Biotechnology		63
		3.4.1	Biotechnology/living subject matter: China	68
		3.4.2	Biotechnology/living subject matter: Europe	69

4 Novelty 75

	4.1	The identity standard for novelty in the US		75
	4.2	Types of prior art		79
	4.3	Exceptions to the first-to-file rule under the AIA		82
	4.4	Pre-AIA novelty		85
	4.5	Pre-AIA patent priority: origins of the "first to invent" system		86
	4.6	Novelty in China		90
		4.6.1	The basic novelty standard	90
		4.6.2	Prior art	91
		4.6.3	International priority and the grace period in China	92
		4.6.4	The prior art defense in China	95
		4.6.5	Disclosure of prior art	99
		4.6.6	The identity requirement in China	102
	4.7	Novelty/state of the art in Europe		106
		4.7.1	Establishing the publication date	109
		4.7.2	Disclosure in a single document in Europe	111
		4.7.3	Prior-filed patent applications: Article 54(3) EPC	115
		4.7.4	Non-prejudicial disclosures: the "grace period" in Europe	117
		4.7.5	Evident abuse of applicant	117
		4.7.6	Note on the Article 54(3) "partial priority" problem	119

5 Inventive step/non-obviousness 122

	5.1	Inventive step in China		129
		5.1.1	Three-step approach	129
		5.1.2	How to decide the technical problem to be solved by the invention	131
	5.2	Inventive step in Europe		135

6 Adequate disclosure and enablement 142

	6.1	Disclosure	142

		6.1.1	Disclosure in China	146
	6.2		Written description requirement	153
		6.2.1	Written description in China	157
	6.3		Adequacy of disclosure in Europe: Article 83 EPC	158

7 Claim interpretation and infringement — 163

- 7.1 Claims in China — 169
  - 7.1.1 Functional limitations — 171
- 7.2 Claim interpretation and infringement in Europe — 179
  - 7.2.1 Claim interpretation in German courts — 186
- 7.3 Indirect infringement — 192

8 Remedies — 196

- 8.1 Injunctions in the US — 196
- 8.2 Injunctions in China — 199
  - 8.2.1 Preliminary injunction — 199
  - 8.2.2 Permanent injunctions in China — 205
- 8.3 Injunctions in Europe — 206
- 8.4 Damages in the US — 217
  - 8.4.1 Lost profits — 218
  - 8.4.2 Reasonable royalty — 222
- 8.5 Damages in China: Article 65 — 224
  - 8.5.1 Enhanced damages proposed by fourth revision of the Patent Law — 229
- 8.6 Damages in Europe — 230

Patent office invalidity trials: the US PTAB as a case study — 240

9 Business aspects of patents — 244

- 9.1 Licensing agreements — 244
  - 9.1.1 Precontractual liability, or *culpa in contrahendo*: protecting disclosures in the pre-contract period — 244
- 9.2 Substantive terms of patent licenses — 250
- 9.3 Enforcing licenses: litigation and arbitration — 256

PART III COPYRIGHT PROTECTION

10 Introduction — 263

Problem: the orphan episode — 263
- 10.1 China — 264
- 10.2 Copyright in other countries: the Berne Convention — 266
- 10.3 Europe — 268

	10.4	United States		271
	10.5	Conclusion: the bottom line		272

11 Subject matter, originality, authorship — 274
    11.1 United States — 274
        11.1.1 Originality — 274
        11.1.2 The fixation requirement — 278
        11.1.3 Specific categories of work — 279
        11.1.4 Authorship — 285
    11.2 China — 291
        11.2.1 Copyrightable criteria: originality and duplicability — 291
        11.2.2 Limitations on copyrightability: the idea/expression dichotomy, the merger doctrine and *scène à faire* — 292
        11.2.3 Specific categories of works — 294
        11.2.4 Authorship — 302
    11.3 Europe — 307
        11.3.1 Originality — 307
        11.3.2 Limitations on copyrightability — 315
        11.3.3 Specific categories of works — 319
        11.3.4 Fixation requirement — 327
        11.3.5 Authorship — 327

12 Rights of the copyright owner — 331
    12.1 Introduction — 331
    12.2 Economic rights — 332
        12.2.1 Right to reproduce — 332
        12.2.2 Right to make derivative works — 351
        12.2.3 Right to distribute and to communicate to the public — 365
    12.3 Moral rights — 383
        12.3.1 Introduction — 383
        12.3.2 Europe — 384
        12.3.3 China — 389
        12.3.4 United States — 391
    12.4 Neighboring rights — 399
        12.4.1 Europe — 399
        12.4.2 China — 407
        12.4.3 United States — 413

13	**Limitations and exceptions**	**417**
	13.1 Introduction	417
	13.2 United States	419
	13.3 Europe	432
	13.3.1 Introduction	432
	13.3.2 Limitations to the right of reproduction	433
	13.3.3 Exhaustion	438
	13.4 China	448
14	**Infringement and remedies**	**457**
	14.1 Introduction	457
	14.2 United States	457
	14.2.1 Note on statutory damages	462
	14.3 China	462
	14.3.1 Direct and indirect infringement	462
	14.3.2 Remedies	463
	14.4 Europe	467
15	**Digital copyright**	**473**
	15.1 Anti-circumvention laws	473
	15.2 Liability of internet service providers	473
	15.2.1 Introduction	473
	15.2.2 United States	474
	15.2.3 Europe	475
	15.2.4 China	476
	15.3 Graduated response	476

PART IV   TRADEMARK LAW

16	**Introduction to trademark protection**	**481**
	Introductory problem	481
17	**Acquisition of trademark rights**	**484**
	17.1 Use vs. registration	484
	17.1.1 US: use in commerce	485
	17.1.2 "Genuine use" in the EU	487
	17.1.3 Registration	490
	17.2 Trademark registrability and rights	503
	17.2.1 Administrative registration	503
	17.2.2 Distinctiveness	512
	17.2.3 Descriptive marks and secondary meaning in the US	521

		17.2.4	Trade dress: product packaging and product configuration	523
		17.2.5	Europe: acquired distinctiveness	527
		17.2.6	China: acquired distinctiveness	532
		17.2.7	China: distinctiveness in three-dimensional mark	535
		17.2.8	Geographic terms	538
		17.2.9	Scandalous marks	544
		17.2.10	Functionality	548
		17.2.11	Meaning in another language	557
	17.3	Incontestability		562
	17.4	Priority		564
		17.4.1	Protection without registration	564
18	**Enforcement**			**584**
	18.1	Infringement		584
		18.1.1	Likelihood of confusion	584
		18.1.2	China: "confusing similarity"	591
		18.1.3	Famous marks	594
	18.2	Defenses		600
		18.2.1	US: Fair use for descriptive marks, non-trademark ("nominative") use, and genericide	600
		18.2.2	Genericide	605
		18.2.3	"Trademark use" and genericness in the EU	611
		18.2.4	Parody: First Amendment/free expression in the US	616
		18.2.5	Nominative (non-trademark) use in China	618
	18.3	Remedies		627
		18.3.1	United States	627
		18.3.2	Europe: damages	636
		18.3.3	Europe: injunctions	642
		18.3.4	China	644
	18.4	International enforcement		646
		18.4.1	Extraterritorial application of US law	646
		18.4.2	Border enforcement: US	649
		18.4.3	Gray market goods: US	651
		18.4.4	Choice of law	652
		18.4.5	Enforcing judgments overseas	656
19	**Licensing issues: quality supervision, exclusive territories, termination**			**658**
	19.1	Territorial rights in the US		659
	19.2	Quality supervision and termination in China		662

PART V TRADE SECRETS

20 Introduction — 669
Introductory problem — 669
20.1 Basic purpose and sources of law — 671
    20.1.1 United States — 672
    20.1.2 China — 673
    20.1.3 The EU — 674

21 What can be protected as a trade secret? — 678
21.1 Defining trade secrets — 678
    21.1.1 United States — 678
    21.1.2 China — 682
    21.1.3 EU countries — 688

22 Reasonable efforts to protect trade secrets — 695
22.1 United States — 695

23 Misappropriation — 702
23.1 Improper means — 702
    23.1.1 United States — 702
    23.1.2 China — 708
    23.1.3 Europe — 712
23.2 Departing employees and noncompetition agreements — 719
    23.2.1 China — 720
23.3 The reverse engineering defense — 724

24 Remedies — 729
24.1 Injunctions: US — 729
24.2 China — 731
24.3 European Union — 731
24.4 Damages — 733
    24.4.1 United States — 733
    24.4.2 China — 734
    24.4.3 European Union — 735

PART VI DESIGN PROTECTION

25 Introduction — 739
25.1 Design and product appeal — 739
    25.1.1 Is IP protection necessary for innovative designs? — 741
    25.1.2 Practicalities of securing protection — 743

26	**Subject matter and originality requirements**		745
	26.1 United States		745
		26.1.1 Design patents	745
		26.1.2 Copyright: product design as "applied art"	753
		26.1.3 Trademark: product packaging and product configuration design	755
	26.2 China		759
	26.3 Europe		759
		26.3.1 Background: traditional design protection in European countries	759
		26.3.2 The EU Design Directive (1998) and Design Regulation (2001)	765
27	**Infringement**		**776**
	27.1 United States		776
		27.1.1 Copyright and trademark	776
		27.1.2 Design patents	776
	27.2 China		779
	27.3 European Union		781
28	**Defenses**		**783**
	28.1 United States: functionality		783
	28.2 Europe		786
		28.2.1 Standards under the Directive	787
	28.3 Functionality in China		789
29	**Remedies**		**790**
	29.1 US: design patents		790
	29.2 Europe/EU		791

Index   795

Preface

The basic facts motivating this book are well known: international trade – the exchange of goods and services that crosses at least one national border – has grown (literally) exponentially in the period from 1800 to 2010. When imports are added to exports, traded goods account for over 50 percent of worldwide economic activity (GDP). *See* Max Roser, Oxford University, https://ourworldindata.org/international-trade. During roughly the same period, the products and services that make up economic activity have become increasingly technology- or information-intensive. Lighter and stronger materials; diverse and effective chemical products (such as polymers and pharmaceuticals); and purely digital products such as video and audio files (*e.g.*, movies and music) are examples of this trend. Because more and more money is required to research and design products, more attention is directed at ways of protecting these investments. One classic mechanism along these lines is intellectual property (IP). It is no surprise that as the technology or information content of economic activity has increased, the importance of IP rights has increased as well. *See, e.g.*, Robert P. Merges, *One Hundred Years of Solicitude: Intellectual Property Law, 1900-2000*, 88 Cal. L. Rev. 2187 (2000). (Some would argue that our thinking about IP – as opposed to basic economic forces – has contributed to or partially caused the growth in IP protection. *See generally* Oren Bracha, Owning Ideas: The Intellectual Origins of American Intellectual Property, 1790–1909 (2017).)

Though based on these important large-scale trends, the topics we cover are decidedly more prosaic. The purpose of this book is to help law students (and lawyers) understand how to coordinate IP protection across multiple jurisdictions. Because many companies, research organizations, and universities are increasingly operating across national boundaries, lawyers must understand how to effectively acquire, deploy, and protect IP rights in multiple national jurisdictions.

This is why we call this "transnational IP law." We chose this label carefully. We meant to distinguish the everyday practice of IP law on behalf of clients that conduct business in multiple countries (transnational IP) from the specialized field of "international IP law." The latter term has as its subject institutions (primarily treaties and the legal entities that administer them) that have been created by multiple sovereign nations to help facilitate or advance IP law across many countries. It is, as the name suggests, a branch of international law. There is no doubt that international institutions (again, particularly treaties) play a significant role in the practice of transnational IP law. Where they are relevant to the workaday practice of transnational IP law, we discuss them at length. But the practice of transnational IP law is concerned more typically with (1) understanding the domestic, national IP laws of those countries or regions where a client does business; and (2) coordinating legal actions and strategies among those different countries. Put briefly, "international IP law" studies the institutions that are set up to coordinate the IP-related activities of sovereign national states; while transnational IP law includes coverage of all laws and institutions required to secure protection of IP rights in multiple countries – including many national, domestic (non-international) laws and institutions. Transnational law is therefore primarily the study of domestic, national (again, non-international) laws and institutions. More particularly, it involves the study of *multiple* national systems – to permit an understanding of how to coordinate IP protection when business is conducted across national boundaries. (Trans- means "across," of course.)

The co-author who initiated this book (Merges) was led to it not by a close study of data, nor by a careful reading of IP scholarship, but by his students. The internationalization of the IP field was borne in by the growing number of students from all over the world showing an interest in IP law. By great good fortune, many excellent students from overseas with a strong IP interest converged on Berkeley Law beginning in the 1990s. (The international tradition long predates this time; there were, for example, Japanese students in among the first classes ever to graduate from the school. And the many esteemed Jewish faculty members who joined in the 1930s, fleeing the Nazi regime in Germany, gave Berkeley long preeminence in the field of Comparative Law.) Indeed, the co-author of this book was among the growing numbers of students. Many of these students returned to their home country (or at least region), but to practice law effectively they felt the need to understand US IP law. It was in watching the career trajectories of these many outstanding students that Merges first hatched the idea for this book. One of the authors of this volume (Professor Song) is a prime example of these trajectories. She practiced at the largest law firm in China, as well as at Walt Disney Company in Shanghai, before beginning her teaching career at Loyola in Los Angeles. And today, Professor Song continues her transnational practice with the large international law firm of Hogan Lovells, with a particular emphasis on Trans-Pacific clients in the entertainment field.

It is commonplace for writers of textbooks or casebooks to thank their students in the Preface. Without students, there are no such books. But in the case of this volume, the many international students, who have come to study in the US are the *sine qua non*, the primary motive cause.

A special mention here is due for Professor Stefan Bechtold of the Swiss Federal Institute of Technology (ETH) in Zurich, Switzerland. Professor Bechtold contributed very significantly to the European portion of Part III, Copyright Law, and to portions of Part IV on Trademark Law. The original plan was for Professor Bechtold to be a full co-author of this volume. Although that plan did not work out, the remaining co-authors are grateful for his contributions.

Of course, some students were directly involved in producing this volume. Among them (and apologizing in advance for errors and omissions – as Shakespeare said, "some smack of age in [me], some relish of the saltiness of time" (Henry IV, Part II)) are: Michael Kuhn and Alicia Roy at UC Berkeley, for assistance with German translations; Mo Wang, Yao Mou, Angela He, Diana Martinez, Lifan Liu and Kelin Zhang at Loyola Law School as well as Mona Liao and Yabing (Robert) Cui at UC Berkeley, for assistance with Chinese translations and help understanding fine points of Chinese law.

Merges thanks also his chief research assistant Jingyuan Luo and assistant Vika Mukha for the heavy lifting phase of the book; Fang Liu of Broad and Bright, Beijing, China, for her first-hand accounts of how to maintain a successful transnational business law practice; the outstanding team at the Advanced Degree Programs office at Berkeley, which annually recruits, assembles, and assists the many overseas students who come to Berkeley; and the staff of the Berkeley Center for Law and Technology, who have kept Berkeley Law on top of the heap in the IP world for more than 20 years. Finally, on the home front, Merges thanks his sons, Robert and James, and his wife Jo, for providing all kinds of support and diversions to sustain the weary author in the course of his labors.

Song thanks her brother Haining Song, a patent lawyer at Fangda Law Firm in Beijing, for his insight and comments on the China section of the patent chapter. Song also thanks her parents, and Hai, for their support and love during this journey.

Unless otherwise stated, all websites were accessed in November 2017.

Please see the companion website containing resources and legal texts for this title: https://www.e-elgar.com/textbooks/merges

Robert Merges
Seagull Haiyan Song

Table of cases

Canada

Eli Lilly and Company v. Government of Canada, NAFTA arbitration (17 March 2017) 67
Harvard College v. Canada (Commissioner of Patents), 2002 SCC 76, 2002 CarswellNat
   3434 (Sup Ct Can, 21 May 2002) 74

China

*Abbot Trading (Shanghai) Ltd. v. Taizhou Huangyan Yilong Ltd. and Beijing Yiyangjie
   Trading Ltd.*, Beijing Third Intermediate People's Court, San Zhong Min Bao Zi No.
   01933 (2013) 203
Andrew, Inc. v. Patent Reexamination Board and Wu Huiyin, Beijing No. 1 Intermediate
   People's Court, Xing Chu Zi [2008] No. 631 (20 August, 2008) aff'd on appeal,
   Beijing High People's Court, Xing Zhing Zi No. 682 (19 December 2008) 169–71
Arctic Food v. Arctic Frozen Food, Beijing First Intermediate People's Court
   yizhongminzhongzi No. 10822 (2013) 662–5
BAI Xian-Yong v. Shanghai Film Group, Shanghai No. 2 Intermediate Court,
   Huerminwuzhichuzi No. 83 (2014) 356–60
Baidu v. TRAB, Beijing High People's Court, Gaoxingzhongzi No. 1081 (2012) 569–72
Baili v. Apple, Beijing IP Office Decision (24 March 2017) 779–81
Beijing Dongda Zhengbao Technology Ltd. v. SUN Weijie, Shandong Qingdao Intermediate
   People's Court, Qinminchuzi No. 105 (2010) 292
Beijing Founder Electronics v. P&G Guangzhou Ltd, Beijing No. 1 Intermediate People's
   Court, Yizhongminzhongzi No. 5969 (2011) 298–302
Beijing Huaqi Data Technology Ltd. v. Shenzhen Langke Technology Ltd.,
   yizhongzhixingchuzi No. 2631 (2010) 538
Beijing RongXingHe Information Consulting Ltd. v. Kewen Info., Beijing 2nd Intermediate
   People's Court, Erzhongminchuzi No. 3960 (2007) 389–90
Beijing Yingtelai Technologies Co. Ltd. v. China Resources and Sinoshield Ltd. (Supreme
   People's Court 2015), Min Shen Zi No. 1541 (2015) 91
BestBuy v. TRAB, Chinese Supreme People's Court, Xingtizi No. 9 (2011) 532–5
Blizzard Entertainment, Inc., NetEase, Inc. v. QiYou, etc. Yue Zhi Fa Zhu Min Chu Zi No. 2
   (2015) Yue Zhi Fa Shang Min Chu Zi No. 2 (2015) 202
BONPIE Sound System v. TRAB, Beijing High People's Court, Jingxingzhong No. 1973
   (2016) 547–8
CEInet Data v. CDC International Network, Beijing High People's Court, Gaominzhongzi
   No. 368 (2002) 293–4

China Friendship Publishing Co., v. Zhejiang Taobao Network Ltd, Beijing 2nd Intermediate
  Court, Erzhongminzhongzi No. 15423 (2009) 466
China Tianfu Coke v. Pepsi Tianfu, Chongqing No. 4 Interim Ct. Yuwuzhongfaminchuzi
  No. 299 (2009) 682–8, 701, 731
China Wenlian Audio-Visual Publishing v. Chang-Jin Audio-Visual Ltd., Chinese Supreme
  People's Court, Minsanzhongzi No. 5 (2008) 410–411
CHIUNG Yao v. YU Zheng, Beijing 3rd Interim Ct. Sanzhongminchuzi No. 07916 (2014)
  aff 'd Beijing High Ct. Gaominzhizhongzi No. 1039 (2015) 263–4, 342–5
Coca-Cola v. TRAB, Beijing High People's Court, Gaoxingzhongzi No. 348 (2011) 535–8
DANJAQ v. TRAB, Beijing High People's Court, Gaoxingzhongzi No. 374 (2011) 580–83
DreamWorks v. TRAB, Beijing High Court, Gaoxingzhizhongzi No. 1969 (2015) 582
Eli Lilly v. Patent Reexamination Board and Haosen Pharmaceutical Ltd., Beijing No. 1
  Intermediate People's Court, Xing Chu Zi No. 540, (2008) aff 'd on appeal, Beijing
  High People's Court, Xing Zhong Zi (20 March 2009) 131–5
Ellison Technologies v. Patent Re-examination Board (SIPO), Court: Beijing Municipal
  Higher People's Court, Gao Xing Zhong Zi No. 1548 (2013) 157–8
Focker v. Yahuan, Chinese Supreme People's Court, Mintizi No. 38 (2014) 622–6
Founder v. Blizzard Entertainment Chinese Supreme People's Court, Minsanzhongzi No. 6
  (2010) 302
Guang Ri Group v. ZHOU Chong-Tai, Guangdong High Court, Yuegaofa Minsanzhongzi
  No. 323 (2006) 305–7
Guangdong Zoke Culture v. Guangzhou Shulian Software, Shanghai High People's Court
  Hugaominsan(zhi)zhongzi No. 7 (2008) 476
Guangmei Fobao Beverages Ltd. v. TRAB, gaoxingzhongzi. No 1224 (2012) 548
Hainan Jingtian Information Ltd. v. Shanghai Xuxi Business Consulting Ltd., Shanghai High
  People's Court, Hugaominsan-zhichuzi No. 122 (2004) 297
*Hou Wanchun v. Patent Re-examination Board of the State Intellectual Property Office of the
  People's Republic of China and Tencent,* Zhi Xing Zi No. 100 (2015) 104
Huawei Technologies Co., Ltd. v. ZTE Corporation, Chinese Supreme Court, Min Shen Zi
  No. 2720 (2015)... 176–9
Huawei v. InterDigital, Shenzhen Intermediate Court, Shen Zhong Fa Zhi Min Chu Zi No.
  857 (2011) aff 'd on appeal, Guangdong High Court, (2013) 226–9
*Interlego AG. (Switzerland) v. Ke Gao Toys Ltd. and Beijing Fuxing Commercial Center Co.,
  Ltd.,* Beijing High People's Court, Gaominzhongzi No. 279 (2002) 295–7
Jean Paul Gaultier v. ZHAO Lingting Beijing No. 2 Intermediate People's Court, Erzhong
  minchuzi No. 7070 (2006) 297
JIANG Ya-Mei v. Sichuan Zhangfei Beef Ltd., Beijing Changping District Court,
  hangminchuzi No. 3064 (2012) 594
Jing Brand v. TRAB, Chinese Supreme People's Court, Xintizi No. 4 (2010) 518–21, 548
*JuLi Integrated Chip Design Co. v. US SigmaTel, Inc., Dongguan City Gemei Electronic
  Technology Co. Ltd. and huang Zhongda,* Shanxi Province Xi'an Intermediate People's
  Court, Li Jun Zi No. 1 (2007) 200–202
Kaiping Weishida Seasonining v. Nestlé, Beijing High People's Court gaoxingzhongzi No.
  1750 (2012) 552–7
Kohler Co. v. Bravat Sanitary Equip. Co., Ltd. (Shanghai), Beijing No. 2 Intermediate

People's Court, Min Chu Zi No. 13842 (2008),aff'd on appeal, Beijing High People's Court, Min Zhong Zi No. 1553 (2009) 96–9
Lacoste v. Jiangyin Hongxin Clothing Ltd., (2007) Suminsanzhongzi No. 0034 626
Land Rover v. TRA B, Beijing High People's Court, Gaoxingzhongzi No. 1151(2011) 566–9
LI Shu-Xian v. LI Wen-Da, Beijing Intermediate People's Court 1989, cert-granted and rejected by Chinese Supreme People's Court 1988, on remand Beijing High People's Court, Gaozhizhongzi No. 18 (1995) 302–5
LIU Bokui v. LI Xia et al, Shanghai No. 2 Intermediate Court Huerzhongminwuzhichuzi No. 115 (2013) 466
LUO Yonghao v. Beijing Silicon Valley E-Commerce Ltd., Beijing Haidian District Court, Haiminchuzi No. 9749 (2006) 292
Mega Blocks, Inc. v. CHEN Daiguang Shantou Intermediate People's Court, Shanzhongfa zhichuzi No. 19 (2005) 297
Microsoft (China) Ltd. v. Patent Reexamination Board, Zheng Long, Beijing Intermediate People's Court Xing Chu Zi No. 1021 (2008) 104
Motie v. Apple, Beijing High People's Court (2014) 476
NBA v. HUANG gaoxingzhongzi No. 343 (2013) 583
Nike v. Yin Xing Clothing Ltd., Shenzhen Intermediate Court Shenzhongfa zhichanchuzi No. 55 (2001) 626
Nokia v. Huaqin, Shanghai Intermediate Court, Hu Yi Zhong Min Wu (Zhi) Chu Zi No. 47 (2011) aff'd by Shanghai High Court, Hu Gao Min San Zhong Zi No. 96 (2013) 172–6
OK Baby Ltd. v. Ci Xi Jiabao Children Products Ltd. Beijing No. 2 Intermediate People's Court, Erzhong minchuzi No. 12293 (2008) 297
Pien Tze Huang v. Hong Ning, Chinese Supreme People's Court Minshenzi No. 1310 (2009) 619–22
Samsung v. TRAB, Beijing High People's Court, Gaoxingzhongzi No. 2015 (2013) 592–4
SARFT Movie Channel v. CETV, Beijing First Intermediate Court Yi Zhong Min Zhong Zi No. 13332 (2006) 449–50
Seiko Epson v. Patent Examination Board, Zheng Yali, (Epson II), Chinese Supreme People's Court, Zhixingzi No. 53 (2010) 148–50
Shaanxi Maozhi Entertainment Ltd. v. DreamWorks Gaomingzhongzi No. 3027 (2013) 621–2
Shanghai Furi Group Ltd. v. HUANG Ziyu, Chinese Supreme People's Court Minshenzi No. 122 (2011) 720–24
Shanghai Hantao Information Consulting Ltd. v. Ai Ju Bang Tech Ltd., Beijing 1st Intermediate People's Court, Yizhongminchuzi No. 5031 (2009) 297
Shanghai Shenda Sound Equipment Ltd. v. JOLIDA (Shanghai) Ltd., Shanghai High People's Court Hugaominsan zhizhongzi No. 65 (2009) 626
Shimano, Inc. v. Patent Reexamination Board, Ningbo Saiguan Bicycle Co., Chinese Supreme People's Court, Xing Ti Zi No. 21 (2013) 150–53
Sotheby's v. Sichuan Sotheby, Beijing High People's Court Gaominzhongzi No. 322 (2008) 597–600
Wan Lian Internet Company v. ZHOU Huimin, Shanghai High People's Court Hugaominsanzhizhongzi No. 100 (2011) 708–12
WANG Jianmin v. LI Hongqi, Xuelin Publishing House, aff'd on appeal, Shanghai High People's Court Hugaominsanzhizhongzi No. 20 (2004) 408–10

WANG Shen v. Google, Beijing High People's Court Gaominzhongzi No. 1221 (2013) 452–6
Xu Yan, Beijing Dong Fang Jing Ning Construction Materials Tech. Ltd. v. Beijing Rui Chang
    Wei Ye Real Estate and Tech. Devel. Co., Ltd., Beijing No. 2 Intermediate People's
    Court, Min Chu Zi No. 120 (2008) aff 'd on appeal, Beijing High People's Court, Min
    WZhong Zi No. 1165 (2008) 102–6
YANG Luo-Shu v. China Pictorial Publishing House, Shandong High People's Court Lu Min
    San Zhong Zi No. 94 (2007) 450–52
YU De-Xin v. SOYODA SA, Suzhiminzhongzi No. 0297 (2012) 626
Yunan Red River v. TRAB, Beijing High People's Court, Gaoxingzhongzi No. 65 (2002) 543–4
ZHANG Bin v. Beijing Huaye Weicheng Culture Development Ltd., Ximinchuzi No. 848
    (2008) 390
Zheng Yali v. Seiko Epson Corp. (Epson I), Patent Reexamination Board, Chinese Supreme
    People's Court, Zhixingzi No. 53 (2010) 146–8
Zhenjiang Yingfang Plastic & Electric Co., Ltd. v. Patent Reexamination Board, Guangdong
    Kejin Nylon Piping Manufacturing Co., Ltd, Beijing No.1 Intermediate People's Court,
    Zhi Xing Chu Zi No. 3085 (2010) aff 'd on appeal, Beijing High People's Court, Xing
    Zhong Zi No. 31 (2011) Revoked in retrial, Supreme People's Court, Xing Ti Zi No. 25
    (32012) 99–102

European Union: Court of Justice of the European Union

Airfield NV and Canal Digitaal, Joined Cases C-431/09 and C-432/09, [2011] ECR
    I-9363 .... 376, 378–9
Anheuser-Busch v. Budějovicky Budvar, narodni podnik, Case C-96/09 [2011] ECR
    I-2131 .... 543, 576–80
Ansul BV v Ajax Brandbeveiliging BV, Case No. C-40/01 [2003] ECR I- 2439 .... 488–90, 589
Apple Inc v. Deutsches Patent-und Markenamt Case C-421/13 [2014] BusLR 962 .... 552, 762–4
Art & Allposters Int'l v. Stichting Pictoright, Case C-419/13, ECLI:EU:C.2015:27 448
Backaldrin Osterreich The Kornspitz Company GmbH v. Pfahnl Backmittel GmbH, C-409/12
    ECLI:EU:C:2014:130 612
Bezpečnostni soft warova asociace, Case C-393/09 [2010] ECR I-13971 .... 313, 317
British Horseracing Board et al. v. William Hill Organization, Case C-203/02 [2004] ECR
    I-10415 404–7
Celaya Emparanza y GaldosInternacional SA v. Proyectos Integrales de Balizamiento SL, Case
    C-488/10 ECLI:EU:C:2012:88 787–8
Daimler Chrysler Corp v. OHIM Case T-128/01 [2003] ECR II-701 761
Dart Industries Inc v. Office for Harmonisation in the Internal Market (Trade Marks and
    Designs) Case T-360/00 [2002] ECR II-3867 531
Deutsche Grammophon Gesellschaft v. Metro-SB-Grossmärkte, Case 78/70 [1971] ECR 487 438–41
El Corte Ingles, SA v. OHIM (EUIPO), Case T-420/03 [2008] ECR II-00837 564–5
Ellos v. OHIM, Case T-219/00 [2002] ECR II-00753 560–61
Eva-Maria Painer v. Standard Verlags GmbH, Case C-145/10 [2011] ECR I-12533 312–15
Fixtures Marketing, Case C-444/02 [2004] ECR I-10549 324
Football Association Premier League and Others, Joined Cases C-403/08 and C-429/08
    [2011] ECR I-9083 .... 313–14, 324–5, 377, 381, 434, 436–8

Football Dataco Ltd. v. Yahoo! UK Ltd., Case C-604/10, ECLI:EU:C:2012:115 322–7
Genentech Inc. v. Hoechst GmbH, Case C-567/14, ECLI:EU:C:2016:526 239
Google Inc. v. Louis Vuitton Malletier SA, Case C-236/08 [2010] ECR I-2417 613–15
Heidelberger Bauchemie GmbH v. DPMA, Case C-49/02 [2014] ETMR 1289 517
Henkel KGaA v. OHIM and Procter & Gamble Co v. OHIM Joined Cases T-335/99 to
  T-337/99; T-30/00; T-117/00 to T-121/00; T-128/00 and T-129/00 [2001] ECR
  II-2723 760–61
Hölterhoff, Case C-2/00 [2002] ECR I-4187; [2002] All ER (EC) 665 [2002] ETMR 79
  [2002] FSR 52 589–91
Huawei v. ZTE Case 170/13 ECLI:EU:C:2015:477 209–13
Infopaq International v. Danske Dagblades Forening, Case C-5/08 [2009] ECR
  I-6569 .... 312–14, 324, 346–51, 403
Infopaq International v. Danske Dagblades Forening, (Infopaq II), Case C-302/10,
  ECLI:EU:C:2012:16 433–8
ITV Broadcasting et al. v. TVCatchup, Case C-607/11, ECLI:EU:C:2013:147 .... 376–9, 381
Koninklijke KPN Nederland [2004] ECR I-01619 763–4
Koninklijke Philips v. Remington, Case C-299/99 [2002] ECR I-05475 551
Libertel v. Benelux Merkenbureau, Case C-104/01 [2003] ECR I-03793 517
Linde, Winward and Rado, Joined Cases C-53/01 to C-55/01 [2003] ECR I-3161 .... 760, 763
L'Oréal SA v. Bellure NV, Case C-487/07 [2009] ECR I-5185 589–91
Martin Luksan v. Petrus van der Let, Case C-277/10, ECLI:EU:C:2012:65 .... 269, 328
Matratzen Concord AG v. Hukla Germany SA, Case C-421/04 [2006] ECR I-2303 561
Nils Svensson et al. v. Retreiever Sverige, Case C-466/12, ECLI:EU:C:2014:76 380–83
Nintendo Co. Ltd. v. BigBen Interactive GmbH, Case C-24/16 ECLI:EU:C:2017:146 770
Painer, Case C-145/10 [2011] ECR I-12533 324
Peek & Cloppenburg KG v. Cassina SpA, Case C-456/06 [2008] ECR I-0273 308–11
Pepsico v. GrupoPromer, Case C-281/10 P [2011] ECR I-10153 .... 774–5, 781
Procter & Gamble Co v. OHIM (Trade Marks and Designs) Case C-383/99 P [2001] ECR
  I-6251 .... 514, 531
SAS Institute v. World Programming, Case C-406/10, ECLI:EU:C:2012:259 315–19
SGAE, Case C-306/05, [2006] ECR I-11519 376–8
Sieckmann v. Deutsche Patent und Markenamt (DPMA), Case C-273/100 [2002] ECR
  I-11737 .... 509, 515–17
Silberquelle GmbH v. Maselli-Strickmode GmbH, Case No. C-495/07 [2009] ECR
  I-00137 490
Storck v OHIM, C-25/05 P, [2006] ECR I-5719 763
Tea Board v. OHIM (Trade Marks and Designs) Case T-624/13 [2015] ETMR 52 531–2
Titus Donner, Case C-5/11, ECLI:EU:C:2012:370 372–5
UsedSoft v. Oracle Int'l, Case C-128/11, ECLI:EU:C:2012:407 441–8
Verein Radetzky-Orden v. Bundesvereinigigung Kameradschaft Case No. C-442/07 [2008]
  ECR I-9223 490
Vuitton Malletier v OHIM, C-97/12 P, EU:C:2014:324 763
*Windsurfing Chiemsee Produktions- und Vertriebs GmbH (WSC) v. Boots- und Segelzubehor
  Walter Huber*, Cases C-108/97 and C-109/97 [1999] ECR I-2779 .... 514, 527–32

European Union: Office of Harmonization in the Internal Market (OHIM)

Julius Samann, Ltd. v. Kubispol., Case no. R1999/2013-3 (OHIM Bd. Appeal, Jan. 20, 2016) 771–4
Kenneth Jebaraj t/a Screw You, . Decision R 495/2005-G (2005) OHIM Bd. Of App. (2005) 546

European Union: European Patent Office

Active inductor/Alcatel Lucent, Case No. T 2297/12 (Euro. Pat. Off. Bd. App. 2 June 2017) 161
Coatex v. Rhodia, "Polymers useful as pH responsive thickeners and monomers" Case No. T 0041/02 (Bd. App. EPO, 19 Jan. 2006) 119
CODIS core STR loci forensic human identification/PROMEGA, Case No. T 1634/15 (Euro. Pat. Off. Bd. App., 14 October 2016), ... 111
Computer program product/IBM, Case No. T 1173/97 (Euro. Pat. Off . Tech. Bd. App., 1 July 1998) 59–63
File search method/FUJITSU, Case No. T 1351/04 (Euro. Pat. Off. Bd. App., 18 April 2007) . 62–3
Fischer-Tropsch Catalysts/SASOL TECHNOLOGY II, Case No. G 1/15 (Eur. Pat. Off. En. Bd. App., 25 November 2014) 120–21
Hakoune/Inadequate description, Case No. T 0219/85 (Eur. Pat. Off . Bd. App., 14 July 1986) 159–62
Henkel KgAA v. Unilever, Case No. T 606/89 (Euro. Pat. Off. Bd. App., 27 July 1989) 139
Hepatitis A virus, Case No. G 2/93 (Euro. Pat. Off. En. Bd. App., 21 December 1994) 160–61
Hydrogen-rich mixture/SHELL (Johnson Matthey Public Limited Company v. Shell Int'l Research), Case No. T 0951/15 (Euro. Pat. Off. Bd. App., 3 April 2017) 111–13
Immunoglobulin preparations/GENENTECH, Case No. T 1212/97 (Euro. Pat. Off. Bd. App., 14 May 2001) 110–111
Metaltech V.O.F. v. Alcan Deutschland GmbH, Case No. T 0033/99 (Tech. Bd. App. EPO, 4 Oct. 2001) 118
Munters Europe A.B. v. KyotoCooling B.V., Case No. T 0353/14 (Eur. Pat. Off . Bd. App., 15 Sept 2016) 107–9
Paper surface sizing/AVEBE (AVEBE B.A. v. Zuckerforschung Tulln GmbH), Case No. T 0035/04 (Euro. Pat. Off . Bd. App., 18 January 2006) 135–41
Porous inorganic oxide/W.R.GRACE & CO.-CONN, Case No. T 2026/10 (Euro. Pat. Off. Bd. App., 2 May 2014) 113–15
Portable device and method of providing menu icons/SAMSUNG Case No. T 0781/10 (Euro. Pat. Off. Tech. Bd. App., 19.9.2013) 62
Simethicone Tablet/Rider, Case No. T-83 (Euro. Pat. Off. Bd. App., 15 March 1984) 140–41
Touch interface reconfiguration/APPLE, Case No. T 0543/14 (Euro. Pat. Off. Tech. Bd. App., 10 October 2016) 62
Transgenic animals/HARVARD, Case No. T 0315/03 (Euro. Pat. Off . Bd. App., 6 July 2004) 70–74
University Patents, Inc. v. Smithkline Beecham Biologicals SA, Case No. G 3/98 (OJ EPO, 2001, 062) (En. Bd. App, EPO, 12 July 2000) 117–19
WARF/stem cells, Case No. G2/06 (Euro. Pat. Off. En. Bd. App, 25 November 2008), ... 74

Table of cases · **xxv**

France

Plon SA v. Hugo, ECDR, Cour de Cassation, 2007, 9 386–7
Samuel Beckett, heirs of, Tribunal de Grande Instance de Paris, 3rd chamber, Oct. 15, 1992,
 R.I.D.A. 1993, 225 387–8

Germany

Articulation Arrangement (Gelenkanordnung), Case No. Xa ZR 36/08 (BGH 4 February
 2010) 187–92
Assertion of standard essential patents (Geltendmachung standardessentieller Patente), Case
 No. 7 O 209/15, BeckRS 2016, 18389 (District Court (Landesgericht), Mannheim, 1
 July 2016) 209–13
Berechnung des Schadens bei Warenzeichenverletzungen Mesmer- Tee II, BGH, GRUR 1966,
 375..................638
BGH, Decision 10 May 1995 – 1 StR 764/94 (LG Nurnberg-Furth) 716–18
Bicycle helmet rotary lock, Case No. 7 O 184/06, NJOZ 2008, 2391, GRUR-RR 2008, 333
 (Mannheim District Court (Landesgericht), 19 October 2007) 231–4
Breach of Secrecy of Representative as Wine Consultant Case No. I ZR 119/00 (19 December
 2002)(Koblenz) Verwertung von Kundenlisten 688–92
Change-Speed Hub (Mehrgangnabe), Case No. X ZR 153/05 (Federal Supreme Court
 (BGH), 12 February 2008), ...189–90
Formstein Case No. X ZR 28/85, 29 April 1986, GRUR 1986, 803..................191
Füllanlage Case No. ZR 133/82, BGH, 19 February 1984 (OLG Karlsruhe)..................692–4
Fußball-Stecktabelle, GRUR 2014, 1199 OLG Nurnberg..................320, 760
Geburtstagszug 'Birthday Train,' GRUR 2014, 175 ....320–21, 760
German Patent Application, DE 102 32 674.6-53, In re (GBH) German Federal Court of
 Justice, Patents, 22 April 2010, ...63
Kunstoffrohrteil [2002] GRUR 511..................185
Meinhard van Gerkan, Case 16 O 240/05, Landgericht Berlin, 28 November 2006, GRUR
 2007, 964 388–9
Metal on Metal, ("Metall auf Metall"), case 1 BvR 1585/13, 2016 German Federal
 Constitutional Court..................400–403
Metrosex, Case No. I ZR 151/05 Decision Federal Supreme Court (BGH) 13 March 2008,
 2008 GRUR 912..................642
Pankreaplex II, KZR 7/79, GRUR 1980, 750, [1980] IIC 695..................727
Pearl Driver (Perlentaucher), Case No. I ZR 12/08, IIC 2011, 978 (BGH)..................360–65
Reichweite des Schutzes einer Farbmarke – Gelbe Worterbucher, Case No. I ZR 228/12
 (BGH), 18 September 2014 642
Schneidmesser I, Decision of 12 March 2002 (Case No. X ZR 168/00), GRUR 2002,
 515..................185, 191
Schneidmesser II, Decision of 12 March 2002 (Case No. X ZR 135/01), GRUR 2002,
 519 – 191
Silberdistel, GRUR 1995, 581 320
Spielbankaffaire, BGH 2 OCtober 1997, 1999 GRUR 152..................268–9

Tripp Trapp Chair, case No. I ZR 98/06, IIC 20101, 236, German Federal Court of Justice..467–72
Viosulfal v. Vitasulfal, BGH, Case No. I ZR 83/59 24 February 1961.........................637–8

United Kingdom

32Red Plc v WHG (International) Ltd [2013] EWHC 815 (Ch) 639–42
Aerotel Limited v Telco Limited; Macrossan's Application [2007] RPC 7 62–3
Alfrank Designs Ltd v Exclusive (UK) Ltd [2015] EWHC 1372 (IPEC)..........................237
Baigent v. Random House Group [2007] EWCA Civ 247 [2007] FSR 24........................268
Bud?jovicky Budvar Narodni Podnik v Anheuser-Busch Inc [2012] EWCA Civ 880 [2012] 3 All ER 1405 580
Cartier Int'l v. Sky [2014] EWHC 3354 (Ch)..643
Catnic Components Ltd v Hill & Smith Ltd [1982] RPC 183.....................................182–6
Celanese Int'l Corp. v. BP Chemicals Ltd. [1999] RPC 203...238
Cescinsky v. George Routledge & Sons, Ltd [1916] 2 KB 325..291
Clark v Adie (1877) 2 App Cas 315...184
Coco v. AN Clark (Engineers) Ltd [1968] FSR 415.......................................701, 712–16
Cosmetic Warriors Ltd & Lush Ltd v. Amazon.co.uk Ltd & Amazon EU Sarl [2014] EWHC 181 (Ch)...615
Eastman Photographic Materials Co. v. John Griffiths Cycle Corp (1898)15 RPC 105 595
Force India Formula One Team Ltd v. 1 Malaysia Racing Team Sdn Bhd [2012] EWHC 616 (Ch) [2012] RPC 29...640
Foskett v. McKeown [2000] 2 WLR 1299 (HL) 461
Gimex International Groupe Import Export v. Chill Bag Co Ltd [2012] EWPCC 31 793
GlaxoSmithKline UK Ltd v Wyeth Holdings LLC [2016] EWHC 1045 (Ch).................186
Gyles v Wilcox, Barrow, and Nutt 1740 2 Atk 143 417–18
Kirin-Amgen v. Hoechst Marion Rousel Ltd., [2004] UKHL 46 [2005] RPC 9.........180–86
L'Oreal SA v Bellure NV, [2010] RPC 23 590
Lucasfilm Ltd. v. Ainsworth [2011] UKSC 39..319
Magmatic Ltd v. PMS International Ltd [2014] EWCA Civ 181 [2014] ECDR 20 781–2
Magnesium Elektron Ltd v. Molycorp Chemicals and Oxides (Europe) Ltd, [2016] RPC 18 [2015] EWHC 3596 (Pat),...217
Michael Baigent v. The Random House Group Ltd. [2016] EWHC 719 (Ch)................345
Millar v Taylor (1769) 98 ER 201 417
Nestec SA & Ors v Dualit Ltd & Ors [2013] EWHC 923 (Pat).....................................120
Nikken Kosakusho Works v. Pioneer Trading Company [2003] EWHC 2006 (Ch).........643
Norwich Pharmacal Co v. Customs & Excise Commissioners [1974] AC 133 [1973] 3 WLR 164...643–4
Ocular Sciences Ltd v Aspect Vision Care Ltd (No.2) [1997] RPC 289..........................736
OOO Abbott v. Design & Display, Ltd., [2017] EWHC 932......................................234–9
Powell v. Head, (1879) 12 Ch D 686..291
Proctor v. Bayley [1889] 6 RPC 538 (Ct App) (1889) 42 ChD 390................................217
Research In Motion UK Ltd v Motorola Inc, [2010] EWHC 118 (Pat).........................186
Royal Brunei Airlines Sdn Bhd v Tan [1995] 2 AC 378...693–4

Saltman Engineering Co. Ltd. v. Campbell Engineering Co. Ltd. (1948) 65 RPC 203................713–14
Seager v. Copydex Ltd. [1967] 1 WLR 923 [1967] RPC 349..713–14
Societe des Produits Nestle SA v Cadbury UK Ltd, [2016] EWHC 50 (Ch) [2016] FSR 19..........761
Stoke-on-Trent City Council v W & J Wass Ltd [1988] 1 WLR 1406..639
Symbian Ltd. v. Comptroller General of Patents, Designs and Trademarks [2008] EWCA Civ
    1066...63
Technip France SA's Patent, [2004] RPC 46...186
Terrapin Ltd. v. Builders' Supply Co. (Hayes) Ltd. [1960] RPC 128..713
Tonson v Walker (1752) 3 Swans (App) 762...417
United Horse-Shoe & Nail Co. v. John Stewart & Co. (1888) LR 13 App Cas 401.....................238
Unwired Planet Int'l Ltd. v. Huawei Technologies Co. Ltd., [2017] EWHC 1304 (Pat)...........213–17
Van Der Lely NV v Bamfords Ltd [1963] RPC 61..184
Vercoe v Rutland Fund Management Ltd [2010] EWHC 424 (Ch)...736
Vestergaard Frandsen A/S v. Bestnet Europe Ltd. [2013] UKSC 31 [2013] RPC 33...................694
Vestergaard Frandsen A/S (now called MVF 3 Aps) v. Bestnet Europe Ltd [2017] FSR 5
    [2016] EWCA Civ 541..736
Warner-Lambert Co LLC v Actavis Group PTC EHF [2015] EWCA Civ 556 [2015] RPC
    25..217

United States

1-800 Contacts, Inc. v. Lens.com, Inc., 722 F.3d 1229 (10th Cir. 2013)..603
24 Hour Fitness USA, Inc. v. 24/7 Tribeca Fitness, LLC, 277 F. Supp. 2d 356, 68 U.S.P.Q. 2d
    1031 (S.D.N.Y. 2003)...521
Aalmuhammed v. Lee, 202 F.3d 1227 (9th Cir. 2000)..289–91
Abercrombie & Fitch Co. v. Hunting World, Inc., 537 F.2d 4, 9 (2nd Cir. 1976)............512, 522, 525,
    608, 755, 758
Ability Search, Inc. v. Lawson, 556 F.Supp. 9, 16 (S.D.N.Y. 1981)...725
Aimster Copyright Litigation, In re, 334 F.3d 643 (7th Cir. 2003)..475
A.J. Canfield Co. v. Honickman, 808 F.2d 291 (3d Cir. 1986)...607
Akamai Techs., Inc. v. Limelight Networks, Inc., 797 F.3d 1020, 1022 (Fed. Cir. 2015)................193
Aladdin Mfg. Co. v. Mantle Lamp Co. of America, 116 F.2d 708 (7th Cir. 1941)..........................633
Alappat, In re, 33 F.3d 1526 (Fed. Cir. 1994)..50
Alexander Milburn Co. v. Davis Bournonville Co., 270 US 390 (1926)..82
Alice Corp. Pty. Ltd. v. CLS Bank International 134 S.Ct. 2347 (2014)..................44–9, 52–3, 64–5
Allarcom Pay Television, Ltd. v. General Instrument Corp., 69 F.3d 381 (9th Cir. 1995).............415
Altvater Gessler-J.A. Baczewski Intern. (USA) Inc. v. Sobieski Destylarnia S.A., 572 F.3d 86
    (2d Cir. 2009)..656
A&M Records v. Napster, 239 F.3d 1004 (9th Cir. 2001)..475
Amazon.com, Inc. v. Barnesandnoble.com, Inc., 239 F.3d 1343 (Fed. Cir. 2001).........................199
American Broadcast Companies, Inc. v. Aereo, Inc., 134 S. Ct. 2498 (2014)....................365–71, 379
American Dental Ass'n v. Delta Dental Plans Ass'n, 126 F.3d 977 (7th Cir. 1997)........................277
American Medical Systems Inc. v. Medical Engineering Corp., 794 F. Supp. 1370 (ED. Wis.
    1992), aff'd in part, rev'd in part & remanded, 6 F.3d 1523 (Fed. Cir. 1993), cert.
    denied, 511 US 1070 (1994)..218

American Rice, Inc. v. Ark. Rice Growers Coop. Ass'n, 701 F.2d 408 (5th Cir. 1983) 648–9
American Scientific Chemical, Inc. v. American Hospital Supply Corp., 690 F.2d 791 (9th Cir. 1982) 523
AMF, Inc. v. Sleekcraft Boats, 599 F.2d 341 (9th Cir. 1979) 588
Analogic Corp. v. Data Translation, Inc., 371 Mass. 643 N.E.2d 804 (1976), 358 N.E.2d 804 730
Anderson v. Stallone, 11 U.S.P.Q. 2d 1161 (1989) 353
Anheuser-Busch, Inc. v Andy's Sportswear, Inc., 40 U.S.P.Q. 2d 1542 (N.D. Cal. 1996) 596
Apple Computer, Inc. v. Franklin Computer Corp., 714 F.2d 1240 (3d Cir. 1983); 282
Applied Elastomerics, Inc. v. Z-Man Fishing Products, Inc., 521 F. Supp. 2d 1031 (N.D. Cal. 2007) 256
Applied Med. Distribution Corp. v. Surgical Co., 587 F.3d 909 (9th Cir. 2009) 258–9
Ariad Pharm., Inc. v. Eli Lilly & Co., 598 F.3d 1336 (Fed. Cir. 2010) 156
Ariosa Diagnostics, Inc. v. Sequenom, Inc., 788 F.3d 1371 (Fed. Cir. 2015), *cert. denied*, 136 S. Ct. 2511 (2016) 67
Armento v. Laser Image, Inc., 950 F. Supp. 719 (WDNC 1996) 288
Arnstein v. Porter, 154 F.2d 464 (2d Cir. 1946) 333–5
Aro Mfg. Co. v. Convertible Top Replacement Co., 377 US 476 (1964) 194
Arrow Fastener Co., Inc. v. Stanley Works, 59 F.3d 384 (2d Cir 1995) 522–3
ART+COM Innovationpool GmbH v. Google Inc., 155 F. Supp. 3d 489 (D. Del. 2016) 224
Ashley Furniture Industries, Inc. v. Sangiacomo N. A., Ltd., 187 F.3d 363 (C.A.4 1999) 757
Association for Molecular Pathology v. Myriad Genetics, Inc., 133 S.Ct. 2107 (2013) 46, 65–8
Ateliers de la Haute-Garonne v. Broetje Automation-USA Inc., 817 F.Supp.2d 394 (D. Del. 2011) 191–2
Authors Guild v. Google, Inc., 804 F.3d 202 (2d Cir. 2015) 423–7
Authors Guild v. HathiTrust 755 F.3d 87 (2d Cir. 2014) 425
Autogiro Co. of America v. United States, 181 Ct.Cl. 55, 384 F.2d 391 (1967) 165–6
Automotive Technologies Int'l, Inc. v. BMW of North America, Inc., 501 F.3d 1274 (Fed. Cir. 2007) 142–5
AutoZone, Inc. v. Tandy Corp., 373 F.3d 786 (6th Cir. 2004) 597
Avtec Systems, Inc. v. Peiffer, 21 F.3d 568 (4th Cir. 1994) 680
B & B Hardware, Inc. v. Hargis Indus., Inc., 135 S. Ct. 1293 (2015) 588
B& R Choiniere Ltee. v. Art's-Way Mfg. Co., 207 U.S.P.Q. 969 (N.D.N.Y. 1979) 650
Baik, 84 U.S.P.Q. 2d 1921 (T.T.A.B. 2007) 543
Baker v. Selden, 101 US 99 (1879) 282–5, 294
Balt. Orioles, Inc. v. Major League Baseball Players Ass'n, 805 F.2d 663 (7th Cir. 1986) 413
Bandag, Inc.v. Al Bolser's Tire Stores, Inc., 750 F.2d 903 (Fed. Cir.1984) 632
BanxCorp v. Costco Wholesale Corp., 978 F. Supp. 2d 280 (S.D.N.Y. 2013) 277
Baseload Energy, Inc. v. Roberts, 619 F.3d 1357 (Fed. Cir. 2010) 256
Bayer Consumer Care AG v. Belmora LLC, 90 U.S.P.Q. 2d 1587 (T.T.A.B. 2009) 501
Bellsouth Advertising & Publishing Corp v. Donnelley Information Publishing, Inc, 999 F. 2d 1436 (11th Cir. 1993) 298
Belmora LLC v. Bayer Consumer Care AG., 84 F.Supp.3d 490 (E.D. Va. 2015) 501
Benthin Management GmbH, In re, 37 U.S.P.Q. 2d 1332 (T.T.A.B. 1995) 542
Berry Sterling Corp. v. Pescor Plastics, Inc., 122 F.3d 1452 (Fed. Cir. 1997) 746–7
Best Lock Corp. v. IlcoUnican Corp., 94 F.3d 1563 (Fed. Cir. 1996) 748

Big Island Candies, Inc. v. Cookie Corner, 269 F. Supp. 2d.1236 (D. Haw. 2003) 757
Bilski v. Kappos, 561 US 593 (2010) 44, 46–9, 51–3
Binion, In re, 93 U.S.P.Q. 2d 1531 (T.T.A.B. 2009) 543
Blinded Veterans Ass'n v. Blinded American Veterans Found., 872 F.2d 1035 (D.C. Cir. 1989) 607
Bliss Salon Day Spa v. Bliss World LLC, 268 F.3d 494 (7th Cir. 2001) 522
BMG Music v. Gonzales, 430 F.3d 888 (7th Cir. 2005) 462
Borden, In re, 90 F.3d 1570 (Fed.Cir. 1996) 751
Brandir International, Inc. v. Cascade Pacific Lumber Co., 834 F. 2d 1142 (2d. Cir. 1987) 297
Bright Tunes Music Corp. v. Harrisongs Music, Ltd., 420 F. Supp. 177 (S.D.N.Y. 1976) aff'd
    sub nom. ABKCO Music, Inc. v. Harrisongs Music, Ltd., 722 F.2d 988 (2d Cir. 1983) 336–8
Brown v. Barbacid (Brown I) 276 F.3d 1327 (Fed. Cir. 2002) 88
Brown v. Barbacid (Brown II) No. 103,586 (Bd. Pat. App. & Interf. Sept. 28, 2004) 88
Brown v. Barbacid, 436 F.3d 1376 (Fed. Cir. 2006) 87–90
Brown v. Duchesne, 60 US 183 (1856) 6
Brownstein v. Lindsay, 742 F.3d 55 (3d Cir. 2014) 291
Broz v. Cellular Info. Sys., Inc., 673 A.2d 148 (Del. 1996) 707
Buffets, Inc. v. Kline, 73 F.3d 965 (9th Cir. 1996) 681
Buildex Inc. v. Kason Indus., Inc., 849 F.2d 1461 (Fed. Cir. 1988) 81–2
Burger King Corp. v. Mason, 710 F.2d 1480 (11th Cir. 1983), cert. denied, 465 US 1102
    (1984) 665
Burger King Corp. v. Weaver, 169 F.3d 1310 (11th Cir. 1999), cert. dismissed, 528 US 948
    (1999) 659
Burrow-Giles Lithographic Co. v. Sarony, 111 US 53 (1884) 279–82
Buti v. Impressa Perosa S.R.L., 139 F.3d 98 (2d Cir. 1998) 487
Cairns v. Franklin Mint Co., 292 F.3d 1139 (9th Cir. 2002) 601–2
California Innovations, Inc.. In re, 329 F.3d 1334 (Fed.Cir.2003) 540
Cameron Int'l Corp. v. Vetco Gray Inc., No. 14-07-00656-CV, 2009 WL 838177 (Tex. App.
    Mar. 31, 2009) 251–6
Campbell v. Acuff-Rose Music, Inc., 510 US 569 (1994) 417, 419–23, 425–6, 617
Capitol Records, Inc. v. Thomas-Rasset, 692 F.3d 899 (8th Cir. 2012) 462
Carbo Ceramics, Inc. v. Keefe, 166 F. App'x 714 (5th Cir. 2006) 733
Cariou v. Prince, 714 F.3d 694 (2d Cir. 2013) 422–3
Carnegie Mellon Univ. v. Marvell Tech. Group, Ltd., 807 F.3d 1283 (Fed. Cir. 2015) 222–4
Carnival Cruise Lines, Inc. v. Shute, 499 US 585 (1991) 653
Carter, In re, 673 F.2d 1378 (CCPA 1982) 752
Cartoon Network LP, LLLP v. CSC Holdings, Inc., 536 F.3d 121 (2008) 366
Cataphote Corp. v. Hudson, 444 F.2d 1313 (5th Cir. 1971) 680
Cazes, In re, 21 U.S.P.Q. 2d 1796 (T.T.A.B. 1991) 542
CCC Information Services, Inc v. Maclean Hunter Market Reports, Inc., 44 F.2d 61 (2d Cir.
    1994), cert. denied, 516 US 817 (1995) 298
CCNV v. Reid, 490 US 730 (1989) 278, 285–9
CDN Inc. v. Kapes, 197 F.3d 1256 (9th Cir. 1999) 298
Celsis In Vitro, Inc. v. Cellz/Direct, Inc., 664 F.3d 922 (Fed. Cir. 2012) 199
Cemen Tech, Inc. v. Three D Indus., L.L.C., 753 N.W.2d 1 (Iowa 2008) 697
Century 21 Real Estate Corp. v. Lendingtree, Inc., 425 F.3d 211 (3d Cir. 2005) 605

Certain Cube Puzzles, In re, 219 U.S.P.Q. 322 (ITC 1982) 651
Chance v. Pac-Tel Teletrac Inc., 242 F.3d 1151 (9th Cir. 2001) 487
Christian Louboutin S.A. v. Yves Saint Laurent Am. Holdings, Inc., 696 F.3d 206 (2d Cir. 2012), ...550
Cliff's Notes, Inc. v. Bantam Doubleday Dell Publishing, 886 F.2d 490 (2d Cir. 1989) 617
Co-Rect Products, Inc. v. Marvy! Advertising Photography, Inc., 780 F.3d 1324 (8th Cir. 1985).....523
Coach Services, Inc. v. Triumph Learning LLC, 668 F.3d 1356 (Fed. Cir. 2012) 596
Cockerham v. Kerr-McGee Chemical Corp., 23 F.3d 101 (5th Cir. 1994) 680
Commil USA, LLC v. Cisco Sys., Inc., 135 S. Ct. 1920 (2015), ...194
Compagnie, Generale Maritime, In re, 993 F.2d 841 (Fed. Cir.1993) 497
Compare Capitol Records, Inc. v. Thomas-Rasset, 692 F.3d 899 (8th Cir. 2012), cert. denied 133 S. Ct. 1584 (2013) 370–71
Comprehensive Technologies Int'l v. Software Artisans, Inc., 3 F.3d 730 (4th Cir. 1993) 719
Computer Associates International, Inc. v. Altai, Inc., 982 F.2d 693 (2d Cir. 1992) 285
Computerland Corp. v. Microland Computer Corp., 586 F.Supp. 22, 25 (N.D. Cal. 1984)...............610
Conmar Prods. Corp. v. Universal Slide Fastener Co., 172 F.2d 150, (2d Cir.1949) 246
Conmar Products Co. v. Universal Slide Fastener Co., 172 F.2d 150 (2d Cir. 1949) 716
Consolidated Electric Light Co v. McKeesport Light Co. ("The Incandescent Lamp Patent"), 159 US 465 (1895) 142–6
Constant v. Advanced Micro–Devices, Inc, 848 F.2d 1560 (Fed. Cir. 1988) 80–81
Continental Paper Bag Co. v. Eastern Paper Bag Co., 210 US 405 (1908), ...197
Craft v. Kobler, 667 F. Supp. 120 (S.D.N.Y. 1987) 277
Cuozzo Speed Techs., LLC v. Lee, 136 S. Ct. 2131 (2016) 240–43
Curtis, In re, 354 F.3d 1347 (Fed. Cir. 2004) 153–7
Dastar Corp. v. Twentieth Century Fox Film Corp., 539 US 23 (2003), ...399
Data General Corp. v. Grumman Sys. Support Corp., 36 F.3d 1147 (1st Cir. 1994) 458
David Netzer Consulting Eng'r LLC v. Shell Oil Co., 824 F.3d 989, (Fed. Cir. 2016) 168–9
Davis v. United Artists, Inc., 547 F. Supp. 722 (S.D.N.Y. 1982) 282
Dawn Donut Co. v. Hart's Food Stores, Inc., 267 F.2d 358 (2d Cir. 1959) 494
Deckers Outdoor Corp. v. Romeo & Juliette, Inc., No. 215CV02812ODWCWX, 2016 WL 7017219 (C.D. Cal. Dec. 1, 2016) 750
Deepsouth Packing Co. v. Laitram Corp., 406 US 518 (1972) 6
Dembiczak, In re, 175 F.3d 994 (Fed. Cir. 1999), ...129
Den-Tal-Ez, Inc. v. Siemens Capital Corp., 389 Pa.Super. 219, 566 A.2d 1214 (1989) 708
Diamond v. Chakrabarty, 447 US 303 (1980) 44, 51, 63–4
Diamond v. Diehr, 450 US 175 (1981) 46, 49–51, 56
Dolbear v. American Bell Telephone Co., 126 US 1 (1888) 44
Door-Master Corp. v. Yorktowne, Inc., 256 F.3d 1308 (Fed. Cir. 2001) 748–50
Dorpan, S.L. v. Hotel Melia, Inc., 728 F.3d 55, 108 U.S.P.Q. 2d 1093 (1st Cir. 2013) 493
Dorr-Oliver, Inc. v. Fluid-Quip, Inc., 94 F.3d 376 (7th Cir. 1996) 586
Dow Chem. Co. v. United States, 226 F.3d 1334 (Fed. Cir. 2000) 166
Dow Chemical Co. v. Astro-Valcour, Inc., 267 F.3d 1334 (Fed. Cir. 2001), cert. denied, 535 US 989 (2002) 89–90
Duluth News–Tribune, a Div. of Nw. Pub'ns, Inc. v. Mesabi Publ'g Co., 84 F.3d 1093 (8th Cir.1996) 514

DuPont Cellophane Co. v. Waxed Products Co., 85 F.2d 75 (2d Cir. 1936), cert. denied, 299 US 601 (1936), cert. denied, 304 US 575 (1938), reh'g denied, 305 US 672 (1938) 606
Durling v. Spectrum Furniture Co., 101 F.3d 100 (Fed. Cir. 1996) 751
E. & J. Gallo Winery v. Andina Licores S.A., 446 F.3d 984
  (9th Cir. 2006) 258
E. & J. Gallo Winery v. Consorzio del Gallo Nero, 782 F.Supp. 472 (N.D.Cal. 1992) 631
E. I. Du Pont de Nemours & Co., In re, 476 F.2d 1357 (C.C.P.A. 1973) 588
E. I. Du Pont deNemours & Co. v. Christopher, 431 F.2d 1012 (5th Cir. 1970) 707–8
Eastman Kodak Co. v. Ricoh Co., No. 12 Civ. 3109 DLC, 2013 WL 4044896 (S.D.N.Y. Aug. 9, 2013) 255
eBay, Inc. v. MercExchange, L.L.C., 547 US 388 (2006) 196–9, 628
Echo Travel, Inc. v. Travel Associates, Inc., 870 F.2d 1264 (7th Cir. 1989) 523
ECI Division of E-Systems, Inc. v. Environmental Communications Incorporated, 207 U.S.P.Q. 443 1980 (T.T.A.B. 1980) 585
Eden Toys, Inc. v. Florelee Undergarment Co., 697 F.2d 27 (2d Cir.1982) 353–4
Edwards v. Arthur Andersen LLP, 81 Cal. Rptr. 3d 282 (Sup Ct California 2008) 719
Egyptian Goddess, Inc. v. Swisa, Inc., 543 F.3d 665 (Fed. Cir. 2008) 776–9
Elcor Chem. Corp. v. Agri-Sul, Inc., 494 S.W.2d 204, (Tex.App.-Dallas 1973) 733
Eli Lilly & Co. v. Natural Answers, Inc., 233 F.3d 456 (7th Cir. 2000) 585–8
Elliott v. Google, Inc., 860 F.3d 1151 (9th Cir. 2017) 610–611
Enhanced Security Research, LLC, In re, 739 F.3d 1347 (Fed. Cir. 2014) 80–82
Enterprise Leasing Co. of Phoenix v. Ehmke, 3 P.3d 1064 (Arizona Court of Appeals 1999) 678–82
Erickson v. Trinity Theatre, Inc., 13 F.3d 1061 (7th Cir. 1994) 289–91
Etablissements Darty et Fils, In re, 759 F.2d 15 (Fed. Cir.1985) 496
Ethicon Endo-Surgery, Inc. v. Covidien, Inc., 796 F.3d 1312 (Fed. Cir. 2015) 745–7
Euromarket Designs, Inc. v. Crate & Barrel Ltd., 96 F. Supp. 2d 824 (N.D. Ill. 2000) 649
Experience Hendrix v. Hendrixlicensing. com, 762 F.3d 829 (9th Cir. 2014) 631
Fairchild Semiconductor Corp. v. Third Dimension (3D) Semiconductor, Inc., 589 F.Supp.2d 84 (D. Me. 2008) 656
Favela v. Fritz Cos., 29 U.S.P.Q. 2d 1694 (C.D. Cal. 1993) 288
Fedders Corp. v. Elite Classics, 268 F. Supp. 2d 1051 (S.D. Ill. 2003), ...527
Feist Publications, Inc. v. Rural Tel. Serv. Co., 499 US 340 (1991) 275–7, 294
Ferrero, Application of, 479 F.2d 1395 (C.C.P.A.1973) 587
Fifty-Six Hope Rd. Music, Ltd. v. A.V.E.L.A., Inc., 778 F.3d 1059 (9th Cir.), cert. denied, 136 S. Ct. 410 (2015) 630–32
Filipino Yellow Pages, Inc. v. Asian Journal Publications, Inc., 198 F.3d 1143 (9th Cir. 1999)...606–11
Finjan, Inc. v. Secure Computing Corp., 626 F.3d 1197 (Fed. Cir. 2010) 224
Flagstar Bank, FSB v. Freestar Bank, N.A., 687 F. Supp. 2d 811 (C.D. Ill. 2009) 494
Folsom v. Marsh, 9 F. Cas. 342 (C.C.D. Mass. 1841) (No. 4901) 418
Fortnightly Corp. v. United Artists Television, Inc., 392 US 390 (1968) 366–7
FragranceNet.com, Inc. v. FragranceX.com, Inc., 679 F. Supp. 2d 312 (E.D.N.Y. 2010) 281
Frank Music Corporation. v. Metro-Goldwyn-Mayer, Inc., 886 F.2d 1545 (9th Cir. 1989) 272
Frosty Treats Inc. v. Sony Computer Entm't Am. Inc., 426 F.3d 1001 (8th Cir.2005) 514
Funk Bros. Seed Co. v. Kalo Inoculant Co., 333 US 127 (1948) 44

G. Heileman Brewing Co., Inc. v. Anheuser-Busch, Inc., 873 F.2d 985 (7th Cir. 1989) 586
Gap, Inc. v. G.A.P. Adventures Inc., 100 U.S.P.Q. 2d 1417 (S.D. N.Y. 2011) 513
Gaylord v US, 777 F.3d 1363 (Fed. Cir. 2015) 223
GE Lighting Solutions LLC v. AgiLight, Inc., 750 F.3d 1304 (Fed. Cir. 2014) 167
Geneva Pharmaceuticals, Inc. v. GlaxoSmithKline PLC, 349 F.3d 1373 (Fed. Cir. 2003) 126
Gentry Gallery, Inc. v. Berkline Corp., 134 F.3d 1473 (Fed. Cir. 1998) 155–6
Georgia–Pacific Corp. v. United States Plywood Corp., 318 F.Supp. 1116 (S.D.N.Y. 1970) 224
Gilead Sciences, Inc. v. Natco Pharma Limited, 753 F.3d 1208, 1212 (Fed. Cir. 2014), cert. denied, 135 S. Ct. 1530 (2015) 126
Gilliam v. American Broadcasting Companies, Inc., 538 F.2d 14 (2d Cir. 1976) 399
Glaverbel Societe Anonyme v. orthlake Mktg. & Supply, Inc., 45 F.3d 1550 (Fed. Cir. 1995) 77
Global-Tech Appliances, Inc. v. SEB S.A., 563 US 754 (2011) 194, 694
Gorham Co. v. White, 14 Wall. 511, 81 US 511 (1871) 777
Gorham Mfg. Co. v. White, 81 US (14 Wall.) 511 (1871) 749
Gottschalk v. Benson, 409 US 63 (1972) 44, 46–7, 49–50
Government Employees Ins. Co. (GEICO) v. Google, Inc., 77 U.S.P.Q.2d 1841 (E.D. Va. 2005) 603
Graham v. John Deere Co. of Kansas City, 383 US 1 (1966) 123–6, 129
Granz v. Harris, 198 F.2d 585 (2d Cir. 1952) 399
Green River Bottling Co. v. Green River Corp., 997 F.2d 359 (7th Cir. 1993) 635
Grupo Gigante SA De CV v. Dallo & Co., 391 F.3d 1088 (9th Cir. 2004) 497–501, 564
Guantanamera Cigar Co. v. Corporacion Habanos, S.A. 729 F. Supp. 2d 246 (D.D.C. 2010) 539–43
H-D Michigan, LLC v. Hellenic Duty Free Shops S.A., 694 F.3d 827 (7th Cir. 2012), ... 655–6
Hall, In re, 781 F.2d 897 (Fed. Cir. 1986) 80–82
Harley-Davidson, Inc. v. Grottanelli, 164 F.3d 806 (2d Cir. 1999) 617
Harper & Row, Publishers, Inc. v. Nation Enters., 471 US 539 (1985) 417
Haymaker Sports, Inc. v. Turian, 581 F.2d 257 (C.C.P.A. 1978) 658
Henry Hope X-Ray Products, Inc. v. Marron Carrel, Inc., 674 F.2d 1336 (9th Cir. 1982), ... 680
Herman Miller v. Palazzetti Imports and Exports, Inc., 270 F.3d 298 (6th Cir. 2001) 756
Hill-Rom Co. v. Gen. Elec. Co., No. 2:14CV187, 2014 WL 3544990, (E.D. Va. July 15, 2014) 199
Hoehling v. Universal City Studios, Inc., 618 F.2d 972, (2d Cir.), cert. denied, 449 US 841 (1980) 277
Hokto Kinoko Co. v. Concord Farms, Inc., 738 F.3d 1085 (9th Cir. 2013) 651
Hotchkiss v. Greenwood, 52 US (11 How.) 248 (1850) 122
Hotels Corp. v. Choice Hotels Int'l, 995 F.2d 1173 (2nd Cir. 1993) 724
Hunt v. Pasternack, 192 F.3d 877 (9th Cir. 1999) 282
Hupp v. Siroflex of Am., Inc., 122 F.3d 1456 (Fed. Cir. 1997) 746, 749
Industrie Pirelli Societa per Azioni, In re, 9 U.S.P.Q. 2d 1564 (T.T.A.B. 1988) 543
Infinity Headwear & Apparel, LLC v. Jay Franco & Sons, Inc., No. 15-CV-1259 (JPO), 2016 WL 5372843, (S.D.N.Y. Sept 26, 2016) 167–8
Integra Lifesciences I v. Merck, KGaA, 331 F.3d 860 (Fed. Cir. 2003) 259
Inwood Laboratories, Inc. v. Ives Laboratories, Inc., 456 US 844 (1982) 524, 758, 785
Itar-Tass Russian News Agency v. Russian Kurier, Inc., 153 F.3d 82 (2d Cir. 1998), ... 653
Iwahashi, In re, 888 F.2d 1370 (Fed. Cir. 1989) 50
Joint-Stock Co. "Baik," In re, 84 U.S.P.Q. 2d 1921 (T.T.A.B. 2007) 542–3

Juicy Couture, Inc. v. Bella Intern. Ltd., 930 F. Supp. 2d 489 (S.D. N.Y. 2013) 647
Jules Berman & Associates, Inc. v. Consolidated Distilled Products, Inc., 202 U.S.P.Q. 67, 1979 WL 24832 (T.T.A.B. 1979) 585
Jurin v. Google Inc., 695 F. Supp. 2d 1117, 95 U.S.P.Q. 2d 1803 (E.D. Cal. 2010), ... 603
JustMed, Inc. v. Byce, 600 F.3d 1118 (9th Cir. 2010) 288
K Mart Corp. v. Cartier, Inc., 486 US 281 (1988) 651–2
Kadant, Inc. v. Seeley Machine, Inc., 244 F. Supp. 2d 19 (N.D.N.Y. 2003) 724–5
Kaneka Corp. v. Xiamen Kingdomway Group. Co., 790 F.3d 1298, 1305 (Fed. Cir. 2015) 168
Kelley v. Chicago Park Dist., 635 F.3d 290 (7th Cir. 2011) 391–9
Kelley v. Southern Pacific Co., 419 US 318 (1974) 287
Kendall-Jackson Winery v. E. & J. Gallo Winery, 150 F.3d 1042 (9th Cir. 1998) 610
Kern River Gas Transmission Co. v. Coastal Corp., 899 F.2d 1458 (5th Cir.), cert. denied, 498 US 952 S. Ct. 374, 112 L. Ed. 2d 336 (1990) 285
Kewanee Oil Co., 416 US 481, 94 S.Ct. 1879 680–81
Key West Hand Print Fabrics, Inc. v. Serbin, Inc., 269 F. Supp. 605 (S.D. Fla. 1965) 458
KeyStone Retaining Wall Sys., Inc. v. Westrock, Inc., 997 F.2d 1444 (Fed. Cir. 1993) 749
Kieselstein-Cord v. Accessories By Pearl, Inc., 623 F. 2d 989 (2d Cir. 1980) 297
King Records, Inc. v. Bennett, 438 F. Supp. 2d 812 (M.D. Tenn. 2006) 355
King-Seeley Thermos Co. v. Aladdin Industries, Inc., 321 F.2d 577, 138 U.S.P.Q. 349 (2d Cir. 1963) 606
Kirtsaeng v. John Wiley & Sons, Inc., 35 ITRD 1049, 133 S. Ct. 1351, 185 L. Ed. 2d 392 (2013) 428–32, 652
Klopfenstein, In re, 380 F.3d 1345, 1347 (Fed. Cir. 2004) 81
Knitwaves, Inc. v. Lollytogs, Ltd., 71 F.3d 996 (C.A.2 1995) 757
KP Permanent Make-Up, Inc. v. Lasting Impression I, Inc., 543 US 111 (2004) 601
KSR Int'l Co. v. Teleflex Inc., 550 US 398 (2007) 126–9, 752
L.A. Gear, Inc. v. Thom McAn Shoe Co., 988 F.2d 1117 (Fed. Cir. 1993) 746
La Societe Anonyme des Parfums le Galion v. Jean Patou, Inc., 495 F.2d 1265 (2d Cir. 1974) 485–7, 572–3
Laboratory Corporation of America Holdings v. Metabolite Laboratories, Inc., 548 US 124 (2006), ... 64
Landscape Forms, Inc. v. Columbia Cascade Co.,113 F.3d 373 (2d Cir. 1997) 551
Larami Corp. v. Amron, No. CIV. A. 91-6145, 1993 WL 69581 (E.D. Pa. Mar. 11, 1993) 163
Le Roy v. Tatham, 55 US 156 (1852) 42–4, 46
Leapfrog, Inc. v. Fisher-Price, Inc., 485 F.3d 1157 (Fed. Cir. 2007) 126
LI Shu-Xian v. LI Wen-Da with Aallmuhammed v. LEE, 202 F. 3d 1227 (9th Cir. 2000) 305
Lindy Pen Co. v. Bic Pen Corp, 982 F.2d 1400, 25 U.S.P.Q. 2d 1570 (9th Cir. 1993) 631
Litton Systems [v. Whirlpool Corp., 728 F.2d 1423 (Fed. Cir. 1984) 777
L.L. Bean, Inc. v. Drake Publishers, Inc., 811 F.2d 26 (1st Cir. 1987) 618
London-Sire Records, Inc. v. Doe 1, 542 F. Supp. 2d 153 (D. Mass. 2008) 371
Lotus v. Borland, 49 F.3d 807 (1st Cir. 1995) 318
Louis Vuitton Malletier, S.A. v. Hyundai Motor Am., No. 10–CV–1611 (PKC), 2012 WL 1022247 (S.D.N.Y. Mar. 22, 2012) 617
Louis Vuitton Malletier, S.A. v. My Other Bag, Inc., 156 F. Supp. 3d 425 (S.D.N.Y. 2016) 616–18
Lucent Techs., Inc. v. Gateway, Inc., 580 F.3d 1301 (Fed. Cir. 2009) 223

M/S Bremen v. Zapata Off-Shore Co., 407 US 1 (1972) 653
McBee v. Delica Co., 417 F.3d 107 (1st Cir. 2005) 648–9
Mackay Radio & Tel. Co. v. Radio Corp. of Am., 306 US 86 (1939) 44
McNeil Nutrition v. Heartland Sweeteners, 566 F. Supp. 2d 378 (E.D. Pa. 2008) 756
McRO, Inc. v. Bandai Namco Games Am. Inc., 837 F.3d 1299 (Fed. Cir. 2016) 51–2, 57–8, 67
McRO, Inc. v. Sony Computer Entm't Am., LLC, 55 F. Supp. 3d 1214 (C.D. Cal. 2014), ... 51
Magi XXI, Inc. v. Stato della Citta del Vaticano, 714 F.3d 714 (2d Cir. 2013), ... 653
Maier Brewing Co. v. Fleischmann Distilling Corp., 390 F.2d 117 (9th Cir. 1968), cert.
 denied, 391 US 966 (1968) 629
Markman v. Westview Instruments, Inc., 517 US 370 (1996) 163–4
Marshak v. Green, 746 F.2d 927, 929 (2d Cir. 1984) 658–9
Martha Graham Sch. & Dance Found. v. Martha Graham Ctr. of Contemporary Dance, Inc.
 380 F.3d 624 (2d Cir. 2004), cert. denied, 544 US 1060 (2005) 288
Mason v. Hepburn, 13 App. D.C. 86 (D.C. Cir. 1898) 89
Mattel, Inc. v. MCA Records, Inc., 296 F.3d 894 (9th Cir. 2002) 597
Mayo Collaborative Services v. Prometheus Laboratories, Inc., 132 S.Ct. 1289 (2012) 46–8, 64–5
Mazer v. Stein, 347 US 201 (1954) 297
MCA Television Ltd. v. Feltner, 89 F.3d 766 (11th Cir. 1996) 271
McNeil-PPC, Inc. v. Walgreen Co., 2013 WL 223400 (T.T.A.B. 2013) 513
MedImmune, Inc. v. Genentech, Inc., 549 US 118 (2007) 256
Metro-Goldwyn-Mayer Distrib. Corp. v. Bijou Theatre Co., 59 F.2d 70 (1st Cir. 1932) 281
MGM v. Grokster, 125 S.Ct. 2764 (2005) 475
Miche Bag, LLC v. Marshall Group, 818 F. Supp. 2d 1098 (N.D. Ind. 2010) 785
Miller's Ale House, Inc. v. Boynton Carolina Ale House, LLC, 702 F.3d 1312 (11th Cir.
 2012) 526–7
Miracle Tuesday, LLC, In re, 695 F.3d 1339 (Fed. Cir. 2012) 542
Mirage Editions, Inc. v. Albuquerque A.R.T. Co., 856 F.2d 1341 (9th Cir. 1988) 353
Moore v. Kulicke & Soffa Indus., Inc., 318 F.3d 561 (3d Cir. 2003) 708
Morrison v. National Australia Bank Ltd., 561 US 247 (2010) 646–7
Mortgage Grader, Inc. v. First Choice Loan Servs. Inc., 811 F.3d 1314 (Fed. Cir. 2016) 51
Moseley v. V Secret Catalogue, Inc., 537 US 418 (2003) 596
MRC Innovations, Inc. v. Hunter Mfg., LLP, 747 F.3d 1326 (Fed. Cir. 2014) 750–52
National Football League v. PrimeTime 24 Joint Venture, 211 F.3d 10, 13 (2d Cir. 2000) 413, 415
nClosures Inc. v. Block & Co., 770 F.3d 598 (7th Cir. 2014) 698–701
Netflix, Inc. v. Rovi Corp., 114 F. Supp. 3d 927 (N.D. Cal. 2015) 51
New Kids on the Block v. News America Pub., Inc., 971 F.2d 302 (9th Cir. 1992) 602, 605
New York City Triathlon, LLC v. NYC Triathlon Club, Inc., 704 F. Supp. 2d 305 (S.D.N.Y.
 2010) 627–8
Nichols v. Universal Pictures Corp., 45 F.2d 119 (2d Cir. 1930) 338–41, 345
Nintendo of America, Inc. v. Aeropower Co., 34 F.3d 246 (4th Cir.1994) 648–9
NLRB v. Amax Coal Co., 453 US 322 (1981) 287
Nobelle.Com, LLC v. Qwest Communications International, Inc., 66 U.S.P.Q. 2d 1300
 (T.T.A.B. 2003) 493
Nystrom v. TREX, 424 F.3d 1136 (Fed. Cir. 2005) 167
Ocean Garden, Inc. v. Marktrade Co., 953 F.2d 500 (9th Cir. 1991) 648–9

Ocean Tomo, LLC v. Barney, 133 F. Supp. 3d 1107 (N.D. Ill. 2015) 256
OddzOn Prods., Inc. v. Just Toys, Inc., 122 F.3d 1396 (Fed. Cir. 1997) 749
Olympia Brewing Co. v. Northwest Brewing Co., 178 Wash. 533, 35 P.2d 104 (1934) 538
On-Line Tech. v. Bodenseewerk Perkin-Elmer, 386 F.3d 1133 (Fed. Cir. 2004) 244–9
Oracle America, Inc. v. Google, Inc., 2016 WL 3181206 (N.D. Cal. 2016) 318
O'Reilly v. Morse, 56 US 62 (1853) 44, 46
Oriental Art Printing, Inc. v. Goldstar Printing Corp., 175 F. Supp. 2d 542 (S.D.N.Y. 2001) 281
Oriental Art Printing Inc. v. GS Printing Corp., 34 F. App'x 401 (2d Cir. 2002) 281
Oriental Daily News, Inc., In re, 230 U.S.P.Q. (BNA) 637 (T.T.A.B.) 557–9
Orthoflex, Inc. v. ThermoTek, Inc., 983 F. Supp. 2d 866 (N.D. Tex. 2013) 727
Pacing Techs., LLC v. Garmin Int'l, Inc., 778 F.3d 1021 (Fed. Cir. 2015) 168
Panduit Corp. v. Stahlin Bros. Fibre Works, Inc., 575 F.2d 1152 (6th Cir. 1978) 222
Park 'N Fly, Inc. v. Dollar Park & Fly, Inc., 469 US 189 (1985), 718 F.2d 327 (9th Cir.1983), 105 S.Ct. 658, 83 L.Ed.2d 582 (1985) 512, 562–4, 609, 756
Parker v. Flook, 437 US 584 (1978) 49–50
Paulik v. Rizkalla, 760 F.2d 1270 (Fed. Cir. 1985) 89
Perfect 10, Inc. v. CCBill, LLC, 488 F.3d (9th Cir. 2007) 475
Peter Schottler Gmbh, In re, 79092036, 2012 WL 5196148 (T.T.A.B.) 542–3
Peters v. Active Mfg. Co., 129 US 530 (1889) 749
Pfaff v. Wells Electronics, Inc., 525 US 5 (1998) 79, 81–2
PHG Technologies v. St. John Companies, 469 F.3d 1361 (Fed. Cir. 2006) 746
Phillips v. AWH Corp., 415 F.3d 1303 (Fed. Cir. 2005) (en banc) 164–9, 171, 191–2
Phillips v. Pembroke Real Estate, Inc., 459 F.3d 128 (1st Cir. 2006) 392, 398
Pickett v. Prince, 207 F.3d 402 (7th Cir. 2000) 353–4
Plastic Contact Lens Co. v. Guaranteed Contact Lenses, Inc., 283 F. Supp. 850 (S.D.N.Y. 1968) 255–6
Platinum Home Mortgage Corp. v. Platinum Financial Group, 149 F.3d 722 (7th Cir. 1998) 522
Playboy Enters., Inc. v. Baccarat Clothing Co., 692 F.2d 1272 (9th Cir. 1982) 631
Plus Products v. Star-Kist Foods, Inc., 220 U.S.P.Q. 541 (T.T.A.B.) 558
PODS Enterprises, LLC v. U-Haul Int'l, Inc., 126 F. Supp. 3d 1263 (M.D. Fla. 2015) 635
Polar Bear Productions, Inc. v. Timex Corp, 384 F.3d 700 (9th Cir. 2004) 271–2
Polaroid Corp. v. Polarad Electronics Corp., 287 F.2d 492 (2d Cir. 1961), cert. denied, 368 US 820, 82 S. Ct. 36, 131 U.S.P.Q. 499 (1961) 587–8
Polo Fashions, Inc. v. Craftex, Inc., 816 F.2d 145 (4th Cir. 1987) 629
Port-a-Pour, Inc. v. Peak Innovations, Inc., No. 13-CV-01511-WYDBNB, 2016 WL 7868828 (D. Colo. June 7, 2016) 727–8
Pro-Football, Inc. v. Blackhorse, 112 F. Supp. 3d 439 (E.D. Va. 2015) 545
Punchgini case, ITC Ltd. v. Punchgini, Inc., 482 F.3d 135 (2d Cir. 2007) 500–501
Qualitex Co. v. Jacobson Products Co., 514 US 159 (1995) 516–17, 524–5, 758
Quality King Distributors, Inc. v. L'anza Research Int'l, Inc., 523 US 135 (1998) 429, 431
Ramada Inns, Inc. v. Gadsden Motel Co., 804 F.2d 1562 (11th Cir. 1986) 633–5
Rates Technology, Inc. v. Speakeasy, Inc., 685 F.3d 163 (2d Cir. 2012) 256
Rath, In re, 402 F.3d 1207 (Fed. Cir. 2005) 495–7

R&B, Inc. v. Needa Parts Mfg., Inc., 418 F. Supp. 2d 684 (E.D. Pa. 2005) 277
Reader's Digest Ass'n v. Conservative Digest, 821 F.2d 800 (D.C. Cir. 1987) 522
Reebok International, Ltd. v. Marnatech Enterprises, Inc., 970 F.2d 552 (9th Cir. 1992) 647
Regents of the Univ. of Cal. v. Eli Lilly & Co., 119 F.3d 1559 (Fed. Cir. 1997) 156
Religious Technology Center v. Netcom On-Line Communication Services, Inc., 923 F. Supp. 1231 (N.D. Cal. 1995) 734
Richardson v. Suzuki Motor Co., 868 F.2d 1226 (Fed. Cir. 1989) 77
Riles v. Shell Expl. & Prod. Co., 298 F.3d 1302 (Fed. Cir. 2002) 223
Rivendell Forest Products, Ltd. v. Georgia-Pacific Corp., 28 F.3d 1042 (10th Cir. 1994) 680–81
Rockwell Graphic Systems Inc. v. DEV Industries, Inc., 925 F.2d 174 (7th Cir. 1991) 700
Rogers v. Koons, 960 F.2d 301 (2d Cir.1992) 281, 587
Rohm & Haas Co. v. Adco Chemical Co., 689 F.2d 424 (3d Cir. 1982) 692
Rosehoff Ltd. v. Cataclean Americas LLC, 2013 WL 2389725 (W.D.N.Y. 2013) 656
Rosen, In re, 673 F.2d 388 (CCPA 1982) 751
S & R Corp. v. Jiffy Lube Int'l, Inc., 968 F.2d 371 (3d Cir. 1992) 665
Salinger v. Colting, 607 F.3d 68 (2d Cir. 2010) 628
Samsung Elecs. Co. v. Apple Inc., 137 S. Ct. 429 (2016) 790–91
Sands, Taylor & Wood v. Quaker Oats Co., 34 F.3d 1340 (7th Cir. 1994) 632
Sanofi-Aventis Deutschland GmbH v. Genentech, Inc., 716 F.3d 586 (Fed. Cir. 2013) 256–60
Sarl Louis Feraud Int'l v. Viewfinder, 489 F.3d 474 (2d Cir. 2007) 656–7
Sasqua Group, Inc. v. Courtney, No. CV 10-528 ADS AKT, 2010 WL 3613855 (E.D.N.Y. Aug. 2, 2010), ... 724–6
Saucy Susan Products, Inc. v. Allied Old English, Inc., 200 F. Supp. 724 (S.D.N.Y. 1961) 656
Schroeder v. Pinterest Inc., 133 A.D.3d 12, 17 N.Y.S.3d 678 (N.Y. App. Div. 2015) 702–8
Sealed Air Corp. v. US International Trade Comm'n, 645 F.2d 976 (C.C.P.A. 1981) 650–51
Sega Enters. Ltd. v. Accolade, Inc., 977 F.2d 1510 (9th Cir. 1992), amended by 1993 US App. LEXIS 78 (9th Cir. Jan. 6, 1993), ... 423
Service Ideas, Inc. v. Traex Corp., 846 F.2d 1118 (7th Cir. 1988) 785
Seven-Up Co. v. Tropicana Prods., Inc., 53 C.C.P.A. 1209, 356 F.2d 567 (1966) 587
Sheldon v. Metro-Goldwyn Pictures Corp., 309 US 390 (1940) 459–62
Shellmar Products Co. v. Allen-Qualley Co., 87 F.2d 104 (7th Cir. 1936) 708
SHI R2 Sols., Inc. v. Pella Corp., 864 N.W.2d 553 (Iowa Ct. App. 2015) 695–8
Shoney's, Inc. v. Schoenbaum, 686 F. Supp. 554, 564 (E.D. Va. 1988), judgment aff'd, 894 F.2d 92 (4th Cir. 1990) 659
Skvorecz, In re, 580 F.3d 1262 (Fed. Cir. 2009) 75–80
Smith Fiberglass Prods., Inc. v. Ameron, Inc., 7 F.3d 1327 (7th Cir.1993) 586
Smith v. Dravo, 203 F.2d 369 (7th Cir. 1953) 708
Smith v. Whitman Saddle Co, 148 US 674 (1893) 777–8
Smollar v. Cawley, 31 U.S.P.Q. 2d 1506 (Bd. Pat. App. & Int'f 1993) 89
So Good Potato Chip Co. v. Frito-Lay, Inc., 462 F.2d 239 (8th Cir. 1972) 660–61
Sobhani v. @Radical.Media Inc., 257 F. Supp. 2d 1234 (C.D. Cal. 2003) 351–5
Societe Civile Succession Guino v. Renoir, 549 F.3d 1182 (9th Cir. 2008) 330
Sony Corp of America v. Universal City Studios, Inc., 464 US 417 (1984) 422–3
Special Devices, Inc. v. OEA, Inc., 270 F.3d 1353 (Fed. Cir. 2002) 81

Specialized Technology Resources, Inc. v. JPS Elastomerics Corp., 80 Mass. App. Ct. 841, 957 N.E.2d 1116 (2011) 720, 729–31
Spirits of New Merced, LLC, In re, 85 U.S.P.Q. 2d 1614 (T.T.A.B. 2007) 538, 540–42
Sport Dimension, Inc. v. Coleman Co., Inc., 820 F.3d 1316 (Fed. Cir. 2016)....................................778
Sportvision v. SportsMedia Tech Corp., 2005 WL 1869350 (N.D. Cal. Aug. 4, 2005).....................786
SquirtCo v. Seven-Up Co., 628 F.2d 1086 (8th Cir. 1980)..588
St. Joseph Iron Works v. Farmers Mfg. Co., 106 F.2d 294 (4th Cir. 1939)..255
Star Athletica, L.L.C. v. Varsity Brands, Inc., No. 15-866, 2017 WL 1066261, (Sup Ct Mar. 22, 2017)...753–5
State Street Bank & Trust Co. v. Signature Financial Group, Inc., 149 F.3d 1368 (Fed. Cir. 1998) 50–51
Steele v. Bulova Watch Co., 344 US 280 (1952)...646–7
Stevo Design, Inc. v. SBR Marketing Ltd., 919 F. Supp. 2d 1112 (D. Nev. 2013) 649
Story Parchment Company v. Paterson Parchment Paper Company, 282 US 555 (1931) 635
Stuart Hall Co., Inc. v. Ampad Corp., 51 F.3d 780 (C.A.8 1995) 757
Studiengesellschaft Kohle m.b.H. v. Novamont Corp., 704 F.2d 48 (2nd Cir.1983),.....................254–5
Sundor Brands, Inc. v. Borden, Inc., 653 F. Supp. 86 (M.D. Fla. 1986) 505
Sunmark, Inc. v. Ocean Spray Cranberries, Inc.,64 F.3d 1055 (7th Cir.1995) 522
Sunrise Jewelry Mfg. Corp. v. Fred, S.A., 175 F.3d 1322 (Fed. Cir. 1999)..610
Surgicenters of America, Inc. v. Medical Dental Surgeries Co., 601 F.2d 1011 (9th Cir. 1979) 608–10
T-Mobile US, Inc. v. AIO Wireless LLC, 991 F. Supp. 2d 888 (S.D. Tex. 2014)..............................517
Tam, In re, 808 F.3d 1321 (Fed. Cir. 2015) 545–6
Tam. Matal v. Tam, 137 S. Ct. 1744 (2017)..546
TAS Distrib. Co. v. Cummins Engine Co., 491 F.3d 625 (7th Cir. 2007) 700
Tax Track Sys. Corp. v. New Investor World, Inc., 478 F.3d 783 (7th Cir. 2007) 700
Teleprompter Corp. v. Columbia Broadcasting System, Inc., 415 US 394 (1974).............................367
Thermo LabSystems Inc., In re, 85 U.S.P.Q. 2d 1285 (T.T.A.B. 2007) 543
Tiffany (NJ) Inc. v. eBay Inc., 600 F.3d 93 (2d Cir. 2010) 603
Tilghman v. Proctor, 102 US 707 (1880) 44
Tillamook Country Smoker, Inc. v. Tillamook County Creamery Ass'n, 465 F.3d 1102 (9th Cir. 2006)..588
Tinseltown, Inc., In re, 212 U.S.P.Q. 863 (T.T.A.B. 1981),..545
Tire Engineering & Distribution, LLC v. Shandong Linglong Rubber Co., 682 F.3d 292 (4th Cir. 2012)..648–9
Titan Tire Corp. v. Case New Holland, Inc., 566 F.3d 1372 (Fed. Cir. 2009) 751
Tommy Hilfiger Licensing, Inc. v. Nature Labs, LLC, 221 F.Supp.2d 410 (S.D.N.Y. 2002), ...618
Toyota Motor Sales, USA., Inc. v. Tabari, 610 F.3d 1171 (9th Cir. 2010) 602
Toys "R" Us, Inc. v. Step Two, S.A., 318 F.3d 446 (3d Cir. 2003) 649
TrafficSchool.com, Inc. v. Edriver Inc., 653 F.3d 820 (9th Cir. 2011)...632
TrafFix Devices, Inc. v. Marketing Displays, Inc., 532 US 23 (2001) 550, 757, 783–6
Twin Peaks Prods., Inc. v. Publications Int'l, Ltd., 996 F.2d 1366 (2d Cir. 1993) 271
Two Men & a Truck/Int'l, Inc. v. Thomas, 908 F. Supp. 2d 1029 (D. Neb. 2012) 514
Two Pesos, Inc. v. Taco Cabana, Inc., 505 US 763 (1992) 512, 524–5, 755–8, 764
Typhoon Touch Technologies v. Dell, Inc. 659 F. 3d 1376 (2011)...176

Ultramercial, Inc. v. Hulu, LLC, 772 F.3d 709 (Fed. Cir. 2014) 51
Ultramercial, LLC v. WildTangent, Inc., 135 S. Ct. 2907 (2015) 51
Underhill v. Hernandez, 168 US 250 (1897) 6
Unisplay, S.A. v. American Elec. Sign Co., 69 F.3d 512 (Fed. Cir. 1995) 224
United States v. Able Time, Inc., 545 F.3d 824 (9th Cir. 2008), cert. denied, 129 S. Ct. 2864 (2009) 650
United States v. American Soc. of Composers, Authors and Publishers, 627 F.3d 64 (C.A.2 2010) 368, 415
United States v. Eighty-Nine (89) Bottles of "Eau de Joy," 797 F.2d 767 (9th Cir. 1986) 652
Universal Elecs., Inc. v. Universal Remote Control, Inc., 943 F. Supp. 2d 1028 (C.D. Cal. 2013) 243
University of Rochester v. G.D. Searle & Co., 358 F.3d 916 (Fed. Cir. 2004) 156
Vacheron Watches, Inc. v. Benrus Watch Co., 155 F. Supp. 932 (S.D.N.Y. 1957), ... 282
Valu Engineering, Inc. v. Rexnord Corp., 278 F.3d 1268 (Fed. Cir. 2002) 549–50, 785
Vanity Fair Mills, Inc. v. T. Eaton Co., 234 F.2d 633 (2d Cir. 1956) 647
Vaudable v. Montmartre, Inc.,[20 Misc.2d 757, 193 N.Y.S.2d 332 (N.Y.Sup. Ct.1959) 499
Viacom Int'l, Inc. v. Youtube, Inc., 676 F.3d 19 (2d Cir. 2012) 475
Victoria Cruises, Inc. v. Changjiang Cruise Overseas Travel Co., 630 F. Supp. 2d 255 (E.D. N.Y. 2008) 633
Video Pipeline, Inc. v. Buena Vista Home Entertainment, Inc., 342 F.3d 191 (3d Cir. 2003) 417
VirtualAgility Inc. v. Salesforce.com, Inc., 2014 BL 191228, 111 U.S.P.Q.2d 1763 (Fed. Cir. July 10, 2014) 243
Vision Sports, Inc. v. Melville Corp., 888 F.2d 609 (9th Cir. 1989) 523
Vita-Mix Corp. v. Basic Holding, Inc., 581 F.3d 1317 (Fed. Cir. 2009) 194–5
Vittoria North America, L.L.C. v. Euro-Asia Imports Inc., 278 F.3d 1076 (10th Cir. 2001) 652
Vylene Enterprises, Inc., In re, 90 F.3d 1472 (9th Cir. 1996) 659
Wada, In re, 194 F.3d 1297, 1300 (Fed.Cir.1999) 540
Wal-Mart Stores, Inc. v. Samara Bros., 529 US 205 (2000) 523–7, 757–9, 764
Wands, In re, 858 F.2d 731, 737 (Fed. Cir. 1988)) 145–6
Warner-Lambert Pharmaceutical Co. v. John J. Reynolds, Inc., 178 F. Supp. 655 (S.D.N.Y. 1959) 716, 727
Warwood v. Hubbard, 218 Mont. 438, 709 P.2d 637, 228 U.S.P.Q. 702 (1985) 538–9
Watec Co., Ltd. v. Liu, 403 F.3d 645, 74 U.S.P.Q.2d 1128 (9th Cir. 2005) 493
Waymark Corp. v. Porta Systems Corp., 245 F.3d 1364 (Fed. Cir. 2001) 193
Westchester Media v. PRL USA Holdings, Inc., 214 F.3d 658, 55 U.S.P.Q.2d 1225 (5th Cir. 2000) 563–4
Whelan Associates, Inc. v. Jaslow Dental Laboratory, Inc., 797 F.2d 1222 (3d Cir. 1986) 285
Williams v. Bridgeport Music, Inc., No. LACV1306004JAKAGRX, 2015 WL 4479500 (C.D. Cal. July 14, 2015) 272
Winston Research Corp. v. Minnesota Mining & Manufacturing Co., 350 F.2d 134 (9th Cir. 1965) 716
Winter v. Natural Resources Defense Council, Inc., 129 S.Ct. 365 (2008) 627
WNET Thirteen v. Aereo, Inc., 712 F.3d 676 (2013) 366
Wolf v. Travolta, No. CV14-938-CAS(VBKX), 2016 WL 3150552 (C.D. Cal. Feb. 4, 2016) 354
Wright v. Palmer, 11 Ariz.App. 292, 464 P.2d 363 681
Xoom, Inc. v. Imageline, Inc., 323 F.3d 279 (4th Cir. 2003) 355

Yale Lock Mfg. Co. v. Sargent, 117 US 536 (1886) 218–22
Yankee Publishing Inc. v. News Am. Publishing Inc., 809 F.Supp. 267 (S.D.N.Y. 1992) 618
Yeti by Molly, Ltd. v. Deckers Outdoor Corp., 259 F.3d 1101 (9th Cir. 2001) 733
YKK Corp. v. Jungwoo Zipper Co., Ltd., 213 F. Supp. 2d 1195, 64 U.S.P.Q.2d 1192 (C.D. Cal. 2002) 513
Zazu Designs v. L'Oreal, S.A., 979 F.2d 499 (7th Cir.1992) 487, 522
Zino Davidoff SA v. CVS Corp., 571 F.3d 238 (2d Cir. 2009) 627

Part I

Introduction

1
What is "transnational" IP law?

1.1 Introduction

This book introduces contemporary intellectual property (IP) law as it is practiced in a global context today. It is designed to be used by students in all three of the major IP regions of the world: China, Europe, and the US. It emphasizes the three primary fields of IP law, patent, copyright, and trademark, with limited coverage of some related areas such as design protection.

Our coverage of IP law is limited to the most important topics, as determined by the frequency with which a typical transnational practitioner encounters issues and problems. This is *not* a book on international IP law, but a book for students whose clients will have business activities across national IP jurisdictions. International IP law is an important tool for transnational practitioners; the primary treaties and international organizations in the IP field provide useful tools. But we are concerned not so much with government-to-government negotiation of treaties, or the running of international organizations, as with the coordination of IP protection by private companies that operate in many jurisdictions around the world. Thus, trans- (across or between) national; not strictly inter-national (government-to-government coordination of national-level IP protection systems).

A word about our jurisdictional coverage: the US; mainland China; and Europe. We realize full well that there are other important markets/legal jurisdictions around the world, including Japan, Korea, countries in South America and Africa, Australia, Canada, etc. We simply cannot cover all countries, so tried to choose major jurisdictions. The skills acquired in comparing and learning how to work across the three jurisdictions we chose should also help you in dealing with other transnational practice issues involving other markets/jurisdictions.

1.1.1 Structures of transnational IP law and practice

This chapter introduces students to the transnational practice of IP law. It begins by distinguishing between (1) legal authority, which exists on several relevant levels; and (2) practices and procedures adopted by business people and lawyers who must manage businesses that depend on IP and whose activities routinely and regularly span multiple national jurisdictions. Transnational IP practice takes legal direction from (1) the levels of legal authority, and turns into (2) a series of decisions and actions that allow for the coordination of a complex business on a global scale.

We note at the outset that our use of "transnational" is meant to be broadly descriptive. It does not necessarily comply with (nor do we wish to engage with) the scholarly debate on the nature of "transnational law," a term of art sometimes used by theorists of international law. *See, e.g.,* Roger Cotterell, *What is Transnational Law?*, 37 L. & Soc. Inquiry 500 (2012) (emphasizing that transnational law involves the extension of the concept of law "beyond the boundaries of the nation-state"); Gregory Shaffer, *Theorizing Transnational Legal Ordering of Private and Business Law*, 1 UC Irvine J. of Int'l, Transnat'l, & Comp. L. 1 (2016) (arguing that laws or norms "are transnational insofar as they transcend and permeate state boundaries"). For us, transnational means what its Latin roots suggest. The prefix "trans-" means, according to the Oxford English Dictionary, "across, to, over, or on the other side of; from one ... state to the another" (OED, 2d ed., 1989, meaning 1). And so, simply put, for us transnational means "*legal practice* that spans across a single nation; to, or over to, other nations; applying from one state (or nation) to another." We are more interested in legal activity that is (mostly) based on national laws, but that spans or relates to multiple legal jurisdictions.

This differs from the way some legal theorists use the term. For them, it means a body of law or source of authority that is itself beyond the origin of a single national legal system. In this sense, it differs from the traditional notion of international law, which implies that sovereign (*i.e.,* self-ruling) countries have come together and decided to create a binding obligation to conform their individual national laws to a single, agreed-upon standard. Transnational law, by comparison, does not originate with the sovereignty of individual countries; its origin transcends national sovereignty. So, for example, an international criminal court is a court whose rules apply to the nationals (or citizens) of many countries. By contrast, a classic international law treaty in the field of criminal law requires all signatory nations to change their *individual, domestic, national* criminal law statutes to adhere to an agreed-upon standard (for example, that financial fraud is punishable by a minimum prison sentence of one year in jail). International law involves coordination of national legal systems. Transnational law – in the theoretical sense used by international law theorists – is not based on individual national legislation. It is based on adherence to an inherently "supra-national" jurisdiction, where some legal rule is created which applies to people in many countries, and which does not require changes in domestic law. It is not rooted in national sovereignty, but in some broader sense of participation in an inherently supranational legal structure.

But to reiterate: this is not what we have in mind. We are interested in legal *practice:* in the practical tasks that business people and lawyers want to accomplish. So for us, transnational law is a form of legal practice, based on conventional legal sources. It has to do with the actions people need to take to coordinate business activities that span multiple individual countries, *i.e.*, multiple legal jurisdictions.

So for the practitioner, there are three levels of legal authority that are encountered on a regular basis: (1) national jurisdictions; (2) regional arrangements (particularly in Europe); and (3) international IP treaties. While in general these three levels are the primary working tools of the transnational IP lawyer, there are two additional sources of law that sometimes come into play. They are both the result of private (non-governmental) arrangements, and they overlay and interact with the three primary levels of authority just described. They are (a) party-to-party, private, bilateral contracts (the source of what is traditionally called "private international law"); and (b) rules and procedures organized by large, international private companies such as Amazon.com, Alibaba, and eBay, which govern the relations between buyers and sellers. These companies do business by bringing buyers and sellers into contact and organizing a massive (and growing) volume of trade. They are (as you know) organized around massive computer systems connected by the internet; because these computer networks provide a foundation or basis for commercial trading, they are known as "platforms" or two-sided platforms (so called because they bring together both sides of a market, buyers and sellers). Increasingly, these large, international "platform companies" are creating and administering a new intermediate level of transnational law – the "law of the platform." *See, e.g.,* Jane K. Winn, *The Secession of the Successful: The Rise of Amazon as Private Global Consumer Protection Regulator,* 58 Ariz. L. Rev. 193 (2016); Orly Lobel, *The Law of the Platform,* 101 Minn. L. Rev. 87 (2016).

The other quasi-level of authority, one rooted in national jurisdictions and historical legal practice, is the sphere of so-called "private international law." (Think of it as another "level 1.5," like law of the platform, because it is in a sense half-way between national law and "public" international law.) This quasi-fourth level, level 1.5, is called private international law because it is used to structure business-to-business transactions through private contracts. One typical aspect of these contracts covers what happens when a dispute arises. Disputes are often handled by private dispute resolution mechanisms (usually, private arbitration); and when they are not, the parties choose by contract both (a) which national jurisdiction may hear and resolve the dispute (*e.g.*, the courts of New York State, or of the Netherlands, or wherever), and (b) which national law (US law, with the New York law of contracts; or Dutch law) will apply in resolving the dispute.

One key point must be emphasized about private international law ("level 1.5"): it typically only applies when parties have a contract. If Party A is making an investment, or licensing some IP right, in a deal with Party B, private international law may well apply. But one of the powerful facts about IP rights is that you do *not* need a preexisting contract to enforce it. IP is true property; it is "good against the world." And this means that even in the absence of a contract you can, if you possess valid IP at the national level, enforce it against infringers whom you have not previously licensed or contracted with. When IP is enforced against "strangers" (people and companies with whom you have had no prior dealings), private international law is generally of no help.

In addition to this basic introduction to the sources or "levels" of law in transnational IP practice, this chapter introduces the major substantive themes that connect the different sections and chapters of the book.

1.1.2 The domestic (national) basis of IP law

As the US Supreme Court first said long ago, "Every sovereign state is bound to respect the independence of every other sovereign state, and the courts of one country will not sit in judgment on the acts of the government of another, done within its own territory" (*Underhill v. Hernandez*, 168 U.S. 250, 252 (1897)). In addition, IP – as an important branch of each country's domestic economic policy – is traditionally and by default highly territorial: IP protection issued by one country extends no further than the border of that country, and impacts beyond that border are viewed with concern. As the US Supreme Court put it in a patent case: "Our patent system makes no claim to extraterritorial effect; 'these acts of Congress do not, and were not intended to, operate beyond the limits of the United States,'" (*Deepsouth Packing Co. v. Laitram Corp.*, 406 U.S. 518, 531 (1972), quoting *Brown v. Duchesne*, 60 U.S. 183, 195 (1856)).

As a consequence, IP law is in general country specific. Unless and until a country surrenders some of its sovereignty voluntarily, that country is the sole arbiter of IP law and policy within its borders.

Countries have, however, at times found it advantageous to adopt regional or truly international arrangements in the IP field. These usually take the form of treaties, though within the EU there is a special form of regional authority called an EU Directive. We will have plenty of opportunity to study these, beginning with the EU Directive on "Orphan Works" under copyright law, from 2012.

In addition there are truly international treaties. Under these countries agree to conform domestic law to an international standard. Some are procedural, such as the Patent Cooperation Treaty, which coordinates multinational patent applications. Others are substantive. The primary substantive treaties are the Paris Convention for patents; the Berne Convention for copyright; the Madrid Protocol for trademarks; and the Agreement on Trade Related Aspects of Intellectual Property (TRIPs) for all of IP. We will have occasion to study each of these.

To understand the difference between transnational and international IP law, it may be helpful to review briefly some history. We will use two important patent law treaties – drafted at different times – as a case study.

1.2 Patent law treaties: the evolution of the international law of patents

Patent law began as a strictly mercantilist policy instrument. *See* Robert P. Merges and John Duffy, Patent Law and Policy (7th ed. 2017) at chapter 1. The granting of rights or privileges by the state was understood to be for the benefit of the granting state and its citizens – and no one else. But by the late nineteenth century, state self-interest expanded to include protection of domestic inventors whose products were increasingly sold on international markets. So in the first wave of international harmonization, culminating in the Paris Convention of 1883, individual nations made common cause to streamline patenting of inventions in multiple jurisdictions. A small degree of state sovereignty was surrendered in exchange for a regime that in theory might benefit inventors in all member states of the Convention. Then in the 1990s, the second wave of patent harmonization crested with TRIPs, part of the Uruguay Round of agreements that created the World Trade Organization. By linking new, substantive standards for IP protection with other trade preferences and policies, TRIPs appealed to the diverging national interests of signatory nations. To bridge this divergence, TRIPs required a greater surrender of sovereignty than the Paris Convention. A more thoroughgoing quid pro quo is latent in the text and background of TRIPs as compared to Paris.

How exactly do international patent treaties constrain the discretion of sovereign nations? In general, they (1) set broad legal standards, required of all signatory nations to the international treaty in question; and (2) they require (in most cases) that the laws of individual nations be changed or amended, through normal procedures of domestic legislation in each country, to conform to those broad standards set in the treaty. They require national law to be *treaty compliant*.

But how powerful are the constraints of compliance in the case of each individual treaty? The answer may differ, depending on the specific treaty under discussion. The Paris Convention was drafted in an era when national sovereignty was a stronger baseline assumption in international patent law. So it should arguably be interpreted in a way that preserves as much sovereign discretion as possible. TRIPs, on the other hand, may require greater surrender of sovereignty. And if harmonization continues in the future – not a sure thing, but entirely possible – the same analysis will apply to any treaties that are signed. In the constant push and pull between patent law's mercantilist roots, and its globalizing aspirations, the historical moment of treaty making will leave a lasting mark.

1.2.1 Paris, 1883; and the Patent Cooperation Treaty of the 1970s

The history of patent harmonization tracks the growth in international trade over time. Until 1800 there was a long period characterized by persistently low international trade flows. According to most estimates, globally the sum of exports and imports throughout the world before 1810 never exceeded more than 10 percent of global annual GDP. *See* https://ourworldindata.org/international-trade#data-sources. This changed over the course of the nineteenth century, when technological advances triggered a period of marked growth in world trade, in what has been called the "first wave of globalization." *See* David S. Jacks, Christopher M. Meissner and Dennis Novy, Trade Costs in the First Wave of Globalization, NBER Working Paper 12602 (Oct. 2006), available at http://www.nber.org/papers/w12602.pdf. *See generally* Angus Maddison, The World Economy: A Millenial Perspective (2001), available at http://theunbrokenwindow.com/Development/MADDISON percent20The percent20World percent20Economy--A percent20Millennial.

pdf, at 95–101 (describing global growth in trade and GDP between 1820 and 1913). The Paris Convention of 1883 was a creature of its time: the coming of globalization to the patent world.

The first wave of globalization came to a screeching halt with the beginning of the First World War. The decline of free trade liberalism, and the rise of nationalism, presaged not only war, but also economic stagnation. There was a sizeable reduction in international trade in the interwar period. After the Second World War trade growth picked up once again. Advances in communications (worldwide phone lines, satellite technology, mobile phones, and the internet) and transportation (containerization, larger ocean transport vessels, road construction) spread the word and paved the way for an ever-growing stream of international trade. Today the sum of exports and imports across nations is higher than 50 percent of global GNP: (https://ourworldindata.org/international-trade#data-sources). Put another way, over half of the goods and services consumed in the world originate somewhere other than the place of consumption.

It was against this broad backdrop that representatives from 11 nations gathered in Paris in 1883. But in this broader context, two more proximate causes precipitated the drafting of the Convention. The first was the wave of international scientific, technical, and cultural "expositions" that so excited and stimulated the developed world in the nineteenth century. And the second was the formation of postal and telegraph unions, at the transnational level, for coordination of transnational communication. *See* Sam Ricketson, The Paris Convention for the Protection of Industrial Property (2015) (hereafter "Ricketson, Paris Convention") at 5–6.

The great expositions of the nineteenth century occurred in London (1851), Vienna (1873), and Paris (1878). The goal of these was to showcase in one place the "state of the art" in many diverse fields, and to teach interested people from many countries the most up-to-date ideas and technologies. Although there was widespread excitement among participants (*see* Petra Moser, *How Do Patent Laws Influence Innovation? Evidence from Nineteenth-Century World's Fairs*, 95 Am. Econ. Rev. 1214 (2005) ("At a time when London had fewer than two million inhabitants, [the 1851 'Crystal Palace' Exhibition] attracted more than six million people")), exhibitors were concerned that their ideas would be shown without any form of legal protection. *See* Ricketson, Paris Convention, at 30. The risk of piracy was explicitly reflected in a number of bilateral and provisional forms of protection, which were put in place prior to the exhibitions in a hasty and ad hoc sort of way (Ricketson, Paris Convention, at 25–30). The inadequacy of these solutions was apparent to all, so a convocation of experts was called in conjunction with the Vienna Exhibition of 1873. This led directly to a parallel meeting in Paris in 1878, which produced the first draft of what would become the Paris Convention of 1883. The elites who ran these meetings – there was usually a Baron this, or Count Von that at the lectern – did not speak explicitly of the need to surrender some degree of national sovereignty to achieve uniformity. They spoke only of protecting inventors and entrepreneurs, and of the obvious need to somehow coordinate parallel national patent filings. But the solutions they arrived at reflected an implicit understanding that they were to solve a limited problem, and that as a result only fairly minimal commitments would be required of the prospective member nations.

It is often said that the Paris Convention reflects only limited substantive harmonization, and that its overall impact falls primarily on patent procedures. There is a sense in which this is true; no country commits to employing an inventive step (or nonobviousness) requirement for example, let alone agrees on how stringently to apply such a standard. At the same time, it is generally understood that a sovereign nation may treat its citizens differently from those of other nations. The very idea of citizenship shows as much. Thus when a country agrees to treat non-nationals just as it treats citizens, it does commit to a restriction in its sovereign prerogatives. Thus the central idea of the Paris Convention, the national treatment principle of Article 2 (*See* Paris Convention for the Protection of Industrial Property, Article 2, 21 U.S.T. 1583 (last revised, July 14, 1967), available at http://www.wipo.int/treaties/en/ip/paris/. does represent the surrender of some national discretion.

Likewise, it is certainly within the purview of a national government to require that legal documents be filed in an office of the government, in order to give those documents effect within the country. And so the concept of international priority in Article 4 (*id.*, at Article 4), perhaps the most widely used feature of the Paris Convention, also represents a small concession of sovereign power.

Yet both these important components of the 1883 Convention can also be seen as fairly minimalist intrusions into sovereignty. National treatment requires no change in the substantive law applied to a nation's citizens; it just requires non-citizens to be treated equally. And the international priority system makes no demands on the details or requirements of patent prosecution. It merely requires that an initial filing in another Convention country be given the same effect as if it were made initially in the national patent office. It should also be mentioned that the Convention adopts a "national option" solution for compulsory working and compulsory licensing. *Id.*, at Article 5(A)(2) and 5(A)(4):

> (2) Each country of the Union shall have the right to take legislative measures providing for the grant of compulsory licenses to prevent the abuses which might result from the exercise of the exclusive rights conferred by the patent, for example, failure to work
>
> . . .
>
> (4) A compulsory license may not be applied for on the ground of failure to work or insufficient working before the expiration of a period of four years from the date of filing of the patent application or three years from the date of the grant of the patent, whichever period expires last; it shall be refused if the patentee justifies his inaction by legitimate reasons.

This was adopted intentionally as a compromise between the forces of "nationalism" and "internationalism" – further sign of the limits of sovereign surrender embedded in the text of the Convention. This is drawn from the very instructive history of the Convention in chapter four of Edith Tilton Penrose, The Economics of the International Patent System (1951), 60–87, at p. 80.

After the successful conclusion of the Paris Convention in the late nineteenth century, further efforts at harmonizing worldwide patent law bore little fruit for nearly another century. This lull in activity was in part due to the success of the Paris Convention, which established a sufficient legal framework so that inventors and their firms could obtain some level of effective protection in most commercially important countries. Yet the process for obtaining protection remained quite cumbersome. Patent applications still had to be filed in every jurisdiction in which protection was desired, and applicants still had to deal with the divergent rules and standards of the world's many individual patent jurisdictions. Nevertheless, the international business community seemed little interested in investing time and resources for further consolidation and harmonization of world patent law. And perhaps, too, the world's nations were not ready in the first half of the twentieth century for the kind of international cooperation necessary to consolidate and harmonize global patent standards.

The next major developments would not occur until the 1970s. That decade saw two international agreements concluded – the Patent Cooperation Treaty or PCT, 28 U.S.T. 7645, T.I.A.S. No. 8733 (opened for signature June 19, 1970; entered into force January 24, 1978), available at http://www.wipo.int/export/sites/www/pct/en/texts/pdf/pct.pdf and the European

Patent Convention or EPC, available at http://www.european-patent-office. org/legal/epc/e/ma1.html. Both of these innovations were directed to the same problem – the burden on applicants of having to file numerous applications to obtain transnational patent protection. Both were also variations of the same solution – consolidation of various national processes into a single international mechanism.

Of the two solutions, the PCT is the less dramatic, though it applies to more countries. It establishes an international application process by which inventors may file a single patent application in any patent office of a jurisdiction bound by the Agreement. The PCT application process has two phases: an "international phase," during which an international searching authority (which can be the national patent office) conducts a prior art search; and the "national phase," during which the applicant must prosecute the application through the patent office of each country where protection is sought. In essence, the PCT provides a uniform procedural framework for filing applications in multiple nations and consolidates one aspect of patent prosecution: prior art searching. The PCT does not, however, eliminate the necessity of separately prosecuting multiple national applications to obtain protection in multiple countries. The PCT has been a modest success. For example, the US PTO received in fiscal year 2006 about 52,000 PCT international applications – a substantial number that is nonetheless dwarfed by the over 417,000 domestic applications filed in the same year. *See* US P.T.O., *Performance and Accountability Report Fiscal Year 2006* (2006), available at https://www.uspto.gov/sites/default/files/about/stratplan/ ar/USPTOFY2006PAR.pdf. But applicants are often drawn to the PCT application process not because of its simplicity, but because of its procedural benefits in delaying patent prosecution at the national level. See the discussion below in Section 1.2.2.

1.2.2 The European Patent Convention and the structure of European IP law

In contrast to the PCT, the European Patent Convention is far more aggressive in establishing a transnational patent process. It establishes a centralized office for patent prosecution for each of its 38 member states, the European Patent Office (EPO), which performs the normal administrative tasks of searching the prior art, examining the application and determining patentability. If the examination process concludes in favor of the applicant, the EPO is authorized to issue a patent that provides rights in *all* EPC countries designated by the applicant. The applicant does not have to go through any additional prosecution in the national offices.

There are two major limitations on the EPC. First, it applies only to 38 European nations; the PCT, by contrast, applies to more than 100 nations. Second, the EPC unifies only the administrative functions of national patent systems. The European patent issued by the EPO is not, in theory, a single transnational patent but a "bundle" of national patents that are enforced through the various national courts of the EPC countries. The nations of Europe are considering other measures that would further unify their patent systems. For example, the proposed Unified Patent and Unified Patent Court (UPC) would establish true European-wide patents, with centralized enforcement. Agreements establishing the unified patent and unified court have been signed in Europe; but neither has yet entered into force because the requisite 13 countries have not yet ratified the agreements (Agreement on a Unified Patent Court and Statute (document 16351/12, of 11.01.2013), available at http://documents.epo.org/projects/babylon/eponet.nsf/0/A10 80B83447CB9DDC1257B36005AAAB8/$File/upc_agreement_en.pdf).

Both the PCT and the EPC were directed to consolidating the international process of patent prosecution. In the 1980s and 1990s, however, the targets of reform changed; the international business community began to tackle the more ambitious project of harmonization, *i.e.*, creating uniform substantive standards of IP protection. The change in goals had a number of catalysts. IP was increasing in value and was beginning to take on a more central role in business planning and strategy. (The establishment of the Federal Circuit in 1982 was both a consequence of this trend, and a partial cause of its continuation.) Moreover, world trade was becoming increasingly important to the economies of the US and other industrialized nations. Markets in developing countries were no longer insignificant, and these countries had traditionally resisted strong IP protection. This led to a new wave of harmonization that culminated in an historical treaty signed in 1995.

1.2.3 Uruguay Round and TRIPs, 1995

To pursue harmonization, the business community in the US and Europe needed a new institutional structure. The existing structure – the World Intellectual Property Organization (WIPO) – would not do. WIPO was created in 1970 as the successor organization to the United International Bureaux for the Protection of Intellectual Property, which had been established in 1893 to administer the Paris Convention and the Berne Convention for the Protection of Artistic and Literary Works, the primary international copyright treaty created in 1886. WIPO's work in patent law had largely been limited to educational efforts; the many newly formed nations from the 1960s and 1970s were thought to need instruction on the ways and means of national patent systems. Then in 1974, WIPO officially became a specialized agency of the United Nations – a forum not thought to be particularly friendly to Western business interests.

Aware of the increasing importance of IP and of WIPO's slow progress in harmonization throughout the 1970s and 1980s, the business community was on the lookout for an alternative institutional structure for harmonization. When influential CEOs from 12 large US companies came together to strengthen IP rights, they settled on a novel solution: grafting IP onto issues of international trade. The reasoning behind formation of this powerful club, known simply as the IP Committee, was sound. The members knew that a major new trade treaty was in the works, under the auspices of the General Agreement on Tariffs and Trade (GATT). And they knew that corporate interests had much greater clout in the GATT negotiation process than they did at WIPO. Thus was born the germ of the idea that later grew into the GATT treaty on TRIPs.

The details of the "IP as trade" campaign are quite interesting. The complex effort to sell the idea to US negotiators, national governments, and professional groups shows just how much the members of the IP Committee valued stronger IP rights. While many argue that negotiators from developing countries did not fully perceive the import of what they were agreeing to in the IP area, it is also true that lowered tariffs for agricultural and manufacturing exports were a powerful incentive to strengthen national IP regimes. Regardless of the process, and putting aside for a moment whether TRIPs was in the self-interest of many of its signatories, the end result is quite significant. TRIPs represents a concession of sovereignty in the IP field on the part of many countries, which goes very far beyond the limited national impact of the Paris Convention of 1883. A good deal of national discretion was traded away in exchange for membership in the TRIPs club.

The catalog of TRIPs minimum requirements is long and well known. The Agreement ended the wide variation in the treatment of pharmaceutical inventions across the world, to name one much-noted example. But perhaps the biggest change to international IP law was in enforcement. The Dispute Settlement Board (DSB) is authorized to receive complaints, arbitrate disputes, and – most important – assess compensatory remedies for violations of TRIPs. The Paris Convention, designed to appeal to national self-interest in a limited sphere, never really needed much enforcement. But the much meatier TRIPs obligations, it was understood, would be a much more tempting target for corner cutting or outright defiance. And so, the DSB.

DSB remedies can take many forms, as can be seen from a sampling of IP-related cases. In the infamous "US – Section 110(5) of the U.S. Copyright Act" case, the passage of a revised public performance provision in US copyright law was successfully challenged by the European Union (Dispute Settlement: Dispute DS160, 9 November 2001; https://www.wto.org/english/tratop_e/dispu_e/cases_e/ds160_e.htm). Shrinking the public performance right, by eliminating royalties from some business establishments, harmed holders of composition copyrights in the EU. *See* the one-page summary of the DSB Panel Report, available at https://www.wto.org/english/tratop_e/dispu_e/cases_e/1pagesum_e/ds160sum_e.pdf. The penalty was a one-time payment of $2.3 million for three years' worth of harm, together with a formal demand that the US amend its Copyright Act to come back into compliance with TRIPs. The EU suspended further arbitration because the parties were working toward a mutually satisfactory agreement. *See id.* ("The United States has thereafter presented status reports to the DSB informing that the US Administration will work closely with the US Congress and will continue to confer with the European Union in order to reach a mutually satisfactory resolution of this matter").

A few years after the DSB decision, the United States Trade Representative (USTR), responsible for TRIPs matters, reported that it was still in consultation with Congress. Presumably those consultations are ongoing in a formal sense, but not in any real sense; there the matter has stood for over 13 years, with the USTR webpage still reporting this as a "pending" matter. *See* https://ustr.gov/issue-areas/enforcement/dispute-settlement-proceedings/united-states-—-section-1105-us-copyright-ac ("Status: Pending."). *See also* World Trade Organization, list of DSB cases by treaty, TRIPs page, available at https://www.wto.org/english/tratop_e/dispu_e/dispu_agreements_index_e.htm?id=A26 (DSB 160: "Current status: Authorization to retaliate requested (including 22.6 arbitration)"). This is all a little like saying that the 1976 US presidential election is still "pending" because the Socialist Workers Party never conceded the result, unhappy that its official 0.2 percent vote tally did not match its own internal calculations that it had instead earned 0.3 percent. The lesson being that, though TRIPs has more teeth than the Paris Convention, it is not exactly a tiger. More like an eight-week-old kitten. Even so, some consequences are better than no consequences. Nations do not yield sovereignty in large dollops but in little dribs and drabs. Such is the pace of progress in the world of IP harmonization.

Although the post-TRIPs amendments in domestic US law are important, they pale in contrast to the revolutionary changes the Agreement makes to the IP regimes of many developing countries. To summarize the highlights, all signatories of the Uruguay Round treaty (which, under the Agreement, become members of the newly created World Trade Organization (WTO)) are obligated to:

- include virtually all important commercial fields within the ambit of patentable subject matter, a major change for those countries that have traditionally refused to enforce pharmaceutical patents on public health/access grounds (TRIPs Article 27);
- test patent applications for the presence of an "inventive step" and "industrial application," which are expressly defined as synonymous with the US requirements of, respectively, nonobviousness and utility (*see* Article 27);
- curtail the practice of granting compulsory licenses for patented technology, by (1) requiring a good-faith attempt to license voluntarily, (2) limiting duration, (3) requiring termination if conditions change, and (4) requiring compensation, subject to judicial review (Article 31). See Final Act Embodying the Results of the Uruguay Round of Multilateral Trade Negotiations, Annex 1C: Agreement on Trade-Related Aspects of Intellectual Property Rights, 33 I.L.M. 1197 (1994), available at http://www.wto.org/english/docs_e/legal_e/27-trips.pdf, at Article 31. This Article has since been amended by the inclusion of new Article 41*bis*, which permits WTO member states greater discretion in requiring compulsory licensing of patents covering drugs that are to be exported to countries meeting the original compulsory licensing criteria of Article 31. TRIPS and Public Health: Members Accepting Amendment of the TRIPS Agreement, World Trade Organization, http://www.wto.org/english/tratop_e/trips_e/amendment_e.htm (last updated January 5, 2012) (list of signatory nations under TRIPs that have to date accepted the Article 31*bis* amendment; when two-thirds of the members accept, it will take effect). See Frederick M. Abbott & Jerome H. Reichman, *The Doha Round's Public Health Legacy: Strategies for the Production and Diffusion of Patented Medicines Under the Amended TRIPS Provisions*, 10 J. Int'l Econ. L. 921, 928 (2007); for critiques, see Dina Halajian, *Inadequacy of TRIPs & the Compulsory License: Why Broad Compulsory Licensing Is Not A Viable Solution to the Access to Medicine Problem*, 38 Brook. J. Int'l L. 1191 (2013); Ann Marie Effingham, *Trips Agreement Article 31(b): The Need for Revision*, 46 Seton Hall L. Rev. 883 (2016).

TRIPs also requires signatory nations to establish certain civil and administrative procedures; to provide parties access to evidence held by opposing parties; to make available injunctions, damages, preliminary relief, and other remedies for acts of infringement; to impose certain border control measures; and to establish criminal penalties in the case of counterfeited copyrighted goods. *See id.* Articles 42–61. In short, TRIPs thoroughly regulates the domestic IP law of the signatory nations.

1.3 Transnational legal strategy: a quick overview

For the most part, transnational legal practice is highly fact- and context-dependent. The specific details of a particular business model; particular facts about the business (such as where a product or service is created or manufactured, and where its largest national markets are); particular facts about a specific IP right (the type and strength of trademark or patent; national rules regarding what is copyrightable, etc., etc.); and particular details of a legal dispute (where the legal opponent has its bases of operation, what its primary markets are, what IP it has in which countries, etc.) will usually be the main determinants of an IP owner's business and IP enforcement strategy.

Even so, a few general points are in order regarding transnational strategy.

First, it is important to recognize the reality that, as we have been saying, different nations have different rules regarding IP rights – their acquisition, maintenance, and enforcement. From a business point of view, these differences raise the cost of running an IP program. Even in a situation where several nations have agreed to recognize one centrally granted IP right (such as in the European Union with respect to EU trademarks, or EPO-granted patents), it costs more to acquire and protect an IP right that is valid in two countries than it does for an IP right in only one country. There are translation costs, perhaps higher maintenance fees for maintaining IP rights in multiple countries, etc.

But where, as is more typical, IP rights are sought in very different countries, those with minimal coordination of formal rules, the costs will usually be even higher. This is because, in addition to higher examination or maintenance fees, there is the extra cost of *finding out what the law is* and *conforming a company's behavior to the requirements of the law*. These are costs that transnational practitioners struggle with every day.

Where two or more legal regimes are involved, there are in general two strategies that may be adopted:

- Uniform strategy: do the same things (with very minor variations) in each country – often taking the most stringent or most restrictive

country's law as the law to which you adapt your behavior. Call this *the lowest-common-denominator* strategy (LCD).
- Country-by-country strategy: adapt your activities to the rules and requirements of each country, without regard to the rules and requirements of other countries. Call this a *strict country-by-country* strategy (C-by-C).

What are the pluses and minuses of each strategy? Consider these issues.

Uniform strategy requires a certain amount of information gathering, usually in the form of legal research, to determine which country has the most restrictive rules and requirements in a certain area. So, for example, if a company is considering different trademarks that might be used on a new line of products, this strategy would involve finding out what country has the most restrictive trademark rules. Perhaps the company is considering seeking trademark protection for a product name that incorporates a geographic place name, such as Half Moon Bay brand beer. The company plans to launch the beer (introduce it on the market) in the US, Germany, France, England, and China. Which country among these is the most restrictive regarding trademarks for geographic place names? Would the company be able to register "Half Moon Bay" for beer and related products in all five countries?

Imagine for a minute that EU trademark law is more restrictive regarding place names than either China or the US. Perhaps in the EU, for example, because Half Moon Bay is a town in California, and because in recent years several beer breweries have been started in that town, EU law would object to Half Moon Bay brand beer because the beer is brewed in Los Angeles, and not actually in Half Moon Bay. Imagine that under US and Chinese trademark law, the rule is different: only place names that are very widely and very closely associated with a product type are prohibited (Idaho Potatoes, for example, or Korean Kimchi).

The transnational practitioner has two choices: (1) choose a name for the beer that will be acceptable even in the EU – for example, choose "Half Moon Beer" as the worldwide trademark; or (2) propose a *different* brand name in the EU, that is, call the beer known as "Half Moon Bay" beer in the US and China, by a different brand name in Europe only – for example, "Half Moon" beer. In either case, to help evoke the same consumer association as "Half Moon Bay," the company could add an additional tag-line or branding as a separate, related (subsidiary) trademark, for example, "Brewed Authentic, on the California Coast."

The first option is an LCD option. To evaluate this option, imagine that market testing establishes that the Half Moon beer brand is less appealing to consumers. It is not as evocative, and does not achieve the same level of positive association, as the Half Moon Bay beer brand. To make the analysis more practical, assume that Half Moon beer, if adopted as the worldwide brand name (*i.e.*, an LCD strategy), would have a worldwide value of $600,000. Now consider brand valuation if the company adopts a C-by-C strategy: using Half Moon Bay beer in the US and China, and Half Moon beer in Europe. World valuation of the overall Half Moon/Half Moon Bay brand family under this scenario would be (we will assume) $800,000. One way to look at this is to say that the business value of a C-by-C strategy, as compared to an LCD strategy, is $200,000: the difference between the Half Moon Bay (for China and the US)-Half Moon (for Europe) brand, and the worldwide Half Moon brand.

To be complete, however, the analysis must take account of the benefits of adopting the LCD strategy. To think this through, it will help to understand that there are considerable benefits to adopting a single worldwide brand. Some of these are business related. Consider, for example, the cost of advertising a global brand. For many advertisements on television, the world wide web, and in print media (newspapers and magazines), a global brand can use the same product pictures and drawings in all countries. Some explanatory text may differ from country to country, because languages differ; but the image itself can remain the same.

In addition to these very concrete benefits, there are more subtle and hard-to-value benefits. When people travel (which is common in the contemporary world), advertising in overseas countries continues to build their image and impression of a brand – if there is a single, recognizable global brand. So a Chinese citizen traveling to Paris and seeing an ad for Half Moon Bay beer would be influenced, however minutely, by the ad. But an ad for a different brand would not have the same effect. Seeing an ad for Half Moon beer in Paris, the Chinese traveler might be confused, wondering if it is the same product or something different from the Half Moon Bay beer known in China. There is a cost to these lost associations. (Note that these costs do not factor into the "brand value" estimates noted earlier. Those estimates relate to the stand-alone value of each brand; the value of the trademark, standing alone. Global advertising benefits relate to the value of having a single brand that can be advertised everywhere. Loss in value from not having a single global brand occurs *regardless* of the brand name itself: the loss for not being able to advertise Half Moon beer globally is the same as the loss for not being able to advertise Half Moon Bay beer globally.)

Where a product does not have a single global brand, there are other costs as well. Different brands, with different logos, raise the cost of advertising. Separate product images must be prepared for each market where the product is sold under a separate brand. So in addition to the inescapable costs of adding text in different languages, separate product images will have to be prepared, which raises costs.

Imagine in our Half Moon Bay beer example that the estimated costs of advertising and promoting a single global brand are $300,000 over the life of the product. Next, assume that it is estimated that, to achieve the same level of consumer association with two brands instead of one, advertising and promotion will cost $400,000. The extra cost of $100,000 can be thought of as the extra money that must be spent to make the same overall impression on consumers when there are two brands. It may mean more ads, or more complex ads (*e.g.*, to explain that Half Moon beer in Europe is the same beer people know as Half Moon Bay beer in the US and China); but in any event, it costs more to achieve a given level of brand awareness when there are two brands instead of only one.

Now consider one last item: legal and administrative costs. In general, it will be simpler and easier, and also cheaper, to maintain a single global brand. In some cases, multiple trademark registrations can be obtained with a single registration (this is explained in more detail in Part IV Trademark Law). In addition, because lawyers have to be on the lookout for new trademark registrations and new products with names that are similar to a valuable brand name, having different brand names raises the cost of monitoring for conflicting or overlapping trademarks. With a single global Half Moon global brand, for example, a new registration or new product for Full Moon beer will draw attention (and maybe a demand letter to the new mark's owner). But a new beer called Crescent Bay beer might not. But with two brands, the cost of this activity goes up. Half Moon Bay beer might be too close to Crescent Bay beer for comfort, so this new trademark or product might justify sending a demand letter. With two brands, in other words, there are more possibilities for confusion. More need for policing activity. More oppositions and potential litigation. In a word: higher costs.

Imagine for simplicity that the lifetime cost of maintaining a single brand worldwide is estimated to be $150,000, while the costs of maintaining two (somewhat similar but not identical) brands are estimated to be $225,000. The extra $75,000 represents a legal-administrative cost of the C-by-C strategy, as compared to an LCD strategy.

We can summarize all this in Table 1.1.

Table 1.1 legal-administrative cost of the C-by-C strategy, as compared to an LCD strategy

Item	LCD Strategy	C-by-C Strategy
Brand Value ($)	600,000	800,000
Advertising/Promotion Costs ($)	300,000	400,000
Administrative/Legal Costs ($)	150,000	225,000
Net ($)	150,000	175,000

Under the assumptions laid out here, you can see that the C-by-C strategy makes sense. So the company will register the trademark Half Moon Bay beer for China and the US, and Half Moon beer for the EU.

Notice that the numbers are close, however. With just a minor change here or there, the LCD strategy would be better. So if, for example, the marketing department decided that in fact the worldwide value of the Half Moon beer trademark would be $650,000 instead of $600,000, then the cost savings of the LCD strategy would be enough to justify adopting Half Moon beer as the single, worldwide brand. (The net under this changed assumption would be $25,000 higher for the LCD strategy: a net value of $200,000 versus a net value of $175,000 for the C-by-C strategy.)

Of course this is a simplified and in some ways unrealistic example. In reality, the analysis can be considerably more complex. Imagine having to think through the possibility of three different brands. And for a copyright situation, the analysis might have to consider whether a particular type of work is protectable in all major jurisdictions; if one jurisdiction does not protect a particular type of work against copying, the risk of piracy or duplication in that jurisdiction will have to be estimated. For patented products, the analysis would include patent validity estimates; enforcement costs and possible outcomes; and differences in potential remedies. The simple example here is meant to just give you a flavor of the type of analysis that transnational IP lawyers are asked to conduct every day.

1.4 Other themes of this book

1.4.1 Formal law vs. practical enforcement

Another feature of this book is that we emphasize the difference between formal law, or "law on the books," and the operational reality of what different legal systems actually deliver in practice. The idea is to teach students to understand that the operational context is crucial to the practical application of legal knowledge. So we will emphasize potential roadblocks to practical deployment of formal law, such as (1) expensive/lengthy litigation, (2) difficult procedures, and (3) low damages (making enforcement actions uneconomical). The idea is to place the formal legal rules in real-world context so as to understand overall context and develop the capacity to shape practical strategies.

1.4.2 Convergence vs. divergence

The overall, high-level trend in the IP field has been toward convergence of the various national and regional systems. Early harmonization (the nineteenth-century Berne and Paris Conventions, primarily) was followed by isolated procedural harmonization efforts, and then the big breakthrough of TRIPs in 1995.

At the same time, many historical differences survived the TRIPs process. In addition, post-TRIPs developments, differences in regional growth rates, and idiosyncratic national issues have led to continued divergence in some areas of IP.

It is crucial for students to understand that both these forces – convergence and divergence – continue to exert significant pressure in IP law. The high-level practice of the field consists in part in understanding how these forces are operating at any particular time with respect to a particular issue or problem. Then, in appropriate cases, the well-trained practitioner can adapt strategy accordingly. Meanwhile students can gain an understanding of those areas where transnational convergence ought to be restored or championed.

Part II

Patent protection

2

Introduction to patent law at the transnational level

⁇ INTRODUCTORY PROBLEM

Sue Yu is the founder and CEO of Red Dragon Security Software, Inc. (Red Dragon), of San Francisco, which has since 2008 been in the business of programming and selling security software for large corporate networks. Red Dragon specializes in custom solutions to security problems, meaning that Sue and her seven programmer colleagues write specialized software code that runs on large corporate computer networks. However, beginning in the summer of 2012, Red Dragon began preparing to enter the market for "mass market" security software. Through an arrangement with one of its largest clients, the massive online retail site Rainforest.com, Red Dragon planned to write and distribute a downloadable security software package for smaller computer networks. The target market was small businesses, such as car dealerships or real estate offices, having an internal corporate network with between two and 100 individual computers attached to it.

Sue of Red Dragon assigned a team of programmers to the new mass-market software project, which she and her team called the Dragon Express Project. The team began coding the new product in September of 2012. By the end of October, the team had a draft of the software specification, which described how the code would work, what modules were required, which team members would program which modules, a master flow chart of how the modules would interact, etc. By the end of February the team had a working prototype of the software – a simplified version of the code that showed its basic functioning. In early March, Red Dragon began working with an outside patent law firm, called Wright, Phile, and Waite, to draft a patent application covering the code developed in the Red Dragon Express project.

In October of 2012 Sue was approached by an independent software company, called Belgium Technical Software (BTS), located in Brussels, Belgium. The BTS CEO, Henri Richard, was an old friend of Sue's. Henri told her that BTS was looking to be acquired by another software company, preferably one in the US. Henri told Sue that BTS had decided it needed access to more capital and to a bigger tool of programming talent than they could find in Belgium. BTS specializes in mass-market, downloadable security software for both individual computer owners and smaller corporate networks. When Sue explained to Henri that Red Dragon was working on the Red Dragon Express project to write similar software, Henri insisted that any corporate acquisition discussions between the two companies be conducted using a "firewall" between the acquisition team at Red Dragon and the software development team working on Red Dragon Express. Such a firewall is common in acquisition negotiations; its purpose is to prevent technical information being transmitted from an acquisition target such as BTS to a competing product development team inside the potential acquiring company.

Sue assured Henri that such a firewall would be put in place and respected. Sue assigned her Vice President of operations, Jack Falltrades, to work with Henri so as to evaluate the BTS acquisition. For the remainder of October and November Jack worked exclusively with Henri, going over the background and experience of the BTS programmer team, evaluating the past sales and technical performance of BTS software products, and discussing BTS's newest products and research plans. Henri told Jack that BTS had just recently developed a new version of its security software that ran at the level of a corporate server computer. Called BTS Prime, it used sophisticated testing techniques to test all incoming data streams, especially downloadable files, at the network server before allowing any file in an incoming message or data stream to reach any individual computer on the network that was being run from and monitored by the server computer. As Henri explained, BTS had been running an experimental version of BTS Prime since January of 2012. It was being tested on the internal BTS corporate network, to fine-tune it for market launch. And it had also been used on servers owned by other companies that BTS maintained at its corporate headquarters, as part of a small business BTS had in running corporate networks for other companies.

Jack thought the BTS Prime software might be an especially valuable product for Red Dragon, and that it might make the BTS acquisition more valuable to Red Dragon. So Jack asked Sue Yu of Red Dragon to sit in on a phone call between Jack and the BTS software development team, which took place on February 15, 2013. During this February 15 phone call, Jack asked detailed questions about BTS Prime and its server-level security functions. The BTS team answered with numerous technical details about how BTS Prime works.

No one on the BTS team knew that Sue Yu was listening to the call. Jack asked if BTS had taken any steps to publicize the BTS Prime software. Henri told him that the software had been demonstrated to a group of technical experts assembled by the EU Directorate for Research and Innovation at a "new directions in computing" workshop on March 19, 2012. The purpose of the demonstration was to compete for funding from the EU, which awarded an "Innovation Grant" to the three companies that were judged most innovative by the panel of experts. The workshop was open to all members of the public, though registration was required in advance and all attendees were informed that the demonstrated software might not include technical features that the software developers considered proprietary.

Shortly after the phone call, Sue Yu informed Jack Falltrades that she had decided against acquiring BTS. No further negotiations were conducted.

The Red Dragon Express team filed a patent application on March 18, 2013, listing three members of the team (all Red Dragon employees), plus Sue Yu, the CEO, as co-inventors and entitled "Computer Security System to Prevent Malware." The US Patent and Trademark Office (USPTO) assigned this application number 70045677 ("the '677 Application"). Sue had been mostly an observer of the product development process for Red Dragon Express until late February of 2013. At that time she began to sit in on final product development and testing meetings of the development team. And she contributed several important ideas regarding how to structure Red Dragon Express so as to test for malware using a network server, before any malware was able to reach an individual computer on the network. This feature had not been part of the draft Red Dragon Express software specification in the fall of 2012.

The written description portion of the '677 Red Dragon patent application includes these passages (this is only part of the written description, not the whole text):

> The invention disclosed herein is an improvement over known prior art systems, which generally test for the presence of malicious software ("malware") at the level of individual computers on a network.
> It is inconvenient for a network administrator to have to canvass all individual computers on a network to construct a master database of all malware received in data elements by computers on the network. One object of the present invention (though not the only object) is to improve on this by enabling a network server to construct a database on its own, by collecting malware code from all incoming data streams (Downloadables) and from this collection assembling a database . . .

In the context of this invention, means for deriving security profile data include but are not limited to use of a software module programmed to test incoming data streams (Downloadables) for the presence of malware. Such a module will be structured so as to call on a stored set of known malware commands; and to conduct a comparison between the code in the Downloadable and all malware commands stored in the Malware database which also forms part of this invention. Programmers skilled in the art of software design will readily recognize that such a comparison may be made using any number of well-known techniques, including but not limited to a "look-up table," where incoming potential malware code is compared with the first few characters in each command stored in the table, and if a match is detected with any command stored in the table, a complete comparison may be conducted with the entire stored command.

The '677 Red Dragon application ends with these claims:

1. A computer-based method, comprising the steps of:
   [a] receiving an incoming Downloadable;
   [b] means for deriving security profile data for the Downloadable, said security profile data including a list of suspicious computer operations that may be attempted by the Downloadable; and
   [c] storing the Downloadable security profile data in a database.
2. The computer-based method of claim 1, wherein the incoming Downloadable [step [a]] is received by a network server before said Downloadable is made accessible to individual computers connected to a network mediated by said Server.
3. The computer-based method of claim 1, wherein the incoming Downloadable is received by an individual dedicated security computer connected to a network of other individual computers and said Downloadable security profile database is contained in said individual dedicated security computer.

Red Dragon Express was introduced on the market in October of 2013. Sales were brisk right from the beginning, with revenues from 2013 totaling $7 million, then growing to $35 million in the first full year of sales (2014).

Meanwhile, after the potential for acquisition by Red Dragon fell apart, Henri of BTS began looking for other potential partners. In June of 2013, BTS agreed to exclusively license the BTS Prime software to Softshell Computers, a large manufacturer of server computers based in Munich, Germany, many of which were used for network administration, *i.e.*, to run corporate networks. The license to Softshell included a substantial investment in the ongoing operations of BTS, and also provided that if sales of Softshell servers increased substantially after the license, Softshell would acquire 100 percent of the outstanding shares of BTS – *i.e.*, a complete acquisition. After June, 2013, Softshell advertised its servers as including "new and improved state of the art security software from BTS." Sales did in fact increase and so Softshell acquired BTS in full in January of 2014. One large customer of Softshell is Bavarian Airlines, a very large German air carrier that runs over 50 separate computer networks in its vast operations. Softshell typically earns $10 million per year by licensing its software to companies that purchase new Softshell servers; Bavarian, for example, will often replace 10 of its 50 servers every year, taking a software license for each of the 10 new servers. In addition, a company such as Bavarian might separately license server software from Softshell. But after the first year, Southeast and other companies are free to license server software from companies other than Softshell, which they often do. So Softshell's $10 million license fee is separate from the cost of the server hardware itself, and is earned on older Softshell servers; but Softshell competes with other companies for this market.

One version of the BTS software sold by Softshell, BTS Prime A, works in the conventional way, with incoming messages screened by the network server before they are allowed to pass to individual computers on the network. BTS Prime A is included as part of Softshell's "Alpha Suite" of programs, its top-of-the-line and most sophisticated systems administration software.

Another version of the BTS software, called BTS Prime B, works differently. BTS Prime B is included in Softshell's less expensive suite of system software, called Softshell Beta Suite. The BTS Prime B program in Softshell Beta Suite installs a short screening program on each individual computer attached to a network. This short program looks for certain patterns in downloaded files that are associated with malware. Because of this, BTS Prime B does not stop each incoming data stream (download) at the server; the server lets each download pass on to whichever individual computer requested it. If the short program on the individual computer detects a potential problem in an incoming data stream (download), it stops the download onto the individual computer and directs it to the server computer, where it undergoes more rigorous malware screening. Most corporate licensees of Softshell Beta Suite software are smaller customers, who typically license the software for $1 million per year.

Finally, Softshell, as part of a push toward "cloud computing," has just rolled out (fall of 2016) a new version of its systems software, called Softshell C Suite (their new ads say "the C is for Cloud"). This software resides on a network server computer, but calls on remote servers in the Softshell corporate headquarters for certain system administration functions. One function is malware screening. If a network server detects a data stream (downloadable) that shows signs of being malware, the server sends the data stream to a special malware detection server in Softshell headquarters. This server keeps a database of all malware sent to it by all network servers belonging to all Softshell customers who are running Softshell C Suite software. Thus, instead of building a database of malware on each system server, Softshell C malware software joins together (aggregates) all reported malware on all Softshell servers connected to the Softshell Cloud.

Beginning in 2015, Red Dragon sales executives began to notice a drop-off in sales of Red Dragon Express. When they checked, they saw that a major reason for this was that owners of older Softshell servers had stopped licensing Red Dragon software and were almost all licensing Softshell Prime A or B. Red Dragon's sales were dropping accordingly; throughout 2015 they continued to lag behind 2014 sales figures.

The '677 Red Dragon patent application issued as US Patent 8,834,033 ("the '033 patent") on March 24, 2015. Prosecution had included one rejection, with the examiner citing mostly older patents and publications (pre-2010) as prior art; Red Dragon's patent lawyers had easily overcome the rejection and the claims in the issued patent were identical to those in the original '677 patent application. In August of 2015, Red Dragon sent a letter to Softshell, enclosing a copy of the '033 patent and informing Softshell that "it is time for our two companies to discuss the potential need for a license to the enclosed patent."

After receipt of this letter, Softshell began investigating ways it might escape from any liability under the '033 patent. A member of the Softshell legal team had discovered a research project that yielded software similar to the Red Dragon Express program. Researchers in the Computer Science Department of Zhuming University in China began in 2011 to work on enhanced security system software. In the fall of 2011, one graduate student at Zhuming, Liu Changchang, began a project for her PhD degree research. Changchang set out to create an enhanced security system that would "learn" about malware coming into a network. Her system worked by diverting each incoming data stream (download) onto a "slave computer," which was connected only to the security system on the main network server computer; it was not in connection with other individual computers on the network. Each downloaded file was permitted to run on the slave computer, and a special monitoring system was in place to detect any behavior from the slave computer that would indicate that the downloaded file was malware. If, for example, the downloaded software attempted to erase files on the slave computer; or attempted to infiltrate the operating system of the slave computer; or attempted to overwrite permissions and restrictions files on the slave computer, the monitoring software would pause all operations, make a safe copy of the download (*i.e.*, a copy that could be read and examined, but that would not run or execute, *i.e.*, could not do any harm), and add that safe copy to a database that was maintained on the network server computer.

Changchang discussed her project at length with other graduate students during the fall of 2011. She also sent emails describing it to her four faculty advisors, three of whom were faculty members at Zhuming, and one of whom worked for a Chinese security software company called Great Wall Security Software, which was based in London, England but which had a research division near the Zhuming campus in China. Finally, on April 1, 2012, Changchang created a demonstration version of her software which she showed at a University Science Fair (a two-day "open house" when members of the public could visit the Zhuming campus and learn about the research that was going on there).

Consider what will happen if Red Dragon acquires patents in the US, Europe and China. And also assume that Changchang Liu may establish a competing company in China, seeking to commercialize the research she began in graduate school.

This exemplifies some of the issues we will cover in this Part. After you have finished this Part, return to this Problem and see if you can spot the relevant issues. Pay attention to the need for transnational practices and strategies.

2.1 Introduction

Patent law began as a legal instrument quite at odds with the goal of transnational coordination. It was originally based on a policy of national economic advancement. The earliest patent systems were designed to promote and maintain technological leadership, at the expense of other nation states in many cases. It was in this sense an example of national legislation designed specifically to enhance national wealth vis-à-vis competitor nations. The shorthand label for these policies is "mercantilism." *See* Thomas Nachbar, *Monopoly, Mercantilism, and the Politics of Regulation*, 91 U. Va. L. Rev. 1313, 1318 (2005), (equating mercantilism with "trade regulation for national wealth").

The first true patent system was in the Venetian Republic – a small, independent city-state whose economic power was based on trade between Europe,

Eastern Europe, the Middle East, and Asia. Venetian patents originated in 1474. The Venetian economy was highly dependent on groups of artisans operating under grants from the Republican government. These "guilds," as they were known, set high standards of workmanship in trades such as shipbuilding, glassblowing, leather tanning, and book printing. *See* Robert P. Merges, *From Medieval Guilds to Open Source Software: Informal Norms, Appropriability Institutions, and Innovation* (Working paper, November, 2004), available at https://www.law.berkeley.edu/files/From_Medieval_Guilds_to_Open_Source_Software.pdf. But the guilds also restricted competition, because only members of a guild were allowed to practice a trade. The Venetian government introduced patents into this economic scene as a way of promoting new entrants. *See* Ted Sichelman and Sean O'Connor, *Patents as Promoters of Competition: The Guild Origins of Patent Law in the Venetian Republic*, 49 U. San Diego L. Rev. 1267 (2012). Even though patents were meant to "disrupt" established economic activity, the goal was still to benefit Venice and the Venetian economy.

Venetian patents were implicitly mercantilist; they fit into a general economic policy meant to develop important technologies for Venice and keep them out of the hands of others. Despite the best efforts of the authorities in Venice and elsewhere, however, technology did spread – and with it came the idea of patents. The best example of this was in the movement of experts in textiles and Venetian glassmaking into England. Under the British crown's aggressive mercantile policy, early artisans received a royal grant of exclusivity in exchange for bringing various technologies from other parts of Europe into England. *See* Sean Bottomley, The British Patent System during the Industrial Revolution 1700–1852: From Privilege to Property (2014), at 1–2; Jeremy Phillips, *The English Patent As a Reward for Invention: The Importation of an Idea*, 3 J. Leg. Hist. 74 (1982). Over time, patents came to be abused by the British royalty because they were a convenient way to raise money for the always cash-hungry monarchy. The king or queen would issue patents on well-known, household items, in exchange for some of the profits derived from these monopoly grants. This brought patents into disrepute and led to the Statute of Monopolies in 1624. This statute outlawed crown-backed monopolies, with one important exception: as a reward for creating a new technology or inventions. After 1624, then, patents survived in Britain as an exception to a general prohibition against state-backed monopolies.

The British patent tradition came to America along with many other ideas and practices from the British legal system. Although the British concern with state monopolies was also felt in the early US (particularly in the writings of Thomas Jefferson), the founding generation in the US was in many ways much more supportive of the idea of patents. There were two main reasons: first, the country itself was new, so a legal instrument designed to "promote progress" by encouraging novel technologies caught the spirit of the times. More practically, the US at its founding was divided into two very different geographic regions. There was the small group of former colonies perched along the east coast; and then there was a vast and seemingly endless stretch of territory to the west, which (to the founders, but not the native peoples) seemed largely uninhabited. These founders felt it their destiny to populate and develop this vast territory. But they realized the population was quite small relative to the task ahead. So they embraced new technologies as a way to better leverage the effort and labor of every person. The imperative for economic development, and the important role of the new federal government in facilitating it, was best articulated by Alexander Hamilton.

As technological development spread among Western countries, and as transportation and communication improved, international trade began to increase. By the late nineteenth century, the fruits of industrialization, in the form of machinery and consumer goods, were being sold on an international scale. This brought the first wave of international patent harmonization. The Paris Convention of 1883 permits a patent application in one country to preserve patent priority in countries all around the world. It also sets basic minimum standards for patent protection in all member countries.

The absence of China from the original Paris Union in 1883 was a result of the long period of inward focus and limited trade in mainland Chinese history. The great scholar Joseph Needham, and associates, exhaustively detailed the thousands of technological and scientific "firsts" originating in China, beginning long before the first millennium of the Common Era. Needham's *Science and Civilization in China* totals 27 volumes and is still being completed. In addition to scientific innovation, many rulers during the dynastic era did promote trade and the projection of power overseas; the most famous example of this is the "treasure fleets," large, technically advanced exploration/military/trading ships that explored the oceans of Asia, Africa, and the Middle East. *See* Louise Levathes, When China Ruled the Seas: The Treasure Fleet of the Dragon Throne, 1405–1433 (1996). But the fleet was disbanded later in the fifteenth century, and China entered a long period of self-sufficiency. Scholars continue to debate the causes and consequences of China's long "inward turn," which has come to be known as the Needham Puzzle. *See* Justin Yifu Lin, *The Needham Puzzle, the Weber Question, and China's Miracle: Long-Term Performance since the Sung Dynasty*, 1 China Economic Journal 63 (2008); Toby E. Huff, The Rise of Early Modern Science: Islam, China, and the West (1993) (exploring unique social/intellectual factors in the West that promoted the "scientific revolution" beginning in the sixteenth century); Benjamin A. Elman, On Their Own Terms: Science in China, 1550–1900 (2005).

The second great wave of international patent harmonization culminated in the TRIPs Agreement of 1995. This coincided with the rise of mainland China as a great industrial and trading power, and formed one pillar in the international trade structure maintained by the WTO. TRIPs further increased international minimum standards, and even included a primitive enforcement mechanism to bring pressure to bear on countries that fail to comply with the standards of protection in the Agreement.

Paris and TRIPs show that world patent systems have come a long way from their early, mercantile roots. Even so, national economic development continues to joust with the demands of world trade. Patent policy must now do a balancing act, promoting internal economic growth, which often depends on robust exports abroad, yet permitting non-nationals access to national patent systems and the domestic markets they are connected with. The results are sometimes uneven. Paris and TRIPs make it possible to obtain patents on a broad international scale. But equal success in asserting and enforcing patents has at times been more elusive. Thus the next frontier in patent harmonization may well be greater efforts to make national patent systems more even-handed when it comes to patent enforcement by nationals and non-nationals.

2.2 Some basic transnational institutions and practices

The heart of the Paris Convention, from a practical perspective, is the right of international priority established in Article 4.A.(1). *See* Paris Convention, available at http://www.wipo.int/treaties/en/text.jsp?file_id=288514. This says: "Any person who has duly filed an application for a patent [or industrial design or trademark] in one of the countries of the [Paris] Union, or his successor in title, shall enjoy, for the purpose of filing in the other countries, a right of priority during the periods hereinafter fixed" (*id.*). The "priority period" for patents is one year from the date of first filing in a Paris Union country (Article 4.C.(1)). Priority applies to any filing that is "equivalent to a regular national filing under the domestic legislation of any country of the Union" (Paris Convention Article 4.A.(2)). Such a filing is defined as "any filing that is adequate to establish the date on which the application was filed in the country concerned..." (Article 4.A.(3)).

Stated simply, the Paris Convention means an inventor can file in any Paris Union country, and if he or she files in any other Union country within one year, the priority date for the other filing(s) will be the original filing date.

Practically speaking, this means that an inventor can "preserve" a priority date without making a series of simultaneous filings in many countries. It gives an inventor time to decide where else, beyond the original country of filing, he or she might want to pursue patent rights.

Two other key concepts in the Paris Convention have significant practical ramifications. First, the priority application establishes a priority date even if that application is later rejected by the national patent office where it was first filed. Second, an applicant who files in country B, relying on his or her priority date from a first filing in country B, must be treated exactly the same as an inventor who lives in country B and files an application there. The first principle is known as "independence of applications"; the second is called "national treatment." *See* Article 4.A.(3); Article 4*bis* (independence); Article 2(1) (national treatment).

2.2.1 Introduction to European patent law

The European patent system is, as of this writing, comprised primarily of the European Patent Convention (EPC), originally adopted in 1973 and last revised in 2016 (16th ed., including Regulations), *see* http://documents.epo.org/projects/babylon/eponet.nsf/0/F9FD0B02F9D1A6B4C1258003004DF610/$File/EPC_16th_edition_2016_en.pdf, and the national patent offices and courts of individual European countries. The EPC created the European Patent Office (EPO), which examines European patent applications according to the rules laid down in the EPC. Prosecution of a single European application in the EPO leads to the issuance of a bundle of national patents in EPC member states; the applicant chooses which countries' national patents will issue. With the important exception of EPO Oppositions, enforcement of patents (including post-EPO invalidation hearings and defenses) takes place in national patent courts. The EPC has been adopted by a total of 38 contracting states, which includes 11 countries that are not members of the EU (including Switzerland, Turkey, Iceland and Norway). *See* https://www.epo.org/about-us/organisation/member-states.html.

The long-awaited (and still not operational) Community Patent Convention (CPC) and unitary Europe-wide patent will change this system when it takes effect, which was originally scheduled for 2017, but delayed. The CPC calls for a Unitary Patent, good throughout all EU Member States, as well as a Unified Patent Court system whose rulings would also have force throughout the EU. See European Patent Office, "Unified Patent Court," available at https://www.epo.org/law-practice/unitary.html. But the pending exit of the UK from the EU ("Brexit") has thrown into doubt the timetable for operation of the new Unitary Patent and Unitary Patent Court systems. See Bardehle Pagenburg (law firm), "The Unitary Patent & Unified Patent Court System – Perspectives after the Brexit Referendum," https://www.bardehle.com/ip-news-knowledge/ip-news/news-detail/the-unitary-patent-unified-patent-court-system-perspectives-after-the-brexit-referendum.html (accessed May 31, 2017); see also Jabeen Bhatti, "Germany Puts Brakes on EU Patent Court Launch," Pat. Copyrt. & Trademark Daily Rep. (BNA), June 14, 2017, available at http://iplaw.bna.com/iprc/5007/split_display.adp?fedfid=114237794&vname=ptdbulallissues&jd=a0m6k8g3f6&split=0 (describing German Constitutional Court challenge to ratification of Unified Patent Court legislation).

Currently the EPO, operating under the EPC, receives roughly 160,000 patent applications per year. See EPO, "European Patent Applications," available at https://www.epo.org/about-us/annual-reports-statistics/annual-report/2016/statistics/patent-applications.html#tab1. This compares favorably with national patent offices in Europe; in Germany, for example, there were slightly more than 72,000 patent applications filed in 2015. See http://www.wipo.int/ipstats/en/statistics/country_profile/profile.jsp?code=DE. There were, by contrast, fewer than 20,000 patent applications filed in the United Kingdom patent office. See http://www.wipo.int/ipstats/en/statistics/country_profile/profile.jsp?code=GB.

Because the EPO is the de facto standard setter for European patent law, we consider below a fair number of decisions from EPO Oppositions. Under the EPC, an opposition may be filed by any party within nine months of issuance of an EPO patent. See EPC (16th ed.), at Article 99, available at http://documents.epo.org/projects/babylon/eponet.nsf/0/F9FD0B02F9D1A6B4C1258003004DF610/$File/EPC_16th_edition_2016_en.pdf. Grounds for oppositions are that: (1) the patent does not meet the requirements of one or more of Articles 52 to 57 ("susceptible of industrial application," similar to US utility; not contrary to "ordre public" (public policy); patentable subject matter; novelty; and inventive step); (2) the specification of the patent does not adequately disclose the invention; or (3) the claims exceed the scope of what was disclosed in the priority application on which the final specification is based (EPC, Article 100).

In addition to EPO oppositions, national patents issued by the EPO may be challenged in various ways in national courts of EU Member States. In some countries, notably Germany, separate judicial invalidation procedures must be pursued; invalidity defenses in patent infringement suits are not permitted. In others, patent challengers may file invalidation procedures or raise invalidity defenses in infringement proceedings. Even in these purely national proceedings, however, EPO validity decisions in Oppositions are important precedents, binding to various degrees.

For claim interpretation, infringement rulings, and remedies, national law is the relevant source of European authority; the EPO does not in general rule on these matters. And so we consider for these topics rulings from various national courts, particularly Germany and Britain.

2.2.2 The basics of Chinese patent law

In 2016, the State Intellectual Property Office (SIPO) in Beijing received 3,465,000 patent applications (for invention patents, utility models ("simple patents"), and design patents). This is the largest volume of patent applications of any national patent office. Of these, 1,339,000 were for invention (or "utility") patents. *See* http://www.sipo.gov.cn/twzb/2016ngjzscqjzygztjsjjy gqkxwfbh/. In that same year, SIPO granted over 400,000 invention (utility) patents. *See* http://english.sipo.gov.cn/statistics/2016/12/201704/ t20170407_1309323.html. As of the end of 2015, the World Intellectual Property Organization (WIPO) estimated that there were over 1,472,000 patents in force in China (*i.e.*, patents not yet expired). *See* http://www.wipo. int/ipstats/en/statistics/country_profile/profile.jsp?code=CN. Because the Chinese economy is large, growing fast, and on a planned trajectory to include more "high-value" or research-intensive products, and because China is such a large manufacturing center, both domestic and overseas patent applicants are increasingly seeing the need for solid patent protection in China. *See* Scott Kennedy, The Fat Tech Dragon, Benchmarking China's Innovation Drive, Center for Strategic and International Studies, Aug. 29, 2017, available at https://www.csis.org/analysis/fat-tech-dragon (summarizing Chinese government policy to increase innovation in the Chinese economy); Daniel R. Cahoy et al., *Global Patent Chokepoints*, 20 Stan. Tech. L. Rev. 213 (2017) (describing growing strategy of challenging technology competitors by obtaining patents in manufacturing centers – "chokepoints" – rather than in multiple countries where product purchasers are located).

2.2.2.1 *Chinese patents: types and strategies*

Besides invention (utility) patents, SIPO in China also issues utility models (UMs) and design patents. UMs, traditionally referred to in some countries as "petty" (or small) patents, can be obtained for many types of inventions, including most inventions that might also qualify for invention patents. The reason so many applicants seek UMs in China is that (1) they issue quickly, with minimal official examination, and (2) therefore they can be enforced quickly, giving a measure of legal protection in a short period of time. This is obviously helpful in an active and competitive economy such as China's. A Chinese UM comes with only a 10-year term of protection (the same as for a Chinese design patent). *See* http://english.sipo.gov.cn/FAQ/200904/t20090408_449726.html. An issued UM cannot be converted into an invention patent in China. It is, however, possible to file parallel UM and invention patent applications if they are filed on the same day. Upon notification of grant of an invention patent, the UM must be abandoned. This means in effect that a UM can be used as "interim protection" during the pendency of an invention patent application.

Design patents are discussed in detail in Chapter 6.

2.2.2.2 *Enforcement options in China*

After a patent is issued the owner may choose to enforce it. There are two primary routes to enforcement in China: administrative enforcement, through regional enforcement offices of SIPO; and through court actions.

SIPO regional offices are located in each of China's 31 provinces. *See* Daniel R. Cahoy et al., *Global Patent Chokepoints*, 20 Stan. Tech. L. Rev. 213, 226 (2017). In general, these proceedings are conducted as administrative investigations, with a target time to resolution of four months. Remedies are limited to injunctions and criminal penalties; these proceedings cannot lead to an award of damages. The outcome of the enforcement action can be appealed to a civil court. Brian J. Love, Christian Helmers & Markus Eberhardt, *Patent Litigation in China: Protecting Rights or the Local Economy?*, 18 Vand. J. Ent. & Tech. L. 713, 722-23 (2016). Appeals begin at the Intermediate People's Court (see below). The SIPO offices handle two types of cases: counterfeiting cases, where a patent owner alleges large-scale identical copying; and patent disputes, where an accused infringer defends its actions more vigorously and the overall proceeding looks more like a patent trial.

According to a 2016 SIPO report, SIPO offices nationwide handled 48,916 patent administrative cases in 2016, of which patent dispute cases amounted to 20,859, up by 42.8 percent from 2015; there were also 28,057 counterfeit patent cases, up by 32.1 percent over 2015. *See* State Intellectual Property Office of the PRC, 2016 Intellectual Property Rights Protection in China

(White Paper), available at http://english.sipo.gov.cn/laws/whitepapers/201709/P020170901588164914494.pdf.

An alternative administrative enforcement route is available through the General Administration of Customs (GAC), a border-enforcement authority that operates in some ways like the International Trade Commission (ITC) and Customs and Border Control agencies in the US. A unique feature of China's GAC is that it has the authority to block exports as well as imports, making it a potentially powerful tool for enforcement against infringing manufacturers in China. See Intellectual Property Rights, Embassy of the US, Beijing (Sept 7, 2017), avail at https://archive.org/details/perma_cc_XLW5-BFZ3 [https://perma.cc/XLW5-BFZ3].

2.2.2.3 Basic Court Structure

The basic structure of civil courts in China looks like this:

Basic People's Courts → Intermediate People's Courts → Higher People's Court → Supreme people's court.

The initial court where a trial is held varies, depending on the parties and the amount in question. In addition, a court of "second instance," such as the Intermediate People's Court acting after an initial trial in a basic People's Court, may re-try a case, rather than simply take a case on appeal. The provisions regarding when retrials are permissible are set out in the Civil Procedure Law of China:

Article 10

When trying civil cases, the people's courts shall apply the collegial bench, disqualification, open trial and "final after two trials" systems in accordance with law.

Article 198

Where the president of a people's court at any level discovers any error in any effective judgment, ruling or consent judgment of the court and deems a retrial necessary, the president shall submit it to the judicial committee for deliberation and decision.
   Where the Supreme People's Court discovers any error in any effective judgment, ruling or consent judgment of a local people's court at any level or a people's court at a higher level discovers any error in any effective judgment, ruling or consent judgment of a people's court at a lower level, the Supreme People's Court

or the court at a higher level shall have the power to directly retry the case or specify a people's court at a lower level to retry the case.

Article 199

A party which deems that an effective judgment or ruling is erroneous may file a petition for retrial with the people's court at the next higher level; and if the parties on one side are numerous or the parties on both sides are citizens, the parties may file a petition for retrial with the original trial people's court. Where a party files a petition for retrial, the execution of the judgment or ruling shall not be discontinued.

To return to issues of court structure, note that the Intellectual Property Courts in Beijing, Shanghai and Guangzhou are at the same hierarchical jurisdiction level as the Intermediate People's Court. An appeal from the Beijing IP court, for example, goes to the Higher People's Court of Beijing. The Supreme People's Court (SPC) takes only major or important cases, though in recent years this has included a fair number of IP cases. To be precise, the SPC accepted 369 civil IP cases in 2016, and concluded 383 total cases (including cases filed in previous years).

Local Chinese courts handled 12,357 initial patent cases in 2016, up by 6.46 percent from 2015.

2.3 Patent validity determinations

In all modern patent systems, patents are applied for in government patent offices. These are often national offices, such as SIPO, the mainland Chinese patent office; and the USPTO. In Europe, most inventors apply for patents at the EPO. In each of these offices, professionals trained in technology and familiar with patent office procedures examine applications to see if they meet the statutory requirements for patentability. To become an issued patent, a patent application must meet all the requirements of patentability. The first requirement is that the invention be the *type of invention* that patent law is meant to cover; that is, the invention must claim something that falls within the bounds of "patentable subject matter." Beyond this first requirement, the invention must also be adequately described to prove the inventor deserves the claims he or she is seeking (the disclosure or description requirement); it must be something new, that is, something that has not appeared in the public record of all prior inventions (the novelty requirement); and it must be a nontrivial advance over what was known before (the inventive step, or nonobviousness, requirement).

Even after a patent issues from a national patent office, it may still be challenged by others who believe the patent does not in fact meet the statutory requirements. This can take place in an administrative challenge to the patent in the patent office where it was issued, or in a separate court proceeding. In many countries, in particular the US, a patent can also be challenged if the owner of the patent alleges that someone is infringing the patent. Invalidity of the patent, in other words, can be raised as a defense by someone accused of patent infringement.

We begin with the requirements of patentability in the US. Some of the cases below arose when an inventor was trying to get a patent and the patent office refused to issue it. These are appeals from rejections in the USPTO. Other cases in the following chapters arose after a patent was issued; the invalidity of the patent was raised as a defense during patent litigation.

3
Patentable subject matter

Section 101 of the US Patent Act of 1952 says:

> Whoever invents or discovers any new and useful process, machine, manufacture, or composition of matter, or any new and useful improvement thereof, may obtain a patent therefor, subject to the conditions and requirements of this title.

This lays out the general categories of patentable subject matter; it has changed little since the original section 1 of the 1790 Patent Act, which allowed patents for any "art, manufacture, engine, machine, or device, or any improvement therein . . ." (Patent Act of 1790, Ch. 7, 1 Stat. 109-112 (April 10, 1790)).

Despite the broad and absolute language ("any . . .") and the wide scope of the categories ("machine, manufacture, or composition of matter . . ."), the US Supreme Court began in the nineteenth century to exclude certain claimed inventions from patentability. Over time, culminating in a series of cases after 2012, these limitations crystallized into three "limitations" on patentability which now dominate the discussion and analysis of patentable subject matter.

The earliest exploration of limits on patentability came as the Court considered some early cases on process patents. In the early case of *Le Roy v. Tatham*, 55 U.S. 156 (1852), for example, the Court considered a patent that disclosed a new way of making lead pipes. Instead of pouring hot lead into a mold, the inventors in the *Le Roy* case put the lead under pressure and high heat in a closed chamber, which made a superior pipe, in particular because pipes formed this way are easier to weld together. The patent claimed as the invention the combination of machinery used, or any variation substantially similar, which would produce the superior result of better lead. The district court had interpreted this to mean that the specific machinery used by the inventors was not important, it was the overall process. The Supreme Court held that this instruction was an error, and reversed the jury verdict below in favor of the inventors: "We think there was error in the above instruction, that the novelty of the combination of the machinery, specifically claimed by the patentees as their invention, was not a material fact for the jury, and that on that ground, the judgment must be reversed" (*Le Roy v. Tatham*, 55 U.S. 156, 177 (1852)).

According to the Supreme Court, the problem with the district court's interpretation of the patent was that it ignored the language chosen by the inventor when drafting his claim:

> What we claim by or invention . . . is the combination of the following parts above described, to wit, the core and bridge or guide-piece, the chamber, and the die, when used to form pipes of metal, under heat and pressure, in the manner set forth, or in any other manner substantially the same (*id.*, at 176).

In addition, the Court pointed out, a claim that was not limited to either specific machinery or a very detailed description of the process would basically cover all ways of achieving the end result or "effect" of superior lead. As the Court said, "A patent is not good for an effect, or the result of a certain process, as that would prohibit all other persons from making the same thing by any means whatsoever. This, by creating monopolies, would discourage arts and manufactures, against the avowed policy of the patent laws" (*Le Roy v. Tatham*, 55 U.S. 156, 175 (1852)). A strong dissent by three Justices disagreed with the majority's interpretation of the claim, arguing that "if the principle is stated to be applicable to any special purpose, so as to produce any result previously unknown, in the way and for the objects described, the patent is good. It is no longer an abstract principle. It becomes to be a principle turned to account . . ." (*Le Roy v. Tatham*, 55 U.S. 156, 185 (1852) (Nelson, J., dissenting)).

In leading up to its holding of unpatentability, the majority opinion of the Court equated the word "effect" with the word "principle," which the district court had used in its jury instruction. It was right at this point that the Supreme Court introduced the idea of implied limitations on the categories of patentable subject matter:

> The word principle is used by elementary writers on patent subjects, and sometimes in adjudications of courts, with such a want of precision in its application, as to mislead. It is admitted, that a principle is not patentable. A principle, in the abstract, is a fundamental truth; an original cause; a motive; these cannot be patented, as no one can claim in either of them an exclusive right. Nor can an exclusive right exist to a new power, should one be discovered in addition to those already known. Through the agency of machinery a new steam power may be said to have

been generated. But no one can appropriate this power exclusively to himself, under the patent laws. The same may be said of electricity, and of any other power in nature, which is alike open to all, and may be applied to useful purposes by the use of machinery (*Le Roy v. Tatham*, 55 U.S. 156, 174–75 (1852)).

As the Court itself said, in a later case, "The mistake has undoubtedly arisen from confounding a patent for a process with a patent for a mere principle" (*Tilghman v. Proctor*, 102 U.S. 707, 726 (1880)). By the later nineteenth century, this misunderstanding had been rectified: "Thus, an art – a process – which is useful, is as much the subject of a patent as a machine, manufacture, or composition of matter" (*Dolbear v. American Bell Telephone Co.*, 126 U.S. 1, 533 (1888)). In the meantime, the holding of *LeRoy* had been boiled down to a simple statement: "[T]he discovery of a principle in natural philosophy or physical science, is not patentable" (*O'Reilly v. Morse*, 56 U.S. 62, 116 (1853)).

Other cases from the late nineteenth and early twentieth centuries repeated the language from *Le Roy*. "[A] scientific truth, or the mathematical expression of it, is not patentable invention" (*Mackay Radio & Tel. Co. v. Radio Corp. of Am.*, 306 U.S. 86, 94 (1939)). "[P]atents cannot issue for the discovery of the phenomena of nature," the Court said, in a case where the inventor combined a series of natural bacteria into a useful combined product (*Funk Bros. Seed Co. v. Kalo Inoculant Co.*, 333 U.S. 127, 130 (1948)).

By the time the first computer program patent appeared before the Supreme Court in 1972, the "exceptions" to the patentable invention categories under §101 had been distilled into a simple three-part statement: "Phenomena of nature, though just discovered, mental processes, and abstract intellectual concepts are not patentable, as they are the basic tools of scientific and technological work" (*Gottschalk v. Benson*, 409 U.S. 63, 67 (1972)). By 1980, the three "exceptions" had been slightly recast, into what are now the well-recognized triad. See *Diamond v. Chakrabarty*, 447 U.S. 303, 309 (1980) ("The laws of nature, physical phenomena, and abstract ideas have been held not patentable"). These three types of claimed inventions were recognized as "exceptions" in 2010 (*Bilski v. Kappos*, 561 U.S. 593, 601 (2010), speaking of the "three specific exceptions").

It is these three "exceptions" – (1) laws of nature, (2) physical phenomena, and (3) abstract ideas – that drive much of the recent, complex, and highly influential case law in this area. In fact, it is accurate to say that US patentability determinations now focus primarily on the *exceptions* rather than the statutory *categories*. To understand the policies behind these exceptions, and the analysis required to apply them, consider first a 2014 case presenting a claim to a computer-based system for lowering the risk of selling things to buyers on credit.

3.1 Software and business methods

Alice Corp. Pty. Ltd. v. CLS Bank International
134 S.Ct. 2347 (2014)

Justice THOMAS delivered the opinion of the Court.

The patents at issue in this case disclose a computer-implemented scheme for mitigating "settlement risk" (*i.e.,* the risk that only one party to a financial transaction will pay what it owes) by using a third-party intermediary. The question presented is whether these claims are patent eligible under 35 U.S.C. §101, or are instead drawn to a patent-ineligible abstract idea. We hold that the claims at issue are drawn to the abstract idea of intermediated settlement, and that merely requiring generic computer implementation fails to transform that abstract idea into a patent-eligible invention. We therefore affirm the judgment of the United States Court of Appeals for the Federal Circuit.

Petitioner Alice Corporation is the assignee of several patents that disclose schemes to manage certain forms of financial risk. [From footnote: The patents at issue are United States Patent Nos. 5,970,479 (the '479 patent), 6,912,510, 7,149,720, and 7,725,375.]

The claims at issue relate to a computerized scheme for mitigating "settlement risk" – *i.e.,* the risk that only one party to an agreed-upon financial exchange will satisfy its obligation. In particular, the claims are designed to facilitate the exchange of financial obligations between two parties by using a computer system as a third-party intermediary.

[From footnote: The parties agree that claim 33 of the '479 patent is representative of the method claims. Claim 33 recites:

> A method of exchanging obligations as between parties, each party holding a credit record and a debit record with an exchange institution, the credit records and debit records for exchange of predetermined obligations, the method comprising the steps of:
> (a) creating a shadow credit record and a shadow debit record for each stakeholder party to be held independently by a supervisory institution from the exchange institutions;
> (b) obtaining from each exchange institution a start-of-day balance for each shadow credit record and shadow debit record;
> (c) for every transaction resulting in an exchange obligation, the supervisory institution adjusting each respective party's shadow credit record or shadow debit record, allowing only these transactions that do not result in the value of the shadow debit record being less

CASE *(continued)*

than the value of the shadow credit record at any time, each said adjustment taking place in chronological order, and

(d) at the end-of-day, the supervisory institution instructing on[e] of the exchange institutions to exchange credits or debits to the credit record and debit record of the respective parties in accordance with the adjustments of the said permitted transactions, the credits and debits being irrevocable, time invariant obligations placed on the exchange institutions.]

The intermediary creates "shadow" credit and debit records (*i.e.,* account ledgers) that mirror the balances in the parties' real-world accounts at "exchange institutions" (*e.g.,* banks). The intermediary updates the shadow records in real [to make sure that the buyer of an item has enough money in its account to pay for it. The Federal Circuit agreed with the district court, finding the claims invalid under §101].

Section 101 of the Patent Act defines the subject matter eligible for patent protection. It provides:

> Whoever invents or discovers any new and useful process, machine, manufacture, or composition of matter, or any new and useful improvement thereof, may obtain a patent therefor, subject to the conditions and requirements of this title. 35 U.S.C. §101.

"We have long held that this provision contains an important implicit exception: Laws of nature, natural phenomena, and abstract ideas are not patentable." *Association for Molecular Pathology v. Myriad Genetics, Inc.,* [133 S.Ct. 2107 (2013)]. We have interpreted §101 and its predecessors in light of this exception for more than 150 years. *Bilski, supra,* at 601–602; see also *O'Reilly v. Morse,* 15 How. 62 (1854); *Le Roy v. Tatham,* 14 How. 156 (1853).

We have described the concern that drives this exclusionary principle as one of pre-emption. See, *e.g., Bilski, supra,* at 611–612 (upholding the patent "would pre-empt use of this approach in all fields, and would effectively grant a monopoly over an abstract idea"). Laws of nature, natural phenomena, and abstract ideas are "the basic tools of scientific and technological work." *Myriad, supra,* [at 2116]. At the same time, we tread carefully in construing this exclusionary principle lest it swallow all of patent law. Thus, an invention is not rendered ineligible for patent simply because it involves an abstract concept. See *Diamond v. Diehr,* 450 U.S. 175, 187 (1981). "[A]pplication[s]" of such concepts "to a new and useful end," we have said, remain eligible for patent protection. *Gottschalk v. Benson,* 409 U.S. 63, 67 (1972).

In *Mayo Collaborative Services v. Prometheus Laboratories, Inc.,* [132 S.Ct. 1289 (2012)], we set forth a framework for distinguishing patents that claim laws of nature, natural phenomena, and abstract ideas from those that claim patent-eligible applications of those concepts. First, we determine whether the claims at issue are directed to one of those patent-ineligible concepts. If so, we then ask, "[w]hat else is there in the claims before us?" *Id.,* at [1297]. To answer that question, we consider the elements of each claim both individually and "as an ordered combination" to determine whether the additional elements

CASE *(continued)*

"transform the nature of the claim" into a patent-eligible application. *Id.,* at [1298]. We have described step two of this analysis as a search for an "inventive concept" – *i.e.,* an element or combination of elements that is "sufficient to ensure that the patent in practice amounts to significantly more than a patent upon the [ineligible concept] itself." *Id.,* at [1294].

We must first determine whether the claims at issue are directed to a patent-ineligible concept. We conclude that they are: These claims are drawn to the abstract idea of intermediated settlement.

The "abstract ideas" category embodies "the longstanding rule that '[a]n idea of itself is not patentable.'" *Benson, supra.* In *Benson,* for example, this Court rejected as ineligible patent claims involving an algorithm for converting binary-coded decimal numerals into pure binary form, holding that the claimed patent was "in practical effect . . . a patent on the algorithm itself." 409 U.S., at 71–72.

We most recently addressed the category of abstract ideas in *Bilski v. Kappos,* 561 U.S. 593 (2010). The claims at issue in *Bilski* described a method for hedging against the financial risk of price fluctuations. Claim 1 recited a series of steps for hedging risk, including: (1) initiating a series of financial transactions between providers and consumers of a commodity; (2) identifying market participants that have a counter risk for the same commodity; and (3) initiating a series of transactions between those market participants and the commodity provider to balance the risk position of the first series of consumer transactions. *Id.,* at 599. Claim 4 "pu[t] the concept articulated in claim 1 into a simple mathematical formula." *Ibid.* The remaining claims were drawn to examples of hedging in commodities and energy markets.

"[A]ll members of the Court agree[d]" that the patent at issue in *Bilski* claimed an "abstract idea." *Id.,* at 609. Specifically, the claims described "the basic concept of hedging, or protecting against risk." *Id.,* at 611. The Court explained that "[h]edging is a fundamental economic practice long prevalent in our system of commerce and taught in any introductory finance class." *Ibid.*

It follows from our prior cases, and *Bilski* in particular, that the claims at issue here are directed to an abstract idea. Petitioner's claims involve a method of exchanging financial obligations between two parties using a third-party intermediary to mitigate settlement risk. The intermediary creates and updates "shadow" records to reflect the value of each party's actual accounts held at "exchange institutions," thereby permitting only those transactions for which the parties have sufficient resources. At the end of each day, the intermediary issues irrevocable instructions to the exchange institutions to carry out the permitted transactions.

On their face, the claims before us are drawn to the concept of intermediated settlement, *i.e.,* the use of a third party to mitigate settlement risk. Like the risk hedging in *Bilski,* the concept of intermediated settlement is "a fundamental economic practice long prevalent in our system of commerce." *Ibid.* Thus, intermediated settlement, like hedging, is an "abstract idea" beyond the scope of §101.

CASE *(continued)*

[W]e need not labor to delimit the precise contours of the "abstract ideas" category in this case. It is enough to recognize that there is no meaningful distinction between the concept of risk hedging in *Bilski* and the concept of intermediated settlement at issue here. Both are squarely within the realm of "abstract ideas" as we have used that term.

Because the claims at issue are directed to the abstract idea of intermediated settlement, we turn to the second step in *Mayo*'s framework. We conclude that the method claims, which merely require generic computer implementation, fail to transform that abstract idea into a patent-eligible invention.

At *Mayo* step two, we must examine the elements of the claim to determine whether it contains an "inventive concept" sufficient to "transform" the claimed abstract idea into a patent-eligible application. [132 S.Ct. at 1294]. A claim that recites an abstract idea must include "additional features" to ensure "that the [claim] is more than a drafting effort designed to monopolize the [abstract idea]." *Id.*, at [1297]. *Mayo* made clear that transformation into a patent-eligible application requires "more than simply stat[ing] the [abstract idea] while adding the words 'apply it.'" *Id.*, at [1294].

Mayo itself is instructive. The patents at issue in *Mayo* claimed a method for measuring metabolites in the bloodstream in order to calibrate the appropriate dosage of thiopurine drugs in the treatment of autoimmune diseases. The respondent in that case contended that the claimed method was a patent-eligible application of natural laws that describe the relationship between the concentration of certain metabolites and the likelihood that the drug dosage will be harmful or ineffective. But methods for determining metabolite levels were already "well known in the art," and the process at issue amounted to "nothing significantly more than an instruction to doctors to apply the applicable laws when treating their patients." [*id.*, at 1298].

[T]he mere recitation of a generic computer cannot transform a patent-ineligible abstract idea into a patent-eligible invention. There is no dispute that a computer is a tangible system (in § 101 terms, a "machine"), or that many computer-implemented claims are formally addressed to patent-eligible subject matter. But if that were the end of the § 101 inquiry, an applicant could claim any principle of the physical or social sciences by reciting a computer system configured to implement the relevant concept.

[T]he relevant question is whether the claims here do more than simply instruct the practitioner to implement the abstract idea of intermediated settlement on a generic computer. They do not.

Taking the claim elements separately, the function performed by the computer at each step of the process is "[p]urely conventional." *Mayo, supra,* at [1299]. Using a computer to create and maintain "shadow" accounts amounts to electronic recordkeeping – one of the most basic functions of a computer. The same is true with respect to the use of a computer to obtain data, adjust account balances, and issue automated instructions; all of these computer functions are "well-understood, routine, conventional activit[ies]" previously known to the industry. *Mayo*, [at 1297]. In short, each step does no more than require a generic computer to perform generic computer functions.

> **CASE** *(continued)*
>
> Petitioner's claims to a computer system and a computer-readable medium fail for substantially the same reasons. As to its system claims, petitioner emphasizes that those claims recite "specific hardware" configured to perform "specific computerized functions." But what petitioner characterizes as specific hardware – a "data processing system" with a "communications controller" and "data storage unit," for example – is purely functional and generic. Nearly every computer will include a "communications controller" and "data storage unit" capable of performing the basic calculation, storage, and transmission functions required by the method claims.
>
> Put another way, the system claims are no different from the method claims in substance. The method claims recite the abstract idea implemented on a generic computer; the system claims recite a handful of generic computer components configured to implement the same idea.
>
> Because petitioner's system and media claims add nothing of substance to the underlying abstract idea, we hold that they too are patent ineligible under §101.
>
> * * *
>
> For the foregoing reasons, the judgment of the Court of Appeals for the Federal Circuit is affirmed.
>
> It is so ordered.

NOTES

1. The Court refers to its 2010 decision in *Bilski v. Kappos*, 561 U.S. 593 (2010). There an inventor sought a patent on a process for hedging risks – making coordinated investments that "cancel out" the risk of changing prices in some product that sellers sell and buyers need. The dependent claims in the patent in *Bilski* described specific applications in the field of energy. So, for example, an intermediary company enters into "fixed-price" contracts with coal mining companies, and at the same time enters into fixed-price contracts with power companies that burn coal in their power-generation plants. If the price of coal goes way up, the power plants are protected; if it goes way down, the mining companies are protected. The intermediary takes a small cut to pay for its trouble.

   The Court rejected the claims as covering an unpatentable abstract idea, citing three of its earlier software patent cases from the 1970s and 1980s:

   > [T]he Court resolves this case narrowly on the basis of this Court's decisions in *Benson, Flook,* and *Diehr*, which show that petitioners' claims are not patentable processes because they are attempts to patent abstract ideas. Indeed, all members of the Court agree that the patent application at issue here falls outside of §101 because it claims an abstract idea (561 U.S., at 609).

   The three cited cases claimed different types of computer-related inventions; in two, the Court found the inventions too abstract to be patentable, and in one the patent was upheld:

   - *Gottschalk v. Benson*, 409 U.S. 63 (1972) presented a claim to a computer algorithm that converted numbers from a simple, space-saving format (binary-coded decimal [BCD], where numbers are stored as simple strings of text) into true binary form (which can be added, subtracted, multiplied, etc.); the Court held:

     > It is conceded that one may not patent an idea. But in practical effect that would be the result if the formula for converting BCD numerals to pure binary numerals were patented in this case. The

mathematical formula involved here has no substantial practical application except in connection with a digital computer, which means that if the judgment below is affirmed, the patent would wholly pre-empt the mathematical formula and in practical effect would be a patent on the algorithm itself (409 U.S. at 71–72).

The *Benson* case introduced two concepts into §101 analysis: (1) the (simplistic) view that computer programs = algorithms = mathematics = abstract ideas; and (2) the notion of "pre-emption," modified from earlier cases, where patents are considered inappropriate for "basic truths" or "basic building blocks" useful in many applications.

- *Parker v. Flook*, 437 U.S. 584 (1978), which found unpatentable a claim to a process for updating an "alarm limit" in a process typically used in oil refineries for converting the heavy molecules of crude oil into the lighter molecules of gasoline. The process is called catalytic conversion because it contacts the crude oil with a catalyst (for promoting a chemical reaction) under certain pressure, temperature and flow rate conditions. The Court said the alarm limit updating process was unpatentable because (1) it involved a mathematical algorithm (found unpatentable in *Benson*) and (2) the other components of the alarm limit process were old and conventional: "Even though a phenomenon of nature or mathematical formula may be well known, an inventive application of the principle may be patented. Conversely, the discovery of such a phenomenon cannot support a patent unless there is some other inventive concept in its application" *id.*, at 594).
- *Diamond v. Diehr*, 450 U.S. 175 (1981) reversed course. On facts quite similar to those in *Flook*, the Court found the claimed invention, which included use of a computer algorithm, patentable. The claim was to a process for curing rubber in an industrial setting. Several steps in the process included use of a computer algorithm that took as inputs measurements inside the rubber-curing mold. The algorithm helped to determine whether the rubber was cured adequately, and thus when it was time to pop open the mold to remove the finished rubber. The Court said:

> [T]he [inventors] here do not seek to patent a mathematical formula. Instead, they seek patent protection for a process of curing synthetic rubber. Their process admittedly employs a well-known mathematical equation, but they do not seek to pre-empt the use of that equation. Rather, they seek only to foreclose from others the use of that equation in conjunction with all of the other steps in their claimed process. These include installing rubber in a press, closing the mold, constantly determining the temperature of the mold, constantly recalculating the appropriate cure time through the use of the formula and a digital computer, and automatically opening the press at the proper time. Obviously, one does not need a "computer" to cure natural or synthetic rubber, but if the computer use incorporated in the process patent significantly lessens the possibility of "overcuring" or "undercuring," the process as a whole does not thereby become unpatentable subject matter (*id.*, at 187).

It is noteworthy that the personnel on the Supreme Court had changed between 1978 (*Flook*) and 1981 (*Diehr*), and also that *Flook* was a 6–3 majority opinion while *Diehr* was 5–4.

2. For many years, inventors navigated the terrain laid out in the early triad of *Benson*, *Flook*, and *Diehr*. Patent applications related to software stressed their relationship to industrial processes and computer hardware, in an attempt to look more like the patentable software-related invention in *Diehr* than the "pure" algorithm claims of *Benson*. *See, e.g., In re Iwahashi*, 888 F.2d 1370 (Fed. Cir. 1989) (finding patentable claim to specialized process for calculating "autocorrelation coefficients" for use in voice recognition; emphasizing two "hardware limitations" in the claimed circuitry, a RAM and ROM chip); *In re Alappat*, 33 F.3d 1526 (Fed. Cir. 1994) (en banc) (finding patentable a process using a brightness shading algorithm to smooth the appearance of a wave display on an oscilloscope).

A major liberalization of §101 case law came in 1998 with a decision holding that a new mutual fund system was patentable, even though the system was implemented on a computer. In *State Street Bank & Trust Co. v. Signature Financial Group, Inc.*, 149 F.3d 1368 (Fed. Cir. 1998), the Federal Circuit (per Judge Rich) laid down an expansive reading of §101 that specifically rejected both the "business method" exception that had been suggested by scholars (i.e., no patents on methods of doing business), and the special prohibition on claims that include an "algorithm." As in cases such as *Alappat*, the court brought the claims under the broadening umbrella of *Diehr* (*id.*, at 1371, emphasizing hardware components, such as the need for a central processing unit (CPU) to conduct the money market investment process claimed). In general,

State Street represents perhaps the strongest statement of the idea that the statutory categories, and not the Supreme Court-developed "exceptions," should dominate patentability analysis:

> The repetitive use of the expansive term "any" in §101 shows Congress's intent not to place any restrictions on the subject matter for which a patent may be obtained beyond those specifically recited in §101. Indeed, the Supreme Court has acknowledged that Congress intended §101 to extend to "anything under the sun that is made by man" (*Diamond v. Chakrabarty*, 447 U.S. 303, 309 (1980)).

See also *Diamond v. Diehr*, 450 U.S. 175, 182 (1981). Thus, it is improper to read limitations into §101 on the subject matter that may be patented where the legislative history indicates that Congress clearly did not intend such limitations. See *Chakrabarty*, 447 U.S. at 308 ("We have also cautioned that courts 'should not read into the patent laws limitations and conditions which the legislature has not expressed'" (*State Street Bank*, 149 F.3d 1368, at 1373 (citations omitted))). Note that *State Street Bank* is definitively inconsistent with the recent Supreme Court cases of *Bilski* and *Alice*, which elevate the "exceptions" over the statutory categories, as discussed above.

3. In the immediate wake of *Alice*, commentators struggled with the two-step test, but courts were consistent: whatever the two-step test means, software patent claims are invalid. So in cases such as *Ultramercial, Inc. v. Hulu, LLC*, 772 F.3d 709 (Fed. Cir. 2014), *cert. denied sub nom. Ultramercial, LLC v. WildTangent, Inc.*, 135 S. Ct. 2907 (2015) (patent claims invalidated under §101); *Mortgage Grader, Inc. v. First Choice Loan Servs. Inc.*, 811 F.3d 1314 (Fed. Cir. 2016) (claims invalid); *Netflix, Inc. v. Rovi Corp.*, 114 F. Supp. 3d 927 (N.D. Cal. 2015) (claims invalid). See generally Jasper L. Tran, *Software Patents: A One-Year Review of Alice v. CLS Bank*, 97 J. Pat. & Trademark Off. Soc'y 532, 545 (2015) ("With few decisions upholding patent-eligibility, the post-*Alice* trend has been overwhelmingly against software-based patent claims with an average invalidation rate of 81.7%" in the Patent Office and the courts). See also James Cosgrove, §101 Rejections in the Post-Alice Era, IP Watchdog Blog, Mar. 7, 2017, available at http://www.ipwatchdog.com/2017/03/07/101-rejections-post-alice-era/id=78635/ (documenting very large increase in §101 final rejections in US software patent prosecution post-*Alice*).

4. A slight correction in the post-*Alice* reported cases may be detectable. In one closely watched case, Judge George H. Wu of the Central District of California invalidated a patent as an abstract idea under §101. *McRO, Inc. v. Sony Computer Entm't Am., LLC*, 55 F. Supp. 3d 1214 (C.D. Cal. 2014), rev'd and remanded sub nom. *McRO, Inc. v. Bandai Namco Games Am. Inc.*, 837 F.3d 1299, 1315 (Fed. Cir. 2016). (Fed. Cir. 2016). But a close look at the technology involved, and the overall context of the case, shows an invention that only by a great stretch might be deemed "abstract." The nature of the technology in *McRO* is far removed from the business methods of *Bilski* and *Alice*, and forms part of such an innovative sector of the animation field that the case was simply begging to be reversed by the Federal Circuit. This the Federal Circuit did. See *McRO, Inc. v. Bandai Namco Games Am. Inc.*, supra.

The technology in the *McRO* case comes from the animation field. It translates spoken words into mouth movements in three-dimensional animated images. This technology helps to automate the process of adapting an animated image to mouth words without having to draw or manually program the animated movements of a character's mouth. The software takes as its input recordings of spoken speech, and provides as output a sequence of animated images of a mouth speaking the words in the recorded input.

According to a story in the trade press, automated mouth and lip animation is an important aspect of the "holy grail" of pure, automated facial animation. Debra Kaufman, *Facial Animation: It's Ready for Its Close-up, Mr. DeMille*, hollywoodindustry.com, September, 2002. This field presents formidable challenges:

> With its complexity, nuance and sophistication, the human face – its expressions and speech – poses seemingly insurmountable challenges to replicate in CGI. Nonetheless, software developers and visual effects facilities have focused resources, research and development to conquer the difficulties of both generating believable facial expressions and lip synching – in a way that's flexible, realistic and cost-effective (*id.*, at 1).

This same story quotes one experienced animator:

> Three years ago, Maury Rosenfeld, president of Los Angeles visual effects facility Planet Blue created Tulip, a combination facial animation and speech modeling system. "At the core of our system is speech recognition," said Rosenfeld. "We take an extraction of both the phonetic content of what people are saying, along with pitch and rhythm." A facial expression model, which integrates with the speech rec-

ognition model, is guided by the animator who "directs" the mood, with the system automatically doing the rest.

"Our interface is an indefinite number of live tracks – you can layer the animation in real time," Rosenfeld explained. "The animator may want to add detail to the left eyebrow for a moment and, on the next pass, he can make it twitch a little. Our system lets the animator get very detailed." Projects include an hour and a half of speech for the James Bond game "The World Is Not Enough," and on tap for the future, said Rosenfeld, is work on "interactive media with next-generation communication technologies."

Planet Blue, the company cited by animator Rosenfeld, is the operating division of the plaintiff in the *McRO* case, McRO, Inc. And Tulip is the commercial embodiment of the invention claimed in the two McRO patents asserted in *McRO v. Acivision*. To get a sense of the technology involved, consider one of the McRO patents, US Patent 6,307,576, "Method for Automatically Animating Lip Synchronization and Facial Expression of Animated Characters," issued October 23, 2001, with a priority date of October 2, 1997.

In the language of this patent, a spatial model of an image of a mouth begins with an initial position, and undergoes a change in shape – a "morph" – during the animation sequence. The animator can input a value that affects the magnitude of the morph; this is called a morph "weight." The end state of an animation sequence is called a "morph target" – it is the mouth shape at the end of a particular sound.

All sounds in spoken language are broken down into simple units called "phonemes," and each phoneme is associated with a certain mouth shape. (Think of the round mouth of an "Ohhh" sound versus the pursed lips of a "Ppppp" sound.) A stream of recorded spoken words is broken down into phonemes, and these are associated with mouth shapes; the transitions from one mouth shape (phoneme) to the next are the morphs.

With this in mind consider claim 1 of the '576 patent, which reads as follows:

1. A method for automatically animating lip synchronization and facial expression of three-dimensional characters comprising:

> obtaining a first set of rules that define output morph weight set stream as a function of phoneme sequence and time of said phoneme sequence;
> obtaining a timed data file of phonemes having a plurality of sub-sequences;
> generating an intermediate stream of output morph weight sets and a plurality of transition parameters between two adjacent morph weight sets by evaluating said plurality of sub-sequences against said first set of rules;
> generating a final stream of output morph weight sets at a desired frame rate from said intermediate stream of output morph weight sets and said plurality of transition parameters; and
> applying said final stream of output morph weight sets to a sequence of animated characters to produce lip synchronization and facial expression control of said animated characters.

U.S. Patent 6,307,576, at col. 11.

Note the specificity of the claim: it requires that the software operator set parameters ("rules that define output morph weight set stream") for the transitions that are automated; it requires the creation of sub-sequences from the timed spoken word ("phoneme") files; and it applies only to "three dimensional character[s]." The Federal Circuit, speaking in terms of the "preemption" language from cases such as *Alice*, emphasized these limits in holding that the claim satisfies §101:

> The narrower concern here is whether the claimed genus of rules preempts all techniques for automating 3–D animation that rely on rules. Claim 1 requires that the rules be rendered in a specific way: as a relationship between sub-sequences of phonemes, timing, and the weight to which each phoneme is expressed visually at a particular timing (as represented by the morph weight set). The specific structure of the claimed rules would prevent broad preemption of all rules-based means of automating lip synchronization, unless the limits of the rules themselves are broad enough to cover all possible approaches. There has been no showing that any rules-based lip-synchronization process must use rules with the specifically claimed characteristics (*McRO, Inc. v. Bandai Namco Games Am. Inc.*, 837 F.3d 1299, 1315 (Fed. Cir. 2016), footnote omitted).

5. Prior to the Supreme Court opinions in *In re Bilski* and *CLS Bank v. Alice*, the US had fewer restrictions on software patents than many other countries. After *Alice*, however, things have changed. If we compare

Chinese patent law and current US law in terms of software-related technologies, we can see that the US law now goes too far in restricting software patents. *See* Robert P. Merges and Renjun Bian, Software Patents after CLS Bank: US – China Comparison, Patent ExpressO Blog, available at http://www.patentexp.com/wp-content/uploads/2014/12/Software-Patents-after-CLS-Bank-US-and-China-Comparison.pdf.

3.2 Introduction to patentable subject matter in China

Since China, unlike the US, is only now beginning to accumulate decided cases in this area, the chief basis used to examine a Chinese patent is its Patent Act, its Implementing Regulations and its Examination Guidelines. The operative Patent Act in China was adopted in 2008 (in the third revision of the original "modern era" Patent Act of 1984). *See* Jennifer Wai-Shing Maguire, *Progressive IP Reform in the Middle Kingdom: An Overview of the Past, Present, and Future of Chinese Intellectual Property Law*, 46 Int'l Law 893, 900 (2012) (summarizing the 1984 Act and the three major revisions since that time).

Article 2.2 of the Chinese Patent Act states that patentable subject matter is limited to "technical solutions." Article 25.2 excludes "rules and methods for mental activities" from patentability. A software-related technology must overcome these two hurdles to be patentable.

3.2.1 Technical solution of Article 2.2

In the Chinese Patent Law (2008), it stipulates that an invention refers to a technical solution.

Article 2

The "inventions" as used in this Law means inventions, utility models and designs.
 The term "invention" refers to any new *technical solution* relating to a product, a process or an improvement thereof.
 The term "utility model" refers to any new technical solution relating to a product's shape, structure, or a combination thereof, which is fit for practical use.

The Examination Guidelines define a "technical solution" as a program designed "to solve a technical problem by a technical means to produce a technical effect." But there is no further definition of "technical problem," "technical means," or "technical effect." In practice, examiners have some flexibility when applying these rules. There are also requirements that people should try to meet when drafting a patent. Thus to some extent, the patentability of a software-related technology relies on its examiner's point of view and how the patent lawyer drafts it.

3.2.2 A computer program itself is not a patentable subject matter but invention relating to a computer program can be a patentable subject matter

The newly passed Guidelines for Patent Examination of 2017 clearly clarify that a computer program itself is not a patentable subject matter but invention relating to a computer program can be a patentable subject matter.

Under the revised Guidelines, software claims may now include a computer program product, a machine-readable medium, or a Beauregard type of claim, which focuses on "an apparatus comprising a processor configured to execute instructions on a computer-readable medium to perform steps of . . ."

An applicant should pursue all new possibilities and include as many claim types as needed in the patent application; among other things, it will make it easier to enforce software patents once they are granted (Chapter 9 of Part II, Guidelines for Patent Examination (2017)).

In Article 25, the Patent Act implicates several exceptions to patentable subject matter. One of them is "rules and methods for mental activities." According to the Examination Guidelines, Part II, Chapter 9, 2.2, "if all the contents of a claim include not only rules and methods for mental activities but also technical features, . . . the claim as a whole is not rules and methods for mental activities, and shall not be excluded from patentability in accordance with Article 25." That is to say, a patent will not be excluded from patentability as long as it includes "technical features." In practice, a claim must have at least one "technical feature" distinctive from the prior art to overcome this hurdle.

It is generally believed that the "rules and methods for mental activities" standard is lower than the "technical solutions" standard. According to the Examination Guidelines Part I, Chapter 2, 6.3, "[t]he technical means is usually embodied by technical features." Therefore, a patent application can easily overcome the "rules and methods for mental activities" hurdle as long as it uses "technical means" and overcomes the "technical solutions" hurdle.

The Examination Guidelines have enumerated several examples of software-related patent applications to make these two standards more understandable. Some are simplified and listed below:

Statutory non-patentable subject matter under Articles 5 and 25

Chinese Patent Law also excludes certain subject matters for patents in Articles 5 and 25.

Article 5

No patent shall be granted for an invention that contravenes any law or social moral or that is detrimental to public interests.

No patent will be granted for an invention based on genetic resources if the access or utilization of the said genetic resources is in violation of any law or administrative regulation.

Article 25

For any of the following, no patent right shall be granted:

(1) scientific discoveries;
(2) rules and methods for mental activities;
(3) methods for the diagnosis or for the treatment of diseases;
(4) animal and plant varieties;
(5) substances obtained by means of nuclear transformation; and
(6) the design, which is used primarily for the identification of pattern, color or the combination of the two on printed flat works.

For processes used in producing products referred to in items (4) of the preceding paragraph, a patent may be granted in accordance with the provisions of this Law.

> [Example 4]
> A method for controlling a die-forming process for rubber by using computer programs, characterized in that it includes the following steps:
>> sampling rubber vulcanization temperature through temperature sensor;
>> computing positive vulcanization period in the vulcanization process for rubber product in response to the vulcanization temperature;
>> determining whether the said positive vulcanization time reaches required positive vulcanization time;
>> sending vulcanization halt signal if the said positive vulcanization time reaches required positive vulcanization time.

This solution is a method for controlling a die-forming process of rubber by using computer programs in order to solve the problem of over-vulcanization and under-vulcanization of rubber, which is a *technical problem*. (Note that the claim is drawn almost directly from the US case of *Diamond v. Diehr*, noted earlier.) The solution is a method by which a die-forming process of rubber is controlled through execution of computer programs. Therefore what it reflects is the accurate and real-time control over rubber vulcanization time based on rubber vulcanization principles, and what it utilizes is the *technical means* in conformity with the laws of nature. Because of the accurate and real-time control over vulcanization time, the quality of rubber product is improved greatly. Therefore, what are obtained by the method are *technical effects*. Thus, this invention application is a solution performing industrial process control through execution of computer programs, which belongs to technical solutions as provided for in Article 2.2 and is the subject matter of patent protection.

> [Example 6]
> A method of removing image noise characterized in that it includes the following steps:
>> obtaining every pixel data of the image to be processed in a computer;
>> computing the grey mean value and the grey variance of the said image from the grey value of all the image pixels;
>> reading the grey values of all the image pixels, and determining whether the gray value of every pixel is within three times variance above or below the mean value, if yes, then not modifying the said pixel gray value, otherwise, regarding the pixel as a noise, removing it by modifying its grey value.

What this solution solves is the *technical problem* of how to remove the image noise effectively and meanwhile reduce the image blur phenomenon due to image noise processing. This solution is a method by which noises of image data are removed through execution of computer programs. Therefore, what it reflects is the approach of taking pixels whose gray value are greater or less than mean value with more than three times variance as noises and removing them, and taking pixels whose gray value are within three times variance above or below the mean value as image signal and not modifying their gray value, thus avoiding the drawback of replacing all the pixels with mean value in the prior art. What it utilizes is *technical means* – a mathematical formula that produces valuable real-world results. This invention very effectively removes image noise and decreases image blur. In the meantime, the system computing effort is reduced due to a decrease of replaced pixels, and the speed and quality of image processing are thereby increased. Thus, what is obtained by the method of the invention is a *technical effect*. Therefore, the invention application is a solution using external technical data processing through execution of computer programs, which makes it a technical solution as provided in Article 2.2 and is the subject matter of patent protection. (Translation modified by authors.)

Consider the patent at issue in the *McRO* case. If it were filed as a patent application in China, chances are it would also be found to be patentable subject matter. Under the "technical solution" test of Article 2.2 of the Chinese Patent Act, "facial expression and lip synchronization" applied in animation technology would likely be considered a technical problem. Though the Chinese Patent Act does not define what constitutes a "technical problem," several issued Chinese patents seem to be in the same technical field as McRO's patent, such as Patent CN101482976 (owned by Tencent Technology (Shenzhen) Co. Ltd.), which discloses a method for driving change of lip shape by voice, method and apparatus for acquiring lip cartoons; and Patent CN101777116 (owned by Chinese Academy of Sciences, Institute of Automation) which discloses a method for analyzing facial expressions on the basis of motion tracking. Thus, the problem McRO's patent is trying to solve by automatically and time-efficiently animating lip synchronization and facial expression of three-dimensional characters compromises what would appear to be a *technical problem* under the Chinese Patent Act.

This solution is also a method by which lip synchronization and facial expression are animated through execution of computer programs. What it reflects is the approach of breaking down a timed sound file into phonemes, generating a morph weight set for each of them, and producing corresponding lip synchronization and facial expression according to that weight set. What it utilizes is *technical means* in conformity with mathematical principles. Since heavy hand operation for arranging different mouth shapes to match spoken words is replaced by a computer program, it is more time efficient and cost effective. Thus, what is obtained by the method of the invention is most definitely a *technical effect*. Therefore, the invention application is a solution realizing external technical data processing through execution of computer programs, which belongs to technical solutions as provided in Article 2.2 and is the subject matter of patent protection.

Meanwhile, each limitation in claim 1 of the '576 patent can be divided into one or more "technical features" if rewritten more technically. For example, part of the second limitation can be rewritten as "obtaining a timed data file of phonemes having a plurality of sub-sequences to be processed in a computer" like the first limitation in Example 6 listed above. Among these technical features, the only thing distinctive from the prior art is the use of a computer, rather than an artist, to set the morph weights and transitions between phonemes. The computer is used to apply certain rules when setting the morph weights, but this is far more concrete and technical than pure "rules or methods for mental activities" such as the basic idea of animating different mouth shapes when pronouncing different words. Therefore, the invention in *McRO* surely has a "technical feature" distinctive from the prior art and thus should overcome the hurdle of "rules and methods for mental activities."

In China, as in the US, examiners will consider whether all features distinct from the prior art are technical or not. As the Federal Circuit said, what McRO's claimed invention does is to automate techniques found in the prior art: "The invention ... uses rules to automatically set a keyframe at the correct point to depict more realistic speech, achieving results similar to those previously achieved manually by animators" (*McRO, Inc. v. Bandai Namco Games Am. Inc.*, 837 F.3d 1299 (Fed. Cir. 2016)). For a Chinese examiner, the "technical feature" requirement is satisfied if the claimed software invention uses computers to implement a specific algorithm to solve an actual technical problem – which appears to be the case here.

In this sense, it seems that China's patent law is closer to the US "tied to a machine" requirement from older cases such as *Iwahashi* and *Alappat*, and which was mentioned in the *Bilski* case in the Supreme Court.

3.3 Subject matter patentability: Europe

European law on subject matter patentability begins with the EPC's relevant Articles, Article 52 and 53:

Article 52
Patentable Inventions

(1) European patents shall be granted for any inventions, in all fields of technology, provided that they are new, involve an inventive step and are susceptible of industrial application.

(2) The following in particular shall not be regarded as inventions within the meaning of paragraph 1:

(a) discoveries, scientific theories and mathematical methods;
(b) aesthetic creations;
(c) schemes, rules and methods for performing mental acts, playing games or doing business, and programs for computers;
(d) presentations of information.

(3) Paragraph 2 shall exclude the patentability of the subject-matter or activities referred to therein only to the extent to which a European patent application or European patent relates to such subject-matter or activities as such.

Article 53
Exceptions to patentability

European patents shall not be granted in respect of:

(a) inventions the commercial exploitation of which would be contrary to "ordre public" or morality; such exploitation shall not be deemed to be so contrary merely because it is prohibited by law or regulation in some or all of the Contracting States;

(b) plant or animal varieties or essentially biological processes for the production of plants or animals; this provision shall not apply to microbiological processes or the products thereof;

(c) methods for treatment of the human or animal body by surgery or therapy and diagnostic methods practised on the human or animal body; this provision shall not apply to products, in particular substances or compositions, for use in any of these methods.

The "susceptible of industrial application" requirement of Article 52(1) is equivalent to the U.S. "utility" requirement. Next, consider Article 52(2)(a) and (c), which exclude, respectively, "mathematical models" and "programs for computers," as modified by Article 52(3) ("... only to the extent to which [a patent] ... relates to such subject-matter or activities as such"). What does it mean to exclude computer programs only "as such"; what more must be claimed before a software invention becomes something other than a computer program in and of itself? The cases below consider this important issue.

CASE

Computer program product/IBM, Case No. T 1173/97 (Euro. Pat. Off. Tech. Bd. App., 1 July 1998), available at https://www.epo.org/law-practice/case-law-appeals/pdf/t971173ex1.pdf.

The appeal was lodged against a decision of the examining division dated 28 July 1997 refusing European patent application No. 91 107 112.4 (publication number 0 457 112) on the grounds that the subject matter of independent claims 20 and 21 was a computer program as such and was therefore excluded from patentability under Article 52(2)(c) and (3) EPC.

The independent claims read as follows:

CASE *(continued)*

1. A method for resource recovery in a computer system running an application which requests a work operation involving a resource, said method comprising the steps of:

implementing a commit procedure for said work request; in case the said commit procedure is not completed due to a failure, notifying said application after some time that it can continue to run, whereby said application need not wait for resynchronization; and while said application continues to run, resynchronizing said incomplete commit procedure for said resource asynchronously relative to said application.

[The rejected claim 20 reads as follows:]

20. A computer program product directly loadable into the internal memory of a digital computer, comprising software code portions for performing the steps of claim 1 when said product is run on a computer.

[Rejected claim 21 covered "A computer program product stored on a computer usable medium" and including "computer readable program means for causing the computer to implement a commit procedure, especially a two-phase commit procedure for said application," and other similar "program means" versions of the elements recited in claim 1.]

[Only claims 20 and 21 were rejected.]

Article 52(2)(c) EPC gives a non-exhaustive list of negative examples, including computer programs. Since this paragraph also mentions activities which are clearly outside the realm of technology, the exclusion of computer programs as such can only be understood as intending to exclude these programs to the same extent as these other activities, which all concern nontechnical subject-matter. A "program as such" (excluded from patentability) would therefore in fact be a nontechnical program.

The combination of the two provisions (Article 52(2) and (3) EPC) demonstrates that the legislators did not want to exclude from patentability all programs for computers. In other words the fact that only patent applications relating to programs for computers as such are excluded from patentability means that patentability may be allowed for patent applications relating to programs for computers where the latter are not considered to be programs for computers as such.

In order to establish the scope of the exclusion from patentability of programs for computers, it is necessary to determine the exact meaning of the expression "as such." This may result in the identification of those programs for computers which, as a result of not being considered programs for computers as such, are open to patentability.

The exclusion from patentability of programs for computers as such (Article 52(2) and (3) EPC) may be construed to mean that such programs are considered to be mere abstract creations, lacking in technical character. The use of the expression "shall not be regarded as inventions" seems to confirm this interpretation. This means that programs for computers must be considered as patentable inventions when they have a technical character.

CASE *(continued)*

[It has been argued that] physical modifications of the hardware (causing, for instance, electrical currents) deriving from the execution of the instructions given by programs for computers cannot per se constitute the technical character required for avoiding the exclusion of those programs.

Although such modifications may be considered to be technical, they are a common feature of all those programs for computers which have been made suitable for being run on a computer, and therefore cannot be used to distinguish programs for computers with a technical character from programs for computers as such.

It is thus necessary to look elsewhere for technical character in the above sense: It could be found in the further effects deriving from the execution (by the hardware) of the instructions given by the computer program. Where said further effects have a technical character or where they cause the software to solve a technical problem, an invention which brings about such an effect may be considered an invention, which can, in principle, be the subject-matter of a patent.

Consequently a patent may be granted not only in the case of an invention where a piece of software manages, by means of a computer, an industrial process or the working of a piece of machinery, but in every case where a program for a computer is the only means, or one of the necessary means, of obtaining a technical effect within the meaning specified above, where, for instance, a technical effect of that kind is achieved by the internal functioning of a computer itself under the influence of said program. In other words, on condition that they are able to produce a technical effect in the above sense, all computer programs must be considered as inventions within the meaning of Article 52(1) EPC, and may be the subject-matter of a patent if the other requirements provided for by the EPC are satisfied.

The Board takes this opportunity to point out that, for the purpose of determining the extent of the exclusion under Article 52(2) and (3) EPC, the said "further" technical effect may, in its opinion, be known in the prior art.

[A] computer program product having the potential to cause a predetermined further technical effect is, in principle, not excluded from patentability under Article 52(2) and (3). Consequently, computer program products are not excluded from patentability under all circumstances. In contrast to the reasons given in the decision under appeal, the Board has derived the technical character of the computer program product from the potential technical effect the program possesses, which effect is set free and may reveal itself when the program is made to run on a computer.

[N]ow that the Board has decided that not all computer program products are prima facie to be excluded from patentability, a thorough examination of the exact wording of ... claims [20 and 21] has to be carried out. In order to preserve the appellant's right to have this determined at two instances, the case is remitted to the first instance for further examination of this point.

The decision under appeal is set aside ... [and] [t]he case is remitted to the first instance for further prosecution.

NOTES

1. The identification of a "technical character" has become the touchstone for patentability in the EPO when it comes to software-related claims. This principle has many applications. It has been held, for example, by the EPO Boards that the visual display of information related to the technical conditions of a machine qualifies as a "technical character," and hence many software inventions related to the display of information are valid under this principle. *See, e.g.,* Portable device and method of providing menu icons/SAMSUNG, Case No. T 0781/10 (Euro. Pat. Off. Tech. Bd. App., 19.9.2013), available at http://www.epo.org/law-practice/case-law-appeals/recent/t100781eu1.html#q (changing focus among icons on device such as mobile phone constitutes an invention having technical character); Touch interface reconfiguration/APPLE, Case No. T 0543/14 (Euro. Pat. Off. Tech. Bd. App., 10 October 2016), available at http://www.epo.org/law-practice/case-law-appeals/recent/t140543eu1.html#q (same holding as to similar invention). On the general characteristics of the technical character test, and a call for harmonization with US law, see Victor Siber, *The Technical Character of Software Invention: Why Continental and United States Patent Law Should Be Consistent in Analyzing Patentability*, 9 Fed. Circuit B.J. 555 (2000).

2. Whatever else can be said for the "technical character" requirement, it excludes inventions that are clearly directed toward methods of doing business. Because this is one of the most active areas of litigation under section 101 of the US Patent Act, it might seem that the technical character test could be a useful guide in the US. The problem with this is that those who have studied "technical character" and the case law under it come away with the same conclusion as those who study section 101 in the US: that it is not in fact an easily predictable test, and therefore provides dubious guidance for courts. *Compare* Dina Roumiantseva, *The Eye of the Storm: Software Patents and the Abstract Idea Doctrine in* CLS Bank v. Alice, 28 Berkeley Tech. L.J. 569, 569 (2013) (critiquing Federal Circuit case law prior to the Supreme Court opinion in *CLS Bank*) and Robert Merges, "Go ask Alice – what can you patent after Alice v. CLS Bank?", SCOTUSblog, June 20, 2014, available at http://www.scotusblog.com/2014/06/symposium-go-ask-alice-what-can-you-patent-after-alice-v-cls-bank/ (critiquing the lack of useful guidance in the Supreme Court opinion in *CLS Bank*) *with* Susan J. Marsnik & Robert E. Thomas, *Drawing a Line in the Patent Subject-Matter Sands: Does Europe Provide a Solution to the Software and Business Method Patent Problem?*, 34 B.C. Int'l & Comp. L. Rev. 227, 230, 320 (2011) ("Instead of serving as a panacea for US patent examiners and courts, the European technical requirement fails to provide a meaningful constraint for software patents and many business method patents on either side of the Atlantic").

3. The European case law continues to evolve, sometimes in ways that cause confusion. *See, e.g.,* File search method/FUJITSU, Case No. T 1351/04 (Euro. Pat. Off. Bd. App., 18 April 2007), available at http://www.epo.org/law-practice/case-law-appeals/recent/t041351eu1.html#q (suggesting that any program claimed as part of a computer-executable medium is capable of directing computer operations and hence is of technical character, *i.e.,* patentable subject matter). Under procedures included in the EPC, the then-President of the EPO referred the issue of computer program patents to the EPO Enlarged Board of Appeal. For questions referred by the EPO President, the Enlarged Board consists of "five legally and two technically qualified members" (EPC, Article 22). In the case so referred, however, the Enlarged Board refused in effect to rule on the request. Although the Enlarged Board identified one issue on which EPO case law was divergent – whether computer program claims to programs stored on a computer-readable medium were per se unpatentable – this was a "legitimate development of the case law and there is no divergence which would make the referral of this point to the Enlarged Board of Appeal by the President admissible" (Programs for computers, Case No. G 0003/08 (Euro. Pat. Off. Enlarged Bd. App., 12 May 2010), available at http://documents.epo.org/projects/babylon/eponet.nsf/0/DC6171F182D8B65AC125772100426656/$File/G3_08_Opinion_12_05_2010_en.pdf, at par. 6). The latter case having not created any crucial divergence, the Enlarged Board dismissed the request (*id.*, at par. 7).

4. National courts have at times struggled to apply EPO case law under national patent statutes. In fact, despite the Enlarged Board's refusal to address divergences in the case law, several courts have held or hinted that the EPO case law is not clear enough to provide useful guidance. The national courts have stepped in with tests and guidelines of their own. For example, in the UK, *Aerotel Limited v. Telco Limited; Macrossan's Application* [2007] RPC 7 (R. Jacob L.J.) laid down a four-part test for patentability in the UK which has been influential. The test is as follows:

(1) Properly construe the claim.
(2) Identify the actual contribution.
(3) Ask whether it falls solely within the excluded subject matter.
(4) Check whether the contribution is actually technical in nature
(*id.*, at par. 40).

The *Aerotel* application was central to the later UK case of *Symbian Ltd. v. Comptroller General of Patents, Designs and Trademarks*, 2008 WL 4125353, [2008] EWCA Civ 1066 (England and Wales Court of Appeals, 8 October 2008), which explicitly declined to follow EPO case law on the grounds that it was inconsistent and not settled enough to compel the UK courts to move away from their own well-settled test. As the *Symbian* court said, at par. 46:

> [T]here is no decision of the Enlarged Board [of the EPO]. Not only does that mean that the view of the Board is not as authoritative as it could be; it also suggests that the Board does not consider that the time has arrived for the point to be conclusively determined. Secondly, the approaches [of the EPO] in [several] decisions since [*Aerotel*] [*e.g.*, the *File search method/FUJITSU* case cited above] are not identical: in particular, one of them appears more consistent with the view preferred in *Aerotel*. Thirdly, we are concerned that, particularly if the passage quoted from *File search method/Fujitsu* represents the Board's view, the computer program exclusion may have lost all meaning. Fourthly, it is not as if the English courts are alone in their concern about the approach of the Board, as . . . observations from the German judiciary . . . demonstrate. Fifthly, if this court is seen to depart too readily from its previous, carefully considered, approach, it would risk throwing the law into disarray.

5. Although the UK court in *Symbian* cited some dissent among German courts, it appears that those courts have in fact hewed more closely to the EPO "technical character" test, and in general find it workable. *See e.g.*, In re German Patent Application, DE 102 32 674.6-53 (Bundespatentgericht [German Federal Court of Justice, Patents], 22 April 2010), trans. available at http://www.online-translator.com//url/translation.aspx?direction=ge&template=General&autotranslate=on&transliterate=&showvariants=&sourceURL=http://news.swpat.org/2010/05/german-court-ruling-upholding-siemens-patent-as-text/. This case held, in reversing the rejection of a computer software patent application at the German Patent Office, that software in general is not excluded as a program for data-processing systems if it solves a concrete technical problem using technical means. In the specific case, a program related to database management was found patentable, as the court applied both German national and EPO case law.

3.4 Biotechnology

The three exceptions to patentable categories (natural laws, phenomena of nature, and abstract ideas) all arguably involve things that are more "found" than they are "made." Because biotechnology deals with the isolation, enhancement, and practical applications of biomolecules and other features of living things, this area of science has featured in many §101 cases since the 1980s.

The biotechnology era got off to a pro-patent start in the early and influential decision of *Diamond v. Chakrabarty*, 447 U.S. 303 (1980). There the Supreme Court confronted a claim to an early version of genetic engineering. The inventor isolated a series of "plasmids" (independent strands of DNA found inside bacteria cells, but not part of the primary genome of those cells). His purpose was to assemble bacteria that can be used to break down complex chemicals found in crude oil; these bacteria were spread onto oil spills in nature, to help clean them up. The Court held that the claims before it were patentable. Though a living thing resulted from creation of the claimed invention ("a bacterium from the genus Pseudomonas containing therein at least two stable energy-generating plasmids, each of said plasmids providing a separate hydrocarbon degradative pathway") (*id*. at 305), that living thing was human-made, and not found in nature: "[The inventor's] claim is not to a hitherto unknown natural phenomenon, but to a nonnaturally occurring manufacture or composition of matter – a product of human ingenuity . . ." (*id*., at 309). Citing the legislative history of the 1952 Patent Act, the Court said that "Congress intended statutory subject matter [under §101] to 'include anything under the sun that is made by man'" (*id*., at 309).

By 2006, the Supreme Court was beginning to show signs that it was rethinking the expansive, pro-patent regime established in *Chakrabarty*. In *Laboratory Corporation of America Holdings v. Metabolite Laboratories, Inc.*, 548 U.S. 124 (2006), the Court first granted certiorari in a §101 case in the life sciences field, and then dismissed the case. But a three-Justice dissent from the dismissal made clear that at least some members of the Court wanted to tighten §101, at least in the case of the medical diagnostic claim at issue there. In 2012, the hints from *Laboratory Corporation of America* came to fruition when the Court decided *Mayo Collaborative Services v. Prometheus Laboratories, Inc.*, 132 S. Ct. 1289 (2012), which held that a claim to a method of adjusting the dosage of certain drugs, by looking for evidence of a chemical response to the drugs in the human body, was invalid as a "law of nature" under §101. "[T]o transform an unpatentable law of nature into a patent-eligible application of such a law," the Court stated, "one must do more than simply state the law of nature while adding the words 'apply it'" (*id*., at 1294). In the course of its opinion, the Court stated what has come to be known as the "two-step test" for §101 patentable subject matter:

> [T]he claims inform a relevant audience about certain laws of nature; any additional steps consist of well-understood, routine, conventional activity already engaged in by the scientific community; and those steps, when viewed as a whole, add nothing significant beyond the sum of their parts taken separately. For these reasons we believe that the steps are not sufficient to transform unpatentable natural correlations into patentable applications of those regularities (*id*., at 1298 (2012)).

Looking back on *Mayo* when it decided *Alice*, the Supreme Court said that the *Mayo* opinion was the origin of the two-step test:

> [In *Mayo*] we set forth a framework for distinguishing patents that claim laws of nature, natural phenomena, and abstract ideas from those that claim patent-eligible

applications of those concepts. First, we determine whether the claims at issue are directed to one of those patent-ineligible concepts. If so, we then ask, "[w]hat else is there in the claims before us?" 132 S.Ct., at 1297. To answer that question, we consider the elements of each claim both individually and "as an ordered combination" to determine whether the additional elements "transform the nature of the claim" into a patent-eligible application. 132 S.Ct., at 1298, 1297. We have described step two of this analysis as a search for an "inventive concept" – i.e., an element or combination of elements that is "sufficient to ensure that the patent in practice amounts to significantly more than a patent upon the [ineligible concept] itself." 132 S.Ct., at 1294. (*Alice Corp. Pty. v. CLS Bank Int'l*, 134 S. Ct. 2347, 2355 (2014)).

This is the same test that drives the result in the next case, which involved a claim to isolated DNA sequences:

CASE

Ass'n for Molecular Pathology v. Myriad Genetics, Inc. 133 S. Ct. 2107 (2013)

Thomas, J.
Respondent Myriad Genetics, Inc. (Myriad), discovered the precise location and sequence of two human genes, mutations of which can substantially increase the risks of breast and ovarian cancer. Myriad obtained a number of patents based upon its discovery. This case involves claims from three of them and requires us to resolve whether a naturally occurring segment of deoxyribonucleic acid (DNA) is patent eligible under 35 U.S.C. §101 by virtue of its isolation from the rest of the human genome. We also address the patent eligibility of synthetically created DNA known as complementary DNA (cDNA), which contains the same protein-coding information found in a segment of natural DNA but omits portions within the DNA segment that do not code for proteins. For the reasons that follow, we hold that a naturally occurring DNA segment is a product of nature and not patent eligible merely because it has been isolated, but that cDNA is patent eligible because it is not naturally occurring.

This case involves patents filed by Myriad after it made one such medical breakthrough. Myriad discovered the precise location and sequence of what are now known as the BRCA1 and BRCA2 genes. Mutations in these genes can dramatically increase an individual's risk of developing breast and ovarian cancer. Myriad's patents would, if valid, give it the exclusive right to isolate an individual's BRCA1 and BRCA2 genes (or any strand of 15 or more nucleotides within the genes) by breaking the covalent bonds that connect the DNA to the rest of the individual's genome.

CASE *(continued)*

It is undisputed that Myriad did not create or alter any of the genetic information encoded in the BRCA1 and BRCA2 genes. The location and order of the nucleotides existed in nature before Myriad found them. Nor did Myriad create or alter the genetic structure of DNA. Instead, Myriad's principal contribution was uncovering the precise location and genetic sequence of the BRCA1 and BRCA2 genes.

Myriad explains that the location of the gene was unknown until Myriad found it among the approximately eight million nucleotide pairs contained in a subpart of [the] chromosome [on which it is located]. Myriad seeks to import these extensive research efforts into the §101 patent-eligibility inquiry. But extensive effort alone is insufficient to satisfy the demands of §101. Nor are Myriad's claims saved by the fact that isolating DNA from the human genome severs chemical bonds and thereby creates a nonnaturally occurring molecule. Myriad's claims are simply not expressed in terms of chemical composition, nor do they rely in any way on the chemical changes that result from the isolation of a particular section of DNA. Instead, the claims understandably focus on the genetic information encoded in the BRCA1 and BRCA2 genes. If the patents depended upon the creation of a unique molecule, then a would-be infringer could arguably avoid at least Myriad's patent claims on entire genes by isolating a DNA sequence that included both the BRCA1 or BRCA2 gene and one additional nucleotide pair. Such a molecule would not be chemically identical to the molecule "invented" by Myriad. But Myriad obviously would resist that outcome because its claim is concerned primarily with the information contained in the genetic sequence, not with the specific chemical composition of a particular molecule.

cDNA does not present the same obstacles to patentability as naturally occurring, isolated DNA segments. [C]reation of a cDNA sequence from mRNA [*i.e.*, messenger RNA, which carries an "edited" copy of the natural DNA, with non-coding regions (introns) removed, from the cell nucleus to the ribosome, the protein-producing locus inside the cell] results in an exons-only molecule that is not naturally occurring. Petitioners concede that cDNA differs from natural DNA in that "the non-coding regions have been removed." They nevertheless argue that cDNA is not patent eligible because "[t]he nucleotide sequence of cDNA is dictated by nature, not by the lab technician." That may be so, but the lab technician unquestionably creates something new when cDNA is made. cDNA retains the naturally occurring exons of DNA, but it is distinct from the DNA from which it was derived. As a result, cDNA is not a "product of nature" and is patent eligible under §101, except insofar as very short series of DNA may have no intervening introns to remove when creating cDNA. In that situation, a short strand of cDNA may be indistinguishable from natural DNA.

[W]e [do not] consider the patentability of DNA in which the order of the naturally occurring nucleotides has been altered. Scientific alteration of the genetic code presents a different inquiry, and we express no opinion about the application of §101 to such endeavors. We merely hold that genes and the information they encode are not patent eligible under §101 simply because they have been isolated from the surrounding genetic material.

NOTES

1. The passage above that emphasizes the "informational" content of the BRCA genes, as opposed to the chemical structure of the genes, rejects the "chemical" orientation of the Federal Circuit's opinion below. The Federal Circuit had stated:

   Isolated DNA . . . is a free-standing portion of a larger, natural DNA molecule. Isolated DNA has been cleaved (*i.e.*, had covalent bonds in its backbone chemically severed) or synthesized to consist of just a fraction of a naturally occurring DNA molecule. [The genes claimed here] in their isolated states are different molecules from DNA that exists in the body; isolated DNA results from human intervention to cleave or synthesize a discrete portion of a native chromosomal DNA, imparting on that isolated DNA a distinctive chemical identity as compared to native DNA. (*Ass'n for Molecular Pathology v. U.S. Patent & Trademark Office*, 689 F.3d 1303, 1328 (Fed. Cir. 2012)).

2. In *Ariosa Diagnostics, Inc. v. Sequenom, Inc.*, 788 F.3d 1371 (Fed. Cir. 2015), *cert. denied*, 136 S. Ct. 2511 (2016), the Federal Circuit followed *Myriad* in finding unpatentable a claim to a technology that was hailed by many as an important medical advance. The claims there covered detection of a fetus's DNA circulating in the bloodstream of the pregnant mother, called "cell free fetal DNA" (cffDNA). Fetal DNA circulates in the mother's bloodstream, separate from her own blood cells. Isolating this fetal DNA allows doctors to test for genetic problems in the fetus – a major breakthrough that saves the mother from the previous alternative, called amniocentesis, which involves piercing the fetus's amniotic sack with a long needle, which sometimes endangered fetus and/or mother. The Federal Circuit invalidated the claims to cffDNA detection because they violated §101. They did this notwithstanding the fact that the medical contribution in the case was significant:

   While [the inventors'] discovery regarding cffDNA may have been a significant contribution to the medical field, that alone does not make it patentable. We do not disagree that detecting cffDNA in maternal plasma or serum that before was discarded as waste material is a positive and valuable contribution to science. But even such valuable contributions can fall short of statutory patentable subject matter, as it does here (*Ariosa Diagnostics, Inc. v. Sequenom, Inc.*, 788 F.3d 1371, 1379–80 (Fed. Cir. 2015), *cert. denied*, 136 S. Ct. 2511 (2016)).

3. Before cases like *McRO* were decided, the post-*Alice* treatment of software patents made it appear that in effect, the US might have eliminated patents for software. It is worth considering, in this connection, whether a near-total ban on patents for an entire subject matter area would constitute a violation of the TRIPs agreement. TRIPs Article 27.1 reads:

   Subject to the provisions of paragraphs 2 and 3, patents shall be available for any inventions, whether products or processes, in all fields of technology, provided that they are new, involve an inventive step and are capable of industrial application . . . (TRIPs Article 27.1, available at https://www.wto.org/english/docs_e/legal_e/27-trips_01_e.htm).

   Article 27.3 include specific types of subject matter which, at each member country's discretion, may be excluded from patent protection. Software is not among them. *See* TRIPs Article 27.3 (allowing exclusion of "diagnostic, therapeutic and surgical methods for the treatment of humans or animals"; and various other plant- and animal-related patents).

   How could a country or company affected by a de facto exclusion from patentability challenge the exclusionary, court-made doctrine under TRIPs? *See* John McDermid, A NAFTA Challenge to Canada's Patent Utility Doctrine is Necessary, IP Watchdog Blog, June 11, 2014; Eli Lilly and Company v. Government of Canada, North American Free Trade Agreement (NAFTA) arbitration, available at http://www.international.gc.ca/trade-agreements-accords-commerciaux/topics-domaines/disp-diff/eli.aspx?lang=eng (description of challenge by Eli Lilly, a US pharmaceutical company, to Canadian court decisions creating a "promise utility" doctrine, which Lilly argues is contrary to the conventional utility doctrine Lilly says was incorporated in the NAFTA Agreement, which Canada joined). The TRIPs Agreement contains language similar to NAFTA, and also includes the possibility of challenges to national laws inconsistent with TRIPs. *See* United States: Section 110(5) of the US Copyright Act, Report of the Panel, June 15, 2000, (00-2284), WT/DS160/R, available at https://www.wto.org/english/tratop_e/dispu_e/1234da.pdf (successful challenge to US legislation on copyright "public performance right"; European nations successfully argued that US law was in violation of TRIPs).

What percentage of software patents would have to be invalidated for the US to be found in violation of the TRIPs Agreement? Would a finding of a violation be an intrusion on US sovereignty? Would a finding of no TRIPs violation be a signal that international agreements in the IP field cannot be effectively enforced?

3.4.1 Biotechnology/living subject matter: China

As mentioned earlier, Chinese Patent Law also excludes certain subject matter for patents in Articles 5 and 25.

Article 5

No patent shall be granted for an invention that contravenes any law or social moral or that is detrimental to public interests.

No patent will be granted for an invention based on genetic resources if the access or utilization of the said genetic resources is in violation of any law or administrative regulation.

Article 25

For any of the following, no patent right shall be granted:

(1) scientific discoveries;
(2) rules and methods for mental activities;
(3) methods for the diagnosis or for the treatment of diseases;
(4) animal and plant varieties;
(5) substances obtained by means of nuclear transformation; and
(6) the design, which is used primarily for the identification of pattern, color or the combination of the two on printed flat works.

For processes used in producing products referred to in items (4) of the preceding paragraph, a patent may be granted in accordance with the provisions of this Law.

There are as yet few cases applying these provisions, but the general consensus seems to be that the controversies that have engulfed biotechnology/living subject matter claims in the US (see above) and Europe (see below) have so far been mostly absent in China. *Cf.* Gregory C. Ellis, *Intellectual Property Rights and the Public Sector: Why Compulsory Licensing of Protected Technologies Critical for Food Security Might Just Work in China*, 16 Pacific Rim L. & Pol'y J. 699 (2007) (discussing agricultural biotechnology products and the prospects for compulsory licensing).

3.4.2 Biotechnology/living subject matter: Europe

The following case involves a second area of controversy in Europe, biotech-related inventions, or inventions touching on living subject matter. In addition to the EPC, the case also makes reference to patent-relevant provisions of Directive 98/44/EC of the European Parliament and of the Council of 6 July 1998, on the legal protection of biotechnological inventions, Official Journal L 213, 30/07/1998 P. 0013 0021 (the EU Biotech Directive). The most important provision of the Biotech Directive was the section specifically on patentability of biotech-related inventions (Article 6 of the Directive), which had been implemented in EPC Rule 23 (now, in the 16th edition of the EPC, this has become Rule 28). The general introduction to this section of the Rules (derived from the Directive) comes in current Rule 26, which states:

> (1) For European patent applications and patents concerning biotechnological inventions, the relevant provisions of the Convention shall be applied and interpreted in accordance with the provisions of this Chapter. Directive 98/44/EC of 6 July 1998, on the legal protection of biotechnological inventions shall be used as a supplementary means of interpretation.
> (2) "Biotechnological inventions" are inventions which concern a product consisting of or containing biological material or a process by means of which biological material is produced, processed or used.
> (3) "Biological material" means any material containing genetic information and capable of reproducing itself or being reproduced in a biological system (EPC Rules, Chapter V, Biotechnological Inventions, Rule 26).

Then, Rules 27 and 28 state conditions of patentability:

Rule 27
Patentable biotechnological inventions

Biotechnological inventions shall also be patentable if they concern:

(a) biological material which is isolated from its natural environment or produced by means of a technical process even if it previously occurred in nature;
(b) plants or animals if the technical feasibility of the invention is not confined to a particular plant or animal variety;
(c) a microbiological or other technical process, or a product obtained by means of such a process other than a plant or animal variety.

Rule 28
Exceptions to patentability

Under Article 53(a), European patents shall not be granted in respect of biotechnological inventions which, in particular, concern the following:

(a) processes for cloning human beings;
(b) processes for modifying the germ line genetic identity of human beings;
(c) uses of human embryos for industrial or commercial purposes;
(d) processes for modifying the genetic identity of animals which are likely to cause them suffering without any substantial medical benefit to man or animal, and also animals resulting from such processes.

CASE

Transgenic animals/HARVARD, Case No. T 0315/03 (Euro. Pat. Off. Bd. App., 6 July 2004), available at http://www.epo.org/law-practice/case-law-appeals/pdf/t030315ex1.pdf.

[Patent applicant sought a European patent for claims such as this one:
1. A method for producing a transgenic eukaryotic animal having an increased probability of developing neoplasms [*i.e.*, tumors], said method comprising introducing into an animal embyro an activated oncogene sequence.]

The focus of this case is a very small animal, namely a mouse – to use a poet's description, a "Wee, sleekit, cowrin, tim'rous beastie" (R. Burns, "To a Mouse", 1785). In all other respects however, this case is not small.

The wording of Article 53(a) EPC is clear: "European patents shall not be granted in respect of: (a) inventions the publication or exploitation of which would be contrary to "ordre public" or morality . . ."

It is, in the Board's opinion, only possible to read the words "contrary to 'ordre public' or morality" as qualifying "publication or exploitation". Accordingly, the Article raises no question of the morality of patenting a particular invention or of the morality of that invention *per se*. This conclusion, of course, applies to the particular animal invention claimed in the patent in suit: this case is concerned neither with the morality of genetically manipulating a mouse nor with the morality of the oncomouse thereby produced nor with the morality of patenting either the oncomouse or the genetic manipulation method but only with the morality of publication or exploitation the oncomouse or that method.

Second, this case is not . . . concerned with "the patenting of animals" or "whether or not animals are patentable under the EPC". Such a decision quite simply cannot, as the EPC

CASE *(continued)*

is currently formulated, ever fall to any of its first instance departments or to the Boards of Appeal. The EPC has a clear set of basic rules as to patentability. First, the fundamental principle is that inventions shall be patentable if they fulfill three criteria – novelty, inventive step and industrial application (Articles 52(1), 54 to 57 EPC). As use of the word "shall" clearly indicates, there is a prima facie presumption in favour of patentability. Second, certain categories of subject-matter (for example, aesthetic creations) are not regarded as inventions at all – these are sometimes called the exclusions (Article 52(2)(3) EPC). Third, certain other categories of subject-matter, while being acknowledged as capable of being inventions, are denied the protection of patents – these are sometimes called the exceptions (Article 53 EPC).

The categories of exclusions and exceptions may, depending on one's moral, social or other point of view, appear acceptable or unacceptable, quixotic or outdated, liberal or conservative. There may certainly be scope within the express wording of certain of those categories for interpretation in order to establish the exact boundaries of the categories but, subject to such interpretative scope, the law is clear: there is no excluded or excepted category of "animals in general". The only provisions which relate to patents for or concerning animals are in Article 53 EPC. The second limb of this Article (Article 53(b) EPC) denies patents to "animal varieties" (a term which certainly requires interpretation and to which the Board returns below) but which, on even the most rudimentary analysis, cannot mean animals in general. The first limb of the same Article (Article 53(a) EPC) denies patents to inventions the publication or exploitation of which would be contrary to "ordre public" or morality and, subject to interpretation which has largely been supplied already by existing case-law and supplementary legislation, this can be invoked to stop a patent being granted for an invention which causes suffering to animals without some counterbalancing benefit.

[A]s regards Article 53(a) EPC, Rule 23d(d) EPC must be taken into account. The relevant text of that Rule reads:

> Under Article 53(a) European patents shall not be granted in respect of biotechnological inventions which, *in particular*, concern the following: . . . (d) processes for modifying the genetic identity of animals which are likely to cause them suffering without any substantial medical benefit to man or animal, and also animals resulting from such processes". (Emphasis added)

To the extent that there may be some biotechnological inventions which "fail" the Rule 23d(d) EPC test and are thus denied a patent at that point while other such inventions may "pass" that test and therefore have to proceed to an Article 53(a) EPC assessment, [the] argument that there is a "two-stage test" is correct.

[T]he Rule 23d(d) EPC test [modifying EPC Article 53(a)] requires three matters to be established: likely animal suffering, likely substantial medical benefit, and the necessary correspondence between the two in terms of the animals in question. The level of proof is

CASE (continued)

the same for both animal suffering and substantial medical benefit, namely a likelihood. Since only a likelihood of suffering need be shown, other matters such as the degree of suffering or the availability of non-animal alternatives need not be considered. Evidence need not be limited to that available at the filing or priority date but evidence becoming available thereafter must be directed to the position at that date.

[Turning to EPC Article 53(b), and the question of what is meant by the exclusion of patents for "animal varieties":] While neither the jurisprudence of the Boards nor Rule 23b EPC (which is concerned with interpretation of the EPC as regards biotechnological inventions) provides a . . . definition for "animal varieties" (or "species" or "races" [the terms used in the German and French translations, respectively, of this Article]), the Board considers that a definition by reference to taxonomical rank would be both consistent with the position in relation to plant varieties and in the interest of legal certainty. With such a definition, an assessment could be made as to whether the claimed subject-matter is excluded from patentability under Article 53(b) EPC as interpreted by Rule 23c(b) EPC . . .

[I]n the taxonomic hierarchy, both "variety" and "race" clearly appear below the category of "species" [*i.e.*, constitutes a "subspecies"].

To summarise the Board's views regarding Article 53(b) EPC . . .: a patent should not be granted for a single animal variety . . . but can be granted even if varieties may fall within the scope of its claims. The definition of animal variety (or species or race) by reference to taxonomical rank would be consistent with the position in relation to plant varieties and in the interest of legal certainty, allowing assessment under Article 53(b) EPC as interpreted by Rule 23c(b) EPC to be made by considering whether, in a case concerning animals, the technical feasibility of the invention is not confined to a particular animal variety.

The claimed method pertains to the field of genetic engineering and the transgenic animals produced by that method may be used as appropriate models for studying different aspects of cancer, such as the development of tissue-specific tumours and the effect of suspected carcinogens . . . They represent technical tools just as other means – such as bacterial tests and culture cell lines – are also technical tools. Thus, both the claimed method and the transgenic animals directly derived therefrom have a technical character. Similarly, the technical feature characterising these transgenic animals – the presence of an activated oncogene which confers an increased probability of developing neoplasm – is also found in their offspring. Therefore, this progeny would also be used as an appropriate technical tool. Thus, the subject-matter of claims 1 and 19 is an invention within the meaning of Article 52 EPC.

[Applying Article 53(b),] it was not in dispute – indeed it was agreed by the parties – that the [claimed] process is likely to cause . . . animals suffering.

The two questions which thus arise are first, whether there is also a likelihood of a substantial medical benefit to man or animal and second, whether that benefit is obtained in the case of all the animals which are likely to suffer *i.e.* whether there is the necessary correspondence between likely suffering and likely benefit. There is no evidence on file,

CASE *(continued)*

either in the patent itself or elsewhere, that any such benefit, let alone a substantial medical benefit, is likely to be derived from applying the claimed process to all rodents, or indeed to any animals of the order *Rodentia* apart from mice. The necessary correspondence, in terms of the animals in question, between the likely suffering and the likely benefit is absent. The respondent has referred to the advantageous provision of several model systems for studying cancer without being restricted to the limited physiology, metabolism, etc. of mice. However, there is quite simply no evidence to show that all the various animals in the category of rodents are so different that each of them would provide a contribution to cancer studies, such as being specifically suited as a model for studying a specific type of cancer. Thus the respondent's argument appears to be no more than argument – it is purely hypothetical and unsubstantiated by any evidence. Therefore, the Board concludes that the likelihood of substantial medical benefit required by Rule 23d(d) EPC has not been satisfied for rodents.

Accordingly, the main request discloses a likelihood of animal suffering but not a likelihood of medical benefit in the case of all animals embraced by the claims. Consequently, the main request fails the balancing test of Rule 23d(d) EPC and must therefore be refused under Article 53(a) EPC. The main request [regarding the broadest claims covering all transgenic "rodents"] is accordingly not allowable.

[As to the narrower claims, limited specifically to transgenic mice:] [T]he Board considers that the subject-matter of claims 1 and 19 of the first auxiliary request "passes" the test in Rule 23d(d) EPC [*i.e.*, the balancing test described above] and thus does not fall within the category of inventions for which patents shall not be granted under that Rule. The request must therefore be assessed under Article 53(a) EPC without reference to that Rule. [The Board also found that these claims pass muster under the more general, *i.e.*, non-biotechnology-specific, balancing test developed in other Board precedent pertaining to Article 53(a) "ordre public" cases.]

The Board has obtained and considered the decision of the Supreme Court of Canada in the corresponding case in that jurisdiction. As appellant 1 mentioned, and as the respondent observed, the decision turned on the meaning of terms present in the Canadian patent legislation but not in the EPC. After three previous appeals following the examiner's decision, the Supreme Court finally decided that the terms "manufacture" and "composition of matter" excluded higher life forms. In summary, not only did this decision arise in a non-European country, not only did it concern legislative terms which do not exist in the patent law of the EPC, not only were the views of the Supreme Court expressed in 2002, but the decision quite clearly does not establish that animal patents arouse public unease.

Having thus considered all the "public perception" arguments, with or without evidence to support them, the only conclusion the Board can make is that in current European culture animals are on the one hand respected as sentient beings which are not to be gratuitously abused or misused; and, on the other hand, animals are accepted as being important in the testing of medicaments and curative methods prior to human application.

[The Board held also that the claims at issue did not in effect attempt to patent an "animal variety," and hence were not unpatentable under Article 52(b).]

NOTES

1. The Canadian decision referred to in the EU *Oncomouse* Opinion just above held that the Harvard claims were unpatentable in Canada because they were not patentable subject matter, being neither a "manufacture" nor a "composition of matter" under the Canadian statute. *See Harvard College v. Canada (Commissioner of Patents)*, 2002 SCC 76, 2002 CarswellNat 3434 (Supreme Court of Canada, May 21, 2002).

2. For detailed analysis of this opinion, see David Thomas, *Technical Board of Appeal decision in the Oncomouse case*, 28 Euro. Intell. Prop. Rev. 57, 60 (2006). (Noting that the opinion's "dismissive treatment of opinion polls, and case law and evidence from other jurisdictions in relation to the oncomouse, is . . . regrettable. Many people do not accept that "inventions" of animals should be patentable in the first place. However, if one starts from the premise that they can be, the [court's] legal analysis [here] is reasonably robust."); Fiona Murray, "Patenting Life: How the Oncomouse Patent Changed the Lives of Mice and Men," in Making and Unmaking Intellectual Property: Creative Production in Legal and Cultural Perspective 399 (Mario Biagioli et al. eds., 2011). For more on Article 53 in EU jurisdictions, see Emir Aly Crowne-Mohammed, *The EPC Exceptions to Patentable Subject Matter in the United Kingdom*, 92 J. Pat. & Trademark Off. Soc'y 435 (2010). For a comparative look at public policy and morality elements of patentable subject matter jurisprudence, see Laura A. Keay, *Morality's Move Within U.S. Patent Law: From Moral Utility to Subject Matter*, 40 AIPLA Q.J. 409 (2012) (charting the rise and fall of morality as an element in US section 101 cases since 1790). For a discussion of the US approach, *see* Robert P. Merges, *Intellectual Property in Higher Life Forms: The Patent System and Controversial Technologies*, 47 Md. L. Rev. 1051 (1988) ("[In general,] [p]atents on new technology should be granted, reserving the right to regulate specific applications. This is the only sensible course.")

3. Another important EU case concerned patents for stem cells. *See WARF/stem sells*, Case No. G2/06 (European Patent Office, Enlarged Body of Appeals, 25 November 2008), available at http://www.epo.org/law-practice/case-law-appeals/pdf/g060002ex1.pdf, at par. 31:

> For the reasons given above, the Enlarged Board of Appeal comes to the conclusion that the legislators (both the legislator of the Implementing Regulations to the EPC and of the [Biotech] Directive) wanted to exclude inventions such as the one underlying this referral from patentability and that in doing so, they have remained within the scope of Article 53(a) EPC and of the TRIPS Agreement.

4

Novelty

To be valid, a patented invention must be both "new" and "nonobvious" (or showing evidence of an "inventive step," which is the same as nonobviousness). In this chapter we consider these requirements.

Novelty is defined under the Patent Act in post-AIA §102, which reads:

> (a) **NOVELTY; PRIOR ART.** – A person shall be entitled to a patent unless –
>
> (1) the claimed invention was patented, described in a printed publication, or in public use, on sale, or otherwise available to the public before the effective filing date of the claimed invention . . . (35 U.S.C. §102(a)).

This novelty provision applies to all post-AIA patents – those filed on or after March 16, 2013. The pre-AIA version of §102 is a bit different; we discuss that a little later in this section.

How to determine whether "the claimed invention" was "patented" before the filing date of the claimed invention? How similar do the claims of the claimed invention have to be to something which was patented before the inventor filed for the claimed invention? That is the topic we take up now.

4.1 The identity standard for novelty in the US

 CASE

In re Skvorecz, 580 F.3d 1262, 1263 (Fed. Cir. 2009)

Newman, Circuit Judge.
[A "chafer" is a tray for holding food, such as at a buffet table. The chafer is typically supported by a stand; sometimes, the stand has space for some kind of heating element

CASE *(continued)*

to keep the food warm. In transporting food service equipment, the chafers are stacked together and the chafing stands are put into a separate stack. The inventor in this case, Robert J. Skvorecz, noticed that when food service workers tried to pull apart a large stack of chafing stands, to take out the stands one by one, they often got stuck together. The stands would wedge or jam into each other, and become very tightly stacked. To solve this problem, he designed a chafing stand that could be easily stacked without jamming, making each stand much easier to pull off the stack. His solution was quite simple: he put a little "wiggle" in the vertical part of the stand, which he calls an "offset" in his patent. This wiggle keeps the stands from jamming. For this simple but useful idea, Mr. Skvorecz received U.S. patent 5,996,948.]

The [Skvorecz patent] specification explains that wire chafing stands are transported and stored nested together in multiple units, and that the nested stands tend to wedge into one another and are then difficult to separate. The invention is an improved structure whereby nested stands are readily separated. The specification describes the improved stand whereby the wire legs have an indent (also called an "offset") located adjacent to the upper ends of the legs, serving to laterally displace each leg relative to the point of attachment of the leg to the upper rim of the stand. The result is that the wire legs of one stand can nest within another stand, without significant wedging of the nested stands into each other. [The "wiggle" or offset is shown in the partial Figure 1 [4.1] below as element number 30. The circular elements 12 and 15 are the ends of the other wires that make up the chafing stand; these wires are welded at 90 degree angles to the legs (18) which includes the offset 30.]

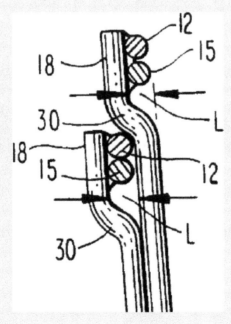

Figure 4.1 Patented Skvorecz design

CASE (continued)

[Claim 1 of the patent reads in part:
1. A wire chafing stand comprising an upper rim of wire steel . . ., a lower rim of wire steel . . . and having a plurality of wire legs with each wire leg . . . being affixed to the upper rim adjacent one end thereof and to said lower rim at a relatively equal distance below the point of attachment to said upper rim and further comprising a plurality of offsets . . . for laterally displacing each wire leg relative to said upper rim to facilitate the nesting of a multiplicity of stands into one another without significant wedging.]

The examiner rejected claim 1 [and other claims] for anticipation based on Figure 2 of United States Patent No. 5,503,062 (the Buff patent), shown [in part] below [Figure 4.2]:

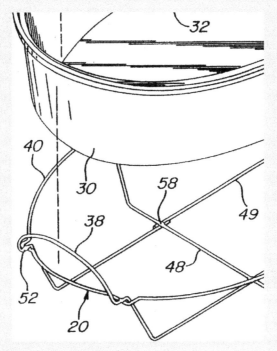

Figure 4.2 Buff patent, prior art design

A rejection for "anticipation" means that the invention is not new. Anticipation requires that all of the claim elements and their limitations are shown in a single prior art reference. See *Richardson v. Suzuki Motor Co.*, 868 F.2d 1226, 1236 (Fed. Cir. 1989) (anticipation requires that the identical invention is described in the reference); *Glaverbel Societe Anonyme v. Northlake Mktg. & Supply, Inc.*, 45 F.3d 1550, 1554 (Fed. Cir. 1995) (same). Anticipation is a question of fact, and is reviewed accordingly. *Glaverbel*, 45 F.3d at 1554. The Board found that the examiner established a prima facie case of anticipation based on the structural similarity between the Skvorecz invention and the Buff drawing, and that Mr.

CASE *(continued)*

Skvorecz "failed to demonstrate that the functional characteristics of his claimed invention are not inherent in the structure disclosed by Buff." The Board stated that "[a]lthough the legs in Buff run [horizontally] along the long axis of the base [as in the drawing, the long leg running underneath the point labeled 58] rather than [downward from the] long axis as disclosed by applicant, such is not precluded by claim language." [That is, the examiner argued that the claim language "each wire leg . . . being affixed . . . to said lower rim" includes, or reads on, the Buff horizontal leg.]

Mr. Skvorecz argues that his device is not the same as that of Buff, and that his claims require that each wire leg has a laterally displacing offset, while the Buff wire leg does not have an offset that laterally displaces the leg from the rim. The Board agreed that "Buff's offset in the rim was not shown to be 'for laterally displacing each wire leg relative to said upper rim' as required by claim 1," but nonetheless maintained the rejection. On rehearing the Board stated that Buff's wire 48 [element 48 in the diagram for the Buff patent, above] is a "transverse member" and not a wire leg [*i.e.*, the cross member 48 in the Buff diagram is separate from the legs which run under element 58 in the diagram] and therefore that it need not have a displacing offset. Mr. Skvorecz states, and we agree, that Buff's wire 48 is a leg of the Buff structure. The Board's contrary statement is unsupported by any evidence.

The Buff device does not have an offset located in each wire that serves as a leg to support the device. In the Buff structure both the transverse wire 48 and the longitudinal wire [running under point 58] provide the bottom support analogous to wire legs, and it is undisputed that wire segment 48 does not have an offset. Anticipation cannot be found, as a matter of law, if any claimed element or limitation is not present in the reference. The "anticipation" rejection is reversed.

NOTES

1. This case is about whether the Skvorecz patent application meets the standard of §102, the novelty provision of the US Patent Act. Notice that the Federal Circuit in this opinion compared the elements of Skvorecz's claim 1 to the features depicted in the diagram from the Buff patent. No attention is paid to the *claims* of the Buff patent; it appears in this case as a reference, an individual piece of prior art. For purposes of applying §102 to the Skvorecz patent application, the claims of the Buff patent are irrelevant; what matters is the *disclosure* in the Buff patent – the detailed description and drawing of the invention in the Buff patent. For §102 purposes, every detail of a prior patent or published patent application is relevant, just as with every detail of a scientific or technical article, or an openly marketed product. Patents, published patent applications, technical articles, sold products, and many other individual references collectively make up the entirety of the prior art.

2. As we will see below, for the most part, the novelty analysis pre- and post-AIA is mostly the same. (Pre-AIA refers to the law prior to March 16, 2013 when the America Invents Act took effect; post-AIA refers to the current law, in effect since that date.) The main difference is with respect to timing: *when* does a prior art reference (a patent, publication, etc.) have to become available for it to count as prior art against a claimed invention? The US AIA, in tune with most other countries, uses the patent application filing date as the cutoff; a patent, publication, etc. (*i.e.*, any prior art "reference") must become available before the filing date to count as prior art. (There are a few exceptions; see below.) For pre-AIA patents (those issued or filed before March 16, 2013), a prior art reference must become available before the

invention date of the invention claimed in a patent application. The difference in relevant dates (or, as patent people call them, "critical dates") explains why the pre-AIA rule is called "first to invent" and the post-AIA rule "first to file." As mentioned, virtually every other patent office in the world conforms to the "first to file" rule, so the AIA simply brought the US into alignment with the world standard.

3. One important way that the AIA maintained continuity with the pre-AIA novelty rule is that the AIA retained many of the traditional words and phrases used to describe prior art references: "patents," "printed publications," "public use," and "on sale" are all found in the pre-AIA Patent Act as well as the AIA. Thus the pre-AIA case law that defines these well-recognized categories of prior art continues to be relevant even now. The same is true of the standard of novelty; the *Skvorecz* case, though decided pre-AIA, may still be cited for the idea that if a single prior art reference discloses every element of a claimed invention, that invention lacks novelty.

4.2 Types of prior art

The Patent Act lists five categories of prior art: (1) patents, (2) printed publications, (3) things "in public use," (4) things "on sale," and (5) information "otherwise available to the public."

Of these the first two are by far the most common types of prior art. These are, for example, very typically the types of prior art that a patent examiner will cite when issuing a rejection of a patent application. And they are the only type of prior art that may be cited when a third party, challenging the validity of an issued patent, requests an "Inter Partes Review" (IPR) proceeding before the Patent Office's Patent Trial and Appeal Board. For the average, everyday prior art search, patents and printed publications are in effect a fairly good approximation of "the prior art" for any given invention.

The next category, things "in public use," can be a fruitful source of prior art, but may be harder to discover and verify. Although an Internet search may turn up products that have features similar to a claimed invention, it can be difficult to tell with precision what the product features are. In addition, if an invention is made for personal use or use by a company for its own purpose, it may not be documented or widely publicized in any way. And most importantly, it may be hard to verify exactly when an invention was first "publicly used." This makes it hard to date exactly when the invention in question entered the prior art.

The fourth category, things that are "on sale," can be the most difficult of all to discover. This is because, as this category has been defined, an invention may simply be (a) *offered* for sale, with no actual resulting sale; and (b) the sale can be completely confidential (at least under pre-AIA law, and under the better reading of the AIA as well) (*Pfaff v. Wells Electronics, Inc.*, 525 U.S. 55 (1998)).

Practically speaking, then, most on sale prior art is discovered during litigation.

The *Skvorecz* case, earlier, dealt with an issued patent as prior art. The following case involves a reference that is a printed publication.

 CASE

In re Enhanced Security Research, LLC, 739 F.3d 1347 (Fed. Cir. 2014)

Dyk, Circuit Judge.
[Enhanced Security Research, or ESR, held U.S. Patent No. 6,119,236 ("the '236 patent"), which was subjected to a USPTO ex parte reexamination by a third-party requestor. In the reexamination, the Board of Patent Appeals and Interferences – predecessor to the current Patent Trial and Appeal Board – found the claims obvious under 35 USC §103. One of the references the third party submitted was a user's manual for a software product called "Netstalker." ESR appealed to the Federal Circuit.]

[Patent owner ESR] contends that the Board erred in treating the Manual as prior art. Whether a document qualifies as a "printed publication" that is "available to the public" for the purposes of 35 U.S.C. §102(a)(1) is a question of law based on underlying findings of fact. *See In re Hall*, 781 F.2d 897, 899 (Fed. Cir. 1986). Under 35 U.S.C. §102(a)(1), prior art encompasses any matter that "was patented, described in a printed publication, or in public use, on sale, or otherwise available to the public before the effective filing date of the claimed invention." This court has interpreted §102 broadly, explaining that even relatively obscure documents qualify as prior art so long as the public has a means of accessing them. Our leading case on public accessibility is *In re Hall*, 781 F.2d 897 (Fed. Cir. 1986). In *Hall* we concluded that "a single cataloged thesis in one university library" constitutes "sufficient accessibility to those interested in the art exercising reasonable diligence." *Id.* at 900.

Thereafter, in *Constant v. Advanced Micro-Devices, Inc.*, we explained that "[a]ccessibility goes to the issue of whether interested members of the relevant public could obtain the information if they wanted to." 848 F.2d 1560, 1569 (Fed. Cir. 1988). Therefore, "[i]f accessibility is proved, there is no requirement to show that particular members of the public actually received the information." *Id.* In this case, the title page of the Manual contains an inscription dating it to May 1996. ESR, however, challenges the Manual's claimed date of priority, arguing that the version of the Manual that the examiner relied on may not have been available in May 1996 and that there are indications that this version was a draft rather than a final document available to the public. However, Stephen Smaha, the Chief Executive Officer of the company that produces the NetStalker software, filed a declaration ("Smaha Declaration") with the PTO averring that the version of the Manual before the examiner was available in May 1996. Smaha explained that "[m]embers of

CASE (continued)

the public showing an interest in buying or licensing the NetStalker product could have obtained a copy of the manual by contacting Haystack or Network Systems Corporation and requesting one," and, indeed, "[t]he NetStalker product was sold to or installed for approximately a dozen customers."

In view of the Manual's inscription date, the Smaha Declaration, and evidence of NetStalker advertisements published in 1995, we conclude that substantial evidence supports the Board's finding that the Manual constituted publically-available prior art under §102(a)(1). ESR also argues that the Manual should not be considered in the circumstances of this case because it was missing pages. We conclude that the PTO's own rules permit the consideration of selected portions of prior art references so long as the missing portions are not necessary to fully understand the submitted portions. ESR cites no authority for the proposition that the PTO is categorically precluded from considering a reference if it is incomplete. We agree that missing pages may sometimes be necessary for understanding a prior art reference. But nothing in the Manual here suggests that the missing pages were necessary to an understanding of the pertinent parts of the reference. As the examiner explained, "[w]hen the source is reviewed as a whole, there is no evidence whatsoever that the missing pages detract in any way from the NetStalker manual's disclosures and teachings." JA 9157.14. The Board reached a similar conclusion, and we agree.

NOTES

1. Although the phrase "printed publication" calls to mind a formally published journal, magazine, book, newspaper, etc., the *Enhanced Security Research* case shows that far more "informal" publications will qualify. In the leading case, a different type of publication was involved:

   In October 1998, [three scientists] presented a printed slide presentation entitled "Enhancement of Cholesterol–Lowering Activity of Dietary Fibers By Extrusion Processing" at a meeting of the American Association of Cereal Chemists ("AACC"). The fourteen-slide presentation was printed and pasted onto poster boards. The printed slide presentation was displayed continuously for two and a half days at the AACC meeting. (*In re Klopfenstein*, 380 F.3d 1345, 1347 (Fed. Cir. 2004)).

   The "poster session" poster board was held to be a publication under 35 U.S.C. §102. In finding that the poster session was a publication, the court emphasized that "public accessibility . . . [is] the criterion by which a prior art reference will be judged." The court then listed four important factors in assessing public accessibility: "[T]he length of time the display was exhibited, the expertise of the target audience, the existence (or lack thereof) of reasonable expectations that the material displayed would not be copied, and the simplicity or ease with which the material displayed could have been copied" (*In re Klopfenstein*, 380 F.3d 1345, 1350 (Fed. Cir. 2004)).

2. The language of AIA §102(a) is slightly different from the pre-AIA language: the AIA added the fifth category of prior art mentioned above, the category "or otherwise available to the public." Some argued that this means that *all* categories of prior art under AIA §102 must be "available to the public," which would be a change. Under the pre-AIA §102, for example, it had long been held that items that were "on sale" could be sold confidentially, in a manner not at all public. *See, e.g., Special Devices, Inc. v. OEA, Inc.*, 270 F.3d 1353, 1357 (Fed. Cir. 2002) ("the on-sale bar would apply even if a patentee's commercial activities took place in secret."); *Buildex Inc. v. Kason Indus., Inc.*, 849 F.2d 1461, 1464 (Fed. Cir. 1988) (holding that a firm offer

sent to prospective purchaser was an "on sale" event, despite the fact that the offer was marked "confidential"); *Pfaff v. Wells Elec., Inc.*, 525 U.S. 55 (1998) (nowhere mentioning whether the purchase order that constituted the on sale event was ever made public; presumably it was not).

The better interpretation, however, is that "or otherwise available to the public" describes a "residual category" of prior art disclosures that were not captured cleanly by any of the pre-AIA prior art categories, such as an oral public presentation. On this view, then, the AIA has almost exactly the same definition of prior art as pre-AIA law.

3. Filed patent applications make up a special category of prior art. Section 102(b) is where this issue is addressed:

(a) **NOVELTY; PRIOR ART.** – A person shall be entitled to a patent unless –

(1) [see above]; or
(2) the claimed invention was described in a patent issued under section 151, or in an application for patent published or deemed published under section 122(b), in which the patent or application, as the case may be, names another inventor and was effectively filed before the effective filing date of the claimed invention (35 U.S.C. §102(b)).

This is a long sentence. It seems complex. And perhaps redundant: isn't "patented" one of the prior art categories under §102(a)? Why do we need this special §102(b) at all?

The key is in the last phrase: "the claimed invention was described in a [patent or application] *effectively filed before the effective filing date of the claimed invention*." The §102(a) category "patented" means *issued patents* – those that have matured from a patent application into an actual, patent office-issued patent. But this section, §102(b), applies not to issued patents, but to patent applications that are filed before an inventor files his or her patent application. In other words: If a later-filing inventor seeks a patent, an earlier-filed but *not yet issued* patent application forms part of the prior art. Even though patent applications are held in confidence (secrecy) until published or issued, they can be prior art as of their filing date.

But note: For a patent application to be prior art against a later-filed invention, the earlier-filed application has to eventually be published or issued. This is a strange feature of AIA §102(b) (and of pre-AIA §102(e), which it is based on). An application can be in the prior art – but only if it is *eventually* published or issued. When an earlier-filed application is published or issued, it becomes prior art *as of its filing date*. Publication or issuance puts it in the prior art, but it "back dates" this prior art reference to the filing date. Weird science, patent law style. The origins of this category of prior art can be found in an opinion by the esteemed Justice Oliver Wendell Holmes, *Alexander Milburn Co. v. Davis Bournonville Co.*, 270 U.S. 390 (1926).

One more feature worth noting: In the long sentence that makes up §102(b), you see this phrase: "the claimed invention was described in a patent [or application which] ... *names another inventor* ..." This means that an inventor who files a series of patent applications need not worry that his or her earlier-filed applications will count as prior art against his or her later-filed applications. It should also be noted that, even when an earlier application is filed by a different inventor, if both that earlier-filer and a later-filer work for the same company or research organization, the earlier-filed application will not be prior art against the later-filed one. *See* AIA §102(b)(2)(C).

4.3 Exceptions to the first-to-file rule under the AIA

The AIA moved the US much closer to the worldwide standard of "first to file" novelty. By shifting the "critical date" in §102 from the date of invention (as under pre-AIA law) to the filing date, the AIA now provides a simple rule for determining whether an invention is new: if a prior art reference appeared in the prior art before the inventor's filing date, the invention is not novel. "Newness" is measured with respect to the filing date of a patent application.

There are two general exceptions to this rule. The exceptions are covered in §102(b). Because this section of the Patent Act can be confusing, we explain it first. Then we introduce the actual text of the statute.

The first exception, §102(b)(1)(A), relates to disclosures made by the inventor him- or herself. An inventor has one year within which to file after making a disclosure. So an inventor who discloses an invention on June 1, 2016 (by publishing an article about it, or putting it on a website, or making a presentation at a conference), may file a patent application anytime up until June 1, 2017, and still maintain his or her right to a patent. This example shows why the §102(b) exceptions are known as a "grace period": Unlike the usual rule, where an inventor must file before a disclosure appears in the prior art, the inventor has an extra year to file.

The second exception is in §102(b)(1)(B). An inventor gets a one-year grace period against *any prior art* if he or she "publicly disclose[s]" the invention earlier than the date of the prior art. While the (b)(1)(A) exception, described just above, prevents the inventor's own disclosures from entering the prior art for one year, the (b)(1)(B) exception applies to all disclosures, no matter who makes them. Thus if on June 1 person B obtains a patent, or publishes an article, or starts publicly using an invention, inventor A can file a patent application *later than* person B's patent, article, or other disclosure. But inventor A must meet two requirements:

- inventor A must make a "public disclosure" *prior to* person B's disclosure; and
- inventor A must file a patent application within one year of his or her public disclosure.

So, with this background in mind, here is the full exceptions provision, in all its glory:

(a) **NOVELTY; PRIOR ART.** – A person shall be entitled to a patent unless –

(1) [invention in prior art]
(2) [special rule for patent applications filed before the claimed invention].

(b) **EXCEPTIONS.** –
(1) DISCLOSURES MADE 1 YEAR OR LESS BEFORE THE EFFECTIVE FILING DATE OF THE CLAIMED INVENTION. – A disclosure made 1 year or less before the effective filing date of a claimed invention shall not be prior art to the claimed invention under subsection (a)(1) if –

(A) the disclosure was made by the inventor or joint inventor or by another who obtained the subject matter disclosed directly or indirectly from the inventor or a joint inventor; or

(B) the subject matter disclosed had, before such disclosure, been publicly disclosed by the inventor or a joint inventor or another who obtained the subject matter disclosed directly or indirectly from the inventor or a joint inventor.

As we note, this can be confusing. A shortened version, with paraphrasing, may help matters:

§102(b)(1) A disclosure made one year or less before the effective filing date of a claimed invention shall NOT be prior art under section (a)(1) if –

(A) the disclosure was made by the inventor [or joint inventor or third party who obtained the invention]; or

(B) the subject matter disclosed [by a third party] had, before such disclosure, been publicly disclosed by the inventor [or joint inventor or third party who obtained the invention].

Several notes may help clarify further:

- A "disclosure" under this provision is any prior art reference. The pre-AIA Patent Act uses "disclosure" in this way, and it also follows from the structure of the statute. Section 102(a) is entitled "Novelty; Prior Art," while §102(b) is entitled "Exceptions." The language at the beginning of §102(b)(1) ("Disclosures made one year or less . . .") clearly refers to the subject of §102(a), which again is prior art.
- A "public disclosure" must logically be distinct from a disclosure. Because this is a new statute, the precise detours of this "publicness" requirement are not yet known. Of course it stands to reason that cases on "printed publications" and "public use" may help in this definition.
- Section 102 consistently uses the (cumbersome) phrase "the inventor or a joint inventor or another who obtained the subject matter disclosed directly or indirectly from the inventor or a joint inventor." Two points here:
  - The acts of a joint inventor are attributable to the other joint inventor(s); they invented as a team and their actions affect the team. They are legal "alter egos" of each other, and of the joint inventive entity considered as a whole.
  - Third parties who have obtained knowledge of an invention from an inventor or joint inventor will have their actions attributed the inventor as well. Although the meaning is not clear, this would certainly

seem to apply to one who surreptitiously, and without the inventor's consent (*i.e.*, "indirectly"), learns of the invention. It also may well apply to associates, colleagues, or coworkers of an inventor who obtain knowledge of the invention "directly" from the inventor.

4.4 Pre-AIA novelty

The categories of prior art discussed so far, for AIA §102, are essentially the same as those used under pre-AIA §102. The difference is the *critical date*: the date from which novelty is measured. Under the AIA, as we have seen, that is the filing date for a patent application. For pre-AIA patents (those filed before March 16, 2013), the critical date is the *date of invention*. Only prior art that becomes available before an inventor's date of invention is available under pre-AIA §102 as prior art against that invention.

One of the primary complexities of pre-AIA novelty is that the "date of invention" is a bit of a misnomer. Under case law from many years, three different events actually enter into a determination of the "date of invention." These are, in order:

- the *conception date*: the first date an inventor can prove he or she had the fully formed idea for an invention;
- the date of *reduction to practice*: the date a working version of the invention was first actually constructed or assembled; or, in the alternative, the date a fully descriptive and workable patent application was filed for an invention (called "constructive reduction to practice"); and
- the date when a patent application was filed (*filing date*).

These three dates, plus one additional rule that applies only in one special situation (the rule of *diligence*), are used to test for pre-AIA "first to invent" novelty. Under regulations applied by the Patent Office, an inventor "may submit an appropriate oath or declaration to establish invention of the subject matter of the rejected claim prior to the effective date of the reference" (37 C.F.R. §1.31). The specific rule applied is as follows:

> [The inventor must] establish reduction to practice prior to the effective date of the reference, or conception of the invention prior to the effective date of the reference coupled with due diligence from prior to said date to a subsequent reduction to practice or to the filing of the application (*id*).

According to the rule, an inventor who established reduction to practice before the effective date of a prior art reference can knock that reference out of the prior art – this shows he or she invented before the date of the reference. Because conception happens before (or at least, at the same time as) reduction to practice, this also necessarily means that an inventor who both conceives and reduces to practice before the effective date of a reference removes that reference from the prior art.

An inventor can also show first invention by showing (1) conception prior to the date of a reference, (2) combined with diligence in moving toward reduction to practice, and then (3) actual reduction to practice (or filing, which constitutes constructive reduction to practice). The key, however, as Rule 131 states, is that the diligence must begin no later than just before the effective date of the reference. This means that an inventor can predate a reference with evidence of conception *only* if he or she can connect that conception to a later reduction to practice by showing diligence in moving toward reduction to practice.

4.5 Pre-AIA patent priority: origins of the "first to invent" system

The rules for novelty as stated just now may seem a bit strange. While perhaps it makes sense to break invention into the stages of conception, reduction to practice, and filing, why should the rules have the precise structure they do – for example, the special role of diligence when connecting an earlier conception to a later reduction to practice?

The answer is that the rules for novelty evolved from cases where two inventors were both seeking a patent. These cases, strictly speaking, are cases of *priority*: the question is, which inventor, as between the two (or sometimes more) seeking a patent, ought to be awarded the patent? The "first to invent" rules began in this setting and were later applied to the simpler problem of novelty. Put simply, priority involves a dispute between two inventors who want a patent. Novelty involves a dispute over whether an invention is new compared to a prior art reference.

The basic rule of priority is often stated this way:

> [W]hen two inventors claim to have invented the same subject matter, priority of invention goes to the first inventor to reduce the invention to practice, unless the other inventor can show that he was the first to conceive the invention and that he exercised reasonable diligence in later reducing that invention to practice (*Monsanto Co. v. Mycogen Plant Science, Inc.*, 61 F. Supp. 2d 133, 180 (D. Del. 1999), later appeal, 261 F.3d 1356 (Fed. Cir. 2001)).

This simple rule covers four common variations:

(1) Where A is first to conceive and first to reduce to practice, A wins.
(2) Where A is first to conceive but last to reduce to practice, A wins but *only if* A can show diligence.
(3) Diligence only matters in this one situation (where an inventor is first to conceive and last to reduce to practice); in other words, in our example, B's diligence does not matter.
(4) The diligence that A must show is for the period beginning just before B entered the field; A must show continuous diligence (as you will see in the *Barbacid* case below) from a time just prior to when B entered the field until A's reduction to practice.

It will help to see how these rules apply in practice. The next case is an example.

 CASE

Brown v. Barbacid, 436 F.3d 1376 (Fed. Cir. 2006)

Newman, Circuit Judge.
This appeal of an invention priority determination, called a patent "interference" proceeding, returns to the Federal Circuit from the Board of Patent Appeals and Interferences (the "Board") of the United States Patent and Trademark Office. The parties are Michael Brown, Joseph Goldstein and Yuval Reiss (together "Brown") [of the University of Texas] and Mariano Barbacid and Veeraswamy Manne (together "Barbacid") [of the E.R. Squibb Pharmaceutical Co.]. The invention common to Brown and Barbacid is a method or assay for identifying compounds that inhibit farnesyl transferase ("FT"), an enzyme involved in the control of cell growth. [FT is an enzyme that catalyzes reactions associated with cell growth. Uncontrolled cell growth is a primary characteristic of cancer, so the ultimate purpose of the test or assay invention at stake in this priority contest is to identify chemical agents that might block FT's activity, and thereby help to treat cancer.]

[The claimed invention can be summarized as: a method for identifying a candidate substance having the ability to inhibit FT, comprising the steps of: (1) making or isolating a composition capable of transferring part of the FT molecule to another composition; (2) interacting the first composition with a "candidate substance" – the chemical being tested for anti-cancer activity; and (3) determining if the substance reduced the transfer of part of the FT molecule, and therefore might be useful in blocking the action of the FT enzyme, thus helping to treat cancer.]

The Barbacid filing date is May 8, 1990; the Brown application has an effective filing date

CASE *(continued)*

of April 18, 1990. [For this reason, Brown is known as the "senior party" – the first filer. Barbacid is the junior party.]

[The Board of Patent Appeals and interferences awarded priority to Barbacid. Brown appealed, and in a first Federal Circuit decision, it reversed the Board. 276 F.3d 1327 (Fed. Cir. 2002) ("*Brown I*") The Federal Circuit in *Brown I* found that, contrary to the Board's decision, the laboratory notebooks and autoradiograph images – images produced by adding radioactive material to material within a cell, to determine the distribution of the material within the cell – produced by Brown co-inventor Yuval Reiss were complete enough to credibly establish a date of conception for Brown. The Federal Circuit remanded to the Board after its *Brown I* decision.]

On remand, the Board held that Brown had established conception no later than November 15, 1989, but had failed to provide corroborated evidence of diligence. Barbacid v. Brown, Interf. No. 103,586 (Bd. Pat. App. & Interf. Sept. 28, 2004) ("*Brown II*"). The Board again awarded priority to Barbacid, and Brown again appealed.

The party that is first to conceive the invention in interference, if last to reduce the invention to practice, is entitled to the patent based on prior conception if, as first to conceive, he exercised reasonable diligence from a time before the other party's conception date to his own reduction to practice date. The purpose of requiring reasonable diligence by the first to conceive the invention but second to reduce to practice is to assure that the invention was not abandoned or unreasonably delayed by the first inventor during the period after the second inventor entered the field.

The first Board decision found Barbacid's date of actual reduction to practice; the Board did not decide Barbacid's conception date. Barbacid, the junior party, had been accorded its date of actual reduction to practice of March 6, 1990. Thus this court instructed that on remand the Board should determine whether Brown showed reasonable diligence from March 6, 1990, until Brown's filing date as constructive reduction to practice on April 18, 1990.

Brown provided evidence from inventor Dr. Reiss and laboratory technician Ms. Morgan concerning the exercise of reasonable diligence during the period from Barbacid's accorded date to Brown's filing date. Dr. Reiss stated that after September 1989 he worked on the farnesyl transferase project "on a daily basis." For the period following Barbacid's actual reduction to practice on March 6, 1990, Dr. Reiss stated that his experiments were directed at further characterizing the FT enzyme, improving the methodology for purifying the enzyme, and improving the overall performance of the assay. He provided laboratory notebook pages recording this work.

The Board rejected Dr. Reiss' testimony for lack of corroboration, and also observed that even if his notebook records showing this work were deemed to corroborate his testimony, they recorded work on only ten of the thirty-one days from March 6 to April 18, and thus were insufficient to establish reasonable diligence. Precedent requires that an inventor's testimony concerning his diligence be corroborated. The basic inquiry is whether, on all of the evidence, there was reasonably continuing activity to reduce the invention to practice.

CASE (continued)

Brown provided evidence of laboratory work during this period performed by Debra Morgan, a scientist working in the Brown laboratory, as evidence of diligence and as corroboration of Dr. Reiss' testimony. Her declaration was accompanied by copies of thirty-eight laboratory notebook pages [describing tests and studies she performed at the direction of Dr. Reiss during the contested diligence period]. Each of the thirty-eight notebook pages was associated with tests specified in her declaration.

The Board found that Ms. Morgan's notebook records along with those of Dr. Reiss filled all but six days of the critical period, and that each of the six remaining days was a single-day gap; this was deemed sufficient to show substantially continuing activity. The Board found that Ms. Morgan "worked for the inventors" and that "her work could inure to the benefit of the inventors to establish reasonable diligence over the entire period." However, the Board refused to credit any of Ms. Morgan's evidence, criticizing what it described as the absence of explanation of the content and purpose of [her] experiments.

We conclude that the Board erred in law, in failing to view the proffered evidence as it would be viewed by persons experienced in the field of the invention. It is undisputed that the subject matter recorded on the Morgan notebook pages and described in her declaration concerns the subject matter of the count. The Board agreed that Ms. Morgan's activity during the critical period, if accepted into evidence, established diligence. We conclude that the Board erred in refusing to accept this evidence, and that reasonable diligence is deemed established.

[Reversed on the question of priority, with priority going to the senior party Brown.]

NOTES

1. The senior party – *i.e.*, first filer – has a number of procedural advantages in a patent interference under pre-AIA law. For example, the junior party has the burden of proof in proving priority. *Smollar v. Cawley*, 31 USPQ2d 1506, 1507 (Bd. Pat. App. & Int'f 1993) ("[T]he burden is on . . . the junior party, to prove their case by a preponderance of the evidence"). The senior party, however, also has the burden of proof if it wants to show conception and/or reduction to practice dates earlier than its filing date. *Id.* So even under a "first to invent" system, there were advantages to filing first.

2. The concept of diligence applies when a first-conceiver reduces to practice later. What happens when there is a long delay between reduction to practice and any further activity, such as filing or commercialization of an invention? This is handled by the statutory concept of "abandonment, suppression or concealment." The rule here is that even one who is first to reduce to practice may lose out to a later inventor if the first inventor takes no action for a long period of time. *See Mason v. Hepburn*, 13 App. D.C. 86 (D.C. Cir. 1898). In general a long delay between reduction to practice and filing of a patent application may raise a concern with abandonment. But if the inventor has a good explanation for the delay – such as that he or she continued to perfect the invention and was working on implementing it – that will excuse the delay. *See, e.g., Dow Chemical Co. v. Astro-Valcour, Inc.*, 267 F.3d 1334 (Fed. Cir. 2001), cert. denied, 535 U.S. 989 (2002) (two-and-one-half year delay between reduction to practice and commercialization; no abandonment found); *Paulik v. Rizkalla*, 760 F.2d 1270, 1273 (Fed. Cir. 1985) (en banc) ("Intentional suppression occurs when an inventor 'designedly, and with the view of applying it indefinitely and exclusively for his own profit, withholds his invention from the public'"; permitting first inventor, who had abandoned invention, to "resuscitate" case for priority by showing that inventor resumed work before second inventor entered the scene).

3. The court in *Barbacid* quotes from the statute, pre-AIA §102(g). This section of the Patent Act reads as follows:

> A person shall be entitled to a patent unless –
>
> . . .
>
> (1) during the course of an interference conducted under section 135 or section 291, another inventor involved therein establishes, to the extent permitted in section 104, that before such person's invention thereof the invention was made by such other inventor and not abandoned, suppressed, or concealed, or
> (2) before such person's invention thereof, the invention was made in this country by another inventor who had not abandoned, suppressed, or concealed it. In determining priority of invention under this subsection, there shall be considered not only the respective dates of conception and reduction to practice of the invention, but also the reasonable diligence of one who was first to conceive and last to reduce to practice, from a time prior to conception by the other.

§102(g)(1) authorizes interferences. An interference is usually brought in the US PTO (under §135), but may be brought as a civil action in a federal district court (§291). The reference to §104 in §102(g)(1) means that evidence of inventive work (conception, reduction to practice, and diligence) may be introduced if the inventive work takes place in any WTO country, which effectively covers the world. The final sentence in §102(g)(2) ("In determining priority of invention under this subsection . . .") is the statutory basis for all the priority rules we have reviewed.

The second part of §102(g), section (g)(2), is not a true priority provision. It is a special source of prior art for novelty purposes. It says that an inventor cannot obtain a patent if "before [the inventor's] invention [date], the invention was made" (a) in this country (b) by another inventor (c) who has not abandoned the invention. The purpose of §102(g)(2) is to prevent the grant of a patent to one who was second to invent, but is the only inventor seeking a patent. By excluding inventions "made in this country by another" but not involved in an interference under pre-AIA §102 (g)(1), this provision insures the integrity of the "first to invent" principle of pre-AIA §102.

As a practical matter, this section usually applies only when a prior invention does not result in a printed publication, on sale event, or public use; these other prior art events are much easier to discover, and simpler to prove, than a §102(g)(2) prior invention by another. In addition, because (g)(2), like (g)(1), requires that the prior invention must not have been abandoned, suppressed, or concealed, this section applies primarily to prior inventions that have been commercialized in way that does not create publicly accessible evidence of the invention. The very difficulty of discovering this sort of evidence makes pre-AIA §102(g)(2) a fairly rare source of prior art. On occasion, however, it has proven useful to patent challengers. *See, e.g., Dow Chemical Co. v. Astro-Valcour, Inc.*, 267 F.3d 1334 (Fed. Cir. 2001), cert. denied, 535 U.S. 989 (2002) (defendant Astro-Valcour was sued for infringer by patentee Dow; Astro-Valcour invalidated the Dow patent by showing that it, Astro-Valcour, had invented the subject matter of the patent before the patentee did; held, this was valid §102(g)(2) prior art, and Astro-Valcour did not abandon, suppress or conceal the invention though it did take over two years to work out a commercially viable way to apply it).

Note that pre-AIA §(g)(2) requires the prior invention to have been made "in th[e] [US]"; this, along with a few other provisions of pre-AIA §102 was eliminated in the AIA; all categories of prior art are now worldwide in scope.

4.6 Novelty in China

4.6.1 The basic novelty standard

The Chinese patent system traditionally employed a "relative novelty" standard with respect to certain types of prior art. Specifically, to qualify as "public use" prior art under the old Chinese law, the public use had to occur domestically (within China). On the other hand, "publication"-type prior art has a worldwide scope. After the 2008 revision of the Chinese Patent Law, the standard of novelty is raised to a so-called "absolute novelty" standard. After 2008, "public use" occurring either domestically or abroad constitutes prior art. *See, e.g., Beijing Yingtelai Technologies Co. Ltd. v. China Resources and Sinoshield Ltd.* (Supreme People's Court 2015), Min Shen Zi No. 1541 ((2015)民申字第1541号) available at wenshu.court.gov.cn/content/content?DocID=99c42318-d75b-4f29-8d6e-792b6c128870 (transl. on 6/2/2017).

Article 22(1)

Inventions and utility models for which patent rights are to be granted shall be ones which are novel, inventive and of practical use.

Article 22(2)

Novelty means that the invention or utility model concerned does not belong to the prior art, and no patent application for the identical invention or utility model has been filed by any entity or individual with the patent administration department under the State Council before the date of application, and recorded in the patent application documents or the patent documentations which are published or announced after the date of application.

Article 22(5)

The term "prior art" as mentioned in this Law refers to the technologies known to the general public both at home and abroad prior to the date of application.

4.6.2 Prior art

Further explanation of the term "prior art" as mentioned in the Chinese Patent Law is described in the Rules of the Implementation of the Chinese Patent Law. The relevant statutory language is:

Rules for the Implementation of the Patent Law of the People's Republic of China (2002 Revision)

Article 30

The existing technology referred to in Article 22, paragraph three of the Patent Law means any technology which has been publicly disclosed in domestic or foreign publications, or has been publicly and domestically used or made known to the public by any other means, before the date of filing (or the priority date where priority is claimed), that is, prior art.

4.6.3 International priority and the grace period in China

There are two exceptions for prior art that can be patentable in China. The determination of these exceptions is based on the filing date. The first exception is based on the Paris Convention priority right owned by an inventor, which falls under Article 29 of the Chinese Patent Law.

Article 29

Where, within twelve months from the date on which any applicant first filed in a foreign country an application for patenting an invention or utility model, or within six months from the date on which any applicant first filed in a foreign country an application for patenting a design, he or it files in China an application for patenting the same, he or it may, in accordance with any agreement concluded between the said foreign country and China, or in accordance with any international treaty to which both countries are a party, or on the basis of the principle of mutual recognition of the right to priority, enjoy the right to priority.

Where, within twelve months from the date on which any applicant first filed in China an application for patenting an invention or utility model, he or it files with the patent administrative department of the State Council an application for patenting the same, he or it may enjoy the right to priority.

An invention or utility model published after the priority date does still own the novelty in application. There are two different categories of the priority right in China, which are the international priority right and domestic priority right owned by inventors.

The second exception for prior art is the extension of a six-month period prior to the filing date. It is the grace period for non-prejudicial disclosures. This rule is similar to the grace period of one year under the AIA Law of the United States. The relevant statutory language falls in Article 24 of Chinese Patent Law:

Article 24 [Grace Period]

An invention for which a patent is applied for does not lose its novelty where, within six months before the date of application, one of the following events occurred:

(1) where it was first exhibited at an international exhibition sponsored or recognized by the Chinese government;

(2) where it was first made public at a prescribed academic or technological meeting;
(3) where it was disclosed by any person without the consent of the applicant.

The following notes will help clarify some issues with respect to the grace period in China.

1. *The practical value of the six-month grace period.* The effect of the grace period is different from the effect of priority. The grace period means that some kinds of disclosure are merely regarded as non-prejudicial to the novelty and inventive step of the application, including some disclosures by the applicant (including inventor) or a third party who obtained knowledge of the invention from the applicant or inventor by legal or illegal means. Nevertheless, this does not mean the date of disclosure of the invention is regarded as the filing date of the application. Therefore, if any third party (say, Party B) makes an identical invention independently and files a patent application earlier than the application by the inventor/applicant (Party A), then, according to the principle of first-to-file, Party A's application will fail, because of Party B's priority. On the other hand, Party B's application may also lack novelty, because the "grace period"-qualifying disclosure by Party A will still be part of the prior art for the third party, Party B (Chapter 3, Section 5 of Part II, Guidelines for Patent Examination (2010)). The grace period in this sense is "personal" to an inventor: A disclosure which qualifies for the grace period under Chinese patent law will be removed from the prior art *for that inventor,* but not for other inventors/applicants. This grace period is, therefore, similar to the "inventor's own" grace period under US law, specifically AIA §102(b)(1)(A). See Jing Wang et. al., *Comparison of United States AIA First-Inventor-to-File with Chinese First-to-File,* 38 U. Dayton L. Rev. 251, 260 (2013).

    If, within six months from the date on which any of the events described in Article 24 occurred and before the applicant files the application, the invention was disclosed once again, provided that the disclosure does not belong to any of the prescribed events, the later disclosure will take away the novelty of the application. If the later disclosure also falls into any of the three prescribed events, the application does not lose novelty because of this later disclosure, but the grace periods shall be calculated from the date of the first disclosure.

    Therefore, inventors in China enjoy limited protection during the grace period. Only the inventor's own disclosure is removed from the prior art, and thus from the novelty analysis. Any third party who independently discloses prior to an applicant's application will anticipate that application. This is especially important when one considers that it may be difficult to prove that a third party obtained knowledge of an invention from an inventor/applicant. See Cui Guobin, Patent Law Cases and Materials, 2nd ed. (2016), at 251. This is a well-known feature of patent law: Proving copying of a patented invention, or proving that information was obtained from an inventor, present significant difficulties. See, e.g., Robert P. Merges, *A Few Kind Words for Absolute Infringement Liability in Patent Law*, 31 Berkeley Tech. L.J. 1, 22–28 (2016) (examining the stringency of proof required to prove "derivation" so as to invalidate a patent under pre-AIA 35 U.S.C. §102(f)).

2. Article 24(1) and (2) exempts certain public presentations from counting as prior art for up to six months. It is crucial to understand that these provisions are narrowly interpreted, however. One scholar who has studied the matter had this to say:

> Between April 1985 and December 2006, out of a total number of 3,334,376 applications, only 1,311 or about 0.039% of all patent applications invoked a grace period. The number of domestic applications was 2,727,626, but only 1,296 of these, or 0.048%, invoked a grace period. By comparison, more use of the grace period was made for patent inventions in the academic sector, where the grace period was invoked in 5.7% of all cases... Further, the grace period seems to be of some importance to small and medium-sized enterprises (Wan Xiaoli, *The Patent Novelty Grace Period in China in Comparative Perspective*, 40 Int'l Rev. of Intell. Prop. & Comp. L. (IIC) 182, 183 (2009)).

A presentation at a general "trade show" that is not a government-approved exhibition, or at a non-government-sanctioned academic conference, does not qualify for this grace period. See Wan Xiaoli, *supra*, at 183. The just-cited article recounts a case from China's Patent Reexamination Board (PRB) involving a design patent held by Rowland Corp.:

> On 9 September 2000, the Patent Re-examination Board upheld the decision of the Patent Office [for the following reasons:] although the disclosure occurred within six months prior to the filing date, the trade fair [at which the disclosure was made] was a commodity fair, not a prescribed academic or technological meeting as claimed by Rowland Corporation (citing Patent Reexamination Board of SIPO, No. FS1867, available at http://www.sipo-reexam.gov.cn/fushen/search/decidedetail.asp?jdh=FS1867&lx=FS (last accessed June 3, 2008).

The moral of the story is that it is essential to have proof that an academic meeting or technology exhibition is government sanctioned before making a public presentation – unless of course a priority patent application is on file (either in China or elsewhere) before the date of the presentation.

3. Article 24(3) removes from the prior art disclosures made by "any person without consent of the applicant." This is the equivalent of provisions in the US and Europe ("evident abuse" of the applicant), which prevent derived information from being used against the true inventor. Note that in China, at least some argue that the language in Article 24(3) might be interpreted to include the filing of a patent application. If such a filing is counted within the meaning of "disclose" then it would appear that Article 24(3) allows a later-filing inventor to obtain a patent, so long as he or she can prove that the earlier filer derived and filed an unauthorized application. *See* Jing Wang et. al., *Comparison of United States AIA First-Inventor-to-File with Chinese First-to-File*, 38 U. Dayton L. Rev. 251, 265 (2013) (Article 24(3) "seems to allow an inventor to avoid the consequence of losing out on the rights to the invention without going through what in the US would [be] require[d] in a derivation proceeding.").

4.6.4 The prior art defense in China

The prior art defense is a legal rule developed by the Chinese courts to solve challenges in patent litigation. Under the conventional Chinese patent system, an accused product or process that falls within the scope of protection of a granted patent is said to be infringing, even if it only uses techniques available in the public domain. Such a ruling is clearly unfair. To solve this problem, the prior art defense was established, where the accused infringer can assert a non-infringement defense by proving that the accused technical solution is a prior art.

The prior art defense was codified into the Chinese Patent Law as part of the 2008 revision. Article 62 of the Patent Law stipulates, in a patent infringement dispute, if the accused infringer has evidence to prove that an accused technical solution *belongs to the prior art*, it shall not constitute an infringement.

Article 62

In a patent infringement dispute, if the accused infringer has evidence to prove that the technology or design exploited is a technology or design of the prior art, the exploitation shall not constitute a patent right infringement.

As to how to decide whether "an accused technical solution belongs to the prior art," Article 14 of *Interpretation of the Supreme People's Court on Several Issues concerning the Application of Law in the Trial of Patent Infringement Dispute Cases, Fa Shi [2009] 21*, states that:

Where all the technical features which are alleged to fall into the scope of protection of a patent are *identical to or are not substantively different from* the corresponding technical features of a technical solution in the prior art, the people's court shall determine that the technology implemented by the alleged infringer as a prior art as provided for in Article 62 of the Patent Law (emphasis in original).

CASE

Kohler Co. v. Bravat Sanitary Equip. Co., Ltd. (Shanghai), Beijing No. 2 Intermediate People's Court, Min Chu Zi [2008] No. 13842, Dec. 18, 2008, aff'd on appeal, Beijing High People's Court, Min Zhong Zi [2009], No. 1553, April 20, 2009

Kohler Co. is the patentee of Chinese invention patent ZL01814674.0, titled "Overflowing soaker bath tub" (hereinafter, "the Subject Patent"), filed on June 25, 2001 and issued on September 7, 2005.

The asserted claims of the Subject Patent read as follows.

1. A bath tub, comprising:
   a bathing basin having a bottom wall and side walls extending to an upper rim;
   an overflow trough having a bottom wall spaced below the upper rim of the basin and above the bottom wall of the basin;
   a conduit providing fluid communication between the overflow trough and basin; and
   a pump associated with the conduit for delivering water from the trough to the basin, wherein said overflow trough is disposed radially outward around at least a majority of a perimeter of the basin for collecting water falling from the upper rim.
2. The bath tub of claim 1, wherein the upper rim of the basin is higher than an uppermost part of the overflow trough.
9. The bath tub of claim 1, wherein an overflow drain opening is disposed in a wall of the trough.
16. The bath tub of claim 9, it further comprises a drain control that operates a drain plug disposed in a drain opening in the bottom wall of the basin, wherein the drain control is mounted to an inner side wall of the overflow trough.

[Kohler Co. asserted that Shanghai Bravat Co. and Guangzhou Bravat Co. infringed the Subject Patent through the manufacture and sale of the accused infringing bathtub. Regarding evidence, Kohler Co. made a notarized purchase of a bathtub (model type B25001W-4). Documents pertaining to the bathtub include: (1) Inspection Report

CASE *(continued)*

stamped with a seal of Beijing Office of Bravat Sanitary Equipment Co., Ltd.; (2) Retailer Authorization stamped with a seal of Bravat (Shanghai) Sanitary Equipment Co. Ltd. (referred to as "Shanghai Bravat Co."); (3) Product Specification; (4) User Manual; and (5) a Warranty Card.]

[Shanghai Bravat Co. and Guangzhou Bravat Co. defended that they did not infringe the subject patent because: (1) the Subject Patent was anticipated by prior art; and (2) the technical solution used by the accused bathtub was prior art. For the prior art defense, defendants collectively submitted seven prior art documents to prove that the technique used by the accused product was publicly known well before the filing date of the subject patent. The main prior art document is DE3610823, which is a German patent, filed on April 1, 1986.]
Claim 1 of DE3610823 reads:

> ... [A] pool, ... and at least one overflow trough to discharge at least a part of the overflow through the upper edge of [the] pool ... characterized in that ... if necessary, the water into the pool [may be resupplied] at least partially via the circulation system in at least one of the following ways, preferably [using] at least one circulation pump and the water circulation line and at least one jet nozzle ...

Claim 4 of DE3610823 reads:

> [The] [p]ool according to claim 1 or 2, characterized in that the edge of pool which is surrounded by the overflow trough or recess is higher than the overflow edge of the pool, and is at least partially higher than the trough or recess.

The description of DE3610823 describes at least one safety overflow, installed on the overflow trough or recess, connected to a water discharging line. Figure 1 of DE3610823 shows the safety overflow is connected to the side wall of the overflow trough.

[Regarding the prior defense proposed by Defendants, Beijing No. 2 Intermediate People's Court made the following findings,]
Claim 1 of the Subject Patent has the following essential technical features:

(1) a bathing basin having a bottom wall and side walls extending to an upper rim;
(2) an overflow trough having a bottom wall spaced below the upper rim of the basin and above the bottom wall of the basin;
(3) a conduit providing fluid communication between the overflow trough and basin;
(4) a pump associated with the conduit for delivering water from the trough to the basin,
(5) wherein said overflow trough is disposed radially outward around at least a majority of a perimeter of the basin for collecting water falling from the upper rim.

CASE *(continued)*

Claim 2 further defines another essential technical feature:

(6) the upper rim of the basin is higher than an uppermost part of the overflow trough.

Claim 9 further defines another essential technical feature:

(7) an overflow drain opening is disposed in a wall of the trough.

Claim 16 further defines another essential technical feature:

(8) a drain control that operates a drain plug disposed in a drain opening in the bottom wall of the basin, wherein the drain control is mounted to an inner side wall of the overflow trough.

[Relying upon the submitted German patent DE3610823, the Court found that:]

(i) claim 1 of DE3610823 disclosed features (1)–(5) of the Subject Patent;
(ii) claim 4 of DE3610823 disclosed feature (6) of the Subject Patent by defining "the edge of pool which is surrounded by the overflow trough or recess is higher than the overflow edge of the pool"; and
(iii) Figure 1 of DE3610823 disclosed feature (7) of the Subject Patent by showing a safety overflow (14) connected to the side wall of the overflow trough and connected to a water discharging line.

[Accordingly, the Court accepted the defendants' prior art defense against asserted claims 1, 2 and 9 of the Subject Patent.]

[Regarding the asserted claim 16, the court found that the "drain control" defined in claim 16 of the Subject Patent was not read on the accused bathtub.]

The plaintiff's request is thus rejected by the Court.

Beijing No. 2 Intermediate People's Court

Judge Wei LIU
Judge Yufeng HAN
Juror Wei ZHANG
Dec. 18, 2008

NOTES

1. **The rationale behind the prior art defense.** If the asserted patent does not have novelty, which is a substantial patentable condition of the patent law, it should be invalidated after an invalidation request is raised. However, the invalidation proceeding is costly and often lasts for years, so the prior art defense creates a faster and cheaper option.
2. **Prior art defense and novelty.** The current standard for the prior art defense in Chinese patent litigation is largely consistent with the "novelty" test standard adopted in patent prosecution. It is important that the prior

art defense test standard in patent litigation does not apply the "inventiveness" test standard adopted in patent prosecutions. For example, to apply the prior art defense, he defendant should not be allowed to look at the combinations of multiple technical solutions, or any "technical inspiration" for making such a combination.

In *Kohler Co. v. Bravat Sanitary Equip. Co., Ltd.*, the court adopts an "identical with or are not substantially different from" test to apply the prior art defense. Assume the involved patent has five essential technical features – (A), (B), (C), (D), and (E) – and the accused product has five corresponding features – (a), (b), (c), (d), and (e). If the said features (a), (b), (c), (d), and (e) are found to be "identical with or are not substantially different from" the corresponding technical features of a technical solution in the prior art, then the prior art defense is satisfied. It should be noted that it is not necessary to examine all the technical features of an accused product or process, but only the technical features alleged to fall within the scope of the subject patent would suffice.

3. Note that the prior art invalidity defense is closely related to a similar defense: the "practicing the prior art" defense. *See* Timothy Lau, *Offensive Use of Prior Art to Invalidate Patents in U.S. and Chinese Patent Litigation*, 30 UCLA Pac. Basin L.J. 201, 203 (2013). An accused infringer who is "practicing the prior art" is free of infringement liability because prior designs are by definition not protectable by a patent. On this principle generally, *see* Robert P. Merges, Justifying Intellectual Property 141–43 (2011) (describing a general principle of IP rule, called the "nonremoval principle," under which public domain material may not be the subject of a property right). The invalidity defense, on the other hand, does *not* require that the accused infringer argue that it is itself practicing the prior art. It is simply an argument that there is prior art somewhere (not necessarily reflected in the infringer's own products) that predates the patent owner's patent, thus rendering it invalid.

4.6.5 Disclosure of prior art

CASE

Zhenjiang Yingfang Plastic & Electric Co., Ltd. v. Patent Reexamination Board, Guangdong Kejin Nylon Piping Manufacturing Co., Ltd, Beijing No.1 Intermediate People's Court, Zhi Xing Chu Zi [2010] No. 3085. Aff'd on appeal, Beijing High People's Court, Xing Zhong Zi [2011] No. 31. Revoked in retrial, Supreme People's Court, Xing Ti Zi [2012] No. 25, November 20, 2012.

Guangdong Kejin Nylon Piping Manufacturing Co., Ltd (hereinafter "Kejin") is the patentee of Chinese Utility Model Patent ZL03274825.6, tilted as "A cast nylon flanged pipe" (hereinafter "the Subject Patent"), which was filed on September 28, 2003.

Claims 1–7 of the Subject Patent read as follows.

1. A cast nylon flanged pipe, including a flange (1) and a straight tube (2), characterized in that the flange (1) and the straight tube (2) are formed into one integral piece, a surface of the flange is provided with a cylindrical support (11), a surface of the cylindrical support is provided with a plurality of grooves (12).

CASE *(continued)*

2. The cast nylon flanged pipe of claim 1, characterized in that the surface of the cylindrical support provided on the surface of the flange has several pieces of "V" shaped grooves (12), the bottom of which forms an angle.
3. The cast nylon flanged pipe of claim 2, characterized in that the "V" shaped grooves have an angle of 60 to 120 degrees formed at the bottom.
4. The cast nylon flanged pipe of claim 2, characterized in that the "V" shaped grooves have an angle of 90 degrees formed at the bottom.
5. The cast nylon flanged pipe of claim 1, characterized in that a space is provided between grooves (12) on the surface of the cylindrical support, and an annular projection (13) is provided on the space, and a recess (14) is provided at a corresponding position on the surface of the other end of the flange.
6. The cast nylon flanged pipe of claim 1, wherein an annular structure (15) is provided around the cylindrical support on the surface of the flange, and the inner diameter of the annular structure (15) matches the outer diameter of the cylindrical support at the other end of the flange, and the height of the annular structure (15) is greater than the thickness of a sealing gasket.
7. The cast nylon flanged pipe of claims 1–6, wherein an "L"-shaped enforcing rib (21) is provided at the connection of the pipe and the flange.

The Subject Patent also has the following figure[] to illustrate the claimed article.

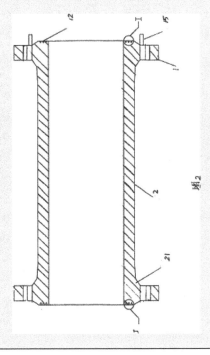

CASE *(continued)*

[In a previous invalidation Decision No. 9751 made by the PRB, claim 1 was declared to be invalid, claims 2–7 were maintained as valid.]

[On April 10, 2009, Zhenjiang Yingfang Plastic & Electric Co., Ltd. (hereinafter "Yingfang Plastic & Electric") filed another invalidation request with the PRB to invalidate claims 2–4 and 7 of the Subject Patent. One of the invalidation grounds is that the Subject Patent has no inventiveness in view of Chinese patent literature CN3205299D (hereinafter "D1") and the national standard HG5005-58 "Pipe, Connection part, and Flange tight faces of pipes" (hereinafter "D2").]

D1 is a Chinese design patent ZL01314886 titled as "tube", which claims an integral tube made of MC nylon material as shown in the following figures.

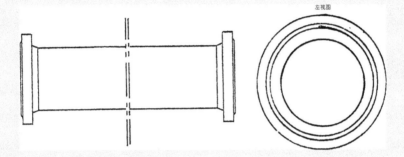

[The PRB made the invalidation Decision No.15012, declaring that claims 2–4 have no inventiveness over D1 and D2, and thus are invalid. Claims 5–7 are maintained as valid.]

[Kejin filed an administrative lawsuit against PRB's Decision No. 15012. On appeal, Beijing No. 1 Intermediate Court revoked the PRB's Decision. PRB appealed, Beijing High Court affirmed. PRB appealed again, and the Supreme Court decided to hear ("retry") the case.]

[The Supreme Court held that,] there are two key issues in question: (1) from the drawings of D1, whether the cylindrical projection shown in Figure 1 can be directly and unambiguously considered as a flange or other tube-connecting component? (2) Whether D1 teaches the forming of a flange and a tube as one integral piece?

[Regarding the first issue, the Supreme Court explained the technical meaning of the term "flange" from both its ordinary meaning and the context of the Subject Patent. Then, the Supreme Court held that,] it is true that D1 does not explicitly describe the cylindrical projection as a flange. However, in view of the structural features shown in the figures of D1, combining the common knowledge of a person of ordinary skill in the art, it is clear the cylindrical projection is actually used as a flange. Thus, the lower courts erred in concluding that "the cylindrical projection shown in Figure 1 of D1 cannot be directly and unambiguously considered as a flange or other tube-connecting component".

[Regarding the second issue, the Supreme Court also held that the lower courts erred in concluding there is no teaching of forming a flange and a tube as an integral piece, on the basis of the Court's finding that there is a flange present in D1.]

CASE *(continued)*

The Court made the following rulings:

(1) Revoking Beijing No. 1 Intermediate People's Court, Zhi Xing Chu Zi [2010] [Order] No. 3085, Beijing High People's Court, Xing Zhong Zi [2011] No. 31.
(2) Sustaining PRB's Decision No. 15012.

This is the final judgement.

Judge Yongchang WANG
Judge Jian LI
Judge Shuhua SONG
November 30, 2012

NOTE

1. In *Yingfang Plastic & Electric Co., Ltd. v. PRB, Kejin Nylon Piping Manufacturing Co., Ltd.*, the Supreme Court held that common knowledge of a person of ordinary skill in the art can be used in interpreting the disclosure of a prior art reference. This extends the disclosure of prior art and thus raises the threshold of establishing novelty or inventiveness of a patent.

4.6.6 The identity requirement in China

Xu Yan, Beijing Dong Fang Jing Ning Construction Materials Tech. Ltd. v. Beijing Rui Chang Wei Ye Real Estate and Tech. Devel. Co., Ltd., Beijing No. 2 Intermediate People's Court, Min Chu Zi [2008] No. 120, June 20, 2008. Aff'd on appeal, Beijing High People's Court, Min WZhong Zi [2008] No. 1165, November 20, 2008

Xu Yan is the patentee of Chinese utility model patent ZL200420077923.9 entitled "Light foaming material filling member with reinforced hard coating" (hereinafter, "the Subject Patent"), filed on July 16, 2004 and granted on August 10, 2005.

(continued)

On July 15, 2007, Xu Yan granted a non-exclusive license to Dong Fang Jing Ning Construction Materials Technology Co., Ltd. (hereinafter, "Dong Fang Jing Ning Ltd."). The term of the non-exclusive license was seven years.

Beijing Rui Chuang Wei Ye Real Estate Development Co., Ltd. (hereinafter, "Rui Chuang Real Estate Ltd.") and Beijing Rui Chuang Wei Ye Science and Technology Development Co., Ltd. (hereinafter, "Rui Chuang Science and Technology Ltd.") were contracted constructors for the Light-Weight porous material (LPM) hollow floor construction project of Zhongguancun Electronic City West District (Wang Jing Technology Park) E6/E7 plots R&D center.

[For this project, Rui Chuang Real Estate Ltd. and Rui Chuang Science and Technology Ltd. used a Phase Change Material (PCM) inner membrane manufactured and sold by Beijing Rui Da Hua Tong Chemical Material Technology Co., Ltd. (hereinafter, "Rui Da Hua Tong Ltd."). These PCM membranes are made of materials that change from liquid to solid and back again, and in the process can store and release energy. They are thus used as part of "passive" heating systems.]

[Xu Yan and Dong Fang Jing Ning Ltd. asserted that the PCM inner membrane infringed the Subject Patent and therefore they brought a lawsuit before Beijing No. 2 Intermediate People's Court. Rui Da Hua Tong Ltd. defended on the grounds that the Subject Patent does not have inventiveness over the prior art and should not reap the benefits offered by the patent law.]

[After the court trial, Beijing No. 2 Intermediate People's Court made the following findings:]

Claim 1 of the Subject Patent reads as follows.

1. A light foaming material filling member with reinforced hard coating, comprising a body part (1), characterized in that the body part (1) is surrounded by a sealing layer (2), and a reinforced layer (3) is between the body part (1) and the sealing layer (2).

[According to Beijing No. 2 Intermediate People's Court,] technical features of the accused PCM inner membrane are as follows: (a) the body part, which is a light foaming material filling member; (b) the body part is wound with tapes; (c) a combination of slurry and grid-like fabrics are provided between the body part and the tapes. The patent owner/plaintiffs asserted that this structure infringed the three-part structure of claim 1 of the patent in suit; with the inner material being inside the "body part", the slurry and grid-like fabrics are the reinforced layer, and the tape wound around this combination forming the sealing layer.]

[As a prior art defense, Rui Da Hua Tong Ltd. provided a prior art document, Chinese Utility Model Patent ZL02293406.5, titled "Light porous material filled with multiple section shapes used in concretes" (hereinafter, "D1"), which was filed on December 24, 2002 and granted on February 25, 2004.]

[The Court found that,] In D1, there are the following technical features: (A) the body part, which is a light porous material; (B) an isolation layer partially made of plastic tapes

(continued)

winding around the outer wall of the body part, and then an intermediate layer combining slurry and fabrics inside the winding tapes.]

[The Court stated that,] the issue presented here is whether the technical solution employed by the allegedly infringing product belongs to the prior art D1.

[The Court first stated the legal standard for making a prior art defense,] according to the patent law, if the defendant proves that the allegedly infringing product belongs to the prior art, then there is no infringement. This is called the prior art defense. Pursuant to the *Supreme Court's Judicial Interpretations Fa Shi [2009] No. 21*, if an allegedly infringing product is "identical to or not substantively different from" a piece of prior art, it is considered to belong to the prior art.

[Then the Court conducted a specific comparison as follows,] in the present case, D1 has a publication date earlier than the filing date of the subject patent, and thus is prior art. Feature (A) of D1 is identical to feature (a) of the allegedly infringing product, feature (B) of D1 is not substantively different (or, is equivalent to) to both features (b) and (c) of the allegedly infringing product. Accordingly, the technical solution of the allegedly infringing product belongs to the prior art D1, and the manufacture and selling of the allegedly infringing product by Rui Da Hua Tong Ltd. does not constitute infringement of the Subject Patent.

Relying on the above facts and reasoning, the Court ruled in favor of the defendants.

NOTES

1. **"Identical to or not substantively different from" test for prior art defense.** Article 62 of the Chinese Patent Law of 2008 defines "prior art defense":

    "In a patent infringement dispute, if the accused infringer has evidence to prove that the technology or design exploited is a technology or design of the prior art, the exploitation shall not constitute a patent right infringement."

    Further, according to the SPC's judicial rules, if an allegedly infringing product is "identical or not substantively different from" a piece of prior art, it is considered to belonging to the prior art.

    Article 14

    Where all the technical features which are alleged to fall into the scope of protection of a patent are *identical to or are not substantively different from* the corresponding technical features of a prior art technical solution, the people's court shall determine the technology implemented by the alleged infringer as a prior art technology as provided for in Article 62 of the Patent Law." (Interpretation of the Supreme People's Court on Several Issues concerning the Application of Law in the Trial of Patent Infringement Dispute Cases (promulgated by the Supreme People's Court, December 28, 2009, effective January 1, 2010, available at http://www.law-lib.com/law/law_view.asp?id=305372).

2. Another case that applies the "identical or not substantively different" test for novelty is *Microsoft (China) Ltd. v. Patent Reexamination Board, Zheng Long,* Beijing No. 1 Intermediate People's Court, Xing Chu Zi [2008] No. 1021, Nov. 21, 2008. There the court held that a prior art software technique for interpreting keystrokes as Mandarin characters did not anticipate (*i.e.*, destroy the novelty of) claims in a patent held by Zheng Long. The order of keystroke entry, together with how the keystroke recognition software identified positional information, was too different in the prior art patent. This meant that Zheng Long's infringement claim against Microsoft could proceed.

3. **"Substantially identical" test for deciding novelty**. When deciding on the issue of "novelty," if the two technical solutions are "substantially identical" they will be considered as the same invention, thus destroying the novelty. This is generally agreed to be a more stringent novelty requirement than we see under US law. *See, e.g.,* Timothy Lau, *Offensive Use of Prior Art to Invalidate Patents in U.S. and Chinese Patent Litigation*, 30 UCLA Pac. Basin L.J. 201, 203 (2013) ("Unlike its U.S. counterpart, which regards an invention as lacking novelty only if the prior art reads on the invention, the Chinese novelty inquiry incorporates an equivalence-type analysis that expands the exact teachings of the prior art to encompass inventions that have the same structure, technical effects, and role"). According to the Examination Guidelines, the "substantial[ly] identical" test involves three elements, *e.g.,* technical field, technical means, and technical effects.

> Section 3.1, Chapter 3, Part II, Examination Guidelines
> Comparing the application being examined with the relevant contents of the prior art or of the invention or utility model filed previously by another person with the Patent Office and published on or after the filing date of the application being examined (hereafter "previously filed and later published" application), if their technical fields, technical problems to be solved, technical solutions, and their expected effects are substantially the same, they shall be regarded as identical inventions or utility models. It should be noted that, in determining the novelty of an application, the examiner shall first of all determine whether the technical solution of the application being examined is *substantially the same* as that of the reference document. When an application is compared with the contents disclosed in a reference document, if the technical solution defined in a claim therein and the technical solution disclosed in the reference document are substantially the same, and the person skilled in the art of the solutions can conclude that both of them can be applied to *the same technical field, solve the same technical problem, and have the same expected effects,* then they can be regarded as identical inventions or utility models.

As one commentator notes, this bears a strong resemblance to the analysis of infringement under the US doctrine of equivalents. *See* Timothy Lau, *supra*, at 222 ("This language used by the people's courts in the novelty analysis mirrors that of equivalence . . .").

4. **Separate comparison**. Further, the technical solution defined by the claim will be compared with that disclosed in one single prior art document.

> Section 3.1, Chapter 3, Part II, Examination Guidelines
> When determining novelty, the examiner shall compare each claim of the application separately with the relevant technical contents disclosed in each item of the prior art or each previously filed and later published invention or utility model, rather than with a combination of the contents disclosed in several items of the prior art or several previously filed and later published applications or with a combination of several technical solutions disclosed in one reference document. That is, the principle of separate comparison shall be applied in the determination of novelty of an invention or utility model application, which is different from the approach to the determination of inventive step of an invention or utility model application (see Chapter 4 Section 3.1 of this Part).

Separate comparison means the prior art defense shall be based on a single piece of prior art, rather than a combination of multiple pieces of prior art (referred to as "combined comparison"). There are proponents of both, but the prevailing opinion in judicial practice is to adopt the "separate comparison" (single reference) approach. "The prior art used for a non-infringement defense shall be a single piece of prior art, that is, a one-by-one comparison shall be made between the accused technical solution and the piece of prior art. It is prohibited to combine multiple pieces of prior art and use such a combined technical solution for prior art defense" (Cheng Yong Shun, Practices in Patent Infringement Judgment (2002), at 87). For a case that appears to permit analysis of multiple prior art references in this defense, see *Hou Wanchun v. Patent Re-examination Board of the State Intellectual Property Office of the People's Republic of China and Tencent* (2015) Zhi Xing Zi No. 100 ((2015) 知行字第100号) available at http://wenshu.court.gov.cn/content/content?DocID=d7ede1a9-ced0-4ad1-9904-252199984670 (transl. on 6/1/2017). The plaintiff here, Hou, is a famous plaintiff in China, having brought a series of cases against Tencent, the cutting-edge technology company in China, and other leading technology corporations in the past four years. But Hou failed in all the cases, mostly because his patents were found invalid. Hou's activities have been discussed in China. See, *e.g.,* (2017) Lu Zhi Fu 39, available at http://wenshu.court.gov.cn/

content/content?DocID=0a0388cd-0913-4cf1-ae50-a744017c34db; (2016) Supreme Court Xing Shen 3313, available at http://wenshu.court.gov.cn/content/content?DocID=c6766687-3081-448e-b970-a7470121ce4c.

5. **Scope of Prior Art**. Claim 1 of D1 defines: (A) Light porous material; (B) An isolation layer, made by coating or winding one or more layers of mortar-like material (such as water slurry), fiber (such as fiber cloth), tapes (such as plastic tape) or the combination thereof; (C) *An enforced layer* made of spiral rib or steel cage, surrounding the outer wall of the isolation layer. Comparing the accused product with claim 1 of D1, the prior art defense will not succeed because there is no "enforced layer" in the accused product. Fortunately, D1 also discloses an embodiment that does not require said "enforced layer". This embodiment of D1 is compared with the accused product by the Court, and thus the Court supported the plaintiff's prior art defense.

4.7 Novelty/state of the art in Europe

The basic provisions on novelty under the EPC are found in Article 54 (Novelty) and Article 55 (Non-prejudicial Disclosures). They are out set out here:

Article 54
Novelty

(1) An invention shall be considered to be new if it does not form part of the state of the art.
(2) The state of the art shall be held to comprise everything made available to the public by means of a written or oral description, by use, or in any other way, before the date of filing of the European patent application.
(3) Additionally, the content of European patent applications as filed, the dates of filing of which are prior to the date referred to in paragraph 2 and which were published on or after that date, shall be considered as comprised in the state of the art. . . .

Article 55
Non-prejudicial disclosures

(1) For the application of Article 54, a disclosure of the invention shall not be taken into consideration if it occurred no earlier than six months preceding the filing of the European patent application and if it was due to, or in consequence of:

(a) an evident abuse in relation to the applicant or his legal predecessor, or
(b) the fact that the applicant or his legal predecessor has displayed the invention at an official, or officially recognised, international exhibition falling within the terms of the Convention on international exhibitions signed at Paris on 22 November 1928 and last revised on 30 November 1972.

(2) In the case of paragraph 1(b), paragraph 1 shall apply only if the applicant states, when filing the European patent application, that the invention has been

so displayed and files a supporting certificate within the time limit and under the conditions laid down in the Implementing Regulations.

The key issues in any novelty decision are: (1) timing: to establish that the document, prior use, or other piece of prior art (in US parlance, the prior art "reference") was within the state of the art before the patent applicant's priority date; (2) identity: to establish that the single prior art document, etc. (reference) discloses every element of the claimed invention whose novelty is at issue; and (3) sufficiency: to establish that the reference disclosed the information contained in it with adequate sufficiency to teach one of skill in the art about the claimed invention. Then it must be determined if one of the exceptions in Article 55 applies, *i.e.*, whether the disclosure, though timely and adequate, is "non-prejudicial" because it meets a statutory exception (evident abuse; display at a qualified international exhibition). We take up each of these issues in the sections that follow.

Munters Europe A.B. v. KyotoCooling B.V., Case No. T 0353/14 (Eur. Pat. Off. Bd. App., 15 Sept 2016)

[The opposed patent covered use of recycled air in a cooling system for large collections of computer servers. The opposing party, Munters Europe, relied in part on a technical white paper (denoted "document D10" in the opinion) that disclosed the elements of the claimed invention. Patent owner KyotoCooling argued in the opposition that this white paper document did not form part of the state of the art, because Munters could not prove that it was available on the Internet at a date earlier than the patent owner's filing date. The Internet website involved in this case is that of the American Power Conversion Corporation, or "APC," and the priority date of the patent owner's patent is September 6, 2006. As noted in the case, APC was acquired by Schneider Electric in 2007. The opinion also makes reference to a publicly available Internet archive called "the Wayback Machine", which allows a user to check the complete contents of the public Internet for any given date in history since roughly 2005; see http://archive.org/web/ ("Internet archive Wayback Machine").]

The opposition division held in the decision under appeal that – on the balance of probabilities – document D10 had not been made available on the Internet before the priority date of the opposed patent. In particular, the opposition division referred to several variations of document D10, namely document D19 and two further documents annexed to the decision under appeal ("Annex I" and "Annex II").

The appellant [opposer, Munters] argued that document D10 had been made available

CASE *(continued)*

on the Internet, specifically on the APC website. The appellant's submissions in this respect can be divided into two main lines of arguments. The first concerns the alleged uploading of document D10 to the APC website, while the second concerns the alleged archiving of D10 on the Wayback Machine.

As indicated above, the opposition division applied the usual standard of proof "balance of probabilities" when assessing whether document D10 had been made available on the Internet before the relevant date.

[The opposer/appellant in this case introduced] a printout of an email dated 15 January 2014 of Mr. Avelar, an employee of Schneider Electric (which had acquired APC in 2007), stating that the file "WP113rev1SN1.pdf" attached to the email was "first released" on 26 October 2005 to the "document reference library" (DRL) database. Annexed to the email printout is a printout of the attached file, which corresponds to document D10.

APC maintains an internal database, the document reference library (DRL), which is accessible to employees of APC and contains a wide variety of documents, e.g. white papers and user manuals. When the status of a document in the DRL is changed to "released", a link to the document is automatically created on APC's public website. Once a white paper is released in this way, it is publicly accessible through an APC website (apc.com, whitepapers.apc.com, apcmedia.com).

Mr. Avelar's statement that the file "WP113rev1SN1.pdf" was "first released" on 26 October 2005 concerns the action of another person, namely Mr. Menon, and was made more than eight years after that date, *i.e.*, in [an] email of 15 January 2014 [pertaining to the opposition], without providing any indication on how this particular file was recovered after so many years and how the link to the log file could be established.

[After reviewing certain other discrepancies in the evidence,] the board is not convinced that the sequence of events in relation to the uploading of document D10 to the APC website transpired in fact as asserted by the appellant.

The board notes that it is well known that links in a website archived by the Wayback Machine may not be preserved or – if intact – may connect to different material than at the time of capture. It is therefore not possible to access, using the Wayback Machine, White Paper 113 as it was available on the APC website at the time of archiving (12 December 2005).

Consequently, the board is not convinced that document D10 was publicly available on the APC website at the time of archiving indicated in document D11 (12 December 2005). In view of the above the board concludes that document D10 cannot be considered as having been made available on the Internet before the priority date of the opposed patent.

NOTES

1. Because of the fluid nature of the Internet, problems of proof such as those that faced the opposing party in this case are common, and may be expected to grow over time. Various "time stamping" solutions to this problem have emerged. One, for example, is available from the same archiving website referred to in the case, the Wayback Machine, *See* www.archive.org/web/ at "Capture a web page as it appears now for use as a

trusted citation in the future." *See generally* WikiPedia Entry, "Trusted Timestamping," available at https://en.wikipedia.org/wiki/Trusted_timestamping.

2. It should be noted, however, that it was a confusion over the specific *version* of the document that mostly concerned the Board in this case. In general, where there is only one version of a disclosure at issue, the redundancy of the Internet makes it difficult to falsify dates, so that a posting date or archive date will usually suffice to establish the state of the art. The Guidelines for Examination in the European Patent Office, November 2016 Edition, available at https://www.epo.org/law-practice/legal-texts/guidelines.html, at Part G – Chapter IV-11, section 7.5, regarding Internet disclosures:

> As a matter of principle, disclosures on the internet form part of the state of the art according to Art. 54(2). Information disclosed on the internet or in online databases is considered to be publicly available as of the date the information was publicly posted. Internet websites often contain highly relevant technical information. Certain information may even be available only on the internet from such websites. This includes, for example, online manuals and tutorials for software products (such as video games) or other products with a short life cycle. Hence for the sake of a valid patent it is often crucial to cite publications only obtainable from such internet websites.

4.7.1 Establishing the publication date

Establishing a publication date has two aspects. It must be assessed separately whether a given date is indicated correctly and whether the content in question was indeed made available to the public as of that date.

The nature of the internet can make it difficult to establish the actual date on which information was made available to the public: for instance, not all web pages mention when they were published. Also, websites are easily updated, yet most do not provide any archive of previously displayed material, nor do they display records which enable members of the public – including examiners – to establish precisely what was published and when.

Neither restricting access to a limited circle of people (*e.g.* by password protection) nor requiring payment for access (analogous to purchasing a book or subscribing to a journal) prevent a web page from forming part of the state of the art. It is sufficient if the web page is in principle available without any bar of confidentiality.

Finally, it is theoretically possible to manipulate the date and content of an internet disclosure (as it is with traditional documents). However, in view of the sheer size and redundancy of the content available on the internet, it is considered very unlikely that an internet disclosure discovered by an examiner has been manipulated. Consequently, unless there are specific indications to the contrary, the date can be accepted as being correct.

Another issue concerning date of availability of a document arises when a printed document is made public *after* a patent applicant's priority date; but is said to report facts first publicly presented *before* that priority date.

This was the situation in *Immunoglobulin preparations/GENENTECH*, Case No. T 1212/97 (Euro. Pat. Off. Bd. App., 14 May 2001). This case involved a claim to recombinant techniques for making specific antibodies. The opposing parties (Roche, Celltech, and others) introduced evidence of a public lecture by a colleague (Dr. Shulman) of one of the discoverers of the basic monoclonal antibody technique (Georges J.F. Kohler). Slides used at the lecture were introduced during the opposition as evidence of what was publicly disclosed at the time of the lecture. The Board discussed the slides (and related testimony of Dr. Shulman) in the following passage:

> For the evidence to be regarded as safe and satisfactory, it must unequivocally relate to what was made available to the public at the lecture. This is not a matter which this Board considers capable of being put beyond reasonable doubt by any evidence of the lecturer alone. The lecturer will have had the knowledge prior to the lecture, and will have prepared the lecture. His or her knowledge will not change as a result of the lecture, that of the audience may. The lecturer's evidence can be taken as defining the maximum amount of knowledge that may have been conveyed to the audience, but cannot be relied on to establish even what minimum of new knowledge was necessarily conveyed to the audience . . . Information appearing in each of the contemporary written notes made at the lecture by at least two members of the audience can usually be regarded as sufficient, whereas information in the notes of a single member of the audience might be inadequate as reflecting the thoughts of the listener rather than solely the content of the lecture. If the lecturer read his lecture from a typescript or manuscript, or the lecturer wrote up his lecture subsequently, and the lecture was subsequently published in this form as part of the proceedings, then the written version might be taken as some evidence of the contents of the lecture, though with some caution as there would be no guarantee that a script was completely and comprehensibly read, or that a write-up was not amplified . . . Most useful would be a handout given to the public at the lecture, containing a summary of the most important parts of the lecture and copies of the slides shown. None of these types of evidence are available for Dr Shulman's lecture . . .
>
> As there is no other evidence that supports the Respondent's case as to what was made publicly available at the lecture, the Board is already forced to the conclusion that there is no safe and satisfactory evidence that the information content of Dr Shulman's lecture as outlined in his declaration and exhibits thereto can be treated as having been made publicly available. Dr Shulman undoubtedly gave the lecture, but insofar as its information content went beyond what was already known in the art, or the comprehensible showing of any of the five slides specifically relied on is concerned, the Board is not satisfied on this on balance of probabilities, let alone beyond reasonable doubt (*id.*, at Reasons 4–6.)

The claims at issue were not, as a consequence, invalidated on the basis of the public lecture.

A similar case, with the opposite result, is *CODIS core STR loci forensic human identification/PROMEGA*, Case No. T 1634/15 (Euro. Pat. Off. Bd. App., 14 October 2016), where the Board concluded, at Reason 8:

> [T]he evidence on file is appropriate and credible to overcome any possible doubt. The board is certain beyond reasonable doubt that the information concerning the [claimed invention] was made available to the public at "The Ninth International Symposium on Human Identification" [of October 8–10, 1998] which took place before the claimed priority date [, and which was reported on in a document called "Meeting Report," which was made public after the priority date].
>
> In this case, there was ample evidence from numerous participants that the claimed invention was disclosed and discussed by numbers of experts in the field at the cited Conference. And the post-Conference report supported the contentions of participants regarding what was discussed, and in what depth. So the claims at issue were invalidated, on the ground that the Conference presentations placed the claimed invention in the state of the art before the patent applicant's priority date.

4.7.2 Disclosure in a single document in Europe

As with novelty worldwide, a single disclosure (document, publicly used product, etc. – *i.e.*, a prior art "reference" in US patent parlance) must contain all elements of a claimed invention for that disclosure to defeat the novelty of the claim. It is important to note, however, that the information in a disclosure must be seen in light of the general knowledge of one skilled in the art. This means that a good deal of information may at times be found to be "implicit" in a disclosure. In addition, the *range* of information in a disclosure need only overlap one or a few embodiments covered by a claim to render that claim non-novel under EPC Article 54.

Both these rules were at issue in the case of *Hydrogen-rich mixture/SHELL* (Johnson Matthey Public Limited Company v. Shell Int'l Research), Case No. T 0951/15 (Euro. Pat. Off. Bd. App., 3 April 2017). There the patentee claimed a process used in the "gasification" of coal, *i.e.*, conversion of coal into a fuel-gas mixture for cleaner combustion or to produce industrial chemicals such as ammonia. The claim included a number of limitations, and read in part:

> 1. Process to prepare a hydrogen rich gas mixture from a halogen containing gas mixture [*i.e.*, gas mixture that includes a halogen, meaning the elements

chlorine, fluorine, bromine, etc.] ... by [contacting the halogen-containing gas mixture with water at very high temperatures, to rid the mixture of most of the halogen]; [passing the mixture through one or more "fixed bed reactors" to further transform it]; wherein the halogen containing gas mixture has a content of halogen compounds of between 50 and 1000 ppm [*i.e.*, "parts per million" – a very low concentration, where for example 1000 ppm is equal to .1 percent].

The opponent, Johnson Matthey, cited an article in a Chinese technical journal (Xu Banghao, Journal of the Chemical Fertilizer Industry, 2006 – the "Xu reference") as the closest prior art. To quote the Board:

> The appellant asserted in particular that the halogen content of the raw coal gas fed to the process illustrated in Figure 1 of [the Xu reference] would implicitly fall within the range defined in claim 1. This assertion was derived from the data in [another reference, setting out well known information], from which it could be calculated that the HCl [*i.e.*, hydrochloric acid] content [which shows the presence of the halogen chlorine] in the raw gas from the Shell gasification process using [two standard types of coal] as feed materials was 294 ppm and 315 ppm, respectively. [Because either of these concentrations falls within the range in claim 1, and because the process described in the Xu reference discloses all the other elements of the claim, use of the Xu reference method with these standard types of coal would include halogen content that falls within the claim and thus renders it non-novel.]
>
> For the board these calculations are irrelevant for the assessment of the novelty of claim 1 of the main request, since [the Xu reference] is silent as to the origin of the coal used in the gasification process. Consequently no conclusion can be drawn ... regarding the halogen content of the coal gasification product used ... for the ... reaction [in the Xu reference].
>
> On the contrary, the board is led to the conclusion that the "raw coal gas" fed via line (1) to the water-gas shift conversion process illustrated in the figure at page 4 of [the Xu reference] is actually halogen-depleted [*i.e.*, has essentially no halogen content]. Removing halogens is in fact a conventional operation, as can be seen from [other documents that form part of the state of the art], wherein the halogens are scrubbed out by water-washing, or alternatively [by] dry chloride removal ...
>
> In any case, in the absence of an indication of the origin of the coal used in the process of [the Xu reference], it follows from the above considerations that the subject-matter of claim 1 at issue is distinguished from the disclosure of [the Xu reference] at least in that the amount of halogen in the gas mixture fed to the water-gas shift conversion process [of the claimed invention] is between 50 and 1000 ppm [, while no such halogen range is definitively disclosed by the Xu reference.]

One point here is that, because the standard types of coal known in the prior art have 294 and 315 ppm of halogen, the halogen range in claim 1 would not be novel. The claimed range is "from 50 to 1000 ppm," and even though the standard coal types are on the lower end of this range, they do fall within the range, rendering it non-novel. The second point is that the single reference in this case, the Xu reference, did not in fact disclose which types of coal were used, and even implied (the Board said) that Xu had removed the halogens from the coal gas feed in his process. This meant that the Xu process in effect included halogens at a level of 0 ppm, which is outside the claimed range of 50–1000; hence the reference did not negate novelty for the claim 1 process. Another point to note is that the Xu reference was written in Chinese (Mandarin), and had to be translated before it could be analyzed by the examiner and the Board – an increasingly common occurrence, as Chinese research and development, and hence published research results in Mandarin, continue to grow.

4.7.2.1 Adequacy of disclosure in a prior art document, etc. (i.e., a reference)

The rules regarding adequate disclosure in a prior art reference are well explained in a Board case from 2014, *Porous inorganic oxide/W.R.GRACE & CO.-CONN*, Case No. T 2026/10 (Euro. Pat. Off. Bd. App., 2 May 2014). Here the applicant, W.R. Grace, invented a new variant of "porous inorganic oxide particles," typically taking the form of a silica gel, which are used in water-absorbing applications such as desiccants, little water-absorbing beads or powders contained in small envelopes that are placed in boxes and other product packaging to absorb water during storage and transport, and therefore keep products from sustaining damage from moisture. The main claim to Grace's invention was as follows:

> 1. A dispersion comprising porous inorganic oxide particles, wherein the particles have:
>
> a) a median particle size in the range of 0.05 to 3 microns; and
> b) porosity such that when an aqueous dispersion of the particles is dried at least 0.5 ml/g of pore volume as measured by BJH nitrogen porosimetry is from pores having a pore size of 50 nm (600 Å) or smaller.

The examiner found an issued US Patent, No. 4,235,716, which included an example (example 2) that disclosed, according to the Board,

> a porous silica gel having an average particle size of 0.5 microns, a pore volume of 1.0 ml/g, a pore width of 10 nm, and a [certain] specific surface [measurement] (see column 5, lines 1 to 10). Although [this patent] discloses neither a method of manufacturing nor a supplier for said porous silica gel, the examining division argued that the inventors . . . had either bought the product or produced it

themselves. It was therefore considered as comprised in the state of the art and anticipated the subject-matter of claim 1.

Notice the parameters of this reference: (1) The particle size of 0.5 microns is within the range of 0.05 to 3 microns; and (2) the pore volume is 1.0 ml/g, *i.e.*, 1 milliliter per gram (a measure of how much absorbent volume is found in each gram of material), which is within the claimed range of "at least 0.5 ml/g." Because all the elements of the claim are found in the prior art document, the claim lacks novelty – *if* the prior art reference discloses the relevant information sufficiently. But does it? That was the question here. To decide the issue, the Board relies on standard patent principles. The test for adequacy of disclosure in a prior art reference is the same test as is used for an inventor who has filed a patent application. This is found in Article 83 of the EPC, as the Board makes clear:

> Article 83 EPC states that a European patent application must disclose the invention in a manner sufficiently clear and complete to be carried out by a person skilled in the art. In accordance with the case law, for the requirement of Article 83 EPC to be met, the skilled person must be able to carry out the invention without undue burden and without the exercise of inventive skill, on the basis of what is disclosed in the application and by using the general knowledge.
>
> According to the jurisprudence . . . the same criteria are to be applied for judging sufficiency of disclosure of a patent application or of a piece of prior art. A prior art document whose teaching does not meet the sufficiency criteria is not enabling and must be disregarded as a prior art (*id.*, at Reasons 2.2.1 to 2.2.2.).

The patent applicant, Grace, had introduced evidence pertinent to this topic. Grace argued, according to the Board, that the prior art patent

> disclosed neither a method of manufacturing said porous silica gel nor another origin therefore. The appellant [Grace] argued that the disclosure in [the prior art patent] of the porous silica gel was not enabling. Its preparation was non-trivial and beyond common knowledge, in particular not before the [appellant/applicant's] priority date of 25 November 1980. It had taken the appellant's experts numerous years of research to develop a process for manufacturing a product having the claimed properties and parameters. In this context, the appellant pointed to claim 19 of the present application which defined a process for the preparation of the claimed dispersions of porous inorganic particles, which process includes the steps of forming a slurry, milling of said slurry, creating a supernatant phase and a settled phase and removing the supernatant phase to separate the two phases and to obtain the settled phase as a final product having

the specified parameter values. The appellant argued that in 1978 (date of filing of [prior art patent]) no method was known which could have resulted in such a material. The appellant was also not aware of a product such as the silica gel of example 2 of [the prior art patent] being or having been offered or sold on the market. Consequently, such a porous silica gel could not have been obtained by purchase, contrary to the finding in the contested decision (at Summary of Facts and Submissions, par. V).

In ruling for the applicant Grace on this issue, the Board emphasized the lack of evidence introduced by the examiner to rebut Grace's points:

It would have been incumbent on the examining division to produce evidence for their assertions, for instance by showing that the product in question was indeed commonly available, or that its manufacture (or at least the manufacture of porous inorganic particles having very similar characteristics) belonged to the general knowledge. A decision on novelty should not be taken on the basis of plausibility considerations and assumptions which are not supported by evidence or arguments. Secondly, even assuming the product was bought – for which there is no evidence –, it is clear that in the absence of information about the source, the document would still not be enabling (*id.*, at Reasons pars. 2.3.1–2.3.2).

And so, the Board reaffirmed the enablement standard for prior art, and provided a lesson in the evidentiary burden of proving enabling disclosure.

4.7.3 Prior-filed patent applications: Article 54(3) EPC

The EPO Guidelines for Examination, available at https://www.epo.org/law-practice/legal-texts/html/guidelines/e/g_iv_5_1.htm, at section 5.1, explain the basic rule regarding prior-filed EPO applications and their availability in the state of the art against later-filed applications:

State of the art pursuant to Art. 54(3)

The state of the art also comprises the content of other European applications filed or validly claiming a priority date earlier than – but published under Art. 93 on or after – the date of filing or valid date of priority of the application being examined. Such earlier applications are part of the state of the art only when considering novelty and not when considering inventive step. The "date of filing" referred to in Art. 54(2) and (3) is thus to be interpreted as meaning the date of priority in appropriate cases. By the "content" of a European application is meant the whole disclosure, i.e. the description, drawings and claims, including:

(i) any matter explicitly disclaimed (with the exception of disclaimers for unworkable embodiments);
(ii) any matter for which an allowable reference to other documents [*i.e.*, incorporation by reference] is made; and
(iii) prior art insofar as explicitly described.

To be clear, this passage refers to patent applications as relevant prior art under both Article 54(2) and Article 54(3). The former is included because a published patent application of course is included in the phrase "everything made available to the public by means of a written or oral description . . . before the date of filing of the European patent application." A published patent application, in other words, is no different from any other published document.

The distinct content of Article 54(3) makes prior-filed EPO applications prior art not as of their publication date (typically 18 months after filing), but as of their *filing date*. (This is the same as the old 35 U.S.C. §102(e) in pre-AIA US law, now covered by AIA §102(a)(2).) Article 54(3) reads:

(3) Additionally, the content of European patent applications as filed, the dates of filing of which are prior to the date referred to in paragraph 2 and which were published on or after that date, shall be considered as comprised in the state of the art.

As the excerpt from the EPO Examination Guidelines above says, the relevant date for a prior-filed EPO application is the priority date of an EPO filing (*i.e.*, any international filing date given effect under the EPC), and not the actual filing date in the EPO. Thus an EPO application that claims priority to an earlier national filing (*e.g.*, in Germany or China) will be counted as part of the prior art as of its German or Chinese priority date (as long as that date is preserved by taking appropriate actions in the EPO, *i.e.*, filing within international treaty deadlines, providing translation as required, etc.).

In addition, note the crucial requirement that, to be prior art, the earlier-filed application must eventually be made public, either by publication of the application or issuance of the patent. In either case, the prior-filed application will have been "published on or after" the priority date of the patent application whose claims are being challenged for novelty, and hence the requirement of Article 54(3) will be met. Article 54(3) has the same temporal structure as pre-AIA U.S. §102(e), AIA §102(a)(2): when a prior-filed application is made public, it becomes prior art *as of its filing date*. The later event activates prior art effect as of the earlier date – in the Latin phrase, *nunc pro tunc* ("now for then").

One additional point: Article 54(3) prior art is available against a patent application *only* for purposes of novelty. Unlike in the US, it is not considered in the determination of inventive step. So in Europe, there is no equivalent of US pre-AIA §102(e)/103 prior art (AIA §102(a)(2)/103 prior art). This is stated clearly in the EPO Examination Guidelines excerpt earlier in this section.

4.7.4 Non-prejudicial disclosures: the "grace period" in Europe

The US is unique in providing a fairly extensive grace period for certain disclosures made more than a year before a US application is filed. The grace period prevents an otherwise invalidating disclosure from being considered; it effectively removes references from the prior art. The European equivalent, labeled "non-prejudicial disclosures," is much narrower. It encompasses only (1) disclosures made via an evident abuse of the applicant (*e.g.*, disclosure after theft of applicant's idea), and (2) exhibits at authorized international fairs, if the exhibit occurred less than six months prior to the priority filing.

It is well established under European law that the six-month grace period for public displays of an invention under Article 55 is counted *not* from the EPO filing date, but from the priority filing date. This means that, if the EPO filing is made after a priority filing (*e.g.*, a national filing prior to EPO filing), the six-month period begins running from the initial priority date and not the EPO filing date. So the applicant may well have less than six months prior to EPO filing to file. This has caused problems for more than a few EPO applicants. *See, e.g., Metaltech V.O.F. v. Alcan Deutschland GmbH*, Case No. T 0033/99 (Tech. Bd. App. EPO, 4 Oct. 2001) (earlier filing in the Netherlands triggered the six-month grace period of EPC Article 55(1)(a); thus use at a trade fair more than six months prior to EPO filing was counted as part of the state of the art under Article 54, and hence the patent was invalid).

4.7.5 Evident abuse of applicant

 CASE

University Patents, Inc. v. Smithkline Beecham Biologicals SA, Case No. G 3/98 (OJ EPO, 2001, 062) (En. Bd. App, EPO, 12 July 2000)

The Opposition Division had revoked the patent in suit for lack of novelty on grounds of public prior use, ruling that a device corresponding to its subject-matter had been handed

CASE *(continued)*

over to a customer. In the appeal proceedings, this prior use and its subject-matter were no longer contested. The proprietor however claimed that the prior use was due to an evident abuse in relation to the original applicant, arguing that the sales manager of a company belonging to the original applicant's wife had handed over the device contrary to the applicant's express instructions. The opponent confirmed this account and thereupon withdrew its opposition. The sales manager subsequently also confirmed the facts in an affidavit.

[The Board] found that the other prior art was not an obstacle to maintaining the patent. On the other hand, the subject-matter of the specified prior use was identical to the subject-matter of claim 1 of the patent in suit, that prior use being the result of an evident abuse in relation to the earlier applicant. The earlier applicant had been the de facto head of his wife's company. By handing over the device contrary to instructions, the sales manager had acted in breach of contract and trust. As the prior use had taken place more than six months before the filing of the application itself, but less than six months before the filing of the priority application, the decision in the case depended on how the six-month period under Article 55(1) EPC should be calculated.

According to Article 89 EPC, which governs the effects of the right of priority, the date of priority counts as the date of filing of the European patent application for the purposes of Article 54(2) and (3) EPC and Article 60(2) EPC [relating to priority between independent inventors]; there is no reference to Article 55 EPC. Thus neither the wording of Article 55 EPC nor that of Article 89 EPC provides for the period for non-prejudicial disclosures to be calculated from the priority date . . . [numerous other arguments on both sides were then considered].

For the calculation of the six-month period referred to in Article 55(1) EPC, the relevant date is the date of the actual filing of the European patent application; the date of priority is not to be taken account of in calculating this period.

NOTES AND QUESTIONS

1. Outright theft of an idea, particularly if accomplished through criminal acts (*e.g.*, breaking and entering) would seem to constitute a textbook case of abuse in relation to an applicant. How did the facts differ here? The disclosure was made by a customer of the inventor's wife's company (with which the inventor himself was associated), who had been given access to the invention by the wife. All involved later admitted that the wife's transfer of the invention to the customer was against the express wishes of the inventor. Compare this to the textbook case. Consider also whether the customer in this scenario could be considered to have misappropriated a trade secret – *i.e.*, would a misappropriation cause of action have been successful against the customer? Should the definition of abuse be more or less broad than the definition of trade secret misappropriation?

2. Abuse of the applicant is argued fairly often, which stands to reason: if successful, it allows the applicant to remove otherwise invalidating prior art for a period up to six months prior to filing, which may often be the difference between validity and invalidity. Looking at the cases, however, it is apparent that the abuse argument rarely succeeds. In that regard consider *Metaltech V.O.F. v. Alcan Deutschland GmbH*, Case No. T 0033/99 (Tech. Bd. App. EPO, 4 Oct. 2001), a Technical Board of Appeal decision described a public use case that may be instructive. As the Board describes the case:

The opposition division revoked the patent after finding an allegation of public prior use proven, namely that in April 1991 on the CEBAL stand at the MACROPAK 91 packaging fair at Utrecht in the Netherlands, Mr Herber showed Mr Heitkamp an apparatus as shown in the patent without obliging Mr Heitkamp to secrecy. The appellant (patentee) maintained that if a visitor to the fair had tried to use the apparatus or if Mr Herber had demonstrated it, then this would have been an evident abuse in relation to the patentee and should not be taken into account since the patent's priority date of 7 August 1991 was less than six months after the packaging fair (Article 55(1)(a) EPC). [Putting aside the issue of priority filing versus EPO filing, the Board considered this evidence.]

The apparatus of the claim "was not only present at the Macropak 91 packaging fair in Utrecht but could also have been seen and handled in its assembled state by a member of the public present at the fair. The respondent has not claimed, nor has Mr Heitkamp testified that the apparatus was dismantled [, negating the idea that the salesperson, Herber, and/or customer, Heitkamp, perpetrated an evident abuse of the applicant by wrongfully assembling, testing or using the apparatus]. The Board must therefore assume that the apparatus at the fair could only be looked at and worked in a manner showing a visitor its ease of handling and the resulting package. The Board therefore only considers those features to have been available to the public which could be seen or detected by a skilled person looking at and handling the apparatus.

And one final point regarding "evident abuse." Though circumstantial evidence may be introduced that a disclosure violated some sort of legal agreement, this by itself may not be enough to establish evident abuse of the applicant. In *Coatex v. Rhodia*, "Polymers useful as pH responsive thickeners and monomers therefor," Case No. T 0041/02 (Bd. App. EPO, 19 Jan. 2006), at par. I, the Board described an argument along these lines made by the patent owner Rhodia, which was contesting an opposition filed by Coatex.

European patent No. 705 854, in respect of European patent application no. 95 402 1994 in the name of Rhone-Poulenc Inc. (later transferred to Rhodia Inc.), [was] filed on 2 October 1995 and claiming a US priority of 3 October 1994 (US 317261).

The Board set forth an argument regarding evident abuse that was made by patent owner Rhodia, at par. VI(a):

[The prior art patent, document "D1"] should be recognized as a non-prejudicial disclosure within the meaning of Article 55(1)(a) EPC. There existed a secrecy agreement between Rheox Inc., the applicant of D1, and Rhone-Poulenc Inc., the legal predecessor of the respondent, relating to the field of rheological additives. This agreement covered the monomer DV-4343 disclosed in D1 [which was said to render the claimed invention of patent owner Rhodia non-novel]. The filing of D1 without prior consultation and/or information of Rhone-Poulenc Inc. was considered to be a breech of the secrecy agreement. To support this argument, [various] declarations ... were submitted.

But the Board rejected this argument regarding evident abuse, at pars. V.(a) and (b):

There was no evidence of any fraud or abuse associated with the filing of D1, let alone an evident abuse. In fact, there were several plausible scenarios (eg misunderstanding, clerical error about a common date of filing, change of mind of the patentee) which did not support an evident abuse. Furthermore, the proprietor neither tried to regain control or ownership of D1 nor sued Rheox Inc. for fraudulent filing of D1. This was definitely not the behaviour of a party discovering an alleged fraudulent filing creating a novelty bar.

4.7.6 Note on the Article 54(3) "partial priority" problem

A highly technical issue arose under Article 55(3) that perplexed courts and practitioners alike until it was resolved. Recall that Article 55(2) defines the state of the art as encompassing all publicly accessible information that becomes available "before the date of filing of the European patent application" whose novelty is in question. Article 54(3) says: "(3) Additionally, the content of European patent applications as filed, the dates of filing of which are prior to the date referred to in paragraph 2 and which were published on or after that date, shall be considered as comprised in the state of the art." Under what conditions might a patent applicant file an application, but amend it so substantially that the original filing is found to form part of the prior art against a later, revised version of the same application – i.e., the "content of [an] . . . application *as filed*" becomes prior art against a later version of the same application?

The scenario arises this way: An applicant files a priority application, then broadens the initially filed claims in a subsequent, related application. When an individual claim was broadened, the argument ran, the broadening of the terms of the claim between the priority document and the second application means that the claim as a whole is not entitled to priority. This was the ruling in cases such as *Nestec SA & Ors v. Dualit Ltd & Ors* [2013] EWHC 923 (Pat) (22 April 2013). Practitioners were upset by this, noting that it should be possible for alternative embodiments covered by a broadened claim to be broken into two groups: those that were supported by the disclosure in the priority application, and those that were not. *See, e.g.,* The IPKat Blog, Poisonous Priorities: How Many Ways Can a Patent Be Toxic?, Tuesday, 7 May 2013, available at http://ipkitten.blogspot.com/2013/05/poisonous-priority-how-many-ways-can.html.

The problem was solved when an Enlarged Board of Appeals panel took a case with these issues. *Fischer-Tropsch Catalysts/SASOL TECHNOLOGY II*, Case No. G 1/15 (Eur. Pat. Off. En. Bd. App., 25 November 2014) involved a referral on this question:

> Where a claim of a European patent application or patent encompasses alternative subject-matters by virtue of one or more generic expressions or otherwise (generic "OR"-claim), may entitlement to partial priority be refused under the EPC for that claim in respect of alternative subject-matter disclosed . . . in the priority document?

The answer, as common sense might suggest, is to split the subject matter of the broadened claim into two parts: that which is supported by the original priority filing (and hence can claim priority from the priority filing date), and that which is not so supported – i.e., a case of "partial priority":

> Under the EPC, entitlement to partial priority may not be refused for a claim encompassing alternative subject-matter by virtue of one or more generic expressions or otherwise [e.g., a generic "this or that" claim, claiming in the alternative]

provided that said alternative subject-matter has been disclosed . . . in an enabling manner in the priority document. No other substantive conditions or limitations apply in this respect.

The reasoning is stated concisely in the opinion, at par. 5.1.3:

> If a claim in the later application is broader than an element disclosed in the priority document, then priority may be claimed for such element but not for all other embodiments encompassed by the claim or claims. This principle applies for each individual element disclosed in a priority document [as well as for claims based in multiple prior-filed applications].

5

Inventive step/ non-obviousness

Early in the history of US patent law, courts came to understand that novelty alone was not enough of a limit on the issuance of patents. Novelty is an important first step, making sure a patented invention is not already available "as is." But it is often easy to make a very minor change to an existing design or product. Without some other requirement "beyond novelty," too many narrow and minor patents would issue.

This was the impetus behind the 1850 case of *Hotchkiss v. Greenwood*, 52 U.S. (11 How.) 248 (1850). In that case, a minor variation on existing designs for doorknobs was rejected by the Supreme Court. The small variation did not deserve a patent because "there was an absence of that degree of skill and ingenuity which constitute essential elements of every invention" (*id.*, at 267). Thus was born the "invention test," which became a requirement for every invention. Though courts consistently applied this "beyond novelty" requirement, it was not codified into the Patent Act until 1952, when §103, the "nonobviousness" requirement, was added. The current version of §103 reads as follows:

> **35 U.S.C. §103 – Conditions for patentability; non-obvious subject matter**
> A patent for a claimed invention may not be obtained, notwithstanding that the claimed invention is not identically disclosed as set forth in section 102, if the differences between the claimed invention and the prior art are such that the claimed invention as a whole would have been obvious before the effective filing date of the claimed invention to a person having ordinary skill in the art to which the claimed invention pertains. Patentability shall not be negated by the manner in which the invention was made.

Although the wording is a bit awkward, the first part of this section reflects the idea that nonobviousness goes "beyond novelty." The statute says a patent may not be obtained "notwithstanding that the claimed invention is not identically disclosed as set forth in section 102." To understand this, you need to see that the drafters of §103 used the phrase "not identically disclosed as set forth in section 102" to represent novelty. So the statute really says "a patent may not be obtained, even if the invention is novel . . ."

The heart of §103 is in what comes after this. It says that a novel invention will not be patentable "if the differences between the claimed invention and the prior art . . . would have been obvious." In the cases that follow we will see how this requirement has been explained and applied by the Supreme Court.

 CASE

Graham v. John Deere Co. of Kansas City, 383 U.S. 1 (1966)

Clark, Justice
The invention [in this case], a combination of old mechanical elements, involves a device designed to absorb shock from plow shanks as they plow through rocky soil and thus to prevent damage to the plow.

Congress may not authorize the issuance of patents whose effects are to remove existent knowledge from the public domain, or to restrict free access to materials already available. Innovation, advancement, and things which add to the sum of useful knowledge are inherent requisites in a patent system which by constitutional command must "promote the Progress of * * * useful Arts."

Within the limits of the constitutional grant, the Congress may, of course, implement the stated purpose of the Framers by selecting the policy which in its judgment best effectuates the constitutional aim. It is the duty of the Commissioner of Patents and of the courts in the administration of the patent system to give effect to the constitutional standard by appropriate application, in each case, of the statutory scheme of the Congress.

The pivotal section around which the present controversy centers is §103. The section is cast in relatively unambiguous terms. Patentability is to depend, in addition to novelty and utility, upon the "non-obvious" nature of the "subject matter sought to be patented" to a person having ordinary skill in the pertinent art.

It is undisputed that this section was, for the first time, a statutory expression of an additional requirement for patentability, originally expressed in *Hotchkiss* [*v. Greenwood*]. [T]he [1952] revision was not intended by Congress to change the general level of patentable invention. We conclude that the section was intended merely as a codification of judicial precedents embracing the *Hotchkiss* condition.

While the ultimate question of patent validity is one of law the §103 condition lends itself to several basic factual inquiries. Under §103, the scope and content of the prior art are to be determined; differences between the prior art and the claims at issue are to be ascertained; and the level of ordinary skill in the pertinent art resolved. Against this

CASE *(continued)*

background, the obviousness or nonobviousness of the subject matter is determined. Such secondary considerations as commercial success, long felt but unsolved needs, failure of others, etc., might be utilized to give light to the circumstances surrounding the origin of the subject matter sought to be patented. As indicia of obviousness or nonobviousness, these inquiries may have relevancy. See Note, *Subtests of 'Nonobviousness': A Nontechnical Approach to Patent Validity*, 112 U. Pa. L. Rev. 1169 (1964).

[The patent in this case,] No. 2,627,798 (hereinafter called the '798 patent) relates to a spring clamp which permits plow shanks to be pushed upward when they hit obstructions in the soil, and then springs the shanks back into normal position when the obstruction is passed over. The mechanism around which the controversy centers is basically a hinge. The top half of it, known as the upper plate is a heavy metal piece clamped to the plow frame and is stationary relative to the plow frame. The lower half of the hinge, known as the hinge plate, is connected to the rear of the upper plate by a hinge pin [D in the diagram] and rotates downward with respect to it. The shank, which is bolted to the forward end of the hinge plate, runs beneath the plate and parallel to it for about nine inches, passes through a stirrup [at C], and then continues backward for several feet curving down toward the ground. As the plow frame is pulled forward, the chisel rips through the soil, thereby plowing it. In the normal position, the hinge plate and the shank are kept tight against the upper plate by a spring, which is atop the upper plate. A rod runs through the center of the spring, extending down through holes in both plates and the shank. Its upper end is bolted to the top of the spring while its lower end is hooked against the underside of the shank.

When the chisel hits a rock or other obstruction in the soil, the obstruction forces the chisel and the rear portion of the shank to move upward. The shank is pivoted against the rear of the hinge plate and pries open the hinge against the closing tendency of the spring. This closing tendency is caused by the fact that, as the hinge is opened, the connecting rod is pulled downward and the spring is compressed. When the obstruction is passed over, the upward force on the chisel disappears and the spring pulls the shank and hinge plate back into their original position. The lower, rear portion of the hinge plate is constructed in the form of a stirrup [at D] which brackets the shank, passing around and beneath it.

Originally, the shanks were rigidly attached to the plow frames. When such plows were used in the rocky, glacial soils of some of the Northern States, they were found to have serious defects. As the chisels hit buried rocks, a vibratory motion was set up and tremendous forces were transmitted to the shank near its connection to the frame. The shank would break. Graham, one of the petitioners, sought to meet that problem, and in 1950 obtained a [prior art] patent, U.S. No. 2,493,811 (hereinafter '811), on a spring clamp which solved some of the difficulties. [The Graham '811 patent is prior art to the '798 patent whose validity is being considered in this case.]

The Graham '811 and '798 patent devices are similar in all elements, save two: (1) the stirrup and the bolted connection of the shank to the hinge plate do not appear in '811; and (2) the position of the shank is reversed, being placed in patent '811 above the hinge plate,

CASE *(continued)*

sandwiched between it and the upper plate. The shank is held in place by the spring rod which is hooked against the bottom of the hinge plate passing through a slot in the shank.

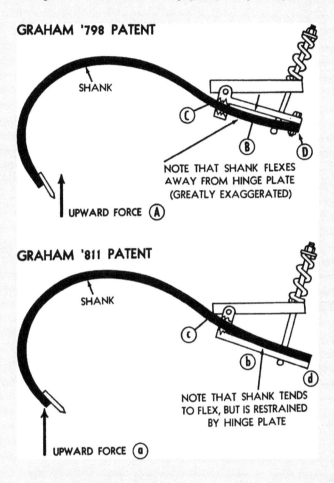

[W]e do not believe that the [patentee's] argument [establishes] the validity of the patent. The tendency of the shank to flex is the same in all cases. If free-flexing, as petitioners now argue, is the crucial difference above the prior art, then it appears evident that the desired result would be obtainable by not boxing the shank within the confines of the hinge. The only other effective place available in the arrangement was to attach it below the hinge plate and run it through a stirrup or bracket that would not disturb its flexing qualities. Certainly a person having ordinary skill in the prior art, given the fact that the flex in the shank could be utilized more effectively if allowed to run the entire length of the shank, would immediately see that the thing to do was what Graham did, *i.e.*, invert the shank and the hinge plate.

We find no nonobvious facets in the '798 arrangement.

NOTES

1. The Graham '811 patent was prior art to the '798 patent even though it was developed by the same team and assigned to the same company as the '798 patent. Graham filed the application for what became the '811 patent in 1947. The patent was issued in 1950. Graham's application for what became the '798 patent was filed in 1951. This is a common scenario; after all, an inventor working in a small field will often contribute ideas against which that inventor's own later inventions were judged with respect to novelty and nonobviousness. If Graham had developed both designs – the '811 prior art design, and the '798 design in the patent at issue – at the same time, then he might have been able to combine them into a single patent application or at least coordinate the prosecution of the two applications.

   A doctrine called "double patenting" can be helpful here: an inventor can file an application on an obvious variant of an earlier-filed patent application; if the inventor agrees to tie the patent term of the later patent application to the patent term for the earlier one, he or she may be able to receive both patents. *See, e.g., Gilead Sciences, Inc. v. Natco Pharma Limited,* 753 F.3d 1208, 1212 (Fed. Cir. 2014), cert. denied, 135 S. Ct. 1530 (2015):

   > The prohibition against double patenting is a longstanding doctrine of patent law. It is based on the core principle that, in exchange for a patent, an inventor must fully disclose his invention and promise to permit free use of it at the end of his patent term. . . . The bar against double patenting was created to preserve that bargained-for right held by the public. . . . If an inventor could obtain several sequential patents on the same invention, he could retain for himself the exclusive right to exclude or control the public's right to use the patented invention far beyond the term awarded to him under the patent laws.

   An obvious variant of a pending application may be claimed in a later-filed application, so long as the patent resulting from the later-filed application has the same termination date as the patent resulting from the first application. This is achieved by a "terminal disclaimer" – a surrender of the right to any patent term from the second patent that would otherwise extend later than the term of the first patent. *See Geneva Pharmaceuticals, Inc. v. GlaxoSmithKline PLC,* 349 F.3d 1373, 1378 (Fed. Cir. 2003) ("With . . . double patenting, a terminal disclaimer may restrict [a second patent's] slight variation to the term of [an] original patent and cure [a] double patenting rejection").

2. The "secondary considerations" mentioned by the court – commercial success of the invention; failure of others to achieve the invention; and long-felt need in the field for the invention – can be important in a close case on nonobviousness. They will not, however, sway a court where the invention in question seems a very minor advance over the prior art. *See, e.g., Leapfrog, Inc. v. Fisher-Price, Inc.,* 485 F.3d 1157 (Fed. Cir. 2007) (clear case of obvious invention overrides secondary consideration evidence). Commercial success evidence has been criticized as unhelpful because the success of commercial products is often the result of multiple factors, not simply superior technology. Robert P. Merges, *Commercial Success and Patent Standards: Economic Perspectives on Innovation,* 76 Cal. L. Rev. 803 (1988) (suggesting that the most persuasive evidence of nonobvious invention is the failure of other competitors to achieve a desirable result).

KSR Int'l Co. v. Teleflex Inc., 550 U.S. 398 (2007)

Justice Kennedy

Teleflex Incorporated and its subsidiary Technology Holding Company – both referred to here as Teleflex – sued KSR International Company for patent infringement. The patent at issue, United States Patent No. 6,237,565, is entitled "Adjustable Pedal Assembly With

CASE (continued)

Electronic Throttle Control." The patentee is Steven J. Engelgau, and the patent is referred to as "the Engelgau patent." Teleflex holds the exclusive license to the patent.

Claim 4 of the Engelgau patent describes a mechanism for combining an electronic sensor with an adjustable automobile pedal so the pedal's position can be transmitted to a computer that controls the throttle in the vehicle's engine. When Teleflex accused KSR of infringing the Engelgau patent by adding an electronic sensor to one of KSR's previously designed pedals, KSR countered that claim 4 was invalid under the Patent Act, 35 U.S.C. §103, because its subject matter was obvious.

[The invention of the Engelgau patent is set forth in the diagram below; the sensor is element 24.]

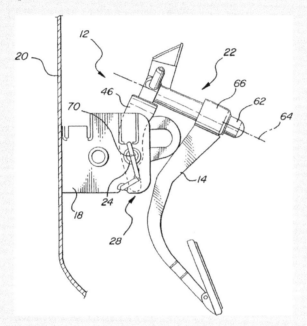

Seeking to resolve the question of obviousness with more uniformity and consistency, the Court of Appeals for the Federal Circuit has employed an approach referred to by the parties as the "teaching, suggestion, or motivation" test (TSM test), under which a patent claim is only proved obvious if "some motivation or suggestion to combine the prior art teachings" can be found in the prior art, the nature of the problem, or the knowledge of a person having ordinary skill in the art.

[I]nventors, beginning in the 1970s, designed pedals that could be adjusted to change their location in the footwell. Important for this case [is a] pedal disclosed in U.S. Patent No. 5,010,782 (filed July 28, 1989) (Asano). The Asano patent reveals a support structure that houses the pedal so that even when the pedal location is adjusted relative to the driver, one

> **CASE** *(continued)*
>
> of the pedal's pivot points stays fixed. [One pivot point in the Engelgau design is shown by the number 70 in the diagram above.]
>
> [KSR is a competitor of Teleflex. KSR supplied moveable pedals to car companies such as Ford and GM. Teleflex sued for infringement of the Engelgau patent.] [The district court,] [f]ollowing *Graham's* direction, compared the teachings of the prior art to the claims of Engelgau. It found "little difference." 298 F.Supp.2d, at 590. Asano taught everything contained in claim 4 except the use of a sensor to detect the pedal's position and transmit it to the computer controlling the throttle. That additional aspect was revealed in [several prior art] sources [the "sensor references]". [The Federal Circuit reversed, applying the "TSM" test it had developed.]
>
> We begin by rejecting the rigid approach of the Court of Appeals. Throughout this Court's engagement with the question of obviousness, our cases have set forth an expansive and flexible approach inconsistent with the way the Court of Appeals applied its TSM test here.
>
> When a work is available in one field of endeavor, design incentives and other market forces can prompt variations of it, either in the same field or a different one. If a person of ordinary skill can implement a predictable variation, §103 likely bars its patentability. For the same reason, if a technique has been used to improve one device, and a person of ordinary skill in the art would recognize that it would improve similar devices in the same way, using the technique is obvious unless its actual application is beyond his or her skill. [A] court must ask whether the improvement is more than the predictable use of prior art elements according to their established functions.
>
> [An] error of the Court of Appeals [was] its assumption that a person of ordinary skill attempting to solve a problem will be led only to those elements of prior art designed to solve the same problem. Common sense teaches that familiar items may have obvious uses beyond their primary purposes, and in many cases a person of ordinary skill will be able to fit the teachings of multiple patents together like pieces of a puzzle. Regardless of Asano's primary purpose, the design provided an obvious example of an adjustable pedal with a fixed pivot point; and the prior art was replete with patents indicating that a fixed pivot point was an ideal mount for a sensor. The idea that a designer hoping to make an adjustable electronic pedal would ignore Asano makes little sense. A person of ordinary skill is also a person of ordinary creativity, not an automaton.
>
> The District Court was correct to conclude that, as of the time Engelgau designed the subject matter in claim 4, it was obvious to a person of ordinary skill to combine Asano with a pivot-mounted pedal position sensor. There then existed a marketplace that created a strong incentive to convert mechanical pedals to electronic pedals, and the prior art taught a number of methods for achieving this advance.
>
> For a designer starting with Asano, the question was where to attach the sensor. The consequent legal question, then, is whether a pedal designer of ordinary skill starting with Asano would have found it obvious to put the sensor on *425 a fixed pivot point. The prior art discussed above leads us to the conclusion that attaching the sensor where both KSR and Engelgau put it would have been obvious to a person of ordinary skill.

NOTES

1. The "TSM" test discussed by the Court in its *KSR* opinion made it easier to obtain patents. That is because, as the Court suggests, it is often difficult to find specific statements in the prior art that it would be a good idea to combine different elements or components to arrive at a certain invention. A notorious case was *In re Dembiczak*, 175 F.3d 994 (Fed. Cir. 1999), where the Federal Circuit reversed a Patent Board of Appeals and Interferences decision denying the applicant a patent on a trash bag with a "pumpkin face" on it. Though trash bags and pumpkin faces were plentiful in the prior art, no one had ever suggested (in a findable reference, anyway) that the two should be combined. *KSR* put an end to this line of cases by reintroducing the basic approach of *Graham v. John Deere*, in which straightforward borrowing from one field into another may be found obvious.

2. *KSR*, as predicted, results in more patents being invalidated for obviousness under §103:

   [P]rior to KSR, when the Federal Circuit reached a final determination on the question of obviousness, the court concluded that the patent was obvious 43% of the time in appeals arising from the district courts and ITC. After KSR, the court reached a conclusion of "obvious" in appeals arising from these tribunals 57% of the time. This difference is statistically significant ... (Jason Rantanen, *The Federal Circuit's New Obviousness Jurisprudence: An Empirical Study*, 16 Stan. Tech. L. Rev. 709, 738 (2013)).

5.1 Inventive step in China

5.1.1 Three-step approach

In accordance with Article 22.1 of the Chinese Patent Law, any invention or utility model for which a patent right may be granted must possess novelty, inventiveness, and practical applicability. Therefore, inventiveness is one of the essential requirements to be satisfied for an invention or utility model application to be granted a patent right.

Inventiveness of an invention means that, as compared with the prior art before the date of filing, the invention has prominent substantive features and represents notable progress. The "notable progress" standard has been the subject of some debate. The phrase is drawn from now-outdated Soviet-era patent law, and appears to set a high standard of patentability. *See* Bu Yuanshi, "Prerequisites for Protection," Chapter 3 in Patent Law in Greater China (Stefan Lugenbuehl and Peter Ganea, eds., 2014), at §3.36, p. 53. At the same time, experienced commentators state that this is no more than a rephrasing of the traditional nonobviousness requirement recognized in various patent systems around the world (and usually said to be synonymous with the "inventive step" requirement). *See id.*, at §3.36, p. 53 ("the notion of prominent substantive features calls for nothing [more than the] non-obviousness of the invention for a person of ordinary skill in the relevant technical domain").

To determine whether an invention has prominent substantive features is to determine, to the person skilled in the art, whether the claimed invention is non-obvious as compared with the prior art. If the claimed invention is obvious as compared with the prior art, it does not have prominent substantive features. On the contrary, if the result of comparison shows that the claimed invention is non-obvious as compared with the prior art, it has prominent substantive features.

To decide the inventiveness of a patent application, the SIPO's Examination Guidelines define a three-step approach.

> **Section 3.2.1.1, Chapter 4, Part II of Examination Guidelines (2010)**
>
> (i) Determining the closest prior art;
> The closest prior art refers to a technical solution in the prior art which is the most closely related to the claimed invention, which shall be the basis for determining whether or not the claimed invention has prominent substantive features.
>
> (ii) Determining the distinguishing feature of the invention and the *technical problem* actually solved by the invention;
> During examination, the examiner shall objectively analyze and determine the technical problem actually solved by the invention. For this purpose, the examiner shall first determine the distinguishing features of the claimed invention as compared with the closest prior art and then determine the technical problem that is actually solved by the invention on the basis of the technical effect of the distinguishing features. The technical problem actually solved by the invention, in this sense, means the technical task in improving the closest prior art to achieve a better technical effect.
>
> (iii) Determining whether or not the claimed invention is obvious to a person skilled in the art;
> At this step, the examiner shall make a judgment, starting from the closest prior art and the technical problem actually solved by the invention, as to whether or not the claimed invention is obvious to a person skilled in the art. In the course of judgment, what is to be determined is whether or not there exists such a technical motivation in the prior art as to apply the said distinguishing features to the closest prior art in solving the existing technical problem (that is, the technical problem actually solved by the invention), where such motivation would prompt a person skilled in the art, when confronted with the technical problem, to improve the closest prior art and thus reach the claimed invention. If there exists such a technical motivation in the prior art, the invention is obvious and thus fails to have prominent substantive features.

As the three-step approach is defined in the SIPO's Examination Guidelines, it actually has no binding power for judges. However, in practice, it is widely used by both Beijing No. 1 Intermediate Court and Beijing High Court in reviewing the PRB's decisions.

In addition, the three-step approach is not the exclusive test for deciding inventiveness.

> **Section 5, Chapter 4, Part II of Examination Guidelines (2010)**
> Usually, whether or not an invention involves an inventive step shall be examined according to the criterion set forth in Section 3.2 of this Chapter. It should be stressed that where an application falls into one of the following circumstances, the examiner shall take the *corresponding factors* into account and avoid making a rash determination that the invention does not involve an inventive step.

Examination Guidelines lists five alternative factors to be considered in deciding inventiveness, including "solving a long-felt but unsolved technical problem," "overcoming a technical prejudice," "producing unexpected technical effect," and, "achieving commercial success."

5.1.2 How to decide the technical problem to be solved by the invention

Eli Lilly v. Patent Reexamination Board and Haosen Pharmaceutical Ltd., Beijing No. 1 Intermediate People's Court, Xing Chu Zi [2007] No. 540, June 20, 2008, aff'd on appeal, Beijing High People's Court, Xing Zhong Zi (2009), No. 122, March 20, 2009

Eli Lilly and Company (hereinafter, "Eli Lilly") is the patentee of Chinese Patent ZL90110125.7 titled "Method for manufacturing N-(pyrrolo [2, 3-d] pyrimidine-3-ylacyl) – glutamic acid derivatives" (hereinafter, "the Subject Patent"). The Subject patent was filed on December 11, 1990, claiming a priority date of December 11, 1989, and was granted and published on January 3, 1996.
Claim 1 reads as follows.

1. A method for preparing a glutamic acid derivative having the formula:

CASE (continued)

$$\begin{array}{c}\text{structure: } H-N(R^5)-C(=O)-\text{ring}-C-C-CH_2CH(R^4)-R^3-C(=O)NH-CH(C(=O)OH)-CH_2CH_2-C(=O)OH\end{array}$$

or a pharmaceutically acceptable salt thereof, in which:

R^3 is thienediyl; furanediyl, lower alkanediyl, or 1,4-phenylene unsubstituted or substituted with halogen;

R^4 is hydrogen;

R^5 is hydrogen, alkyl having 1 to 6 carbon atoms, or amino;

the configuration about the carbon atom designated * is S,

which comprises hydrogenating a compound of the following formula through acidic and/or basic catalysis,

$$\begin{array}{c}\text{structure with } R^6, R^{5'}, R^{4'}, R^3, OR^{2'}\end{array}$$

in which:

$R^{2'}$ is hydrogen or a carboxy-protecting group;

R^3 is defined as above;

$R^{4'}$ is hydrogen;

$R^{5'}$ is hydrogen, alkyl having 1 to 6 carbon atoms, amino, or alkanoylamino; and

R^6 is hydrogen or alkanoyloxy having 1 to 6 carbon atoms;

wherein at least one of $R^{2'}$ is a carboxy-protecting group, or $R^{5'}$ is alkanoylamino, or R^6 is alkanoyloxy,

$R^{2'}$ is converted to hydrogen or a carboxylic acid salt when $R^{2'}$ is a carboxy-protecting group, $R^{5'}$ is converted to amino when $R^{5'}$ is alkanoylamino, and R^6 is converted to hydrogen when R^6 is alkanoyloxy.

CASE (continued)

[On June 20, 2005, Jiangsu Province Haosen Pharmaceutical Co., Ltd. (hereinafter, "Haosen") filed an invalidation request to the PRB of the SIPO to invalidate the Subject Patent.]

[The PRB ruled], Evidence 4 (CN1037513A, U.S. counterpart US5539113A) discloses a method of preparing a composition of the following formula or its salts:

$$\underset{H_2N}{\overset{X}{\underset{N}{\bigvee}}} \overset{R}{\underset{|}{-(CH)_n}} - \underset{}{\bigcirc} - CONHCHCOOR^1 \quad (I)$$
$$CH_2CH_2COOR^2$$

In addition, in REFERENCE EXAMPLE 8 of Evidence 4, it discloses production of methyl 4-[3-(2-amino-7-benzyl-3-isopropyloxymethyl-4(3H) – oxopyrrolo [2,3-d]pyrimidin-5-yl)-1-oxo-2-propenyl] benzoate.

[Based on the disclosure of Evidence 8,] the PRB concluded that claim 1 of the Subject Patent has only one *distinguishing feature*: in the compound of claim 1, the connecting group between the phenylene and pyrrolo-pyrimindin ring is ethylidene; in example 8 of Evidence 4, the connecting group is propylidene.

[The PRB held, in view of the above distinguishing feature,] the *technical problem* actually solved by the Subject Patent is to provide "a manufacturing method for producing a compound which connects phenylene and pyrrolo-pyrimindin ring by ethylidene, instead of propylidene."

[Lastly, the PRB held that the above distinguishing feature is obvious for an ordinary person skilled in the art in view of the above technical problem. Accordingly, the PRB ruled that claims 1–3 are invalid under Article 22(3) of the Patent Law due to a lack of inventiveness.]

[Eli Lilly appealed to Beijing No. 1 Intermediate People's Court.]

[Beijing No. 1 Intermediate People's Court held that,] in evaluating the inventiveness step, the PRB erred to recognize the technical problem to be solved by the present invention. Starting from the distinguishing feature of claim 1, in view of Example 8 of Evidence 4, the court found that the technical problem actually solved by the subject patent is referenced in the language: "in order to obtain a better anti-tumor effect, the propylidene group in Evidence 4 is substituted with ethylidene group, resulting in the same manufacturing method and compound of claim 1."

[Accordingly, Beijing No. 1 Intermediate People's Court revoked the PRB's decision and remanded it for retrial. The PRB appealed to Beijing High People's Court.]

[Beijing High People's Court held that,] it is necessary to first discuss the technical problem, which is defined in §3.2.1.1, Chapter 4, Part II, Guidelines for Patent Examination (hereinafter, "the Guidelines"):

CASE *(continued)*

The technical problem actually solved by the invention means the technical task in improving the closest prior art in order to achieve a better technical effect. . . . As a principle, any technical effect of an invention may be used as basis to determine the technical problem, as long as the technical effect could be recognized by a person skilled in the art from the contents set forth in the description.

Comparing this subject patent with Example 8 of Evidence 4, claim 1 has only one distinguishing feature: in the compound of claim 1, the connecting group between phenylene and the pyrrolo-pyrimindin ring is ethylidene; while in Example 8, the connecting group is propylidene.

In the 1st instance decision made by Beijing No. 1 Intermediate People's Court, the court held that, with respect to the distinguishing technical feature, the technical problem actually solved by the subject patent is described as: "for a better anti-tumor effect, the propylidene group in Evidence 8 of Evidence 4 is substituted with ethylidene group, resulting in the same manufacturing method and compound of claim 1." The court's assertion of "better anti-tumor effect" is based on the comparison between compound C manufactured by the method claim 1 and compound B of Example 8, where a difference of 4.3 times IC_{50} of leukemia cells is found.

However, another question is whether such a comparison is sufficient to prove prominent progresses made by compound C over compound B in inhibiting activity of leukemia cells. This question should be answered with further investigation conducted by the PRB based on the description and other relevant evidence.

As noted, the distinguishing feature of claim 1, as found by Beijing No. 1 Intermediate People's Court, is insufficient to support the court's finding of the technical problem. Instead, the court or the PRB should reconsider what the technical problem is after a sufficient examination of the relevant evidence. A correct finding of the technical problem is a prerequisite for an inventiveness assessment.

[Accordingly, Beijing High Court concluded that] Beijing No. 1 Intermediate People's Court was correct to revoke the PRB's Decision, even though it failed to make a correct finding of the technical problem either.

Beijing High People's Court affirmed the judgment made by Beijing No. 1 Intermediate People's Court.

Judge Bisheng SHI

NOTES

1. **Correct finding of the technical problem is a prerequisite for deciding inventiveness.** In this case, the Beijing High Court pointed out that both the PRB and the Intermediate Court erred in identifying the technical problem to be solved by the Subject Patent. As this step is a prerequisite for deciding the inventiveness step, the PRB's decision was revoked and remanded.
2. **Objective technical problem.** It is common that the inventor's finding of the technical problem might not be identical to that recognized by a person skilled in the art. For example, after conducting a prior art search, the examiner's finding of the closest prior art might also be different from the inventor's finding.

In order to assess inventiveness in an objective manner, the technical problem should be *objectively* determined without being limited by the inventor's knowledge. The concept of "objective technical problem," as explained by Judge Bisheng SHI, is supported by the SIPO's Examination Guidelines:

> In the course of examination, because the closest prior art identified by the examiner may be different from that asserted by the applicant in the description, the technical problem actually solved by the invention, which is re-determined on the basis of the closest prior art, may not be the same as that described in the description. Under such a circumstance, the technical problem actually solved by the invention should be *re-determined* on the basis of the closest prior art identified by the examiner.

3. **Motivation factor in deciding "inventiveness."** As to the issue of "inventiveness," the essential question is whether the patent is inventive (or, obvious) in the context of one or more pieces of prior art documents. In particular, courts will inquire into whether any technical "motivation" exists in the prior art as a whole that would motivate a person skilled in the relevant art to improve the prior art (*e.g.*, to combine prior art documents) so as to obtain the technical solution of the patent in order to solve the technical problem.

5.2 Inventive step in Europe

EPC Article 56 reads:

Article 56
Inventive step

An invention shall be considered as involving an inventive step if, having regard to the state of the art, it is not obvious to a person skilled in the art. If the state of the art also includes documents within the meaning of Article 54, paragraph 3, these documents shall not be considered in deciding whether there has been an inventive step.

Although the connection to nonobviousness in the US is apparent, there are some distinct features in the European approach to inventive step issues – in particular, (1) the emphasis on identifying the single "closest" prior art reference, and (2) the problem-solution approach.

The best way to understand these two features of EU law is through a specific case, as with this one:

 CASE

Paper surface sizing/AVEBE (AVEBE B.A. v. Zuckerforschung Tulln GmbH), Case No. T 0035/04 (Euro. Pat. Off. Bd. App., 18 January 2006)

This appeal is from the decision of the Opposition Division revoking European patent No. 0 737 777 concerning a method for surface sizing paper using a size based on amylopectin

CASE *(continued)*

potato starch (hereinafter "APS") and the paper thus obtained. ["Sizing" is the process of treating the surface of paper to make it less susceptible to ink blotting, or to make it more water-resistant, or to strengthen it.]
Claim 1 [of the issued patent] read:

> 1. A method for surface sizing paper, characterized in that an aqueous solution of a degraded amylopectin potato starch is applied to the paper and the sized paper is thereafter dried.

Claims 2 to 5 defined preferred embodiments of the method of claim 1.
Claim 6 read:

> 6. Surface-sized paper with the layer of size consisting entirely or substantially entirely of degraded amylopectin potato starch.

[Amylopectin is a chemical compound closely related to glucose (sugar); it is one of the two chemical constituents of common starch. Amylopectin potato starch is made from potatoes, and the patentee, Avebe, sells a trademarked form of it that was the product of traditional or "classical" plant breeding techniques (as opposed to recombinant genetic techniques). It is described by Avebe as "a waxy potato starch containing more than 95% amylopectin," and is sold under the trademark "Eliane." *See* http://www.avebe.com/products/eliane/.]
 [Among the documents cited in the opposition were:
E1 = [US Patent 3,931,422] . . .
E6 = C.T. Beals "Surface Applications," in Dry Strength Additives (W. F. Reynolds ed., 1980), pp. 35–65.]
 The Opposition division considered that document E1 disclosed at column 3, lines 29 to 32 a list of degraded starches suitable as basis for surface sizes for paper (hereinafter "the list of E1"). This list comprised inter alia "potato starch", "waxy corn starch" and ended with the wording "wheat starch and the amylopectin fraction therefrom".
 [There was controversy during the Opposition over whether the last phrase in the last item in the E1 list, "and the amylopectin fraction therefrom", applied to *only* the last list item, wheat item, or to each item on the list, viz., "the amylopectin fraction of potato starch, waxy corn starch" etc. Because it could not be established convincingly that the amylopectin fractions of all the list members had been intended, it was decided that claim 1 was novel; neither E1 nor any other single reference recited all the elements of the claim.]
 The Board observes that the patent in suit aims at obtaining surface-sized paper with improved strength (see paragraphs 12, 28 and 30), in particular with improved IGT dry pick resistance, and that also document E1 mentions that surface sizing aims at increasing the paper strength (see column 1 lines 11 to 15). Hence the Board has no reason to depart from the finding in the decision under appeal that the prior art disclosed in this citation

CASE *(continued)*

represents a reasonable starting point for the assessment of inventive step. This has not been disputed by the parties.

[As part of its case, the patent owner, Avebe, introduced a Report demonstrating that its sizing method produced surprisingly superior surface-sized paper in comparison to that treated with sizes based on alternative techniques such as native potato starch ("native PS"), waxy corn starch or fractionated-amylopectin potato starch (fractionated-APS"). This Report is referred to as "the data of 2004."]

As conceded by the Appellant at the oral proceedings before the Board, the data of 2004 prove that the paper surface sized with fractionated-APS according to the method claimed displays worse IGT dry pick resistance than that sized with native-PS. ["Picking" is the term for damage to the surface of paper; "dry pick resistance" is the quality of resisting surface damage or picking when the paper is dry – *e.g.*, resistance to surface damage from the impact of inkjet printing or handling. IGT Testing Systems, Inc. is a company that makes testing equipment, including a machine that is used to test paper surface strength, *i.e.*, "pick resistance."] Therefore, the Board must conclude that the embodiments of the claimed method based on degraded fractionated-APS do not result in the technical advantage stated in the patent in suit when compared with the prior art disclosed in document E1.

Under these circumstances the technical problem credibly solved by the method claimed vis-à-vis the prior art disclosed in document E1 boils down to that of providing another surface sizing method, *i.e.*, an alternative to this prior art.

The Appellant has argued that fractionated-APS has never been disclosed to be suitable for surface sizing paper and, thus, that the skilled person would have no reasons for replacing the conventional starches used in the surface sizing method of document E1 by this APS.

The Board considers that, in view of the technical problem posed, the critical question is whether or not the skilled person would have replaced the conventional starches used in the surface sizing method of document E1 by fractionated-APS in the reasonable expectation that this modification would produce an acceptable surface-sized paper. Since the list of E1 discloses several different starches as equally suitable for surface sizes, this citation teaches implicitly to the skilled reader that the surface-sized paper produced by using any of them must display acceptable properties. Hence, the skilled person would reasonably expect, in the absence of any reason to the contrary, that any other available starch similar to those mentioned in the list of E1 is basically also suitable for surface sizing paper, regardless as to whether *e.g.*, the product label accompanying such a starch and/or the relevant publications in which it is disclosed contain an explicit reference specifically to such use.

For the person skilled in the art of paper production fractionated-APS is a conventional product. This fact has not been disputed by the Appellant. Moreover, it is expected to be similar to both the native-PS from which it is derived, and the "waxy" corn starch, another native starch but which is substantially free from amylose. Both these starches are explicitly mentioned in the list of E1. Hence, even in the absence of a document explicitly suggesting that degraded fractionated-APS is suitable for surface sizing, it required no inventive

CASE *(continued)*

ingenuity for the skilled person to foresee that the amylopectin fraction of potato starch might also be used for surface sizing paper in the method of document E1.

Hence, the Board finds that the skilled person would consider it obvious to replace the starches mentioned in the list of E1 with fractionated-APS, in the expectation of a surface-sized paper with acceptable properties.

The Board comes, therefore, to the conclusion that the subject-matter of process claim 1 of the main request does not involve an inventive step and, hence, that this request is not allowable because it does not comply with the requirements of Article[] . . . 56 EPC. The same applies to the subject-matter of claim 6 relating to the product obtained from the process of claim 1.

[During the Opposition, in keeping with EPO Opposition practice, the patentee had filed an "auxiliary request" – a proposal to amend its claims so as to narrow them and thus avoid the grounds of the opposition. In this auxiliary request, Amended claim 1 reads as follows:

> 1. A method for surface sizing paper wherein amylopectin potato starch granules isolated from potato tubers obtained from genetically modified potato plants which form said starch granules in the potato tubers, said starch granules comprising more than 95% by weight, based on dry substance, of amylopectin, are degraded, and wherein an aqueous solution of the degraded amylopectin potato starch is applied to the paper and the sized paper is thereafter dried.]

The Respondent has contested the patentability of [this] auxiliary request, only in view of its obviousness vis-à-vis the prior art method disclosed in document E1 in combination with the disclosure in document E4 that native-APS was an increasingly important ingredient for the production of paper.

The Board notes that claim 1 of the present request requires the use of an aqueous solution of degraded granules of native-APS, a starch that is undisputedly not disclosed in document E1.

The Board finds convincing the submission of the Appellant at the oral proceedings that the data of 2004 credibly demonstrate that the feature distinguishing the method according to claim 1 from the relevant prior art disclosed in document E1, actually results in the superior strength stated in paragraph 12 of the patent in suit. This is evident when considering, in particular, that the IGT dry pick resistance values reported for the native-APS-based samples in Tables 4 to 6 are superior to those for the waxy corn starch-based and for the native-PS-based samples respectively reported in each of these tables, *i.e.*, the two sizes explicitly disclosed in the list of E1 having the closest structural proximity to the size of the invention.

The Board concludes therefore that the subject-matter of claim 1 of the second auxiliary request has credibly solved in view of the prior art disclosed in document E1 as most suitable starting point, the technical problem of providing surface-sized paper with strength superior to that obtainable by the use of the prior art starch sizes.

CASE (continued)

Hence, the assessment of inventive step boils down to establishing whether or not the skilled person would have replaced the starch sizes used in the method of E1 for surface sizing paper by a similar size obtained from native-APS, in the expectation that this modification would increase the strength of the obtained surface-sized paper.

The Board observes that E4 and the other citations considered by the Respondent as relevant for the assessment of inventive step do not mention at all that native-APS might be suitable for surface sizing paper. Hence, the same citations cannot possibly suggest that this starch may actually provide surface-sized paper with superior strength. On the contrary, the skilled person would rather expect, in view the general prejudice reported in the textbook E2, that any amylose-free starch, *i.e.*, any starch made substantially only of amylopectin, cannot possibly provide a paper strength superior to that already achieved in the prior art.

The Board concludes, therefore, that the skilled person would have expected that the desired superior strength of the surface-sized paper could not be achieved by using any APS consisting substantially of amylopectin only and, thus, that also the native-APS disclosed *e.g.*, in document E4 would not be suitable for obtaining the desired effect. Hence, the combination of the disclosure in documents E1 and E4 does not render predictable the superior strength of the surface-sized paper obtained with the method of present claim 1.

The Board finds also that the subject-matter of claim 1 is not rendered obvious by any of the other combinations of documents.

The Board comes therefore to the conclusion that the subject-matter of claim 1 of the second auxiliary request involves an inventive step and, hence, complies with the requirements of Article 56 EPC.

NOTES

1. As mentioned, the "closest art" component of EPO analysis is distinctive. In general, the closest prior art is that whose use is similar to the claimed invention, and which requires the minimum of structural and functional modifications to arrive at the claimed invention. *See Henkel KgAA v. Unilever*, Case No. T 606/89 (Euro. Pat. Off. Bd. App., 27 July 1989), at Reasons par. 2:

    It is the established jurisprudence of the Boards of Appeal that the objective assessment of inventive step has to be preceded by the determination of the technical problem which the invention addresses and solves and that the technical problem is to be formulated in the light of the closest state of the art. Therefore, in order to apply this approach for objectively assessing inventive step, it is essential to establish the closest prior art. Generally, this requires that the claimed invention should be compared with the art concerned with a similar use which requires the minimum of structural and functional modifications. Thus, in the present case, this involves not only comparing the claimed compositions with those of the prior art, but also giving consideration to the particular properties which render the compositions suitable for the desired use.

2. The problem-solution approach may seem straightforward, because many patent specifications are drafted with an eye toward the problem encountered by the inventor, and the reasons why the claimed invention solves the problem. In many cases, however, this discussion in the patent may be quite general (*e.g.*, "the invention saves money," or "the invention is an improvement in the way task X is performed" or the like). There may be no specific "framing" of the problem in terms of the closest prior art. Because of this, the EPO

permits an inventor to reframe the problem solved by the patent in terms keyed specifically to the closest prior art. As long as the problem (as well as the solution) is identifiable (though not explicitly stated) in the originally filed specification, this is permitted. *See, e.g.*, at Reasons par. 2:

> It belongs to the well-established jurisprudence of the Boards of Appeal that where a specific problem is identified in the description, the applicant or patentee may be allowed to put forward a modified version of the problem particularly if the issue of inventiveness has to be considered on an objective basis against a new prior art which comes closer to the invention than that considered in the original patent application or granted patent specification. Reference is made in this respect to the decision T 184/82 (OJEPO 1984, 261) where the Board allowed a re-definition of the problem to such an extent that the skilled person "could recognize the same as implied or related to the problem initially suggested" (see point 5 of the reasons) ... [T]he Board [has] held that the reformulation of the problem is [permitted] if the problem could be deduced by a person skilled in the art from the application as originally filed when seen in the light of the nearest prior art ...

3. Board and court opinions interpreting EPC Article 56 often grapple with the ultimate issue of obviousness. As the EPO Examination Guidelines state, at Part G, Chapter VII-2, par. 5: "In order to assess inventive step in an objective and predictable manner, the so-called "problem-and-solution approach" should be applied. Thus deviation from this approach should be exceptional."

In the problem-and-solution approach, there are three main stages:

(i) determining the "closest prior art",
(ii) establishing the "objective technical problem" to be solved, and
(iii) considering whether or not the claimed invention, starting from the closest prior art and the objective technical problem, would have been obvious to the skilled person.

Emphasis is often placed on the phrasing of point (iii): whether the claimed invention "*would* have been obvious" from the closest prior art. This leads to a well-known formulation, the "could-would" distinction, which is also discussed in the EPO Examination Guidelines, at Part G, Chapter VII-2, par. 5.3 (emphasis in original):

> In the third stage the question to be answered is whether there is any teaching in the prior art as a whole that *would* (not simply could, but would) have prompted the skilled person, faced with the objective technical problem, to modify or adapt the closest prior art while taking account of that teaching, thereby arriving at something falling within the terms of the claims, and thus achieving what the invention achieves. In other words, the point is not whether the skilled person could have arrived at the invention by adapting or modifying the closest prior art, but whether he *would have done* so because the prior art incited him to do so in the hope of solving the objective technical problem or in expectation of some improvement or advantage. Even an implicit prompting or implicitly recognizable incentive is sufficient to show that the skilled person would have combined the elements from the prior art. This must have been the case for the skilled person before the filing or priority date valid for the claim under examination.

See, e.g., Simethicone Tablet/Rider, Case No. T-83 (Euro. Pat. Off. Bd. App., 15 March 1984), which involved the addition of a "barrier" level in a multi-tiered or "layered" pharmaceutical tablet, with the goal to slow the release of the ingredient placed behind the barrier. The prior art (represented by a Yen reference) involved a different (and in itself considered effective at the time) solution, which was to embed the ingredient in a large volume of carrier material. Based on this record, the Board discussed whether one skilled in the art would have been led to the barrier solution of the claimed invention, at Reasons par. 7:

> The question regarding the inventive step, in relation to the modification of the layered tablet of the state of the art as suggested by the present applicants, is not whether the skilled man could have inserted a barrier between the layers but whether he would have done so in expectation of some improvement or advantage. Since the Yen tablet was, on the face of it and from what was assumed in view of its commercialisation, a satisfactory answer to the problem of undesirable migration, the addition of a barrier would have appeared superfluous, wasteful and devoid of any technical effect. In view of the recognition that a barrier has, after all, a substantial effect [*i.e.*, it provides superior performance after storage – a defect

in the Yen carrier solution that was discovered by the barrier inventor whose patent is at issue here], the outcome was not predictable and the claimed modification involves an inventive step on this basis.

For those accustomed to discussions of nonobviousness under US patent law (35 U.S.C. §103), this is familiar reasoning. The possibility that a technical solution "could" work implies that it is plausible; that it is not beyond the realm of possibilities. But, by contrast, a belief that a certain solution *would* work is tantamount to a prediction that the solution is not only plausible but very likely to achieve its goal. The entire question of obviousness has been modeled on this basis, with the key emphasis on the assessment of a skilled person of the probability of success for a certain solution at a time just before the solution is attempted. *See* Robert P. Merges, *Uncertainty and the Standard of Patentability*, 7 [Berkeley] High Tech. L.J. 1 (1992).

6

Adequate disclosure and enablement

6.1 Disclosure

 CASE

Consolidated Electric Light Co. v. McKeesport Light Co. ("The Incandescent Lamp Patent"), 159 U.S. 465 (1895)

Justice Brown
[Infringement suit by the Consolidated Electric Light Company against the McKeesport Light Company, to recover damages for the infringement of letters patent No. 317,076, issued May 12, 1885, to the Electro-Dynamic Light Company, assignee of the two inventors, Sawyer and Man, for an electric light. Defendant was a licensee of a rival light bulb technology, covered by patent no. 223,898 and invented by Thomas Edison. Only the validity of the Sawyer and Man '076 patent is at issue in this opinion.]
For many years prior to 1880, experiments had been made by a large number of persons, in various countries, with a view to the production of an incandescent light which could be made available for domestic purposes, and could compete with gas in the matter of expense. Owing partly to a failure to find a proper material, which should burn but not consume, partly to the difficulty of obtaining a perfect vacuum in the globe in which the light was suspended, and partly to a misapprehension of the true principle of incandescent lighting, these experiments had not been attended with success; although it had been demonstrated as early as 1845 that, whatever material was used, the conductor must be enclosed in an airtight bulb, to prevent it from being consumed by the oxygen in the atmosphere. The chief difficulty was that the carbon burners were subject to a rapid disintegration or evaporation, which electricians assumed was due to the disrupting action of the electric current, and hence the conclusion was reached that carbon contained in itself the elements of its own destruction, and was not a suitable material for the burner of an incandescent lamp. [Sawyer and Man discovered that a certain type of partially burned paper, carbonized paper, makes

CASE *(continued)*

an effective incandescing element in a light bulb. In the diagram from their patent, below, the carbonized paper is the semicircular material between the two vertical terminals, most easily seen in Figure 3 on the left.]

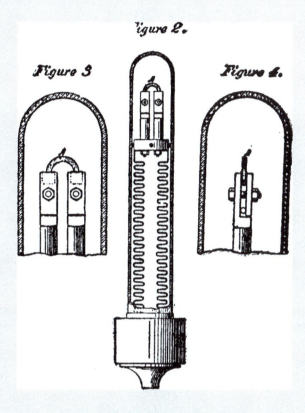

It is admitted that the lamp described in the Sawyer and Man patent is no longer in use, and ... that the lamp manufactured by the [patentee], and put upon the market, is substantially the Edison lamp; but it is said that, in the conductor used by Edison (a particular part of the stem of the bamboo, lying directly beneath the siliceous cuticle, the peculiar fitness for which purpose was undoubtedly discovered by him), he made use of a fibrous or textile material covered by the patent to Sawyer and Man, and is therefore an infringer. It was admitted, however, that the third claim – for a conductor of carbonized paper – was not infringed. [A diagram of the Edison light bulb, taken from his '260 patent, is reproduced below. The thin strand of bamboo used for the incandescing element in marked A in the diagram.]

CASE *(continued)*

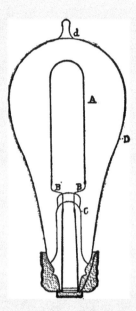

Is the complainant entitled to a monopoly of all fibrous and textile materials for incandescent conductors? If the patentees had discovered in fibrous and textile substances a quality common to them all, or to them generally, as distinguishing them from other materials, such as minerals, etc., and such quality or characteristic adapted them peculiarly to incandescent conductors, such claim might not be too broad. Sawyer and Man supposed they had discovered in carbonized paper the best material for an incandescent conductor. Instead of confining themselves to carbonized paper, as they might properly have done, and in fact did in their third claim, they made a broad claim for every fibrous or textile material, when in fact an examination of over 6,000 vegetable growths showed that none of them possessed the peculiar qualities that fitted them for that purpose. Was everybody, then, precluded by this broad claim from making further investigation? We think not.

The injustice of so holding is manifest in view of the experiments made, and continued for several months, by Mr. Edison and his assistants, among the different species of vegetable growth, for the purpose of ascertaining the one best adapted to an incandescent conductor. Of these he found suitable for his purpose only about three species of bamboo, one species of cane from the valley of the Amazon (impossible to be procured in quantities on account of the climate), and one or two species of fibers from the agave family. [W]hile experimenting with a bamboo strip which formed the edge of a palm-leaf fan, cut into filaments, he obtained surprising results. After microscopic examination of the material, he dispatched a man to Japan to make arrangements for securing the bamboo in quantities. It seems that the characteristic of the bamboo which makes it particularly suitable is that the fibers run more nearly parallel than in other species of wood. Owing to this, it can be cut

CASE *(continued)*

up into filaments having parallel fibers, running throughout their length, and producing a homogeneous carbon. There is no generic quality, however, in vegetable fibers, because they are fibrous, which adapts them to the purpose. Indeed, the fibers are rather a disadvantage. [T]here is no such quality common to fibrous and textile substances generally as makes them suitable for an incandescent conductor. The question really is whether the imperfectly successful experiments of Sawyer and Man, with carbonized paper and wood carbon, conceding all that is claimed for them, authorize them to put under tribute the results of the brilliant discoveries made by others.

It is required by Rev. St. §4888, that the application shall contain "a written description of the device, and of the manner and process of making constructing, compounding, and using it in such full, clear, concise, and exact terms as to enable any person, skilled in the art or science to which it appertains or with which it is most nearly connected, to make, construct, compound, and use the same." If the description be so vague and uncertain that no one can tell, except by independent experiments, how to construct the patented device, the patent is void.

Under these circumstances, to hold that one who had discovered that a certain fibrous or textile material answered the required purpose should obtain the right to exclude everybody from the whole domain of fibrous and textile materials, and thereby shut out any further efforts to discover a better specimen of that class than the patentee had employed, would be an unwarranted extension of his monopoly, and operate rather to discourage than to promote invention. If Sawyer and Man had discovered that a certain carbonized paper would answer the purpose, their claim to all carbonized paper would, perhaps, not be extravagant; but the fact that paper happens to belong to the fibrous kingdom did not invest them with sovereignty over this entire kingdom, and thereby practically limit other experimenters to the domain of minerals.

NOTES

1. The *Incandescent Lamp* standard – often described as the "undue experimentation test" – continues to dominate enablement cases. For example, in *Automotive Technologies Int'l, Inc. v. BMW of North America, Inc.*, 501 F.3d 1274 (Fed. Cir. 2007), the inventor claimed a sensor mounted inside the side door of a car. The sensor is used to signal that a crash has occurred; it initiates the inflation of an airbag to protect passengers. The claim covered a mass suspended inside a housing, and a mechanism to sense the movement of the mass in the event of a crash. The specification only described mechanical movement and sensing techniques, however. Typically the mass shifts inside the housing and closes an electrical circuit, setting off the airbag. The claim covers other sensing techniques, however, including various ways of detecting movement of the mass by electronic sensing: the motion of the mass causes a change in some electrical property inside the housing, and this sets off the airbag. The court held that the electronic sensing approaches were not enabled, because "undue experimentation would have been required to make and use an electronic side impact sensor . . ." (*id.*, at 1284).

2. A useful eight-factor test for determining undue experimentation issues has been set forth by the Federal Circuit:

    (1) the quantity of experimentation necessary, (2) the amount of direction or guidance presented, (3) the presence or absence of working examples, (4) the nature of the invention, (5) the state of the prior

art, (6) the relative skill of those in the art, (7) the predictability or unpredictability of the art, and (8) the breadth of the claims
(*In re Wands*, 858 F.2d 731, 737 (Fed. Cir. 1988)).

6.1.1 Disclosure in China

Chinese Supreme Court's Trilogy on Applying Article 33 of the Patent Law (deciding "New Matter")

Article 33 of the Patent Law stipulates that an applicant may amend his or her patent application documents, provided that the amendment to the invention or utility model patent application documents does not exceed *the scope specified in the original written descriptions and claims*, or that the amendment to the design patent application documents does not exceed the scope shown in the original drawings or pictures.

In prosecution and invalidation practice, SIPO examiners used to apply a quite rigid standard to interpret "the scope specified in the original written descriptions and claims." It has become common that an amended feature will not be accepted unless it has been literally described in the original disclosure.

In the following three patent invalidation cases involving Article 33, which were appealed to the Supreme Court from 2011 to 2013, the Supreme Court judges rejected the SIPO's standard and proposed a more flexible approach.

 CASE

i. Epson 1

Zheng Yali v. Seiko Epson Corp., Patent Reexamination Board, Chinese Supreme People's Court, Zhixingzi No. 53 (2010)

Seiko Epson Corporation ("Seiko Epson") is the patentee of the No. 00131800.4 invention patent named "Inkjet Box" ("the Subject Patent"). The Subject Patent is a divisional application of the patent application No. 99800780.3, which is a PCT application PCT/JP99/02579 entering the National Phase.
   The granted claim 1 reads as follows:

> **CASE** *(continued)*
>
> 1. An ink cartridge for mounting on an ink jet printing apparatus, which supplies ink to a printhead of said ink jet printing apparatus via an ink supplying needle, the ink cartridge comprising:
> a plurality of walls;
> an ink supply port formed on one of the plurality walls for receiving the ink supply needle of the printing apparatus;
> a storage device disposed on said cartridge, used for storing information related to ink;
> a circuit board mounted on a second wall intersecting with a first wall of said plurality of walls, said circuit board is located in the center line of the ink supply port; and
> a plurality of contacts provided on the exterior of said cartridge, used for connecting said storage device to said ink-jet printing apparatus, wherein the contacts forming a plurality of columns.
>
> [During prosecution of the Subject Patent, Seiko Epson uses "storage device" to replace the original term "semiconductor storage device". Seiko Epson admits that the revised term "storage device" has not occurred in the original disclosure.]
>
> [Zheng Yali, etc. filed invalidity request against the Subject Patent to the PRB. The PRB made the No. 11291 Decision to declared claim 1 (and other claims as well) of Subject Patent invalid, on the grounds that Seiko Epson's amendment of "storage device" exceeds the original scope, which does not comply with Article 33 of the Chinese Patent Law.]
>
> [Seiko Epson was not satisfied with the PRB's decision and brought administrative litigation. Beijing No. 1 Intermediate People's Court made a first instance judgment affirming the No. 11291 decision. Seiko Epson appealed to Beijing Higher People's Court, which vacated the judgment of the first instance, holding that Seiko Epson's amendment of "storage device" in claim 1 was acceptable. Zheng Yali filed a retrial request to the Supreme People's Court, which rejected the application.]
>
> [The Supreme People's Court interprets Article 33 of the Patent Law as follows:] ... the "scope of the original disclosure" should comprise the following contents:
>
> 1. The contents explicitly described in the original specification, drawings and claims, either in the form of text or graphics;
> 2. The contents that can be *directly and explicitly derived* by a person of ordinary skills in the art through comprehensive consideration of the original specification, drawings and claims. As long as the derived contents are *obvious* for those skilled in the art in view of the original disclosure, it shall be considered as in the scope of the original disclosure.
>
> ...
>
> When applying Article 33, it shall not be mechanically interpreted in such a way that only when revised contents can be deduced from original disclosure via a *one-to-one mathematical logic mapping* by a person of ordinary skills in the art, it meets said "directly and explicitly derivation" standard.

CASE *(continued)*

[After establishing the above standard, the Supreme Court further explained:] for those skilled in the art, it is obvious to figure out that said semiconductor storage device of the Subject Patent can be easily replaced by other types of storage devices, including non-semiconductor storage devices. . . . Thus, the replacement of "semiconductor storage device" by "storage device" does not exceed the original disclosure.

[The Supreme Court confirmed the holding of the second instance, ruling that Seiko Epson's amendment of "storage device" is in conformity with Article 33 of the Patent Law. The retrial request by Zheng Yali is rejected.]

Judge Zhonglin HE
Judge Li ZHU
Judge Yuanming QIN
Dec. 25, 2011

CASE

ii. Epson 2

Seiko Epson v. Patent Reexamination Board, Zheng Yali, Chinese Supreme People's Court, Zhixingzi No. 53-1 (2010)

[Seiko Epson Corporation ("Seiko Epson") is the patentee of the No. 00131800.4 invention patent named "Inkjet Box" ("the Subject Patent"). The Subject Patent is a divisional application of the No. 99800780.3 invention patent application, which is a PCT application PCT/JP99/02579 entering the National Phase in China.]
The granted claim 8 reads as follows:

> 8. An ink cartridge for mounting on an ink jet printing apparatus, which supplies ink to a printhead of said ink jet printing apparatus via an ink supplying needle, the ink cartridge comprising:
> a plurality of walls;
> an ink supply port formed on one of the plurality walls for receiving the ink supply needle of the printing apparatus;
> a <u>memory device</u> disposed on said cartridge, used for storing information related to ink;
> a plurality of contacts used for connecting said memory device to said ink-jet printing apparatus, wherein the contacts forming a plurality of columns, wherein one of said plurality

CASE *(continued)*

of columns being closer to the ink supply port than other columns, and the column of contacts being closest to the ink supply port is longer than the column of contacts being furthest to the ink supply port.

[During the prosecution of the Subject Patent, Seiko Epson uses "memory device" to replace the original term "semiconductor storage device."]

[Zheng Yali, etc. filed invalidity request against the Subject Patent to the PRB. The PRB made the No. 11291 Decision to declared claim 8 (and other claims as well) of Subject Patent invalid, on the grounds that Seiko Epson's amendment of "memory device" exceeds the original scope, which does not comply with Article 33 of the Chinese Patent Law.]

[Seiko Epson was not satisfied with the PRB's decision and brought administrative litigation. Beijing No. 1 Intermediate People's Court made a first instance judgment affirming the No. 11291 decision. [Seiko Epson appealed to Beijing Higher People's Court.]

[Beijing Higher People's Court held in the second instance that, "memory device", which is newly added, exceeds the original disclosure and thus is not in conformity with Article 33 of the Patent Law.] . . . Although Seiko Epson stated during prosecution that "memory device" shall be interpreted as "semiconductor storage device 61 of Fig 7(b)," such a statement is still irrelevant for applying Article 33. . . . Therefore, claims 8, 12 and 29 are not in conformity with Article 33 of the Patent Law, and should be invalid. [Seiko Epson was not satisfied and filed a retrial request to the Supreme People's Court.]

[The Supreme People's Court ruled:] . . . As to how to take into consideration the patentee's own statement made during prosecution when deciding whether an amendment exceeds the original disclosure or not. . . . *In particular, if the patentee's own statement exceeds the original disclosure, it becomes irrelevant and shall not be considered when deciding whether an amendment complies with Article 33 or not.*

[Next, the Supreme Court tries to decide the meaning of "memory device."] First, the ordinary meaning of "memory device" for those skilled in the art is an equivalent of "storage device." However, in the context of the Subject Patent, as the Subject Patent uses the terms "storage device" and "memory device" in a distinguishing manner, "memory device" and "storage device" shall have distinct meanings.

[Lastly, the Supreme Court stated,] the scope of the original specification and claims should comprise the following contents: (1) the contents explicitly expressed in the original specification, drawings and claims, either in text or graphics; (2) the contents that can be *directly and explicitly derived* by the people with ordinary skills in the art through comprehensive consideration of the original specification, drawings and claims . . .]

[Applying the above standard, the Supreme Court ruled that] "memory device" is neither explicitly described in the original application documents, nor can be directly and explicitly derived by a person of ordinary skill in the art from the original specification, drawings and claims. Therefore, the amendment of "memory device" in claim 8 violates Article 33 of the Patent Law.

CASE *(continued)*

[The Supreme Court maintained that claim 8 of the Subject Patent is invalid and rejected the retrial request of Seiko Epson.]

Judge Kesheng JIN
Judge Li ZHU
Judge Guimei LANG
Sep. 23, 2013

iii. Shimano v. PRB

Shimano, Inc. v. Patent Reexamination Board, Ningbo Saiguan Bicycle Co., Chinese Supreme People's Court, Xing Ti Zi No. 21 (2013)

Shimano, Inc. ("Shimano") is the patentee of Chinese invention patent No. ZL02127848.2 tilted "back gearshifter" ("the Subject Patent"), which is a divisional application of the original application No. 94102612.4. The original application was filed on February 3, 1994, claiming priority date February 3, 1993.

The granted claims 1 and 2 of the Subject Patent read as follows:

> 1. A rear derailleur (100), comprising:
> a bracket member (5);
> a support member (4), for supporting a chain guide (3) having a guide wheel (1) and a tension pulley (2);
> a pair of connecting members (6,7) for connecting the support member (4) and the bracket member (5);
> the bracket body (8), which comprises a first connecting structure (8a), a second connecting structure (8b) and a positioning structure (8c), wherein said first connecting structure (8a) is provided in the holder body (8) near one end and is used for connecting said bracket member (5) pivotally to said bracket member (8) around a first axis (91), said second connecting means (8b) is provided in the holder body (8) near the other end; and a tension spring (12) mounted on said bracket member (5);
> characterized in that:
> said holder body (8) is made by a substantially L-shaped plate;

CASE (continued)

    the shape of the second connecting means (8b) of the bracket body (8) is a substantially circular hole;

    the bracket body (8) having a hole (8d) formed close to said first connecting structure (8a), used for receiving an end of the tension spring (12), so as to connect the tension spring (12) to the a bracket body (8);

    the shape of the positioning structure (8c) is formed as an extending part out of the surface of the plate, wherein the extending part is adjacent said second connecting means (8b).

  2. The rear derailleur according to claim 1, characterized in that said positioning structure (8c) is formed by pressing.

At filing the divisional application and during prosecution, Shimano made the following amendments:

    (i) in claims 1, it replaces "circular bolt hole" with "circular hole";
    (ii) in claim 2, it replaces "molding" with "pressing";
    (iii) in the specification, it replaces "molding" with "pressing."

[Shimano admits that said revised terms "round hole" or "pressing" are not described in the original specification or claims.]

On December 11, 2009, Saiguan Company ("Saiguan") filed an invalidity request to the PRB against the Subject Patent on the ground that the above amendments exceed the original disclosure, and thus do not comply with Article 33 of the Patent Law.

On May 13, 2010, the PRB made the No. 15307 Decision, declaring the Subject Patent completely invalid.

[Shimano was not satisfied, and brought an administrative suit before Beijing No.1 Intermediate People's Court. The court affirmed the No. 15307 Decision. Shimano then appealed to Beijing High Court. The High Court affirmed. Shimano filed a retrial request to the Supreme Court.]

[The Supreme Court ruled the following:]

    ... The scope of the original specification and claims should cover: (1) all contents directly described in the original specification and claims, figures, either in text or graphics, and (2) contents that *can be determined* by a person of ordinary skill in the art based on the original specification, drawings and claims. When deciding whether an amendment exceeds the original disclosure, it should comprehensively consider: technical characteristics and common expression in the related technical field, knowledge level and cognitive ability of a person with ordinary skills in the art, the internal essential requirements of the claimed technical solution itself and other elements...

[Applying the above standard to the present case, the Supreme Court comments on the above amendments in question one by one:]

CASE *(continued)*

Regarding amendment (i), the court concluded that, in claim 1, the replacement of "circular bolt hole" by "circular hole" does not comply with Article 33 of the Patent Law . . . However, granted dependent claim 6 defines that "circular hole" is "circular bolt hole" . . . Therefore, granted claim 6 does not exceed the original disclosure and is in conformity with Article 33 of the Patent Law.

Regarding amendments (ii) and (iii), the court concluded that, in mechanical field, "molding" and "pressing" are two terms have different technical meanings. Shimano's above amendments (ii) and (iii) are not contents that can be determined from the original application documents. Thus the amendment to claim 2 exceeds the scope recorded in the original specification and claims, and is not in conformity with the provisions of Article 33 of the Patent Law.

[However, the Court further commented that amendments (ii) and (iii) are actually not material to the allowance of the Subject Patent, as both amendments make no contribution to the novelty or non-obviousness of the Subject Patent. Yet such amendments render the patent invalid, which might not be fair for the patentee. The Court raised the issue that Article 33 fails to distinguish between an "inventiveness-step contributing" amendment and a "non-inventiveness contributing" amendment, and suggests future legislation will address this issue.]

[In conclusion, the Supreme Court ruled that the amendment to claim 6 of the Subject Patent was in conformity with the provisions of Article 33 of the Patent Law, and remanded PRB's Decision in part.]

This is the final ruling.

Judge Yongchang WANG
Judge Jian LI
Judge Rong WU
Dec. 27, 2013

NOTES AND QUESTIONS

1. In *Epson 1* and *Epson 2*, in view of the original term "semiconductor storage device," the amended term "storage device" is acceptable, but amended term "memory device" is not. Why?
2. **"One-to-one mathematical/logic correspondence" standard v. Obvious test Standard**. In *Epson 1*, the Supreme Court rejected the rigid "one-to-one mathematical/logic correspondence" standard of PRB in applying Article 33 (*e.g.*, deciding "new matter"), but proposed an "obvious test standard." However, after *Epson 1*, SIPO publicly criticized the "obvious test standard." This might explain why the Supreme Court stepped back from the "obvious test standard" in *Epson 2*.
3. **Prosecution history is irrelevant**. Further, in *Epson 2*, the Supreme Court stated that prosecution history is irrelevant for deciding whether an amendment is "new matter."
4. In *Shimano*, the Supreme Court did not adopt either PRB's "One-to-one mathematical/logic correspondence" standard, or the "obvious test standard" in *Epson 1*. Instead, the Court emphasized that "original disclosure" shall cover "contents [that] can be determined by an ordinary person skilled in the art."
5. **Legislation advice by Supreme Court**. In *Shimano*, the Supreme Court suggests that, when applying

Article 33 in invalidation, it is more reasonable to first evaluate whether an amendment is material to the allowance during prosecution. If not, it might be unfair to invalidate a patent on the basis of a non-material amendment. However, the Supreme Court further says it is the Congress's responsibility to revise Article 33 in future legislation.

6. **Judge Li ZHU's Article**. Judge Li ZHU, who tried both *Epson 1* and *Epson 2*, published *Legal Standard and Remedies for Applying Article 33 in Patent Trial Cases*, 2 Chinese Patent and Trademark (2015). In this article, Judge Li ZHU concluded that, instead of focusing on whether an amendment has been literally described in the original disclosure in applying Article 33, it shall focus on whether an amendment substantially exceeds the original disclosure for those skilled in the art. This matches the legislation spirit of Article 33, which is to strike a balance between the patentee's amendment right and the public's reliance interest on the original disclosure.

6.2 Written description requirement

In re Curtis, 354 F.3d 1347 (Fed. Cir. 2004)

Clevenger, J.

John P. Curtis [et al.] seek review of the decision of the United States Patent and Trademark Office ("PTO") Board of Patent Appeals and Interferences ("Board") affirming the final rejections [of most claims of] U.S. Patent No. 5,209,251 (the "'251 Patent"), entitled "Dental Floss." The Board determined that Curtis could not [claim] the benefit of an earlier patent application because the disclosure therein failed to adequately describe the subject matter encompassed by the rejected claims under 35 U.S.C. §112, ¶ 1. Because the Board's decision is supported by substantial evidence and otherwise is in accordance with law, we affirm.

Dental floss should not require a user to apply substantial force in order to get the floss to pass through the spaces between teeth. Otherwise, it may cause the user's gums to bleed during flossing. Dental floss must also be easily grasped by a user so that it can be readily manipulated for flossing. Therefore, the commercial acceptability of a dental floss depends on the coefficient of friction ("COF") of the material from which it is made. A dental floss made from a material with a COF that is too high will stick to teeth and will have to be used with substantial force. Material with too low a COF will yield a dental floss that slips easily through a user's hands and will be difficult to manipulate. Thus, the ideal dental floss is made from a material that has a COF in a particular "sweet spot" such that it is neither too sticky nor too slippery.

On March 29, 1988, Curtis filed U.S. Patent Application No. 07/174,757 (the '757 Application) claiming an improved dental floss made of expanded polytetrafluoroethylene ("PTFE") filaments coated with microcrystalline wax ("MCW") having a COF between 0.08 and 0.25. The inventors stated:

> [I]t has been unexpectedly discovered that floss made of porous, high strength Expanded PTFE is extremely effective to provide hygienic tooth and gum care. Moreover, excellent effect is also provided when the floss is coated with microcrystalline wax (MCW). The MCW, surprisingly,

CASE *(continued)*

adheres to the porous, high strength PTFE which without a coating has a very low COF... and when coated with MCW generally has a COF intermediate between prior art floss white and uncoated PTFE...

[After an initial continuation in part (a patent application adding some material to the specification of a previously filed application) was filed,] Curtis filed a second continuation-in-part application which was assigned application number 07/729,834 (the '834 Application) and which ultimately issued as the '251 Patent. The written description of the '834 Application contains statements which are not found in the [original] '962 Application. For example, the '834 Application states:

> It has been found that the polytetrafluoroethylene floss can be coated or otherwise treated with a friction coating, such as a wax, to increase the coefficient of friction to a level where the floss is easier to handle and does not slip through the fingers of the user as easily as the untreated floss. It has further been found that the thinner polytetrafluoroethylene [sic] flosses of 600 to 800 denier that are coated with a friction enhancing coating are easy to handle and comfortable to use.

It also discloses that this genus of "friction enhancing coatings" is comprised of materials that adhere well to PTFE and that increase the COF of a PTFE dental floss to about 0.08 or greater. The disclosure in the '834 Application also states that "water soluble coating[s] such as polyvinyl alcohol or polyethyleneoxide" are suitable alternative friction enhancing coatings. [The PTO combined a reexamination request and a reissue filing by the patentee into a single new patent application; the reexamination requestor had cited a European application, European Patent 90/003,885 (the EP 355,466, the EP '466 patent), as prior art against Curtis' filing.]

Curtis attempted to remove EP '466 as prior art by claiming the benefit of the December 2, 1988 filing date of the '962 Application pursuant to 35 U.S.C. §120. [Because Curtis' original US application came before the issue date of EP '466, the EP '466 patent would not be prior art against Curtis – *if* Curtis could legitimately claim his original filing date, *i.e.*, the filing date of his original '962 Application.] The examiner determined that Curtis was not entitled to the earlier filing date because the disclosure in the '962 Application did not enable a person of ordinary skill in the art to practice the claims of the '251 Patent without undue experimentation and issued a final rejection accordingly.

Curtis appealed this decision to the Board. The Board reversed the examiner's enablement rejection and stated:

> [W]e agree with the appellants that when all the factors are considered the disclosure of the parent application is such that undue experimentation is not required to practice the claimed invention. Accordingly, we find that the examiner has not established a prima facie case of lack of enablement under 35 U.S.C. §112, first paragraph.

CASE (continued)

However, the Board ruled that Curtis was not entitled to the benefit of the '962 Application filing date in any event because that application did not provide an adequate written description of the later-claimed genus of friction enhancing coatings. The Board determined that MCW was the only friction enhancing coating disclosed expressly or inherently in the '962 Application and, therefore, "it did not provide written description support for the later-claimed, generic subject matter of the claims under appeal."

Claims found in a later-filed application are entitled to the filing date of an earlier application if, inter alia, the disclosure in the earlier application provides an adequate written description of the later-filed claims under 35 U.S.C. §112, ¶ 1. This requires the disclosure in the earlier application to reasonably convey to one of ordinary skill in the art that the inventors possessed the later-claimed subject matter when they filed the earlier application. [*See*] *Gentry Gallery, Inc. v. Berkline Corp.*, 134 F.3d 1473, 1479 (Fed. Cir. 1998) ("To fulfill the written description requirement, the patent specification 'must clearly allow persons of ordinary skill in the art to recognize that [the inventor] invented what is claimed.'").

The Board's conclusion that a particular disclosure does or does not comply with the written description requirement is a determination of fact. We review the Board's findings of fact for substantial evidence in the administrative record.

The single example Curtis provided in the '962 Application is further evidence that the appellants conveyed only MCW as a suitable friction enhancing coating for a PTFE dental floss. The example "set[s] forth [the] test results of the COF of the flosses of the present invention compared to leading brands of commercial dental floss now on the U.S. market and to Expanded PTFE floss having no MCW coating." The record before us also indicates that, at the time the '962 Application was filed, the inventors did not convey any other material that could adhere to PTFE in such a way so as to yield a commercially acceptable dental floss.

[A] patentee will not be deemed to have invented species sufficient to constitute the genus by virtue of having disclosed a single species when, as is the case here, the evidence indicates ordinary artisans could not predict the operability in the invention of any species other than the one disclosed.

For the reasons stated above, the decision of the Board denying Curtis the benefit of the filing date of the '962 Application and affirming the final rejections of the examiner was supported by substantial evidence in the record. Therefore the decision of the Board is affirmed.

NOTES

1. This opinion is helpful in pointing out the difference between enablement and written description. The Board found that Curtis had taught enough to enable a person of skill in the art to make a dental floss with a variety of anti-friction coatings. The single example of such a dental floss coating in the specification, microcrystalline wax (MCW), was enough to teach people in this field how to make and use flosses

with various other coatings. And yet: The Board held that the applicant Curtis had consistently indicated that MCW was the *only* floss coating that Curtis had really considered. Curtis' statements, in other words, indicated that Curtis himself had not considered any other coatings. The specification, as the court puts it, did not "reasonably convey to one of ordinary skill in the art that the inventor[ ] possessed the later-claimed subject matter." This idea of possession comes up frequently in written description cases. In these cases, it is crucial to understand the difference between "teaching" (which is the essence of enablement) and "possession" (which is the essence of written description).

2. What if Curtis had included a description of multiple low-friction coatings in his original patent application; would the original application still be susceptible to the charge that it failed the written description requirement? The Federal Circuit has ruled yes: Even originally filed applications which are not changed by amendment or a continuation in part are susceptible to written description defenses. *See, e.g., Regents of the Univ. of Cal. v. Eli Lilly & Co.*, 119 F.3d 1559, 1567–68 (Fed. Cir. 1997). *See generally* Janice M. Mueller, *The Evolving Application of the Written Description Requirement to Biotechnological Inventions*, 13 Berkeley Tech. L.J. 615 (1998). Some experienced scholars have criticized this move, but it is now the established law in the Federal Circuit. *See* Timothy R. Holbrook, *Possession in Patent Law*, 59 SMU L. Rev. 123, 161 (2006).

3. The case of *Gentry Gallery, Inc. v. Berkline Corp.*, 134 F.3d 1473 (Fed. Cir. 1998), cited in *In re Curtis*, demonstrates another application of the written description requirement. In that case the original claims covered a sofa with two reclining seats on it. The button to control the reclining seats was located on a box between two sections of the sofa (the "console" it was called). When a competitor introduced a double reclining seat sofa, the competitor placed the control button on the armrest – not on the console. The applicant then amended its claims to cover this new variation. Two things were clear: The original application enabled furniture designers skilled in the art to locate the control button anywhere; there was no structural or mechanical reason it had to be on the console. Thus the amended claim was enabled under §112. Second, there is no rule per se prohibiting claims from being amended to cover the products of a competitor. Cases had noted in the past that this was not itself contrary to any provision of patent law. Even so, the court invalidated the amended claim under the written description requirement. But why? One author explained:

> In some cases, a patentee has filed a specification that hones in on a particular set of embodiments, which are claimed in an initial application. Then one or more claims is amended to cover either a competitor's product or an item suggested by the prior art. In each of these, the original application, by failing to claim initially the technology later claimed in an amendment, signals that these embodiments are not particularly important or even relevant to the inventor. It is the actions of a third party that give them salience. When a third party introduces the disclosed but unclaimed variant, it suddenly acquires salience for the applicant. This seems unfair to the courts involved. By virtue of a claim amendment, a patentee attempts to encompass embodiments he or she did not envision as belonging to the real heart of the invention.
>
> This type of unfairness might be described as "misappropriation by amendment." The patentee attempts to appropriate the effort of a competitor or the contributions of a prior art reference, such as an earlier technical article or patent. The unfairness is straightforward: these embodiments are more properly attributed to the labor of others. They are not rightfully within the ambit of an inventor's patent right (Robert P. Merges, *Software and Patent Scope: A Report from the Middle Innings*, 85 Tex. L. Rev. 1627, 1653–54 (2007).)

4. Another line of written description cases involves biotechnology inventions. In these cases, the Federal Circuit has held that claims to biological mechanisms, which lack examples of compounds that trigger or work under those mechanisms, fail the written description requirement. *See Ariad Pharm., Inc. v. Eli Lilly & Co.*, 598 F.3d 1336 (Fed. Cir. 2010) (discoverers of mechanism by which harmful cellular process is initiated understood that molecules could be identified that would act to stop this harmful process; but lack of disclosure of any of these molecules meant that the patent failed the written description requirement); *Univ. of Rochester v. G.D. Searle & Co.*, 358 F.3d 916 (Fed. Cir. 2004) (developers of screening test, to identify molecules which inhibited production of one [harmful] bodily product, without inhibiting production of second [beneficial] bodily product, obtained patent; was ruled invalid under written description requirement because it did not identify any actual compounds that satisfied the test, but only described the test itself).

It might be pointed out that under the traditional "undue experiment" standard of *Incandescent Lamp* and other enablement cases, these cases reach the same outcome. In this sense it might be argued that the written description requirement, at least in some cases, merely duplicates the enablement requirement.

6.2.1 Written description in China

 CASE

Ellison Technologies v. Patent Re-examination Board (SIPO), Court: Beijing Municipal Higher People's Court No.: (2013) Gao Xing Zhong Zi 1548 ((2013) 高行终字第1548号) available at https://www.itslaw.com/detail?judgementId=4d35d1aa-0bbc-4a12-98c0-efc2ba058a36&area=1&index=1&sortType=1&count=27&conditions (transl. on 6/2/2017)

Facts:
Ellison Technologies Inc. ("Ellison"), the Plaintiff, is a Delaware company of the United States. Defendants are Huawei Technologies Co. Ltd. ("Huawei") and Patent Re-examination Board of the State Intellectual Property Office of the People's Republic of China (SIPO).

The patent at issue is Ellison's CN1264024 C patent, which was filed in 1999 and issued in 2006. Ellison made an amendment to the patent application, broadening the claimed patented scope. In 2013, Huawei sued Ellison on two bases, (1) that the amendment made by Ericsson during prosecution is much broader than the claims as originally filed; and (2) the claim is invalid for lack of novelty.

Issues:
Whether an applicant can amend his patent application documents to broaden the scope specified in the original written descriptions and claims.

Holding and Reasoning:
No. According to Article 33 of Chinese Patent Law, an applicant can amend his patent application documents but the amendment should not exceed the scope specified in the original written descriptions and claims.

Article 33 of Chinese Patent Law:
An applicant may amend his patent application documents, provided that the amendment

CASE *(continued)*

to the invention or utility model patent application documents does not exceed the scope specified in the original written descriptions and claims, or that the amendment to the design patent application documents does not exceed the scope shown in the original drawings or pictures.

The claims involved acquisition of a global positioning satellite (GPS) transmission signal by a cell phone or computer (called a "mobile station" (MS)). Ericsson amended the application documents to broaden the initial claim scope. In the original written description and claims, a "base transmission station" (BTS) such as a cell phone tower communicates an approximate geographic location to the mobile phone or computer (the MS); then the MS uses this location to home in on a more precise GPS location, calculated from special GPS satellites. Later on, Ericcson amended its claims to cover a wider range of initial location estimation procedures, such as a pre-programmed estimate of GPS satellite locations based on historical data or estimated satellite elevation angles.

The Court held that the amendment of application documents is limited by the scope of the original description in the specification, including all stated purposes and limitations. Broadened claims are thus invalid.

6.3 Adequacy of disclosure in Europe: Article 83 EPC

The skilled person must be able to carry out the invention without undue burden and without the exercise of inventive skill, on the basis of what is disclosed in the application and by using the general knowledge (see T 694/92, OJ EPO 1997, 408; and T 612/92 of 28 February 1996, Reasons points 11 to 13).

Article 83
Disclosure of the invention

The European patent application shall disclose the invention in a manner sufficiently clear and complete for it to be carried out by a person skilled in the art.

Article 84
Claims

The claims shall define the matter for which protection is sought. They shall be clear and concise and be supported by the description.

CASE

Hakoune/Inadequate description, Case No. T 0219/85 (Eur. Pat. Off. Bd. App., 14 July 1986), available at http://www.epo.org/law-practice/case-law-appeals/recent/t850219ep1.html#q

[The applicant, Hakoune, appealed a rejection of claims related to the invention at issue, a technique for etching identifying information onto a gem stone, such as a diamond. The technique involved coating the surface of the diamond with a photoresist resin, a chemical coating that reacts with light. A miniaturized serial number, or other unique identifying symbol, is written on a thin film, which is placed over the diamond and exposed to light. The photoresist resin on the diamond reacts to the light chemically, except where it blocked by the identifying image in the film. A solution is then passed over the diamond, which washes away the photo-activated resin. Only the symbol that was on the film remains on the diamond. Then the diamond is subject to bombardment by cathode rays, which react with the image on the diamond and cause it to burn or etch into the diamond's surface.]

The claim read as follows: "A process for treating a gem stone to provide it with an inscription on one side or facet . . . in order to render the stone identifiable, characterised in that the stone is coated with a photoresist resin to which a photographic film bearing the desired inscription is applied, the resin is developed by exposing it to a light source, the exposed portions of the resin are removed by conventional means and the portion of the stone thus treated is subjected to cathode bombardment in such a manner that the stone becomes etched wherever it is not protected by the resin."

While examination was in progress, the applicant, in a letter received on 28 September 1984, proposed a new wording for Claim 1, hereinafter referred to as "alternative Claim 1", which [among other changes substituted for the phrase "in such a manner that the stone becomes etched," the replacement phrase "characterised in that the portion of the stone thus treated is subjected to cathode bombardment under conditions such that the stone becomes etched to a depth of 50 to 500 angströms wherever it is not protected by the resin."]

[The Examining Division rejected the claim on the basis that, as disclosed, it was impossible to tell how to perform the desired etching, and therefore due to the lack of disclosure it could not be ascertained whether the invention really represented an inventive step over the prior art. The closest prior art was a Belgian patent, BE 868 383, which taught transfer of an identifying mark using a similar technique, and cathode ray bombardment; but the bombardment was solely for the purpose of cleaning the gemstone after the photo-transfer process involving the identifying mark.]

The same treatment applied to the same surface results, according to the state of the art in the diamond being cleaned and, according to the European application (in so far as it is explained) in the diamond being etched. The essential difference between the two

CASE *(continued)*

processes, which gives rise to the different results, is enshrined in the vague term "under conditions such", which can be accepted only if it can be shown that it is sufficiently clear to enable a person skilled in the art to carry out the invention disclosed in the application (Article 83 EPC). Either, therefore, the purport of these words must emerge clearly from a reading of the original text of the patent application or the conditions that give rise to this different result must be so apparent to the skilled person as to require no further explanation.

According to the original text of the European patent application, the etching is effected at stage 5 of the process by cathode bombardment with an ionised gas. The only amplification given is that cathode bombardment results in etching of the parts not protected by the resin. No further information is therefore given which would enable a skilled person to use the known process to attain this different result. This fact is confirmed by an explanatory memo from the applicant's technical staff annexed to the applicant's letter received on 28 September 1984 which states that "details of the actual production process have been kept secret to prevent them being copied straight from the patent".

There remains the question of what general information was available to the skilled person on the priority date of the European patent application. In a letter received [by the EPO] on 11 March 1986, the appellant argues that in view of the literature existing on the subject the mere use of the terms "etching" and "cathode bombardment" in the application would enable a person skilled in the art to carry out the engraving on the diamond. The Board is unable to accept this contention: – firstly, because precisely the same terms are used in the documents concerning treatment that results merely in the diamond being cleaned, and – secondly because the documentation relating to the treatment of materials other than diamond simply shows the complexity of the problem according to the material to be attacked and nowhere considers the treatment of diamond. Vague references such as "in such a manner that" or "under conditions such that" would therefore not on their own enable a skilled person to establish the conditions required to achieve the desired result.

The Board concludes that Claim 1, both in its original and alternative forms, was not clear within the meaning of Article 84 EPC and furthermore that the invention was not disclosed in the original application in a manner sufficiently clear and complete for it to be carried out by a person skilled in the art, as required by Article 83 EPC. There is therefore no way in which the lack of clarity of the claims could be remedied without extending the subject-matter of the application beyond its content as filed, which would contravene Article 123(2) EPC. Neither version of the claim, therefore, is allowable.

NOTES

1. The general standard applied in the *Hakoune* case has been restated on a number of occasions, including in *Hepatitis A virus*, Case No. G 2/93 (Euro. Pat. Off. En. Bd. App., 21 December 1994), available at http://www.epo.org/law-practice/case-law-appeals/recent/g930002ep1.html#q, at Reasons par. 4:

Pursuant to Article 83 EPC, a European patent application "must disclose the invention in a manner sufficiently clear and complete for it to be carried out by a person skilled in the art". In order to meet the requirements of Article 83 EPC, a European patent application must therefore contain sufficient information to allow a person skilled in the art, using his common general knowledge, to perceive the technical teaching inherent in the claimed invention and to put it into effect accordingly.

This test is routinely applied by examiners, and the Board of Appeal takes care to review Article 83 rejections according to the detailed facts of each case. So in *Active inductor/Alcatel Lucent*, Case No. T 2297/12 (Euro. Pat. Off. Bd. App. 2 June 2017), for example, the applicant had disclosed and claimed an "active inductor" circuit. This is a circuit that emulates the performance of a traditional inductor (sometimes called a "coil": usually a magnetic core component with wires wrapped around it, which emits a magnetic field signal when current is passed through the wires). The claim recited as an element a "metal oxide semiconductor (MOS) transistor." The EPO examiner rejected the claim on the grounds that the disclosure did not adequately teach one skilled in the art to construct all the claimed embodiments of such a circuit. The prior art showed that inductor circuits had traditionally required two transistors, and the single-transistor invention as claimed deviated from this principle, but was not (the examiner said) supported by adequate disclosure in the specification. The Board of Appeals reversed the rejection. It relied on the following argument presented by the applicant, at p. 5:

> A skilled person having studied the present application and availing himself of general technical knowledge was not unduly burdened to put into practice the present invention defined by claim 1 according to the main request [on appeal]. Based on the teaching of the present application, the skilled person would have . . . easily fabricated and used "active inductors" as described in the claims and shown in the figures. It was possible to reproduce the claimed circuit using the original application documents without any inventive effort over and above the ordinary skills of a practitioner . . . Thus, the application as a whole provided sufficient disclosure enabling the skilled person to carry out the present invention defined by claim 1 according to the main request, as required by Article 83 EPC.

On this basis, the Board held:

> A person skilled in the art is not unduly burdened to connect a MOS transistor with a resistor and a supply voltage in order to arrive at a circuit for use as an active inductor according to claim 1. Consequently the objection according to Article 83 EPC has no basis (Reasons, par. 3.3, p. 8).

2. A common issue involving Article 83 arises when a patent applicant amends his or her claims during prosecution at the EPO, as in the *Hakoune* case. Claim amendments are permissible, so long as the newly amended claim is supported by the disclosure in the original application on the date of filing, *i.e.*, the priority date. This is set out in EPC Article 123(2), which says:

Article 123
Amendments

(1) The European patent application or European patent may be amended in proceedings before the European Patent Office, in accordance with the Implementing Regulations. In any event, the applicant shall be given at least one opportunity to amend the application of his own volition.
(2) The European patent application or European patent may not be amended in such a way that it contains subject-matter which extends beyond the content of the application as filed.

An important issue in some EPO decisions has been whether the applicants disclosed "at least one way" of carrying out the claimed invention. The authoritative Case Law of the Boards of Appeal of the European Patent Office (8th ed. 2016), at Chapter II.C.4.2., pp. 333–34:

> An invention is in principle sufficiently disclosed if at least one way is clearly indicated enabling the person skilled in the art to carry out the invention. If this is the case, the non-availability of some particular variants of a functionally defined component feature of the invention is immaterial to sufficiency as long as there are suitable variants known to the skilled person through the disclosure or common general knowledge which provide the same effect for the invention. This has been confirmed by many decisions . . .

An important related point concerns the range or scope of disclosure, as compared to the scope of the claims:

> The disclosure of one way of performing an invention is only sufficient if it allows the invention to be performed in the whole range claimed rather than only in some members of the claimed class to be obtained. This is considered a question of fact. Sufficiency of disclosure thus presupposes that the skilled person is able to obtain substantially all embodiments falling within the ambit of the claims. This view has been taken by the board in numerous decisions . . . This principle applies to any invention irrespective of the way in which it is defined, be it by way of a functional feature or not. The peculiarity of the functional definition of a technical feature resides in the fact that it is defined by means of its effect. That mode of definition comprises an indefinite and abstract host of possible alternatives, which is acceptable as long as all alternatives are available and achieve the desired result. With respect to a claimed process defined in a functional manner, i.e. by its outcome, the board [has] concluded that what was lacking was a generalisable teaching applicable within the scope of the claims, i.e. beyond the specific examples.

More technical details and more than one example may be necessary in order to support claims of a broad scope. This must be decided on a case-by-case basis. The board must also be satisfied first that the patent specification put the skilled person in possession of at least one way of putting the claimed invention into practice, and secondly that the skilled person could put the invention into practice over the whole scope of the claim. If the board was not satisfied on the first point that one way existed, the second point did not need to be considered

The authoritative Case Law of the Boards of Appeal of the European Patent Office (8th ed. 2016), at Chapter II.C.4.4, p. 335 (citations omitted).

Enabling the full range of embodiments covered by a claim is particularly important when it comes to chemical patents, where large classes or "families" of chemical compounds are frequently claimed. *See* Paul England, *Novelty and Sufficiency in A Single, Pan-European Standard*, 32 Euro. I.P. Rev. 467 (2010):

> [The scope of disclosure] point is of particular importance in circumstances where a class is claimed that is so large it would be impossible to disclose in the confines of a patent specification specific means by which every member in the class can be obtained. The classic example of this is a patent which claims a so-called "Markush formula" covering millions of compounds. In this respect, it is suggested here that the different compounds across the class, the embodiments, can be pictured as variations on a theme, the theme being the underlying principle of general application, the invention.

7

Claim interpretation and infringement

A patent claim uses words to carve out a technological space for ownership by the patentee. The size and shape of that space is determined by the precise words in the claim. And the boundaries of the space dictate which products fall within the claim, and which fall outside. So, for example, an early claim to oversized toy squirt guns, for launching a stream of water great distances, described (1) a central body of the squirt gun, and (2) a water "chamber" (or tank) placed "therein." The owner of this patent was not alone in the market; it had a competitor. This competitor designed a new-generation squirt gun with a large, detachable, water tank. This tank sat on top of the central body of the squirt gun. The patentee sued the competitor for patent infringement. The court found no infringement, holding in essence that a tank "thereon" (on top of) the body did *not* fall within the boundaries of the patentee's claim. "Thereon" was different from "therein" – and millions of dollars of squirt guns could be sold without being subject to legal liability to the patentee. *See Larami Corp. v. Amron*, No. CIV. A. 91-6145, 1993 WL 69581, at *4 (E.D. Pa. Mar. 11, 1993) (because the accused product, the competitor water gun, has an external tank on top of the central body, "there is no 'chamber' for liquid contained within the housing of the water gun).

As the *Larami* case shows, a good deal of money can be at stake in a legal determination over the precise meaning of a single word ("therein"). As a result, the fights over the precise meaning of a claim term or terms are among the most hard fought in the law of patents. Two absolutely central features of these fights are (1) who gets to decide on the meaning of patent claim terms, judge or jury?; and (2) what precise steps, procedures and legal sources are to be followed when finding the meaning of a claim term?

The first question was answered by the Supreme Court in *Markman v. Westview Instruments, Inc.*, 517 370 (1996): claim interpretation is a matter of law. Ever since, a crucial early battleground in almost all patent cases has been the *Markman* hearing, where the contesting parties argue over the precise meaning of specific claim terms.

The second issue is dealt with in the influential case that follows.

 CASE

Phillips v. AWH Corp., 415 F.3d 1303 (Fed. Cir. 2005) (en banc)

Bryson, J.
Edward H. Phillips invented modular, steel-shell panels that can be welded together to form vandalism-resistant walls. The panels are especially useful in building prisons because they are load-bearing and impact-resistant, while also insulating against fire and noise. Mr. Phillips obtained a patent on the invention, U.S. Patent No. 4,677,798 ("the '798 patent"), and he subsequently entered into an arrangement with AWH Corporation ("AWH") to market and sell the panels. That arrangement ended in 1990. In 1991, however, Mr. Phillips received a sales brochure from AWH that suggested to him that AWH was continuing to use his patented technology without his consent. [Two diagrams showing the design of the '798 patent are reproduced below. The first shows how the modular steel panels are fitted together to form structures, *e.g.*, a building. The second is a highly enlarged view of the inside of the steel walls, looking from above.]

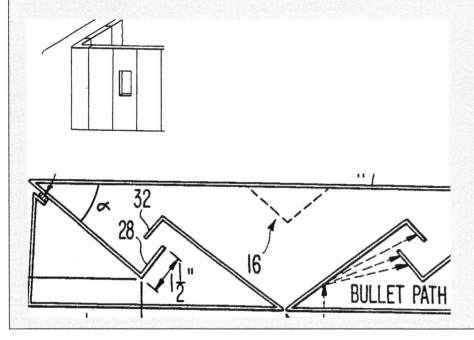

CASE *(continued)*

[Phillips sued for infringement; the district court found that defendant AWH did not infringe, because the steel panels the defendant was selling did not fall within the language of the patentee's claims. Specifically, the defendant AWH sold steel walls with internal metal supports (or "baffles", as the claim calls them) that went straight across the inside of the walls, *i.e.*, they were at 90 degree angles to the outside steel walls, while the patentee's claims were found to require interior metal supports (marked 28 and 32 in the diagram above) that were at angles greater than or less than 90 degrees. A first Federal Circuit decision affirming this district court opinion was vacated, and the full Federal Circuit took the case en banc (*i.e.*, the entire court) to consider important questions of claim construction.]

Claim 1 of the '798 patent is representative of the asserted claims with respect to the use of the term "baffles." It recites:

> Building modules adapted to fit together for construction of fire, sound and impact resistant security barriers and rooms for use in securing records and persons, comprising in combination, an outer shell . . ., sealant means . . . and further means disposed inside the shell for increasing its load bearing capacity comprising *internal steel **baffles** extending inwardly from the steel shell walls*.

We have frequently stated that the words of a claim "are generally given their ordinary and customary meaning." We have made clear, moreover, that the ordinary and customary meaning of a claim term is the meaning that the term would have to a person of ordinary skill in the art in question at the time of the invention, *i.e.*, as of the effective filing date of the patent application.

Importantly, the person of ordinary skill in the art is deemed to read the claim term not only in the context of the particular claim in which the disputed term appears, but in the context of the entire patent, including the specification.

In many cases that give rise to litigation, determining the ordinary and customary meaning of the claim requires examination of terms that have a particular meaning in a field of art. Because the meaning of a claim term as understood by persons of skill in the art is often not immediately apparent, and because patentees frequently use terms idiosyncratically, the court looks to "those sources available to the public that show what a person of skill in the art would have understood disputed claim language to mean." Those sources include "the words of the claims themselves, the remainder of the specification, the prosecution history, and extrinsic evidence concerning relevant scientific principles, the meaning of technical terms, and the state of the art."

This court and its predecessors have long emphasized the importance of the specification in claim construction. In *Autogiro Co. of America v. United States*, 181 Ct.Cl. 55, 384 F.2d 391, 397–98 (1967), the Court of Claims characterized the specification as "a concordance for the claims," based on the statutory requirement that the specification "describe the manner and process of making and using" the patented invention.

Consistent with that general principle, our cases recognize that the specification may reveal a special definition given to a claim term by the patentee that differs from the meaning

CASE *(continued)*

it would otherwise possess. In such cases, the inventor's lexicography governs. In other cases, the specification may reveal an intentional disclaimer, or disavowal, of claim scope by the inventor. In that instance as well, the inventor has dictated the correct claim scope, and the inventor's intention, as expressed in the specification, is regarded as dispositive.

In addition to consulting the specification, we have held that a court "should also consider the patent's prosecution history, if it is in evidence." The prosecution history, which we have designated as part of the "intrinsic evidence," consists of the complete record of the proceedings before the PTO and includes the prior art cited during the examination of the patent. *Autogiro*, 384 F.2d at 399. Like the specification, the prosecution history provides evidence of how the PTO and the inventor understood the patent.

Although we have emphasized the importance of intrinsic evidence in claim construction, we have also authorized district courts to rely on extrinsic evidence, which "consists of all evidence external to the patent and prosecution history, including expert and inventor testimony, dictionaries, and learned treatises." However, while extrinsic evidence "can shed useful light on the relevant art," we have explained that it is "less significant than the intrinsic record in determining 'the legally operative meaning of claim language.'"

In sum, extrinsic evidence may be useful to the court, but it is unlikely to result in a reliable interpretation of patent claim scope unless considered in the context of the intrinsic evidence. Nonetheless, because extrinsic evidence can help educate the court regarding the field of the invention and can help the court determine what a person of ordinary skill in the art would understand claim terms to mean, it is permissible for the district court in its sound discretion to admit and use such evidence.

[Returning to the Phillips patent at issue in this case:] The critical language of [the word "baffles" in] claim 1 of the '798 patent imposes three clear requirements with respect to the baffles. First, the baffles must be made of steel. Second, they must be part of the load-bearing means for the wall section. Third, they must be pointed inward from the walls. Both parties, stipulating to a dictionary definition, also conceded that the term "baffles" refers to objects that check, impede, or obstruct the flow of something. The intrinsic evidence confirms that a person of skill in the art would understand that the term "baffles," as used in the '798 patent, would have that generic meaning.

The other claims of the '798 patent specify particular functions to be served by the baffles. For example, dependent claim 2 states that the baffles may be "oriented with the panel sections disposed at angles for deflecting projectiles such as bullets able to penetrate the steel plates." The inclusion of such a specific limitation on the term "baffles" in claim 2 makes it likely that the patentee did not contemplate that the term "baffles" already contained that limitation. *See Dow Chem. Co. v. United States*, 226 F.3d 1334, 1341–42 (Fed. Cir. 2000) (concluding that an independent claim should be given broader scope than a dependent claim to avoid rendering the dependent claim redundant). Independent claim 17 further supports that proposition. It states that baffles are placed "projecting

CASE (continued)

inwardly from the outer shell at angles tending to deflect projectiles that penetrate the outer shell."

That limitation would be unnecessary if persons of skill in the art understood that the baffles inherently served such a function.

[Another function of the baffles, discussed in the patent specification, is to make the walls stronger, *i.e.*, to increase the load-bearing capacity of the walls.]

The fact that the written description of the '798 patent sets forth multiple objectives to be served by the baffles recited in the claims confirms that the term "baffles" should not be read restrictively to require that the baffles in each case serve all of the recited functions. We have held that "[t]he fact that a patent asserts that an invention achieves several objectives does not require that each of the claims be construed as limited to structures that are capable of achieving all of the objectives." Although deflecting projectiles is one of the advantages of the baffles of the '798 patent, the patent does not require that the inward extending structures always be capable of performing that function. Accordingly, we conclude that a person of skill in the art would not interpret the disclosure and claims of the '798 patent to mean that a structure extending inward from one of the wall faces is a "baffle" if it is at an acute or obtuse angle, but is not a "baffle" if it is disposed at a right angle.

Because we disagree with the district court's claim construction, we reverse the summary judgment of noninfringement. In light of our decision on claim construction, it is necessary to remand the infringement claims to the district court for further proceedings.

NOTES

1. The basic message of the *Phillips* case is that the specification tops all other sources for interpreting a patent claim – especially dictionaries. After *Phillips*, a key guide to interpreting a word or phrase in a claim is the way the word or phrase appears *in context* in the patent specification. One example of many comes from the case of *Nystrom v. TREX*, 424 F.3d 1136 (Fed. Cir. 2005). The inventor claimed a "board" that was curved so as to shed water; the boards were combined to form a deck. Each mention of a "board" in the specification explicitly mentioned boards made of wood, but the patentee argued that the patent covered the defendant's "composite" board made from a mix of wood and plastic. The court disagreed; consistent contextual evidence showed that in this patent, a "board" was limited to wood. This was despite the fact that a few dictionaries defined "board" broadly to include long structural items made of material other than wood.

2. One subsidiary point from *Phillips* is also important: an inventor may provide an explicit definition of a claim term; if so, this meaning will prevail over "plain meaning," dictionary definitions, and pretty much anything else. *See, e.g., GE Lighting Solutions LLC v. AgiLight, Inc.*, 750 F.3d 1304, 1309 (Fed. Cir. 2014). An example of this "lexicographer rule" comes from *Infinity Headwear & Apparel, LLC v. Jay Franco & Sons, Inc.*, No. 15-CV-1259 (JPO), 2016 WL 5372843, at *1 (S.D.N.Y. Sept 26, 2016). This *Infinity Headwear* case had as its core U.S. Patent No. 8,864,544 ("the '544 patent"), which covers a cape-like children's costume toy that can be stored in the hood of the costume, as the following diagram shows:

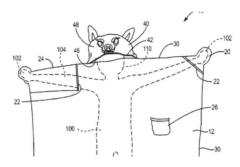

The relevant claim in the '544 patent says:

> A hooded blanket and stuffed toy combination device that includes a blanket having a perimeter defining an area, a hood attached to the perimeter and positioned externally to the area, and an ornamental surface comprising an outer surface of the hood, wherein the hood comprises an outer shell and an interior volume whereby the blanket is stored within the interior volume of the hood to provide a stuffed toy.

The cape-like part of the costume is claimed as a "blanket" in several claims of the patent. The accused infringer Jay Franco & Sons argued, in contrast, that the plain (dictionary) meaning of the term "blanket" (i.e., a warmth-adding layer of bedding) should be applied. The patentee Infinity proposed a claim construction based on the specification's explicit definition of the term blanket. The relevant part of the specification reads:

> As used herein, the term "blanket" may include a blanket, a comforter, a sheet, a jacket, a windbreaker, a parka, a poncho, a towel, a beach towel, a bath towel, a coat, a wrap, a scarf, a shawl, a cloak, a shirt, a sweatshirt, a hooded shirt and/or a hooded sweatshirt. In general, one having skill in the art will appreciate that the teachings of the present invention may be applied to any piece of clothing or other material compatible with the underlying methodologies and principles disclosed herein.

'544 patent col. 2 l. 62–col. 3 l. 3. The court applied the "lexicographer rule" mentioned in *Phillips* in resolving whether Infinity's preferred meaning would be applied:

> The Court concludes that this is an explicit definition of the term "blanket" contained in the specification that meets the "exacting" standard for finding lexicography. GE Lighting Solutions, [supra], at 1309. The phrase "[a]s used herein," as well as setting off the term-at-issue in quotation marks, clearly indicates an intent by the drafter to provide a particular definition of the term "blanket" that is contrary to its plain and ordinary meaning (*Infinity Headwear & Apparel, LLC v. Jay Franco & Sons, Inc.*, No. 15-CV-1259 (JPO), 2016 WL 5372843, at *9 (S.D.N.Y. Sept. 26, 2016)).

Based on this holding, Infinity won the case on this point.

Many times, a "contextual" finding regarding a claim term's meaning shades into a sort of "implied lexicographer" notion. *See, e.g., Kaneka Corp. v. Xiamen Kingdomway Group. Co.*, 790 F.3d 1298, 1305 (Fed. Cir. 2015) ("Although the specification does not specifically define the term "sealed," the appropriate definition can be ascertained from the specification"; rejecting use of dictionary definition, and instead using inferred definition based on examples and diagrams from the specification).

3. In addition to the "lexicographer rule," *Phillips* makes a second important subsidiary point. When an inventor explicitly *rules out* certain meanings of a claim term, judges interpreting claims should hold those inventors to those statements. This is known as "disavowal," which means "to disclaim, disown or repudiate." This represents a sort of "negative lexicographer rule": a definition that excludes certain meanings. Courts have taken these negative statements seriously. *See, e.g., Pacing Techs., LLC v. Garmin Int'l, Inc.*, 778 F.3d 1021, 1024 (Fed. Cir. 2015) ("We have found disavowal or disclaimer based on clear and unmistakable statement, such as 'the present invention includes . . .,' 'the present invention is . . .,' and 'all embodiments of the present invention are . . .'"). *See also David Netzer Consulting Eng'r LLC v. Shell Oil Co.*, 824 F.3d 989, 994 (Fed. Cir. 2016) (in patent specification, inventor consistently distinguished "present invention" from

a conventional method, which the inventor said was no longer required due to a shift in market demand; held, these statements amount to a disavowal of the conventional method as being within the scope of the patentee's claims).

7.1 Claims in China

 CASE

Andrew, Inc. v. Patent Reexamination Board and Wu Huiyin, Beijing No. 1 Intermediate People's Court, Xing Chu Zi [2008] No. 631, Aug. 20, 2008, aff'd on appeal, Beijing High People's Court, Xing Zhing Zi [2008] No. 682, Dec. 19, 2008

Andrew, Inc. is the patentee of Chinese Patent ZL.95196544.1, titled "An antenna control system," filed on October 16, 1995 (hereinafter, "the Subject Patent"). Claim 14 of the subject patent, which is an independent claim, reads as follows:

> 14. An antenna system, comprising:
> An antenna, comprising two or more radiating elements and an electromechanical means for moving *at least one phase shifting element's components* to vary the phase of signals supplied to the respective radiating elements to vary downtilt of the beam of the antenna; and
> a controller, external to the antenna, for supplying drive signals to the electromechanical means for adjusting downtilt of the beam of the antenna.

In addition, Page 7 of the description of the Subject Patent describes the "relatively moving parts of one or more phase shifting elements," which are related to the antenna system of claim 14.

[On November 29, 2006, Wu Huiying filed an invalidation request to the PRB, asserting that claims 14–24 of the Subject Patent do not comply with Article 26(4) of the Chinese Patent Law (hereinafter, "the Law") and Rule 21(1) of the Implementing Regulations (hereinafter, "the Regulations").

[After reviewing the patent, the PRB made the following findings.]

> There is more than one phase shifting element, and there is more than one component in a phase shifting element. However, relying on the description of the subject patent, it is not immediately apparent whether the term "at least one" is used to modify the terms "the phase shifting element"

CASE *(continued)*

or "component of said phase shifting element." (This ambiguity is partially caused by the Chinese translation. In the U.S. counterpart Patent US6198458, the corresponding wording of claim 14 is "moving components of at least one phase shifting element.") In addition, claim 14 fails to give a clear and definite description of the connections between the elements in the electromechanical means, or connections between the electromechanical means and other means in the antenna system. Accordingly, claim 14 is not clear, and its dependent claims 15–24 are unclear as well. This does not comply with Rule 20(1) of the Regulations.

[In view of the aforesaid reasoning, the PRB made Decision No. 10009 to declare claims 14–24 invalid.]

[Andrew, Inc. appealed this Decision to Beijing No. 1 Intermediate People's Court, contending that claims 14–24 are adequately clear to meet the requirements of the related provisions of the law, and that Decision No.10009 should be revoked.]

[Beijing No. 1 Intermediate People's Court made the following findings:]

According to Chinese grammar, the phrase "at least one" should be interpreted as describing the immediate following phrase "phase shift element," rather than the word "components." Therefore, the language "for moving at least one phase shifting element's components" in claim 14 is clear. As stated in claim 14, electromechanical means are used for "moving at least one phase shifting element's components," and a controller are used "for supplying drive signals to the electromechanical means." This language explains the function of the electromechanical means, including its interaction with the phase shifting element and the controller. Relying on the claims and descriptions, the technical solution sought for protection by claim 14 is clear to those skilled in the relevant art.

Moreover, as long as the descriptions of a claim can clearly define the protection scope of a patent, the "clear" requirement is met; and it is irrelevant whether the claim breadth is excessive or not. Rather, excessive claim breadth is an issue to be decided under Article 26(4) of the Patent Law and Rule 21(2) of the Regulations. There are no laws or regulations that render a claim unclear if it is drafted based on its functional definitions, nor has it been established that a product claim must not contain any functional definitions. If a broad claim breadth is based on functional definitions, it exceeds the disclosure of the descriptions. In that case, the issue is not whether the claim is clear or not, but rather whether the claim is supported by the descriptions or not.

[With this reasoning, Beijing No. 1 Intermediate Court found that the PRB erred in concluding that claims 14–24 are unclear, therefore revoking and remanding the PRB's Decision. The PRB and Wu Huiying both appealed to the Beijing High Court. After the court trial, the High Court affirmed the first instance judgment.]

NOTES

1. **"A person of ordinary skill in the art"**. In *Andrew Inc. v. PRB*, the Court made it clear that, when deciding whether a claim term is clear or not, the decision should be made by an ordinary person skilled in the relevant art. Further, according to the Examination Guidelines of SIPO, "a person of ordinary skill in the art" is presumed to be aware of the customary technical knowledge and also to have access to all the technologies and experiment tools existing before the application date in the technical field, all in relation to the technical field of the invention.
2. **Intrinsic evidence v. extrinsic evidence**. In *Andrew Inc. v. PRB*, when deciding the meaning of the claim term in question, "at least one phase shifting element's components," the judge did both an ordinary grammar analysis and a technical context analysis on the basis of the description and drawings of the Subject Patent. What if two such interpretations conflict with each other? In the Judicial Rules issued by the Supreme Court in 2009, Article 3 stipulates that the application documents (specification, claims, drawings) and prosecution history shall have a higher weight in interpreting claim terms than extrinsic evidence (*e.g.*, textbooks, dictionaries, etc.). This echoes the similar US rule established in *Phillips v. AWH Corp.*, 415 F.3d 1303 (Fed. Cir. 2005).
3. The Judgment also touches upon another issue, *i.e.*, the relationship between requirements of a clear claim and a claim supported by its description. According to the comments of Judge Bo XU, who tried the first instance of the case, the "claim clarity" requirement focuses on claim drafting, where the definite claim breadth may be obtained from clear claim drafting. The requirement of a "claim being supported by the description," on the other hand, focuses on the relationship between the claims and the descriptions, which aim to achieve the legislative purpose of patent law, *i.e.* "protection in exchange for disclosure."

7.1.1 Functional limitations

In 2009, the Supreme Court issued Interpretation of the Supreme People's Court on Several Issues concerning the Application of Law in the Trial of Patent Infringement Dispute Cases [Fa Shi (2009) No.21], which stipulates how to interpret a functional claim feature.

Article 4

> For technical features described by function or effect in a claim, the people's court shall determine the content of these technical features according to the specific implementation of the functions or effects described in the specification and drawings or an equivalent thereof.

Similar to Paragraph 6, Article 112 of the US Patent Law, Article 4 of the SPC's 2009 judicial rules proposes a two-step approach to interpret a functional claim feature: (i) recognize a functional feature; (ii) decide the scope of the functional feature on the basis of the embodiments and equivalents thereof.

On the other hand, SIPO's examiners adopt an approach similar to "broadest reasonable interpretation" (BRI) in interpreting functional features during prosecution.

In Chapter 2, Part 2, Section 3.2.1 of SIPO's Examination Guidelines (2010), it says:

> *Technical features defined by function in a claim shall be construed as embracing all the means that are capable of performing the function.* For claims containing a feature defined by function, whether the definition by function can be supported by the description shall be examined. If the function is carried out in a particular way in the embodiments of the description, and the person skilled in the art would not appreciate that the function can be carried out by other alternative means not described in the description, or the person skilled in the art can reasonably doubt that one or more means embraced in the definition by function cannot solve the technical problem aimed to be solved by the invention or utility model and achieve the same technical effect, then the definition by function as embracing the other alternative means or means incapable of solving the technical problem shall not be allowed in the claim.

As there seems to be a split between the SIPO and the courts regarding how to interpret (or, even how to recognize) a functional feature of a claim, it raises concerns among patentees, in particular in the computer and software industry. The following case *Nokia v. Huaqin* reflects the above split, and further triggers the following question: How to draft and enforce a claim with functional limitation.

CASE

Nokia v. Huaqin, Shanghai Intermediate Court, Hu Yi Zhong Min Wu (Zhi) Chu Zi No. 47 [2011], June 2013; aff'd by Shanghai High Court, Hu Gao Min San Zhong Zi No. 96 [2013]

Nokia, Inc. is the patentee of CN Patent ZL Patent ZL200480001590.4, titled "Selecting a data transfer method" (the Subject Patent). In 2011, Nokia filed a patent infringement lawsuit against Huaqin, Inc., demanding 20 million RMB damages as total, on the basis of the Subject Patent.

Huaqin filed an invalidity request to the Subject Patent and successfully invalidated claims 1, 3, 5, 6, 8, and 10. It shall be noted that claim 7 is maintained as valid by the PRB. In particular, the PRB held that claim 7 is supported by the specification, and does not have an excessive claim breadth.

Claims 6 and 7 of the Subject Patent read as follows:

CASE *(continued)*

>Claim 6. A terminal device configured to determine a message to be transmitted on the basis of inputs received from a user, the terminal device is further configured to check at least one piece of property information concerning the message being entered or already entered, and the terminal device is configured to select, in order to transmit the message, a data transfer method associated in predetermined selection conditions with the property information, characterized in that the property information is one of the following information: information types which designating format of information entered into and/or selected for the message, identifier of the receiver, type of the identifier of the receiver.
>
>Claim 7: A terminal device of claim 6,
>> the terminal device is *further configured to*: apply the data transfer method selection to a message editor used for entering messages;
>>
>> the terminal device is configured to: transmit the message, based on the selection of the data transfer method carried out in the message editor, to a data transfer application supporting the selected data transfer method;
>>
>> the terminal device is configured to: transmit the message, according to a data transfer protocol used by the data transfer application, to a telecommunications network.

The Subject Patent has four drawings, which are illustrated below [Figure 7.1].
[In 2013, Shanghai No. 1 Intermediate Court held claim 7 of the Subject Patent is not construable, and ruled that Nokia's patent cannot be enforced.]

[Nokia appealed, Shanghai High Court ruled that,] there are two key issues: (1) whether claim 7 contains a functional technical feature; (2) whether the scope of claim 7 can be determined on the basis of the embodiments described in the specification and figures.

[Regarding the first issue, the court ruled that the feature "the terminal device is configured to: *apply the data transfer method selection to a message editor used for entering messages*" is a functional feature, based on the following reasons:]

- Secondly, according to the literal meaning of the term "being configured to/for", it defines the function or effect that is supposed to be achieved by the claimed device or component. Therefore, it is clear that said technical feature defined by the term "being configured to . . ." uses a functional language.
- Thirdly, regarding a technical feature using a functional language, if its meaning as understood after reading the claims, specification and figures, is same as its meaning for a person of ordinary skill in the art, then such a technical feature is not a functional feature. The contents of said technical feature shall be determined according to its reasonable meanings.
- However, Nokia also argued that the feature "message editor" in claim 7 is a distinguished feature in view of the prior art, which contributes the inventiveness step of the Subject Patent. Thus, Nokia at least admitted the feature "message editor" shall not be simply understood as a conventional means in the art for achieving said function

CASE *(continued)*

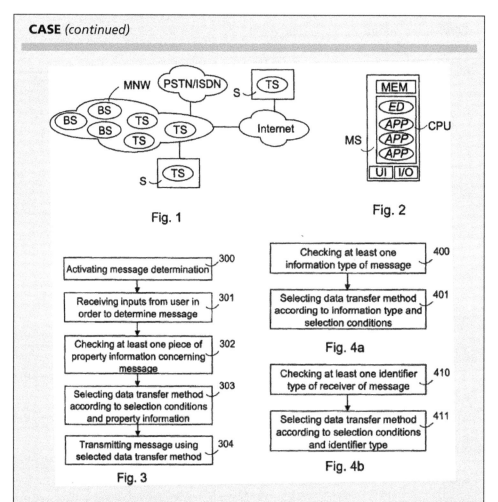

Figure 7.1 Nokia Patented Software System

or effect, but shall have a meaning which is differernt from common understanding of a person with ordinary skill in the art.
- For the above reasons, the court finds the feature in question is a functional feature.

[Regarding the second issue, the court ruled that,]

- It is clear that the embodiments described in the specification and Figures 3, 4a, 4b are all related to methods, steps and functions. The Subject patent merely states that the above mentioned method steps can be applied in a mobile station (MS) or a message editor, and further states that it could be achieved by software, hardware, or a cominbation of both. However, there is no disclosure of any specific technical means in the specification or figures as to how to apply the above method steps into a mobile terminal or a message

CASE *(continued)*

editor. In other words, the specification and figures fail to disclose an embodiment of how the the function "... configured to ..." is achieved in a mobile terminal or a message editor. According to Article 4 of the SPC's 2009 judicial rules, the court cannot decide the contents of claim 7, and thus cannot decide the scope of claim 7.

[In conclusion, the Shanghai High court agreed with the lower court that the asserted claim 7 of the Subject Patent is not construable, and affirmed.]

Shanghai High Court
Judge Dan ZHU
Judge Jianfeng MA
Judge Guangwei WANG
February, 24, 2014

NOTES AND QUESTIONS

1. **Is "configure to ..." an indicator of a functional feature?** Following Shanghai High Court's reasoning, the term "configured to ..." is a functional language, and thus the feature defined by such a term is presumed to be a functional feature. However, such a presumption is rebuttable "if the meaning of the feature in question as understood after reading the claims, specification and figures, is same as its meaning for a person of ordinary skill in the art." In *Nokia v. Huaqin*, the feature in question, "message editor," is alleged by Nokia to be a distinguishing feature contributing to the inventiveness step, and thus shall not have a common meaning for a person of ordinary skill in the art. (Otherwise, such a feature will be obvious.) Accordingly, the court ruled that Nokia fails to rebut the presumption.
2. **For a functional feature of a device claim, what kind of description is qualified as an embodiment?** In *Nokia v. Huaqin*, the court stated "the embodiments described in the specification and Figures 3, 4a, 4b are all related to methods, steps and functions." Does it mean flowcharts of algorithm or process are not considered as "embodiments" of a device claim under Article 4 of Supreme Court's Judicial Rules (Fashi [2009] No. 21)?
3. **Beijing High Court's definition of a functional feature.** In October 2013, Beijing High Court issued *Guidelines for Determination of Patent Infringement*, which stipulate how to decide a functional feature.

   Article 16

   The contents of a functional feature expressed through a function or effect in a claim shall be determined in view of the specific embodiments for carrying out the function or effect described in the description and drawings or the equivalents thereof.

   A functional feature refers to a technical feature in a claim that defines component of a product, or the cooperative relationship between the components, or steps of a method, with the role they play, the function they perform or the effect they achieve in the invention.

   The technical feature in the following circumstances shall not be regarded as functional technical means:

   (1) Technical features which are expressed in the language of functions or effects and which have become the technical nouns commonly known by a person having ordinary skill in the art, such as a conductor, heat radiator, adhesive, amplifier, transmitter, filter; and

(2) Technical features which are expressed in the language of functions or effects but which are also described with corresponding features relating to structure, material, steps or the like.

4. **Beijing High Court's Comments on *Nokia v. Huaqin***. In *Interpretations and Applications of Guidelines for Determination of Patent Infringement* (2014.9), Beijing High Court gives comments on *Nokia v. Huaqin* (pp. 82–84), conveying the following key messages:

(1) For the software industry, sometimes it is difficult to draw a line between function/effect and specific operations.

(2) In US practice, software algorithm or flowcharts are considered by the CAFC [US Court of Appeals for the Federal Circuit] as a type of "structure" (see *Typhoon Touch Technologies v. Dell, Inc.* Case No. 2009-1589).

(3) For software patents, Art. 4 of the SPC's 2009 Judicial Rules (Fashi [2009] No. 21) might not necessarily be triggered. Instead, Article 2 and 3 of the SPC's 2009 Judicial Rules (Fashi [2009] No. 21) might be applied for claim construction.

(4) Lastly, for software patent drafting, sufficient disclosure of specific embodiments (flowchart, detailed illustration of structure/modules, etc.) is recommended.

CASE

Huawei Technologies Co., Ltd. v. ZTE Corporation, Chinese Supreme Court (2015) Min Shen Zi No. 2720 ((2015) 民申字第 2720 号) available at http://wenshu.court.gov.cn/content/content?DocID=38c5b718-89d1-4e3b-bf50-20b91eead75e (transl. on 9/17/2017)

Against the judgment (2014) Zhezhizhongzi No. 161, delivered by the Higher People's Court of Zhejiang Province on 13th Feb., 2015, deciding the infringement dispute of a patent for invention among ZTE Corporation (ZTE), the respondent of this retrial, and Hangzhou Alibaba Advertising Co., Ltd. (Alibaba), the defendant of the first instance, Huawei Technologies Co., Ltd. (Huawei), the applicant of this retrial, filed a petition for retrial to this court. A collegial bench has been formed by this court accordance with law. Now the case has been concluded. [For information on retrials and procedure in China, see in this Part, Section 2.2.2.3, *supra*.]

The Court recognizes that the major issue of this case is whether the technical solution in dispute falls into the scope of the rights conferred under the claim 1 of Huawei's patent.

According to Article 59 paragraph 1 of China's Patent Law, the scope of the patent right for an invention or utility model shall be determined by the terms of the claims. The description and the appended drawings can be used to interpret the claims. The purpose of claims is to identify the scope and boundaries of a patent right. The function of the description and drawings are to describe a technical solution clearly and completely, so that skilled persons in the relevant field of technology can understand it and carry it out. Since it

CASE *(continued)*

is impossible to require a description to list all modes of carrying out an invention, it is not proper to narrow down the scope of a patent right [unduly by limiting the claimed invention to examples and drawings].

The patent in dispute is a patent for invention titled "A method for preventing IP address deceit in dynamic address distribution". Patent No. ZL02125007.3. Huawei Technologies Co., Ltd. is the right holder. Claim 1 includes these features [or elements]: (1) add end-users MAC [media access control] address [uniquely assigned to each device connected to a local network such as WiFi], source IP address information for a valid-user's (legal subscriber's) address table; (2) the subscriber terminal sends an ARP [address Resolution Protocol] message packet to a switch [in the Internet system, *i.e.*, in the general network to which the WiFi hub and devices ("terminals") are connected]; (3) the switch checks the source MAC address and source IP address in the ARP message packet, detecting whether there is a matching item in the legal subscriber's address table; if so, the system adds the source MAC address and source IP address sent by the subscriber terminal into [the list of users who can permissibly connect to the network, in a software] address table, so that end-user can access the network and communicate through the network; otherwise, [if there is no match between a requesting user's MAC address and source IP address, the system] discards the ARP packet.

According to the text of claim 1, firstly, it doesn't include the phrase "whether a DHCP [Dynamic Host Configuration Protocol – a local network software function that assigns a unique IP address to each user on the network, to allow the user to communicate over the Internet] is switched on", and each feature of the claim doesn't imply the requirement of a switched-on DHCP repeater [which permits a WiFi range extender to work in the same network with users who receive IP addresses from the DHCP system]. Thus, the text of claim 1 doesn't limit the method for preventing IP address deceit in dynamic address distribution only to the one situation in which a DHCP repeater is switched on.

Secondly, according to the background technology written in the description and present technologies known to the inventor, whether a DHCP repeater is switched on or off depends on whether the DHCP server is in the same network segment with the subscriber terminal. Both situations are possible. Therefore, claim 1 in this case doesn't exclude the situation in which a DHCP is switched off. Additionally, a switched-off situation can exist during the network-constructing process. [To limit the claim to the situation where it covers only the "repeater-on" mode] will [unduly and unfairly] narrow down the scope of the patent [by limiting it to the situation depicted in the disclosure and drawings of the patent specification].

The patented process is [meant] to prevent possible IP address deceit in dynamic address assignment and distribution, [and] the communication between a DHCP server and a subscriber terminal is inevitable [in this situation], thus the DHCP server [can either be] in [or] not in the same network segment with the subscriber terminal. [Because repeater mode is required only when the server and terminal are in the same network segment, limiting the claim to cover only this mode would unduly limit its scope].

CASE *(continued)*

[With claim interpretation settled, the court next turns to the question of infringement by defendant ZTE.]

Huawei and ZTE both agreed during the trial that the product under infringement challenge provides different technical process in different network constructions. Under the testing process presented by ZTE, which is the ideal network application environment for the patent in this case with the DHCP switched on, the process to prevent IP address deceit offered by the product [accused of infringement] is different from the process in claim 1 of the patent in this case; it does not fall into the rights scope of Huawei's patent. This court affirms [this].

[A]ccording to Article 11, paragraph 1 of Patent Law, after the granting of patent for an invention of process, unless it is otherwise prescribed by this Law, no entity or individual is entitled to, without permission of the patentee, use the patented process and use, promise the sale of, sell or import the product directly obtained from the patented process, for production or business purposes. That is to say, a patent right, as a monopoly right, excludes and prohibits the unauthorized use of a patented process. Hence, the key of this case is to consider whether ZTE inevitably and necessarily applies Huawei's network-constructing process and thus actually uses the patent in dispute.

Though the product under infringement challenge can repeat the patented process [*i.e.*, is capable of performing the process], we cannot presume that ZTE builds the same network application environment and actually uses the patent in this case in its process of developing and pre-delivery testing its product.

[T]hough users used the product under infringement challenge and realized its function of preventing IP address deceit, we cannot presume that they used the [claimed process to do so]. [C]onsidering the practical purpose of the product under infringement challenge, it has various function sets ... [including several that would not infringe claim 1]. Huawei failed to prove that ZTE provides their users any [instructions directing them to follow a procedure that would infringe claim 1]. Therefore, the existing evidence is not sufficient to prove the inevitability and necessity that once users purchased the product under infringement challenge the [claimed process] in this case is used.

The judgment of the second trial is clear in fact finding and correct in application of law. This court sustains the judgment.

NOTES

1. Notice that there were two relevant infringement inquiries in this case. The first concerned direct infringement by ZTE: here the question was whether, in setting up, configuring, and testing its switch, ZTE infringed claim 1 of Huawei's patent? The court did not believe the evidence was sufficient to establish infringement by ZTE. An interesting question – *if* infringement had been established – would remain regarding damages in such a case. Assume that ZTE infringed claim 1 just one time for each product that it sold to end users. Assume further that these end users did *not* perform the claimed process when using the device purchased from ZTE. Could all the end user activity in such a case be considered to flow from or result from the single, initial act of infringement by ZTE? And if so, could Huawei obtain damages for all

the units purchased and used, and all the benefits received, by end users? In other words, could the single act of infringement be enough to warrant extensive damages due to the "downstream" use of the device after the infringing set-up? On this topic generally, see Mark Lemley, The Fruit of the Poisonous Tree in IP Law (November 9, 2016) (Stanford Public Law Working Paper No. 2867099), available at SSRN: https://ssrn.com/abstract=2867099 or http://dx.doi.org/10.2139/ssrn.2867099.

2. The second alleged infringement here was on the part of end users. If end users were the direct infringers, and ZTE was limited only to selling a product that invited and permitted end users to infringe, ZTE would be liable as an indirect infringer. The discussion in the case to the effect that ZTE never instructed or directed end users to use the purchased ZTE product in an infringing way can be seen as a rejection of the argument that ZTE indirectly infringed. In the US this type of activity by a party such as ZTE is called "active inducement" and is covered by 35 U.S.S. §271(b).

7.2 Claim interpretation and infringement in Europe

EPC Article 69
Extent of protection

(1) The extent of the protection conferred by a European patent or a European patent application shall be determined by the claims. Nevertheless, the description and drawings shall be used to interpret the claims.

From the Protocol on the Interpretation of Article 69 EPC, adopted June 28, 2001 (see OJ EPO 2001, Special edition No. 4, p. 55), part of the Convention pursuant to EPC Article 164, paragraph 1 (on the significance of Regulations and Protocols):

[Protocol Article 1] **General Principles:** Article 69 should not be interpreted as meaning that the extent of the protection conferred by a European patent is to be understood as that defined by the strict, literal meaning of the wording used in the claims, the description and drawings being employed only for the purpose of resolving an ambiguity found in the claims. Nor should it be taken to mean that the claims serve only as a guideline and that the actual protection conferred may extend to what, from a consideration of the description and drawings by a person skilled in the art, the patent proprietor has contemplated. On the contrary, it is to be interpreted as defining a position between these extremes which combines a fair protection for the patent proprietor with a reasonable degree of legal certainty for third parties.

[Protocol Article 2] **Equivalents:** For the purpose of determining the extent of protection conferred by a European patent, due account shall be taken of any element which is equivalent to an element specified in the claims.

The cases that follow are drawn mainly from the UK and Germany, in keeping with the overall design of this volume. Validity in the EU, as you know at this point, is handled by both the EPO and national courts, with the EPO Boards leading the way in the interpretation of most aspects of the EPC. Infringement – which necessitates an examination of claims (and claim scope), is different: the EPO stays out of these matters (pending launch of a truly Europe-wide enforcement mechanism). So a word about the progression of patent cases in the UK and Germany is therefore in order.

In the UK, patent cases follow this progression: Patents County Court, the Patents Court at the High Court, the Court of Appeal, and finally the Supreme Court of the UK (formerly the House of Lords). For details, and statistics on patent cases between the years 2000 and 2008, see Christian Helmers and Luke McDonagh, Patent Litigation in the UK, London School of Econ. Wkg. Pap. 12/2012 (Sept 23, 2012), available at https://www.lse.ac.uk/collections/law/wps/WPS2012-12_Mcdonagh.pdf; and https://papers.ssrn.com/sol3/papers.cfm?abstract_id=2154939.

In Germany, 12 district courts have jurisdiction over first instance (trial) patent infringement matters (Düsseldorf, Hamburg, Munich I, Braunschweig, Freiburg, Mannheim, Berlin, Erfurt, Leipzig, Saarbrücken, Nuremberg-Fürth and Magdeburg). Their respective superior Higher Regional Courts rule on appeals. Appeals from the Higher Regional courts are to the Federal Court of Justice, the Bundesgerichtshof (BGH), which is, for civil law matters, the Supreme Court of Germany.

 CASE

Kirin-Amgen v. Hoechst Marion Rousel Ltd., [2004] UKHL 46, [2005] R.P.C. 9

[Speech (opinion) of Hoffmann, Lord Justice.]
[Plaintiff Kirin-Amgen developed a recombinant version of the useful protein erythropoietin (EPO), which is made naturally in the human kidney. They used conventional genetic engineering techniques, viz., identification of the gene sequence, isolation and purification of this sequence, transfer of this "exogenous" EPO DNA to a bacterial host cell, and then multiplication of the host cell so as to induce expression of large quantities of EPO.]

The accused infringer, Transkaryotic Therapies (TKT), or its British licensee Hoechst Marion Rousel Ltd., also produced EPO for therapeutic purposes. But the TKT approach uses a natural ("endogenous") DNA sequence coding for EPO in a human cell, into which an exogenous upstream control sequence has been inserted whose purpose is to "activate"

CASE *(continued)*

or turn on the natural EPO gene. (This is called GA-EPO, or "gene activated" EPO.) This causes the gene to express EPO for therapeutic purposes. The TKT could not have been done at the time of the patent but can now be done by using a phenomenon called "homologous recombination". It is fully described by Neuberger J. and I need say no more than that it enables TKT to activate or "switch on" the EPO gene in a human cell which would not ordinarily express that protein and then to select for commercial use those descendants of the manipulated cells in which the relevant genes have been amplified to produce a high level of expression.

The [plaintiff's patent] specification explains the relevant science, the nature of EPO and the difficulties which stood in the way of identifying the gene. It then describes the methods which Dr Lin [plaintiff's inventor] used to find the gene in the DNA of monkeys and humans and sets out the full sequences for both species. In a series of 12 examples it describes what Dr Lin was able to do with this information. There are 31 claims but we need concern ourselves only with claims 1, 19 and 26. To summarise them very briefly and leaving out qualifications to which I shall later return, they are for (1) a DNA sequence for use in securing the expression of EPO in a host cell, (19) EPO which is the product of the expression of an exogenous DNA sequence and (26) EPO which is the product of the expression in a host cell of a DNA sequence according to claim 1. Only claims 19 and 26 are alleged to have been infringed because TKT do not make any GA-EPO in this country. The alleged infringement is by importation. But claim 26 cannot be understood without first construing claim 1.

I shall now set out the precise terms of the three relevant claims. Claim 1 is for:

> A DNA sequence for use in securing expression in a procaryotic or eucaryotic host cell of a polypeptide product having at least part of the primary structural [conformation] of that of erythropoietin to allow possession of the biological property of causing bone marrow cells to increase production of reticulocytes and red blood cells and to increase [haemoglobin] synthesis or iron uptake, said DNA sequence selected from the group consisting of:
> (a) the DNA sequences set out in Tables V and VI or their complementary strands;
> (b) DNA sequences which hybridize under stringent conditions to the protein coding regions of the DNA sequences defined in (a) or fragments thereof; and
> (c) DNA sequences which, but for the degeneracy of the genetic code, would hybridize to the DNA sequences defined in (a) and (b).

Claim 19 is for:

> A recombinant polypeptide having part or all of the primary structural conformation of human or monkey erythropoietin . . . or any allelic variant or derivative thereof possessing the biological property of causing bone marrow cells to increase production of reticulocytes and red blood cells to increase haemoglobin synthesis or iron uptake

CASE *(continued)*

and characterised by being the product of eucaryotic expression of an exogenous DNA sequence and which has a higher molecular weight by SDS-PAGE from erythropoietin isolated from urinary sources.

Finally, claim 26 is for:

> A polypeptide product of the expression in a eucaryotic host cell of a DNA sequence according to any of claims 1, 2, 3, 5, 6 and 7.

Until the [UK] Patents Act 1977, which gave effect to the European Patent Convention ("EPC") there was nothing in any UK statute about the extent of protection conferred by a patent. It was governed by the common law, the terms of the royal grant and general principles of construction. It was these principles which Lord Diplock expounded in the leading case of *Catnic Components Ltd v. Hill & Smith Ltd* [1982] R.P.C. 183, which concerned a patent granted before 1977. But the EPC and the Act deal expressly with the matter in some detail. Article 84 specifies the role of the claims in an application to the European Patent Office for a European patent: "The claims shall define the matter for which protection is sought. They shall be clear and concise and be supported by the description."

For present purposes, the most important provision is Art. 69 of the EPC, which applies to infringement proceedings in the domestic courts of all Contracting States: "The extent of the protection conferred by a European patent or a European patent application shall be determined by the terms of the claims. Nevertheless, the description and drawings shall be used to interpret the claims." In stating unequivocally that the extent of protection shall be "determined" (in German, "bestimmt") by the "terms of the claims" (den Inhalt der Patentansprüche) the Convention followed what had long been the law in the United Kingdom.

In Germany, however, the practice before 1977 in infringement proceedings (validity is determined by a different court) was commonly to treat the claims as a point of departure ("Ausgangspunkt") in determining the extent of protection, for which the criterion was the inventive achievement ("erfinderische Leistung") disclosed by the specification as a whole. Likewise in the Netherlands, Professor Jan Brinkhof, former Vice-President of the Hague Court of Appeals, has written that the role of the claims before 1977 was "extremely modest": see *Is there a European Doctrine of Equivalence?* (2002) 33 IIC 911, 915. What mattered was the "essence of the invention" or what we would call the inventive concept.

Although the EPC thus adopted the United Kingdom principle of using the claims to determine the extent of protection, the Contracting States were unwilling to accept what were understood to be the principles of construction which United Kingdom courts applied in deciding what the claims meant. These principles, which I shall explain in greater detail in a moment, were perceived as having sometimes resulted in claims being given an unduly narrow and literal construction. The Contracting Parties wanted to make it clear that legal technicalities of this kind should be rejected. On the other hand, it was accepted

CASE *(continued)*

that countries which had previously looked to the "essence of the invention" rather than the actual terms of the claims should not carry on exactly as before under the guise of giving the claims a generous interpretation.

This compromise was given effect by the "Protocol on the Interpretation of Article 69":

> Article 69 should not be interpreted in the sense that the extent of the protection conferred by a European patent is to be understood as that defined by the strict, literal meaning of the wording used in the claims, the description and drawings being employed only for the purpose of resolving an ambiguity found in the claims. Neither should it be interpreted in the sense that the claims serve only as a guideline and that the actual protection conferred may extend to what, from a consideration of the description and drawings by a person skilled in the art, the patentee has contemplated. On the contrary, it is to be interpreted as defining a position between these extremes which combines a fair protection for the patentee with a reasonable degree of certainty for third parties.

It is often said, on the basis of the words "a position between these extremes", that the Protocol represents a compromise between two different approaches to the interpretation of claims. Both art. 69 and the Protocol are given effect in United Kingdom law, in relation to infringement, by ss. 60 and 125 of the Act.

[As against the earlier UK approach of sometimes rather strict and narrow interpretations of legal documents, such as patent claims or commercial contracts, the UK courts in the 1970s began to take the view that] the author of a document such as a contract or patent specification is using language to make a communication for a practical purpose and that a rule of construction which gives his language a meaning different from the way it would have been understood by the people to whom it was actually addressed is liable to defeat his intentions. It is against that background that one must read the well known passage in the speech of Lord Diplock in *Catnic Components Ltd v Hill & Smith Ltd* [1982] R.P.C. 183, 243 when he said that the new approach should also be applied to the construction of patent claims:

> A patent specification should be given a purposive construction rather than a purely literal one derived from applying to it the kind of meticulous verbal analysis in which lawyers are too often tempted by their training to indulge.

"Purposive construction" does not mean that one is extending or going beyond the definition of the technical matter for which the patentee seeks protection in the claims. The question is always what the person skilled in the art would have understood the patentee to be using the language of the claim to mean. And for this purpose, the language he has chosen is usually of critical importance. The conventions of word meaning and syntax enable us to express our meanings with great accuracy and subtlety and the skilled man will ordinarily assume that the patentee has chosen his language accordingly.

CASE *(continued)*

At the time when the rules about natural and ordinary meanings were more or less rigidly applied, the United Kingdom and American courts showed understandable anxiety about applying a construction which allowed someone to avoid infringement by making an "immaterial variation" in the invention as described in the claims. In England, this led to the development of a doctrine of infringement by use of the "pith and marrow" of the invention (a phrase invented by Lord Cairns in *Clark v Adie* (1877) 2 App Cas 315, 320) as opposed to a "textual infringement". The pith and marrow doctrine was always a bit vague ("necessary to prevent sharp practice" said Lord Reid in *C Van Der Lely NV v Bamfords Ltd* [1963] R.P.C. 61, 77) and it was unclear whether the courts regarded it as a principle of construction or an extension of protection outside the claims. In the United States, where a similar principle is called the "doctrine of equivalents", it is frankly acknowledged that it allows the patentee to extend his monopoly beyond the claims.

The *Catnic* principle of construction is, therefore, in my opinion, precisely in accordance with the Protocol. It is intended to give the patentee the full extent, but not more than the full extent, of the monopoly which a reasonable person skilled in the art, reading the claims in context, would think he was intending to claim. Of course it is easy to say this and sometimes more difficult to apply it in practice, although the difficulty should not be exaggerated. The vast majority of patent specifications are perfectly clear about the extent of the monopoly they claim. Disputes over them never come to court. In borderline cases, however, it does happen that an interpretation which strikes one person as fair and reasonable will strike another as unfair to the patentee or unreasonable for third parties. That degree of uncertainty is inherent in any rule which involves the construction of any document.

Although art. 69 prevents equivalence from extending protection outside the claims, there is no reason why it cannot be an important part of the background of facts known to the skilled man which would affect what he understood the claims to mean. That is no more than common sense. It is also expressly provided by the new art. 2 added to the Protocol by the Munich Act revising the EPC, dated November 29, 2000 (but which has not yet come into force): "For the purpose of determining the extent of protection conferred by a European patent, due account shall be taken of any element which is equivalent to an element specified in the claims."

[**Construction of Claims in this Case**]
It will be recalled that claim 1 is to a DNA sequence, selected from the sequences set out in Table VI or related sequences, for securing the expression of EPO in a "host cell". The chief question of construction is whether the person skilled in the art would understand "host cell" to mean a cell which is host to the DNA sequence which coded for EPO. The alternative, put forward by Amgen, is that it can include a sequence which is endogenous to the cell, like the human EPO gene which expresses GA-EPO, as long as the cell is host to some exogenous DNA. In the TKT process, it is host to the control sequence and other machinery introduced by homologous recombination.

The German courts have their own guidelines for dealing with equivalents, which

CASE *(continued)*

have some resemblance to the Protocol questions. In the "quintet" of cases before the Bundesgerichtshof (see, for example, *Kunstoffrohrteil* [2002] G.R.U.R. 511 and *Schneidemesser* 1 [2003] E.N.P.R. 12 309) which concerned questions of whether figures or measurements in a claim allow some degree of approximation (and, if so, what degree), the court expressly said that its approach was similar to that adopted in *Catnic* [, though there are some minor differences as well, particularly with respect to the fact that in German courts the question is less whether the accused device works "in the same way" as the claimed invention, and more whether it "solves the same problem" addressed by the invention.]

The effect of the construction for which Amgen contends is that claim 1 should be read as including any DNA sequence, whether exogenous or endogenous, which expresses EPO in consequence of the application to the cell of any form of DNA recombinant technology. It would have been easy to draft such a claim. Whether the specification would have been sufficient to support it, in the sense of enabling expression by any form of DNA recombinant technology, is another matter . . .

Amgen submit that although homologous recombination was a known phenomenon in 1983, its use to achieve "gene activation" was unknown. The method of manufacture by DNA recombinant technology referred to in the claim was the only one known at the priority date. At the time, it was in practice equivalent to a general claim for manufacture by recombinant DNA technology. It should therefore be construed as such. Amgen say that if the claims cannot be construed in terms sufficiently general to include methods unknown at the priority date, the value of a patent would be destroyed as soon as some new technology for achieving the same result was invented.

I do not dispute that a claim may, upon its proper construction, cover products or processes which involve the use of technology unknown at the time the claim was drafted. The question is whether the person skilled in the art would understand the description in a way which was sufficiently general to include the new technology. There is no difficulty in principle about construing general terms to include embodiments which were unknown at the time the document was written. One frequently does that in construing legislation, for example, by construing "carriage" in a 19th century statute to include a motor car. In such cases it is particularly important not to be too literal. It may be clear from the language, context and background that the patentee intended to refer in general terms to, for example, every way of achieving a certain result, even though he has used language which is in some respects inappropriate in relation to a new way of achieving that result . . .

In the present case, however, I agree with the Court of Appeal . . . that the man skilled in the art would not have understood the claim as sufficiently general to include gene activation. He would have understood it to be limited to the expression of an exogenous DNA sequence which coded for EPO.

For these reasons I would hold that TKT did not infringe any of the claims and dismiss Amgen's appeal.

[Lord Hoffmann went on to say that he would find claim 19, to recombinant EPO, invalid for lack of enablement; and EPO characterized as in claim 26 lacking in novelty, in

> **CASE** *(continued)*
>
> both cases because the inventor had not in fact invented EPO however derived, but instead had invented recombinant EPO produced by conventional genetic engineering techniques. The four other Lord Justices concurred in the views of Lord Justice Hoffmann.]

NOTES

1. *Kirin-Amgen* has become a cornerstone case on claim interpretation and infringement under UK law, and has accordingly been cited in many subsequent cases. *See, e.g., GlaxoSmithKline UK Ltd v. Wyeth Holdings LLC*, [2016] EWHC 1045 (Ch), 2016 WL 02641917, where the court was asked to consider infringement of claims to proteins useful in treating meningitis. Claim 1 recited: "A composition containing at least one protein comprising an amino acid sequence having sequence identity greater than 95% to the amino acid sequence of any one of [three specified sequences] . . .". Claim 3 of the patent was dependent on claim 1, and claimed as a composition "the amino acid sequence of [one of the three specified proteins]." Citing *Kirin-Amgen*, as well as the Protocol to EPC Article 69, the court said with respect to claim 3:

   > [Accused infringer] Wyeth's construction of claim 3 does not provide reasonable certainty to the public, as required by the Protocol to Article 69 of the European Patent Convention, as it is not clear what percentage identity would satisfy claim 3. It may be that this claim would be satisfied by anything more than 95% or 97% identity, or perhaps 99% identity would be required. If claim 3 does not mean 100% identity, then it would be of uncertain scope . . . (*id.*, at par. 80).

   See also Research In Motion UK Ltd v. Motorola Inc, [2010] EWHC 118 (Pat), 2010 WL 308564 (applying *Kirin-Amgen* principles to interpretation of claims in mobile telecommunications field). *Kirin-Amgen* itself cites two important prior cases: (1) *Catnic Components Ltd v. Hill & Smith Ltd*, [1982] RPC 183; and (2) *Technip France SA's Patent*, [2004] RPC 46 (Jacob, LJ). The former case, in a speech (or opinion) by the noteworthy jurist Lord Diplock, was an early harbinger of the shift from literalistic interpretation to more open-textured "purposive" construction. The latter case laid down some specific principles to work in conjunction with EPC Article 69 and its Protocol. *See generally* Christian Von Drathen, *Patent scope in English and German law under the European Patent Convention 1973 and 2000*, 39 Int'l Rev. I.P. & Comp. L. 384 (2008). For more comparative analysis of the UK and Germany, see Jan Klink, *Cherry Picking in Cross-Border Patent Infringement Actions: A Comparative Overview of German and UK Procedure and Practice*, 26 Eur. I.P. Rev. 493 (2004).

2. Lord Hoffmann's discussion of "purposive" claim interpretation, and the reasons why it is consistent with the EPC Article 69 Protocol on claim interpretation, have been particularly influential in patent law. This is part of a wider jurisprudence on purposive interpretation, which itself has been the subject of serious study. *See, e.g.*, Justine Pila, "Lord Hoffmann and Purposive Interpretation in Intellectual Property Law," in The Jurisprudence of Lord Hoffmann: A Festschrift in Honour of Lord Leonard Hoffmann (Paul S Davies and Justine Pila, eds., 2015), at Chapter 10. *See generally* Aharon Barak, Purposive Interpretation in Law (Sari Bashi, trans., 2005).

7.2.1 Claim interpretation in German courts

Historically, German courts have had a distinctive approach to claim interpretation. The emphasis is on (1) finding the inventive heart or essence of a claimed invention, and (2) interpreting claims liberally, with the inventive contribution in mind. Though there has been significant trimming of this traditional approach in light of EPC Article 69 and its Protocol, traces of the historical practice can at times be detected in German opinions on infringement. Consider the following case.

"Articulation Arrangement" (Gelenkanordnung), Case No. Xa ZR 36/08 (Federal Supreme Court (Bundesgerichtshof – BGH) 4 February 2010)

[The invention relates to collision dampening in the joints or connections between railway cars – an invention spurred by the tragic train derailment in Eschede, Germany, in 1988. *See* https://en.wikipedia.org/wiki/Eschede_derailment. The basic idea is to provide dampening under normal conditions, *i.e.*, some way to allow force to be transmitted between railway cars during normal operation; and then a dampening device that is activated under extreme conditions, such as a collision or derailment. The extreme condition part of the device is "destructive," meaning that it breaks or is destroyed when activated. Its job is to dampen severe shocks, to keep them from being transmitted directly and intensely between railway cars. These devices have a common general structure, but can be constructed in a number of different variations on this basic theme. The general structure is X – x – X, where the large X's are called "articulated arms", and the small x is a "bearing." The large X's are there to handle the extreme condition, *e.g.*, the collision, while the small x, the bearing, absorbs normal levels of force during normal operation of the train. The articulated arm contains a "destructive energy-dissipating member" which breaks upon impact, lessening the transmission of force between cars.

This invention is described in European Patent 1,312,527, filed on September 17, 2001. Claim 1 reads as follows (with elements renumbered from those in the reported case):

[1] An articulation arrangement for the articulated connection of boxes of a multi-unit vehicle [*i.e.*, railways cars], comprising
 [a] a first articulated arm and
 [b] a second articulated arm,
[2] which cooperate in an articulated manner by means of a bearing, and
[3] at least one destructive energy-dissipating member which dissipates the energy arising from an impact transferred by one box to a neighbouring connected box,
[4] characterised in that the energy-dissipating member is
 [a] integrated free from play in one of the articulated arms.

The patent was issued, then successfully opposed; but it was reinstated by an EPO Technical Board of Appeals decision, T 1269/05. When the patent owner asserted it against the defendant, the owner prevailed; that decision was overturned on appeal, which led to the opinion set forth here.

The key infringement issue was the meaning of claim element [4][a], which requires the energy-dissipating member to be "integrated free from play in one of the articulated arms."

> **CASE** *(continued)*
>
> The patentee's device featured an integrated structure in which the articulated arms push against metal brackets that are flared at the ends, so when the arms are forced against the brackets the brackets bend outward and then break. The accused infringer constructed its device differently; its articulation arm includes a plate that is set 10–15 millimeters (.4–.6 of an inch) from a series of metal tubes designed to compress when the plate contacts them, which occurs during a collision or derailment.]
>
> The appeal court dismissed the action on the grounds that the contested embodiment did not implement Feature [[4][a]], since the energy-dissipating member was not integrated free from play in the articulated arm. This assessment cannot be upheld on appeal [, and is therefore reversed].
>
> The patent at issue states *inter alia* that the known articulation arrangements should be further developed such that the energy transferred by an extreme impact is "also" absorbed. This implies that the impacts occurring during normal running operations should also be absorbed, as was the case in the previously known designs. Corresponding with this, a significant advantage of the patented device is seen in the fact that both the impacts that arise during normal running operations – such as in the case of moderate acceleration – and those that occur in extreme situations – such as in the event of a collision – are largely absorbed by the energy-dissipating member. The description of a "preferred embodiment" – the only example embodiment that is set out in more detail in the patent at issue – states, on the other hand, that the articulation arrangement contains, in addition to the energy-dissipating member according to the invention, a spherelastic bearing [a specific type of small "x" in the X – x – X arrangement] that, as known from the state of the art, serves to absorb the impacts and vibrations occurring during normal running operations.
>
> According to [various] statements [in the specification], the function of the energy-dissipating members is to absorb the energy that is transferred via the articulation arrangement from box to box by means of the plastic deformation [*i.e.*, breaking or "destruction"] of the energy-dissipating members if a predetermined response force such as occurs in the event of a collision, is exceeded. In the defined working range below the response force of the energy-dissipating members, the [middle] bearing should, according to its function as known from the state of the art, absorb pressure and tension elastically, thus attenuating the impacts arising during normal running operations.
>
> Patent claim 1 does not expressly mention attenuation measures for the impacts occurring during normal running operations. From this, the appeal court concluded that the (destructive) energy-dissipating member must be designed in such a way that it can also absorb these impacts. The description of the object in the patent at issue showed that the attenuation effect known from the state of the art was naturally to be retained during normal running operations. Of the components specified in patent claim 1, only the energy-dissipating member would implement this purpose. The energy-dissipating member had the attenuation characteristics needed for this by not being integrated somehow or other but rather "free from play" in the articulated arm.

CASE *(continued)*

This conclusion is incorrect. Admittedly, the patent at issue discloses that the attenuation effect according to the patent for the event of an extreme impact is not intended to replace the attenuation effect for normal running operations known from the state of the art, but rather is intended to supplement it. However, the fact that patent claim 1 does not mention any components that serve this purpose does not permit the conclusion that this function must be performed by the energy-dissipating member specified in [claim element 4].

The appeal court was essentially guided by the assumption that the object of the invention was to provide an articulation arrangement that: –

- was also capable of absorbing the energy transferred by an extreme impact; [and]
- could dissipate the impacts occurring during normal running operations in the known manner . . .

In this approach, the appeal court failed to take account of the fact that the determination of the technical problem is part of the construction of the patent claim. The technical problem results from what the invention actually accomplishes. This is to be developed by construing the patent claim. The function of the individual features in the context of the patent claim is to be used to derive what technical problem these features of themselves and in their totality actually solve. What is designated as the object of the invention can contain an indication of the correct interpretation. However, the details of the description concerning the object of the invention are, as otherwise for the description, subject to the priority of the patent claim as against the other contents of the patent specification. The consultation of description and drawings must not lead to a substantive restriction of the subject matter as determined by the wording of the patent claim.

The fact that the defendant [accused infringer] has in the meantime been granted a patent for a device corresponding with the contested embodiment [*i.e.*, a patent on the defendant's own design] could only be of relevance if a feature of the patent at issue had been replaced [in the defendant's patent] by an equivalent substitute and patent claim 1 was therefore only implemented in equivalent form. However, the contested embodiment implements all features of patent claim 1 literally [, so this principle is not relevant].
[Appeals court reversed; judgment for plaintiff patent owner.]

 NOTES

1. The emphasis on the problem solved by the claimed invention – and the importance of this for claim interpretation – is a recurring theme in the German law of infringement and claim interpretation. For another example, consider *Change-Speed Hub (Mehrgangnabe)*, Case No. X ZR 153/05 (Federal Supreme Court (Bundesgerichtshof – BGH), 12 February 2008), at pars. 30–37, where the court said:

    The assessment of the question whether a patent infringement has taken place must first address the technical teaching that, from the point of view of the person skilled in the art addressed by the patent at issue, results from the features of the patent claim seen individually and in their totality [citation omitted].

The semantic content of the patent claim seen in its totality and the contribution made by the individual features to the result achieved by the invention are to be determined by means of interpretation, making use of the description and drawings that elucidate the patent claim (Art. 69(1) second sentence, European Patent Convention; Sec. 14 second sentence, [German] Patent Act). The function of the interpretation of the patent claim is thus not to be left to the court expert but instead is the responsibility of the court.

[It is the role of the expert to inform the court of facts, not to substitute for the court's judgment. Experts are for example prone to over-emphasizing actual embodiments, rather than the abstract words of patent claims; this led the expert in this case to interpret a claim element too restrictively, as the expert was influenced by an embodiment on the market and by an example in the specification.]

Nor was the appeal court entitled to waive [its own] examination [of the claims] to the extent that the expert's statements were consistent with the example embodiments explained and set out in the patent descriptions. A restriction of the interpretation to this effect would be incompatible with the principle that an example embodiment as a rule does not permit a restrictive interpretation of a patent claim that characterises the invention generally. If thus the technical teaching of the patent claims has not been determined, this means that the necessary basis is missing to permit an appropriate examination whether the contested product falls within the scope of protection of the plaintiff's patents either literally or as an equivalent embodiment.

Accordingly, the contested decision is set aside and the case returned to the appeal court for rehearing. In its interpretation of the plaintiff's patents, the appeal court shall, in particular, examine how far its previous assumptions on the design and effect of the change-speed hub in accordance with the invention merely concern possible embodiments of the claimed technical teachings or whether they characterise such teachings themselves in the general form in which they are protected for the plaintiff in the relevant patent claim. A narrower interpretation of the patent claim than the wording of itself might suggest can result from the consultation of the description and the drawings that is always necessary [citation omitted]. However, this requires a careful examination in the individual case and in particular must not be derived from the fact that the description and drawings only concern some of the embodiments that fall within the wording of the patent claim. The decisive factor is, on the contrary, whether the interpretation of the patent claim using the description and drawings shows that only such a narrower technical teaching will achieve the technical result that according to the invention is to be achieved with the means specified in the claim.

See also Klett/Sonntag/Wilske, Intellectual Property Law in Germany, Auflage 2008 (Beck-online):

> In German legal practice it has been stressed again and again that every patent and utility model is entitled to the widest conceivable scope of protection. This extent is situated in the area between the disclosure of the patent specification and the state of the art. The upper limit should be set, according to general opinion, by the entitlement of third parties to adequate legal security. This balance of interest between a maximum reward for the inventor, on the one hand, and legal security for thirds on the other, is also implied in the sense of the Protocol on the Interpretation of Art. 69 EPC.

The German practice, then, is (historically anyway) closer to "central claiming" than to the contemporary US style of "peripheral claiming." See, e.g., Toshiko Takenaka, *Interpreting Patent Claims: The United States, Germany and Japan*, 17 IIC Studies 1, 3 (1995):

> The central definition theory requires that the scope of the patent protection be determined by defining the principle forming the inventive idea or solution underlying the claim language. Courts use the wording of the claim as a guideline to determine the scope of protection, but are not strictly bound by the claim limitations.

But of course, with the adoption of the Protocol to Article 69 of the EPC, there has been a major push to harmonize claim interpretation in Europe – resulting in a practice that might be described as "flexible but peripheral." *Cf.* David L. Cohen, *Article 69 and European Patent Integration*, 92 Nw. U. L. Rev. 1082 (1998). *See also* White & Case (law firm), The case law of the German courts of lower instance for patent law and utility model law since the year 2013, December 2014 in GRUR-RR, reprinted at https://www.whitecase.com/publications/article/case-law-german-courts-lower-instance-patent-law-and-utility-model-law-year (posted Mar. 6, 2015; visited June, 2017) (describing in detail lower court cases in Germany that overall try to strike the balance suggested in the Protocol to Article 69). *See also* Dr. Holger Glas and Thomas Mayer, "Germany," Chapter 10 in Patent Claim Interpretation – Global Edition (Dec. 2016 Update), at §10:7 ("In

Germany, there is no file history estoppel. The claim or the language used in the claim must not be narrowly construed for the sole purpose of avoiding invalidity.")

2. Traditionally, in accordance with their liberal approach to claim interpretation, German courts have recognized a version of the doctrine of equivalents (DOE), as it is known and practiced in the US. This emerged from and was an integral part of the traditional German approach, known as the "tripartite" (or three-part) doctrine. A helpful historical survey puts it this way:

> Toward the end of the 1930s, German courts began attempting to make the scope of protection more predictable by imposing an analytical framework with which it could be measured. The courts developed a German "tripartite doctrine" . . . Under that doctrine, a patent provided three areas of protection for: (1) the direct subject matter of the invention; (2) the subject matter of the invention; and (3) the general inventive idea. The first part – the direct subject matter – corresponded to the American and British concepts of literal and "textual" infringement, respectively . . . The second part – the subject matter of the invention – comprised the inventive idea or technical teaching that a skilled person would derive from the claims, without inventive effort, in light of the description, drawings, prior art, and general knowledge available to skilled persons. To identify the subject matter of the invention, a court would analyze the problem and solution underlying the invention and derive the combination of elements that embodied the inventive idea. The scope of protection then included at least evident equivalents and inferior embodiments of that subject matter. Equivalence was measured by whether an accused feature had the same technical function as the claimed element and could replace it within the inventive idea for solving the underlying problem. To be an "evident" equivalent, that replaceability had to be immediately evident to the skilled person . . . The third part of the German "tripartite" doctrine – the "general inventive idea" – was relevant only where the accused device fell outside the technical teaching of the patent. In such a case the court would examine whether a common inventive idea encompassed both the accused device and the technical teaching of the patent, as evidenced by the claims, description, and drawings. Any such common, inventive idea was termed the "general inventive idea." German courts protected the general inventive idea in order to provide the inventor a monopoly commensurate with the extent to which he or she enriched the art . . . Protection of the general inventive idea represented the broadest protection available to German patents (Ray D. Weston, Jr., *A Comparative Analysis of the Doctrine of Equivalents: Can European Approaches Solve an American Dilemma?*, 39 IDEA 35, 54–56 (1998).)

Vestiges of this practice remain, particularly the emphasis (evident in the *Articulation Arrangement (Gelenkanordnung)* case, the main excerpt above) on the technical problem solved by the claimed invention. Consider also how these ideas carry through in the application of the DOE in Germany. So, for example, in Federal Court of Justice (BGH), Decision of 12 March 2002 (Docket No. X ZR 168/00), GRUR 2002, 515 – *Schneidmesser I*, and the Decision of 12 March 2002 (Docket No. X ZR 135/01), GRUR 2002, 519 – *Schneidmesser II*, the court made the point that, under German law, an embodiment is to be regarded as an equivalent of the patented invention if the following three preconditions are fulfilled: (1) the accused variant solves the problem underlying the invention with modified means which objectively have the same effect as the invention (Gleichwirkung); (2) a person skilled in the art is able by means of his general technical knowledge to find, without inventive effort, the modified means as having the same effect (Naheliegen); and (3) the considerations to be applied by the skilled person in this regard must be so closely oriented to the essence of the technical teaching described in the patent claim that the person skilled in the art considers the variant with its modified means as equivalent to the solution provided by the invention as defined in the claim (Gleichwertigkeit). At the same time, the court noted that the prior art imposes a limitation on the application of the doctrine of equivalents, preventing claims from covering equivalents that are present in, or obvious in light of, the prior art. *See* Federal Court of Justice (BGH), Decision of 29 April 1986 (Docket No. X ZR 28/85), GRUR 1986, 803 – *Formstein*.

3. For more on the comparison between US, German, and other nations' analysis of patent infringement, *see Ateliers de la Haute-Garonne v. Broetje Automation-USA Inc.*, 2011 Markman 722937, 2011 WL 722937, *5 (D. Del. 2011) (ruling that claim constructions given by a German court in construing a German patent which was a counterpart to the patent in suit would be treated as extrinsic evidence and only given little weight:

> At the hearing, the Court inquired into a comparison between German patent law and U.S. patent law. Counsel for [defendant] Broetje responded that '[a]fter [the US decision in] *Phillips* . . . they're much

closer in that the specification is used to help instruct what the claims mean as opposed to merely looking at an abstract meaning like the way we would have in the old days [prior to *Phillips*].' Aside from attorney argument, however, there is no concrete evidence in the record concerning the similarities or differences between U.S. patent law and German patent law. The German court's opinion is at most extrinsic evidence. The determination of what the claim language means in light of the specifications at issue here, under the governing law, is the duty of this Court, and the constructions offered by another court, applying foreign law, have little relevance to that determination. Accordingly, the Court affords little weight to the constructions provided by the German court and will proceed to construe the claim terms at issue here without deference to the German court's decision.

For earlier comparative analysis, see Stefan A. Riesenfeld, *The New American Patent Act in the Light of Comparative Law: Part II*, 102 U. Pa. L. Rev. 723, 757 (1954) (German patent claims differ from the usual American forms in that they customarily commence with a generic reference to the invention and then introduce and specify the novel feature with the clause "characterized by," which may be couched in functional terms; and they are more expansively interpreted in some cases); Kurt Legner, *The Interpretation of a German Patent in an Infringement Action*, 17 J. Pat. Off. Soc'y 393 (1935); Georg Benjamin, *Interpretation of German Patents*, 17 J. Pat. Off. Soc'y 585 (1935); Georg Benjamin, Interpretation of a Patent in Germany, 18 J. Pat. Off. Soc'y 365 (1936).

4. We consider here primarily claim interpretation as the threshold for patent infringement. There are in addition some fine points regarding infringing activities under German law, just as in the US. For example, contributory infringement occurs when someone facilitates direct infringement through the offering and sale of materials which relate to the essential features of a claimed invention. The buyer or user of the materials so supplied is the direct infringer. For more on this and related topics, see the extensive discussion in chapter II.5.A of Toshiko Takenaka, Christopher Rademacher et al., Patent Enforcement in the U.S., Germany and Japan (2015), at pp. 92–99 (acts of direct infringement), and pp. 99–105, and pp. 108–10 (exemptions from infringement for private use, experimental use and use by a pharmacy).

7.3 Indirect infringement

When a single person or company employs all the elements of a claimed invention, that constitutes patent infringement. But what if a person or company merely instructs or directs another, with that other being the one who actually performs the infringing act? Or what if a person or company sells an assembly that is incomplete in some minor respect, knowing that the buyer of the assembly intends to add the missing element to complete the infringing device?

The single actor who clearly infringes is known as a *direct infringer*. One who directs or guides, or sells a just-less-than-complete assembly, is by contrast an *indirect infringer*. Directing or guiding is called "inducement." Selling less than an entire assembly invokes the doctrine of "contributory infringement."

Infringement in all its dimensions is covered in §271 of the Patent Act:

(a) Except as otherwise provided in this title, whoever without authority makes, uses, offers to sell, or sells any patented invention, within the United States or imports into the United States any patented invention during the term of the patent therefor, infringes the patent.

(b) Whoever actively induces infringement of a patent shall be liable as an infringer.

(c) Whoever offers to sell or sells within the United States or imports into the United States a component of a patented machine, manufacture, combination or composition, or a material or apparatus for use in practicing a patented process, constituting a material part of the invention, knowing the same to be especially made or especially adapted for use in an infringement of such patent, and not a staple article or commodity of commerce suitable for substantial noninfringing use, shall be liable as a contributory infringer.

There is an extensive body of case law on what it means to "make," "use," "sell", etc. *See, e.g., Waymark Corp. v. Porta Systems Corp.*, 245 F.3d 1364 (Fed. Cir. 2001) (assembly and testing of less than all the components called for in the patent claim does not constitute a "making" of the claimed invention under §271(a)). One area of particular interest is infringement that is distributed or shared among multiple entities. (Note that §271(a) says "[w]hoever . . ." – denoting a singular subject, meaning only one person or company.) The Federal Circuit has held that even a loose affiliation between two entities can make the acts of one an extension or alter ego of the other, and that therefore in such a "joint enterprise" the actors working together can commit direct infringement even though they are spread among multiple entities. *Akamai Techs., Inc. v. Limelight Networks, Inc.*, 797 F.3d 1020, 1022 (Fed. Cir. 2015) (finding that a joint enterprise includes action by agreement, acts for a common purpose, or actions within a community of pecuniary interest).

Direct infringement does not require any showing of knowledge or intent. One can infringe a patent even if ignorant of the patent, ignorant of infringing the patent, or indeed if ignorant of the fact that patents exist at all. By the same token, independent invention is no defense to patent infringement. Recreating a technology on one's own constitutes patent infringement; the only requirement is that the recreated technology falls within one or more claims of a valid US patent. *See* Robert P. Merges, *A Few Kind Words for Absolute Infringement Liability in Patent Law*, 31 Berkeley Tech. L.J. 1 (2016) (defending this aspect of patent law).

Intent is required for indirect infringement, however.

To "actively induce" infringement under §271(b), one must *intend* to promote or bring about an act of infringement. As mentioned, inducement usually involves guiding or instructing another party to act. The intent requirement under §271(b) means that one who instructs another in a way that results in infringement must do so in a way that is at least very highly likely to result in infringement – *i.e.*, the instructing party must act at least *recklessly*. That is the holding in an important Supreme Court case, *Global-tech Appliances, Inc. v. SEB, S.A.*, 563 U.S. 754 (2011) ("willful blindness" to possibility of infringement, where potential infringer withheld evidence of specific patent from attorney asked to do infringement assessment based on all extant patents, amounted to inducement). Another recent Supreme Court case explores the intent requirement for induced infringement. In *Commil USA, LLC v. Cisco Sys., Inc.*, 135 S. Ct. 1920 (2015), the Court held that a good-faith belief in the invalidity of a patent was not enough to excuse inducement; one must believe in good faith that the instructions or guidance given to a direct infringer will not result in patent infringement. The intent requirement for inducement, in other words, is all about intent to infringe. If you believe the party receiving instructions or guidance will infringe the patent, then you will be liable for inducing infringement. A belief that infringement does not matter, because the patent in question is invalid – that will not excuse liability.

Contributory infringement is the sale of a "component," or of a "material or apparatus used in a process"; the act of selling such a component or material will be contributory infringement if: (1) the sold item is a "material part" of the claimed invention; (2) the seller "know[s] the [component or material] to be especially made or adapted for infringing use"; and (3) the sold item is not a "staple article or commodity of commerce suitable for substantial noninfringing use."

The "Material part" requirement for contributory infringement is in place to prevent patent infringement liability for one who sells a minor component (a bolt or screw, for example) which is incorporated into an infringing assembly (such as an entire machine).

The second requirement, that the seller must "know" the component sold is especially made or adapted for infringing use, supplies the knowledge requirement for contributory infringement. *Aro Mfg. Co. v. Convertible Top Replacement Co.*, 377 U.S. 476 (1964).

In addition to the "material part" and "knowledge" requirements, contributory infringement also requires that the sold item *not* be a "staple article . . . of commerce suitable for substantial noninfringing use." This insures that one cannot be found liable for patent infringement for selling an item that might very well have extensive use outside the context of patent infringement. Even if the component is a "material part" of an infringing device, the component sale will not infringe if it has extensive use in noninfringing devices as well. A good example of how this works comes from the case of *Vita-Mix Corp. v.*

Basic Holding, Inc., 581 F.3d 1317 (Fed. Cir. 2009). In the *Vita-Mix* case, the holder of a process patent for operating a blender without the formation of air pockets around the blender blades sued the seller of a consumer blender. The accused blender reproduced the patentee's blade design, but also sold the blender with a "stirring stick" (much like a long spoon) that could be used, optionally, to stir material in the blender and avoid formation of air pockets that way. The Federal Circuit held that sale of the blender was not contributory infringement. This was because when a consumer used the stirring stick, the blender did not infringe the process patent. And this meant that the blender itself had a "substantial noninfringing use."

8

Remedies

After a patent has been found to be valid and infringed, the next issue is remedies. How will the court give the patentee a remedy that makes up for the infringement of the patent? That is our topic here.

8.1   Injunctions in the US

 CASE

eBay Inc. v. MercExchange, L.L.C., 547 U.S. 388 (2006)

Thomas, Justice

Petitioner eBay operates a popular Internet Web site that allows private sellers to list goods they wish to sell, either through an auction or at a fixed price. Petitioner Half.com, now a wholly owned subsidiary of eBay, operates a similar Web site. Respondent MercExchange, L.L.C., holds a number of patents, including a business method patent for an electronic market designed to facilitate the sale of goods between private individuals by establishing a central authority to promote trust among participants. See U.S. Patent No. 5,845,265. MercExchange sought to license its patent to eBay, but the parties failed to reach an agreement. MercExchange subsequently filed a patent infringement suit against eBay in the United States District Court for the Eastern District of Virginia. A jury found that MercExchange's patent was valid, that eBay had infringed that patent, and that an award of damages was appropriate. Following the jury verdict, the District Court denied MercExchange's motion for permanent injunctive relief. 275 F.Supp.2d 695 (2003). The Court of Appeals for the Federal Circuit reversed, applying its "general rule that courts will issue permanent injunctions against patent infringement absent exceptional circumstances." 401 F.3d 1323, 1339 (2005).

According to well-established principles of equity, a plaintiff seeking a permanent injunction must satisfy a four-factor test before a court may grant such relief. A plaintiff must demonstrate: (1) that it has suffered an irreparable injury; (2) that remedies available at law, such as monetary damages, are inadequate to compensate for that injury; (3) that, considering the balance of hardships between the plaintiff and defendant, a remedy in

CASE *(continued)*

equity is warranted; and (4) that the public interest would not be disserved by a permanent injunction.

Neither the District Court nor the Court of Appeals below fairly applied these traditional equitable principles in deciding respondent's motion for a permanent injunction. Although the District Court recited the traditional four-factor test, it appeared to adopt certain expansive principles suggesting that injunctive relief could not issue in a broad swath of cases. Most notably, it concluded that a "plaintiff's willingness to license its patents" and "its lack of commercial activity in practicing the patents" would be sufficient to establish that the patent holder would not suffer irreparable harm if an injunction did not issue. But traditional equitable principles do not permit such broad classifications. For example, some patent holders, such as university researchers or self-made inventors, might reasonably prefer to license their patents, rather than undertake efforts to secure the financing necessary to bring their works to market themselves. Such patent holders may be able to satisfy the traditional four-factor test, and we see no basis for categorically denying them the opportunity to do so. To the extent that the District Court adopted such a categorical rule, then, its analysis cannot be squared with the principles of equity adopted by Congress. The court's categorical rule is also in tension with *Continental Paper Bag Co. v. Eastern Paper Bag Co.*, 210 U.S. 405, 422–430 (1908), which rejected the contention that a court of equity has no jurisdiction to grant injunctive relief to a patent holder who has unreasonably declined to use the patent.

In reversing the District Court, the Court of Appeals departed in the opposite direction from the four-factor test. The court articulated a "general rule," unique to patent disputes, "that a permanent injunction will issue once infringement and validity have been adjudged." 401 F.3d, at 1338. The court further indicated that injunctions should be denied only in the "unusual" case, under "exceptional circumstances" and "in rare instances . . . to protect the public interest." *Id.*, at 1338–1339. Just as the District Court erred in its categorical denial of injunctive relief, the Court of Appeals erred in its categorical grant of such relief. Because we conclude that neither court below correctly applied the traditional four-factor framework that governs the award of injunctive relief, we vacate the judgment of the Court of Appeals, so that the District Court may apply that framework in the first instance.

Justice Kennedy, with whom Justice Stevens, Justice Souter, and Justice Breyer join, concurring.

In cases now arising trial courts should bear in mind that in many instances the nature of the patent being enforced and the economic function of the patent holder present considerations quite unlike earlier cases. An industry has developed in which firms use patents not as a basis for producing and selling goods but, instead, primarily for obtaining licensing fees. See FTC, To Promote Innovation: The Proper Balance of Competition and Patent Law and Policy, ch. 3, pp. 38–39 (Oct. 2003), available at http://www.ftc.gov/os/2003/10/innovationrpt.pdf. For these firms, an injunction, and the potentially serious sanctions arising from its violation, can be employed as a bargaining tool to charge exorbitant fees to companies that seek to buy licenses to practice the patent. When the patented invention is but a small component of the product the companies seek to produce

> **CASE** *(continued)*
>
> and the threat of an injunction is employed simply for undue leverage in negotiations, legal damages may well be sufficient to compensate for the infringement and an injunction may not serve the public interest. In addition injunctive relief may have different consequences for the burgeoning number of patents over business methods, which were not of much economic and legal significance in earlier times. The potential vagueness and suspect validity of some of these patents may affect the calculus under the four-factor test.
>
> The equitable discretion over injunctions, granted by the Patent Act, is well suited to allow courts to adapt to the rapid technological and legal developments in the patent system. For these reasons it should be recognized that district courts must determine whether past practice fits the circumstances of the cases before them. With these observations, I join the opinion of the Court.

NOTES

1. The *eBay* case marks a major change not only in patent doctrine, but also in the awareness of the courts to the special problems of contemporary patent litigation. To begin, the Federal Circuit's "automatic injunction" rule meant that permanent injunctions were granted in almost every patent infringement case between the founding of the Federal Circuit in 1982 and the *eBay* case in 2006. That changed drastically. According to one detailed study:

    > [P]ermanent injunctions were granted slightly less than three-quarters of the time (72.5%) during the time period studied (May, 2006 to December, 2013). This figure is consistent with previous empirical scholarship on the rate of permanent injunctions following *eBay*, which range between 72% and 75%. However, it represents a decline from the state of play before *eBay*, when injunctions were granted to prevailing patentees in almost all cases (Christopher B. Seaman, *Permanent Injunctions in Patent Litigation After* Ebay: *An Empirical Study*, 101 Iowa L. Rev. 1949, 1983 (2016) (footnotes omitted)).

    See also Kirti Gupta & Jay P. Kesan, Studying the Impact of eBay on Injunctive Relief in Patent Cases 9 fig. 3 (July 10, 2015) (unpublished manuscript), http://papers.ssrn.com/sol3/papers.cfm?abstract_id=2629399 (finding permanent injunctions were granted in 80% of the cases studied after *eBay*).

    Although technically only a concurring opinion, the comments by Justice Kennedy (joined by three other Justices) have proven to be the most influential part of the opinion. This is because the Kennedy concurrence addresses the real heart of the issues that defendants such as eBay were complaining about in the lead-up to the Supreme Court case. The patentee in *eBay*, MercExchange, is not a software company or an online auction company; it does no real research or product development. MercExchange acquired the patents at issue in the *eBay* case, and then sued other companies for patent infringement. Although the patents were obtained by a company that was trying to make a product and sell it on the market, that company and that product never succeeded. So *eBay* raises questions about this general practice, where patents are acquired for the sole purpose of making money by licensing and, if necessary, through patent litigation. Although there is debate about the exact boundaries of the concept, MercExchange is widely thought to be an example of what is known as a "patent troll." Another term often used is "Patent Assertion Entity" (PAE). *See* Robert P. Merges, *The Trouble with Trolls: Innovation, Rent-Seeking, and Patent Law Reform*, 24 Berkeley Tech. L.J. 1583 (2009).

    It is absolutely clear from a study of the cases that the primary impact of *eBay* has been to make injunctions very difficult to obtain for patent trolls, or PAEs:

    > PAEs rarely obtained a permanent injunction after prevailing on liability (16%; 4 of 25 cases), while other patentees are successful in obtaining injunctions in the vast majority of cases (80%; 154 of 193 cases) . . .

This finding appears to lend weight to the view expressed in Justice Kennedy's concurrence that district courts should be reluctant to grant injunctions when the patentee is using the patent "not as a basis for producing and selling goods but, instead, primarily for obtaining licensing fees." . . . Even in the rare cases where a PAE was granted an injunction, the patentee was generally a failing or failed operating company that had previously sought to commercialize the patent and thus was only a non-practicing entity at the time of the injunction decision (Christopher B. Seaman, *Permanent Injunctions, supra*, at 1988–89).

In addition, denial of permanent injunctions is but one of many patent reforms introduced by courts and Congress to address the patent troll problem. The general concern is that patent litigation has grown too quickly, and that patents are being used more to drive law suit settlements than as the basis for innovation, new technologies, new companies, and new jobs – the traditional payoffs associated with patents.

2. The *eBay* case by its terms is only about permanent injunctions: the remedy sought after a patent case is completed. Another form of injunction that can be very important to patentees is the *preliminary* injunction. As its name implies, this form of injunction is sought before a patent case has been completed. It is in fact often sought by a patentee soon after a patent case is filed. In some cases, patentees need to prevent infringement while a patent trial is being conducted.

The standards for issuing a preliminary injunction are similar to those for a permanent injunction, with one important exception. Because this type of injunction is sought at the beginning of the trial, the patentee has to convince the court that it has a high likelihood of success on the merits of the case – that, when the case is completed, the patent will be found valid and infringed. *Celsis In Vitro, Inc. v. Cellz/Direct, Inc.*, 664 F.3d 922, 926 (Fed. Cir. 2012) (four-factor test for grant of preliminary injunction: 1) likelihood of success on the merits; 2) irreparable harm; 3) the balance of hardships; and 4) the public interest.). This means the court must conduct a hearing that provides a synopsis of the overall validity and infringement aspects of the patent trial. Courts are careful to distinguish these determinations from the final and complete resolution of issues after a full trial. *See Amazon.com, Inc. v. Barnesandnoble.com, Inc.*, 239 F.3d 1343, 1359–60 (Fed. Cir. 2001):

> [Defendant] has mounted a serious challenge to the validity of [patentee] Amazon's patent. We hasten to add, however, that this conclusion only undermines the prerequisite for entry of a preliminary injunction. Our decision today on the validity issue in no way resolves the ultimate question of invalidity. That is a matter for resolution at trial . . . All we hold, in the meantime, is that BN cast enough doubt on the validity of the patent to avoid a preliminary injunction, and that the validity issue should be resolved finally at trial).

The same is true for preliminary injunctions that are denied because of doubts about the patentee's ability to prove infringement at trial. *See, e.g., Hill-Rom Co. v. Gen. Elec. Co.*, No. 2:14CV187, 2014 WL 3544990, at *1 (E.D. Va. July 15, 2014) (significant questions regarding infringement led court to deny patentee's preliminary injunction motion).

3. When a permanent injunction is denied, the patentee may still recover "ongoing royalties" – monetary damages adequate to compensate the patentee for continuing infringement post-trial. *See* Christopher B. Seaman, *Ongoing Royalties in Patent Cases After eBay: An Empirical Assessment and Proposed Framework*, 23 Tex. Intell. Prop. L.J. 203 (2015) (reporting the results of an empirical study of ongoing royalty awards after *eBay*).

8.2 Injunctions in China

8.2.1 Preliminary injunction

The Supreme Court's Judicial Rules [Fa Shi No. 20 (2001)] stipulates the legal standard for issuing a preliminary injunction for patent infringement. In particular, it says that the people's court shall examine following aspects:

(1) whether or not the act which is being implemented or will be implemented by the party against whom an preliminary injunction request is filed constitutes an infringement of patent right;

(2) whether or not there will be irremediable harm to the legal rights and interests of the applicant, if a preliminary injunction is not issued;
(3) the applicant's provision of a bond; and
(4) whether or not a preliminary injunction (if issued) would impair the public interests.

The following case is an example showing how the court applied the above standard.

 CASE

Ju Li Integrated Chip Design Co. v. US SigmaTel, Inc., Dongguan City Gemei Electronic Technology Co. Ltd. and Huang Zhongda, Shanxi Province Xi'an Intermediate People's Court, Li Jun Zi [2007] No. 1, May 21, 2007

Ju Li Integrated Chip Design Co., Ltd. (hereinafter, "the applicant") filed an application to Xi'an Intermediate People's Court for a preliminary injunction against SigmaTel Inc., Dongguan City Gemei Electronic Technology Co., Ltd. and Huang Zhongda (hereinafter, collectively, "the respondents").

The applicant owns the Chinese Patent No. ZL01145044.4 titled "Over-sampling digital-analogue converter with variable sampling frequency" (hereinafter, "the Subject Patent"), which was filed on December 31, 2001 and granted on May 11, 2005.

Claim 1 of the Subject Patent reads as follows:

1. An oversampling digital-to-analog converter with variable sampling frequency, characterized by processing an input signal of different sampling frequency, the oversampling digital-to-analog converter comprising:

    a frequency upscaler, for up-scaling the frequency of said input signal with a factor of M so as to produce an oversampled signal;

    a digital low-pass filter, used for filtering out high frequency components of the up-scaled oversampled signal, and outputting data at a first rate;

    a data buffer, used for receiving output data from the digital low-pass filter at said first rate, and outputting data at a second data rate;

    a modulator, used for reading said data from said data buffer at the second data rate, and modulating the data;

    a digital-to-analog converter, for converting the modulated signal into an analog output signal; and

CASE (continued)

an analog low-pass filter, used for filtering out a high-frequency component of the analog signal to generate an output signal.

[The applicant asserts that,]

the U.S. SigmaTel Inc. had exported STMP35xx series multimedia player master chips to China. Dongguan City Gemei Electronic Technology Co., Ltd. imported the said multimedia player master chips, and used the chips to manufacture and sell MP3 players containing said chips. Huang Zhongda sold these MP3 players.

After conducting a technical analysis of the STMP35xx series multimedia player master chips, it finds all the features of the subject patent could be read on the chip, such that the respondents had infringed the subject patent.

[The applicant further asserted that,]

the IC design industry is a capital-intensive industry that requires enormous capital investment, and therefore, enforcement of its intellectual property right is of critical importance. Without the preliminary injunction, the applicant will suffer irreparable harm. In particular, the price of the patented product will plummet, and the petitioner's goodwill and reputation will be damaged.

[Relying on the above factors,] the applicant filed an application for a preliminary injunction. [Xi'an Intermediate People's Court held the following opinions,]

when a patent holder or an interested party can prove that another identity is infringing or is about to infringe his patent right, and such an infringement will cause irreparable harm, he can file a preliminary injunction request before the court. The applicant in the preliminary injunction proceeding must provide the following documents: (1) documents showing that the patent is authentic and valid, such as the certificate of patent right, an official receipt of annual fee payment, and also the claims and description of the patent; (2) the respondent is infringing or is about to infringe the patent, which can be proved by a technical comparison between the allegedly infringing product and the Subject Patent. The applicant also needs to provide a bond to cover the respondents' costs and damages if the application turns out to be filed in error and causing damage to the defendant. If any of the above conditions are not met, the preliminary injunction request will be rejected.

In the present case, Ju Li Ltd. provided the following evidence: a certificate of the patent right, the written claims and description, the official receipt of the annual fee payment, and a technical comparison between the allegedly infringing product and the patent, which constitutes a *prima facie* case of infringement; and finally, a bond.

[Because the application met all of the statutory requirements,] the Court decided to grant the preliminary injunction as follows:

CASE (continued)

1. Effective upon receipt of this ruling, the respondent SigmaTel Inc. shall stop exporting to China the chips that infringe the subject patent ZL01145044.4 "Over-sampling digital-analogue converter with variable sampling frequency."
2. Effective upon receipt of this ruling, the respondent Dongguan City Gemei Electronic Technology Co., Ltd. shall stop importing, using, and selling the chips that infringe the subject patent ZL01145044.4 "Over-sampling digital-analogue converter with variable sampling frequency."
3. Effective upon receipt of this ruling, the respondent Huang Zhongda shall stop selling the MP3 player containing the chips that infringe the subject patent ZL01145044.4 "Over-sampling digital-analogue converter with variable sampling frequency."

Judge Jianjun YAO

NOTES

1. Within 15 days after the preliminary injunction was issued, Ju Li Ltd. brought a lawsuit before the same court. During the trial, Ju Li Ltd. reached a settlement with the respondents, and subsequently, withdrew the litigation. Accordingly, the court lifted its preliminary injunction.
2. **Reconsideration Procedure for preliminary Injunction**. Paragraph 1 of Article 10 of Judicial Interpretations [2001] No. 20 states that "where the interested party is not satisfied with the ruling, he may apply for reconsideration within 10 days from the date of the receipt of the ruling." Thus, the parties can only file a reconsideration request to the same court, rather than appealing to a higher court against a ruling of preliminary injunction.
3. **Recent Development of Legal Standard for Preliminary Injunction**. In 2015, the Supreme Court published a working draft of Judicial Rules regarding preliminary injunction in IP and unfair competition disputes, and asked for public comments. In this draft, one additional factor to be considered is "balances of hardships to the parties."
4. **Preliminary Injunction in IP litigation of Game Industry**. In a recent IP litigation involving copyright, trademark, and unfair competition, *Blizzard Entertainment, Inc., NetEase, Inc. v. QiYou, etc.* ((2015) Yue Zhi Fa Zhu Min Chu Zi No. 2, (2015) Yue Zhi Fa Shang Min Chu Zi No. 2), Blizzard Inc. successfully obtained from Guangzhou IP court a preliminary injunction, which ordered QiYou to stop providing or operating the infringing game. In this case, Blizzard provided a bond of 10 million RMB, which is higher than the actual 6 million RMB damages awarded by the court later.
5. **Preliminary Injunction in IP litigation involving Reality TV Show "The Voice of China"**. In other IP litigation involving Reality TV show "The Voice of China", Beijing IP court issued a preliminary injunction against the 5th season of "The Voice of China" ((2016) Jing 73 Xing Bao No.1). Talpa Content B.V. is the licensor of the "Voice of . . ." TV format. The applicant Zhejiang Tak Television Corp. is the new licensee of the TV format "The Voice of China", while the respondent Shanghai Can Xing Culture Communication Co., Ltd. is the previous licensee. The applicant provided 130 million RMB as a bond. Later, the respondent changed the name of the TV show to "New Song of China."

Abbot Trading (Shanghai) Ltd. v. Taizhou Huangyan Yilong Ltd. and Beijing Yiyangjie Trading Ltd., Beijing Third Intermediate People's Court, (2013) San Zhong Min Bao Zi 01933 ((2013) 三中民保字第 01933), available at http://wenshu.court.gov.cn/content/content?DocID=c92dcd69-f74c-4a4c-b38d-49411dcbc8b7 (transl. on 6/5/2017)

Applicant Abbot Trading (Shanghai) Ltd. ("Abbott") filed an application to Beijing Third Intermediate People's Court for a preliminary injunction against Taizhou Huangyan Yilong Ltd. and Beijing Yiyangjie Trading Ltd. ("two defendants").

The applicant owns the Chinese Patent No. ZL200730158176.0, titled "Container" and was granted the right to file lawsuit against infringers in its own name. Abbot filed a pre-trial preliminary injunction request with the Beijing Third Intermediate People's Court once it found the two Chinese companies infringed the patent. Abbot filed a pre-trial preliminary injunction request with the Beijing Third Intermediate People's Court once it found the two Chinese companies infringed the patent. The standards for issuing a preliminary injunction taken by the Court are as follows:

(1) Whether the conduct of the defendants is being implemented or to be implemented constitute an infringement of the patent;
(2) If not to take any relevant measure, whether irreparable damage would be caused to the applicant;
(3) Whether the order of preliminary injunction would cause larger actual damage to the applicant;
(4) Whether the order of preliminary injunction would harm the public interest;
(5) Whether the applicant has provided security.

The Court analyzed the five-element standard and issued preliminary injunction.
 (1) The conduct of defendants infringed the patent of the applicant.
 Article 11, Section 2 of Chinese Patent Law provides exclusive protection to a design patent that no unit or individual may exploit the patent without permission of the patentee, i.e., it or he may not, for production or business purposes, manufacture, offer to sell, sell or import the design patent products. According to Section 2 of Article 59 of Chinese Patent Law, the scope of protection for the design patent right shall be confined to the design of

CASE *(continued)*

the product as shown in the drawings or pictures, and the brief description may be used to explain the said design as shown in the drawings or pictures.

Article 11 of Supreme People's Court interpretation on the trial of Patent Infringement Cases Application of Laws: The Court should judge the identity or similarity of the designs based on the patented design and the characteristics of the design patented and that alleged as a comprehensive overall visual effect. Those characteristics determined by technical functions or the materials and internal structures cannot affect the overall visual effect of the product should not be considered. There are two circumstances should be highly considered for the more influential roles they play on the design of the overall visual effect: (A) The parts of the product that can be observed more easily compared to the other parts; (B) The features of design distinguish the patented design.

The designs at issue are both container of milk powder within the same category of product. The difference between the patented design and the alleged design is too slight that the Court shall determine that both are the same. The overall visual has no substantial difference between the two designs.

Therefore, the conduct of defendants infringed the patent of the applicant.

(2) Irreparable damage would be caused to the applicant if no relevant measure is taken.

Designed products at issue are milk powder containers. It can be expected that the infringing products of the two Chinese companies will be sold to the consumers together with the milk powder. Each process of the sale sells the infringing products and thus broadens the loss towards the patent owner, Abbott. If no relevant measure is taken, damage caused to Abbott would expand and be hard to calculate.

(3) The failure to order a preliminary injunction would cause larger actual damage to the applicant.

The loss to the two Chinese companies after the order of preliminary injunction is predictable, as the order of preliminary injunction will stop them from benefiting from the infringing conduct. However, the loss to Abbott if it fails to order a preliminary injunction is unpredictable. Once the infringing products run into market, it is hard to calculate the actual damage resulting from the use of the infringing products; much less possible to calculate the irreparable damage towards Abbott. Therefore, remedies available at law, such as monetary damages, are inadequate to compensate for the injury if not to order a preliminary injunction to stop the infringing conduct of the two Chinese companies.

(4) The public interest would not be disserved by a preliminary injunction.

There is nothing to prove any harm will be caused to the public interest if a preliminary injunction is ordered to the two Chinese companies.

(5) The applicant has provided 4,000,000 RMB in cash as security. Thus, considering the balance of hardships between the plaintiff and defendant, a remedy in equity is warranted.

Therefore, the Court granted a preliminary injunction to the two Chinese companies.

NOTES

1. **The Abbott case is the first patent infringement case granting preliminary injunction order in the Beijing area.** Pre-trial preliminary injunction is available under the Chinese Patent Law. Because the application of pre-trial preliminary injunction may stop the infringement quickly, it is usually regarded as an effective means to stop patent infringement in patent infringement cases. However, in the judicial practice in China, it is quite rare that Chinese courts grant pre-trial preliminary injunction in patent infringement cases. For example, in the Beijing area, no preliminary injunction order was ever granted in patent infringement cases before 2013. Except for other reasons, the major reason is that it is difficult to determine whether the "irreparable damage" has been caused as it is a pre-condition to grant the pre-trial preliminary injunction. This situation was changed in 2013 because of the *Abbott* case.

2. **In China, the use of actual losses instead of lost profits when determining the order of preliminary injunction.** According to Article 65 of the Chinese Patent Law,

    > the amount of compensation for patent infringement shall be determined according to the patentee's actual losses caused by the infringement. If it is hard to determine the actual losses, the amount of compensation may be determined according to the benefits acquired by the infringer through the infringement. If it is hard to determine the losses of the patentee or the benefits acquired by the infringer, the amount of compensation may be determined according to the reasonably multiplied amount of the royalties of that patent. The amount of compensation shall include the reasonable expenses paid by the patentee for putting an end to the infringement. If the losses of the patentee, benefits of the infringer, or royalties of the patent are all hard to determine, the Court may, on the basis of the factors such as the type of patent, nature of the infringement, and seriousness of the case, determine the amount of compensation within the range from 10,000 RMB to 1,000,000 RMB.

    In China, the amount of actual losses is used as an element to test whether the order of preliminary injunction should be granted.

3. **The influence of this case.** This case was recognized by the Supreme Court in April 2014 as one of the five typical cases, which shows that the Supreme Court had affirmed and supported the Beijing court's standard on the determination of "irreparable damage." Moreover, in February 2015, the Supreme Court published a proposed judicial interpretation on some legal issues in the Act and invited public input. In the draft interpretation, the Supreme Court tried to clarify the instances of "irreparable damage." For example, in Article 8 of the interpretation, it is pointed out that "irreparable damage" is the situation in which damage could not be cured or calculated by money. Examples may be as follows: (1) occurrence or persistence of the act would seize the petitioner's market share or force the petitioner to sell well below its normal market, thus seriously undermining the petitioner's competitive advantage; (2) occurrence or persistence of the act would lead to subsequent infringements that would be difficult to control, and significantly increase the damage caused to the petitioner; (3) occurrence or persistence of the act would cause harm to the personal right of the petitioner; (4) the adverse party would be unable to compensate the petitioner. The following situations are generally not regarded as "irreparable damage" being caused to the petitioner: (1) the petitioner knows or should know the existence of the act but unreasonably delays in seeking judicial relief; (2) no reasonable grounds for not using or planning to implement the relevant intellectual property rights; (3) damage caused to the petitioner may be easily calculated in money. This is a major test, and a major departure from it should not be lightly implied.

8.2.2 Permanent injunctions in China

"In most of the past cases of China, once a patent is judged to be infringed, a permanent injunction is subsequently granted to end the patent infringement" (Cui Guobin, Patent Law Cases and Materials, Peking University Press, 2nd edition, 2016, at 818). It is obvious that the rule of permanent injunction in China benefits the patent owner much more than that provided by the US permanent injunction. But there exists a tendency to balance the outcomes of granting a preliminary injunction and a permanent injunction after the judgment of patent infringement. (Cui Guobin, *supra*, at 819.) The standard of the four-element test in the *eBay* case seems to have some influence in Chinese jurisdictions.

8.3 Injunctions in Europe

The German Patent Act says this about the availability of an injunction:

> The injured party may, where there is a risk of recurrence, bring an action for an injunction against any person who uses a patented invention in breach of Paragraphs 9 to 13. The injured party shall also have that right if an infringement is liable to be committed for the first time (Paragraph 139(1) of the Law on Patents (Patentgesetz, BGBl. 1981 I, p. 1, at par. 139(1), as amended most recently by Paragraph 13 of the Law of 24 November 2011 (BGBl. 2011 I, p. 2302).

Under this provision, German courts traditionally grant injunctions – both preliminary and permanent – quite liberally and frequently in patent cases. (This is one reason why, post-*eBay* in the US, German courts have become popular venues for patent owners engaged in transnational patent disputes.)

> If infringement is found [by a German court], it will, in the initial infringement action, usually award an injunction and a claim for disclosure of information [pertaining to damages], enabling the patentee to calculate the amount that can be sought as damages. Most parties settle the amount of damages out of court, after either the district court or the appellate court awards an injunction and the claim for information (Toshiko Takenaka, Christopher Rademacher et al., Patent Enforcement in the U.S., Germany and Japan (2015), at 403.)

See also Christopher Rademacher, "Injunctive Relief in Patent Cases in the US, Germany and Japan – Recent Developments and Outlook," in Intellectual Property Systems in Common Law and Civil Law Countries (Toshiko Takenaka, ed., 2013), at 325; Katrin Cremers, Fabian Gaessler, Dietmar Harhoff, Christian Helmers, & Yassine Lefouili, *Invalid but Infringed? An Analysis of the Bifurcated Patent Litigation System*, 131 J. Econ. Beh. & Org. 218 (2016).

The case that follows is an important recent case from Germany, yet its importance rests in part on how its holding diverges from the conventional German practice just described. To understand this case, one needs to be familiar with an earlier decision of the Court of Justice of the EU, *Huawei Technologies Co. Ltd v. ZTE Corp.*, Case C-170/13 (Court of Justice of the

European Union (CJEU) (former European Court of Justice (ECJ)), 16 July 2015), available at http://curia.europa.eu/juris/document/document.jsf?text=&docid=165911&pageIndex=0&doclang=EN&mode=lst&dir=&occ=first&part=1&cid=509527. In this case, the ECJ had to decide whether, under the facts presented, a failure to license the patents in question amounted to an anticompetitive act – the "abuse of a dominant position" as is expressed in German law (and in various other national laws in Europe and elsewhere). The alleged abuse here occurred, the defendant/accused infringer said, because the plaintiff/patentee Huawei had joined a technical standards group in the technology area covered by the patents. Under procedures applied by the group, it was decided that the Huawei patents were necessary to implement the technical standard. In other words, to comply with the technical standard (which related to the transfer of information from a mobile phone to and from mobile base stations, using radio frequency transmissions to encode data), a company had to use procedures that would necessarily infringe the patents. This made those patents so-called "Standard-Essential Patents," or "SEPs."

Part of the obligation that Huawei (and other group members) undertake when joining a standards group is to license all SEPs it owned under "Fair, Reasonable, and Non-discriminatory" terms (often called "FRAND Licensing"). The defendant ZTE here argued that, under the facts, the patent owner Huawei did not comply with its FRAND licensing commitment, and hence that seeking an injunction from the German court would amount to an abuse of a dominant position. The non-compliance was the result, the defendant argued, of the fact that Huawei never offered a clear license setting out the royalty rate to be applied to the patents at issue.

Thus when Huawei initiated infringement litigation without having made this offer, the defendant argued, Huawei violated the Treaty on the Functioning of the European Union (TFEU), Article 102, which reads: "Any abuse by one or more undertakings of a dominant position within the internal market or in a substantial part of it shall be prohibited as incompatible with the internal market in so far as it may affect trade between Member States." TFEU section 102 has been implemented in German law via Paragraphs 19 and 20 of the Law against Restrictions of Competition (Gesetz gegen Wettbewerbsbeschränkungen) of 26 June 2013 (BGBl. 2013 I, p. 1750). The CJEU accepted the referral in this case to clarify this issue, and spoke as follows regarding the abuse of dominant position objection to the grant of an injunction:

> [T]he proprietor of an SEP which considers that that SEP is the subject of an infringement cannot, without infringing Article 102 TFEU, bring an action for a

prohibitory injunction or for the recall of products against the alleged infringer without notice or prior consultation with the alleged infringer, even if the SEP has already been used by the alleged infringer.

Prior to such proceedings, it is thus for the proprietor of the SEP in question, first, to alert the alleged infringer of the infringement complained about by designating that SEP and specifying the way in which it has been infringed...

Secondly, after the alleged infringer has expressed its willingness to conclude a licensing agreement on FRAND terms, it is for the proprietor of the SEP to present to that alleged infringer a specific, written offer for a licence on FRAND terms, in accordance with the undertaking given to the standardisation body, specifying, in particular, the amount of the royalty and the way in which that royalty is to be calculated...

[W]here the proprietor of an SEP has given an undertaking to the standardisation body to grant licences on FRAND terms, it can be expected that it will make such an offer. Furthermore, in the absence of a public standard licensing agreement, and where licensing agreements already concluded with other competitors are not made public, the proprietor of the SEP is better placed to check whether its offer complies with the condition of non-discrimination than is the alleged infringer.

[I]t is for the alleged infringer diligently to respond to that offer, in accordance with recognised commercial practices in the field and in good faith, a point which must be established on the basis of objective factors and which implies, in particular, that there are no delaying tactics.

Should the alleged infringer not accept the offer made to it, it may rely on the abusive nature of an action for a prohibitory injunction or for the recall of products only if it has submitted to the proprietor of the SEP in question, promptly and in writing, a specific counter-offer that corresponds to FRAND terms.

Furthermore, where the alleged infringer is using the teachings of the SEP before a licensing agreement has been concluded, it is for that alleged infringer, from the point at which its counter-offer is rejected, to provide appropriate security, in accordance with recognised commercial practices in the field, for example by providing a bank guarantee or by placing the amounts necessary on deposit. The calculation of that security must include, inter alia, the number of past acts of use of the SEP, and the alleged infringer must be able to render an account in respect of those acts of use.

In addition, where no agreement is reached on the details of the FRAND terms following the counter-offer by the alleged infringer, the parties may, by common agreement, request that the amount of the royalty be determined by an independent third party, by decision without delay (*Huawei Technologies Co. Ltd v. ZTE Corp*, at pars. 60–68).

CASE

Assertion of standard essential patents (Geltendmachung standardessentieller Patente), Case No. 7 O 209/15, BeckRS 2016, 18389 (District Court (Landesgericht), Mannheim, 1 July 2016)

PatG §§ 139, 9; TFEU Art. 102

1. The proprietor of a standard essential patent shall notify the alleged infringer of the infringement, so that the latter can examine the protective right. If the alleged infringer is licensed, the patentee must provide him with an acceptable license agreement on FRAND terms, specifying the method of calculating the license rate.
2. The patent proprietor can not make up these steps, if they are not subject to pre-litigation, in the process. The action must then be dismissed with regard to the claims for omission, recall and removal from the distribution channels. (Conventions of the author)

[This was a patent infringement case involving EU patents 1,062,743 and 1,062,745, both in effect in Germany, both entitled "Radio Communication System," and both assigned to Philips N.V. In the first part of its decision, the court held that the defendant had infringed both patents. The court issued an order for the defendant/accused infringer to produce information to allow the plaintiff/patent owner to calculate damages. In the second part of the opinion, the court turns to the issue of an injunction. Patent owner Philips had requested the grant of an injunction, which as mentioned is routine in patent cases in Germany. But the defendant objected, on the grounds that the normal injunction remedy would, if granted here, violate the CJEU's holding in *Huawei v. ZTE*. The court responded as follows to the plaintiff's request for several traditional remedies under German patent law, including an injunction and the recall of infringing products from the market.]

[T]he complaint must be rejected to the extent that Plaintiff is additionally seeking an injunction, a recall, the removal from distribution channels, and the destruction of patent-infringing products. Access to such remedies is barred by antitrust law in light of the opinion of the Court of Justice of the European Union in *Huawei v. ZTE*.

a) In the [court's] opinion, the [CJEU] stressed that only under very special circumstances is [a patent] unenforceable in an infringement proceeding. As a result, any factual circumstances that allegedly outweigh patent law have to be pled and, if in dispute, proven by the accused infringer.

CASE *(continued)*

The [CJEU] developed in its opinion a concept that is meant to enable courts to assess the behavior of the SEP holder as well as that of the alleged infringer. [The idea is to assess] whether the enforcement of SEP-based injunctive relief and a recall must be deemed an unjustified abuse of a market position – a means of exerting pressure on a negotiating party of a kind that cannot be accepted. [The alternative is to decide] whether [the requested injunction] must be deemed an appropriate response to dilatory tactics employed by the (alleged) infringer. However, the court is convinced that the [CJEU] opinion does not intend to place the burden of a determination of FRAND [licensing] terms on courts hearing infringement cases in which injunctive relief and a recall – but not a collection of FRAND licensing fees as in a subsequent proceeding – are sought.

To achieve this objective, the [CJEU] deems it necessary [for] the patent holder [to satisfy a prerequisite condition, before bringing] a complaint containing a prayer for injunctive relief and a recall. [This is because such a requested remedy] exerts massive pressure on the alleged infringer at the negotiating table. [The prerequisite is this: the plaintiff/patent owner must] notif[y] an alleged infringer of the asserted infringement, specifying the relevant SEP and stating in which way it is allegedly infringed. At a minimum, the patent holder will have to specify the declared-essential patent-in-suit based on its patent number and will have to state that this patent was declared essential to a standard in a notice to the relevant standard-setting organization.

At a minimum, it is required that the patent holder states which technical functionality of the accused devices implements the standard. Normally, the accused infringer will be aware of the fact that the device is designed to comply with the standard. Therefore, a mere reference to the fact that the alleged infringer makes or sells standard-compliant products is an insufficient infringement notice. Much to the contrary, the notice must enable the alleged infringer to perform or outsource an analysis of the legal situation. Due to the great diversity of technical functions that are typically defined in an industry standard and, especially, in light of the [CJEU's] mentioning of the difficulties in assessing the legal situation, it is a requirement that the SEP holder, at a minimum, specify the category of the technical functionality of the standard in such a way that the alleged infringer is enabled to meet its general obligation of analyzing the legal situation.

The level of detail required for this notice can only be adjudicated on a case-by-case and context-specific basis. In this analysis, it must be taken into consideration what level of technical knowledge the infringer has or [how easily] such knowledge can be obtained by him, in the form of professional advice, on a reasonably acceptable basis. In the court's opinion, the [CJEU's] requirements for a substantiation of the infringement allegation is generally met by presenting claim charts of the kind customarily presented in licensing negotiations, provided that they recite the asserted claim of the patent-in-suit or a related claim that also has the determinative elements, structured on the basis of claim limitations compared to the relevant passages of the specification of the standard. [Such claim charts] do not have to meet the requirements that an infringement complaint has to meet in order to survive a motion to dismiss. Therefore, it is usually sufficient that the alleged infringer

> **CASE** *(continued)*
>
> can understand the allegation brought by the SEP holder, at a minimum by externally or internally seeking technical expert advice.
>
> The same applies to the SEP holder's further obligation to submit, prior to bringing a complaint against an alleged infringer who has expressed a willingness in principle to take a license, a specific licensing offer on FRAND terms and to particularly specify the license fee and its derivation. In light of the aforementioned interpretation of the [CJEU] opinion by the court, this entails the requirement that the offer be [in a form that may be formally accepted by the alleged infringer, *i.e.*, a true offer] and contain the essential terms and conditions. The [CJEU's] statement that the patent holder has to submit a specific written licensing offer on FRAND terms does not mean that the court hearing an infringement case has to make a determination as to whether or . . . not the SEP holder's offer is actually fair, reasonable and non-discriminatory. Otherwise the infringement proceedings would . . . face the burden of having to determine which amount of license fees and which other contractual terms precisely meet those criteria. A licensing offer is contrary to antitrust law and evidently not FRAND only if in light of the specific situation in the negotiations between the parties and in light of market conditions it represents exploitative abuse.
>
> In this regard, the patent holder has to state the method of calculating the license fee. In the court's opinion, the SEP holder must enable the alleged infringer to appreciate on the basis of objective criteria the reasons for which the SEP holder is convinced of the proposed terms meeting FRAND criteria. It is insufficient that an SEP holder proposing a license agreement involving a per-unit fee merely states that per-unit fee without explaining why that amount is deemed to meet FRAND criteria. Therefore, the SEP holder has to shed light on the amount in communications with the alleged infringer, such as by reference to a standard licensing program that is commonly practiced and accepted by third parties or by pointing to other figures from which the royalty sought is derived, such as a pool license fee, which is actually paid for a license to a patent pool by third parties, provided that the pool also contains patents relevant to the standard in question.
>
> The [alleged] infringer must respond to this offer even if – as [would be expected] – he does not deem it to meet FRAND criteria . . .
>
> In the court's opinion, an exception herefrom is warranted exclusively in such cases in which the SEP holder's offer is, based on a summary determination, evidently not FRAND and, therefore, constitutes an abuse of a dominant market position by the SEP holder. The counterproposal must be submitted without undue delay, given that the [CJEU] does not support dilatory tactics by alleged infringers. Therefore, the alleged infringer has to respond to the SEP holder's specific written offer as promptly as it can be reasonably expected of him given the specific circumstances of the case and in light of industry practice and the good-faith principle.
>
> If the SEP holder rejects this [the alleged infringer's counterproposal] and the alleged infringer was already implementing the SEP prior to concluding a license agreement, the [CJEU] requires a bond or deposit that stands as reasonable surety from the moment the counterproposal is rejected. The calculation of the amount of the surety must, among other

CASE *(continued)*

things, involve the number of past acts of infringement of the SEP in question, for which the alleged infringer must be able to provide an accounting. The surety furthermore has to meet commonly accepted principles in the relevant field.

b) An application of the test laid out herein precludes Plaintiff, for antitrust reasons, from enforcing the [relevant forms of] relief sought in the present case.

aa) In the present case, ... [p]laintiff has failed to meet its obligation of providing transparency to Defendant as to why it believes the $1 [per-unit] royalty sought to be FRAND or why ... it is within the FRAND-related wiggle room granted to it [under related rulings by other district courts in the wake of the *Huawei v. ZTE* decision]. Instead, Plaintiff merely quantified the $1 per-unit royalty in its offer. The [court here] holds that a mere statement of factors to a multiplication falls short of the [CJEU's] requirements. The general presentation of a UMTS [technical standard; part of the long term evolution or LTE mobile standard package] licensing program ... also fail to provide further information capable of meeting the related [transparency] obligation.

Plaintiff provided [a rationale for its $1 per device royalty demand, by way of an expert's report,] which allegedly proves that Plaintiff is not seeking a discriminatory royalty rate from Defendant. Such pleading and production of evidence occurred after bringing the complaint and is, therefore, not capable of complying with the [CJEU's] intent that negotiations take place without the burden of a litigation aimed at injunctive relief, a recall, or removal and destruction [of infringing products]. Therefore, the [court] interprets the [CJEU's] list of requirements as requiring, prior to bringing a complaint, not only a notice of the accused infringement, but also of the method with which the license fee sought by the SEP holder has been calculated. The alleged infringer cannot make a decision in the course of negotiations as to whether he is willing to accept transparent FRAND terms and to take a license unless the method underlying the royalty computation has been substantiated prior to bringing the complaint ... Even if it should be procedurally possible to meet previously-unmet requirements at a later stage, by withdrawing the original complaint and refiling after meeting the obligations, it must be ensured that in this case there will be a sufficient amount of time between the withdrawal of the original complaint and its refiling for negotiating without the immediate pressure resulting from a pending litigation. Even if the SEP holder makes up for previously, in the original proceedings, failing to provide the required explanation, he will have to grant the alleged infringer, prior to refiling the complaint, a certain amount of time during which Defendant can evaluate the arguments presented to buttress the methodology underlying the royalty calculation and relating to the question of whether the royalty sought meets FRAND criteria.

If we did not impose restrictions on how the SEP holder can, without sanctions, correct for [its failure to] meet [FRAND-related] obligations prior to bringing the complaint, this would run counter to the guiding principle of the [CJEU's] opinion, according to which negotiations must take place without the burden of a pending litigation, but on the basis of having all information enabling an assessment of whether or not a proposed license agreement is FRAND-compliant.

CASE (continued)

In the present case, Plaintiff was not relieved from this obligation on the basis of Defendant having been an unwilling licensee. Even if, in the course of negotiations, Defendant may have occasionally refused to make a payment of license fees, the [court] cannot conclude that Defendant had generally presented itself as an unwilling licensee [citing correspondence from Defendant/accused infringer, in which it requested clarification of the rationale for the patent owner's royalty demand.]. Furthermore, Defendant's willingness to take a license manifests itself in an offer, prior to this litigation, to transfer certain patents from its own portfolio, regardless of the circumstance that Plaintiff rejected that proposal for not considering it attractive. Defendant's willingness to discuss with Plaintiff a license is also proven by the fact that Defendant obtained [an] expert report . . . in order to buttress the license fee it deemed FRAND. While this occurred only after the complaint was brought, it still reflects in the court's opinion a willingness in principle to negotiate a license agreement . . .

The court furthermore views as an indication of Defendant's willingness in principle to take a license the circumstance that Defendant has meanwhile made a significant [monetary] deposit with a court [by way of an escrow or bond payment], allegedly covering its sales [of SEP-covered] products around the globe. Even though this occurred only after the complaint had been brought, this circumstance at least enables us to conclude, on the basis of indicia, that Defendant is a willing licensee, which reinforces the court's holding that Defendant . . . is not generally an unwilling licensee.

[Injunction denied.]

NOTES

1. It is crucial to understand, as emphasized in the introduction to this section, just how unusual the preceding opinion is in the overall context of German patent law. *See* Florian Mueller, "Nokia wins German patent injunction against all HTC Android devices including the One series," FOSSPatents Blog, Dec. 20, 2013, available at http://www.fosspatents.com/2013/12/nokia-wins-german-patent-injunction.html.

    HTC can and undoubtedly will appeal this ruling. But in the meantime, unless HTC manages to convince the appeals court right away that it is more likely than not to succeed with its appeal (a reasonably high hurdle), Nokia can enforce this injunction (including a recall of infringing devices from resellers and commercial users) on a provisional basis by posting a 400 million euro ($550 million) bond or giving security to the same amount. This is a permanent – not preliminary – injunction following an early first hearing held in October 2012 and a full trial held in 2013.

2. The law of preliminary injunctions in Germany has some interesting features. First, urgency or threatened imminent harm is a crucial factor. At the same time, however, courts usually require at least some indication that the patent at issue in the requested injunction is valid. This can be difficult: as explained, validity and infringement are pursued in separate legal actions in Germany. As a consequence, available evidence on a strong indication of validity can be hard to come by. *See* Thomas Cotter, "Hoppe-Jänisch on Important German Patent Cases Since 2013 (Part 2)," available at http://comparativepatentremedies.blogspot.com/2015/02/hoppe-janisch-on-important-german.html (summarizing article on German case law, including the law of preliminary injunctions).

Unwired Planet Int'l Ltd. v. Huawei Technologies Co. Ltd., [2017] EWHC 1304, EWHC (Pat) (UK), No. HP-2014-000005, 6/7/17, 2017 WL 01233380

[Mr. Justice Birss]

Unwired Planet have a worldwide patent portfolio which includes numerous patents which are declared essential to various telecommunications standards (2G GSM, 3G UMTS, and 4G LTE). Most of the relevant portfolio was acquired from Ericsson. Unwired Planet's business is licensing those patents to companies who make and sell telecommunications equipment such as mobile phones and infrastructure. This action began in March 2014 when Unwired Planet sued Huawei, Samsung and Google for infringement of six UK patents from their portfolio. Five were claimed to be SEPs (see below). Unwired Planet contended their patents were infringed and (so far as relevant) essential.

This judgment arises from [a separate case involving the parties which] relates to the patents which are or are said to be Standards Essential Patents or SEPs. Part of the process of standardisation involves holders of patents which are essential to an international telecommunications standard declaring them as essential to the relevant standards body. In this case that body is the European Telecommunications Standards Institute (ETSI). The ETSI IPR Policy requires that a patentee declaring patents as essential to a standard commits to licensing those patents on FRAND terms.

After proceedings began, in April 2014, Unwired Planet made an open offer to the defendants to license its entire global portfolio (SEPs and non-SEPs). The defendants denied infringement/essentiality and contended the patents were invalid, counterclaiming for revocation. So, they said, no licence was needed. They also contended that Unwired Planet's offer was not FRAND. In addition, Huawei and Samsung raised defences and counterclaims based on breaches of competition law. This involved both arguments about Art 101 of the Treaty on the Functioning of the European Union (TFEU) relating to the Master Sale Agreement (MSA) whereby Unwired Planet acquired patents from Ericsson and arguments about Art 102 TFEU concerning abuse of dominant position. The allegation that the offer was not FRAND was pleaded as a breach of competition law.

For a UK SEP portfolio licence Unwired Planet's August 2016 proposals are:

i) for LTE: infrastructure 0.42%; mobile devices 0.55%;
ii) for GSM/UMTS: infrastructure 0.21%; mobile devices 0.28%.

Huawei's . . . [final] licensing proposal . . . proposed a licence under the whole of Unwired Planet's UK SEP portfolio. The UK portfolio rates were:

CASE *(continued)*

i)   for LTE: infrastructure 0.061%; mobile devices 0.059%;
ii) for UMTS: infrastructure 0.046%; mobile devices 0.046%;
iii) for GSM single mode: infrastructure 0.045%; mobile devices 0.045%.

[A]s the owner of SEPs, Unwired Planet is in a dominant position in the market for licences under those SEPs.

Huawei's stance before the court throughout this claim has been that because they were sued before FRAND terms were offered they have a defence to the injunction claim. That stance is founded on a narrow interpretation of Huawei v. ZTE which I have rejected. I am satisfied that the commencement of this action, including the claim for an injunction, was not an abuse of Unwired Planet's dominant position. The same goes for Unwired Planet's conduct during the proceedings. I reject the "premature litigation" [prong or theory] of abuse.

Should an injunction be granted?
The relevant patents have been found valid and infringed. Unwired Planet wish to enter into a worldwide licence. Huawei is willing to enter into a UK portfolio licence but refuses to enter into a worldwide licence. However a worldwide licence is FRAND and Unwired Planet are entitled to insist on it. In this case a UK only licence would not be FRAND. An injunction ought to be granted because Huawei stand before the court without a licence but have the means to become licensed open to them.

Were it not for the fact that Huawei did not engage with the terms of the worldwide draft, I would have been able to hand down this judgment with the worldwide terms fully settled. That has not proved possible. So in the exercise of my discretion I will not grant the injunction on the day this judgment is handed down in public. Normally when a judgment in a case of this complexity is handed down a date some few weeks afterwards is found for the consequential orders. I will deal with the injunction at that later hearing . . . Unwired Planet's legal team will be able to produce a clean copy of the worldwide licence in the form I have approved. They should file it at court and serve it on Huawei well in advance of the later hearing. I do not expect to hear any further argument about the terms since the time for that has passed. I will discuss the directions for this on the day the judgment is handed down.

[From the subsequent decision in this case, opinion of June 7, 2017, available at http://www.bailii.org/ew/cases/EWHC/Patents/2017/1304.html]

[I]n my judgment it is not irrelevant that the undertaking offered by Huawei is only offered now, after many years of litigation and after judgment has been handed down. If, from the outset, Huawei had given an unqualified undertaking to enter into whatever licence the court (including an appellate court) had decided was FRAND, then an injunction at this stage would not have been appropriate. Indeed Huawei argued that the terms of the qualification on the claim for an injunction sought by Unwired Planet from the beginning (main judgment paragraph 679–83) run counter to such an injunction. That would have

CASE *(continued)*

been a better point if Huawei had offered this undertaking at an earlier stage. It is also notable that Huawei argued, and I accepted, that the qualification was ineffective.

On the other hand the patentee's FRAND undertaking does make this situation very different from a normal IP case. The question is whether, given the FRAND undertaking, even a very belated undertaking to take whatever FRAND licence the court settles should mean that the court should refuse a FRAND injunction in the appropriate form. The possibility of an appeal has nothing to do with it because Huawei's ability to appeal is and can be protected whichever approach I take.

Huawei contend that absent an appeal they would sign the Settled Licence now. I do not doubt that but it is no different from the position of any defendant who changes their tune after they have lost a case. Throughout these proceedings Huawei have maintained a determined stance that they would not accept a worldwide licence in this way. It has been a fundamental issue. In my judgment the undertaking offered by Huawei now is too late. By refusing to offer an unqualified undertaking before trial and before judgment Huawei forced Unwired Planet to come to court and vindicate its rights. The right thing to do now is grant a FRAND injunction albeit one which will be stayed on terms pending appeal.

In summary:

i) A FRAND injunction will be granted. That is one which is discharged if the defendant enters into the FRAND licence. It will be stayed pending appeal.

ii) The declaration will provide that the Settled Licence represented the FRAND terms in these circumstances between these parties.

NOTES

1. The notion of a "FRAND injunction" is new with this case, perhaps; but in many ways the decision simply implements general principles that have been emerging from FRAND-related litigation for the past few years. The injunction as granted restrains Huawei from infringing the patents in Unwired Planet's global patent portfolio, but will have no effect once they enter into a FRAND license. It is a contemporary updating of the venerable instrument of an equitable remedy: a solution deemed fair, under the circumstances, by the considered judgment of the court. It might be described as a "contingent injunction": The injunction dissolves upon the contingency of the parties reaching a FRAND-compliant agreement. Notice too that the court has reviewed the non-royalty (non-money-related) terms of the proposed licensing agreement. This is an effort to prevent the prospective licensor, the patent holder, from stretching out the effective period of the injunction and inflicting financial pain on the licensee/defendant as a result.

2. Some of the best commentary on the *Huawei* case comes from Professor Thomas Cotter of the University of Minnesota Law School, author of the book Comparative Patent Remedies (2013). Prof. Cotter operates a blog, also called Comparative Patent Remedies; his commentary on the *Huawei* case can be found at *"Some Thoughts on Unwired Planet v. Huawei,"* April 17, 2017, available at http://comparativepatentremedies.blogspot.com/2017/04/some-thoughts-on-unwired-planet-v-huawei.html. *See also* Norman Siebrasse and Thomas F. Cotter, *The Value of the Standard*, 101 Minnesota L. Rev. 1159 (2017).

3. One of the many issues the court struggles with in the UK case excerpted above is how to handle the fact that it has jurisdiction only over infringement in the UK, whereas the parties operate (and ultimately seek a license for) worldwide sales and operations. Numerous ideas have been put forth on how to handle the

multinational realities of SEP licensing disputes. For one contemporary approach, see Jorge L. Contreras and Michael A. Eixenberger, "The Anti-Suit Injunction – A Transnational Remedy for Multi-Jurisdictional SEP Litigation," in *The Cambridge Handbook of Technical Standardization Law – Patent, Antitrust and Competition Law* (Jorge L. Contreras, ed., 2017, forthcoming), available at SSRN: https://ssrn.com/abstract=2966309:

> An anti-suit injunction is an interlocutory remedy issued by a court in one jurisdiction which prohibits a litigant from initiating or continuing parallel litigation in another jurisdiction or jurisdictions. Anti-suit injunctions thus contain litigation costs and reduce the likelihood of inconsistent results by ensuring that issues are resolved in one jurisdiction before they are litigated elsewhere. In the standards context, anti-suit injunctions can be particularly powerful tools for prospective licensees alleging that SEP holders have failed to comply with their FRAND licensing obligations. Specifically, a court reviewing a SEP holder's compliance with a FRAND licensing commitment may issue an anti-suit injunction to prevent the SEP holder from bringing foreign patent infringement claims (including injunctions against the sale of infringing products) until the FRAND licensing dispute has been resolved in the issuing jurisdiction.

4. As with the German cases discussed earlier, be aware that the SEP cases, particularly in the mobile phone industry, are very much not the norm in UK patent litigation. As one court said, "[W]hile the [UK] Patents Court always retains a discretion whether or not to grant an injunction following a finding of infringement [,] and ... may exercise that discretion for example by delaying the final injunction in some cases, it is very rare for such an injunction to be refused altogether." *Magnesium Elektron Ltd v. Molycorp Chemicals and Oxides (Europe) Ltd*, [2016] R.P.C. 18, [2015] EWHC 3596 (Pat), at par. 38. For a rare exception, see *Proctor v. Bayley* [1889] 6 RPC 538 (Ct. App.), 42 Ch. D. 390 [1889] (final injunction refused in patent case because, although the defendant had been found to infringe, the court did not accept there was any basis to infer that there would be a continuance of the wrongful activity).

5. On preliminary relief in the UK, see *Warner-Lambert Co. LLC v. Actavis Group PTC EHF*, [2015] R.P.C. 25, [2015] EWCA Civ 556 (affirming denial of preliminary relief, i.e., injunction, in pharmaceutical patent infringement case).

8.4 Damages in the US

What harm does a patentee suffer when someone infringes a patent? In general, the harm is the economic loss that results when the patentee experiences competition beyond what he or she would have experienced in the absence of the infringement. In short: It is the dollar value of the loss in exclusivity. The patent was supposed to keep out competitors; but the infringer entered the market. The job of patent damages is to reconstruct what *would have happened* if the infringer had not competed with the patentee.

The simplest version of this scenario is where (1) the patentee's patent covers a single, complete product sold into a discrete economic market; (2) as a result of the patent, the patentee has the right to exclude all competitors from this market; and (3) every sale that is actually made by the infringer after the infringement begins would have been made instead by the patentee, if only there had been no infringement.

In this simple case, patent damages reward a "deserving monopolist" (the patentee) for the wrongful loss of its monopoly profits. A patent infringer enters the patentee's market and competes. This reduces the patentee/

monopolist's profits. In a simple case, the patentee and infringer are the only competitors. As damages, the infringer must pay the difference between (1) the patentee's profits in the presence of the infringer, and (2) the monopoly profits the patentee *would have earned* if the infringer had not been in the market. The market with the patentee and infringer is known as a "duopoly" – *i.e.*, a two-seller market. A duopoly is better for consumers than a monopoly even though the price for a good under duopoly may be higher than it would be under ideal conditions (*i.e.*, "perfect competition") – *i.e.*, with many competitors and with ease of entry.

The best illustration of the simple case is a patent covering a pharmaceutical product or medical device that requires approval by the federal agency charged with drug and device safety, the Food and Drug Administration. For drugs, a single patent (usually on the active ingredient or "small molecule" responsible for treating a disease or medical condition) may well cover a single product, which is sold on a distinct market. In this case, the patent truly does confer a true economic monopoly on the patentee. *See, e.g., American Medical Systems Inc. v. Medical Engineering Corp.*, 794 F. Supp. 1370, 1393 (E.D. Wis. 1992), aff'd in part, rev'd in part & remanded, 6 F.3d 1523 (Fed. Cir. 1993), cert. denied, 511 U.S. 1070 (1994) (no adequate alternative available on the market for the patentee's patented medical device; awarding $906,806 in lost profits due to infringement).

In many other cases, however, the nature of the technology and the market realities governing the conditions under which the patented technology is sold raise questions. Of particular interest are these two: (1) does the patent cover an entire product, or only one part or component of a product?; and (2) what are the competitive conditions under which this product is sold – what is the nature of the market and who competes in it? The following case, though dating from the nineteenth century, provides a good introduction to these issues.

8.4.1 Lost profits

Yale Lock Mfg. Co. v. Sargent, 117 U.S. 536 (1886)

Justice Blatchford.
[The invention in this case, claimed by U.S. Patent RE 4,696, granted to Sargent, January 2,

CASE (continued)

1872, is for a combination lock for use on a strongbox or safe that is hard to break into or "pick." The key to this lock, so to speak, is that the wheels in the combination portion, which are spun to form the right combination to open the lock, are isolated mechanically from the deadbolt that actually opens the safe. Figure 8.1 shows the wheels of the lock; the isolated engagement mechanism that contacts the deadbolt is shown at element E in the diagram.]

Figure 8.1 Patented lock design

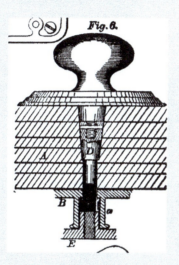

On the question of damages, the defendant contends that there was no sufficient or legal proof that the plaintiff suffered the damages reported and adjudged, or any other damages. The action of the master, the character of the exceptions to his report, and the view taken by the circuit court, are fully shown by its opinion, which [found that, due to the presence of the infringer's competing product on the market, the patentee Sargent lowered the price of one model of lock (the "number 3 model") by $1, and lowered the price on a second model (the "number 5") by $2. The master also found, however, that the infringer's locks included a feature that was not present in the patentee's locks – the "Rosner device" (which permits re-setting the combination by using a small key in the back of the lock; see George Rosner, U.S. Patent No. 30,092, "Permutation Lock," reissued July 25, 1871). Because the Rosner device was popular, the master concluded that only one half of the patentee's reduction in sales was due to the presence of the infringing feature; the other one half is attributable to the non-patented additional feature. And so "the plaintiff is entitled to recover from the defendant, as damages, one-half of the amount of the reduction in prices caused by the defendant since January 2, 1872; that is, on 1,009 No. 3 locks, $1 per lock, being $1,009, and on 13,524 No. 5 locks, at 50c. per lock, $6,762; being a total of $7,771."]

This is a case where the patentee granted no licenses, and had no established license fee, but supplied the demand for his lock himself. The market for the lock was limited to safe makers. No one but a safe maker wanted or would buy such a lock. The master was unable

CASE (continued)

to determine, from the proofs, what profits, if any, the defendant had made from the use of the turning bolt. He disallowed all items of damage from the loss to the plaintiff of the sale of infringing locks sold by the defendant, and confined his award to the enforced reduction of price on the locks which the plaintiff sold, caused by the infringement.

That this is a proper item of damages, if proved, is clear. It is a pecuniary injury caused by the infringement, and is the subject of an award of damages, although the defendant may have made no profits and the plaintiff may have had no established license fee. As the plaintiff, at the time of the infringement, availed himself of his exclusive right by keeping his patent a monopoly, and granting no licenses, the difference between his pecuniary condition after the infringement, and what his condition would have been if the infringement had not occurred, is to be measured, so far as his own sales of locks are concerned, by the difference between the money he would have realized from such sales if the infringement had not interfered with such monopoly, and the money he did realize from such sales. If such difference can be ascertained by proper and satisfactory evidence, it is a proper measure of damages.

The damages to be recovered are 'actual damages;' and they may properly include such losses to the plaintiff as were allowed in this case. The turning bolt was the essential feature of the Sargent lock. The defendant adopted Sargent's arrangement, and then reduced the price of the lock, forcing Sargent to do the same, in order to hold his trade. The evidence shows that the reduction of prices by Sargent was solely due to the defendant's infringement. The only competitor with Sargent in the use of his turning-bolt arrangement, during the period covered by the accounting, was the defendant. We think the master made proper allowances for all other causes which could have affected the plaintiff's prices; that the proper deduction was made for the use of the Rosner device in the defendant's lock; and that the damages awarded are no greater than the testimony warranted. The decision that the plaintiff, as owner of the patent, was entitled to recover the damages, was correct.

NOTES AND QUESTIONS

1. Students of economics are accustomed to think of "monopoly profits" as a bad thing. Monopolies allow a single seller to sell a product at a higher price than it would under competitive conditions. Indeed, one important goal of antitrust law is to root out illicit monopolies, so as to encourage competition and therefore help consumers. When it comes to patent damages, however, monopoly profits are a *good thing*: they are the deserved reward for an inventor who has contributed something valuable to society. The patentee, then, is a sort of "virtuous monopolist" who has earned the right to exclude competitors and therefore enforce the deserved monopoly. Where a patent truly confers an economic monopoly, the goal of patent damages is to figure out how much harm the "virtuous monopolist" suffered at the hands of the "wrongful competitor" (the infringer).

2. In *Yale Lock*, the Supreme Court agreed with the fact finder in the case (a special master) in saying that the safe locks at issue had several features that were important to customers who purchased the plaintiff's safes. This explains why the court did not give the patentee all the damages it had asked for. The patentee had asked the court to give in damages all the profit that was lost due to the lower price for safes when the infringer/competitor entered the market. The court decided, however, that only half of the price reduction

that occurred when the infringer entered the market could be recovered as infringement damages. The other half was attributable not to "wrongful competition" (infringement) for the patented feature, but to another important feature that was not covered by the patent claim (the Rosner device). Consumers purchased safes from the defendant, in other words, for two reasons: (1) the safes included the patented feature (which was wrongful, *i.e.*, infringed a patent); and (2) the safes included the Rosner device, which the patentee's safes did not have and which consumers liked. The special master assigned to the case had to figure out what portion of the harm suffered by the patentee was attributable to the patent infringement, and what portion came from consumers' appreciation for the Rosner device. Only the first component – only the portion of plaintiff's harm that came from patent infringement – was properly compensable under the Patent Act.

As the relatively simple case of *Yale Lock* demonstrates, patents typically cover technological components: small pieces of larger technologies. Today, a patent may cover only one very small component of a very large and complex multi-component product: a part of a mobile phone antenna, for instance; or a technique for compressing data to be sent over a network; or a method for encoding location information in a text or email; or any of millions of other small technological components.

Patents map onto technologies. The invention in an antenna patent may form part of a mobile phone antenna. The compression algorithm may be used in a software program for transmitting digital content such as music, video, or text. Patents often cover bite-sized components or features that form part of larger technologies. Mapping here means figuring out where the patented component fits into a larger technological system such as an electronic component or a part of a machine.

Technologies, in turn, map onto products. The antenna is part of a mobile phone. The compression algorithm is part of a data streaming program used by music streaming companies or video websites. A "product" here means a single thing purchased by consumers. Consumers don't buy components separately, like the combination deadbolt in the *Yale Lock* case; they buy products, such as a combination safe.

Finally, products map onto markets. The combination safe sold by the patentee in *Yale Lock* is sold into the safe market, where other competitors with other models of safes compete. This is the market for high security safes. These safes are sold to banks, large retail stores, financial institutions, and the like. They are related to other security devices and services, such as small home-use safes and armored guards and alarm systems. In our other examples, the mobile phone containing the antenna is sold in competition with other mobile devices, including phones, tablets, and watches. The data streaming program is incorporated into the software of one of several music streaming companies, or is used by one video streaming service (Netflix, say) that competes with others (Amazon Prime or YouTube, for example).

This complex, multi-step "mapping" can be summarized in the following simple diagram:

Patents → Technologies → Products → Markets

And in *Yale Lock*, this relationship looks like this:

Sargent patent → Combination lock → Combination safe → Market for high-security safes

What does this do for us? It illustrates the attenuated relationship between a patent and a product market. At the practical level, it cautions against over-generalized statements such as "patent A grants an economic monopoly in a product market." The right to exclude others from making or selling a portion of a component, in other words, is a long way from giving a legal monopoly over an entire product market. To understand the true economic effects of a given patent, one must do the multi-step mapping just described. Only in this way can one move from the technological exclusivity conferred by a patent to the economic harm caused when the patent is infringed.

3. The principle of *Yale Lock* is contained in Patent Act §284, which deals with damages in patent cases:

> Upon finding for the claimant the court shall award the claimant damages adequate to compensate for the infringement, but in no event less than a reasonable royalty for the use made of the invention by the infringer, together with interest and costs as fixed by the court.
>
> When the damages are not found by a jury, the court shall assess them. In either event the court may increase the damages up to three times the amount found or assessed . . .
>
> The court may receive expert testimony as an aid to the determination of damages or of what royalty would be reasonable under the circumstances (35 U.S.C. §284).

Extensive case law has established that this provision sets out a two-tiered approach to damages: (1) the patentee's lost profits ("damages adequate to compensate for the infringement"), and, as a fallback, (2) "in no event less than a reasonable royalty." Cases such as *Yale Lock* are concerned with lost profits; cases in the following section center on reasonable royalty awards.

4. An important case interpreting the lost profits aspect of §284 is *Panduit Corp. v. Stahlin Bros. Fibre Works, Inc.*, 575 F.2d 1152, 1156 (6th Cir. 1978):

> To obtain as damages the profits on sales he would have made absent infringement, i.e., the sales made by the infringer, a patent owner must prove: (1) demand for the patented product, (2) absence of acceptable noninfringing substitutes, (3) his manufacturing and marketing capability to exploit the demand, and (4) the amount of profit he would have made.
>
> While each factor has been the subject of extensive discussion in the case law, the most important one is often factor (2), absence of noninfringing substitutes. This requires the court to determine if, had the infringer not infringed, the patentee would have made some or all of the sales that the infringer actually did make due to its infringement.
>
> When assessing lost profits, it is important to remember that it is about *profits*, not total sales or revenues. To determine profits, one must calculate:
>
> (1) Sales price x (2) number of units sold, which = (3) total revenue; then (4) minus the costs of production, yields (5) profits.
>
> Calculating the patentee's lost profits usually involves (a) obtaining actual data for values (1) – (5), that is, the price, sales, profit etc. that *actually occurred* in the presence of the infringer, and then (b) adjusting the data to approximate what the numbers *would have looked like* if the infringement had never occurred. Adjustments may include: (1) accounting for "price erosion", the reduction in price that happens when an infringer competes in a market that the patentee would have had to him or herself; (2) adjustment in number of units sold – the higher price that accompanies a single seller usually leads to lower sales (because fewer people buy a thing when it is priced higher); (3) adjustment in revenue based in the prior two adjustments; and (4) adjustment in costs, because the cost per unit might go up if fewer units are made (due to lower economies of scale). All these adjustments to *actual* figures that are obtained after infringement are made to estimate the lost profits damages of a patentee.
>
> What if lost profits cannot be calculated? Then, as §284, the courts fall back on a reasonable royalty measure, as in the case that follows.

8.4.2 Reasonable royalty

 CASE

Carnegie Mellon Univ. v. Marvell Tech. Group, Ltd., 807 F.3d 1283 (Fed. Cir. 2015)

Taranto, Circuit Judge.

[Plaintiff Carnegie-Mellon University (CMU) owns U.S. Patent No. 6,201,839, and related No. 6,438,180. These two patents claim improved methods for reducing errors in the reading of digital data stored on magnetic recording devices such as a computer hard disk.]

CMU sued Marvell Technology Group, Ltd. and Marvell Semiconductor, Inc. (collectively "Marvell") for infringing two patents related to hard-disk drives. A jury found for CMU on infringement and validity, and it awarded roughly $1.17 billion as a reasonable royalty for the infringing acts, using a rate of 50 cents for each of certain semiconductor

CASE (continued)

chips sold by Marvell for use in hard-disk drives. The district court [adjusted the rates for various factors awarded] a continuing royalty at 50 cents per Marvell-sold chip.

35 U.S.C. §284 guarantees to a patent holder "in no event less than a reasonable royalty for the use made of the invention by the infringer." One approach to calculating a reasonable royalty that measures the value of the use of the patented technology posits a "hypothetical negotiation" between a "willing licensor" and a "willing licensee" "to ascertain the royalty upon which the parties would have agreed had they successfully negotiated an agreement just before infringement began." *Lucent Techs., Inc. v. Gateway, Inc.*, 580 F.3d 1301, 1324–25 (Fed. Cir. 2009). That approach, like any reconstruction of the hypothetical world in which the infringer did not actually infringe but negotiated in advance for authority to practice the patents, does not require "mathematical exactness," but a "reasonable approximation" under the circumstances. A key inquiry in the analysis is what it would have been worth to the defendant, as it saw things at the time, to obtain the authority to use the patented technology, considering the benefits it would expect to receive from using the technology and the alternatives it might have pursued. Thus, a "basic premise of the hypothetical negotiation" is "the opportunity for making substantial profits if the two sides [are] willing to join forces" by arriving at a license of the technology.

At the same time, "[t]he economic relationship between the patented method and non-infringing alternative methods, of necessity, would limit the hypothetical negotiation." *Riles v. Shell Expl. & Prod. Co.*, 298 F.3d 1302, 1312 (Fed. Cir. 2002). In the determination of what the negotiation over opportunities and alternatives would have looked like, "the nature of the invention, its utility and advantages, and the extent of the use involved" are important considerations. Past licensing practices of the parties and licenses for similar technology in the industry may be useful evidence. But such evidentiary use must take careful account of any "economically relevant differences between the circumstances of those licenses and the circumstances of the matter in litigation." This court has noted the common (not universal) economic justifications for using per-unit royalties for measuring the value of use of a technology: doing so ties compensation paid to revealed marketplace success, minimizing under- and over-payment risks from lump-sum payments agreed to in advance. *Lucent*, 580 F.3d at 1325–26; see *Gaylord*, 777 F.3d at 1369.

In common-sense terms, a per-unit royalty here allowed Marvell's payments to vary with the sales its infringing activity produced, which are a good way of valuing what it was worth to Marvell to engage in that activity. Marvell nevertheless contends that the evidence of the parties' past practices compels a finding that the parties would have agreed to a flat fee, not a per-unit royalty. CMU explained to the jury that the licensees in each of those instances had longstanding, collaborative research partnerships with CMU and had invested substantial sums over the years in CMU's hard-disk-drive focused research. Significantly, those licenses were granted before CMU ever developed the patentable technology; the licensees gave CMU money with no guarantee that any usable technology would result, sharing the costs of uncertain research in the hope of a future potential benefit.

There also was ample evidence that 50 cents was an appropriate amount for the perchip

CASE *(continued)*

license. CMU offered evidence that, at the time of the hypothetical negotiation, Marvell had no alternative to CMU's technology. There is evidence too, after the fact but still relevant, that CMU's technology is so significant that it is used industry-wide. At the time of the hypothetical negotiation, Marvell faced strong market pressure to improve the performance of its chips, and testimony and internal documents showed (in sometimes-dramatic language) that its previous attempt to produce a new design was failing because the resulting chips produced excessive heat. Finally, the evidence supported a finding that, if Marvell could use CMU's technology, it could pay CMU 50 cents per chip and still meet its reasonable profit goal – indeed, it would end up keeping upwards of three quarters of the per-chip profit. On the evidence presented at trial, the jury could properly find that a royalty of 50 cents per chip reasonably valued Marvell's use of CMU's technology and would have been a good deal in the hypothetical negotiation. Accordingly, the jury's royalty determination must stand.

NOTES

1. A "reasonable royalty" derives from a hypothetical negotiation between the patentee and the infringer when the infringement began. *See, e.g., Unisplay, S.A. v. American Elec. Sign Co.*, 69 F.3d 512, 517 (Fed. Cir. 1995). A comprehensive (but repetitive) list of relevant factors for a reasonable royalty calculation appears in *Georgia-Pacific Corp. v. United States Plywood Corp.*, 318 F.Supp. 1116, 1120 (S.D.N.Y. 1970).
2. The analysis in the *Carnegie-Mellon* case regarding the "comparability" of licenses is quite common, but in many cases it is the *patentee* (and not the infringer) that is challenged on the relevance of the past licenses it introduces into evidence. Often the infringer will argue that the patentee's licenses improperly inflate the royalty rate because those licenses differ in important ways from the infringer's use of the patentee's claimed technology. *See, e.g., Finjan, Inc. v. Secure Computing Corp.*, 626 F.3d 1197, 1211 (Fed. Cir. 2010) (When relying on past licenses, an expert "must account for differences in the technologies and economic circumstances of the contracting parties"; the patentee's effort to introduce evidence of past infringement litigation settlement agreements was rejected because litigation settlement differs from the hypothetical willing licensor/willing licensee scenario appropriate for reasonable royalty determinations). *See also ART+COM Innovationpool GmbH v. Google Inc.*, 155 F. Supp. 3d 489, 512 (D. Del. 2016) (rejecting litigation settlement licenses but permitting introduction of two non-litigation "real-world" licenses as evidence of reasonable royalty rate).

8.5 Damages in China: Article 65

Article 65

The amount of compensation for a patent infringement shall be determined on the basis of the actual losses incurred to the patentee as a result of the infringement. If it is difficult to determine the actual losses, the actual losses may be determined on the basis of the gains which the infringer has obtained from the infringement. If it is difficult to determine the losses incurred to the patentee or the gains obtained by the infringer, the amount shall be reasonably determined by reference to the multiple of the royalties for this patent. In addition, the compensation shall include the reasonable expenses that the patentee has paid for stopping the infringement.

> If it is difficult to determine the losses incurred to the patentee, the gains obtained by the infringer as well as the royalty obtained for the patent, the people's court may, by taking into account such factors as the type of patent, nature and particulars of the infringement, etc., decide a compensation in the sum of not less than 10,000 yuan but not more than 1 million yuan.

This statutory damages provision has been criticized by a number of commentators over the years. One consistent complaint is that the amounts are simply too low to justify litigation in many infringement cases. This is unfortunate because statutory damages are considered essentially the only, or exclusive, remedy in Chinese patent infringement cases. (Of course, the prospect of an injunction also factors into a decision to litigate.) See, e.g., Xiaowu Li and Don Wang, *Chinese Patent Law's Statutory Damages Provision: The One Size that Fits None*, 26 Wash. Int'l L.J. 209, 211 (2017) (footnotes omitted):

> [T]he average damages awarded in patent infringement cases in China from 2006 to 2013 [was] a mere RMB 118,266.00 (approximately $18,253.00). This is only 35% of the average damages claimed by the patentees. One judge from Guangdong People's High Court commented that the damages awarded in intellectual property cases are generally less than 5% of the actual losses suffered by plaintiffs. This turns out to be very problematic. On one hand, there is little incentive for infringers to proactively avoid infringement given the "easy profits" one can make through infringement as compared to the low damages he or she has to pay if found infringing. On the other, the low damages award, as compared to the litigation costs, renders it uneconomical for patentees to enforce patent rights in courts.

Insufficient discovery and problems of proof are the main reason that statutory damages are in effect the only basis of monetary damages in Chinese patent cases. See Xiaowu Li and Don Wang, *supra*, at 214 ("[E]ven though a patentee's loss is the primary calculation method in theory, it is rarely used in practice. In China, plaintiffs bear the burden to produce sufficient evidence to establish the loss of sales as a result of the infringement, and in most cases, they are unable to do so."). The proposal in this article: eliminate the statutory damages provision altogether.

Other contributing factors to the low damage awards in China have also been identified. These include (1) a tradition of employing court-appointed experts to help with damages assessments (problematical because these experts are often not familiar with technical details in various industries), see Yieyie Yang, *A Patent Problem: Can Chinese Courts Compare with the U.S. in Providing Patent Holders with Adequate Monetary Damages*, 96 J. Pat. & Trademark Off. Soc'y 140, 152 (2014); and (2) perhaps some residual of traditional Confucian principles which elevate community interests over individual credit, *see* Rachel T. Wu, *Awaking the Sleeping Dragon: The Evolving Chinese Patent Laws and its Implications for Pharmaceutical Patents*, 34 Fordham Int'l L.J. 549, 553 (2011); William P. Alford, To Steal a Book is an Elegant Offense: Intellectual Property Law in Chinese Civilization (1995). For an instructive counterargument, which claims that "property consciousness" can be found more readily outside of elite imperial court culture, see Jonathan Ocko, *Copying, Culture, and Control: Chinese Intellectual Property Law in Historical Context [Book Review of Alford]*, 8 Yale J. L. & the Humanities 559, 571 (1996) ("I would argue, even if one cannot find it inscribed in codes or litigated in courts, an intellectual property rights consciousness, or sensibility, has probably existed in China for a long time. To uncover and understand this sensibility, we must move outside the sphere of literati painters and scholars").

Huawei v. InterDigital, Shenzhen Intermediate Court, (2011) Shen Zhong Fa Zhi Min Chu Zi No. 857. Aff'd on appeal, Guangdong High Court, (2013) Yue Gao Fa Min San Zhong Zi No. 305

InterDigital and its related entities (collectively "IDC") own more than 19,500 patents and applications, some of which are essential to the communication standards (*e.g.*, 2G, 3G, 4G and IEEE802). Such patents are called "SEP", and SEP owners are required to grant a license based on Fair, Reasonable, and Non-Discriminatory (FRAND) conditions.

[Huawei's products are compliant with the above standards, thus implement IDC's SEPs. IDC and Huawei negotiated but failed to reach agreement on the SEP's licensing terms. In 2011, IDC sued Huawei for patent infringement before the US court and ITC.]

[In 2011, Huawei sued IDC in China for antitrust violation and requested the Chinese court to decide IDC's SEP licensing fees. The lower court ruled that the FRAND licensing rate of IDC's Chinese Standard Essential Patents ("SEPs") should be 0.019 percent of sales revenue of Huawei's involved smart phones. IDC appealed, and the High Court affirmed.]

[On appeal, the High Court reviewed the following issues raised by the IDC:]

(i) Whether InterDigital Communications Inc., InterDigital Technology Corporation, InterDigital Patent Holdings Inc., IPR Licensing Inc., shall be co-defendants.
[The court listed the following facts and then concluded that these four business entities are co-defendants: They call themselves collectively "InterDigital Group"; they are co-plaintiffs in the US litigation against Huawei; they have at least one common senior manager, Lawrence F. Shay; they share the same business interests, though they

(continued)

undertake different responsibilities for obtaining patents, licensing patents, enforcing patents, building SEP into standards.]
(ii) Whether Chinese law shall be applied in this case.
[The court decided that the Chinese law shall be applied here for the following reasons: The patents to be licensed are Chinese Patents; these patents are essential for complying with Chinese standards; Huawei is a company incorporated in China.]
(iii) Whether IDC has violated its FRAND obligations.
[The court found the following acts of IDC had violated its FRAND obligations: InterDigital offered an unfairly high licensing rate to Huawei, in comparison with the rates it offered to Apple, Samsung, etc. IDC asked for a free license of all patents owned by Huawei. The court further pointed out that Huawei has a big patent portfolio. For example, by the end of year 2010, Huawei had over 30,000 Chinese patent applications, over 8,000 PCT applications and 17,000 issued patents (of which 3,000 were foreign patents). Also, IDC offered a tie-in licensing of both its SEPs and non-SEPs.]
[In another ruling, Yue Gao Fa Min San Zhong Zi No. 305 [2013], the same Court concluded that InterDigital's above acts constitute "abuse of predominant market position" and thus violated Anti-Monopoly Law (AML).]
(iv) Whether the Court has the authority to directly decide a FRAND rate of a SEP.
[On appeal, IDC argued that the court should not intervene in such a private licensing negotiation. The court disagreed, at least for the following reasons.]

> In the middle of negotiation, IDC first launched litigation and 337 investigation against Huawei before the U.S. court and USITC. If a Chinese court is excluded from hearing the case, it will create a double-standard, which is unfair to Huawei.
>
> Pursuant to Article 57 of the Chinese Patent Law, the Patent Office can directly decide a compulsory licensing rate, provided two parties cannot reach an agreement. The court admitted the present case relates to deciding FRAND rates of SEPs, rather than compulsory licensing. However, the court asserted that it has the similar authority of the Patent Office, namely, to decide a FRAND rate when two parties cannot reach an agreement through negotiation.

(v) Whether the rate 0.019% set by the lower court is appropriate.
[Based on the evidence provided by Huawei, the court found the following facts:]

> IDC's license to Apple is about 0.0187% of Apple's sales revenue from related iPhones. Specifically, IDC offered a 7-year (2007–2014) non-exclusive, non-transferrable, global license for Apple in exchange for 56 million USD. Based upon the sales information disclosed by Apple and other sources, the court deduced that Apple's related iPhone sales revenue is at least 300 billion USD from 2007 to 2014. By dividing 56 million with 300 billion, the court got the number 0.0187%.
>
> In addition, IDC's license to Samsung is about 0.19% of Samsung's sales revenue from related smart phones. Specifically, IDC offered a 5-year (2007–2012) non-exclusive, non-

(continued)

transferrable, global license for Samsung in exchange for 400 million USD. Based upon the sales information disclosed by Samsung and other sources, the court deduced that Samsung's related smart phone sales revenue is over 210 billion USD from 2007 to 2012. By dividing 400 million with 210 billion, the court got the 0.19%.

[Lastly, the court explained why Apple's rate 0.0187 percent is used as a reference basis to decide a FRAND rate offered to Huawei:]

Apple's rate seems to come out of a fair, equal and voluntary negotiation, which share the same spirits of IDC's FRAND obligations . . . When IDC and Apple reached the licensing agreement in 2007, there was no litigation between the parties. On the other hand, when IDC and Samsung reached the licensing deal in 2009, they were litigating before the court.

[For the above reasons, the High Court affirmed the lower court's ruling.]

Guangdong High People's Court
Judge Xiuping OU
Judge Lihao YUE
Judge Lihua OU
Oct. 16, 2013

NOTES

1. **Injunctions for SEPs**. According to the Supreme Court's Judicial Rules for patent litigation, which became effective on April 1, 2016, an injunction is still available for SEPs, except that patentee has violated its FRAND obligations. Paragraphs 1, 2 of Article 24 state:

    Article 24(1), (2)

    Where the recommended national, industrial or local standards give clear notice of the involved essential patents, if the infringer makes a non-infringement defense that implementation of such standards do not need a license from the patentee, the court shall generally not support it.

    Where the commended national, industrial or local standards give clear notice of the involved essential patents, and in negotiation between the patentee and the alleged infringer on the licensing conditions of such essential patent, if the patentee intentionally violates its obligation for licensing on fair, reasonable and non-discriminatory ("FRAND") terms as promised in the process of standard developing, which causes failure to reach the patent licensing contract, *the people's court shall, in general, not support the patentee's request for an injunction,* provided that the alleged infringer has no obvious fault in the negotiation.

2. **How to calculate a FRAND licensing rate**. Paragraph 3 of Article 24 of the SPC's judicial rules confirms that the court can decide FRAND licensing fees for SEPs, if relevant parties fail to reach an agreement. Further, it lists factors to be considered by the court when deciding FRAND licensing fees for SEPs.

    Article 24(3)

    The licensing conditions as mentioned in Paragraph 2 of this Article shall be determined upon negotiation by the relevant patentee and the alleged infringer. Where no consensus is reached after sufficient negotiation, the parties may request the people's court to determine such conditions, in which case the people's court shall, on fair, reasonable and non-discriminatory (FRAND) terms, take into comprehensive consideration of the following: *extent of innovation of the patent, the role of the patent in relevant standards, the technical field to which the standards belong, the nature and scope of the standards, relevant licensing conditions and other factors, in order to determine such licensing conditions.*

8.5.1 Enhanced damages proposed by fourth revision of the Patent Law

The Chinese Patent Law is in its fourth revision process. The draft has been submitted to the Congress and is pending for approval. In Article 68 of the draft, it introduces significant changes in order to enhance damages for patent infringement. The draft proposes changes in the following three aspects.

1. **Treble damages for Willful Infringement**
   Article 68(1)

The amount of compensation for patent right infringement shall be determined according to the patentee's actual losses caused by the infringement. If it is hard to determine the actual losses, the amount of compensation may be determined according to the benefits acquired by the infringer through the infringement. If it is hard to determine the losses of the patentee or the benefits acquired by the infringer, the amount of compensation may be determined reasonably according to the multiplied amount of the royalties of that patent. *For an act of intentional infringement of patent right, the people's court may determine an amount of compensation equal to 1~3 times the amount determined as described above* according to factors like the seriousness, scale and damage results of the act of infringement. The amount of compensation shall include the reasonable expenses paid by the patentee for putting an end to the infringement.

2. **Maximum Statutory Compensation Raised from 1 Million to 5 Million RMB**
   Article 68(2)

If the losses of the patentee, benefits of the infringer, or royalties of the patent are all hard to determine, the people's court may, on the basis of the factors such as the type of patent right, nature of the infringement, and seriousness of the case, determine an amount of compensation that *ranges from 100,000 yuan to 5,000,000 yuan.*

3. **Burden of Proof Shifting to Defendant**
   Article 68(3)

After the people's court finds that an act of infringing a patent right is established, it may order the infringer to submit the account books and materials related to the act of infringement, if such account books and materials are mainly in the possession of the infringer, in order to determine the amount of compensation, provided that the patentee has done its best to provide evidences. *If the infringer does not submit relevant account books and materials or submits false account books and materials, the people's court may determine the amount of compensation by taking into account the assertions and evidences provided by the patentee.*

8.6 Damages in Europe

The basic provision on damages in German patent cases is set out in §139 of the Patentgesetz (1980, as amended 2013), available at http://www.wipo.int/wipolex/en/text.jsp?file_id=401424:

Legal infringements
Section 139

(1) Any person who uses a patented invention contrary to sections 9 to 13 [on infringement] may, in the event of the risk of recurrent infringement, be sued by the aggrieved party for cessation and desistance. This right may also be asserted in the event of the risk of a first-time infringement.

(2) Any person who performs the act intentionally or negligently shall be obliged to compensate the aggrieved party for the damage caused. When assessing the compensation, consideration may also be given to the profit which the infringer has obtained by infringing the right. The claim for compensation may also be calculated on the basis of the amount which the infringer would have been required to pay as equitable remuneration if he had obtained permission to use the invention.

(3) If the subject-matter of the patent is a process for manufacturing a new product, the same product produced by someone else shall, until there is proof to the contrary, be deemed to have been produced using the patented process. In taking evidence to the contrary, consideration shall be given to the defendant's legitimate interests in protecting his manufacturing and trade secrets.

In the UK, the section on damages (UK Patent Act of 1977, revised as of April, 2014, Chapter 37 Part I, at §61) reads as follows:

61. Proceedings for infringement of patent.

(1) Subject to the following provisions of this Part of this Act, civil proceedings may be brought in the court by the proprietor of a patent in respect of any act alleged to infringe the patent and (without prejudice to any other jurisdiction of the court) in those proceedings a claim may be made –

(a) for an injunction or interdict restraining the defendant or defender from any apprehended act of infringement;

(b) for an order for him to deliver up or destroy any patented product in relation to which the patent is infringed or any article in which that product is inextricably comprised;
(c) for damages in respect of the infringement;
(d) for an account of the profits derived by him from the infringement;
(e) for a declaration or declarator that the patent is valid and has been infringed by him.

(2) The court shall not, in respect of the same infringement, both award the proprietor of a patent damages and order that he shall be given an account of the profits.

We consider below one case of each of these jurisdictions.

Bicycle helmet rotary lock, Case No. 7 O 184/06, NJOZ 2008, 2391, GRUR-RR 2008, 333 (Mannheim District Court (Landesgericht), 19 October 2007)

The parties dispute the amount of compensation for damages resulting from loss of profit due to patent infringement. [The patent involved a novel bicycle helmet which had a built-in helmet lock, useful for securing the helmet in high-theft areas. There were two plaintiffs, related business entities. Plaintiff one had licensed the patent, under which it owned rights, to the second plaintiff, a manufacturing company. Plaintiff two had been manufacturing and supplying bicycle helmet locks for the Defendant's bicycle helmets; defendant took plaintiff's helmet locks and then integrated them into bicycle helmets which it sold in Germany. The defendant had initially complied with its contractual obligations to the two plaintiffs, but then, in an effort to save money, began to buy helmet locks from a third-party supplier based in China. The plaintiffs sued defendant for patent infringement, and the patent was found valid and infringed, which led to this damages action.]

In the period from 1999 to 2003 [licensed units were as follows]: 1999: 60,000 pieces; 2000: 215,000 pieces; 2001: 360,000 pieces; 2002: 170,000 pieces; 2003: 140,000 pieces.

[Infringement began after 2003, and there were a total of 303,400 patent-infringing helmet locks purchased by the defendant from the overseas company.] [Thus, the] calculation of the claim for damages must be based on 303,400 patent-infringing helmet locks.

Under Article 249 of the Civil Code, the injured party can seek compensation for the difference between [its condition] brought about by the infringement and the [condition] which would have been achieved without the infringement. The injured person can,

> **CASE** *(continued)*
>
> therefore, claim compensation for the profit which has escaped him by reducing his own [price] as a result of the infringement of the patent. The burden of proof for the determination of causality between patent infringement and loss of the injured party is borne by the injured party.
>
> In general, it can not be assumed that the revenue of the infringer would have been directly or indirectly in the form of royalties to the plaintiff. It is necessary to establish that the revenue of the injured party [*i.e.*, the patent owner] would have increased with a certain probability [in the absence of infringement] ... according to the usual course of events or according to special circumstances. This is the case here.
>
> It is true that the forensic practice of a patent infringement situation [*i.e.*, reconstruction of what would have happened in the absence of infringement,] [creates challenges] as a viable way of calculating damages. [The problem often occurs in] proof of the causality between patent infringement and loss of sales. [Often, this is in the case where] the injured party [plaintiff/patent owner], like the infringer, competes as a manufacturer or distributor for sales to a third party. It is then a question of whether the third person, instead of acquiring the cheaper, infringing product from the infringer, would really have bought the more expensive product of the patent owner, with the certainty necessary for judicial conviction, or whether he could instead rely on [unpatented] alternatives.
>
> This is not the case [here], however. The plaintiff and infringers are here not competitors in the market for sales to a third party. On the contrary, in this case the [defendant] later infringer, who was at first legally acting, was the customer of the [plaintiff/patentee]. In order not to have to pay the price demanded by the patent owner, the defendants decided to keep making their bicycle helmets according to the [plaintiff's] patented design, [but] to obtain precisely this device designed in this way, but substantially cheaper, [from a third party overseas supplier – resulting in patent infringement]. In this case, the [court] is certainly convinced that, in the ordinary course of events, [the] decision of the defendant [was] unlawful [in replacing their supply of helmet locks from the patentee, by contracting with an unauthorized overseas source].
>
> The fact that [there are alternatives to the patented] technical solution for a bicycle helmet lock does not lead to the denial of causality. It is merely necessary that, according to the ordinary course of events or the particular circumstances, the plaintiff's revenue would have increased with a certain probability without the infringing acts of the defendants.
>
> The customer shall also be entitled to the most recent claim for compensation.
>
> In the case of [the second plaintiff, the patent owner/licensor], the amount claimed shall be in respect of the agreed per unit license rate. This corresponds to a per unit license of €0.033 which, in the case of 303,400 patent-infringing rotary locks, corresponds to the amount of the payment claimed in the action: €10,012.20 plus interest.
>
> [The first plaintiff] is entitled to claim compensation for loss of profit [on sales revenue totaling] €735,745. In the calculation of the loss of profit, the agreed sales price [is] €3.60 per piece.
>
> [Under German law,] the plaintiff must present a profit calculation based on the specific

CASE (continued)

product. [This involves subtracting relevant costs from the total revenue, which was just discussed; revenue minus costs equals profit.] The purchase cost [of] material[s] used to make the helmet locks was €.740 per unit produced. [Relevant parts include the] cable, latch, stop, housing, lock carrier, end piece, stopper, cover, rotating handle, illuminated cover, blinking circuit including button cells and contact element, spring and rope. [The transport cost introduced by the defendant is not disputed.]

For tool costs, [defendant] has stated €.054 per unit. In doing so, it stated that a total of 8 tools had been required. [Labor cost per unit was based on the prevailing hourly wage.] It has taken into account the saved amortization costs proportionally from the components not supplied due to the infringement of the patent in relation to the maximum number of components which can be produced with the respective tools. The maintenance costs during the 7 months of patent infringement are also taken into account. The [plaintiff] has thus provided a comprehensible calculation of the tool costs. Without success, the defendant considers that this cost approach is insufficient. The calculation is based on [prior court-approved procedures] and, moreover, relates to the [infringing] product.

Saved packaging costs [proved to be €.004 per unit.] This means that a reasonable calculation has been made on the basis of which [total costs] of [€1.175] per unit is deducted [from] the contract price of €3.60 [, leaving a profit of €2.425 per unit]. On the basis of 303,400 patent-infringing rotary locks, this results in a loss of profits amounting to €735,745 [or roughly $823,000].

[Defendant is] therefore . . . liable for the payment of €735,745 plus the most recently applied interest to [plaintiff one] and the payment of €10,012.20 with regard to [the second plaintiff].

NOTES

1. Causality is always an important issue in patent damages cases. A patent owner can introduce financial evidence of its condition prior to and then after an infringement; but this by itself is not enough. There is a need, also, for evidence *connecting* the loss to the acts of infringement. The evidence in this case provides a good example of how a patent owner might make this connection. Here, the patent owner had been selling components to the defendant for inclusion in the defendant's commercial product (a bike helmet). The introduction of competition from the unauthorized overseas supplier led to a drop in the patent owner's sales under its contract with the defendant. The earlier purchases helped to establish that the reduced financial position of the patent owner was caused by the infringing devices; without the infringement, the plaintiff/patent owner's profits would have continued at the old, pre-infringement rate. The court's job, then, was simply to calculate what the patentee's profits would have been in the absence of infringement – which was easy, as it was just a matter of extrapolating from the past sales. The licensor plaintiff had an established royalty rate, so its loss was easy to calculate too. Note the requisite standard of proof: it is a matter of probabilities, not certainty: Plaintiff must simply establish that "according to the ordinary course of events or the particular circumstances, the plaintiff's revenue would have increased with a certain probability without the infringing acts of the defendants."

2. The second major approach to damages in Germany is to award the patentee the full profits made by the infringer – a so-called "disgorgement" remedy. As described by commentator Marcus Schönknecht, in his article *Determination of Patent Damages in Germany*, 43 Int'l Rev. Intell. Prop. & Comp. L. (IIC) 309 (2012),

available at https://beck-online.beck.de/Print/CurrentMagazine?vpath=bibdata%5Czeits%5Ciic%5C2012%5Ccont%5Ciic.2012.309.1.htm&hlwords=on&printdialogmode=CurrentDoc&x=48&y=11, at 315–17 (footnotes/citations omitted):

> [As an alternative to its lost profits,] the patentee can claim the infringer's profits. The purpose behind this method is not compensation for the actually incurred damage, but rather a fair settlement of the financial prejudice suffered by the patentee. For the sake of facilitating calculation, German law accepts that the determined amount does not necessarily completely correspond to the damage suffered by the patentee. This method avoids the problems described above. In particular, the patentee can base his calculations on information provided by the infringer. Thus, the patentee does not have to disclose internal business information to his competitor. The amount that must be surrendered to the patentee cannot be calculated in a precise way, but must be estimated under Sec. 287 of the Code of Civil Procedure; the factual basis for this estimation must – if possible – be established in an objective way. The underlying idea of this method is that, if the infringer made profits by using the invention, it can be assumed that the patentee lost corresponding profits. While this is obviously not generally true, the law establishes a legal fiction to that effect, including that the patentee operates a business with the same production and distribution performance as the infringer. Since a legal fiction is not rebuttable, it is not relevant whether the patent holder actually could have realized the same amount of profits. Nor is it relevant whether the patentee actually manufactures or markets patented products or whether he commercializes the patent by granting licenses.
>
> In assessing the amount of damages according to the "infringer's profit" method, the court will consider three elements. The starting point is the infringer's [revenue] of the infringing products. The court will then deduct certain costs to calculate the profits realized from the [revenue]. Finally, the court will multiply the profits with a quota [*i.e.*, apportionment factor] to capture only that part of the profits that is generated by the patent infringement. The formula for damages according to this method is therefore: infringer's profits = ([revenue] – deductible costs) × quota

CASE

OOO Abbott v. Design & Display, Ltd., [2017] EWHC 932, 2017 WL 01435547 (Intell. Prop. Enterprise Ct., 26 April 2017)

In a judgment dated 24 February 2016, [2016] EWCA Civ 95, the Court of Appeal allowed an appeal against an order made by me dated 16 October 2014, in which I assessed sums due to the claimants (collectively referred to as "Abbott"). This followed the trial of an account of profits and my judgment of 4 September 2014, [2014] EWHC 2924 (IPEC) ("the first account judgment").

Earlier HHJ Birss QC had found that Abbott's European Patent (UK) No. 1 816 931 ("the Patent") was valid and had been infringed by the defendants [, a company called "Design & Display"], see judgment of 30 May 2013, [2013] EWPCC 27.

The Patent claimed a display panel of the type used to display goods in shops. The important part of the invention concerns inserts made of a resilient metal, typically aluminium. The inserts are located into horizontal slots cut into the panels. Shelves or hangars for displaying goods are supported by the inserts.

The Order of the Court of Appeal on 24 February 2016 included this: "The Account

CASE *(continued)*

of profits be remitted to the Intellectual Property Enterprise Court for determination of the following issue . . .: (a) What proportion of sales of slatted panels sold together with infringing inserts should be included within the Appellant's account of profits?

Lewison LJ [of the Court of Appeal] quoted from my description of Design & Display's business:

> Design & Display manufactures and sells retail equipment, including display panels for use in shops. . . . [Its] primary business was as a joiner for shopfitters, making bespoke items of shop furniture, . . . called 'equipment'. This equipment included displays, some of which had slatted panels (sometimes referred to as slatboards or slatwalls) sold both in standard sizes and as custom-sized panels. These were the panels with horizontal slots into which the aluminium inserts could be introduced – in the case of the infringing inserts, introduced by a snap-in process. Shelves or hangars for displaying the goods could then be slotted into the inserts.
>
> In the relevant period Design & Display sold the slatted panels in two ways. First, it sold the panels with inserts separately for subsequent assembly by the customer. At the trial these were referred to as 'unincorporated' panels and inserts. Secondly, Design & Display sold pre-assembled displays of which the panels with inserts were part. These were referred to as 'incorporated' panels and inserts. In addition, some unincorporated inserts were sold without slatted panels.
>
> Design & Display did not itself make the inserts but purchased them from an aluminium extruder in the form of lengths which were cut into sections to make the individual inserts. The panels were purchased in the form of plain panels into which the slots were machined by Design & Display.

The Court of Appeal set out the overall task of a court when deciding which part of the profits made by the infringer in the course of his infringing business fall due to the patentee. Lewison LJ, with whom [two other judges] agreed, said:

> Section 61(1)(d) of the Patents Act 1977 entitles a patentee to claim against an infringer an account of the profits 'derived by him from the infringement'. An account of profits is confined to profits actually made, its purpose being not to punish the defendant but to prevent his unjust enrichment. The underlying theory is that the infringer is treated as having carried on his business (to the extent that it infringes) on behalf of the patentee. The broad principle is that the patentee is entitled to profits that have been earned by the use of his invention. If the patentee does not recover those profits, the infringer will have been unjustly enriched. So the purpose of the account is to quantify the extent to which the infringer would be unjustly enriched if he were to retain the profits derived by him from the infringement. That requires the fact finder first to identify the patentee's invention and second to decide what (if any) profits the infringer derived from the use of that invention. The second of these questions may give rise to difficulty where the infringer sells products associated with the subject matter of the patent (often called 'convoyed goods') or products into which the subject matter of the patent is incorporated. The court must

CASE *(continued)*

determine what profit has been earned, in a legal sense, by the infringer's wrongful acts. It is clear, then, that an account of profits looks at the facts through the lens of what the infringer has done; and what the patentee might have suffered by way of loss in the real world is irrelevant.

Thus, there are broadly two steps:

(1) Identify the invention.
(2) Identify the profits (if any) made by the defendant from his use of the invention, taking into account convoyed goods and/or products into which the subject matter of the invention is incorporated.

Generally speaking, an invention disclosed in a patent will be that which is set out in a claim. All the claims of the Patent are product claims for "A display panel..." with stated characteristics of the panel including the presence of an insert which itself has stated features. All the claims after claim 1 are dependent upon claim 1.

At first glance the answer to the first issue remitted by the Court of Appeal is self-evident. The inventions claimed are panels and panels are what Design & Display sold, so it should account for its profits on panels, including the inserts. However, in an inquiry as to damages or an account of profits it is necessary to focus on the 'invention' in a narrower sense.

Generally, as one progresses down the list of claims in a patent the matter set out in each claim becomes successively more extensive and the scope of the monopoly correspondingly more confined.

In his paragraph 7 (see above) Lewison LJ pointed out why the identification of relevant profits may not be straightforward, given that the invention may form only part of the articles sold by the infringer and/or because it may be that convoyed goods must be considered.

Lewison LJ identified two circumstances in which a losing defendant in a patent action should also account for profits from sales of goods other than those which precisely embody the invention:

(1) Where the invention relates to an essential feature of those goods.
(2) Where those goods would not have existed had the defendant not infringed the claimant's patent.

[Where either is true, an apportionment of damages is inappropriate; damages should be measured by the value of the entire product so produced.]

[In prior cases,] the protected feature of the product was functionally and/or commercially the most significant part of the whole. It was in that sense essential. I include the possibility of its being commercially the most significant part because in Dart it might well have been said that the most important function of a plastic kitchen container is to contain its contents and for the most part that is performed by the body of the container.

CASE (continued)

However, it was presumably the lid which gave the canister in question its commercial advantage over competitors and was thus, commercially, the most important part.

Neither test for whether apportionment is appropriate is binary. It could be that from the point of view of some purchasers the relevant feature is essential but from the point of view of others it is not. Similarly, it is possible that if the protected feature had not been available for use, some of the entire goods would have come into existence, but fewer of them. In my view, in such cases the court should make a partial apportionment: the infringer must account for the profit on a proportion of the entire articles.

There is a third test identified by Lewison LJ. If satisfied, it requires an infringer to pay over profits on non-infringing goods or services, *i.e.* convoyed goods or services. Lewison LJ approved the unchallenged proposition contained in the first account judgment that if sales of the products embodying the patent infringed 'drove' the sales of other goods, the latter qualified as sales of convoyed goods and the defendant was accountable for profits on those sales.

I first used the criterion of one set of sales 'driving' another in *Alfrank Designs Ltd v. Exclusive (UK) Ltd* [2015] EWHC 1372 (IPEC), at [29]–[34]. That was a judgment in an inquiry as to damages. There, I stated that I was using the term to mean that there was a causative link in the mind of the purchaser between his decision to purchase the goods protected by the claimant's right and a consequential decision also to buy the convoyed goods.

The inquiry in *Alfrank* followed the admission by the first defendant, a furniture wholesaler, that it had infringed unregistered design rights in the design of two dining room tables. The rights were owned by the claimant, a competing furniture wholesaler. The evidence was that consumers in the market for new household furniture characteristically decide first on the dining room table they like. Having done so, they buy matching furniture. Once the sale of the dining room table had been secured via a furniture retailer, the wholesaler would make sales of other items in the same range via the retailer. In that sense the sales of infringing dining room tables by the first defendant in *Alfrank* 'drove' sales of other convoyed items.

[I]n the first account judgment I found that where customers specified a wish to buy the infringing inserts because of the advantages they offered, the inserts drove associated sales of compatible panels which were thus convoyed sales. This was not challenged on appeal. It would follow that Design & Display is liable for the profits made on such sales of both inserts and panels because the sales of the panels were convoyed sales.

Some of Design & Display's customers who bought the panels and inserts separately will have wanted specifically the infringing insert. Had Design & Display not been able to provide those inserts, it is likely that those customers would have gone elsewhere for panels. I again estimate that in relation to sales of the panels with separate inserts, 10% of the sales of panels were driven by the sales of accompanying inserts in that way. Abbott is entitled to the whole of Design & Display's profit on 10% of its sales of infringing inserts and separate but associated panels.

CASE *(continued)*

That leaves, in each case, the other 90% of panels sold. Where the customer did not specify infringing inserts, Design & Display still made infringing sales. The question to be resolved is what part of the profit on the sales of the panels is to be apportioned to the invention. Design & Display is liable for that part of the profit.

In the first account judgment I said that the part of the invention embodied in the panel was only a modest section of the panels sold, namely the slot into which the infringing inserts were fitted. I had in mind the size of the slot relative to the [physical size of the] panel as a whole, but I do not believe that this resolves the present issue. I have to consider what proportion of profit made on panels sold should be apportioned to the invention, *i.e.* the inserts and the slots in the panels into which the inserts fitted. It makes no difference whether the inserts were incorporated before or after sale.

One, though not necessarily the only way to approach this is by reference to function. The function of the panel is to act as a frame on which goods can be displayed. One of the requirements of the design is to have a slot compatible with the inserts used. That is a minor, but not insignificant part of the whole function.

The best way to estimate the correct figure is to separate the profit on panels and inserts. Abbot is entitled to the whole of the profit made on the relevant inserts plus 10% of the profit made on the panel. [A section of the opinion on deducting overhead costs as part of the profit calculation is omitted.]

The parties were agreed that they would calculate the profit, if any, due to be paid by Design & Display to Abbott, once the principles had been decided. I invite the parties to do so.

NOTES

1. For discussion of the principles in this decision, see Thomas F. Cotter, "A Recent English Decision on Accountings of Profits," Comparative Patent Remedies Blog, Feb. 29, 2016, available at http://comparativepatentremedies.blogspot.com/2016/02/a-recent-english-decision-on.html, where Professor Cotter says:

   In my opinion, Lord Justice Lewison [in the Appeal Court opinion] is right to require apportionment of the defendant's profit where the patent did not drive demand for the defendant's product, because otherwise the defendant is being required to disgorge more than the value of the patented invention to it: it's being required to disgorge profits that are properly attributable to other features. With all due respect, however, the principle actually cuts deeper than the court seems to recognize. From an economic perspective, the value of the invention to the defendant is only the surplus profit the defendant earned over and above what it would have earned from the use of the next-best available noninfringing technology. Unfortunately, the House of Lords over a century ago in *United Horse-Shoe & Nail Co. v. John Stewart & Co.* (1888) L.R. 13 App. Case 401 held that the fact that the defendant could have resorted to a noninfringing alternative is irrelevant to the amount of the plaintiff's lost profit, and in *Celanese Int'l Corp. v. BP Chemicals Ltd.* [1999] R.P.C. 203 Justice Laddie held that the same principle applies to awards of defendant's profits. The principle that noninfringing alternatives are irrelevant necessarily leads to overcompensation, . . . [and] apportionment and the relevance of noninfringing alternatives are "inseparable concepts." At least Lord Justice Lewison's opinion for the court undoes some of the damage of ignoring alternatives.

2. For discussion of this and other recent (and important) damages cases in the Intellectual Property Enterprise Court (IPEC), see Charlotte Scott, *Damages Inquiries and Accounts of Profits in the IPEC*, 38 Euro. Intell. Prop. Rev. 273 (2016). In this article, Ms. Scott describes the initial opinion that was appealed; that initial opinion specified that all panels sold by the defendant should be included in the patentee's profits. The Court of Appeals remanded, resulting in the opinion just above. In that opinion, the judge (Judge Hacon of the IPEC) divided panel sales into two categories: (1) those that were clearly driven by demand for the patented item (the inserts) – 10 percent of all sales, in the judge's estimation; and (2) those that were not. In category (1), full lost profits – the profits from sale of an entire panel – will be paid to the patentee. In category (2), only 10 percent of the profit from panels will be payable to the patent owner. This is the result of Judge Hacon's estimation that 10 percent of the value of panels sold (to those for whom the patented inserts were *not* the "driving force" behind their demand for panels) was attributable to the patented invention. Only category (1) represented true "convoyed" sales: sales of an unpatented item that are driven by, and thus attributable to, the value of the patented invention. In category (2), it can be presumed that customers would have bought panels even without the patented inserts. But because those inserts were included in the panels purchased by this group of buyers, and because those inserts were valuable, the court demands that an appropriate percentage of overall profits be attributable to the patented invention. That invention did not *drive* these sales; but the invention did add value to the panels that were purchased. This is what apportionment is all about.

3. In a related matter, the CJEU decided in *Genentech Inc. v. Hoechst GmbH*, Case C-567/14 (a plant variety protection case) that even when an intellectual property (IP) right is later invalidated, accrued royalties under an IP licensing agreement must still be paid in full. Contractual language that changes this result may well be enforceable; but without this language, the accrued royalties must be paid.

4. On patent litigation generally in the UK, see Christian Helmers & Luke McDonagh, *Patent Litigation in the UK: An Empirical Survey 2000–2008*, 8 J. Intell. Prop. L. & Practice 846 (2013) (finding that over 100 patent suits are filed each year in England and Wales).

5. For discussion of "convoyed sales" damages in US patent cases, see Robert A. Matthews, Jr., Annotated Patent Digest §30:62 (September 2017 Update) "Convoyed sales and derivative sales" (details on many cases in the US).

Patent office invalidity trials: The US PTAB as a case study

In most patent systems around the world, a company that wants to challenge an issued patent can do so in an administrative proceeding. In some countries, this is the only way to challenge a patent's validity; in others, patent validity may be raised as a defense in the context of a patent infringement lawsuit. Administrative invalidity proceedings are called "oppositions" in the European Patent Office. In mainland China, they are called actions before the Patent Review Board. It was not until 1999 that the US adopted a similar method of administrative challenge. And under the AIA of 2011, the US took a big step that brought it closer to Europe, China, and other countries. The following case represents the first US Supreme Court opinion to consider this new system of administrative challenge. We examine it here as an example of an important transnational enforcement issue: coordination between court actions and patent office administrative proceedings.

 CASE

Cuozzo Speed Techs., LLC v. Lee, 136 S. Ct. 2131 (2016)

Justice Breyer delivered the opinion of the Court.
The Leahy-Smith America Invents Act creates a process called "inter partes review" [IPR]. That review process allows a third party to ask the US Patent and Trademark Office to reexamine the claims in an already-issued patent and to cancel any claim that the agency finds to be unpatentable in light of prior art. See §102 (requiring "novel[ty]"); §103 (disqualifying claims that are "obvious"). [The IPR procedure replaced "inter partes reexaminations," initiated in 1999; these permitted significant participation in the patent challenge by the party challenging the patent; they were in turn an addition to "traditional" reexaminations, begun in 1980, under which patent challengers are permitted only to

CASE *(continued)*

request a reexamination, and thereafter play no role in the proceedings. "Traditional" reexaminations are still in effect in the PTO.]

We consider [this provision]:

> "No Appeal. – The determination by the Director [of the Patent Office] whether to institute an inter partes review under this section shall be final and non-appealable." §314(d).

Does this provision bar a court from considering whether the Patent Office wrongly "determin[ed] . . . to institute an inter partes review," ibid., when it did so on grounds not specifically mentioned in a third party's review request?

We conclude that [this] provision, though it may not bar consideration of a constitutional question, for example, does bar judicial review of the kind of mine-run claim at issue here, involving the Patent Office's decision to institute inter partes review.

In 2011, Congress enacted the statute before us. That statute modifies "inter partes reexamination," which it now calls "inter partes review." See H.R. Rep. No. 112-98, pt. 1, pp. 46–47 (2011) (H.R. Rep.) . . . The new statute provides a challenger with broader participation rights. It creates within the Patent Office a Patent Trial and Appeal Board (Board) composed of administrative patent judges, who are patent lawyers and former patent examiners, among others. §6. That Board conducts the proceedings, reaches a conclusion, and sets forth its reasons. See ibid.

The statute sets forth time limits for completing this review. §316(a)(11). It grants the Patent Office the authority to issue rules. §316(a)(4). Like its predecessors, the statute authorizes judicial review of a "final written decision" canceling a patent claim. §319. And, the statute says that the agency's initial decision "whether to institute an inter partes review" is "final and nonappealable." §314(d).

[In 2002, Giuseppe A. Cuozzo applied for a patent for a speedometer that uses GPS technology to indicate when the vehicle exceeds the legal speed limit on a particular road. The PTO granted the patent in 2004 (US Patent No. 6,778,074). In 2012, Garmin sought inter partes review of patent of the Cuozzo Patent's 20 claims.

With respect to claim 17 of Cuozzo's patent, Garmin argued that the claim was obvious in light of three prior art references, known as the Aumayer, Evans, and Wendt patents. Garmin did not assert that particular trio of references as a ground for invalidating claims 10 and 14 of the patent. Nevertheless, the PTO Board decided to review not only claim 17, but also claims 10 and 14, on the basis of that trio of patent references. Even though the inter partes review statute requires petitions to set forth the grounds for challenge "with particularity," §312(a)(3), the Board reasoned that Garmin had "implicitly" challenged claims 10 and 14 on the basis of the three references because "claim 17 depends on claim 14 which depends on claim 10."

The Board held that claims 10, 14, and 17 of the Cuozzo Patent were obvious in light of the three prior art patent references. In appealing to the Federal Circuit, Cuozzo argued that the Board decision to institute review against claims 10 and 14 was legally wrong.

CASE *(continued)*

Like the [Federal Circuit], we believe that Cuozzo's contention that the Patent Office unlawfully initiated its agency review is not appealable. For one thing, that is what §314(d) says. It states that the "determination by the [Patent Office] whether to institute an inter partes review under this section shall be *final and nonappealable*." (Emphasis added.)

For another, the legal dispute at issue is an ordinary dispute about the application of certain relevant patent statutes concerning the Patent Office's decision to institute inter partes review. Cuozzo points to a related statutory section, §312, which says that petitions must be pleaded "with particularity." Those words, in its view, mean that the petition should have specifically said that claims 10 and 14 are also obvious in light of this same prior art. Garmin's petition, the government replies, need not have mentioned claims 10 and 14 separately, for claims 10, 14, and 17 are all logically linked; the claims "rise and fall together," and a petition need not simply repeat the same argument expressly when it is so obviously implied. In our view, the "No Appeal" provision's language must, at the least, forbid an appeal that attacks a "determination . . . whether to institute" review by raising this kind of legal question and little more, §314(d).

Moreover, a contrary holding would undercut one important congressional objective, namely, giving the Patent Office significant power to revisit and revise earlier patent grants. See H.R. Rep., at 45, 48 (explaining that the statute seeks to "improve patent quality and restore confidence in the presumption of validity that comes with issued patents"); 157 Cong. Rec. 9778 (2011) (remarks of Rep. Goodlatte) (noting that inter partes review "screen[s] out bad patents while bolstering valid ones"). We doubt that Congress would have granted the Patent Office this authority, including, for example, the ability to continue proceedings even after the original petitioner settles and drops out, §317(a), if it had thought that the agency's final decision could be unwound under some minor statutory technicality related to its preliminary decision to institute inter partes review. [The Court goes on to say that its decision in this case leaves open the question whether an appeal is possible when a Board decision regarding whether to institute a proceeding raises constitutional issues.]

Affirmed.

NOTES

1. A second issue in the case was whether the PTO was within its rights to pass regulations stipulating the standard for claim construction in an IPR proceeding. The PTO had decreed that the Patent Trial and Appeal Board (PTAB) is to use the "broadest reasonable interpretation" standard, which is the same one that patent examiners use in patent prosecution. The Supreme Court held that the AIA has given the PTO authority to pass regulations such as this one.
2. The IPR proceedings at issue in *Cuozzo Speed* are not the only type of administrative patent challenge initiated by the AIA. Two other important ones are: (1) Post-Grant Review (PGR), available within nine months of patent issuance. A PGR can challenge a patent on more grounds than an IPR, including §§101 and 112; (2) A Covered Business Method (CBM) proceeding, which is similar in some ways to a PGR but which (a) applies only to business method patents, and (b) was made available against all issued patents,

not just patents issued in the prior nine months. For more on PGRs, CBMs, and the other types of AIA administrative challenges, see Robert P. Merges and John F. Duffy, Patent Law and Policy (7th ed., 2017), at Chapter 10.

3. Two other important issues in IPRs are (1) the extent to which a patent challenger is prevented from retrying specific grounds of invalidity in a court-based trial, after the same patent has been challenged in an IPR (called "estoppel"); and (2) the ability of a patent challenger to suspend an ongoing court trial, pending resolution of an IPR proceeding involving the same patent as the trial (called a "stay").

With respect to estoppel, a patent challenger is prevented from arguing in litigation (*i.e.*, in a court case) "that the claim is invalid on any ground that the petitioner raised or reasonably could have raised during" the IPR. See 35 U.S.C. §315(e) (2012) (inter partes review). The same language appears in the estoppel provision relating to PGRs. 35 U.S.C. §325(e) (postgrant review). The statutory estoppel provision for covered business method review is narrower and applies only to invalidity grounds *actually* raised by the petitioner. See AIA §18(a)(1)(D).

The AIA makes the granting of a litigation "stay" discretionary with district courts. Typically, courts will consider three factors (derived from older case law on stay requests in reexaminations): (1) the potential for prejudice or tactical disadvantage; (2) the timing of the desired stay relative to that of the administrative proceeding itself; and (3) the likelihood that resolution of the administrative proceeding may simplify the pending litigation. See *Universal Elecs., Inc. v. Universal Remote Control, Inc.*, 943 F. Supp. 2d 1028, 1030–33 (C.D. Cal. 2013). The Federal Circuit has, at least in some cases, shown a strong preference for the granting of stays. See *VirtualAgility Inc. v. Salesforce.com, Inc.*, 2014 BL 191228, 111 U.S.P.Q.2d 1763 (Fed. Cir. July 10, 2014). Saurabh Vishnubakhat and Jay P. Kesan, *Strategic Decisionmaking in Dual PTAB and District Court Proceedings*, 31 Berkeley Tech. L. J. 45 (2016) (finding that 70 percent of IPRs are initiated by defendants already in litigation with a patent owner, but that 30 percent are not; and noting that many of the parties to IPR that are not in litigation have joined pre-existing IPRs that were initiated by litigation parties – meaning that *groups* of competitors are often joining together to challenge issued patents).

9
Business aspects of patents

9.1 Licensing agreements

Although the acquisition of patent rights ("prosecution") and patent litigation are both specialized fields, patent-related transactions are so common that many general corporate lawyers touch on this part of patent law in their practices. In this section we cover only the basics. For much more detail on these and related topics, see Robert W. Gomulkiewicz, Xuan-Thao Nguyen, and Danielle Conway-Jones, Licensing Intellectual Property: Law and Application (2nd ed., 2011).

For this brief introduction, we follow the three main stages of most licensing transactions: (a) the initial contact and negotiation period, when the prospective parties are exploring the possibility of a licensing deal; (b) the contract drafting stage, when substantive issues are hammered out and memorialized in the licensing agreement; and (3) the enforcement stage, which occurs in only a small fraction of transactions, when the parties pursue legal enforcement of their rights under the license.

9.1.1 Precontractual liability, or *culpa in contrahendo*: protecting disclosures in the pre-contract period

The following case demonstrates several important points. First, it shows that disclosures in the pre-contract period, made while the parties are evaluating the licensing opportunity and negotiating the basic terms of a deal, are usually made under a Non-disclosure Agreement or NDA. Second, it shows the difficulty of *proving* trade secret misappropriation, notwithstanding the presence of the NDA. And third, it shows the crucial importance of patent protection. Even if a disclosing party fails to prove its legal claims for trade secret misappropriation and breach of NDA contract, it can still rely on patent protection as an alternative basis of legal recovery. (The version of the case below reverses the order in which the court addressed the issues in the actual case report. In the actual report patent infringement is considered before trade secret misappropriation.)

CASE

On-Line Tech. v. Bodenseewerk Perkin-Elmer, 386 F.3d 1133 (Fed. Cir. 2004)

Bryson, Circuit Judge.

The dispute in this case involves a device known as a long-path gas cell, which is used in an infrared spectrometer to determine the composition of gases such as emissions from industrial plants. The spectrometer captures the gas to be tested and directs a beam of infrared light through the chamber containing the gas. After the light has passed through the chamber, a detector measures the absorption of the light, from which the properties of the gas can be determined. It has long been understood in the art that lengthening the light path in the gas cell chamber can result in a more accurate absorption reading. One problem encountered in long-path gas cells, however, was that over the long path created by multiple reflections of the light beam within the chamber, the quality of the beam would become degraded, primarily because of astigmatism induced by the mirrors used in the system. Astigmatism is an optical aberration created when an optical element or system has a different focal length in each of two orthogonal planes. K.D. Moeller, Optics (1988), at 448; H.P. Brueggemann, Conic Mirrors (1968), at 15.

In 1995, appellant On-Line Technologies, Inc. obtained a patent, U.S. Patent No. 5,440,143 ("the '143 patent"), on a method for increasing the length of the light path in a gas cell while correcting for astigmatism and thereby reducing the diffusion of the beam of light. On-Line subsequently brought an action in the United States District Court for the District of Connecticut against a group of related parties, [all related to Bodenseewerk Perkin-Elmer GmbH] (collectively, "Perkin-Elmer").

In its complaint, On-Line alleged that Perkin-Elmer had made, used, and sold a device that infringed the '143 patent. In addition, On-Line asserted several state law claims, including misappropriation of trade secrets, violation of the state law of unfair competition, breach of contract, and fraud. In support of the state law claims, On-Line alleged that, pursuant to a nondisclosure agreement, it had revealed its gas cell design to Perkin-Elmer scientists in anticipation of a possible business arrangement between the companies relating to On-Line's device. Rather than pursuing a joint enterprise, however, Perkin-Elmer allegedly copied what it had learned from On-Line and incorporated the disclosed technology into its commercial product, thus breaching the nondisclosure agreement and violating the state law prohibitions against unfair competition, theft of trade secrets, and fraud.

[**Trade Secret Claims**]

In the district court, On-Line alleged that Perkin-Elmer misappropriated confidential information relating to the design of On-Line's long-path gas cell. The district court ruled that On-Line failed to prove actionable misappropriation because the information at issue was disclosed in the '143 patent and because On-Line failed to point to any evidence that

CASE *(continued)*

Perkin-Elmer had improperly used any information relating to the gas cell prior to the issuance of the patent. Based on the summary judgment record, the district court concluded that undisputed evidence showed that Perkin-Elmer did not begin to incorporate the features of On-Line's gas cell into its own product until 1996, after the issuance of the '143 patent. Although On-Line referred to evidence regarding Perkin-Elmer's conduct before the issuance of the '143 patent, the district court held that none of that evidence was probative of misappropriation because the conduct in question all constituted legitimate evaluation of On-Line's product pursuant to the nondisclosure agreement entered into by On-Line and Perkin-Elmer in 1994. As to On-Line's claim that not all of the secrets relating to its gas cell were disclosed in the '143 patent, the court found that claim to be unsupported by any evidence.

After a patent has issued, the information contained within it is ordinarily regarded as public and not subject to protection as a trade secret. See Restatement (Third) of Unfair Competition §39 cmt. f (1995) ("Information that is generally known or readily ascertainable through proper means . . . by others to whom it has potential economic value is not protectable as a trade secret. Thus, information that is disclosed in a patent or contained in published materials reasonably accessible to competitors does not qualify for protection [as a trade secret]."); *Conmar Prods. Corp. v. Universal Slide Fastener Co.*, 172 F.2d 150, 155–56 (2d Cir.1949) (L. Hand). Moreover, the nondisclosure agreement in this case specifically provided that the obligation of confidentiality created by the agreement "will not apply to any information . . . which becomes publicly available other than by breach of this agreement." Consequently, On-Line cannot claim that Perkin-Elmer's activities following the issuance of the '143 patent constituted misappropriation of confidential information unless the activities related to information not disclosed in the patent.

In the district court, On-Line claimed that Perkins-Elmer had misappropriated information relating to the design of the long-path gas cell and had used it to build its own long-path gas cell prior to the issuance of the '143 patent. The district court, however, concluded that the evidence to which On-Line pointed did not create a genuine issue of material fact on that issue, and we agree. As characterized by the district court, the evidence showed that Perkin-Elmer took various steps to evaluate the On-Line technology that it was considering buying, but did not show that Perkin-Elmer began building its own gas cell before 1996. Although On-Line asserts that the evidence of Perkin-Elmer's course of conduct with respect to On-Line's product shows that it made use of On-Line's gas cell trade secret before the issuance of the '143 patent, On-Line's general characterizations do not satisfy the requirement that it point to specific evidence sufficient to create a disputed issue of material fact.

We also reject On-Line's argument that Perkin-Elmer's acts of copying and testing On-Line's gas cell during the period covered by the nondisclosure agreement were not authorized by the agreement and therefore constituted misappropriation. As the district court noted, On-Line did not present any evidence that Perkin-Elmer began to develop

CASE (continued)

its own cell during the period covered by the agreement or otherwise engaged in conduct prohibited by the nondisclosure agreement. Instead, the evidence relating to Perkin-Elmer's conduct with respect to the disclosed technology shows merely that Perkin-Elmer tested and evaluated that technology, which was conduct contemplated by the nondisclosure agreement. Moreover, Robert Hoult, a Perkin-Elmer scientist who visited On-Line's facility following the execution of the nondisclosure agreement, submitted an affidavit in which he averred that he had learned nothing useful about On-Line's gas cell that was not already evident from On-Line's nonconfidential marketing brochure. On-Line did not offer evidence to contradict Dr. Hoult's representation. Because On-Line failed to demonstrate a disputed issue of material fact with respect to the long-path gas cell trade secret claim, we affirm the district court's grant of summary judgment on that issue.

[**Patent Infringement**]

The district court's grant of summary judgment of noninfringement as to claim 1 of the '143 patent was premised on the court's claim construction. On-Line contends that the district court erred in construing the claim and therefore erred in entering summary judgment.

Claim 1 of the '143 patent recites as follows (emphasis added):

> A folded-path radiation absorption gas cell comprising: an enclosure having first and second ends, and defining a substantially closed chamber therewithin; spaced input radiation and output radiation windows formed through said first end of said enclosure and aligned on a first axis; a concave reflective field surface extending at least partially between said windows at said first end of said enclosure; *a pair of substantially spherical, concave reflective objective surfaces* at said second end of said enclosure disposed in confronting relationship to said field surface, said objective surfaces being aligned side-by-side on an axis parallel to said first axis and in optical registry with said windows, *at least one of said objective surfaces having a cylindrical component added thereto to increase coincidence of focii in two orthogonal planes*, thereby to maximize the energy throughput characteristic of said cell; and means for the introduction and withdrawal of gas into and from said chamber of said enclosure.

The invention to which claim 1 is directed is an improvement on a type of gas cell known as a "White cell." A White cell uses several mirrors that are aligned to make the light follow a long path as it passes through the test chamber. In the invention, two mirrors are placed side by side at the opposite end of the main chamber from a third mirror. A beam of light enters the chamber and is repeatedly reflected off the three mirrors until it reaches an exit point. Because the mirrors reflect the light beam back and forth across the chamber multiple times, the path of the beam is much longer than the distance from one end of the chamber to the other.

The '143 patent sought to address the problem of astigmatic diffusion of the light beam passing through the cell. The solution proposed by the '143 patent was to shape the secondary mirrors in a manner that would counteract the astigmatism induced by

CASE *(continued)*

reflections from the spherical mirrors used in White cells and thus keep the beam of light focused during its passage through the cell '143 patent, col. 4, ll. 52–62. To achieve that purpose, each claim of the '143 patent required the mirrors to have "substantially spherical, concave reflective objective surfaces . . . at least one of said objective surfaces having a cylindrical component added thereto to increase coincidence of focii in two orthogonal planes . . ." *Id.*, col. 5, ll. 44–52; col. 6, ll. 14–22, 40–48. On-Line asserted that Perkin-Elmer's commercial long-path gas cells infringed claim 1 of the '143 patent. In particular, On-Line contended that Perkin-Elmer's cells used objective mirrors of the sort recited in the claim to correct for astigmatism. In the district court, Perkin-Elmer did not dispute that its accused gas cells used objective mirrors shaped to correct for astigmatism. Perkin-Elmer argued, however, that its objective mirrors had toroidal surfaces, not "substantially spherical" surfaces "having a cylindrical component added thereto," as required by claim 1 of the '143 patent. For that reason, Perkin-Elmer argued, its gas cells were not within the scope of the patent, either literally or under the doctrine of equivalents. In essence, Perkin-Elmer's argument was that a toroidal surface is different from a substantially spherical surface with a cylindrical component added to it. Because On-Line not only did not claim toroidal mirror surfaces but specifically omitted them from its claims, Perkin-Elmer contended that On-Line had dedicated surfaces of that shape to the public. The district court agreed with Perkin-Elmer and held that Perkin-Elmer's toroidal surface was not covered by the '143 patent. In explaining its claim construction ruling, the district court noted that the specification described the contour of the spherical objective mirrors as "approach[ing] toroidal." '143 patent, col. 4, ll. 8–12. The court stated that "[b]ecause mirrors with a contour which only 'approaches toroidal' cannot be said to be actual toroidal mirrors, toroidal objective mirrors are not spherical objective mirrors with cylindrical corrections."

On appeal, On-Line contends that the district court erred in ruling that objective mirrors having a toroidal surface are not within the scope of claim 1 of the '143 patent. We agree with On-Line that, properly construed, the reference to a "substantially spherical, concave reflective surface . . . having a cylindrical component added thereto to increase coincidence of focii in two orthogonal planes" defines a set of curved surfaces that includes a toroidal surface. We reach that conclusion because the specification makes clear that the claim language referring to spherical surfaces with cylindrical components includes toroidal surfaces.

[T]he specification refers to the curved surfaces in the preferred embodiment of the invention as toroidal surfaces ("the toroids of the surfaces 62, 64," '143 patent, col. 4, line 16), and in doing so it describes those surfaces by using the same language that is used in claim 1 ("generally spherical reflective surfaces," each of which "has a cylindrical component superimposed thereupon," *id.*, col. 4, ll. 7–10). Accordingly, the specification makes it clear that, for purposes of the '143 patent, a toroidal surface is a substantially spherical reflective surface that has a cylindrical component superimposed thereupon. Second, even if the specification were less explicit in equating the term "toroid" with a generally spherical surface having a cylindrical component added thereto, the reference to the preferred

CASE (continued)

embodiment as having mirrors with toroidal surfaces would give rise to a very strong inference that the claim should be construed to include such surfaces.

Accordingly, because the summary judgment of noninfringement was based on an erroneous claim construction, we vacate the judgment of noninfringement and remand the case for further proceedings on the remaining issues pertinent to On-Line's claim of infringement.

NOTES

1. The key claim, claim 1, of the patent in this case was later ruled invalid. See *On-Line Techs., Inc. v. Perkin-Elmer Corp.*, 448 F. Supp. 2d 365 (D. Conn. 2006) (prior art in the form of a prior patent anticipates claim 1 of the '143 patent). Nevertheless, the case teaches some valuable lessons. One important lesson is that it is helpful to have a patent or patent application in hand when approaching another party to negotiate a license. Because the trade secret cause of action was not successful here, On-Line had only one way to recover on its claim that Perkin-Elmer learned about the long-cell technology from On-Line: patent infringement. Without a patent infringement claim, in other words, On-Line would have had no recourse. On the importance of patent protection in encouraging pre-contractual disclosure and negotiation, see Robert P. Merges, *A Transactional View of Property Rights*, 20 Berkeley Tech. L. J. 1477 (2005). And remember, patent infringement does not require proof that the defendant copied from the patent owner. No knowledge of the patent or the invention is required to prove patent infringement. All that is required is to prove that the defendant is making, using, or selling an invention that meets all the claim limitations of at least one of the patent owner's claims. That's it. See Robert P. Merges, *A Few Kind Words for Absolute Infringement Liability in Patent Law*, 31 Berkeley Tech. L.J. 1 (2016).

   On the other hand the case illustrates the trade-off inherent in choosing to patent. Because the patent issued before Perkin-Elmer commercialized its technology, and because On-Line could not prove to the satisfaction of the court precisely what was disclosed to Perkin-Elmer and when, the court held that On-Line could not prove misappropriation of trade secrets. The issuance of the patent meant that all the information in the disclosure was now in the public domain; anyone is free to learn from it. That left only the patent cause of action for On-Line. But because patents are subject to stringent tests of validity, when broad prior art was found it meant that the On-Line patent was found invalid. Thus the disclosure in the patent was no longer subject to any valid patent claim, and it became free to all who might want to copy the disclosed invention.

2. The misappropriation claim in the *On-Line* case might also be addressed in civil law jurisdictions under the doctrine of *culpa in contrahendo* – fault in contemplation of a contract, or, as it is sometimes known in common law countries, "precontractual liability." German law has long recognized liability for fault in contracting under the *culpa in contrahendo* rubric. In both France and Germany this doctrine originated outside the civil codes, pinned at most to abstract provisions in the codes such as a general duty of good faith. But the 2001 revision to the obligations articles of the German Civil Code (the Bürgerliches Gesetzbuch, or "BGB"), now includes this concept explicitly. See BGB, available at http://www.gesetze-im-internet.de/eng lisch_bgb/englisch_bgb.html#p0430. The doctrine derives from BGB §241(2), which requires "each party to take account of the rights, legal interests and other interests of the other party." Under §242, parties have a general obligation "to perform according to the requirements of good faith." Then BGB §311 states the heart of the obligation, when it directs that the duty of good faith "comes into existence by . . . the commencement of contract negotiations" (BGB §311(2)(1)). The scope of the duty of good faith, and its application to disclosure of sensitive information during negotiations, may differ in some respects from the application of US trade secret law. For background and comparison of the legal theories at work in this area of law, see Friedrich Kessler & Edith Fine, *Culpa in Contrahendo, Bargaining in Good Faith, and Freedom of Contract: A Comparative Study*, 77 Harv. L. Rev. 401 (1964); Han Shiyuan, *Culpa in Contrahendo in Chinese Contract Law*, 6 Tsinghua China L. Rev. 157 (2014). See generally Wang Jingen & Larry A. DiMatteo, *Chinese Reception and Transplantation of Western Contract Law*, 34 Berkeley J. Int'l L. 44 (2016).

9.2 Substantive terms of patent licenses

Most licensing agreements are formed around a few core terms. The backbone of the agreement usually centers on:

- the grant: precisely which rights (for example: right to make, right to sell) are granted from the patent owner to the licensee;
- the territory: region, state, province, country, multiple countries;
- the term: how long the agreement remains in effect, either a fixed period of time or renewable by one or both parties at various intervals; and
- the royalty rate, which is determined from a combination of technology value/competitive conditions and the other terms just described.

Each of these terms may be elaborated, expanded, and modified by other terms of the agreement. These other terms can cover a very wide range of issues, including (but by no means limited to): termination rights under various conditions; choice of law provisions and/or arbitration provisions; and accounting and inspection procedures.

The case that follows is one of many examples that might have been chosen to illustrate a dispute over a substantive term of a licensing agreement. The particular term at issue is a "most favored nation" (MFN) clause, which simply says that the licensee of a patent is to receive a royalty rate no higher than the best rate that any other patent licensee receives. It is typically negotiated by the licensee of a patent to insure that the licensee does not end up at a disadvantage compared to other, future licensees. For the licensee, it is a matter of fairness: "adjust my royalty rate down if you give another licensee a better rate in the future."

The license in this case illustrates why licensees ask for MFN clauses. The technology involves an oil well device called a "Christmas tree" – a mechanical structure made up of pipes, valves, spigots, and other oil flow-managing components, which vaguely resembles a Western-style Christmas tree. The plaintiff in the case, Cameron International, held a patent on an improved version of the Christmas tree (the "SpoolTree" design), which was used in wells that are sunk in ocean waters (so-called "subsea wells"). Cameron planned to license the patent to all three of its competitors in the market for subsea Christmas trees: Vetco, Kvaerner, and FMC. The first licensee was Vetco. Vetco accepted the need for a license, but, being first, did not want to end up paying a higher royalty rate than the other two licensees who had not yet signed contracts with Cameron: Kvaerner and FMC. So the parties negotiated an MFN clause.

But license agreements can be complex. When Cameron negotiated with Kvaerner and FMC, the result was a series of contracts with various complex provisions involving the details of what was exchanged and how much was to be paid. These agreements, Vetco said, in effect involved lower royalty rates, which would trigger the MFN clause and lower Vetco's payments to Cameron. Cameron disagreed; it said that the details of the agreements did not lower the effective royalty rate to Kvaerner and FMC, so the MFN clause was not activated. Litigation in a Texas state court followed. Pursuant to the agreement, the parties took their dispute over royalty terms to an expert "economic evaluator" (arbitrator) – Professor Paul Janicke of the University of Houston Law School. Professor Janicke's arbitration award in the case was brought for review before the trial court. The trial court upheld Professor Janicke's findings, and that court decision was appealed to the Texas Court of Appeals, which authored the opinion below. (Note that in this opinion, the patent holder-plaintiff Cameron is referred to as the "appellant" because it filed the appeal to the Court of Appeals; Vetco is the "appellee".)

CASE

Cameron Int'l Corp. v. Vetco Gray Inc., No. 14-07-00656-CV, 2009 WL 838177 (Tex. App. Mar. 31, 2009)

There are four primary manufacturers of subsea Christmas trees worldwide: appellant, appellee, Vetco Gray Inc., Kvaerner Oilfield Products, Inc. ("Kvaerner"), and FMC Technologies, Inc. ("FMC"). Originally, Christmas trees were vertical. Maintenance on subsea wells was an expensive and time-consuming process because the entire vertical Christmas tree had to be removed first. In 1996, appellant patented a new design of Christmas tree, a horizontal tree, which appellant called the SpoolTree. The SpoolTree design was superior to the old vertical tree design because it allowed maintenance to be performed while the tree remained in place and provided better protection against leakage that could endanger workers and harm the environment.

After it patented the SpoolTree, appellant sent notice of its patent to its three competitors: appellee [Vetco], Kvaerner, and FMC. In addition, appellant invited each of the three competitors to negotiate a license to use the SpoolTree design. Of the three competitors, only appellee [Vetco] entered into negotiations with appellant for a license. Kvaerner and FMC entered into litigation with appellant over the design. In 1997 appellee's negotiations with appellant were successful and they entered into a contract, the Cross-License Agreement. Pursuant to the Cross-License Agreement, appellee agreed to pay appellant a royalty rate of 6.5 percent of all revenue obtained from selling products covered

CASE *(continued)*

by appellant's patents retroactive to August 1996. In addition, appellee gave appellant a cross-license for several of appellee's products and received a $3 million credit to be applied to its royalty payments to appellant. In addition, to protect appellee's status as the first to obtain a SpoolTree license, the Cross-License Agreement includes a "most-favored licensee" clause that requires appellant to promptly notify appellee of any SpoolTree licenses appellant might grant to a third party. In addition, paragraph 5.2 of the Cross-License Agreement provides:

> In the event the ROYALTY TERMS of such third-party license are, as a whole, more favorable to the other PARTY than are provided in this CROSS LICENSE AGREEMENT, then for so long as the third-party license is in effect, the other PARTY shall be entitled to elect the more favorable ROYALTY TERMS from the date of notice to the third party or the date of marking, whichever is earlier.

To address the possibility that future SpoolTree licenses might not have an explicit royalty percentage such as appellee's 6.5 percent, the parties included paragraph 5.6 in the Cross-License Agreement, which provides:

> In the event the PARTIES cannot agree on the ROYALTY TERMS of a third party license, the PARTIES shall select within fifteen (15) days after written request by a PARTY one economic evaluator by mutual agreement, which agreement shall not be unreasonably withheld. The PARTIES shall submit in writing to the economic evaluator the issue of the ROYALTY TERMS for the third party license. Each PARTY shall be allowed one written submission and neither party shall be allowed a responsive or other written submission unless specifically requested in writing by the economic evaluator. There shall be no ex parte contact with the economic evaluator concerning the subject matter. The economic evaluator's decision, which must be made within one month of the final submission, shall be binding upon the PARTIES. The PARTIES shall share the cost of the economic evaluator.

Eventually, appellant resolved its litigation and negotiated license agreements with both Kvaerner and FMC. The Kvaerner license involved a fixed sum royalty for each Christmas tree sold using appellant's patents as well as two supply agreements. On August 22, 2003, appellee sent appellant [Cameron, the patent owner] notice of its election of the Kvaerner royalty rate. In response, appellant refused to acknowledge appellee's election, threatened to terminate appellee's license by declaring appellee in default, and refused appellee's requests to take the matter to an economic evaluator. Appellant then initiated the current litigation asking the trial court to declare, among other things, (1) that any election by appellee of the Kvaerner royalty rate must be based upon the economic value exchanged as a whole, and (2) the determination of the effective percentage rate of the Kvaerner royalty rate must take the economic value appellant received from the two Kvaerner supply agreements into account.

CASE *(continued)*

While the current litigation was in progress, appellant, on March 7, 2004, entered into a license agreement with FMC (the "2004 FMC License"). The 2004 FMC License required FMC to make a lump sum payment of $6 million to appellant. In addition, the 2004 FMC License included a cross-license granting appellant a license to certain FMC patents and a supply agreement. Under the 2004 FMC License, once it had paid the $6 million lump sum, FMC had no royalty obligations going forward. After reviewing the 2004 FMC License, appellee notified appellant of its election of the 2004 FMC License's royalty terms and appellant "acknowledg[ed] and accept[ed] [appellee's] election." Despite that acknowledgment and acceptance, the litigation between appellant and appellee continued as the dispute widened to include the 2004 FMC License.

In March 2005, appellant moved to abate the litigation and send the dispute over the royalty rates to arbitration. The trial court granted appellant's motion and ordered the parties to arbitration. The parties selected Professor Paul M. Janicke, a law professor at the University of Houston Law Center, as the neutral arbitrator. Based on the terms of the Cross-License Agreement and the trial court's arbitration order, Professor Janicke was to determine the "royalty terms" of the 2004 FMC License and the Kvaerner license. In October 2005, Professor Janicke issued his report. In his report, Professor Janicke found the 2004 FMC License had an effective royalty rate of 0.76 percent and the Kvaerner license had an effective royalty rate of 6.46 percent, making both more favorable than appellee's 6.5 percent royalty rate. Appellant moved to vacate the arbitration award while appellee asked the trial court to confirm it. On November 18, 2005, the trial court granted appellee's motion and confirmed the arbitration award.

Following the arbitration, appellant and FMC entered into an amended and restated cross-license agreement (the "2005 FMC License"). Appellant then notified appellee that since the 2004 FMC License had been replaced, appellee had lost the 0.76 percent royalty rate and its royalty rate had reverted back to the original 6.5 percent. This issue was then added to the ongoing litigation.

All remaining issues related to the construction of the Cross-License Agreement were resolved through a series of motions for partial summary judgment filed by appellee and which were granted by the trial court. On July 20, 2006 the trial court granted appellee's motion for partial summary judgment contending it had not breached the Cross-License Agreement when it applied the $14 million credit resulting from the arbitrator's award to any amounts due to appellant for the use of appellant's SpoolTree patents. On September 8, 2006 the trial court granted appellee's motion for partial summary judgment asserting any credit generated by appellee's election of the 2004 FMC royalty rate remained in place regardless of the continuing validity or existence of the 2004 FMC License. Finally, on November 22, 2006 the trial court granted appellee's motion for partial summary judgment asserting (1) the Cross-License Agreement was not ambiguous, and (2) that once appellee had elected the 2004 FMC royalty terms, nothing in the language of the Cross-License Agreement allowed appellee's royalty terms to revert back to the original 6.5 percent rate.

CASE *(continued)*

After the parties dismissed their remaining claims, the trial court entered a final judgment incorporating its prior orders. This appeal followed.

[Referring to paragraph 5.2, which says "In the event the ROYALTY TERMS of such third-party license are, as a whole, more favorable to the other PARTY than are provided in this CROSS LICENSE AGREEMENT, then *for so long as the third-party license is in effect*, the other PARTY shall be entitled to elect the more favorable ROYALTY TERMS . . ."], we conclude the phrase "then for so long as the third-party license is in effect" modifies the phrase "the other PARTY shall be entitled to elect the more favorable ROYALTY TERMS." The meaning of the verb "elect" is "to select by vote (as for office or membership)" or "choose, pick." *The Merriam Webster Dictionary New Edition* (2004). Accordingly, we hold the only reasonable construction of paragraph 5.2 of the Cross-License Agreement is that it created a window of time in which appellee could choose the 2004 FMC royalty rate and once chosen, the new rate would remain in effect for the remaining duration of the Cross-License Agreement.

[This ruling favors appellee Vetco; appellant Cameron had argued that the phrase "for so long as the third party license is in effect" meant that if a license with a lower rate were to end, the lower rate for the Cameron-Vetco license would also end. The court rejected this reading and held instead that paragraph 5.2 means that Vetco can choose or "elect" the lower rate at any time the other, lower-royalty, license is in effect; and even if that other, lower-royalty license ends, the lower rate from that license will continue to apply to the Cameron-Vetco license. Which is what happened here, because the FMC license was, for a period, a lower-royalty (0.76 percent) license; even though it ended, Vetco is still to receive the lower rate because Vetco elected this rate while the FMC license was in effect.]

[Cameron argued that the court should take into account the purpose of the MFN clause – which Cameron said was to make sure Vetco did not suffer a competitive disadvantage with any of its competitor/licensees. Because the FMC lower-royalty agreement ended, Cameron said Vetco was no longer at a competitive disadvantage so the higher rate of 6.5 percent should come back into force.] In support of its position that the purpose of a most-favored-licensee clause is to avoid a competitive disadvantage, appellant calls this court's attention to the testimony of its intellectual property counsel explaining his interpretation of the Most-Favored-Licensee clause at issue here. However, because we have determined the Cross-License Agreement is not ambiguous, [this] evidence is not admissible . . .

In addition, appellant cites *Studiengesellschaft Kohle m.b.H. v. Novamont Corp.*, 704 F.2d 48, 53 (2nd Cir.1983), in support of its argument that the purpose of every most-favored-licensee clause is to avoid a competitive disadvantage. However, while the court in *Novamont* did conclude the purpose of the most-favored-licensee clause at issue in that case was to avoid a competitive disadvantage, the *Novamont* clause differs from paragraph 5.2 in two important ways. First, the most-favored-licensee clause in *Novamont* had a specific reversion clause providing that the elected royalty terms would revert back to the original terms if the third party license terminated. Second, the *Novamont* most-favored-licensee clause also had a section providing that the licensor had no obligation to repay to the

CASE *(continued)*

licensee any royalties the licensee had previously paid. The most-favored-licensee clause at issue here does not have a reversion clause and specifically provides that when appellee elected a more favorable royalty rate, it was entitled to a retroactive credit on all royalties paid since the inception of the Cross-License Agreement.

Appellant's proffered construction of the most-favored-licensee clause is further undermined by the retroactive nature of appellee's election of a more favorable royalty rate. By agreeing to make the newly elected royalty rate retroactive to the beginning of the Cross-License Agreement, a period when appellee was not at a competitive disadvantage because there was not a more favorable royalty rate, demonstrates the parties, through paragraph 5.2, rather than avoiding a competitive disadvantage, instead sought to ensure that appellee, the party with the most-favored-licensee status, actually had the best royalty rate throughout the life of the Cross-License Agreement.

After examining the Cross-License Agreement and the arbitrator's award, there is no doubt Professor Janicke followed his contractual instructions and his award falls within the permitted scope of the Cross-License Agreement. [Trial court affirmed.]

NOTES

1. MFN clauses affect the core part of any license agreement – the royalty rate charged for use of the patent(s). It's no surprise then that various nuances of MFN clauses have been raised in disputes over licensing terms. For example, one issue that sometimes arises begins when the actions or behavior of a patent owner *imply* that it is licensing its patents, even though there is no formal licensing agreement. Does an implied license (which usually comes with an implicit royalty rate of zero) constitute a third-party license that triggers an MFN? The court in *St. Joseph Iron Works v. Farmers Mfg. Co.*, 106 F.2d 294, 296 (4th Cir. 1939) said yes. The patent owner had repaired equipment held by one of its customers, and the repair caused the customer's equipment to become infringing embodiments of patents that had been licensed to plaintiff St. Joseph Iron. The court said yes, the implied license that came with the patent owner's repair work did amount to a royalty-free license to use the patents, and hence triggered the plaintiff-licensee's MFN clause.

2. An implied license scenario also arose in another case, but the court reached a different result. The patentee, Eastman Kodak, had been allied with Pentax, Inc. in various business deals. Kodak never enforced its patents against Pentax; but it never gave an outright license, either. Later, Kodak licensed patents to Ricoh Corporation. The licensing agreement included a clause that required Ricoh to pay past royalties if it acquired a company that had "not previously licensed" Kodak's patents. When Ricoh acquired Pentax, Kodak demanded payment under this clause; Ricoh refused, arguing that there had been an implied license between Kodak and Pentax, so the "not previously licensed" provision did not apply. Kodak sued to recover the past royalties. The district court in *Eastman Kodak Co. v. Ricoh Co.*, No. 12 Civ. 3109 DLC, 2013 WL 4044896 (S.D.N.Y. Aug. 9, 2013) held:

    > Kodak has demonstrated that Pentax was "not previously licensed" under Kodak patents, and Ricoh has failed to respond with evidence raising a genuine issue of fact with respect to whether Pentax was so licensed. Accordingly, because Pentax was not previously licensed by Kodak under Kodak patents, Ricoh's failure to pay any royalties on Pentax's digital cameras sold during the term of the PLA constitutes a breach of that agreement (*id.*, at *11.)

3. The details of MFN clauses may matter. In *Plastic Contact Lens Co. v. Guaranteed Contact Lenses, Inc.*, 283 F. Supp. 850 (S.D.N.Y. 1968), the licensor had the foresight to exempt from an MFN clause licenses reached in settlement of prior litigation. The court found that a third party license granted for settlement of counter-

suits for patent infringement was within the exception to the "most favored licensee" clause. So the licensee was out of luck; it could not demand a royalty rate equal to the one in the settlement agreement.

4. One issue that often comes up when parties to a license agreement have a dispute is whether a licensee can challenge the validity of licensed patents while still paying royalties and exploiting the licensed patents. The Supreme Court said in 2007 that a licensee need not terminate or breach the licensing agreement in this situation in order to have standing to challenge the licensed patents. *MedImmune, Inc. v. Genentech, Inc.*, 549 U.S. 118 (2007).

To prevent licensee challenges, patent licensors sometimes insert "no challenge" clauses into licensing agreements. These bar licensees from challenging the validity of the licensed patents. *See* Thomas K. Cheng, *Antitrust Treatment of the No Challenge Clause*, 5 NYU J. Intell. Prop. & Ent. L. 437 (2016). They are thus helpful to licensors; but are they enforceable? The courts have split on this important issue. *Compare Baseload Energy, Inc. v. Roberts*, 619 F.3d 1357 (Fed. Cir. 2010) (unambiguous no-challenge clause in settlement agreement is enforceable) *with Rates Technology, Inc. v. Speakeasy, Inc.*, 685 F.3d 163 (2d Cir. 2012) (no-challenge clause in litigation settlement agreement is enforceable only after the licensee has had an opportunity to discover evidence in its lawsuit with the patent owner; settlements entered into prior to discovery will not be enforced) and *Ocean Tomo, LLC v. Barney*, 133 F. Supp. 3d 1107 (N.D. Ill. 2015) (no-challenge clause in licensing agreement did not fall under post-discovery settlement rule of *Rates Technology*, and so was unenforceable). In this situation, lawyers may still employ no-challenge clauses in licensing agreements. But they may not be enforceable.

One point worth noting here is that a finding of patent invalidity does not entitle a licensee to recoup royalties already paid (*Applied Elastomerics, Inc. v. Z-Man Fishing Products, Inc.*, 521 F. Supp. 2d 1031 (N.D. Cal. 2007)), unless of course the parties negotiate a repayment clause in the licensing agreement. Without such a special clause, however, past royalties need not be repaid.

9.3 Enforcing licenses: litigation and arbitration

Arbitration awards are generally granted the same level of recognition as judgments. The United Nations Convention for the Recognition and Enforcement of Foreign Arbitral Awards of 1958, known as the New York Convention, provides for the recognition of arbitral awards on par with domestic court judgments without review on the merits. See Contracting States, New York Arbitration Convention, http://www.newyorkconvention.org/countries.

CASE

Sanofi-Aventis Deutschland GmbH v. Genentech, Inc., 716 F.3d 586 (Fed. Cir. 2013)

Reyna, J.
In 1992, Genentech entered into an agreement (the "Agreement") with [Sanofi] licensing [Sanofi-owned] intellectual property related to [gene] enhancers, including the [Sanofi patent] applications that ultimately matured into the patents-in-suit. The Agreement specified that in exchange for fixed annual payments, Genentech could practice the patents-in-suit for research purposes. Genentech made these payments from 1992 to 2008. In addition, the Agreement required Genentech to pay a running royalty of 0.5% on the sale

CASE *(continued)*

of commercially marketable goods incorporating a "Licensed Product." The Agreement defined licensed products as "materials (including organisms), the manufacture, use or sale of which would, in the absence of this Agreement, infringe one or more unexpired issued claims of the Licensed Patent Rights." The Agreement was governed by German law and required disputes to be settled by arbitration in accordance with the rules of the International Chamber of Commerce ("ICC").

In the present case, Sanofi alleges that Genentech infringed the patents-in-suit by using the patented enhancers in the manufacture and sale of two drugs: Rituxan and Avastin. Genentech launched Rituxan in December 1997 and Avastin in February 2004. Genentech did not identify Rituxan or Avastin as licensed products, nor did it pay the 0.5% royalty on them. Sanofi accused these products of infringing the asserted patents. Genentech [then] notified Sanofi of its intent to terminate the Agreement. [Sanofi] demanded arbitration before a European arbitrator of the ICC [, and then Genentech's termination became effective].

Genentech [then] filed a complaint for declaratory judgment of invalidity and non-infringement in the United States District Court for the Northern District of California. On the same day, Sanofi filed an infringement complaint in the United States District Court for the Eastern District of Texas. The two actions were consolidated in the Northern District of California and, after a *Markman* hearing, the court granted summary judgment of non-infringement. Sanofi appealed, and this court [the Federal Circuit] affirmed.

While the litigation proceeded in the United States, the ICC arbitration continued abroad. After the *Markman* hearing but before the judgment of non-infringement, Sanofi argued to the arbitrator that the district court's claim construction was wrong. After this court affirmed, Genentech argued to the arbitrator that our judgment disposed of all issues in the arbitration; Sanofi urged the arbitrator to proceed to determine an appropriate amount of royalties. In the Second Partial Award, the arbitrator appeared inclined to agree with [Sanofi], stating that Rituxan "is produced with the help of the [patents-in-suit]." The arbitrator did not, however, decide the issue of liability at that time.

On remand [after the non-infringement decision], Genentech moved the district court to enjoin Sanofi from continuing with the foreign arbitration. The court denied the motion, finding that "an injunction would frustrate the policies of [the United States] in favor of enforcement of forum selection clauses in arbitration agreements," and that the injunction would not be in the interest of international comity. The court observed that as a matter of U.S. law, Rituxan did not infringe the patents-in-suit, but concluded that "[t]o the extent that the arbitration involves the same infringement questions, under U.S. law, Genentech can present its arguments to the arbitrator regarding why the judgment of this court should be respected."

The arbitrator [then] determined that German substantive law, not United States patent law, would be used to determine whether Rituxan was a licensed article under the Agreement. Applying that law, the arbitrator determined that a drug could be a licensed article even though it did not contain the patented enhancers, so long as those enhancers

CASE *(continued)*

were used in its manufacture. Because it concluded that the enhancers were used in making Rituxan, the arbitrator determined that Genentech was liable for damages under the Agreement. Arbitration proceedings to determine a damages amount are ongoing at this time. Genentech appeals the denial of its request for an anti-suit injunction. [Ninth Circuit law applies to this dispute.]

It is well-settled that U.S. courts have the power to enjoin parties from pursuing litigation before foreign tribunals. *See, e.g.,* [*E. & J. Gallo Winery v. Andina Licores S.A.*, 446 F.3d 984 (9th Cir. 2006)], at 989. "[I]n evaluating a request for an antisuit injunction, [the district court] must determine (1) 'whether or not the parties and the issues are the same, and whether or not the first action is dispositive of the action to be enjoined'; (2) whether the foreign litigation would 'frustrate a policy of the forum issuing the injunction'; and (3) 'whether the impact on comity would be tolerable.'" [*Applied Med. Distribution Corp. v. Surgical Co.*, 587 F.3d 909, 913 (9th Cir. 2009)], at 913 (quoting *Gallo*, 446 F.3d at 991, 994).

As to the first factor, [t]he issues need not be identical; it is enough that they are functionally the same such that the result in one action is dispositive of the other. If they are not identical or functionally the same, no injunction will lie. Genentech argues that the issues are functionally the same because the royalty obligation that is the subject of the foreign arbitration depends upon the same alleged patent infringement that the Federal Circuit held did not occur; thus, there is nothing left for the foreign arbitrator to resolve.

Sanofi offers several bases for its counter-argument that the issues are not the same: (1) that the U.S. litigation involves infringement, while the foreign arbitration is a breach of contract dispute; (2) that the U.S. litigation involves only the time after the license was terminated, whereas the foreign arbitration involves the time up until the termination; and (3) that the U.S. dispute involves the application of U.S. patent law, while the foreign arbitration involves the application of German contract law, French procedural law, and the rules of the ICC.

The Ninth Circuit recently addressed anti-suit injunctions in *Applied Medical*. There, a Californian supplier entered into a distribution agreement with a Belgian distributor. Although *Applied Medical* dealt with an agreement under U.S. law and a forum selection clause specifying a U.S. state [California], its reasoning is nevertheless instructive. The Ninth Circuit held that the district court had erred by "requiring that the claims in the domestic and foreign action be 'identical' instead of engaging in the more functional inquiry concerning dispositiveness required by *Gallo*." 587 F.3d at 914. Although the Belgian law claims were not identical to the U.S. claims, which were phrased as concerning the limitation on liability provision of the agreement, the Ninth Circuit determined that they were functionally the same because they arose out of the agreement and were subject to the forum selection clause.

The instant case presents a mirror image of *Applied Medical*. We agree with Sanofi that the U.S. judgment of non-infringement is not dispositive as to breach of the Agreement. As in *Applied Medical*, the dispute arises out of the Agreement and is subject to the Agreement's

CASE *(continued)*

forum selection clause. The issue in the foreign arbitration is breach of the Agreement, not patent infringement. Applying German law, the arbitrator has already deviated from U.S. patent law by concluding that infringement is possible even if the patents are invalid. In addition, the arbitrator has adopted a definition of infringement that includes using the enhancer to produce Rituxan, even if the enhancer is not in the ultimate product.

The district court's denial of the anti-suit injunction is further grounded in the second *Gallo* factor: whether the foreign litigation would frustrate a policy of the forum issuing the injunction. [I]t is undeniable that the United States has a strong policy in favor of forum selection clauses. In both *Gallo* and *Applied Medical*, the Ninth Circuit vindicated this policy by enforcing U.S. forum-selection clauses by means of an anti-suit injunction. Although the forum selection clause in this case weighs against jurisdiction in the United States, the same reasoning applies: enjoining suit would undermine the parties' choice of forum.

As the Ninth Circuit explained in *Applied Medical*:

> [G]lobalization has enhanced the significance of international trade, and those in business who would trade across national lines confront many varying legal systems in different countries. If we do not give primacy to parties' choice of forum and choice of law, there will be insufficient certainty to foster international trade relations. Conversely, so long as the parties have no gross disparity in bargaining power, it is difficult to see how holding them to their agreed forum and law is not beneficent.

587 F.3d at 916. The district court's denial of Genentech's request for an anti-suit injunction was not an abuse of discretion. None of the three *Gallo* factors supports the imposition of the injunction Genentech requests. [Affirmed.]

NOTES AND QUESTIONS

1. Why might German law be different from US law on the question of infringement in this case? In general, US patent law does not consider a final product to infringe a patent claim unless the product itself meets the limitations of the claim. If a claim is infringed *along the way*, during the development of a final product, the most that US law might permit is the awarding of "reach through" damages on sales of that final product. See *Integra Lifesciences I v. Merck, KGaA*, 331 F.3d 860, 871–72 (Fed. Cir. 2003) ("[T]his court does not opine on the applicability of a reach-through royalty in this case, [but there is a possibility] of a hypothetical negotiation between Merck and Integra for access to the [patented] technology . . . which Merck utilized . . . in its drug development process"). On this issue generally under US law, see Mark A. Lemley, "The Fruit of the Poisonous Tree in IP Law" (November 9, 2016), available at SSRN: https://ssrn.com/abstract=2867099.

2. Note also that the court points out that under German law, an invalid patent may nevertheless be infringed. This is a shorthand way of saying that under German law, infringement and validity are considered in completely separate legal actions. Often, the infringement determination comes first. That means that for some period of time, a legal remedy may be in place to compensate for infringement, even though the patent is later invalidated. Infringement suits are heard in Germany's 12 regional courts, such as Düsseldorf or Berlin. Invalidity, however, must be tried before the German Federal Patent Court in Munich. (An alter-

native is to challenge a patent in an opposition in the EPO or German Patent Office.) *See* Charleen Fei, *Justice Delayed is Justice Denied: The Principle of Bifurcation in the German Patent Litigation System*, 14 Wake Forest J. of Bus. and IP Law 619 (2014). The added cost of this two-part proceeding leads to fewer patents being challenged, which is in general a bad thing for society. *See* Katrin Cremers, Fabian Gaessler, Dietmar Harhoff, Christian Helmers, and Yassine Lefouili, "Invalid But Infringed? An Analysis of the Bifurcated Patent Litigation System", Toulouse School of Economics Working Paper 16-698 (July 9, 2016), available at http://www.tse-fr.eu/sites/default/files/TSE/documents/doc/wp/2016/wp_tse_698.pdf (showing there are fewer challenges and more settlements in Germany's bifurcated system).

3. The paramount principle identified by the court in *Sanofi* is respect for contracting parties and their choice of law. The agreement in the case specified both a set of procedural rules (International Chamber of Commerce (ICC) arbitration rules) and the national law to be applied to disputes heard in that forum (German law). There are several popular forums where IP and other business disputes are heard, often (but not always) under ICC rules. See for example Background, WIPO Arbitration & Mediation Center, WIPO, http://www.wipo.int/amc/en/center/background.html; Profile of Cases, Singapore International Arbitration Centre, SIAC, available at http://www.siac.org.sg. *See generally* Marc Jonas Block, *The Benefits of Alternative Dispute Resolution for International Commercial and Intellectual Property Disputes*, 44 Rutgers L. Rec. 1 (2017).

Part III

Copyright protection

10

Introduction

Problem: the orphan episode

CHIUNG Yao is a famous romance novelist. Born in mainland China, now living in Taiwan, her works have been popular with readers for decades. One of her best-known books, translated as "Plum Blossom Scar," was used as the basis of a TV series *The Palace 3: The Lost Daughter*, by a mainland Chinese production company. Because the TV series was produced without authorization, CHIUNG Yao brought a copyright infringement suit against the production company, and won her case. *See CHIUNG Yao v. YU Zheng*, Beijing Third Intermediate Court, Civil Division, Initial Ruling, Case No. 07916 (Dec. 25, 2014), affirmed by Beijing High Court, Civil Division, Case No. 1039 (awarding damages of roughly five million yuan, or $800,000, and issuing an injunction).

Now imagine you are an entertainment lawyer working for that production company, which we will call All China TV (ACTV). Imagine further that ACTV now has acquired authorization (in the form of an assignment of TV production rights) from Ms. CHIUNG, the author, to make multiple TV series based on her romance novels. It is one episode in one of these TV series that will concern you here.

The series is called *The Patient Bride*, and is about a young married woman whose new husband goes off to war for many years, with the wife enduring much waiting for his return. The one episode in question involves a mysterious traveler known only as The Healer, who comes to the young bride's town. The Healer is an older woman who practices traditional medicine, but also tells fortunes. The rumor is that she is a bit of a magician. Our protagonist, the young patient bride, comes to the aid of The Healer when she is accused of witchcraft and of intentionally poisoning the son of the town's mayor. In return for the young bride's help, The Healer uses a magic mirror she has to locate the young bride's husband. For just a few brief moments, the bride is able to *see* that her husband is alive and safe and fighting bravely. The

Healer leaves and the young bride is happy to have some news of her far-away husband.

All well and good; but there is a problem. The writers of this episode, who work for ACTV, apparently drew on a short story for the plot. A production assistant on the TV show saw this right away when he first saw the rough version of the episode, which was then being filmed. "This is taken directly from the story 'Village Healer,' he said. "I recognized it immediately." The short story this assistant referred to, "Village Healer," was written in mainland China in 1991 and published in a small regional literary magazine that year. It is the only story known to have been written by its author, and no one has any idea how to locate her now.

The problem is that the entire season of this TV series has been scripted, and large portions have already been filmed. Several later episodes in the season refer back to the episode with The Healer. It has even been incorporated in rough drafts of several episodes slated for the next season. And the episode itself has already been largely filmed – at a cost of $2.5 million (16,413,000 yuan) already.

The TV series is shown in three major markets: first in mainland China, then the US, then Europe. It is first shown on mandarin-language TV networks, and later shown with subtitles and with "dubbing" (voiceovers) in English, French, and German. The series is also distributed in these markets in the form of pre-recorded DVDs. There are also plans to license the series for "streaming" on video content websites in all three markets (*e.g.*, Netflix in the US, Periscope in Europe, and Youku or CNTV in China).

So the question you have to address is what to do about the unauthorized episode? You must consider this with respect to all three major markets, *i.e.*, all three legal jurisdictions.

10.1 China

The Chinese Copyright Act of 2010, as amended, provides that an author shall have the right to both "publication" (Article 10(11)) and "adaptation, that is, the right to change a work to create a new work of originality" (Article 10(14)). Copyright Law of the PRC, available at: http://www.wipo.int/wipolex/en/details.jsp?id=6062. Thus the TV episode in question might well infringe the copyright in the short story "Village Healer", as it is clearly an "adaptation" of that story. Copies of the episode sold on DVDs will clearly be "video recordings," which are protected as "neighboring rights" under the approach common in China and Europe. In addition, the right to broadcast a work is explicitly enumerated in Article 10(11) of the Copyright Act.

Because the author of the short story cannot be located, there is a chance that no one will complain about the TV adaptation. If the author has died, and has heirs, it is possible they do not even know about the story. But there is always a risk that one or more of them might realize the connection between the TV episode and the story. So broadcasting the TV episode, selling copies on DVD, and streaming the episode on websites surely carries some risk.

One important step in analyzing the problem is to assess the potential magnitude of this risk. If a copyright owner were to emerge and bring suit against ACTV, what would the remedy likely be?

One possibility is that a court might issue an injunction under Article 47 of the 2010 Act. It reads:

> A copyright owner or owner of a copyright-related right who has evidence to establish that another person is committing or will commit an act of infringing his right, which could cause irreparable injury to his legitimate rights and interests if the act is not stopped immediately, may apply to the People's Court for ordering cessation of the related act and for taking the measures for property preservation before instituting legal proceedings.

This would obviously make it difficult for ACTV to honor its contracts to make all episodes available for online streaming, re-showings, etc. On the other hand it is technically feasible to take one episode out of circulation, at least until a settlement can be reached with the copyright owner.

As for damages, that may be difficult to predict. Article 49 says that "the infringer shall compensate for the actual injury suffered by the right holder; where the actual injury is difficult to compute, the damages shall be paid on the basis of the unlawful income of the infringer." There are also statutory damages, though the statute limits these damages to no more than RMB 500,000 (around $80,000), "depending on the circumstances of the infringing act." (Note that statutory damages in such a case may be doubled under the new version of the Chinese Copyright Act.)

Proper compensation under these standards may be difficult to assess, but in any event the "unlawful income" attributable to the TV show episode could conceivably reach a fairly large figure. Millions of Chinese RMB are spent to buy advertising when an episode of the show is first broadcast. It is true that the characters and continuing plot elements add much value to the overall TV series, and that these components of value are distinct from the value of the plot drawn from the "Village Healer" story for the one episode. But even a moderate percentage of the income from one episode, which a court might attribute to the value of the story plot, could amount to a sizeable damages award.

Some data from past cases might be helpful in assessing the risk. One study from 2009 found that "[t]raditionally, more than 90 percent of all IPR damages awarded in China are under $100,000. Highest damages awards in cases during the decade of the 2000s were: $2.78 million (2008–midyear), $44.3 million (2007), $210,000 (2006), $1.1 million (2005), and $50,000 (2004)" (National Economic Research Associates, Inc., "NERA Releases Report on Intellectual Property Litigation and Damages Trends in China, February 13, 2009, available at http://www.nera.com/news-events/press-releases/2009/nera-releases-report-on-intellectual-property-litigation-and-dam.html).

One point worth noting: Even if the damages from infringing a single episode were found to equal the total damages awarded to CHIUNG Yao for the entire original series, this amounts only to $800,000 or RMB 16.5 million. In the end the risk of infringement liability may be seen as reasonable in light of the cost of re-shooting the episode, and in view of the profits to ACTV per episode – assuming (and this is important) that no injunction will issue. If a permanent injunction *does* issue, the entire investment will be lost.

10.2 Copyright in other countries: the Berne Convention

The Berne Convention, adopted originally in 1886, is the most important international copyright treaty. As discussed in Chapter 1, it gives copyright holders in member countries rights over their works in all other countries that have signed the treaty. The treaty originated in Europe, so all countries there are members. And the US joined in 1988. China joined in 1992.

Copies of the episodes sold on DVDs or similar media meet the definition of "cinematographic works" under the Convention. *See* Berne Convention, Article 2(1). Broadcasts are excluded from the Berne Convention, under the Euro-centric tradition which holds that copyright is exclusively associated with the work of individual human authors. As a consequence, rights over broadcasts, referred to as one of the "neighboring rights" under the European tradition, are covered in separate treaties. The most important of these is the 1961 Rome Convention for the Protection of Performers, Producers of

Phonograms and Broadcasting Organizations. *See* http://www.wipo.int/treaties/en/ip/rome/. Germany and France are signatories, *see* http://www.wipo.int/treaties/en/ShowResults.jsp?lang=en&treaty_id=17. In Britain, as in other common law countries, broadcast rights are subsumed under the more general public performance right. *See* UK Copyright, Designs and Patent Act of 1988, section 1(1)(b) (listing "broadcasts" as a protected category of work). Though copyright terms are shorter in many countries for broadcasts and other neighboring rights, the Rome Convention provides for a minimum 20-year term measured from the date of broadcast, so the TV episode in question will still be under protection.

The short story copyright in our scenario originated in China. If it had been written after 1992, when China joined Berne, coverage in other member countries would be automatic and straightforward. One of the most basic aspects of Berne is the principle of National Treatment. *See* Berne Convention Article 5(1) ("Authors shall enjoy, in respect of works for which they are protected under this Convention, in countries of the Union other than the country of origin, the rights which their respective laws do now or may hereafter grant to their nationals....").

But the "Village Healer" story predates China's adoption of Berne by a year. (It was written in 1991 and China joined Berne in 1992.) For works such as this, we look to Berne Article 18(1), which provides retroactive coverage for all works still under copyright protection at the time the treaty is adopted: "This Convention shall apply to all works which, at the moment of its coming into force, have not yet fallen into the public domain in the country of origin through the expiry of the term of protection." And so – as long as the story is still protected by copyright in China – it can be protected in any Berne member country. Because under the 2010 Act, the term of copyright in China is life of the author plus 50 years (Section 3, Article 21), even if the author died immediately after the story was published in 1991, it still has several decades of protection remaining.

What of the fact that the TV show is an adaptation or derivative work, rather than a direct reproduction of the short story? The Berne Convention in Article 2(3) lists among its minimum standards the protection of "[t]ranslations, adaptations, ... and other alterations of a literary or artistic work," so any signatory of the Berne Convention will protect the adaptation right. We have already seen this in the case of China. *See generally* Daniel Gervais, *The Derivative Right, or Why Copyright Law Protects Foxes Better Than Hedgehogs*, 15 Vand. J. Ent. & Tech. L. 785, 820 (2013).

10.3 Europe

The Village Healer is an example of what is known as an orphan work – one whose author cannot be located. The European Commission adopted a Directive to deal with such works, but it only permits public libraries and nonprofit national broadcasters to disseminate works whose authors cannot be found. *See* Council Directive 2012/28, of the European Parliament and of the Council of 25 October 2012 on Certain Permitted Uses of Orphan Works, 2012 OJ L 299/5; Jane C. Ginsburg, *Fair Use for Free, or Permitted-but-Paid?*, 29 Berkeley Tech. L.J. 1383, 1446 (2014). The Directive does not cover the use of orphan works in TV shows.

As an adaptation, the TV show would be found to infringe the original copyright in the major countries of Europe: Germany, the UK, and France. *See, e.g.,* Adolf Dietz, "Germany," in 2 International Copyright Law & Practice, at GER-33 (Paul E. Geller ed., 2011) (describing scope of adaptation right in Germany); Code de la Propriété Intellectuelle, Art. L.112-3 (Fr.) (WIPOLex text, available at http://www.wipo.int/edocs/lexdocs/laws/fr/fr/fr485fr.pdf) (rights include translations and adaptations); *Baigent v. Random House Group* [2007] EWCA Civ. 247, [145], [2007] F.S.R. 24 (Eng. & Wales) (though derivative works are protected under the general right to prevent reproduction, and not a specifically enumerated derivative work right, "UK law thus points to a distinct role for the derivative right, even though it is not named or identified under that rubric in the statute. Its target is the appropriation of originality embodied in the author's expression"). *See generally* Paul Edward Geller, *Hiroshige vs. Van Gogh: Resolving the Dilemma of Copyright Scope in Remedying Infringement*, 46 J. Copyright Soc'y U.S.A. 39, 46–47 (1998) (describing expansion of copyright to embrace derivative works in the nineteenth century).

Under some circumstances in European countries there is a dispute over who is the "author" of a work such as a TV show or film. In particular, the "work for hire" rule, well known to US lawyers, does not in general apply, making assignment contracts from all contributors crucial. *See generally* Seagull HY Song, China's Copyright Protection of Audio-Visual Works, A Comparison with Europe and the US, IIC Max Planck Institute for Innovation and Competition (Volume 46, 2015) (discussing different treatments of film ownership between France, Germany, the US and China). Also *see* the Spielbankaffaire decision, BGH (Federal Court of Justice) (Germany), Oct. 2, 1997, 1999 GRUR 152, and in English translation in 30 I.I.C. 227 (1999) (holding that the laws of the protecting countries respectively determine the initial vestees of copyright in an audiovisual work, while considering that this vesting may be subject to subsequent contractual allocation), on remand, OLG (Intermediate Court), Munich, Jan. 10, 2002, 2003 Zeitschrift für Urheber- u. Medienrecht 141. For this and other purposes, the question of authorship is usually decided in accordance with the law of the country where protection is sought. (On jurisdiction, as opposed to the substantive law of these cases, *see* Convention of 27 September 1968, on Jurisdiction and the Enforcement of Judgments in Civil and Commercial Matters ("Brussels Convention"), available at https://curia.europa.eu/common/recdoc/convention/en/c-textes/brux-idx.htm). Thus the resolution of this issue in Germany would be determined by German law; in France, French law, and so on. Note, however, that the European Court of Justice has held that by default (in the absence of contract) national law in the EU must provide for initial vesting of copyright in the director of a film and not the producer or anyone else. *See* ECJ Case C-277/10, *Martin Luksan v. Petrus van der Let* [2012] ECR I-0000, available at http://curia.europa.eu/juris/document/document.jsf?docid=119322&doclang=EN (holding also that national law may contain a presumption that rights have been transferred from director to producer, so long as the presumption is not irrebuttable). For our purposes, this is important only insofar as ownership (which traces from original authorship) must be established in order to initiate a lawsuit. Thus we will assume that ACTV can establish ownership, making enforcement possible.

Because infringement should, as mentioned, be clear cut here, the main issue once again is remedies. In general the primary risk, as in China, is of an injunction. Since 2004, when the EU adopted the IP Enforcement Directive, a broad range of remedies have been available to European IP holders. These include preliminary and permanent injunctions in appropriate cases. *See* Directive 2004/48/EC of the European Parliament and of the Council, 29 April 2004, On the Enforcement of Intellectual Property rights ("EU Enforcement Directive"), available at http://eur-lex.europa.eu/legal-content/EN/TXT/PDF/?uri=CELEX:32004L0048R(01)&from=EN, at Articles 9 (preliminary injunctions) and 11 (injunctions). One risk here is that the distribution of the episode may be subject to an injunction based only on our plans to broadcast it. In Germany, for example, an injured party may obtain a preliminary injunction even if the infringement is imminent and has not taken place yet (1 International Copyright Law and Practice ch. GER §8[4][a][i] (Paul Edward Geller & Melville B. Nimmer eds., 2005). *See also* Roberto Garza Barbosa, *International Copyright Law and Litigation: A Mechanism for Improvement*, 11 Marq. Intell. Prop. L. Rev. 77, 84 (2007) (describing the law in France and Germany).

It should be noted, however, that the EU Enforcement Directive includes a provision on "alternative measures" which may be helpful, particularly if infringement is found to be innocent, *i.e.*, without knowledge that the acts in question infringe a valid copyright:

> Member States may provide that, in appropriate cases and at the request of the person liable to be subject to the measures provided for in this section, the competent judicial authorities may order pecuniary compensation to be paid to the injured party instead of applying the measures provided for in this section if that person acted unintentionally and without negligence, if execution of the measures in question would cause him/her disproportionate harm and if pecuniary compensation to the injured party appears reasonably satisfactory (EU Enforcement Directive at Article 12).

Because in our scenario we have not yet distributed the infringing episode, the innocent infringer language does not apply. But perhaps we could argue that enjoining a single episode would cause disproportionate harm because it would break the continuity of the TV series, and because this injunction would in effect reach beyond the protected work (the single episode), with wide-ranging effects on the value of the series as a whole. On this *see generally* Robert P. Merges, Justifying Intellectual Property (2011) at Chapter 6 ("The Proportionality Principle").

If an injunction did not issue in one or more countries, we would nevertheless be faced with the prospect of paying damages. While traditionally copyright damages varied considerably among the European countries, the EU Enforcement Directive once again provided some uniformity. Article 13, on Damages, provides:

> When the judicial authorities set the damages:
>
> > (a) they shall take into account all appropriate aspects, such as the negative economic consequences, including lost profits, which the injured party has suffered, any unfair profits made by the infringer and, in appropriate cases, elements other than economic factors, such as the moral prejudice caused to the rightholder by the infringement; or
> > as an alternative to (a), they may, in appropriate cases, set the damages as a lump sum on the basis of elements such as at least the amount of royalties or fees which would have been due if the infringer had requested authorisation to use the intellectual property right in question (EU Enforcement Directive, at Article 13).

To determine the proper level of compensation, a court would look to evidence of how much ACTV has paid outside, independent scriptwriters for other episodes of our series *The Patient Bride*.

10.4 United States

To begin, in the US several cases hold that each episode of a TV series is a separate work. *See MCA Television Ltd. v. Feltner*, 89 F.3d 766 (11th Cir. 1996); *Twin Peaks Prods., Inc. v. Publications Int'l, Ltd.*, 996 F.2d 1366 (2d Cir. 1993).

There is little doubt about either the derivative work issue or the substantial similarity (liability) issue; the episode is undoubtedly a protected work, and it undoubtedly infringes the underlying story. The US, as a member of Berne, would have to recognize the validity of the copyright if an appropriate owner were to emerge. And the status of the TV episode as a potential work made for hire is irrelevant because the infringement is of the short story, which is of course not a work for hire.

Much will turn, then, on the remedies. In the US in recent years, a preliminary injunction was granted in 41 (44.1 percent) of the decisions analyzed in one study. *See* Jiarui Liu, *Copyright Injunctions After Ebay: An Empirical Study*, 16 Lewis & Clark L. Rev. 215, 232 (2012). Likewise, among the 413 decisions studied, a permanent injunction (after liability was established) was granted in 378 (91.5 percent) of copyright decisions (*id.*, at 237). So the risk is very high that a court may well enjoin distribution and broadcast of the infringing episode.

As for damages under 17 U.S.C. §504, the key issues will be (1) establishing an accounting measure of ACTV's gross revenues with respect to the single episode of the series; and (2) how to apportion the value of the plot/story – the portion of the overall production contributed by the underlying story which was infringed.

On both issues, there is a fair amount of guidance. As for the damages "base," §504(b) of the Copyright Act provides:

> The copyright owner is entitled to recover the actual damages suffered by him or her as a result of the infringement, and any profits of the infringer that are attributable to the infringement and are not taken into account in computing the actual damages. In establishing the infringer's profits, the copyright owner is required to present proof only of the infringer's gross revenue, and the infringer is required to prove his or her deductible expenses and the elements of profit attributable to factors other than the copyrighted work.

The short story copyright owner would have to establish CATV's revenues related to this one episode. *See, e.g., Polar Bear Productions, Inc. v. Timex Corp.,*

384 F.3d 700, 711 (9th Cir. 2004) ("Thus, a copyright owner is required to do more initially than toss up an undifferentiated gross revenue number; the revenue stream must bear a legally significant relationship to the infringement"). A strict pro rata apportionment may not always be appropriate; so simply taking CATV's revenues for the entire year related to this TV series might not be enough of a starting point. Particularly exciting or important episodes (a big "reveal" for example, or the first or last episodes of the season) might account for a more than pro rata share of the annual revenue. See, e.g., Frank Music Corporation v. Metro-Goldwyn-Mayer, Inc., 886 F.2d 1545, 1548 (9th Cir. 1989) (District court erred, in apportioning the profits from a musical play, when it held that a 10-minute segment of a 100-minute show pointed automatically to 10 percent of the total profits from the musical; some adjustment for quality and importance was required, according to the Court of Appeals).

In any event, partially because the disgorgement remedy can hit hard, CATV could conceivably be on the hook for some very significant damages. To take one of many recent examples, the heirs of the singer/composer Marvin Gaye recently won a jury verdict totaling $7.3 million against singer/performers Pherell Williams and Robin Thicke. See Williams v. Bridgeport Music, Inc., No. LACV1306004JAKAGRX, 2015 WL 4479500 (C.D. Cal. July 14, 2015); see also Ben Sisario and Noah Smith, 'Blurred Lines' Infringed on Marvin Gaye Copyright, Jury Rules, N.Y. Times, Mar. 10, 2015, available at http://www.nytimes.com/2015/03/11/business/media/blurred-lines-infringed-on-marvin-gaye-copyright-jury-rules.html?_r=0. This included both lost profits (of $4 million) and disgorgement ($3.3 million).

10.5 Conclusion: the bottom line

The episode based on the infringing short story carries significant risk across the major countries where ACTV has deals to show the TV series. At the same time, no copyright holder may ever come forward. The decision whether to proceed with showing the episode comes down to whether management wants to take the risk of copyright infringement liability in this instance.

One consideration, consistent with the framework introduced earlier, is the net benefit of showing the series completely in some jurisdictions (e.g., mainland China) and withholding the risky episode from others (e.g., a potential high-risk [high damages] jurisdiction such as the US). The cost here is a special instance of the general cost of non-uniformity. If the episode is not shown in some countries, audiences in these high-risk countries will have a different overall viewing experience than other audiences. Perhaps this break in continuity, limited to these jurisdictions, will not be too costly to the overall reputation of the series. But perhaps it will create a perception that these Chinese series are confusing or hard to follow – which could affect future ACTV licensing revenues in these countries. The risk of a permanent injunction in each jurisdiction is a key consideration here, as that remedy will prevent the airing of the contested episode.

As you can *see*, these can be difficult decisions. One partial solution, however, is worth mentioning. Companies in the entertainment industry in some countries can buy insurance – in the form of "errors and omissions" (E&O) policies – that covers the risk of IP lawsuits. The premiums for these policies are set carefully, on a case-by-case basis, because entertainment products vary in many ways and thus present highly diverse risk profiles to insurance companies. *See, e.g.,* Paul S. Marks, *Book Review of "Clearance & Copyright" by Michael C. Donaldson and Lisa Callif (*4th edition, Silman-James Press, 2014), L.A. Law, May 2015, at 38 (reviewing book on copyright clearance procedures with extensive coverage of E&O insurance policies). Even so, just getting a quote from several E&O insurers provides useful information. A reasonable quote means the risk is probably not too catastrophic. A very high quote might mean the opposite: It could be a sign that infringement risk is great enough to avoid distributing the episode in at least one jurisdiction of interest. Again, note, however, that E&O insurance is not available in all countries. China, for instance has yet to develop a market for this insurance product.

11

Subject matter, originality, authorship

11.1 United States

11.1.1 Originality

Copyright is available for a vast expanse of works. Music, plays, movies, paintings, books – these are the core of traditional copyright. Some of these traditional categories have been expanded over the years; for example, computer software is now defined under US law as a "literary work," and "pictorial works" now covers most photographs in addition to drawings, paintings, etc. In addition, copyright now covers non-traditional works such as pantomimes, choreography, statues ("sculptural works"), and even architecture.

Regardless of the type of work in question, there is a basic requirement that must be met for *any* work to be included in copyright. This is the requirement of originality. Under the US Copyright Act, originality has two dimensions: first, a work must truly originate with the person claiming to be an author. You cannot copyright someone else's creation. Second, even when a person undoubtedly makes a new work, that work must exhibit at least a tiny degree of creativity. So for example, you cannot simply write down the English language alphabet (A, B, C, etc.) and register it under the Copyright Act. That is just not original enough to merit legal protection.

The practical impact of the originality requirement often hits home when a person or company makes a list of factual information. In some cases making a comprehensive list can be quite useful, and it can take a fair degree of time and effort. The classic example is the phone book – a useful tool, particularly when online searching is not possible. The case below deals with just this question.

CASE

Feist Publications, Inc. v. Rural Tel. Serv. Co., 499 U.S. 340 (1991)

Rural Telephone Service Company, Inc., is a certified public utility that provides telephone service to several communities in northwest Kansas. It is subject to a state regulation that requires all telephone companies operating in Kansas to issue annually an updated telephone directory. Accordingly, as a condition of its monopoly franchise, Rural publishes a typical telephone directory, consisting of white pages and yellow pages. The white pages list in alphabetical order the names of Rural's subscribers, together with their towns and telephone numbers.

Feist Publications, Inc., is a publishing company that specializes in area-wide telephone directories. Unlike a typical directory, which covers only a particular calling area, Feist's area-wide directories cover a much larger geographical range, reducing the need to call directory assistance or consult multiple directories. The Feist directory that is the subject of this litigation covers 11 different telephone service areas in 15 counties and contains 46,878 white pages listings – compared to Rural's approximately 7,700 listings.

As the sole provider of telephone service in its service area, Rural obtains subscriber information quite easily. Persons desiring telephone service must apply to Rural and provide their names and addresses; Rural then assigns them a telephone number. To obtain white pages listings for its area-wide directory, Feist approached each of the 11 telephone companies operating in northwest Kansas and offered to pay for the right to use its white pages listings. Of the 11 telephone companies, only Rural refused to license its listings to Feist. Rural's refusal created a problem for Feist, as omitting these listings would have left a gaping hole in its area-wide directory, rendering it less attractive to potential yellow pages advertisers.

Unable to license Rural's white pages listings, Feist used them without Rural's consent. [Feist sued for copyright infringement. It won in the trial court, the U.S. District Court in Kansas; and it won on appeal to the Tenth Circuit Court of Appeals. Both courts cited a long line of cases under U.S. copyright law holding that phone books were copyrightable subject matter.]

This case concerns the interaction of two well-established propositions. The first is that facts are not copyrightable; the other, that compilations of facts generally are.

The key to resolving the tension [between these two propositions] lies in understanding why facts are not copyrightable. The sine qua non of copyright is originality. To qualify for copyright protection, a work must be original to the author. Original, as the term is used in copyright, means only that the work was independently created by the author (as opposed to copied from other works), and that it possesses at least some minimal degree of creativity. To be sure, the requisite level of creativity is extremely low; even a slight amount will suffice. The vast majority of works make the grade quite easily, as they possess some creative spark. Originality does not signify novelty; a work may be original even though it closely

CASE *(continued)*

resembles other works so long as the similarity is fortuitous, not the result of copying. To illustrate, assume that two poets, each ignorant of the other, compose identical poems. Neither work is novel, yet both are original and, hence, copyrightable.

Originality is a constitutional requirement. The source of Congress' power to enact copyright laws is Article I, §8, cl. 8, of the Constitution, which authorizes Congress to "secur[e] for limited Times to Authors . . . the exclusive Right to their respective Writings."

It is this bedrock principle of copyright that mandates the law's seemingly disparate treatment of facts and factual compilations. This is because facts do not owe their origin to an act of authorship. The distinction is one between creation and discovery: The first person to find and report a particular fact has not created the fact; he or she has merely discovered its existence.

Factual compilations, on the other hand, may possess the requisite originality. The compilation author typically chooses which facts to include, in what order to place them, and how to arrange the collected data so that they may be used effectively by readers. These choices as to selection and arrangement, so long as they are made independently by the compiler and entail a minimal degree of creativity, are sufficiently original that Congress may protect such compilations through the copyright laws. Thus, even a directory that contains absolutely no protectible written expression, only facts, meets the constitutional minimum for copyright protection if it features an original selection or arrangement.

This protection is subject to an important limitation. The mere fact that a work is copyrighted does not mean that every element of the work may be protected. [C]opyright protection may extend only to those components of a work that are original to the author. Thus, if the compilation author clothes facts with an original collocation of words, he or she may be able to claim a copyright in this written expression. Others may copy the underlying facts from the publication, but not the precise words used to present them. Where the compilation author adds no written expression but rather lets the facts speak for themselves, the expressive element is more elusive. The only conceivable expression is the manner in which the compiler has selected and arranged the facts. Thus, if the selection and arrangement are original, these elements of the work are eligible for copyright protection. This inevitably means that the copyright in a factual compilation is thin. Notwithstanding a valid copyright, a subsequent compiler remains free to use the facts contained in another's publication to aid in preparing a competing work, so long as the competing work does not feature the same selection and arrangement.

It may seem unfair that much of the fruit of the compiler's labor may be used by others without compensation. The primary objective of copyright is not to reward the labor of authors, but "[t]o promote the Progress of Science and useful Arts." Art. I, §8, cl. 8. [The Court discusses the so-called "sweat of the brow" theory for protecting compilations, and rejects it as inconsistent with copyright law's purpose and design.]

The question is . . . did Feist, by taking 1,309 names, towns, and telephone numbers from Rural's white pages, copy anything that was "original" to Rural? Certainly, the raw data does not satisfy the originality requirement. [T]hese bits of information are uncopyrightable

CASE (continued)

facts; they existed before Rural reported them and would have continued to exist if Rural had never published a telephone directory.

The selection, coordination, and arrangement of Rural's white pages do not satisfy the minimum constitutional standards for copyright protection. Rural simply takes the data provided by its subscribers and lists it alphabetically by surname. The end product is a garden-variety white pages directory, devoid of even the slightest trace of creativity. Rural's selection of listings could not be more obvious: It publishes the most basic information – name, town, and telephone number – about each person who applies to it for telephone service. This is "selection" of a sort, but it lacks the modicum of creativity necessary to transform mere selection into copyrightable expression.

Because Rural's white pages lack the requisite originality, Feist's use of the listings cannot constitute infringement. This decision should not be construed as demeaning Rural's efforts in compiling its directory, but rather as making clear that copyright rewards originality, not effort.

NOTES

1. *Feist* has been applied to a copyright infringement claim involving a listing service for the interest rates charged by banks on mortgages, and the interest rates paid by banks on various types of deposits. The court held that these were factual matters and that there was no originality in the way they were selected and arranged – so there was no copyright in them. *BanxCorp v. Costco Wholesale Corp.*, 978 F. Supp. 2d 280 (S.D.N.Y. 2013). *See also R&B, Inc. v. Needa Parts Mfg., Inc.*, 418 F. Supp. 2d 684 (E.D. Pa. 2005) (no copyright in numbers assigned to auto parts; simple listing of parts and associated part numbers lacks originality). But *see Am. Dental Ass'n v. Delta Dental Plans Ass'n*, 126 F.3d 977 (7th Cir. 1997) (list of procedure codes for dental work, copyrighted by professional dentists' association, was original copyrightable work; dental insurance company using list for its claims and payment procedures did infringe valid copyright).

2. Because biographies and histories do to some degree list facts about a person's life or about events, the "no copyright for facts" rule has sometimes been applied to cases where an accused copyright infringer cites facts from a person's life or historical events. *See Hoehling v. Universal City Studios, Inc.*, 618 F.2d 972, 978 (2d Cir.), cert. denied, 449 U.S. 841 (1980); *Craft v. Kobler*, 667 F. Supp. 120, 123 (S.D.N.Y. 1987) ("When a biographer or historian, using a copyrighted work as a source, takes historical information from it, he does not infringe the copyright. The law does not recognize private ownership of historical information"). At the same time, the specific textual descriptions of a person or series of events are typically protectable because they usually evince some originality of expression. *See Craft v. Kobler, supra*, 667 F. Supp. 120, at 123 ("What the copyright law protects is rather the author's craftsmanship and art in the presentation of the material. It is the manner of expression and not the factual content that enjoys copyright protection").

3. The "sweat of the brow" theory for protecting compilations appears to embody the notion that property arises from effort or labor – a theory of property acquisition closely associated with the English political theorist John Locke. Yet Locke's theory of property is more complex than a simple "labor equals property" formulation. He wrote that property acquisition through labor was justified only if the laborer leaves "as much, and as good" of what is taken for others who may follow. This "sufficiency proviso" arguably explains the need, expressed in *Feist*, to prevent people from claiming property in facts and in non-original compilations of facts. Facts should be available to all, not just the first person who tries to own them. On Locke's theory and intellectual property, *see* Robert P. Merges, Justifying Intellectual Property (2011), Chapter 2.

11.1.2 The fixation requirement

Original works of authorship under US copyright law must be "fixed in any tangible medium of expression, now known or later developed, from which they can be perceived, reproduced, or otherwise communicated, either directly or with the aid of a machine or device" (17 U.S.C. § 102(a)). Thus a live musical performance which is neither composed nor recorded does not result in a copyrightable work. If the work is recorded on a computer hard drive, USB drive, magnetic tape, etc., however, it is subject to copyright protection.

The fixation requirement is a prerequisite to copyright; but do not confuse this with the idea that the written composition or recorded music is the essence of what copyright protects. These are merely "copies," in the terms of the Copyright Act. (Technically, a single instance of a recorded piece of music is defined as a "phonorecord," *see* 17 U.S.C. 101 (definition of "phonorecord"), but this is just a music-specific type of copy.) What they are copies of is what copyright protects: the underlying, intangible "work." So a work must be embodied in a copy (or phonorecord) to be protected; but it is the work and not the copy that is the subject of protection.

One implication of this is that possession of a copy does not mean that the possessor owns the copyright in the underlying work – *i.e.*, the work that is embodied in the copy. As the statute says,

> Ownership of a copyright, or of any of the exclusive rights under a copyright, is distinct from ownership of any material object in which the work is embodied. Transfer of ownership of any material object, including the copy or phonorecord in which the work is first fixed, does not of itself convey any rights in the copyrighted work embodied in the object; nor, in the absence of an agreement, does transfer of ownership of a copyright or of any exclusive rights under a copyright convey property rights in any material object (17 U.S.C. §202).

This is obvious in the case of a book: Buying a copy of the book does not give you the right to make copies of it and sell them. But it is also true of something like a painting or sculpture: Sale or transfer of the sole copy of a painting or sculpture does not carry with it a transfer of copyright. *See, e.g., CCNV v. Reid*, 1991 U.S. Dist. LEXIS 20227, *1 (D.D.C. Oct. 16, 1991), on remand from 490 U.S. 730 (1989) (permitting sculptor access to sole copy of sculpture held by its owner, who had commissioned it for purposes of making a mold of it to sell copies). *See generally*; 3 Nimmer on Copyright §10.09[C][2].

11.1.3 Specific categories of work

Source: WikiCommons (in public domain, out of copyright).

Figure 11.1 Sarony photo of Oscar Wilde

 CASE

Burrow-Giles Lithographic Co. v. Sarony, 111 U.S. 53 (1884)

The suit was commenced by an action at law in which Sarony was plaintiff and the lithographic company was defendant, the plaintiff charging the defendant with violating his copyright in regard to a photograph, the title of which is "Oscar Wilde, No. 18." [J]udgment in favor of the plaintiff was rendered for the sum of $610. Among the finding of facts made by the court the following presents the principal question raised by the assignment of errors in the case: (3) That the plaintiff, about the month of January, 1882, under an agreement with Oscar Wilde, became and was the author, inventor, designer, and proprietor of the photograph in suit, the title of which is "Oscar Wilde, No. 18"; that the same is a useful, new, harmonious, characteristic, and graceful picture, and that said plaintiff made the same

CASE *(continued)*

entirely from his own original mental conception, to which he gave visible form by posing the said Oscar Wilde in front of the camera, selecting and arranging the costume, draperies, and other various accessories in said photograph, arranging the subject so as to present graceful outlines, arranging and disposing the light and shade, suggesting and evoking the desired expression. Other findings leave no doubt that plaintiff had taken all the steps required by the act of congress to obtain copyright of this photograph. That defendant is liable there can be no question if those sections are valid as they relate to photographs.

[The key question] the court below decided [was] that congress had and has the constitutional right to protect photographs and negatives thereof by copyright.

The constitutional question is not free from difficulty. The argument here is that a photograph is not a writing nor the production of an author. Under the acts of congress designed to give effect to [Article I, section 8, paragraph 8], the persons who are to be benefited are divided into two classes – authors and inventors. The monopoly which is granted to the former is called a copyright: that given to the latter, letters patent. We have then copyright and patent-right, and it is the first of these under which plaintiff asserts a claim for relief. It is insisted, in argument, that a photograph being a reproduction, on paper, of the exact features of some natural object, or of some person, is not a writing of which the producer is the author. Section 4952 of the Revised Statutes places photographs in the same class as things which may be copyrighted with "books, maps, charts, dramatic or musical compositions, engravings, cuts, prints, paintings, drawings, statues, statuary, and models or designs intended to be perfected as works of the fine arts."

The first congress of the United States, sitting immediately after the formation of the constitution, enacted [protection for] the "author or authors of any map, chart, book, or books." This [1790] statute not only makes maps and charts subjects of copyright, but mentions them before books in the order of designation. [In 1802 Congress added protection for] he who shall invent and design, engrave, etch, or work, or from his own works shall cause to be designed and engraved, etched, or worked, any historical or other print or prints. [Then in] 1831, [it added] musical compositions. The construction placed upon the constitution by the first act of 1790 and the act of 1802, by the men who were contemporary with its formation, many of whom were members of the convention which framed it, is of itself entitled to very great weight, and when it is remembered that the rights thus established have not been disputed during a period of nearly a century, it is almost conclusive. Unless, therefore, photographs can be distinguished in the classification of this point from the maps, charts, designs, engravings, etchings, cuts, and other prints, it is difficult to *see* why congress cannot make them the subject of copyright as well as the others.

So, also, no one would now claim that the word 'writing' in this clause of the constitution, though the only word used as to subjects in regard to which authors are to be secured, is limited to the actual script of the author, and excludes books and all other printed matter. By writings in that clause is meant the literary productions of those authors, and congress very properly has declared these to include all forms of writing, printing, engravings, etchings, etc., by which the ideas in the mind of the author are given visible expression.

CASE *(continued)*

The only reason why photographs were not included in the extended list in the act of 1802 is, probably, that they did not exist, as photography, as an art, was then unknown, and the scientific principle on which it rests, and the chemicals and machinery by which it is operated, have all been discovered long since that statute was enacted.

We entertain no doubt that the constitution is broad enough to cover an act authorizing copyright of photographs, so far as they are representatives of original intellectual conceptions of the author. But it is said that a photograph is the mere mechanical reproduction of the physical features or outlines of some object, animate or inanimate, and involves no originality of thought or any novelty in the intellectual operation connected with its visible reproduction in shape of a picture. This may be true in regard to the ordinary production of a photograph, and that in such case a copyright is no protection. On the question as thus stated we decide nothing.

[The factual] findings [below], we think, show this photograph to be an original work of art, the product of plaintiff's intellectual invention, of which plaintiff is the author, and of a class of inventions for which the constitution intended that congress should secure to him the exclusive right to use, publish, and sell, as it has done by section 4952 of the Revised Statutes. The judgment of the circuit court is accordingly affirmed.

NOTES

1. Many cases since *Burrow-Giles* have found photographs copyrightable. *See, e.g., Rogers v. Koons*, 960 F.2d 301, 307 (2d Cir.1992). In a few cases, however, the courts have said that the photographs are so unoriginal or generic that they do not exhibit the requisite degree of originality to be copyrightable. *See, e.g., Oriental Art Printing, Inc. v. Goldstar Printing Corp.*, 175 F. Supp. 2d 542 (S.D.N.Y. 2001) aff'd in part, appeal dismissed in part sub nom. *Oriental Art Printing Inc. v. GS Printing Corp.*, 34 F. App'x 401 (2d Cir. 2002) (photos of Chinese meals included in menu are not copyrightable). *See also FragranceNet.com, Inc. v. FragranceX.com, Inc.*, 679 F. Supp. 2d 312, 322 (E.D.N.Y. 2010) (denying defendant's motion to dismiss: "At this stage, however, this Court lacks sufficient evidence to determine the originality of the images at issue as a matter of law," so the copyright infringement case may proceed for relevant facts surrounding the photos to emerge).

2. Copyright scholars continue to argue about originality and copyright for photos. *See, e.g.*, Joseph Scott Miller, *Hoisting Originality*, 31 Cardozo L. Rev. 451, 464 (2009) (advocating "a patent-inspired approach to copyright's creativity requirement," *i.e.*, raising the originality standard in a way analogous to patent law's nonobviousness doctrine); Eva E. Subotnik, *Originality Proxies: Toward A Theory of Copyright and Creativity*, 76 Brook. L. Rev. 1487, 1552 (2011) (arguing "against a presumption of protectability for photography").

3. By amendment in 1912, the US Congress for the first time included movies within the scope of copyright. *See Metro-Goldwyn-Mayer Distrib. Corp. v. Bijou Theatre Co.*, 59 F.2d 70, 72 (1st Cir. 1932) (interpreting the 1912 Act). Here and elsewhere, copyright law expanded to cover new subject matter as new technologies and entertainment options evolved. *See generally* Paul Goldstein, Copyright's Highway (rev. ed., 2003); Peter S. Menell, *Envisioning Copyright Law's Digital Future*, 46 N.Y.L. Sch. L. Rev. 63 (2003). On the general tendency of IP law to expand over time, both reflecting and helping to bring about greater economic value for the works underlying IP rights, *see* Robert P. Merges, *One Hundred Years of Solicitude: Intellectual Property Law, 1900–2000*, 88 Cal. L. Rev. 2187 (2000).

4. **Computer software**. Computer software was added to copyright in the US in 1980. It is defined as a

type of literary work. *See Apple Computer, Inc. v. Franklin Computer Corp.*, 714 F.2d 1240 (3d Cir. 1983); 1 Nimmer on Copyright §2.04[C][1] (recounting the history of copyright protection for software). *See generally* David Nimmer, *Codifying Copyright Comprehensibly*, 51 UCLA L. Rev. 1233, 1256–68, 1383–85 (2004).

5. Various other creative works have been incorporated into US copyright law over the years:

   (a) **Music**: When a composer writes a piece of music, the resulting composition may be copyrighted. In addition, when musicians play a piece of music and it is recorded, they may have rights in the resulting recording. Composition copyrights have been around for many years; the *Burrow-Giles* case mentions music being added to copyright in the early nineteenth century. But sound recording copyright came much later. It was not until 1972 that the Copyright Act was amended to include sound recording protection.

   (b) **Titles**: In general, copyright may not be claimed in titles. In some cases, however, courts have recognized trademark-like rights in titles, so that the originator of a well-known title may seek protection against a third party's use of the title if it will confuse the public into thinking the originator stands behind the third party's work. *See, e.g., Davis v. United Artists, Inc.*, 547 F. Supp. 722 (S.D.N.Y. 1982).

   (c) **Utilitarian Works**: Mechanical devices that are not sculptures cannot be copyrighted; utilitarian works are properly the subject of patent, and not copyright, protection. *See, e.g., Vacheron Watches, Inc. v. Benrus Watch Co.*, 155 F. Supp. 932 (S.D.N.Y. 1957), aff'd on other grounds, 260 F.2d 637 (2d Cir. 1958) (no copyright protection for mechanical watches).

   (d) **Architecture**: In 1990, in order to comply with accession to the Berne Copyright Convention, the US added explicit protection for architectural works, which are defined as: "[T]he design of a building as embodied in any tangible medium of expression, including a building, architectural plans, or drawings. The work includes the overall form as well as the arrangement and composition of spaces and elements in the design, but does not include individual standard features" (17 U.S.C. §101 (1990)). Thus the underlying architectural design is protected, but this of course does not extend to ownership of the building itself. An architect may build a building for a buyer yet retain copyright in the underlying architectural design, which may then be asserted against other architects who copy the building's design. *See, e.g., Hunt v. Pasternack*, 192 F.3d 877, 880 (9th Cir. 1999).

11.1.3.1 Exclusion of systems, methods, procedures

The US Copyright Act contains an important exclusion, whose scope has been the subject of keen debate. It reads as follows:

> In no case does copyright protection for an original work of authorship extend to any idea, procedure, process, system, method of operation, concept, principle, or discovery, regardless of the form in which it is described, explained, illustrated, or embodied in such a work (17 U.S.C. §102(b)).

The classic case that gave rise to this provision involved an accounting system that used ledger forms such as that in Figure 11.2.

Source: Published federal case (out of copyright).

Figure 11.2 Selden's copyrighted accounting ledger

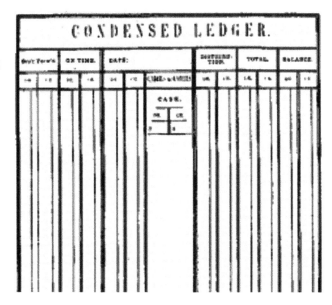

CASE

Baker v. Selden, 101 U.S. 99 (1879)

Charles Selden, the testator of the complainant in this case, in the year 1859 took the requisite steps for obtaining the copyright of a book, entitled "Selden's Condensed Ledger, or Book-keeping Simplified," the object of which was to exhibit and explain a peculiar system of book-keeping. In 1860 and 1861, he took the copyright of several other books, containing additions to and improvements upon the said system. The bill of complaint was filed against the defendant, Baker, for an alleged infringement of these copyrights. The latter, in his answer, denied that Selden was the author or designer of the books, and denied the infringement charged, and contends on the argument that the matter alleged to be infringed is not a lawful subject of copyright.

The book or series of books of which the complainant claims the copyright consists of an introductory essay explaining the system of book-keeping referred to, to which are annexed certain forms or blanks, consisting of ruled lines, and headings, illustrating the system and showing how it is to be used and carried out in practice. This system effects the same results as book-keeping by double entry; but, by a peculiar arrangement of columns and headings, presents the entire operation, of a day, a week, or a month, on a single page, or on two pages facing each other, in an account-book.

The defendant uses a similar plan so far as results are concerned; but makes a different arrangement of the columns, and uses different headings. If the complainant's testator had the exclusive right to the use of the system explained in his book, it would be difficult to contend that the defendant does not infringe it, notwithstanding the difference in his form

CASE *(continued)*

of arrangement; but if it be assumed that the system is open to public use, it seems to be equally difficult to contend that the books made and sold by the defendant are a violation of the copyright of the complainant's book considered merely as a book explanatory of the system.

Where the truths of a science or the methods of an art are the common property of the whole world, any author has the right to express the one, or explain and use the other, in his own way. As an author, Selden explained the system in a particular way. It may be conceded that Baker makes and uses account-books arranged on substantially the same system; but the proof fails to show that he has violated the copyright of Selden's book, regarding the latter merely as an explanatory work; or that he has infringed Selden's right in any way, unless the latter became entitled to an exclusive right in the system.

[T]here is a clear distinction between the book, as such, and the art which it is intended to illustrate. The mere statement of the proposition is so evident, that it requires hardly any argument to support it. The same distinction may be predicated of every other art as well as that of book-keeping. A treatise on the composition and use of medicines, be they old or new; on the construction and use of ploughs, or watches, or churns; or on the mixture and application of colors for painting or dyeing; or on the mode of drawing lines to produce the effect of perspective, – would be the subject of copyright; but no one would contend that the copyright of the treatise would give the exclusive right to the art or manufacture described therein. The copyright of the book, if not pirated from other works, would be valid without regard to the novelty, or want of novelty, of its subject-matter. The novelty of the art or thing described or explained has nothing to do with the validity of the copyright. To give to the author of the book an exclusive property in the art described therein, when no examination of its novelty has ever been officially made, would be a surprise and a fraud upon the public. That is the province of letters-patent, not of copyright. The claim to an invention or discovery of an art or manufacture must be subjected to the examination of the Patent Office before an exclusive right therein can be obtained; and it can only be secured by a patent from the government.

The description of the art in a book, though entitled to the benefit of copyright, lays no foundation for an exclusive claim to the art itself. The object of the one is explanation; the object of the other is use. The former may be secured by copyright. The latter can only be secured, if it can be secured at all, by letters-patent.

The conclusion to which we have come is, that blank account-books are not the subject of copyright; and that the mere copyright of Selden's book did not confer upon him the exclusive right to make and use account-books, ruled and arranged as designated by him and described and illustrated in said book. The decree of the Circuit Court must be reversed, and the cause remanded with instructions to dismiss the complainant's bill.

NOTES

1. One uncontroversial reading of *Baker* is that, where there is only one possible way to express or explain a system, that expression may not be copyrighted. So, for example, if there is only one way to annotate an existing public domain map for purposes of showing the planned location of an oil pipeline, the resulting map is not protectable by copyright. *See Kern River Gas Transmission Co. v. Coastal Corp.*, 899 F.2d 1458 (5th Cir.), cert. denied, 498 U.S. 952, 111 S. Ct. 374, 112 L. Ed. 2d 336 (1990). The rationale is simple: Allowing copyright in the map would in effect confer a monopoly over the right to build the actual pipeline along the planned route. Though this concept, often called "the merger doctrine," is usually described as an aspect of copyright infringement doctrine (*see infra* Section 11.2.2), it also expresses a truth about copyrightable subject matter. Because the particular description of the pipeline's location is the sole way to explain where to locate it, protecting that description would *in effect* protect the "system [or] method of operation" of the pipeline.

2. The more controversial question with regard to *Baker* is how much of a distinct role it creates for functional works, software in particular. One view – perhaps the most common – is that §102(b) of the Copyright Act takes aim quite explicitly at attempts to gain property rights over a "system, method of operation, . . . or discovery," and broadly excludes copyright for expressions that describe such a system or method of operation. The emphasis in *Baker* on drawing a clear and clean line between copyright and patent is the primary thrust behind this approach. Under this view, business people who create functional works such as the accounting system in *Baker* must not be permitted to use copyright law to obtain a "backdoor patent" on the functional aspects of their works. Leading software copyright cases incorporate this view in holding that functional aspects of a computer program must be eliminated before it is subjected to comparison with another program in determining copyright infringement. *See Computer Associates International, Inc. v. Altai, Inc.*, 982 F.2d 693 (2d Cir. 1992); Pamela Samuelson, *Why Copyright Law Excludes Systems and Processes from the Scope of Its Protection*, 85 Tex. L. Rev. 1921 (2007); Lloyd L. Weinreb, *Copyright for Functional Expression*, 111 Harv. L. Rev. 1149 (1998).

   The alternative view, primarily associated with the Nimmer copyright treatise and some early software cases, is that *Baker* is simply one of many cases holding that ideas are not copyrightable, only expression is. *See* 1 Nimmer on Copyright §2.18 (2015); *Whelan Associates, Inc. v. Jaslow Dental Laboratory, Inc.*, 797 F.2d 1222, 1224–25 (3d Cir. 1986). This view might be said to emphasize the words "idea, . . . concept, principle" in §102(b). The main argument is that there is no difference between "functional" and "expressive" works when it comes to §102(b). Ideas are never protectable, but expression always is. So the problem with the *Baker* case was that the plaintiff was trying to protect a broad "idea, concept, [or] principle," in the same way that the author of a book might try to protect broad or generic plot elements. The exclusion of "ideas" from copyright prevents both the accounting system author and the novelist from seeking overexpansive protection – and there is no important difference between these types of works. The fact that one type of work is read for entertainment and the other has a practical "use" is irrelevant. For a thorough review of the argument, *see* Nimmer, *supra*; Pamela Samuelson, *Why Copyright Law Excludes Systems and Processes from the Scope of Its Protection*, 85 Tex. L. Rev. 1921 (2007).

11.1.4 Authorship

11.1.4.1 Work made for hire

CCNV v. Reid, 490 U.S. 730 (1989)

In this case, an artist and the organization that hired him to produce a sculpture contest the ownership of the copyright in that work. To resolve this dispute, we must construe the

CASE *(continued)*

"work made for hire" provisions of the Copyright Act of 1976 (Act or 1976 Act), 17 U.S.C. §§ 101 and 201(b), and in particular, the provision in § 101, which defines as a "work made for hire" a "work prepared by an employee within the scope of his or her employment" (hereinafter § 101(1)).

Petitioners are the Community for Creative Non-Violence (CCNV), a nonprofit unincorporated association dedicated to eliminating homelessness in America, and Mitch Snyder, a member and trustee of CCNV. In the fall of 1985, CCNV decided to participate in the annual Christmastime Pageant of Peace in Washington, D.C., by sponsoring a display to dramatize the plight of the homeless. [They commissioned a statue, to be made by Respondent Reed, in the form of a homeless family posed in the traditional "nativity scene" or crèche scene associated with the Christian celebration of Christmas.]

The parties agreed that the project would cost no more than $15,000, not including Reid's services, which he offered to donate. The parties did not sign a written agreement. Neither party mentioned copyright. After Reid received an advance of $3,000, he made several sketches of figures in various poses. At Snyder's request, Reid sent CCNV a sketch of a proposed sculpture showing the family in a crèche-like setting: the mother seated, cradling a baby in her lap; the father standing behind her, bending over her shoulder to touch the baby's foot. Reid testified that Snyder asked for the sketch to use in raising funds for the sculpture. Snyder testified that it was also for his approval.

[Reid finished the statue.] The statue remained on display for a month. In late January 1986, CCNV members returned it to Reid's studio in Baltimore for minor repairs. Several weeks later, Snyder began making plans to take the statue on a tour of several cities to raise money for the homeless. Reid objected, contending that the material [it was made of] was not strong enough to withstand the ambitious itinerary. [The two filed competing copyright registration certificates; this litigation ensued. The district court held that the statue was a "work for hire" under the Copyright Act, and that CCNV owned the copyright. The Court of Appeals reversed and said the work was not a work for hire, so Reid owned the copyright.]

The Copyright Act of 1976 provides that copyright ownership "vests initially in the author or authors of the work." 17 U.S.C. § 201(a). As a general rule, the author is the party who actually creates the work, that is, the person who translates an idea into a fixed, tangible expression entitled to copyright protection. § 102. The Act carves out an important exception, however, for "works made for hire." If the work is for hire, "the employer or other person for whom the work was prepared is considered the author" and owns the copyright, unless there is a written agreement to the contrary. § 201(b). ["Work for hire" status affects the copyright term, right to renewal, and right to terminate licenses and assignments.]

Section 101 of the 1976 Act provides that a work is "for hire" under two sets of circumstances:

(1) a work prepared by an employee within the scope of his or her employment; or
(2) a work specially ordered or commissioned for use as a contribution to a collective work, as a

CASE *(continued)*

part of a motion picture or other audiovisual work, as a translation, as a supplementary work, as a compilation, as an instructional text, as a test, as answer material for a test, or as an atlas, if the parties expressly agree in a written instrument signed by them that the work shall be considered a work made for hire (17 U.S.C. §101 (definition of "work for hire")).

[A sculpture does not fit any of the categories in §101(2).] The dispositive inquiry in this case therefore is whether "Third World America" is "a work prepared by an employee within the scope of his or her employment" under §101(1).

The Act nowhere defines the terms "employee" or "scope of employment." It is, however, well established that "[w]here Congress uses terms that have accumulated settled meaning under . . . the common law, a court must infer, unless the statute otherwise dictates, that Congress means to incorporate the established meaning of these terms." *NLRB v. Amax Coal Co.*, 453 U.S. 322, 329 (1981).

In the past, when Congress has used the term "employee" without defining it, we have concluded that Congress intended to describe the conventional master-servant relationship as understood by common-law agency doctrine. *See, e.g., Kelley v. Southern Pacific Co.*, 419 U.S. 318, 322–323 (1974). Nothing in the text of the work for hire provisions indicates that Congress used the words "employee" and "employment" to describe anything other than 'the conventional relation of employer and employee." *Kelley*, supra, 419 U.S., at 323. On the contrary, Congress' intent to incorporate the agency law definition is suggested by §101(1)'s use of the term, "scope of employment," a widely used term of art in agency law. See Restatement (Second) of Agency §228 (1958) (hereinafter Restatement). [The Court rejects the view that a "work for hire" is any work that was made when the paying or commissioning party has the right to direct and control the making of the work, or actually exercised that right during the making of the work.]

In determining whether a hired party is an employee under the general common law of agency, we consider the hiring party's right to control the manner and means by which the product is accomplished. Among the other factors relevant to this inquiry are the skill required; the source of the instrumentalities and tools; the location of the work; the duration of the relationship between the parties; whether the hiring party has the right to assign additional projects to the hired party; the extent of the hired party's discretion over when and how long to work; the method of payment; the hired party's role in hiring and paying assistants; whether the work is part of the regular business of the hiring party; whether the hiring party is in business; the provision of employee benefits; and the tax treatment of the hired party. See Restatement §220(2) (setting forth a nonexhaustive list of factors relevant to determining whether a hired party is an employee). No one of these factors is determinative.

Examining the circumstances of this case in light of these factors, we agree with the Court of Appeals that Reid was not an employee of CCNV but an independent contractor. True, CCNV members directed enough of Reid's work to ensure that he produced a sculpture that met their specifications. The extent of control the hiring party exercises

CASE *(continued)*

over the details of the product is not dispositive. Indeed, all the other circumstances weigh heavily against finding an employment relationship. Reid is a sculptor, a skilled occupation. Reid supplied his own tools. He worked in his own studio in Baltimore, making daily supervision of his activities from Washington practically impossible. Reid was retained for less than two months, a relatively short period of time. During and after this time, CCNV had no right to assign additional projects to Reid. Apart from the deadline for completing the sculpture, Reid had absolute freedom to decide when and how long to work. CCNV paid Reid $15,000, a sum dependent on "completion of a specific job, a method by which independent contractors are often compensated." *Holt v. Winpisinger*, 811 F.2d 1532, 1540 (1987). Reid had total discretion in hiring and paying assistants. "Creating sculptures was hardly 'regular business' for CCNV." 846 F.2d, at 1494, n. 11. Finally, CCNV did not pay payroll or Social Security taxes, provide any employee benefits, or contribute to unemployment insurance or workers' compensation funds.

CCNV is not the author of "Third World America" by virtue of the work for hire provisions of the Act. However, as the Court of Appeals made clear, CCNV nevertheless may be a joint author of the sculpture.

NOTES

1. The multi-factor test of *CCNV* has been applied numerous times since the decision came down. *See, e.g., JustMed, Inc. v. Byce*, 600 F.3d 1118, 1128 (9th Cir. 2010) (informal nature of startup company explains loose employment arrangement; but programmer was an employee so his program was a work for hire). One court has applied the "loaned servant doctrine" of workers' compensation cases here to rule that a company that uses a "labor outsourcing" company to hire people was an employer for purposes of the doctrine. *Favela v. Fritz Cos.*, 29 U.S.P.Q.2d 1694, 1697–98 (C.D. Cal. 1993). In another case, the famous dancer and choreographer Martha Graham had done much of her later work as an employee of a corporate entity that was in effect just an alter ego for the dancer herself. The court held that her dance company owned a number of her works as works for hire. *See Martha Graham Sch. & Dance Found. v. Martha Graham Ctr. of Contemporary Dance, Inc.*, 380 F.3d 624 (2d Cir. 2004), cert. denied, 544 U.S. 1060 (2005). For a critique of the current works made for hire doctrine, *see* Anthony J. Casey & Andres Sawicki, *Copyright in Teams*, 80 U. Chi. L. Rev. 1683, 1724 (2013).
2. The categories of works listed as "specially ordered or commissioned" in 17 U.S.C. §202(2) have been explained as all involving many small contributions by multiple individual creators. The rationale for a "work for hire" designation in these cases is that a single owner is more efficient. It saves the cost of requiring and keeping track of many individual assignments or licenses. *See* Litman, *Copyright, Compromise, and Legislative History*, 72 Cornell L. Rev. 857, 890–91 (1987). The writing requirement in §202(2) is in the statute to demonstrate that a creator knowingly parted with the status of original author, by agreeing to a "work for hire" arrangement. Cases hold that there is some flexibility in the content of the writing; it need not, for example, necessarily mention the phrase "work for hire" (*Armento v. Laser Image, Inc.*, 950 F. Supp. 719, 730 (W.D.N.C. 1996)).
3. A controversial and short-lived amendment to the "work for hire" provision in 1999 rendered recording artists as employee/commissioned parties, and thus made all sound recordings works for hire. Numerous musicians reacted violently to this characterization and the statute in question was quickly repealed. *See* 1 Nimmer on Copyright §5.03[B][2][a][ii] (2015).

11.1.4.2 Co-authorship

Aalmuhammed v. Lee, 202 F.3d 1227 (9th Cir. 2000)

In 1991, Warner Brothers contracted with Spike Lee and his production companies to make the movie Malcolm X, to be based on the book, The Autobiography of Malcolm X. Lee co-wrote the screenplay, directed, and co-produced the movie, which starred Denzel Washington as Malcolm X. Washington asked Jefri Aalmuhammed to assist him in his preparation for the starring role because Aalmuhammed knew a great deal about Malcolm X and Islam. Aalmuhammed, a devout Muslim, was particularly knowledgeable about the life of Malcolm X, having previously written, directed, and produced a documentary film about Malcolm X.

Aalmuhammed joined Washington on the movie set. The movie was filmed in the New York metropolitan area and Egypt. Aalmuhammed presented evidence that his involvement in making the movie was very extensive. He reviewed the shooting script for Spike Lee and Denzel Washington and suggested extensive script revisions. Some of his script revisions were included in the released version of the film; others were filmed but not included in the released version. Most of the revisions Aalmuhammed made were to ensure the religious and historical accuracy and authenticity of scenes depicting Malcolm X's religious conversion and pilgrimage to Mecca.

Aalmuhammed submitted evidence that he directed Denzel Washington and other actors while on the set, created at least two entire scenes with new characters, translated Arabic into English for subtitles, supplied his own voice for voice-overs, selected the proper prayers and religious practices for the characters, and edited parts of the movie during post production.

Aalmuhammed never had a written contract with Warner Brothers, Lee, or Lee's production companies, but he expected Lee to compensate him for his work. He did not intend to work and bear his expenses in New York and Egypt gratuitously. Aalmuhammed ultimately received a check for $25,000 from Lee, which he cashed, and a check for $100,000 from Washington, which he did not cash.

During the summer before Malcolm X's November 1992 release, Aalmuhammed asked for a writing credit as a co-writer of the film, but was turned down. When the film was released, it credited Aalmuhammed only as an "Islamic Technical Consultant," far down the list. In November 1995, Aalmuhammed applied for a copyright with the U.S. Copyright Office, claiming he was a co-creator, co-writer, and co-director of the movie. The Copyright Office issued him a "Certificate of Registration," but advised him in a letter that his "claims conflict with previous registrations" of the film. [This litigation ensued.]

Aalmuhammed claimed that the movie Malcolm X was a "joint work" of which he was an author, thus making him a co-owner of the copyright.

CASE *(continued)*

Aalmuhammed argues that he established a genuine issue of fact as to whether he was an author of a "joint work," Malcolm X. The Copyright Act does not define "author," but it does define "joint work":

> A "joint work" is a work prepared by two or more authors with the intention that their contributions be merged into inseparable or interdependent parts of a unitary whole.

17 U.S.C. §101.
The statutory language establishes that for a work to be a "joint work" there must be (1) a copyrightable work, (2) two or more "authors," and (3) the authors must intend their contributions be merged into inseparable or interdependent parts of a unitary whole. A "joint work" in this circuit "requires each author to make an independently copyrightable contribution" to the disputed work. Malcolm X is a copyrightable work, and it is undisputed that the movie was intended by everyone involved with it to be a unitary whole. It is also undisputed that Aalmuhammed made substantial and valuable contributions to the movie, including technical help, such as speaking Arabic to the persons in charge of the mosque in Egypt, scholarly and creative help, such as teaching the actors how to pray properly as Muslims, and script changes to add verisimilitude to the religious aspects of the movie. Speaking Arabic to persons in charge of the mosque, however, does not result in a copyrightable contribution to the motion picture. Coaching of actors, to be copyrightable, must be turned into an expression in a form subject to copyright. The same may be said for many of Aalmuhammed's other activities. Aalmuhammed has, however, submitted evidence that he rewrote several specific passages of dialogue that appeared in Malcolm X, and that he wrote scenes relating to Malcolm X's Hajj pilgrimage that were enacted in the movie. If Aalmuhammed's evidence is accepted, as it must be on summary judgment, these items would have been independently copyrightable. Aalmuhammed, therefore, has presented a genuine issue of fact as to whether he made a copyrightable contribution.

Aalmuhammed established that he contributed substantially to the film, but not that he was one of its "authors." We hold that authorship is required under the statutory definition of a joint work, and that authorship is not the same thing as making a valuable and copyrightable contribution. We recognize that a contributor of an expression may be deemed to be the "author" of that expression for purposes of determining whether it is independently copyrightable. The issue we deal with is a different and larger one: is the contributor an author of the joint work within the meaning of 17 U.S.C. §101.

Who, in the absence of contract, can be considered an author of a movie? *Burrow–Giles* defines author as the person to whom the work owes its origin and who superintended the whole work, the "master mind." In a movie this definition, in the absence of a contract to the contrary, would generally limit authorship to someone at the top of the screen credits, sometimes the producer, sometimes the director, possibly the star, or the screenwriter – someone who has artistic control.

Aalmuhammed did not at any time have superintendence of the work. Warner Brothers

CASE *(continued)*

and Spike Lee controlled it. Aalmuhammed was not the person "who has actually formed the picture by putting the persons in position, and arranging the place . . ." Spike Lee was, so far as we can tell from the record. Aalmuhammed lacked control over the work, and absence of control is strong evidence of the absence of co-authorship.

Because the record before the district court established no genuine issue of fact as to Aalmuhammed's co-authorship of Malcolm X as a joint work, the district court correctly granted summary judgment dismissing his claims for declaratory judgment and an accounting resting on co-authorship.

[The court remanded for findings on the monetary value of Aalmuhammed's contributions to the film, which he can recover under a restitution or *quantum meruit* theory.]

NOTES

1. The opinion says, "A 'joint work' in this circuit 'requires each author to make an independently copyrightable contribution' to the disputed work. Other circuits (in fact, a majority) require joint authors to make at least a substantial contribution, and of course require the resulting overall work to be copyrightable; but they do not require each author contribute independently copyrightable material. *See, e.g., Erickson v. Trinity Theatre, Inc.*, 13 F.3d 1061, 1067–71 (7th Cir. 1994).
2. In general any author of a joint work may license the work to others without the permission or involvement of the work's other author(s). Profits earned, however, must be shared with the other authors of the joint work. *See, e.g., Brownstein v. Lindsay*, 742 F.3d 55, 68 (3d Cir. 2014). It is noteworthy that this arrangement is in general *not* effective in foreign jurisdictions, where involvement of all authors of a joint work is required. *See, e.g.*, United Kingdom: *Powell v. Head*, 12 Ch. D. 686 (1879); *Cescinsky v. George Routledge & Sons, Ltd.*, 2 K.B. 325 (1916); France: Law No. 57-296, §10, Act of March 11, 1957; Italy: Law No. 633, §10, Act of April 22, 1914 as amended.

11.2 China

11.2.1 Copyrightable criteria: originality and duplicability

Based on Article 1 of the Chinese Copyright Law and Article 2 of the Chinese Copyright Implementing Regulations, a work might be subject to copyright protection if it meets the following four criteria: (1) the work must be intellectual creations contributed by human being(s); (2) it must be in the field of literary, artistic and scientific domain; (3) it constitutes original works of authorship; and finally (4) it can be reproduced.

The first element requires a copyright subject matter to be intellectual creations of human beings. This requirement excludes other works created by non-human beings, such as by animals or by nature, no matter how much aesthetic value the work might possess.

The second element highlights the purpose of Chinese copyright law and also draws a fine line between copyrightable subject matter and patentable subject matter. Unlike patent law, which seeks to encourage creativity, research, and development in the field of science and technology, copyright law is more focused on protecting works in the field of literary and artistic domain.

The third element "originality" requires a work to be an original work of authorship. Here, the originality standard is pretty similar to its counterpart under the US copyright law. In other words, it requires a work to be an independent creation of the author, rather than copying from someone else's. Also, the work needs to meet a certain "creativity" standard. As to how "creative" the work needs to be, it is more or less subject to courts' discretion. A review of Chinese case law seems to suggest that the creativity standard required by Chinese judges is similar to the US standard, which requires the creativity to be more than trivial.

The fourth element requires that a copyrightable work can be reproduced. Unlike the US copyright law, which requires the expressions of ideas to be fixed in a tangible medium, Chinese copyright law, as with most jurisdictions, does not pose a fixation requirement to works. In other words, oral works, such as public speeches, live concerts, and spontaneous lectures are all subject to copyright protection so long as such works can be reproduced. (*See Beijing Dongda Zhengbao Technology Ltd. v. SUN Weijie*, Shandong Qingdao Intermediate People's Court, Qinminchuzi No. 105, 2010; *LUO Yonghao v. Beijing Silicon Valley E-Commerce Ltd.*, Beijing Haidian District Court, Haiminchuzi No. 9749, 2006.)

11.2.2 Limitations on copyrightability: the idea/expression dichotomy, the merger doctrine and *scène à faire*

As a general rule, copyright law does not protect ideas, but expressions of such ideas only. This is known as "the idea/expression dichotomy." The challenge in applying the idea/expression dichotomy though is to determine where to draw the line between non-copyrightable ideas and copyrightable expressions. The idea/expression dichotomy also developed an extension doctrine, known as "the merger doctrine," which provides that when there is only one or but a few limited ways of expressing an idea, the expression will merge with the idea and the work becomes non-copyrightable. The following case deals with both of these doctrines.

CEInet Data v. CDC International Network, Beijing High People's Court, Gaominzhongzi No. 368 (2002)

Plaintiff, CEInet Data Co., Ltd., provides economical data analysis, consultation and computer data processing services. Its economic forecast charts, including "CEI Macro-Economic Forecast,", "CEI Prosperity Trend" and "CEI Advance Composition Index," use various circles in different colors and fonts, to indicate its predictions on future economic trends as "overheated, heated, stable, cold and inactive." The aforesaid forecast economic charts are available on Plaintiff's website, with a copyright statement as follows "Copyright work of CEInet Data. Reproduction and Repost of such charts are prohibited without CEInet Data's authorization."

Defendant, CDC International Network Communications Co., Ltd., is an internet company providing internet solutions and advertising services for its clients. Defendant copied 10 economic forecast charts of Plaintiff, without authorization from or attribution to Plaintiff. The charts that Defendant copied and posted on its own website include the logos of CEIdata. Plaintiff sued Defendant for violating the copyright of its economic charts.

The trial court held that the "CEI Prosperity Trend Chart" and "CEI Advance Composition Index Chart" created by CEInet Data are common expressions of charts to indicate changes in economic data, thus lacking sufficient originality to be protected under Chinese copyright law.

[During the appeal process,] this court [the appellate court] holds that, the focus of this case is to determine whether the CEI Prosperity Trend Chart, CEI Advance Composition Index Chart and other economic forecast charts prepared by CEInet Data have enough originality to qualify as copyrightable works under the Chinese Copyright Law.

Although the CEI Prosperity Trend Chart, CEI Advance Composition Index Chart and other forecast charts created by CEInet Data have used common expressions of curve charts to indicate the change of economic indexes, curve chart is not the only way or one of a few limited ways of expressing such economic forecasts.

Originality requires a work to be independently created by its author. It first requires a work not to be a plagiarized work, and must possess a certain degree of creativity (not too much is required though). It secondly requires the work to contain the judgments of its author. In this case, it is undisputed that the economic forecast charts are independently created by CEInet Data, not copying from someone else's work. The dispute, however, lies in whether each chart reflects creative judgment of its author. This court holds that as long as the charts reflect the selection and independent judgment of its author, such charts are copyrightable works.

In this case, the primary difference between CEInet Data's forecast charts and those of its competitors is that CEInet Data exercised its own discretion in filling the gaps where

> **CASE** *(continued)*
>
> economic data was not publicly available, made seasonal adjustment on its charts during holiday seasons, and selected different color backgrounds in the charts to create a better visual effect. These discretional adjustments reflect personal judgments of the charts author. Although curve charts might share similar visual effects due to the chart features, the overall visual effects of curve charts could be still different due to the different choices and judgments of their authors. In addition, the selection of color backgrounds [in CEInet Data's charts] also reflected the aesthetic judgment of its authors, thus distinguishing its charts from others. As such, it is fair to conclude that Plaintiff's forecast charts possess sufficient originality [to be protected by copyright law].

QUESTION

1. Compare the *CEInet Data* case with the US copyright cases *Feist* and *Baker*. Do you think that the Chinese courts hold a similar standard as their US counterparts in terms of the originality threshold for copyrightable works? Do you agree with the Chinese courts that the curve charts, as prepared by CEInet Data, have enough originality to qualify for copyright protection?

11.2.3 Specific categories of works

11.2.3.1 Introduction

In the first version (1990) of the Chinese Copyright Law, 10 categories of works were identified as copyrightable subject matter. Later on, various other works have been added to the list of copyrightable works over the years, including acrobatic works, architectural works, cinematographic (audio-visual) works, works of applied art, computer software etc.

A comparison of the categories of works in the Chinese copyright law and that of the US and other countries seem to suggest that although drafted in different legislative languages, most works have similar definitions and enjoy the same coverage. For example, a "written work" under the Chinese Copyright Law and a "literary work" under the US Copyright Act both refer to the type of work that can be expressed in words, numbers, or other verbal or numerical symbols, such as a book, a poem, a novel etc. Similarly, "musical works, dramatic works, pantomime, choreographic works, pictorial works and graphic works" also have similar meaning and coverage under copyright systems of various jurisdictions.

However, there are also noticeable differences in terms of several special categories of works. The following paragraphs will discuss these special works.

11.2.3.2 Works of applied art

Interlego AG. (Switzerland) v. Ke Gao Toys Ltd. and Beijing Fuxing Commercial Center Co., Ltd., Beijing High People's Court, Gaominzhongzi No. 279 (2002)

Plaintiff Interlego AG. ("Interlego") is a Swiss company producing toys. Interlego's toy products first entered into the Chinese market in 1992. On February 25, 1998, LEGO Overseas A/S and LEGO Future ApS assigned its copyrights to a number of LEGO toy bricks to Interlego, including (1) the copyright and interest in the LEGO toy bricks created, developed and marketed by the employees and designers of Licensor, which under Denmark law encompasses all the sculptures, words, pictures, drawings, photos, scripts, written works and works of the applied art; and (2) all other rights, including the copyright, related rights and interests of the aforesaid works produced and sold in China. Interlego also filed a number of design patents for its LEGO toys in China.

Interlego claimed that Defendant Ke Gao Toys Ltd. ("Ke Gao"), a Chinese company, infringed the copyright of its works of applied art (toy bricks) by manufacturing and selling similar toy bricks of Interlego, without authorization.

[In response, Ke Gao contended that it has obtained design patents for the toy bricks it manufactured and sold in China. Although Interlego had requested that Ke Gao's aforesaid design patents be invalidated by the Chinese Patent Office, such invalidation requests were rejected, and therefore Ke Gao's patents for its toy bricks remain valid. Ke Gao also argued that it had authorization from its licensors – two Korean companies – to manufacture and sell the toy bricks. Ke Gao submitted the following evidence during the trial: (1) Agreement between Ke Gao and its Korean licensors to manufacture and sell the toy bricks in China, and (2) an earlier judgment made by the Korean Intellectual Property Office, which denied LEGO's invalidation request against another prior design patent under no 75644.]

The first instance court held that a work of applied art should first of all, be a copyrightable work as defined under the Chinese Copyright Law, meeting both the originality and duplicability standards. Secondly, a work of applied art should also possess "utilitarian" and "artistic" features. In other words, a work of applied art, [under the Chinese copyright law], needs to meet four criteria: original, duplicable, utilitarian and artistic.

Among the 53 alleged infringed toy bricks owned by Plaintiff, the first instance court held that three of them lacked enough artistic features to qualify as works of applied art, but finding the remaining 50 toy bricks satisfying the requirements of utilitarian, artistic, original and duplicable, thus subject to copyright protection as works of applied art. Further, the court compared the defendant's toy bricks with those of the plaintiff's 50 copyrightable

CASE *(continued)*

toy bricks and concluded that 33 bricks were substantial[ly] similar, thus finding Defendant liable for copyright infringement.

[Both Plaintiff and Defendant appealed before Beijing High People's Court.]

The issues presented before this court [the appellate court] include: (1) the scope and extent of protection for works of applied art in China, (2) whether Interlego's 53 LEGO toy bricks qualify as works of applied art, thus subject to copyright protection; and (3) whether Ke Gao infringed copyright of Interlego with respect to the disputed toy bricks.

As to the first issue, since both Switzerland and China are member states of the Berne Convention, which protects works of applied art under Article 2 of the Berne Convention, China is obliged to protect works of applied art for nationals of member states of the Convention. According to the Berne Convention and *Provisions on the Implementation of the International Copyright Treaties (1992)*, the protection term for works of applied art is 25 years from the works' completion date.

With regard to copyrightability of Interlego's disputed LEGO toy bricks, Ke Gao argued that since Interlego already filed design patents for such toy bricks, it should not be allowed to claim "double protection" under the Copyright Law. However, this court found no legislative language that suggested that works of applied art cannot receive double protection under both the patent law and the copyright law.

Although Interlego had filed design patents in China for its toys' components, this court determined that such patent applications did not prevent the disputed toy components from simultaneously or continuously receiving protection under the Copyright Law as works of applied art. Therefore, the court rejected Ke Gao's contention that Interlego's toy components should not be protectable under the Copyright Law simply because the same components acquired a design patent.

A work of applied art is a work of intellectual creation, which should meet the requirement of a copyrightable work under the Copyright Law [being original and duplicable], but also possessing utilitarian and artistic features. In other words, a work of applied art shall meet all the criteria of being utilitarian, artistic, original and duplicable. The utilitarian aspect of works of applied art means that the work shall have utilitarian functions instead of pure decorative purpose. The artistic aspect requires the work to have a certain degree of artistic values, which should be deemed as an artwork by the general public.

[The court agreed with the first instance court] that among the 53 disputed toy bricks, three did not qualify as works of applied art because they did not attain the appropriate degree of artistic values. But the remaining 50 toy bricks qualify as works of applied art subject to copyright protection.

[As to the third issue, *i.e.* whether Ke Gao's toys were substantially similar to those of Interlego,] the appellate court upheld the trial court's decision that of the 50 disputed Plaintiff's copyrightable toy bricks, 17 bricks were not substantial[ly] similar, while finding the remaining toys bricks similar.

NOTES AND QUESTIONS

1. In *Interlego*, Chinese judges held that the patent application of Interlego for the disputed toy bricks does not prevent it from also claiming copyright protection for the same toy bricks, thus affording "double protection" of both patent and copyright for the same toy bricks. Do you agree with the Chinese court's analysis here?

2. The same standard for works of applied art has also been adopted in later cases decided by Chinese courts, including *Mega Blocks, Inc. v. CHEN Daiguang* (Shantou Intermediate People's Court, Shanzhongfa zhichuzi No. 19, 2005), *Jean Paul Gaultier v. ZHAO Lingting* (Beijing No. 2 Intermediate People's Court, Erzhong minchuzi No. 7070, 2006) and *OK Baby Ltd. v. Ci Xi Jiabao Children Products Ltd.* (Beijing No. 2 Intermediate People's Court, Erzhong minchuzi No. 12293, 2008) etc. In all these cases, Chinese courts have required a work of applied art to meet all the criteria of being original, duplicable, and possessing utilitarian and artistic features.

3. In the US the test of separability (*i.e.* physical separability or conceptual separability) is applied to works of applied art. (*See* H.R. Rep. No. 94-1476, 94th Cong., 2d Sess. 54–55 (1976), reprinted in 1976 U.S.C.C.A.N. 5659, 5667–68; *Mazer v. Stein*, 347 U.S.201 (1954); *Kieselstein-Cord v. Accessories By Pearl, Inc.*, 623 F. 2d 989 (2d Cir. 1980); *Brandir International, Inc. v. Cascade Pacific Lumber Co.*, 834 F. 2d 1142 (2d. Cir. 1987). In other words, a work of applied art is subject to copyright protection only if its utilitarian function can be physically or conceptually separated from its artistic features. If the utilitarian aspect of a work of applied art cannot be separated physically or conceptually from its artistic elements, then the work cannot be protected by the US copyright law. The rationale behind such a separability test, as explained in the House Report, is to ensure that there is a clear line between copyrightable subject matter and patentable subject matter: "In adopting this amendatory language, the Committee is seeking to draw as clear a line as possible between copyrightable works of applied arts and uncopyrighted works of industrial designs . . ." (H.R. Rep. No. 94-1476, 94th Cong., 2d Sess. 54–55 (1976), reprinted in 1976 U.S.C.C.A.N. 5659, 5667–68). Now compare the separability test of the United States with the all-four-criteria test in China with regard to copyrightability of works of applied art. Which approach makes sense to you, and why?

11.2.3.3 Databases

Databases, also known as compilations of data, are protected as compilation works under the Chinese Copyright Law. A compilation work is entitled to copyright protection if there is sufficient originality in the selection, organization, and coordination of the underlying materials. Therefore, to qualify for copyright protection a database also needs to possess sufficient originality in the selection, arrangement, and coordination of the underlying data. (*See Hainan Jingtian Information Ltd. v. Shanghai Xuxi Business Consulting Ltd.*, Shanghai High People's Court, Hugaominsan-zhichuzi No. 122, 2004, finding "enough originality" in the selection, arrangement, and compilation of Plaintiff's database, a compilation of laws, regulations, and cases; *Shanghai Hantao Information Consulting Ltd. v. Ai Ju Bang Tech Ltd.*, Beijing 1st Intermediate People's Court, Yizhongminchuzi No. 5031, 2009, rejecting originality in Plaintiff's database, a compilation of customer reviews arranged by chronological order).

The Chinese approach of protecting databases as compilation works is very similar to that of the US, which also rejects the "sweat of the brow" theory and requires sufficient originality in the selection, organization and coordination of the underlying data. (*See Bellsouth Advertising & Publishing Corp v. Donnelley Information Publishing, Inc.*, 999 F. 2d 1436 (11th Cir. 1993) (en banc), cert. denied, 510 U.S. 1101 (1994); *CCC Information Services, Inc. v. Maclean Hunter Market Reports, Inc.*, 44 F.2d 61 (2d Cir. 1994), cert. denied, 516 U.S. 817 (1995); *CDN Inc. v. Kapes*, 197 F.3d 1256 (9th Cir. 1999).)

There has been discussion among Chinese legislators regarding protection of databases through *sui generis* legislation, such as the EU Database Directive. But so far, no specific legislation has been issued regarding database, and database has been primarily protected in China through the copyright law assuming that the database in dispute deserves copyright protection, and also by contract, tort, anti-unfair completion law, and trade secret law.

11.2.3.4 Typefaces

CASE

Beijing Founder Electronics v. P&G Guangzhou Ltd, Beijing No. 1 Intermediate People's Court, Yizhongminzhongzi No. 5969, 2011

Plaintiff Beijing Founder Electronics Co., Ltd. ("Founder") designs and provides Chinese character typefaces through its computer software. In September 1998, Founder commissioned QI Li, a graphic designer, to design Chinese character fonts, including the Qian-Style font. Later, Founder developed the "Qian-Style Typeface" based on QI's Qian-Style font after digitization and computerization of the fonts with certain adjustments, and recorded the Qian-Style Typeface as works of fine art before the Chinese Copyright Office.

In August 2000, Founder launched the Qian-Style Typeface, as with other 122 Chinese character typefaces, in its disc software. On the cover page of the software, it stated that the typefaces included in the software could be used for multiple purposes, including for graphic design purpose. The software also included a license agreement ("License"). But unlike other click-wrap software agreements, Founder's disputed software did not require any action (such as a "click") from the user before it was installed. Based on the License, the end user is allowed to use the typeface software on one computer terminal only, for computer screen display and print out purposes. Founder specifically reserved a number of rights in the License, including "copying, lending, leasing or disseminating the software via internet, either wholly or partly; re-releasing the Chinese character-inventory (including

CASE *(continued)*

but not limited to releasing via television, movie, picture, webpage, printing for commercial use etc.), either wholly or partly; embedding the typefaces in any portable document format (including but not limited to the PDF format etc.); applying the product to network or multi-users system etc." Founder also stated in the License that prior approval is required for any use of the Qian-Style Typeface should such uses fall outside of the License scope.

Defendant Procter & Gamble (Guangzhou) Ltd. ("P&G"), hired a design company NICOSIA Creative Expresso Ltd. (NICE) to design a product package for its shampoo products under the trademark "Rejoice." NICE purchased the official version of Founder's typeface software and adopted the Qian-Style Typeface to design the Chinese characters "飘柔" (meaning "Rejoice") related to P&G's shampoo product label.

Founder sued P&G for copyright infringement, on the grounds that P&G's unauthorized use of the Qian-Style Typeface for its trademark "飘柔"(Rejoice) on its shampoo product packages violated Founder's copyright to both the Chinese character typeface inventory and also individual character typeface, which should be protected as works of fine art.

The first-instance court found that there was sufficient originality in the selection, scanning, digitalization, manual polishing, integration and processing of Founder's Chinese character typeface inventory. Therefore, the court held that the Chinese character typeface inventory was copyrightable work of fine art under the Chinese Copyright Law.

But the first-instance court rejected Founder's copyright claim for each individual Chinese character typeface. The court held that, works of fine art refer to paintings, calligraphy, sculptures and other two-dimensional or three-dimensional works that are formed by lines, colors or other patterns. Unlike other types of copyrightable works, works of fine art require aesthetic value, with a purpose to convey visual enjoyment.

Among the various types of works of fine art, paintings and sculpture might enjoy the highest degree of originality because its creator has more discretion in creating such works. For instance, different painters could choose different materials and apply different painting styles when painting the same scenic view. As a result, the final works (paintings) created by different authors could look vastly different. However, as far as Chinese calligraphy is concerned, calligraphers are more restrained in their expressions because the characters they write are fixed in a certain way.

Chinese character is composed of structure and strokes (spelling). Its primary purpose is to communicate with others as a tool, and aesthetic value is of only secondary importance. Because the structure and stroke of each Chinese character is fixed, there is little possibility to restructure or reform it, otherwise the character will be mis-spelt. As such, to claim copyright protection for the Chinese character requires additional originality in the presentation of the character, which is distinctive and novel enough to distinguish from other presentations of the same character . . . In this case, the individual typeface for Chinese character lacks such originality to claim for copyright protection. The first-instance court rejected Founder's claim for copyrightability of individual typeface.

[The first instance court also rejected Founder's claim that P&G's use of the Qian-Style Typeface in its shampoo product package constituted copyright infringement. The court

CASE *(continued)*

held that the product package, which incorporated the Qian-Style Typeface, was designed and created by NICE, and therefore, there was no direct nexus between P&G and Founder in terms of use of the typeface software... The court rejected Founder's claims, and Founder appealed.]

[During the appeal, the appellate court summarized the legal issues presented before its court as follows:]

Whether Defendant P&G's use of the Qian-Style Typeface on its trademark Infringed Founder's copyright

To bring a prima facie case of copyright infringement, Plaintiff Founder needs to prove the following elements: (1) the disputed character "Rejoice" in the Qian-Style Typeface is a copyrightable "work" defined under the Chinese Copyright Law; (2) Founder is copyright owner of such copyrightable works; (3) Defendant reproduced and distributed the above works; and (4) the alleged reproduction and distribution was conducted without Plaintiff's consent. Consent could be either explicit or implied.

The appellate court held that Founder has provided "implied consent" with regard to P&G's use of its trademark"飘柔"(Rejoice) in the Qian-Style Typeface. The aforesaid finding was concluded based on how the trademark"飘柔"(Rejoice) in the Qian-Style Typeface was created by NICE, the design company commissioned by P&G. First of all, NICE purchased a legitimate version of Founder's typeface software. Secondly, NICE chose the Qian-Style Typeface included in the software when printing the characters trademark"飘柔"(Rejoice). Based on the aforesaid facts, NICE was entitled to use any individual typeface included in the software when designing character fonts for its clients, and also to license its clients for further reproduction and distribution of such characters. As such, the subsequent reproduction and distribution of the characters "飘柔"(Rejoice) by Defendant did not constitute copyright infringement.

[When addressing Founder's implied consent, the court addressed the following issues:]

Where a legitimate purchaser [*i.e.* NICE] of Founder's typeface software has reasonable expectations to use the intellectual property rights attached in the software in a reasonable way;

Whether the IP owner [*i.e.* FOUNDER] has set out explicit, reasonable and limited restrictions to the use of such IP [*i.e.* typefaces] in its software license agreement with its legitimate purchaser;

Whether the IP owner [*i.e.* Founder] has set out explicit, reasonable and limited restrictions to the continued use of the typefaces by others [P&G].

In this case, it should be interpreted that by purchasing a legitimate version of Founder's typeface software, the purchaser [*i.e.* NICE] has obtained an implied license to use the intellectual property right attached in the software in a reasonable way.

In reaching the above conclusion, the court takes into account two major factors. First, it is a basic principle to balance interests of various parties when protecting intellectual property rights of rights holders. Second, in a market economy, a purchaser pays for a product at a price with reasonable expectations to use the product in a certain way.

CASE *(continued)*

The reasonable expectation of the use of a product is determined by the essential function of the product. In this case, NICE bought a legitimate version of Founder's typeface software, which is designed to produce, generate and display different typefaces of Chinese characters on a computer screen, in order to design a packaging label for his client. Therefore, NICE had reasonable expectations to believe that he was authorized to freely use the typeface characters generated by the software, to incorporate these characters into his design, and to finally deliver the design work product to his client. Apparently, such consumers as NICE had no interests in the software language or the source code of the program. Rather the primary purpose for such a purchase is to use the Chinese typefaces generated by the software. As such, NICE's expectations to freely use the Chinese characters generated by the software are "reasonable expectations."

Moreover, the prevailing purpose of character typeface inventory is to be used as a tool to communicate, with its aesthetic value being secondary. It should be noted that even for typefaces with very distinctive and artistic features, the main motivation behind the purchase of typeface software is still to use it as a tool to communicate. Otherwise, a potential purchaser would purchase calligraphy works instead of typeface software.

As to the second and third issues, whether Founder has set out "explicit, reasonable and limited restrictions" with respect to the use of the intellectual property rights attached in the software and typefaces, the court found that because (1) Founder's software does not come with a click-wrap license agreement, and there was no evidence to show that NICE had agreed to the terms of the use, and (2) Founder never distinguished an "individual/family or private" version of software from a more pricy "enterprise/commercial version," [which would otherwise have allowed the commercial use of the software] in the promotion, distribution and sale of the software, Founder failed to establish explicit, reasonable and limited restrictions regarding the use of its software and its Chinese typefaces.

[In view of the above, the appellate court concluded that because the use of Founder's software and its typeface by NICE and P&G are within "reasonable expectations" of such uses, and that Founder failed to set out explicit, reasonable and limited restrictions for such uses, Defendants were deemed to have obtained "implied consent" from Founder, and therefore were not found liable for copyright infringement.]

NOTES AND QUESTIONS

1. The first instance court rejected Founder's copyright claim for individual character typeface on the grounds that it lacks sufficient originality, but found that the collective character inventory meets the copyrightability standard. Do you agree? How does the originality standard of individual typeface differ from a collection of typefaces?
2. Both the first instance court and the appellate court mentioned calligraphy (*i.e.* works of fine art) when addressing the copyrightability of typefaces. Do you think that calligraphy and typefaces are similar types of works, and if so, why?

   In *Founder v. P&G*, the appellate court did not address the copyrightability of typefaces in its ruling, but instead ruled in favor of P&G on the theory of "implied consent." In another case, *Founder v. Blizzard Entertainment* (Chinese Supreme People's Court, Minsanzhongzi No. 6, 2010), the Chinese Supreme Court held that Founder's Chinese character inventory does not fall into the category of works of fine art, but might be subject to copyright protection as computer software. Do you agree with the reasoning of the Chinese Supreme Court?

In the US, typefaces are not copyrightable works. Volume 37 of the Code of the U.S. Federal Regulations clearly excludes typefaces as copyrightable works: "The following are examples of works *not* subject to copyright and applications for registration of such works cannot be entertained: . . . typeface as typeface." This is consistent with the House of Representatives report that accompanied the passing of the 1976 Copyright Law:

> The Committee has considered, but chosen to defer, the possibility of protecting the design of typefaces. A "typeface" can be defined as a set of letters, numbers, or other symbolic characters, whose forms are related by repeating design elements consistently applied in a notational system and are intended to be embodied in articles whose *intrinsic utilitarian function* is for use in composing text or other cognizable combinations of characters. The Committee does not regard the design of typeface, as thus defined, to be a copyrightable "pictorial, graphic, or sculptural work" within the meaning of this bill and the application of the dividing line in section 101.

(*See* H. R. Rep. No. 94-1476, 94th Congress, 2d Session at 55 (1976), reprinted in 1978 U.S. Cong. and Admin. News 5659, 5668.) The US Copyright Office also made similar comments in its *Policy Decision on Copyrightability of Digitized Typefaces*: "Digitized representations of typeface designs are not registrable under the Copyright Act because they do not constitute original works of authorship . . ." (*see* 53 Fed. Reg. 38110 (Sept. 29, 1988)). Do you agree with the US approach of rejecting typefaces as copyrightable works, and why? *See* Jacqueline D Lipton, *To © or Not to ©? Copyright and Innovation in the Digital Typeface Industry*, 43 U.C. Davis L. Rev. 143 (2009).

11.2.4 Authorship

11.2.4.1 Co-authorship

CASE

LI Shu-Xian v. LI Wen-Da, decided by Beijing Intermediate People's Court 1989, cert-granted and rejected by Chinese Supreme People's Court 1988, on remand Beijing High People's Court, Gaozhizhongzi No. 18, 1995

Plaintiff LI Shu-Xian was the widow of Aisin-Gioro Pu Yi ("Pu Yi"), the last emperor in China. During his last years as a prisoner at the Fushun War Criminal Administrative Office ("War Criminal Office"), Pu Yi dictated a draft of his autobiography ("Draft") to show repentance for his former life.

The Draft explored Pu Yi's life story, from a child emperor of the Qing Dynasty to the puppet emperor during the Japanese invasion, and finally ended up being as a prisoner and

CASE *(continued)*

an ordinary citizen in the new People's Republic of China. The draft was first distributed as an internal document among the government. The central government soon arranged the Draft to be published. During the process, Peoples Publishing House ("Peoples") was assigned to assist Pu Yi in finalizing the Draft and getting it published.

Defendant LI Wen-Da was an editor at Peoples during that time. He was assigned by Peoples to assist Pu Yi in the compilation and modification of the Draft into a publishable book. The book "*The First Half of My Life*" (also known as *From Emperor to Citizen*, hereinafter referred as the "Book") was finally published by Peoples, under the name of Pu Yi, in 1964.

[Between 1960 and 1964, Defendant contributed the following efforts in the publication of the Book]:

(1) Between April and May 1960, LI Wen-Da took notes and compiled Pu Yi's dictation, while Pu Yi developed the outline and made comments on LI Wen-Da's draft script. During this period, the first half of the Draft was abridged, while the second half of the Draft was mostly overhauled.

(2) Between July and August 1960, LI Wen-Da made a few field trips to places where Pu Yi once lived, verifying some basic facts and correcting a number of factual errors in the Draft.

(3) In late March 1961, LI Wen-Da submitted an "Outline for the Second Draft of the Book" to Peoples. The outline included a revision plan for rewriting, expanding and editing several chapters in the Book. On August 15, 1961, LI Wen-Da submitted his revision proposal and provided additional advice regarding the theme of the Book at a seminar organized by Peoples. After the seminar, LI Wen-Da continued to collect related information, introduced memorabilia in the Draft, and worked on the manuscript and compilation of the Draft.

(4) During the same period, Pu Yi continued to dictate his life story, share his experiences and review the manuscript.

After the publication of the Book, Pu Yi sent Defendant a handwritten "Thank you" note, expressing his gratitude for Defendant's help and support in completing the Book. Additionally, Pu Yi mentioned Defendant's assistance with the revision and compilation of the Book several times in his diary.

[In 1984, two studios approached both Plaintiff and Defendant, trying to get permission to make a movie based on the Book. Plaintiff refused to grant the permission, while Defendant agreed on the grounds that he was the co-author of the Book. Plaintiff sued Defendant for copyright infringement, arguing that Defendant was not the co-author of the Book, and Pu Yi was the sole author of the Book.]

Beijing High People's Court held that: Pu Yi and Defendant were co-authors of the Book for the following reasons: (1) An author is the one who creates the work directly. Because the Book was quite different from the original Draft, Defendant had contributed enough

CASE (continued)

time and creativity in finishing the Book; (2) the Court rejected Plaintiff's claim that the Book was published in Pu Yi's name alone thus Pu Yi should be the sole author of the book, on the grounds that the author may publish his work anonymously. Defendant's waiver of his name on the Book does not necessarily indicate his waiver of copyright to the Book. (3) Pu Yi and Defendant received equal remuneration for the royalty of the Book; (4) The Book should be considered as a "biography literature" rather than an "autobiography." As such, LI Wen-Da can be the author of a biography literature.

[The aforesaid opinion was rejected by Chinese Supreme Court in its panel opinion in 1991. The Supreme Court held that Defendant was not the author of the Book, on the following grounds:]

(1) There was no agreed intent from Pu Yi to co-author the Book with Defendant. The Book was first created as an autobiography of Pu Yi to show his repentance for his former life. Defendant was assigned by Peoples to work with Pu Yi to finalize and publish the book. All the evidence, including the job assignment, Pu Yi's thank you note and his diary etc., indicated that there was no shared intent between Pu Yi and Defendant to be co-authors of the Book.
(2) The Book is an autobiography, written in Pu Yi's first narrative, reflecting Pu Yi's own thoughts and published in his name alone. Pu Yi himself would bear the outcome and public response of the Book. Therefore, it differs from other biographic literature.
(3) [The Court also rejected Defendant's claim that because he was compensated equally with Pu Yi in receiving the royalty of the Book, he should be considered as co-author of the Book. The Supreme Court held that 50% of royalty compensation only meant that Defendant was compensated appropriately, but was no indication of his 50% authorship to the Book.]

NOTES AND QUESTIONS

1. Compare *LI Shu-Xian v. LI Wen-Da* with *Aallmuhammed v. LEE*, 202 F. 3d 1227 (9th Cir. 2000). Do you think that the Chinese courts and their counterparts in the US hold the same standard in terms of co-authorship of works?
2. For some autobiographical works, success in completion of the book is partially, if not mostly, attributed to those behind the scenes, who actually write the book or assist in revising and editing the book. These people are known as "ghost writers." Do you think that ghost writers deserve to be recognized as co-authors of such books? Why?
3. In 2002, the Chinese Supreme People's Court issued a *Judicial Interpretation Regarding Application of Law Related to Copyright Disputes*, which addressed copyright authorship for works prepared by ghost writers and those of autobiographic literature in detail. Article 13 provided that "For speeches and presentations that are prepared by people other than the speaker or presenter himself, copyright ownership for such works vests in the speaker and presenter, who reviews the work and release the work in his or her name. Those who prepare the works (*i.e.* ghost writer) should be compensated accordingly." Article 14 addresses copyright authorship for autographic works: "copyright ownership for autobiographic work vests in the narrator in the work, unless the contract provides otherwise. The person who assists in preparing and

writing the autobiographic work should be compensated accordingly." Note that although China is not a case law jurisdiction, the judicial interpretations issued by the Chinese Supreme People's Court do have legally binding power over all lower courts in China. In other words, this Judicial Interpretation has made it law to vest copyright authorship of an autobiography with the biographee him- or herself, provided that the autobiography is written in the first-person narrative and published in his or her own name. Do you agree with such an approach?

4. In a joint work, permission of all co-authors is required for an assignment or an exclusive license. However, as far as a non-exclusive license is concerned, different countries have different approaches. For example, in the US, any author of a joint work may grant a non-exclusive license without his or her co-authors' consent, subject to a duty to account to the co-authors for any profits arising from the license. In contrast, some civil law countries, such as France, require consent from all the co-authors for such a non-exclusive license. In China, if a joint work includes contributions that are not separable, consent from all the co-authors is required although the law provides safeguards against unreasonable withholding of such consent by co-authors. Which approach do you think is more likely to promote progress and creativity?

11.2.4.2 Work for hire

CASE

Guang Ri Group v. ZHOU Chong-Tai, Guangdong High Court, Yuegaofa Minsanzhongzi No. 323, 2006

Plaintiff, ZHOU Chongtai ("ZHOU"), was an employee of Defendant Guangzhou Elevator Factory ("Guangzhou Elevator") from 1982 to 1986. ZHOU's job description included: designing advertisement and brochure, attending exhibition and decorating retail departments.

In 1982, ZHOU was asked by Defendant to design a trademark for the company. ZHOU created a few drafts and submitted six of them to Defendant for its review. Defendant picked one of the designs as its trademark and registered the subject mark successfully in 1984. The subject trademark "Guangri & device" was later awarded "20th Golden Award for the Best Trade Name" and "22nd International Award for the Best Trade Name" in 1996, and named "Famous Trademark of Guangdong Province" in 1999.

In 2005, Plaintiff ZHOU filed a declaratory judgment before Guangzhou Intermediate Court, asking the court to confirm that (1) the subject mark "Guangri & device" was not a work for hire but a commissioned work, and ZHOU alone should be the copyright owner of the subject trademark; and (2) ZHOU was entitled to both the honor and monetary benefits of the awards granted to the subject mark.

[Defendant contended that (1) it also contributed in the creation of the subject mark; (2) the subject mark was a work for hire, created by ZHOU during his course of employment with Defendant.]

The first-instance court summarized the legal issues as follows: (1) Whether the work (i.e. trademark "Guangri & device") was independently created by ZHOU or jointly created

CASE *(continued)*

by ZHOU and Defendant; (2) whether the work was a work for hire; and (3) who should own the copyright for the work.

[The first instance court concluded that the trademark "Guangri & device" was created by ZHOU alone; the work was a work for hire created by ZHOU during his course of employment with Defendant. Based on Article 16(1) of the Chinese Copyright Law (1991) and Article 11 of the Chinese Copyright Law Implementing Regulations (2002), "Authorship for a work for hire vests with the employee who creates the work, but the employer has a 2-year exclusive period to exploit the work," thus holding that ZHOU was the author of the work . . .]

Affirmed.

NOTES AND QUESTIONS

1. Under the Chinese Copyright Law, in the general case the author of a work is the person who creates it. There is, however, a special provision for works made for hire, as stated in Article 11 of the Chinese Copyright Act:

    Article 11

    [1] Except otherwise provided in this Law, the copyright in a work shall belong to its author. The author of a work is the citizen who has created the work.
    [2] Where a work is created according to the will and under the supervision and responsibility of a legal entity or another organization, such legal entity or organization shall be treated as the author of the work.
    [3] The citizen, legal entity or organization whose name is affixed to a work shall, without the contrary proof, be the author of the work.

2. The Chinese Copyright Act contains a further provision specifically on derivative works:

    Article 16

    [1] A work created by a citizen when fulfilling the tasks assigned to him by a legal entity or another organization shall be deemed to be a work made for hire. Unless otherwise provided in Paragraph 2 of this Article, the copyright of such a work shall be enjoyed by the author, but the legal entity or organization shall have a priority right to exploit the work within the scope of its professional activities. During the two years after the completion of the work, the author shall not, without the consent of the legal entity or organization, authorize a third party to exploit the work in the same way as the legal entity or organization does.
    [2] In the following cases the author of a service work shall enjoy the right of authorship, while the legal entity or organization shall enjoy other rights included in the copyright and may reward the author:
        (1) drawings of engineering designs and product designs, maps, computer software and other service works, which are created mainly with the materials and technical resources of the legal entity or organization and under its responsibility;
        (2) service works of which the copyright is, in accordance with the laws or administrative regulations or as agreed upon in the contract, enjoyed by the legal entity or organization.

    In the first group of works made for hire, Article 16[1], the author/creator has a copyright in the work he or she creates. There is no "automatic" assignment of his or her copyright to the employer. Even so, the employer retains "a priority right to exploit the work within the scope of its professional activities." In addition, this "priority exploitation" right is exclusive for the first two years after creation of the work; the creator/owner cannot license or assign the copyright to a third party in a way that undermines the employer's exclusivity for this two-year period. The structure of this entitlement is similar to the "shop right" in US patent law, wherein an employee retains ownership of a patented invention, but the employer has a right to exploit the invention in a way consistent with its normal business operations (*i.e.,* it cannot radically expand the business related to the invention). *See* Robert P. Merges, *The Law and Economics of Employee Inventions,* 13 Harv. J.L. & Tech. 1 (1999).

The second paragraph of Article 16 defines a related but distinct category of works: the category of "service work" copyrights. Although this provision has occasioned a fair amount of controversy in Chinese cases, the basic arrangement is this: the author of these enumerated works ("engineering designs, maps, computer software" etc.) automatically transfers all rights in such works to his or her employer – with one exception: the "right of authorship." This has been interpreted to mean that the employee retains the "attribution right" for these works, while all other rights, in particular all "economic" rights (reproduction, adaptation, etc.) automatically pass to the employer. *See* Xinqiang (David) Sun, *Authorship in China (and Beyond): Authorship and Related Issues Under the Chinese Copyright Law of 1990,* 54 Hous. L. Rev. 469, 489 (2016). Standing alone, this provision is interesting but poses no insurmountable challenges; it is in many ways similar to the rule in patent law, under which inventors must always be natural persons (not corporations), and an inventor retains the right to be identified as such regardless of who owns the patent covering his or her invention.

The problem comes in the conflict between Article 11[2] and Article 16[2]. The former, covering works "created according to the will and under the supervision and responsibility of" an employer – a definition which surely covers many works, including "drawings of engineering designs and product designs, maps, computer software and other service works" (Article 16[2](1)) as well as works dealt with in "laws or administrative regulations or as agreed upon in [a] contract" (Article 16[2](2)). Put simply, many works fall under *both* Article 11[2] *and* Article 16[2], yet there is nothing in the law to help decide which of the different legal outcomes applies to such works. As one commentator put it:

> Article 11, Paragraph 3 and Article 16, Paragraph 2, appl[y] the creator-as-author rule and the deemed-to-be-author rule [respectively] to the same category of works made for hire at the same time. But the deemed-to-be-author rule is not a rule free-standing, but only an exception to the creator-as-author rule. Accordingly, they cannot apply together side-by-side. Otherwise, conflicts will arise between the principle and its exception. Recent chaotic Chinese judicial practice has proved this. In solving disputes over the initial ownership of a work made for hire where an employer or legal person is involved, some courts have treated the work as a legal person's work by applying Article 11 . . . and rendered a judgment in favor of the employer. Other courts, to the contrary, by applying Article 16, Paragraph 2 have made a judgment favorable to the employee (Xinqiang (David) Sun, *Authorship in China (and Beyond): Authorship and Related Issues Under the Chinese Copyright Law of 1990,* 54 Hous. L. Rev. 469, 495 (2016)).

See also LIU Yinliang, *Revising the Principles of Copyright Ownership: A Simplify Approach from A Comparative Perspective,* Politics and Law, No. 11, (2007); CUI Guobin, Copyright Law: Cases and Materials, (2014), at 315 (arguing for narrow construction of Article 16[2](1), to at least minimize the problem).

3. Because of the different treatments of "work for hire" doctrine among various jurisdictions, multinational companies that have overseas operations need to draft their employment contracts accordingly to reflect such variations. Assuming that you are an in-house counsel of an international tech company, headquartered in the United States, but with operations in China and other countries, how would you advise your company and their overseas operations to draft such employment contracts?

11.3 Europe

11.3.1 Originality

While the EU has increasingly harmonized copyright laws across EU Member States over the last 25 years, the European *acquis communautaire* (*i.e.,* all legislation, legal acts, and court decisions that form part of the legal order of the EU) does not cover all areas of copyright law. One of the areas of European copyright law that has not been generally harmonized by the legislator is the required standard of originality.

For a small number of work categories, particular EU copyright Directives provided for standards of originality. Art. 1(3) of the EU Software Directive 2009/24/EC provides that a computer program shall receive copyright protection if "it is original in the sense that it is the author's own intellectual creation. No other criteria shall be applied to determine its eligibility for protection." Art. 6 of the EU Term Directive 2006/110/EC provides a similar provision with regard to the copyrightability of photographs. And Art. 3(1) of the EU Database Directive 96/9/EC extends copyright protection to databases "which, by reason of the selection or arrangement of their contents, constitute the author's own intellectual creation."

Apart from these select cases, for a long time, EU copyright law left the definition of originality standards to the individual Member States. One of the reasons for this lack of harmonization may be that originality standards lie at the heart of a country's copyright system. Across Europe, the approaches towards originality standards have taken very different paths. In the United Kingdom, copyright originality has traditionally been based on a modified "sweat of the brow" doctrine which focuses on the "own skill, labour, judgment and effort" of the copyright author (*see* Jonathan Griffiths et al., "United Kingdom," in 2 International Copyright Law & Practice, at §2[1][b] (Paul E. Geller ed., 2015). In continental Europe, most copyright laws had adopted some version of an "author's own intellectual creation" standard. These differences are not only of conceptual importance. They also had practical consequences. Consider the following case concerning the copyrightability of furniture design, which was referred to the Court of Justice of the European Union by the German Bundesgerichtshof (the Federal Court of Justice, the highest German court in civil matters):

Case C-456/06, Peek & Cloppenburg KG v. Cassina SpA, Court of Justice of the European Union [2008] E.C.R. I-0273E.C.R. I-0273

14 Cassina manufactures chairs. Its collection includes furniture manufactured according to the designs of Charles-Édouard Jeanneret (Le Corbusier). That furniture includes

CASE *(continued)*

armchairs and sofas in categories LC 2 and LC 3 and the table system LC 10-P. Cassina has concluded a licensing agreement for the manufacture and sale of that furniture.

15   Peek & Cloppenburg operates menswear and womenswear shops throughout Germany. It has set up in one of its shops a rest area for customers, fitted out with armchairs and sofas from the LC 2 and LC 3 range and a low table from the LC 10-P table system. In a display window of its outlet, Peek & Cloppenburg placed an armchair from the LC 2 range for decorative purposes. Those items of furniture did not come from Cassina but were manufactured without Cassina's consent by an undertaking in Bologna (Italy). According to the referring court, such furniture was not protected at the time by copyright in the Member State in which it was manufactured.

16   As it considered that Peek & Cloppenburg had infringed its rights by so doing, Cassina brought an action against it before the Landgericht Frankfurt (Frankfurt Regional Court) (Germany) seeking an order that it must desist from that practice and provide Cassina with information, in particular as regards the distribution channels for those items of furniture. In addition, Cassina sought an order that Peek & Cloppenburg pay damages.

17   After the Landgericht Frankfurt had granted Cassina's application and the appeal court had, essentially, confirmed the judgment given at first instance, Peek & Cloppenburg brought an appeal on a point of law before the Bundesgerichtshof (Federal Court of Justice) (Germany).

18   That court states that, since Cassina has an exclusive right of distribution for the purpose of Paragraph 17 of the Law on copyright of 9 September 1965, its decisions turn on whether the conduct of Peek & Cloppenburg referred to above infringed that right.

. . .

28   . . . [T]he referring court is essentially asking whether the concept of distribution to the public otherwise than through the sale of the original of a work or a copy thereof, for the purpose of Article 4(1) of Directive 2001/29, must be interpreted as meaning that it includes, first, granting to the public the right to use reproductions of a work protected by copyright without that grant of use entailing a transfer of ownership and, secondly, exhibiting those reproductions to the public without actually granting a right to use them.

29   Neither Article 4(1) of Directive 2001/29 nor any other provision of that directive gives a sufficient explanation of the concept of distribution to the public of a work protected by copyright. That concept is, on the other hand, defined more clearly by the CT [WIPO Copyright Treaty] and the PPT [WIPO Performances and Phonograms Treaty].

. . .

32   Article 6(1) of the CT defines the concept of the right of distribution enjoyed by the authors of literary and artistic works as the exclusive right of authorising the making available to the public of the original and copies of their works through sale or 'other transfer of ownership'. Moreover, Articles 8 and 12 of the PPT contain the same definitions of the right of distribution enjoyed by performers and producers of phonograms. Thus, the relevant international Treaties link the concept of distribution exclusively to that of transfer of ownership.

CASE *(continued)*

33   Since Article 4(1) of Directive 2001/29 provides, in such a context, for 'distribution by sale or otherwise', that concept should be interpreted in accordance with those Treaties as a form of distribution which entails a transfer of ownership.

34   The wording of the provisions relating to the exhaustion of the right of distribution in the CT and Directive 2001/29 also points to that conclusion. Exhaustion is dealt with in Article 6(2) of the CT, which links it to the acts referred to in Article 6(1). Thus, paragraphs 1 and 2 of Article 6 of the CT form a whole and should be interpreted together. Those two provisions refer expressly to acts entailing a transfer of ownership.

35   Article 4(1) and (2) of Directive 2001/29 follow the same scheme as Article 6 of the CT and are intended to implement it. Like Article 6(2) of the CT, Article 4(2) of the directive provides for the exhaustion of the distribution right within the Community in respect of the original or copies of the work on the first sale or other transfer of ownership of that object. Since Article 4 implements Article 6 of the CT and should be interpreted, like Article 6 of the CT, as a whole, it follows that the term 'otherwise' in Article 4(1) of Directive 2001/29 must be interpreted in accordance with the meaning given to it in Article 4(2), that is to say, as entailing a transfer of ownership.

36   It follows that the concept of distribution to the public, otherwise than through sale, of the original of a work or a copy thereof, for the purpose of Article 4(1) of Directive 2001/29, covers acts which entail, and only acts which entail, a transfer of the ownership of that object. The information provided by the referring court shows that that clearly does not apply to the acts at issue in the main proceedings.

37   Contrary to what Cassina asserts, those findings are not affected by recitals 9 to 11 in the preamble to Directive 2001/29, which state that harmonisation of copyright must take as a basis a high level of protection, that authors have to receive an appropriate reward for the use of their work and that the system for the protection of copyright must be rigorous and effective.

38   That protection can be achieved only within the framework put in place by the Community legislature. Therefore, it is not for the Court to create, for authors' benefit, new rights which have not been provided for by Directive 2001/29 and by so doing to widen the scope of the concept of distribution of the original of a work or a copy thereof beyond that envisaged by the Community legislature.

39   It would be for the Community legislature to amend, if necessary, the Community rules on protection of intellectual property if it considered that protection of authors is not assured to an adequate level by the legislation in force and that uses such as those at issue in the main proceedings should be subject to authors' consent.

40   For the same reasons, Cassina's arguments according to which the concept of distribution of the original of a work or a copy thereof should be interpreted widely, on the ground that the actions at issue in the main proceedings are objectionable because the copyright owner obtained no remuneration for the use of copies of his work, which is protected under the legislation of the Member State where those copies are used, cannot be accepted.

...

CASE (continued)

On those grounds, the Court (Fourth Chamber) hereby rules:

The concept of distribution to the public, otherwise than through sale, of the original of a work or a copy thereof, for the purpose of Article 4(1) of Directive 2001/29/EC of the European Parliament and of the Council of 22 May 2001 on the harmonisation of certain aspects of copyright and related rights in the information society, applies only where there is a transfer of the ownership of that object. As a result, neither granting to the public the right to use reproductions of a work protected by copyright nor exhibiting to the public those reproductions without actually granting a right to use them can constitute such a form of distribution.

NOTES

1. For a long time, furniture design could not receive copyright protection under Italian copyright law, whereas furniture was copyrightable under German law. Such differences in copyrightability standards can lead to problems in case of transnational commerce. In the case above, Cassina had problems suing the Italian manufacturer of the "counterfeit" armchairs, sofas, and table in Italy because of the lack of copyright protection. Therefore, it sued a German department store chain which displayed the furniture in their stores. Under German copyright law, the problem was not whether Cassina's furniture was copyrightable. The problem was whether the German distribution right covered also the display of copyrighted works without transfer of ownership.

2. This case demonstrates that the lack of harmonization of originality standards may lead to problems in the EU-wide definition of exploitation rights. In the *Peek & Cloppenburg v. Cassina* case, the ECJ held that it is the job of the EU legislature, not the Court, to increase copyright protection for furniture if the legislature deems this appropriate. However, in later decisions, the Court has adopted a more active role. As we will see below, it has increasingly harmonized originality requirements without waiting for the EU legislature to take action.

3. However, legislatures of EU Member States have become active as well. The exemption of furniture design from copyright protection could be justified as furniture can still receive protection under EU and national design protection systems. However, various practical and theoretical reasons exist why European countries have an interest in including furniture design into their copyright systems. (Can you think of some reasons?) In 2014, the Italian Parliament amended its Intellectual Property Code to include furniture design as copyrightable subject matter. As a result, the problem raised in the case above would no longer occur today.

4. Can you think of reasons why it has been so difficult to harmonize originality standards across the EU?

5. Furniture is not the only category of works whose copyright protection may differ across European countries. A classic example is perfumes. Dutch courts have granted copyright protection to perfumes, while some French courts have refused it. See Tania Su Li Cheng, *Copyright Protection of Haute Cuisine: Recipe for Disaster?*, 30 Eur. Intell. Prop. Rev. 93, 98 (2008); Herman Cohen Jehoram, *The Dutch Supreme Court Recognises Copyright in the Scent of a Perfume the Flying Dutchman: All Sails, No Anchor*, 28 Eur. Intell. Prop. Rev. 629 (2006); Catherine Seville, *Copyright in Perfumes: Smelling a Rat*, 66 Cambridge L.J. 49 (2007); Sergio Balañá, *Urheberrechtsschutz für Parfüms*, 54 Gewerblicher Rechtsschutz und Urheberrecht: Internationaler Teil 979 (2005) (analyzing reasons why perfume manufacturers became interested in claiming intellectual property protection on their perfumes in France and the Netherlands).

No EU Directive has established a general standard of originality that is applicable to all copyrightable works. In recent years, the ECJ has begun to harmonize the originality requirement in European copyright law through judicial interpretation. The justification for such harmonization is that it is impossible to determine the scope of exploitation rights, which are harmonized at the European level, unless the originality standard is also harmonized.

Starting in 2009 (Case C-5/08, *Infopaq Int'l v. Danske Dagblades Forening*, E.C.R. 2009, I-06569, the ECJ became more active in harmonizing the standard of originality in EU copyright law. A later case deals with the originality standard as applied to a portrait photography of an Austrian child who was later kidnapped for eight years and made worldwide news after her escape in 2006.

CASE

Case C-145/10, Eva-Maria Painer v. Standard Verlags GmbH, European Court of Justice [2011] E.C.R. I-12533

27   Ms Painer has for many years worked as a freelance photographer, photographing, in particular, children in nurseries and day homes. In the course of that work, she took several photographs of Natascha K. designing the background, deciding the position and facial expression, and producing and developing them ('the contested photographs').

28   Ms Painer has, for more than 17 years, labelled the photographs she produces with her name. That labelling has been done in different ways which have varied over the years, by stickers and/or impressions in decorative portfolios or mounts. Those indications have always stated her name and business address.

29   Ms Painer sold the photographs which she produced, but without conferring on third parties any rights over them and without consenting to their publication. The price she charged for photographs corresponded solely to the price of the prints.

30   After Natascha K., then aged 10, was abducted in 1998, the competent security authorities launched a search appeal in which the contested photographs were used.

31   The defendants in the main proceedings are newspaper and magazine publishers. Only Standard is established in Vienna (Austria). The other defendants in the main proceedings are established in Germany.

...

34   Following Natascha K.'s escape and prior to her first public appearance, the defendants in the main proceedings published the contested photographs in the abovementioned newspapers, magazines and websites without, however, indicating the name of the photographer, or indicating a name other than Ms Painer's as the photographer.

...

36   Several of those publications also published a portrait, created by computer from the

CASE *(continued)*

contested photographs, which, since there was no recent photograph of Natascha K. until her first public appearance, represented the supposed image of Natascha K. ('the contested photo-fit').

...

40   ... [T]he Oberster Gerichtshof held, applying the relevant national rules, that the defendants in the main proceedings did not need Ms Painer's consent to publish the contested photo-fit.

...

86   ... [T]he referring court's question must be understood as asking, in essence, whether Article 6 of Directive 93/98 [today Art. 6 of the EU Terms Directive 2006/116/EC] must be interpreted as meaning that a portrait photograph can, under that provision, be protected by copyright and, if so, whether, because of the allegedly too minor degree of creative freedom such photographs can offer, that protection, particularly as regards the regime governing reproduction of works provided for in Article 2(a) of Directive 2001/29 [EU InfoSoc Directive], is inferior to that enjoyed by other works, particularly photographic works.

87   As regards, first, the question whether realistic photographs, particularly portrait photographs, enjoy copyright protection under Article 6 of Directive 93/98, it is important to point out that the Court has already decided, in Case C-5/08 *Infopaq International* [2009] ECR I-6569, paragraph 35, that copyright is liable to apply only in relation to a subject-matter, such as a photograph, which is original in the sense that it is its author's own intellectual creation.

88   As stated in recital 17 in the preamble to Directive 93/98, an intellectual creation is an author's own if it reflects the author's personality.

89   That is the case if the author was able to express his creative abilities in the production of the work by making free and creative choices (see, *a contrario*, Joined Cases C-403/08 and C-429/08 *Football Association Premier League and Others* [2011] ECR I-9083, paragraph 98).

90   As regards a portrait photograph, the photographer can make free and creative choices in several ways and at various points in its production.

91   In the preparation phase, the photographer can choose the background, the subject's pose and the lighting. When taking a portrait photograph, he can choose the framing, the angle of view and the atmosphere created. Finally, when selecting the snapshot, the photographer may choose from a variety of developing techniques the one he wishes to adopt or, where appropriate, use computer software.

92   By making those various choices, the author of a portrait photograph can stamp the work created with his 'personal touch'.

93   Consequently, as regards a portrait photograph, the freedom available to the author to exercise his creative abilities will not necessarily be minor or even non-existent.

94   In view of the foregoing, a portrait photograph can, under Article 6 of Directive 93/98, be protected by copyright if, which it is for the national court to determine in each case,

CASE *(continued)*

such photograph is an intellectual creation of the author reflecting his personality and expressing his free and creative choices in the production of that photograph.

95 As regards, secondly, the question whether such protection is inferior to that enjoyed by other works, particularly photographic works, it is appropriate to point out straightaway that the author of a protected work is, under Article 2(a) of Directive 2001/29, entitled to, among other things, the exclusive right to authorise or prohibit its direct or indirect, temporary or permanent reproduction by any means and in any form, in whole or in part.

96 In that regard, the Court has held that the protection conferred by that provision must be given a broad interpretation (see *Infopaq International*, paragraph 43).

97 Moreover, nothing in Directive 2001/29 or in any other directive applicable in this field supports the view that the extent of such protection should depend on possible differences in the degree of creative freedom in the production of various categories of works.

98 Therefore, as regards a portrait photograph, the protection conferred by Article 2(a) of Directive 2001/29 cannot be inferior to that enjoyed by other works, including other photographic works.

. . .

On those grounds, the Court (Third Chamber) hereby rules:

. . .

2. Article 6 of Council Directive 93/98/EEC of 29 October 1993 harmonising the term of protection of copyright and certain related rights must be interpreted as meaning that a portrait photograph can, under that provision, be protected by copyright if, which it is for the national court to determine in each case, such photograph is an intellectual creation of the author reflecting his personality and expressing his free and creative choices in the production of that photograph. Since it has been determined that the portrait photograph in question is a work, its protection is not inferior to that enjoyed by any other work, including other photographic works.

NOTES

1. The decision is important for the harmonization of EU originality requirements, as it not only repeats the statement from the CJEU's *Infopaq* decision and earlier European copyright Directives that originality should be understood as the "author's own intellectual creation." The decision also notes that an intellectual creation should reflect the author's personality and that the author's capability to express his creative abilities requires him to make free and creative choices. However, the extent of the degrees of creative freedom does not have an impact on the level of copyright protection a work enjoys.

2. The decision should be seen as part of a line of case law in which the ECJ attempts to harmonize originality standards in EU copyright law. This line of case law started with a decision concerning the copyrightability of a news clipping service (*Infopaq Int'l A/S v. Danske Dagblades Forening* (Case C-5/08, [2009] E.C.R. I-6569). Later cases include a decision concerning the copyrightability of graphical user interfaces (Case C-393/09, *Bezpečnostní Softwarová Asociace (BSA) – Svaz Softwarové Ochrany v. Ministerstvo Kultury*, [2010] E.C.R. I-13971) and broadcasting rights for sporting events (Joint Cases C-403/08 & C-429/08, *Football Association Premier League Ltd. v. QC Leisure & Murphy v. Media Prot. Servs. Ltd.*, [2011] E.C.R. I-09083).

3. In none of its decisions has the ECJ been clear about the scope of its harmonization efforts. Given its language and its general style of adjudication, it seems reasonable to assume, however, that the Court is interpreting the European copyright Directives as containing an autonomous standard of originality which covers all conceivable categories of works. While the ECJ is thereby de facto creating an EU-wide originality standard, it is still the task of national courts to determine whether a particular work fulfills these standards. This raises the question how national originality standards are affected by the case law of the ECJ. In the United Kingdom, it remains to be seen how the "own skill, labour, judgment and effort" test of copyright originality will be affected (*see* Eleonora Rosati, Originality in EU Copyright (2013); Andreas Rahmatian, *Originality in UK Copyright Law: The Old "Skill and Labour" Doctrine Under Pressure*, 44 International Review of Intellectual Property and Competition Law, 29 (2013)). The European case law may also decrease the willingness of national courts to vary the originality standard for different work categories (for an example from German copyright law as applied to works of applied art, *see infra* Section 11.3.3.2

11.3.2 Limitations on copyrightability

In both US and Chinese copyright law, the idea/expression dichotomy as well as the *scène-à-faire* doctrines put important limitations on copyrightability. In Europe, neither of these doctrines has been expressively recognized in European Directives in a way that would apply to all copyrightable subject matter. The European project on copyright harmonization is still ongoing, and limitations on copyrightability are often still a matter of national copyright law. There are, however, special cases in which European law deals with such limitations. One important example is the idea/expression dichotomy as applied to copyrightable computer programs: According to Art. 1(2) of the Computer Programs Directive, "[i]deas and principles which underlie any element of a computer program, including those which underlie its interfaces, are not protected by copyright under this Directive."

Case C-406/10, SAS Institute v. World Programming, Court of Justice of the European Union, ECLI:EU:C:2012:259

23   SAS Institute is a developer of analytical software. It has developed an integrated set of computer programs over a period of 35 years which enables users to carry out a wide range of data processing and analysis tasks, in particular, statistical analysis ('the SAS System'). The core component of the SAS System, called 'Base SAS', enables users to write and run their own application programs in order to adapt the SAS System to work with their data (Scripts). Such Scripts are written in a language which is peculiar to the SAS System ('the SAS Language').

24   WPL perceived that there was a market demand for alternative software capable of

CASE *(continued)*

executing application programs written in the SAS Language. WPL therefore produced the 'World Programming System', designed to emulate the SAS components as closely as possible in that, with a few minor exceptions, it attempted to ensure that the same inputs would produce the same outputs. This would enable users of the SAS System to run the Scripts which they have developed for use with the SAS System on the 'World Programming System'.

25   The High Court of Justice of England and Wales, Chancery Division, points out that it is not established that, in order to do so, WPL had access to the source code of the SAS components, copied any of the text of that source code or copied any of the structural design of the source code.

26   The High Court also points out that two previous courts have held, in the context of separate proceedings, that it is not an infringement of the copyright in the source code of a computer program for a competitor of the copyright owner to study how the program functions and then to write its own program to emulate that functionality.

27   SAS Institute, disputing that approach, has brought an action before the referring court. Its principal claims are that WPL:

– copied the manuals for the SAS System published by SAS Institute when creating the 'World Programming System', thereby infringing SAS Institute's copyright in those manuals;
– in so doing, indirectly copied the computer programs comprising the SAS components, thereby infringing its copyright in those components;
– used a version of the SAS system known as the 'Learning Edition', in breach of the terms of the licence relating to that version and of the commitments made under that licence, and in breach of SAS Institute's copyright in that version; and
– infringed the copyright in the manuals for the SAS System by creating its own manual.

. . .

29   By these questions, the national court asks, in essence, whether Article 1(2) of Directive 91/250 must be interpreted as meaning that the functionality of a computer program and the programming language and the format of data files used in a computer program in order to exploit certain of its functions constitute a form of expression of that program and may, as such, be protected by copyright in computer programs for the purposes of that directive.

30   In accordance with Article 1(1) of Directive 91/250, computer programs are protected by copyright as literary works within the meaning of the Berne Convention.

31   Article 1(2) of Directive 91/250 extends that protection to the expression in any form of a computer program. That provision states, however, that the ideas and principles which underlie any element of a computer program, including those which underlie its interfaces, are not protected by copyright under that directive.

32   The 14th recital in the preamble to Directive 91/250 confirms, in this respect, that, in

CASE *(continued)*

accordance with the principle that only the expression of a computer program is protected by copyright, to the extent that logic, algorithms and programming languages comprise ideas and principles, those ideas and principles are not protected under that directive. The 15th recital in the preamble to Directive 91/250 states that, in accordance with the legislation and jurisprudence of the Member States and the international copyright conventions, the expression of those ideas and principles is to be protected by copyright.

33 With respect to international law, both Article 2 of the WIPO Copyright Treaty and Article 9(2) of the TRIPs Agreement provide that copyright protection extends to expressions and not to ideas, procedures, methods of operation or mathematical concepts as such.

34 Article 10(1) of the TRIPs Agreement provides that computer programs, whether in source or object code, are to be protected as literary works under the Berne Convention.

35 In a judgment delivered after the reference for a preliminary ruling had been lodged in the present case, the Court interpreted Article 1(2) of Directive 91/250 as meaning that the object of the protection conferred by that directive is the expression in any form of a computer program, such as the source code and the object code, which permits reproduction in different computer languages (judgment of 22 December 2010 in Case C-393/09 *Bezpečnostní softwarová asociace* [2010] ECR I-13971, paragraph 35).

36 In accordance with the second phrase of the seventh recital in the preamble to Directive 91/250, the term 'computer program' also includes preparatory design work leading to the development of a computer program, provided that the nature of the preparatory work is such that a computer program can result from it at a later stage.

37 Thus, the object of protection under Directive 91/250 includes the forms of expression of a computer program and the preparatory design work capable of leading, respectively, to the reproduction or the subsequent creation of such a program (*Bezpečnostní softwarová asociace*, paragraph 37).

38 From this the Court concluded that the source code and the object code of a computer program are forms of expression thereof which, consequently, are entitled to be protected by copyright as computer programs, by virtue of Article 1(2) of Directive 91/250. On the other hand, as regards the graphic user interface, the Court held that such an interface does not enable the reproduction of the computer program, but merely constitutes one element of that program by means of which users make use of the features of that program (*Bezpečnostní softwarová asociace*, paragraphs 34 and 41).

39 On the basis of those considerations, it must be stated that, with regard to the elements of a computer program which are the subject of Questions 1 to 5, neither the functionality of a computer program nor the programming language and the format of data files used in a computer program in order to exploit certain of its functions constitute a form of expression of that program for the purposes of Article 1(2) of Directive 91/250.

40 As the Advocate General states in point 57 of his Opinion, to accept that the functionality of a computer program can be protected by copyright would amount to making it possible to monopolise ideas, to the detriment of technological progress and industrial development.

CASE *(continued)*

41 Moreover, point 3.7 of the explanatory memorandum to the Proposal for Directive 91/250 [COM(88) 816] states that the main advantage of protecting computer programs by copyright is that such protection covers only the individual expression of the work and thus leaves other authors the desired latitude to create similar or even identical programs provided that they refrain from copying.

42 With respect to the programming language and the format of data files used in a computer program to interpret and execute application programs written by users and to read and write data in a specific format of data files, these are elements of that program by means of which users exploit certain functions of that program.

43 In that context, it should be made clear that, if a third party were to procure the part of the source code or the object code relating to the programming language or to the format of data files used in a computer program, and if that party were to create, with the aid of that code, similar elements in its own computer program, that conduct would be liable to constitute partial reproduction within the meaning of Article 4(a) of Directive 91/250.

44 As is, however, apparent from the order for reference, WPL did not have access to the source code of SAS Institute's program and did not carry out any decompilation of the object code of that program. By means of observing, studying and testing the behaviour of SAS Institute's program, WPL reproduced the functionality of that program by using the same programming language and the same format of data files.

45 The Court also points out that the finding made in paragraph 39 of the present judgment cannot affect the possibility that the SAS language and the format of SAS Institute's data files might be protected, as works, by copyright under Directive 2001/29 if they are their author's own intellectual creation (*see Bezpečnostní softwarová asociace*, paragraphs 44 to 46).

46 Consequently, the answer to Questions 1 to 5 is that Article 1(2) of Directive 91/250 must be interpreted as meaning that neither the functionality of a computer program nor the programming language and the format of data files used in a computer program in order to exploit certain of its functions constitute a form of expression of that program and, as such, are not protected by copyright in computer programs for the purposes of that directive.

. . .

On those grounds, the Court (Grand Chamber) hereby rules:

1. Article 1(2) of Council Directive 91/250/EEC of 14 May 1991 on the legal protection of computer programs must be interpreted as meaning that neither the functionality of a computer program nor the programming language and the format of data files used in a computer program in order to exploit certain of its functions constitute a form of expression of that program and, as such, are not protected by copyright in computer programs for the purposes of that directive.

NOTES AND QUESTIONS

It has always been an important question how copyright protection for computer software should affect competition between different software companies. In *Lotus v. Borland*, 49 F.3d 807 (1st Cir. 1995), the US Court of Appeals for the First Circuit held that software user interfaces cannot be protected by copyright (the US Supreme Court later affirmed in 516 U.S. 233 (1996), but did not set precedent because of Justice Steven's recusal). After the Court of Appeals for the Federal Circuit held in 2014 that some Java APIs were copyrightable (750 F.3d 1339 (Fed. Cir. 2014)) and the US Supreme Court had denied certioriari (135 S.Ct. 2887 (U.S. 2015)), a US district court upheld a jury decision in 2016 according to which Google's use and modification of the Java APIs in the development of the Android operating system was fair use (*Oracle America, Inc. v. Google, Inc.*, 2016 WL 3181206 (N.D. Cal. 2016)). How do these decisions relate to the CJEU decision in *SAS v. World Programming*?

11.3.3 Specific categories of works

11.3.3.1 Introduction

As mentioned before, copyright law in Europe has still not been fully harmonized by the EU. The varying approaches of what constitutes a copyrighted "work" in different European jurisdictions is another example of such lack of harmonization. Under UK law, copyright

> subsists . . . in the following descriptions of work –
>
> (a) original literary, dramatic, musical or artistic works,
> (b) sound recordings, films or broadcasts, and
> (c) the typographical arrangement of published editions (Sec. 1(1)Copyright, Designs and Patents Act (CDPA)),

and Sections 3 to 8 CDPA elaborate on those work categories. This has created problems for unconventional works which do not easily fall in one of the categories of works provided by the UK CDPA. The UK Supreme Court ruled in 2011 that Stormtrooper helmets from Lucasfilm's Star Wars universe are not protected by copyright under UK law, as they could not be considered a sculpture under the closed list of work categories (*Lucasfilm Ltd. v. Ainsworth* [2011] UKSC 39). The closed list may not only mean that some subject matter is not eligible for copyright protection. It may also lead to varying scopes of protection. Section 21(1) CDPA provides the adaptation right to literary, dramatic, or musical works, but does not mention artistic works; Sec. 17(3) CDPA notes that the three-dimensional reproduction of a two-dimensional artistic work is an act of copying, but does not talk about three-dimensional reproductions of other than artistic works. Different categories of work may, therefore, receive different levels of protection under UK copyright law (Eleonora Rosati, *Closed National Systems of Copyright-protectable Works are No Longer Compatible with EU Law*, GRUR Int. 1112, 1117 (2014)).

By contrast, while German copyright law provides a similar list in Article 2 Copyright Act, it makes clear that such list is open-ended:

Protected works in the literary, scientific and artistic domain include, *in particular*:

1. Literary works, such as written works, speeches and computer programs;
2. Musical works;
3. Pantomimic works, including works of dance;
4. Artistic works, including works of architecture and of applied art and drafts of such works;
5. Photographic works, including works produced by processes similar to photography;
6. Cinematographic works, including works produced by processes similar to cinematography;
7. Illustrations of a scientific or technical nature, such as drawings, plans, maps, sketches, tables and three-dimensional representations (Article 2(1) German Copyright Act, emphasis added by the authors).

Article L112-2 of the French Intellectual Property Code includes a provision which is similar to the German one. Compared to UK copyright law, the French and German copyright laws tend to create fewer problems with regard to protecting unconventional works via copyright law. As the CJEU is increasingly applying a uniform originality standard to all copyrighted works under EU copyright law, it could be that, at some point, closed lists of eligible copyright subject matter may become incompatible with EU copyright law (on this discussion, *see* Rosati, *supra*).

11.3.3.2 *Works of applied art*

Works of applied art may be protected by both copyright and design protection. In order to differentiate between the protection of copyrighted works and aesthetic (not functional) designs (formerly called "Geschmacksmuster" in German law), German courts used to require a substantial degree of originality for works of applied art: Only those objects were copyrightable whose artistic quality was substantially higher than what the ordinary designer was able to produce. In a decision from 2014, the German Bundesgerichtshof abandoned this strict standard. See GRUR 2014, 175 – *Geburtstagszug* (the "Birthday Train" copyright case, English version reported in International Intellectual Prop. & Competition Law (Max Planck) 2014, at 831), abandoning cases such as BGH GRUR 1995, 581 – *Silberdistel*; and OLG Nürnberg GRUR 2014, 1199 – *Fußball-Stecktabelle*), partly under the rationale that the old standard was meant to distinguish copyright from design protection, while the new European Directive now awards a separate and distinct design right so German law need not be concerned with the copyright/design interface. (The litigation here involved employee compensation for valuable creations; and the holding permitted a claim to profits by the employee, which can be made under copyright law – which applied now that the originality standard had been lowered – but not under design protection.) The birthday train design in the case may have been simple, but it was original enough to warrant copyright protection.

NOTES

1. If an author licenses his work to a licensee, both parties to the contract will have certain – often diverging – predictions of how successful the commercial exploitation of the copyrighted work under the license agreement will be. If it later turns out that the author underestimated the commercial value of his work, the additional surplus will fully remain with the licensee, according to standard contract doctrines. German copyright law has important exceptions to this rule. According to Art. 32a German Copyright Act, the author may demand a further equitable share of the additional surplus if the agreed remuneration in the original license agreement was "conspicuously disproportionate to the proceeds and benefits derived from the exploitation of the work." In the case about the birthday train, the author demanded such additional remuneration as the sale figures of the birthday train were much higher than expected.
2. The German "Birthday Train" decision has a significant impact on the relationship between German copyright and design protection law. From a legal perspective, it may have become easier to protect aesthetic designs not only through design protection, but also through copyright law. The overlap between both areas of intellectual property law has thereby increased. Can you think of strategic reasons why design companies may want to rely on copyright protection rather than design protection? For more information on the impact of the decision on German copyright law, see Karl-Nikolaus Peifer, *"Individualität" or Originality? Core Concepts in German Copyright Law*, 63 Gewerblicher Rechtsschutz und Urheberrecht: Internationaler Teil, 1100 (2014).

11.3.3.3 Databases

When the Database Directive was adopted in 1996, it implemented a two-tiered protection system. According to the Directive, databases shall be protected by copyright if the selection or arrangement of data constitute the author's own intellectual creation (Art. 3(1) Database Directive). In this case, it is only the selection or arrangement of data which is copyrighted, not the data itself (Art. 3(2) Database Directive). Databases can also be protected by a *sui generis* database protection right in which case the database does not have to meet copyright's originality standard. For information on the *sui generis* database protection right under the Database Directive, *see infra* Section 12.4.1.2.

Case C-604/10, Football Dataco Ltd. v. Yahoo! UK Ltd., Court of Justice of the European Union, ECLI:EU:C:2012:115

Creation of the fixture lists of the English and Scottish football leagues

12 According to the order for reference, the creation of the annual fixture lists of the football leagues in England and Scotland follows, on the whole, comparable rules and procedure.

13 It involves having regard to several rules, which are called 'the golden rules', the most important of which are:

- no club shall have three consecutive home or away matches;
- in any five consecutive matches no club shall have four home matches or four away matches;
- as far as possible, each club should have played an equal number of home and away matches at all times during the season, and
- all clubs should have as near as possible an equal number of home and away matches for mid-week matches.

14 The procedure for drawing up a fixture list such as those in question in the main proceedings consists of several stages. The first stage, which begins during the previous season, is the preparation by employees of the leagues concerned of the Premier League fixture schedule and an outline fixture list for other leagues. That stage consists of establishing a list of possible dates for the fixtures on the basis of a series of basic parameters (the dates of the start and the end of the season, the number of fixtures which must be played, the dates reserved to other national, European or international competitions).

15 The second stage is the sending out, to the clubs concerned, of questionnaires prior to the fixing of the schedule and the analysis of the responses to these questionnaires, in particular 'specific date' requests (a request by a club to play its fixture against another club at home or away on a particular date), 'non-specific date' requests (a request by a club to play a certain match on a certain day of the week at a certain time, for example, Saturday after 1.30 pm), and 'pairing' requests (a request that two or more clubs not play at home on the same day). Around 200 requests are made per season.

16 The third stage, which, in the case of the English football leagues, is undertaken by Mr Thompson of Atos Origin IT Services UK Ltd, comprises two tasks, 'sequencing' and 'pairing'.

17 Sequencing aims to achieve the perfect home-away sequence for every club, having regard to the golden rules, a series of organisational constraints and, as far as possible, the requests made by the clubs. Mr Thompson then produces a pairing grid on the basis of the

CASE *(continued)*

requests made by the teams. He gradually inserts the names of the teams into that grid and attempts to resolve a maximum amount of problem cases until a satisfactory draft fixture list is completed. For that purpose, he uses a computer program, to which he transfers information from the sequencing sheet and the pairing grid to produce a readable version of the fixture list.
18 The final stage involves Mr Thompson working with employees of the professional leagues concerned to review the content of the fixture lists. That review is carried out manually with the assistance of computer software to find solutions to outstanding problems. Two meetings then take place, one with a fixtures working party and the other with police representatives, in order to finalise the fixture list. In the 2008/2009 season, 56 changes were made during that final stage.
19 According to the findings of fact made by the judge at first instance reproduced in the order for reference, the process of preparing the football fixture lists in question in the main proceedings is not purely mechanistic or deterministic; on the contrary, it requires very significant labour and skill in order to satisfy the multitude of competing requirements while respecting the applicable rules as far as possible. The work needed is not mere application of rigid criteria, and is unlike, for instance, the compilation of a telephone directory, in that it requires judgment and skill at each stage, in particular where the computer program finds no solution for a given set of constraints. With regard to the partial computerisation of the process, Mr Thompson states that it does not eliminate the need for judgment and discretion.

The facts in the main proceedings and the questions referred for a preliminary ruling
20 Football Dataco and Others claim that they own, in respect of the English and Scottish football league fixture lists, a 'sui generis' right pursuant to Article 7 of Directive 96/9, a copyright pursuant to Article 3 of that directive, and a copyright under United Kingdom intellectual property legislation.
21 Yahoo and Others do not accept that such rights exist in law, arguing that they are entitled to use the lists in the conduct of their business without having to pay financial compensation.
22 The judge at first instance held that those lists are eligible for protection by copyright under Article 3 of Directive 96/9, on the ground that their preparation requires a substantial quantum of creative work. However, he refused to recognise either of the two other rights claimed.
23 The referring court confirmed the judgment at first instance as regards the ineligibility of the lists in question in the main proceedings for protection by the 'sui generis' right under Article 7 of Directive 96/9. By contrast, the referring court raises the question of whether the lists are eligible for protection by copyright under Article 3 of that directive. The referring court also has doubts regarding the possibility of the lists being protected by the copyright pursuant to United Kingdom legislation prior to that directive under conditions which are different to those which are set out in Article 3 of Directive 96/9.
...

CASE *(continued)*

26 First of all, it is to be noted that, on the one hand, the Court has already held that a football league fixture list constitutes a 'database' within the meaning of Article 1(2) of Directive 96/9. The Court essentially held that the combination of the date, the time and the identity of the two teams playing in both home and away matches has autonomous informative value which renders them 'independent materials' within the meaning of Article 1(2) of Directive 96/9, and that the arrangement, in the form of a fixture list, of the dates, times and names of teams in the various fixtures of a football league meets the conditions set out in Article 1(2) of Directive 96/9 as to the systematic or methodical arrangement and individual accessibility of the data contained in the database (see Case C-444/02 *Fixtures Marketing* [2004] ECR I-10549, paragraphs 33 to 36).

27 On the other hand, it is apparent from both a comparison of the terms of Article 3(1) and Article 7(1) of Directive 96/9 and from other provisions or recitals of Directive 96/9, in particular Article 7(4) and recital 39 to that directive, that the copyright and the 'sui generis' right amount to two independent rights whose object and conditions of application are different.

...

29 Under Article 3(1) of Directive 96/9, 'databases' within the meaning of Article 1(2) of that directive are protected by copyright if, by reason of the selection or arrangement of their contents, they constitute the author's own intellectual creation.

30 Firstly, it is apparent from reading Article 3(2) in conjunction with recital 15 of Directive 96/9 that the copyright protection provided for by that directive concerns the 'structure' of the database, and not its 'contents' nor, therefore, the elements constituting its contents.

...

32 In that context, the concepts of 'selection' and of 'arrangement' within the meaning of Article 3(1) of Directive 96/9 refer respectively to the selection and the arrangement of data, through which the author of the database gives the database its structure. By contrast, those concepts do not extend to the creation of the data contained in that database.

...

37 ... [A]s is apparent from recital 16 of Directive 96/9, the notion of the author's own intellectual creation refers to the criterion of originality (see, to that effect, Case C-5/08 *Infopaq International* [2009] ECR I-6569, paragraphs 35, 37 and 38; Case C-393/09 *Bezpečnostní softwarová asociace* [2010] ECR I-13971 paragraph 45; Joined Cases C-403/08 and C-429/08 *Football Association Premier League and Others* [2011] ECR I-9083, paragraph 97; and Case C-145/10 *Painer* [2011] ECR I-12533, paragraph 87).

38 As regards the setting up of a database, that criterion of originality is satisfied when, through the selection or arrangement of the data which it contains, its author expresses his creative ability in an original manner by making free and creative choices (see, by analogy, *Infopaq International*, paragraph 45; *Bezpečnostní softwarová asociace*, paragraph 50; and *Painer*, paragraph 89) and thus stamps his 'personal touch' (*Painer*, paragraph 92).

39 By contrast, that criterion is not satisfied when the setting up of the database is dictated

CASE *(continued)*

by technical considerations, rules or constraints which leave no room for creative freedom (see, by analogy, *Bezpečnostní softwarová asociace*, paragraphs 48 and 49, and *Football Association Premier League and Others*, paragraph 98).

40 As is apparent from both Article 3(1) and recital 16 of Directive 96/9, no other criteria than that of originality is to be applied to determine the eligibility of a database for the copyright protection provided for by that directive.

41 Therefore, on the one hand, provided that the selection or arrangement of the data – namely, in a case such as the one in the main proceedings, data corresponding to the date, the time and the identity of teams relating to the different fixtures of the league concerned (see paragraph 26 of the present judgment) – is an original expression of the creativity of the author of the database, it is irrelevant for the purpose of assessing the eligibility of the database for the copyright protection provided for by Directive 96/9 whether or not that selection or arrangement includes 'adding important significance' to that data, as mentioned in section (b) of the referring court's first question.

42 On the other hand, the fact that the setting up of the database required, irrespective of the creation of the data which it contains, significant labour and skill of its author, as mentioned in section (c) of that same question, cannot as such justify the protection of it by copyright under Directive 96/9, if that labour and that skill do not express any originality in the selection or arrangement of that data.

43 In the present case, it is for the referring court to assess, in the light of the factors set out above, whether the football fixture lists in question in the main proceedings are databases which satisfy the conditions of eligibility for the copyright protection set out in Article 3(1) of Directive 96/9.

44 In that respect, the procedures for creating those lists, as described by the referring court, if they are not supplemented by elements reflecting originality in the selection or arrangement of the data contained in those lists, do not suffice for the database in question to be protected by the copyright provided for in Article 3(1) of Directive 96/9.

45 In light of the considerations above, the answer to the first question is that Article 3(1) of Directive 96/9 must be interpreted as meaning that a 'database' within the meaning of Article 1(2) of that directive is protected by the copyright laid down by that directive provided that the selection or arrangement of the data which it contains amounts to an original expression of the creative freedom of its author, which is a matter for the national court to determine.

46 As a consequence:

- the intellectual effort and skill of creating that data are not relevant in order to assess the eligibility of that database for protection by that right;
- it is irrelevant, for that purpose, whether or not the selection or arrangement of that data includes the addition of important significance to that data, and
- the significant labour and skill required for setting up that database cannot as such justify such a protection if they do not express any originality in the selection or arrangement of the data which that database contains.

CASE *(continued)*

The second question submitted for a preliminary ruling

47 By its second question, the referring court is essentially asking whether Directive 96/9 must be interpreted as precluding national legislation which grants databases, as defined in Article 1(2) of that directive, copyright protection under conditions which are different to those set out in Article 3(1) of the directive.

48 In that respect, it must be pointed out that Directive 96/9 aims, according to recitals 1 to 4 of the directive, to remove the differences which existed between national legislation on the legal protection of databases, particularly as regards the scope and conditions of copyright protection, and which adversely affected the functioning of the internal market, the free movement of goods or services within the European Union and the development of an information market within the European Union.

49 In that context, as is apparent from recital 60 of Directive 96/9, Article 3 of that directive carries out a 'harmonization of the criteria for determining whether a database is to be protected by copyright'.

...

52 In light of the above considerations, the answer to the second question is that Directive 96/9 must be interpreted as meaning that, subject to the transitional provision contained in Article 14(2) of that directive, it precludes national legislation which grants databases, as defined in Article 1(2) of the directive, copyright protection under conditions which are different to those set out in Article 3(1) of the directive.

...

On those grounds, the Court (Third Chamber) hereby rules:

1. Article 3(1) of Directive 96/9/EC of the European Parliament and of the Council of 11 March 1996 on the legal protection of databases must be interpreted as meaning that a 'database' within the meaning of Article 1(2) of that directive is protected by the copyright laid down by that directive provided that the selection or arrangement of the data which it contains amounts to an original expression of the creative freedom of its author, which is a matter for the national court to determine.
    As a consequence:
    – the intellectual effort and skill of creating that data are not relevant in order to assess the eligibility of that database for protection by that right;
    – it is irrelevant, for that purpose, whether or not the selection or arrangement of that data includes the addition of important significance to that data, and
    – the significant labour and skill required for setting up that database cannot as such justify such a protection if they do not express any originality in the selection or arrangement of the data which that database contains.
2. Directive 96/9 must be interpreted as meaning that, subject to the transitional provision contained in Article 14(2) of that directive, it precludes national legislation which grants databases, as defined in Article 1(2) of the directive, copyright protection under conditions which are different to those set out in Article 3(1) of the directive.

> This decision is interesting in various respects. First, the decision demonstrates that the CJEU has moved towards a general originality standard that applies to all kinds of copyrightable subject matter. Second, the Court notes that Member States are preempted from granting copyright protection to databases under conditions that diverge from those set out in the Directive. Thereby, the Court effectively imposes a harmonized originality standard for databases on EU Member States as they are not allowed to deviate from this standard in their national copyright laws. Third, the Court does not provide a final answer whether the football fixture lists are actually protected by copyright law. Rather, it is for the referring court to assess this question (note 43). This is because the CJEU became active in response to a reference from a preliminary ruling (Art. 267 TFEU) from the Court of Appeal of England and Wales (Civil Division). In essence, the UK Court has asked the CJEU to provide a legal interpretation of an EU Directive, which lies in the ultimate competence of the CJEU. Once the CJEU has provided such interpretation, it is for the court of the EU Member State to apply that interpretation to the national implementation of the EU Directive and the facts of the case.

11.3.4 Fixation requirement

Fixation requirements have not been harmonized by the EU. Rather, fixation requirements stem from Member States' copyright laws. According to Sec. 3(2) of the UK CDPA, "[c]opyright does not subsist in a literary, dramatic or musical work unless and until it is recorded, in writing or otherwise." Other categories of works (sound recordings, films, broadcasts, typographical arrangements) are not subject to this express fixation requirement, but can often only exist in some material form.

By contrast, German copyright law does not impose a fixation requirement as a prerequisite of copyright protection. French copyright law stresses in Art. L111-1 CPI [Code Propriété Intellectuel, *i.e.*, Intellectual Property Code] that the author of a work shall, "by the mere fact of its creation," enjoy an exclusive incorporeal property right. In both jurisdictions, copyright arises by the mere creative act of the author. Neither is fixation nor any other formality required to receive copyright protection. This can have implications for live performances, jazz improvisations, and similar artistic expressions.

11.3.5 Authorship

11.3.5.1 Introduction

There is no EU-wide harmonization of who a copyright author is. Some EU copyright Directives define authorship and initial ownership in special cases: Art. 1(5) Satellite and Cable Directive, Art. 2(2) Rental Right Directive and Art. 2(1) Term Directive, note that the principal director of a cinematographic or audiovisual work is also a copyright author as far as these Directives are concerned. This has led the CJEU to conclude that the satellite broadcasting right vests in the principal director as author of the movie. As a result, Member States (Austria) are not allowed to allocate the satellite broadcasting right directly and exclusively to the movie producer, while they are allowed to provide for a statutory rebuttable presumption of transfer (CJEU, Case C-277/10, Feb. 9, 2012, *Martin Luksan v. Petrus van der Let*, ECLI:EU:C:2012:65).

Sometimes, European law seems to harmonize authorship, but then leaves substantial freedom to Member States with regard to implementation. Art. 2(1) Computer Programs Directive and Art. 4(1) Database Directive define the author of a computer program or database as either the natural person or group of natural persons who has created the program/database "or, where the legislation of the Member State permits, the legal person designated as the rightholder by that legislation."

Apart from these limited provisions, EU law is silent on copyright authorship, leaving allocation of authorship to Member States. This is another sign of the limited extent of European copyright harmonization.

11.3.5.2 *Work made for hire*

In general, EU copyright law does not prescribe how to allocate authorship in employment relationships. The only exception is Art. 2(3) Computer Programs Directive, according to which the employer of a computer programmer is exclusively entitled to exercise all economic rights in the computer program. Other Directives are silent on this issue (*see, e.g.*, Recital 29 of the Database Directive). As a result, apart from computer programs, it is the national laws of Member States which allocate authorship in employment relationships.

In Germany, copyright authorship always vests with the natural person who has created the work. German copyright theory follows a monistic tradition according to which the economic and personal interests of an author vis-à-vis his or her work are inseparably interwoven. As German copyright law recognizes the special bond between an author and his or her work, no equivalent to the "work made for hire" doctrine exists. Rather, works created in an employment relationship or on commission are always initially owned by the natural person who created the work. At least in theory, German copyright law thereby strengthens the position of the author. It is then the task of German contract law and employment law to resolve potential conflicts between authors and their employers. However, following the impression that authors require additional protection against publishers and other intermediaries, the German Parliament has increasingly added provisions to the Copyright Act which limit freedom of contract between authors and licensees in order to protect the authors. Copyright licenses with vague types of exploitation, for example, are restricted to the purpose pursued by both parties of the license contract (Sec. 31(5) Copyright Act). If the extent of a copyright license is unclear, the author retains certain rights (publication, adaptation, audiovisual rights; Sec. 37 Copyright Act). Publishers of periodicals (other than newspapers) receive an exclusive right to reproduce the licensed work, to distribute it and to make it available to the public. However, authors may use their work otherwise, one year after the publication of the periodical, absent contrary agreement (Sec. 38(1) Copyright Act).

In France, authors are the natural persons who created the work. Legal persons may hold a copyright, but only after an express or implied transfer. Art. L113-1 CPI provides a rebuttable presumption that the person under whose name a work has been divulged is its author. This can lead to a rebuttable presumption that a legal person owns a copyright in a work (*see* J.-L. Goutal, *Présomption de titularité des droits d'exploitation au profit des personnes morales*, 175 R.I.D.A., 65 (1998)). Also, French copyright law knows "collective works" which are created by several authors under the direction of an entrepreneur who then publishes them under his or her name, without the possibility to attribute individual contributions to individual authors (Art. L113-2 CPI). For such works, the entrepreneur is considered as the initial copyright owner (Art. L113-5 CPI). Absent contractual agreements, the contributing authors can neither prevent commercial exploitation of the collective work, nor are they entitled, by copyright law, to any share of the profit. Apart from collective works, employed authors retain copyright. However, some employment contracts pre-assign all rights in the works an employee creates on the job to the employer, thereby mimicking a "work made for hire" doctrine on a contractual basis.

Compared to France and Germany, UK copyright law is more willing to allocate authorship of copyrighted works that have been created in an employment relationship to the employer. By default, Sec. 11(2) CDPA allocates authorship in literary, dramatic, musical or artistic work, or film to the employer. Again, UK copyright law provides various rebuttable presumptions concerning authorship. The person named as an author on a published literary, dramatic, musical, or artistic work is, for example, presumed to be the author (Sec. 104(2)(a) CDPA).

11.3.5.3 Co-authorship

Under German copyright law, several co-authors jointly own a work if they have jointly created it and if their respective contributions cannot be separately exploited (Sec. 9 Copyright Act). Exploitation rights are then owned jointly by the co-authors, so that, in principle, all of them must give their consent to an exploitation (Sec. 8(2) Copyright Act). Under French law, a collaborative work is a work to whose creation several natural persons have contributed together (Art. L113-2 CPI). It is common property of its co-authors, and any exploitation requires the consent of all co-authors (Art. L113-3 CPI). Similar rules exist in UK copyright law, with special rules for movie co-authorship (Sec. 10 CDPA).

A famous French case of co-authorship involved renowned French artist Pierre-August Renoir and an assistant, Richard Guino. The two collaborated on a series of sculptures in Renoir's later years. Guino's family challenged the authorship in the statues after Guino's death (and long after Renoir's death), resulting in a finding by a French court that the two were in fact co-authors. Important details included evidence that Guino worked very closely with Renoir, and contributed many ideas to the execution of the statues. *See* Alix Kirsta, *The Renoir Wars*, The Telegraph, May 5, 2007, available at http://www.telegraph.co.uk/culture/3664946/The-Renoir-wars.html. A later US case pitted Renoir's estate against Guino's heirs, when the Renoir family violated a settlement agreement by selling unauthorized copies of the co-authored statues to a US art dealer. *See Societe Civile Succession Guino v. Renoir*, 549 F.3d 1182, 1184 (9th Cir. 2008).

12
Rights of the copyright owner

12.1 Introduction

Traditionally, world copyright systems are divided into those following the European "author's rights" model, and those adhering more to the common law view typified by the US.

The author's rights approach stresses the very close affinity between an author and his or her works. Support for this conception comes from the continental philosophers Immanuel Kant and Georg Wilhelm Friedrich Hegel, together with a host of legal theorists and modern-day scholars. Authors' rights under the European model are classified as either economic rights or moral rights. Economic rights include the crucial right to prevent copying, together with other rights such as the adaptation and translation right, the right to distribute or make publicly available, etc. Certain rights are usually classified as "neighboring rights" because although they may be important economically they are slightly different conceptually from the more basic economic rights. These neighboring rights include broadcast rights, performance rights, and the rights of record companies (*i.e.*, "phonogram" rights). Though they concern economic interests, they are not directly associated with authors per se. Performers, under this view, differ from the "intellectual" creators of songs, plays, etc.; while broadcasters and record labels (or phonogram companies) are only disseminators, rather than creators, of authors' works.

Apart from economic rights, European legal systems have historically also protected moral rights. Indeed, the moral or "noneconomic" rights are central to the author's rights tradition. Moral rights include the right of an artist to have his or her name associated with a creative work ("paternity right"); the right to prevent mutilation or distortion of the work ("right of integrity"); and the right to withdraw or disown a work. Other rights are also included in many countries.

The common law approach, again exemplified by the US, conceives of copyright as a unified set of rights. Thus there is no distinction between author's rights proper and neighboring rights; and there is no division between economic rights and moral rights. (Indeed, there is scant protection for moral rights, a point considered below.) The traditional explanation for this is that in the US, the goal of copyright is to maximize the creation and dissemination of new works, consistent with maximum access by the public to creative expression. This "utilitarian" approach is not in itself directly concerned with the rights of authors; authors are given rights only as a means to an end, viz., the creation of new expressive works for the benefit of the public.

12.2 Economic rights

12.2.1 Right to reproduce

12.2.1.1 United States

Source: Wikimedia; public domain.

Figure 12.1 American composer Cole Porter

Arnstein v. Porter, 154 F.2d 464 (2d Cir. 1946)

[Jerome] FRANK, Circuit Judge.

The principal question on this appeal is whether the lower court properly deprived plaintiff of a trial of his copyright infringement action. The answer depends on whether 'there is the slightest doubt as to the facts.' In applying that standard here, it is important to avoid confusing two separate elements essential to a plaintiff's case in such a suit: (a) that defendant copied from plaintiff's copyrighted work and (b) that the copying (assuming it to be proved) went to far as to constitute improper appropriation.

As to the first – copying – the evidence may consist (a) of defendant's admission that he copied or (b) of circumstantial evidence – usually evidence of access – from which the trier of the facts may reasonably infer copying. Of course, if there are no similarities, no amount of evidence of access will suffice to prove copying. If there is evidence of access and similarities exist, then the trier of the facts must determine whether the similarities are sufficient to prove copying. On this issue, analysis ('dissection') is relevant, and the testimony of experts may be received to aid the trier of the facts. If evidence of access is absent, the similarities must be so striking as to preclude the possibility that plaintiff and defendant independently arrived at the same result.

If copying is established, then only does there arise the second issue, that of illicit copying (unlawful appropriation). On that issue (as noted more in detail below) the test is the response of the ordinary lay hearer; accordingly, on that issue, 'dissection' and expert testimony are irrelevant.

In some cases, the similarities between the plaintiff's and defendant's work are so extensive and striking as, without more, both to justify an inference of copying and to prove improper appropriation. But such double-purpose evidence is not required; that is, if copying is otherwise shown, proof of improper appropriation need not consist of similarities which, standing alone, would support an inference of copying.

Each of these two issues – copying and improper appropriation – is an issue of fact.

We turn first to the issue of copying. After listening to the compositions as played in the phonograph recordings submitted by defendant, we find similarities; but we hold that unquestionably, standing alone, they do not compel the conclusion, or permit the inference, that defendant copied. The similarities, however, are sufficient so that, if there is enough evidence of access to permit the case to go to the jury, the jury may properly infer that the similarities did not result from coincidence.

Summary judgment was, then, proper if indubitably defendant did not have access to plaintiff's compositions. Plainly that presents an issue of fact. On that issue, the district judge, who heard no oral testimony, had before him the depositions of plaintiff and defendant. The judge characterized plaintiff's story as 'fantastic'; and, in the light of the references in his opinion to defendant's deposition, the judge obviously accepted defendant's denial of access and copying. Although part of plaintiff's testimony on

> **CASE** *(continued)*
>
> deposition (as to 'stooges' and the like) does seem 'fantastic,' yet plaintiff's credibility, even as to those improbabilities, should be left to the jury. If evidence is 'of a kind that greatly taxes the credulity of the judge, he can say so, or, if he totally disbelieves it, he may announce that fact, leaving the jury free to believe it or not.' We should not overlook the shrewd proverbial admonition that sometimes truth is stranger than fiction.
>
> But even if we were to disregard the improbable aspects of plaintiff's story, there remain parts by no means 'fantastic.' On the record now before us, more than a million copies of one of his compositions were sold; copies of others were sold in smaller quantities or distributed to radio stations or band leaders or publishers, or the pieces were publicly performed. If, after hearing both parties testify, the jury disbelieves defendant's denials, it can, from such facts, reasonably infer access. It follows that, as credibility is unavoidably involved, a genuine issue of material fact presents itself. With credibility a vital factor, plaintiff is entitled to a trial where the jury can observe the witnesses while testifying. Plaintiff must not be deprived of the invaluable privilege of cross-examining the defendant – the 'crucial test of credibility' – in the presence of the jury. Plaintiff, or a lawyer on his behalf, on such examination may elicit damaging admissions from defendant; more important, plaintiff may persuade the jury, observing defendant's manner when testifying, that defendant is unworthy of belief.
>
> With all that in mind, we cannot now say – as we think we must say to sustain a summary judgment – that at the close of a trial the judge could properly direct a verdict.
>
> Defendant asked the judge to take judicial notice of five previous copyright infringement actions [the plaintiff Arnstein has filed]. Defendant, in his brief in this court says, 'This is perhaps the most significant' argument in 'this case,' and presses us to hold that affirmance of the dismissal should be based thereon. But we regard it as entirely improper to give any weight to other actions lost by plaintiff. Absent the factors which make up res judicata (not present here), each case must stand on its own bottom, subject, of course, to the doctrine of stare decisis. Succumbing to the temptation to consider other defeats suffered by a party may lead a court astray. When a particular suit is vexatious, sometimes at its conclusion the court can give some redress to the victorious party. Perhaps the Legislature can and should meet this problem more effectively. But we surely must not do so, as defendant here would have us do, by prejudging the merits of the case before us.
>
> Reversed and remanded.
>
> CLARK, Circuit Judge (dissenting).
>
> After repeated hearings of the records, I could not find therein what my brothers found. In our former musical plagiarism cases we have, naturally, relied on what seemed the total sound effect; but we have also analyzed the music enough to make sure of an intelligible and intellectual decision. [O]ne may look to the total impression to repulse the charge of plagiarism where a minute 'dissection' might dredge up some points of similarity. Hence one cannot use a purely theoretical disquisition to supply a tonal resemblance which does not otherwise exist. Certainly, however, that does not suggest or compel the converse – that one must keep his brain in torpor for fear that otherwise it would make clear differences which do exist. Music is a matter of the intellect as well as the emotions; that is why

CASE (continued)

eminent musical scholars insist upon the employment of the intellectual faculties for a just appreciation of music.

Consequently I do not think we should abolish the use of the intellect here even if we could. When, however, we start with an examination of the written and printed material supplied by the plaintiff in his complaint and exhibits, we find at once that he does not and cannot claim extensive copying, measure by measure, of his compositions. He therefore has resorted to a comparative analysis – the 'dissection' found unpersuasive in the earlier cases – to support his claim of plagiarism of small detached portions here and there, the musical fillers between the better known parts of the melody. And plaintiff's compositions, as pointed out in the cases cited above, are of the simple and trite character where small repetitive sequences are not hard to discover. It is as though we found Shakespeare a plagiarist on the basis of his use of articles, pronouns, prepositions, and adjectives also used by others. The surprising thing, however, is to note the small amount of even this type of reproduction which plaintiff by dint of extreme dissection has been able to find.

Source: Gerald Ford Presidential Library; US Government work, public domain

Figure 12.2 George Harrison of *The Beatles*

Source: Gerald Ford Presidential Library; US Government work, public domain

Figure 12.3 American composer/musician Billy Preston

> **CASE**
>
> ## Bright Tunes Music Corp. v. Harrisongs Music, Ltd., 420 F. Supp. 177 (S.D.N.Y. 1976) aff'd sub nom. ABKCO Music, Inc. v. Harrisongs Music, Ltd., 722 F.2d 988 (2d Cir. 1983)
>
> OWEN, District Judge.
> This is an action in which it is claimed that a successful song, My Sweet Lord, listing George Harrison as the composer, is plagiarized from an earlier successful song, He's So Fine, composed by Ronald Mack, recorded by a singing group called the "Chiffons," the copyright of which is owned by plaintiff, Bright Tunes Music Corp.
> He's So Fine, recorded in 1962, is a catchy tune consisting essentially of four repetitions of a very short basic musical phrase, "sol-mi-re," (hereinafter motif A), altered as necessary to fit the words, followed by four repetitions of another short basic musical phrase, "sol-la-do-la-do," (hereinafter motif B). While neither motif is novel, the four repetitions of A, followed by four repetitions of B, is a highly unique pattern. In addition, in the second use of the motif B series, there is a grace note inserted making the phrase go "sol-la-do-la-re-do."
> My Sweet Lord, recorded first in 1970, also uses the same motif A (modified to suit the words) four times, followed by motif B, repeated three times, not four. In place of He's So Fine's fourth repetition of motif B, My Sweet Lord has a transitional passage of musical attractiveness of the same approximate length, with the identical grace note in the identical second repetition. The harmonies of both songs are identical.
> George Harrison, a former member of The Beatles, was aware of He's So Fine. In the United States, it was No. 1 on the billboard charts for five weeks; in England, Harrison's home country, it was No. 12 on the charts on June 1, 1963, a date upon which one of the Beatle songs was, in fact, in first position. For seven weeks in 1963, He's So Fine was one of the top hits in England.
> According to Harrison, the circumstances of the composition of My Sweet Lord were as follows. Harrison and his group, which include an American black gospel singer named Billy Preston, were in Copenhagen, Denmark, on a singing engagement. There was a press conference involving the group going on backstage. Harrison slipped away from the press conference and went to a room upstairs and began "vamping" some guitar chords, fitting on to the chords he was playing the words, "Hallelujah" and "Hare Krishna" in various ways. During the course of this vamping, he was alternating between what musicians call a Minor II chord and a Major V chord.
> At some point, germinating started and he went down to meet with others of the group, asking them to listen, which they did, and everyone began to join in, taking first "Hallelujah" and then "Hare Krishna" and putting them into four part harmony. Harrison obviously started using the "Hallelujah," etc., as repeated sounds, and from there developed the lyrics,

CASE *(continued)*

to wit, "My Sweet Lord," "Dear, Dear Lord," etc. In any event, from this very free-flowing exchange of ideas, with Harrison playing his two chords and everybody singing "Hallelujah" and "Hare Krishna," there began to emerge the My Sweet Lord text idea, which Harrison sought to develop a little bit further during the following week as he was playing it on his guitar. Thus developed motif A and its words interspersed with "Hallelujah" and "Hare Krishna."

Approximately one week after the idea first began to germinate, the entire group flew back to London because they had earlier booked time to go to a recording studio with Billy Preston to make an album. In the studio, Preston was the principal musician. Harrison did not play in the session. He had given Preston his basic motif A with the idea that it be turned into a song, and was back and forth from the studio to the engineer's recording booth, supervising the recording "takes." Under circumstances that Harrison was utterly unable to recall, while everybody was working toward a finished song, in the recording studio, somehow or other the essential three notes of motif A reached polished form.

"Q. (By the Court): . . . you feel that those three notes . . . the motif A in the record, those three notes developed somewhere in that recording session?"

"Mr. Harrison: I'd say those three there were finalized as beginning there."

"Q. (By the Court): Is it possible that Billy Preston hit on those (notes comprising motif A)?

"Mr. Harrison: Yes, but it's possible also that I hit on that, too, as far back as the dressing room, just scat singing."

The Billy Preston recording, listing George Harrison as the composer, was thereafter issued by Apple Records. The music was then reduced to paper by someone who prepared a "lead sheet" containing the melody, the words and the harmony for the United States copyright application.

Seeking the wellsprings of musical composition why a composer chooses the succession of notes and the harmonies he does whether it be George Harrison or Richard Wagner is a fascinating inquiry. It is apparent from the extensive colloquy between the Court and Harrison covering forty pages in the transcript that neither Harrison nor Preston were conscious of the fact that they were utilizing the He's So Fine theme. However, they in fact were, for it is perfectly obvious to the listener that in musical terms, the two songs are virtually identical except for one phrase. There is motif A used four times, followed by motif B, four times in one case, and three times in the other, with the same grace note in the second repetition of motif B.

What happened? I conclude that the composer, in seeking musical materials to clothe his thoughts, was working with various possibilities. As he tried this possibility and that, there came to the surface of his mind a particular combination that pleased him as being one he felt would be appealing to a prospective listener; in other words, that this combination of sounds would work. Why? Because his subconscious knew it already had worked in a song his conscious mind did not remember. Having arrived at this pleasing combination of sounds, the recording was made, the lead sheet prepared for copyright and the song became

CASE *(continued)*

an enormous success. Did Harrison deliberately use the music of He's So Fine? I do not believe he did so deliberately. Nevertheless, it is clear that My Sweet Lord is the very same song as He's So Fine with different words, and Harrison had access to He's So Fine. This is, under the law, infringement of copyright, and is no less so even though subconsciously accomplished. *Sheldon v. Metro-Goldwyn Pictures Corp.*, 81 F.2d 49, 54 (2d Cir. 1936); *Northern Music Corp. v. Pacemaker Music Co., Inc.*, 147 U.S.P.Q. 358, 359 (S.D.N.Y.1965).

Source: Harvard University Library, public domain, copyright expired

Figure 12.4 US Judge Learned Hand, around 1910

 CASE

Nichols v. Universal Pictures Corp., 45 F.2d 119 (2d Cir. 1930)

Learned HAND, Circuit Judge.
The plaintiff is the author of a [copyrighted] play, "Abie's Irish Rose." The defendant produced publicly a motion picture, 'The Cohens and The Kellys,' which the plaintiff alleges was taken from it.

'Abie's Irish Rose' presents a Jewish family living in prosperous circumstances in New York. The father, a widower, is in business as a merchant, in which his son and only child

CASE *(continued)*

helps him. The boy has philandered with young women, who to his father's great disgust have always been Gentiles, for he is obsessed with a passion that his daughter-in-law shall be [Jewish]. When the play opens the son, who has been courting a young Irish Catholic girl, has already married her secretly before a Protestant minister, and is concerned to soften the blow for his father, by securing a favorable impression of his bride, while [making the father believe she is Jewish]. The girl somewhat reluctantly falls in with the plan; the father takes the bait, becomes infatuated with the girl, concludes that they must marry, and assumes that of course they will, if he so decides. He calls in a rabbi, and prepares for the wedding according to the Jewish rite.

Meanwhile the girl's father, also a widower, who lives in California, and is as intense in his own religious antagonism as the Jew, has been called to New York, supposing that his daughter is to marry an Irishman and a Catholic. Accompanied by a priest, he arrives at the house at the moment when the marriage is being celebrated, but too late to prevent it and the two fathers, each infuriated by the proposed union of his child to a heretic, fall into unseemly and grotesque antics. The priest and the rabbi become friendly, exchange trite sentiments about religion, and agree that the match is good. Apparently out of abundant caution, the priest celebrates the marriage for a third time, while the girl's father is inveigled away. The second act closes with each father, still outraged, seeking to find some way by which the union, thus trebly insured, may be dissolved.

The last act takes place about a year later, the young couple having meanwhile been abjured by each father, and left to their own resources. They have had twins, a boy and a girl, but their fathers know no more than that a child has been born. At Christmas each, led by his craving to see his grandchild, goes separately to the young folks' home, where they encounter each other, each laden with gifts, one for a boy, the other for a girl. After some slapstick comedy, depending upon the insistence of each that he is right about the sex of the grandchild, they become reconciled when they learn the truth, and that each child is to bear the given name of a grandparent. The curtain falls as the fathers are exchanging amenities.

'The Cohens and The Kellys' presents two families, Jewish and Irish, living side by side in the poorer quarters of New York in a state of perpetual enmity. The wives in both cases are still living, and share in the mutual animosity, as do two small sons, and even the respective dogs. The Jews have a daughter, the Irish a son; the Jewish father is in the clothing business; the Irishman is a policeman. The children are in love with each other, and secretly marry, apparently after the play opens. The Jew, being in great financial straits, learns from a lawyer that he has fallen heir to a large fortune from a great-aunt, and moves into a great house, fitted luxuriously. Here he and his family live in vulgar ostentation, and here the Irish boy seeks out his Jewish bride, and is chased away by the angry father. The Jew then abuses the Irishman over the telephone, and both become hysterically excited. The extremity of his feelings make the Jew sick, so that he must go to Florida for a rest, just before which the daughter discloses her marriage to her mother.

On his return the Jew finds that his daughter has borne a child; at first he suspects the lawyer, but eventually learns the truth and is overcome with anger at such a low alliance.

> **CASE** *(continued)*
>
> Meanwhile, the Irish family who have been forbidden to see the grandchild, go to the Jew's house, and after a violent scene between the two fathers in which the Jew disowns his daughter, who decides to go back with her husband, the Irishman takes her back with her baby to his own poor lodgings. The lawyer, who had hoped to marry the Jew's daughter, seeing his plan foiled, tells the Jew that his fortune really belongs to the Irishman, who was also related to the dead woman, but offers to conceal his knowledge, if the Jew will share the loot. This the Jew repudiates, and, leaving the astonished lawyer, walks through the rain to his enemy's house to surrender the property. He arrives in great defection, tells the truth, and abjectly turns to leave. A reconciliation ensues, the Irishman agreeing to share with him equally.
>
> It is of course essential to any protection of literary property, whether at common-law or under the statute, that the right cannot be limited literally to the text, else a plagiarist would escape by immaterial variations. That has never been the law, but, as soon as literal appropriation ceases to be the test, the whole matter is necessarily at large, so that the decisions cannot help much in a new case. When plays are concerned, the plagiarist may excise a separate scene; or he may appropriate part of the dialogue. Then the question is whether the part so taken is 'substantial,' and therefore not a 'fair use' of the copyrighted work. But when the plagiarist does not take out a block in suit, but an abstract of the whole, decision is more troublesome.
>
> Upon any work, and especially upon a play, a great number of patterns of increasing generality will fit equally well, as more and more of the incident is left out. The last may perhaps be no more than the most general statement of what the play is about, and at times might consist only of its title; but there is a point in this series of abstractions where they are no longer protected, since otherwise the playwright could prevent the use of his 'ideas,' to which, apart from their expression, his property is never extended. Nobody has ever been able to fix that boundary, and nobody ever can. In some cases the question has been treated as though it were analogous to lifting a portion out of the copyrighted work; but the analogy is not a good one, because, though the skeleton is a part of the body, it pervades and supports the whole. In such cases we are rather concerned with the line between expression and what is expressed. As respects plays, the controversy chiefly centers upon the characters and sequence of incident, these being the substance.
>
> We do not doubt that two plays may correspond in plot closely enough for infringement. How far that correspondence must go is another matter. Nor need we hold that the same may not be true as to the characters, quite independently of the 'plot' proper, though, as far as we know such a case has never arisen. If Twelfth Night were copyrighted, it is quite possible that a second comer might so closely imitate Sir Toby Belch or Malvolio as to infringe, but it would not be enough that for one of his characters he cast a riotous knight who kept wassail to the discomfort of the household, or a vain and foppish steward who became amorous of his mistress. These would be no more than Shakespeare's 'ideas' in the play, as little capable of monopoly as Einstein's Doctrine of Relativity, or Darwin's theory of the Origin of Species. It follows that the less developed the characters, the less

CASE *(continued)*

they can be copyrighted; that is the penalty an author must bear for marking them too indistinctly.

In the two plays at bar we think both as to incident and character, the defendant took no more – assuming that it took anything at all – than the law allowed. The stories are quite different. One is of a religious [person] who insists upon his child's marrying no one outside his faith; opposed by another who is in this respect just like him, and is his foil. Their difference in race is merely an obbligato to the main theme, religion. They are reconciled through the honesty of the Jew and the generosity of the Irishman; the grandchild has nothing whatever to do with it. The only matter common to the two is a quarrel between a Jewish and an Irish father, the marriage of their children, the birth of grandchildren and a reconciliation.

If the defendant took so much from the plaintiff, it may well have been because her amazing success seemed to prove that this was a subject of enduring popularity. Even so, granting that the plaintiff's play was wholly original, and assuming that novelty is not essential to a copyright, there is no monopoly in such a background. Though the plaintiff discovered the vein, she could not keep it to herself; so defined, the theme was too generalized an abstraction from what she wrote. It was only a part of her 'ideas.'

Nor does she fare better as to her characters. It is indeed scarcely credible that she should not have been aware of those stock figures, the low comedy Jew and Irishman. The defendant has not taken from her more than their prototypes have contained for many decades. If so, obviously so to generalize her copyright, would allow her to cover what was not original with her. But we need not hold this as matter of fact, much as we might be justified. Even though we take it that she devised her figures out of her brain de novo, still the defendant was within its rights.

The Plaintiff's Jew is quite unlike the defendant's. His obsession in his religion, on which depends such racial animosity as he has. He is affectionate, warm and patriarchal. None of these fit the defendant's Jew, who shows affection for his daughter only once, and who has none but the most superficial interest in his grandchild. The Irish fathers are even more unlike; the plaintiff's a mere symbol for religious fanaticism and patriarchal pride, scarcely a character at all. Neither quality appears in the defendant's, for while he goes to get his grandchild, it is rather out of a truculent determination not to be forbidden, than from pride in his progeny. For the rest he is only a grotesque hobbledehoy, used for low comedy of the most conventional sort, which any one might borrow, if he chanced not to know the exemplar.

12.2.1.2 China

CHIUNG Yao v. YU Zheng, Beijing 3rd Interim Ct. [2014] Sanzhongminchuzi No. 07916, aff'd Beijing High Ct. [2015] Gaominzhizhongzi No. 1039

Plaintiff CHIUNG Yao, a well-known author of romance novels, claimed that she is the author to the novel *Plum Blossom Scar* (1993) and also the script writer for the television series produced under the same title. Defendant YU Zheng wrote a script and directed a television series between 2012–2013, entitled *Palace III: the Lost Daughter* . . . CHIUNG claimed that YU's television series *Palace III* and its underlying script violated the copyright of her prior novel and script for *Plum Blossom Scar* . . . CHIUNG submitted twenty-one specific plot elements from her work to support her contention that the plot elements between the two works are strikingly similar . . .

[The Court first reviewed Plaintiff's work *Plum Blossom Scar* and summarized its synopsis as follows:

"[Plaintiff's] story was set in the background of a royal family in China's Qing dynasty. The emperor had always hoped to have a son, who could inherit his title, but his wife already had three daughters and a fourth one on the way . . . During his birthday celebration, the emperor was introduced to a beautiful young woman, with whom he immediately fell in love and decided to marry. Out of fears of losing her power and status in the royal family, the empress followed her sister's advice and switched her newborn baby girl with a baby boy they found outside the palace.

Before abandoning her baby girl in a basket, the empress tattooed a picture of a plum blossom on her daughter's shoulder, hoping that the blossom scar could help her identify her daughter in the future . . . The abandoned princess was later found by a creek and adopted by an indigent couple . . .

The switched baby boy was raised as the prince of the royal family. Years later, as fate would have it, he met the abandoned princess upon saving her from trouble. In true fairy tale fashion, he fell in love with her. However, the prince was already arranged to marry another princess. Despite the objections from his royal family, the prince insisted on taking the abandoned princess as his concubine as a condition to entering into the arranged marriage. Eventually, the truth about the true identity of the fake prince and the abandoned princess is revealed. The royal family is punished for the lies and cover up. The story ends tragically with the princess committing suicide and the prince leaving the palace forever . . ."]

[The court then turned to Defendant's work *Palace III: the Lost Daughter* and found a

CASE *(continued)*

number of similar plot elements between two works, in particular in the beginning of the story. The court noted that Defendant's story diverged in the following ways: (1) instead of a *plum blossom tattoo* on the baby girl's shoulder, Defendant's baby girl had a natural birth mark; (2) rather than being adopted by a couple, the baby girl was adopted by a single woman operating a brothel; (3) the young couple met for the first time in different circumstances; and (4) defendant's story ended with a much more complicated plot including a revenge and the birth of a grandchild, etc.] . . .

Issue 3: Whether Plaintiff's work *Plum Blossom Scar* is a valid copyrighted work
[I]t is crucial to protect plot elements in literary works . . . .. Consequently, copyright protection extends to character settings, plot elements and logical sequences that are sufficiently specific.

Idea-Expression Dichotomy: Special Experience Test
The distinction between idea and expression is necessary but often difficult to grasp. This Court finds that an abstract analogy can be used to analyze the idea-expression dichotomy. If a literary work is a Pyramid, the bottom of the Pyramid would be expressions with sufficient details, and the top of the Pyramid would be the most abstract, and therefore a generalized idea. When a copyright owner of a literary work sues others for copyright infringement, such a Pyramid analysis should be applied to determine whether the similar parts between the plaintiff's works and the defendant's works are copyrightable expressions or uncopyrightable ideas – the closer to the top, the more likely to be an idea; the closer to the bottom, the more likely to be an expression.

This Court also employs a "source-identifying special experience test" to distinguish idea from expression, dictating that one shall determine whether the plot elements in question are general and abstract or detailed enough to elicit a special aesthetic experience that is sufficient to identify the source of the works. If such plot elements are detailed enough, then they can be categorized as expressions . . . Likewise, if the identities, relationships and role/plot correspondence of characters are specific enough, then such character settings and relationships should be considered as copyrightable expressions.

Scènes à faire, the merger doctrine and public knowledge
. . . This Court rules that after applying the scènes à faire, the merger doctrine and public domain doctrine, the remaining original contributions of the author will be protected. For example, specific story elements such as character setting, role relationships, scenes, plot elements and logical arrangement of the plot might be subject to copyright protection. Although an author cannot prevent others from using specific scenes, limited expression or public knowledge, he can prevent others from using his original contributions to the work. Therefore, when determining whether works based on original expressions but with specific scenes, limited expression and public knowledge are subject to copyright protection, it is essential to see whether an author used such elements to develop originality in his work. In copyright infringement cases, it is the defendant's burden to prove that the scènes à faire

> **CASE** *(continued)*
>
> doctrine, merger doctrine or public domain theory bars copyright protection for the subject work, and that the author (Plaintiff), is not the original creator of the work.
>
> **Issue 4: Whether Defendant's Work copied copyrightable elements in Plaintiff's prior Work *Plum***
>
> *Whether Defendant YU had access to Plaintiff's prior work*
> Two elements are required to establish that Defendant copied Plaintiff's copyrightable work: access and substantial similarity. Access can be proved by two means: either by direct evidence that proves Defendant has actual access to the unpublished prior work, or by circumstantial evidence that shows the prior work has been published and made available to the public before Defendant created his work. Based on Article 9 of the *Interpretation of the Supreme People's Court Concerning the Application of Laws in the Trial of Civil Disputes over Copyright*, the term "making it known to the public" means that a work is disclosed to the public (to an unspecified group of people) by the copyright holder or with the permission from the copyright holder. Here, it can be presumed that Plaintiff's work was made to the public because the TV drama *Plum Blossom Scar* based on Plaintiff's script was broadcast to the public, [and] thus [was] available to Defendant.
>
> *Relationship between adaptation and reasonable reference*
> The difference between copyright infringement and reasonable reference is the distinction between copying copyrightable expression of ideas as opposed to borrowing a [non-copyrightable] idea. When evaluating whether idea reference is fair, it is crucial to evaluate how much and to what extent the latter work referenced the original author's prior work. A case-by-case analysis, both qualitatively and quantatively, is required.
>
> *Substantial Similarity Test*
> When [applying the substantial similarity test in literature works,] it is inappropriate to simply compare two works word by word, and reject similarities between two works simply because of the differences in texts. An effective comparison should examine whether the later work is substantially similar to the prior work although it could be a challenging task in derivative works because a derivative work is often similar but not identical with the prior underlying work...
>
> *Comparison regarding character setting and relationships*
> ... [In this case, when we compare] the specific character setting and plot of the works in question, it appears that the characters from Plaintiff's script and novel *Plum Blossom Scar* also existed in Defendant's work *The Palace*.... The aforesaid characters not only corresponded with the character setting and the roles' relationships [in Defendant's work], but also correlated to specific plot and development of the story. In the absence of Defendant's counter-evidence, this Court determined that Defendant's script *The Palace* adapted character settings and character relationships from Plaintiff's prior work *Plum Blossom Scar*.

CASE *(continued)*

Comparison regarding plot elements
To facilitate the comparison between Plaintiff's prior work and Defendant's latter work, Plaintiff submitted twenty-one plot elements from both works to demonstrate the substantial similarity between the two works. This Court finds that the *Plum Blossom Scar* and *The Palace* script shared similar arrangements of details in the plot. A few of the aforesaid plot elements are not copyrightable because they are in the public domain, and Plaintiff's work *Plum Blossom Scar* lacks sufficient originality in the creation and arrangement of events. But, nine plot arrangements in Defendant's work *The Palace* were substantially similar to the original arrangement in Plaintiff's work *Plum Blossom Scar*, with only minor differences.

Total evaluation of works
Plaintiff claimed that twenty-one plot elements from her script *Plum Blossom Scar* and seventeen plot elements from her novel *Plum Blossom Scar* were substantially similar to Defendant's work. [This Court finds that] the plot arrangement and development in Defendant's Work *The Palace* script were nearly identical to that of Plaintiff's work, with only slight variations in the sequence of certain plot. However, such variations in the sequence did not ultimately change the underlying logic and plot development in Defendant's work

. . .

To conclude, this Court finds that the disputed plot in Defendant's work *The Palace* were substantially similar to Plaintiff's work of *Plum Blossom Scar*, and thus constituting an adaptation of Plaintiff's works without authorization.

NOTES

1. Compare *CHIUNG Yao v. YU Zheng* with *Nichols v. Universal Pictures Corp*. Do you think that the Chinese courts applied similar copyright principles, including the idea/expression dichotomy, the merger doctrine and the substantial similarity test, as their counterparts in the United States? How?
2. The abstraction test proposed in *Nichols v. Universal Pictures Corp.*, which tries to distinguish non-copyrightable ideas from copyrightable expressions of such ideas, also found its influence elsewhere, although with variations and uncertainty. In *Michael Baigent v. The Random House Group Ltd*. EWHC 719 (Ch) (2006), the British judges were asked to determine whether the best-seller novel *The Da Vinci Code* was an infringement of the copyright in an earlier publication *The Holy Blood and The Holy Grail*. After a lengthy discussion and comparison of the story elements, structure, and character relationships between the two books, the British judges eventually found there was no infringement. Judge Hand once described the challenge of applying the abstraction test as, "Nobody has ever been able to fix that boundary, and nobody ever can." If you were asked to draft a formula for the substantial similarity test involving copying of literature works, what would that be?

12.2.1.3 Europe

For a long time, the copyright systems of individual European countries have provided a right of reproduction to copyright authors. With the Information

Society Directive of 2001, the EU adopted a definition of the right of reproduction that all EU Member States were required to adopt. Article 2 of the Directive reads:

> Member States shall provide for the exclusive right to authorise or prohibit direct or indirect, temporary or permanent reproduction by any means and in any form, in whole or in part:
>
> (a)   for authors, of their works;
> (b)   for performers, of fixations of their performances;
> (c)   for phonogram producers, of their phonograms;
> (d)   for the producers of the first fixations of films, in respect of the original and copies of their films;
> (e)   for broadcasting organisations, of fixations of their broadcasts, whether those broadcasts are transmitted by wire or over the air, including by cable or satellite.

This provision not only provided a harmonized basis for the reproduction right across the EU, it also enabled the CJEU to decide cases on the relationship between the reproduction right and new technologies that would set standards across the EU.

 CASE

Case C-5/08, Infopaq Int'l v. Danske Dagblades Forening, Court of Justice of the European Union, ECLI:EU:C:2009:465 ("Infopaq I")

13   Infopaq operates a media monitoring and analysis business which consists primarily in drawing up summaries of selected articles from Danish daily newspapers and other periodicals. The articles are selected on the basis of certain subject criteria agreed with customers and the selection is made by means of a 'data capture process'. The summaries are sent to customers by email.
14   DDF is a professional association of Danish daily newspaper publishers, whose function is inter alia to assist its members with copyright issues.
15   In 2005 DDF became aware that Infopaq was scanning newspaper articles for commercial purposes without authorisation from the relevant rightholders. Taking the view that such consent was necessary for processing articles using the process in question, DDF complained to Infopaq about this procedure.
16   The data capture process comprises the five phases described below which, according to DDF, lead to four acts of reproduction of newspaper articles.

CASE *(continued)*

17 First, the relevant publications are registered manually by Infopaq employees in an electronic registration database.

18 Secondly, once the spines are cut off the publications so that all the pages consist of loose sheets, the publications are scanned. The section to be scanned is selected from the registration database before the publication is put into the scanner. Scanning allows a TIFF ('Tagged Image File Format') file to be created for each page of the publication. When scanning is completed, the TIFF file is transferred to an OCR ('Optical Character Recognition') server.

19 Thirdly, the OCR server translates the TIFF file into data that can be processed digitally. During that process, the image of each letter is translated into a character code which tells the computer what type of letter it is. For instance, the image of the letters 'TDC' is translated into something the computer can treat as the letters 'TDC' and put in a text format which can be recognised by the computer's system. These data are saved as a text file which can be understood by any text processing program. The OCR process is completed by deleting the TIFF file.

20 Fourthly, the text file is processed to find a search word defined beforehand. Each time a match for a search word is found, data is generated giving the publication, section and page number on which the match was found, together with a value expressed as a percentage between 0 and 100 indicating how far into the text it is to be found, in order to make it easier to read the article. Also in order to make it easier to find the search word when reading the article, the five words which come before and after the search word are captured ('extract of 11 words'). At the end of the process the text file is deleted.

21 Fifthly, at the end of the data capture process a cover sheet is printed out in respect of all the pages where the relevant search word was found. The following is an example of the text of a cover sheet:

'4 November 2005 – *Dagbladet Arbejderen*, page 3:
TDC: 73% "a forthcoming sale of the telecommunications group TDC which is expected to be bought"'.

22 Infopaq disputed the claim that the procedure required consent from the rightholders and brought an action against DDF before the Østre Landsret (Eastern Regional Court), claiming that DDF should be ordered to acknowledge that Infopaq is entitled in Denmark to apply the abovementioned procedure without the consent of DDF or of its members. After the Østre Landsret dismissed that action, Infopaq brought an appeal before the referring court.

23 According to the Højesteret, it is not disputed in this case that consent from the rightholders is not required to engage in press monitoring activity and the writing of summaries consisting in manual reading of each publication, selection of the relevant articles on the basis of predetermined search words, and production of a manually prepared cover sheet for the summary writers, giving an identified search word in an article and its position in the newspaper. Similarly, the parties in the main proceedings do not dispute that genuinely independent summary writing per se is lawful and does not require consent from the rightholders.

CASE *(continued)*

24 Nor is it disputed in this case that the data capture process described above involves two acts of reproduction: the creation of a TIFF file when the printed articles are scanned and the conversion of the TIFF file into a text file. In addition, it is common ground that this procedure entails the reproduction of parts of the scanned printed articles since the extract of 11 words is stored and those 11 words are printed out on paper.

25 There is, however, disagreement between the parties as to whether there is reproduction as contemplated by Article 2 of Directive 2001/29 . . . .

26 In those circumstances, the Højesteret a decided to stay the proceedings and to refer the following questions to the Court of Justice for a preliminary ruling:

> (1) Can the storing and subsequent printing out of a text extract from an article in a daily newspaper, consisting of a search word and the five preceding and five subsequent words, be regarded as acts of reproduction which are protected (see Article 2 of [Directive 2001/29]?
> . . .

30 By its first question, the national court asks, essentially, whether the concept of 'reproduction in part' within the meaning of Directive 2001/29 is to be interpreted as meaning that it encompasses the storing and subsequent printing out on paper of a text extract consisting of 11 words.

31 It is clear that Directive 2001/29 does not define the concept of either 'reproduction' or 'reproduction in part'.

32 In those circumstances, those concepts must be defined having regard to the wording and context of Article 2 of Directive 2001/29, where the reference to them is to be found and in the light of both the overall objectives of that directive and international law (see, to that effect, *SGAE*, paragraphs 34 and 35 and case-law cited).

33 Article 2(a) of Directive 2001/29 provides that authors have the exclusive right to authorise or prohibit reproduction, in whole or in part, of their works. It follows that protection of the author's right to authorise or prohibit reproduction is intended to cover 'work'.

34 It is, moreover, apparent from the general scheme of the Berne Convention, in particular Article 2(5) and (8), that the protection of certain subject-matters as artistic or literary works presupposes that they are intellectual creations.

35 Similarly, under Articles 1(3) of Directive 91/250, 3(1) of Directive 96/9 and 6 of Directive 2006/116, works such as computer programs, databases or photographs are protected by copyright only if they are original in the sense that they are their author's own intellectual creation.

36 In establishing a harmonised legal framework for copyright, Directive 2001/29 is based on the same principle, as evidenced by recitals 4, 9 to 11 and 20 in the preamble thereto.

37 In those circumstances, copyright within the meaning of Article 2(a) of Directive 2001/29 is liable to apply only in relation to a subject-matter which is original in the sense that it is its author's own intellectual creation.

CASE *(continued)*

38 As regards the parts of a work, it should be borne in mind that there is nothing in Directive 2001/29 or any other relevant directive indicating that those parts are to be treated any differently from the work as a whole. It follows that they are protected by copyright since, as such, they share the originality of the whole work.

39 In the light of the considerations referred to in paragraph 37 of this judgment, the various parts of a work thus enjoy protection under Article 2(a) of Directive 2001/29, provided that they contain elements which are the expression of the intellectual creation of the author of the work.

40 With respect to the scope of such protection of a work, it follows from recitals 9 to 11 in the preamble to Directive 2001/29 that its main objective is to introduce a high level of protection, in particular for authors to enable them to receive an appropriate reward for the use of their works, including at the time of reproduction of those works, in order to be able to pursue their creative and artistic work.

41 Similarly, recital 21 in the preamble to Directive 2001/29 requires that the acts covered by the right of reproduction be construed broadly.

42 That requirement of a broad definition of those acts is, moreover, also to be found in the wording of Article 2 of that directive, which uses expressions such as 'direct or indirect', 'temporary or permanent', 'by any means' and 'in any form'.

43 Consequently, the protection conferred by Article 2 of Directive 2001/29 must be given a broad interpretation.

44 As regards newspaper articles, their author's own intellectual creation, referred to in paragraph 37 of this judgment, is evidenced clearly from the form, the manner in which the subject is presented and the linguistic expression. In the main proceedings, moreover, it is common ground that newspaper articles, as such, are literary works covered by Directive 2001/29.

45 Regarding the elements of such works covered by the protection, it should be observed that they consist of words which, considered in isolation, are not as such an intellectual creation of the author who employs them. It is only through the choice, sequence and combination of those words that the author may express his creativity in an original manner and achieve a result which is an intellectual creation.

46 Words as such do not, therefore, constitute elements covered by the protection.

47 That being so, given the requirement of a broad interpretation of the scope of the protection conferred by Article 2 of Directive 2001/29, the possibility may not be ruled out that certain isolated sentences, or even certain parts of sentences in the text in question, may be suitable for conveying to the reader the originality of a publication such as a newspaper article, by communicating to that reader an element which is, in itself, the expression of the intellectual creation of the author of that article. Such sentences or parts of sentences are, therefore, liable to come within the scope of the protection provided for in Article 2(a) of that directive.

48 In the light of those considerations, the reproduction of an extract of a protected work which, like those at issue in the main proceedings, comprises 11 consecutive words thereof,

CASE *(continued)*

is such as to constitute reproduction in part within the meaning of Article 2 of Directive 2001/29, if that extract contains an element of the work which, as such, expresses the author's own intellectual creation; it is for the national court to make this determination.

49 It must be remembered also that the data capture process used by Infopaq allows for the reproduction of multiple extracts of protected works. That process reproduces an extract of 11 words each time a search word appears in the relevant work and, moreover, often operates using a number of search words because some clients ask Infopaq to draw up summaries based on a number of criteria.

50 In so doing, that process increases the likelihood that Infopaq will make reproductions in part within the meaning of Article 2(a) of Directive 2001/29 because the cumulative effect of those extracts may lead to the reconstitution of lengthy fragments which are liable to reflect the originality of the work in question, with the result that they contain a number of elements which are such as to express the intellectual creation of the author of that work.

51 In the light of the foregoing, the answer to the first question is that an act occurring during a data capture process, which consists of storing an extract of a protected work comprising 11 words and printing out that extract, is such as to come within the concept of reproduction in part within the meaning of Article 2 of Directive 2001/29, if the elements thus reproduced are the expression of the intellectual creation of their author; it is for the national court to make this determination.

. . .

On those grounds, the Court (Fourth Chamber) hereby rules:

1. An act occurring during a data capture process, which consists of storing an extract of a protected work comprising 11 words and printing out that extract, is such as to come within the concept of reproduction in part within the meaning of Article 2 of Directive 2001/29/EC of the European Parliament and of the Council of 22 May 2001 on the harmonisation of certain aspects of copyright and related rights in the information society, if the elements thus reproduced are the expression of the intellectual creation of their author; it is for the national court to make this determination . . ..

NOTES

1. This case is important as it expands the applicability of the standard of originality (author's own intellectual creation) beyond the limited cases in which this standard has been used by European Directives (computer programs, photographs, databases). It started a phase of unprecedented judicial activism in European copyright law. The CJEU found that important building blocks of copyright law had not been harmonized on a European level. It was not realistic that such harmonization would be achieved, at least in the short term, by the complex interaction of the European Commission, the European Parliament and the Council that leads to the adoption of new Directives. As a result, the CJEU apparently decided to do the job itself.

2. The case is also important because it shows that even copying an 11-word extract from a copyrighted work can be a violation of the reproduction right if the excerpt itself fulfills the European standard of originality. At the same time, the case shows the limited role of the CJEU in resolving conflicts. The court has the

authority to resolve conflicts in the legal interpretation of primary and secondary EU law. But the application of the legal rules to a particular case is left to national courts. In 2013, the Danish Supreme Court affirmed that Infopaq had violated the copyright of the Danish newspaper because the 11-word extracts would, from time to time, contain copyrighted sentences or part thereof.
3. There are two *Infopaq* CJEU decisions. The first one, which you have just read ("*Infopaq I*"), deals with the originality standard and the right of reproduction. The second one ("*Infopaq II*") deals with copyright limitations and Art. 5(1) Information Society Directive, *see infra* Section 13.3.2).
4. While Art. 5 Information Society Directive harmonizes the right to reproduce in EU law across most work categories, the reproduction right vis-à-vis computer programs is still governed by Art. 4(1)(a) Computer Programs Directive. This Directive was originally adopted in 1991 and predates the Information Society Directive by 10 years. A similar overlap exists with the Database Directive.

12.2.2 Right to make derivative works

12.2.2.1 United States

 CASE

Sobhani v. @Radical.Media Inc., 257 F. Supp. 2d 1234 (C.D. Cal. 2003)

WILSON, District Judge.
Plaintiff Babak Sobhani ("Sobhani") is an aspiring commercial director. In late 2000 and early 2001, Sobhani conceived, directed and produced five short video advertisements ("Spec Commercials") as a means of promoting himself to prospective employers.

The Spec [*i.e.*, "speculative," meaning not prepared with prior authorization, done at the creator's own initiative] Commercials were styled along the lines of then preexisting commercials for Jack-in-the-Box restaurants, but contained new elements in that they spoofed the popular motion picture Cast Away, starring Tom Hanks. In the movie, Hanks's character becomes stranded alone on a small island following an airplane crash. Hanks's character battles his isolation by speaking to a "Wilson" volleyball that survived the crash, and to which Hanks ascribes anthropomorphic characteristics.

Certain Jack-in-the-Box advertisements feature a "Jack head" which speaks during the commercials, and some include a smaller "Jack antenna ball head," which does the same. Plaintiff's Spec Commercials portray a man (who looks much like Hanks's character) apparently stranded on a small island (which looks much like the beachfront from Cast Away). In certain spots, the man is clean-shaven and apparently newly arrived, while others portray the man as bearded and somewhat grizzled. Instead of a mute Wilson volleyball, however, Plaintiff's character interacts with a small, talking Jack head antenna ball, and discusses with the head certain Jack-in-the-Box products, such as the "Sourdough Jack" burger. Integrated into most, and at the end of all, of the Spec Commercials is actual footage copied from previously-aired Jack-in-the-Box commercials (including footage of the Sourdough Jack burger and dropping Jack-in-the-Box bags).

CASE (continued)

Plaintiff sent his Spec Commercials to between five and ten companies, including Defendant @radical.media ("Radical"). Radical received the tape containing the spots on November 2, 2001, and at least two Radical employees viewed the Spec Commercials on November 9, 2001. In January and February of 2002, Radical produced a commercial similar in many respects to Plaintiff's spots. In it, a bearded, haggard man is apparently stranded on a small island. As in Plaintiff's spots, the man and island closely resemble those in Cast Away. The man is antagonized by a Jack-in-the-Box antenna ball head, which extols the virtues of Jack-in-the-Box products, including the Sourdough Jack burger. The ad includes almost identical footage of the burger, and "dropping bags" at its conclusion. In a notable similarity, the antenna ball is at one point portrayed as affixed to the top of a stick the bearded man is attempting to use to start a fire – as it is in one of Plaintiff's spots.

Radical contends that the commercial it produced was independently conceived by an employee of advertising agency Kowloon Wholesale Seafood Company d/b/a/ Secret Weapon Marketing ("Secret Weapon") in late November 2001. Radical argues that it was hired simply to produce the commercial, which was created, written and directed by Secret Weapon, and that Radical contributed in no way to its creative content. Moreover, Radical maintains that those Radical employees who worked on the Secret Weapon commercial had no knowledge of or exposure to Plaintiff's Spec Commercials.

Plaintiff alleges that he registered both the Spec Commercials and Teleplays with the U.S. Copyright Office, and now sues for infringement of both.

Radical moves for summary judgment on two bases. First, it argues that the evidence of independent creation rebuts any inference of copying Sobhani may have raised. Second, Radical contends that Sobhani's Spec Commercials are unauthorized derivative works for which no copyright obtains.

[The court denied summary judgment in favor of defendant on the access/copying question, stating that defendant's evidence of independent creation would only be persuasive at this stage of the proceeding if it had shown creation prior to the alleged access to plaintiff's works.]

Radical also claims that Plaintiff's Spec Commercials are unauthorized derivative works, and thus that Plaintiff cannot sue for their infringement.

A copyright holder's rights include the exclusive right to prepare derivative works. 17 U.S.C. 106(2). Under the Copyright Act:

> A "derivative work" is a work based upon one or more preexisting works, such as a translation, musical arrangement, dramatization, fictionalization, motion picture version, sound recording, art reproduction, abridgment, condensation, or any other form in which a work may be recast, transformed, or adapted. A work consisting of editorial revisions, annotations, elaborations, or other modifications which, as a whole, represent an original work of authorship, is a "derivative work."

17 U.S.C. §101.

To determine whether derivative works are within the definition of the statute, the Ninth

CASE *(continued)*

Circuit has imported the similarity standard used to determine infringement. In essence, a "derivative work" under the Copyright Act is one which "would be considered an infringing work if the material which it has derived from a preexisting work had been taken without the consent of the copyright proprietor of such preexisting work." *Mirage Editions, Inc. v. Albuquerque A.R.T. Co.*, 856 F.2d 1341 (9th Cir. 1988). Accordingly, if a work is derived from a previous work, and the new work thereby infringes a copyright in the previous work, then the new work is an unauthorized (and infringing) derivative work.

Because the Spec Commercials are derivative of the Jack-in-the-Box commercials, and in fact use a copyrighted character (the Jack-in-the-Box head), as well as actual footage from those commercials, they seem clearly to fall within the Act's broad definition of "derivative works."

[The plaintiff tried to invoke the fair use defense to show his right to ownership of the new material on the derivative works. The court noted this was a "novel" theory – novel because plaintiff was using fair use not as a defense to an infringement action by Jack-in-the-Box, but as a justification for its rights in the material it added to Jack-in-the-Box's copyrighted characters.] The pertinent question is whether Plaintiff's works are unauthorized, derivative works under the Copyright Act. The derivative nature of the Spec Commercials, combined with the substantial unauthorized use of copyrighted Jack-in-the-Box elements, demonstrate that they are. This is true regardless whether Plaintiff could avoid liability under the Act [as a fair use] if sued for infringement.

Because Plaintiff's Spec Commercials are unauthorized derivative works, the disputed question before the Court is whether Plaintiff is entitled to copyright protection in the new elements of his works. Plaintiff cites section 103(a) of the Copyright Act, which provides in pertinent part that "protection for a work employing preexisting material in which copyright subsists does not extend to any part of the work in which such material has been used unlawfully." Plaintiff construes this provision to mean that his "original contributions" to the commercials are entitled to copyright protection, even if the work as a whole is an unauthorized derivative work.

The Second Circuit (in dicta) and Nimmer on Copyright appear to agree substantially with Plaintiff's construction of the statutory language. See *Eden Toys, Inc. v. Florelee Undergarment Co.*, 697 F.2d 27, 34 n. 6 (2d Cir.1982); 1–3 Nimmer on Copyright §3.06 (2002). However, there is an important limitation suggested by both authorities and ignored entirely by Plaintiff: copyright protection does not extend "to derivative works if the pre-existing work tends to pervade the entire derivative work." Nimmer at §3.06 (emphasis added); Eden Toys, 697 F.2d at 34 n. 6 (quoting Nimmer).

Thus, the court in *Anderson v. Stallone* held that a spec script for a fourth Rocky movie (building from the characters and plot of the previous three) was pervaded by copyrighted characters from the first three movies, and thus not entitled to copyright protection. 1989 WL 206431, at *5, 8–11 (April 25, 1989).

Likewise, the Seventh Circuit recently suggested that no copyright obtains in any portion of an unauthorized derivative work. *Pickett v. Prince*, 207 F.3d 402 (7th Cir. 2000). Writing

CASE *(continued)*

for a unanimous panel, Judge Posner concluded that section 103(a) should not be read "as qualifying the exclusive right of the owner of a copyright of the original work to make derivative works based on that work . . ." Id. at 406. Rather, "[s]ection 103(a) means only . . . that the right to make a derivative work does not authorize the maker to incorporate into it material that infringes someone else's copyright." The *Pickett* court explicitly rejected the dicta in *Eden Toys, Inc.*, 697 F.2d at 34 n. 6 (suggesting that copyright might subsist in a derivative work making unauthorized use of other copyrighted work, provided the original work does not "pervade" the derivative work). Id. Judge Posner concluded that this principle, "if taken seriously (which it has not been), would inject enormous uncertainty into the law of copyright and undermine the exclusive right that section 106(2) gives the owner of the copyright on the original work." Id.

The Court need not reconcile these potentially conflicting authorities. Copyrighted Jack-in-the-Box commercial footage, and, particularly, the Jack antenna ball head character, are integrated into and integral to Plaintiff's Spec Commercials. Indeed, Plaintiff's counsel at hearing on this Motion specifically stated that it would be impossible to compare the works at issue in this case without reference to the Jack head.

Because copyrighted work pervades the derivative work, and because Plaintiff used the previous work without authorization, no copyright protection is afforded under either *Eden Toys* or *Pickett*.

This conclusion highlights an additional reason why Plaintiff's claims likely fail. Even assuming Plaintiff is entitled to copyright protection in certain remaining elements of his Spec Commercials, the residuum seem insufficient to allow Plaintiff to prevail on his claims. If the proprietary Jack-in-the-Box elements are ignored, all that remains is a largely unoriginal and elementary spoof of the (copyrighted) Cast Away movie. Since Plaintiff does not argue that the dialog employed in Radical's commercial is similar in any respect to that authored by Plaintiff, the only remaining similarities owe to the commercials' common Cast Away derivation. And since the mere *idea* of placing Jack-in-the-Box characters and footage in a Cast Away context is, of course, not copyrightable, there would remain virtually no independent similarity. Because this issue is not necessary to the Court's holding, however, the Court refrains from deciding it.

NOTES AND QUESTIONS

1. One aspect of the case turns on the distinction between two types of derivative works: those where the new material is easily severable or removable from the material derived from an underlying work; and those where the new material pervades the entire work. For the former, consider an example: Imagine a new episode of the *Star Wars* films where a new character, not found in any previous movies, is introduced. The first scene involves the new character interacting with old, established characters from the earlier films. Say, for example, the new character is given a commission to conduct a secret mission, with various characters from the old films explaining the mission and its importance. Then the other scenes

from the movie involve only the new character and new situations; none of the old characters reappear, and none of the old background, space ships, settings, etc., are used again; all the action, dialogue, and setting are new. This would clearly be a protectible derivative work under the test announced in *Sobhani* (do you see why?). In many cases, however, it can be very difficult to distinguish between a derivative work that is "separable" and one that "pervades the entire original" material. *See, e.g., Wolf v. Travolta*, No. CV14-938-CAS(VBKX), 2016 WL 3150552, at *17 (C.D. Cal. Feb. 4, 2016) (denying summary judgment on this issue, because it is a factually intensive inquiry that can be decided only after a full trial on the merits).

2. The issue in this case often arises when works are done speculatively, or "on spec." An aspiring creator uses an established underlying work to show his or her talent, and to "audition" for a creative position on the authorized team of people doing creative projects related to the underlying work. Is the legal treatment of the aspiring creative person fair? Would it be more fair to give the aspiring creator some kind of rights in his or her contribution, regardless of whether that contribution was severable from the underlying work or pervades that work? Would the aspiring creator's rights have to be a property right? Are there other ways to recognize their contributions or at least prevent the unauthorized use of those contributions?

3. A *compilation* is defined as:

> a work formed by the collection and assembling of preexisting materials or of data that are selected, coordinated, or arranged in such a way that the resulting work as a whole constitutes an original work of authorship... (17 U.S.C. §101).

In addition, a special type of compilation is known as a collective work. These are works "such as a periodical issue, anthology, or encyclopedia, in which a number of contributions, constituting separate and independent works in themselves, are assembled into a collective whole" (*id.*). Thus the difference between a compilation and a collective work is that the former involves the assemblage of material which may or may not be copyrighted or copyrightable; while the latter involves assemblage of works which are copyrighted or copyrightable. A book listing the names of authors and their home towns would be a compilation, while a book with excerpts from the authors' greatest works would be a collective work. Note that because registration of a copyright is a prerequisite to a court enforcement action, it sometimes occurs that a registration for a collective work is argued to be insufficient to permit enforcement of copyright in one constituent work contained in the collective work. Courts have generally held that, where the copyright owner of the collective work is also the copyright owner of a separate constituent work, the collective copyright registration will suffice. *See Xoom, Inc. v. Imageline, Inc.*, 323 F.3d 279, 283 (4th Cir. 2003) (adopting view "that where owner of a collective work also owns the copyright for a constituent part of that work, registration of the collective work is sufficient to permit an infringement action of the constituent part"); *King Records, Inc. v. Bennett*, 438 F. Supp. 2d 812, 841 (M.D. Tenn. 2006) (applying this rule to a collection of musical works).

4. **Fair use defense**: The Nimmer on Copyright treatise notes: "The House Report comments on the fact that ... Section 103(a) conditions copyright in a derivative or collective work upon the pre-existing material not having been used 'unlawfully' rather than merely without the consent of the copyright owner of such pre-existing material" 1–3 Nimmer on Copyright §3.06, citing House Report, 1976 Copyright Act). From this, the treatise says that a derivative work which qualifies for the fair use exemption may give rise to a valid copyright in the new material that is added. In the *Sobhani* case, this would mean that, if the aspiring director's use of the copyrighted material from Jack-in-the-Box *and* the film Cast Away were both fair use, the director might have a valid copyright in the added material. How did the judge in *Sobhani* handle this issue? Is it also necessary that the new added material be independently copyrightable?

12.2.2.2 China

BAI Xian-Yong v. Shanghai Film Group, [2014] Shanghai No. 2 Intermediate Court, Huerminwuzhichuzi No. 83

Plaintiff BAI Xian-Yong ("BAI") sued Co-defendants Shanghai Film Group Co. ("SFG"),Shanghai Yi-Xiang Culture Communication Ltd. ("Yi-Xiang"), and Shanghai Jun-Zheng Culture and Arts Development Ltd. ("Jun-Zheng") regarding a copyright infringement dispute.

Plaintiff BAI is a well-known writer in Taiwan and also the author of the novel *Goddess in Exile* ("Novel"). The Novel was first published in the twenty-fifth issue of the magazine *Contemporary Literature* in 1965 in Taiwan. In 2005, the Novel was published in the *Collections of Awarded Authors in The First Beijing Literature Festival – BAI Xian-Yong* in Mainland China and later included in other publications in Mainland China.

In 1989, with BAI's authorization, Shanghai Film Studio, a subsidiary of SFG, adapted the Novel into a movie titled *The Last Aristocrats* ("Movie"). The Movie was directed by the acclaimed director Mr. XIE Jin and released within a year. In 2013, Co-defendant Yi-Xiang prepared to adapt the Movie into a stage drama ("Drama") under the same title. On August 31, 2013, Yi-Xiang held a press conference to announce the production of the Drama in commemoration of XIE Jin's 90th Birthday. Mr. GE Hongwei ("Mr. GE"), General Manager of Yi-Xiang, discussed the production of the Drama at the press conference. Plaintiff's photo was also used as the background during the press conference.

On October 16, 2013, SFG reached a license agreement (License Agreement) with Yi-Xiang, which includes the following provisions:

> SFG hereby licenses Yi-Xiang to use its Movie under the following terms: (1) SFG authorizes Yi-Xiang to use elements of the Movie *inter alia*, the plot, script, setting, music, stage design and other elements in the Movie that Yi-Xiang deems necessary to prepare for the Drama; (2) SFG guarantees that it owns the copyright and right of images to the Movie, and that the Movie does not infringe any other party's copyright or other rights; (3) SFG guarantees that Yi-Xiang will not be involved in any copyright or other IP disputes when adapting the Drama based on the Movie, and that no other third party will impose liability against Yi-Xiang . . .

Since early December 2013, the Drama has been promoted under the joint names of SFG, Yi-Xiang and Jun-Zheng. SFG allegedly co-hosted a promotional event at Shanghai People's Grand Stage ("Shanghai Stage") with Yi-Xiang and Jun-Zheng. Pamphlets and posters for the Drama indicated that the Drama was made "[i]n honor of Director XIE Jin's 90th Birthday" and that the performance was hosted by SFG and sponsored by Yi-Xiang and

CASE *(continued)*

Jun-Zheng. The promotional materials also indicated that the Drama would be performed six times at Shanghai Stage from December 17–22, 2013.

On December 16, 2013, Plaintiff BAI issued a public notice to the media and a warning letter to Yi-Xiang and Shanghai Stage, requesting Co-defendants to immediately stop the infringement. However, BAI's letter did not receive much attention from Co-defendants, and the alleged infringing Drama continued its performance at Shanghai Stage from December 17 to 22. The Drama turned out to be a big success, grossing over 1,849,320 RMB [$278,395] revenue at the box office, and also attracted wide media coverage.

Plaintiff claimed that, Co-defendants' Drama was an unauthorized derivative work made based on his prior Novel. Since Plaintiff owns copyright to the Novel and never authorized Co-defendants to produce the Drama based on the Novel, Co-defendants violated his copyright to the Novel. Plaintiff also claimed that SFG, producer of the Movie, also infringed his copyright by authorizing a third party (Yi-Xiang and Jun-Zheng) to make a derivative work (the Drama) based on his underlying Novel, without his permission.

Co-defendant SFG counterclaimed that: SFG obtained permission from the copyright owner of the Movie – Shanghai Film Studio – before it authorized Yi-Xiang to produce the Drama based on the Movie; [and that] [t]he Drama was produced not for commercial purpose, but as a tribute to the acclaimed director XIE Jin, Director of the Movie. Also, SFG derived no economic benefits from the Drama.

Co-defendants Yi-Xiang and Jun-Zheng counterclaimed that: (1) they obtained permission from SFG to adapt the Movie into the Drama. They also attempted to acquire authorization from BAI through an intermediary person, which showed their good faith efforts; (2) The Drama was made as a tribute to the Movie's director XIE Jin; and (3) since most of the tickets to the Drama were distributed as gifts for free, they did not earn profits from producing and performing the Drama, but actually suffered an economic loss instead.

Shanghai No. 2 Intermediate Court found that there was no dispute that Co-defendants Yi-Xiang and Jun-Zheng adapted the Movie into the Drama bearing the same title. The issues of this case can be summarized as follows: (1) whether Yi-Xiang and Jun-Zheng obtained appropriate authorization from BAI and SFG to prepare the Drama based on the underlying works; (2) whether SFG had authority to license Yi-Xiang the right of adaptation to produce the Drama; and (3) allocation of civil liabilities among Co-defendants should copyright infringement be established.

1. Whether Yi-Xiang and Jun-Zheng's adaptation was authorized by BAI and SFG
Pursuant to Item 2 Article 37 of Chinese Copyright Law, "To perform a work created by adaptation, translation, annotation or arrangement of a pre-existing work, the party shall obtain permission from and pay remuneration to both the owner of the copyright in the work created by adaptation, translation, annotation or arrangement, and the owner of the copyright in the original work." The dispute here arose from Yi-Xiang and Jun-Zheng's stage adaptation of the Movie. Since the Movie was adapted based on the prior Novel authored by BAI, thus the Movie is a derivative work based on Plaintiff's underlying Novel.

CASE *(continued)*

A derivative work is a work created based on an original, copyrightable pre-existing work. Copyright protection in a derivative work only extends to the new, original materials in the derivative work that is contributed by the latter author. Therefore, the copyright to the pre-existing materials in a derivative work remains with the original author of the underlying work. As such, to prepare a second derivative work based on the first derivative work, permission needs to be obtained from both copyright owner of the first derivative work and also copyright owner of the underlying original work.

Here, SFG owns copyright to the Movie after it got permission from BAI, copyright owner of the underlying Novel, to prepare the Movie based on the Novel. However, since the Movie was a derivative work based on the prior Novel, when Yi-Xiang and Jun-Zheng decided to make another work "the Drama" based on the Movie, they should get authorization from both the copyright owner of the underlying Novel – BAI, and also the copyright owner of the Movie – SFG, in order to adapt the Movie into the Drama.

(1) Authorization from the copyright owner of the Movie

Since SFG, producer and copyright owner of the Movie, authorized Yi-Xiang in the License Agreement, to use original elements from the Movie to create the Drama, this Court finds that Yi-Xiang has obtained necessary authorization from the copyright owner of the Movie when adapting the Movie into the Drama.

(2) Authorization from the copyright owner of the underlying Novel

BAI argued that although SFG was authorized to make the Movie based on the Novel, SFG did not have the permission to authorize other people to make other derivative works based on the Novel.

SFG responded that, as copyright owner to the Movie, SFG only authorized Yi-Xiang to use elements from the Movie, and such an authorization did not extend to copyrightable elements in the underlying Novel. SFG agreed that Yi-Xiang should obtain authorization from BAI separately. (The fact that Yi-Xiang failed to get consent from BAI was not SFG's responsibility).

Yi-Xiang and Jun-Zheng argued that, according to the provisions in the Licensing Agreement that they signed with SFG, they were authorized to prepare derivative works based on the Novel and the Movie.

This Court finds that, pursuant to Article 15 of Chinese Copyright Law, "director, screenwriter, lyricist, composer and cameraman in a cinematographic work shall enjoy the right of authorship in the work, while the copyright of the work vests with its producer." Article 12 also stipulates that where a work is created by adaptation, translation, annotation or arrangement of a pre-existing work, the copyright in the derivative work belongs to the adapter, translator or arranger, provided that the exercise of such copyright shall not prejudice the copyright in the underlying original work.

Based on the above facts and evidence, this Court rules as follows:

(1) The Licensing Agreement between SFG and Yi-Xiang was drafted by GE's lawyer and signed by SFG's representative. The Licensing Agreement indicates that SFG was the producer of the Movie, thus enjoyed copyright to the Movie. However, SFG did not have

CASE *(continued)*

authority to grant a license on behalf of BAI. Nor did the existing evidence suggest that SFG intended to grant a license on behalf of BAI to use the underlying materials in the underlying Novel. In other words, in addition to SFG's permission, Yi-Xiang still needed to obtain authorization from BAI to prepare the Drama.

(2) Mr. GE's testimony suggested that Yi-Xiang was fully aware that it needed to obtain authorization from the author of the underlying Novel – BAI, because Yi-Xiang had tried to contact BAI for authorization several times, both before and after it entered the Licensing Agreement with SFG.

(3) BAI failed to provide sufficient evidence to prove that SFG was involved in the adaptation or performance of the infringing Drama. Also Yi-Xiang and Jun-Zheng both testified that they completed the adaptation of the Drama independently without participation from SFG.

In view of the above, this court finds that, first of all, Yi-Xiang and Jun-Zheng prepared the Drama, a derivative work based on the Novel, without BAI's authorization. Such activities infringed BAI's copyright to the Novel, including the right of authorship, the right of adaptation and the right to remuneration. Second, SFG's license to Yi-Xiang to authorize them to make the Drama based on the Movie did not constitute infringement of BAI's copyright, thus SFG was not found liable in the copyright dispute.

NOTES AND QUESTIONS

1. Unlike the 1976 Copyright Act in the US, Chinese copyright law does not have one specific provision addressing "the right to prepare derivative works." Instead, it is discussed in a number of provisions related to "the right to adapt, the right to translate, the right to prepare cinematographic works and the right to compile." *See* Article 10(13)–(16) of PRC Copyright Law (2010).
2. The *BAI v. SFG* opinion did not expressly tell us what kind of authorization that SFG received from BAI, *i.e.* a license or an assignment, when SFG made the Movie based on BAI's prior underlying Novel. As you might recall from your contract class, a license means permission to use, but does not usually involve change of ownership for the underlying property; while an assignment, on the other hand, involves transfer of ownership in the underlying property. In the entertainment industry, when a studio decides to make a movie based on an underlying literature work, they will always try to secure an assignment, versus a license, for the right to make a movie. Why do you think this is the case?
3. In the US during the 1930s, there was a debate between writers and movie studios as to whether copyrights were "divisible rights." Writers proposed to "lease or license" their scripts to studios, instead of "selling or assigning" the entire copyright, in the belief that by leasing the script, they could retain the right to develop a script if the studio decided not to put it into production. This idea was rejected by the studios who were concerned that a license to use the copyright might void the copyright entirely. The debate ended in the 1950s, with the conclusion of the Writers Guild of America Theatrical and Television Basic Agreement ("MBA"), which recognized that copyrights were divisible rights and can be assigned separately. Under the MBA, studios agree to pay separate consideration to writers if they were to acquire the publication, stage and radio rights of the script, in addition to the movie right. Nowadays, the concept that copyrights are divisible and can be assigned separately also extends to other categories of rights, such as theme park rights, merchandise rights and gaming rights, etc. *See* Seagull Haiyan Song, *China's Copyright Protection for Audio-Visual Works: A Comparison with Europe and the U.S.*, IIC – 46(4) International Review of Intellectual Property and Competition Law (2015). Note that a writer or actor with market power can

insist on payment whether a movie is made or not, in what is called a "pay or play" agreement. *See* Victor P. Goldberg, *Bloomer Girl Revisited or How to Frame an Unmade Picture*, 1998 Wis. L. Rev. 1051 (1998). Now let us take one of the best-seller book series *Harry Potter* for example, do you know which companies have obtained the book rights, movie rights, theme park rights and gaming rights for this underlying work?

12.2.2.3 Europe

CASE

German Federal Court of Justice (Bundesgerichtshof), Case I ZR 12/08, IIC 2011, 978: "Pearl Driver" ("Perlentaucher")

The plaintiff publishes the Frankfurter Allgemeine Zeitung (FAZ) [the premier daily newspaper in Germany]. It is the holder of the word trade marks "Frankfurter Allgemeine Zeitung" and "FAZ" registered *inter alia* for newspapers and magazines. The defendant operates a culture magazine on the website "perlentaucher.de", where it also placed summaries (abstracts) of book reviews from various well-known newspapers. These include book reviews from the FAZ, which the defendant reproduces in considerably abbreviated form under the title "Notiz zur FAZ (Notes on the FAZ)". The abstracts are written by the defendant's employees and contain particularly informative passages from the original reviews, mostly indicated by the use of quotation marks. The defendant has granted the internet bookstores "amazon.de" and "buecher.de" licences to reproduce these summaries. The following sets out an example of an original review ("Revolution im Schlafsack") and the corresponding summary ("Notiz zur FAZ dated 23 December 2004"): ...

The plaintiff regards this exploitation of the abstracts by means of the grant of licences to third parties as an infringement of its copyright in the reviews published in the FAZ, an infringement of the rights to the trade marks "Frankfurter Allgemeine Zeitung" and "FAZ" and an infringement of competition law from the point of view of an avoidable deception as to origin, unreasonable exploitation of reputation and dishonest impediment.

The plaintiff has petitioned that the defendant be ordered, on pain of a penalty, to refrain

1. primarily (main petition): from distributing and/or permitting the distribution of summaries of book reviews (abstracts) from the "Frankfurter Allgemeine Zeitung" that reproduce the content of the original review above all, but not only exclusively by adopting sections of the original text, and to refrain from licensing and/or permitting the licensing of the rights to such to the said third parties, . . .
2. alternatively to 1: from distributing and/or permitting the distribution of summaries of book reviews (abstracts) that reproduce the content of the original review by adopting original sections of the text that are placed next to each other merely using filler words or partial sentences and to refrain from licensing and/or permitting the licensing

CASE *(continued)*

of the rights to such to the said third parties, in particular if such occurs as in the "Perlentaucher reviews";
3. alternatively to 2: from distributing and/or permitting the distribution of summaries of book reviews (abstracts) from the "Frankfurter Allgemeine Zeitung" that reproduce the content of the original reviews by [specific] authors by adopting sections of the original text, and to refrain from licensing and/or permitting the licensing of the rights to such to the said third parties;
4. alternatively to 3: from distributing and/or permitting the distribution of the "Perlentaucher reviews" via third-party internet websites such as "amazon.de" and "buecher.de" and licensing and/or permitting the licensing of the rights to such to the said third parties;

In addition, the plaintiff has also claimed the disclosure of information and a finding of damages, in each case related to the petitions for injunctions referred to above and the actions identified therein.

The district court dismissed the action. The plaintiff's appeal was unsuccessful. In its appeal on the law, admitted by the appeal court, the plaintiff pursues its petition, the dismissal of which is requested by the defendant.

. . .

The appeal on the law is partially successful to the extent that it objects to the appeal court's decision against the plaintiff with respect to the second, third and fourth petitions.

I. Claims based on copyright.
1. The appeal court rightly assumed that the claims asserted by the plaintiff in the second and third petitions are unfounded to the extent that they are based on an infringement of the copyright in the original reviews.

. . .

This assessment can be upheld on appeal on the law. The admissibility under copyright law of an exploitation of the abstracts depends on whether these are to be regarded as dependent adaptations (Sec. 23 Copyright Act) or as free use (Sec. 24 of the Act) of the original reviews . . . The decisive factor here is the extent to which the new work agrees with the work used in features on which the creative individuality of the work used is based. The mere fact that the new work contains sections of the original text of the work used that are only separated by filler words or partial sentences (second petition) or contains sections of the original text of the works by specific authors (third petition) therefore does not mean that the new work is a dependent adaptation of the older work. This for instance is not the case if the sections of the original text adopted are common expressions. Where the second and third petitions are based on an infringement of copyright, they therefore do not address the specific form of the infringement and are thus unfounded as a whole.

. . .

2. The appeal court rightly assumed that the fourth petition did not go too far because its

CASE *(continued)*

subject matter was the contested Perlentaucher reviews and hence the concrete form of the infringement. The appeal on the law rightly objects that the appeal court regarded the fourth petition as unfounded to the extent that it is based on an infringement of the copyright in the entire text of the relevant original review.

a) The appeal court rightly assumed that the original reviews were personal intellectual creations in the light of their literary quality (Sec. 2(2) Copyright Act) and hence were protected literary works (Sec. 2(1) No. 1 of the Act). . . .

c) The appeal court also assumed that the abstracts in question were not adaptations or transformations of the original reviews; on the contrary, the abstracts were to be regarded as independent works that had been created in free use of the original reviews and that pursuant to Sec. 24(1) of the Act could be published and exploited without the consent of the author of the work used. The objections put forward in the appeal on the law to this assessment are upheld.

aa) The provision of Sec. 24 of the Act is applicable to the case at issue, since the abstracts are works within the meaning of the Copyright Act, *i.e.* personal intellectual creations (Sec. 2(2) of the Act). . . ..

This assessment by the appeal court is susceptible to legal reservations. The appeal court wrongly assumed that the determination whether an abstract is to be regarded as a dependent adaptation or a free use of an original work is subject not to the conventional but rather to special standards (see 1). In addition, the appeal court's view that the abstracts in question were to be assumed to be a free use of the original reviews is based on incomplete findings (see 2).

(1) According to the established judicial practice of this court, the answer to the question whether an independent new work has been created in free use of a protected older work depends decisively on the distance that the new work maintains to the individual features borrowed from the work used. As the appeal court still rightly assumed, a free use requires that the individual features borrowed from the protected older work pale into insignificance in the light of the individuality of the new work. As a rule, this precondition is satisfied if the individual features borrowed from the protected older work fade into the background with the result that the use of the older work by the newer one only appears as a stimulus for the creation of a new and independent work.

The distance to the borrowed individual features of the work used as required for a free use can, even where there are considerable adoptions, also be satisfied if the new work maintains such a large internal distance to the individual features borrowed from the older work that it is to be regarded as independent by its nature. In such a case, too, it can be said, contrary to the appeal court's opinion, that the individual features borrowed from the older work "pale into insignificance" in the more recent work. [Parodies are an example of this.]

The copyrighted creative individuality of a book review is as a rule not to be found in its content but rather in its form and in particular its phrasing. In a literary work, the

CASE *(continued)*

copyrighted individual intellectual creation can be expressed both in the composition of the language molded by the line of thoughts and in the collection, selection, classification and arrangement of the material. Where on the other hand the creative force of a literary work is to be found solely in the innovative character of its content, there can be no possibility of copyright protection. The notional content of a literary work must be accessible to free intellectual discussion. The idea underlying a literary work is therefore as a matter of principle not protected by copyright. The case may be different if this idea has been given an individual form, such as for instance is the case in the individual intellectual composition of the material of a novel.

According to general experience, it is certainly possible to summarise the notional content of a literary work, and hence the content of a book review, in the writer's own words. If the literary work, like a book review as a rule, enjoys copyright protection solely on the basis of its linguistic composition, such a summary as a matter of principle constitutes a free use of this literary work that cannot be contested under copyright law within the meaning of Sec. 24(1) of the Copyright Act. If such a summary also contains phrasing on which the creative individuality of the literary work is based, it must be examined whether the result is a dependent adaptation or a free use. This examination, which is primarily the function of the trial judge, requires no special criteria but instead the conventional principles apply. According to these, the decisive factor is whether the summary, despite these agreements, maintains, in an overall view, so great an external distance to the literary work that it is to be regarded as an independent new work.

(2) The appeal on the law rightly objects to the incompleteness of the findings on which the appeal court based its decision that the abstracts at issue were to be assumed to be a free use of the original reviews.

The appeal court's finding that the word-for-word adoption of text passages from the original reviews in the abstracts was limited to individual words or brief sequences of words is correct to the extent that the sections adopted word for word only constitute a small extract from the original reviews. However, the appeal court ought to have taken account of the share of the abstracts accounted for by the sections adopted. The comparison of abstracts and original reviews submitted by the plaintiff shows that many abstracts consisted to a large extent or even for the most part of original sections of the text adopted word for word. Even if the word-for-word adoption, as the appeal court assumed, was in part hardly avoidable given the descriptive nature of text passages, numerous abstracts adopted to a considerable extent the particularly informative and inventively worded phrases of the original reviews.

The appeal court's finding that the defendant had compressed into six to nine lines the original reviews that were often many times as long, does not take sufficient account of the fact that the abstracts often do not summarise the original reviews in their own words but simply shorten them by firstly omitting entire sections and sentences of the original reviews (mainly those that reproduce the content of the work reviewed) and secondly retain word for word particularly informative and striking phrases (mainly those that contain an evaluation of the book discussed).

CASE *(continued)*

It cannot be assumed that the application of the general rules would not in most cases permit the writing of brief summaries of another's works, without which the flood of information could not be mastered. In general, the author of the summary of a literary work is able to maintain a sufficient distance to the original work. As a matter of principle, he can make use of the entire bandwidth of linguistic means of expression, with the result that he is in most cases capable of summarising the other's literary work in his own words. He is not prevented from adopting phrases that are common in the field in question. He is at liberty to reproduce the general content of the original. . . .

Admittedly, small parts of the work can also enjoy copyright protection provided that they themselves constitute personal intellectual creations within the meaning of Sec. 2(2) of the Copyright Act. Subject to these conditions, even small parts of a literary work can enjoy copyright protection (cf. Art. 2a of Directive 2001/29 of the European Parliament and Council dated 22 May 2001 on the approximation of certain aspects of copyright and related rights in the information society). However, in the case of very small parts of a literary work – such as individual words or brief sequences of words – copyright protection will in most cases fail due to these of themselves not being sufficiently individual.

According to these criteria, there can be no objection, contrary to the view put forward in the appeal on the law, based on legal reasons to the appeal court's opinion that individual words and sequences of words in the original reviews were not of themselves protected by copyright.

. . .

D. Accordingly, on appeal on the law by the plaintiff, the appeal decision is set aside. [T]he appeal court will again have to examine whether the abstracts at issue are adaptations or transformations of the original reviews, which pursuant to Sec. 23 sentence 1 of the Copyright Act cannot be published and exploited without the consent of the author of the original reviews. This decision can lead to different results for different abstracts, since this question cannot be answered generally but only on the basis of an assessment of each individual case.

NOTES AND QUESTIONS

1. While the Information Society Directive has harmonized the right of reproduction, distribution, and of communication to the public across all copyrightable subject matter, the right to make derivate works has not received comparable attention on an EU level. As a result, Member State copyright law and cases still play an important role.
2. German copyright law distinguishes between "free uses" of a copyrighted work, which do not require a license (Sec. 24 German Copyright Act), and "dependent uses," which do require a license (Sec. 23 German Copyright Act). In the decision you have just read, the court follows its established case law that, in order to qualify as a free use, a new work has to demonstrate sufficient distance from the original work. Does this spatial metaphor of the "distance" between an original work and a follow-on work make the issues more easily understood? Do you find it natural to apply this metaphor to questions of copyright infringement?
3. Sec. 12(1) German Copyright Act grants authors "a right to determine whether and how his work shall be

published." It is part of Germany's strong protection for authors' moral rights (*see infra* 12.3.2). Sec. 12(2) goes even further by granting an author "the right to communicate or describe the content of his work to the public as long as neither the work nor the essential content or a description of the work has been published with his consent." The court had to deal with the argument that one could conclude from this provision that authors do not have any exclusive right to communicate the content of their work once it has been published. What are arguments supporting such an *argumentum e contrario*, and what would the policy implications of such limitation on moral rights be?

12.2.3 Right to distribute and to communicate to the public

12.2.3.1 United States

American Broadcast Companies, Inc. v. Aereo, Inc., 134 S. Ct. 2498 (2014)

Breyer, J.
The Copyright Act of 1976 gives a copyright owner the "exclusive righ[t]" to "perform the copyrighted work publicly." 17 U.S.C. §106(4). The Act's Transmit Clause defines that exclusive right as including the right to

> transmit or otherwise communicate a performance . . . of the [copyrighted] work . . . to the public, by means of any device or process, whether the members of the public capable of receiving the performance . . . receive it in the same place or in separate places and at the same time or at different times.

§101. We must decide whether respondent Aereo, Inc., infringes this exclusive right by selling its subscribers a technologically complex service that allows them to watch television programs over the Internet at about the same time as the programs are broadcast over the air. We conclude that it does.

For a monthly fee, Aereo offers subscribers broadcast television programming over the Internet, virtually as the programming is being broadcast. Much of this programming is made up of copyrighted works. Aereo neither owns the copyright in those works nor holds a license from the copyright owners to perform those works publicly.

Aereo's system is made up of servers, transcoders, and thousands of dime-sized antennas housed in a central warehouse. It works roughly as follows: First, when a subscriber wants to watch a show that is currently being broadcast, he visits Aereo's website and selects, from a list of the local programming, the show he wishes to see.

Second, one of Aereo's servers selects an antenna, which it dedicates to the use of that subscriber (and that subscriber alone) for the duration of the selected show. A server then tunes the antenna to the over-the-air broadcast carrying the show. The antenna begins to

CASE *(continued)*

receive the broadcast, and an Aereo transcoder translates the signals received into data that can be transmitted over the Internet.

Third, rather than directly send the data to the subscriber, a server saves the data in a subscriber-specific folder on Aereo's hard drive. In other words, Aereo's system creates a subscriber-specific copy – that is, a "personal" copy – of the subscriber's program of choice.

Fourth, once several seconds of programming have been saved, Aereo's server begins to stream the saved copy of the show to the subscriber over the Internet. (The subscriber may instead direct Aereo to stream the program at a later time, but that aspect of Aereo's service is not before us.) The subscriber can watch the streamed program on the screen of his personal computer, tablet, smart phone, Internet-connected television, or other Internet-connected device. The streaming continues, a mere few seconds behind the over-the-air broadcast, until the subscriber has received the entire show. See A Dictionary of Computing 494 (6th ed. 2008) (defining "streaming" as "[t]he process of providing a steady flow of audio or video data so that an Internet user is able to access it as it is transmitted").

Petitioners are television producers, marketers, distributors, and broadcasters who own the copyrights in many of the programs that Aereo's system streams to its subscribers. They brought suit against Aereo for copyright infringement in Federal District Court.

The District Court denied the preliminary injunction. 874 F.Supp.2d 373 (S.D.N.Y.2012). Relying on prior Circuit precedent, a divided panel of the Second Circuit affirmed. *WNET, Thirteen v. Aereo, Inc.*, 712 F.3d 676 (2013) (citing *Cartoon Network LP, LLLP v. CSC Holdings, Inc.*, 536 F.3d 121 (2008)). In the Second Circuit's view, Aereo does not perform publicly within the meaning of the Transmit Clause because it does not transmit "to the public." Rather, each time Aereo streams a program to a subscriber, it sends a private transmission that is available only to that subscriber.

This case requires us to answer two questions: First, in operating in the manner described above, does Aereo "perform" at all? And second, if so, does Aereo do so "publicly"? We address these distinct questions in turn.

Does Aereo "transmit . . . a performance" when a subscriber watches a show using Aereo's system, or is it only the subscriber who transmits? In Aereo's view, it does not perform. It does no more than supply equipment that "emulate[s] the operation of a home antenna and [digital video recorder (DVR)]." Like a home antenna and DVR, Aereo's equipment simply responds to its subscribers' directives. So it is only the subscribers who "perform" when they use Aereo's equipment to stream television programs to themselves.

When read in light of its purpose, the Act is unmistakable: An entity that engages in activities like Aereo's performs.

History makes plain that one of Congress' primary purposes in amending the Copyright Act in 1976 was to overturn this Court's determination that community antenna television (CATV) systems (the precursors of modern cable systems) fell outside the Act's scope. In *Fortnightly Corp. v. United Artists Television, Inc.*, 392 U.S. 390 (1968), the Court considered a CATV system that carried local television broadcasting, much of which was copyrighted, to its subscribers in two cities. The CATV provider placed antennas on hills

CASE *(continued)*

above the cities and used coaxial cables to carry the signals received by the antennas to the home television sets of its subscribers.

Asked to decide whether the CATV provider infringed copyright holders' exclusive right to perform their works publicly, the Court held that the provider did not "perform" at all. The Court drew a line: "Broadcasters perform. Viewers do not perform." 392 U.S., at 398. And a CATV provider "falls on the viewer's side of the line." Id., at 399.

The Court reasoned that CATV providers were unlike broadcasters:

"Broadcasters select the programs to be viewed; CATV systems simply carry, without editing, whatever programs they receive."

In *Teleprompter Corp. v. Columbia Broadcasting System, Inc.*, 415 U.S. 394 (1974), [the Court reached the same conclusion where the CATV system captured broadcasts and transmitted them to subscribers hundreds of miles away].

In 1976 Congress amended the Copyright Act in large part to reject the Court's holdings in *Fortnightly* and *Teleprompter*. Congress enacted new language that erased the Court's line between broadcaster and viewer, in respect to "perform[ing]" a work. The amended statute clarifies that to "perform" an audiovisual work means "to show its images in any sequence or to make the sounds accompanying it audible." §101. Under this new language, both the broadcaster and the viewer of a television program "perform," because they both show the program's images and make audible the program's sounds.

Congress also enacted the Transmit Clause, which specifies that an entity performs publicly when it "transmit[s] . . . a performance . . . to the public." §101. Cable system activities, like those of the CATV systems in *Fortnightly* and *Teleprompter*, lie at the heart of the activities that Congress intended this language to cover. The Clause thus makes clear that an entity that acts like a CATV system itself performs, even if when doing so, it simply enhances viewers' ability to receive broadcast television signals.

This history makes clear that Aereo is not simply an equipment provider. Rather, Aereo, and not just its subscribers, "perform[s]" (or "transmit[s]"). Aereo's activities are substantially similar to those of the CATV companies that Congress amended the Act to reach. Aereo's equipment may serve a "viewer function"; it may enhance the viewer's ability to receive a broadcaster's programs. It may even emulate equipment a viewer could use at home. But the same was true of the equipment that was before the Court, and ultimately before Congress, in *Fortnightly* and *Teleprompter*.

We recognize, and Aereo and the dissent emphasize, one particular difference between Aereo's system and the cable systems at issue in *Fortnightly* and *Teleprompter*. The systems in those cases transmitted constantly; they sent continuous programming to each subscriber's television set. In contrast, Aereo's system remains inert until a subscriber indicates that she wants to watch a program. Only at that moment, in automatic response to the subscriber's request, does Aereo's system activate an antenna and begin to transmit the requested program.

This is a critical difference, says the dissent. It means that Aereo's subscribers, not Aereo, "selec[t] the copyrighted content" that is "perform [ed]," post, at 2513 (opinion of SCALIA, J.), and for that reason they, not Aereo, "transmit" the performance.

CASE (continued)

Given Aereo's overwhelming likeness to the cable companies targeted by the 1976 amendments, this sole technological difference between Aereo and traditional cable companies does not make a critical difference here. The subscribers of the *Fortnightly* and *Teleprompter* cable systems also selected what programs to display on their receiving sets. The same is true of an Aereo subscriber. Of course, in *Fortnightly* the television signals, in a sense, lurked behind the screen, ready to emerge when the subscriber turned the knob. Here the signals pursue their ordinary course of travel through the universe until today's "turn of the knob" – a click on a website – activates machinery that intercepts and reroutes them to Aereo's subscribers over the Internet. But this difference means nothing to the subscriber. It means nothing to the broadcaster. We do not see how this single difference, invisible to subscriber and broadcaster alike, could transform a system that is for all practical purposes a traditional cable system into "a copy shop that provides its patrons with a library card."

Next, we must consider whether Aereo performs petitioners' works "publicly," within the meaning of the Transmit Clause. Under the Clause, an entity performs a work publicly when it "transmit[s] . . . a performance . . . of the work . . . to the public." §101. Aereo denies that it satisfies this definition. It reasons as follows: First, the "performance" it "transmit[s]" is the performance created by its act of transmitting. And second, because each of these performances is capable of being received by one and only one subscriber, Aereo transmits privately, not publicly. Even assuming Aereo's first argument is correct, its second does not follow.

We begin with Aereo's first argument. Petitioners say Aereo transmits a *prior* performance of their works. Thus when Aereo retransmits a network's prior broadcast, the underlying broadcast (itself a performance) is the performance that Aereo transmits. Aereo, as discussed above, says the performance it transmits is the *new* performance created by its act of transmitting. That performance comes into existence when Aereo streams the sounds and images of a broadcast program to a subscriber's screen.

We assume *arguendo* that Aereo's first argument is correct. Thus, for present purposes, to transmit a performance of (at least) an audiovisual work means to communicate contemporaneously visible images and contemporaneously audible sounds of the work. Cf. *United States v. American Soc. of Composers, Authors and Publishers*, 627 F.3d 64, 73 (C.A.2 2010) (holding that a download of a work is not a performance because the data transmitted are not "contemporaneously perceptible"). When an Aereo subscriber selects a program to watch, Aereo streams the program over the Internet to that subscriber. And those images and sounds are contemporaneously visible and audible on the subscriber's computer (or other Internet-connected device). So under our assumed definition, Aereo transmits a performance whenever its subscribers watch a program.

But what about the Clause's further requirement that Aereo transmit a performance "to the public"? As we have said, an Aereo subscriber receives broadcast television signals with an antenna dedicated to him alone. Aereo's system makes from those signals a personal copy of the selected program. It streams the content of the copy to the same subscriber and to no one else. One and only one subscriber has the ability to see and hear each Aereo

CASE *(continued)*

transmission. The fact that each transmission is to only one subscriber, in Aereo's view, means that it does not transmit a performance "to the public."

In terms of the Act's purposes, these differences do not distinguish Aereo's system from cable systems, which do perform "publicly." Viewed in terms of Congress' regulatory objectives, why should any of these technological differences matter? They concern the behind-the-scenes way in which Aereo delivers television programming to its viewers' screens. They do not render Aereo's commercial objective any different from that of cable companies. Nor do they significantly alter the viewing experience of Aereo's subscribers. Why would a subscriber who wishes to watch a television show care much whether images and sounds are delivered to his screen via a large multisubscriber antenna or one small dedicated antenna, whether they arrive instantaneously or after a few seconds' delay, or whether they are transmitted directly or after a personal copy is made? And why, if Aereo is right, could not modern CATV systems simply continue the same commercial and consumer-oriented activities, free of copyright restrictions, provided they substitute such new technologies for old? Congress would as much have intended to protect a copyright holder from the unlicensed activities of Aereo as from those of cable companies.

The Transmit Clause must permit this interpretation, for it provides that one may transmit a performance to the public "whether the members of the public capable of receiving the performance . . . receive it . . . at the same time or at different times." §101. Were the words "to transmit . . . a performance" limited to a single act of communication, members of the public could not receive the performance communicated "at different times." Therefore, in light of the purpose and text of the Clause, we conclude that when an entity communicates the same contemporaneously perceptible images and sounds to multiple people, it transmits a performance to them regardless of the number of discrete communications it makes.

Aereo communicates the same contemporaneously perceptible images and sounds to a large number of people who are unrelated and unknown to each other. This matters because, although the Act does not define "the public," it specifies that an entity performs publicly when it performs at "any place where a substantial number of persons outside of a normal circle of a family and its social acquaintances is gathered." *Ibid.* The Act thereby suggests that "the public" consists of a large group of people outside of a family and friends.

Neither the record nor Aereo suggests that Aereo's subscribers receive performances in their capacities as owners or possessors of the underlying works. This is relevant because when an entity performs to a set of people, whether they constitute "the public" often depends upon their relationship to the underlying work. When, for example, a valet parking attendant returns cars to their drivers, we would not say that the parking service provides cars "to the public." We would say that it provides the cars to their owners. We would say that a car dealership, on the other hand, does provide cars to the public, for it sells cars to individuals who lack a pre-existing relationship to the cars. Similarly, an entity that transmits a performance to individuals in their capacities as owners or possessors does not perform

> **CASE** *(continued)*
>
> to "the public," whereas an entity like Aereo that transmits to large numbers of paying subscribers who lack any prior relationship to the works does so perform.
>
> Aereo and many of its supporting *amici* argue that to apply the Transmit Clause to Aereo's conduct will impose copyright liability on other technologies, including new technologies, that Congress could not possibly have wanted to reach. We agree that Congress, while intending the Transmit Clause to apply broadly to cable companies and their equivalents, did not intend to discourage or to control the emergence or use of different kinds of technologies. But we do not believe that our limited holding today will have that effect. We have interpreted the term "the public" to apply to a group of individuals acting as ordinary members of the public who pay primarily to watch broadcast television programs, many of which are copyrighted. We have said that it does not extend to those who act as owners or possessors of the relevant product. And we have not considered whether the public performance right is infringed when the user of a service pays primarily for something other than the transmission of copyrighted works, such as the remote storage of content. See Brief for United States as *Amicus Curiae* 31 (distinguishing cloud-based storage services because they "offer consumers more numerous and convenient means of playing back copies that the consumers have *already* lawfully acquired" (emphasis in original)). In addition, an entity does not transmit to the public if it does not transmit to a substantial number of people outside of a family and its social circle.
>
> Justice SCALIA, with whom Justice THOMAS and Justice ALITO join, dissenting.
>
> The Networks sued Aereo for several forms of copyright infringement, but we are here concerned with a single claim: that Aereo violates the Networks' "exclusive righ[t]" to "perform" their programs "publicly." 17 U.S.C. §106(4). That claim fails at the very outset because Aereo does not "perform" at all. The Court manages to reach the opposite conclusion only by disregarding widely accepted rules for service-provider liability and adopting in their place an improvised standard ("looks-like-cable-TV") that will sow confusion for years to come. [The dissent emphasizes that Aereo, as a service provider, does not make the requisite volitional choices or intentional acts that cause performances to occur, so should not be held liable direct for copyright infringement.]

NOTES AND COMMENTS

1. **Distribution right.** Section 106(3) of the Copyright Act incorporates an exclusive right for the copyright owner "to distribute copies or phonorecords of the copyrighted work to the public by sale or other transfer of ownership, or by rental, lease, or lending." The distribution right entered US law in an attempt to override the large and confusing body of case law that had accumulated over the publication right under the 1909 Copyright Act. By far the most contentious aspect of the right to distribute has been the many cases dealing with internet computer-based file sharing. This is an issue that has divided the courts. Some have read the distribution right broadly to encompass merely making copies available to other file sharers. Others have imposed a strict requirement that plaintiffs go beyond proof of mere making available; they require in addition proof that a copyrighted work was, in fact, distributed to third parties. *Compare Capitol Records, Inc. v. Thomas-Rasset*, 692 F.3d 899 (8th Cir. 2012), cert. denied 133 S. Ct. 1584 (2013) (finding

that making available is tantamount to distribution) with *London-Sire Records, Inc. v. Doe 1*, 542 F. Supp. 2d 153 (D. Mass. 2008) (distribution requires actual receipt and use by third parties). *See generally* 2 Melville Nimmer and David Nimmer, Nimmer on Copyright §8.11[D][1] (2016) ("[T]he intent of Congress was to incorporate a 'make available' right into the copyright owner's arsenal"). A further point: The distribution right does not permit a copyright owner to prevent the sale or other transfer of a lawfully owned copy of the owner's work; resale is specifically permitted under 17 U.S.C. §109(a).

2. **Excluded works: sound recordings.** Section 106(4) of the Copyright Act sets out the types of works that come with a right to public performance: "The copyright owner shall have the right . . . in the case of literary, musical, dramatic, and choreographic works, pantomimes, and motion pictures and other audiovisual works, to perform the copyrighted work publicly." When one compares this with §102, which lays out all types of copyrightable works (*see* §102(a)(1)–(8)), two exclusions become apparent: (1) pictorial, graphic, and sculptural works; and (2) sound recordings. Category (1) makes sense, because it is hard to imagine how one might "perform" a statue, for example; but note that the right to public display, in §106(5), specifically applies to statues. (It says: The copyright owner shall have the right . . . in the case of literary, musical, dramatic, and choreographic works, pantomimes, and pictorial, graphic, or sculptural works, including the individual images of a motion picture or other audiovisual work, to display the copyrighted work publicly"). But the second exclusion, sound recordings, is more noteworthy.

In general, traditional or "terrestrial" broadcasters in the US are exempt from paying a public performance right for sound recordings. The rationale goes back to the early days of radio and TV broadcasting, when a song played over the air was said to receive a boost in sales of copies of the song on records, and later, on cassettes, CDs, etc. – on "phonorecords" in the words of the Copyright Act. Note that this applies only to the recorded music: the author or owner of the written song, *i.e.*, the owner of rights to the sheet music and lyrics (if any) of the song *do* have a public performance right, because sheet music (unlike a sound recording) is a literary work, which does qualify for the public performance right under 17 U.S.C. §106(4).

The historic rule of no public performance right for sound recordings was revised, however. Under the Digital Performance Right in Sound Recordings Act of 1995 (DPRSRA), codified at 17 U.S.C. §106(6), 114–115, broadcasters of digital performances – webcasters, satellite radio, cable subscriber channels – must now pay royalties to music performers. Under the DPRSRA, digital performances are divided into two categories: subscription interactive services (in which listeners can choose which songs to listen to – *e.g.*, Spotify), for which service companies must pay royalties to performers through privately negotiated deals; and subscription noninteractive services (where the listener simply listens to a stream of music with no choice over what is played; *e.g.*, Sirius Satellite Radio). For these latter performances, the DPRSRA created a compulsory license (*i.e.*, government-mandated payment schedule) and a collective rights organization called SoundExchange, which distributes the compulsory royalty payments directly to performers (45 percent) and to the sound recording copyright owner, most often a record label (50 percent). Non-featured performers receive five percent of the royalties, via a royalty pool. *See* http://www.soundexchange.com. The DPRSRA also expanded another compulsory license, but it has nothing do with performance rights. That other license is a compulsory license to music rights owners (*i.e.*, owners of rights to sheet music) whenever a copy of a phonorecord embodying their music is made. Such a "digital phonorecord delivery" results in royalties to sheet music copyright holders for digital downloads, *e.g.*, the sale of copyrighted "ringtones" for mobile phones. *See* Daniel M. Simon, *Cell Phone Ringtones: A Case Study Exemplifying the Complexities of the §115 Mechanical License of the Copyright Act of 1976*, 57 Duke L.J. 1865 (2008).

12.2.3.2 Europe

 CASE

Case C-5/11, Titus Donner, Court of Justice of the European Union, ECLI:EU:C:2012:370

11 Mr Donner, a German national, was, at the time of the facts in the main proceedings, the principal director and shareholder of In.Sp.Em. Srl ('Inspem'), a freight forwarding company established in Bologna (Italy) and essentially conducted his business from his place of residence in Germany.

12 Inspem ensured the transport of goods sold by Dimensione Direct Sales Srl ('Dimensione'), a company also established in Bologna, the head office of which was situated in immediate proximity of that of Inspem. Dimensione used advertisements and supplements in newspapers, direct publicity letters and a German-language internet website to offer replicas of furnishings in the so-called 'Bauhaus' style for sale to customers residing in Germany, without having a licence to market them in Germany. These included replicas of [various lamps, chairs, etc.].

13 According to the findings of the Landgericht München II, all of the said items are copyright-protected in Germany as works of applied art. In Italy, however, there was no copyright protection or, alternatively, no enforceable copyright protection as against third parties during the period of relevance, namely from 1 January 2005 to 15 January 2008.

14 The furnishings at issue in the main proceedings, sold by Dimensione, were stored, in their packaging on which the name and address of the purchaser were indicated, in Dimensione's delivery warehouse in Sterzing (Italy). Under the general sales conditions, if customers residing in Germany did not wish to collect the goods they had ordered, or nominate their own freight forwarder, Dimensione recommended that Inspem be instructed. In the cases in the main proceedings the customers instructed Inspem to transport the furnishings that they had purchased. The Inspem drivers collected the items at the warehouse in Sterzing and paid the relevant purchase price to Dimensione.

CASE *(continued)*

Inspem collected the purchase price and freight charges from the customer on delivery to the person who had placed the order in Germany. Whenever a customer failed to accept or make payment for a delivery of furnishings, the goods were returned to Dimensione, which reimbursed Inspem for the purchase price already advanced and also paid the freight charges.

15 According to the Landgericht München II, Mr Donner thereby committed the criminal offence of aiding and abetting the prohibited commercial exploitation of copyright-protected works, contrary to Paragraphs 106 and 108a of the UrhG and also Paragraph 27 of the Criminal Code.

16 Dimensione was [therefore] found to have distributed copies of protected works in Germany.

17 Mr Donner appealed on a point of law (revision) against that judgment to the Bundesgerichtshof. He argues, first, that 'distribution to the public' under Article 4(1) of Directive 2001/29 and, consequently, under Paragraph 17 of the UrhG, presupposes a transfer of ownership of the goods, which in the main proceedings took place in Italy, the transfer of possession of the goods, that is to say, the actual power of disposal over those goods, not being necessary in that regard. He argues, secondly, that a conviction of him based on any other interpretation would be contrary to the principle of free movement of goods guaranteed under Article 34 TFEU because it would lead to an unjustified and artificial partitioning of the markets. Lastly and thirdly, he argues that, in any event, the handing-over of the goods in Italy to the carrier, which accepted them on behalf of ascertained customers, gave rise to a change of possession so that, from that point of view as well, the relevant facts occurred in Italy.

18 The Bundesgerichtshof concurs in the interpretation adopted by the Landgericht München II, to the effect that 'distribution to the public' by sale under Article 4(1) of Directive 2001/29 presupposes that not just ownership but also *de facto* power of disposal of the copyright-protected reproduction is transferred to a third party. In order to be considered as being distributed to the public, the reproduction of a work has to be transferred from the manufacturer's internal sphere of operation into the public sphere or into the free trade arena. As long as such a reproduction remains within the manufacturer's internal sphere of operation or the same group of companies, it cannot be deemed to have reached the public, since the existence of a business transaction based on genuine external dealings is lacking in such a scenario.

19 On the other hand, the Bundesgerichtshof considers that Articles 34 TFEU and 36 TFEU may preclude upholding Mr Donner's conviction should the application of the national criminal law provisions to the facts of the main proceedings be found to give rise to an unjustified restriction on the free movement of goods.

20 In those circumstances the Bundesgerichtshof decided to stay the proceedings before it and to refer the following question to the Court for a preliminary ruling:

'Are Articles 34 and 36 TFEU governing the free movement of goods to be interpreted as precluding the criminal offence of aiding and abetting the prohibited distribution of

CASE *(continued)*

copyright-protected works resulting from the application of national criminal law where, on a cross-border sale of a work that is copyright protected in Germany,

- that work is taken to Germany from a Member State of the European Union and de facto power of disposal thereof is transferred in Germany,
- but the transfer of ownership took place in the other Member State in which copyright protection for the work did not exist or was unenforceable as against third parties?'

The question referred for a preliminary ruling . . . .

The interpretation of Article 4(1) of Directive 2001/29

26   It must be observed that the distribution to the public is characterised by a series of acts going, at the very least, from the conclusion of a contract of sale to the performance thereof by delivery to a member of the public. Thus, in the context of a cross-border sale, acts giving rise to a 'distribution to the public' under Article 4(1) of Directive 2001/29 may take place in a number of Member States. In such a context, such a transaction may infringe on the exclusive right to authorise or prohibit any forms of distribution to the public in a number of Member States.

27   A trader in such circumstances bears responsibility for any act carried out by him or on his behalf giving rise to a 'distribution to the public' in a Member State where the goods distributed are protected by copyright. Any such act carried out by a third party may also be attributed to him, where he specifically targeted the public of the State of destination and must have been aware of the actions of that third party.

. . .

30   Accordingly, the answer to the first part of the question referred is that a trader who directs his advertising at members of the public residing in a given Member State and creates or makes available to them a specific delivery system and payment method, or allows a third party to do so, thereby enabling those members of the public to receive delivery of copies of works protected by copyright in that same Member State, makes, in the Member State where the delivery takes place, a 'distribution to the public' under Article 4(1) of Directive 2001/29.

. . .

On those grounds, the Court (Fourth Chamber) hereby rules:

A trader who directs his advertising at members of the public residing in a given Member State and creates or makes available to them a specific delivery system and payment method, or allows a third party to do so, thereby enabling those members of the public to receive delivery of copies of works protected by copyright in that same Member State, makes, in the Member State where the delivery takes place, a 'distribution to the public' under Article 4(1) of Directive 2001/29/EC of the European Parliament and of the Council of 22 May 2001 on the harmonisation of certain aspects of copyright and related rights in the information society.

NOTES AND QUESTIONS

1. The *Donner* case is a good example of why the CJEU has become more active in harmonizing core copyright concepts through judicial decisions over the last years. At least between 2005 and 2008, there was a difference between German and Italian copyright law as far as the copyrightability of furniture design is concerned. As the EU had not harmonized originality standards at that time, it was up to the CJEU to decide whether the distribution of the furniture only took place in Italy (where the furniture was not copyright-protected) or also in Germany (where it was protected). The CJEU takes this case (and other cases) as an opportunity to develop an autonomous concept of the right of distribution whose interpretation does not depend on the individual copyright systems of EU Member States.
2. Why is it so hard for the EU to harmonize originality standards in copyright law? Why did it require the CJEU to step in, instead of the European legislators (European Parliament and the Council, with support from the European Commission), to harmonize originality standards?
3. Arts. 2–4 Information Society Directive harmonize the right of reproduction, the right of communication to the public, the right of making available to the public and the right to distribute on an EU level. Furthermore, the Rental Rights Directive harmonizes a rental and lending right. As Directives only require EU Member States to change their national laws according to the Directive, but leaves them the choice of form and method of implementation (Art. 288 TFEU), the provisions of the Information Society Directive do not mean that these exploitation rights are identical across all EU Member States.
4. In the UK, Sec. 16 CDPA lists the various exploitation rights granted to authors: the right to copy the work; to issue copies of the work to the public; to rent or lend the work to the public; to perform, show or play the work in the public; to communicate the work to the public; and to make an adaptation of the work. Sec. 15 German Copyright Act distinguishes between the right to exploit a work "in material form" and the right to communicate it publicly in "non-material form." Under both umbrella rights, specific exploitation rights (material: reproduction, distribution, rental, exhibition; non-material: recitation, performance, representation, broadcasting, cablecasting, communicating via sound or visual recordings, retransmission of broadcasts or cablecasts, making available to the public) are then listed. According to Sec. 122-1 French CPI, the author's economic exploitation rights include the right of performance ("representation") and the right of reproduction. This structure dates back to the eighteenth century, and courts have construed both rights broadly (André Lucas et al., "France," in 1 International Copyright Law & Practice, at §1[3] (Paul E. Geller ed., 2015) (describing the historic distinction between the right to stage works publicly and the right to print and publish works). In French copyright law, the right to reproduce also includes the adaptation right and a right to control to whom copies of a work may be communicated ("droit de destination"). The right of performance encompasses the right to communicate to the public. These differences in implementation can have practical consequences. In Germany, the list of rights under "material" and "non-material form" is not considered exhaustive. Rather, if new technological developments enable a new method of exploitation, at least theoretically, this could be covered by the umbrella rights of Sec. 15 German Copyright Act without having to adapt the statute. More importantly, the statutory distinction between material and non-material rights of exploitation has led some German commentators and courts to conclude that the exhaustion principle only applies to material rights of exploitation (*i.e.* the distribution right) and not non-material rights (*i.e.* the right to communicate to the public). In France, following the adoption of a right of distribution in the EU Information Society Directive, the legislator has decided to not expressly implement a distribution right in French copyright law. Rather, the "right of destination" is often conceived as a functional equivalent to the distribution right (Lucas et al., *supra*, at §8[1][b][i][A]).
5. In addition to the exploitation rights mentioned, the Resale Rights Directive has introduced a "droit de suite" in the EU. Once an artist has sold his or her artwork, he or she is entitled to receive a royalty based on the sale price of any resale of the work. The marginal royalty rate decreases as the sale price increases. It ranges between 4 percent for sale prices up to €50,000 and 0.25 percent for the portion of the sale price exceeding €500,000. The resale right is neither alienable nor waivable. This Directive has affected, particularly, art dealers and auction houses located in London, in their competition with New York and other cities; *see* Jonathan Collins, *Droit de suite: An Artistic Stroke of Genius? A Critical Exploration of the European Directive and its Resultant Effects*, EIPR, 305–12 (2002).

Case C-607/11, ITV Broadcasting et al. v. TVCatchup, Court of Justice of the European Union, ECLI:EU:C:2013:147

8 The claimants in the main proceedings are commercial television broadcasters who own copyright under national law in the television broadcasts themselves and in films and other items which are included in their broadcasts. They are funded by advertising carried in their broadcasts.

9 TVC offers an internet television broadcasting service. The service permits its users to receive, via the internet, 'live' streams of free-to-air television broadcasts, including television broadcasts transmitted by the claimants in the main proceedings.

10 TVC ensures that those using its service can obtain access only to content which they are already legally entitled to watch in the United Kingdom by virtue of their television licence. The terms to which users must agree thus include the possession of a valid TV licence and a restriction of use of TVC services to the United Kingdom. The TVC website has the facility to authenticate the user's location and to refuse access where the conditions imposed on users are not satisfied.

11 The TVC service is funded by advertising. Audiovisual advertising is shown before the user is able to view the live stream. The advertisements already contained in the original broadcasts are left unchanged and sent to the user as part of the stream. There is also 'in-skin' advertising, which appears on the user's computer or other equipment

...

16 The claimants in the main proceedings instituted proceedings against TVC before the High Court of Justice (England and Wales) (Chancery Division) for breach of their copyright in their broadcasts and films, alleging, inter alia, that there is a communication of the works to the public prohibited by section 20 of the Copyright, Designs and Patents Act 1988, in the version applicable to the facts in the main proceedings, and by Article 3(1) of Directive 2001/29.

17 The High Court takes the view that it is not clear from the judgments in Case C-306/05 *SGAE* [2006] ECR I-11519 and in Joined Cases C-431/09 and C-432/09 *Airfield NV and Canal Digitaal* [2011] ECR I-9363 whether there is a 'communication to the public' within the meaning of Article 3(1) of Directive 2001/29 in [this case].

18 In those circumstances the High Court of Justice (England and Wales) (Chancery Division) decided to stay the proceedings and to refer the following questions to the Court for a preliminary ruling:

'1. Does the right to authorise or prohibit a "communication to the public of their works by wire or wireless means" in Article 3(1) of [Directive 2001/29] extend to a case where:

CASE *(continued)*

(a) Authors authorise the inclusion of their works in a terrestrial free-to-air television broadcast which is intended for reception either throughout the territory of a Member State or within a geographical area within a Member State;

(b) A third party ([that is to say,] an organisation other than the original broadcaster) provides a service whereby individual subscribers within the intended area of reception of the broadcast who could lawfully receive the broadcast on a television receiver in their own homes may log on to the third party's server and receive the content of the broadcast by means of an internet stream?

2. Does it make any difference to the answer to the above question if:

(a) The third party's server allows only a "one-to-one" connection for each subscriber whereby each individual subscriber establishes his or her own internet connection to the server and every data packet sent by the server onto the internet is addressed to only one individual subscriber?

(b) The third party's service is funded by advertising which is presented "pre-roll" ([that is to say,] during the period of time after a subscriber logs on but before he or she begins to receive the broadcast content) or "in-skin" ([that is to say,] within the frame of the viewing software which displays the received programme on the subscriber's viewing device but outside the programme picture) but the original advertisements contained within the broadcast are presented to the subscriber at the point where they are inserted in the programme by the broadcaster?

(c) The intervening organisation is:
  (i) providing an alternative service to that of the original broadcaster, thereby acting in direct competition with the original broadcaster for viewers; or
  (ii) acting in direct competition with the original broadcaster for advertising revenues?'

Consideration of the questions referred
Question 1 and Question 2(a)
19 By Question 1 and Question 2(a), the referring court asks, in essence, whether the concept of 'communication to the public', within the meaning of Article 3(1) of Directive 2001/29, must be interpreted as meaning that it covers a retransmission of the works included.
20 First of all, it is to be noted that the principal objective of Directive 2001/29 is to establish a high level of protection of authors, allowing them to obtain an appropriate reward for the use of their works, including on the occasion of communication to the public. It follows that 'communication to the public' must be interpreted broadly, as recital 23 in the preamble to the directive indeed expressly states (*SGAE*, paragraph 36, and Joined Cases C-403/08 and C-429/08 *Football Association Premier League and Others* [2011] ECR I-9083, paragraph 186).

...

CASE *(continued)*

23 [T]he author's right of communication to the public covers any transmission or retransmission of a work to the public not present at the place where the communication originates, by wire or wireless means, including broadcasting. In addition, it is apparent from Article 3(3) of that directive that authorising the inclusion of protected works in a communication to the public does not exhaust the right to authorise or prohibit other communications of those works to the public.

24 It follows that, by regulating the situations in which a given work is put to multiple use, the European Union legislature intended that each transmission or retransmission of a work which uses a specific technical means must, as a rule, be individually authorised by the author of the work in question.

...

26 Given that the making of works available through the retransmission of a terrestrial television broadcast over the internet uses a specific technical means different from that of the original communication, that retransmission must be considered to be a 'communication' within the meaning of Article 3(1) of Directive 2001/29. Consequently, such a retransmission cannot be exempt from authorisation by the authors of the retransmitted works when these are communicated to the public.

27 That conclusion cannot be undermined by TVC's objection that the making of the works available over the internet, as was done in the case in the main proceedings, is merely a technical means to ensure or improve reception of the terrestrial television broadcast in its catchment area.

...

30 In the present case . . . the intervention by TVC consists in a transmission of the protected works at issue which is different from that of the broadcasting organisation concerned. TVC's intervention is in no way intended to maintain or improve the quality of the transmission by that other broadcasting organisation. In those circumstances, that intervention cannot be considered to be a mere technical means within the meaning specified in paragraph 28 above.

31 In the second place, in order to be categorised as a 'communication to the public' within the meaning of Article 3(1) of Directive 2001/29, the protected works must also in fact be communicated to a 'public'.

32 In that connection, it follows from the case-law of the Court that the term 'public' in Article 3(1) of Directive 2001/29 refers to an indeterminate number of potential recipients and implies, moreover, a fairly large number of persons (see, to that effect, *SGAE*, paragraphs 37 and 38 and the case-law cited).

33 As regards that last criterion specifically, the cumulative effect of making the works available to potential recipients should be taken into account. In that connection, it is in particular relevant to ascertain the number of persons who have access to the same work at the same time and successively (*SGAE*, paragraph 39).

34 In that context, it is irrelevant whether the potential recipients access the

CASE (continued)

communicated works through a one-to-one connection. That technique does not prevent a large number of persons having access to the same work at the same time.

...

37 However, TVC contends that the retransmission at issue in the main proceedings does not satisfy the requirement that there must be a new public, which is none the less necessary within the meaning of the judgments in *SGAE* (paragraph 40), *Football Association Premier League and Others* (paragraph 197), and *Airfield and Canal Digitaal* (paragraph 72). The recipients of the retransmission effected by TVC are, it submits, entitled to follow the televised broadcast, identical in content, using their own television sets.

38 In that connection, it should be noted that the situations examined in the cases which gave rise to the abovementioned judgments differ clearly from the situation at issue in the case in the main proceedings. In those cases, the Court examined situations in which an operator had made accessible, by its deliberate intervention, a broadcast containing protected works to a new public which was not considered by the authors concerned when they authorised the broadcast in question.

...

On those grounds, the Court (Fourth Chamber) hereby rules:

1. The concept of 'communication to the public', within the meaning of Article 3(1) of Directive 2001/29/EC of the European Parliament and of the Council of 22 May 2001 on the harmonisation of certain aspects of copyright and related rights in the information society, must be interpreted as meaning that it covers a retransmission of the works included in a terrestrial television broadcast

- where the retransmission is made by an organisation other than the original broadcaster,
- by means of an internet stream made available to the subscribers of that other organisation who may receive that retransmission by logging on to its server,
- even though those subscribers are within the area of reception of that terrestrial television broadcast and may lawfully receive the broadcast on a television receiver.

2. The answer to Question 1 is not influenced by the fact that a retransmission, such as that at issue in the main proceedings, is funded by advertising and is therefore of a profit-making nature.

3. The answer to Question 1 is not influenced by the fact that a retransmission, such as that at issue in the main proceedings, is made by an organisation which is acting in direct competition with the original broadcaster.

NOTES AND QUESTIONS

The decision is similar to the *Aereo* decision of the US Supreme Court (*see supra* Section 12.2.3.1). In what respects do the products both cases are about differ? How do the outcomes and the approaches of the Supreme Court and the CJEU differ? What is the impact of both decisions on innovation in distribution technologies?

CASE

Case C-466/12, Nils Svensson et al. v. Retriever Sverige, Court of Justice of the European Union, ECLI:EU:C:2014:76

8 The applicants in the main proceedings, all journalists, wrote press articles that were published in the *Göteborgs-Posten* newspaper and on the *Göteborgs-Posten* website. Retriever Sverige operates a website that provides its clients, according to their needs, with lists of clickable Internet links to articles published by other websites. It is common ground between the parties that those articles were freely accessible on the *Göteborgs-Posten* newspaper site. According to the applicants in the main proceedings, if a client clicks on one of those links, it is not apparent to him that he has been redirected to another site in order to access the work in which he is interested. By contrast, according to Retriever Sverige, it is clear to the client that, when he clicks on one of those links, he is redirected to another site.
9 The applicants in the main proceedings brought an action against Retriever Sverige before the Stockholms tingsrätt (Stockholm District Court) in order to obtain compensation on the ground that that company had made use, without their authorisation, of certain articles by them, by making them available to its clients.
10 By judgment of 11 June 2010, the Stockholms tingsrätt rejected their application. The applicants in the main proceedings then brought an appeal against that judgment before the Svea hovrätt (Svea Court of Appeal).
11 Before that court, the applicants in the main proceedings claimed, inter alia, that Retriever Sverige had infringed their exclusive right to make their respective works available to the public, in that as a result of the services offered on its website, Retriever Sverige's clients had access to the applicants' works.
12 Retriever Sverige contends, in defence, that the provision of lists of Internet links to works communicated to the public on other websites does not constitute an act liable to affect the copyright in those works. Retriever Sverige also contends that it did not carry out any transmission of any protected work; its action is limited to indicating to its clients the websites on which the works that are of interest to them are to be found.
13 In those circumstances, the Svea hovrätt decided to stay the proceedings and to refer the following questions to the Court of Justice for a preliminary ruling:
"(1) If anyone other than the holder of copyright in a certain work supplies a clickable link to the work on his website, does that constitute communication to the public within the meaning of Article 3(1) of Directive [2001/29]?
(2) Is the assessment under question 1 affected if the work to which the link refers is on a website on the Internet which can be accessed by anyone without restrictions or if access is restricted in some way?
(3) When making the assessment under question 1, should any distinction be drawn between a case where the work, after the user has clicked on the link, is shown on another

CASE *(continued)*

website and one where the work, after the user has clicked on the link, is shown in such a way as to give the impression that it is appearing on the same website?
(4) Is it possible for a Member State to give wider protection to authors' exclusive right by enabling communication to the public to cover a greater range of acts than provided for in Article 3(1) of Directive 2001/29?"

Consideration of the questions referred

The first three questions

16 [T]he concept of communication to the public includes two cumulative criteria, namely, an "act of communication" of a work and the communication of that work to a "public" (see, to that effect, Case C-607/11 *ITV Broadcasting and Others* [2013] ECR, paragraphs 21 and 31).

17 As regards the first of those criteria, that is, the existence of an "act of communication", this must be construed broadly (see, to that effect, Joined Cases C-403/08 and C-429/08 *Football Association Premier League and Others* [2011] ECR I-9083, paragraph 193), in order to ensure, in accordance with, inter alia, recitals 4 and 9 in the preamble to Directive 2001/29, a high level of protection for copyright holders.

18 In the circumstances of this case, it must be observed that the provision, on a website, of clickable links to protected works published without any access restrictions on another site, affords users of the first site direct access to those works.

...

26 The public targeted by the initial communication consisted of all potential visitors to the site concerned, since, given that access to the works on that site was not subject to any restrictive measures, all Internet users could therefore have free access to them.

27 In those circumstances, it must be held that, where all the users of another site to whom the works at issue have been communicated by means of a clickable link could access those works directly on the site on which they were initially communicated, without the involvement of the manager of that other site, the users of the site managed by the latter must be deemed to be potential recipients of the initial communication and, therefore, as being part of the public taken into account by the copyright holders when they authorised the initial communication.

28 Therefore, since there is no new public, the authorisation of the copyright holders is not required for a communication to the public such as that in the main proceedings.

29 Such a finding cannot be called in question were the referring court to find, although this is not clear from the documents before the Court, that when Internet users click on the link at issue, the work appears in such a way as to give the impression that it is appearing on the site on which that link is found, whereas in fact that work comes from another site.

30 That additional circumstance in no way alters the conclusion that the provision on a site of a clickable link to a protected work published and freely accessible on another site has the effect of making that work available to users of the first site and that it therefore constitutes a communication to the public. However, since there is no new public,

> **CASE** *(continued)*
>
> the authorisation of the copyright holders is in any event not required for such a communication to the public.
>
> 31 On the other hand, where a clickable link makes it possible for users of the site on which that link appears to circumvent restrictions put in place by the site on which the protected work appears in order to restrict public access to that work to the latter site's subscribers only, and the link accordingly constitutes an intervention without which those users would not be able to access the works transmitted, all those users must be deemed to be a new public, which was not taken into account by the copyright holders when they authorised the initial communication, and accordingly the holders' authorisation is required for such a communication to the public. This is the case, in particular, where the work is no longer available to the public on the site on which it was initially communicated or where it is henceforth available on that site only to a restricted public, while being accessible on another Internet site without the copyright holders' authorisation.
>
> *The fourth question*
>
> 33 By its fourth question, the referring court asks, in essence, whether Article 3(1) of Directive 2001/29 must be interpreted as precluding a Member State from giving wider protection to copyright holders by laying down that the concept of communication to the public includes a wider range of activities than those referred to in that provision.
>
> . . .
>
> 35 [T]he objective pursued by Directive 2001/29 would inevitably be undermined if the concept of communication to the public were to be construed in different Member States as including a wider range of activities than those referred to in Article 3(1) of that directive.
>
> . . .
>
> 41 Therefore, the answer to the fourth question is that Article 3(1) of Directive 2001/29 must be interpreted as precluding a Member State from giving wider protection to copyright holders by laying down that the concept of communication to the public includes a wider range of activities than those referred to in that provision.
>
> . . .
>
> On those grounds, the Court (Fourth Chamber) hereby rules:
>
> 1. Article 3(1) of Directive 2001/29/EC of the European Parliament and of the Council of 22 May 2001 on the harmonisation of certain aspects of copyright and related rights in the information society, must be interpreted as meaning that the provision on a website of clickable links to works freely available on another website does not constitute an "act of communication to the public", as referred to in that provision.
>
> 2. Article 3(1) of Directive 2001/29 must be interpreted as precluding a Member State from giving wider protection to copyright holders by laying down that the concept of communication to the public includes a wider range of activities than those referred to in that provision.

NOTES

1. Since the commercialization of the internet, courts have had to deal with the question whether providing hyperlinks to copyrighted web pages can lead to copyright liability themselves. In the *Svenson* decision, the CJEU had to address this question not with regard to the reproduction right, but with regard to the right of communication to the public. In denying copyright liability, it is noteworthy that the court follows its earlier case law by not resorting to national definitions of this exploitation right, but rather developing an autonomous concept of the right to communicate to the public.
2. The court notes in par. 17 that this right must be construed broadly in order to achieve a high level of copyright protection. This indicates that the normative foundations for copyright protection on a European level may vary from those in the US.
3. Furthermore, the court reiterates its position that a re-communication of a copyrighted work infringes the right to communicate to the public only if the communication is directed at a new public, *i.e.* at a public that was not taken into account when the copyright owner authorized the initial communication to the public. By introducing a "new public" requirement, the court attempts to link the scope of the exploitation right to the economic value of the exploitation. The exact scope and implications of this "new public" requirement are still in flux and will probably lead to further case law, both at the European and the national level.
4. Finally, the court also stresses that the Information Society Directive set both a lower and an upper bound when creating the right to communicate to the public: Member States are not allowed to create a national version of this right that would go further than what the Directive prescribes. This is another signal that the CJEU is doing what it can to harmonize copyright law across the EU.

12.3 Moral rights

12.3.1 Introduction

Moral rights (or "droit morale" in French) are a separate bundle of rights that attach to works of authorship. They are often distinguished from "economic rights" in copyright law and scholarship. Moral rights, according to the Berne Convention, exist "[i]ndependently of the author's economic rights" and protect against certain acts that "would be prejudicial to [the author's] honor or reputation" (Berne Convention, Article *6bis*, available at http://www.wipo.int/wipolex/en/treaties/text.jsp?file_id=283693). Moral rights in continental Europe have a very long provenance, and have achieved a high level of development in various national copyright laws in Europe. *See* Stig Strmholm, Le droit moral de l'auteur en droit allemand, franais et scandinave, 3 vols. (1967).

Economic rights include the right to make copies; to make derivative works (or adaptations); right to distribute, perform, make publicly available, etc. Moral rights are more "personal" to authors, in two senses. First, they cover aspects of a work that are closely connected to the reputation and personal contribution of the author: the right of an author to have his or her name attached to a work ("attribution"); to not have the work destroyed, mangled, or mutilated ("integrity"); and the rights to first disseminate ("divulgation") and later remove ("withdrawal") a work, according to the author's wishes.

Because moral rights are so personal to the creator of a work, they may have different terms (*i.e.*, last longer) than pure economic rights. At the limit, they may be indefinite: inuring first to an author and later to his or her heirs. In addition, moral rights are often said to be inalienable: Because they protect the personality interest and reputation of the single original author, they cannot be bought and sold so that others might exercise them or waive them. As one observer has said:

> If the economic faculties serve to guarantee to authors a share in the income from work exploitation, droit moral and its faculties serve to guarantee protection for the personal, intellectual and spiritual interests of authors; in view of the fundamental importance of protection of personality in modern society, they cannot be signed away. Moral rights, in short, guarantee that it is the author and only the author who decides on the moment, place, extent, destination and time of dissemination of his work, on the concrete configuration, form and content of his work, and under what name – his true name or a pseudonym, the name of another person (perhaps also a ghostwriter) or else, in anonymous form – the work shall enter the public scene (Adolf Dietz, *The Moral Right of the Author: Moral Rights and the Civil Law Countries*, 19 Colum.-VLA J.L. & Arts 199, 207–08 (1995)).

For an account of Kantian philosophy and its normative implications for IP law, see Robert P. Merges, Justifying Intellectual Property (2011), at Chapter 3, pp. 68ff. The key elements are: (1) the importance of individual people and their characters and contributions ("human agency"); (2) the role of property as an institution in protecting expressions of a person's individual character; and (3) the grounding of property in individual rights, and the important relationship between property and legitimate government. For an excellent recent account of moral rights, and a well-reasoned appeal to them adopted more widely in the US, see Roberta Rosenthal Kwall, The Soul of Creativity: Forging a Moral Rights Law for the United States (2009). *See also* Thomas F. Cotter, *Pragmatism, Economics, and the Droit Moral*, 76 N.C. L. Rev. 1 (1997); Natalie C. Suhl, *Moral Rights Protection in the United States Under the Berne Convention: A Fictional Work?*, 12 Fordham Intell. Prop. Media & Ent. L.J. 1203, 1228 (2002).

12.3.2 Europe

France is generally acknowledged to be the cradle of moral rights. Current French law, in its Copyright Code, includes specific reference to these rights. *See* Loi relative au code de la propriété intellectuelle (partie legislative), Loi No. 95-597 of July 1, 1992, J.O. July 3, 1992, at 8801, codified in Code de la Propriété Intellectuelle (Fr.), English trans. available at https://www.legifrance.gouv.fr/content/download/1959/13723/version/3/../Code_35.

pdf, at sections L121-1 through L121-9. The most important of these rights are attribution; divulgement (right to disseminate a work); integrity; and withdrawal (right to disavow or remove a work that no longer accurately represents one's artistic vision).

Under Article L123-1, the moral rights granted to authors in France are perpetual. One well-known treatise, however, states that the right of withdrawal may only be exercised during the life of a work's original author. *See* A. Lucas and H.-J. Lucas, Traité de la Propriété Littéraire et Artistique (4th ed., 2010), at pars. 466, 540.

Moral rights also found a solid foothold in German law. Most theorists locate the intellectual origins of German moral rights law in the writings of the great philosophers Immanuel Kant and G.W.F. Hegel. The emphasis on property as an institution that assists individual people to invest and project their will or self into the world led naturally to the view that intellectual creations are imbued with the distinctive marks of their authors. This is especially associated with German theorist Otto Freidrich von Gierke. *See* Cheryl Swack, *Safeguarding Artistic Creation and the Cultural Heritage: A Comparison of Droit Moral Between France and the United States*, 22 Colum.-VLA J.L. & Arts 361, 371 (1998).

Today, German copyright law includes a subsection on moral rights, which includes specifically protection for the right of divulgement, attribution and integrity. *See* German Copyright Act of 1965 (last amended 2016), at §§11–13, available at http://www.wipo.int/wipolex/en/text.jsp?file_id=423012 (automatic English translation version).

Unlike in France, where moral rights are perpetual, moral rights in Germany expire with the other "economic" rights of the author – generally 70 years after the death of the author. *See* German Copyright Act §64, *supra*.

Despite the historically distinctive tradition of utilitarian (vs. personality-based) copyright in the United Kingdom, UK copyright law does recognize three primary moral rights: the right to be identified as author or director (CDPA 1988, as amended, at Sec. 77), the right to object to derogatory treatment of the work (CDPA, Sec. 80), and the right not to have a work falsely attributed to another (CDPA, Sec. 84). *See* J.A.L. Sterling, "United Kingdom" [Moral Rights], at section 8.24, in World Copyright Law (J.A.L. Sterling & Trevor Cook, eds., 4th ed., 2008 & Supp. 2017).

With this background in mind, consider now some actual cases under moral rights provisions of various national laws in Europe.

Plon SA v. Hugo, E.C.D.R., Cour de Cassation (French Court of Cassation), 2007, 9

Mr Ceresa, a writer and journalist, is the author of two novels entitled "Cosette, or the Time of Illusions" and "Marius, or the Fugitive" published by Plon SA and presented as sequels to "Les Misérables" written by Victor Hugo; Pierre Hugo, Victor Hugo's heir, has brought a claim in damages for violation of the respect due to the work by his ancestor; the French writers' society (SGDL) joined in to support the action of its own volition, asking for payment of the symbolic sum of one euro for violation of the collective interests of the profession; the Appeal Court allowed the claims.

...

First, in the light of the finding that the devolution of moral rights in this case followed the normal rules of succession, it was by way of a definitive assessment of the wishes of Victor Hugo, as expressed in his wills dated April 9 and September 23, 1875, and not by reference to the distinctions established by the Law of March 11, 1957 on the devolution of various privileges in relation to moral rights that the Appeal Court ruled that the author had intended to dissociate the publication of his work (which he had entrusted to third parties) from the right to respect and to authorship thereof (of which he had not intended to deprive his heirs); the first part of this ground of appeal is therefore unfounded on the facts.

Plon SA and Mr Ceresa did not mention at the Appeal Court stage the failure to accept rights of succession under which Pierre Hugo is asserting his status as heir; the second part of the ground of appeal, which is new and a mixture of fact, is inadmissible.

Finally, although the right to respect for a work passes to the heirs under the normal rules of succession a co-heir has the capacity to take unilateral action to safeguard that right; since this ground of appeal is substituted for the ground of appeal upheld by the Appeal Court the judgment is justified in law.

...

Having found that the SGDL, which is a recognised association formed in the public interest, had authority under its deed of association to "generally safeguard the moral and material interests of its members" (Art. 1) and the capacity to join in any proceedings concerning a professional point of law of general interest (Art. 44(4)) the Appeal Court – which had established that this case concerns an issue of principle as to the legitimacy of "sequels" to literary works liable to constitute a violation of the collective interests of the profession – rightly found that the said association's involvement in the action of its own volition was admissible; however, the ground of appeal is not valid.

...

Having regard to Arts L.121-1 and L.123-1 of the Intellectual Property Code, together with Art. 10 of the Convention for the Protection of Human Rights and Fundamental Freedoms;

Whereas the "sequel" to a literary work is concerned with the right of adaptation; subject

CASE *(continued)*

to respect for a right to the name and integrity of the adapted work, the concept of creative freedom prevents the author of a work or his heirs from banning a sequel to it after their monopolistic exploitation rights have expired.

Whereas, in holding that – by editing and publishing the two works at issue and presenting them as sequels to Les Misérables – Plon SA had violated the moral rights of Victor Hugo over that work, the Appeal Court judgment states that although the latter never took offence at, let alone opposed, theatrical adaptations of his books or even the adoption of his characters by other authors, it was nevertheless established that the writer would not have agreed to another author writing a sequel to Les Misérables; hence it was of little consequence that the characters (one of whom had been resurrected whilst others had been revived) should remain in the books wrongly presented as adaptations of the original work since Plon SA were claiming outside the judicial arena that they were a continuation (faithful or otherwise) of those brought into the world for literary eternity by Victor Hugo; to ban any sequel to Les Misérables could not, as wrongly claimed, constitute a violation of the principle of creative freedom as, in this case, this work (being a veritable monument of world literature) was not a simple novel in that it originated in a philosophical and political approach, as explained by Victor Hugo himself; it was also complete; it therefore follows that no sequel to a work such as Les Misérables could be permitted without violating the moral rights of Victor Hugo.

In ruling in this way on spurious grounds based on the genre and merits of the work or on its complete nature without examining the disputed works or establishing that they would have changed Victor Hugo's work or that confusion would arise as to their authorship, the Appeal Court (which did not therefore establish the violation of moral rights and made its ruling in disregard of creative freedom) was in breach of the aforementioned legislation.

On these grounds, [the Cour de Cassation] *Overturns and annuls* the judgment pronounced between the parties by the Paris Appeal Court on March 31, 2004 save insofar as it declares Pierre Hugo's action and SGDL's voluntary joinder admissible; consequently, on all other points, restores the proceedings and the parties to the position in which they were in before the said Appeal Court judgment was pronounced and, for the purposes thereof, refers the case back to the Paris Appeal Court sitting with different judges.

CASE

Tribunal de Grande Instance de Paris (High Court of Paris), 3rd chamber, Oct. 15, 1992, R.I.D.A. 1993, 225

In 1991, French director Bruton Boussagol produced Samuel Beckett's "Waiting for Godot" for the annual Avignon Festival. He decided to cast the four lead male roles with four

CASE (continued)

actresses. When contacted, the heirs of the deceased author would not grant the necessary copyright licenses because it had been the desire of Samuel Beckett that the play should not be performed by female actresses. When the play was performed nevertheless, the heirs sued the director and his theater company for an alleged infringement of Becket's post-mortal moral rights. The High Court of Paris held in 1992 that the production had violated Beckett's right of integrity as enshrined in French copyright law, and that it was not upon the judge to scrutinize the desire of the author. It ordered the director and his theater company to pay a symbolic damage of one Franc to the heirs, and to publish the judgment in three newspapers at a cost of up to 36,000 Francs.

NOTES

As you can see from this and other cases, moral rights law often requires an inquiry into what the original author would have wished or wanted with respect to subsequent performances or adaptations of a work. Who in these cases is given authority to speak for the author? Why are family members privileged over others, such as contemporary creators in the same medium (authors, in this case), or scholars who have studied the lives and works of the original author? Does it make sense to assume that the wishes of an author are "frozen in time," or would it be possible to try to imagine how the author's intentions might have evolved over time?

CASE

Landgericht Berlin (Regional Court Berlin), Nov. 28, 2006, case 16 O 240/05, GRUR 2007, 964

After the fall of the Berlin Wall, the German government decided to build a new main railway station for Berlin close to the Brandenburg Gate at a cost of about 1 billion Euros. The well-known German architect Meinhard van Gerkan was commissioned by the German railway company Deutsche Bahn to design the station. When the railway company later decided to replace a planned vaulted ceiling with a flat ceiling, the architect objected. The dispute went to court and the Berlin regional court held that the unauthorized change in the station design by Deutsche Bahn was a violation of the architect's moral right of integrity under German copyright law. Even though the contract between the railway company and the architect included a provision according to which the company could apply changes to the design, replacing the ceiling was not covered by the provision as it defaced the copyrighted work. The court held that Deutsche Bahn was required to remove the flat ceiling at an estimated cost of 44.5 million Euros.

NOTES

1. It is interesting that, even though the architect and the railway company had a contract including a provision concerning design changes, the contract could not prevent the dispute, as moral rights cannot be waived or transferred by contract under German law.
2. The parties later settled the dispute out of court at an undisclosed sum without the ceiling being replaced. Although moral rights are conceptualized as "non-pecuniary" and "non-economic" in nature, they may have important financial consequences in the end.

12.3.3 China

CASE

Beijing RongXingHe Information Consulting Ltd. v. Kewen Info., (2007) Beijing 2nd Intermediate People's Court, Erzhongminchuzi No. 3960

Plaintiff, RongXinHe Information Consulting Co., Ltd. ('RXH'), launched a promotional campaign on its website www.starhave.com ('Starhave') in May 2005, featuring crystal constellation articles and related designs to promote crystal jewelry products. During the same period, RXH also commissioned Beijing Shu-Guang Design Company to design images for this promotional campaign. Based on the commission agreement, all the copyrights and interests related to the designs were assigned to RXH. Later, Shu-Guang assigned the copyright to the twelve pictures they designed for RXH, including pictures of *Aquarius, Pisces, Aries, Taurus, Gemini, Cancer, Leo, Virgo, Libra, Scorpio, Sagittarius* and *Capricornus* accordingly. RXH posted the twelve pictures on its website, each accompanied with a digitized watermark "starhave" to indicate its origin, also with a copyright notice.

Defendants, Kewen Information Ltd. ('Kewen') and Dang Dang Kewen E-Commerce Co., Ltd. ('Dang Dang') are the operators of the website www.dangdang.com. On November 24, 2005, Plaintiff found its twelve pictures posted on Defendant's website in the 'Swarovski Crystals Series' column, a promotion webpage launched by Defendant for Swarovski crystal products. None of the twelve pictures on Defendant's website carried Plaintiff's digitized watermarks or mentioned Plaintiff. Among the twelve pictures, six pictures were cropped, also without watermark or attribution to Plaintiff.

Plaintiff RXH alleged that Defendants Kewen and Dang Dang posted Plaintiff's twelve copyrighted pictures on its own website without permission. Plaintiff also alleged that Defendant maliciously deleted the digital rights management information (*i.e.* watermarks) on the original pictures, revised some of the pictures and failed to give credit to Plaintiff, therefore violating Plaintiff's right of authorship, right of revision, right of reproduction and right of communication through information network. As such, RXH requested the court

CASE (continued)

to enjoin Defendants from continuing to use the disputed pictures online, to issue a public apology and also to pay damages.

In their joint defense, Kewen and Dang Dang contended that the disputed pictures were provided by Zhong Shen and were originated from www.sohu.com ('Sohu'). They further contended RXH had not suffered financial losses from the alleged infringement.

This Court acknowledged that in a statement made by Zhong Shen on December 8, 2005, Zhong Shen claimed that it had acquired the disputed pictures from Sohu and then provided them to Defendants. [The Court also noted in a related judgment issued] on September 22, 2006, Beijing Haidian District Court found Sohu liable for copyright infringement against RXH's copyright to the twelve pictures that Sohu distributed without RXH's permission.

According to Chinese Copyright Law, copyright ownership for commissioned works can be determined between the commissioner and the commissioned party in the contract. In this case, based on the commission agreement between RXH and Shu Guang, RXH owns the copyright to the disputed pictures.

Defendants alleged that the disputed pictures originated from Sohu. However, since Sohu was found to be liable for infringing the copyright of RXH by using the pictures without authorization, and given that Defendants failed to provide evidence for the lawful origin of the pictures, Defendants were found to have used the pictures without permission.

To conclude, because Defendants used the twelve pictures on its website without Plaintiff's permission, revised six of the pictures, removed the digitized watermarks and did not attribute the origin to Plaintiff, this Court held that Defendant violated Plaintiff's right of authorship, right of revision, right of reproduction and the right of communication through information network.

NOTES AND QUESTIONS

1. The current PRC copyright law includes four categories of moral rights, the right to claim authorship, the right to divulge, the right to revise, and also the right to protect the work's integrity (Article 10(1)–(4) PRC Copyright Law). With regard to the last two categories of moral rights, *i.e.* "the right to revise" and "the right to protect the work's integrity," there has been confusion and uncertainty as to where to draw the line distinguishing the two. For instance, In *RXH v. Kewen*, Beijing No. 2 Intermediate Court held that Kewen's "cropping of the 6 constellation pictures" violated plaintiff's right to revise, but was not "defamatory enough" to violate plaintiff's right to protect the work's integrity. Yet in *ZHANG Bin v. Huaye Weicheng Culture Ltd.*, Beijing West District Court found that by changing the background of the plaintiff's original painting "White Hair" and also replacing the original faces in plaintiff's painting, defendant significantly altered the style and aesthetic value of plaintiff's work, thus finding defendant liable for infringing plaintiff's right to the work's integrity. See *ZHANG Bin v. Beijing Huaye Weicheng Culture Development Ltd.*, (2008) Ximinchuzi No. 848. What do you think should be the standard distinguishing these two causes of action?

2. In the current 3rd Revision of the PRC Copyright Law, it is suggested that "the right to revise" and "the right to protect work's integrity" be combined into one clause "the right to protect the work's integrity" so as to be more consistent with the Berne Convention. Do you think that such changes might resolve the confusion discussed earlier?

12.3.4 United States

Copyright law in the US adopts a very different position. Traditionally, the US Copyright Act did not include any specific protection of moral rights. With the accession of the US to the Berne Convention for the Protection of Literary and Artistic Works, a limited protection of moral rights was created for visual artists in the Visual Artists Rights Act (VARA) of 1990. Authors of works of visual art have a right of attribution, a right to protect the integrity of their work, and a right to prevent the destruction in case of works of a recognized stature (17 U.S.C. §106A(a)). These rights are inalienable, but can be waived (17 U.S.C. §106A(e)). They expire when the author dies (17 U.S.C. §106A(d)). Authors other than visual artists do not benefit from a similar protection of moral rights. Outside the limited scope of VARA, various doctrines in US federal and state law may protect some moral interests of authors on a case-by-case basis. However, US law generally provides far less protection of moral rights than its European counterparts.

CASE

Kelley v. Chicago Park Dist., 635 F.3d 290 (7th Cir. 2011)

SYKES, Circuit Judge.
Chapman Kelley is a nationally recognized artist known for his representational paintings of landscapes and flowers – in particular, romantic floral and woodland interpretations set within ellipses. In 1984 he received permission from the Chicago Park District to install an ambitious wildflower display at the north end of Grant Park, a prominent public space in the heart of downtown Chicago. "Wildflower Works" was thereafter planted: two enormous elliptical flower beds, each nearly as big as a football field, featuring a variety of native wildflowers and edged with borders of gravel and steel.

Promoted as "living art," Wildflower Works received critical and popular acclaim, and for a while Kelley and a group of volunteers tended the vast garden, pruning and replanting as needed. But by 2004 Wildflower Works had deteriorated, and the City's goals for Grant Park had changed. So the Park District dramatically modified the garden, substantially reducing its size, reconfiguring the oval flower beds into rectangles, and changing some of the planting material.

Kelley sued the Park District for violating his "right of integrity" under the Visual Artists Rights Act of 1990 ("VARA"), 17 U.S.C. §106A, and also for breach of contract. The contract claim is insubstantial; the main event here is the VARA claim, which is novel and tests the boundaries of copyright law. Congress enacted this statute to comply with the nation's obligations under the Berne Convention for the Protection of Literary and

CASE *(continued)*

Source: Public domain: from Federal Judicial Opinion.

Figure [12.5] Chapman Kelley's Wildflower Works

Artistic Works. VARA amended the Copyright Act, importing a limited version of the civil-law concept of the "moral rights of the artist" into our intellectual-property law. In brief, for certain types of visual art – paintings, drawings, prints, sculptures, and exhibition photographs – VARA confers upon the artist certain rights of attribution and integrity. The latter include the right of the artist to prevent, during his lifetime, any distortion or modification of his work that would be "prejudicial to his . . . honor or reputation," and to recover for any such intentional distortion or modification undertaken without his consent. See 17 U.S.C. §106A(a)(3)(A).

The district court held a bench trial and entered a split judgment. The court rejected Kelley's moral-rights claim for two reasons. First, the judge held that although Wildflower Works could be classified as both a painting and a sculpture and therefore a work of visual art under VARA, it lacked sufficient originality to be eligible for copyright, a foundational requirement in the statute. Second, following the First Circuit's decision in Phillips v. Pembroke Real Estate, Inc., 459 F.3d 128 (1st Cir. 2006), the court concluded that site-specific art like Wildflower Works is categorically excluded from protection under VARA.

There is reason to doubt several of the district court's conclusions: that Wildflower Works is a painting or sculpture; that it flunks the test for originality; and that all site-specific art is excluded from VARA. But the court was right to reject this claim; for reasons relating to copyright's requirements of expressive authorship and fixation, a living garden like Wildflower Works is not copyrightable.

For the next several years, Kelley's permit was renewed and he and his volunteers tended the impressive garden. Of course, the forces of nature – the varying bloom periods of the plants; their spread habits, compatibility, and life cycles; and the weather – produced constant change. Some wildflowers naturally did better than others. Some spread

CASE *(continued)*

aggressively and encroached on neighboring plants. Some withered and died. Unwanted plants sprung up from seeds brought in by birds and the wind. Four years after Wildflower Works was planted, the Park District decided to discontinue the exhibit.

Kelley responded by suing the Park District in federal court, claiming the termination of his permit violated the First Amendment. The parties quickly settled; in exchange for dismissal of the suit, the Park District agreed to extend Kelley's permit for another year. [The Park District renewed the permit until 1994 and after that Kelley and his associates continued as before without a formal permit. In 2004 the Park District proposed changes culminating in a plan to cut the garden's size by half.] Kelley then sued the Park District for violating his moral rights under VARA. He claimed that Wildflower Works was both a painting and a sculpture and therefore a "work of visual art" under VARA, and that the Park District's reconfiguration of it was an intentional "distortion, mutilation, or other modification" of his work and was "prejudicial to his . . . honor or reputation." See 17 U.S.C. §106A(a)(3)(A). Kelley sought compensation for the moral-rights violation, statutory damages, and attorney's fees. He later quantified his damages, requesting a staggering $25 million for the VARA violation. [The Park District won at trial and Kelley appealed.]

That artists have certain "moral rights" in their work is a doctrine long recognized in civil-law countries but only recently imported into the United States. Moral rights are generally grouped into two categories: rights of attribution and rights of integrity.

Originating in nineteenth-century France, moral rights – *le droit moral* – are understood as rights inhering in the artist's personality, transcending property and contract rights and existing independently of the artist's economic interest in his work. VARA introduced a limited version of this European doctrine into American law, but it is not an easy fit.

VARA was enacted as a consequence of the United States' accession to the Berne Convention for the Protection of Literary and Artistic Works. After many years of resistance, the Senate ratified the treaty in 1988, bringing the United States into the Berne Union effective the following year. [I]n 1928 Article *6bis* was added [to the Berne Convention], incorporating the concept of moral rights. Article *6bis* provides:

> (1) Independently of the author's economic rights, and even after the transfer of the said rights, the author shall have the right to claim authorship of the work and to object to any distortion, mutilation or other modification of, or other derogatory action in relation to, the said work, which would be prejudicial to his honor or reputation.
>
> . . .
>
> (3) The means of redress for safeguarding the rights granted by this Article shall be governed by the legislation of the country where protection is claimed.

Berne Convention for the Protection of Literary and Artistic Works, art. *6bis,* Sept. 9, 1886, *as revised at* Paris on July 24, 1971, S. TREATY DOC. NO. 99–27 (1986).

When the United States joined the Berne Union in 1989, the concept of moral rights was largely unknown in American law. Article *6bis* was a major obstacle to Berne ratification.

> **CASE** *(continued)*
>
> *See* Roberta Rosenthal Kwall, *How Fine Art Fares Post VARA*, 1 MARQ. INTELL. PROP. L.REV.V. 1, 1–4 (1997).
>
> American unease with European moral-rights doctrine – more particularly, the obligations imposed by Article 6bis – persisted beyond Berne ratification. VARA was enacted to fill this perceived gap, but its moral-rights protection is quite a bit narrower than its European counterpart.
>
> **VARA's scope**
> VARA amended the Copyright Act and provides a measure of protection for a limited set of moral rights falling under the rubric of "rights of attribution" and "rights of integrity" – but only for artists who create specific types of visual art. 17 U.S.C. §106A(a). The statutory coverage is limited to paintings, drawings, prints, sculptures, and photographs created for exhibition existing in a single copy or a limited edition of 200 or less. *See id.* §101 (defining "work of visual art"). The rights conferred by the statute exist independently of property rights; the artist retains them even after he no longer holds title to his work. *Id.* §106A(a).
>
> More specifically, VARA's attribution and integrity rights are as follows:
>
>> (a) **Rights of attribution and integrity.** Subject to section 107 and independent of the exclusive rights provided in section 106, *the author of a work of visual art –*
>> (1) shall have the right –
>>   (A) to claim authorship of that work, and
>>   (B) to prevent the use of his or her name as the author of any work of visual art which he or she did not create;
>> (2) shall have the right to prevent the use of his or her name as the author of the work of visual art in the event of distortion, mutilation, or other modification of the work which would be prejudicial to his or her honor or reputation; and
>> (3) subject to the limitations set forth in section 113(d), *shall have the right –*
>>   (A) to prevent any intentional distortion, mutilation, or other modification of that work which would be prejudicial to his or her honor or reputation, and any intentional distortion, mutilation, or modification of that work is a violation of that right, and
>>   (B) to prevent any destruction of a work of recognized stature, and any intentional or grossly negligent destruction of that work is a violation of that right.
>
> 17 U.S.C. §106A(a) (emphasis added).
> At issue here is the right of integrity conferred by subsection (a)(3)(A), which precludes any intentional modification or distortion of a work of visual art that "would be prejudicial to [the artist's] honor or reputation."
>
> A qualifying "work of visual art" is defined as:
>
>> (1) *a painting,* drawing, print, *or sculpture,* existing in a single copy, in a limited edition of 200 or fewer that are signed and consecutively numbered by the author, or, in the case

CASE *(continued)*

of a sculpture, in multiple cast, carved, or fabricated sculptures of 200 or fewer that are consecutively numbered by the author and bear the signature or other identifying mark of the author; or

(2) a still photographic image produced for exhibition purposes only, existing in a single copy that is signed by the author, or in a limited edition of 200 copies or fewer that are signed and consecutively numbered by the author.

Id. §101 (emphasis added). This definition also contains a number of specific exclusions: *e.g.,* posters, maps, and globes; books, newspapers, magazines, and other periodicals; "motion picture[s] or other audiovisual work [s]"; merchandising and promotional materials; "any work made for hire"; and "any work not subject to copyright protection under this title." *Id.*

[U]nder VARA, a work must first satisfy basic copyright standards. Under the Copyright Act of 1976, copyright subsists in "original works of authorship fixed in any tangible medium of expression, now known or later developed, from which they can be perceived, reproduced, or otherwise communicated." *Id.* §102(a). "Works of authorship" include "pictorial, graphic, and sculptural works." *Id.* §102(a)(5). VARA's definition of "work of visual art" is limited to a narrow subset of this broader universe of "pictorial, graphic, and sculptural works" that are otherwise eligible for copyright; only a select few categories of art get the extra protection provided by the moral-rights concept.

Several exceptions limit the scope of the rights granted under the statute:

(c) Exceptions. (1) The modification of a work of visual art which is a result of the passage of time or the inherent nature of the materials is not a distortion, mutilation, or other modification described in subsection (a)(3)(A).

(2) The modification of a work of visual art which is the result of conservation, or of the public presentation, including lighting and placement, of the work is not a destruction, distortion, mutilation, or other modification described in subsection (a)(3) unless the modification is caused by gross negligence.

17 U.S.C. §106A(c) (emphasis added). The second of these – the "public presentation" exception – is at issue here. Another exception invoked by the Park District is found in a different section of the Copyright Act that defines the scope of a copyright owner's rights:

(d)(1) In a case in which –

(A) *a work of visual art has been incorporated in or made part of a building* in such a way that removing the work from the building will cause the destruction, distortion, mutilation, or other modification of the work as described in section 106A(a)(3), and

(B) the author consented to the installation of the work in the building either before the effective date set forth in section 610(a) of the Visual Artists Rights Act of 1990, or in a written instrument executed on or after such effective date that is signed by the owner of the building and the author and that specifies that installation of the work may subject the work to destruction, distortion, mutilation, or other modification, by reason of its removal,

CASE *(continued)*

then the rights conferred by paragraphs (2) and (3) of section 106A(a) shall not apply. *Id.* §113 (emphasis added). This is known as the "building exception."

VARA rights cannot be transferred or assigned, but they can be waived in a writing signed by the artist and "specifically identify[ing] the work, and uses of that work, to which the waiver applies." *Id.* §106A(e)(1). Absent a written waiver, the artist retains VARA rights during his lifetime even if he transfers ownership of the work or assigns his copyright. *Id.* §106A(d)(1), (e)(2).

Is Wildflower Works a painting or sculpture?

The district court held that Wildflower Works was both a painting and a sculpture but was insufficiently original to qualify for copyright. Alternatively, the court concluded that it was site-specific art and held that all site-specific art is implicitly excluded from VARA.

VARA's definition of "work of visual art" operates to narrow and focus the statute's coverage; only a "painting, drawing, print, or sculpture," or an exhibition photograph will qualify. These terms are not further defined, but the overall structure of the statutory scheme clearly illuminates the limiting effect of this definition. Copyright's broad general coverage extends to "original works of authorship," and this includes "pictorial, graphic, and sculptural works." 17 U.S.C. §102(a)(5). The use of the adjectives "pictorial" and "sculptural" suggests flexibility and breadth in application. In contrast VARA uses the specific nouns "painting" and "sculpture." To qualify for moral-rights protection under VARA, Wildflower Works cannot just be "pictorial" or "sculptural" in some aspect or effect, it must actually *be* a "painting" or a "sculpture." Not metaphorically or by analogy, but *really*.

That Kelley considered the garden to be both a painting and a sculpture – only rendered in living material – is not dispositive.

Kelley's expert, a professor of art history, reinforced his view that Wildflower Works was both a painting and a sculpture, but the district court largely disregarded her testimony as unhelpful. If a living garden like Wildflower Works really counts as both a painting and a sculpture, then these terms do no limiting work at all.

This case raises serious questions about the meaning and application of VARA's definition of qualifying works of visual art – questions with potentially decisive consequences for this and other moral-rights claims. But the Park District has not challenged this aspect of the district court's decision, so we move directly to the question of copyrightability, which is actually where the analysis should start in the first place.

Is Wildflower Works copyrightable?

To merit copyright protection, Wildflower Works must be an "original work [] of authorship fixed in a[] tangible medium of expression . . . from which [it] can be perceived, reproduced, or otherwise communicated." 17 U.S.C. §102(a). The district court held that although Wildflower Works was both a painting and a sculpture, it was ineligible for copyright because it lacked originality. [However,] the law is clear that a work can be original even if it is not novel. No one argues that Wildflower Works was copied; it plainly possesses more than a little creative spark.

> **CASE** *(continued)*
>
> The real impediment to copyright here is not that Wildflower Works fails the test for originality (understood as "not copied" and "possessing some creativity") but that a living garden lacks the kind of authorship and stable fixation normally required to support copyright. Unlike originality, authorship and fixation are *explicit* constitutional requirements; the Copyright Clause empowers Congress to secure for "authors" exclusive rights in their "writings."
>
> We fully accept that the artistic community might classify Kelley's garden as a work of postmodern conceptual art. We acknowledge as well that copyright's prerequisites of authorship and fixation are broadly defined. But the law must have some limits; not all conceptual art may be copyrighted. In the ordinary copyright case, authorship and fixation are not contested; most works presented for copyright are unambiguously authored and unambiguously fixed. But this is not an ordinary case. A living garden like Wildflower Works is neither "authored" nor "fixed" in the senses required for copyright.
>
> Simply put, gardens are planted and cultivated, not authored. A garden's constituent elements are alive and inherently changeable, not fixed. Most of what we see and experience in a garden – the colors, shapes, textures, and scents of the plants – originates in nature, not in the mind of the gardener. At any given moment in time, a garden owes most of its form and appearance to natural forces, though the gardener who plants and tends it obviously assists. All this is true of Wildflower Works, even though it was designed and planted by an artist.
>
> Of course, a human "author" – whether an artist, a professional landscape designer, or an amateur backyard gardener – determines the initial arrangement of the plants in a garden. This is not the kind of authorship required for copyright. To the extent that seeds or seedlings can be considered a "medium of expression," they originate in nature, and natural forces – not the intellect of the gardener – determine their form, growth, and appearance. Moreover, a garden is simply too changeable to satisfy the primary purpose of fixation; its appearance is too inherently variable to supply a baseline for determining questions of copyright creation and infringement. If a garden can qualify as a "work of authorship" sufficiently "embodied in a copy," at what point has fixation occurred? When the garden is newly planted? When its first blossoms appear? When it is in full bloom? How – and at what point in time – is a court to determine whether infringing copying has occurred?
>
> In contrast, when a landscape designer conceives of a plan for a garden and puts it in writing – records it in text, diagrams, or drawings on paper or on a digital-storage device – we can say that his intangible intellectual property has been embodied in a fixed and tangible "copy." This writing is a sufficiently permanent and stable copy of the designer's intellectual expression and is vulnerable to infringing copying, giving rise to the designer's right to claim copyright. The same cannot be said of a garden, which is not a fixed copy of the gardener's intellectual property. Although the planting material is tangible and can be perceived for more than a transitory duration, it is not stable or permanent enough to be called "fixed."

CASE *(continued)*

Site-specific art, and the public-presentation and building exceptions
This case also raises some important questions about the application of VARA to site-specific art, as well as the statute's public-presentation and building exceptions. Though we need not decide these questions, we do have a few words of caution about the district court's treatment of the issue of VARA and site-specific art. The court classified Wildflower Works as a form of site-specific art; we see no reason to upset this factual finding. The court then adopted the First Circuit's holding in *Phillips* that site-specific art is categorically excluded from VARA. This legal conclusion is open to question.

Phillips involved a VARA claim brought by artist David Phillips in a dispute over a display of 27 of his sculptures in Boston's Eastport Park across from Boston Harbor. *Phillips v. Pembroke Real Estate, Inc.*, 459 F.3d 128, 130 (1st Cir. 2006). A planned redesign of the park called for the removal and relocation of Phillips's sculptures; he sought an injunction under VARA, claiming the removal of his sculptures would violate his right of integrity. *Id.* at 131.

There are a couple of reasons to question [the *Phillips*] interpretation of VARA. First, the term "site-specific art" appears nowhere in the statute. Nothing in the definition of a "work of visual art" either explicitly or by implication excludes this form of art from moral-rights protection. Nor does application of the public-presentation exception operate to eliminate *every* type of protection VARA grants to creators of site-specific art; the exception simply narrows the scope of the statute's protection for all qualifying works of visual art. The exception basically provides a safe harbor for ordinary changes in the public presentation of VARA-qualifying artworks; the artist has no cause of action unless through gross negligence the work is modified, distorted, or destroyed in the process of changing its public presentation.

Second, *Phillips*'s all-or-nothing approach to site-specific art may be unwarranted. Site-specific art is not *necessarily* destroyed if moved; modified, yes, but not always utterly destroyed. Moreover, some of VARA's protections are unaffected by the public-presentation exception. An artist's right of integrity can be violated in ways that do not implicate the work's location or manner of public presentation; site-specific art – like any other type of art – can be defaced and damaged in ways that do not relate to its public display. And the public-presentation exception does nothing to limit the right of attribution, which prevents an artist's name from being misappropriated.

Then there is the matter of the building exception, which applies to works "incorporated in or made part of a building in such a way that removing the work from the building will cause the destruction, distortion, mutilation, or other modification of the work." 17 U.S.C. §113(d)(1)(A). These works do not get moral-rights protection if the artist: (1) consented to the installation of his work in the building (if pre-VARA); or (2) executed a written acknowledgment that removal of the work may subject it to destruction, distortion, mutilation, or modification (if post-VARA). *Id.* §113(d)(1)(B). On its face this exception covers a particular kind of site-specific art. Its presence in the statute suggests that site-specific art is not categorically excluded from VARA.

These observations are of course general and not dispositive. Because we are resolving

> **CASE** *(continued)*
>
> the VARA claim on other grounds, we need not decide whether VARA is inapplicable to site-specific art.
>
> [The court also dismissed a contract-based claim by the artist Chapman Kelley, based on periodic representations by the Park District.]

NOTES AND COMMENTS

1. **Moral rights in the US pre-VARA.** The opinion quotes commentary to the effect that, prior to US accession to the Berne Convention, "some Berne co-Unionists . . . expressed doubts regarding the accuracy or sincerity of the U.S. declaration that its law already afforded a degree of moral rights protection equivalent to Berne standards" (Jane C. Ginsburg, *Copyright in the 101st Congress: Commentary on the Visual Artists Rights Act and the Architectural Works Copyright Protection Act of 1990*, 14 COLUM.-VLA J.L. & ARTS 477, 478–79 (1990)). The moral rights "tradition" in the US consisted primarily of one federal court case, *Gilliam v. American Broadcasting Companies, Inc.*, 538 F.2d 14 (2d Cir. 1976). *Gilliam* was a claim by the creators of the *Monty Python's Flying Circus* series in Britain that adaptation of the series for the US market resulted in a mutilation of the works (due to the shortening or various routines to account for commercials in the US version; the original skits were broadcast commercial-free on the state funded BBC network in Britain). But the holding in *Gilliam* was arguably more contract based than moral rights oriented. The court there emphasized that the agreement between Gilliam and the US broadcast network ABC did not include the right to modify the original content. Thus the case can be seen as an extension or application of earlier US case law, based on state contract causes of action, in situations where a licensor claimed "misrepresentation" where a licensee modified (read: mutilated) a licensed work. *See, e.g., Granz v. Harris*, 198 F.2d 585 (2d Cir. 1952) (substantial cutting of original work constitutes misrepresentation).

2. **Right to attribution in the US: still in search of a firm foundation.** The Supreme Court of the US passed on a golden opportunity to firmly establish the right of attribution in the US. In the trademark case of *Dastar Corp. v. Twentieth Century Fox Film Corp.*, 539 U.S. 23 (2003), that Court held that the reproducing a public domain work without attribution to the original authors was not a violation of federal trademark law (the Lanham Act). For an expert assessment of the remaining shortcomings in US protection for moral rights, *see* Jane C. Ginsburg, *Moral Rights in the U.S.: Still in Need of a* Guardian Ad Litem, 30 Cardozo Arts & Ent. L.J. 73 (2012).

12.4 Neighboring rights

12.4.1 Europe

12.4.1.1 *Performing artists, producers, audiovisual communication enterprises*

Continental-European copyright law makes a strict distinction between the rights of copyright authors and the rights of performers, producers of sound and video recordings, and broadcasting organizations. The latter group are not part of copyright protection in a narrow sense, but constitute so-called "neighboring rights" ("droits voisins"). These rights are not granted to authors who create copyrighted works themselves, but to other individuals or companies who are facilitating the dissemination of copyrighted works in one way or the other. Neighboring rights differ from authors' copyrights in that they are typically narrower in scope and shorter in term (*see* Art. 3 Term Directive). At the EU level, neighboring rights have been harmonized in the Rental Rights Directive (granting distribution rights, broadcasting and communication to the public rights, fixation rights as well as rental and lending rights to performers, sound and video recording producers, and broadcasting organizations) and in the Information Society Directive (granting a reproduction right and the right to make available to the public to neighboring rights holders). At the level of EU Member States, the implementation of neighboring rights varies. In France and Germany, neighboring rights are implemented as Part 2 of the respective Copyright Acts (Arts. L211-1 to L217-3 CPI and Secs. 70–87h German Copyright Act). In the UK, as in other common law countries, the producers of a sound recording and of a film as well as a broadcasting organization are considered normal copyright authors (Sec. 9(2) CDPA), while performers' rights are implemented as Part 2 of the CDPA.

While the Rental Rights and the Information Society Directives provide for certain neighboring rights, this does not prevent EU Member States from adding further neighboring rights to their national copyright law. The German legislator, for example, introduced a neighboring right for press publishers in 2013 (Sec. 87f–87h German Copyright Act). It is questionable whether this attempt to protect news publishers against Google News and similar enterprises will be successful. For a related empirical investigation, *see* Lesley Chiou & Catherine Tucker, Content Aggregation by Platforms: The Case of the News Media, 2015, available at http://ssrn.com/abstract=1864203; *see also* Eleonora Rosati, *Neighbouring Rights for Publishers: Are National and (Possible) EU Initiatives Lawful?*, 47 International Review of Intellectual Property and Competition Law, 569–94 (2016).

German Federal Constitutional Court (Bundesverfassungsgericht), case 1 BvR 1585/13, 2016 – "Metal on Metal" ("Metall auf Metall")

The constitutional complaint concerns the question to what extent musicians can invoke artistic freedom when facing copyright-related claims of phonogram producers in which they challenge that parts of their phonogram are used by way of the so-called sampling.

CASE (continued)

Complainants are, among others, two composers and the singer of the song "*Nur mir*", which was published in 1997 in several versions on the album "*Die neue S-Klasse*" and on an EP ("extended play"), as well as the music production company that produced the album and the EP. According to the facts established in the civil court proceedings, to produce two versions of the song "*Nur mir*", a two-second rhythm sequence from the soundtrack of the composition "*Metall auf Metall*" from the "Trans Europa Express" album by the German band "*Kraftwerk*" from 1977 was sampled from the original and embedded, with minor changes only, in the two versions as continuously repeated rhythm ("loop").

Following an action brought by two founding members of the band "*Kraftwerk*", the composers and the music production company were ordered to cease and desist from producing and selling phonograms with the two concerned versions of the song "*Nur mir*" and hand over already existing phonograms to the plaintiffs for destruction. In addition, the complainants (in the present constitutional complaint proceedings) were found liable to pay damages to the original plaintiffs. The Federal Court of Justice, which dealt with the matter twice, upheld the decision (Judgment of 20 November 2008 – I ZR 112/06, Metall auf Metall I – and Judgment of 13 December 2012 – I ZR 182/11, Metall auf Metall II –). It held that even the use of extremely short parts of a soundtrack produced by another party constituted an interference with the phonogram producer's right to protection of his work pursuant to §85 sec. 1 sentence 1 UrhG and generally required the latter's approval. By applying the provision of §24 sec. 1 UrhG, the court recognised free use as an exception to this requirement. But the prerequisite for such free use was that the sequence concerned could not be reproduced in a way that sounded like the original. According to the findings by the Hamburg Higher Regional Court (*Oberlandesgericht*) (Judgment of 17 August 2011 – 5 U 48/05 –) this was, however, possible in the present case so that the complainants could not invoke the right to free use.

With their constitutional complaint the composers and the music production company claim in particular a violation of their fundamental right to artistic freedom under Art. 5 sec. 3 sentence 1 of the Basic Law (*Grundgesetz* – GG).

Key Considerations of the Senate:
The challenged decisions violate the freedom of artistic activity of three of a total of twelve complainants (Art. 5 sec. 3 sentence 1 of the Basic Law, *Grundgesetz* – GG). . . .

2. The challenged decisions violate the freedom of artistic activity of the two composers and the music production company of the song "*Nur mir*" guaranteed by Art. 5 sec. 3 sentence 1 GG.

a) When interpreting and applying copyright laws, civil courts must reproduce the balance struck in the Act between the property interests of phonogram producers and the conflicting fundamental rights, thereby avoiding that fundamental rights are disproportionately restricted. The point at which the Federal Constitutional Court has to rectify a violation of constitutional law is reached only if the interpretation

CASE *(continued)*

by the civil courts reveals errors that are, also due to their substantial significance, of considerable relevance for the specific case.

b) In a legal assessment of the use of works protected by copyright, the copyright holders' interest to prevent commercial exploitation of their works by third parties without their consent conflicts with the interest of other artists to induce a creative process by an artistic dialogue with existing works without being subject to financial risks or restrictions in terms of content. If the creative development of an artist is measured against an interference with copyrights that only slightly limits the possibilities of exploitation, the exploitation interests of the copyright holders may have to cede in favour of the freedom to enter into an artistic dialogue. These principles are also applicable if phonograms protected under §85 sec. 1 sentence 1 UrhG are used for artistic purposes.

c) The presumption by the Federal Court of Justice that even the inclusion of very brief sound sequences constitutes an interference with the plaintiffs' right to protection as phonogram producers if the used sequence can be reproduced so as to sound like the original, does not take sufficient account of the right to artistic freedom. Where a musical artist who intends to use samples to create a new work does not want to refrain from including a sample in his new piece of music, the strict interpretation of free use by the Federal Court of Justice puts him in the position of having to decide whether to obtain a sample license from the phonogram producer or to reproduce the sample himself. In both cases, however, the freedom of artistic activity and hence also the further cultural development would be restricted.

Emphasising the possibility to obtain a license does not provide an equivalent degree of protection of the freedom of artistic activity: The process of granting rights is extremely difficult in case of works which assemble many different samples in a collage-like manner.

Nor is the reproduction of sounds by the artist himself an equivalent substitute. The use of samples is a typical style element of hip-hop. The necessary consideration of specific artistic criteria requires that such aspects defining this music genre not be ignored. In addition, reproducing a sample cover by the artist himself can be very laborious, and the assessment whether such a sound is equivalent to the original leads to considerable insecurity among artists.

d) In the present case of a license-free use of sampling, these restrictions of the freedom of artistic activity are measured against an only minor interference with the claimants' rights as phonogram producers, which does not entail considerable economic disadvantages. There is no evident risk that the plaintiffs in the initial proceedings will suffer from a decline in sales through the adoption of the sound sequence into the two versions of the song "*Nur mir*" that are at issue here. Such a risk might possibly occur at most in individual cases in which the newly created work shows such similarity to the phonogram with the original sound sequence that one could actually presume that the new work will compete with the original phonogram. In this context one must consider

CASE *(continued)*

the artistic and temporal distance to the original work, the significance of the borrowed sequence, the impact of the economic damage for the creator of the original work as well as its prominence. The fact that §24 sec. 1 UrhG deprives the phonogram producer of the possibility to charge license fees does not automatically – and particularly not in the case at hand – entail a considerable economic disadvantage for the phonogram producer. The Constitution does not require the protection of small and tiny (sound) elements by a copyright-related right, which in the course of time could further complicate or even render impossible the use of existing cultural assets.

e) As a consequence, the exploitation interests of the phonogram producers must stand back when measured against the interests of free use for artistic activity. The additional criterion that a used sequence cannot be covered in a way that it sounds like the original, which was introduced by the Federal Court of Justice for the applicability of §24 sec. 1 UrhG to interferences with the rights of rights as phonogram producers, is not suitable for achieving a proportionate balance between the interest of an unrestricted continuing development of artistic activity and the property interests of the phonogram producers.

NOTES

1. It is a not often that a European constitutional court deals with an issue of copyright law. In this case, the German Constitutional Court had to deal with a tension between the neighboring right of a phonogram producer over a sound recording and the interest of a hip hop producer to freely use a two-second sample from the earlier recording in his own song. While the phonogram producer's interests are constitutionally protected as property (Art. 14 German Basic Law (the German Constitution)), the hip hop producer can benefit from the constitutionally protected artistic freedom enshrined in Art. 5(3) German Basic Law.

2. We have seen in the *Infopaq I* decision that the CJEU held that the copy of an extract of a protected work violates the reproduction right only if the extract contains an element of the work which fulfills copyright's originality standards. According to the case law of the German Federal Court of Justice, this is not the required standard for the neighboring right of the phonogram producer. The court argues that, while the copyright in a song intends to protect the personal creation of a composer, the phonogram producer's neighboring right is intended to reward the economic, organizational, and technical achievements of the producer. As a result, if a short sample from a song, which is used in another song, does not fulfill the originality standard, such reuse may not violate the copyright of the original composer, but may violate the neighboring right of the phonogram producer (German Federal Court of Justice (Bundesgerichtshof), case I ZR 112/06, GRUR 2009, 403 – "Metal on Metal I" ("Metall auf Metall I")). This explains why German sampling cases are litigated under the phonogram producer's neighboring rights, not the composer's copyright.

12.4.1.2 Databases

CASE

Case C-203/02, British Horseracing Board et al. v. William Hill Organization, Court of Justice of the European Union, ECLI:EU:C:2004:695

10   The BHB [British Horseracing Board] and Others manage the horse racing industry in the United Kingdom and in various capacities compile and maintain the BHB database which contains a large amount of information supplied by horse owners, trainers, horse race organisers and others involved in the racing industry. The database contains information on inter alia the pedigrees of some one million horses, and "pre-race information" on races to be held in the United Kingdom. That information includes the name, place and date of the race concerned, the distance over which the race is to be run, the criteria for eligibility to enter the race, the date by which entries must be received, the entry fee payable and the amount of money the racecourse is to contribute to the prize money for the race.

11   Weatherbys Group Ltd, the company which compiles and maintains the BHB database, performs three principal functions, which lead up to the issue of pre-race information.

12   First, it registers information concerning owners, trainers, jockeys and horses and records the performances of those horses in each race.

13   Second, it decides on weight adding and handicapping for the horses entered for the various races.

14   Third, it compiles the lists of horses running in the races. This activity is carried out by its own call centre, manned by about 30 operators. They record telephone calls entering horses in each race organised. The identity and status of the person entering the horse and whether the characteristics of the horse meet the criteria for entry to the race are then checked. Following those checks the entries are published provisionally. To take part in the race, the trainer must confirm the horse's participation by telephone by declaring it the day before the race at the latest. The operators must then ascertain whether the horse can be authorised to run the race in the light of the number of declarations already recorded. A central computer then allocates a saddle cloth number to each horse and determines the stall from which it will start. The final list of runners is published the day before the race.

15   The BHB database contains essential information not only for those directly involved in horse racing but also for radio and television broadcasters and for bookmakers and their clients. The cost of running the BHB database is approximately £4 million per annum. The fees charged to third parties for the use of the information in the database cover about a quarter of that amount.

...

17   William Hill, which is a subscriber to [BHB services], is one of the leading providers of off-course bookmaking services in the United Kingdom, to both UK and international

CASE *(continued)*

customers. It launched an on-line betting service on two internet sites. Those interested can use these sites to find out what horses are running in which races at which racecourses and what odds are offered by William Hill.

18 The information displayed on William Hill's internet sites is obtained, first, from newspapers published the day before the race and, second, from the [BHB].

19 According to the order for reference, the information displayed on William Hill's internet sites represents a very small proportion of the total amount of data on the BHB database, given that it concerns only the following matters: the names of all the horses in the race, the date, time and/or name of the race and the name of the racecourse where the race will be held. Also according to the order for reference, the horse races and the lists of runners are not arranged on William Hill's internet sites in the same way as in the BHB database.

20 In March 2000 the BHB and Others brought proceedings against William Hill in the High Court of Justice of England and Wales, Chancery Division, alleging infringement of their *sui generis* right. They contend, first, that each day's use by William Hill of racing data taken from the newspapers or the RDF is an extraction or re-utilisation of a substantial part of the contents of the BHB database, contrary to Article 7(1) of the directive. Secondly, they say that even if the individual extracts made by William Hill are not substantial they should be prohibited under Article 7(5) of the directive.

21 The High Court of Justice ruled in a judgment of 9 February 2001 that the action of BHB and Others was well founded. William Hill appealed to the referring court.

22 In the light of the problems of interpretation of the directive, the Court of Appeal decided to stay proceedings and refer the following questions to the Court of Justice for a preliminary ruling:

. . .

The second and third questions, concerning the concept of investment in the obtaining or verification of the contents of a database within the meaning of Article 7(1) of the directive

28 By its second and third questions the referring court seeks clarification of the concept of investment in the obtaining and verification of the contents of a database within the meaning of Article 7(1) of the directive.

29 Article 7(1) of the directive reserves the protection of the *sui generis* right to databases which meet a specific criterion, namely to those which show that there has been qualitatively and/or quantitatively a substantial investment in the obtaining, verification or presentation of their contents.

31 Against that background, the expression 'investment in . . . the obtaining . . . of the contents' of a database must, as William Hill point[s] out, be understood to refer to the resources used to seek out existing independent materials and collect them in the database, and not to the resources used for the creation as such of independent materials. The purpose of the protection by the *sui generis* right provided for by the directive is to promote the establishment of storage and processing systems for existing information and not the creation of materials capable of being collected subsequently in a database.

. . .

CASE *(continued)*

37 In the case in the main proceedings, the referring court seeks to know whether the investments described in paragraph 14 of this judgment can be considered to amount to investment in obtaining the contents of the BHB database. The plaintiffs in the main proceedings stress, in that connection, the substantial nature of the above investment.

38 However, investment in the selection, for the purpose of organising horse racing, of the horses admitted to run in the race concerned relates to the creation of the data which make up the lists for those races which appear in the BHB database. It does not constitute investment in obtaining the contents of the database. It cannot, therefore, be taken into account in assessing whether the investment in the creation of the database was substantial.

...

41 [T]he resources used to draw up a list of horses in a race and to carry out checks in that connection do not represent investment in the obtaining and verification of the contents of the database in which that list appears.

42 In the light of the foregoing, the second and third questions referred should be answered as follows:

- The expression "investment in . . . the obtaining . . . of the contents" of a database in Article 7(1) of the directive must be understood to refer to the resources used to seek out existing independent materials and collect them in the database. It does not cover the resources used for the creation of materials which make up the contents of a database.
- The expression "investment in . . . the . . . verification . . . of the contents" of a database in Article 7(1) of the directive must be understood to refer to the resources used, with a view to ensuring the reliability of the information contained in that database, to monitor the accuracy of the materials collected when the database was created and during its operation. The resources used for verification during the stage of creation of materials which are subsequently collected in a database do not fall within that definition.
- The resources used to draw up a list of horses in a race and to carry out checks in that connection do not constitute investment in the obtaining and verification of the contents of the database in which that list appears.

...

On those grounds, the Court (Grand Chamber) rules as follows:

1. The expression "investment in . . . the obtaining . . . of the contents" of a database in Article 7(1) of Directive 96/9/EC of the European Parliament and of the Council of 11 March 1996 on the legal protection of databases must be understood to refer to the resources used to seek out existing independent materials and collect them in the database. It does not cover the resources used for the creation of materials which make up the contents of a database . . .

NOTES

1. The history of European database protection is a typical example of efforts to harmonize European copyright law. Prior to the adoption of the European Database Directive, some EU Member States (UK, Denmark, Sweden, and the Netherlands) protected non-original data compilations, while other Member States did not or only in special circumstances, such as under unfair competition rules. When the Database Directive was adopted in 1996, it implemented a two-tiered protection system. According to the Directive, databases shall be protected by copyright if the selection or arrangement of data constitute the author's own intellectual creation (Art. 3(1) Database Directive, see supra Section 11.3.3.3 In this case, it is only the selection or arrangement of data which is copyrighted, not the data itself (Art. 3(2) Database Directive). Databases can also be protected by a *sui generis* database protection right if "there has been qualitatively and/or quantitatively a substantial investment in either the obtaining, verification or presentation of the contents to prevent extraction and/or re-utilization of the whole or of a substantial part ... of the contents of that database" (Art. 7(1) Database Directive). In this case, the mere investment in the data collection may be protected; see Matthias Leistner, "The Protection of Databases," in Research Handbook on the Future of EU Copyright 427–57 (Estelle Derclaye ed., 2009). In this subsection, we are looking at this *sui generis* database protection right.
2. One of the policy goals of introduction of a *sui generis* database protection in the EU was to strengthen the European database industry vis-à-vis their international competition, in particular from the US. In 2005, the European Commission published a report evaluating the impact of the Database Directive on the European database industry. The report was based on a survey among European database producers and publishers as well as on a directory of international databases which, among other things, counted the number of available databases. The report found that the economic impact of the *sui generis* right on database production is unproven, but that the European publishing industry argued the right was crucial to them. See Commission of the European Communities, First Evaluation of Directive 96/9/EC on the Legal Protection of Databases, December 12, 2005, available at http://ec.europa.eu/internal_market/copyright/docs/databases/evaluation_report_en.pdf. What do you think about the methodological approach of the report? How would a sound analysis to measure the impact of the Database Directive on database productivity in Europe look?

12.4.2 China

12.4.2.1 Introduction

The Chinese Copyright Law affords neighboring rights protection to the following related parties: publishers (Arts. 30–36), performing artists (Arts. 37–39), producers of phonograms (Arts. 40–42) and broadcasting organizations (Arts. 43–46). As briefly explained in the Introduction, the "copyright" concept, in a broad sense, as interpreted by many civil law jurisdictions, includes both author's rights (*droit d'auteur*) and also neighboring rights (*droits voisins*, also known as "related rights").

Author's rights refers to the rights of an author who *creates* the work, by writing a poem, composing a song, drawing a painting, creating a sculpture or taking a photograph. Neighboring rights holders, on the other hand, do not necessarily participate in the creation of the works. Instead, they act more like the "middlemen" of the entire pipeline – with authors on the one side of the pipe line and the general public on the other side – who invest time, capital, and energy to distribute the works created by authors to the general public. Although neighboring rights holders are not authors per se, the value and importance of their work cannot be underestimated. As such, a different set of rights, *i.e.* neighboring rights, is created to ensure that the rights and interests of neighboring rights holders are sufficiently protected, thus providing them with incentive to further disseminate the works.

Note that we used a metaphor "middlemen" to describe the role of neighboring rights holders. First of all, neighboring rights holders are not authors, thus they do not enjoy the exclusive rights that are granted to copyright owners of the works. In other words, before neighboring rights holders could disseminate a work by publishing, performing, producing a phonogram of or broadcasting it, they first need to get permission from the copyright owner of the underlying work. This is known as "copyright clearance" in the industry. Then, after the neighboring rights holders receive permission from the copyright owners of the underlying work to create their own "works," be they either publications, performances, phonograms, or broadcasts of the underlying works, they are now entitled to prevent others from using their works without authorization.

12.4.2.2 Publishers

CASE

WANG Jianmin v. LI Hongqi, Xuelin Publishing House, aff'd on appeal, Shanghai High People's Court (2004) Hugaominsanzhizhongzi No. 20

Plaintiff WANG Jingmin ("WANG") entered into a publishing contract with Defendant LI Hongqi ("LI") on September 1, 2001, aka "First Contract". The first Contract includes the following provisions: (1) LI, the copyright owner of the book *The Code of Chinese Character: Story of the Invention of Chinese Character* (the "Book"), agrees to authorize WANG, an exclusive right to publish the Book in simplified Chinese characters within the territory of Mainland China for five years; (2) LI warrants that the Book does not infringe intellectual property rights of any other third party, and further guarantees that he will not assign or resell the publication rights to other parties; and (3) WANG agrees to pay LI a flat fee of RMB 100,000 as the royalty of the Book.

    A few days after the execution of the First Contract, LI issued a letter, authorizing WANG to be in charge of the publication and distribution of the Book. On the same day of September 5, 2001, LI also signed a receipt, confirming the receipt of the royalty at RMB 100,000 from WANG.

CASE *(continued)*

On October 5, 2001, LI entered into another publishing contract with Xuelin Publishing House ("Xuelin"), aka "Second Contract". The Second Contract provides that Xuelin would enjoy the exclusive right of publication for the Book for five years, while LI was entitled to a royalty-based remuneration. In March 2002, the Book was published by Xuelin in the first edition of eight thousand copies. In September 2002, the Book was reprinted by Xuelin in three thousand copies.

[WANG sued both LI and Xuelin for violating his exclusive right of publication. LI argued that because WANG was an individual and did not have the publication permit necessary to publish the Book, the Court should invalidate the First Contract] . . .

[Reasoning of the Court as follows . . .]

Issue 2: Validity of the First Contract between WANG and LI

This Court held that the First Contract between WANG and LI was concluded through mutual consultation and reflected the true intent of each party. Also, none of the stipulations under the First Contract are conflicting with existing laws or regulations. Therefore, the court found the First Contract to be legitimate and valid.

As to Defendant's argument that WANG, as an individual, does not have a publication permit to publish books, thus requesting the First Contract be voided, the Court does not agree with such an argument. [It is true that] publication should be subject to administrative regulations such as *Regulations on Publication Administration*, and a publication permit is required to publish books. However, the exclusive right of publication as specified in the First Contract was private right in nature. Based on the copyright law, copyright owner has right to dispose his copyrighted work, [including the right to publish his work or authorize others to publish his work.] [In this case,] even if the licensee [WANG] does not have a publication permit, therefore could not publish the book himself, he could entrust a third party to publish LI's Book. In other words, it is possible for a natural person [WANG], to acquire the publication right from the copyright owner [LI], and then entrust a third publishing house who has a publication permit to publish the Book. Therefore, the exclusive right of publication provided in the First Contract is valid . . .

Issue 4: Whether defendants LI and Xuelin violated the publication right of WANG

Pursuant to the First Contract, LI agreed and guaranteed that WANG was granted with an exclusive right of publication within the term of the contract. Therefore, by entering into a second competing contract with Xuelin without WANG's permission, LI breached the contract with WANG and also committed copyright infringement against WANG's exclusive right of publication. Since WANG based his legal claim on the ground of copyright infringement, Li should be held liable for copyright infringement accordingly.

As to Co-defendant Xuelin, it was unaware of the existence of the First Contract when it entered into the publishing contract with LI. From Xuelin's perspective, it obtained permission from LI, the copyright owner, to publish the Book. The contract was concluded in accordance with the general practice of the publishing industry and was consistent with

> **CASE** *(continued)*
>
> the relevant laws and regulations. As such, Xuelin was not at fault when entering into the Second Contract and publishing the Book. As a result, the Court found Xuelin not liable for copyright infringement...
> [LI's appeal was rejected, and the court so affirmed.]

12.4.2.3 Performers, phonogram producers, and broadcasters

Problem hypo

A start-up media company based in Los Angeles would like to distribute DVDs of a popular Beijing opera *Farewell, My Concubine*. The CEO of this company just returned from China a month ago. He was so intrigued by the opera experience he had in Beijing that he wants to distribute this particular opera in DVD format in North America.

Now they come to you for advice, both business and legal related. What options does this company have in order to achieve this goal? What rights or authorization does the company need to obtain from various rights holders?

NOTES AND QUESTIONS

1. In the Hypo described above, what could be the implication that your client is a "start up" company? How would that affect your consulting approach with the client?
2. From the business perspective, what are the possible options of "distributing DVDs of an opera"? Would each business option result to different legal implications? How?
3. Assuming that there is already an existing DVD recording of the Beijing opera *Farewell, My concubine* produced by SONG Entertainment Ltd., if your client would like to distribute that particular recording, what should he do (or probably what should you do if you represent him)? What are the key terms that should be included in your due diligence check list?
4. Or, assuming that there is no existing DVD recording of the Beijing Opera that your client is interested in, but instead he would like to start from scratch and organize a team of professional artists to perform that opera and then record that performance into phonograms for distribution purposes what rights does he need to clear then?
5. Following on Question 4, is there any difference between hiring local talent (performers) from California and hiring international talent from China when performing that opera? What are the legal considerations that your client should be mindful of?
6. Finally, assuming that your client has successfully cleared all the rights and successfully distributed the DVD recordings of the Beijing Opera *Farewell, My concubine*, and now that a local broadcasting station 888 would like to broadcast this opera during their lunch hour session every Tuesday for three months, what permission does this station need to get in order to broadcast this phonogram?
7. The Hypo was based on an earlier case *China Wenlian Audio-Visual Publishing v. Chang-Jin Audio-Visual Ltd.*, decided by the Chinese Supreme People's Court in 2008. *See* (2008) Chinese Supreme People's Court, Minsanzhongzi No. 5. In this case, the Chinese Supreme court held that Plaintiff Chang Jin, producer and distributor of three local operas, having obtained permission from the copyright owners of the

operas (including writers and composers) and also the performing entity, thus enjoyed the neighboring rights protection, including the distribution right and reproduction right, granted under Article 41 of the PRC Copyright Law. Defendant Wenlian, having reproduced and distributed the same recordings made by Chang Jin, thus violated Chang Jin's neighboring rights.

12.4.2.4 Audio-visual works or audio-visual recordings: copyrightable subject matter or neighboring rights subject matter?

Warner Music Hong Kong Ltd. v. Chongqing Taiqing Real Estate Development Co., Ltd., Yinhe Xuangong Entertainment Ltd., (2005) Chongqing High People's Court, Yu Gao Fa Min Zhong Zi No. 112

In 2002, Plaintiff Warner Music HK Ltd. ("Warner Music HK"), distributed a Karaoke VCD collection, titled "Sammi Cheng Love Is Affectation" (the "VCD"). The VCD collection includes three music videos ("MTVs"): "808," "Seamless'" and "Show Off the Beauty" among others. On the back cover of the VCD, there was a copyright statement, which reads as follows: "(p) + (c) 2002 Warner Music Hong Kong Limited." The '(P)' stands for Warner Music HK's rights as the producer of the sound recordings, and '(c)' stands for its ownership of the copyrights with the songs included in the collection.

In 2003, Warner Music HK learned that the VCDs were performed at Yinhe Xuangong Karaoke Bar ("Yinhe KTV") in Chongqing, a subsidiary of Chongqing Taiqing Real Estate Ltd. ("Taiqing") without permission. Warner Music HK shortly brought an action against Yinhe KTV and Taiqing suing for copyright infringement.

The trial court found that the three disputed MTVs were audio-visual works created by a process analogous to cinematography, thus finding defendants liable for infringing the public performance right of Warner Music HK by performing the MTVs in public for commercial purpose without authorization.

In the appeal, Defendant Yinhe KTV made the following counter-arguments. First, it argued that it already paid a statutory license fee to China Music Copyright Society, a copyright collective management organization representing song writers, thus should not be found liable for copyright infringement. Second, the disputed MTVs should be treated as audio-visual recordings, rather than audio-visual works, and therefore should only receive limited neighboring rights protection.

Warner Music HK responded with three arguments. First, whether the disputed MTVs are 'works' under Copyright Law or works created by a process analogous to cinematography should be determined based on its originality and reproducibility. If the

CASE *(continued)*

MTVs are works under Copyright Law, Warner Music HK is the holder of the presentation right. Second, how a MTV is created is an important criterion in determining its legal characterization. Video recordings are created by mechanical video shooting, the producer of which entitles the copyright-related rights and interests rather than the presentation right. In contrast, MTVs are created by a process analogous to cinematography because it is the product of creative activities such as play writing, directing, acting, shooting, film editing and post-producing, and the producer of which entitles the presentation right. Finally, the copyright to a work exists from the date of completion and is not conditioned upon the administrative approval.

The key issue in the case is how to define MTV works, as audio-visual works or audio-visual recordings. As a form of expression, MTV is a combination of musical work and video work. Musical work refers to the melody that can be sung or played either with or without lyrics. Video work refers to series of pictures and images that are recorded on certain medium and can be projected with the aid of proper instruments. Under the Chinese Copyright Law, video works are works created by a process analogous to cinematography and falls into copyrightable subject matter [under Article 3]. Musical and video works are different forms of artistic expressions. Although they both exist in MTV works, they represent different creative efforts of contributors [*i.e.* lyricists, composers, directors], thus deserving separate protection under the Copyright Law.

In this case, Warner Music HK alleged that Yinhe KTV infringed its copyright of the underlying three MTVs. Yinhe KTV argued that that it had paid royalties to China Music Copyright Society, and thus should be free to use the disputed MTVs. This Court does not think so. China Music Copyright Society, [as a right management organization], only manages copyright of the music works on behalf of their members, mostly song writers (*i.e.* lyricists and composers), but they do not represent producers of phonograms. [Therefore, permission from China Music Copyright Society is not sufficient to publicly perform the disputed MTV works in a Karaoke bar.]

To qualify as an audio-visual work under the Chinese Copyright Law, there needs to be certain originality and intellectual creativity in the creation of such works. A simple audio-visual recording, which is made through mechanical video shooting of live performances or scenery, or a mechanical combination of music plus camera images, would not be original enough to qualify as works created by a process analogous to cinematography under Chinese Copyright Law. Thus, for video recordings that lack enough originality, they can only receive limited neighboring rights protection; and their owners should only be treated as producers of phonograms, rather than authors of cinematographic works.

In this case, the three disputed MTVs demonstrate a theme reflected by the selection of songs; the video part includes images of scenery, stages, lighting and other effects. The MTVs also include performances from the singer and actors, with actions and facial expressions, followed with a story plot. All of these show the intellectual creations of the screenwriters, director, actors, screen editor and other members of the team. Besides,

CASE *(continued)*

the disputed MTVs were recorded on certain medium and can be presented with the aid of proper instruments. Therefore, the court determined that the disputed MTVs qualify as copyrightable works [audio-visual works] created by a process analogous to cinematography, and thus entitled to copyright protection under the Copyright Law.

NOTES AND QUESTIONS

1. In the current Chinese Copyright Law (2010 version), there is a distinction between "audio-visual works" and "audio-visual recordings," as with Germany. The former category, such as cinematographic works, is considered as "creative works with sufficient originality," thus falling into copyrightable subject matter under Article 3 of the PRC Copyright Law. The latter, such as a surveillance video-recording in a supermarket, is considered as "mechanical recordings without much creativity," thus only subject to neighboring rights protection. However, to draw a clear line between these two often turns out to be a challenge. For instance, would a telecast of an Oscar night be an audio-visual work or an audio-visual recording? What about the telecast of the Olympic Games or the FIFA World Cup? Should the judges consider how many cameras are used in the telecast? What about the commercials inserted in the telecasts?

2. In the US, the House Report 94-1976 states that "[w]hen a football game is being covered by four television cameras, with a director guiding the activities of the four cameramen and choosing which of their electronic images are sent out to the public and in what order, there is little doubt that what the cameramen and director are doing constitutes 'authorship.'" See House Report 94-1476 at 52 (1976); *see also Balt. Orioles, Inc. v. Major League Baseball Players Ass'n*, 805 F.2d 663, 668 (7th Cir. 1986); *Nat'l Football League v. PrimeTime 24 Joint Venture*, 211 F.3d 10, 13 (2d Cir. 2000). But remember that the US Copyright Act does not protect neighboring rights, thus making no distinction between copyrightable subject matter (*i.e.* audio-visual works) and neighboring rights subject matter (*i.e.* audio-visual recordings.) The only criteria to determine whether the telecast of a sports game or a music event is subject to copyright protection in the US area whether there is sufficient originality in the work and whether the work is fixed. Now compare this with the Chinese approach: Do you think that the US approach, which makes no distinction between audio-visual works and audio-visual recordings, but rather focuses the criteria on the "originality" of the underlying work, makes more sense? *See* Seagull Haiyan Song, *How Should China Respond to Online Piracy of Sports Telecasts? A Comparative Study of Chinese Copyright Legislation to the US and European Legislation*, University of Denver Sports and Entertainment Law Journal (2011).

3. In the current third revision of the Chinese Copyright Law, the provisions addressing "audio-visual recordings" in the neighboring rights section (Chapter 4) will be deleted, thus removing the distinction between audio-visual works and audio-visual recordings. Under the new proposed legislative language, the primary criteria to determine whether an audio-visual product, such as a sports telecast, a concert telecast, or a gala dinner telecast, can be protected as audio-visual works subject to copyright protection, are whether such telecasts have sufficient originality and also can be duplicated. Do you think this approach makes more sense? What are some of the reasons that might justify the protection of sports telecasts or telecasts of similar big events through the copyright law? What might be the concerns to protect these telecasts through the copyright law?

12.4.3 United States

In addition to the rights to make and distribute copies and adaptations of a work, copyright owners possess the exclusive right to perform or display their works publicly (17 U.S.C. §106(4), (5)). The performance and display rights roughly parallel each other, and most types of copyrighted works are covered by one or the other of the two rights. Paintings, sculptures, photographs, single photo frames from movies or video games, and physical copies of books are displayed. Plays, dances, movies, copyrighted combinations of still photographs (such as slide shows), and readings of books are performed publicly. Importantly, no public display right exists in architectural works, and only a limited public performance right (discussed below) exists in sound recordings.

There is also generally a copyright in the musical composition that is infringed by public performance unless a royalty is paid to the composer or the music publisher to whom the composer transferred the relevant rights to the musical composition. These are typically handled through blanket licenses – permission to publicly perform a song from a vast catalog in exchange for a fee based on the scale of the business activity – administered by the American Society of Composers, Authors and Publishers (ASCAP), Broadcast Music Inc. (BMI), or Society of European Stage Authors and Composers (SESAC).

The definitions of both performance and display are quite broad. The limitation to "public" performances and displays, however, prevents many commonplace activities from infringing performance and display rights. The definition of a public performance or display is set forth in section 101:

> To perform or display a work "publicly" means –
>
> (1) to perform or display it at a place open to the public or at any place where a substantial number of persons outside of a normal circle of a family and its social acquaintances is gathered; or
> (2) to transmit or otherwise communicate a performance or display of the work to a place specified by clause (1) or to the public, by means of any device or process, whether the members of the public capable of receiving the performance or display receive it in the same place or in separate places and at the same time or at different times.

Under this definition, the owner of a copy of a piece of music can have a (small) gathering at which he or she plays a CD or video. Large parties – if they go beyond the amorphous definition of your "social acquaintances" – may pose problems. Furthermore, if the place of performance or display is "open to the public," it does not appear to matter how many people actually view the performance. Clause (2) appears to cover all broadcasts to the "public" even if members of the public do not view the copyrighted work at the same place or time. Thus, a television broadcast is a performance, even though no one may watch it at all, or if people watch it only in the privacy of their own homes. The scope of what constitutes a "performance" has become particularly complex in the area of broadcasting and cable television. A "performance" has a communicative element that must be met to establish an infringing act: the "mere act of input into a computer or other retrieval system would not appear to be a performance, nor would other internal operations of a computer, such as the scanning of a work to determine whether it contains material the user is seeking" (Nimmer on Copyright §8.14[B]). In the 1976 Act, Congress determined that "a cable television system is performing when it retransmits the broadcast to its subscribers" (H.R. Rep. No. 94-1476, at 63 (1976)); *see also National Football League v. PrimeTime 24 Joint Venture*, 211 F.3d 10, 13 (2d Cir. 2000) (holding that "a public performance or display includes each step in the process by which a protected work wends its way to the audience"); but *see Allarcom Pay Television, Ltd. v. General Instrument Corp.*, 69 F.3d 381, 387 (9th Cir. 1995) (holding that copyright infringement did not occur until the signal was received by the viewing public). The Second Circuit has also held that downloading a music file from one computer to another does not constitute a performance. *See United States v. ASCAP*, 627 F.3d 64 (2d Cir. 2010). *See generally* 2 Melville Nimmer and David Nimmer, Nimmer on Copyright §8.14 (2016).

Sound recordings did not come under the protection of federal copyright law until 1972. Even then, the political strength of broadcasters persuaded Congress to deny public performance rights to the owners of sound recordings. Broadcasters did not want to pay royalties to sound recording owners as well as musical composition owners. Musical composition copyright owners, and their collecting societies (ASCAP, BMI, and SESAC) were also concerned that public performance royalties paid to sound recording owners would cut into their share of licensing revenues paid by broadcasters.

The introduction of digital transmission technology in the 1990s altered this balance. Recording artists feared that transmission of near-perfect quality recordings that could be recorded on digital audio devices posed a significant risk of piracy. Traditional broadcasters partially aligned with sound recording owners in favoring some protection for digital performance rights in sound recordings because of the competitive threat posed by new broadcasting entities such as digital audio subscription and interactive services. The resulting compromise became the Digital Performance Right in Sound Recordings Act (DPRSRA) of 1995, codified at §§106(6), 114. The Digital Millennium Copyright Act (DMCA), enacted in 1998, modified the DPRSRA. The net effect of the DPRSRA and DMCA was to create significant complexity in the licensing of digital public performance rights for sound recordings.

To simplify, noninteractive services are very generally defined as those in which the user experience mimics a radio broadcast. That is, the users may not choose the specific track or artist they wish to hear, but are provided a pre-programmed or semi-random combination of tracks. Colloquially, this means streaming. Royalties are paid to performing artists – the musicians who record music that is performed – through a compulsory licensing organization known as SoundExchange.

The Section 114 statutory license covers public performances by four classes of digital music services: eligible nonsubscription services (*i.e.,* noninteractive webcasters and simulcasters that charge no fees), preexisting subscription services (*i.e.,* residential subscription services which began providing music over digital cable or satellite television before July 1998), new subscription services (*i.e.,* noninteractive webcasters and simulcasters that charge a fee, as well as residential subscription services providing music over digital cable or satellite television since July 1998), and preexisting satellite digital audio radio services (*e.g.,* SiriusXM Radio).

As required by 17 U.S.C. §112 and 17 U.S.C. §114, SoundExchange, along with other interested parties, participates in each periodic rate-making proceedings to establish rates that compensate copyright owners and performers for the use of copyrighted sound recordings. Such rate setting proceedings may be resolved through arbitration proceedings or through voluntary multi-party settlements.

Through SoundExchange, US musicians now have a counterpart to the neighboring rights organizations long known in other countries around the world. But the US public performance right applies only to digital transmissions, whereas neighboring rights organizations in roughly 80 countries pay royalties to musicians for all public performances, including those transmitted by traditional broadcasters.

13
Limitations and exceptions

13.1 Introduction

Seagull HY Song, *Reevaluating Fair Use in China – A Comparative Copyright Analysis of Chinese Fair Use Legislation, the U.S. Fair Use Doctrine, and the European Fair Dealing Model*, IDEA: The Intellectual Property L.R. Volume 51 (2011)

The origin of fair use doctrine lies in the judge-made law of "fair abridgement" that was developed in a number of eighteenth century cases in which the English courts took a liberal view of how a person other than the author could "abridge" a work without permission from the author. See *Gyles v. Wilcox, Barrow, and Nutt.* 1740 2 Atk 143; *Tonson v. Walker* 1752 3 Swans (App) 762; *Millar v. Taylor* (1769) 98 ER 201. To date the fair use doctrine, also known as fair dealing doctrine in the Commonwealth and Continental European countries, has been codified under the Berne Convention, Rome Convention, TRIPS agreement, WCT and WPPT treaties, and widely accepted in many countries although with certain variations.

Generally speaking, fair use/fair dealing has been presented in three models: 1) the United States fair use model that allows an open-ended list of permissible uses based on consideration of statutory factors; 2) the fair dealing model in most Commonwealth and Continental European countries represented by the United Kingdom featuring an enumerated list of defined copyright limitations and exceptions; and 3) a combination of the U.S. and U.K. models currently found in the Taiwanese Copyright Act and the recently revised South Korean Copyright Act, which offers both an enumerated list of permissible uses (as with the U.K.) and a number of factors to be considered in determining whether the particular use is fair (as with the U.S.) . . .

Under the U.S. Copyright law, fair use is a limitation on the exclusive rights granted to the copyright owner. In case of copyright infringement, the defendant must prove fair use as an affirmative defense. *Campbell v. Acuff-Rose Music, Inc.*, 510 U.S. 569, 590 (1994); *Harper & Row, Publishers, Inc. v. Nation Enters.*, 471 U.S. 539, 561 (1985); *Video Pipeline, Inc. v. Buena Vista Home Entm't, Inc.*, 342 F.3d 191, 197 (3d Cir. 2003). The doctrine originated from judicial interpretation of Great Britain's first copyright law, the Statute of Anne of 1710, in cases including *Gyles v. Wilcox.* Justice Story drew on these English cases when he introduced the fair use concept under U.S. copyright law in his 1841 opinion in *Folsom v. Marsh*, 9 F. Cas. 342 (C.C.D. Mass. 1841) (No. 4901). Fair use was later codified into the Copyright Act of 1976, 17 U.S.C. §107.

Section 107 includes three parts: 1) a preamble that identifies the fair use of a copyrighted work as an exception to the copyright owner's exclusive rights and provides non-exclusive examples of potentially permissible uses such as "criticism, comment, news reporting, teaching (including multiple copies for classroom use), scholarship, or research" for illustrative purpose, 2) a list of four factors that courts must consider in determining whether or not a particular use is fair; and 3) an additional statement added in 1992 regarding unpublished books. Section 107 does not provide a rule to be automatically applied in deciding whether a particular use is fair or not. Instead, all four factors must be considered in each specific fair-use case

. . .

Similar to fair use, fair dealing is a doctrine of limitations and exceptions to copyright in a number of the Commonwealth and Continental European countries represented by the United Kingdom, Canada, Germany, France and China etc. Unlike the fair use doctrine in the U.S., fair dealing is an enumerated list of copyright exceptions and cannot apply to actions that do not fall within such categories. Therefore, fair dealing doctrine has been criticized for being too restrictive and not flexible. See Justice Laddie, *Copyright: Over-Strength, Over-regulated, Over-rated*, 18 European Intellectual Property Review (1996) 253, 258–259. *Report of the Committee to Consider the Law on Copyright and Designs, 1977* (Cmnd 6732) (which recommended the U.K. adopt a general purpose fair use defense. The proposal was eventually rejected by the legislature.) . . .

The advantage of the U.S. fair use model seems to be that by allowing an open-ended list of permissible uses based on consideration of statutory factors, it is more flexible and robust compared to its counterpart in the Commonwealth and European countries, thus more ready to accommodate to the development of new technology. The different outcomes of the Google thumbnail litigation cases and [Google Library Project] decided by the U.S., European and [Chinese] courts set a good example illustrating such divergences. On the other hand, the "flexibility" of the U.S. fair use model has its own disadvantage, where it has been criticized for creating significant ex ante uncertainty. See Melville B. Nimmer & David Nimmer, *Nimmer on Copyright* §13.05 [A][1][b], Paul Goldstein, Goldstein on Copyright §12.2.2, at 12.34 (3d ed. 2005). Having examined many fair use cases, David Nimmer concluded that "the four factors fail to drive the analysis, but rather serve as convenient pegs on which to hang antecedent conclusions." David Nimmer, *"'Fairest of Them All' and Other Fairy Tales of Fair Use"* (2003) 66 Law & Contemp. Probs. Professor Barton Beebe's statistical analysis of more than two hundred fair use cases is also consistent with this conclusion. Barton Beebe, *An Empirical Study of U.S. Copyright Fair Use Opinions, 1978–2005*, 156 U. Pa. L. Rev. 549 (2008). Critics of the current U.S. fair use model, therefore, argue that because of lacking bright-line rule and high costs of litigation plus potentially enormous statutory damages, potential fair users might be deterred from engaging fair uses of copyrighted works, thus creating a culture of "clearing for fear." See Marjorie Heins & Tricia Beckles, Brennan Ctr. for Justice, N.Y. Univ. Sch. Of Law, *Will Fair Use Survive: Free Expression in the Age of Copyright Control* 5–6 (2005).

13.2 United States

Campbell v. Acuff-Rose Music, Inc., 510 U.S. 569 (1994)

Souter, J.

We are called upon to decide whether 2 Live Crew's commercial parody of Roy Orbison's song, "Oh, Pretty Woman," may be a fair use within the meaning of the Copyright Act of 1976, 17 U.S.C. §107. Although the District Court granted summary judgment for 2 Live Crew, the Court of Appeals reversed, holding the defense of fair use barred by the song's commercial character and excessive borrowing. Because we hold that a parody's commercial character is only one element to be weighed in a fair use enquiry, and that insufficient consideration was given to the nature of parody in weighing the degree of copying, we reverse and remand.

In 1964, Roy Orbison and William Dees wrote a rock ballad called "Oh, Pretty Woman" and assigned their rights in it to respondent Acuff-Rose Music, Inc. *See* Appendix A, *infra*, at 1179. Acuff-Rose registered the song for copyright protection.

Petitioners Luther R. Campbell [et al.] are collectively known as 2 Live Crew, a popular rap music group. In 1989, Campbell wrote a song entitled "Pretty Woman," which he later described in an affidavit as intended, "through comical lyrics, to satirize the original work. . ." 2 Live Crew's manager informed Acuff-Rose that 2 Live Crew had written a parody of "Oh, Pretty Woman," that they would afford all credit for ownership and authorship of the original song to Acuff-Rose, Dees, and Orbison, and that they were willing to pay a fee for the use they wished to make of it. Acuff-Rose's agent refused permission.

In 1989, 2 Live Crew released records, cassette tapes, and compact discs of "Pretty Woman" in a collection of songs entitled "As Clean As They Wanna Be." [Acuff-Rose sued.]

It is uncontested here that 2 Live Crew's song would be an infringement of Acuff-Rose's rights in "Oh, Pretty Woman," under the Copyright Act, but for a finding of fair use through parody. From the infancy of copyright protection, some opportunity for fair use of copyrighted materials has been thought necessary. Fair use remained exclusively judge-made doctrine until the passage of the 1976 Copyright Act:

CASE (continued)

§107. Limitations on exclusive rights: Fair use

Notwithstanding the provisions of sections 106 and 106A, the fair use of a copyrighted work, including such use by reproduction in copies or phonorecords or by any other means specified by that section, for purposes such as criticism, comment, news reporting, teaching (including multiple copies for classroom use), scholarship, or research, is not an infringement of copyright. In determining whether the use made of a work in any particular case is a fair use the factors to be considered shall include –

(1) the purpose and character of the use, including whether such use is of a commercial nature or is for nonprofit educational purposes;
(2) the nature of the copyrighted work;
(3) the amount and substantiality of the portion used in relation to the copyrighted work as a whole; and
(4) the effect of the use upon the potential market for or value of the copyrighted work.

The fact that a work is unpublished shall not itself bar a finding of fair use if such finding is made upon consideration of all the above factors.

The first factor in a fair use enquiry is "the purpose and character of the use, including whether such use is of a commercial nature or is for nonprofit educational purposes." §107(1). The enquiry here may be guided by the examples given in the preamble to §107, looking to whether the use is for criticism, or comment, or news reporting, and the like. The central purpose of this investigation is to see, in Justice Story's words, whether the new work adds something new, with a further purpose or different character, altering the first [work] with new expression, meaning, or message; it asks, in other words, whether and to what extent the new work is "transformative." [Judge Pierre Leval, *Toward a Fair Use Standard*, 103 Harv. L. Rev. 1105, 1111 (1990).] Although such transformative use is not absolutely necessary for a finding of fair use, the goal of copyright, to promote science and the arts, is generally furthered by the creation of transformative works.

Parody has an obvious claim to transformative value, as Acuff-Rose itself does not deny. Like less ostensibly humorous forms of criticism, it can provide social benefit, by shedding light on an earlier work, and, in the process, creating a new one. We thus line up with the courts that have held that parody, like other comment or criticism, may claim fair use under §107.

While we might not assign a high rank to the parodic element here, we think it fair to say that 2 Live Crew's song reasonably could be perceived as commenting on the original or criticizing it, to some degree.

The second statutory factor, "the nature of the copyrighted work," §107(2), calls for recognition that some works are closer to the core of intended copyright protection than others, with the consequence that fair use is more difficult to establish when the former works are copied. We agree with both the District Court and the Court of Appeals that the Orbison original's creative expression for public dissemination falls within the core of the copyright's protective purposes. This fact, however, is not much help in this case, since parodies almost invariably copy publicly known, expressive works.

CASE *(continued)*

The third factor asks whether "the amount and substantiality of the portion used in relation to the copyrighted work as a whole," §107(3). Parody presents a difficult case. Parody's humor, or in any event its comment, necessarily springs from recognizable allusion to its object through distorted imitation. Its art lies in the tension between a known original and its parodic twin. When parody takes aim at a particular original work, the parody must be able to "conjure up" at least enough of that original to make the object of its critical wit recognizable. Once enough has been taken to assure identification, how much more is reasonable will depend, say, on the extent to which the song's overriding purpose and character is to parody the original or, in contrast, the likelihood that the parody may serve as a market substitute for the original. But using some characteristic features cannot be avoided.

It is true, of course, that 2 Live Crew copied the characteristic opening bass riff (or musical phrase) of the original, and true that the words of the first line copy the Orbison lyrics. But if quotation of the opening riff and the first line may be said to go to the "heart" of the original, the heart is also what most readily conjures up the song for parody, and it is the heart at which parody takes aim.

This is not, of course, to say that anyone who calls himself a parodist can skim the cream and get away scot free. In parody, the question of fairness asks what else the parodist did besides go to the heart of the original. It is significant that 2 Live Crew not only copied the first line of the original, but thereafter departed markedly from the Orbison lyrics for its own ends. 2 Live Crew not only copied the bass riff and repeated it, but also produced otherwise distinctive sounds, interposing "scraper" noise, overlaying the music with solos in different keys, and altering the drum beat. This is not a case, then, where "a substantial portion" of the parody itself is composed of a "verbatim" copying of the original. It is not, that is, a case where the parody is so insubstantial, as compared to the copying, that the third factor must be resolved as a matter of law against the parodists.

Suffice it to say here that, as to the lyrics, we think the Court of Appeals correctly suggested that "no more was taken than necessary," but just for that reason, we fail to see how the copying can be excessive in relation to its parodic purpose, even if the portion taken is the original's "heart." As to the music, we express no opinion whether repetition of the bass riff is excessive copying, and we remand to permit evaluation of the amount taken, in light of the song's parodic purpose and character, its transformative elements, and considerations of the potential for market substitution sketched more fully below.

The fourth fair use factor is "the effect of the use upon the potential market for or value of the copyrighted work." §107(4).

The court reasoned that because "the use of the copyrighted work is wholly commercial, . . . we presume that a likelihood of future harm to Acuff-Rose exists." In so doing, the court resolved the fourth factor against 2 Live Crew, just as it had the first, by applying a presumption about the effect of commercial use, a presumption which as applied here we hold to be error.

No "presumption" or inference of market harm that might find support in [*Sony Corp.*

CASE (continued)

of America v. Universal City Studios, Inc., 464 U.S. 417 (1984)] is applicable to a case involving something beyond mere duplication for commercial purposes. *Sony*'s discussion of a presumption contrasts a context of verbatim copying of the original in its entirety for commercial purposes, with the noncommercial context of Sony itself (home copying of television programming). In the former circumstances, what *Sony* said simply makes common sense: when a commercial use amounts to mere duplication of the entirety of an original, it clearly serves as a market replacement for it, making it likely that cognizable market harm to the original will occur. Sony, *supra*, 464 U.S., at 451. But when, on the contrary, the second use is transformative, market substitution is at least less certain, and market harm may not be so readily inferred. Indeed, as to parody pure and simple, it is more likely that the new work will not affect the market for the original in a way cognizable under this factor, that is, by acting as a substitute for it. This is so because the parody and the original usually serve different market functions.

Reversed and remanded.

NOTES AND COMMENTS

1. **Outcome.** Though the case was remanded back to the district court, the parties settled before further proceedings. *See* Acuff-Rose Settles Suit with Rap Group, The Commercial Appeal (Memphis), June 5, 1996.
2. **Time shifting and transaction costs.** The case of *Sony Corp. of America v. Universal City Studios, Inc.*, 464 U.S. 417 (1984), cited and discussed in *Campbell*, was a major watershed in US copyright law. This case held that home copying of copyrighted television shows broadcast in the US is protected by fair use, where the purpose of the copying is not to archive the show but merely to watch it at a later time. This case also held that the sellers of home VHS tape copiers were not liable for any copyright infringement by consumers of the home taping machines, because those machines were capable of substantial noninfringing use (*i.e.*, the protected home copying). *Sony* is therefore a major case in the area of fair use as well as indirect copyright infringement.

   The *Sony* case gave birth to a very influential theory of fair use. Copyright scholar Wendy Gordon wrote that fair use should often be invoked when licensing markets do not form; that is, a finding of fair use should follow when desirable transfers of copyrights are frustrated because licensing is too expensive or otherwise unavailable (Wendy J. Gordon, *Fair Use as Market Failure: A Structural and Economic Analysis of the Betamax Case and Its Predecessors*, 82 Colum. L. Rev. 1600 (1982)). For follow-on work in this vein, *see* Robert P. Merges, *The End of Friction? Property Rights and Contract in the "Newtonian" World of on-Line Commerce*, 12 Berkeley Tech. L.J. 115 (1997) (speculating about the future of fair use in a world of zero or very low transaction costs); Lydia Pallas Loren, *Redefining the Market Failure Approach to Fair Use in an Era of Copyright Permission Systems*, 5 J. Intell. Prop. L. 1, 58 (1997). One specific point relevant to licensing, and emphasized by the Court in *Campbell*, is that it may be unusual for copyright holders to voluntarily license their works to a parodist, knowing that doing so will open them to ridicule. *See* Robert P. Merges, *Are You Making Fun of Me? Notes on Market Failure and the Parody Defense in Copyright*, 21 AIPLA Q.J. 305, 305 (1993) (describing refusals to license for "non-economic" reasons, *i.e.*, refusing licenses that would profit both parties).
3. **The transformative use revolution.** Many cases after *Campbell* turn on whether the infringing work "transforms" the original copyrighted work, in the manner the Court discussed in *Campbell*. *See, e.g., Cariou v. Prince*, 714 F.3d 694 (2d Cir. 2013) (where one artist cut out copyrighted pictures from a book, and added varying amounts of additional creative material, court held that 25 out of 30 works incorporating photos were transformative, and hence protected by fair use; remanding case for determination of whether remain-

ing five works were also transformative). Empirical studies confirm that this is now perhaps the crucial factor in fair use analysis. *See* Matthew Sag, *Predicting Fair Use*, 73 Ohio St. L.J. 47, 79 (2012) ("The evidence presented here that transformative use and partial copying are both strong indicators of fair use makes it difficult to sustain the common charge [that fair use doctrine is characterized by] incoherence and unpredictability"). Some argue in fact that it has become not only too important but also unpredictable. *See* Matthew D. Bunker & Clay Calvert, *The Jurisprudence of Transformation: Intellectual Incoherence and Doctrinal Murkiness Twenty Years After* Campbell v. Acuff-Rose Music, Duke L. & Tech. Rev., June 9, 2014, at 92, 93.

As for the statutory factors, a comprehensive study found that in general factor four (market impact) was the important factor in determining the outcome of fair use cases, followed by factor one (nature of the work):

> [T]he outcome of factor four coincided with the outcome of the overall test in 83.8% of the 297 dispositive opinions while the outcome of factor one coincided with the outcome of the overall test in 81.5% of these same opinions. By comparison, the outcome of factor two coincided with the outcome of the overall test in 50.2% of these opinions. As for the combined influence of factors one and four, in 214 (or 72.1%) of the opinions, factors one and four either both favored or both disfavored fair use. In all but one of these opinions, the outcome of the fair use test followed the outcome of these two factors. What happened when, if ever, factor one favored (or disfavored) fair use while factor four disfavored (or favored) fair use? Did one of these leading factors consistently trump the other? Factors one and four pointed in opposite directions in only 20 of the opinions. In 14 of these opinions, the outcome of the test followed the outcome of factor four, while in 6, the outcome of the test followed the outcome of factor one. Though hardly conclusive, this breakdown is consistent with the conventional view that factor four exerts the stronger influence on the outcome of the test (Barton Beebe, *An Empirical Study of U.S. Copyright Fair Use Opinions, 1978–2005*, 156 U. Pa. L. Rev. 549, 584–85 (2008).

Cases now emphasize that at times, an alleged fair use can actually *benefit* the owner of the copyright in the infringed-upon work. *See* Jeanne C. Fromer, *Market Effects Bearing on Fair Use*, 90 Wash. L. Rev. 615 (2015) (collecting cases showing a positive post-infringement impact on the market for the copyrighted work). And an empirical study specifically concerned with copying short excerpts of musical works ("sampling") confirmed this possibility:

> Collecting and comparing sales information for [350 sampled] songs [on one sampling-intensive album, called "Girl Talk"] found that – to a 92.5% degree of statistical significance – the copyrighted songs sold better in the year after being sampled relative to the year before. To the extent the Copyright Act instructs courts to analyze (among other considerations) the effect an alleged fair use has on the potential market for the original work, these findings favor the conclusion that digital sampling is a fair use, though each statutory fair use consideration should still be considered (W. Michael Schuster, *Fair Use, Girl Talk, and Digital Sampling: An Empirical Study of Music Sampling's Effect on the Market for Copyrighted Works*, 67 Okla. L. Rev. 443, 444 (2015)).

4. **Reverse engineering.** In *Sega Enters. Ltd. v. Accolade, Inc.*, 977 F.2d 1510 (9th Cir. 1992), amended by 1993 U.S. App. LEXIS 78 (9th Cir. Jan. 6, 1993), the court found that it was fair use to reverse engineer copyrighted access codes that allowed video game cartridges to operate in hardware consoles. The consoles were sold by companies that tried to use the access codes to keep out unauthorized video game cartridges. The case, and others like it, is described in Pamela Samuelson, *Unbundling Fair Uses*, 77 Fordham L. Rev. 2537, 2621 (2009).

CASE

Authors Guild v. Google, Inc., 804 F.3d 202 (2d Cir. 2015)

LEVAL, Circuit Judge:

This copyright dispute tests the boundaries of fair use. Plaintiffs, who are authors of

CASE *(continued)*

published books under copyright, sued Google, Inc. ("Google") for copyright infringement in the United States District Court for the Southern District of New York (Chin, J.). They appeal from the grant of summary judgment in Google's favor. Through its Library Project and its Google Books project, acting without permission of rights holders, Google has made digital copies of tens of millions of books, including Plaintiffs', that were submitted to it for that purpose by major libraries. Google has scanned the digital copies and established a publicly available search function. An Internet user can use this function to search without charge to determine whether the book contains a specified word or term and also see "snippets" of text containing the searched-for terms. In addition, Google has allowed the participating libraries to download and retain digital copies of the books they submit, under agreements which commit the libraries not to use their digital copies in violation of the copyright laws. These activities of Google are alleged to constitute infringement of Plaintiffs' copyrights. Plaintiffs sought injunctive and declaratory relief as well as damages.

Google defended on the ground that its actions constitute "fair use," which, under 17 U.S.C. §107, is "not an infringement." The district court agreed. *Authors Guild, Inc. v. Google Inc.*, 954 F.Supp.2d 282, 294 (S.D.N.Y.2013). Plaintiffs brought this appeal.

Google's making of a digital copy to provide a search function is a transformative use, which augments public knowledge by making available information about Plaintiffs' books without providing the public with a substantial substitute for matter protected by the Plaintiffs' copyright interests in the original works or derivatives of them. The same is true, at least under present conditions, of Google's provision of the snippet function. Plaintiffs' contention that Google has usurped their opportunity to access paid and unpaid licensing markets for substantially the same functions that Google provides fails, in part because the licensing markets in fact involve very different functions than those that Google provides, and in part because an author's derivative rights do not include an exclusive right to supply information (of the sort provided by Google) about her works. Google's profit motivation does not in these circumstances justify denial of fair use.

[The court summarized the four fair use factors, plus the "transformative use" idea, from the *Campbell* case.] The word "transformative" cannot be taken too literally as a sufficient key to understanding the elements of fair use. It is rather a suggestive symbol for a complex thought, and does not mean that any and all changes made to an author's original text will necessarily support a finding of fair use. The Supreme Court's discussion in *Campbell* gave important guidance on assessing when a transformative use tends to support a conclusion of fair use. The would-be fair user of another's work must have justification for the taking. A secondary author is not necessarily at liberty to make wholesale takings of the original author's expression merely because of how well the original author's expression would convey the secondary author's different message. Among the best recognized justifications for copying from another's work is to provide comment on it or criticism of it. A taking from another author's work for the purpose of making points that have no bearing on the original may well be fair use, but the taker would need to show a justification. This part of the Supreme Court's discussion is significant in assessing Google's claim of fair use because

CASE *(continued)*

Google's claim of transformative purpose for copying from the works of others is to provide otherwise unavailable information about the originals.

We have no difficulty concluding that Google's making of a digital copy of Plaintiffs' books for the purpose of enabling a search for identification of books containing a term of interest to the searcher involves a highly transformative purpose, in the sense intended by *Campbell*. Our court's exemplary discussion in [*Authors Guild v.*] *HathiTrust* [755 F.3d 87 (2d Cir. 2014)] informs our ruling. That case involved a dispute that is closely related, although not identical, to this one. Authors brought claims of copyright infringement against HathiTrust, an entity formed by libraries participating in the Google Library Project to pool the digital copies of their books created for them by Google. The suit challenged various usages HathiTrust made of the digital copies. Among the challenged uses was HathiTrust's offer to its patrons of "full-text searches," which, very much like the search offered by Google Books to Internet users, permitted patrons of the libraries to locate in which of the digitized books specific words or phrases appeared. 755 F.3d at 98. (HathiTrust's search facility did not include the snippet view function, or any other display of text.) We concluded that both the making of the digital copies and the use of those copies to offer the search tool were fair uses. *Id.* at 105. Notwithstanding that the libraries had downloaded and stored complete digital copies of entire books, we noted that such copying was essential to permit searchers to identify and locate the books in which words or phrases of interest to them appeared. *Id.* at 97.

Plaintiffs correctly point out that this case is significantly different from *HathiTrust* in that the Google Books search function allows searchers to read snippets from the book searched, whereas HathiTrust did not allow searchers to view any part of the book. Snippet view adds important value to the basic transformative search function, which tells only whether and how often the searched term appears in the book. Merely knowing that a term of interest appears in a book does not necessarily tell the searcher whether she needs to obtain the book, because it does not reveal whether the term is discussed in a manner or context falling within the scope of the searcher's interest.

Google's division of the page into tiny snippets is designed to show the searcher just enough context surrounding the searched term to help her evaluate whether the book falls within the scope of her interest (without revealing so much as to threaten the author's copyright interests). Snippet view thus adds importantly to the highly transformative purpose of identifying books of interest to the searcher. With respect to the first factor test, it favors a finding of fair use (unless the value of its transformative purpose is overcome by its providing text in a manner that offers a competing substitute for Plaintiffs' books, which we discuss under factors three and four below).

[With respect to factor two:] To the extent that the "nature" of the original copyrighted work necessarily combines with the "purpose and character" of the secondary work to permit assessment of whether the secondary work uses the original in a "transformative" manner, as the term is used in *Campbell*, the second factor favors fair use not because Plaintiffs' works are factual, but because the secondary use transformatively provides

CASE *(continued)*

valuable information about the original, rather than replicating protected expression in a manner that provides a meaningful substitute for the original.

The third statutory factor instructs us to consider "the amount and substantiality of the portion used in relation to the copyrighted work as a whole." The clear implication of the third factor is that a finding of fair use is more likely when small amounts, or less important passages, are copied than when the copying is extensive, or encompasses the most important parts of the original. The obvious reason for this lies in the relationship between the third and the fourth factors. The larger the amount, or the more important the part, of the original that is copied, the greater the likelihood that the secondary work might serve as an effectively competing substitute for the original, and might therefore diminish the original rights holder's sales and profits.

While Google *makes* an unauthorized digital copy of the entire book, it does not reveal that digital copy to the public. The copy is made to enable the search functions to reveal limited, important information about the books. With respect to the search function, Google satisfies the third factor test, as illuminated by the Supreme Court in *Campbell*. Google has constructed the snippet feature in a manner that substantially protects against its serving as an effectively competing substitute for Plaintiffs' books. In addition, Google does not provide snippet view for types of books, such as dictionaries and cookbooks, for which viewing a small segment is likely to satisfy the searcher's need. The result of these restrictions is, so far as the record demonstrates, that a searcher cannot succeed, even after long extended effort to multiply what can be revealed, in revealing through a snippet search what could usefully serve as a competing substitute for the original.

The fourth fair use factor, "the effect of the [copying] use upon the potential market for or value of the copyrighted work," focuses on whether the copy brings to the marketplace a competing substitute for the original, or its derivative, so as to deprive the rights holder of significant revenues because of the likelihood that potential purchasers may opt to acquire the copy in preference to the original. Because copyright is a commercial doctrine whose objective is to stimulate creativity among potential authors by enabling them to earn money from their creations, the fourth factor is of great importance in making a fair use assessment.

[W]e conclude that the snippet function does not give searchers access to effectively competing substitutes. Snippet view, at best and after a large commitment of manpower, produces discontinuous, tiny fragments, amounting in the aggregate to no more than 16% of a book. This does not threaten the rights holders with any significant harm to the value of their copyrights or diminish their harvest of copyright revenue.

We recognize that the snippet function can cause *some* loss of sales. There are surely instances in which a searcher's need for access to a text will be satisfied by the snippet view, resulting in either the loss of a sale to that searcher, or reduction of demand on libraries for that title, which might have resulted in libraries purchasing additional copies. But the possibility, or even the probability or certainty, of some loss of sales does not suffice to make the copy an effectively competing substitute that would tilt the weighty fourth factor

CASE *(continued)*

in favor of the rights holder in the original. There must be a meaningful or significant effect "upon the potential market for or value of the copyrighted work."

[Plaintiff Authors Guild argued that, because the book snippets provided by Google were derivative works that would otherwise be available only via licenses granted by book copyright owners, the snippet function was not protected by fair use.] Plaintiffs seek to support their derivative claim by a showing that there exist, or would have existed, paid licensing markets in digitized works, such as those provided by the Copyright Clearance Center or the previous, revenue-generating version of the Google Partners Program. Plaintiffs also point to the proposed settlement agreement rejected by the district court in this case, according to which Google would have paid authors for its use of digitized copies of their works. The existence or potential existence of such paid licensing schemes does not support Plaintiffs' derivative argument. The access to the expressive content of the original that is or would have been provided by the paid licensing arrangements Plaintiffs cite is far more extensive than that which Google's search and snippet view functions provide. Those arrangements allow or would have allowed public users to read substantial portions of the book. Such access would most likely constitute copyright infringement if not licensed by the rights holders. Accordingly, such arrangements have no bearing on Google's present programs, which, in a non-infringing manner, allow the public to obtain limited data about the contents of the book, without allowing any substantial reading of its text.

Plaintiffs also seek to support their derivative claim by a showing that there is a current *unpaid* market in licenses for partial viewing of digitized books, such as the licenses that publishers currently grant to the Google Partners program and Amazon's Search Inside the Book program to display substantial portions of their books.

[The court dismissed plaintiff's argument that this case was governed by cases on the licensing of short excerpts of musical works for mobile phone ringtones: Unlike cases involving copyrighted "ringtones," the court said that the purpose of the Google books service was not to provide a "meaningful experience of the expressive content of the book," but instead "to give some minimal contextual information to help the searcher learn whether the book's use of [a search] term will be of interest to her."]

In sum, we conclude that Google's unauthorized digitizing of copyright-protected works, creation of a search functionality, and display of snippets from those works are non-infringing fair uses. The purpose of the copying is highly transformative, the public display of text is limited, and the revelations do not provide a significant market substitute for the protected aspects of the originals. Google's commercial nature and profit motivation do not justify denial of fair use.

NOTE

For a deep and comprehensive analysis of this case and its many ramifications, *see* Pamela Samuelson, *The Google Books Settlement as Copyright Reform*, 2011 Wisconsin L. Rev. 479 (2011).

13.2.2.1 First sale

CASE

Kirtsaeng v. John Wiley & Sons, Inc., 35 ITRD 1049, 133 S. Ct. 1351, 185 L. Ed. 2d 392 (2013)

Justice BREYER delivered the opinion of the Court.

Section 106 of the Copyright Act grants "the owner of copyright under this title" certain "exclusive rights," including the right "to distribute copies . . . of the copyrighted work to the public by sale or other transfer of ownership." 17 U.S.C. §106(3). These rights are qualified, however, by the application of various limitations set forth in the next several sections of the Act, §§107 through 122. Those sections, typically entitled "Limitations on exclusive rights," include, for example, the principle of "fair use" (§107), permission for limited library archival reproduction, (§108), and the doctrine at issue here, the "first sale" doctrine (§109).

Section 109(a) sets forth the "first sale" doctrine as follows:

> Notwithstanding the provisions of section 106(3) [the section that grants the owner exclusive distribution rights], the owner of a particular copy or phonorecord *lawfully made under this title* . . . is entitled, without the authority of the copyright owner, to sell or otherwise dispose of the possession of that copy or phonorecord." (Emphasis added.)

Thus, even though §106(3) forbids distribution of a copy of, say, the copyrighted novel Herzog without the copyright owner's permission, §109(a) adds that, once a copy of Herzog has been lawfully sold (or its ownership otherwise lawfully transferred), the buyer of that *copy* and subsequent owners are free to dispose of it as they wish. In copyright jargon, the "first sale" has "exhausted" the copyright owner's §106(3) exclusive distribution right.

What, however, if the copy of Herzog was printed abroad and then initially sold with the copyright owner's permission? Does the "first sale" doctrine still apply? Is the buyer, like the buyer of a domestically manufactured copy, free to bring the copy into the United States and dispose of it as he or she wishes?

To put the matter technically, an "importation" provision, §602(a)(1), says that "[i]mportation into the United States, without the authority of the owner of copyright under this title, of copies . . . of a work that have been acquired outside the United States is an infringement of the exclusive right to distribute copies . . . *under section 106* . . . ." 17 U.S.C. §602(a)(1) (2006 ed., Supp. V) (emphasis added).

Thus §602(a)(1) makes clear that importing a copy without permission violates the owner's exclusive distribution right. But in doing so, §602(a)(1) refers explicitly to the *§106(3)* exclusive distribution right. As we have just said, §106 is by its terms "[s]ubject to" the various doctrines and principles contained in §§107 through 122, including §109(a)'s "first sale" limitation. Do those same modifications apply – in particular, does

CASE (continued)

the "first sale" modification apply – when considering whether §602(a)(1) prohibits importing a copy?

In *Quality King Distributors, Inc. v. L'anza Research Int'l, Inc.,* 523 U.S. 135, 145 (1998), we held that §602(a)(1)'s reference to §106(3)'s exclusive distribution right incorporates the later subsections' limitations, including, in particular, the "first sale" doctrine of §109. Thus, it might seem that, §602(a)(1) notwithstanding, one who buys a copy abroad can freely import that copy into the United States and dispose of it, just as he could had he bought the copy in the United States.

But *Quality King* considered an instance in which the copy, though purchased abroad, was initially manufactured in the United States (and then sent abroad and sold). This case is like *Quality King* but for one important fact. The copies at issue here were manufactured abroad. That fact is important because §109(a) says that the "first sale" doctrine applies to "a particular copy or phonorecord *lawfully made under this title.*" And we must decide here whether the five words, "lawfully made under this title," make a critical legal difference.

Putting section numbers to the side, we ask whether the "first sale" doctrine applies to protect a buyer or other lawful owner of a copy (of a copyrighted work) lawfully manufactured abroad. Can that buyer bring that copy into the United States (and sell it or give it away) without obtaining permission to do so from the copyright owner? Can, for example, someone who purchases, say at a used bookstore, a book printed abroad subsequently resell it without the copyright owner's permission?

In our view, the answers to these questions are, yes. We hold that the "first sale" doctrine applies to copies of a copyrighted work lawfully made abroad.

[T]here are two essentially equivalent versions of a Wiley textbook, each version manufactured and sold with Wiley's permission: (1) an American version printed and sold in the United States, and (2) a foreign version manufactured and sold abroad. And Wiley makes certain that copies of the second version state that they are not to be taken (without permission) into the United States.

Petitioner, Supap Kirtsaeng, a citizen of Thailand, moved to the United States in 1997 to study mathematics at Cornell University. Kirtsaeng successfully completed his undergraduate courses at Cornell, successfully completed a PhD program in mathematics at the University of Southern California, and then, as promised [under the terms of his Thai government grant], returned to Thailand to teach. While he was studying in the United States, Kirtsaeng asked his friends and family in Thailand to buy copies of foreign edition English-language textbooks at Thai book shops, where they sold at low prices, and mail them to him in the United States. Kirtsaeng would then sell them, reimburse his family and friends, and keep the profit.

[The district court and court of appeals both held that the "under this title" language referred to the place of first sale, which meant that the first sale doctrine did not apply to textbooks first purchased overseas.]

Under any of [the "geographical interpretations" of §109(a), the] "first sale" doctrine would not apply to the Wiley Asia books at issue here. And, despite an American copyright

CASE *(continued)*

owner's permission to *make* copies abroad, one who *buys* a copy of any such book or other copyrighted work – whether at a retail store, over the Internet, or at a library sale – could not resell (or otherwise dispose of) that particular copy without further permission.

Kirtsaeng, however, reads the words "lawfully made under this title" as imposing a *non*-geographical limitation. He says that they mean made "in accordance with" or "in compliance with" the Copyright Act. In that case, §109(a)'s "first sale" doctrine would apply to copyrighted works as long as their manufacture met the requirements of American copyright law. In particular, the doctrine would apply where, as here, copies are manufactured abroad with the permission of the copyright owner. See §106 (referring to the owner's right to authorize).

In our view, §109(a)'s language, its context, and the common-law history of the "first sale" doctrine, taken together, favor a *non*-geographical interpretation. We also doubt that Congress would have intended to create the practical copyright-related harms with which a geographical interpretation would threaten ordinary scholarly, artistic, commercial, and consumer activities. We consequently conclude that Kirtsaeng's nongeographical reading is the better reading of the Act.

The language of §109(a) read literally favors Kirtsaeng's nongeographical interpretation, namely, that "lawfully made under this title" means made "in accordance with" or "in compliance with" the Copyright Act. The language of §109(a) says nothing about geography. [T]he nongeographical reading is simple, it promotes a traditional copyright objective (combatting piracy), and it makes word-by-word linguistic sense.

The geographical interpretation, however, bristles with linguistic difficulties. It gives the word "lawfully" little, if any, linguistic work to do. (How could a book be *un*lawfully "made under this title"?) It imports geography into a statutory provision that says nothing explicitly about it. And it is far more complex than may at first appear.

[One problem is that "under" does not mean "where".] A far more serious difficulty arises out of the uncertainty and complexity surrounding the second step's effort to read the necessary geographical limitation into the word "applicable" (or the equivalent). Where, precisely, is the Copyright Act "applicable"? The Act does not instantly *protect* an American copyright holder from unauthorized piracy taking place abroad. But that fact does not mean the Act is *inapplicable* to copies made abroad.

[O]rdinary English permits us to say that the Act "applies" to an Irish manuscript lying in its author's Dublin desk drawer as well as to an original recording of a ballet performance first made in Japan and now on display in a Kyoto art gallery.

In sum, we believe that geographical interpretations create more linguistic problems than they resolve. And considerations of simplicity and coherence tip the purely linguistic balance in Kirtsaeng's, nongeographical, favor.

[Statutory context and the common law history of the "first sale" doctrine also favor a non-geographic interpretation.]

Associations of libraries, used-book dealers, technology companies, consumer-goods retailers, and museums point to various ways in which a geographical interpretation would

CASE *(continued)*

fail to further basic constitutional copyright objectives, in particular "promot[ing] the Progress of Science and useful Arts." U.S. Const., Art. I, §8, cl. 8.

The American Library Association tells us that library collections contain at least 200 million books published abroad; that many others were first published in the United States but printed abroad because of lower costs; and that a geographical interpretation will likely require the libraries to obtain permission (or at least create significant uncertainty) before circulating or otherwise distributing these books. How, the American Library Association asks, are the libraries to obtain permission to distribute these millions of books?

Used-book dealers tell us that, from the time when Benjamin Franklin and Thomas Jefferson built commercial and personal libraries of foreign books, American readers have bought used books published and printed abroad. Technology companies tell us that "automobiles, microwaves, calculators, mobile phones, tablets, and personal computers" contain copyrightable software programs or packaging. Many of these items are made abroad with the American copyright holder's permission and then sold and imported (with that permission) to the United States. A geographical interpretation would prevent the resale of, say, a car, without the permission of the holder of each copyright on each piece of copyrighted automobile software. Retailers tell us that over $2.3 trillion worth of foreign goods were imported in 2011. American retailers buy many of these goods after a first sale abroad. And, many of these items bear, carry, or contain copyrighted "packaging, logos, labels, and product inserts and instructions for [the use of] everyday packaged goods from floor cleaners and health and beauty products to breakfast cereals."

These examples, and others previously mentioned, help explain *why* Lord Coke considered the "first sale" doctrine necessary to protect "Trade and Traffi[c], and bargaining and contracting," and they help explain *why* American copyright law has long applied that doctrine.

Justice KAGAN, concurring:

At bottom, John Wiley (together with the dissent) asks us to misconstrue §109(a) in order to restore §602(a)(1) to its purportedly rightful function of enabling copyright holders to segment international markets. I think John Wiley may have a point about what §602(a)(1) was designed to do; that gives me pause about *Quality King*'s holding that the first-sale doctrine limits the importation ban's scope. But the Court today correctly declines the invitation to save §602(a)(1) from *Quality King* by destroying the first-sale protection that §109(a) gives to every owner of a copy manufactured abroad. That would swap one (possible) mistake for a much worse one, and make our reading of the statute only less reflective of Congressional intent. If Congress thinks copyright owners need greater power to restrict importation and thus divide markets, a ready solution is at hand – not the one John Wiley offers in this case, but the one the Court rejected in *Quality King*.

Justice GINSBURG, dissenting:

[The dissent extensively reviews the linguistic, legislative, and historical arguments in favor of the "geographical interpretation" of "first sale."] [I]f, as the Court suggests, there are a multitude of copyright owners champing at the bit to bring lawsuits against libraries, art

> **CASE** *(continued)*
>
> museums, and consumers in an effort to exercise perpetual control over the downstream distribution and public display of foreign-made copies, might one not expect that at least a handful of such lawsuits would have been filed over the past 30 years? The absence of such suits indicates that the "practical problems" hypothesized by the Court are greatly exaggerated. They surely do not warrant disregarding Congress' intent, expressed in §602(a)(1), to grant copyright owners the authority to bar the importation of foreign-made copies of their works.

13.3 Europe

13.3.1 Introduction

As we have already seen, European copyright law is a combination of partial harmonization at the EU level through EU Directives and – in recent years – through judicial activism of the CJEU and of national copyright systems that have developed over centuries. Typically, legislative harmonization at the EU level occurred if there was a pressing need for such harmonization and a political solution seemed within reach. When the EU adopted the Information Society Directive, harmonizing limitations to copyright protection were an important policy goal. The Directive has fallen short of this goal. Art. 5 of the Directive implements an exhaustive list of exceptions which EU Member States must or may provide in their national copyright laws. The only mandatory limitation that all Member States have to implement according to Art. 5 is a limitation of the right of reproduction in Art. 5(1). All other 20 limitations to the right of reproduction in Art. 5(2), to the rights of reproduction, communication and making available to the public in Art. 5(3), and to the right of distribution in Art. 5(4), are optional. Due to the broad latitude left to the Member States regarding which limitation to implement in what way, the provision has not led to true harmonization of copyright limitations across the EU.

At the same time, Recital 32 of the Directive points out that Art. 5 provides an exhaustive enumeration of limitations to the right of reproduction and the right of communication to the public. Member States are not allowed to implement any copyright limitations that are not listed in Art. 5. Once the Directive came into effect, existing limitations in national copyright laws had to be modified or revoked insofar as they did not fall within the scope of the exhaustive list of Art. 5. As a result, Art. 5 Information Society Directive is an interesting combination of an exhaustive harmonization (in terms of types of limitations) without a true substantive harmonization (in terms of comparability of limitations across countries).

13.3.2 Limitations to the right of reproduction

CASE

Case C-302/10, Infopaq Int'l v. Danske Dagblades Forening, Court of Justice of the European Union, ECLI:EU:C:2012:16 ("Infopaq II")

...

23 Following [the CJEU's judgment in *Infopaq I*, however, the Højesteret found that it could still be called upon to decide whether Infopaq infringed Directive 2001/29 by carrying out th[e] [book review extracting] process, with the exception of the extract of 11 words, that is to say by confining itself to the implementation of the first three acts of reproduction. The Højesteret therefore referred the following questions to the Court for a preliminary ruling:

'1. Is the stage of the technological process at which temporary acts of reproduction take place relevant to whether they constitute "an integral and essential part of a technological process", within the meaning of Article 5(1) of Directive 2001/29?
2. Can temporary acts of reproduction be an "integral and essential part of a technological process" if they consist of manual scanning of entire newspaper articles whereby the latter are transformed from a printed medium into a digital medium?
3. Does the concept of "lawful use", within the meaning of Article 5(1) of Directive 2001/29, include any form of use which does not require the copyright holder's consent?
4. Does the concept of "lawful use", within the meaning of Article 5(1) of Directive 2001/29, include the scanning by a commercial business of entire newspaper articles and subsequent processing of the reproduction, for use in the business's summary writing, even where the rightholder has not given consent to those acts, if the other requirements in the provision are satisfied?
   Is it relevant to the answer to the question whether the 11 words are stored after the data capture process is terminated?
5. What criteria should be used to assess whether temporary acts of reproduction have "independent economic significance", within the meaning of Article 5(1) of Directive 2001/29 if the other requirements in the provision are satisfied?
6. Can the user's efficiency gains from temporary acts of reproduction be taken into

CASE *(continued)*

account in assessing whether the acts have "independent economic significance", within the meaning of Article 5(1) of Directive 2001/29?

7. Can the scanning by a commercial business of entire newspaper articles and the subsequent processing of the reproduction, be regarded as constituting "certain special cases which do not conflict with a normal exploitation" of the newspaper articles and "not unreasonably [prejudicing] the legitimate interests of the rightholder", pursuant to Article 5(5) of Directive 2001/29, if the requirements in Article 5(1) of the directive are satisfied?

Is it relevant to the answer to the question whether the 11 words are stored after the data capture process is terminated?'

...

25 Under Article 5(1) of Directive 2001/29, an act of reproduction is exempted from the reproduction right provided for in Article 2 thereof provided that it fulfils five conditions, namely, where

- the act is temporary;
- it is transient or incidental;
- it is an integral and essential part of a technological process;
- its sole purpose is to enable a transmission in a network between third parties by an intermediary or a lawful use of a work or protected subject-matter; and
- the act has no independent economic significance.

26 First, it must be borne in mind that those conditions are cumulative in the sense that non-compliance with any one of them will lead to the act of reproduction not being exempted, pursuant to Article 5(1) of Directive 2001/29, from the reproduction right provided for in Article 2 of that directive (*Infopaq International*, paragraph 55).

27 Secondly, it is apparent from the Court's case-law that the conditions listed above must be interpreted strictly because Article 5(1) of that directive is a derogation from the general principle established by that directive, namely the requirement that the rightholder authorise any reproduction of a protected work (see *Infopaq International*, paragraphs 56 and 57, and Cases C-403/08 and C-429/08 *Football Association Premier League and Others* [2011] ECR I-9083, paragraph 162).

Questions 1 and 2 relating to the condition that the acts of reproduction must constitute an integral and essential part of a technological process

33 In the present case, it should be recalled that the technological process in question consists of carrying out electronic and automatic research in newspaper articles and identifying and extracting predefined key words from those articles, in order to render the drafting of summaries of newspaper articles more efficient.

34 In that context, there are three successive acts of reproduction involved. They

CASE *(continued)*

materialise through the creation of the TIFF file, then that of the text file and, finally, through that of the file containing the extract of 11 words.

35 In that context, first, it is not in dispute that none of those acts are completed outside of that technological process.

36 Secondly, it is irrelevant that such a technological process is activated by the manual insertion of newspaper articles into a scanner, in order to achieve a first temporary reproduction – the creation of a TIFF file – and that it is terminated by an act of temporary reproduction, namely the creation of a file containing an extract of 11 words.

37 Finally, it should be noted that the technological process in question could not function correctly and efficiently without the acts of reproduction concerned.

...

39 In view of the above, the answer to the first and second questions is that Article 5(1) of Directive 2001/29 must be interpreted as meaning that the acts of temporary reproduction carried out during a data capture process, such as those in issue in the main proceedings, fulfil the condition that those acts must constitute an integral and essential part of a technological process, notwithstanding the fact that they initiate and terminate that process and involve human intervention.

Questions 3 and 4 relating to the condition that the acts of reproduction must pursue a sole purpose, namely to enable either the transmission of a protected work or a protected subject-matter in a network between third parties by an intermediary, or the lawful use of such a work or such a subject-matter

41 It must be noted at the outset that the acts of reproduction concerned are not intended to enable a transmission in a network between third parties by an intermediary. In those circumstances, it should be examined whether the sole purpose of those acts is to enable the lawful use of a protected work or a protected subject-matter.

...

43 In the case in the main proceedings, it should be noted, first, that in the situation outlined by the referring court, where the last act of the technological process of data capture, namely the printing of the extract of 11 words, is not performed, the technological process concerned, including therefore the creation of the TIFF file, that of the text file and that of the file containing the extract of 11 words, is intended to enable a more efficient drafting of summaries of newspaper articles and, therefore, a use of those articles. Secondly, there is nothing in the file before the Court to indicate that the result of that technological process, namely the extract of 11 words, is intended to enable another use.

44 In respect of the lawful or unlawful character of the use, it is not disputed that the drafting of a summary of newspaper articles is not, in the present case, authorised by the holders of the copyright over these articles. However, it should be noted that such an activity is not restricted by European Union legislation. Furthermore, it is apparent from the statements of both Infopaq and the DDF that the drafting of that summary is not an activity which is restricted by Danish legislation.

45 In those circumstances, that use cannot be considered to be unlawful.

CASE (continued)

46 In view of the foregoing, the answer to the third and fourth questions is that Article 5(1) of Directive 2001/29 must be interpreted as meaning that the acts of temporary reproduction carried out during a data capture process, such as those in issue in the main proceedings, fulfil the condition that those acts must pursue a sole purpose, namely the lawful use of a protected work or a protected subject-matter.

Questions 5 and 6 relating to the condition that the acts of reproduction must not have independent economic significance

48 [It] should be recalled that the acts of temporary reproduction, within the meaning of Article 5(1), aim to make access to the protected works and their use possible. Since those works have a specific economic value, access to them and their use necessarily has economic significance (see, to that effect, *Football Association Premier League and Others*, paragraph 174).

49 Furthermore, as is apparent from Recital 33 in the preamble to Directive 2001/29, the acts of temporary reproduction – like the acts enabling 'browsing' and 'caching' – have the purpose of facilitating the use of a work or making that use more efficient. Thus, an inherent feature of those acts is to enable the achievement of efficiency gains in the context of such use and, consequently, to lead to increased profits or a reduction in production costs.

50 However, those acts must not have independent economic significance, in that the economic advantage derived from their implementation must not be either distinct or separable from the economic advantage derived from the lawful use of the work concerned and it must not generate an additional economic advantage going beyond that derived from that use of the protected work (see, to that effect, *Football Association Premier League and Others*, paragraph 175).

51 The efficiency gains resulting from the implementation of the acts of temporary reproduction, such as those in issue in the main proceedings, have no such independent economic significance, inasmuch as the economic advantages derived from their application only materialise during the use of the reproduced subject matter, so that they are neither distinct nor separable from the advantages derived from its use.

. . .

54 Consequently, the answer to the fifth and sixth questions is that Article 5(1) of Directive 2001/29 must be interpreted as meaning that the acts of temporary reproduction carried out during a data capture process, such as those in issue in the main proceedings, fulfil the condition that those acts must not have an independent economic significance provided, first, that the implementation of those acts does not enable the generation of an additional profit, going beyond that derived from lawful use of the protected work and, secondly, that the acts of temporary reproduction do not lead to a modification of that work.

Question 7 relating to the condition that the acts of reproduction must neither conflict with the normal exploitation of the work nor unreasonably prejudice the legitimate interests of the rightholder

56 [I]f those acts of reproduction fulfil all the conditions of Article 5(1) of Directive 2001/29, as interpreted by the case-law of the Court, it must be held that they do not

CASE *(continued)*

conflict with the normal exploitation of the work or unreasonably prejudice the legitimate interests of the rightholder (*Football Association Premier League and Others*, paragraph 181).

57   Consequently, the answer to the seventh question is that Article 5(5) of Directive 2001/29 must be interpreted as meaning that, if they fulfil all the conditions laid down in Article 5(1) of that directive, the acts of temporary reproduction carried out during a 'data capture' process, such as those in issue in the main proceedings, must be regarded as fulfilling the condition that the acts of reproduction may not conflict with a normal exploitation of the work or unreasonably prejudice the legitimate interests of the rightholder.

...

On those grounds, the Court (Third Chamber) hereby rules:

(1) Article 5(1) of Directive 2001/29/EC of the European Parliament and of the Council of 22 May 2001 on the harmonisation of certain aspects of copyright and related rights in the information society must be interpreted as meaning that the acts of temporary reproduction carried out during a 'data capture' process, such as those in issue in the main proceedings,
   - fulfil the condition that those acts must constitute an integral and essential part of a technological process, notwithstanding the fact that they initiate and terminate that process and involve human intervention;
   - fulfil the condition that those acts of reproduction must pursue a sole purpose, namely to enable the lawful use of a protected work or a protected subject-matter;
   - fulfil the condition that those acts must not have an independent economic significance provided, first, that the implementation of those acts does not enable the generation of an additional profit going beyond that derived from the lawful use of the protected work and, secondly, that the acts of temporary reproduction do not lead to a modification of that work.

(2) Article 5(5) of Directive 2001/29 must be interpreted as meaning that, if they fulfil all the conditions laid down in Article 5(1) of that directive, the acts of temporary reproduction carried out during a 'data capture' process, such as those in issue in the main proceedings, must be regarded as fulfilling the condition that the acts of reproduction may not conflict with a normal exploitation of the work or unreasonably prejudice the legitimate interests of the rightholder.

NOTES AND QUESTIONS

1. After the CJEU had provided some guidance to the Danish Supreme Court (Højesteret) in *Infopaq I*, the court referred the case back to the CJEU to receive a more detailed interpretation of copyright limitations in Art. 5 Information Society Directive. The decision is noteworthy, among other issues, as it demonstrates how the copyright limitations of Art. 5(1)–(3) Information Society Directive also have to pass the three-step test of Art. 5(5) of the Directive.

2. The judgment is a good example of a copyright decision operating under an enumerated list of copyright exceptions. How would a US court, operating under a system of fair use defense, have addressed the issue?
3. Traditionally, the CJEU noted that copyright exceptions must be interpreted narrowly. This is not only due to the three-step test as laid down in Art. 5(5) Information Society Directive, but also because the court viewed it as a general norm that provisions which deviate from a general principle in a Directive should be interpreted narrowly. This very formalistic approach has been softened up. In later decisions, however, the CJEU has deviated from a very strict interpretation of copyright exceptions, noting that the interpretation may not hamper the development of new technologies and must achieve a fair balance between the interests of right holders, users, and society at large (*see, e.g.*, CJEU, Joined Cases 403/08 & 429/08, *Football Association Premier League et al. v. QC Leisure*, ECLI:EU:C:2011:631, at 164; CJEU, Case 360/13, *Public Relations Consultations Assoc. v. Newspaper Licensing Agency*, ECLI:EU:C:2014:1195, at 24).

13.3.3 Exhaustion

Case 78/70, Deutsche Grammophon Gesellschaft v. Metro-SB-Grossmärkte, Court of Justice of the European Union, E.C.R. 1971, 487

1   By an order of 8 October 1970, which was received at the court registry on 7 December 1970, the Hanseatisches Oberlandesgericht, Hamburg [Hamburg Court of Appeals], referred to the Court of Justice, under Article 177 of the Treaty Establishing the European Economic Community, certain questions on the interpretation of the second paragraph of Article 5, Article 85(1) and Article 86 of the treaty.

The first question
2   In the first question the Court is asked to rule whether it is contrary to the second paragraph of Article 5 or Article 85 (1) of the EEC Treaty to interpret Articles 97 and 85 of the German law of 9 September 1965 on copyright and related rights to mean that a German undertaking manufacturing sound recordings may rely on its exclusive right of distribution to prohibit the marketing in the Federal Republic of Germany of sound recordings which it has itself supplied to its French subsidiary which, although independent at law, is wholly subordinate to it commercially.

...

4   It is clear from the facts recorded by the Hanseatisches Oberlandesgericht, Hamburg, that what it asks may be reduced in essentials to the question whether the exclusive right of distributing the protected articles which is conferred by a national law on the manufacturer of sound recordings may, without infringing community provisions, prevent the marketing on national territory of products lawfully distributed by such manufacturer or with his consent on the territory of another member state. The court of justice is asked to define the tenor and the scope of the relevant community provisions, with particular reference to the second paragraph of Article 5 or Article 85(1).

CASE *(continued)*

5   According to the second paragraph of Article 5 of the Treaty, member states "shall abstain from any measure which could jeopardize the attainment of the objective of this treaty". This provision lays down a general duty for the member states, the actual tenor of which depends in each individual case on the provisions of the treaty or on the rules derived from its general scheme.

6   According to article 85(1) of the treaty "the following shall be prohibited as incompatible with the common market: all agreements between undertakings, decisions by associations of undertakings and concerted practices which may affect trade between member states and which have as their object or effect the prevention, restriction or distortion of competition within the common market". The exercise of the exclusive right referred to in the question might fall under the prohibition set out by this provision each time it manifests itself as the subject, the means or the result of an agreement which, by preventing imports from other member states of products lawfully distributed there, has as its effect the partitioning of the market.

7   If, however, the exercise of the right does not exhibit those elements of contract or concerted practice referred to in Article 85 (1) it is necessary, in order to answer the question referred, further to consider whether the exercise of the right in question is compatible with other provisions of the treaty, in particular those relating to the free movement of goods.

8   The principles to be considered in the present case are those concerned with the attainment of a single market between the member states, which are placed both in part two of the treaty devoted to the foundations of the Community, under the free movement of goods, and in article 3(g) of the Treaty which prescribes the institution of a system ensuring that competition in the common market is not distorted.

9   Moreover, where certain prohibitions or restrictions on trade between member states are conceded in Article 36, the treaty makes express reference to them, providing that such derogations shall not constitute "a means of arbitrary discrimination or a disguised restriction on trade between member states".

10   It is thus in the light of those provisions, especially of articles 36, 85 and 86, that an appraisal should be made as to how far the exercise of a national right related to copyright may impede the marketing of products from another member state.

11   Amongst the prohibitions or restrictions on the free movement of goods which it concedes Article 36 refers to industrial and commercial property. On the assumption that those provisions may be relevant to a right related to copyright, it is nevertheless clear from that article that, although the treaty does not affect the existence of rights recognized by the legislation of a member state with regard to industrial and commercial property, the exercise of such rights may nevertheless fall within the prohibitions laid down by the Treaty. Although it permits prohibitions or restrictions on the free movement of products, which are justified for the purpose of protecting industrial and commercial property, article 36 only admits derogations from that freedom to the extent to which they are justified for the purpose of safeguarding rights which constitute the specific subject-matter of such property.

> **CASE** *(continued)*
>
> 12 If a right related to copyright is relied upon to prevent the marketing in a member state of products distributed by the holder of the right or with his consent on the territory of another member state on the sole ground that such distribution did not take place on the national territory, such a prohibition, which would legitimize the isolation of national markets, would be repugnant to the essential purpose of the treaty, which is to unite national markets into a single market.
>
> That purpose could not be attained if, under the various legal systems of the member states, nationals of those states were able to partition the market and bring about arbitrary discrimination or disguised restrictions on trade between member states.
>
> 13 Consequently, it would be in conflict with the provisions prescribing the free movement of products within the common market for a manufacturer of sound recordings to exercise the exclusive right to distribute the protected articles, conferred upon him by the legislation of a member state, in such a way as to prohibit the sale in that state of products placed on the market by him or with his consent in another member state solely because such distribution did not occur within the territory of the first member state.
>
> . . .
>
> **The court**
>
> In answer to the question referred to it by the Hanseatisches Oberlandesgericht, Hamburg, pursuant to an order of that court of 8 October 1970, hereby rules:
>
> 1. It is in conflict with the provisions prescribing the free movement of products within the common market for a manufacturer of sound recordings to exercise the exclusive right to distribute the protected articles, conferred upon him by the legislation of a member state, in such a way as to prohibit the sale in that state of products placed on the market by him or with his consent in another member state solely because such distribution did not occur within the territory of the first member state.
>
> . . .

NOTES

1. This classic case demonstrates the origin of the doctrine of European-wide exhaustion in EU copyright law. When the record company Deutsche Grammophon attempted to prevent the import of its records from France to Germany, arguing that it had not given consent to their distribution in Germany, the Court created the principle of EU-wide exhaustion, showing that the record company had, in fact, consented to their distribution in France. Copyright protection had come into conflict with the freedom of movement of goods, a foundational principle of EU law. In this conflict, the free movement principle won, and copyright protection became restricted. Following this decision, the principle of regional exhaustion became an important aspect of European intellectual property legislation and jurisprudence. Today, Art. 4(2) Information Society Directive provides that the copyright owner's distribution right is subject to EU-wide exhaustion.

2. According to the wording of Art. 4(2) Information Society Directive, the right of distribution is exhausted "within the Community", *i.e.* within the territory of the EU. However, there are special rules in the agree-

ment of the European Economic Area (Annex 17 No. 9(e) and Protocol 28 to Art. 2) according to which the effect of exhaustion extends to member states of the EEA as well. Member states of the EEA include not only EU Member States, but also Norway, Iceland, and Liechtenstein. So, strictly speaking, there is no EU-wide, but EEA-wide exhaustion in European copyright law.

Case C-128/11, UsedSoft v. Oracle Int'l, Court of Justice of the European Union, ECLI:EU:C:2012:407

20   Oracle develops and markets computer software. It is the proprietor of the exclusive user rights under copyright law in those programs. It is also the proprietor of the German and Community word marks Oracle, which are registered inter alia for computer software.
21   Oracle distributes the software at issue in the main proceedings, namely databank software, in 85% of cases by downloading from the internet. The customer downloads a copy of the software directly to his computer from Oracle's website. The software is what is known as 'client-server-software'. The user right for such a program, which is granted by a licence agreement, includes the right to store a copy of the program permanently on a server and to allow a certain number of users to access it by downloading it to the main memory of their work-station computers. On the basis of a maintenance agreement, updated versions of the software ('updates') and programs for correcting faults ('patches') can be downloaded from Oracle's website. At the customer's request, the programs are also supplied on CD-ROM or DVD.
22   Oracle offers group licences for the software at issue in the main proceedings for a minimum of 25 users each. An undertaking requiring licences for 27 users thus has to acquire two licences.
23   Oracle's licence agreements for the software at issue in the main proceedings contain the following term, under the heading 'Grant of rights':
'With the payment for services you receive, exclusively for your internal business purposes, for an unlimited period a non-exclusive non-transferable user right free of charge for everything that Oracle develops and makes available to you on the basis of this agreement.'
24   UsedSoft markets used software licences, including user licences for the Oracle computer programs at issue in the main proceedings. For that purpose UsedSoft acquires from customers of Oracle such user licences, or parts of them, where the original licences relate to a greater number of users than required by the first acquirer.
25   In October 2005 UsedSoft promoted an 'Oracle Special Offer' in which it offered for sale 'already used' licences for the Oracle programs at issue in the main proceedings. In doing so it pointed out that the licences were all 'current' in the sense that the maintenance agreement concluded between the original licence holder and Oracle was still in force, and that the lawfulness of the original sale was confirmed by a notarial certificate.
26   Customers of UsedSoft who are not yet in possession of the Oracle software in question

CASE *(continued)*

download a copy of the program directly from Oracle's website, after acquiring such a used licence. Customers who already have that software and then purchase further licences for additional users are induced by UsedSoft to copy the program to the work stations of those users.

27 Oracle brought proceedings in the Landgericht München I (Regional Court, Munich I) seeking an order that UsedSoft cease the practices described in paragraphs 24 to 26 above. That court allowed Oracle's application. UsedSoft's appeal against the decision was dismissed. UsedSoft thereupon appealed on a point of law to the Bundesgerichtshof (Federal Court of Justice).

28 According to the Bundesgerichtshof, the actions of UsedSoft and its customers infringe Oracle's exclusive right of permanent or temporary reproduction of computer programs within the meaning of Article 4(1)(a) of Directive 2009/24. UsedSoft's customers cannot, in that court's view, rely on a right validly transferred to them by Oracle to reproduce the computer programs. Oracle's licence agreements state that the right to use the programs is 'non-transferable'. Oracle's customers are not therefore entitled to transfer to third parties the right of reproduction of those programs.

29 The outcome of the dispute depends, according to that court, on whether the customers of UsedSoft can successfully rely on Paragraph 69d(1) of the UrhG, which transposes Article 5(1) of Directive 2009/24 into German law.

30 The question arises, first, whether a person who, like UsedSoft's customers, does not hold a user right in the computer program granted by the rightholder, but relies on the exhaustion of the right to distribute a copy of the computer program, is a 'lawful acquirer' of that copy within the meaning of Article 5(1) of Directive 2009/24. The referring court considers that that is the case. It explains that the marketability of a copy of the computer program which arises from the exhaustion of the distribution right would be largely meaningless if the acquirer of such a copy did not have the right to reproduce the program. The use of a computer program, unlike the use of other works protected by copyright, generally requires its reproduction. Article 5(1) of Directive 2009/24 thus serves to safeguard the exhaustion of the distribution right under Article 4(2) of Directive 2009/24.

31 Next, the referring court considers whether, in a case such as that in the main proceedings, the right to distribute a copy of a computer program is exhausted under the second sentence of Paragraph 69c(3) of the UrhG, which transposes Article 4(2) of Directive 2009/24.

32 There are several possible interpretations. First, Article 4(2) of Directive 2009/24 could be applicable if the rightholder allows a customer, after the conclusion of a licence agreement, to make a copy of a computer program by downloading that program from the internet and storing it on a computer. That provision attaches the legal consequence of exhaustion of the distribution right to the first sale of a copy of the program and does not necessarily presuppose the putting into circulation of a physical copy of the program. Secondly, Article 4(2) of Directive 2009/24 could be applicable by analogy in the case of the sale of a computer program by means of on-line transmission. According

CASE *(continued)*

to the supporters of that view, there is an unintended lacuna in the law ('planwidrige Regelungslücke') because the authors of the directive did not regulate or contemplate on-line transmission of computer programs. Thirdly, Article 4(2) of Directive 2009/24 is inapplicable because the exhaustion of the distribution right under that provision always presupposes the putting into circulation of a physical copy of the program by the rightholder or with his consent. The authors of the directive deliberately refrained from extending the rule on exhaustion to the on-line transmission of computer programs.

33   Finally, the referring court raises the question whether a person who has acquired a used licence may, for making a copy of the program (as UsedSoft's customers do in the dispute in the main proceedings by downloading a copy of Oracle's program onto a computer from Oracle's website or uploading it to the main memory of other work stations), rely on exhaustion of the right of distribution of the copy of the program made by the first acquirer, with the consent of the rightholder, by downloading it from the internet, if the first acquirer has deleted his copy or no longer uses it. The referring court considers that the application by analogy of Articles 5(1) and 4(2) of Directive 2009/24 can be ruled out. Exhaustion of the distribution right is intended solely to guarantee the marketability of a copy of a program which is incorporated in a particular data carrier and sold by the rightholder or with his consent. The effect of exhaustion should not therefore be extended to the non-physical data transmitted on-line.

34   In those circumstances the Bundesgerichtshof decided to stay the proceedings and to refer the following questions to the Court for a preliminary ruling:

'1. Is the person who can rely on exhaustion of the right to distribute a copy of a computer program a "lawful acquirer" within the meaning of Article 5(1) of Directive 2009/24?

2. If the reply to the first question is in the affirmative: is the right to distribute a copy of a computer program exhausted in accordance with the first half-sentence of Article 4(2) of Directive 2009/24 when the acquirer has made the copy with the rightholder's consent by downloading the program from the internet onto a data carrier?

3. If the reply to the second question is also in the affirmative: can a person who has acquired a "used" software licence for generating a program copy as "lawful acquirer" under Article 5(1) and the first half-sentence of Article 4(2) of Directive 2009/24 also rely on exhaustion of the right to distribute the copy of the computer program made by the first acquirer with the rightholder's consent by downloading the program from the internet onto a data carrier if the first acquirer has erased his program copy or no longer uses it?'

Consideration of the questions referred
Question 2
35   By its second question, which should be addressed first, the referring court essentially seeks to know whether and under what conditions the downloading from the internet of a copy of a computer program, authorised by the copyright holder, can give rise to exhaustion of the right of distribution of that copy in the European Union within the meaning of Article 4(2) of Directive 2009/24.

CASE *(continued)*

36   It should be recalled that under Article 4(2) of Directive 2009/24 the first sale in the European Union of a copy of a computer program by the rightholder or with his consent exhausts the distribution right within the European Union of that copy.

37   According to the order for reference, the copyright holder itself, in this case Oracle, makes available to its customers in the European Union who wish to use its computer program a copy of that program which can be downloaded from its website.

38   To determine whether, in a situation such as that at issue in the main proceedings, the copyright holder's distribution right is exhausted, it must be ascertained, first, whether the contractual relationship between the rightholder and its customer, within which the downloading of a copy of the program in question has taken place, may be regarded as a 'first sale . . . of a copy of a program' within the meaning of Article 4(2) of Directive 2009/24. . . .

42   According to a commonly accepted definition, a 'sale' is an agreement by which a person, in return for payment, transfers to another person his rights of ownership in an item of tangible or intangible property belonging to him. It follows that the commercial transaction giving rise, in accordance with Article 4(2) of Directive 2009/24, to exhaustion of the right of distribution of a copy of a computer program must involve a transfer of the right of ownership in that copy.

43   Oracle submits that it does not sell copies of its computer programs at issue in the main proceedings. It says that it makes available to its customers, free of charge, on its website a copy of the program concerned, and they can download that copy. The copy thus downloaded may not, however, be used by the customers unless they have concluded a user licence agreement with Oracle. Such a licence gives Oracle's customers a non-exclusive and non-transferable user right for an unlimited period for that program. Oracle submits that neither the making available of a copy free of charge nor the conclusion of the user licence agreement involves a transfer of the right of ownership of that copy.

44   In this respect, it must be observed that the downloading of a copy of a computer program and the conclusion of a user licence agreement for that copy form an indivisible whole. Downloading a copy of a computer program is pointless if the copy cannot be used by its possessor. Those two operations must therefore be examined as a whole for the purposes of their legal classification.

. . .

46   [T]he operations mentioned in paragraph 44 above, examined as a whole, involve the transfer of the right of ownership of the copy of the computer program in question.

. . .

48   Consequently, in a situation such as that at issue in the main proceedings, the transfer by the copyright holder to a customer of a copy of a computer program, accompanied by the conclusion between the same parties of a user licence agreement, constitutes a 'first sale . . . of a copy of a program' within the meaning of Article 4(2) of Directive 2009/24.

. . .

53   [I]t must also be examined whether, as argued by Oracle, the governments which have submitted observations to the Court, and the Commission, the exhaustion of the

CASE *(continued)*

distribution right referred to in Article 4(2) of Directive 2009/24 relates only to tangible property and not to intangible copies of computer programs downloaded from the internet.

...

55 On this point, it must be stated, first, that it does not appear from Article 4(2) of Directive 2009/24 that the exhaustion of the right of distribution of copies of computer programs mentioned in that provision is limited to copies of programmes on a material medium such as a CD-ROM or DVD. On the contrary, that provision, by referring without further specification to the 'sale ... of a copy of a program', makes no distinction according to the tangible or intangible form of the copy in question.

...

59 In those circumstances, it must be considered that the exhaustion of the distribution right under Article 4(2) of Directive 2009/24 concerns both tangible and intangible copies of a computer program, and hence also copies of programs which, on the occasion of their first sale, have been downloaded from the internet onto the first acquirer's computer.

...

61 It should be added that, from an economic point of view, the sale of a computer program on CD-ROM or DVD and the sale of a program by downloading from the internet are similar. The on-line transmission method is the functional equivalent of the supply of a material medium. Interpreting Article 4(2) of Directive 2009/24 in the light of the principle of equal treatment confirms that the exhaustion of the distribution right under that provision takes effect after the first sale in the European Union of a copy of a computer program by the copyright holder or with his consent, regardless of whether the sale relates to a tangible or an intangible copy of the program.

...

64 [I]t must also be examined whether, as Oracle claims, the maintenance agreement concluded by the first acquirer prevents in any event the exhaustion of the right provided for in Article 4(2) of Directive 2009/24, since the copy of the computer program which the first acquirer may transfer to a second acquirer no longer corresponds to the copy he downloaded but to a new copy of the program.

65 According to the order for reference, the used licences offered by UsedSoft are 'current', in that the sale of the copy of the program by Oracle to its customer was accompanied by the conclusion of a maintenance agreement for that copy.

66 It must be observed that the exhaustion of the right of distribution of a copy of a computer program under Article 4(2) of Directive 2009/24 only concerns copies which have been the subject of a first sale in the European Union by the copyright holder or with his consent. It does not relate to contracts for services, such as maintenance agreements, which are separable from such a sale and were concluded, possibly for an unlimited period, on the occasion of the sale.

67 None the less, the conclusion of a maintenance agreement, such as those at issue in the main proceedings, on the occasion of the sale of an intangible copy of a computer program has the effect that the copy originally purchased is patched and updated. Even if

CASE *(continued)*

the maintenance agreement is for a limited period, the functionalities corrected, altered or added on the basis of such an agreement form an integral part of the copy originally downloaded and can be used by the acquirer of the copy for an unlimited period, even in the event that the acquirer subsequently decides not to renew the maintenance agreement.

68   In such circumstances, the exhaustion of the distribution right under Article 4(2) of Directive 2009/24 extends to the copy of the computer program sold as corrected and updated by the copyright holder.

69   It should be pointed out, however, that if the licence acquired by the first acquirer relates to a greater number of users than he needs, as stated in paragraphs 22 and 24 above, the acquirer is not authorised by the effect of the exhaustion of the distribution right under Article 4(2) of Directive 2009/24 to divide the licence and resell only the user right for the computer program concerned corresponding to a number of users determined by him.

70   An original acquirer who resells a tangible or intangible copy of a computer program for which the copyright holder's right of distribution is exhausted in accordance with Article 4(2) of Directive 2009/24 must, in order to avoid infringing the exclusive right of reproduction of a computer program which belongs to its author, laid down in Article 4(1)(a) of Directive 2009/24, make his own copy unusable at the time of its resale. In a situation such as that mentioned in the preceding paragraph, the customer of the copyright holder will continue to use the copy of the program installed on his server and will not thus make it unusable.

71   Moreover, even if an acquirer of additional user rights for the computer program concerned did not carry out a new installation – and hence a new reproduction – of the program on a server belonging to him, the effect of the exhaustion of the distribution right under Article 4(2) of Directive 2009/24 would in any event not extend to such user rights. In such a case the acquisition of additional user rights does not relate to the copy for which the distribution right was exhausted at the time of that transaction. On the contrary, it is intended solely to make it possible to extend the number of users of the copy which the acquirer of additional rights has himself already installed on his server.

72   On the basis of all the foregoing, the answer to Question 2 is that Article 4(2) of Directive 2009/24 must be interpreted as meaning that the right of distribution of a copy of a computer program is exhausted if the copyright holder who has authorised, even free of charge, the downloading of that copy from the internet onto a data carrier has also conferred, in return for payment of a fee intended to enable him to obtain a remuneration corresponding to the economic value of the copy of the work of which he is the proprietor, a right to use that copy for an unlimited period.

Questions 1 and 3

73   By its first and third questions the referring court seeks essentially to know whether, and under what conditions, an acquirer of used licences for computer programs, such as those sold by UsedSoft, may, as a result of the exhaustion of the distribution right under Article 4(2) of Directive 2009/24, be regarded as a 'lawful acquirer' within the meaning of Article 5(1) of Directive 2009/24 who, in accordance with that provision, enjoys the right

CASE *(continued)*

of reproduction of the program concerned in order to enable him to use the program in accordance with its intended purpose.

74 Article 5(1) of Directive 2009/24 provides that, in the absence of specific contractual provisions, the reproduction of a computer program does not require authorisation by the author of the program where that reproduction is necessary for the use of the computer program by the lawful acquirer in accordance with its intended purpose, including for error correction.

...

80 Since the copyright holder cannot object to the resale of a copy of a computer program for which that rightholder's distribution right is exhausted under Article 4(2) of Directive 2009/24, it must be concluded that a second acquirer of that copy and any subsequent acquirer are 'lawful acquirers' of it within the meaning of Article 5(1) of Directive 2009/24.

81 Consequently, in the event of a resale of the copy of the computer program by the first acquirer, the new acquirer will be able, in accordance with Article 5(1) of Directive 2009/24, to download onto his computer the copy sold to him by the first acquirer. Such a download must be regarded as a reproduction of a computer program that is necessary to enable the new acquirer to use the program in accordance with its intended purpose.

...

87 [However,], a copyright holder such as Oracle is entitled, in the event of the resale of a user licence entailing the resale of a copy of a computer program downloaded from his website, to ensure by all technical means at his disposal that the copy still in the hands of the reseller is made unusable.

88 It follows from the foregoing that the answer to Questions 1 and 3 is that Articles 4(2) and 5(1) of Directive 2009/24 must be interpreted as meaning that, in the event of the resale of a user licence entailing the resale of a copy of a computer program downloaded from the copyright holder's website, that licence having originally been granted by that rightholder to the first acquirer for an unlimited period in return for payment of a fee intended to enable the rightholder to obtain a remuneration corresponding to the economic value of that copy of his work, the second acquirer of the licence, as well as any subsequent acquirer of it, will be able to rely on the exhaustion of the distribution right under Article 4(2) of that directive, and hence be regarded as lawful acquirers of a copy of a computer program within the meaning of Article 5(1) of that directive and benefit from the right of reproduction provided for in that provision.

...

On those grounds, the Court (Grand Chamber) hereby rules:

1. Article 4(2) of Directive 2009/24/EC of the European Parliament and of the Council of 23 April 2009 on the legal protection of computer programs must be interpreted as meaning that the right of distribution of a copy of a computer program is exhausted if the copyright holder who has authorised, even free of charge, the downloading of that copy from the internet onto a data carrier has also conferred, in return for payment of

CASE *(continued)*

a fee intended to enable him to obtain a remuneration corresponding to the economic value of the copy of the work of which he is the proprietor, a right to use that copy for an unlimited period.

2. Articles 4(2) and 5(1) of Directive 2009/24 must be interpreted as meaning that, in the event of the resale of a user licence entailing the resale of a copy of a computer program downloaded from the copyright holder's website, that licence having originally been granted by that rightholder to the first acquirer for an unlimited period in return for payment of a fee intended to enable the rightholder to obtain a remuneration corresponding to the economic value of that copy of his work, the second acquirer of the licence, as well as any subsequent acquirer of it, will be able to rely on the exhaustion of the distribution right under Article 4(2) of that directive, and hence be regarded as lawful acquirers of a copy of a computer program within the meaning of Article 5(1) of that directive and benefit from the right of reproduction provided for in that provision.

NOTES

1. In various jurisdictions, the relationship between property rights attached to computer software (copyright) and contractual agreements pertaining to its use (software licenses) is a complex one. Courts around the globe have to struggle with questions such as: Who owns software? Is software sold, or licensed, or both? Can the author of a software program impose use covenants running with the property? The emergence of secondary markets for used computer software licenses highlights many of these problems. Some argue that the control over the distribution and redistribution of software programs should reside with the copyright owner, while others want to enable an open market on which software licenses can be freely traded. With the *UsedSoft* decision, the CJEU enabled secondary markets for used computer programs within the EU.

2. While the CJEU held in UsedSoft that the exhaustion of the distribution right in Art. 4(2) Computer Programs Directive concerns both tangible and intangible copies of a computer program, it neither drew conclusions for the general right of communication to the public nor the general distribution right as laid down in the Information Society Directive, both of which apply to copyrightable subject matter but not to computer programs. Rather, the Court treats the Computer Programs Directive, which does not know a separate right of communication to the public, as *lex specialis* to the Information Society Directive. More recent case law by the CJEU suggests that the court might not be willing to extend the exhaustion principle to online transmissions (*see* CJEU, Case C-419/13, *Art & Allposters Int'l v. Stichting Pictoright*, ECLI:EU:C.2015:27).

13.4 China

As with the UK model, China also adopts the fair dealing doctrine that allows users to use copyrighted works without seeking permission from rights holders. Article 22 of the PRC Copyright Law provides an enumerated list of 12 exceptions to copyright, including, for example, for purposes of private study and research, comments, and reporting of current events. In order to accommodate fair use in the digital world, Article 6 of the Regulations for the Protection of Rights of Communication through Information Networks ("2006 Regulations") extends the list of permissible uses provided under Article 22 of the PRC Copyright Law to the internet.

SARFT Movie Channel v. CETV, Beijing First Intermediate Court [2006] Yi Zhong Min Zhong Zi No. 13332

In April 2001, Plaintiff, Movie Channel of State Administration of Radio, Film and Television (SRAFT Channel), entered into a co-production agreement with Bayi Film Studio. The two parties agreed to the following terms among others: (1) both parties agreed to co-produce a movie, *Charging Out Amazon* (the "*Movie*"); (2) SARFT Channel exclusively owns the television right and internet right of the Movie . . .

In April 2002, the Movie was approved by Chinese Film Bureau and was released shortly [thereafter]. The movie achieved a great success and won several film awards between 2001–2003. On September 10, 2005, Defendant China Education Television ('CETV'), broadcasted the Movie on its movie channel "Weekend Theatre" without Plaintiff's permission. Several commercial[s] were included during the broadcast of the Movie.

[Plaintiff SARFT Channel brought a lawsuit against CETV, claiming that Defendant violated its exclusive copyright (the television right) to the Movie. In its defense, CETV contended that the broadcast of the Movie was fair use, which falls under Article 22(6), which provides that "translation, or reproduction in a small quantity of copies of a published work by teachers or scientific researchers for use in classroom teaching or scientific research, is exempted from getting permission from, or making payment of remuneration to, the copyright owner."]

The first-instance court rejected Defendant's in-classroom teaching exception argument, holding that Article 22(6) only applies to face-to-face in-classroom teaching, and does not extend to remote training or teaching by radio, television or other media.

[Defendant appealed. Defendant also added another defense "use of a work by a state agency for the purpose of fulfilling its duty" under Article 22(7) in the appeal.]

The issue presented before this court is whether Defendant's broadcast of the Movie falls into any exceptions or limitations provided under Article 22 of PRC Copyright Law.

Article 22(7) of PRC Copyright Law provides that, *where a state agency used a published work, within a reasonable extent, for performing its official duty, the work might be used without authorization from the copyright owner and without payment of remuneration thereto, provided that the author's name and the title of the work shall be indicated and other rights to which the copyright owner are not infringed.*

With regard to the legislative purpose of this provision, "state agency" refers to an official state institution that is in charge of governmental affairs, and the term "performing official

CASE *(continued)*

duty" refers to performing duties that are directly related to its state function. A liberal interpretation of this provision would not be appropriate or recommend[ed].

In this case, Defendant CETV, as with other media companies, has a responsibility to [broadcast programs] to inform the public. However, CETV's broadcast of the Movie didn't fall under Article 22(7) for the following reasons: First, there is no conflict between implementing the policy and guideline of Chinese Communist Party and respecting the Chinese Copyright Law at the same time. The two share the same goal of encouraging creativity and disseminating works that promote the progress of socialist culture and values. Second, Defendant CETV was not a stage agency in charge of public affairs. Also, broadcasting the Movie was not performing an official duty that was directly related to a state purpose. Third, media companies should not use the advocacy of patriotism or promotion of traditional virtues as an excuse to freely exploit copyrightable works of other parties without permission or compensation. Otherwise, the purpose of the copyright law would be defeated. Last, CETV admitted that commercials were inserted during the broadcast of the Movie, which proved the commercial nature of Defendant's use. Therefore, CETV's broadcast of the Movie didn't fall under Article 22(7) of Chinese Copyright Law.

[With regard to the other defense "in classroom teaching exception" that defendant raised, the Court affirmed with the first-instance court, that defendant's use – broadcast of the Movie at its movie channel – did not fall in the exception of in-classroom teaching under Article 22(6).]

Affirmed.

YANG Luo-Shu v. China Pictorial Publishing House, Shandong High People's Court [2007] Lu Min San Zhong Zi No. 94

Plaintiff YANG Luo-Shu ("YANG") is a well-known painter and also heir of the renowned YANG family, who enjoys reputation with respect to paintings under the theme of Chinese New Year. In January 2006, YANG learned that Defendant China Pictorial Publishing House ("CPPH"), published a book entitled *"A Journey of New Year Paintings from the YANG Family"* (the "Book") authored by YANG Fu-Yuan, in which more than fifty of Plaintiff's paintings were included without permission or compensation. Among these fifty paintings, sixteen works did not accredit YANG as the author.

YANG soon filed a copyright infringement case against both CPPH and YANG Fu-Yuan,

CASE *(continued)*

author of the Book, requesting the defendants to cease the infringement immediately, make a public apology and also request for monetary damages.

The first-instance court found that Plaintiff YANG and his family enjoyed great reputation in paintings with Chinese lunar year theme. On October 11, 2006, YANG registered his works, including *The Collection of Woodcut Based on Water Margin*, *The Collection of Woodcut Based on Journey to the West*, and *The Collection of Woodcut Based on a Dream of Red Mansions*, with the local Shandong Copyright Office. The sixteen works at issue were taken from YANG's three book collections.

[It was not disputed that YANG owns copyright to the paintings used in defendant's Book. It was equally undisputed that the disputed paintings were copyrighted works. However, defendants raised fair use defense.]

CPPH argued that, the paintings used in the Book were for purpose of "introducing, commenting and promoting YANG's works." Therefore, such a use falls into the exceptions and limitations provided under Article 22 (2) of PRC Copyright Law, and thus constituting fair use.

The issues presented before this court include: (1) whether the exploitation of YANG's works by CPPH constituted fair use as defined under Article 22 of PRC Copyright Law; and (2) determination of liability issue should an infringement be established.

With regard to the first issue, Article 22(2) of PRC Copyright Law provides that

> [I]n the following cases, a work may be used without permission from, and without payment of remuneration to, the copyright owner, provided that the name of the author and the title of the work are mentioned and the other rights enjoyed by the copyright owner in accordance with this Law are not prejudiced . . .
> (2) if appropriate quotation was made from another person's published work in one's own work for the purpose of introducing or commenting a certain work or explaining a certain point.

In this case, the court [made the following findings and analysis]. First, the main purpose of the Book was not to comment or introduce YANG's paintings. Instead, the Book was focused on introducing the renowned YANG family, its family members, the historical events surrounding the family and also the travel stories of the author himself. As such, the purpose of the Book was not to "comment or introduce a certain work or explain a certain point."

Second, the chapters in which the paintings were included had little relevance to the paintings themselves. Also, the amount of the paintings that were used and included in the Book exceeded the extent that was appropriate.

Finally, with respect to the impact of the use, it is clear that the inclusion of YANG's paintings in the Book added aesthetic value to the Book. Therefore, Defendant's use of Plaintiff's works without permission or payment deprived Plaintiff's opportunity to exploit the works in a license market. As such, the court held that Defendant's use of YANG's works in the Book did not fall into Article 22(1)(ii) of Chinese Copyright Laws, thus finding Defendant liable for copyright infringement . . .

[Partially affirmed, partially revoked].

NOTES AND COMMENTS

1. Compare *SARFT Movie Channel* with *YANG Luo-Shu*. Do you think that Chinese courts have stringently followed the "fair dealing" model, which only examines the enumerated list of exceptions and limitations, in their fair use analysis?
2. In *YANG Luo-Shu v. Shanghai Pictorial Publishing House*, the Chinese court analyzed the purpose of use; amount of use and also potential impact of defendant's use on plaintiff's work. Do you find such reasoning similar to the multi-factor analysis of the US fair use analysis?

CASE

WANG Shen v. Google, Beijing High People's Court [2013] Gaominzhongzi No. 1221

The appellant Google Inc. ("Google") appealed Beijing No. 1 Intermediate Court's decision (No. 1321, 2011) regarding a copyright infringement dispute against the appellee WANG Shen ("WANG"). Co-defendant Beijing Gu-Xiang Information Technology Ltd. ("Gu-Xiang"), which managed and operated Google China's website, is no longer a party to this suit. This Court accepted this case on February 26, 2013 and held a public trial on April 24, 2013. This Court made a final ruling.

1. **Facts regarding copyright of the disputed Book**
   In March 2000, Shanghai Sanlian Publishing House ("Sanlian") published the disputed book *Acid Lover* ("Book"). The Book has 130,000 words in total and consists of eleven essays. The Book credited "Mian Mian" as the author. WANG submitted the original copy of her Household Registration, which showed that Mian Mian was her former name.
2. **Facts regarding Google China's website**
   WANG submitted a notarized certificate indicating that WANG's attorney conducted the following activities on Google China's website (http://www.google.cn) on October 30, 2009:
   (1) Upon entering the keyword "Mian Mian" in Google China's book search page, the Book would appear as the first search result.
   (2) After clicking on the search result of the Book, it linked into another webpage displaying the Book's summary, excerpts, frequently used terms and phrases as well as its copyright information. This whole process occurred under Google China's website, with no other websites involved.
   (3) On this new webpage, clicking on the frequently used terms and phrases led to relevant excerpts of the Book. This whole process occurred under Google China's website, with no other websites involved.

WANG claimed that during the aforesaid search process, the Book was made available over the internet without authorization from Plaintiff. Also the entire search process, as evidenced by the Notary Public, was completely conducted under Google China's

CASE *(continued)*

website, without linking or redirecting to other websites, thus Google and Gu-Xiang violated WANG's copyright to the Book. Gu-Xiang countered that the search process described by WANG was merely a preview of the Book, rather than dissemination of information over the internet. Gu-Xiang also argued that because of a new search model that Google recently implemented, search result failed to show or redirect to other websites, but remained with Google China's website.

3. **Facts regarding Google's scanning of the Book**

   Google explained its Library Project [and how the Book was scanned] in the following statement, "Google obtained a paper copy of the Book according to its agreement with Stanford University. Google scanned the Book on March 14, 2008 in the United States. Then it legally digitalized the Book under the US law. The digital copy of the Book was only saved in Google's U.S. server."

   Google further explained that "the Library allowed the public to preview limited content (*i.e.* 'excerpts') of its scanned books through the Google China (google.cn) search engine . . . With this preview feature, users may scroll through the excerpts and decide whether to purchase the book or not. Users will not be able to download or read the complete book on Google China's website without purchasing it."

   Beijing No. 1 Intermediate Court found that the scanning, digitalization and distribution of the Book through the internet occurred within the territory of People's Republic of China. Therefore, Chinese courts exercised jurisdiction over this case, and Chinese law should apply. The court also held that WANG's former name was Mian Mian, and therefore WANG has a valid copyright ownership to the Book.

   [With regard to Defendant's scanning, digitalization, and distribution of the Book], the court held that Gu-Xiang's distribution of the Book over the internet constituted fair use, and therefore Gu-Xiang and Google were not held liable for violating WANG's right to distribute or make the work available over the internet. But as far as Google's scanning and digitalization is concerned, the court held that, Google's reproduction of the Book did not constitute fair use, and therefore Google was liable for violating WANG's exclusive right to reproduce. Since Gu-Xiang was not directly involved in the reproduction process, Gu-Xiang was not liable for violating WANG's exclusive reproduction right to the Book. As such, the court ordered Google to immediately stop the infringement and to compensate WANG for the economic losses and litigation costs . . .

   [Google appealed before the Beijing High Court, raising the issues of jurisdiction, application of law, fair use defense, and also the amount of monetary damages.]
   [With regard to the issues presented before us], this Court found as follows:

1. *Whether Chinese Courts Have Jurisdiction Over This Case*

   Pursuant to Article 243 of Civil Procedure Law of the People's Republic of China, "In a contract dispute or other dispute involving property rights, against a defendant who has no domicile within the territory of China, if the contract is signed or performed

CASE *(continued)*

within the territory of China, or if the object of the action is located within the territory of China, or if the defendant has distrainable property within the territory of China, or if the defendant has its representative office within the territory of China, then the people's court of the place where the contract is signed or performed, or where the object of the action is, or where the defendant's distrainable property is located, or where the tort occurs, or where the defendant's representative office is located, shall have jurisdiction." Also, pursuant to Article 28 of Judicial Interpretation Regarding PRC Civil Procedure Law issued by the Chinese Supreme Court, the "location of tort" could either be the place where "the tort is conducted" or where "the result of the tort occurred."

In this case, WANG claimed that Google unlawfully scanned and digitalized the Book [authored by a Chinese writer] in China. Gu-Xiang, [a Chinese company which operates and manages Google's China website,] distributed the Book over the internet to Chinese audience. Also, the notarization process, which showed the consequence of the tort behavior, also occurred in China. Since Google failed to provide evidence to prove that the scanning and digitalization of the Book occurred elsewhere, this Court affirms with the lower court's ruling that, Chinese courts have jurisdiction over this case, and Chinese law should apply because the infringement tort and its consequences both occurred within the territory of China.

2. *Whether Google's Scanning and Digitalization of the Book Constituted Copyright Infringement*

Pursuant to Article 47 of PRC Copyright Law, "individuals who reproduce copyrighted work without the copyright owner's authorization should bear civil liabilities . . . unless provided otherwise." The term "reproduce" here means the act of reproducing one or more copies of a work by printing, photocopying, copying, lithographing, making a sound recording or video recording, duplicating a recording, or duplicating a photographic work, or by other means. Scanning and digitalizing a copyrighted work certainly constitutes reproduction of a work.

In this case, Google reproduced the Book without WANG's authorization, thus violating the reproduction right to WANG's book. Google should cease the infringement and pay for damages, unless certain limitations and exceptions apply. Google argued that its reproduction of the Book constituted fair use. But since Google's use of the Book does not fit squarely within the [enumerated list of 12] permissible uses defined under Article 22 of PRC Copyright Law, it should be presumed that Google's reproduction without authorization constituted copyright infringement [unless exceptions apply]. However, in view of the fact that Chinese courts have recognized fair uses that do not fall exactly under the enumerated list of permissible uses under Article 22 in recent years, if Google could prove its use is fair, [we do not rule out such possibility] that its use might be considered as fair use under special circumstances [even if it does not fall into any of the 12 enumerated exceptions in the list under the existing law].

CASE *(continued)*

When determining whether Defendant's use constitutes fair use, the Court should apply a multi-factor analysis based on a case-by-case approach. The list of factors that courts should consider include: the purpose and nature of the use, the nature of [plaintiff's] copyrighted work, the amount and substantiality of the use of the work, the impact of the use (*i.e.* whether Defendant's use affects the normal exploitation of the copyrighted work,) and finally whether Defendant's use unreasonably prejudices the legal rights and interests of the copyright holder. [It should be noted that] Defendant should bear the burden of proof in the aforesaid multi-factor analysis. Here, Google did not provide evidence to prove that its use met any of the factors above, so its argument for fair use cannot be established. This Court hereby dismisses it.

Actual or potential damage to the market of Plaintiff's copyrighted work is not a prerequisite to establish copyright infringement liability under Chinese Copyright Law. Unless exception applies, unauthorized reproduction of a copyrighted work constitutes copyright infringement. The legislative purpose behind this is that most copyright infringements involve "reproduction" of the work as a first step before other rights are violated, and it is not merely because "reproducing" a copyrighted work may cause financial harm to Plaintiff's work. Therefore by prohibiting unauthorized reproduction of a copyrighted work, the law can effectively prohibit violation of other exclusive rights reserved for copyright holders. As such, we do not agree with the reasoning of the first instance court, which found liability because [defendant's infringement activity] would necessarily harm the copyright owner's economic interests. Therefore, the first instance court's reasoning should be corrected [although we agree with its conclusion].

[As discussed above], unauthorized reproduction of a copyrighted work generally constitutes copyright infringement. But certain [fair] uses of a work requires reproduction of the work, as the first step, before other uses of such a work could take place. Under such circumstances, the "use" of the work should be considered as a whole, and the "reproduction" of the work, [as one of such uses], should not be treated independently from other uses in the fair-use analysis. For example, unauthorized reproduction of a copyrighted work for the purpose of research and education, or reproduction of a copyrighted work by governmental agency for the purpose of fulfilling the government duty, should be deemed as fair use and not constituting copyright infringement. Here, Google reproduced the textual content and all pages of the Book to develop its Library Project. If the public dissemination of the Book over the internet constituted fair use, then the reproduction of the Book, [a prerequisite step before the distribution use occurs,] should also be deemed as fair use. Therefore, the first instance court was incorrect to hold that the fair-use analysis of the distribution of the Book over the internet has no relevance to the fair use analysis of Google's reproduction of the Book. The first instance court's ruling on this issue should be corrected.

. . .

CASE (continued)

In summary, the court of first instance did not err in the fact finding. Also, the application of the law was basically correct [with minor adjustments.] Google's claims and reasoning could not be established. Pursuant to Article 170, Paragraph 1, Item 1 of the *Civil Procedure Law of People's Republic of China*, the appellate court hereby rejects the claims on appeal and affirms the original verdict.

NOTES AND QUESTIONS

1. Professor Seagull Haiyan Song categorized the fair use model in the world into three categories: (1) an open-ended list of permissible uses based on multi-factor analysis (*e.g.* the US); (2) an enumerated list of permissible uses defined under the copyright law(*e.g.* most continental European models); and (3) a hybrid model where judges will first look at the enumerated list to see whether defendant's use falls into any specific category; and in the negative case, they will then apply the multi-factor analysis to determine whether such a use is fair (*e.g.* the South Korean model). Which model do you think the *WANG v. Google* case falls into? Does this approach of determining fair use make sense to you? Why?
2. In the *WANG v. Google* opinion, Chinese judges seem to suggest that direct or potential harm to the market of plaintiff's copyrighted work is not important, or at least, "not a prerequisite to establish liability of defendant." Do you agree with this reasoning? Recall that under the US Copyright law, the first and the last statutory factors, *i.e.* the nature and purpose of the use and the impact of such a use to the market of Plaintiff's work, are the most important factors to a fair use analysis. Which approach makes more sense to you? Why?
3. Chinese judges acknowledged in *WANG v. Google* that use of a copyrighted work might touch on a number of exclusive rights of the copyright holder, such as the right to reproduce, the right to distribute, and the right to make the work available over the internet. In terms of fair use analysis, Chinese judges seem to believe that if one use of the work is found fair, the other uses should be found fair too. Do you agree with this reasoning? Can you think of scenarios where one use of a particular copyrighted work might be fair, but other uses of the same copyrighted work are not considered as fair use?
4. In the third revision of the Chinese Copyright Law, the legislators adopt the hybrid model that combines an enumerated list of permissible uses with a multifactor analysis. In addition to the original list of 12 permissible exceptions and limitations, a new provision is suggested in the new draft, "Other circumstances. [If] such a use does not conflict with a normal exploitation of the work, and does not unreasonably prejudice the legitimate interests of the copyright owner, [such a use might be deemed as fair use]." This newly added provision, also known as the "three-step test," is expected to provide more flexibility to potential fair uses.

14

Infringement and remedies

14.1 Introduction

This section moves past validity and subject matter issues. We turn now to questions of copyright infringement (standards and legal tests), as well as remedies for acts found to be infringing.

14.2 United States

To prove infringement, a copyright owner must show: (1) that his or her copyright was validly registered; (2) that the party accused of infringement violated one of the statutory rights in §106 either directly or indirectly; and (3) that the infringing act occurred within the US or at least affected the copyright owner's interests in the US.

Proof of infringement follows the outlines laid out in the *Arnstein v. Porter* case in Chapter 12. That is, the scope of the reproduction right requires that the work accused of infringement be "substantially similar" to the copyrighted work. Substantial similarity therefore provides a dual-purpose test: it limits the reproduction right under §106(1), and also provides a ready-made test of infringement for all the rights in §106.

An infringer is one not authorized to perform the acts in §106. At times the question is not whether an act occurred; it is whether a particular accused infringer was authorized or not. A license from the copyright owner will shield the accused infringer from liability. One who is licensed, but performs acts outside the scope of his or her license, may be an infringer, however. One statutory rule that comes into play here is the "first sale" provision of 17 U.S.C. §109. This says that once a copyrighted item is sold, the person who buys it may resell it (or otherwise transfer it) to a third party without that third party incurring any liability for copyright infringement. The copyright owner's rights are "cut off" after the first sale, and any subsequent owner or possessor of the copyrighted work need not worry about infringement.

Note that the rule generally applies *only* to actual sales of the copyrighted item: a license from the copyright owner to a licensee may mean that a third party who takes a work from a licensee may still face liability for copyright infringement.

Where the defendant committed the infringing act itself, it is referred to as direct infringement. At times, however, a defendant participates in some way in an act of infringement without directly, itself, performing a prohibited act. A defendant that rents space to an infringer with knowledge of infringement, for example, will be liable under a theory of vicarious liability. More difficult cases arise when a defendant sells a product or provides a service that enables others to make copies. Various online filesharing systems have created some complex law in this area, as the *Grokster* case below illustrates.

Under the US Copyright Act, a prevailing copyright owner "is entitled to recover the actual damages suffered by him or her as a result of the infringement, and any profits of the infringer that are attributable to the infringement …" (17 U.S.C. §504(b)). This has been interpreted to mean that, where the defendant made more money from infringing than the plaintiff lost, the plaintiff may receive both its lost profits and the difference between those profits and what the defendant earned. Despite what the statute might seem to say, a prevailing copyright owner cannot recoup all of its lost profits plus all of the infringer's profits.

The most important language in §504(b) is the phrase "as a result of the infringement," together with the phrase "attributable to the infringement." Whether it is the copyright owner's lost profits or the infringer's profits, the statute requires that the damages to be paid were caused by the infringing acts. This causation requirement creates a significant burden for copyright owners. See *Key West Hand Print Fabrics, Inc. v. Serbin, Inc.*, 269 F. Supp. 605, 613 (S.D. Fla. 1965) (plaintiff's lost profits: The plaintiff has the burden "of establishing with reasonable probability the existence of a causal connection between defendant's infringement and loss of anticipated revenue"); *Data General Corp. v. Grumman Sys. Support Corp.*, 36 F.3d 1147, 1171, 1175 (1st Cir. 1994) (defendant's profits: plaintiff must prove that defendant's profits were caused by infringement). In practical terms, this usually boils down to a requirement that the copyright owner show total profits; the burden then shifts to the defendant to prove what portion of the proven profits are *not* the result of copyright infringement. This is the general approach whether damages are based on the copyright owner's lost profits or the infringer's actual profits. See generally 5 Nimmer on Copyright §§14.02, 14.03 (2016).

The following case is a foundational one on the topic of apportionment. It deals with recovery of defendant's profits by the plaintiff copyright owner, and was decided under the 1909 Copyright Act, but the basic reasoning is sound and instructive.

CASE

Sheldon v. Metro-Goldwyn Pictures Corp., 309 U.S. 390 (1940)

Mr. Chief Justice HUGHES delivered the opinion of the Court.
The questions presented are whether, in computing an award of profits against an infringer of a copyright, there may be an apportionment so as to give to the owner of the copyright only that part of the profits found to be attributable to the use of the copyrighted material as distinguished from what the infringer himself has supplied, and, if so, whether the evidence affords a proper basis for the apportionment decreed in this case.

Petitioners' complaint charged infringement of their play 'Dishonored Lady' by respondents' motion picture 'Letty Lynton', and sought an injunction and an accounting of profits. The Circuit Court of Appeals, reversing the District Court, found and enjoined the infringement and directed an accounting. Thereupon the District Court confirmed with slight modifications the report of a special master which awarded to petitioners all the net profits made by respondents from their exhibitions of the motion picture, amounting to $587,604.37. The Circuit Court of Appeals reversed, holding that there should be an apportionment and fixing petitioners' share of the net profits at one-fifth.

Petitioners' play 'Dishonored Lady' was based upon the trial in Scotland, in 1857, of Madeleine Smith for the murder of her lover, – a cause célèbre included in the series of 'Notable British Trials' which was published in 1927. The play was copyrighted as an unpublished work in 1930, and was produced here and abroad. Respondents took the title of their motion picture 'Letty Lynton' from a novel of that name written by an English author, Mrs. Belloc Lowndes, and published in 1930. That novel was also based upon the story of Madeleine Smith and the motion picture rights were bought by respondents. There had been negotiations for the motion picture rights in petitioners' play, and the price had been fixed at $30,000, but these negotiations fell through.

As the Court of Appeals found, respondents in producing the motion picture in question worked over old material; 'the general skeleton was already in the public demesne. A wanton girl kills her lover to free herself for a better match; she is brought to trial for the murder and escapes'. But not content with the mere use of that basic plot, respondents resorted to petitioners' copyrighted play. They were not innocent offenders. From comparison and analysis, the Court of Appeals concluded that they had 'deliberately lifted the play'; their 'borrowing was a deliberate plagiarism'. It is from that standpoint that we approach the questions now raised.

Respondents contend that the material taken by infringement contributed in but a small

> **CASE** *(continued)*
>
> measure to the production and success of the motion picture. They say that they themselves contributed the main factors in producing the large net profits; that is, the popular actors, the scenery, and the expert producers and directors. Both courts below have sustained this contention.
>
> [The court agreed that a reasonable analogy to this case comes from patent infringement cases, where apportionment of damages is appropriate.]
>
> Petitioners stress the point that respondents have been found guilty of deliberate plagiarism, but we perceive no ground for saying that in awarding profits to the copyright proprietor as a means of compensation, the court may make an award of profits which have been shown not to be due to the infringement. That would be not to do equity but to inflict an unauthorized penalty. To call the infringer a trustee ex maleficio merely indicates 'a mode of approach and an imperfect analogy by which the wrongdoer will be made to hand over the proceeds of his wrong'. He is in the position of one who has confused his own gains with those which belong to another. He 'must yield the gains begotten of his wrong'. Where there is a commingling of gains, he must abide the consequences, unless he can make a separation of the profits so as to assure to the injured party all that justly belongs to him. When such an apportionment has been fairly made, the copyright proprietor receives all the profits which have been gained through the use of the infringing material and that is all that the statute authorizes and equity sanctions.
>
> The controlling fact in the determination of the apportionment was that the profits had been derived, not from the mere performance of a copyrighted play, but from the exhibition of a motion picture which had its distinctive profit-making features, apart from the use of any infringing material, by reason of the expert and creative operations involved in its production and direction. In that aspect the case has a certain resemblance to that of a patent infringement, where the infringer has created profits by the addition of non-infringing and valuable improvements. And, in this instance, it plainly appeared that what respondents had contributed accounted for by far the larger part of their gains.
>
> The testimony showed quite clearly that in the creation of profits from the exhibition of a motion picture, the talent and popularity of the 'motion picture stars' generally constitutes the main drawing power of the picture, and that this is especially true where the title of the picture is not identified with any well-known play or novel. Here, it appeared that the picture did not bear the title of the copyrighted play and that it was not presented or advertised as having any connection whatever with the play. It was also shown that the picture had been 'sold', that is, licensed to almost all the exhibitors as identified simply with the name of a popular motion picture actress before even the title 'Letty Lynton' was used. In addition to the drawing power of the 'motion picture stars', other factors in creating the profits were found in the artistic conceptions and in the expert supervision and direction of the various processes which made possible the composite result with its attractiveness to the public.
>
> Upon these various considerations, with elaboration of detail, respondents' expert witnesses gave their views as to the extent to which the use of the copyrighted material had

CASE *(continued)*

contributed to the profits in question. The underlying facts as to the factors in successful production and exhibition of motion pictures were abundantly proved, but, as the court below recognized, the ultimate estimates of the expert witnesses were only the expression 'of their very decided opinions'. These witnesses were in complete agreement that the portion of the profits attributable to the use of the copyrighted play in the circumstances here disclosed was very small. Their estimates given in percentages of receipts ran from five to twelve per cent; the estimate apparently most favored was ten per cent as the limit. One finally expressed the view that the play contributed nothing. There was no rebuttal. But the court below was not willing to accept the experts' testimony 'at its face value'. The court felt that is must make an award 'which by no possibility shall be too small'. Desiring to give petitioners the benefit of every doubt, the court allowed for the contribution of the play twenty per cent of the net profits.

Petitioners are not in a position to complain that the amount thus allowed by the court was greater than the expert evidence warranted. Nor is there any basis for attack, and we do not understand that any attack is made, upon the qualifications of the experts. Nor can we say that the testimony afforded no basis for a finding. What is required is not mathematical exactness but only a reasonable approximation. That, after all, is a matter of judgment and the testimony of those who are informed by observation and experience may be not only helpful but, as we have said, may be indispensable. Equity is concerned with making a fair apportionment so that neither party will have what justly belongs to the other. Confronted with the manifest injustice of giving to petitioners all the profits made by the motion picture, the court in making an apportionment was entitled to avail itself of the experience of those best qualified to form a judgment in the particular field of inquiry and come to its conclusion aided by their testimony. We *see* no greater difficulty in the admission and use of expert testimony in such a case than in the countless cases involving values of property rights in which such testimony often forms the sole basis for decision.

 NOTES AND COMMENTS

1. **Copyright infringement as wrongful gain.** The rationale for permitting recovery of the defendant's profits has roots in the law of restitution. In that body of law, plaintiffs are permitted to recovery when their efforts have led to the "unjust enrichment" of another. For a classic account of the restitutionary foundations of IP law, *see* Wendy J. Gordon, *Of Harms and Benefits: Torts, Restitution, and Intellectual Property*, 21 J. Leg. Studies 449 (1992). Note, however, that strict application of restitution sometimes results in the recovery of all the defendant's "ill-gotten" gains, as fruit of the forbidden (infringing) tree – a theory which precludes accounting for any contribution made by the infringer. *See, e.g., Foskett v. McKeown* [2000] 2 W.L.R. 1299 (H.L.) (appeal taken from Eng. (UK)) (stating that a person who buys a lottery ticket with intentionally stolen money, and wins the lottery, must give the entire lottery winnings to the person from whom the money was stolen). *See generally* Daniel Friedmann, *Restitution for Wrongs: The Measure of Recovery*, 79 Tex. L. Rev. 1879 (2001).
2. **"Efficient infringement."** By permitting an infringing defendant to keep any profit it makes, *after* fully compensating the copyright owner for infringement, the Copyright Act opens space for the idea of "efficient infringement." This concept borrows from the well-known contracts literature on "efficient breach,"

which begins with the premise that breach of contract is not wrong itself, and ought to occur whenever the breaching party can fully compensate the other party to the contract, while still coming out ahead. *See* Robert Cooter & Melvin Aron Eisenberg, *Damages for Breach of Contract*, 73 Calif. L. Rev. 1432 (1985).

14.2.1 Note on statutory damages

Because damages may be difficult to calculate, and to deter infringement, copyright owners may obtain statutory damages in an amount between $750 and $30,000 per work, at the discretion of the court (17 U.S.C. §504. Plaintiffs who can show willful infringement may be entitled to damages up to $150,000 per work.(*id.*, §504(c)(2)). On the other hand, defendants who can show that they were "not aware and had no reason to believe" they were infringing copyright may have the damages reduced to $200 per work (*id*). Note that according to 17 U.S.C. §412, statutory damages are only available in the US for works that were registered with the Copyright Office prior to infringement, or within three months of publication of the work.

These provisions have given rise to some controversy, particularly in the area of filesharing, *i.e.*, music downloading. *See, e.g., Capitol Records, Inc. v. Thomas-Rasset*, 692 F.3d 899 (8th Cir. 2012) (reinstating original jury award of $222,000 in case in which district court judge capped damages at $54,000; noting that subsequent jury had awarded $1.9 million in statutory damages, but the record label plaintiffs had decided not to seek this amount on appeal for "tactical reasons," presumably terrible public relations). *See also BMG Music v. Gonzales*, 430 F.3d 888 (7th Cir. 2005) (upholding statutory damages award of $22,500 against defendant liable for copyright infringement from downloaded songs). On proposals for reform of statutory damages, *see* Pamela Samuelson & Tara Wheatland, *Statutory Damages in Copyright Law: A Remedy in Need of Reform*, 51 Wm. & Mary L. Rev. 439 (2009).

14.3 China

14.3.1 Direct and indirect infringement

To bring a prima facie case of copyright infringement, plaintiff needs to prove (1) ownership of a valid copyright; and (2) defendant violates one or more of the exclusive rights granted under Article 10 of the PRC Copyright Law directly or indirectly.

The standard to determine direct infringement in China is more or less the same as that of other jurisdictions. The indirect liability theory, on the other hand, is slightly different from some jurisdictions. For instance, unlike the US, which specifies indirect liability as contributory liability, vicarious liability and inducement theory, China does not distinguish such but generally refers to it as the "joint-liability" theory. *See* Articles 8 and 9 of the PRC Tort Law (2009). Yet it should be noted that in the indirect infringement analysis, the same factors, such as defendant's material contribution to the infringement activity, actual or constructive knowledge of the infringement, the right and ability to control the infringement, and whether defendant derives direct financial benefits arising from the direct infringement, will all be taken into consideration in determining whether defendant's acts constitute indirect infringement.

14.3.2 Remedies

Because intellectual property is protected through a combination of property and liability rules, its legal remedies also reflect a mixture of both. Article 47 of the PRC Copyright Law provides that anyone who commits copyright infringement, "depending on the circumstances, must bear civil liabilities for such remedies as ceasing the infringement act, eliminating the effects of the act, making a public apology or compensating for damages . . ." In other words, the remedies available to a prevailing copyright owner in China include injunctive relief, monetary damages, and apology.

14.3.2.1 Injunctive relief

Both preliminary and permanent injunctive relief are available to the plaintiff copyright owners in copyright infringement cases, although with various standards. With regard to preliminary injunction, the Chinese Supreme Court lists the following factors for consideration, "(1) Plaintiff's likelihood of success in the litigation; (2) whether the non-issuance of a preliminary injunction will bring irreparable harm to Plaintiff; (3) the bond posted by the Plaintiff; and finally (4) balance of the public interest" (Article 11, Chinese Supreme Court's Judicial Interpretation Regarding Preliminary Injunction and Evidence Preservation Requests in Trademark Related Cases, 2002).

In terms of permanent injunction, as with the current practice in the US, permanent injunction is not an automatic relief after finding an infringement. Instead, the following factors are usually taken into consideration by the courts: (1) whether non-issuance of a permanent injunction will cause irreparable harm to plaintiff; (2) balance of hardship to defendant; (3) balance of public interest; and (4) whether defendant is at fault with regard to infringement.

The following case deals with both the joint liability theory and the standard for granting a permanent injunction in Chinese copyright cases.

CHIUNG Yao v. YU Zheng, Beijing 3rd Intermediate Court [2014] Sanzhongminchuzi No. 7916

Plaintiff CHIUNG Yao, a well-known author of romance novels, claimed that she is the author to the novel *Plum Blossom Scar* (1993) and also the script writer for the television series produced under the same title. Defendant YU Zheng wrote a script and directed a television series between 2012–2013, entitled *Palace III: the Lost Daughter* . . .

[CHIUNG claimed that YU's television series *Palace III* and its underlying script violated the copyright of her prior novel and script for *Plum Blossom Scar*.]

[After applying the idea/expression dichotomy, the merger doctrine, and the substantial similarity test, the court held that defendant YU had copied the copyrightable elements of Plaintiff's work, thus finding defendants liable for copyright infringement.]

Issue 6: Joint-Liability of Co-Defendants

[With regard to joint liability among co-defendants, this court held that], pursuant to Article 8 of PRC Tort Law, joint tort liability can be found when two or more persons committed a tortious activity and caused harm to others. Joint tortfeasance can be established through the following elements: (1) more than one party jointly engage in the tortious activity; (2) co-defendants share fault in committing the tort; (3) the tortious activity is directed at the same target; and (4) the tort is the proximate and actual cause of Plaintiff's losses.

As such, Co-Defendants Dongyang Huanyu, Hunan eTV, Dongyang Xingrui and Wanda Group, who co-produced the infringing TV series *The Palace*, shall be found jointly liable for the infringement of Plaintiff's cinematographic right to the work . . .

[Co-defendant Wanda Group argued that it was only a financial investor of the alleged infringing drama and did not participate in the production or distribution of the drama, thus should not be found jointly liable for the infringement.]

[The court rejected Wanda's argument, holding that] the Joint Investor and Production Agreement signed between Wanda and producer of the infringing drama suggests that, Wanda received producer's credit and also financial returns from the infringing television drama. As such, Wanda should be found jointly liable for infringing Plaintiff's right of adaptation and cinematographic right, as with other co-defendants in this case.

[With regard to Plaintiff's request for permanent injunction,] the court held that the purpose of copyright law is to protect the rights and interests [of] copyright holders so as to promote the creativity and the general public welfare. In this case, if Defendant's infringement continues [by allowing the infringing drama to continue its public performance and distribution], Plaintiff will be deprived of an opportunity to exploit her own copyrighted work in the actual and potential derivative market. Such a result will be against the principle of fair use.

> **CASE** *(continued)*
>
> Up to now, Defendant's infringing drama has been distributed over multiple networks for over eight months. Although co-defendants refused to submit the writer agreement and distribution agreement before this court, based on the fair market value and commercial practice of this industry, [it is reasonable to conclude that] Defendant YU already received a decent amount of the writer's fee, and other co-defendants also have benefited handsomely from the distribution and public performance of the infringing drama during the past few months. As such, the grant of a permanent injunction enjoining the further distribution and performance of the infringing drama will not cause unreasonable hardship to Defendant or imbalance between Plaintiff and Defendant.
>
> In view of the default of Defendants, the extent of infringement, consequence of the infringement and the social impact that it caused, we hold that a permanent injunction should be issued to stop the reproduction, distribution and further performance of the infringing drama . . .

NOTES AND QUESTIONS

1. The joint-liability theory and permanent injunction issued in *CHIUNG Yao v. YU Zheng* came as a surprise to the Chinese entertainment industry. It is not uncommon for financial investors in this industry to sign a Joint Investor and Production Agreement that would allow the investor to receive producer credit and financial returns. Depending on the investment amount and leverage between the two parties, investors may have between some to no control over the artistic process of the project, such as casting and story development. Typically, when the investors are purely financial investors with limited industry knowledge, they usually take a hands-off approach to the artistic process. By finding Wanda Group jointly liable in the infringement case, Beijing courts had drawn attention to a range of newly arisen issues surrounding investment in films, television, and other entertainment-related projects in China.

2. Critics claim that the *CHIUNG Yao* decision will have a chilling impact on future investment in the Chinese entertainment industry. They argue that the joint-liability theory imposed on financial investors will drive away investment, thus slowing the development of China's entertainment industry. They also feel that enjoining this 65-episode TV series seems to be a colossal waste of resources and investment, because, unless defendants obtain permission from the copyright owner of the original work to prepare derivative works, the TV series would be frozen for good. Do you agree with the critics that such a ruling might be too harsh? Or do you think this is necessary to curtail the rampant piracy and to promote creativity in the long run?

14.3.2.2 Damages

In general, monetary damages are available to a prevailing plaintiff if he or she could prove the actual losses that he or she suffers from the infringement or the illegal gains that defendant derives from the infringement. But in reality, it is often difficult to prove either, especially given that discovery is not available in the Chinese legal system. As such, statutory damages, the maximum amount at RMB 500,000, becomes the most frequently adopted damages standard in the recent case law. Under the third revision of the

PRC Copyright law, the new threshold for statutory damage is suggested to increase to RMB 1 million.

14.3.2.3 Apology

Apology is a unique remedy provided by the Chinese Civil Law and also the Tort Law. Articles 47 and 48 of the PRC Copyright Law also specify "apology" as one of the remedies available for a prevailing copyright owner upon finding of the copyright infringement. See Xuan-Thao Nguyen, *Apologies as Intellectual Property Remedies: Lessons from China*, 44 Connecticut L. R. (2012) (comparing and discussing apology as a legal remedy in IP-related cases between the US and China.)

Nonetheless, as a special remedy under the Chinese Copyright Law, apology has its own limitations in its application. First, apology as a remedy is only available when the moral rights of an author (*i.e.* natural person) are infringed. In other words, if the litigation is filed based upon violation of economic rights or if the prevailing copyright owner is not a natural person, apology is not available as a legal remedy. In *LIU Bokui v. LI Xia et al.*, the defendant was sued for infringing on the plaintiff's right of revision of the copyrighted work. The court supported the plaintiff's request for apology as a legal remedy, holding that "apology is applicable, when the infringing act leads to the depreciation and humiliation of the author's social image and personal feelings, so as to remedy the author's psychological sufferings and to restore his self-evaluation and dignity . . ." (Shanghai No. 2 Intermediate Court [2013] Huerzhongminwu(zhi)chuzi No. 115). However, in another case, *China Friendship Publishing Co., v. Zhejiang Taobao Network Ltd.*, the court rejected plaintiff's request for public apology, because "as a legal person, Plaintiff does not enjoy moral rights to the work. . ." (Beijing 2nd Intermediate Court [2009] Erzhongminzhongzi No. 15423). Also *see* generally Chen Ruwen & He Huawen, *Apology as Remedy under Chinese Copyright Law*, 2 Chinese Patents & Trademarks (2015).

Second, apology as a legal remedy is only available when the author of the work is still alive. According to the PRC Copyright Law and PRC Copyright Implementing Regulations, when the author of a work is deceased, "the moral rights, including the right of authorship, the right of revision and the right to protect the work's integrity, should be protected (enforced) by his successor or legatee. If there is no such a successor or legatee, the moral rights of the deceased author should be protected by the copyright administration . . ." As interpreted by the recent case law, this provision means that the successor of a deceased author can enforce the moral rights of the deceased, but with limited remedy. For instance, in *China Unicom v. Hua et al.*, the appellate court held that

> the moral rights that are infringed [in this case] are the right of authorship and the right to revise . . . Since the author of the work is deceased, apology as a legal remedy is no longer appropriate in this case [because] the infringement of the moral rights will no longer harm the [deceased author's] personality or mentality. As such, it is inappropriate to grant apology as a remedy . . . (*China Unicom v. Hua et al.*, Shanghai No. 1 Intermediate Court [2013] Huyizhongminwu (zhi) zhongzi No. 51).

14.4 Europe

Copyright remedies reside at the intersection of copyright and tort law in most European jurisdictions. While the European harmonization of copyright law is relatively advanced, the core of tort law is still largely a matter of national law in the EU. As a result, many of the doctrines governing copyright remedies were originally developed in the copyright systems of each individual EU Member State.

In 2004, the EU adopted the Enforcement Directive, which harmonized questions of enforcement across all IP rights. As far as damages are concerned, Art. 13 Enforcement Directive states that damages should be calculated according to (a) the actual harm caused by the infringement, or (b) a hypothetical license fee the infringer would have been required to pay had he or she requested authorization, or, in case of non-willful infringement, (c) the profits made by the infringer or some pre-calculated amount of damages. The Directive also includes provisions on (preliminary and permanent) injunctive relief, on measures to preserve evidence, on rights of information, on the publication of judicial decisions against infringers, and similar measures.

 CASE

German Federal Court of Justice (Bundesgerichtshof), case I ZR 98/06, IIC 2010, 236 – "Tripp Trapp Chair"

The plaintiff is the holder of the exclusive user rights to the "Tripp-Trapp" children's highchair it manufactures and markets. From 1997 to 2002, the defendant marketed the "Alpha" children's highchair, which is similar in appearance to the Tripp-Trapp chair. The

CASE *(continued)*

Alpha chairs were purchased by the defendant from Hauck Ltd. Hong Kong and Hauck GmbH & Co. KG. The two chairs are reproduced below [Figures 14.1 and 14.2]:

Figure [14.1] Tripp-Trapp chair

The plaintiff is of the opinion that the defendant's marketing of the Alpha chairs infringes its user rights to the Tripp-Trapp chair. In preceding litigation, it brought a claim – which was largely successful – against Hauck GmbH & Co. KG and its general partner and the general partner's managing director for a cease-and-desist order, and additionally against Hauck GmbH & Co. KG for information and a finding of damages [citation omitted]. It claims damages in a separate action, in which the present Court has likewise rendered a decision today [citation omitted]. In the present case, it claims damages from the defendant in the form of the surrender of the infringer's profits.

Figure [14.2] Alpha chair

CASE *(continued)*

At first instance the plaintiff claimed €576,053.75. The district court upheld the claim to the amount of €567,208.31. In its appeal, the defendant petitioned that the claim be dismissed in full, while the plaintiff in cross-appeal pursued its claim to the full amount. After expiry of the cross-appeal deadline, the plaintiff increased its claim to €679,114.15. The appeal court held the amended claim to be inadmissible and upheld the award of damages to the amount of €357,253.52. Both parties were granted leave to appeal by the appeal court. The defendant petitions that the claim be dismissed in full while the plaintiff pursues its petition for payment to the extent that it was dismissed at the previous instances. Each party petitions that the opposing party's appeal on the law be dismissed.

Findings:
I. The appeal court assumed that the amendment of the claim in the appeal instance was inadmissible. The defendant was ordered to pay the plaintiff damages to the amount of €357,253.52 according to the calculation method of the surrender of the infringer's profits as selected by the plaintiff on the grounds of the infringement of the plaintiff's user rights pursuant to Sec. 97(1) of the Copyright Act (old version). . . .
II. The defendant's appeal on the law against this decision is upheld, the plaintiff's appeal on the law is upheld in part. . . .
2. As the appeal court rightly assumed, the defendant is liable for damages to the plaintiff pursuant to Sec. 97(1) of the old version of the Copyright Act for having unlawfully and culpably infringed the plaintiff's exclusive user right to the copyright Tripp-Trapp chair. . . .
3. The plaintiff is entitled to a claim for damages to the amount of up to €361,654.82 – without taking into account the amendment of the claim – against the defendant on the grounds of its marketing of the Alpha chairs purchased from Hauck Ltd. Hong Kong that infringed the plaintiff's exclusive user rights to the Tripp-Trapp chair pursuant to Sec. 97(1) second sentence of the old version of the Copyright Act, such damages being determined according to the calculation method of the surrender of the infringer's profits as selected by the plaintiff. . . .
The plaintiff's appeal on the law unsuccessfully objects that the appeal court deducted marketing costs of €1 per chair from the total profits (see below, II 3 a). The appeal court's view that the lack of a causal relationship between the breach of copyright and the infringer's profit meant that a deduction of 10% was appropriate is, on the other hand, not free of errors in law (see below II 3 b). In calculating the claim for damages, the appeal court wrongly applied the discount for causality first and only then deducted the marketing costs; if calculated correctly, the claim for damages is justified to the amount of up to €361,654.82 (see below II 3 c).
a) The appeal court rightly reduced the total profits by the costs of €44,013 (€1 per chair sold) as assumed by the plaintiff itself.
aa) In order to determine the infringer's profits, the total profits are to be reduced by all costs that are directly ascribable to the production and marketing of the infringing objects [citations omitted].

CASE *(continued)*

bb) From the profits obtained, the appeal court deducted a lump-sum of €1 per chair sold. This expenditure – confusingly referred to by the appeal court as overheads – is undisputedly a lump-sum cost for the carriage and marketing of an Alpha chair. Such costs are directly ascribable to the Alpha chairs that infringe the plaintiff's user rights and are therefore deductible as a matter of principle. The objections raised by the plaintiff against the amount of this deduction in its appeal on the law are unsuccessful. . . .

b) The appeal court's finding that a discount of 10% is appropriate on the grounds of a lack of a causal relationship between the copyright infringement and the infringer's profits is on the other hand not free of errors in law.

aa) However, the appeal court rightly assumed that the infringer's profits are only to be surrendered to the extent that they are based on the infringement of the right [citation omitted]. In the case of the infringing exploitation of an adaptation, the decisive factor is the extent to which the purchaser's decision to acquire the contested embodiment is due precisely to the fact that the embodiment discloses the features on which the copyright protection of the work used is based. This is to be interpreted not in the sense of adequate causality but rather – comparable with the calculation of the extent of contributory negligence within the framework of Sec. 254 of the Civil Code – in the sense of a value-judgement-based attribution [citations omitted]. This is dependent not solely on the quantitative extent but even more on the qualitative value of the borrowed elements [citation omitted].

The extent to which the profits obtained are based on the infringement of the rights is to be assessed by the trial judge at his discretion pursuant to Sec. 287 of the Code of Civil Procedure unless, in exceptional cases, there is no indication whatsoever for an estimate [citations omitted]. This Court is only required to examine whether the trial judge's estimate is based on fundamentally incorrect or obviously inappropriate considerations or whether essential facts have been neglected and, in particular whether facts underlying the estimate that have been submitted by the parties or result from the nature of the matter have not been assessed [citation omitted]. That is the case here.

bb) The defendant's appeal rightly argues that the appeal court's assumption that the defendant's profits could not in the present case be apportioned according to the extent of the technical and design shares is based on errors in law.

(1) In the light of the fact that the Alpha chair is an admittedly close but not identical imitation of the Tripp-Trapp chair, the appeal court considered that the deduction of 10% of the total infringer's profits was appropriate. Accordingly, it obviously assumed that if the Tripp-Trapp chair had been imitated identically the total profits achieved through the sale of the Alpha chair would be based on the infringement of copyright. However, this cannot be assumed automatically, at the least in the case of an infringement – as here – of copyright user rights to a work of applied art.

(2) Works of applied art differed from works of "pure" art in that they serve a utilitarian purpose [citation omitted]. As the appeal court rightly assumed, the decision to buy a utilitarian object – such as a child's highchair in the present case – is as a rule not

CASE *(continued)*

determined merely by the aesthetic design but also by technical functionality. It can therefore not be assumed automatically that the profits obtained through the identical imitation of a copyright utilitarian object are based to the full extent on the fact that each purchase decision – and hence the entire profits – are caused solely by the imitated appearance and not by other essential factors such as technical functionality or a lower price [citation omitted]. A specific justification is therefore needed as to why the decision to buy the non-free adaptation of a copyright work of applied art is solely or even merely primarily determined by the fact that this adaptation discloses features that form the basis of the copyright protection of the work used. The appeal court, logically from its point of view, did not adopt any findings on this point. It is a matter for the plaintiff, which bears the burden of presentation and proof for showing that the infringer's profits are based on the copyright infringement, to submit on this point.

Indications for a weighting of the aesthetic and functional features that are decisive for the purchase decision can in particular be derived from the type of utilitarian object. Thus in the case of furniture, experience suggests that function will be of greater importance for the purchase decision than in the case of jewellery. Accordingly, the appeal court will have to examine the defendant's submission in the appeal instance, argued by the defendant in the appeal on the law as having been ignored, that the design element of a child's chair is by no means the only and not even the main motivation for the purchase of a specific chair, and that parents concerned about the well-being of their child place more attention on the function and safety of the chair, which are also the main reason for the purchase of a Tripp-Trapp or Alpha highchair.

cc) The justification provided so far by the appeal court does not support its assumption that the different visual impression of the Alpha chair meant that a causality discount of 10% was sufficient. . . .

(2) These remarks by the appeal court do not show sufficiently clearly why a causality discount of only 10% should be sufficient in order to take account of the fact that the Alfa chair has not adopted the "L" shape of the Tripp-Trapp chair. . . .

4. Contrary to the appeal court's view, the claims for damages derived from Sec. 97(1) second sentence of the old version of the Copyright Act asserted by the plaintiff against the defendant on the grounds on the marketing of the Alpha chairs supplied by Hauck GmbH & Co. KG cannot be dismissed on the grounds that the plaintiff has already successfully brought an action for damages against Hauck GmbH & Co. KG as supplier. The plaintiff is entitled to a claim against the defendant for damages according to the calculation method selected by it of the surrender of the infringer's profits to the amount of – without taking account of the amendment of the action – up to €156,545.39. . . .

bb) The injured party is, as a matter of principle, entitled to claim as damages from each infringer within a chain of infringers the surrender of the profits obtained by it. . . .

In the case of an infringement of user rights, the mere encroachment upon the uses permitted only to the rightholder as such leads to damage in the sense of damages law [citations omitted]. Each infringer within a chain of infringers intervenes in the right of

CASE *(continued)*

distribution reserved exclusively to the rightholder by putting the protected object into circulation without authorisation [citations omitted]. Contrary to the appeal court's point of view, the constellation at issue here is not to be assessed differently on the grounds that the infringements at all distribution stages were in terms of manner and scope identical in content in that both Hauck GmbH & Co. KG as manufacturer and supplier and the defendant as purchaser and vendor of the chairs each act for the purpose of putting them into circulation [citations omitted]. The joint and several liability of a plurality of infringers in a chain of infringers does not depend on whether the infringements are of the same kind or of the same effect but merely on whether they cause the same damage. ...

(a) The claim to the surrender of the infringer's profits is not a claim to compensation for the specific damage incurred but instead aims differently at providing equitable compensation for the financial disadvantage that the injured rightholder has suffered. It would be inequitable to leave the infringer with profits based on the unauthorised use of the exclusive right. The confiscation of the infringer's profits also serves to punish the damaging conduct and in this way to prevent an infringement of intellectual property rights that deserve special protection [citations omitted].

It would be in conflict with this legal principle on which the compensation of damage through the surrender of infringer profits is based if individual infringers within a chain of infringers should be allowed to retain the profits obtained through the unlawful and culpable infringement of a right if the injured party had already demanded the surrender of infringer profits from other infringers. The infringer of an intellectual property right has no claim worthy of protection to obtain or retain profits from acts that infringe intellectual property rights. Each infringer must therefore surrender his entire profits irrespective of whether the injured party could himself have obtained the profits achieved by the infringers [citations omitted].

III. Accordingly, on appeal on the law by the parties, the appeal court's decision is set aside and the plaintiffs more extensive appeal dismissed to the extent that the appeal court ordered the defendant to pay €357,253.52 and dismissed the plaintiff's claims pursued in the cross-appeal including the amendment of the claim to the amount of €253,701.05 plus interest. The plaintiff is entitled to damages of up to €610,954.57. It can claim up to €361,654.82 on the grounds of the marketing of the Alpha chairs supplied by Hauck Hong Kong Ltd. and up to €156,545.39 on the grounds of the marketing of the Alpha chairs supplied by Hauck GmbH & Co. KG. In addition, the claims for damages pursued in the amendment of the claim for up to €92,754.36 are well founded (increase of the defendant's profits by up to €103,060.40 less a causality deduction of at least 10%). To the extent that the decision has been set aside, the case is returned to the appeal court for rehearing and a new decision.

15
Digital copyright

15.1 Anti-circumvention laws

In the EU, anti-circumvention laws are split between two EU Directives. Art. 6 Information Society Directive provides protection against the circumvention of effective technological protection measures and prohibits certain preparatory activities such as the manufacturing or sale of anti-circumvention devices. Art. 6(4) includes a complicated provision which attempts to balance technological protection measures with copyright limitations. It adopts a "key escrow approach" under which a beneficiary of a copyright limitation would not be allowed to develop, distribute, or obtain circumvention devices from the market. Rather, he or she would be entitled to obtain appropriate means, such as circumvention devices or decryption keys, from a particular institution. Equipped with these means, he or she would be allowed to circumvent the technological protection. While this approach is an interesting theoretical alternative to the approach adopted by the US Digital Millennium Copyright Act, it has been hampered by various conceptual and practical shortcomings (*see* Stefan Bechtold, *Digital Rights Management in the United States and Europe*, 52 Am. J. Comp. L. 323, 368–81 (2004)), and its practical impact has remained negligible.

In addition to the copyright-related Art. 6 Information Society Directive, Article 4 of the Conditional Access Directive of 1998 prohibits the production, distribution, and promotion of illicit devices that circumvent technological protection measures. Although the Directive stems from the pay TV and broadcasting sector, it may apply to a wide variety of internet-based Digital Rights Management (DRM) systems as well.

15.2 Liability of internet service providers

15.2.1 Introduction

How to determine the liability of internet service providers (ISPs) has been one of the most debated issues in the discussion of internet law and policy during the past two decades. Liability of ISPs can arise in a number of legal fields including trademark, trade secrets, unfair competition, defamation, privacy, and of course copyright law.

Under the context of copyright law, ISPs might become vulnerable to charges of copyright infringement, whether direct or indirect, during the process of hosting web pages, forwarding and processing messages, newsgroups, and emails, providing online chat venues, and linking users to sites and services in the internet world. Where an ISP directly infringes copyright of rights holders, such as serving as an intent content provider (ICP) instead of a mere conduit, a copyright holder can certainly bring a direct infringement claim against such ISP/ICPs. More often, ISPs might be held secondarily liable for copyright infringement attributed to the direct infringement activities of its end-users. To strike a balance between protecting rights of copyright holders and shielding liability of ISPs, a number of countries have developed specific ISP legislation and secondary liability theories to restrict ISPs' liabilities from infringement activities conducted by others.

Generally speaking, there have been no universally accepted secondary liability theories worldwide. Nonetheless, an overall review of copyright infringement cases in the US, Europe, and China shows that courts will generally consider the following factors when determining the liability of ISPs: an ISP's knowledge of infringing activities by its end-users, its intent to infringe, material contribution to the infringing activity, ability and rights to control the access or infringing activities, and direct financial benefits arising from infringing activities. *See generally* Seagull Haiyan Song, *A Comparative Copyright Analysis of ISP Liability in China Versus the United States and Europe*, 27 The Computer & Internet Lawyer, (2010).

15.2.2 United States

The Online Copyright Infringement Liability Limitation Act (OCILLA) is a US federal law that creates a conditional safe harbor for online service providers (OSPs) including ISPs and other internet intermediaries by shielding them from liability for the infringing acts of others. OCILLA was passed as a part of the 1998 Digital Millennium Copyright Act (DMCA) and is sometimes referred to as the "Safe Harbor" provision or as "DMCA Section 512".

DMCA Section 512 provides that an ISP might be exempt from liability for copyright infringement stemming from transmitting, caching, hosting, or linking to infringing materials. To trigger the safe harbor provisions, an ISP must satisfy two threshold requirements. First, the ISP must "adopt and reasonably implement a policy" of addressing and terminating accounts of users who are "repeat infringers." Second, the ISP must accommodate and not interfere with "standard technical measures." See 17 U.S.C. §512.

Over the years, the US courts have developed contributory liability, vicarious liability, and inducement theories holding ISPs secondarily liable for copyright infringement. See *A&M Records v. Napster*, 239 F.3d 1004 (9th Cir. 2001), *In re Aimster Copyright Litigation*, 334 F.3d 643 (7th Cir. 2003), *Perfect 10, Inc. v. CCBill, LLC*, 488 F.3d 1102 (9th Cir. 2007), *Viacom Int'l, Inc. v. Youtube, Inc.*, 676 F.3d 19 (2d Cir. 2012). In *MGM v. Grokster*, the Supreme Court borrowed the "inducement liability" concept from patent law, holding that "[O]ne who distributes a device with the object of promoting its use to infringe copyright, as shown by clear expression or other affirmative steps taken to foster infringement, is liable for the resulting acts of infringement by third parties." See *MGM v. Grokster*, 125 S.Ct. 2764 (2005).

15.2.3 Europe

The EU E-commerce Directive 2000/31/EC adopts the definition of "Information Society Service" under Article 1.2 of Directive 98/34/EC to refer to ISPs and addresses the civil and criminal liabilities of ISPs acting as intermediaries. The Directive provides that ISPs will not be held liable under any field of law where an application of strict liability would impair the expansion of electronic commerce within the EU. This approach is called "horizontal" because it addresses liability regardless of the grounds for liability; it therefore applies not only to copyright law, but also to other areas of law such as defamation and obscenity.

Although a number of secondary liability cases have been decided under the specific provisions of Articles 12–14 of the Directive, there seem to be no clearly labeled secondary liability theories applicable to ISPs under the EU case law. Based on the Directive, an ISP is exempt from liability when it serves as a "mere conduit" (Article 12) or provides "temporary caching" (Article 13) for the sole purpose of making the transmission of content more efficient, is of a mere technical, automatic, and passive nature, and where the ISP has neither knowledge nor control over the content being transmitted or stored. For ISPs who provide content storage, *i.e.* "hosting services" (Article 14), they are exempt from liability provided that they do not have "actual knowledge or are aware of facts or circumstances" of illegal activities, and "expeditiously remove or disable" access to content upon receipt of such knowledge or awareness. Although Article 15 of the Directive prevents Member States from posing a "general duty to monitor," it does not prevent courts or administrative agencies of Member States from imposing a monitoring obligation in a specific, defined, individual case.

15.2.4 China

China adopted the Regulations for the Protection of Rights of Communication through Information Networks ("2006 Regulations") in 2006 to address increasing concerns over online piracy. The Regulations follow a number of principles set out in the US DMCA, including the safe harbor provisions for ISPs. *See* Articles 20–23 of 2006 Regulations.

The legal basis for finding an ISP secondarily liable lies in the PRC Civil Code and the PRC Tort Law with respect to the "joint-liability" theory. The Supreme Court Judicial Interpretation (2012), a legally binding document, also discussed the standard of "joint-liability" theory for an ISP in 2012.

Although China does not have specific secondary liability theories such as contributory, vicarious, or inducement theories like those developed in the U.S., Chinese courts would look to similar factors in their legal reasoning, including: an ISP's knowledge of infringement, its intent, the ability and right to control infringing activity, financial benefits arising from infringing activities, and contribution to the infringing activity etc. *See Guangdong Zoke Culture v. Guangzhou Shulian Software*, Shanghai High People's Court [2008] Hugaominsan(zhi)zhongzi No. 7 (finding defendant Shulian Software jointly liable for copyright infringement by providing its users with P2P software to download copyrighted movies without authorization and also for directing users to the movie section on its website for download); *Motie v. Apple*, Beijing High People's Court [2014] (finding defendant Apple jointly liable for copyright infringement by providing content of the disputed book series on its App store, without authorization).

15.3 Graduated response

The graduated response (GR) program is also known as "Three Strikes Policy." End-users who keep ignoring repeated notices on copyright infringement risk losing access to the internet. The GR program was originally initiated in France (Elysee/Olivenness Agreement) as a result of a three-way deal between the government, ISPs and right holders. To date, jurisdictions around the world including France, South Korea, and Taiwan have enacted GR laws. Others jurisdictions, including the US, are also working toward implementing such rules either in law or in practice. When we look at the GR programs adopted in each jurisdiction, we notice interesting variations from place to place. *See generally* Seagull Haiyan Song, *A Comparative Copyright Analysis of ISP Liability in China Versus the United States and Europe*, 27 The Computer & Internet Lawyer (2010).

The French version of GR, known as the HADOPI Law or Creation and Internet Law, was introduced in 2009. The law attempts to regulate and control internet access as a means to encourage compliance with copyright laws. The French GR system produced mixed results. In the first three years of its existence, the HADOPI agency only finalized three proceedings against infringers. However, empirical research found that consumer awareness around copyright infringement created by the HADOPI discussions led to an increase in authorized online music sales of between 22 and 25 percent (Brett Danaher et al., *The Effect of Graduated Response Anti-Piracy Laws on Music Sales*, J. Indu. Econ. 62 (2014), 541–53). In 2013, the part of HADOPI that allowed for suspension of internet access to repeat offenders was revoked. And the French government has announced plans to dissolve the HADOPI agency altogether.

In South Korea, the due process undertaken by an impartial review body before revoking the end-user's internet subscription service is processed by an administrative agency, *i.e.* the Korea Copyright Commission (KCC) rather than a judicial court. The KCC was established to conduct mediation of disputes on copyright infringement. It may also deliberate on copyright infringement and request injunction orders before courts.

The three-strikes legislation implemented in Korea not only targets end-users who repeatedly reproduce or upload unauthorized copyrighted content, it also prevents message boards that receive more than three warnings for not sincerely carrying out deletion orders if such message boards are deemed to have impaired the healthy-use culture of copyrighted works over the internet.

The amendments to Taiwan's Copyright Law in May 2009 mandated a three-strike policy for ISPs against their customers in respect of copyright infringement. The Taiwan Intellectual Property Office (TIPO) subsequently issued Implementing Regulations in November 2009. Based on the Revised Copyright Law and Implementing Regulations, safe harbor provisions will be denied to ISPs if they fail to implement the three-strike infringement requirement. Therefore, in a P2P context, if an ISP fails to forward a right holder's notices of initial and repeat infringements or to terminate (in whole or in part) the subscription of a repeat infringer following the third instance of infringement, it will be deprived of safe harbor protection.

Part IV

Trademark law

16

Introduction to trademark protection

INTRODUCTORY PROBLEM

Kwami Durango, nicknamed KD, is one of the best and best-known basketball players in the National Basketball Association (NBA). He was a previous Most Valuable Player (MVP) award winner who only added to his fame by recently changing teams in search of his first NBA championship. He has a line of basketball shoes, sportswear, and related goods sold by the huge international sporting goods company Ariadne, Inc. Among the 20 trademarks Ariadne has registered for KD are (1) "KD," a simple word mark (*i.e.*, with no color or style added) for sporting goods, clothing, hats, shoes, hosted athletic camp services, and leisure tours; and (2) a stylized KD mark, against a background consisting of a certain shade of blue and gold coloring.

Köln-Düsseldorfer Steamship Lines, GmbH (KDSL) is one of the oldest and best-known tourism companies in Europe. Based in Germany, it has also expanded into Asia in recent years with a line of luxury cruise ships. The company has a number of trademarks that are widely registered in the US and European countries (via a Community Trademark registered in Alicante, Spain), including K-DSL, KD Steam, and simply K-D. One of KDSL's registered Community trademarks, which is based on a much earlier (nineteenth-century) German priority use dating to its early days as a steamship line, is the mark KD against a blue and gold background. A variation of this mark shows the lettering KD Steam against the same background.

KayDee Cosmetics (KDC) was founded in Shanghai in 1999 as a subsidiary of a small chemical company that also makes food additives, pesticides, and industrial chemicals for various manufacturing industries, including the women's cosmetics industry. Until recently, it had never registered its "KayDee" trademark in China, but on June 1, 2016, it filed a Chinese trademark application with the State Administration for Industry and Commerce (SAIC) in Beijing.

Ariadne is working with Kwami Durango to advance his brand and increase income from merchandising and licensing activities. As part of the brand extension strategy, Ariadne is negotiating licenses of the KD trademarks with outside vendors in a number of fields beyond athletic clothing and athletic shoes. The new markets include: (1) luxury cruises sponsored by and attended by Kwami himself; and (2) sunscreen and lip balm products carrying the KD brand.

As you go through this Part, be thinking about what problems the KD brand may encounter in its expansion efforts, and how you might resolve any resulting legal disputes.

As the Introductory Problem to this Part ("KD Brands") shows, trademark law provides protection for a crucial corporate asset. And it is in many cases an inherently transnational form of IP rights, because so much commerce today spans national boundaries.

Trademark law at its heart protects consumers against deceit. The deceit it guards against happens when a product, with a seemingly familiar label, does not in fact come from the company that makes and sells the familiar product, but from someone else. Consumers come to believe that a familiar label or logo means a familiar company, or, as trademark texts put it, a "single source."

From a company's point of view, the law's protection of consumers encourages certain investments. Investments in establishing, promoting, and extending a company's "brand" have been to shown to be an important determinant of profitability for many companies. In one study, "brand equity" was measured using past investments in trademark registrations. The study found a strong positive relationship between trademark-related investments and a company's profit margin in the sale of its products. *See* Dirk Crass, Dirk Czarnitzki and Andrew A. Toole, The Dynamic Relationship between Investments in Brand Equity and Firm Profitability: Evidence using Trademark Registrations USPTO Economic Working Paper No. 2016-1, January 2016, at 2, available at https://www.uspto.gov/about-us/organizational-offices/office-policy-and-international-affairs/office-chief-economist-5 ("Our approach reveals the dynamic profile between past brand-related investments and current profitability.").

Because these investments take many forms, and because consumers at times develop very elaborate "relationships" with brands, trademark law has been changing in recent years. One way to describe it to say that it is adapting to the growth of the idea of a brand itself. *See* Deven R. Desai, *From Trademarks to Brands*, 64 Fla. L. Rev. 981 (2012). A brand is a logo, word, product characteristic, and/or design which evokes a suite of associations and feelings in the mind of a consumer. Because these associations are the font of great value, trademark law has become increasingly important. These are the topics we explore and discuss in this Part.

17
Acquisition of trademark rights

17.1 Use vs. registration

The national trademark systems of the world fall into two major groupings, common law and civil law. A number of features distinguish the two, but the most important has to do with when a person or company can acquire trademarks rights. In common law systems, acquisition generally requires *use*: actual sale of goods or services. In civil law systems, one acquires rights by *registering* a trademark with a governmental trademark office. This historical division continues to exert significant influence on the trademark systems of countries around the world.

At the same time, registration matters even in common law countries. And use is far from irrelevant in civil law countries. Registration can secure greater rights, for example, for trademarks first recognized through use. And the scope of use, or lack of use (abandonment) can be significant in civil law countries. Later in this Part, we will see how these concepts play out in the details of trademark law.

The US, as a common law country, serves as a good example of the way that the use of a trademark determines acquisition of legal rights. So we start with the US "use in commerce" requirement.

17.1.1 US: use in commerce

 CASE

La Societe Anonyme des Parfums le Galion v. Jean Patou, Inc., 495 F.2d 1265, 1269 (2d Cir. 1974)

Friendly, J.

Plaintiff LeGalion, a French perfume manufacturer, has for years sold its perfume under the trademark 'SNOB' in a number of foreign countries. The sales have been substantial, amounting in one recent five-year period to almost $2,000,000. LeGalion has been unable to sell SNOB in the United States, however, because in 1951 defendant Patou, an American perfume manufacturer, obtained a trademark registration for SNOB in this country. Pursuant to §42 of the Lanham Act, 15 U.S.C. §1124, Customs officials subsequently refused to permit LeGalion to import its SNOB perfume because of the conflict with defendant's registered mark. In spite of the registration, Patou has never made a serious effort to merchandise SNOB; between 1950 and 1971, it sold only some 89 bottles of SNOB, and it engaged in no advertising or other sales efforts on behalf of the product. Patou's sales of SNOB between 1951 and 1969 generated a 'gross profit' of only about $100, on retail sales of less than $600.

[After an initial legal complaint in 1956 was abandoned,] LeGalion sought to force the Collector of Customs to permit the importation of its SNOB perfume and requested . . . cancellation of Patou's SNOB registration. In a six-page memorandum decision [in 1972], Judge Gagliardi held that although Patou's sales of SNOB were minimal, they were sufficient to maintain its trademark rights, and thus to block the importation of LeGalion's product. The court based its conclusion on three grounds. First, it found that the sales program was not a sham: each sale was profitable, and each was effected on order from a bona fide customer . . . Second, it held that Patou's minimal use of its SNOB trademark was sufficient 'in the light of the customary practice of perfumers to "reserve" a name and to carry on trademark maintenance programs,' 353 F.Supp. at 293. The court noted that the difficulty of finding new and attractive trade names for perfumes had caused manufacturers to hold a number of potential trade names in reserve until such time as the company might decide to begin large-scale distribution of the product under that name. Minimal bona fide use for the purpose of trademark protection, the court wrote, is all the law requires. Finally, the district court held that the [prior legal actions] constituted a valid defense to LeGalion's claim that Patou's use of the mark had been only token in nature.

The difficulties relating to trademark law [in this case] stem from the tension between providing relative security to a business in maintaining its trademarks and preventing a business with only a nominal claim to a valuable trademark from barring its use by a party with a substantial financial stake in using the mark.

CASE *(continued)*

Under familiar trademark principles, the right to exclusive use of a trademark derives from its appropriation and subsequent use in the marketplace. The user who first appropriates the mark obtains an enforceable right to exclude others from using it, as long as the initial appropriation and use are accompanied by an intention to continue exploiting the mark commercially, . . . *United Drug Co. v. Theodore Rectanus Co.*, 248 U.S. 90 (1918).

There is no such thing as property in a trademark except as a right appurtenant to an established business or trade in connection with which the mark is employed. The law of trademarks is but a part of the broader law of unfair competition; the right to a particular mark grows out of its use, not is mere adoption; its function is simply to designate the goods as the product of a particular trader and to protect his good will against the sale of another's product as his; and it is not the subject of property except in connection with an existing business.

Plaintiff claims that the minimal use in this case was not sufficient to constitute the bona fide use of the trademark necessary to confer rights upon Patou, particularly since by obtaining its registration Patou succeeded in completely excluding LeGalion's established product from the American market.

While the district court termed the 89 sales in 20 years 'bona-fide,' we cannot agree that such a meager trickle of business constituted the kind of bona fide use intended to afford a basis for trademark protection. The court found that the sales were profitable in that they produced a total 'gross profit' of $100 over the twenty-year period. However, it is inconceivable that Patou could actually have experienced anything but a substantial per unit loss in bottling, labeling, handling, and shipping its SNOB perfume at the rate of one and two bottles per order. Simply maintaining accurate records of the sales of SNOB would easily have eaten up the $100 'gross profit' over the twenty-year period. Even if it should happen that by some touch of managerial or accounting wizardry Patou has managed to turn a net profit of a few dollars on its sales of SNOB, its use of the trademark would still not constitute good faith commercial exploitation. It is true, as defendant contends, that trademark rights have often been upheld in spite of modest sales programs . . . In those cases, however, the trademark usage, although limited, was part of an ongoing program to exploit the mark commercially. In numerous other cases, where no present intent has been found to market the trademarked product, minimal sales have been held insufficient to establish trademark rights.

The district court recognized, as Patou virtually concedes, that Patou's real purpose in making its meagre sales of SNOB was to establish and maintain rights in the SNOB trademark. Patou representatives testified that the company maintained the program in order to preserve the option of someday producing SNOB in large volume. In fact, it seems much more likely that Patou regarded the program as a relatively painless way to keep a potential competitor at bay. The disincentives to develop its own perfume under the SNOB label were strong – it would not be able to expand into many foreign markets, and the likely confusion between it and its foreign competitor might work to its disadvantage. In any event, we disagree with the district court's conclusion that because of the custom in

CASE *(continued)*

the perfume industry of 'reserving' trade names and 'carrying on trademark maintenance programs,' Patou's conduct was sufficient to establish rights to the SNOB mark. The token sales program engaged in here is by its very nature inconsistent with a present plan of commercial exploitation.

[The case was remanded for consideration of jurisdictional issues, and for clarification of the effect of the earlier, 1956, lawsuit between the parties.]

NOTES

1. For another case showing no "bona fide use in commerce," see *Zazu Designs v. L'Oreal, S.A.*, 979 F.2d 499 (1992), where two interstate shipments of hair products to friends in other states was found insufficient use to establish US trademark rights.
2. What exactly constitutes "use"; does advertising in preparation for product introduction count? In most cases, no. So, for example, in *Buti v. Impressa Perosa S.R.L.*, 139 F.3d 98 (2d Cir. 1998), a restaurant in Milan, Italy, named "Fashion Café" advertised its business in the US. Just before Buti opened restaurants with the same name in the US, the court held that the Milan restaurant could not obtain US trademark rights through its advertising because the services they planned to introduce were not yet in operation within the US. There are, however, a few cases that go the other way. Under the rubric of "analogous use," a trademark user can establish priority through "use analogous to trademark use," provided that the user makes actual use of the mark within a reasonable period of time following the analogous use. See, e.g., *Chance v. Pac-Tel Teletrac Inc.*, 242 F.3d 1151 (9th Cir. 2001) (finding that defendant's pre-launch marketing campaign, including distribution of press releases and presentations to prospective customers, soon followed by launch of service, established priority over a competing user of the mark under the doctrine of analogous use).
3. With the very minor exception of "analogous use" described in Note 2, trademark rights in the US are established by use rather than registration. A major change to this traditional rule was introduced in 1989 with the advent of ITU registration. See Trademark Law Revision Act of 1989, Pub. L. No. 100-667, 102 Stat. 3935, codified at 15 U.S.C. §1051. This section says that "[a] person who has a bona fide intention, under circumstances showing the good faith of such person, to use a trademark in commerce may apply to register the trademark . . . on the principal register." The Trademark Office issues a "notice of allowance" to the trademark owner upon registration of a mark that meets the requirements of the Lanham Act (U.S.C. §1063(b)(2)). After the notice of allowance is granted, the trademark owner has six months (extendable to one year automatically and to three years when the applicant can show a good cause) to submit a verified statement that the trademark has been used in commerce; the mark is then added to the Principal Register. In the absence of a timely statement, the trademark is considered abandoned (15 U.S.C. §1051(d)). When use is shown within the deadline, however, the ITU application is considered "constructive use" under 15 U.S.C. §1057(c), which gives the mark owner nationwide priority from the date of the ITU application.
4. What happens when the first user of a mark has been using the mark in commerce for some time, and then a later user of the same mark comes along and registers it under the Lanham Act? Conflict between such "common law use" and federal registration are described in Section 17.1.3.1.1, just below.

17.1.2 "Genuine use" in the EU

As mentioned, trademark experts often contrast registration systems with those requiring trademark "use" (such as the US). The differences may be overstated, however. In Europe, for example, though registration by itself may begin the process by which legal rights attach to a mark, failure to actively use the mark for an appreciable period of time will result in the invalidation of the mark. This is the "genuine use" requirement.

Under the EU Trademark Directive of 2015, Directive 2015/2436, 16 December 2015 (modifying the 2008 EU Trademark Directive), Article 16 on "Use of Trademarks" provides as follows:

1. If, within a period of five years following the date of the completion of the registration procedure, the proprietor has not put the trade mark to genuine use in the Member State in connection with the goods or services in respect of which it is registered, or if such use has been suspended during a continuous five-year period, the trade mark shall be subject to the limits and sanctions provided for in Article 17 [Non-use as a defense to infringement], Article 19(1) [absence of genuine use as ground for revocation], Article 44(1) and (2) [non-use as defense in opposition], and Article 46(3) and (4) [absence of proof of non-use, and use in less than all registered classes] of registered classes], unless there are proper reasons for non-use.
2. Where a Member State provides for opposition proceedings following registration, the five-year period referred to in paragraph 1 shall be calculated from the date when the mark can no longer be opposed or, in the event that an opposition has been lodged, from the date when a decision terminating the opposition proceedings became final or the opposition was withdrawn.
3. With regard to trade marks registered under international arrangements and having effect in the Member State, the five-year period referred to in paragraph 1 shall be calculated from the date when the mark can no longer be rejected or opposed. Where an opposition has been lodged or when an objection on absolute or relative grounds has been notified, the period shall be calculated from the date when a decision terminating the opposition proceedings or a ruling on absolute or relative grounds for refusal became final or the opposition was withdrawn.

CASE

Ansul BV v Ajax Brandbeveiliging BV, Case No. C-40/01 (ECJ[CJEU], 11 March 2003)

[Ansul was an authorized seller of fire extinguishers marketed in the Netherlands under the trademark "Minimax". Defendant Ajax was a subsidiary of the German company named Minimax that manufactures these fire extinguishers, and that owns trademark registrations for the "Minimax" brand in various countries, including the Netherlands. After Ajax/

CASE *(continued)*

Minimax terminated its arrangement with Ansul, and began selling Minimax brand fire extinguishers directly in the Netherlands, Ansul applied for its own trademark for Minimax, limited to the class of services concerned with repairing and maintaining Minimax brand fire extinguishers. A Dutch court granted Ajax's motion to revoke the Ansul trademark for repair and maintenance, on the ground that Ajax had not made a "genuine use" of the mark under the Netherlands national statute embodying EU Trademark Directive of 1988, Directive 89/104/EEC of 1988. A genuine use, in the view of this court, involves placing new products on the market and selling them to consumers. So service of repair of existing products could not, the court thought, be a genuine use. The Netherlands Supreme Court received an appeal from this decision and referred the issue to the ECJ (now CJEU).]

"Genuine use" must . . . be understood to denote use that is not merely token, serving solely to preserve the rights conferred by the mark. Such use must be consistent with the essential function of a trade mark, which is to guarantee the identity of the origin of goods or services to the consumer or end user by enabling him, without any possibility of confusion, to distinguish the product or service from others which have another origin. It follows that "genuine use" of the mark entails use of the mark on the market for the goods or services protected by that mark and not just internal use by the undertaking concerned. The protection the mark confers and the consequences of registering it in terms of enforceability vis-à-vis third parties cannot continue to operate if the mark loses its commercial raison d'être, which is to create or preserve an outlet for the goods or services that bear the sign of which it is composed, as distinct from the goods or services of other undertakings. Use of the mark must therefore relate to goods or services already marketed or about to be.

Assessing the circumstances of the case may thus include giving consideration, *inter alia*, to the nature of the goods or service at issue, the characteristics of the market concerned and the scale and frequency of use of the mark. Use of the mark need not, therefore, always be quantitatively significant for it to be deemed genuine, as that depends on the characteristics of the goods or service concerned on the corresponding market.

Use of the mark may also in certain circumstances be genuine for goods in respect of which it is registered that were sold at one time but are no longer available. That applies, inter alia, where the proprietor of the trade mark under which such goods were put on the market sells parts which are integral to the make-up or structure of the goods previously sold, and for which he makes actual use of the same mark . . . Since the parts are integral to those goods and are sold under the same mark, genuine use of the mark for those parts must be considered to relate to the goods previously sold and to serve to preserve the proprietor's rights in respect of those goods.

The same may be true where the trade mark proprietor makes actual use of the mark, under the same conditions, for goods and services which, though not integral to the make-up or structure of the goods previously sold, are directly related to those goods and intended to meet the needs of customers of those goods. That may apply to after-sales services, such as the sale of accessories or related parts, or the supply of maintenance and repair services.

> **CASE** *(continued)*
>
> [T]here is "genuine use" of a trade mark where the mark is used in accordance with its essential function, which is to guarantee the identity of the origin of the goods or services for which it is registered, in order to create or preserve an outlet for those goods or services
> . . .

 NOTES

1. When is use of a trademark by a nonprofit entity a "genuine use"? That issue was addressed in *Verein Radetzky-Orden v. Bundesvereingigung Kameradschaft "Feldmarschall Radetzky"* [*Verein Radetzky-Orden*], Case No. C-442/07 (CJEU, 9 December 2008), at par. 24:

   > [A] trade mark is put to genuine use where a non-profit-making association uses the trade mark, in its relations with the public, in announcements of forthcoming events, on business papers and on advertising material and where the association's members wear badges featuring that trade mark when collecting and distributing donations.

   For comparative US-EU analysis, *see* Tara M. Aaron & Axel Nordemann, *The Concepts of Use of A Trademark Under European Union and United States Trademark Law*, 104 Trademark Rep. 1186, 1240 (2014).

2. If a mark is placed on goods that are not sold, but given away instead, does that constitute "genuine use" under Article 16 of the 2015 EU Trademark Directive? Usually not, the ECJ (now CJEU) has said. *See Silberquelle GmbH v. Maselli-Strickmode GmbH*, Case No. C-495/07 (ECJ, 15 January 2009), at pars. 19–20:

   > [I]t is essential, in the light of the number of marks that are registered and the conflicts that are likely to arise between them, to maintain the rights conferred by a mark for a given class of goods or services only where that mark has been used on the market for goods or services belonging to that class.
   >
   > [T]hat condition is not fulfilled where promotional items are handed out as a reward for the purchase of other goods and to encourage the sale of the latter.

   Given that many online businesses do not charge a direct fee for their services (*e.g.*, web search, music streaming, etc.), where does this leave these businesses? Is it realistic to say that a company that relies on advertising, but draws users through use of a well-advertised brand, is not making "genuine use" of its mark? Note that extensive advertising is a separate factor that might work in favor of a mark owner even if its product (such as a mobile phone app) is given away and not sold directly. *See generally* William Robinson, Giles Pratt, & Ruth Kelly, *Trademark Law Harmonization in the European Union: Twenty Years Back and Forth*, 23 Fordham Intell. Prop. Media & Ent. L.J. 731, 770 (2013) (arguing that the overall successful harmonization of substantive EU trademark law may face challenges with respect to online trademark use and other "new media" issues).

3. For updates on "genuine use" cases, *see* Paul Bicknell, *The CJEU's Extension of* Nestle *in* Colloseum Holding AG v. Levi Strauss & Co: *Genuine Use of a Registered Trade Mark as Part of a Composite Mark or in Conjunction with Another Mark*, 35 E.I.P.R. 616 (2013).

17.1.3 Registration

17.1.3.1 National registration

Traditionally, in civil law registration systems, formal rights begin when a trademark is registered with a national trademark office, or with a regional or international office of which the relevant country is a member. Even in the US, as we will see, trademark rights based on use can be registered (and thereby strengthened in various ways) by registering them with the US Patent and Trademark Office. Registration forms require information about the trademark owner; the type (or "class") of goods or services the trademark is used on; and a sample (or "specimen") of the mark. Figure 17.1 shows cover pages for two countries, Germany and China.

What if a trademark application looks the same as or similar to a previously issued trademark or a prior-filed trademark application? Resolving these issues constitutes a good portion of the work of national trademark offices, and the lawyers who practice before them. Generally speaking, when there is conflict between two trademark users who are both seeking trademark registration, the fight comes down to the similarity of the marks and the degree of overlap in the markets for the products covered by the marks. Markets are broken down into specific "classes" that are described at a highly detailed level; there is even an international Convention, the Nice Convention, for harmonization of trademark classes between national trademark offices.

The Problem that began this Part gives an example of conflict over trademark classifications. The "KD" mark for athletic shoes was said to conflict with a prior registration for "Sports Shoes," Nice classification 250132; but the KD word mark was registered before in some European countries for provision of tourist guide and touring services, including tours for sporting events (such as European Champion's League soccer matches) which includes, in some cases, classification number 410059, the organization of sports competitions (*i.e.*, organizing outings and competitions among tour members, *e.g.*, holding a "mini Tour de France" for participants in a group tour, which involves staging a bicycle race over part of the same terrain traveled the previous day by actual Tour de France competitors). Are athletic shoes close enough to sporting competitions to cause confusion among consumers? That is the question that must be resolved before the junior user (KD for athletic shoes) can register its mark in the face of the senior user's mark for a related class (organizing athletic competitions).

17.1.3.1.1 Common law use and federal (national) registration

As mentioned, the US is a common law or "use-based" trademark country. Yet the US has elaborate mechanisms for registering trademarks in a federal (national) trademark office, as do almost all other countries in the world. What happens if there is a conflict between these principles? What if one user uses a trademark in commerce first (the "senior user"), but then a second ("junior") user registers the trademark with the US Patent and Trademark Office? Who then has priority?

Figure 17.1 German and Chinese national trademark applications

Sources: https://www.dpma.de (Germany); http://sbj.saic.gov.cn (China).

US trademark law has worked out an elaborate set of compromise rules in these cases. Stated simply, priority in these cases looks like this:

1. If the common law user is the senior user, but its use is limited to some portion or region of the US, the junior user will be allowed to register the mark and gain trademark rights to all parts of the US *except* the senior user's common law area of use. See *Dorpan, S.L. v. Hotel Melia, Inc.*, 728 F.3d 55, 63, 108 U.S.P.Q.2d 1093 (1st Cir. 2013) (territorial rights of a federal registrant are always subject to the prior common law rights of a senior user); 2 McCarthy on Trademarks and Unfair Competition §16:18.50 (4th ed. & Supp., 2016).
   a. The prior user must be able to show *continuous use*; senior common law rights require no breaks in the period of use.
   b. The common law use area of the senior user is determined with reference to the senior user's commercial use of the mark prior to the junior user's registration. Where the senior user can establish prior use throughout the US, the junior user's federal registration gives no rights. See *Watec Co., Ltd. v. Liu*, 403 F.3d 645, 74 U.S.P.Q.2d 1128 (9th Cir. 2005) (court affirmed jury verdict that foreign manufacturer was the owner of the trademark and that the former US importer infringed the mark; importer's registration was defeated under Lanham Act §15 by the foreign manufacturer's prior nationwide advertising and promotion). Where the senior user's use is limited, its continuing rights will also be limited.
   c. Those who filed their own application to register prior to the junior user's application also receive priority; a junior user gains no additional rights by filing a federal registration if that registration comes after a prior application. Under the common law, parties using the same mark but in separate areas of use, can continue their separate uses if no confusion is likely to result. As for federal trademark rights, a Patent and Trademark Office procedure called a "concurrent use proceeding" permits two parties using the same mark, but in different areas of use, to each acquire federal registration of their marks. See, e.g., *Nobelle.com, LLC v. Qwest Communications International, Inc.*, 66 U.S.P.Q.2d 1300, 1307 (T.T.A.B. 2003) (Original and familiar "Bell Telephone" trademark was assigned to each regional phone company when the Bell System was split up under a consent decree, and reissued as a series of concurrent registrations: "A concurrent use registration, by its very nature, contemplates that the registered mark can and does function to identify more than one source.") For specifics on concurrent use registration, *see* 3 McCarthy on Trademarks and Unfair Competition §20:81 (4th ed. & Supp., 2016).

2. A US applicant who has previously filed a foreign application to register, and whose foreign application qualifies under Lanham Act §44(d), is also accorded priority as against a later US applicant. (*See* the related discussion of Lanham Act §44(e), in Section 17.1.3.1.2, just below.)
3. If the federal registrant is the senior user, the junior user's use gives it no solid rights at all. This is because a valid federal registration serves as "constructive notice" of the rights of the senior user/registrant throughout the entire territory of the US. At the same time, although the senior user/federal registrant can acquire nationwide *rights*, it will not actually be able to exclude a junior common law user unless and until the federal registrant can show that it is about to enter the junior user's actual territory of use; until it is ready to enter the junior user's territory, the senior user/registrant cannot obtain a *remedy* to realize its federal rights. *Dawn Donut Co. v. Hart's Food Stores, Inc.*, 267 F.2d 358, 365 (2d Cir. 1959); *Flagstar Bank, FSB v. Freestar Bank, N.A.*, 687 F. Supp. 2d 811, 830 (C.D. Ill. 2009) (No evidence of likely expansion of federal registrant banking chain, active in Michigan, Indiana, and Georgia, into junior user's Illinois territory and thus no likelihood of confusion until entry into Illinois is imminent). Note that with the rise of the internet, and more mobile customers for many products, the *Dawn Donut* rule may be less important than in the past. De facto national use or presence is easier to achieve now than in the era when *Dawn Donut* was decided. This makes junior common law use in the face of a senior user's federal registration a perilous project indeed.

17.1.3.1.2 International filing in lieu of use in commerce

The US Lanham Act, through Section 44(e), covers foreign applicants for US trademarks who have previously registered in their home country:

> **44(e) Registration on principal or supplemental register; copy of foreign registration**
> A mark duly registered in the country of origin of the foreign applicant may be registered on the principal register if eligible, otherwise on the supplemental register in this chapter provided. Such applicant shall submit, within such time period as may be prescribed by the Director, a true copy, a photocopy, a certification, or a certified copy of the registration in the country of origin of the applicant. The application must state the applicant's bona fide intention to use the mark in commerce, but use in commerce shall not be required prior to registration (Lanham Act §44(e), 15 U.S.C. §1126(e)).

This section of the Lanham Act has occasioned controversy over the degree to which it modifies US trademark law as applied to marks filed first in other countries. At a minimum, it is quite clear that §44(e) dispenses with proof of US use in commerce; it thus provides equal treatment for foreign mark owners, putting them on the same footing as domestic ITU registrants. The debate is joined at another point: whether §44(e) modifies other substantive trademark rules. Some judges (and scholars) take the view that this section was meant to codify, in US law, article 6*quinquies* of the Paris Convention, which addresses the protection of marks registered first in one member country when they are later registered in other member countries:

> A(1) Every trademark duly registered in the country of origin shall be accepted for filing and protected as is in the other countries of the [Paris] Union, subject to the reservations indicated in this Article. Such countries may, before proceeding to final registration, require the production of a certificate of registration in the country of origin, issued by the competent authority. No authentication shall be required for this certificate.
>
> ...
>
> B. Trademarks covered by this Article may be neither denied registration nor invalidated except in the following cases:
>
> 1. when they are of such a nature as to infringe rights acquired by third parties in the country where protection is claimed;
> 2. when they are devoid of any distinctive character, or consist exclusively of signs or indications which may serve, in trade, to designate the kind, quality, quantity, intended purpose, value, place of origin, of the goods, or the time of production, or have become customary in the current language or in the bona fide and established practices of the trade of the country where protection is claimed;
> 3. when they are contrary to morality or public order and, in particular, or such a nature as to deceive the public. It is understood that a mark may not be considered contrary to public order for the sole reason that it does not conform to a provision of the legislation on marks, except if such provision itself relates to public order (Paris Convention for the Protection of Industrial Property, July 14, 1967, art. 6*quinquies*, 21 U.S.T. 1583, 1643–44).

The argument is that §44(e) states the *sole and exclusive* grounds for refusing to register a trademark first registered outside the US. When the Paris Convention criteria are compared to Lanham Act §2(e), it is clear that the §2(e) list of reasons to refuse registration is longer than the Paris Convention. So, for example, §2(e) says that a US trademark can be refused registration on the grounds that it is "primarily merely a surname" (Lanham Act §2(e)(4), 15 U.S.C. §1052(e)(4)). An example of this thinking comes from *In re*

Rath, 402 F.3d 1207, 1209 (Fed. Cir. 2005), where the registrant relied on §44(e) to obtain its US rights:

> Rath argues that he is exempt from the surname rule because it does not fall within any of the three enumerated exceptions to the registration of foreign marks within the Paris Convention, and he is therefore entitled to registration of his mark on the principal register. The PTO urges that surname marks are descriptive, and therefore "devoid of any distinctive character" within the meaning of the Paris Convention, such that no conflict exists between the requirements of the Lanham Act and the Paris Convention.

But the Federal Circuit in this case rejected the idea that §44(e) was meant to codify the Paris Convention: "We need not decide whether the surname rule conflicts with the Paris Convention because we find that the Paris Convention is not a self-executing treaty and requires congressional implementation" (*id*, at 1209). And the court concluded that §44(e) did not straightforwardly adopt Article 6*quinquies* of the Paris Convention. In particular, when §44(e) says "A mark duly registered in the country of origin of the foreign applicant may be registered on the principal register if eligible," the phrase *if eligible* does not by itself enact the limitations of Article 6*quinquies*:

> We specifically noted in [*In re Etablissements Darty et Fils*, 759 F.2d 15 (Fed. Cir.1985)] that "[s]ection 44(e) specifically directs issuance of registration on the Principal Register only 'if eligible.'" 759 F.2d at 18. The language of section 44(e) itself makes clear that the reference to eligibility pertains to eligibility for registration on the principal register, rather than eligibility under the Paris Convention. The leading treatise confirms this interpretation. McCarthy states that the requirement of eligibility necessarily means "that the mark is subject to all the recognized statutory bars to U.S. registration." 4 J. Thomas McCarthy, *McCarthy on Trademarks and Unfair Competition* §29:13 (4th ed. 2004). Section 2(e)(4) of the Lanham Act – prohibiting the registration of a mark that "is primarily merely a surname" on the principal register – is such an eligibility requirement. 15 U.S.C. §1052(e)(4) . . .
> [W]e conclude that while section 44(e) . . . affects United States priority or prior use rules, it is impossible to read section 44(e) to require the registration of foreign marks that fail to meet United States requirements for eligibility. Section 44 applications are subject to the section 2 bars to registration, of which the surname rule is one (*In re Rath*, 402 F.3d 1207, 1213–14 (Fed. Cir. 2005)).

The alternative view is summarized by Judge Bryson, concurring in the *Rath* case:

In light of (1) our treaty obligations; (2) the fact that section 44 was viewed as a distinct piece of legislation implementing those treaty obligations; (3) the legislative purpose behind the Lanham Act; and (4) our decision in [*In re Compagnie Generale Maritime,* 993 F.2d 841 (Fed. Cir.1993) (refusing to deny registration for a foreign mark that was geographically descriptive, because geographic descriptiveness was not a ground of refusal under the Paris Convention)], the term "if eligible" is more appropriately read to refer to the explicit eligibility requirements set forth in section 44(b), which incorporates the eligibility requirements of applicable international agreements, including the Paris Convention. In other words, the applicant must be a person whose country of origin is a party to a convention relating to trademarks, the restrictions set forth in section 44 must not apply, and registration must be allowable under the applicable conventions. In the event those requirements are satisfied, the person is "eligible" for the benefits conferred by section 44. In sum, the more natural reading of the "if eligible" language of section 44(e) is that it refers to eligibility under section 44 of the Lanham Act and thus incorporates the requirements of the Paris Convention for foreign applications (*In re Rath,* 402 F.3d 1207, 1220 (Fed. Cir. 2005) (Bryson, J., concurring)).

Given the importance of trans-national trademarks and branding in contemporary commerce, this is perhaps an issue the US Supreme Court will eventually address.

17.1.3.1.3 The "well-known mark" doctrine in the US

An exception to the "first use in commerce" rule is recognized in at least some US courts in the case of "well-known marks" that have been in long use outside the US Note that this doctrine, where it applies, is effective for trademarks that have not been registered in the US; *i.e.,* it applies in Lanham Act §43(a) cases. The doctrine was recognized in the following case from the Ninth Circuit Court of Appeals:

Grupo Gigante SA De CV v. Dallo & Co., 391 F.3d 1088, 1091 (9th Cir. 2004)

Kleinfeld, Circuit Judge.
This is a trademark case. The contest is between a large Mexican grocery chain that has long used the mark, but not in the United States, and a small American chain that was the first to use the mark in the United States, but did so, long after the Mexican chain began

CASE *(continued)*

using it [in Mexico], in a locality where [the small American chain operated and where] shoppers were familiar with the Mexican mark.

Grupo Gigante S.A. de C.V. ("Grupo Gigante") operates a large chain of grocery stores in Mexico, called "Gigante," meaning "Giant" in Spanish. Grupo Gigante first called a store "Gigante" in Mexico City in 1962. In 1963, Grupo Gigante registered the "Gigante" mark as a trade name in Mexico, and has kept its registration current ever since. The chain was quite successful, and it had expanded into Baja California, Mexico by 1987. By 1991, Grupo Gigante had almost 100 stores in Mexico, including six in Baja, all using the mark "Gigante." Two of the Baja stores were in Tijuana, a city on the U.S.-Mexican border, just south of San Diego.

As of August 1991, Grupo Gigante had not opened any stores in the United States. That month, Michael Dallo began operating a grocery store in San Diego, using the name "Gigante Market." In October 1996, Dallo and one of his brothers, Chris Dallo, opened a second store in San Diego, also under the name Gigante Market. The Dallo brothers – who include Michael, Chris, and their two other brothers, Douray and Rafid – have since controlled the two stores through various limited liability corporations.

In 1998, Grupo Gigante decided that the time had come to enter the Southern California market. It arranged a meeting with Michael Dallo in June 1998 to discuss the Dallos' use of the name "Gigante." Grupo Gigante was unsuccessful at this meeting in its attempt to convince Dallo to stop using the "Gigante" mark. Also in June 1998, Grupo Gigante registered the "Gigante" mark with the state of California. The Dallos did likewise in July 1998. Neither has registered the mark federally.

About one year later, in May 1999, Grupo Gigante opened its first U.S. store. That store was followed by a second later that year, and then by a third in 2000. All three stores were in the Los Angeles area. All were called "Gigante," like Grupo Gigante's Mexican stores.

In July 1999, after learning of the opening of Grupo Gigante's first U.S. store, the Dallos sent Grupo Gigante a cease-and-desist letter, making the same demand of Grupo Gigante that Grupo Gigante had made of them earlier: stop using the name Gigante. [A declaratory judgment action from the Dallos followed.]

The [district] court recognized that under the "territoriality principle," use of a mark in another country generally does not serve to give the user trademark rights in the United States. Thus, the territoriality principle suggests that the Dallos' use of the mark, which was the first in the United States, would entitle them to claim the mark. But it held that because Grupo Gigante had already made Gigante a well-known mark in Southern California by the time the Dallos began using it, an exception to the territoriality principle applied. As the district court interpreted what is known as the "famous-mark" or "well-known mark" exception to the territoriality principle, Grupo Gigante's earlier use in Mexico was sufficient to give it the superior claim to the mark in Southern California. The court held, therefore, that Grupo Gigante was entitled to a declaratory judgment that it had a valid, protectable interest in the Gigante name.

There is no circuit-court authority – from this or any other circuit – applying a famous-

CASE *(continued)*

mark exception to the territoriality principle. At least one circuit judge has, in a dissent, called into question whether there actually is any meaningful famous-mark exception. We hold, however, that there is a famous mark exception to the territoriality principle. While the territoriality principle is a long-standing and important doctrine within trademark law, it cannot be absolute. An absolute territoriality rule without a famous-mark exception would promote consumer confusion and fraud. Commerce crosses borders. In this nation of immigrants, so do people. Trademark is, at its core, about protecting against consumer confusion and "palming off." There can be no justification for using trademark law to fool immigrants into thinking that they are buying from the store they liked back home.

It might not matter if someone visiting Fairbanks, Alaska from Wellington, New Zealand saw a cute hair-salon name – "Hair Today, Gone Tomorrow," "Mane Place," "Hair on Earth," "Mary's Hair'em," or "Shear Heaven" – and decided to use the name on her own salon back home in New Zealand. The ladies [sic] in New Zealand would not likely think they were going to a branch of a Fairbanks hair salon. But if someone opened a high-end salon with a red door in Wellington and called it Elizabeth Arden's, women might very well go there because they thought they were going to an affiliate of the Elizabeth Arden chain, even if there had not been any other Elizabeth Ardens in New Zealand prior to the salon's opening. If it was not an affiliate, just a local store with no connection, customers would be fooled. The real Elizabeth Arden chain might lose business if word spread that the Wellington salon was nothing special.

[A prior case, *Vaudable v. Montmartre, Inc.,* [20 Misc.2d 757, 193 N.Y.S.2d 332 (N.Y.Sup. Ct.1959)] stands for the principle that even those who use marks in other countries can sometimes – when their marks are famous enough – gain exclusive rights to the marks in this country, the case itself tells us little about just how famous or well-known the foreign mark must be. The opinion states in rather conclusory terms that the [famous] Paris [restaurant] Maxim's "is, of course, well known in this country," and that "[t]here is *no doubt* as to its unique and eminent position as a restaurant of international fame and prestige." This language suggests that Maxim's had achieved quite a high degree of fame here, and certainly enough to qualify for the exception to the territoriality principle, but it suggests nothing about just how much fame was necessary. It does not suggest where the line is between "Shear Heaven" and Maxim's.

To determine whether the famous-mark exception to the territoriality rule applies, the district court must determine whether the mark satisfies the secondary meaning test. The district court determined that it did in this case, and we agree with its persuasive analysis. But secondary meaning is not enough.

In addition, where the mark has not before been used in the American market, the court must be satisfied, by a preponderance of the evidence, that a *substantial* percentage of consumers in the relevant American market is familiar with the foreign mark. The relevant American market is the geographic area where the defendant uses the alleged infringing mark. In making this determination, the court should consider such factors as the intentional copying of the mark by the defendant, and whether customers of the American

> **CASE** *(continued)*
>
> firm are likely to think they are patronizing the same firm that uses the mark in another country. While these factors are not necessarily determinative, they are particularly relevant because they bear heavily on the risks of consumer confusion and fraud, which are the reasons for having a famous-mark exception.
>
> Because the district court did not have the benefit of this additional test, we vacate and remand so that it may be applied. We intimate no judgment on whether further motion practice and some additions to what the district court has already written in its published opinion will suffice, or whether trial will be needed to apply this new test. Nor do we intimate what the result should be.
>
> Reversed and remanded.

NOTES

1. The well-known mark rule is required under the Paris Convention and the TRIPs Agreement.

    Paris Convention Article 6bis: Marks: *Well-Known Marks*

    (1) The countries of the Union undertake, ex officio if their legislation so permits, or at the request of an interested party, to refuse or to cancel the registration, and to prohibit the use, of a trademark which constitutes a reproduction, an imitation, or a translation, liable to create confusion, of a mark considered by the competent authority of the country of registration or use to be well known in that country as being already the mark of a person entitled to the benefits of this Convention and used for identical or similar goods. These provisions shall also apply when the essential part of the mark constitutes a reproduction of any such well-known mark or an imitation liable to create confusion therewith.

    (2) A period of at least five years from the date of registration shall be allowed for requesting the cancellation of such a mark. The countries of the Union may provide for a period within which the prohibition of use must be requested.

    (3) No time limit shall be fixed for requesting the cancellation or the prohibition of the use of marks registered or used in bad faith.

    TRIPS Agreement, Article 16

    2. Article 6*bis* of the Paris Convention (1967) shall apply, *mutatis mutandis*, to services. In determining whether a trademark is well-known, Members shall take account of the knowledge of the trademark in the relevant sector of the public, including knowledge in the Member concerned which has been obtained as a result of the promotion of the trademark.

    3. Article 6*bis* of the Paris Convention (1967) shall apply, *mutatis mutandis*, to goods or services which are not similar to those in respect of which a trademark is registered, provided that use of that trademark in relation to those goods or services would indicate a connection between those goods or services and the owner of the registered trademark and provided that the interests of the owner of the registered trademark are likely to be damaged by such use.

2. The Second Circuit rejected the well-known mark rule in the *Punchgini* case, *ITC Ltd. v. Punchgini, Inc.*, 482 F.3d 135 (2d Cir. 2007). There plaintiff had operated a restaurant called BUKHARA in four locations in Asia. It had also had a New York restaurant by that name, but it had closed some years earlier. The court refused to find that the well-known marks rule was a part of federal law so as to give plaintiff a ground to assert infringement after some of its former employees opened their own Bukhara restaurant in New York City in 1999 and copied the plaintiff's décor and menu. The court refused to recognize that the Lanham Act incorporated the well-known mark doctrine, and said that the Plaintiff's recourse was to Congress and

not the courts. The court reviewed §44 of the Act, which the *Grupo Gigante* court had relied on to find US recognition of well-known marks, which reads:

> Any person whose country of origin is a party to any convention or treaty relating to trademarks, trade or commercial names, or the repression of unfair competition, to which the United States is also a party, or extends reciprocal rights to nationals of the United States by law, shall be entitled to the benefits of this section under the conditions expressed herein to the extent necessary to give effect to any provision of such convention, treaty or reciprocal law, in addition to the rights to which any owner of a mark is otherwise entitled by this chapter (Lanham Act §44, 15 U.S.C. §1126(b)).

The TTAB follows the Second Circuit, and not the Ninth Circuit, in failing to recognize the well known marks doctrine. *See Bayer Consumer Care AG v. Belmora LLC*, 90 U.S.P.Q.2d 1587, 1591 (T.T.A.B. 2009), later proceedings *Belmora LLC v. Bayer Consumer Care AG.*, 84 F.Supp.3d 490 (E.D. Va. 2015) (Agreeing with the Trademark Trial and Appeal Board (TTAB) that the Lanham Act does not does not incorporate the Paris Convention's well-known marks rule and it is not a ground for challenging a trademark registration).

17.1.3.2 *International treaties and registration*

Traditionally, trademarks were usually pursued first in the home country of the mark's owner. As a product became more successful and an international market developed, the product would be introduced into other countries and trademark protection would then be sought. This typically took the form of a sequential series of national filings. So a trademark lawyer representing a client with a successful product sold on world markets would have to manage and coordinate a broad series of independent national filings.

With the expansion of international trade in the nineteenth century, trademark lawyers recognized that an international regime might be useful to coordinate multiple national filings. Thus was born the trademark component of the Paris Convention of 1886. Under the Paris Convention, a trademark application filed in one of the 175 countries that recognize the Convention gives the applicant six months within which to file in any of the other countries that recognize it. Any of these subsequent applications will be regarded as if they had been filed on the same day as the first application. This means they have priority over applications for the same mark filed by others during that six-month period.

The Paris Convention remains in force, and some trademark applicants still rely on it to coordinate international filings. But another international system has since come to prominence, the Madrid System, which substantially expands a trademark owner's ability to coordinate international filings. Under the Madrid System, a trademark applicant first files in any Madrid member country (*i.e.*, most countries in the world) – typically, in the trademark owner's home country. *See* Ash Nagdev, *Statistical Analysis of the United States' Accession to the Madrid Protocol*, 6 Nw. J. Tech. & Intell. Prop. 211,

225 (2008), at Table 5 (showing the vast majority of international applications first filed in trademark owner's home country trademark office). This becomes what is called the "basic" application. Next a Madrid application is filed in the international trademark office of the World Intellectual Property Organization (WIPO). This Madrid application designates which of the Madrid member countries the applicants would like to apply to for trademark rights. Each national office then treats the Madrid application as the equivalent of a valid national filing. In this way, a single application, in one language (English or French), paying a single fee in one currency, can serve as the basis of a series of worldwide national filings.

Despite the convenience of the Paris and Madrid Systems, few trademark applicants make use of these systems. Those that do tend to be large, sophisticated, usually multinational corporations whose lines of business are inherently global. *See, e.g.*, US Patent and Trademark Office, Trademark Dashboard, available at https://www.uspto.gov/dashboards/trademarks/main.dashxml (accessed Aug. 29, 2016) (showing that in 2015, 83 percent of trademark applications were based on either use in commerce, or ITU, in the US; with 10.8 percent of applications coming through the Paris Convention and 6.2 percent coming through the Madrid System).

17.1.3.2.1 The Madrid System

The Protocol Relating to the Madrid Agreement Concerning the International Registration of Marks (Madrid Protocol) is one of two treaties comprising the Madrid System for international registration of trademarks. *See* Madrid Agreement Concerning the International Registration of Marks, April 14, 1891, 175 Consol. T.S. 57. This is an agreement under the Paris Convention for the Protection of Industrial Property, Stockholm Revision, done July 14, 1967, Art. 2(1), 21 U.S.T. 1629, 1631, 828 U.N.T.S. 305, 313. The other treaty, the Madrid Protocol, is a scaled-down version of the Madrid Agreement. *See* Protocol Relating to the Madrid Agreement Concerning the International Registration of Marks, adopted at Madrid on June 27, 1989, available at http://www.wipo.int/treaties/en/text.jsp?file_id=283484. It is this version, the Protocol, that the US joined in 2002. *See* 3 McCarthy on Trademarks and Unfair Competition §19:31.20 (4th ed. & Supp., 2016).

The Madrid Protocol is a filing treaty and not a substantive harmonization treaty. It provides a cost-effective and efficient way for trademark holders – individuals and businesses – to ensure protection for their marks in multiple countries through the filing of one application with a single office, in one language, with one set of fees, in one currency. Each member country decides on trademark registration in its own national trademark office. Once the trademark office in a designated country grants protection, the mark is protected in that country just as if the application had originated in that office. The Madrid Protocol also provides for continuing management of the mark after it has been registered; WIPO's International Bureau maintains records regarding ownership and renewal. The International Bureau administers the Madrid System and coordinates the transmittal of requests for protection, renewals, and other relevant documentation to all members.

Despite the administrative inconvenience, trademark applications filed under the Madrid Protocol have some distinct disadvantages. Madrid registrations are limited for all time to the original list of product categories entered in the "basic" application (in the home country); because the US requires narrower and more specific product categories than many other countries, this limits the future scope of a Madrid-registered mark. In addition, there is a five-year initial period during which international rights remain dependent on the fate of the "basic" (home country) application:

> For a period of five years from the date of its registration, an international registration under the Protocol remains dependent on the status of the basic application or registration in its office of origin. During this period of "dependency," if the basic application or registration in the office of origin ceases to have effect for any reason, the international registration also fails and will be cancelled (3 McCarthy on Trademarks and Unfair Competition §19:31.65 (4th ed. & Supp., 2016)).

17.1.3.2.2 Community trademarks and the EUIPO

As described later in this Part, the EU now employs a regional (EU-wide) trademark registration system, administered by the EU Intellectual Property Office in Alicante, Spain. This is a successor to the Office for Harmonisation in the Internal Market (OHIM), which was the name of the trademark registry before 2016.

17.2 Trademark registrability and rights

17.2.1 Administrative registration

Administrative proceedings concerning trademarks in the US are among the most stringent in the world. Unlike most foreign registration systems, which review applications only for compliance with formal requirements, the US Patent and Trademark Office (PTO) reviews applications to ensure that they meet both formal requirements (which are largely set forth in §1 of the Lanham

Act) and substantive requirements (largely found in §2 of the Lanham Act). For marks already being used in commerce, the application process consists of five basic stages: (1) application, (2) examination, (3) publication in the PTO's Official Gazette, (4) opposition, and (5) registration. For marks which the applicant intends to use in commerce in the near future, the process consists of two additional stages following opposition and preceding registration: (4.a) the issuance by the PTO of a "Notice of Allowance" and (4.b) the filing by the applicant of a Statement of Use. We review each of these stages below.

Registration in the European IP Office in Alicante, Spain, confers Europe-wide rights, as described earlier. It is, overall, similar in many respects to the US registration procedure, though examination by the office is not as stringent. (In Europe, there is more reliance on private party policing of published trademark oppositions – *i.e.*, oppositions). In addition, of course, there is the added complexity of language requirements.

Registration in SIPO, the Chinese national trademark office, follows similar contours. Oppositions are important for published SIPO applications as well. Later sections in this Part detail some of the substantive requirements applied by SIPO and the courts charged with enforcing Chinese trademark law.

17.2.1.1 Principal vs. Supplemental Register in the US

Although registration is not a prerequisite to trademark protection, trademarks registered on the Principal Register enjoy a number of significant advantages. The primary advantages are: (1) nationwide constructive use and constructive notice, which cut off rights of other users of the same or similar marks (Lanham Act §22 (15 U.S.C. §1072) and Lanham Act §7(c) (15 U.S.C. §1057(c))); (2) the possibility of achieving incontestable status after five years, which greatly enhances rights by eliminating a number of defenses (Lanham Act §15 (15 U.S.C. §1065)); and (3) a prima facie presumption of the validity of the mark and the registrant's ownership of the mark, Lanham Act §33(a) (15 U.S.C. §1115(a)).

Trademark applications are filed at the PTO and made available for public scrutiny soon after filing. This procedure is different from patent applications, the contents of which are kept secret for 18 months after filing in most cases.

The Supplemental Register was established by the 1946 Lanham Act to enable US applicants to domestically register trademarks so that they might obtain registration under the laws of foreign countries. Under the Paris Convention, foreign registration could not be granted in the absence of domestic registration. Because there are countries where trademark registration is granted to marks that would not qualify for the US Principal Register, the Supplemental Register was created. Thus, even if a US mark cannot gain the advantages of registration on the Principal Register, it may obtain protection in foreign countries. See Lanham Act §23, 15 U.S.C.A. §1091.

To be eligible for the Supplemental Register a mark need only be capable of distinguishing goods or services. There is no need to prove that it actually functions in that capacity. The Supplemental Register is not available for clearly generic names, but it is available for the registration of trade dress. Unlike the Principal Register, registration on the Supplemental Register confers no substantive trademark rights. As one court explained,

> Plaintiff's supplemental registration of its container design does not create substantive rights or in itself give plaintiff an exclusive right to use the bottle shape. Likewise, plaintiff's application for principal registration of its container creates no presumptions in its favor because plaintiff has not completed the registration process. However, plaintiff may be entitled to protection from use by defendant of this particular bottle configuration if plaintiff can establish that the configuration has acquired secondary meaning or if plaintiff can show that defendant's use of the bottle configuration in its overall trade dress constitutes unfair competition (*Sundor Brands, Inc. v. Borden, Inc.*, 653 F. Supp. 86, 91 (M.D. Fla. 1986)).

17.2.1.2 Applications

Trademark applications may be filed electronically or, at additional cost, in paper form. In 2015, 80 percent of trademark applications at the PTO were processed electronically. See United States Patent and Trademark Office, Citizen Centric Report, Fiscal Year 2015, at 1 (2015). The application is relatively simple. See Lanham Act §§1(a) & 1(b) (setting out the required contents of use-based and intent-to-use applications, respectively).

The Lanham Act establishes five bases for filing a trademark application: (1) actual use of the mark in commerce (Lanham Act §1(a)); (2) bona fide intent to use the mark in commerce (Lanham Act §1(b)); (3) a claim of priority based on an earlier-filed foreign application to register the mark (Lanham Act §44(d)); (4) registration of the mark in a foreign applicant's country of origin (Lanham Act §44(e)); and (5) extension of protection of an international registration under the Madrid System for the international registration of trademarks (Lanham Act §66(a)), which is discussed in the following Note. Most trademark applications at the PTO are now filed under the Lanham Act §1(b) ITU basis.

The applicant must identify the particular goods or services on or in connection with which it uses or intends to use the mark. The applicant should also identify the international class number(s) of the identified goods or services. *See* Trademark Manual of Examining Procedure ("TMEP") §805. The identification of goods or services in the application does not by itself limit the breadth of the applicant's exclusive rights. But the classes named in the final registration do bear significantly on the mark owner's rights.

The applicant must submit a drawing or image of the trademark. If the mark consists of colors, the drawing must as well. For word marks, a typed representation of the mark is sufficient. For nonvisual marks, such as sound or scent marks, the applicant need not submit a drawing. The PTO relies instead on the applicant's description of the mark given elsewhere in the application and on the applicant's specimen of use (TMEP §807.09).

Applicants filing a "1(a)" use-based application must submit a specimen showing use of the mark in commerce. For electronic applications, this specimen typically takes the form of digital photographs of the mark attached to goods or .pdf images of materials promoting services. Applicants filing a "1(b)" IUT application need not (because they very likely cannot) submit a specimen of use with their application, but must do so instead when they file their Statement of Use. *See* Lanham Act §1(d)(1) (15 U.S.C. 1051(d)(1)).

To give a sense of scale, the PTO received 503,889 trademark applications in 2015. During the same year, it issued 208,660 trademark registrations. Average total pendency of trademark applications at the PTO in 2015 was approximately 10 months. WIPO estimates that there are 1,853,874 active trademark registrations in force in the US. Another estimate puts the total at 2,094,051. *See* Barton Beebe and Jeanne C. Fromer, *Are We Running Out of Trademarks? An Empirical Study of Trademark Depletion and Congestion*, 131 Harv. L. Rev. 945, 956 (2018). By comparison, there are over eight million in China, and 941,736 in Germany. *See* www.ipstats.wipo.int.

17.2.1.3 Absolute vs. relative grounds for refusal in Europe

The EU Trademark Directive, 2015 Revision, Dir. No. 2015/2436 (16 Dec. 2016), follows the earlier versions of the Directive in dividing the grounds of unregistrability (*i.e.*, "refusal") or invalidity into two categories: "absolute" and "relative." The first describes bases for unregistrability which do not depend on the existence or priority dates of other trademarks. The latter category covers unregistrability based on the existence and priority of other, conflicting trademarks; the registration is "relative" to competing marks, in other words.

Here are the relevant provisions:

SECTION 2
Grounds for refusal or invalidity
Article 4
Absolute grounds for refusal or invalidity

1. The following shall not be registered or, if registered, shall be liable to be declared invalid:
   (a) signs which cannot constitute a trade mark;
   (b) trade marks which are devoid of any distinctive character;
   (c) trade marks which consist exclusively of signs or indications which may serve, in trade, to designate the kind, quality, quantity, intended purpose, value, geographical origin, or the time of production of the goods or of rendering of the service, or other characteristics of the goods or services;
   (d) trade marks which consist exclusively of signs or indications which have become customary in the current language or in the bona fide and established practices of the trade;
   (e) signs which consist exclusively of:
      (i) the shape, or another characteristic, which results from the nature of the goods themselves;
      (ii) the shape, or another characteristic, of goods which is necessary to obtain a technical result;
      (iii) the shape, or another characteristic, which gives substantial value to the goods;
   (f) trade marks which are contrary to public policy or to accepted principles of morality;
   (g) trade marks which are of such a nature as to deceive the public, for instance, as to the nature, quality or geographical origin of the goods or service;
   (h) trade marks which have not been authorised by the competent authorities and are to be refused or invalidated pursuant to Article 6ter of the Paris Convention;
   (i) trade marks which are excluded from registration pursuant to Union legislation or the national law of the Member State concerned, or to international agreements to which the Union or the Member State concerned is party, providing for protection of designations of origin and geographical indications;

(j) trade marks which are excluded from registration pursuant to Union legislation or international agreements to which the Union is party, providing for protection of traditional terms for wine;

(k) trade marks which are excluded from registration pursuant to Union legislation or international agreements to which the Union is party, providing for protection of traditional specialities guaranteed;

(l) trade marks which consist of, or reproduce in their essential elements, an earlier plant variety denomination registered in accordance with Union legislation or the national law of the Member State concerned, or international agreements to which the Union or the Member State concerned is party, providing protection for plant variety rights, and which are in respect of plant varieties of the same or closely related species.

2. A trade mark shall be liable to be declared invalid where the application for registration of the trade mark was made in bad faith by the applicant. Any Member State may also provide that such a trade mark is not to be registered.

Article 5
Relative grounds for refusal or invalidity

1. A trade mark shall not be registered or, if registered, shall be liable to be declared invalid where:

(a) it is identical with an earlier trade mark, and the goods or services for which the trade mark is applied for or is registered are identical with the goods or services for which the earlier trade mark is protected;

(b) because of its identity with, or similarity to, the earlier trade mark and the identity or similarity of the goods or services covered by the trade marks, there exists a likelihood of confusion on the part of the public; the likelihood of confusion includes the likelihood of association with the earlier trade mark.

2. 'Earlier trade marks' within the meaning of paragraph 1 means:

(a) trade marks of the following kinds with a date of application for registration which is earlier than the date of application for registration of the trade mark, taking account, where appropriate, of the priorities claimed in respect of those trade marks:
  (i) EU trade marks;
  (ii) trade marks registered in the Member State concerned or, in the case of Belgium, Luxembourg or the Netherlands, at the Benelux Office for Intellectual Property;
  (iii) trade marks registered under international arrangements which have effect in the Member State concerned;

(b) EU trade marks which validly claim seniority, in accordance with Regulation (EC) No 207/2009, of a trade mark referred to in points (a)(ii) and (iii), even when the latter trade mark has been surrendered or allowed to lapse;

(c) applications for the trade marks referred to in points (a) and (b), subject to their registration;

(d) trade marks which, on the date of application for registration of the trade mark, or, where appropriate, of the priority claimed in respect of the application for registration of the trade mark, are well known in the Member State concerned, in the sense in which the words 'well-known' are used in Article 6bis of the Paris Convention.

3. Furthermore, a trade mark shall not be registered or, if registered, shall be liable to be declared invalid where:

(a) it is identical with, or similar to, an earlier trade mark irrespective of whether the goods or services for which it is applied or registered are identical with, similar to or not similar to those for which the earlier trade mark is registered, where the earlier trade mark has a reputation in the Member State in respect of which registration is applied for or in which the trade mark is registered or, in the case of an EU trade mark, has a reputation in the Union and the use of the later trade mark without due cause would take unfair advantage of, or be detrimental to, the distinctive character or the repute of the earlier trade mark;

. . .

4. Any Member State may provide that a trade mark is not to be registered or, if registered, is liable to be declared invalid where, and to the extent that:

(a) rights to a non-registered trade mark or to another sign used in the course of trade were acquired prior to the date of application for registration of the subsequent trade mark, or the date of the priority claimed for the application for registration of the subsequent trade mark, and that non-registered trade mark or other sign confers on its proprietor the right to prohibit the use of a subsequent trade mark;

(b) the use of the trade mark may be prohibited by virtue of an earlier right, other than the rights referred to in paragraph 2 and point (a) of this paragraph, and in particular:
  (i) a right to a name;
  (ii) a right of personal portrayal;
  (iii) a copyright;
  (iv) an industrial property right.

(c) the trade mark is liable to be confused with an earlier trade mark protected abroad, provided that, at the date of the application, the applicant was acting in bad faith . . .

On the important threshold requirement in Article 2 of the EU Trademark Directive, "capable of distinguishing," *see* the case of *Sieckmann v. Deutsche Patent und Markenamt (DPMA)*, below this Part. Likewise *see* Section 17.2.2 *infra* on acquired distinctiveness.

17.2.1.4 Registration in China (CTMO)

Unlike common law jurisdictions, which recognize trademark rights arising from both common law use and national registrations, Chinese trademark law adopts the first-to-file principle, thus granting the exclusive rights to trademarks only to those who file and register the trademarks first. A non-registered trademark will not receive trademark protection in China, except under certain circumstances, such as when the non-registered mark is a well-known trademark or when the prior registration was filed in bad faith by a trademark squatter.

In China, trademark applications are filed before the Chinese Trademark Office under the State Administration of Industry and Commerce (SAIC). The Chinese Trademark Office conducts both formality and substantial examination against the applied mark, in particular with its registrability and availability. Assuming that the applied mark is both registrable (*i.e.* "distinctive" and we will talk more about trademark distinctiveness a little later) and available (meaning that "no prior similar trademarks are revealed in terms of similar goods or services"), then the applied trademark will be preliminarily approved for registration and then published in the Trademark Gazette for opposition purpose. If no opposition is filed within the three-month publication period, then the applied mark will mature into registration.

Things do not always go that smoothly of course. An applied trademark might be blocked from registration for several reasons: (1) it might be rejected by the Chinese Trademark Office for lacking distinctiveness (See Articles 9–12 of Chinese Trademark Law); or (2) the mark might be distinctive enough, but is blocked by another similar prior trademark covering similar goods or services. Whatever the obstacle might be, the applicant always has a chance to file an appeal before the Trademark Review and Adjudication Board (TRAB), a parallel trademark administrative agency responsible for reviewing decisions made by the Chinese Trademark Office.

Decisions made by the TRAB used to be final decisions. This has changed since China joined the WTO in 2002. Based on China's commitment to enter the WTO, all administrative decisions have to be reviewed by the judicial system – the peoples' courts in China. As such, now the interested parties could continue their journey of appeal, first to the Beijing Intermediate People's Court (*i.e.* court of first instance), then to the Beijing High People's Court (appellate court), and sometimes to the Chinese Supreme People's Court (the highest court of China).

Article 8 of the Chinese Trademark Law (recently revised in 2013) allows a trademark for registration, either a word mark, device mark, mark composed of letters or numbers, three-dimensional mark, color combination mark, or a sound mark, as long as such a mark can distinguish the origin of its related goods and/or services. Articles 10–11 then provide a negative list of trademarks that cannot be registered as trademarks.

Article 10 of the Chinese Trademark Law reads:

> The following signs shall not be used as trademarks:
>
> (1) Those identical with or similar to the State name, national flag, national emblem, national anthem, military flag, army emblem, military songs, medals and others of the People's Republic of China; those identical with the names and signs of central state organs, names of the specific locations thereof, or those identical with the names or device of landmark buildings;
> (2) Those identical with or similar to the state names, national flags, national emblems or military flags of foreign countries, unless permitted by the government of the country;
> (3) Those identical with or similar to the names, flags, or emblems of international inter-governmental organizations, unless permitted by the organization concerned or unlikely to mislead the public;
> (4) Those identical with or similar to an official sign or inspection seal that indicates control and guarantee, unless it is authorized;
> (5) Those identical with or similar to the names or signs of the Red Cross or the Red Crescent;
> (6) Those of discrimination against any race;
> (7) Those of fraud that may easily mislead the public in the characteristics such as the quality of goods, or place of production; and
> (8) Those detrimental to socialist morals or customs, or having other unhealthy influences.
>
> The geographical names of administrative divisions at or above the county level and foreign geographical names well-known to the public shall not be used as trademarks, except for geographical names that contain other meanings or constitute parts of a collective mark or certification mark. Where a trademark bearing any of the above-mentioned geographical names has been registered, it shall continue to be valid.

Later in this Part we discuss the registrability standard under the Chinese Trademark Law with respect to the use of a state name in a trademark, geographic term in a trademark, scandalous mark, distinction between inherent distinctiveness and acquired distinctiveness, and also the functionality issue.

17.2.2 Distinctiveness

17.2.2.1 United States: the spectrum from arbitrary/fanciful to descriptive/generic

Trademarks are traditionally classified and arrayed along a "spectrum." The legal treatment of a trademark depends in part on how it is classified. The Supreme Court summarized the classifications in these terms:

> A trademark is defined in 15 U.S.C. §1127 as including "any word, name, symbol, or device or any combination thereof" used by any person "to identify and distinguish his or her goods, including a unique product, from those manufactured or sold by others and to indicate the source of the goods, even if that source is unknown." In order to be registered, a mark must be capable of distinguishing the applicant's goods from those of others. §1052. Marks are often classified in categories of generally increasing distinctiveness; following the classic formulation set out by Judge Friendly, they may be (1) generic; (2) descriptive; (3) suggestive; (4) arbitrary; or (5) fanciful. See *Abercrombie & Fitch Co. v. Hunting World, Inc.,* 537 F.2d 4, 9 ([2nd Cir.] 1976)... The latter three categories of marks, because their intrinsic nature serves to identify a particular source of a product, are deemed inherently distinctive and are entitled to protection. In contrast, generic marks – those that "refe[r] to the genus of which the particular product is a species," *Park 'N Fly, Inc. v. Dollar Park & Fly, Inc.,* 469 U.S. 189, 194 (1985), citing *Abercrombie & Fitch, supra,* at 9 – are not registrable as trademarks. *Park 'N Fly, supra,* 469 U.S., at 194.
>
> Marks which are merely descriptive of a product are not inherently distinctive. When used to describe a product, they do not inherently identify a particular source, and hence cannot be protected. However, descriptive marks may acquire the distinctiveness which will allow them to be protected under the Act. Section 2 of the Lanham Act provides that a descriptive mark that otherwise could not be registered under the Act may be registered if it "has become distinctive of the applicant's goods in commerce." §§2(e), (f), 15 U.S.C. §§1052(e), (f). See *Park 'N Fly, supra,* at 194, 196. This acquired distinctiveness is generally called "secondary meaning" (*Two Pesos, Inc. v. Taco Cabana, Inc.,* 505 U.S. 763, 768–69 (1992)).

The following sections give some examples of each type of trademark.

17.2.2.1.1 Fanciful marks

These are made-up words. Famous examples include Kodak, for camera film and cameras, and Xerox for photocopiers. Another example is Zyrtec, for an allergy medication. *McNeil-PPC, Inc. v. Walgreen Co.*, 2013 WL 223400 (T.T.A.B. 2013) (not precedential; sustaining opposition brought by owner of Zyrtec mark to registration of competing mark, WAL-ZYR, meant to denote "Walgreen's version of Zyrtec").

17.2.2.1.2 Arbitrary marks

These are words that have standard meanings, but are used to signify products that have nothing to do with the standard meaning. Examples here include "Gap" and "Google." The word "gap" has a meaning, of course (a space or opening between two proximate things), but as applied to the sale of clothing, shoes and accessories, it is arbitrary (*Gap, Inc. v. G.A.P. Adventures Inc.*, 100 U.S.P.Q.2d 1417, 2011 WL 2946384 (S.D. N.Y. 2011)). Google has a fanciful sound, but it is in fact a word (taken from the sport of cricket, and meaning "to throw a ball with a sharp break or curve," which ball is known as a "googly"). Google is also close to the term "Googol," made up by a mathematician's child, to describe a very large number, namely, the number one with one hundred zeroes after it. *See* Oxford English Dictionary (2d. ed., 1989 and Supp., 2009), at "google" and "googol," respectively.

Another example is "Apple" for computers and mobile phones. These products have nothing to do with fruit.

Initials can also be arbitrary (*YKK Corp. v. Jungwoo Zipper Co., Ltd.*, 213 F. Supp. 2d 1195, 64 U.S.P.Q.2d 1192, 1195 (C.D. Cal. 2002)) (entering summary judgment for plaintiff, owner of "YKK" trademark for zippers; finding likelihood of confusion with proposed registration of mark "YPP" for same products, after classifying "YKK" as arbitrary; "YKK is derived from 'Yoshida Kogyo Kabushikikaisha,' the original company name, and is in no way either descriptive or suggestive of the company's products).

17.2.2.1.3 Suggestive marks

Suggestive marks are those that imply or suggest some feature or attribute of a product, but do not come right out and *describe* the product. One example is "Coppertone" for tanning lotion. For light-skinned people, a copper tone or color often follows from exposure to the sun, and is associated with outdoor activity and good health. Therefore "Coppertone" suggests an even suntan, but does not describe it. A trademark like "Good Tan", however, would be descriptive. Courts sometimes describe the difference between suggestive and descriptive marks by asking whether the mark requires any imagination to go from the mark to the nature of the product. Consider this passage from a case involving the trademark TWO MEN AND A TRUCK, which was used by a moving company:

> [T]he TWO MEN AND A TRUCK Mark seems to be "suggestive"; it "requires some measure of imagination to reach a conclusion regarding the nature of the" services offered. *Duluth News–Tribune, a Div. of Nw. Pub'ns, Inc. v. Mesabi Publ'g Co.,* 84 F.3d 1093, 1096 (8th Cir.1996). Therefore, Plaintiff is likely to show that its TWO MEN AND A TRUCK Mark is conceptually strong. See *Frosty Treats Inc. v. Sony Computer Entm't Am. Inc.,* 426 F.3d 1001, 1005 (8th Cir.2005) ("Suggestive marks . . . are entitled to protection regardless of whether they have acquired secondary meaning.") (*Two Men & a Truck/Int'l, Inc. v. Thomas,* 908 F. Supp. 2d 1029, 1037 (D. Neb. 2012)).

The reason companies fight over the suggestive–descriptive distinction is that it is much easier to gain protection for a suggestive mark. These marks, like those that are arbitrary or fanciful, are "strong" marks that are said to be inherently distinctive. They can be protected as soon as they are used in commerce. But a descriptive mark is less strong; to protect it, a company must show that it has become associated in the minds of an appreciable number of buyers with a particular source.

17.2.2.2 *"Capability of being represented graphically" and "capability of distinguishing" in Europe (CTM/EUIPO)*

In Europe, there is less emphasis on the spectrum concept, and more on the distinction between inherent and acquired distinctiveness. This is discussed in depth in the cases on inherent distinctiveness covered below, especially *Windsurfing Chiemsee Produktions- und Vertriebs GmbH (WSC) v. Boots- und Segelzubehör Walter Huber,* as well as the case of *Procter & Gamble Co v. Office for Harmonisation in the Internal Market (Trade Marks and Designs) (OHIM)* (Case C-383/99 P) [2001] E.C.R. I-6251 (ECJ [EUIPO]), discussed in the notes after *Windsurfing*. Meanwhile, consider two other important threshold issues in European trademark law, the "graphic representation" requirement and the "capability of distinguishing" criterion.

CASE

Sieckmann v. Deutsche Patent und Markenamt (DPMA), Case C-273/100 (Court of Justice of the European Union, 12 December, 2002)

[Plaintiff Ralf Sieckmann attempted to register a trademark for a perfume scent. With his application, he sent a verbal description of the scent; a chemical formula for the liquid perfume; a referral to places where samples of the perfume could be found; and finally, an offer to deposit samples of the perfume at the DPMA, the German national trademark office. The DPMA refused registration, and Sieckmann appealed to the Bundespatentgericht (Federal Patents Court), which referred the case to the European Court of Justice, now the CJEU.]

Article 2 of the [EU Trademark] Directive contains a list of examples of signs of which a trade mark may consist. It is worded as follows:

> 'A trade mark may consist of any sign capable of being represented graphically, particularly words, including personal names, designs, letters, numerals, the shape of goods or of their packaging, provided that such signs are capable of distinguishing the goods or services of one undertaking from those of other undertakings.'

[Conforming German national legislation passed in 1995.]

[T]he Bundespatentgericht held that in theory odours may be capable of being accepted in trade as an independent means of identifying an undertaking, in accordance with Paragraph 3(1) of the Markengesetz [the German national trademark law]. The referring court found that the mark deposited would be capable of distinguishing the abovementioned services and would not be regarded as purely descriptive of the characteristics of those services.

By contrast, that court found that there are doubts as to whether an olfactory mark, such as that at issue in the case before it, can satisfy the requirement of graphic representability [under Article 4 of the Community Trademark Regulations, and Article 2 of the EU Trademark Directive].

Article 2 of the Directive must be interpreted as meaning that a trade mark may consist of a sign which is not in itself capable of being perceived visually, provided that it can be represented graphically. That graphic representation must enable the sign to be represented visually, particularly by means of images, lines or characters, so that it can be precisely identified. Such an interpretation is required to allow for the sound operation of the trade mark registration system.

[T]he competent authorities must know with clarity and precision the nature of the signs of which a mark consists in order to be able to fulfil their obligations in relation to the prior examination of registration applications and to the publication and maintenance of

CASE *(continued)*

an appropriate and precise register of trademarks. On the other hand, economic operators must, with clarity and precision, be able to find out about registrations or applications for registration made by their current or potential competitors and thus to receive relevant information about the rights of third parties.

Article 2 of the Directive must be interpreted as meaning that a trade mark may consist of a sign which is not in itself capable of being perceived visually, provided that it can be represented graphically, particularly by means of images, lines or characters, and that the representation is clear, precise, self-contained, easily accessible, intelligible, durable and objective.

As regards a chemical formula . . . few people would recognise in such a formula the odour in question. Such a formula is not sufficiently intelligible. In addition, . . . a chemical formula does not represent the odour of a substance, but the substance as such, and nor is it sufficiently clear and precise. It is therefore not a representation for the purposes of Article 2 of the Directive. In respect of the description of an odour, although it is graphic, it is not sufficiently clear, precise and objective.

As to the deposit of an odour sample, it does not constitute a graphic representation for the purposes of Article 2 of the Directive. Moreover, an odour sample is not sufficiently stable or durable.

NOTES

1. The key holding here concerns "capability of being represented graphically"; the registrant's use of a verbal description, and offer to deposit a sample of the perfume, were deemed inadequate under this requirement. The question remains, given the difficulty of representing the scent graphically, how a scent may properly be registered. Notice the comments in the decision regarding chemical formulas – which suggests that in some cases this might do the trick.

    The 2015 Trademark Directive changed the provision at issue in this case. Article 3 of the 2015 Directive, entitled "Signs of which a trademark might consist," now provides:

    > A trade mark may consist of any signs, in particular words, including personal names, or designs, letters, numerals, colours, the shape of goods or of the packaging of goods, or sounds, provided that such signs are capable of:
    > (a) distinguishing the goods or services of one undertaking from those of other undertakings; and
    > (b) being represented on the register in a manner which enables the competent authorities and the public to determine the clear and precise subject matter of the protection afforded to its proprietor.

2. The CJEU did *not* hold that a scent does not have the "capability of distinguishing" goods. For more insight into "capability of distinguishing," consider Jan Klink, *Germany: trade marks – letter Z – capable of distinguishing*, 25(8) Euro. I.P. Rev. (2003), at N129–130 (describing German Federal Supreme Court case finding no evidence to suggest that the single letter "Z" would not be capable of distinguishing cigarettes and related products; there is no per se prohibition on registering a single letter as a trademark). This is in general a liberal standard, with the "represented graphically" requirement as a practical constraint on its breadth.

3. In the US, as in the EU, a single color can be protected as an indication of origin. As the Supreme Court has said, "Since human beings might use as a 'symbol' or 'device' almost anything at all that is capable of carrying meaning, th[e statutory] language, read literally, is not restrictive" (*Qualitex Co. v. Jacobson Products Co.*, 514 U.S. 159, 162 (1995)) (upholding protection for a dry cleaning press pad with a distinctive color, after proof

that specific color had acquired "secondary meaning" with purchasing public). *See also T-Mobile US, Inc. v. AIO Wireless LLC*, 991 F. Supp. 2d 888 (S.D. Tex. 2014) (granting preliminary injunction to plaintiff prohibiting defendant from using registered shade of magenta/pink in connection with wireless subscriber services; finding likelihood that plaintiff will succeed at trial in proving secondary meaning for color and likelihood of confusion). In the EU, the case of *Libertel v. Benelux Merkenbureau*, Case C-104/01 (ECJ (CJEU), 6 May 2003), available at http://curia.europa.eu/juris/showPdf.jsf?text=&docid=48237&pageIndex=0&doclang=EN&mode=lst&dir=&occ=first&part=1&cid=949195, dealt directly with protection of a single color as a trademark. Plaintiff Libertel attempted to register the color orange for telecommunications services. The Benelux trademark office (which handles registrations for the "Benelux" countries, Belgium, the Netherlands, and Luxembourg) rejected the application for failure to show "acquisition of a distinctive character" (the equivalent to "secondary meaning" under US law). Libertel appealed, the case went to the Netherlands Supreme Court, and it was referred to the ECJ (now the CJEU). The court held that it is possible, in principle, for a single color to be registered as a trademark, when it is "capable of distinguishing" the goods or services of an individual company (*id.*, at pars. 40–42). After noting that there are only a limited number of readily perceived colors, and that "depleting" the colors available to competitors through trademark protection might harm consumers, the court said: "In the case of a colour per se, distinctiveness without any prior use is inconceivable save in exceptional circumstances, and particularly where the number of goods or services for which the mark is claimed is very restricted and the relevant market very specific." Thus, in the vast majority of cases, protection for a color will require proof of acquisition of distinctive character, *i.e.*, "secondary meaning" as it is called in US law:

> [A color] may acquire [a distinctive] character in relation to the goods or services claimed following the use made of it, pursuant to Article 3(3) of the Directive. That distinctive character may be acquired, *inter alia*, after the normal process of familiarising the relevant public has taken place. In such cases, the competent authority must make an overall assessment of the evidence that the mark has come to identify the product concerned as originating from a particular undertaking, and thus to distinguish that product from goods of other undertakings . . . (*id.*, at par. 67).

A variation on the theme in *Libertel* is covered by *Heidelberger Bauchemie GmbH v. DPMA*, Case C-49/02 (ECJ (CJEU), 24 June, 2004), available at http://curia.europa.eu/juris/showPdf.jsf?text=&docid=49315&pageIndex=0&doclang=EN&mode=lst&dir=&occ=first&part=1&cid=949195, which establishes that color combinations may be protected if they are systematically arranged in a set pattern. This case dealt with the German codification of Articles 2 and 3 of the Community Trademark Directive of 1988, which was in effect when it was decided. The registration document showed the plaintiff's two corporate colors (specific shades of blue and yellow), with one color on the top half of the page and the other on the bottom, and claimed the use of the two colors in any combination. The rejection by the German national trademark office (DPMA) was upheld by the court's interpretation of Article 2:

> The mere juxtaposition of two or more colours, without shape or contours, or a reference to two or more colours "in every conceivable form", as is the case with the trade mark which is the subject of [this case], does not exhibit the qualities of precision and uniformity required by Article 2 of the Directive . . .

17.2.2.3 China: inherent distinctiveness

As with "novelty" to patent law and "originality" to copyright law, "distinctiveness" is the key element in the context of trademark law, which determines whether a mark is eligible for trademark registration. A trademark can either be inherently distinctive or later acquires distinctiveness through long-term use. Inherently distinctive marks usually refer to either "fanciful marks" that are made-up words, such as "Lenovo" for computers, or "arbitrary marks" that have standard meaning but have little relevance to the features of the products, such as "Panda" for restaurants and catering services. Acquired-distinctive marks, on the other hand, refer to "suggestive or descriptive marks," which do not have the strongest distinctive features but have later acquired distinctiveness, typically through long-term use and promotional efforts, so as to be able to identify the origin of the goods and services (*see* Article 11 Chinese Trademark Law).

CASE

Jing Brand v. TRAB, Chinese Supreme People's Court, Xintizi No. 4 (2010)

Applicant, Jing Brand, filed a trademark application for its trademark "China Jing Wine" ("applied mark") to the Chinese Trademark Office on October 20, 2005, under filing No. 4953206, in Class 33 of alcoholic beverages (except beers). On February 26, 2008, the Chinese Trademark Office rejected Jing Brand's trademark application, on the grounds that the applied mark contained the words "China", which are identical with the state name of People's Republic of China, and therefore cannot be used or registered as a trademark, based on Article 10(1) and Article 28 of *Trademark Law of the People's Republic of China* ("Chinese Trademark Law").

[Unsatisfied with the rejection decision from the Chinese Trademark Office,] Jing Brand filed an appeal before the Trademark Review and Adjudication Board (TRAB), with the following arguments: First, the primary element in the applied mark is the character "Jing", which is part of Jing Brand's famous house brand. The character "China" in the applied mark is different from, *i.e.* much smaller in terms of font and style than, the prominent character "Jing" in the applied mark. Also, the applicant only included the word "China" in the mark to identify the source country of its wine. Second, according to the *Standard for Examination of Trademarks* ("The Examination Standard"), an internal examination guideline issued by the Chinese Trademark Office, the applied mark should not be prohibited for registration because the mark as a whole has enough distinctiveness.

Figure 17.2 Jing Brand's proposed trademark

CASE *(continued)*

On November 24, 2008, the TRAB rejected Jing Brand's trademark appeal, holding that Article 10(1) of the Chinese Trademark Law clearly prohibits state names from being used or registered as trademarks. Since the applied mark included the state name "China", the mark should not be approved for registration.

[Shortly afterward, Jing Brand filed an administrative review lawsuit before Beijing First Intermediate Court against the TRAB. Jing Brand claimed that, although the applied mark contained the word "China," the applied mark as a whole was not identical with or similar to the state name of China, and therefore should be approved for registration.]

During the trial, Beijing First Intermediate Court held that: the applied mark is a combination of word characters and device[s], including three Chinese characters "China," "Jing" and "Wine" and also a device of a square stamp. The Chinese character "Jing" in the applied mark is in Xing-Style font, which is vastly different from and much bigger than the other two characters in the mark. Also, the character "Jing" is prominently located on the left side of the square stamp, while the character "China" looks different from the character "Jing" in terms of font and style. The court found that TRAB's rejection decision was only based on the fact that the applied mark contained the character "China," but failed to consider the overall distinctiveness of the applied mark. As such, the court reversed the TRAB decision.

[TRAB soon filed an appeal before Beijing High People's Court]. During the appeal, Beijing High Court held that: Article 10(1) of Chinese Trademark Law prohibits marks that are identical with or similar to the state name of Peoples' Republic of China from being used or registered as trademarks. However, when a trademark includes multiple elements, and the state name is only one of such elements, the mark might be registrable as a whole [if the mark has distinctive character as a whole.] In this case, Beijing High Court concurred with Beijing First Intermediate Court's findings that the applied mark is a combination of Chinese characters and device[s], and thus possesses distinctiveness as a whole.

[TRAB soon petitioned for a retrial before the Chinese Supreme People's Court, claiming that the applied mark, which contains characters that are identical with or similar to the state name of China, should not be allowed for trademark registration based on Article 10(1) of the Chinese Trademark Law. TRAB also argued that the Examination Standard also makes clear that any mark containing words that are identical with or similar to the state name of China are prohibited from trademark use or registration, except for three scenarios.]

In the retrial before Chinese Supreme Court, TRAB also explained in great details as to why such marks should not be allowed for registration:

(1) First, the legislative purpose of Chinese Trademark Law is not only to protect the interests of trademark rights holders and that of the public, but also to uphold the dignity of the nation. The state name, national flag, national emblem, national anthem and other signs of the People's Republic of China are the symbols of national dignity. To ensure that the market participants use the state name in a reasonable and lawful way

CASE *(continued)*

in commercial activities, marks that contain the state name often receive strict scrutiny during trademark examination. In fact, most marks that contain the state name will not pass the examination standard and will not be allowed for trademark registration.

(2) Under exceptional circumstances, the combination of "China" with other distinctive marks may be used together to serve as a trademark, identifying the source of its goods and services. But such cases are rare and need to go through careful scrutiny.

In this case, the company name of the applicant is "Jing Brand," and does not include the character "China". The applied trademark includes the character "China," which purpose [based on the applicant] is to identify the source of its products. As such, such a use does not fall into the exceptions under which a state name might be used for a trademark. Therefore, the applicant's use of "China" in its applied mark with the enterprise name "Jing" constitutes an inappropriate use of the state name.

[As such, TRAB concluded that the trial court and appellate court erred in their rulings, which decisions would loosen the registration requirements for state names and allow ineligible trademarks for registration.]

[During the re-examination,] the Supreme People's Court held that: trademarks are used to identify the source of goods and services from various manufacturers and service providers. According to Article 10(1) of Chinese Trademark Law, the words or devices that are identical with or similar to the state name of People's Republic of China shall not be used or registered as trademarks. The legislative language "*identical with or similar to the state name of People's Republic of China*" in this provision refers to circumstances, under which a trademark as a whole is identical with or similar to the state name of China. As to those trademarks, which contain a state name but do not resemble with a state name overall when combined with other elements, they should not be deemed as "identical with or similar to the state name of China."

Here, the applied mark includes three Chinese characters "China," "Jing" and "Wine." Although it contains the word "China," the mark as a whole is not identical with or similar to the state name of China, due to the inclusion of other elements in the mark such as "Jing" and "Wine." Therefore, this Court rejects TRAB's argument on appeal.

However, this Court recognizes that state name is the symbol of a country, and therefore, the [inappropriate] use of a state name in a trademark for commercial purpose may eventually diminish the value of the state name, which in turn, might tarnish the dignity of the nation or bring other adverse effect to the public interest and social order. Therefore, for trademarks that contain words identical with or similar to a state name, in addition to Article 10(1) of Chinese Trademark Law, the TRAB should also consider other applicable clauses in the Chinese Trademark Law, when deciding its registrability. For example, if such marks might have adverse effect to the state's image and public order, they shall not be used or registered as trademarks.

This Court finds that Beijing First Intermediate Court and Beijing High Court were correct to revoke TRAB's decision but erred in their reasoning. In this case, TRAB still

> **CASE** *(continued)*
>
> needs to examine whether the applied mark violates other relevant provisions of the Chinese Trademark Law. This Court hereby (1) affirms the Beijing High Court's final administrative judgment, and (2) requests the TRAB to re-examine Jing Brand's application for trademark registration.
> This is the final ruling.

17.2.3 Descriptive marks and secondary meaning in the US

Descriptive marks are those which describe the products they refer to. A good example is the trademark 24 HOUR FITNESS for a gym. *See 24 Hour Fitness USA, Inc. v. 24/7 Tribeca Fitness, LLC*, 277 F. Supp. 2d 356, 68 U.S.P.Q.2d 1031, 1034 (S.D. N.Y. 2003) (24 Hour Fitness is descriptive but still protectable, because the mark owner has established secondary meaning).

Other marks characterized as descriptive include CHAP STIK (for lip balm), CAR FRESHNER (for car air freshener), and BEER NUTS (for nuts often served with beer). *See* 2 Thomas J. McCarthy, *McCarthy on Trademarks and Unfair Competition* §11:24 (4th ed. & Supp., 2016). Further descriptive marks would include "WRITES WELL" for pens, and "DURABLE TREAD" for car tires.

Judge Frank Easterbrook of the Seventh Circuit Court of Appeals provides a good account of how courts draw the line between suggestive and descriptive marks:

> Bliss Salon argues that . . . the word "bliss" is "suggestive," and all "suggestive" marks are protected automatically, without need to prove secondary meaning or likely confusion. "Bliss" is not generic, and it does not describe any attribute of hair styling or shampoo. Emotions are not product attributes; if one could achieve "bliss" by washing one's hair many religious leaders and psychoanalysts would be out of business. Thus [Bliss argues] the word must be "suggestive," and a suggestive mark creates an entitlement to protection from usurpers, the argument wraps up.
> Suggestive ("Tide" laundry detergent), arbitrary ("Apple" computers), and fanciful ("Exxon" gasoline) marks collectively are distinctive in the sense that secondary meaning is likely to develop, as a result of which any duplicate use of the name is likely to breed confusion about the product's source. Generic marks, on the other hand, designate the products themselves rather than any particular maker, and descriptive marks might (but usually won't) acquire distinctiveness.

A court cannot choose between the "descriptive" and "suggestive" categories on the basis of a dictionary; Judge Friendly's continuum [in *Abercrombie & Fitch*] is functional, and placement must be functional too. This is why we held in *Platinum Home Mortgage Corp. v. Platinum Financial Group*, 149 F.3d 722, 730 (7th Cir.1998), that the word "platinum" is descriptive rather than suggestive in the financial-services industry. Platinum, like the phrase "gilt-edged," suggests high quality or elegance, and issuers of credit cards or mortgage loans may choose it because of the association with the upper crust; in this *linguistic* sense the word is suggestive. But because so many firms use the word (and the color) for financial products, it cannot be inherently distinctive; quite the contrary, it is no more distinctive than a "gold card" or "born with a silver spoon in his mouth." Functionally, therefore, the word had to go in the descriptive category. "Tide" detergent is linguistically suggestive (it suggests the cleansing action of water), but this mark is and remains *legally* suggestive only because it has retained distinctiveness as a product identifier. Bliss marks are a glut on the market in hair styling and beauty care. They are not distinctive, so the word does not belong in the "suggestive" cubbyhole. If Bliss Salon wants to get anywhere in this litigation, it will have to prove that its mark has acquired secondary meaning and that Bliss World's use of the same mark is likely to cause confusion about source in or near Wilmette. See *Sunmark, Inc. v. Ocean Spray Cranberries, Inc.*,64 F.3d 1055 (7th Cir.1995); cf. *Zazú Designs v. L'Oréal, S.A.*, 979 F.2d 499 (7th Cir.1992) (*Bliss Salon Day Spa v. Bliss World LLC*, 268 F.3d 494, 496–97 (7th Cir. 2001) (Easterbrook, J.)).

When a mark is classified as descriptive, the mark owner must prove that the mark is associated with a single source in order for it be protected under the Lanham Act. This is the secondary meaning requirement. There is no single way to prove secondary meaning.

One traditional way of proving secondary meaning is by circumstantial evidence, in particular the seller's efforts in advertising the mark throughout a wide group of prospective buyers (*Reader's Digest Ass'n v. Conservative Digest*, 821 F.2d 800 (D.C. Cir. 1987)). The court there said that evidence of substantial sales and promotion, while probative of secondary meaning, is not dispositive, because the company's promotional efforts and high sales may not in fact succeed in establishing secondary meaning in the public mind. However, the court was clear that this can be powerful circumstantial evidence of secondary meaning: "But to say that proof of extensive advertising and substantial sales may not be probative of secondary meaning is to defy both logic and common sense" (*id*, at 805).

Other circumstantial evidence can include the number of actual sales made, see, *e.g.*, *Arrow Fastener Co., Inc. v. Stanley Works*, 59 F.3d 384, 393 (2d Cir.

1995), and the size of the seller. *See American Scientific Chemical, Inc. v. American Hospital Supply Corp.*, 690 F.2d 791 (9th Cir. 1982); *Echo Travel, Inc. v. Travel Associates, Inc.*, 870 F.2d 1264 (7th Cir. 1989).

More direct evidence takes the form of survey evidence. *See Vision Sports, Inc. v. Melville Corp.*, 888 F.2d 609 (9th Cir. 1989) (expert surveys are the best evidence of secondary meaning). *See also Co-Rect Products, Inc. v. Marvy! Advertising Photography, Inc.*, 780 F.2d 1324, n.9 (8th Cir. 1985) ("Consumer surveys are recognized by several circuits as the most direct and persuasive evidence of secondary meaning").

17.2.4 Trade dress: product packaging and product configuration

CASE

Wal-Mart Stores, Inc. v. Samara Brothers, Inc., 529 U.S. 205 (2000)

Justice Scalia delivered the opinion of the Court.

In this case, we decide under what circumstances a product's design is distinctive, and therefore protectible, in an action for infringement of unregistered trade dress under §43(a) of the Trademark Act of 1946 (Lanham Act), 60 Stat. 441, as amended, 15 U.S.C. §1125(a). Respondent Samara Brothers, Inc., designs and manufactures children's clothing. Its primary product is a line of spring/summer one-piece seersucker outfits decorated with appliques of hearts, flowers, fruits, and the like. A number of chain stores, including JCPenney, sell this line of clothing under contract with Samara.

Petitioner Wal-Mart Stores, Inc., is one of the nation's best known retailers, selling among other things children's clothing. In 1995, Wal-Mart contracted with one of its suppliers to manufacture a line of children's outfits for sale in the 1996 spring/summer season. Wal-Mart sent photographs of a number of garments from Samara's line, on which [Wal-Mart's] garments were to be based; 16 of Samara's garments, many of which contained copyrighted elements [were copied]. In 1996, Wal-Mart briskly sold the so-called knockoffs, generating more than $1.15 million in gross profits...

[Walmart sued for, among other things,] infringement of unregistered trade dress under §43(a) of the Lanham Act, 15 U.S.C. §1125(a). After a weeklong trial, the jury found in favor of Samara on all of its claims. The Second Circuit affirmed, and we granted certiorari.

The Lanham Act provides for the registration of trademarks, which it defines in §45 to include "any word, name, symbol, or device, or any combination thereof [used or intended to be used] to identify and distinguish [a producer's] goods... from those manufactured or sold by others and to indicate the source of the goods..." 15 U.S.C. §1127. In addition to protecting registered marks, the Lanham Act, in §43(a), gives a producer a cause of action

CASE *(continued)*

for the use by any person of "any word, term, name, symbol, or device, or any combination thereof... which... is likely to cause confusion... as to the origin, sponsorship, or approval of his or her goods." 15 U.S.C. §1125(a). It is the latter provision that is at issue in this case.

The breadth of the definition of marks registrable under §2, and of the confusion-producing elements recited as actionable by §43(a), has been held to embrace not just word marks, such as "Nike," and symbol marks, such as Nike's "swoosh" symbol, but also "trade dress" – a category that originally included only the packaging, or "dressing," of a product, but in recent years has been expanded by many courts of appeals to encompass the design of a product. These courts have assumed, often without discussion, that trade dress constitutes a "symbol" or "device" for purposes of the relevant sections, and we conclude likewise. "Since human beings might use as a 'symbol' or 'device' almost anything at all that is capable of carrying meaning, this language, read literally, is not restrictive." *Qualitex Co. v. Jacobson Products Co.*, 514 U.S. 159, 162 (1995). This reading of §2 and §43(a) is buttressed by a recently added subsection of §43(a), §43(a)(3), which refers specifically to "civil action[s] for trade dress infringement under this chapter for trade dress not registered on the principal register." 15 U.S.C.A. §1125(a)(3) (Oct. 1999 Supp.).

The text of §43(a) provides little guidance as to the circumstances under which unregistered trade dress may be protected. It does require that a producer show that the allegedly infringing feature is not "functional," see §43(a)(3), and is likely to cause confusion with the product for which protection is sought, see §43(a)(1)(A), 15 U.S.C. §1125(a)(1)(A). Nothing in §43(a) explicitly requires a producer to show that its trade dress is distinctive, but courts have universally imposed that requirement, since without distinctiveness the trade dress would not "cause confusion... as to the origin, sponsorship, or approval of [the] goods," as the section requires. Distinctiveness is, moreover, an explicit prerequisite for registration of trade dress under §2, and "the general principles qualifying a mark for registration under §2 of the Lanham Act are for the most part applicable in determining whether an unregistered mark is entitled to protection under §43(a)." *Two Pesos, Inc. v. Taco Cabana, Inc.*, 505 U.S. 763, 768 (1992) (citations omitted).

In evaluating the distinctiveness of a mark under §2 (and therefore, by analogy, under §43(a)), courts have held that a mark can be distinctive in one of two ways. First, a mark is inherently distinctive if "[its] intrinsic nature serves to identify a particular source." Ibid. In the context of word marks, courts have applied the now-classic test originally formulated by Judge Friendly, in which word marks that are "arbitrary" ("Camel" cigarettes), "fanciful" ("Kodak" film), or "suggestive" ("Tide" laundry detergent) are held to be inherently distinctive. See *Abercrombie & Fitch Co. v. Hunting World, Inc.*, 537 F.2d 4, 10-11 (C.A.2 1976). Second, a mark has acquired distinctiveness, even if it is not inherently distinctive, if it has developed secondary meaning, which occurs when, "in the minds of the public, the primary significance of a [mark] is to identify the source of the product rather than the product itself." *Inwood Laboratories, Inc. v. Ives Laboratories, Inc.*, 456 U.S. 844, 851, n. 11 (1982).

CASE *(continued)*

Nothing in §2 demands the conclusion that *every* category of mark necessarily includes some marks "by which the goods of the applicant may be distinguished from the goods of others" *without* secondary meaning – that in every category some marks are inherently distinctive.

Indeed, with respect to at least one category of mark – colors – we have held that no mark can ever be inherently distinctive. See *Qualitex*, 514 U.S., at 162–163. In *Qualitex*, petitioner manufactured and sold green-gold dry-cleaning press pads. After respondent began selling pads of a similar color, petitioner brought suit under §43(a), then added a claim under §32 after obtaining registration for the color of its pads. We held that a color could be protected as a trademark, but only upon a showing of secondary meaning. Reasoning by analogy to the *Abercrombie & Fitch* test developed for word marks, we noted that a product's color is unlike a "fanciful," "arbitrary," or "suggestive" mark, since it does not "almost *automatically* tell a customer that [it] refer[s] to a brand," ibid., and does not "immediately. . .signal a brand or a product 'source,'" id., at 163. However, we noted that, "over time, customers may come to treat a particular color on a product or its packaging . . . as signifying a brand." Id., at 162–163. Because a color, like a "descriptive" word mark, could eventually "come to indicate a product's origin," we concluded that it could be protected *upon a showing of secondary meaning.* Ibid.

It seems to us that design, like color, is not inherently distinctive. The attribution of inherent distinctiveness to certain categories of word marks and product packaging derives from the fact that the very purpose of attaching a particular word to a product, or encasing it in a distinctive packaging, is most often to identify the source of the product. Although the words and packaging can serve subsidiary functions – a suggestive word mark (such as "Tide" for laundry detergent), for instance, may invoke positive connotations in the consumer's mind, and a garish form of packaging (such as Tide's squat, brightly decorated plastic bottles for its liquid laundry detergent) may attract an otherwise indifferent consumer's attention on a crowded store shelf – their predominant function remains source identification.

In the case of product design, as in the case of color, we think consumer predisposition to equate the feature with the source does not exist. Consumers are aware of the reality that, almost invariably, even the most unusual of product designs – such as a cocktail shaker shaped like a penguin – is intended not to identify the source, but to render the product itself more useful or more appealing.

The fact that product design almost invariably serves purposes other than source identification not only renders inherent distinctiveness problematic; it also renders application of an inherent-distinctiveness principle more harmful to other consumer interests. Consumers should not be deprived of the benefits of competition with regard to the utilitarian and esthetic purposes that product design ordinarily serves by a rule of law that facilitates plausible threats of suit against new entrants based upon alleged inherent distinctiveness.

Respondent contends that our decision in *Two Pesos* forecloses a conclusion that

CASE *(continued)*

product-design trade dress can never be inherently distinctive. In that case, we held that the trade dress of a chain of Mexican restaurants, which the plaintiff described as "a festive eating atmosphere having interior dining and patio areas decorated with artifacts, bright colors, paintings and murals," 505 U.S., at 765 (internal quotation marks and citation omitted), could be protected under §43(a) without a showing of secondary meaning, see id., at 776. *Two Pesos* unquestionably establishes the legal principle that trade dress can be inherently distinctive, see, e.g., id., at 773, but it does not establish that *product-design* trade dress can be. *Two Pesos* is inapposite to our holding here because the trade dress at issue, the decor of a restaurant, seems to us not to constitute product *design*. It was either product packaging – which, as we have discussed, normally *is* taken by the consumer to indicate origin – or else some tertium quid [third thing, i.e., other thing] that is akin to product packaging and has no bearing on the present case.

Respondent replies that this manner of distinguishing *Two Pesos* will force courts to draw difficult lines between product-design and product-packaging trade dress. There will indeed be some hard cases at the margin: a classic glass Coca-Cola bottle, for instance, may constitute packaging for those consumers who drink the Coke and then discard the bottle, but may constitute the product itself for those consumers who are bottle collectors, or part of the product itself for those consumers who buy Coke in the classic glass bottle, rather than a can, because they think it more stylish to drink from the former. We believe, however, that the frequency and the difficulty of having to distinguish between product design and product packaging will be much less than the frequency and the difficulty of having to decide when a product design is inherently distinctive. To the extent there are close cases, we believe that courts should err on the side of caution and classify ambiguous trade dress as product design, thereby requiring secondary meaning. The very closeness will suggest the existence of relatively small utility in adopting an inherent-distinctiveness principle, and relatively great consumer benefit in requiring a demonstration of secondary meaning.

We hold that, in an action for infringement of unregistered trade dress under §43(a) of the Lanham Act, a product's design is distinctive, and therefore protectible, only upon a showing of secondary meaning. The judgment of the Second Circuit is reversed, and the case is remanded for further proceedings consistent with this opinion.

NOTES AND QUESTIONS

1. The Supreme Court establishes that product packaging can be inherently distinctive while product design cannot. Are you convinced that the Court is correct that close cases (such as the Coca-Cola bottle) should be characterized as product design and hence subject to the higher threshold of secondary meaning? Obviously, after *Wal-Mart*, the parties will fight over the issue of whether the design claimed as trade dress is product design or packaging. Secondary meaning is always required for product design but only sometimes required for product packaging. For an example of a product "package" (or perhaps "tertium quid," Justice Scalia calls it), see *Two Pesos, Inc. v. Taco Cabana, Inc.*, 505 U.S. 763 (1992) (restaurant appearance and décor were inherently distinctive); *Miller's Ale House, Inc. v. Boynton Carolina Ale House, LLC*, 702 F.3d 1312, 1323–1324 (11th Cir. 2012) (restaurant décor, menu, and server attire were product packaging,

not product design; but they lacked secondary meaning). For an example of product design, *see Fedders Corp. v. Elite Classics*, 268 F. Supp. 2d 1051 (S.D. Ill. 2003), related reference, 279 F. Supp. 2d 965 (S.D. Ill. 2003) (curved front piece on air conditioner unit; no secondary meaning proven: preliminary injunction denied).

17.2.5 Europe: acquired distinctiveness

 CASE

Windsurfing Chiemsee Produktions- und Vertriebs GmbH (WSC) v. Boots- und Segelzubehör Walter Huber, Cases C-108/97 and C-109/97 (ECJ (CJEU) 4 May 1999), available at http://curia.europa.eu/juris/showPdf.jsf?text=&docid=44567&pageIndex=0&doclang=EN&mode=lst&dir=&occ=first&part=1&cid=347091

[Two] questions [under Article 3 of the EU Trademark Directive of 1988, in effect at the time of this decision] were raised in two sets of proceedings between Windsurfing Chiemsee Produktions- und Vertriebs GmbH (hereinafter 'Windsurfing Chiemsee'), on the one hand, and Boots- und Segelzubehör Walter Huber (hereinafter 'Huber') and Franz Attenberger, on the other, relating to the use by Huber and Mr Attenberger of the designation 'Chiemsee' for the sale of sportswear.
[Article 3 is entitled "Grounds for Invalidity." Article 3.1 says in relevant part: "3.1. The following shall not be registered or if registered shall be liable to be declared invalid: . . .

(b) trade marks which are devoid of any distinctive character;
(c) trade marks which consist exclusively of signs or indications which may serve, in trade, to designate the kind, quality, quantity, intended purpose, value, geographical origin, or the time of production of the goods or of rendering of the service, or other characteristics of the goods or service;
(d) trade marks which consist exclusively of signs or indications which have become customary in the current language or in the bona fide and established practices of the trade . . ."

Article 3.3 then says:]
  "3. A trade mark shall not be refused registration or be declared invalid in accordance

CASE *(continued)*

with paragraph 1 (b), (c) or (d) if, before the date of application for registration and following the use which has been made of it, it has acquired a distinctive character. Any Member State may in addition provide that this provision shall also apply where the distinctive character was acquired after the date of application for registration or after the date of registration".

[The court then addressed the implementation of this Article of the Directive in German law, which was the basis for the trademark infringement suit in this case.]

Pursuant to [the] Markengesetz [German Trademark law in effect at the time of this decision], Section 8(2)(2) [prevents registration of marks which "consist exclusively of . . . indications which may serve in trade to designate the . . . geographical origin . . . or other characteristics of the goods," i.e., which are descriptive of the goods. Under Article 8(3), however, this provision] does not apply "if the mark, before the time of the decision on registration, as a result of its use for the goods . . . in respect of which registration has been applied for, has gained acceptance among the relevant class of persons".

The Chiemsee is the largest lake in Bavaria, with an area of 80 km^2. It is a tourist destination and surfing is one of the activities carried on there. The surrounding area, called the 'Chiemgau', is primarily agricultural. Windsurfing Chiemsee, which is based near the shores of the Chiemsee, sells sports fashion clothing, shoes and other sports goods which are designed by a sister company based in the same place, but are manufactured elsewhere. The goods bear the designation 'Chiemsee'. Between 1992 and 1994, Windsurfing Chiemsee registered that designation in Germany as a picture trade mark in the form of various graphic designs, in some cases with additional features or words such as "Chiemsee Jeans" and "Windsurfing – Chiemsee – Active Wear".

Huber has been selling sports clothing such as T-shirts and sweat-shirts since 1995 in a town situated near the shores of the Chiemsee. The clothing bears the designation 'Chiemsee', but this is depicted in a different graphic form from that of the trade marks which identify Windsurfing Chiemsee's products. Mr Attenberger sells the same type of sports clothing in the Chiemsee area, also bearing the designation "Chiemsee", but using different graphic forms and, for certain products, additional features different from those of Windsurfing Chiemsee.

In the main proceedings, Windsurfing Chiemsee challenges the use by Huber and Mr Attenberger of the name "Chiemsee", claiming that, notwithstanding the differences in graphic representation of the marks on the products in question, there is a likelihood of confusion with its designation "Chiemsee" with which, it claims, the public is familiar and which has in any case been in use since 1990. The defendants in the main proceedings, on the other hand, contend that, since the word "Chiemsee" is an indication which designates geographical origin and must consequently remain available, it is not capable of protection, and that using it in a different graphic form from that used by Windsurfing Chiemsee cannot create any likelihood of confusion.

[T]he national court is essentially asking in what circumstances Article 3(1)(c) of the

CASE *(continued)*

Directive precludes registration of a trade mark which consists exclusively of a geographical name. In particular, it is asking:

- if the application of Article 3(1)(c) depends on whether there is a real, current or serious need to leave the sign or indication free; and
- what connection there must be between the geographical location and the goods in respect of which registration of the geographical name for that location as a trade mark is applied for.

Article 3(1)(c) of the Directive pursues an aim which is in the public interest, namely that descriptive signs or indications relating to the categories of goods or services in respect of which registration is applied for may be freely used by all, including as collective marks or as part of complex or graphic marks. Article 3(1)(c) therefore prevents such signs and indications from being reserved to one undertaking alone because they have been registered as trade marks.

Article 3(1)(c) of the Directive is not confined to prohibiting the registration of geographical names as trade marks solely where they designate specified geographical locations which are already famous, or are known for the category of goods concerned, and which are therefore associated with those goods in the mind of the relevant class of persons, that is to say in the trade and amongst average consumers of that category of goods in the territory in respect of which registration is applied for. Indeed, it is clear from the actual wording of Article 3(l)(c), which refers to '. . . indications which may serve . . . to designate . . . geographical origin', that geographical names which are liable to be used by undertakings must remain available to such undertakings as indications of the geographical origin of the category of goods concerned.

Thus, under Article 3(1)(c) of the Directive, the competent authority must assess whether a geographical name in respect of which application for registration as a trade mark is made designates a place which is currently associated in the mind of the relevant class of persons with the category of goods concerned, or whether it is reasonable to assume that such an association may be established in the future. In the latter case, when assessing whether the geographical name is capable, in the mind of the relevant class of persons, of designating the origin of the category of goods in question, regard must be had more particularly to the degree of familiarity amongst such persons with that name, with the characteristics of the place designated by the name, and with the category of goods concerned.

[I]t cannot be ruled out that the name of a lake may serve to designate geographical origin within the meaning of Article 3(l)(c), even for goods such as those in the main proceedings, provided that the name could be understood by the relevant class of persons to include the shores of the lake or the surrounding area. It follows from the foregoing that the application of Article 3(1)(c) of the Directive does not depend on there being a real, current or serious need to leave a sign or indication free ('Freihaltebedürfnis') under German case-law.

CASE *(continued)*

[W]hilst an indication of the geographical origin of goods to which Article 3(1)(c) of the Directive applies usually indicates the place where the goods were or could be manufactured, the connection between a category of goods and a geographical location might depend on other ties, such as the fact that the goods were conceived and designed in the geographical location concerned.

[J]ust as distinctive character is one of the general conditions for registering a trade mark under Article 3(1)(b), distinctive character acquired through use means that the mark must serve to identify the product in respect of which registration is applied for as originating from a particular undertaking, and thus to distinguish that product from goods of other undertakings.

It follows that a geographical name may be registered as a trade mark if, following the use which has been made of it, it has come to identify the product in respect of which registration is applied for as originating from a particular undertaking and thus to distinguish that product from goods of other undertakings. Where that is the case, the geographical designation has gained a new significance and its connotation, no longer purely descriptive, justifies its registration as a trade mark. Windsurfing Chiemsee and the Commission are therefore right to assert that Article 3(3) does not permit any differentiation as regards distinctiveness by reference to the perceived importance of keeping the geographical name available for use by other undertakings.

In determining whether a mark has acquired distinctive character following the use made of it, the competent authority must make an overall assessment of the evidence that the mark has come to identify the product concerned as originating from a particular undertaking, and thus to distinguish that product from goods of other undertakings.

In that connection, regard must be had in particular to the specific nature of the geographical name in question. Indeed, where a geographical name is very well known, it can acquire distinctive character under Article 3(3) of the Directive only if there has been long-standing and intensive use of the mark by the undertaking applying for registration. A fortiori, where a name is already familiar as an indication of geographical origin in relation to a certain category of goods, an undertaking applying for registration of the name in respect of goods in that category must show that the use of the mark – both long-standing and intensive – is particularly well established.

In assessing the distinctive character of a mark in respect of which registration has been applied for, the following may also be taken into account: the market share held by the mark; how intensive, geographically widespread and long-standing use of the mark has been; the amount invested by the undertaking in promoting the mark; the proportion of the relevant class of persons who, because of the mark, identify goods as originating from a particular undertaking; and statements from chambers of commerce and industry or other trade and professional associations.

If, on the basis of those factors, the competent authority finds that the relevant class of persons, or at least a significant proportion thereof, identify goods as originating from a particular undertaking because of the trade mark, it must hold that the requirement for

> **CASE** *(continued)*
>
> registering the mark laid down in Article 3(3) of the Directive is satisfied. However, the circumstances in which that requirement may be regarded as satisfied cannot be shown to exist solely by reference to general, abstract data such as predetermined percentages. [At the same time, use of an opinion poll is an accepted method, if permitted by national law.]

NOTES

1. There has been some tension in the EU case law following the *Windsurfing* case. In *Procter & Gamble Co. v. Office for Harmonisation in the Internal Market (Trade Marks and Designs) (OHIM)* (Case C-383/99 P) [2001] E.C.R. I-6251 (ECJ [EUIPO]), the ECJ (now CJEU) directed attention away from the per se rule of unregistrability stressed in *Windsurfing*. Rather than categorize Article 7 of the Community Trademark Regulation as a categorical prohibition on registering descriptive marks (which had been the emphasis in *Windsurfing*), the *Procter & Gamble* court highlighted the fact that registration is only prohibited until the point where a registrant can show acquired distinctiveness. This is in contrast to *Windsurfing*. As one commentator said,

   > The Baby-Dry [*Procter & Gamble*] approach allows a greater number of trade marks to be registered because the criterion of registrability is the ability to act as a trade mark, so anything that can function in this way could be registered. In contrast, the rationale behind Windsurfing, which recognises the German idea of Freihaltebedürfnis ("real, current or serious need to keep an indication free") leads to a narrower range of registrable marks, because what must be kept free is, to some extent, subjective and so can lead to a greater number of exclusions. Additionally, there is a degree of speculation in deciding what must be kept free, as there is a need to protect in the public interest not only signs that other traders are currently using, but also those that other traders might need to use in order to compete in the future. Such guesswork may result in an overbroad estimate of what will be needed by others many years down the line (Ilanah Simon, *What's Cooking at the CFI? More Guidance on Descriptive and Non Distinctive Trade Marks*, 25 Euro. I.P. Rev. 322, 322–23 (2003)).

   To the extent there is tension between *Windsurfing* and *Procter and Gamble*, it was resolved to a great degree in *Dart Industries Inc v. Office for Harmonisation in the Internal Market (Trade Marks and Designs) (OHIM)* (Case T-360/00) [2002] E.C.R. II-3867 (CFI (2nd Chamber)), available at http://curia.europa.eu/juris/showPdf.jsf?text=&docid=47751&pageIndex=0&doclang=EN&mode=lst&dir=&occ=first&part=1&cid=552023. *Dart Industries* reversed an OHIM (now EUIPO) panel finding that the mark "UltraPlus" (for ovenware, microwave and convection oven dishes, etc.) was descriptive, and incapable of serving as a trademark. The Court of First Instance of the EU held instead that while "Ultra-pure" or "Ultra-strong" might be descriptive (with the "ultra" simply highlighting a quality or feature of the product), "Ultra-pure" could not be descriptive because it was a made-up word. Both parts were "exemplary," or evocative of "going beyond the standard." Taken together, the word "Ultra-pure" is a "made-up word" (*i.e.*, fanciful), and is therefore fully capable of serving as a trademark. The *Freihaltebedürfnis* rationale featured in *Windsurfing* was not mentioned, as the concern for "trademark depletion" was not implicated in the case of a made-up word.

2. On the closely related topic of trademark-like protection for food and wine products associated with particular regions ("Geographical Indications"), *see* Bernard O'Connor, *The Legal Protection of Geographical Indications*, 1 I.P.Q. (2004); Council Regulation (EC) no. 510/2006, Article 13, March 20, 2006, on the protection of geographical indications and designations of origin for agricultural products and foodstuffs, available at http://eur-lex.europa.eu/legal-content/en/ALL/?uri=CELEX:32006R0510; Dev Gangjee, *Relocating the Law of Geographical Indications* (2012).

3. What if a trademark identifies a geographic area well known for one type of product, but the mark itself is used on other products? *See, e.g., Tea Board v. Office for Harmonisation in the Internal Market (Trade Marks and Designs) (OHIM)* (Case T-624/13), [2015] E.T.M.R. 52. There a registrant registered the name

"Darjeeling" (well known as a locale for growing tea) for use on clothing, footwear, headgear, and other goods) and faced an opposition from the operator of the collective mark for Darjeeling tea. The General Court agreed with the OHIM (now EUIPO) in rejecting the opposition: "The mere possibility that the average consumer might believe that the goods and services provided under a trade mark were connected with goods originating in the geographical area of the same name was not sufficient to establish similarity or identity between the goods and services."

17.2.6 China: acquired distinctiveness

As mentioned earlier, non-inherent-distinctive marks can also acquire distinctiveness through later use. The following cases explain the standards in determining secondary meaning in trademark registrability cases.

CASE

BestBuy v. TRAB, Chinese Supreme People's Court, Xingtizi No. 9 (2011)

The appellant Best Buy filed a trademark application for mark "BEST BUY and device" ("applied mark") to the Chinese Trademark Office on February 12, 2004, under filing No. 3909917, in Class 35 covering services such as advertising (for others), import and export agency, etc. The applied mark consists of English words "BEST," "BUY" and also a yellow square-shaped logo, with the two English words lining vertically inside the logo.
On February 28, 2006, the Chinese Trademark Office rejected Best Buy's trademark application on the grounds that the applied mark was descriptive to the quality and characteristic of the service provided.
 On March 17, 2006, Best Buy filed an appeal before the TRAB, claiming that (1) the applied mark as a whole possesses certain distinctive character in its visual design, word combination and meaning, thus satisfying the distinctiveness requirement of trademark registration; and (2) that the applied mark has also acquired distinctiveness through extensive and continuous commercial use. [On June 16, 2006, Best Buy submitted new evidence to prove that its applied mark has acquired distinctiveness through commercial use, including evidence of its retail stores located in San Francisco and other cities in California, its successful trademark registrations in other countries, its trademark logos posted on its website, and also a report prepared by a consulting firm, which shows the number of visitors from mainland China on its official website.]
 On May 28, 2008, the TRAB rejected Best Buy's appeal, holding that the word "BEST" in the applied mark means "the best, most excellent and most beneficial," and the word "BUY" in the mark means "to purchase, sales and trade, etc." As such, "BEST BUY" in the applied mark can be interpreted as "the best trade or the best sale." When the applied mark is used in connection with its specific services, TRAB held that "Best Buy" indicated the

CASE *(continued)*

quality and characteristic of its services, thus lacking the distinctiveness required for a trademark. Pursuant to Article 11 Item 1(2), 1(3) and Article 28 of Chinese Trademark Law, the TRAB rejected the appellant's appeal.

[Best Buy shortly filed an administrative lawsuit before the Beijing First Intermediate Court against the TRAB's decision.]

During the trial, Beijing First Intermediate Court held that: the applied mark is a combination of word characters and device, including the English words "BEST" and "BUY" and a device of a yellow-shaded square. The two English words, which are vertically aligned inside the yellow-shaded square, are more conspicuous to the consumers, and thus more distinctly identifiable. Given the fact that Chinese customers are quite familiar with the commonly used English words "BEST" and "BUY," they will interpret the mark as "the best deal" or "the best bargain." As such, the applied mark describes the characteristics of the designated services, and lacks the distinctiveness required for a trademark to identify the sources of goods and services. Therefore, Beijing First Intermediate Court affirmed the TRAB's decision to reject the applied mark for registration.

[Later, Best Buy appealed before Beijing High Court.]

Beijing High Court found that, pursuant to Article 11(1)(2) of the Chinese Trademark Law, TRAB correctly rejected the appellant's trademark application for "BEST BUY," which mark directly described the quality and characteristics of its designated services. From the overall visual effect of the applied mark, "BEST" and "BUY" are more conspicuous to the consumers. The former word means "the best/superior", while the latter means "deal/bargain." Therefore, the applied mark directly describes the quality and characteristics of the relevant services.

In addition, Beijing High Court held that the new evidence submitted by Best Buy – proof of its retail stores in California, its trademark registrations in other countries, trademarks posted on its website, and data of its website traffic – was insufficient to prove that the applied mark has acquired distinctiveness in China through long-time commercial use. Therefore, Beijing High Court rejected Best Buy's appeal and affirmed the lower court's ruling.

Best Buy continued to request for a re-trial before the Chinese Supreme People's Court, claiming that:

(1) The applied mark has acquired distinctiveness [through long-time commercial use and promotional efforts.] First, the applied mark is a unique combination of a square shape logo in bright yellow color, and the English words "BEST" and "BUY." The yellow square logo in the applied mark was originally created by Best Buy, and is the most distinctive part of the applied mark and has already been approved for registration in China in Class 35 and other classes. Best Buy then added the words of "BEST" and "BUY" to the foreground of the registered yellow square logo, thus creating a new mark including a device, color and letters. As such, the applied mark has distinctive

CASE *(continued)*

character as a whole and can serve to identify the sources of goods or services. Further, the applied mark has been approved for registration in many English-speaking countries, [which also proves the distinctiveness of the mark as a whole]. Moreover, in China, to Chinese consumers whose native language is not English, the logo in the applied mark, rather than the English letters "BEST" and "BUY," is the more prominent and identifiable element. Because the yellow square logo is a registered mark in China, the applied mark, which has the distinctive yellow square log plus the applicant's business name "BEST BUY," should also be approved for trademark registration.

(2) The applied mark has also acquired distinctiveness through extensive use in China and can serve to identify the source of its services, thus should be granted for trademark registration.

[Best Buy also submitted 531 pages of supplemental evidence in the trial proceeding to establish that the applied mark has acquired secondary meaning through extensive use and commercial promotions in China, and that it has become the only identification linking between the trademark and its service provider.]

Chinese Supreme People's Court confirmed the facts found by the trial court and the appellate court. In addition, this Court found that Best Buy submitted 75 pieces of evidence, proving its commercial use of the applied mark in Mainland China. This Court also recognized that Best Buy ranked No. 1 in electric appliance retails in North America and was named one of the Fortune Global 500 companies. In January 2007, Best Buy opened its first store in Shanghai and attracted wide coverage and attention from the industry . . .

This Court held that, it is reasonable for the interested parties to request an opportunity to present their claims and submit evidence before a decision is made, especially when such a decision might be an unfavorable decision to the interested party. Likewise, in the trademark appeal process, TRAB should also give the applicant an opportunity to present its arguments and submit new evidence if TRAB decides to reject the subject appeal on different legal grounds from those of the Chinese Trademark Office in its rejection decision.

During the judicial review of trademark registration related disputes, all the new evidence should be considered because the trademark registration procedure is not finished yet . . . Here, Best Buy submitted abundant evidence in the trial proceeding that was relevant to the determination of the distinctiveness of the applied mark. If such evidence was not considered, Best Buy would have lost its opportunity for relief. Therefore, such evidence should be taken into consideration when determining whether the applied mark has acquired distinctiveness.

The primary purpose of a trademark is to identify the source of its designated goods and services. To achieve this purpose, the applied trademark must be distinctive enough so that the relevant public would be able to associate the mark with the source of goods and

CASE *(continued)*

services. Marks that are generic names, shapes or models of the goods, or marks that have direct reference to the quality, main materials, function, usage, weight, amount and other characteristics of the goods, and marks that lack distinctive character, cannot be registered as trademarks. When dealing with administrative cases of trademark registration, people's courts should determine whether the applied mark as a whole has acquired distinctiveness, based on the relevant public's association of the goods with the disputed trademark. If the descriptive element in the mark does not affect the overall distinctiveness of the mark such that the relevant public can still identify the source of the goods, then courts should find distinctiveness in such a mark.

Here, the applied mark is comprised of two English words "BEST" and "BUY," and a square yellow logo. Although the words "BEST" and "BUY" are descriptive of the associated service to some extent, the mark as a whole is distinctive due to its additional elements with the square logo and its bright color. In addition, the applied mark enjoys global recognition, including recognition in China through actual use. As such, the applied mark can help the relevant public to identify the source of its services. The TRAB, the trial court and the appellate court failed to consider the applied mark's overall distinctiveness and disregarded new evidence submitted by Best Buy. This Court hereby reversed those rulings.

This is the final ruling.

17.2.7 China: distinctiveness in three-dimensional mark

CASE

Coca-Cola v. TRAB, Beijing High People's Court, Gaoxingzhongzi No. 348 (2011)

On October 8, 2002, Coca-Cola filed a trademark application for its "Three-Dimensional Mark," in the shape of a bottle design ("applied mark"), before the Chinese Trademark Office, under filing No. 3330291 in Class 32 covering goods such as mineral water and other non-alcoholic beverages. On November 20, 2003, the Chinese Trademark Office rejected Coca-Cola's three-dimensional trademark application on the grounds that the applied three-dimensional mark was merely a packaging design for a common beverage container, thus lacking distinctiveness required to be registered as a trademark.

CASE *(continued)*

Figure [17.3] Coca-Cola's proposed bottle-shaped trademark

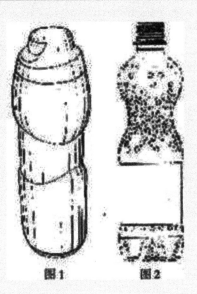

[Coca-Cola shortly filed an appeal before the TRAB. On March 8, 2010, the TRAB also rejected Coca-Cola's appeal on similar grounds as those of the Chinese Trademark Office. Coca-Cola soon filed an administrative review suit before Beijing First Intermediate Court.]

[During the trial,] Beijing First Intermediate Court held that: the applied three-dimensional mark is a three-dimensional cylinder, with a nipped-in waist and polka dot in the middle, and also several separate standing legs at the bottom. From the perspective of consumers, the applied mark resembles a beverage container more than a trademark, the latter of which identifies the source of goods and services.

Also, most of the use evidence submitted by Coca Cola were dated after the application date of the applied mark, thus cannot prove that the applied mark has acquired distinctiveness through long-term use. As such, Beijing First Intermediate Court affirmed the TRAB's decision.

[Coca-Cola appealed before Beijing High Court on the following grounds: First, the TRAB failed to prove that the bottle shape of the applied mark was commonly used in the relevant market. As a matter of fact, no other enterprise or individuals had used or applied to register the bottle-design mark similar to that of Coca-Cola's "Fanta" bottle design. Second, the applied three-dimensional mark is both inherently distinctive and also has acquired distinctiveness though Coca-Cola's intensive promotional campaign.]

This Court held that, pursuant to Article 11(3) of the Chinese Trademark Law, marks that lack distinctive characteristics are not permitted to be registered as trademarks. Trademark distinctiveness means that the mark needs to have characteristics that could help

CASE (continued)

consumers to identify and distinguish the source of its related goods or services. Whether a trademark possesses distinctiveness is determined by the relevance between the mark and its designated goods and services: the less relevance between the mark and its goods/services, the stronger the mark's distinctiveness is; and the more relevance between the mark and its goods and services, the weaker the mark's distinctiveness is.

When deciding whether a trademark has distinctiveness (*i.e.* its relationship with its goods and services, and also to which degree they are related), TRAB and peoples courts should refer to Chinese Trademark Law and its regulations for guidance. As such, actual evidence regarding the use of a trademark in the market place could be helpful, but is not a prerequisite in making such a determination. Therefore, this Court dismisses Coca-Cola's claim that TRAB did not provide sufficient evidence in reaching its rejection decision.

Here, Coca-Cola's applied mark is a three-dimensional mark that resembles the shape of beverage containers. Three-dimensional marks are registrable if such marks, *i.e.* the container's shape, possess enough distinctiveness that could identify the source of its goods and services. Further, the existence of distinctiveness is not determined by the unique design of the container, but rather by how such a trademark design could distinguish its origin from other manufacturers. If a container design is merely unique in design, but cannot serve to identify the source of its goods, then such a container design has not acquired distinctiveness in the trademark law context. As such, the fact that the applied mark is unique in design and no other enterprise or individual has used such a similar container design only suggests that this mark may be protected by copyright law or patent law, but [such evidence] is not enough to establish the distinctiveness required for a trademark registration. That is because the requirement for trademark distinctiveness is not to identify the function of different goods, but rather to identify the sources of goods and services.

Most of the evidence submitted by Coca-Cola was related to the use of the applied mark in conjunction with its other trademark "Fanta" since 2003. Therefore, none of the aforesaid evidence could prove that the applied mark [alone, without the word mark "Fanta"] has acquired distinctiveness [to identify the source of goods.]

To summarize, this Court finds that Beijing First Intermediate Court and TRAB were correct in their findings, and therefore, rejecting the appeal and affirming the original judgment.

This is the final ruling.

NOTES AND QUESTIONS

1. In *Coca-Cola v. TRAB*, Gaoxingzhongzi No. 348 (2011), the three-dimensional trademark case deals with the bottle shape of Coco-Cola's Fanta drink, instead of its more iconic rounded-shape of the classic Coke bottle. Now compare the two three-dimensional marks, *i.e.* Fanta drink bottle and Coke's bottle, in Figure 17.4. Do you agree with the court's reasoning that the bottle shape of Fanta drink is less distinctive than that of the Coke bottle?

Source: Chinese reported decision; U.S. Trademark Register.

Figure 17.4 Comparing bottle shapes

2. **Maintain distinctiveness**: It should be noted that distinctive character in a trademark might also get lost if it is not maintained appropriately. For example, "Aspirin," a former trademark owned by Bayer, later lost its trademark status in the US because it has become a generic term for acetylsalicylic acid products. The Chinese Trademark Law also addresses the scenario where a former distinctive trademark might be invalidated if it later becomes a generic name to its designated goods or services due to inappropriate use (Art. 49(2) Chinese Trademark Law). In *Beijing Huaqi Data Technology Ltd. v. Shenzhen Langke Technology Ltd.*, (2010) yizhongzhixingchuzi No. 2631, Beijing courts invalidated the registered trademark "优盘" (meaning "U drive") under no. 1509704, which was registered in 2001 in class 9 covering goods "computer discs and computers," on the grounds that the mark has become a generic name referring to "USB drives." Can you think of any other trademark examples that might also be at risk of losing distinctive character because of the inappropriate use by the public or media?

17.2.8 Geographic terms

17.2.8.1 United States

Geographic terms can be adopted as trademarks. However, because these terms refer to a feature of the product – where it is made – they are treated just like any other descriptive mark. They require secondary meaning in order to be registered. Examples include Olympia, for beer brewed in Olympia, Washington State; *see Olympia Brewing Co. v. Northwest Brewing Co.*, 178 Wash. 533, 35 P.2d 104 (1934) (secondary meaning found); *In re Spirits of New Merced, LLC*, 85 U.S.P.Q.2d 1614 (T.T.A.B. 2007) (finding Yosemite Beer, which was advertised as brewed near Yosemite National Park, primarily geographically descriptive of applicant's beer); Yellowstone, for outfitting services located near Yellowstone National Park, *see Warwood v. Hubbard*, 218 Mont. 438, 709 P.2d 637, 228 U.S.P.Q. 702 (1985) (no secondary meaning found); and American for truck bodies, *see McCabe-Powers Auto Body Co. v. American Truck Equipment Co.*, 150 F. Supp. 194, 113 U.S.P.Q. 217 (D. Or. 1957) (secondary meaning found).

Even though geographic terms can be descriptive, usually because they are connected to goods originating from or sold in the geographic place, they can also be arbitrary. The Amazon is a real geographic location, for example, but Amazon.com, the large internet retailer, is not particularly associated with the Amazonian jungle. So in this case it is an arbitrary name. The same is true of other trademarks. Chevrolet auto makes a truck named the Sonoma, which is an actual county in California; yet no one would assume the truck is produced in the county (which is largely rural), so Sonoma for trucks is arbitrary.

17.2.8.1.1 "Deceptively misdescriptive" geographic names

The general rule just stated is that a geographic place name can serve as a valid trademark, if the owner of the mark proves secondary meaning. But what if it appears that the trademark owner is referencing a place name famous for a certain type of goods, and those goods do not in fact come from that place? That is the domain of Lanham Act §2(e)(3), and the subject of the following case.

CASE

Guantanamera Cigar Co. v. Corporacion Habanos, S.A., 729 F. Supp. 2d 246 (D.D.C. 2010)

ROYCE C. LAMBERTH, District Judge.

This case comes before the Court on cross motions for summary judgment filed by plaintiff Guantanamera Cigar Company's ("GCC") and defendant Corporacion Habanos, S.A. ("Habanos"). Upon reviewing the motions, the Court concludes that the Trademark Trial and Appeal Board ("TTAB") erred as a matter of law in applying the three-part test for primarily geographically deceptively misdescriptive marks, which are barred from registration by the Lanham Act, 15 U.S.C. §1052(e)(3) (2006).

The TTAB improperly denied registration of GUANTANAMERA for cigars because it used an incorrect legal standard. The TTAB must deny registration of marks "which when used on or in connection with the goods of the applicant is primarily geographically deceptively misdescriptive of them." 15 U.S.C. §1052(e)(3). A mark is "primarily geographically deceptively misdescriptive" when:

CASE (continued)

(1) the primary significance of the mark is a generally known geographic location, (2) the consuming public is likely to believe the place identified by the mark indicates the origin of the goods bearing the mark, when in fact the goods do not come from that place, and (3) the misrepresentation was a material factor in the consumer's decision.

In re California Innovations, Inc., 329 F.3d 1334, 1341 (Fed.Cir.2003). The TTAB cited the proper legal standard, but erred in its application of the third part. The Court reviews the three parts of the test – geographic location, goods-place association, and materiality – as applied by the TTAB.

a. Geographic Location

There is significant evidence in the record to find that Cuba or Guantanamo, Cuba is the primary significance of GUANTANAMERA. The primary significance of a mark is a finding of fact. *See In re Wada*, 194 F.3d 1297, 1300 (Fed.Cir.1999). Guantanamera literally means "girl from Guantanamo." The Plaintiff argues that the primary meaning of GUANTANAMERA is the famous Cuban song by Joseito Fernandez. The TTAB recognized that the folk song's history reinforces the geographic connection to Guantanamo and Cuba. (Op. U.S.P.T.O. at 14.) Based on the deferential standard of review, the Court finds that the Plaintiff produced insufficient evidence to disturb the TTAB's factual finding that GUANTANAMERA's primary significance is a geographic location.

b. Goods–Place Association

There is sufficient evidence to find that the consuming public is likely to believe that the Plaintiff's cigars originate from Cuba. If consumers are likely to believe that the place identified on the mark is the origin of the goods, when in fact the goods do not come from that place, the element is satisfied. *California Innovations*, 329 F.3d at 1341; *see also In re Spirits International N.V.*, 563 F.3d 1347, 1350–51 (Fed.Cir.2009) (leaving the TTAB's analysis of the goods-place association unaltered when the TTAB found that Moscow was well known for vodka). The Federal Circuit characterized this element as a "relatively easy burden of showing a naked goods-place association." *California Innovations*, 329 F.3d at 1340.

The plaintiff argues that GUANTANAMERA fails the goods-place association test because Guantanamo is not known for the cigars. In support of this argument, the Plaintiff cited a quotation from *Spirits* that neither opposing counsel nor this Court could locate. The record contains ample evidence that cigar tobacco is produced in the Guantanamo province. There is also ample evidence to support the finding that Cuba is well-known for cigars. Beyond the evidence that Guantanamo produces cigars, the plaintiff insists the goods-place association element is not satisfied because the place named in the mark is not known for producing the product. (*See* Pl.'s Mot. Summ. J. 25–20.) The Court finds this argument unpersuasive because there is sufficient evidence in the record to support a finding that Guantanamo is known for producing cigar tobacco. The TTAB did not err in finding that the goods-place association was met.

CASE *(continued)*

c. Materiality

The TTAB erred as a matter of law in its analysis of materiality. To establish a *prima facie* case, the TTAB or the opposition must show that "a significant portion of the relevant consumers would be materially influenced in the decision to purchase the product or service by the geographic meaning of the mark." *Spirits*, 563 F.3d at 1357. Accordingly, the Court holds that Habanos never established a *prima facie* case for the third part of the test before the TTAB.

In *Spirits*, the TTAB refused to register the mark MOSKOVSKAYA for vodka because it was primarily geographically deceptively misdescriptive. *Id.* at 1350. MOSKOVSKAYA literally means "of or from Moscow," but the registrant admitted that the vodka is not manufactured, produced, or sold in Moscow and has no connection to Moscow. *Id.* The TTAB found that the primary significance of the mark was a generally known geographic location and recognized that Moscow is renowned for vodka. *Id.* Thus, the first two elements of the test were satisfied. *Id.* The Court took issue with the TTAB's application of the third element, the materiality requirement. *Id.* at 1350–51.

The TTAB reasoned that because 706,000 people in the United States speak Russian, and because 706,000 is "an appreciable number," the materiality requirement was satisfied. *Id.* at 1351. The Court remanded the case without ruling on the merits because the TTAB failed to consider whether Russia speakers were a "substantial portion" of the intended audience. *Id.* at 1357. The Court noted that only 0.25% of the U.S. population speaks Russian. *Id.* To satisfy the materiality requirement, a substantial portion of relevant consumers must be likely to be deceived, not an absolute number or particular segment (such as foreign language speakers). *Id.* at 1353.

Here, the TTAB erred as a matter of law in applying the materiality requirement. The TTAB decided this case before the Federal Circuit decided *Spirits*. The portion of the TTAB's opinion that addressed the materiality factor was only four sentences and did not make any findings regarding a "substantial proportion" of materially deceived consumers. The TTAB stated two reasons why the misrepresentation is material in the minds of consumers: (1) Cuba's "renown and reputation for high quality cigars" and (2) the plaintiff's subjective intent to deceive customers evidenced by previously placing "Guantanamera, Cuba" and "Genuine Cuban Tobacco" on the packaging.

Spirits plainly demands more than a finding of Cuba's reputation for high quality cigars. In *Spirits,* Moscow's renown reputation for vodka was not enough to affirm the TTAB's legal conclusion; likewise, Cuba's renown reputation for cigars is not enough in this case.

The Court finds the plaintiff's false claims on the packaging equally inadequate to satisfy *Spirits*. First, the registrant's subjective intent provides little, if any, insight into the minds of consumers. Consumers could have numerous reasons as to why they purchase Guantanamera cigars, but without any objective findings, it is difficult to make an accurate conclusion as to whether the geographic misdescription will materially affect a "substantial portion" of consumers. Second, the Court does not consider extraneous and out-dated marketing material particularly relevant in determining a mark's ability to satisfy the §1052(e)(3) registration bar. The Lanham Act bars registration of *marks* that are primarily

CASE *(continued)*

geographically deceptively misdescriptive, not marks that are accompanied by deceptive packaging material. *See* 15 U.S.C. §1052.

Habanos attempts to distinguish *Spirits* by asserting that this case meets the "substantial proportion" requirement. It argues that there are millions of Spanish speakers in the U.S., that the English speaking public recognizes "guantanamera" to mean Guantanamo, Cuba, and that GCC targeted Spanish speaking consumers. Nevertheless, this evidence fails to determine that a substantial proportion of the target audience would be deceived into purchasing the cigars *because of* the false goods-place association. Habanos never introduced evidence that suggested material deception of a substantial proportion of the relevant consuming public.

[The TTAB is reversed and the case remanded back to the US Patent and Trademark Office.]

NOTES

1. A similar case involves the trademark JPK Paris 75, which its owner attempted to register for handbags and related goods (*In re Miracle Tuesday, LLC*, 695 F.3d 1339 (Fed. Cir. 2012)). The Federal Circuit affirmed a rejection of the mark on the ground that a substantial portion of relevant consumers would associate the mark with the city of Paris, and that the goods in question were not in fact manufactured in Paris.

2. The law pertaining to family names or surnames is quite similar to the law for geographic place names. For example, consider *In Re Peter Schöttler Gmbh*, 79092036, 2012 WL 5196148 (TTAB, Sept. 28, 2012). According to the TTAB opinion,

   > Applicant requests extension of protection for the mark SCHÖTTLER (in standard characters) to be used on or in connection with a variety of metal products, metalworking and forging services, and engineering services in International Classes 6, 40, and 42. The examining attorney issued a final refusal to register, alleging that the mark is primarily merely a surname. Trademark Act §2(e)(4); 15 U.S.C. §1052(e)(4) (at *1).

   Section 2(e)(4) of the Trademark Act prohibits registration on the Principal Register if the proposed mark is "primarily merely a surname." The TTAB noted that if there is any doubt whether a proposed mark is primarily a surname, it must resolve that doubt in favor of the trademark applicant, citing *In re Benthin Management GmbH*, 37 USPQ2d 1332, 1334 (TTAB 1995). In *Benthin*, the TTAB identified five factors to consider in determining whether a mark is primarily merely a surname:

   1. the degree of the surname's "rareness";
   2. whether anyone connected with the applicant has the involved term as a surname;
   3. whether the mark has any recognized meaning other than as a surname;
   4. whether the mark has the "look and sound" of a surname; and
   5. whether the manner in which the mark is displayed might negate any surname significance.

   In the *Schöttler* case, the trademark examiner identified over 40 telephone listings of people with the surname "Schöttler"; she cited this as evidence that the mark was primarily a surname. The TTAB reversed her finding. Turning first to the "rareness" element of the *Benthin* factors, the Board said:

   > While the examining attorney is correct that there is no minimum number of listings required to show surname significance, *In re Cazes*, 21 USPQ2d 1796, 1797 (TTAB 1991), it is not the case that any number of listings will do, no matter how small. The issue is whether the surname in question is common or rare, and in each case, the rareness of the surname must be considered as a part of all the record evidence pertaining to the *Benthin* factors. Nonetheless, it is fair to say that the rareness of the name at issue often plays an important role in determining whether the proposed mark is primarily merely a surname. E.g., *In re Joint-Stock Co. "Baik"*, 84 USPQ2d 1921, 1923–24 (TTAB 2007) (at *2).

   The Board continued:

We find that the forty listings of record put SCHÖTTLER in the category of very rare surnames, particularly in the absence of any other evidence showing that the public would recognize it as a surname notwithstanding its rareness. On factor 2, the TTAB recognized that "The applicant firm" was founded in 1840 by a man named Peter Schöttler"(*id*, at *3).

As for factor 3, the trademark examiner "submitted two searches of online dictionaries (one English, one German) for the term 'Schöttler.' Final Office Action (July 1, 2011). Inasmuch as neither search found a definition for Schöttler, the examining attorney argues that the term has no recognized meaning other than that of a surname . . ."

With respect to factor 4, the trademark examiner argued that SCHÖTTLER has the look and sound of a surname, because there are a number of surnames used in the US that begin with the letters "Sch." In addition, many surnames used and heard in the US contain accent marks such as the umlaut over the "O" in Schöttler. The TTAB found that this determination was not well supported by the evidence in the case:

> This *Benthin* factor is somewhat subjective. *In re Binion*, 93 USPQ2d 1531, 1537 (TTAB 2009). However, even subjective determinations must be based on some evidence. As applicant points out, the examining attorney has submitted no evidence in support of her argument about common surnames in the United States. *See e.g., Baik*, 84 USPQ2d 1921, 1924 (TTAB 2007) (evidence from Yahoo People Search "to show that 'more common' surnames . . . are similar in appearance and sound"); *In re Thermo LabSystems Inc.*, 85 USPQ2d 1285 (TTAB 2007) ("examining attorney's evidence from about.com shows that . . . many surnames end with 'son'"); *In re Industrie Pirelli Societa per Azioni*, 9 USPQ2d 1564, 1566 (TTAB 1988) (PIRELLI, though rare, resembles common surnames in the *American Surnames* book).
>
> While we agree that SCHÖTTLER could *possibly* be perceived as a surname, that conclusion is not inevitable . . . We conclude that in the absence of evidence to support it, we are not able to give the [trademark examiner's] unsupported opinion on this factor any weight (*id.*, at *4).

The TTAB ultimately reversed the examiner's refusal to register the mark: "On balance, we find the degree of rareness of the surname SCHÖTTLER to be a factor which weighs heavily in favor of reversal, outweighing the fact that the mark has no other meaning and that applicant's founder was named Schöttler"(*id*)

17.2.8.2 Europe

For treatment of a geographical place name, and the relationship to two other important issues (geographic indications of origin in Europe, and the "of more than mere local significance" requirement), see *Anheuser-Busch v. Budějovický Budvar, národní podnik*, Case C-96/09 (ECJ [CJEU], 29 March 2011, covered later in this Part.

17.2.8.3 China

Yunan Red River v. TRAB, Beijing High People's Court, Gaoxingzhongzi No. 65 (2002)

On December 4, 1995, Daxinganling Beiqishen Health Product Co. Ltd. ("DXAL Health Product Co.") filed a trademark application for mark "红河" ("Red River in Chinese," referred as "the subject mark") with the Chinese Trademark Office under filing No.

CASE *(continued)*

1022719. On June 7, 1997, the subject mark was approved for registration in class 32 in terms of beer and alcoholic drinks. On November 28, 2000, DXAL Health Product Co. assigned the subject mark to Red River Distribution Department ("Red River DD").

On August 13, 2001, Yunnan Red River filed a trademark cancellation against the subject mark before the TRAB on the grounds that the subject mark is the geographic name of a local county, thus violating Article 10 of Chinese Trademark Law, and should not be allowed for registration.

[The TRAB rejected Yunnan Red River's arguments, holding that the subject mark is a valid trademark because the mark "Red River" also has other meanings, in addition to its reference to the geographic county. Yunnan Red River shortly filed an administrative trademark review before Beijing First Intermediate Court.]

Beijing First Intermediate Court held that, Article 10 of Chinese Trademark Law states that "[t]he geographical names of administrative divisions at or above the county level and foreign geographical names well-known to the public shall not be used as trademarks, except for geographical names that have other meanings . . .". A geographical name has other meanings if: (1) its other meanings are specific and well-known; or (2) it has been used as an idiomatic expression. In this case, the court found that the subject mark also has other meanings, such as "a river in red color," thus holding that the subject mark is a valid trademark registration and rejecting Yunnan Red River's cancellation arguments.

[Yunnan Red River soon appealed before Beijing High Court, the appellate court.]

Beijing High People's Court held that, Article 10 states that "geographical names of administrative divisions at or above the county level well-known to the public shall not be used as trademarks, except for geographical names that contain other meanings . . .". The reason behind such legislative language is that trademarks that refer to geographical names usually cannot serve to identify the source of its goods and services. Thus, by allowing such trademarks for registration would be misleading to the consumers.

In this case, the evidence shows that "Red River" also refers to a river located in Vietnam. In addition, "Red River" also literally means "a river in red color." As such, the subject mark meets the criteria for having additional meanings in addition to its reference to a local county, thus should be allowed for registration.

17.2.9 Scandalous marks

17.2.9.1 United States

Lanham Act §2(a) (15 U.S.C. §1052) reads in part:

> No trademark by which the goods of the applicant may be distinguished from the goods of others shall be refused registration on the principal register on account of its nature unless it –

(a) Consists of or comprises immoral, deceptive, or scandalous matter; or matter which may disparage or falsely suggest a connection with persons, living or dead, institutions, beliefs, or national symbols, or bring them into contempt, or disrepute.

Under this part of the Lanham Act, a wide array of trademark applications have been rejected over the years if they would be perceived as scandalous by a "substantial composite of the general public" at the time the registration of the matter is sought. So, for example, in *In re Tinseltown, Inc.*, 212 U.S.P.Q. 863 (T.T.A.B. 1981), the word mark BULLSHIT was refused registration as "scandalous" despite the applicant's contention that the purpose of the mark was to make fun of designer names and logos. In another contentious case, *Pro-Football, Inc. v. Blackhorse*, 112 F. Supp. 3d 439 (E.D. Va. 2015), appeal filed, oral argument scheduled for 2016, a long series of legal proceedings culminated in affirmance of the T.T.A.B.'s cancellation of federal registrations for trademarks to the "Washington Redskins" National Football League team name.

One issue raised in the *Blackhorse* case, among others, is this: Is Section 2(a) unconstitutional? In *In re Tam*, 808 F.3d 1321 (Fed. Cir. 2015), *as corrected* (Feb. 11, 2016), the Federal Circuit issued an *en banc* opinion saying "yes." The court held that Section 2(a) fails to satisfy the strict scrutiny review imposed on any restriction related to speech, and therefore that this section of the Lanham Act is null and void because it violates the US Constitution.

The *Tam* case grew out of some interesting facts. Simon Tam is part of an Asian-American dance rock band called *The Slants*. Tam named the band *The Slants* with the specific idea of challenging stereotypes and slurs against Asian people. The idea is that when an Asian band uses the name, they call attention to it and also "take it back," turning what is meant to be an attack into a positive statement: yes, we are Asian-American, and we are not ashamed of that and in fact we are proud of who we are. In 2011, Tam filed for trademark registration of *The Slants*. The PTO denied registration on the ground that the name was disparaging of a substantial composite of persons of Asian descent. The T.T.A.B. affirmed (*In re Tam*, No. 85472044, 2013 WL 5498164 (T.T.A.B. Sept. 26, 2013)). On appeal, the Federal Circuit initially affirmed, but then *sua sponte* ordered rehearing *en banc*. That led to the final opinion finding §2(a) of the Lanham Act unconstitutional.

The basic idea behind the opinion is that trademark protection encourages a certain type of speech, the use of a word or symbol to describe a business, product, or service. Under the strong guarantees for free speech embodied in the first amendment to the US Constitution, if the government promotes or restricts speech that favors one side or the other on some issue of interest, the government must justify this under a very demanding standard (strict scrutiny). The Federal Circuit said that §2(a) is used to suppress certain attempts to "speak" – it stops registrants from gaining protection for a trademark that would help promote its use. It is thus unconstitutional under the First Amendment. The court treated §2(a) as an instance of what is known as "viewpoint discrimination." If, for example, Tam had attempted to register a trademark for the band name "The Virtuous Asians," the Trademark Office would not have rejected his application under §2(a). But because he tried to register "The Slants," his application was rejected. The Trademark Office thus discriminated against one particular viewpoint: the "negative" or disparaging viewpoint. This, the Federal Circuit said, is not permitted under the First Amendment. *See generally Recent Case, First Amendment – Offense-Based Bar on Trademark Registration – Federal Circuit Holds the Lanham Act's Antidisparagement Provision Unconstitutional. – In Re Tam*, 808 F.3d 1321 (Fed. Cir. 2015) (En Banc), 129 Harv. L. Rev. 2265 (2016).

The Supreme Court affirmed the Federal Circuit opinion in *Tam. Matal v. Tam*, 137 S. Ct. 1744 (2017). The Court followed the basic rationale that had been laid out by the Federal Circuit: "We ... hold that [the disparagement] provision [Lanham Act §2(a)] violates the Free Speech Clause of the First Amendment. It offends a bedrock First Amendment principle: Speech may not be banned on the ground that it expresses ideas that offend" (137 S.Ct. at 1751).

17.2.9.2 Europe

Under Article 4.1(f) of the EU Trademark Directive, it is an absolute ground of refusal to register a mark that is "contrary to public policy or to accepted standards of morality." This provision is rarely applied, however. For example, the OHIM (now EUIPO) Trademark Office Board of Appeal reversed an initial rejection of the trademark "Screw You," arguing that "[t]he office should not refuse to register a trade mark which is only likely to offend a small minority of exceptionally puritanical citizens" (*Kenneth Jebaraj trading as Screw You*, OHIM Bd. Of App. Decision R 495/2005-G (2005)).

17.2.9.3 China

> **CASE**
>
> # BONPIE Sound System v. TRAB, Beijing High People's Court, Jingxingzhong No. 1973 (2016)
>
> Applicant, BONPIE Sound System filed a trademark application for mark "帮派BONPIE" (referred as "applied mark") on December 2, 2013 under filing no. 13650899, in Class 9 covering goods "computers, phones and chargers etc."
>
> On November 8, 2014, the applied mark was rejected by the Chinese Trademark Office, on the grounds that the applied mark "帮派," which literally means "mafia and gang" in Chinese, has improper influence to the social public, if used as a trademark, and therefore should not be allowed for registration.
>
> [BONPIE shortly thereafter filed an appeal before the TRAB. The TRAB reaffirmed the Chinese Trademark Office's rejection, finding the applied mark to have a negative impact on the social public interest, and that it thus should not be allowed for registration. BONPIE then continued to appeal before Beijing Intellectual Property Court.]
>
> Beijing Intellectual Property Court [the court of first instance] held that, based on the evidence submitted by the parties involved in this case and also the common understanding of the general public, the characters "帮派" in the applied mark is more likely to be interpreted as referring to "mafia group or gang group" by the general public, thus having negative meaning as a trademark. [As such, Beijing Intellectual Property Court affirmed the decisions made by the TRAB and Chinese Trademark Office, and rejected the applied mark for registration.]
>
> [During the administrative review before Beijing High Court], the court held that, according to Article 10(8) of the Chinese Trademark Law, trademarks that are detrimental to social morals or customs or having other adverse effects, shall not be used as trademarks. The term "social morals and customs" refers to the universal social value and standard that the majority of the society observes and complies with. The "adverse effect" refers to negative factors or influences that might cause to China's politics, economy, culture, religion, ethnic groups and other such public interest and public order etc.
>
> In this case, the applied mark includes the Chinese characters "帮派" and Roman letters "BONPIE." To most consumers, whose native language is Chinese, the most distinguishable part in the applied mark is its Chinese characters "帮派." The term "帮派" [in the Chinese language], refers to a small group that is established and connected for the purpose of achieving their common (mostly illegitimate) goals and interests. The rules of such a group and its social values are usually different from the universal social values shared by the general public, and such a group is understood to bring negative and adverse impact to the society. As such, the applied mark, which contains the characters "帮派," if used as a trademark, will likely bring negative and adverse effect to the social public interests and public order, and therefore should not be registered as a trademark.
>
> Article 10(8) of Chinese Trademark Law is an absolute prohibition clause. If a trademark

> **CASE** *(continued)*
>
> falls into this category, then it is strictly prohibited from trademark use or registration, and the evidence of long-time use of the mark will not overcome the registration obstacle. As such, we also reject BONPIE's argument that the applied mark has acquired distinctiveness after long-time use.
> We hereby reject the appeal and reaffirm the lower court's ruling.
> This is the final ruling.

NOTES AND QUESTIONS

1. In most jurisdictions, if a trademark includes the name of a state, names of foreign countries, names of international inter-governmental organizations or the Red Cross, it will not be allowed for registration. What might be the rationale behind such a rule?
2. In *Jing Brand v. TRAB*, the TRAB stated in its rejection decision (and also in its appeal) that marks that contain the name of a state might be allowed for trademark registration but only under special circumstances. For example, the trademark "Bank of China" is a registered trademark owned by Bank of China, one of the four largest Chinese state-owned banks in terms of banking service. Why do you think that the mark "Bank of China" could be allowed for trademark registration? Can you think of any other examples that might fit with this special criterion described by the TRAB?
3. In *Jing Brand v. TRAB*, the Chinese Supreme People's Court rejected TRAB's reliance on Article 10(1) of the Chinese Trademark Law, finding the applied mark "Chinese Jing Wine and device" to be distinctive as a whole. But at the end of its opinion, it also noted that other provisions of the Chinese Trademark Law might also be relevant in considering whether a trademark that contains the name of a state should be allowed for trademark registration. Consider possible examples in which a trademark containing the name of a country could damage the image of the state, and therefore should not be allowed for registration. (For more discussion, *see* ZHOU Yun-Chuan, Rules and Cases, Litigation Involving the Authorization and Determination of Trademark Rights (2014), chapter 2.)
4. As with the Lanham Act §2(a) (15 U.S.C §1052), Article 10(8) of the Chinese Trademark Law also addresses trademarks that might have a negative influence or impact on social morals or customs. The term "social morals and customs" generally refers to the universal social values observed and respected by society. The "adverse effect" refers to negative influences that would be detrimental to China's politics, economy, culture, religion, ethnic groups, and other such public interest and public order etc. In *Guangmei Fobao Beverages Ltd. v. TRAB*, (2012) gaoxingzhongzi. No 1224, Beijing High Court affirmed by the lower court and TRAB, holding that the applied mark "佛宝Fobao," which contains the Chinese character "佛" (meaning "Buddha"), would be improper to be used as a trademark for the goods "beer and alcoholic drinks." The courts found that since one of Buddhism's Precepts is to "avoid alcoholic drinking," to allow a trademark that contains the character "Buddha" for registration in terms of "alcoholic drinks" would bring negative influence to the religion, and thus should be prohibited.

17.2.10 Functionality

17.2.10.1 United States

Trademark law protects words, signs, symbols, etc., that signify to buyers that goods or services come from a certain source. Because buyers also associate product shapes and packaging with individual sources, these elements of "trade dress" can also be protected as trademarks. We discussed this earlier in this chapter. There is, however, an important limit on trade dress protection. It may not extend to the features of a product that make it work, *i.e.*, useful features that contribute to its function. So, for example, the shape of a bottle (such as the iconic rounded shape of the classic Coke bottle) might be protected as trade dress; but if a certain opening size or diameter in the neck of a bottle made it perform better, no individual seller of products in bottles with that dimension could protect the neck opening size as a feature of trade dress.

An example of a "functional" and therefore non-trade-dress-protectable element of a product comes from the case of *Valu Eng'g, Inc. v. Rexnord Corp.*, 278 F.3d 1268 (Fed. Cir. 2002). There the seller of industrial machinery tried to register three different designs for guardrails on assembly lines; these rails keep the products being manufactured from falling off an assembly line as the products move along from one stage of production to the next. The three shapes are shown in Figure 17.5.

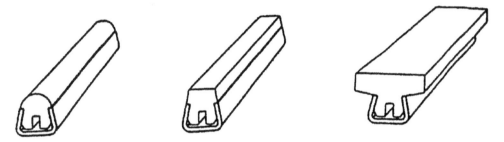

Source: reported case opinion.

Figure 17.5 Proposed registration for assembly line guardrail shapes

> The T.T.A.B. denied registration of the rail guide designs on the basis of functionality, and the Federal Circuit agrees. Specifically, according to the Federal Circuit, the Board made these findings:
>
>> [T]he Board found that: an abandoned utility patent application filed by Valu but rejected under 35 U.S.C. §103 "disclose[d] certain utilitarian advantages of [Valu's] guide rail designs, and that those advantages . . . result from the shape of the guide rail designs," . . .; Valu's advertising materials "tout the utilitarian advantages of [Valu's] guide rail design[s]," . . .; the "limited number of basic guide rail designs . . . should not be counted as 'alternative designs'" because they are "dictated solely by function," . . .; and Valu's guide rail designs "result[] in a comparatively simple or cheap method of manufacturing," . . . Accordingly, the Board sustained Rexnord's

opposition and refused to register Valu's guide rail designs (*Valu Engineering, Inc. v. Rexnord Corp.,* 278 F.3d 1268, 1272 (Fed. Cir. 2002)).

These are the basic factors that have often been cited in functionality cases. The first, the significance of a patent (either attempted, as in *Valu Engineering,* or expired), was the subject of a Supreme Court opinion in *TrafFix Devices, Inc. v. Marketing Displays, Inc.,* 532 U.S. 23 (2001). *TrafFix Devices* held that courts must consider an expired utility patent when analyzing functionality. The concern is that trade dress protection should not be used to in effect extend a patent indefinitely after the patent has expired. (Recall that trademark protection is in theory indefinite; as long as consumer associations connect a mark or trade dress with a single source, the mark or trade dress is protectable, while a patent expires in general 20 years after it is filed.)

Another line of cases deals with a different dimension of the functionality doctrine. Sometimes a product feature is not exactly useful, in the sense of the guide rails from the *Valu Engineering* case, yet it makes a product more appealing to consumers. Can an individual seller that employs such a feature protect it under trade dress law? The answer is a bit complex. In general, courts have said that any product feature that is not related to a single seller's "reputation" may be excluded from protectable trade dress. Even though such a feature might not be useful, in the sense of contributing to the product's actual function, it might be necessary to leave that feature unprotected so as to foster robust competition. Because the basic idea behind excluding product features from protectability comes from cases such as *Valu Engineering,* this rule is included in the functionality doctrine. But because it is not truly related to utility, it is called "aesthetic functionality."

This can be a confusing idea, so an example will help. In *Christian Louboutin S.A. v. Yves Saint Laurent Am. Holdings, Inc.,* 696 F.3d 206 (2d Cir. 2012), the Second Circuit Court of Appeals held that a fashion designer could not fully protect its distinctive bright red shoe-bottom (or "outsole") under Lanham Act trade dress protection. The seller, Christian Louboutin, had designed a distinctive line of women's shoes with the striking bright red sole. Yves Saint Laurent introduced a competing line of shoes, and Christian Louboutin sued for infringement of its trade dress. The Second Circuit held that Christian Louboutin could protect *only* those shoes in which the outsole was placed next to a contrasting color; so a black leather shoe with the distinctive red outsole was protected, while an all-red shoe (leather upper and outsole) could not be.

If a design feature such as a color is not truly functional, why limit trademark protection with respect to that feature? The answer is that courts have come to believe that some design features add to the desirability of a product as much or more than the actual useful features of the product. When this is so, allowing a single seller of such a product to protect a desirable design feature through trademark law would effectively "lock up" that feature for that single seller. Competition would suffer. And this means of course that consumers would ultimately suffer.

Courts have held to this doctrine of "aesthetic functionality" despite the fact that sometimes, a single seller who promotes a desirable feature may come to be associated with that feature in the minds of at least some consumers. In these cases courts choose the competition-preserving path, and reject trademark protection for a design feature, even though that feature may have come to serve as a signifier of source for at least some consumers. *See Landscape Forms, Inc. v. Columbia Cascade Co.*, 113 F.3d 373, 379–80 (2d Cir. 1997) ("The functionality defense, moreover, by denying an otherwise valid claim of trade dress infringement if its recognition would create an unwarranted monopoly, protects competition even at the cost of potential consumer confusion").

17.2.10.2 Europe

Three-dimensional designs that are purely functional cannot be protected as a trademark under the EU Trademark Directive. *See* EU Trademark Directive, Article 4.1(e) (marks are excluded from protection if they consist of "(i) the shape, or another characteristic, which results from the nature of the goods themselves; (ii) the shape, or another characteristic, of goods which is necessary to obtain a technical result; [or] (iii) the shape, or another characteristic, which gives substantial value to the goods"). *See Philips v. Remington*, Case C-299/99 (ECJ [CJEU] (18 June 2002) (rejecting trademark registration of picture mark for three-bladed shaver).

The EU Design Directive also provides for a functionality defense which is similar in scope to the defense as applied under trademark principles in the US and China. *See* EU Design Directive (1998), at Article 7.

Article 7
Designs dictated by their technical function and designs of interconnections:

1. A design right shall not subsist in features of appearance of a product which are solely dictated by its technical function.
2. A design right shall not subsist in features of appearance of a product which must necessarily be reproduced in their exact form and dimensions in order to permit the product in which the design is incorporated or to which it is applied

to be mechanically connected to or placed in, around or against another product so that either product may perform its function.

3. Notwithstanding paragraph 2, a design right shall, under the conditions set out in Articles 4 and 5, subsist in a design serving the purpose of allowing multiple assembly or connection of mutually interchangeable products within a modular system.

Can a distinctive retail store layout be registered as a trademark, in and of itself (without the presence of an accompanying logo or word mark)? Yes, said the CJEU, in a case originating with a rejection of a trademark application in Germany. *See Apple Inc v. Deutsches Patent-und Markenamt* (Case C-421/13), [2014] Bus. L.R. 962 (ECJ (3rd Chamber)), available at http://curia.europa.eu/juris/document/document.jsf?text=&docid=154829&pageIndex=0&doclang=EN&mode=lst&dir=&occ=first&part=1&cid=793165 (excerpted and discussed in Part VI of this book, on Design Protection). *See generally* Graeme B. Dinwoodie, *Federalized Functionalism: The Future of Design Protection in the European Union*, 24 Am. Intell. Prop. L. Ass'n Q. J. 611 (1996).

17.2.10.3 China

Article 12 of Chinese Trademark Law reads:

> Where a three-dimensional mark is applied for registration as a trademark, application shall be rejected if the three-dimensional mark merely indicates the shape inherent in the nature of the goods concerned, or if the three-dimensional sign is only dictated by the need to achieve technical effects or the need to give the goods substantive value.

This provision is understood to be an important limitation on trade dress protection. In other words, a three-dimensional mark might be registrable as a trademark only if the feature of the three-dimensional mark adds no aesthetic value or technical functions to the goods.

 CASE

Kaiping Weishida Seasoning v. Nestlé, Beijing High People's Court (2012) gaoxingzhongzi No. 1750

The appellant Nestlé Products Co., Ltd. ("Nestlé") appealed to this Court after Beijing First Intermediate Court ruled in favor of the appellee Kaiping Weishida Seasoning Co., Ltd.

CASE (continued)

("Weishida") in a trademark dispute. TRAB was the defendant in the first instance trial. On November 8, 2012, this Court accepted this case and opened the court session on February 28, 2013. This Court made a final ruling.

On March 14, 2002, Nestlé filed an international trademark application designating China, for the mark "Three-Dimensional Mark" ("disputed mark"), a brown and yellow bottle-shaped design, under No. 640537 in Class 30 covering goods such as "seasonings, flavorings and condiments."

Weishida filed a cancellation action against Nestlé's disputed mark before the TRAB on the grounds that: (1) Nestlé's disputed trademark lacks distinctiveness because the mark has been widely used by other seasoning product manufacturers in China, thus violating Article 11 of Chinese Trademark Law; and (2) the disputed mark is also aesthetically functional, thus violating Article 12 of Chinese Trademark Law . . .

Figure 17.6 Bottle shape trademark application

Nestlé responded that: (1) The disputed mark was created by Mr. Julius Maggi back in 1886 and has been used on seasoning products since then. As such, this three-dimensional mark has acquired secondary meaning through long-term use; (2) The disputed mark has been successfully registered in other countries, and therefore has proved its distinctiveness; and (3) The disputed mark is unique in its design and thus distinguishable from other brands in the same field . . .

[During the cancellation proceeding, the TRAB rejected Weishida's cancellation grounds, and Weishida shortly thereafter filed an administrative lawsuit against TRAB in the Beijing First Intermediate Court.]

During the trial, Beijing First Intermediate Court summarized the issues presented

CASE *(continued)*

before the court as the following: (1) legal procedures of the TRAB; (2) whether the disputed mark is distinctive; and (3) whether the disputed mark is aesthetically functional
...

Issue 2: Whether the disputed mark is distinctive
Article 11 of Chinese Trademark Law provides that,

> (1) the following marks shall not be registered as trademarks: (a) generic names, designs or models for the goods in connection with which it is used; (b) descriptive marks that identify the quality, raw materials, function, use, weight, quantity or other features of the goods; and (c) those lacking distinctive features;
> (2) the marks in the preceding paragraphs may be registrable if they acquire distinctiveness through secondary meaning, where marks become readily identifiable through actual use.

Trademarks are registrable if they are either inherently distinctive or have acquired distinctiveness (*i.e.* secondary meaning) through long-time use. The marks listed in Article 11(1) of Chinese Trademark Law are not inherently distinctive, but might be eligible for trademark registration if they have acquired distinctiveness later.
[The court then provided a detailed analysis, as follows, as to how to determine whether a trademark, in particular a three-dimensional mark, is either inherently distinctive or has acquired distinctiveness through later use.]

1. *Whether the disputed mark is inherently distinctive*
In order to assess the distinctive character of a mark, courts typically consider the degree of recognition between the relevant public and the mark. A trademark does not have distinctive feature if it cannot help the consumers to identify the source of its goods. In general, marks that directly describe the features of goods or services (such as quality, function, packaging, and color) cannot serve to identify the source of the goods because such marks will be considered by the relevant public as elements or features of the products. As such, descriptive marks lack inherent distinctiveness.
In this case, the trial court held that the disputed mark lacked distinctiveness based on the following considerations:

(1) Generally speaking, three-dimensional marks are less likely to be inherently distinctive.

Three-dimensional marks are normally used in the following three ways: (a) as the shape of the goods itself; (b) as the packaging of the goods; or (c) as ornamentation. If a three-dimensional mark is used in the first two ways, the relevant public is more likely to view the mark as the packaging of the goods or the shape of the goods, instead of as a trademark to identify its source.

In addition, unlike two-dimensional marks, whose distinctive feature is closely related to the uniqueness of the mark (for instance, fanciful marks or arbitrary marks usually enjoy the highest degree of distinctiveness), uniqueness of a three-dimensional mark, on

CASE *(continued)*

the other hand, has little influence on the overall distinctiveness of the mark. As long as the three-dimensional mark is represented in the package design or shape of the product, even if such a mark is novel in design and has never been used by other marker players before, the relevant public would still consider the three-dimensional mark as part of the product package, instead of as a trademark – the source identifier. As such, the inherent distinctiveness of a three-dimensional mark has little relevance to such factors as the novelty or fancifulness of the mark.

(2) The disputed mark is likely to be viewed as the packaging design or the container shape of the specific goods associated with the mark.
Since the disputed mark is used on its designated seasoning goods, the relevant public is more likely to view the mark as the packaging design/container shape of its goods rather than a trademark. As such, the disputed mark cannot help consumers identify the source of the product. Therefore, the disputed mark lacks inherent distinctiveness required for a trademark.

2. *Whether the disputed mark has acquired distinctiveness*
Pursuant to Article 11(2) of Chinese Trademark Law, if a mark that lacks inherent distinctiveness becomes well-known for its designated goods or services through extensive use, and that the relevant public can associate the mark with the source of its corresponding goods or services, then this mark is considered as having acquired distinctiveness through secondary meaning. As a result, this mark becomes registrable.
In practice, the acquired distinctiveness of a trademark is closely related to its reputation. If it can be established that there is wide recognition among the relevant public to the trademark and that there has been a unique relationship between the trademark and the source of its goods and services, then it should be concluded that such a mark has acquired distinctiveness.

Here, the trial court held that the current evidence cannot prove that the disputed mark has acquired distinctiveness because: (1) Before Nestlé applied to register the disputed mark in 2002, other seasoning companies in China had already started using identical or similarly shaped bottles with that of Nestle in seasoning products; (2) Nestlé failed to provide sufficient evidence to prove the reputation of the disputed mark.

Issue 3: Whether the disputed mark is aesthetically functional
Pursuant to Article 12 of the Chinese Trademark Law, "Where a three-dimensional mark is applied for registration as a trademark, application shall be rejected if the three-dimensional mark merely indicates the shape inherent in the nature of the goods concerned, or if the three-dimensional sign is only dictated by the need to achieve technical effects or the need to give the goods substantive value."

If a disputed mark violates Article 12, then it cannot be registered, regardless of its distinctive features. In other words, if a trademark is rejected because of lacking distinctiveness based on Article 11, it might still become registrable in the future should it acquire distinctiveness through extensive use. But if a trademark is deemed as violating

CASE *(continued)*

Article 12, then it is barred from trademark registration for good. Given that the legal consequences of the two articles (Article 11 and 12) are different, a separate consideration of the disputed mark under Article 12 is also necessary in this case.

Article 12 essentially bars trademark registration of a three-dimensional mark that is aesthetically functional. A three-dimensional mark is aesthetically functional if it has an "aesthetic" element and provides "substantive value" to the goods. Because the substantive value of goods is usually realized through the relevant public's purchase, it is only reasonable to determine the "substantive value" of goods from the perspective of its purchasers or consumers. If consumers make their purchase decisions based on the "aesthetic values" of the three-dimensional mark, rather than the manufacturer or service provider behind such products – the source of the goods, then this three-dimensional mark is deemed to have "substantive value" to its goods.

There are several policy reasons as to why the Chinese Trademark Law does not protect three-dimensional marks with aesthetic functionality.

First of all, the Chinese Trademark Law protects the interests of trademark owners that derive from the source-identifying function of trademarks. But as far as three-dimensional marks with aesthetic values are concerned, their values are more often aesthetically-oriented, and have little relevance with the source-identifying function of trademarks. Therefore, protecting three-dimensional marks with aesthetic values are not consistent with the legislative purpose of trademark law.

Second, protection of three-dimensional marks with aesthetical values would also confuse the boundaries between Chinese trademark law, patent law and copyright law. It is not uncommon to find a three-dimensional mark that might be eligible for both design patent protection, trademark protection and also copyright protection. But because the patent law, trademark law and copyright law serve different purposes, require different registrability criteria and implement different protection mechanisms, with different valid periods, it would be unfair for an applicant to arbitrage the different systems, by registering the three-dimensional mark with aesthetic values as a design patent first, and then instead of releasing the design patent to the public after the patent expires, but continues to enjoy the exclusive right to the mark for an indefinite period by registering it as a trademark. Such a result defeats the purpose of intellectual property system and conflicts with the legislative intent of legislators.

Third, such protection [if granted] will put competitors in the same industry at an unreasonable disadvantage. When three-dimensional marks with aesthetic functionality enter into the public domain after their patent/copyright periods expire, competitors should be allowed to freely use the mark. However, if Chinese Trademark Law were to protect such marks, competitors' use of the mark would infringe the trademark holder's exclusive right. As such, the extended protection would result in unreasonable use of public resources and an unfair competitive advantage to competitors.

In this case, the disputed mark, in the form of a square-shaped bottle with designated colors, is used for seasoning products. From the consumers' point of view, if their purchase decisions to buy the seasoning product is primarily based on the unique design of the

CASE *(continued)*

product container, then the three-dimensional mark will be deemed to have aesthetic functionality. However, the general consensus is that consumers usually make purchase decisions of seasoning products based on factors such as the quality or manufacturer of such products. Even if the unique design of a container shape might be taken into consideration during the purchase process, such a factor is clearly not determinative. Therefore, the disputed mark does not have aesthetic functionality, and thus does not violate Article 12 of Chinese Trademark Law.

In sum, this court hereby rejects Nestlé's appeal, pursuant to Article 61(1) of the Chinese Administrative Procedure Law, and affirms the Beijing First Intermediate Court's judgment. [Beijing High Court affirms the decision and reasoning made by the first instance court, and rejects the disputed mark for registration.]

NOTES

1. In *Weishida v. Nestlé*, the first instance court provided a detailed analysis on the distinctiveness and functionality of Nestlé's three-dimensional mark. On the distinctiveness issue, the courts seemed to believe that a three-dimensional mark is usually "less-distinctive" compared with a two-dimensional mark because most three-dimensional marks are the shape of a product configuration or packaging design, thus lacking distinctiveness. Do you agree?
2. On the issue of functionality, the court in *Weishida v. Nestlé* explains the legislative rationale as to why marks with functionality should not be registered as trademarks. Do you find such rationale compelling? In this specific case, the Chinese courts did not find Nestlé's three-dimensional bottle design mark to be functional, but can you think of other examples where the three-dimensional mark is "functional?" In other words, the motivation of purchases is driven not only by the product itself, but also by the aesthetic feature or functionality of the mark?

17.2.11 Meaning in another language

17.2.11.1 US: doctrine of foreign equivalents; "exclusively descriptive" in another language (EU)

CASE

In Re Oriental Daily News, Inc., 230 U.S.P.Q. (BNA) 637 (TTAB July 23, 1986)

Oriental Daily News, Ltd., a corporation of Hong Kong, has appealed from the final refusal of the Trademark Examining Attorney to register the Chinese characters shown below for newspapers. The Examining Attorney has refused registration under Section 2(e)(1) of the [Lanham] Act, 15 U.S.C. §1052(e)(1), because, under the doctrine of foreign equivalents,

CASE *(continued)*

**Figure
[17.7]** Oriental Daily
News

We affirm.

Applicant argues that the Chinese symbols it seeks to register, whose direct transliteration is "Tung Fong Jih Pao," translate into ORIENTAL DAILY NEWS "in only a very loose sense." More particularly, applicant argues that the Chinese characters or ideographs sought to be registered are distinctive creations which identify applicant as a source of the goods. In contrast to the phonetic English language, composed of letters of the alphabet which indicate sound, applicant explains, the written Chinese language is composed of units which are picture symbols for things and concepts. When such characters are drawn, each symbol becomes a unique, distinctive creation, according to applicant's attorney. Because of the nature of the Chinese language, precise translation into English is difficult. Accordingly, applicant's attorney argues that conventional trademark rules and especially the doctrine of foreign equivalents should not apply. Even assuming that the doctrine of foreign equivalents is applicable to Chinese characters, applicant argues that the translated English words are not merely descriptive of any feature or characteristic of its newspapers but are at most suggestive of the goods.

We have carefully considered applicant's arguments but find them unpersuasive. First, as the Examining Attorney has pointed out, the newspapers submitted as specimens of record show the words "ORIENTAL DAILY NEWS" at the top thereof. In addition, the promotional brochure (front and back cover) in both Chinese and English, submitted by applicant with its appeal brief (and treated by the Examining Attorney as of record),

CASE *(continued)*

also indicates that applicant translates the Chinese characters as ORIENTAL DAILY NEWS. Finally, in applicant's Canadian registration of the same symbols, made of record by applicant, it is unequivocally indicated that the translation of the Chinese characters is ORIENTAL DAILY NEWS. Accordingly, on this record we must consider that the characters sought to be registered are translated as ORIENTAL DAILY NEWS.

With respect to the issue of descriptiveness, applicant has submitted and the Examining Attorney eventually accepted a disclaimer of the last two characters, said by applicant to represent the words DAILY NEWS. This disclaimer is, of course, an admission of the descriptiveness of those symbols. *Plus Products v. Star-Kist Foods, Inc.*, 220 USPQ 541, 543 (TTAB 1983). Citing the definition of the word "oriental" as "pertaining to the countries or region of the Orient or to their peoples, languages or culture" (*The American Heritage Dictionary*, College Edition, 1976), the Examining Attorney argues that the term "Oriental" is descriptive of not only the language in which the paper is published but also the general subject matter of the newspaper, that is, its content of daily news about the Orient, the Oriental people and their affairs. Since the doctrine of foreign equivalents should encompass the ideographic symbols of the Chinese language, the Examining Attorney concludes that the mark sought to be registered merely describes a feature or characteristic of applicant's goods.

We agree. While the Board has apparently never considered the applicability of the doctrine of foreign equivalents to the Chinese language, we see no reason why descriptive words represented by Chinese characters should be treated any differently from descriptive words in other contemporary languages. See the discussion of the rationale for this doctrine in *In re Le Sorbet, Inc.*, 228 USPQ 27, 30-31 (TTAB 1985). The foreign equivalent of a merely descriptive or generic English word is no more registrable than the English-language term. McCarthy, *Trademarks and Unfair Competition* §12.13A(2d ed., 1984).

Given that the symbols sought to be registered translate as ORIENTAL DAILY NEWS, it seems to us that the relevant purchasing public is likely to attribute to this combination the significance which the Examining Attorney indicates. For a daily newspaper in the Chinese language apparently printed in Hong Kong, readers in this country (including a sizable number of readers familiar with both the Chinese and English languages) are likely to perceive applicant's mark as merely descriptive of the general focus of the content or the subject matter of applicant's publication, that is, daily news concerning the Orient, the people of that region, their languages, culture and affairs.

Decision: The refusal of registration is affirmed.

17.2.11.2 EU: descriptive in another language

Ellos v. OHIM, Case T-219/00 (EU General Court, 27 Feb. 2002), available at http://curia.europa.eu/juris/showPdf.jsf?text=&docid=46752&pageIndex=0&doclang=EN&mode=lst&dir=&occ=first&part=1&cid=959041

The trade mark in respect of which registration was sought was the term ELLOS [for clothing, footwear, headgear; and for "customer services for mail order sales"]. [Registration was denied and the applicant Ellos appealed.] The Board of Appeal [of the Community Trademark Office] considered, essentially, that the term ELLOS was exclusively descriptive in Spain, given that ELLOS is the third person plural pronoun in the Spanish language and is frequently used as a collective term designating all members of the male sex. The Board of Appeal concluded that the word ELLOS cannot be registered as a trade mark . . . because it designates the type or purpose of those goods [*i.e.*, for male customers, goods sold to men].

The applicant maintains that the word ELLOS is sufficiently 'distinctive' in character to become a Community trade mark. According to the applicant, even if the word 'ellos' is the third person plural of the personal pronoun in the Spanish language, it is not devoid of 'distinctive' character per se.

The Office submits that the word ELLOS, when used in connection with the goods and services referred to by the applicant in its application, will immediately, and without further thought or any other reasoning being necessary, inform Spanish-speaking consumers that those goods and services are intended especially for men.

Under Article 7(1)(c) of Regulation No 40/94, 'trade marks which consist exclusively of signs or indications which may serve, in trade, to designate the kind, quality, quantity, intended purpose, value, geographical origin or the time of production of the goods or of rendering of the service, or other characteristics of the goods or service' are not to be registered.

As regards the question whether, for the section of the public targeted, there is a direct and specific relationship between the sign in question and 'clothing, footwear, headgear', the Board of Appeal rightly considered that the word ELLOS, as the third person plural pronoun in the Spanish language, may be used, in the Spanish-speaking part of the Community, to designate the purpose of those goods, namely 'clothing, footwear, headgear' for male customers.

As regards the question whether, for the section of the public targeted, there is a direct and specific relationship between the sign in question and 'clothing, footwear, headgear', the Board of Appeal rightly considered that the word ELLOS, as the third person plural

CASE *(continued)*

pronoun in the Spanish language, may be used, in the Spanish-speaking part of the Community, to designate the purpose of those goods, namely 'clothing, footwear, headgear' for male customers.

Given the differences which usually exist between clothing for men and clothing for women, the conveying of the information that the clothing is intended for male customers represents an essential characteristic of the goods in question which is taken into account by the section of the public targeted.

[T]he relationship between the word ELLOS and 'customer services for mail-order sales', as described by the Board of Appeal in the contested decision, is too indeterminate and vague to be caught by the prohibition laid down in Article 7(1)(c) of Regulation No 40/94. It follows that the Board of Appeal was wrong in holding that the word ELLOS is exclusively descriptive as regards 'customer services for mail-order sales' and that the present plea should therefore be upheld to that extent [*i.e.*, plaintiff wins on this aspect of the appeal.]

NOTES

1. The holding is premised on the idea that for a large number of consumers (men who speak Spanish), registering "Ellos" for clothing and the like would be descriptive of the goods. "Men" brand "men's clothing" is incapable of distinguishing the brand; it describes a type of goods instead. If Ellos also sells women's clothing, then for women the brand might not be descriptive. (It might sound strange, but would not be descriptive.) However, the fact that for a major segment of consumers (men) Ellos would be descriptive is enough to bar registration of the mark in the Community Trademark Office (now called the EUIPO).

2. Does the same rule of "descriptive in another language" apply to *national* (as opposed to the EU) trademark offices? No, according to the ECJ (now CJEU) in *Matratzen Concord AG v. Hukla Germany SA*, Case C-421/04 (CJEU, 9 March 2006), available at http://curia.europa.eu/juris/showPdf.jsf?text=&docid=57330&pageIndex=0&doclang=EN&mode=lst&dir=&occ=first&part=1&cid=964207. Hukla owned a Spanish national trademark registration for the mark "Matratzen." Plaintiff Matratzen Concord (MC) filed an EU trademark application in the OHIM (now EUIPO). Hukla opposed MC's EU application; and then MC brought a cancellation action in a Spanish court to cancel Hukla's Spanish national registration. MC's argument was that a national registration of a mark with a descriptive meaning in another language might restrict the free movement of goods, which is prohibited under the basic EU treaty. But the court rejected this notion, stating that nothing in Article 3 of the Trademark Directive of 1988 then in effect prevented registration in this situation:

> [T]he Directive does not preclude the registration in a Member State, as a national trade mark, of a term borrowed from the language of another Member State in which it is devoid of distinctive character or descriptive of the goods or services in respect of which registration is sought, unless the relevant parties in the Member State in which registration is sought are capable of identifying the meaning of the term.

17.3 Incontestability

Park'N Fly, Inc. v. Dollar Park and Fly, Inc., 469 U.S. 189 (1985)

Justice O'Connor delivered the opinion of the Court.

In this case we consider whether an action to enjoin the infringement of an incontestable trade or service mark may be defended on the grounds that the mark is merely descriptive. We conclude that neither the language of the relevant statutes nor the legislative history supports such a defense.

Petitioner operates long-term parking lots near airports. After starting business in St. Louis in 1967, [p]etitioner applied in 1969 to the United States Patent and Trademark Office (Patent Office) to register a service mark consisting of the logo of an airplane and the words "Park'N Fly." The registration issued in August 1971. Nearly six years later, petitioner filed an affidavit with the Patent Office to establish the incontestable status of the mark. As required by §15 of the Trademark Act of 1946 (Lanham Act), 60 Stat. 433, as amended, 15 U.S.C. §1065, the affidavit stated that the mark had been registered and in continuous use for five consecutive years, that there had been no final adverse decision to petitioner's claim of ownership or right to registration, and that no proceedings involving such rights were pending. Incontestable status provides, subject to the provisions of §15 and §33(b) of the Lanham Act, "conclusive evidence of the registrant's exclusive right to use the registered mark . . ." §33(b), 15 U.S.C. §1115(b).

Respondent also provides long-term airport parking services, but only has operations in Portland, Oregon. Respondent calls its business "Dollar Park and Fly." Petitioner filed this infringement action in 1978 in the United States District Court for the District of Oregon and requested the court permanently to enjoin respondent from using the words "Park and Fly" in connection with its business. Respondent counterclaimed and sought cancellation of petitioner's mark on the grounds that it is a generic term. See §14(c), 15 U.S.C. §1064(c). Respondent also argued that petitioner's mark is unenforceable because it is merely descriptive. See §2(e), 15 U.S.C. §1052(e).

This case requires us to consider the effect of the incontestability provisions of the Lanham Act in the context of an infringement action defended on the grounds that the mark is merely descriptive. With respect to incontestable trade or service marks, §33(b) of the Lanham Act states that "registration shall be conclusive evidence of the registrant's exclusive right to use the registered mark" subject to the conditions of §15 and certain enumerated defenses. Section 15 incorporates by reference subsections (c) and (e) of §14, 15 U.S.C. §1064. An incontestable mark that becomes generic may be canceled at any time pursuant to §14(c). That section also allows cancellation of an incontestable mark at any time if it has been abandoned, if it is being used to misrepresent the source of the goods or

CASE *(continued)*

services in connection with which it is used, or if it was obtained fraudulently or contrary to the provisions of §4, 15 U.S.C. §1054, or §§2(a)–(c), 15 U.S.C. §§1052(a)–(c) . . .

The language of the Lanham Act also refutes any conclusion that an incontestable mark may be challenged as merely descriptive. A mark that is merely descriptive of an applicant's goods or services is not registrable unless the mark has secondary meaning. Before a mark achieves incontestable status, registration provides prima facie evidence of the registrant's exclusive right to use the mark in commerce. §33(a), 15 U.S.C. §1115(a). The Lanham Act expressly provides that before a mark becomes incontestable an opposing party may prove any legal or equitable defense which might have been asserted if the mark had not been registered. Ibid. Thus, §33(a) would have allowed respondent to challenge petitioner's mark as merely descriptive if the mark had not become incontestable. With respect to incontestable marks, however, §33(b) provides that registration is conclusive evidence of the registrant's exclusive right to use the mark, subject to the conditions of §15 and the seven defenses enumerated in §33(b) itself. Mere descriptiveness is not recognized by either §15 or §33(b) as a basis for challenging an incontestable mark.

Respondent argues, however, that enforcing petitioner's mark would conflict with the goals of the Lanham Act because the mark is merely descriptive and should never have been registered in the first place . . .

The dissent [by Justice Stevens; omitted] echoes arguments made by opponents of the Lanham Act that the incontestable status of a descriptive mark might take from the public domain language that is merely descriptive. As we have explained, Congress has already addressed concerns to prevent the "commercial monopolization" of descriptive language. The Lanham Act allows a mark to be challenged at any time if it becomes generic, and, under certain circumstances, permits the nontrademark use of descriptive terms contained in an incontestable mark [under the trademark "fair use" defense for descriptive marks, described later in this Part]. Finally, if "monopolization" of an incontestable mark threatens economic competition, §33(b)(7), 15 U.S.C. §1115(b)(7), provides a defense on the grounds that the mark is being used to violate federal antitrust laws. At bottom, the dissent simply disagrees with the balance struck by Congress in determining the protection to be given to incontestable marks . . .

We conclude that the holder of a registered mark may rely on incontestability to enjoin infringement and that such an action may not be defended on the grounds that the mark is merely descriptive.

NOTES

1. Incontestable status does not relieve the plaintiff from proving likelihood of confusion, as seen in Lanham Act §33(b): "Such conclusive evidence of the right to use the registered mark shall be subject to proof of infringement as defined in section 32." Section 32 of the Lanham Act defines the test of infringement as unauthorized use which is likely to cause confusion, mistake, or deception.
2. Incontestability applies only to the use of the mark as first registered and as confirmed in the five-year affi-

davit to secure incontestable status; it does not extend to related use of the mark on a product other than one originally associated with the mark. *Westchester Media v. PRL USA Holdings, Inc.*, 214 F.3d 658, 55 U.S.P.Q.2d 1225 (5th Cir. 2000) (attempt to rely on incontestability for POLO mark, originally applied to participants in the sport of Polo, cannot be used to defend attack on a new registration for use of POLO for a general consumer-oriented magazine).

17.4 Priority

17.4.1 Protection without registration

17.4.1.1 Well-known marks

17.4.1.1.1 United States

As we saw earlier, in the US, registration of a trademark first used in commerce overseas can qualify as use under the Lanham Act. *See* Lanham Act §44(e). As discussed earlier in connection with the case of *Grupo Gigante SA De CV v. Dallo & Co.*, 391 F.3d 1088, 1091 (9th Cir. 2004), where the well-known mark doctrine is applied in the US, it grants effective priority to "well-known" or famous marks even before they have been formally used in commerce in the US. But as noted, this is a controversial doctrine and has not been universally embraced.

17.4.1.1.2 Europe

In *El Corte Inglés, SA v. OHIM (EUIPO)*, Case T-420/03 (General Court, 17 June, 2008), available at http://curia.europa.eu/juris/document/document.jsf?text=&docid=69030&pageIndex=0&doclang=EN&mode=lst&dir=&occ=first&part=1&cid=656647, The General Court dealt with an opposition to a Community trademark application submitted by Sanchez and Saugar. The mark was for a stylized version of the word "Boomerang," for telecommunications services such as TV broadcasting. The opposer, plaintiff El Corte Inglés, argued that its trademarks were registered for various classes of goods in Spain and certain other countries, and that even if the classes of goods did not overlap with those listed in the application it was opposing, the Boomerang mark had become famous or well known, and hence the application must be rejected on that basis. The General Court disagreed, citing a WIPO study group document listing stringent requirements for proof that a mark is well known – requirements the court said were not proven in this case:

> Under Article 2 of the joint recommendation concerning the provisions on the protection of well-known trademarks, adopted by the Assembly of the Paris Union and the General Assembly of the World Intellectual Property Organisation

[sic] (WIPO) at the 34th series of meetings of assemblies of the Member States of the WIPO (of 20 to 29 September 1999) [available at http://www.wipo.int/edocs/pubdocs/en/marks/833/pub833.pdf], in determining whether a mark is a well-known mark within the meaning of the Paris Convention, the competent authority can take into account any circumstances from which it may be inferred that the mark is well known, including: the degree of knowledge or recognition of the mark in the relevant sector of the public; the duration, extent and geographical area of any use of the mark; the duration, extent and geographical area of any promotion of the mark, including advertising or publicity and the presentation, at fairs or exhibitions, of the goods and/or services to which the mark applies; the duration and geographical area of any registrations, and/or any applications for registration, of the mark, to the extent to which they reflect use or recognition of the mark; the record of successful enforcement of rights in the mark, in particular, the extent to which the mark has been recognised as well known by competent authorities; the value associated with the mark.

In the present case, it is apparent from the case-file that, in order to establish the existence of its earlier well-known marks in Spain, Ireland, Greece and the United Kingdom, the applicant produced before the Opposition Division, first, extracts from catalogues of its goods, showing that the trade name 'Boomerang' is used for a variety of sports clothing, accessories and equipment, secondly, a photograph of two zeppelin-shaped balloons which bear the word 'Boomerang' taken at a sporting event and, thirdly, various articles from Spanish newspapers relating to an indoor-soccer club called 'Boomerang Interviú' and, later, 'Boomerang', sponsored by the applicant.

It must therefore be held, as the Opposition Division rightly stated and the Board of Appeal confirmed . . ., that those documents do not prove that the trade marks at issue were used or even known or recognised in Ireland, Greece and/or the United Kingdom. Moreover, although those documents prove that at least some of the marks at issue were used by the applicant in Spain, they contain no information as to the duration and the extent of that use, the degree of knowledge or recognition of the trade marks at issue in Spain or any other information from which it might be inferred that the marks at issue are well known in Spain or in a substantial part of Spanish territory.

Thus, the "well-known" mark basis for the opposition was rejected.

Note that "well-known" is different, under EU law, from the important concept of "of more than local significance," which is treated below.

17.4.1.1.3 China

As a member of the Paris Convention, China grants protection to well-known trademarks, as provided by Articles 13–14 of the Chinese Trademark Law (2013), *Provisions on Recognition and Protection of Well-Known Marks* (2014) and also several Judicial Opinions issued by the Chinese Supreme People's Court.

Based on *Provisions of Recognition and Protection of Well-Known Marks*, a well-known trademark refers to a mark, whose reputation has been widely recognized by the relevant public in the territory of China (Article 2). And if a trademark is fortunate enough to be recognized as a well-known trademark, then it will receive "stronger (extra)" protection than ordinary trademarks, primarily in the following two ways: (1) If the well-known trademark is a registered trademark in China, then its protection will extend to other dissimilar goods and services from its own; or (2) if the well-known trademark is a non-registered trademark in China, then it will be treated as a "registered trademark" in China and enjoy protection for goods and services similar to its own (See Article 13 of Chinese Trademark Law.)

A number of factors will be taken into consideration by the Chinese Trademark Office, TRAB and people's courts, the three institutions that have jurisdiction over well-known trademark cases, including: (1) popularity of the mark in its own industry; (2) duration of the mark in use; (3) duration, extent, and geographical range of the advertisement and promotional efforts related to the mark; (4) previous records showing that the mark has been recognized as a well-known trademark, and any other factors that might be relevant. (See Article 14 Chinese Trademark Law and Article 9 *Provisions on Recognition and Protection of Well-Known Marks*.)

The following two cases demonstrate how well-known trademarks are protected in China, one as a non-registered trademark (*Land Rover*) and the other as a registered trademark (*Baidu*).

Land Rover v. TRAB, Beijing High People's Court, Gaoxingzhongzi No. 1151(2011)

On November 10, 1999, Geely filed a trademark application for the mark "陆虎" (meaning "land tiger" in Chinese and pronounced as "lu hu") under application No. 1535599 in Class

CASE *(continued)*

12 with respect to "[v]ehicles; apparatus for locomotion by land, air or water; wheelchairs; motors and engines for land vehicles; vehicle body parts and transmissions," (referred as the "disputed mark.") The application was approved by Chinese Trademark Office on March 7, 2001, with a valid term until March 6, 2021.

On April 26, 2004, Jaguar Land Rover Ltd. ("Land Rover") filed a petition to cancel the disputed mark, alleging violations of Article 31 of Chinese Trademark Law. On July 19, 2010, TRAB rejected the cancellation. Land Rover then appealed to Beijing First Intermediate People's Court.

Beijing First Intermediate Court reasoned as follows: Article 13 of Chinese Trademark Law provides that, "[t]he trademark application shall neither infringe upon another party's prior existing rights, nor be an improper means to register a trademark that is already in use by another party and enjoys substantial influence." Article 3 of *the Regulation for the Implementation of the Trademark Law of the People's Republic of China* ("Implementing Regulations") further specifies that, for purposes of trademark law, the "use of trademark" refers to uses, such as "affixing trademarks to commodities, commodity packages or containers as well as commodity exchange documents or using trademarks to advertisements, exhibitions and other commercial activities." Therefore, trademark squatting arises when a trademark squatter files an application for a mark that: 1) is a prior trademark owned by others; 2) enjoys certain influence; and 3) has been actively used by the legitimate brand owner itself in commerce.

[Land Rover submitted news articles and editorials to show that its SUVs were commonly referred to as "路虎" (identical with the disputed mark) prior to the application date of the disputed mark. In particular, in one of the interview articles with a representative from BMW, the former right holder of Land Rover, the representative also referred the mark "LAND ROVER" as "路虎." Land Rover also submitted over 40 news articles and editorials to prove that the disputed mark was widely recognized as the Chinese name for "LAND ROVER" by the relevant public, and there was a one-to-one relationship between the disputed mark and BMW, the right holder at the time. Therefore, Land Rover concluded that the mark "路虎" had obtained wide recognition among consumers and could serve to identify the source and quality level of the goods.]

[Land Rover also argued that,] as a professional automobile manufacturer, Geely should have known the one-to-one relationship between the mark "路虎" and "LAND ROVER," especially considering the sufficient influence that Land Rover's mark enjoys among the relevant public. Therefore, Geely's conduct was improper because it violated Article 31 of the Trademark Law.

[In the administrative review, Beijing First Intermediate Court found that TRAB failed to consider the evidence provided by Land Rover, thus revoking TRAB's decision and remanding it back for reexamination.]

[Both dissatisfied with the judgment, TRAB and Geely appealed to Beijing High Court.]

During the appeal, TRAB argued that, for the purposes of Article 31 of the Trademark Law, the mark "already in use by another party and enjoys sufficient influence" only refers

CASE *(continued)*

to the *unregistered well-known trademarks* that have gained reputation before the filing date of the disputed mark within certain territories (emphasis added). In addition, according to Article 3 of the Implementing Regulations, the disputed mark must also have been actually used by the legitimate brand owner in its own commerce. TRAB argued that, the news articles and editorials submitted by Land Rover were not created by Land Rover itself, and also were insufficient to prove that Land Rover actually used the disputed mark on automotive products and advertising in Mainland China prior to the application date of the disputed mark. Therefore, TRAB concluded that there was insufficient evidence to prove that Land Rover actively used or advertised the disputed mark. Accordingly, it did not give arise to the bad-faith filing scenario illustrated in Article 31 of the Trademark Law.

Geely argued that: 1) the disputed mark was legally registered by Geely, and Land Rover did not own the disputed mark in any form; 2) Land Rover did not use the disputed mark in the course of its commercial activities prior to the application date of the disputed mark; and 3) there was not a one-to-one relationship between "Land Rover" and the disputed mark because "LAND ROVER" has many versions of Chinese translations, such as "罗孚" or "陆华" and Land Rover never confirmed that the disputed mark was the official Chinese translation for the mark "LAND ROVER."

This court held that, Article 31 of the Trademark Law provides that, "[t]he trademark application shall neither infringe upon another party's prior existing rights, nor be an improper means to register a trademark that is already in use by another party and enjoys substantial influence." The crux of the case is whether the disputed mark "路虎" was used by Land Rover prior to the application date of the disputed mark, and whether the mark enjoyed sufficient reputation among the relevant public in China at that time.

Article 3 of the Implementing Regulation specifies that, for purposes of trademark law, the use of trademark refers to uses such as "affixing trademarks to commodities, commodity packages or containers as well as commodity exchange documents or using trademarks to advertisements, exhibitions and other commercial activities." According to the news articles and editorials submitted by Land Rover during the administrative review procedure, Land Rover's SUVs were referred to as "路虎," in identical Chinese characters with the disputed mark. Although these news articles and editorials did not necessarily demonstrate that the right holder at the time, BMW, actively used the disputed mark for brand communication and media promotion purposes, they were sufficient to prove that the disputed mark was commercialized and pointed to the same product indicated by "LAND ROVER." In addition, during an interview, a BMW representative specifically referred to "LAND ROVER" as "路虎," which should also constitute as active use of the mark.

Granted, there are various ways to translate "LAND ROVER" into Chinese language. However, that does not negate the prior use by BMW or the fact that "路虎" is the Chinese name for "LAND ROVER." Additionally, after considering the number of the news article and editorials submitted by Land Rover and the professional level of such media, [we agreed that] the mark "路虎" enjoyed sufficient influence among the automobile industry prior to the application date of the disputed mark.

CASE *(continued)*

Geely, as a professional automobile manufacturer, should have known the one-to-one relationship between "LAND ROVER" and the mark "路虎," as well as the good reputation that "路虎" enjoyed within the industry. However, it still attempted to register the disputed mark "路虎" [in terms of automobile products in China]. Such conduct was apparently improper.

In summary, Beijing First Intermediate Court gathered the correct evidence, applied the right law, and followed the right procedure. TRAB and Geely's request and reasoning for appeals lacked sufficient evidentiary support, and therefore were not accepted. Pursuant to Article 61(i) of the Chinese Rules of Civil Procedure, we affirm the decision of the court of first instance.

CASE

Baidu v. TRAB, Beijing High People's Court, Gaoxingzhongzi No. 1081 (2012)

The appellant, Trademark Review and Adjudication Board of the State Administration for Industry & Commerce of the People's Republic of China ("TRAB"), appealed to this Court [Beijing High Court] after Beijing First Intermediate Court ruled in favor of the appellee Baidu Online Network Technology (Beijing) Co., Ltd. ("Baidu") in a trademark dispute. Shenzhen Tuberose Dietary Supplement Co. Ltd. ("Tuberose") was the third party in the first-instance trial. On June 18, 2012, this Court accepted this case and opened the court session. This Court hereby made a final ruling.

Both Beijing First Intermediate Court and this Court confirmed the following facts: On March 16, 2000, Baidu filed a trademark application for its mark "Baidu" in Class 42 covering services such as "computer programming, and computer information provided through computer information network" ("subject mark.") The subject mark was approved for registration on May 28, 2001, under registration No. 1579950, with a valid period until May 27, 2021.

On April 13, 2005, Tuberose applied to register the disputed trademark "Baidu" ("the disputed trademark") with the Chinese Trademark Office. On February 14, 2008, the disputed trademark was approved for registration under no. 4599043, in Class 10 of condom and non-chemical contraceptives, with a valid term until February 13, 2018. [Baidu filed a trademark cancellation action against Tuberose's disputed trademark before the TRAB.]

Baidu claimed that as the largest Chinese search engine service provider, the company has registered the mark "Baidu" in numerous classes since 2000. Through years of promotion and commercial use, the subject mark Baidu has obtained a strong recognition

CASE *(continued)*

and reputation among the public, including in the industry of medical products and dietary supplements. Also, the subject trademark "Baidu" was recognized as a well-known trademark in 2008. As such, Baidu concluded that, Tuberose's registration of the disputed trademark in terms of condom products will cause confusion among the public, thus diluting the well-known reputation of Baidu's trademark. Baidu further argued that the disputed trademark, which is identical with the trade name of Baidu, also violated Baidu's prior rights to trade name.

On December 2, 2011, TRAB rejected Baidu's cancellation, finding that the evidence submitted by Baidu could only prove that its Baidu trademark was famous in terms of internet search engine services, but failed to establish that the mark had obtained its well-known status before the application date of the disputed mark. TRAB also concluded that since the disputed mark was registered in a different class from that of Baidu, the registration and use of the disputed trademark would not cause confusion among the public or damage the interests of Baidu.

[Baidu soon filed an administrative lawsuit against the TRAB before Beijing First Intermediate Court.]

[During the trial, Beijing First Intermediate Court summarized the issues of the case as: (1) whether Baidu's "Baidu" trademark is a well-known trademark; and (2) whether the registration of the disputed trademark would confuse the public and cause potential harm to Baidu's corporate interests.]

Beijing First Intermediate Court held that, the term "Baidu" first appeared in an ancient Chinese poem, but otherwise does not have any specific meaning in Chinese language. Because the term has little relevance to the internet search services, the mark "Baidu" should be treated as an arbitrary mark, thus having strong distinctive character as a trademark. Further, [evidence suggested that] the mark "Baidu" has become a well-known trademark among the relevant public through extensive and continuous use. The relevant public can easily associates the mark "Baidu" with the provider of its internet search services – Baidu. Given the well-known status of Baidu's mark and the fact that the disputed mark is identical with Baidu's well-known mark, consumers are likely to be confused even though the goods and services covered by two marks are different. The use of the disputed mark in terms of condom products would still remind consumers of Baidu – the internet search engine company, and such an association would dilute the distinctiveness of Baidu trademark.

Although the condom belongs to the category of daily necessities, it still remains a taboo to some Chinese consumers and is rarely discussed in public life due to the influence of Chinese traditional values. The association between the well-known "Baidu" trademark with condoms therefore might tarnish Baidu's well-known trademark status, thus diminishing consumers' recognition and harming Baidu's interests.

In addition to the disputed trademark, Tuberose also applied for another 147 trademark registrations for its "condom" products, many of which are identical with or similar to other preexisting registered trademarks. This suggests that Tuberose has been fully aware of other companies' prior trademarks, especially well-known trademarks. Here, Baidu's

CASE *(continued)*

"Baidu" trademark is a distinctive mark and also a well-known trademark. One may infer that Tuberose purposefully registered the disputed trademark in order to benefit from the goodwill and reputation of Baidu's well-known trademark. Furthermore, Tuberose used a combination of logos and word marks on its product packages that are highly similar to Baidu's website logo, which is also indicative of Tuberose's ill intention.

As such, the Beijing First Intermediate Court found that the registration of the disputed trademark violated Article 13(2) of Chinese Trademark Law, and thus should be invalidated. The TRAB erred in its findings and its decision should be overruled.

[TRAB was unsatisfied with the trial ruling and then appealed to Beijing High People's Court.]

[Beijing High People's Court started its inquiry with a reading of Article 13(2) of the Chinese Trademark law, *i.e.* whether Baidu's trademark is a well-known trademark registered in China; and if so, whether its protection might extend to dissimilar goods and services.] Article 13(2) of Chinese Trademark Law provides that,

> Where a mark is a reproduction, imitation, or translation of a third-party's famous trademark, which has been registered in China and where the goods are not identical or dissimilar with, and thus may mislead the public and cause injury to the interests of the registrant of the famous trademark, no registration shall be granted and the use of the mark shall be prohibited.

This provision was drafted with the legislative intent to provide relatively stronger and broader protection for well-known trademarks, so as to promote the goodwill and recognition associated with well-known trademarks and to deter bad-faith registration by trademark squatters.

[The main issues are:]

(1) Was Baidu's trademark a well-known trademark before the application date of the disputed trademark?

A well-known trademark refers to a trademark that has obtained wide recognition among the relevant public in China. Article 14 of Chinese Trademark Law lists out the following factors for consideration in determining whether a mark is a well-known trademark: (1) the degree of public recognition of the mark in its own industry; (2) the length of the mark in use; (3) the duration, extent and geographic area of the advertisement and publicity related to the mark; (4) prior records of the mark being recognized as a well-known trademark; and (5) other factors. This court does not require evidence for each of the five factors, but instead will consider all the factors as a whole.

Here, [based on the evidence submitted by Baidu, we found that] the trial court was correct in finding that Baidu registered its trademark in search engine services in China and also that the trademark Baidu had obtained its well-known status before Tuberose applied to register the disputed trademark.

(2) Would the registration of the disputed trademark confuse the public and potentially damage Baidu's legitimate interests?

> **CASE** *(continued)*
>
> The public associates the trademark "Baidu" with the internet search engine company – Baidu. When consumers see the disputed trademark on condoms, they may wrongfully associate such goods with Baidu, thus diminishing the distinctiveness of the well-known trademark.
>
> The evidence also suggests that Tuberose willfully tried to profit from Baidu's good reputation. Tuberose also applied to register another 147 trademarks, such as "BMW," "Nestle," "Nike," "IKEA," "Seven-Up," "Carrefour," "Yahoo" and "Alibaba" etc., on its condom products, many of which are identical with or similar to other preexisting registered trademarks. In addition, the packaging on Tuberose's products included a combination of logos and word marks that also highly resembles Baidu's logo on its website, which also suggests Tuberose's ill intention to free-ride on Baidu's good will.
>
> Tuberose submitted evidence to show that other companies had also registered the mark "Baidu," but failed to prove that these "Baidu" trademarks were in actual use and might cause confusion among the relevant public. In addition, trademark examination is conducted on a case-by-case basis, and registrations of other trademarks are not the reasons to justify that the disputed trademark in this case should also be registered.
>
> Therefore, the trial court was correct in finding that Tuberose's registration of the disputed mark might cause confusion among the public and damage the interests of Baidu. As such, the registration of the disputed trademark should be cancelled.
>
> This is the final ruling.

NOTES

> While it is standard to select up to 10 product classifications in a Chinese trademark application, this still makes it impossible to register for all potential product classes to which a trademark might be attached. This case shows the "famous mark" doctrine may protect an earlier registrant (such as the Baidu search engine) from a competing, later registration in a product class that the earlier registrant did not include in its registration. *See* Stan Abrams, "Prophylactic Filing and Baidu's Victory Over Condom Trademark Squatter," China Hearsay Blog, April 10, 2012, available at http://www.chinahearsay.com/prophylactic-filing-and-baidus-victory-over-condom-trademark-squatter/.

17.4.1.2 Non-well-known marks

17.4.1.2.1 United States

For most trademarks (those that are not famous or well known), priority for non-registered marks is decided according to traditional common law rules. In the earlier section in this chapter on "Use in Commerce," we described those rules and their application. Aside from so-called "token use," *see La Societe Anonyme des Parfums le Galion v. Jean Patou, Inc.*, 495 F.2d 1265, 1269 (2d Cir. 1974), priority is determined according to who first used a mark in commerce. And as described earlier, where two users of the same mark operate in distinct territories (typically states in the US), they may each continue using the mark, and even expand their territorial use, so long as there is no resulting confusion. It is even possible, as discussed earlier, for two registrants to obtain "concurrent use" registration for the same mark.

17.4.1.2.2 EU/Europe

Article 5 of the 2015 Trademark Directive, entitled "Relative Grounds for Invalidity," reads as follows:

1. A trade mark shall not be registered or, if registered, shall be liable to be declared invalid where:
   (a) it is identical with an earlier trade mark, and the goods or services for which the trade mark is applied for or is registered are identical with the goods or services for which the earlier trade mark is protected;
   (b) because of its identity with, or similarity to, the earlier trade mark and the identity or similarity of the goods or services covered by the trade marks, there exists a likelihood of confusion on the part of the public; the likelihood of confusion includes the likelihood of association with the earlier trade mark.
2. 'Earlier trade marks' within the meaning of paragraph 1 means:
   (a) trade marks of the following kinds with a date of application for registration which is earlier than the date of application for registration of the trade mark, taking account, where appropriate, of the priorities claimed in respect of those trade marks:
      (i) EU trade marks;
      (ii) trade marks registered in the Member State concerned or, in the case of Belgium, Luxembourg or the Netherlands, at the Benelux Office for Intellectual Property;
      (iii) trade marks registered under international arrangements which have effect in the Member State concerned;
   (b) EU trade marks which validly claim seniority, in accordance with Regulation (EC) No 207/2009, of a trade mark referred to in points (a)(ii) and (iii), even when the latter trade mark has been surrendered or allowed to lapse;
   (c) applications for the trade marks referred to in points (a) and (b), subject to their registration;
   (d) trade marks which, on the date of application for registration of the trade mark, or, where appropriate, of the priority claimed in respect of the application for registration of the trade mark, are well known in the Member State concerned, in the sense in which the words 'well-known' are used in Article 6bis of the Paris Convention.

3. Furthermore, a trade mark shall not be registered or, if registered, shall be liable to be declared invalid where:
   (a) it is identical with, or similar to, an earlier trade mark irrespective of whether the goods or services for which it is applied or registered are identical with, similar to or not similar to those for which the earlier trade mark is registered, where the earlier trade mark has a reputation in the Member State in respect of which registration is applied for or in which the trade mark is registered or, in the case of an EU trade mark, has a reputation in the Union and the use of the later trade mark without due cause would take unfair advantage of, or be detrimental to, the distinctive character or the repute of the earlier trade mark;
   . . .
   (c) and to the extent that, pursuant to Union legislation or the law of the Member State concerned providing for protection of designations of origin and geographical indications: (i) an application for a designation of origin or a geographical indication had already been submitted in accordance with Union legislation or the law of the Member State concerned prior to the date of application for registration of the trade mark or the date of the priority claimed for the application, subject to its subsequent registration; (ii) that designation of origin or geographical indication confers on the person authorised under the relevant law to exercise the rights arising therefrom the right to prohibit the use of a subsequent trade mark.
4. Any Member State may provide that a trade mark is not to be registered or, if registered, is liable to be declared invalid where, and to the extent that:
   (a) rights to a non-registered trade mark or to another sign used in the course of trade were acquired prior to the date of application for registration of the subsequent trade mark, or the date of the priority claimed for the application for registration of the subsequent trade mark, and that non-registered trade mark or other sign confers on its proprietor the right to prohibit the use of a subsequent trade mark;
   (b) the use of the trade mark may be prohibited by virtue of an earlier right, other than the rights referred to in paragraph 2 and point (a) of this paragraph, and in particular:
      (i) a right to a name;
      (ii) a right of personal portrayal;
      (iii) a copyright;
      (iv) an industrial property right;
   (c) the trade mark is liable to be confused with an earlier trade mark protected abroad, provided that, at the date of the application, the applicant was acting in bad faith.

17.4.1.2.2.1   *"Of more than mere local significance"*

A related concept comes from the Community Trademark Regulation, which, unlike a Directive, bound all Member States upon issuance by the European Parliament and Council, and which is the operational legal authority for the EUIPO. The latest version of this Regulation was enacted on 14 June 2017, *see* https://euipo.europa.eu/ohimportal/en/eu-trade-mark-regulation. The provision in question relates to oppositions to registration brought by owners of unregistered marks.

[Article 8: Relative Grounds for Refusal]

1. Upon opposition by the proprietor of an earlier trade mark, the trade mark applied for shall not be registered:
   (a) if it is identical with the earlier trade mark and the goods or services for which registration is applied for are identical with the goods or services for which the earlier trade mark is protected;
   (b) if because of its identity with, or similarity to, the earlier trade mark and the identity or similarity of the goods or services covered by the trade marks there exists a likelihood of confusion on the part of the public in the territory in which the earlier trade mark is protected; the likelihood of confusion includes the likelihood of association with the earlier trade mark.

2. For the purposes of paragraph 1, 'earlier trade marks' means:

(a) trade marks of the following kinds with a date of application for registration which is earlier than the date of application for registration of the Community trademark, taking account, where appropriate, of the priorities claimed in respect of those trade marks:
   (i) Community trade marks;
   (ii) trade marks registered in a Member State, or, in the case of Belgium, the Netherlands or Luxembourg, at the Benelux Office for Intellectual Property;
   (iii) trade marks registered under international arrangements which have effect in a Member State;
   (iv) trade marks registered under international arrangements which have effect in the Community;
   (b) applications for the trade marks referred to in subparagraph (a), subject to their registration;
   (c) trade marks which, on the date of application for registration of the Community trade mark, or, where appropriate, of the priority claimed in respect of the application for registration of the Community trade mark, are well known in a Member State, in the sense in which the words 'well known' are used in Article 6bis of the Paris Convention.

. . .

4. Upon opposition by the proprietor of a non-registered trade mark or of another sign used in the course of trade of more than mere local significance, the trade mark applied for shall not be registered where and to the extent that, pursuant to the Community legislation or the law of the Member State governing that sign:
   (a) rights to that sign were acquired prior to the date of application for registration of the Community trade mark, or the date of the priority claimed for the application for registration of the Community trade mark;
   (b) that sign confers on its proprietor the right to prohibit the use of a subsequent trade mark.

What does it mean for a mark to be "of more than mere local significance" under Article 8(4)?

CASE

Anheuser-Busch v. Budějovický Budvar, národní podnik, Case C-96/09 (ECJ [CJEU]), 29 March 2011), available at http://curia.europa.eu/juris/document/document.jsf?text=&docid=80814&pageIndex=0&doclang=EN&mode=lst&dir=&occ=first&part=1&cid=665595

[Plaintiff is the well-known US company that makes and sells Budweiser beer; one trademark it owns is for "Bud." Defendants opposed plaintiff's attempt to register "BUD" as a Community trademark.]

By its appeal, Anheuser-Busch Inc. ("Anheuser-Busch") seeks to have set aside the judgment of the Court of First Instance of the European Communities (now "the General Court"), by which the General Court upheld the actions brought by Budějovický Budvar, národní podnik ("Budvar") [upholding opposition to] Anheuser-Busch's applications for registration as a Community trade mark of the sign "BUD".

Article 43(2) and (3) of [the Community Trademark] regulation [of 1993] provides:

2. If the applicant so requests, the proprietor of an earlier Community trade mark who has given notice of opposition shall furnish proof that, during the period of five years preceding the date of publication of the Community trade mark application, the earlier Community trade mark has

CASE *(continued)*

been put to genuine use in the Community in connection with the goods or services in respect of which it is registered and which he cites as justification for his opposition, or that there are proper reasons for non-use, provided the earlier Community trade mark has at that date been registered for not less than five years. In the absence of proof to this effect, the opposition shall be rejected. If the earlier Community trade mark has been used in relation to part only of the goods or services for which it is registered it shall, for the purposes of the examination of the opposition, be deemed to be registered in respect only of that part of the goods or services.
3. Paragraph 2 shall apply to earlier national trade marks . . ., by substituting use in the Member State in which the earlier national trade mark is protected for use in the Community.

In support of its opposition, Budvar relied, first of all, under Article 8(1)(b) of Regulation No 40/94, on the existence of an earlier trade mark, namely international figurative mark 'Bud' (No 361 566), registered for beer, effective in Austria, Benelux and Italy.

By decisions of 23 December 2004 and 26 January 2005, the Opposition Division [of OHIM] dismissed the oppositions filed against the registration of the trade marks covered by the other three trade mark applications; it considered, in essence, that evidence had not been adduced to establish that the appellation of origin 'bud', in the case of France, Italy, Austria and Portugal, was a sign used in the course of trade of more than mere local significance.

[T]he Board of Appeal held that the evidence provided by Budvar to show use of the appellation of origin 'bud' in France, Italy, Austria and Portugal was insufficient. The General Court held that the Board of Appeal was not competent to determine whether Budvar had established the validity of the earlier rights that it relied on under Article 8(4) of Regulation No 40/94 when there were serious doubts as to their validity.

[T]he notion of use of a sign of 'more than mere local significance' is an autonomous requirement of EU law which must be satisfied, as must the other requirements laid down in Article 8(4)(a) and (b) of Regulation No 40/94 and, more generally, all the requirements laid down in Article 8, 'prior to the date of application for registration of the Community trade mark, or the date of the priority claimed for the application for registration of the Community trade mark'.

Anheuser-Busch claims that the General Court also infringed Article 8(4) of Regulation No 40/94 by interpreting incorrectly the words 'of more than mere local significance' contained in that provision.

Anheuser-Busch maintains, in particular, that the 'significance' of a sign within the meaning of Article 8(4) of Regulation No 40/94 must be assessed in relation to the territory in which it is protected, in this case France and Austria.

Moreover, a sign can have significance within the meaning of that provision only if it is used in the markets of the Member States under whose laws it is protected. Such significance cannot stem from the mere fact that the sign is protected under the law of two or more Member States.

Anheuser-Busch concludes that the words 'more than mere local significance' are to be

CASE *(continued)*

interpreted as constituting an autonomous EU law requirement which cannot be subject to national law but which must result from use of the sign in question in the markets of the Member States in whose territory it is protected.

OHIM maintains that, by linking, the 'significance' of the sign to the territorial scope of the protection recognised by the national law relied on, the General Court overlooked the fact that the requirement laid down in Article 8(4) of Regulation No 40/94 that the sign be of more than mere local significance is an EU law requirement that cannot be assessed by reference to national law.

The General Court erred in law by holding that the earlier rights are of more than mere local significance, within the meaning of Article 8(4) of Regulation No 40/94, solely because their protection extends beyond their territory of origin.

According to OHIM, the 'significance' criterion is meant to put an effective limit on all the potential signs, other than trade marks, which could be relied on in order to challenge the registrability of a Community trade mark. Accordingly, this notion must relate to the economic importance and the geographical ambit of the '[use] in the course of trade'.

Budvar maintains, by contrast, that the expression 'more than mere local significance', within the meaning of Article 8(4) of Regulation No 40/94, refers to the geographical extent of the protection of the sign at issue, namely the territory in which the opponent may assert its earlier right, in the present case all French and Austrian territories in which the rights relied on are protected.

That expression therefore refers to the territory in which the sign is protected, not that in which it is used. A contrary interpretation would conflict with the very wording of Article 8(4) of Regulation No 40/94 and, in addition, would amount to imposing on the opponent an additional requirement which, moreover, would not be consistent with Article 107 of Regulation No 40/94, which makes the territory in which the prior right is protected, and not the territory in which it is used, a criterion for implementation of an earlier right.

Where the geographical extent of the protection of a sign is merely local, the sign must indeed be regarded as of mere local significance. However, it does not follow that the condition laid down in Article 8(4) of Regulation No 40/94 is met in every case simply because the sign in question is protected in a territory which cannot be regarded as merely local, in the present case because the territory of protection extends beyond the territory of origin.

The common purpose of the two conditions laid down in Article 8(4) of Regulation No 40/94 is to limit conflicts between signs by preventing an earlier right which is not sufficiently definite – that is to say, important and significant in the course of trade – from preventing registration of a new Community trade mark. A right of opposition of that kind must be reserved to signs which actually have a real presence on their relevant market.

Accordingly, the significance of a sign cannot be a function of the mere geographical extent of its protection, since, if that were the case, a sign whose protection is not merely local could, by virtue of that fact alone, prevent registration of a Community trade mark – and could do so even though the sign is used only to a very limited extent in the course of trade.

It follows that, in order to be capable of preventing registration of a new sign, the sign

CASE *(continued)*

relied on in opposition must actually be used in a sufficiently significant manner in the course of trade and its geographical extent must not be merely local, which implies, where the territory in which that sign is protected may be regarded as other than local, that the sign must be used in a substantial part of that territory.

In order to ascertain whether that is the case, account must be taken of the duration and intensity of the use of that sign as a distinctive element vis-à-vis its addressees, namely purchasers and consumers as well as suppliers and competitors. In that regard, the use made of the sign in advertising and commercial correspondence is of particular relevance.

Since it is necessary to examine the use of the sign concerned in the course of trade in a part – not merely local – of the territory of protection, the General Court also made an error of law in holding that Article 8(4) of Regulation No 40/94 does not require that the sign concerned be used in the territory in which it is protected and that use in a territory other than that in which it is protected may suffice, even where there is no use at all in the territory of protection.

It is in fact only in the territory in which the sign is protected, whether the whole or only part of it is concerned, that the applicable law confers on the sign exclusive rights which may enter into conflict with a Community trade mark.

It follows from the foregoing that [t]he General Court erred in holding, first, that the significance of the sign concerned, which cannot be merely local, must be evaluated exclusively by reference to the extent of the territory in which the sign is protected, without taking account of its use in that territory, second, that the relevant territory for the purpose of evaluating the use of that sign is not necessarily the territory in which the sign is protected and, finally, that the use of the sign does not necessarily have to occur before the date of the application for registration of the Community trade mark.

On those grounds, the Court (Grand Chamber) hereby: . . . Sets aside the judgment of the Court of First Instance of the European Communities.

NOTES

1. The holding here deals with evidence of earlier use of a trademark that is unregistered in some states as evidence that a later-filed Community mark should not be registered. To succeed, an opponent must show that earlier use of the mark has "more than merely local significance." The court says "the use made of the sign in advertising and commercial correspondence is of particular relevance" in this inquiry. Why might this be so? The reason, the court says, is that mere national *registration* is not enough to block a subsequent community trademark application. There must be evidence of *use*:

   > [I]n order to be capable of preventing registration of a new sign, the sign relied on in opposition must actually be used in a sufficiently significant manner in the course of trade and its geographical extent must not be merely local, which implies, where the territory in which that sign is protected may be regarded as other than local, that the sign must be used in a substantial part of that territory.

2. This case is part of a long-running and wide-ranging trademark battle between the giant US beer concern, Anheuser-Busch (AB), and the smaller but older Czech Republic beer maker Budějovický Budvar ("Budvar"). An important subsequent chapter in the conflict resulted in a finding that, at least in some EU states, AB and Budvar *both* had the right to register the "Bud" mark and use them in parallel: a so-

called concurrent use situation. *See Budějovický Budvar Národní Podnik v. Anheuser-Busch Inc.*, 2012 WL 2499981, [2012] EWCA Civ 880; [2012] 3 All E.R. 1405 (UK Court of Appeal, Civ. Division, 3 July 2012) (UK concurrent use upheld). But with respect to the trademark "Budweiser," neither company holds worldwide rights. AB must rely on its "Bud" mark in Europe, because Budvar holds European priority for that mark in many countries. On the other hand, Budvar's beer is sold under the trademark "Czechvar," because of AB's long-standing use in the US. Still another dimension of the case concerns geographical indications: Budweiser means literally (in the Czech language) "beer from the town of Budweis," which lies in the region known as Bohemia. But AB's long-standing use (and long-ago acquired secondary meaning or distinctiveness) renders the mark unfit for designation as an appellation of origin. *See generally* Benjamin Cunningham, "Where a Budwesier Isn't Allowed to Be a Budweiser," Time, Jan. 27, 2014.

3. As this case shows, prior unregistered national use of a trademark can be the basis of national rights, and of an opposition in the EUIPO, but cannot be used to establish EU-wide rights. (Famous or well-known marks might be an exception.) On this general topic, see Verena von Bomhard & Artur Geier, *Unregistered Trademarks in EU Trademark Law*, 107 Trademark Rep. 677, 699 (2017) ("Th[e 2015] Directive has, however, once again stopped short of harmonizing unregistered trademark rights, which continue to remain in the domain of the Member States. The EUTMR [EU Trademark Regulation] recognizes these rights as grounds for both opposition and invalidity, but it does not grant any EU-wide rights based on mere use... Greater harmonization in this respect would be desirable from the perspective of global trademark owners.").

17.4.1.2.3 China

CASE

DANJAQ v. TRAB, Beijing High People's Court, Gaoxingzhongzi No. 374 (2011)

Applicant, XIE filed a trademark application for its trademark "邦德007 Bond" (referred to as "disputed mark") on March 22, 2002, under filing no. 3121466 in Class 10 covering goods condoms and contraception products. [The disputed mark was soon preliminarily approved for registration and published for opposition purpose.]

Figure 17.8 Proposed Bond trademark application

DANJAQ timely filed an opposition against the disputed mark based on its own prior registrations for the mark "007 and device" in Class 28 and also the mark "JAMES BOND" in Class 41.

CASE *(continued)*

During the opposition proceeding, the Chinese Trademark Office rejected DANJAQ's opposition claims on the following grounds: (1) DANJAQ's copyright claim for the title "James Bond 007" is not valid because copyright law protects expressions of a work, but not the title of a work; (2) DANJAQ owns trademark rights for marks "James Bond" and "007" in classes 28 and 41, but not in the same class (Class 10) that XIE's mark was filed; and (3) DANJAQ's claim that XIE maliciously preempted its trademark registration in bad faith is not supported by the existing evidence. Therefore, the Chinese Trademark Office rejected DANJAQ's opposition and approved XIE's trademark No. 3121466 for registration.

DANJAQ soon filed an appeal before TRAB, arguing that: (1) "007" and "JAMES BOND" are both well-known character names of James Bond, a very popular agent character, in the same-title movie franchise series owned by DANJAQ. Therefore, in addition to the copyright and trademark protection for the mark "James Bond" and "007," James Bond should also be protected as a merchandise right associated with the character; (2) The disputed mark is confusingly similar to DANJAQ's well-known James Bond and 007 trademarks, and the co-existence of two marks will cause confusion among the public as to the origin of the goods and services. Thus, the disputed mark should not be allowed for registration. [DANJAQ also submitted evidence to the TRAB, proving the long-term use and reputation of its James Bond trademark in China.]

On March 1, 2010, the TRAB rejected DANJAQ's appeal and affirmed the Chinese Trademark Office's decision, holding that, the disputed trademark was filed under a different class (Class 10) from those goods covered by DANJAQ's prior trademarks in Class 28(*e.g.* toys) and Class 41 (*e.g.* entertainment services.) Therefore, the disputed trademark and DANJAQ's prior trademarks do not constitute similar trademarks in terms of similar goods or services. [As to DANJAQ's copyright claim, TRAB also rejected its claim], holding that although the disputed trademark might remind people of the "007" movie franchise, yet the movie title alone does not have enough originality to be protected as a copyrightable work, thus rejecting DANJAQ's copyright claim. The TRAB also rejected DANJAQ's claim to the merchandise right, on the grounds that such claims have no legal ground in China. As for DANJAQ's claim for well-known trademark protection, the TRAB held that it is difficult to determine whether DANJAQ's marks had become well known in the territory of mainland China in terms of toys and educational services before the application date of the disputed mark. Therefore, the TRAB concluded that the registration of the disputed trademark in Class 10 would not mislead or confuse consumers as to DANJAQ's trademarks in Class 28 and 31.

[DANJAQ was not satisfied with TRAB's decision and soon filed an administrative review suit before Beijing First Intermediate Court.]

Beijing First Intermediate Court partially affirmed and partially revoked the TRAB's decision, holding that, there was insufficient evidence to prove that DANJAQ's trademarks in Class 28 and 41 were well-known trademarks in China before the application date of the disputed mark, thus rejecting DANJAQ's claim for well-known trademark protection. However, the court did find that the disputed mark "邦德 007 Bond" violated the principle

CASE *(continued)*

of good faith and public order, provided under Article 10 (8) of Chinese Trademark Law, thus revoked the TRAB's decision and remanded the case for reexamination by the TRAB.

[The TRAB shortly thereafter appealed before Beijing High People's Court].
This court held that, according to Article 10(8) of the Chinese Trademark Law, trademarks that are detrimental to social morals or customs or having other adverse effects, shall not be used as trademarks. This "unhealthy social influence" clause refers to scenarios under which a trademark could have caused negative effect to China's politics, economy, culture, religions, ethnic groups and other such public interests and public order etc. Because the disputed trademark "邦德007 Bond" in Class 10 does not fall into this category, the court of first instance erred in citing this provision to revoke the TRAB's decision.

This Court found that, before the disputed trademark was filed in China in 2002, the marks "James Bond," "Bond" and "007" have already gained wide reputation and recognition among the relevant public in China, as a result of the world-wide distribution of James Bond movie series. The reputation of the marks "James Bond," "Bond" and "007" is attributed by DANJAQ's creative work, and the commercial value associated with such marks is also attributed to DANJAQ's significant labor and capital investment. Therefore, the names of the characters in the franchise movies should be protected as prior rights.

The TRAB erred in its holding that DANJAQ lacked legal ground to claim merchandise right for the characters "James Bond," "Bond" and "007." This Court hereby reversed its ruling. Also, Beijing First Intermediate Court erred in relying on Article 10(8) of Chinese Trademark Law to reach its decision although its final ruling is correct. As such, this Court affirmed the trial court's final ruling and dismissed the appeals by the TRAB and XIE.

NOTES AND QUESTIONS

1. **Character rights and merchandise rights:** *DANJAQ v. TRAB* might be the first case in China where Beijing courts addressed the concept of "character rights" as prior rights although not so explicitly. A few years later in *DreamWorks v. TRAB*, Gaoxingzhizhongzi No. 1969 (2015), Beijing High Court was asked to address the same issue again – protection of character rights/merchandise rights as prior rights – this time with DreamWorks' *Kung Fu Panda* at stake. At the beginning of the trials, both TRAB and Beijing First Intermediate Court rejected DreamWorks' prior rights claim for merchandise rights and character rights, holding that such prior rights do not have formal legal basis in China. During the appeal, Beijing High Court overruled the lower court's ruling and recognized that names and characters in movies might possess distinctive character and commercial value that are different from the mere box office revenue, thus constituting prior rights under Article 32 of Chinese Trademark Law. In its Opinion, Beijing High Court also contemplated a list of factors for consideration in determining whether a trademark could benefit from "merchandise rights or character rights," such as: (1) the reputation and influence of the mark – the more famous the movie name or the name of the character is, the broader the scope of protection for the merchandising rights; and (2) likelihood of confusion among the public. For example are the goods or services between two parties closely related? Is the later application merely free riding on the reputation or business value of the movie characters? Do you agree with Beijing High Court's decision in *DreamWorks*? Do you think that "character rights or merchandise rights" should be recognized and protected as a separate "prior right"? Why?

2. **Other prior rights:** The Chinese courts have also attempted to protect other prior rights, such as prior

patent rights, prior copyrights, prior trade names and prior rights of people's names etc., in their trademark case law (Article 32 of Chinese Trademark Law). For example, names of celebrities such as "Britney" (singer), "Giorgio Armani" (fashion designer) and "GUO Jing-jing" (former Olympic gold medalist) have been protected in various trademark disputes. (See (2011) Gaoxingzhongzi No. 1640; (2010) gaoxingzhongzi No. 1387 and (2010) yizhongzhixingchuzi No. 382). Also, prior copyrights to paintings and designs were also afforded with protection, (2012) gaoxingzhongzi No. 1255, where the court held that the disputed trademark "Tiger and device" was confusingly similar to the tiger painting created by Tiger Corp.; also *see NBA v. HUANG*, (2013) gaoxingzhongzi No. 343 (holding that the disputed mark "Bull device" is confusingly similar to the NBA's Chicago Bull design).

18
Enforcement

18.1 Infringement

18.1.1 Likelihood of confusion

In the US, Europe, and China, a key concept for determining infringement is the "likelihood of confusion." This brief chapter introduces the concept from the point of view of US law, but the general comments apply to all three major jurisdictions.

We see below how specific standards have been developed for this crucial concept. As an introductory matter, however, it is best to start with the simple idea that confusion between two marks attached to two products is a function of two factors: (1) similarity of the marks; and (2) similarity of the goods. Case law makes this clear. In *In re Majestic Distilling Co., Inc.*, 315 F.3d 1311 (Fed. Cir. 2003), the US Federal Circuit dealt with a case where a trademark applicant appealed from a decision of the Patent and Trademark Office (PTO) Trademark Trial and Appeal Board (TTAB) affirming the examining attorney's refusal to register the mark "RED BULL" for tequila. The Federal Circuit held that substantial evidence supported Board's finding that applicant's mark for tequila was likely to be confused with previously registered "RED BULL" marks for energy drinks. Here the marks were identical, and the products were fairy close (both types of beverages).

The more closely related are the goods, the less similarity between the marks is required to support the ultimate conclusion that confusion is likely. This is evident from a wide variety of cases. See, e.g. *Nautilus Group, Inc. v. ICON Health and Fitness, Inc.*, 372 F.3d 1330 (Fed. Cir. 2004) (where the parties' goods are functionally almost identical, less similarity between their marks is required to justify a finding of likelihood of confusion; the court here affirmed the grant of a preliminary injunction against products sold under the name CrossBow, as likely to be confused with plaintiff's BowFlex mark, where both marks were used on home exercise machines; using law of Ninth Circuit).

When the products are identical, less similarity between marks is required. *See Jules Berman & Associates, Inc. v. Consolidated Distilled Products, Inc.,* 202 U.S.P.Q. 67, 70, 1979 WL 24832 (T.T.A.B. 1979). (Kahlua – Chula both for coffee liqueur); *ECI Division of E-Systems, Inc. v. Environmental Communications Incorporated*, 207 U.S.P.Q. 443, 449, 1980 WL 30140 (T.T.A.B. 1980) ("where as here, the goods of the parties are similar in kind and/or closely related and travel in the same trade channels where they can be encountered by the same purchasers, the degree of similarity of the marks under which these products are sold need not be as great as in the case of diverse or different goods").

These concepts are quite familiar from the European context. We have seen earlier in the section on "Absolute vs. Relative Grounds for Refusal or Invalidity" under the EU Trademark Directive, Article 4, that the same basic principles apply in Europe. Identical marks for identical goods are per se to be refused (or invalidated), while the standard for similar marks and goods is the familiar "likelihood of confusion." *See* earlier section 18.1.1. A simple interpretation of this two-part standard is that confusion is presumed in the case of an identical mark for identical goods, while it must be affirmatively shown in the case of similar marks/goods.

18.1.1.1 United States

Eli Lilly & Co. v. Natural Answers, Inc., 233 F.3d 456 (7th Cir. 2000)

Terence T. Evans, Circuit Judge.
When Internet start-up Natural Answers, Inc. began marketing a line of herbal products called Herbscriptions, we assume it hoped to avoid getting embroiled in a nasty court fight, especially one with a global pharmaceutical giant like the Eli Lilly company. But no such luck, for here it is (along with its founder Brian Feinstein), asking us to reverse a district court order, granted on Lilly's motion for a preliminary injunction, which stopped Natural Answers from marketing its herbal "mood elevator" HERBROZAC. Although Natural Answers does its best to paint this case as David versus Goliath, and hopes for a result similar to that achieved by David, it doesn't have much of a slingshot to carry into the battle.

The basis of Lilly's claim is that the name HERBROZAC comes unfairly close to Lilly's protected mark for PROZAC®, a prescription drug used to treat clinical depression. PROZAC® has received considerable media attention since its rollout in 1988.

CASE *(continued)*

Natural Answers develops, markets, and sells a line of herbal dietary supplements that it calls Herbscriptions. Herbscriptions are positioned as "drug alternatives" and include supplements called HerbenolPM, HERBALIUM, HERBASPIRIN, and HERBADRYL. Natural Answers' Feinstein testified that each name was chosen to call to mind the function of a famous drug from which its name is derived.

Before Natural Answers could get HERBROZAC off the ground, Lilly sued to enjoin use of that name, claiming infringement under the Lanham Trademark Act, 15 U.S.C. §1125(a) [and other causes of action]. [The district court judge granted a preliminary injunction to plaintiff Eli Lilly.]

We turn first to the Lanham Act, enacted in 1946. In the Act, Congress explicitly stated it intended to protect registered marks from interference by state legislation, prevent unfair competition, and protect against fraud "by the use of reproductions, copies, counterfeits, or colorable imitations of registered marks . . ." 15 U.S.C. §1127. Against this background suggesting a broad legislative purpose, courts have come to a consensus that a Lanham Act plaintiff need only establish that its mark is protectable and that the junior mark is likely to cause confusion among consumers. Because Lilly registered the PROZAC® mark in 1985 and has used it continuously for more than 5 years, it is incontestable. *See* 15 U.S.C. §1065. As a result, Natural Answers cannot – and does not – argue that the PROZAC® mark is outside the protection of the Lanham Act.

Natural Answers does contend, however, that consumers are unlikely to be confused by the HERBROZAC name. In assessing the likelihood of consumer confusion, we generally consider seven factors: (1) the similarity between the marks in appearance and suggestion, (2) the similarity of the products, (3) the area and manner of concurrent use of the products, (4) the degree of care likely to be exercised by consumers, (5) the strength of the complainant's mark, (6) any evidence of actual confusion, and (7) the defendant's intent (or lack thereof) to palm off its product as that of another. *Smith Fiberglass Prods., Inc. v. Ameron, Inc.*, 7 F.3d 1327, 1329 (7th Cir.1993). As the district court recognized, these factors are not a mechanical checklist, and "[t]he proper weight given to each . . . will vary from case to case." *Dorr-Oliver, Inc. v. Fluid-Quip, Inc.*, 94 F.3d 376, 381 (7th Cir. 1996). At the same time, although no one factor is decisive, the similarity of the marks, the intent of the defendant, and evidence of actual confusion are the most important considerations. *G. Heileman Brewing Co., Inc. v. Anheuser-Busch, Inc.*, 873 F.2d 985, 999 (7th Cir. 1989).

After an exhaustive analysis of each of the relevant factors, Judge Hamilton concluded that use of the HERBROZAC name was likely to confuse consumers. Specifically, he found that the similarity between the two marks and products, the strength of the PROZAC® mark, consumers' degree of care in choosing between PROZAC® and HERBROZAC, alleged evidence of actual confusion, and Natural Answers' intent to palm off all created a likelihood of confusion. The conclusion regarding likelihood of confusion is a finding of fact which will not be reversed unless it is clearly erroneous.

The similarity between the names PROZAC® and HERBROZAC is obvious: HERBROZAC contains five of the six letters in PROZAC®, and the "B" in HERBROZAC

CASE *(continued)*

sounds similar to the "P" in PROZAC®. Natural Answers argues that the two marks are dissimilar because HERBROZAC may be pronounced with an emphasis on the first syllable (HERBrozac), thus rendering the "B" and "P" sounds less similar than when the second syllable of HERBROZAC is emphasized (herBROzac). Even under Natural Answers' preferred pronunciation (which seems contrary to the natural pronunciation of a combination of the root words "herb" and "Prozac"), however, the two words are strikingly similar.

Natural Answers next argues that the HERBROZAC name merely "calls to mind" PROZAC®, while at the same time distinguishing itself. The mere fact that one mark brings another mark to mind is not sufficient to establish a likelihood of confusion as to the source of the product. *Application of Ferrero,* 479 F.2d 1395, 1397 (C.C.P.A.1973). In addition, Natural Answers asserts that its adaptation of the PROZAC® name is a parody and implies that, as such, it is entitled to some heightened form of protection from trademark liability. In any case, the HERB prefix, according to Natural Answers, so significantly distinguishes HERBROZAC from PROZAC® that consumer confusion is unlikely.

As the district court found, however, "HERBROZAC does much more than merely 'call to mind' the PROZAC® mark." Unlike the mark at issue in *Ferrero*, PROZAC® is a fanciful word that has no meaning independent of Lilly's mark. Such marks are entitled to the highest protection. *See Seven-Up Co. v. Tropicana Prods., Inc.,* 53 C.C.P.A. 1209, 356 F.2d 567, 568 (1966) ("with coined words which are meaningless so far as the English language is concerned, slight variations in spelling or arrangement of letters are often insufficient to direct the buyer's attention to the distinction between marks"). In addition, the district court received evidence that other pharmaceutical companies have expanded their product lines to include dietary supplements based on "St. John's Wort" (the principal herbal component of HERBROZAC), increasing the likelihood that consumers would mistakenly believe that HERBROZAC is affiliated with or sponsored by Lilly. Moreover, HERBROZAC is not a parody of PROZAC®. A parody is a humorous or satirical imitation of a work of art that "creates a new art work that makes ridiculous the style and expression of the original." *Rogers v. Koons,* 960 F.2d 301, 309–10 (2d Cir. 1992). Natural Answers does not even attempt to point out any humor or satire in its imitation of the PROZAC® mark. Given the strong similarity in the marks and the potential overlap in Lilly's and Natural Answers' product lines, the mere addition of the HERB prefix does not go far enough to distinguish Natural Answers' product from PROZAC®. Accordingly, the strong similarity of the marks weighs heavily in favor of a finding of likelihood of confusion. [Preliminary injunction affirmed.]

NOTES

1. The seven-factor test used by the Seventh Circuit in *Eli Lilly* is typical of the tests used by the various circuits, even though those tests often involve a few more factors. *See, e.g., Polaroid Corp. v. Polarad Electronics Corp.,* 287 F.2d 492 (2d Cir. 1961), cert. denied, 368 U.S. 820, 82 S. Ct. 36, 131 U.S.P.Q. 499 (1961) (setting

out eight-factor test still used in the Second Circuit); *AMF, Inc. v. Sleekcraft Boats*, 599 F.2d 341 (9th Cir. 1979) (similar eight-factor test); *In re E. I. Du Pont de Nemours & Co.*, 476 F.2d 1357 (C.C.P.A. 1973) (13-point test still used by the Federal Circuit). The Supreme Court has recognized, in a decision that makes TTAB similarity decisions binding on court actions involving the same parties, that "the [likelihood of confusion] factors are not fundamentally different" in the Federal Circuit (which reviews TTAB findings) and the Eighth Circuit. *B & B Hardware, Inc. v. Hargis Indus., Inc.*, 135 S. Ct. 1293, 1307 (2015). This despite the fact that the Federal Circuit employs 13 factors under the *DuPont* test, while the Eighth Circuit employs a six-factor test. See *SquirtCo v. Seven-Up Co.*, 628 F.2d 1086 (8th Cir. 1980) (six-factor test).

2. Likelihood of confusion is not only relevant in trademark infringement litigation; it is also the standard used by the TTAB in making registration decisions, and conducting oppositions and cancellation proceedings. Lanham Act §2, 15 U.S.C.A. §1052. See *B & B Hardware, Inc. v. Hargis Indus., Inc.*, 135 S. Ct. 1293, 1307 (2015); *Tillamook Country Smoker, Inc. v. Tillamook County Creamery Ass'n*, 465 F.3d 1102, 1111 (9th Cir. 2006) ("Under §2(d) of the Lanham Act, 15 U.S.C.A. §1052(d), the test for trademark registration uses the same 'likelihood of confusion' standard as the test for trademark infringement").

3. Notice that "strength of the mark" uses the same spectrum as the Trademark Office uses for registration: arbitrary/fanciful; suggestive; descriptive; and (unprotectable) generic marks.

18.1.1.2 Europe

Article 5 of the EU Trademark Directive of 1998 (as amended and restated in 2015) says this about the standard for trademark infringement:

Article 5
Rights Conferred by a Trademark

1. The registered trade mark shall confer on the proprietor exclusive rights therein. The proprietor shall be entitled to prevent all third parties not having his consent from using in the course of trade:
   (a) any sign which is identical with the trade mark in relation to goods or services which are identical with those for which the trade mark is registered;
   (b) any sign where, because of its identity with, or similarity to, the trade mark and the identity or similarity of the goods or services covered by the trade mark and the sign, there exists a likelihood of confusion on the part of the public, which includes the likelihood of association between the sign and the trade mark.

We have already covered what is meant by the phrase "an earlier mark" (which is detailed in Article 5.2), in the earlier section on registration, Section 17.1.

This provision differs from the US Lanham Act in that it separates infringement into two types: (1) identical (as to the mark and the goods); and (2) similar. The second category is handled under the same standard as the US Lanham Act – likelihood of confusion. For the first, there is either no requirement that confusion be proven; or, alternatively, confusion is presumed from the identical nature of the goods and the mark. In such cases, because of the identity of the mark and the products, the only remaining issue will often be the question of "genuine use" under EU law. *See, e.g., Ansul BV v. Ajax Brandbeveiliging BV*, Case C-40/01 (ECJ [CJEU], 11 March 2003), in Chapter 17.

When it comes to non-identical marks and products, how does European law work? Consider the following case.

 CASE

L'Oréal SA v. Bellure NV, Case C-487/07 (ECJ [CJEU]), 18 June 2009), available at http://curia.europa.eu/juris/document/document.jsf?text=&docid=75459&pageIndex=0&doclang=EN&mode=lst&dir=&occ=first&part=1&cid=1139685

[Defendant Bellure sells low-cost imitations of plaintiff's expensive branded perfumes.] In marketing perfumes . . ., [Bellure] use[s] comparison lists which they provide to their retailers and which indicate the word mark of the fine fragrance of which the perfume being marketed is an imitation ("the comparison lists"). [Thus, Bellure's list says, for example, that its "La Veleur" perfume imitates L'Oréal's "Tresor" perfume. L'Oréal says the comparison lists infringe its trademarks directly; that defendant's similar-looking packaging infringes its packaging trademarks; and that the comparison list is illicit comparative advertising.]

The protection conferred by Article 5(1)(a) of Directive 89/104 is . . . broader than that provided by Article 5(1)(b), the application of which requires that there be a likelihood of confusion and accordingly the possibility that the essential function of the mark may be affected. [T]he protection afforded by the registered trade mark is absolute in the case of identity between the mark and the sign and also between the goods or services, whereas, in case of similarity between the mark and the sign and between the goods or services, the likelihood of confusion constitutes the specific condition for such protection.

It is apparent from the case-law . . . that the proprietor of the mark cannot oppose the use of a sign identical with the mark on the basis of Article 5(1)(a) of Directive 89/104 if that use is not liable to cause detriment to any of the functions of that mark.

Thus, the Court has already held that certain uses for purely descriptive purposes are excluded from the scope of application of Article 5(1) of Directive 89/104, because they do not affect any of the interests which that provision is intended to protect and accordingly do not constitute "use" within the meaning of that provision (see, to that effect, Case C-2/00 *Hölterhoff* [2002] ECR I-4187, paragraph 16).

It must, however, be made clear that the situation described in the main proceedings is

CASE *(continued)*

fundamentally different from that which gave rise to the judgment in *Hölterhoff*, in that the word marks belonging to L'Oréal are used in the comparison lists distributed by [Bellure] not for purely descriptive purposes, but for the purpose of advertising.

It is for the referring court to determine whether, in a situation such as that which arises in the main proceedings, the use which is made of the marks belonging to L'Oréal is liable to affect one of the functions of those marks, such as, in particular, their functions of communication, investment or advertising.

NOTES

1. With the ECJ's opinion here in hand, the UK Court of Appeal (Civil Division) found that Bellure had in fact infringed L'Oréal's trademarks by virtue of Bellure's "comparison list." *L'Oréal SA v. Bellure NV*, 2010 WL 1990595, [2010] R.P.C. 23; (2010). The Court of Appeal was, however, doubtful about the rationale provided by the ECJ:

   [T]he [ECJ] has indicated the answer as to whether the use is within Art.5(1)(a). According to the Court the use goes beyond "purely descriptive" use because it is used for advertising. A line is apparently to be drawn between something like a discussion between a would-be seller and his potential customer ("I can supply a diamond cut in the same shape as Spirit Sun"), which is apparently not "advertising" even though "Spirit Sun" is being used to gain a sale, and an out-and-out general purpose advertising aid such as a comparison list. I confess I do not know where that line is, but this case falls the wrong side of it. Why? Because the Court has said so. It regards the use as affecting the communication, advertising and investment functions of the mark (*L'Oréal SA v. Bellure NV*, [2010] R.P.C. 23, at par. 31).

2. A second issue in the *L'Oréal* case was comparative advertising. L'Oréal claimed that the comparison list was a comparative ad that violated the terms of the EU Directive on Comparative Advertising, Directive 2006/114/EC of 12 December 2006 concerning misleading and comparative advertising (previously Directive 84/450/EEC of 10 September 1984), as amended by Directive 97/55/EC (6 October 1997). The operative section of this Directive was Article 3a, which reads:

   Comparative advertising shall, as far as the comparison is concerned, be permitted when the following conditions are met:
   (a) it is not misleading according to Articles 2(2), 3 and 7(1);
   . . .
   (d) it does not create confusion in the market place between the advertiser and a competitor or between the advertiser's trade marks, trade names, other distinguishing marks, goods or services and those of a competitor;
   (e) it does not discredit or denigrate the trade marks, trade names, other distinguishing marks, goods, services, activities, or circumstances of a competitor;
   . . .
   (g) it does not take unfair advantage of the reputation of a trade mark, trade name or other distinguishing marks of a competitor or of the designation of origin of competing products;
   (h) it does not present goods or services as imitations or replicas of goods or services bearing a protected trade mark or trade name.

   The ECJ (CJEU) stated that the purpose of this Article 3a was to prohibit an advertiser from stating in comparative advertising that its product is an imitation or replica of the product covered by the trade mark. The comparison list had the function of implicitly communicating that the listed products were imitations or replicas of L'Oréal's trademarked perfumes. This was so, the ECJ said, even though the comparison list was keyed to the fragrance of each perfume and not necessarily the overall trade impression of the perfume. The end result was that the list allowed Bellure to take unfair advantage of the reputation of L'Oréal's marks within the meaning of Article 3(1)(g) of the Directive.

3. The case of *Holterhoff v. Freiesleben*, Case C-2/00 (ECJ [CJEU]14 May 2002), [2002] E.C.R. I-4187; [2002] All E.R. (EC) 665; [2002] E.T.M.R. 79; [2002] F.S.R. 52 (ECJ), cited in the ECJ opinion, dealt with a diamond cutter who supplied cut stones to the trademark owner Freiesleben. The dealer, when describing his services to a third party, said that he would supply stones with the type of cut of the precious stones covered by the trademark. The ECJ held that this description was not intended to suggest that the stones originated in Mr. Freiesleben's company, and that therefore he had not used the trademarked terms as an indicator of source (*i.e.*, in a trademark sense), and hence there should be no finding of trademark infringement.

18.1.2 China: "confusing similarity"

To bring a prima facie trademark infringement case before Chinese courts, plaintiff needs to prove: (1) ownership of a valid trademark registration; (2) defendant's mark is confusingly similar to plaintiff's mark in terms of similar goods and/or services; (3) defendant's mark is used in the context of trademark law; and (4) likelihood of confusion among the relevant public. (*See* Article 57 Chinese Trademark Law; Supreme People's Court Judicial Interpretation Regarding Application of Law in Trademark Disputes (2002) No. 32, referred to as "Judicial Interpretation No. 32".)

With regard to the standard in determining "identical or similar marks in terms of similar goods/services," the Judicial Interpretation No. 32 issued by the Chinese Supreme Court and the related case law have helped to provide certain guidance in clarifying this issue. As a general rule, two marks will be deemed as "identical marks" if they are "visually indistinguishable." Likewise, two marks will be deemed as "confusingly similar marks," if: (1) they are similar with respect to visual effect, pronunciation, and concept in terms of word marks; or in terms of device marks, three-dimensional marks or color marks, they share overall similarity when viewed as a whole; and (2) the similarity between two marks is likely to cause confusion among the relevant public with respect to the origin of the goods and services (Art. 9 of Judicial Interpretation No. 32).

When determining the similarity between "the goods and services" covered by two marks, courts usually consider the following factors, including whether the goods serve similar purposes and functions, whether they come from similar production lines, whether they share similar distribution channels and consumer groups, and lastly whether the relevant public might associate one product with the other (Art. 11 of Judicial Interpretation No. 32).

The following case provides an interesting example of how Chinese courts apply the "similarity standard" with respect to similar marks in terms of similar goods or services.

Samsung v. TRAB, Beijing High People's Court, Gaoxingzhongzi No. 2015 (2013)

Applicant, Samsung Electronics Ltd., filed a trademark application for mark "三星" ("Samsung" in Chinese characters, herein referred as "the applied mark") to the Chinese Trademark Office under filing No. 8494295 in Class 9, covering goods such as television, telephone, mobile phone, laptop, videophone, copying machine, battery charger, etc.

The applied mark was partially rejected by the Chinese Trademark Office on the grounds that it was confusingly similar to two prior trademark applications in terms of similar goods in Class 9. Among the two cited trademarks, one is a pending trademark application for mark "三星" (identical with the applied mark) filed by China Shanxing Ltd. in Class 9 under no. 4814059 ("Cited Mark No. 1"). The other one is an existing trademark registration for mark "三星 Shanxing and device" under no. 214738 in Class 9 covering goods "screens," filed by Zhangjiagang Electronic Instructional Equipment ("ZEIE") on March 7, 1984. ("Cited Mark No. 2") Cited Mark No. 2 was later approved for registration on October 30, 1984, with a valid period until October 29, 2014. As a result, the Chinese Trademark Office rejected the applied mark for registration in terms of the following goods "battery, camera, solar cell and battery chargers," which are considered as similar goods with those of the two prior trademarks, and only approved the applied mark for registration in terms of the goods "videophone, telephone, smart phone, mobile phone and laptop etc."

[Dissatisfied with the Trademark Office's decision, Samsung filed an appeal before the TRAB, arguing that: (1) because Cited Mark No. 1 is still pending and has not been approved for registration, it should not constitute an obstacle for the registration of the applied mark; and (2) the goods "screens" covered by the Cited Mark No. 2 are not similar to the rejected goods "cameras" covered by the applied mark, and thus, they are not similar marks in terms of similar goods.]

On October 8, 2012, TRAB partially approved and partially rejected Samsung's appeal, holding that: (1) because Cited Mark No. 1 was rejected for registration during the opposition procedure, it no longer constitutes an obstacle to the registration of the applied mark. Therefore, the goods "battery products" designated by the applied mark can now proceed into registration; (2) the applied mark is similar to the Cited Mark No. 2 in terms of visual effect, pronunciation and concept because both marks contain the Chinese characters "三星." Also, the goods "camera" covered by the applied mark fall into the same subgroup 0909 with the goods "screens" designated and approved by the Cited Mark No. 2, and therefore, two marks are similar marks in terms of similar goods, and the goods "camera" filed by Samsung cannot be approved for registration.

Beijing First Intermediate Court held that, the "Classification Chart for Similar Products and Services" ("Classification Chart") was drafted by the Chinese Trademark Office based on *Nice Agreement Concerning the International Classification of Goods and Services for the Purposes of the Registration of Marks*. According to the Judicial Interpretation Regarding

CASE *(continued)*

Application of Law Related to Trademark Disputes issued by the Chinese Supreme People's Court (2002) No. 32, when considering the similarity between the goods covered by the applicant's mark and the prior marks, the courts may refer to the Classification Chart for reference.

Here, Cited Mark No. 2 was registered in Class 9 covering goods "screens," which falls into subgroup 0909. The applied mark was filed in Class 9 covering goods "camera product," which also falls into subgroup 0909. Because "screens" and "camera products" share similar purposes, usage, distribution channels and consumer groups, they constitute similar products. As such, Beijing First Intermediate Court rejected Samsung's argument that its "camera products" are not similar goods with the screen products covered by the Cited Mark No. 2, thus affirming TRAB's ruling.

Samsung shortly filed a review before Beijing High Court, arguing that: (1) the goods covered by the Cited Mark No. 2 "screens" and the goods "camera products" covered by the applied mark significantly differ in terms of function, material, distribution channels, market and consumer groups, and therefore, they are not similar goods. (2) Samsung was established in 1969, and its house mark "SAMSUNG" has been a well-known trademark due to its extensive use and promotional efforts. In China, as early as in 2006, the mark "Samsung" was already recognized as a well-known trademark. There has been a one-to-one relationship between the applied mark "Samsung" in Chinese characters and Samsung – the origin of the goods, and therefore, the registration of the applied mark in terms of "cameras" in class 9 would not mislead consumers as to the origin of such products.

[Samsung also submitted evidence, during the trial, regarding the product categories related to "cameras" and "screens" on various e-commerce websites, such as Amazon, Taobao and JD etc. The evidence showed that "screens" belong to the category of "office supplies," whereas "camera products" belong to the category of "digital products" as listed by various websites. Samsung also submitted evidence regarding the well-known status of its house mark "Samsung."]

The issue presented before this court is whether the applied mark is similar to the Cited Mark No. 2 in terms of similar goods according to Article 28 of Chinese Trademark Law.

Similar goods refer to those goods that share similarities in terms of function, usage, production units, distribution channels and markets etc., or that they share special connections and therefore might allow the consumers to associate one with the other. The Classification Chart might be used for reference when determining whether the goods or services filed by two marks are similar, but at the same time, equal emphasis should also be focused on the actual market practice, the general perspective of the relevant public, and other factors that might also be relevant.

Here, the material for the screen products designated by Cited Mark No. 2 is fabric or plastic; its function is to serve the projection purpose, and its consumer groups are usually cinemas and education institutions. The primary distribution channel for screen products is through non-electronics products. As such, the "screens" approved for the Cited Mark No. 2 are different products from "cameras" designated by the applied mark from the

> **CASE** *(continued)*
>
> perspective of the relevant public. As such, the goods covered by two marks are not similar goods.
>
> Also, [in terms of two marks], the primary element in the applied mark is the Chinese characters "三星" (Samsung in Chinese translation), while Cited Mark No. 2 is a combination mark, including Chinese characters "三星," Roman letters "Shanxing" and also a device. Therefore, the two marks are visually different from each other too. As such, the co-existence of two marks will not cause confusion among the consumers.
>
> To summarize, this court hereby reversed Beijing First Intermediate Court's decision and the TRAB's ruling.
>
> This is the final ruling.

NOTES AND QUESTIONS

1. In the Judicial Interpretation No. 32, Chinese Supreme Court also included three principles in determining whether two marks constitute identical or similar marks. First, the examination should be based on "the relevant public" standard. Here, the "relevant public" refers to the consumers and industry players (such as competitors, vendors and distributors), who are associated in the field of the relevant goods and services. Second, the similarity comparison should be conducted against the prominent elements of the two marks. Third, the reputation of two marks should also be taken into consideration. With regard to the first principle, why do you think that the Chinese Supreme Court applied the "relevant public" standard versus the "general public" standard when making the similarity determination?
2. In trademark infringement cases, plaintiff also needs to prove the likelihood of confusion among the relevant public. In *JIANG Ya-Mei v. Sichuan Zhangfei Beef Ltd.*, (2012) changminchuzi No. 3064, Beijing Changping District Court acknowledged that defendant's mark "Zhang Fei" is similar to Plaintiff's prior trademark registration "Zhang Fei and device" in terms of similar services (*i.e.* restaurant business), but nonetheless found no trademark infringement. The court ruled that there was "no likelihood of confusion" among the relevant public due to the different geographic coverage, the consumer groups and how the marks were actually used by two parties, thus rejecting plaintiff's claims for trademark infringement.

18.1.3 Famous marks

18.1.3.1 United States

We have seen that trademarks can be protected against infringing uses on identical or similar goods. Now we explore federal Lanham Act protection for use of a trademark on a completely unrelated good. This is known as antidilution protection.

The difference between traditional trademark infringement and protection against dilution can be seen in the names themselves. To infringe a right is to break in on it, to encroach on it; the word "infringe" has a strong physical connotation, which suggests that a transgressor has stepped onto or over the edge of some type of physical boundary. ("Fringe," after all, means a border, edging or margin.)

Dilution has an altogether different connotation. This word generally means "to weaken or reduce the consistency" of something, typically by adding water. A common idiom is "watered down."

Antidilution protection arose in trademark law (first at the state level, then only later in the federal Lanham Act) as a way of providing protection for a trademark when another user was using the mark on goods completely unrelated to those sold by the trademark owner. It originated in Germany, and made its way to the US. *See* Walter Derenberg, *The Problem of Trademark Dilution and the Antidilution Statutes*, 44 Cal. L. Rev. 439 (1956); 4 McCarthy on Trademarks and Unfair Competition §24:67 (4th ed. & Supp., 2016). *See* Frank I. Schechter, *The Rational Basis of Trademark Protection*, 40 Harv. L. Rev. 813 (1927) (proposing antidilution protection in the US).

So in a famous early case, the well-known maker of camera film, Kodak, brought suit against a bicycle shop that had begun selling bicycles under the trademark "Kodak Brand Bicycles," even though the bicycle shop had no connection whatsoever to the well-known film and camera maker. Cameras are very different from bicycles, and it is highly likely that no appreciable number of consumers would believe that the bike shop was part of Kodak. Thus there is probably no likelihood of confusion in this case. Even so, Kodak the film and camera company argued that the mere use of the Kodak name on a product other than camera and film would reduce the distinctiveness of the Kodak mark, and therefore cause an economic injury. *Eastman Photographic Materials Co. v. John Griffiths Cycle Corp.*, 15 R.P.C. 105 (High Ct. of Justice, Ch. 1898). The idea behind the lawsuit was that Kodak is a very distinctive word. If many companies began using the trademark on all kinds of products, Kodak would cease to be uniquely associated with the well-known film and camera company.

It is this "reduction in overall distinctiveness" that leads to one of two common categories of dilution: dilution by "blurring." The blurring metaphor is very close to the original "watering down" metaphor associated with the concept of antidilution protection. The basis idea is that the uniqueness of a mark is undermined when it is used on a range of products other than the ones originally associated with the trademark. *See* Monica Hof Wallace, *Using the Past to Predict the Future: Refocusing the Analysis of A Federal Dilution Claim*, 73 U. Cin. L. Rev. 945 (2005).

The other branch of antidilution applies when a mark is used on a product or in a way that would tend to create negative associations in the minds of consumers: something in poor taste, or "unwholesome", or associated with low moral standards. Thus a seller of t-shirts using the trademark "Buttweiser" was enjoined from further sales by the owner of the famous BUDWEISER beer trademark. *Anheuser-Busch, Inc. v. Andy's Sportswear, Inc.,* 40 U.S.P.Q.2d 1542 (N.D. Cal. 1996). *See generally* 4 McCarthy on Trademarks and Unfair Competition §24:89 (4th ed. & Supp., 2016) (tarnishment occurs when "the effect of the defendant's unauthorized use is to dilute by tarnishing or degrading positive associations of the mark and thus, to harm the reputation of the mark").

It is essential to any dilution claim that the trademark in question must be very well known or, under the Lanham Act, "famous." In order to be "famous," a mark must be "widely recognized by the general consuming public of the United States" as a designation indicating a single source of goods or services (Lanham Act §43(c)(2), 15 U.S.C.A. §1125(c)(2)). Fame, for purposes of a federal antidilution claim, can be quite difficult to prove. *See, e.g., Coach Services, Inc. v. Triumph Learning LLC,* 668 F.3d 1356, 1373 (Fed. Cir. 2012) (evidence did not prove that COACH for high-end handbags and leather goods was a "famous" mark for purposes of federal antidilution claim.)

The Supreme Court read the new federal antidilution statute to require proof of actual dilution resulting from the defendant's use of the mark (*Moseley v. V Secret Catalogue, Inc.,* 537 U.S. 418 (2003)). Because this was considered a very stringent (and hard-to-meet) standard, Congress quickly amended the statute in the Trademark Dilution Reform Act of 2006 (TDRA), Pub. L. No. 109-312, 120 Stat. 1730, 1730. The TDRA now requires merely that the trademark owner show that a defendant's use of the trademark is "likely to cause dilution by blurring or dilution by tarnishment":

> Dilution by Blurring; Dilution by Tarnishment. (1) Injunctive Relief. Subject to the principles of equity, the owner of a famous mark that is distinctive, inherently or through acquired distinctiveness, shall be entitled to an injunction against another person who, at any time after the owner's mark has become famous, commences use of a mark or trade name in commerce that is likely to cause dilution by blurring or dilution by tarnishment of the famous mark, regardless of the presence or absence of actual or likely confusion, of competition, or of actual economic injury (TDRA, §2(1)).

Even after this amendment, however, the federal courts remain somewhat at odds with each other as regards the proper test for dilution. *See* Keith C. Rawlins, *Likelihood of Dilution by Blurring: A Circuit Comparison and Empirical*

Analysis, 16 Tex. Intell. Prop. L.J. 385, 410 (2008) (showing that the regional federal circuits in the US employ three different tests for determining "likelihood of dilution" under federal dilution law). As a consequence, it can be difficult to prove dilution even for a trademark that is famous. *See, e.g., AutoZone, Inc. v. Tandy Corp.*, 373 F.3d 786 (6th Cir. 2004) (retail automotive parts seller failed to establish dilution of its famous "AutoZone" mark by consumer electronics seller's use of "PowerZone" mark; marks were insufficiently similar to cause actual dilution and there was no other evidence of actual dilution).

Finally, because "tarnishment" can contain an element of satire or humor, and because using a trademark to make a joke at the expense of the mark owner is protected under the first amendment law of parody (see below), dilution by tarnishment can be further limited. *See, e.g., Mattel, Inc. v. MCA Records, Inc.*, 296 F.3d 894 (9th Cir. 2002) (use of the mark BARBIE in a song by a rock band was permitted as it parodied and made fun of the brainless, passive image that has evolved from the trademarked BARBIE doll sold by plaintiff Mattel).

18.1.3.2 China

Sotheby's v. Sichuan Sotheby, Beijing High People's Court (2008) Gaominzhongzi No. 322

Plaintiff Sotheby's, Inc. ("Sotheby's") was established in London in 1744. It is one of the oldest and most reputable international auction houses for fine and decorative art, jewelry, real estate and collectibles.

On January 21, 1995, Sotheby's registered its English-word mark "Sotheby's" under registration No. 776055 in Class 35 in China in terms of auction services. Later, Sotheby's also registered the same English-word mark in Classes 36 and 37. Between 1999 and 2000, Sotheby's also filed and registered its Chinese mark "苏富比" (Sotheby in Chinese characters) in Classes 16, 19, 21, 24, and 27 in China. In Class 35 "auction services", Sotheby's owns a pending application for the Chinese word mark "苏富比" (Sotheby in Chinese characters) filed on May 15, 2006, [which remains pending at the time of the litigation].

Sotheby's Hong Kong, Ltd. ("Sotheby's Hong Kong") is a wholly-owned subsidiary of Sotheby's. It was founded in Hong Kong on May 7, 1974, with the sole purpose to promote plaintiff's auction services in Asia. Sotheby's Hong Kong was authorized to use both the English-word mark "Sotheby's" and its Chinese character mark "苏富比" by its parent company in Hong Kong and mainland China.

CASE *(continued)*

On June 5, 1988, Sotheby's Hong Kong held the "Return of Marco Polo" auction in the Forbidden City in Beijing. *People's Daily*, [a major national newspaper], covered the event both on May 27 and June 6, 1988. The May 27 article specifically referred to the host of the auction as "the UK auction house Sotheby's." The June 6 article referred to the host of the auction as "the world-renowned auction house – International Sotheby's Auction Company." Both the English word and Chinese character marks "苏富比" and "Sotheby's" were used in the promotional materials for the auction.

On May 17, 1994, Sotheby's Hong Kong opened its Shanghai office. Since then, the Shanghai office hosted biannual spring and fall exhibition previews in Beijing and Shanghai. The marks "Sotheby's," "苏富比" and the calligraphy version of "苏富比" have been used by Sotheby's Hong Kong and its Shanghai Office in the catalogues, promotional materials and invitation letters distributed at various exhibitions.

On August 22, 2006, Sotheby's filed a complaint to the Online Dispute Resolution Center of China International Economic and Trade Arbitration Commission ("Resolution Center"), alleging that Ningbo Huiya Investment Ltd. ("Huiya Investment") registered the domain names <sotheby's.cn> and <sotheby's.co> in bad faith. On December 15, 2006, the Resolution Center issued the verdict No. 0205, holding that the Chinese character mark "苏富比" has earned certain recognition in China, and therefore, the disputed domain names were registered in bad faith by Huiya Investment and should be transferred to Sotheby's.

Defendant Sichuan Sotheby Auction Company ("Sichuan Sotheby") was established on December 5, 2003. [During the trial preparation stage, Plaintiff's counsel went to China's Auction Exhibition and notarized various documents and promotional materials distributed by the defendant. In the pamphlet distributed by the defendant, the words "中国苏富比"(meaning "China Sotheby's") and "苏富比及图" (meaning "Sotheby's & device") appeared on every page of the brochure. In addition, the words "苏富比拍卖" (meaning "Sotheby's Auction") and the calligraphy version of "苏富比" ("Sotheby" in Chinese) were also included on many pages in the pamphlet. In particular, in the introduction paragraph, the defendant Sichuan Sotheby was described to be a subsidiary of China Sotheby Auction Ltd, which owns a number of companies, including Defendant's company, Sichuan Sotheby Media, China Sotheby Publishing (Holdings) Ltd., Hong Kong Sotheby International Auction Ltd., Hong Kong Sotheby Capital Investment Ltd., and Guangxi Beihai Sotheby E-Commerce Co. Ltd. Further, the pamphlet described Defendant's trademark as "a world-renowned brand with 280 years of history."]

Beijing No. 2 Intermediate Court found that: The Chinese character mark "苏富比" in terms of auction services is an unregistered trademark in China. Plaintiff and its subsidiaries in Hong Kong and Shanghai have used the mark "苏富比" in mainland China since 1988. Through continuous use and promotions, the mark "苏富比" has enjoyed sufficient recognition and reputation among the relevant public, as evidenced by the articles, news reports and advertisements published by books, magazines, online media and paper media. The Resolution Center also acknowledged the reputation of the mark "苏富比" through a domain name dispute case. Accordingly, the court held that the mark "苏富比" has

CASE *(continued)*

obtained enough reputation among the relevant public in China, and therefore, should be protected as an unregistered well-known trademark in China.

Plaintiff authorized its Hong Kong Office to use the subject mark "苏富比," which has used and promoted the mark in mainland China since. Due to the legal restrictions [that foreign auction companies are prohibited from directly hosting auctions within mainland China], Plaintiff and its subsidiaries have never hosted any auctions in mainland China. However, Plaintiff has engaged in other activities related to the auction services, such as advertising and hosting charity auctions, which are allowed within the current legal structure in mainland China. These activities are essential to promote the brand name of Sotheby, attract buyers and expand the market in mainland China. Therefore, although Sotheby's has not hosted any official auctions within mainland China, its other promotional activities together with the use of the mark "苏富比" still constitute as use of the trademark in mainland China.

Defendant Sichuan Sotheby is specialized in the auction of personal property, real property and common art items; whereas Plaintiff Sotheby's is focused on the auction market of fine arts. Although the auction items that two parties focus on vary a bit, both are in the business of auctions, and therefore, the services that they provide fall into the same category of services. Defendant blatantly used the marks "苏富比" (Sotheby in Chinese characters), the calligraphy version of "苏富比," "苏富比拍卖" (Sotheby Auction), "中国苏富比" (China Sotheby) and "苏富比及图" (Sotheby and device) in its auctions, promotional materials, websites and also the business cards of its legal representatives. All these marks are either identical with or similar to Plaintiff's unregistered well-known mark "苏富比" (Sotheby in Chinese). Therefore, defendant is liable for trademark infringement.

[Dissatisfied with the decision, defendant filed an appeal to Beijing High Court, arguing that plaintiff does not have a valid claim over the mark "苏富比" because plaintiff has never actually used the subject mark in mainland China in the context of trademark law, as a result of the restriction imposed by the Chinese Auction Law.]

Beijing High Court held that, *Article 2 of Judicial Interpretation on the Application of Law in Trademark Disputes* provides that: "[I]mitating or translating another's registered well-known trademark or its main part and using it as a trademark on non-identical or dissimilar goods thereby misleading the public and potentially prejudicing the interests of the registrant of the well-known trademark, constitute acts causing other harm to another's exclusive right to use a registered trademark." Trademark use, refers to usages that could identify the source of services and distinguish different service providers among the relevant public.

In this case, although Sotheby's has not directly engaged in commercial auctions in mainland China due to the restrictions imposed by Chinese Auction Law and *Regulation for the Implementation of the Cultural Relics Protection Law of the People's Republic of China*, its mark "苏富比" still obtains recognition and reputation among the relevant public due to other activities it provided, such as charity auctions, fundraising auctions, exhibition previews and advertising activities. Therefore, such activities were sufficient to demonstrate the actual use of the mark "苏富比" in mainland China.

> **CASE** *(continued)*
>
> Plaintiff Sotheby's is commonly referred to as "苏富比" by Chinese media in various news reports covering its commercial activities in mainland China. In addition, Plaintiff has been using the word "苏富比" as its Chinese company name since 1995. Through the trademark license agreement, Sotheby's Hong Kong and its Shanghai Office have also used the mark "苏富比" as its mark and trade name for a long time. Therefore, the use of the mark "苏富比" by its Hong Kong subsidiary and the Shanghai office should also be attributed to Sotheby's.
>
> In view of the above, we affirm the Beijing No. 2 Intermediate Court's decision that the mark "苏富比" constitutes an unregistered well-known mark with respect to auctioneering services. Defendant's use of various trademarks that contain the characters "苏富比" will cause confusion among the relevant public as to the origin of the services, thus diluting the reputation of Plaintiff's mark and constituting trademark infringement.
>
> This is the final ruling.

NOTES

We have discussed in previous chapters that to claim well-known mark protection, plaintiff has to prove: (1) popularity of the mark in its own industry; (2) duration of the mark in use; (3) duration, extent, and geographical range of the advertisement and promotional efforts related to the mark; and (4) previous records showing that the mark has been recognized as a well-known trademark, and any other factors that might be relevant. (See Article 14 Chinese Trademark Law and Article 9 *Provisions on Recognition and Protection of Well-Known Marks*.) In *Sotheby's*, plaintiff had not held any auction events in mainland China, thus had not actually "used" the mark by itself in China, due to the restrictions imposed on foreign auction houses within mainland China. But the courts recognized the use of the marks by its licensee and subsidiaries in Hong Kong and Shanghai. Do you think that such uses should be considered in determining the well-known status of the mark?

18.2 Defenses

18.2.1 US: Fair use for descriptive marks, non-trademark ("nominative") use, and genericide

18.2.1.1 Fair use for descriptive marks

For descriptive trademarks (which includes (1) marks which describe a product, *e.g.*, STRONG brand metal cables; (2) geographically descriptive marks, *e.g.*, CENTRAL VALLEY grapes from the Central Valley of California; and (3) personal names, *e.g.*, MILLER'S Department Store, for a store founded by Mr. Miller and run by the Miller family), it has long been the rule that use of a word or phrase which happens to be a trademark is not infringement if the word or phrase is used merely to describe a product. Generally a use to describe does not violate trademark rights. So, for example, a seller that competes with the STRONG brand in the market for cables, and which says that its cables are "durable and strong" does not infringe the STRONG brand trademark. So, too, a seller who truthfully says its grapes are from "the Central Valley of California" does not infringe the CENTRAL VALLEY mark for grapes. And a competitor that says its new department store, the SPECTRUM store, will be "run by Mrs. Megan Miller," does not infringe the MILLER Department Store trademark.

Classic fair use remains a defense even when a trademark owner can prove that the defendant's use of the descriptive word or phrase does in fact cause some degree of consumer confusion. See *KP Permanent Make-Up, Inc. v. Lasting Impression I, Inc.*, 543 U.S. 111 (2004) (case involving the descriptive mark "microcolor" for makeup products; a defendant raising the "fair use" defense has no burden to negate a likelihood of confusion; yet the court indicated that evidence of a likelihood of confusion can be factored into the overall balancing of evidence to determine if the use is indeed "fair").

18.2.1.2 Nominative use

What if the seller of mobile phone covers sold under the name SLEEKSKIN wanted to tell potential buyers that its phone covers fit both Apple® and Samsung® brand mobile phones? Could an advertisement say "SLEEKSKIN – just the choice for either Apple or Samsung mobile phones" without infringing the Apple and Samsung trademarks? The answer is yes. The Apple and Samsung trademarks here are being used to name the mobile phones; they are not being used in a way that tries to convince potential buyers that SLEEKSKIN covers originate with the Apple Company or Samsung. This is an example of nominative use: use of a trademark to name a product, rather than as an indicator of source. It is not trademark infringement because it is not likely to confuse a consumer. The obvious goal of this advertisement would be to promote SLEEKSKIN mobile phone covers, and as long as the SLEEKSKIN mark was being used by its rightful owner, there is no likelihood of confusion.

One court described nominative use of a trademark in these terms, comparing it to "classical" descriptive fair use. *Cairns v. Franklin Mint Co.*, 292 F.3d 1139, 1151 (9th Cir. 2002):

> The nominative fair use analysis is appropriate where a defendant has used the plaintiff's mark to describe the plaintiff's product, even if the defendant's ultimate goal is to describe his own product. Conversely, the classic fair use [of a descriptive

mark] analysis is appropriate where a defendant has used the plaintiff's mark only to describe his own product, and not at all to describe the plaintiff's product.

The Ninth Circuit found nominative use in a well-known case. A newspaper ran a contest asking its readers to name their favorite member of a then-popular teenage-oriented rock band called *The New Kids on the Block*. The band sued the newspaper for infringement, but the court found for the defendant newspaper. In its decision, the court laid down a three-part test that has proven useful in nominative use cases:

> [W]here the defendant uses a trademark to describe the plaintiff's product, rather than its own, we hold that a commercial user is entitled to a nominative fair use defense provided he meets the following three requirements. First, the product or services in question must be one not readily identifiable without use of the trademark; second, only so much of the mark or marks may be used as is reasonably necessary to identify the product or service; and third, the user must do nothing that would, in conjunction with the mark, suggest sponsorship or endorsement by the trademark holder (*New Kids on the Block v. News America Pub., Inc.*, 971 F.2d 302, 308 (9th Cir. 1992)).

To constitute trademark infringement, then, the defendant's use of the trademark must be to indicate the origin of a product for purposes of selling a product. In a classic case of "passing off," this is clear enough: Unauthorized seller B puts A's trademark on goods in an attempt to convince buyers that B's goods really come from A. But as with the *New Kids* case, other uses of a trademark are different. If a news reporter writes a story about hiring practices at Google, Inc., he or she naturally uses a trademarked term ("Google"). But readers of the news story will not be led to think that the reporter is trying to pass him- or herself off as Google, Inc., or even an authorized Google representative. This was the same logic behind the *New Kids on the Block* case. See also *Toyota Motor Sales, U.S.A., Inc. v. Tabari*, 610 F.3d 1171, 1178 (9th Cir. 2010) (use of trademarked term "Lexus" in dealer's website name, Lexusbroker.com, was nominative (fair) use of Lexus name and thus did not infringe Lexus trademark).

18.2.1.3 Keyword purchases and "trademark use"

Perhaps the most contentious issue in the area of "non-trademark use" (*i.e.*, nominative fair use) is Google's use of trademarks as so-called "Keywords." Under Google's AdSense service, any company can pay to have its own product advertising appear in the "sponsored search" area when a Google user types the trademarked term into the search box. This is in fact how Google makes much of its money. So, for example, General Motors Company can pay to have ads for its Cadillac luxury cars appear any time a user types "Mercedes Benz" into the search box. The questions this raises under trademark law are: (1) Is Google making a "trademark use" of the Mercedes Benz mark when it sells advertising space to General Motors when users type in "Mercedes Benz"; and (2) Is General Motors making a trademark use of the Mercedes mark in such a case?

Generally, the courts in the US and Europe have held that *both* parties in these circumstances have no liability under trademark law. So in *Jurin v. Google Inc.*, 695 F. Supp. 2d 1117, 95 U.S.P.Q.2d 1803 (E.D. Cal. 2010), the court dismissed an infringement claim by the plaintiff, saying that sale of ad space to plaintiff's competitor was unlikely to cause confusion, because the competitor's products were clearly sold under their own trademark and not the plaintiff's. So, too, in *Government Employees Ins. Co. (GEICO) v. Google, Inc.*, 77 U.S.P.Q.2d 1841 (E.D. Va. 2005) (same, except as to some competitor ads that used the GeiGeico name in the text of the ads and not just in the search terms that generated display of ads).

Competitor companies themselves have also been found not to use trademarks in a trademark sense when they purchase ad space triggered by a search for the trademarked term. This was the main holding in *1-800 Contacts, Inc. v. Lens.com, Inc.*, 722 F.3d 1229 (10th Cir. 2013). For product auction sites, in addition, re-sellers of used products may use the trademarked term for those products without fear of trademark infringement. *See Tiffany (NJ) Inc. v. eBay Inc.*, 600 F.3d 93, 103 (2d Cir. 2010) ("We agree with the district court that eBay's use of Tiffany's mark on its website and in sponsored links was lawful.").

Commentators emphasize, however, that the details of the paid advertising display matter quite a bit in this context. If "sponsored" or paid ads in any way appear to be associated with the plaintiff's trademark term, nominative or non-trademark use may not save the defendant company from liability. *See* Jacoby and Sableman, *Keyword-Based Advertising: Filling in Factual Voids*, 97 Trademark Rep. 681 (2007); 5 Thomas J. McCarthy, McCarthy on Trademarks and Unfair Competition, at §25A:7 ("Search engines selling targeted advertising – Is confusion likely?), (4th ed. & Supp., 2017). *See generally* David J. Franklyn & David A. Hyman, *Trademarks As Search Engine Keywords: Much Ado About Something?*, 26 Harv. J.L. & Tech. 481, 516 (2013); David A. Hyman & David J. Franklyn, *Trademarks As Search-Engine Keywords: Who, What, When?*, 92 Tex. L. Rev. 2117, 2117 (2014):

> Most Internet searches result in unpaid (organic or algorithmic) results, and paid ads. The specific ads that are displayed are dictated by the user's search terms ("keywords"). In 2004, Google began offering trademarks for use as keywords on an unrestricted basis, followed in due course by other search engines. Once that happened, any entity (including sellers of competing products) could have their ads appear in response to a search for the trademarked product. Trademark owners responded by filing more than 100 lawsuits in the United States and Europe, making the dispute the hottest controversy in the history of trademark law. Litigation has focused on purchases by competitors – giving the impression that competitors account for a large portion of such purchases. We find that competitors account for a relatively small percentage of keyword purchases, and many trademark owners purchase their own marks as keywords. We also find a high degree of fluctuation in the number of paid ads and the domain names to which those ads are linked. We conclude that the risk of widespread abuse is low. Trademark owners' objections seem to have more to do with objections to free riding than with the zone of interests currently protected by U.S. trademark law.

Can you see what this "free riding" concern is about? When General Motors invests in ads keyed to a user's search for Mercedes Benz, General Motors (and Google) are in some sense building on the many years of effort Mercedes has expended in making quality cars, and on decades of advertising to associate the Mercedes mark with that reputation of quality. The question is: Should General Motors and Google profit (however indirectly) from these investments by Mercedes? If there is harm here, or any degree of unfairness, the consensus seems to be that it cannot be redressed by conventional trademark law. As long as General Motors is not representing its cars as Mercedes cars, this is not a matter that trademark law can address. What other theories can you think of to address it? *See* Robert P. Merges, *Justifying Intellectual Property* 89 (2011) ("[Professor Wendy] Gordon's restitutionary theory of IP shows how a simple duty not to take wrongfully can serve as the footing for a true property right, good against the world. Gordon's theory, seen this way, has a thoroughly Kantian spirit"), citing Wendy J. Gordon, *On Owning Information: Intellectual Property and the Restitutionary Impulse*, 78 Va. L. Rev. 149 (1992). *See also* James Gordley, Foundations of Private Law: Property, Tort, Contract, Unjust Enrichment 15 (2006). On the other hand, if the public benefits (in the form of price competition for quality cars) from the sale of trademarked keywords, perhaps this can be justified. In other words, if the public is better off, and Mercedes has not suffered a harm cognizable under traditional trademark principles, why not permit this practice?

NOTES

1. The Third Circuit modified the three-factor *New Kids on the Block* test in the case of *Century 21 Real Estate Corp. v. Lendingtree, Inc.*, 425 F.3d 211, 228 (3d Cir. 2005). The Third Circuit's factors are:

    1. Is the use of plaintiff's mark necessary to describe (1) plaintiff's product or service and (2) defendant's product or service?
    2. Is only so much of the plaintiff's mark used as is necessary to describe plaintiff's products or services? [and]
    3. Does the defendant's conduct or language reflect the true and accurate relationship between plaintiff and defendant's products or services?

    According to the court, "[i]f each of these questions can be answered in the affirmative, the use will be considered a fair one, regardless of whether likelihood of confusion exists." In the Third Circuit, in other words, nominative fair use is not conducted as a special version of the traditional likelihood of confusion test; it is a separate *affirmative defense* that applies even if likelihood of confusion is proven.

2. **Applied to antidilution claims**. The Trademark Dilution Reform Act of 2006 (mentioned earlier) added statutory defenses that connect closely to the concept of nominative use. Lanham Act §43(c) codifies these; it reads in part:

    (3) Exclusions.
       The following shall not be actionable as dilution by blurring or dilution by tarnishment under this subsection:
    (A) Any fair use, including a nominative or descriptive fair use, or facilitation of such fair use, of a famous mark by another person other than as a designation of source for the person's own goods or services, including use in connection with – (i) advertising or promotion that permits consumers to compare goods or services; or (ii) identifying and parodying, criticizing, or commenting upon the famous mark owner or the goods or services of the famous mark owner.
    (B) All forms of news reporting and news commentary.
    (C) Any noncommercial use of a mark (Lanham Act §43(c)(3), 15 U.S.C.A. §1125(c)(3)).

    The third, "any noncommercial use of a mark," corresponds to the nominative use defense.

18.2.2 Genericide

There is no such thing as a generic trademark. A supposed mark that is used to describe a product category, a type of thing, cannot be protected as a trademark. So there can be no PANTS brand for pants; this is a type of product and not a source.

The PANTS attempted mark is an example of a trademark that is "born generic." It cannot be, and never could have been, used as a trademark. There is another type of generic mark, however: one which comes, *over time*, to be associated in the minds of the purchasing public as a type of product. Such a mark is not "born generic"; it may in fact have been a fanciful mark when born. But if it comes to be associated with a genus or product type, it is said to have been killed as a trademark. It has suffered from "genericide" – death by becoming generic.

Two famous examples from the annals of consumer products in the US are "Cellophane" and "Thermos." Both were originally fanciful, made-up words;

both came to be used to describe a type of product; and both were eventually found to be generic. *See DuPont Cellophane Co. v. Waxed Products Co.*, 85 F.2d 75 (2d Cir. 1936), cert. denied, 299 U.S. 601 (1936), cert. denied, 304 U.S. 575 (1938), reh'g denied, 305 U.S. 672 (1938) (CELLOPHANE is generic); *King-Seeley Thermos Co. v. Aladdin Industries, Inc.*, 321 F.2d 577, 579, 138 U.S.P.Q. 349 (2d Cir. 1963) ("The word 'thermos' became a part of the public domain . . . because of the plaintiff's lack of reasonable diligence in asserting and protecting its trademark rights in the word 'Thermos' . . .").

The key to genericness is how the average consumer uses the trademark. A buyer who says "I need to keep my coffee warm, I'd like to buy a Thermos and I don't care which manufacturer makes it" has indicated that Thermos is a type of product. But a buyer who says "I want to buy an insulated drink container. Do you carry the Thermos brand?" has indicated that Thermos is a trademark indicating a single source.

If you are introducing a new type of product, how can you insure your trademark does not suffer from genericide down the line? J. Thomas McCarthy recommends several strategies to prevent genericide: (1) introduce useful descriptive terms in advertising at the same time as the trademark term (*e.g.*, Xerox brand of photocopiers); and (2) educational advertising that makes clear the trademark should never be used to denote another seller's product ("do not say 'a Xerox machine'; say 'a XEROX brand photocopier"). *See* 2 J. Thomas McCarthy, McCarthy on Trademarks and Unfair Competition §12:26 (4th ed. & Supp., 2016).

To see how courts analyze genericide, consider this case; it concerns an asserted trademark that the defendant says was "born generic":

 CASE

Filipino Yellow Pages, Inc. v. Asian Journal Publications, Inc., 198 F.3d 1143 (9th Cir. 1999)

O'Scannlain, Circuit Judge.
We must decide whether the publisher of a telephone directory for the Filipino-American community can establish that the term "Filipino Yellow Pages" is protectible under trademark law.

Fil-Am Enterprises, Inc. ("Fil-Am"), published the Filipino Directory of California, a telephone directory directed primarily at the Filipino-American community of Southern California. In December 1986, Oriel and Jornacion [, co-owners of Fil-Am] terminated

CASE *(continued)*

their business relationship and divided up their business interests through execution of a "Shareholders' Buy Out Agreement" ("the Agreement"). Under the Agreement, Oriel acquired complete ownership of Fil-Am's telephone directory business, and Jornacion agreed not to compete "in the Filipino Directory (Filipino Yellow Pages) [market] in California" for three years. Oriel, as owner of Fil-Am, continued to publish the Filipino Directory of California until 1991. Between 1991 and 1993, Fil-Am joined two partners to publish a telephone directory known as the Filipino Directory of the U.S.A. and Canada. In 1993, Fil-Am sold its interest in the Filipino Directory of the U.S.A. and Canada. Oriel and his wife, Cora Macabagdal Oriel, then formed a new corporate entity, Asian Journal Publications, Inc. ("AJP"). Since 1994, AJP has published a telephone directory called the Filipino Consumer Directory. Pursuant to the Agreement's non-compete provision, Jornacion did not participate in the Filipino-American telephone directory market between December 1986 and December 1989. Jornacion reentered the market in 1990 by forming the Filipino Yellow Pages, Inc. ("FYP"), publisher of a directory called the Filipino Yellow Pages. FYP's Filipino Yellow Pages, AJP's Filipino Consumer Directory, and the Filipino Directory of the U.S.A. and Canada currently compete in the Filipino-American telephone directory market in California. A directory unaffiliated with FYP's directory, also called the Filipino Yellow Pages, is marketed to the Filipino-American community in the eastern United States by Kayumanggi Communications, Inc. AJP's Filipino Consumer Directory has a white-pages section, which contains general reference information as well as a listing of people and organizations affiliated with the Filipino-American community. The Filipino Consumer Directory also has a yellow pages section containing information about businesses serving the Filipino-American community. AJP periodically uses the term "Filipino Consumer Yellow Pages" in print advertisements directed at potential advertisers. These advertisements either reference the full name of the directory or are found within the Filipino Consumer Directory itself.

If [a potential trademark] term is generic, it cannot be the subject of trademark protection under any circumstances, even with a showing of secondary meaning. Before proceeding to the merits, a word on the burden of persuasion is appropriate. In cases involving properly registered marks, a presumption of validity places the burden of proving genericness upon the defendant. See 15 U.S.C. §1057(b) ("A certificate of registration of a mark . . . shall be prima facie evidence of the validity of the registered mark. . ."). If a supposedly valid mark is not federally registered, however, the plaintiff has the burden of proving nongenericness once the defendant asserts genericness as a defense. *See, e.g., Blinded Veterans Ass'n v. Blinded American Veterans Found.*, 872 F.2d 1035, 1041 (D.C. Cir. 1989); *A.J. Canfield Co. v. Honickman*, 808 F.2d 291, 297 (3d Cir. 1986).

The case at bar involves a claimed mark that is unregistered; FYP has not yet been successful in its attempts to register "Filipino Yellow Pages" with the PTO. Thus FYP, as trademark plaintiff, bears the burden of showing that "Filipino Yellow Pages" is not generic.

AJP contends that "Filipino Yellow Pages" is a generic term and as such incapable of trademark protection, while FYP argues that the term is protectible as a descriptive term

CASE *(continued)*

with secondary meaning. "A 'generic' term is one that refers, or has come to be understood as referring, to the genus of which the particular product or service is a species. It cannot become a trademark under any circumstances." *Surgicenters*, 601 F.2d at 1014 (citing *Abercrombie*, 537 F.2d at 9–10). As explained by one commentator, a generic term is "the name of the product or service itself – what [the product] is, and as such . . . the very antithesis of a mark." 2 J. Thomas McCarthy, Trademarks and Unfair Competition §12:1[1] (4th ed. 1997). A descriptive term, unlike a generic term, can be a subject for trademark protection under appropriate circumstances. Although descriptive terms generally do not enjoy trademark protection, a descriptive term can be protected provided that it has acquired "secondary meaning" in the minds of consumers, *i.e.*, it has "become distinctive of the [trademark] applicant's goods in commerce." *Abercrombie*, 537 F.2d at 10 (quoting 15 U.S.C. §1052(f)).

Here the parties do not dispute that "Filipino" and "yellow pages" are generic terms. The word "Filipino" is a clearly generic term used to refer to "a native of the Philippine islands" or "a citizen of the Republic of the Philippines." Webster's Ninth New Collegiate Dictionary 462 (1986). The term "yellow pages" has been found to be a generic term for "a local business telephone directory alphabetized by product or service." *AmCan Enters., Inc. v. Renzi*, 32 F.3d 233, 234 (7th Cir. 1994) (Posner, J.) (citing cases, and noting that "yellow pages," which originally was not a generic term, has become generic over time); see also Webster's Ninth New Collegiate Dictionary 1367 (defining "yellow pages" as "the section of a telephone directory that lists businesses and professional firms alphabetically by category and that includes classified advertising").

The issue then becomes whether combining the generic terms "Filipino" and "yellow pages" to form the composite term "Filipino Yellow Pages" creates a generic or a descriptive term. AJP argues, and the district court concluded, that "Filipino Yellow Pages" is generic based on this court's analysis in *Surgicenters of America, Inc. v. Medical Dental Surgeries Co.*, 601 F.2d 1011 (9th Cir. 1979). In *Surgicenters*, we held that the term "surgicenter" was generic and that the plaintiff's registered service mark had to be removed from the trademark register. In our discussion in *Surgicenters*, we summarized (but did not explicitly adopt) the analysis of the district court in that case, which reasoned that "surgicenter," created by combining the generic terms "surgery" and "center," retained the generic quality of its components. *Id.* at 1015. Nowhere in *Surgicenters* did we hold, however, that a composite term made up of generic components is automatically generic unless the combination constitutes a "deviation from normal usage" or an "unusual unitary combination."

In reaching our conclusion of genericness in *Surgicenters*, we placed significant but not controlling weight on the dictionary definitions and generic nature of "surgery" and "center." We explained that "[w]hile not determinative, dictionary definitions are relevant and often persuasive in determining how a term is understood by the consuming public, the ultimate test of whether a trademark is generic." *Id.* at 1015 n. 11. But we also based our genericness finding upon detailed information in some 45 exhibits that, taken collectively,

CASE *(continued)*

suggested that the consuming public considered the composite term "surgicenter" to mean a surgical center generally speaking, as opposed to a surgical center maintained and operated by the plaintiff specifically. See *id.* at 1017. These exhibits included letters from potential consumers and several publications that used the term "surgicenter" in a clearly generic sense. The finding of genericness in *Surgicenters* cannot be separated from the uniquely well-developed record in that case.

In this case, the district court cited *Surgicenters* for the proposition that "a combination of two generic words is also generic, unless the combination is a 'deviation from natural usage' or an 'unusual unitary combination.'" The court then stated that "[u]nder this analysis, the term 'Filipino Yellow Pages' seems to be neither a 'deviation from natural usage,' nor an 'unusual unitary combination.'" The district court's reading of *Surgicenters* appears somewhat troubling insofar as it oversimplifies our opinion. First, it overlooks our explicit recognition that "words which could not individually become a trademark may become one when taken together." 601 F.2d at 1017 (internal quotation marks omitted). Second, it effectively makes dictionary definitions the crucial factor in assessing genericness, even though Surgicenters makes clear that such definitions are "not determinative" and that the "ultimate test" of genericness is "how a term is understood by the consuming public." *Id.* at 1015 n. 11.

Several of our more recent cases have taken a fairly integrative approach to evaluating composite terms, rejecting the breaking down of such terms into their individual (and often generic) parts. In *Park'N Fly, Inc. v. Dollar Park and Fly, Inc.*, 718 F.2d 327 (9th Cir.1983), rev'd on other grounds, 469 U.S. 189, 105 S.Ct. 658, 83 L.Ed.2d 582 (1985), the defendant challenged the validity of the plaintiff's trademark by arguing that "Park'N Fly" was generic with respect to airport parking lots. The defendant made an argument "based on the words themselves," contending that because "park" and "fly," the component parts of the plaintiff's trademark, are ordinary words, their combination was also generic. Id. at 330. We declined to invalidate the plaintiff's trademark as generic based on this analysis.

When *Surgicenters* is examined in light of [various] later cases, it becomes clear that *Surgicenters* should not be read overbroadly to stand for the simple proposition that "generic plus generic equals generic." Rather, *Surgicenters* must be read in its proper context. First, it must be noted that *Surgicenters* explicitly recognizes that generic individual terms can be combined to form valid composite marks. See 601 F.2d at 1017. Second, it must be recalled that we found the term "surgicenter" generic based in large part on a well-developed record of 45 exhibits showing that the term "surgicenter," considered as a whole, was generic (*i.e.*, understood by the consuming public as referring simply to a center at which surgery was performed).

In light of the foregoing discussion, the district court here may have oversimplified matters somewhat when it stated that "[t]he Ninth Circuit has held that a combination of two generic words is also generic, unless the combination is a 'deviation from natural usage' or an 'unusual unitary combination.'" Any arguable imprecision in the district court's application of Surgicenters was harmless, however, because the term "Filipino Yellow Pages"

CASE *(continued)*

would be unprotectible in any event. In finding "Filipino Yellow Pages" generic, the district court did not rely solely upon the generic nature and presence in the dictionary of "Filipino" and "yellow pages." The district court also considered other evidence tending to suggest that "Filipino Yellow Pages," even when considered as an entire mark, is generic with respect to telephone directories.

An important difference between *Surgicenters* and the instant case should be noted, however. The mark at issue in *Surgicenters* was a federally-registered mark, and thus the burden of proving genericness rested upon the party challenging the mark's validity. See *id.* at 1012, 1014. The mark at issue in this case, in contrast, is not registered; thus FYP, as trademark plaintiff, must prove that "Filipino Yellow Pages" is not generic. It does not appear that FYP has offered evidence of nongenericness sufficient to rebut even the fairly modest evidence of genericness offered by AJP. In light of the evidence presented by AJP, it would seem that under the "who-are-you/what-are-you" test, the term "Filipino Yellow Pages" is generic. If faced with the question "What are you?", FYP's Filipino Yellow Pages, AJP's Filipino Consumer Directory, and the Filipino Directory of the U.S.A. and Canada could all respond in the same way: "A Filipino yellow pages." Giving FYP exclusive rights to the term "Filipino Yellow Pages" might be inappropriate because it would effectively "grant [FYP as] owner of the mark a monopoly, since a competitor could not describe his goods as what they are." *Surgicenters*, 601 F.2d at 1017 (internal quotation marks omitted).

Even assuming that AJP's other evidence of genericness would be insufficient to sustain a genericness finding by itself, it certainly suggests that "Filipino Yellow Pages," if descriptive, would be the feeblest of descriptive marks — in the words of one court, "perilously close to the 'generic' line." *Computerland Corp. v. Microland Computer Corp.*, 586 F.Supp. 22, 25 (N.D. Cal. 1984). Such a weak descriptive mark could be a valid trademark only with a strong showing of strong secondary meaning.

NOTES

1. On the use of dictionaries to prove genericness, *see* Ralph H. Folsom & Larry L. Teply, *Trademarked Generic Words*, 89 Yale L.J. 1323, 1346–47 n. 110 (1980) (describing organized efforts of trademark attorneys to pressure dictionary publishers into excluding trademarked words and/or including disclaimers, and arguing that inclusion in a dictionary should not bear on genericide issue). *See also* William M. Landes & Richard A. Posner, *Trademark Law: An Economic Perspective*, 30 J.L. & Econ. 265, 296 (1987) ("Thus, although words held to be generic are more likely to show up in the dictionary than those held not to be generic, the difference in probabilities is small – 54% versus 41%").
2. Trade dress and product configurations can also be generic. *See, e.g., Kendall-Jackson Winery v. E. & J. Gallo Winery*, 150 F.3d 1042 (9th Cir. 1998), holding that an autumn-season grape leaf featured on both plaintiff's and defendant's wine bottles was generic in the wine industry. *See also Sunrise Jewelry Mfg. Corp. v. Fred, S.A.*, 175 F.3d 1322 (Fed. Cir. 1999) (holding that generic product configuration may be cancelled notwithstanding "incontestable" status; remanding for determination of genericness).
3. One common technique used to prove genericness (or its absence) is the consumer survey. Using this technique, a court found that the well-known search company Google is identified as a company or source, and not a general type of online search; and so the Google trademark was found not to be generic. *Elliott v.*

Google, Inc., 860 F.3d 1151, 1162 (9th Cir. 2017) (noting (1) that genericness inquiry must be directed at specific product category such as internet search engines; and (2) the fact that "google" was often used as a verb in a generic sense ("to google" something, meaning to search for it on the internet), does not by itself establish that the primary association of "Google" in the minds of most consumers is with a generic action rather than a specific source or company, *i.e.*, Google, Inc.).

18.2.3 "Trademark use" and genericness in the EU

As can be seen from the *Filipino Yellow Pages* case, the listing of words in dictionaries has important implications for a finding of genericness. The EU Trademark Directive has an interesting provision dealing with this; it purports to require dictionaries to include notation of the fact that a term in the dictionary is a registered trademark:

Article 12

Reproduction of trade marks in dictionaries

> If the reproduction of a trade mark in a dictionary, encyclopaedia or similar reference work, in print or electronic form, gives the impression that it constitutes the generic name of the goods or services for which the trade mark is registered, the publisher of the work shall, at the request of the proprietor of the trade mark, ensure that the reproduction of the trade mark is, without delay, and in the case of works in printed form at the latest in the next edition of the publication, accompanied by an indication that it is a registered trade mark (EU Trademark Directive, 2015 Revision, Dir. No. 2015/2436 (16 Dec. 2016), at Article 12).

The provision does not specify how a trademark owner can force a publisher to add this notation; it would seem to raise questions of press freedom. Again, however, from a strictly trademark point of view, it shows the power of dictionary listings to render a term generic. And at least some dictionary listings seem to comply with the provision. *See, e.g.*, "Jello" in the Oxford English Dictionary (2d ed. 1989) ("A *proprietary* name for the powder used to make a fruit-flavored gelatin dessert" (emphasis added)).

The admonition to dictionary publishers is one aspect of the emphasis in the Directive on what might be termed "at fault" genericide: the loss of trademark distinctiveness when the trademark owner helps bring about (by acts or "inactivity") the generic use of the mark. This is made explicit in the Community Trademark Regulation, No. 207/2009 (26 Feb. 2009), at Article 51.1.(b):

Grounds for Revocation

1. The rights of the proprietor of the Community trade mark shall be declared to be revoked on application to the Office or on the basis of a counterclaim in infringement proceedings:

. . .

(b) if, in consequence of acts or inactivity of the proprietor, the trade mark has become the common name in the trade for a product or service in respect of which it is registered. . .

This provision was applied in the case of *Backaldrin Österreich The Kornspitz Company GmbH v. Pfahnl Backmittel GmbH*, C-409/12 (CJEU, 6 March 2014), available at http://curia.europa.eu/juris/document/document.jsf?text=&docid=148746&pageIndex=0&doclang=EN&mode=lst&dir=&occ=first&part=1&cid=1000080, where plaintiff's trademark KORNSPITZ, for "a bakery product, namely for bread rolls which are oblong in shape and have a point at both ends," was said by its competitors (including defendant Pfahnl) to be generic. Backaldrin argued to the referring court that some users of its products were bakers, and some were consumers, or "end users." The CJEU held that

in a case such as that at issue in the main proceedings, a trade mark is liable to revocation in respect of a product for which it is registered if, in consequence of acts or inactivity of the proprietor, that trade mark has become the common name for that product from the point of view solely of end users of the product. (at par. 30).

The court also commented on what "inactivity" on the part of the trademark owner means. In this case, the trademark owner supplied baking materials to bakers, but did not insist that the bakers attach the KORNSPITZ name to the end products made and sold by the bakers. When, the courts said,

the sellers of the product made using the material supplied by the proprietor of the trade mark do not generally inform their customers that the sign used to designate the product in question has been registered as a trade mark and thus contribute to the transformation of that trade mark into the common name, that proprietor's failure to take any initiative which may encourage those sellers to make more use of that mark may be classified as inactivity within the meaning of Article 12(2)(a) of Directive 2008/95.

It is for the referring court to examine whether, in the present case, Backaldrin took any initiative to encourage the bakers and foodstuffs distributors selling the bread rolls made using the baking mix it had supplied to make more use of the trade mark KORNSPITZ in their commercial contact with customers (*id.*, at pars. 34–35).

Google Inc. v. Louis Vuitton Malletier SA, Case C-236/08 (ECJ [CJEU] 23 March 2010)

[The court begins by explaining the Google AdWords program, *i.e.*, the sale of keywords to advertisers.]

A number of advertisers can reserve the same keyword. The order in which their advertising links are then displayed is determined according to, in particular, the maximum price per click, the number of previous clicks on those links and the quality of the ad as assessed by Google. The advertiser can at any time improve its ranking in the display by fixing a higher maximum price per click or by trying to improve the quality of its ad. Google has set up an automated process for the selection of keywords and the creation of ads. Advertisers select the keywords, draft the commercial message, and input the link to their site.

At the beginning of 2003, Vuitton became aware that the entry, by internet users, of terms constituting its trade marks into Google's search engine triggered the display, under the heading 'sponsored links', of links to sites offering imitation versions of Vuitton's products. It was also established that Google offered advertisers the possibility of selecting not only keywords which correspond to Vuitton's trade marks, but also those keywords in combination with expressions indicating imitation, such as 'imitation' and 'copy'. Vuitton brought proceeding against Google with a view, inter alia, to obtaining a declaration that Google had infringed its trade marks. [Louis Vuitton prevailed in the French court of first instance in Paris, then on appeal. Google appealed to the Cour de cassation (French Court of Cassation), which joined this to another, related case, and referred several questions to the ECJ, now the CJEU.]

Must Article 5(1)(a) and (b) of [Directive 89/104] [of 1988] and Article 9(1)(a) and (b) of [Regulation No 40/94] [of 1993] be interpreted as meaning that a provider of a paid referencing service [*e.g.*, Google] who makes available to advertisers keywords reproducing or imitating registered trade marks and arranges by the referencing agreement to create and favourable display, on the basis of those keywords, advertising links to sites offering infringing goods is using those trade marks in a manner which their proprietor is entitled to prevent?

In the event that the trade marks have a reputation, may the proprietor oppose such use under Article 5(2) of [Directive 89/104] and Article 9(1)(c) of [Regulation No 40/94]?
Article 5(1)(a) and (b) of Directive 89/104 and Article 9(1)(a) and (b) of Regulation No 40/94 entitle proprietors of trade marks, subject to certain conditions, to prohibit third parties from using signs identical with, or similar to, their trade marks for goods or services identical with, or similar to, those for which those trade marks are registered.
The use of a sign identical with a trade mark constitutes use in the course of trade where it occurs in the context of commercial activity with a view to economic advantage and not as a private matter.

CASE *(continued)*

From the advertiser's point of view, the selection of a keyword identical with a trade mark has the object and effect of displaying an advertising link to the site on which he offers his goods or services for sale. Since the sign selected as a keyword is the means used to trigger that ad display, it cannot be disputed that the advertiser indeed uses it in the context of commercial activity and not as a private matter.

With regard, next, to the referencing service provider, it is common ground that it is carrying out a commercial activity with a view to economic advantage when it stores as keywords, for certain of its clients, signs which are identical with trade marks and arranges for the display of ads on the basis of those keywords.

It is also common ground that that service is not supplied only to the proprietors of those trade marks or to operators entitled to market their goods or services, but, at least in the proceedings in question, is provided without the consent of the proprietors and is supplied to their competitors or to imitators.

Although it is clear from those factors that the referencing service provider operates 'in the course of trade' when it permits advertisers to select, as keywords, signs identical with trade marks, stores those signs and displays its clients' ads on the basis thereof, it does not follow, however, from those factors that that service provider itself 'uses' those signs within the terms of Article 5 of Directive 89/104 and Article 9 of Regulation No 40/94.

In that regard, suffice it to note that the use, by a third party, of a sign identical with, or similar to, the proprietor's trade mark implies, at the very least, that that third party uses the sign in its own commercial communication. A referencing service provider allows its clients to use signs which are identical with, or similar to, trade marks, without itself using those signs.

That conclusion is not called into question by the fact that that service provider is paid by its clients for the use of those signs. The fact of creating the technical conditions necessary for the use of a sign and being paid for that service does not mean that the party offering the service itself uses the sign.

[T]he proprietor of the mark cannot oppose the use of a sign identical with the mark if that use is not liable to cause detriment to any of the functions of that mark . . . Those functions include not only the essential function of the trade mark, which is to guarantee to consumers the origin of the goods or services ('the function of indicating origin'), but also its other functions, in particular that of guaranteeing the quality of the goods or services in question and those of communication, investment or advertising.

The function of indicating the origin of the mark is adversely affected if the ad does not enable normally informed and reasonably attentive internet users, or enables them only with difficulty, to ascertain whether the goods or services referred to by the ad originate from the proprietor of the trade mark or an undertaking economically connected to it or, on the contrary, originate from a third party (see, to that effect, Céline, paragraph 27 and the case-law cited).

In such a situation, which is, moreover, characterised by the fact that the ad in question appears immediately after entry of the trade mark as a search term by the internet user

CASE (continued)

concerned and is displayed at a point when the trade mark is, in its capacity as a search term, also displayed on the screen, the internet user may err as to the origin of the goods or services in question. In those circumstances, the use by the third party of the sign identical with the mark as a keyword triggering the display of that ad is liable to create the impression that there is a material link in the course of trade between the goods or services in question and the proprietor of the trade mark.

Having regard to the important position which internet advertising occupies in trade and commerce, it is plausible that the proprietor of a trade mark may register its own trade mark as a keyword with a referencing service provider in order to have an ad appear under the heading 'sponsored links'. Where that is the case, the proprietor of the mark must, as necessary, agree to pay a higher price per click than certain other economic operators if it wishes to ensure that its ad appears before those of those operators which have also selected its mark as a keyword. Furthermore, even if the proprietor of the mark is prepared to pay a higher price per click than that offered by third parties which have also selected that trade mark, the proprietor cannot be certain that its ad will appear before those of those third parties, given that other factors are also taken into account in determining the order in which the ads are displayed.

Nevertheless, those repercussions of use by third parties of a sign identical with the trade mark do not of themselves constitute an adverse effect on the advertising function of the trade mark.

[T]he proprietor of a trade mark is entitled to prohibit an advertiser from advertising, on the basis of a keyword identical with that trade mark which that advertiser has, without the consent of the proprietor, selected in connection with an internet referencing service, goods or services identical with those for which that mark is registered, in the case where that ad does not enable an average internet user, or enables that user only with difficulty, to ascertain whether the goods or services referred to therein originate from the proprietor of the trade mark or an undertaking economically connected to it or, on the contrary, originate from a third party; [and] an internet referencing service provider which stores, as a keyword, a sign identical with a trade mark and organises the display of ads on the basis of that keyword does not use that sign within the meaning of Article 5(1) of Directive 89/104 or of Article 9(1)(a) and (b) of Regulation No 40/94.

NOTES

1. The court's analysis breaks trademark "use" into two components: (1) use in a commercial (*i.e.*, non-private) sense; and trademark-oriented use, as opposed to use for a non-trademark purpose. This creates the possibility of non-private commercial activity which is nonetheless free of trademark infringement. Which is exactly what the court seems to recommend as a finding in this case.
2. The key to the holding here is the principle that there will be trademark infringement liability under the EU Directive of 1988 –

    where [an] ad does not enable an average internet user, or enables that user only with difficulty, to ascertain whether the goods or services referred to therein originate from the proprietor of the trade mark or an undertaking [*i.e.*, company] economically connected to it or, on the contrary, originate from a third party...

Put differently, so long as the advertising that is triggered by the user's search is clearly demarcated as (1) not affiliated with the owner of the trademark that was used in the search, and (2) not meant to imply that the goods advertised are affiliated with or sponsored by the trademark owners, the sale of keywords and resulting display of competitor ads will not constitute trademark infringement. This provides a clear "safe harbor" for Google, other search engine companies, and advertisers who buy trademarked keywords. *See Cosmetic Warriors Ltd & Lush Ltd v. Amazon.co.uk Ltd & Amazon EU Sàrl* [2014] EWHC 181 (Ch) (Lush's Community trade mark was held to be infringed by Amazon's purchase and use of "lush" as a keyword through Google AdWords, where Amazon's sponsored link showed the trade mark in its ad; but Amazon's use of the same keyword was found non-infringing when the word "lush" was not displayed in its online ad). *See generally* Georgios Psaroudakis, *In Search of the Trade Mark Functions: Keyword Advertising in European Law*, 34 Euro. I.P. Rev. 33 (2012).

18.2.4 Parody: First Amendment/free expression in the US

Louis Vuitton Malletier, S.A. v. My Other Bag, Inc., 156 F. Supp. 3d 425 (S.D.N.Y. 2016)

JESSE M. FURMAN, United States District Judge

The Court concludes as a matter of law that MOB's bags are protected as fair use – in particular, that its use of Louis Vuitton's marks constitutes "parody." As noted, a successful parody communicates to a consumer that "an entity separate and distinct from the trademark owner is poking fun at a trademark or the policies of its owner." 6 J. Thomas McCarthy, McCarthy on Trademarks and Unfair Competition §31:153 (4th ed., updated Dec. 2015) ("McCarthy"). In other words, a parody clearly indicates to the ordinary observer "that the defendant is not connected in any way with the owner of the target trademark." Id. That is precisely what MOB's bags communicate. Indeed, the whole point is to play on the well-known "my other car . . ." joke by playfully suggesting that the carrier's "other bag" – that is, not the bag that he or she is carrying – is a Louis Vuitton bag. That joke – combined with the stylized, almost cartoonish renderings of Louis Vuitton's bags depicted on the totes – builds significant distance between MOB's inexpensive workhorse totes and the expensive handbags they are meant to evoke, and invites an amusing comparison between MOB and the luxury status of Louis Vuitton. Further, the image of exclusivity and refinery that Louis Vuitton has so carefully cultivated is, at least in part, the brunt of the joke: Whereas a Louis Vuitton handbag is something wealthy women may handle with reverent care and display to communicate a certain status, MOB's canvas totes are utilitarian bags "intended to be stuffed with produce at the supermarket, sweaty clothes at the gym, or towels at the beach." (Mem. Law Def. My Other Bag, Inc. Supp. Mot. Summ. J. (Docket No. 56) ("MOB's Mem.")) 24). Louis Vuitton protests that, even if MOB's totes are a parody of something, they are not a parody of its handbags and, relatedly, that MOB's argument is a post hoc fabrication for purposes of this litigation. (Louis Vuitton's Mem. 17–20, 23). The company notes that MOB's Chief Executive Officer, Tara Martin, has referred to its bags as

CASE *(continued)*

"iconic" and stated that she never intended to disparage Louis Vuitton. (Id. at 18–19; see also Calhoun Decl., Ex. 25, at LVMA0001390 (MOB website describing its bags as "an ode to handbags women love"). Thus, Louis Vuitton argues, the "My Other Bag . . ." joke mocks only MOB itself or, to the extent it has a broader target, "any humor is merely part of a larger social commentary, not a parody directed towards Louis Vuitton or its products." (Id. at 19). In support of those arguments, Louis Vuitton relies heavily on its victory in an unpublished 2012 opinion from this District: Louis Vuitton Malletier, S.A. v. Hyundai Motor Am., No. 10–CV–1611 (PKC), 2012 WL 1022247 (S.D.N.Y. Mar. 22, 2012). In that case, Hyundai aired a thirty-second commercial titled "Luxury," which included "a four-second scene of an inner-city basketball game played on a lavish marble court with a gold hoop." Id. at *1. The scene also included a basketball bearing marks meant to evoke the Louis Vuitton Toile Monogram. See id. The Court rejected Hyundai's parody defense based in large part on deposition testimony from Hyundai representatives that conclusively established that the car company had no intention for the commercial to make any statement about Louis Vuitton at all. See id. at *17–19 (excerpting deposition testimony establishing that Hyundai did not mean to "criticize" or "make fun of" Louis Vuitton, or even "compare the Hyundai with [Louis Vuitton]"). On the basis of that testimony, the Court concluded that Hyundai had "disclaimed any intention to parody, criticize or comment upon Louis Vuitton" and that the ad was only intended to make a "broader social comment" about "what it means for a product to be luxurious." Id. at *17 (internal quotation marks omitted). The Hyundai decision is not without its critics, see, e.g., 4 McCarthy §24:120, but, in any event, this case is easily distinguished on its facts. Here, unlike in Hyundai, it is self-evident that MOB did mean to say something about Louis Vuitton specifically. That is, Louis Vuitton's handbags are an integral part of the joke that gives MOB its name and features prominently on every tote bag that MOB sells. In arguing otherwise, Louis Vuitton takes too narrow a view of what can qualify as a parody. The quip "My Other Bag . . . is a Louis Vuitton," printed on a workhorse canvas bag, derives its humor from a constellation of features – including the features of the canvas bag itself, society's larger obsession with status symbols, and the meticulously promoted image of expensive taste (or showy status) that Louis Vuitton handbags have, to many, come to symbolize. The fact that MOB's totes convey a message about more than just Louis Vuitton bags is not fatal to a successful parody defense. See Campbell v. Acuff–Rose Music, Inc., 510 U.S. 569, 580, 114 S.Ct. 1164, 127 L.Ed.2d 500 (1994) (holding that a copyright parodist must show that his parody, "at least in part, comments on [the parodied] author's work" (emphasis added)); Harley-Davidson, Inc. v. Grottanelli, 164 F.3d 806, 813 (2d Cir. 1999) (applying that standard to trademark parody). And the fact that Louis Vuitton at least does not find the comparison funny is immaterial; Louis Vuitton's sense of humor (or lack thereof) does not delineate the parameters of its rights (or MOB's rights) under trademark law. See, e.g., Cliffs Notes, 886 F.2d at 495–96 ("[T]he district court apparently thought that the parody here had to make an obvious joke out of the cover of the original in order to be regarded as a parody. We do not see why this is so. It is true that some of the covers of the parodies brought to our attention, unlike

CASE *(continued)*

that of [the defendant], contain obvious visual gags. But parody may be sophisticated as well as slapstick; a literary work is a parody if, taken as a whole, it pokes fun at its subject." (footnote omitted)); cf. Yankee Publ'g Inc. v. News Am. Publ'g Inc., 809 F.Supp. 267, 280 (S.D.N.Y. 1992) ("Although [the defendant's] position would probably be stronger if its joke had been clearer, the obscurity of its joke does not deprive it of First Amendment support. First Amendment protections do not apply only to those who speak clearly, whose jokes are funny, and whose parodies succeed."). In those regards, another decision from this District, *437 Tommy Hilfiger Licensing, Inc. v. Nature Labs, LLC, 221 F.Supp.2d 410, 415 (S.D.N.Y. 2002), is more on point. That case involved a line of parody perfume products for use on pets. In particular, the defendant had created a pet perfume called Tommy Holedigger, which resembled a Tommy Hilfiger fragrance in name, scent, and packaging. See id. at 412–13. Hilfiger, like Louis Vuitton here, argued (albeit in connection with a claim of trademark infringement rather than dilution) that the defendant was not entitled to protection as a parody because "its product admittedly makes no comment about Hilfiger." Id. at 415. In support of that argument, Hilfiger cited testimony from the defendant's general partner that his product was not intended to make any comment about Hilfiger or its products. See id. Noting that the general partner had also testified that "he was intending to create a 'parody . . . target[ing] . . . Tommy Hilfiger,' 'a fun play on words,' or 'spoof . . . [t]o create enjoyment, a lighter side,'" Judge Mukasey rejected Hilfiger's argument as follows: Although [the general partner] had difficulty expressing the parodic content of his communicative message, courts have explained that: Trademark parodies . . . do convey a message. The message may be simply that business and product images need not always be taken too seriously; a trademark parody reminds us that we are free to laugh at the images and associations linked with the mark. The message also may be a simple form of entertainment conveyed by juxtaposing the irreverent representation of the trademark with the idealized image created by the mark's owner. Id. (quoting *L.L. Bean, Inc. v. Drake Publishers, Inc.*, 811 F.2d 26, 34 (1st Cir. 1987)). He added, in a comment that applies equally well here: "One can readily see why high-end fashion brands would be ripe targets for such mockery." Id.

18.2.5 Nominative (non-trademark) use in China

Pien Tze Huang v. Hong Ning, Chinese Supreme People's Court (2009) Minshenzi No. 1310

Plaintiff, Zhangzhou Pientzehuang Pharmaceutical Co. Ltd., ("PTH") was founded in December 1999. It was the successor to Zhangzhou Pientzuhuang Group (founded in

CASE *(continued)*

1993), formerly Zhangzhou Pharmaceuticals Company (founded in December 1957). PTH filed and registered the trademarks for "PIEN TZE HUANG" and its Chinese characters "片仔癀" in Class 3 (cosmetics and toothpaste) and Class 5 (pharmaceuticals) in China (referred as "Disputed Mark"). PIEN TZE HUANG was also a unique and traditional Chinese medicine that was exclusively produced by PTH. On January 5, 1999, the Chinese Trademark Office recognized the disputed marks as well-known trademarks in its (1999) No. 45 Decision. The Chinese Ministry of Commerce also recognized PTH's trademark "片仔癀" as a "Chinese Old Brand."

Defendant, Zhangzhou Hongning Household Chemicals Co., Ltd. ("Hongning"), manufactures and sells cosmetic products. Defendant was established on July 6, 1998 and co-founded by HCC and Zhangzhou Hongning Canned Food Company.

HCC was established in 1979, and its product "Lychee Brand PIEN TZE HUANG Pearl Cream" has been recognized as an *Excellent Product of Fujian Province* since December 1988. In 1990, HCC registered the trademark "Lychee Brand" under No. 525083 in 1990. In March 1999, HCC transferred its trademark "Lychee Brand" to Hongning. Hongning continued to produce and sell over twenty types of cosmetics and other household chemical products, including "Lychee Brand PIEN TZE HUANG Pearl Cream" and "PIEN TZE HUANG Special Effect Toothpaste." All of defendant's products included the disputed trademark on their packaging labels, which were in identical fonts with the registered trademarks of plaintiff.

On April 20, 2007, Plaintiff brought a trademark infringement case against the defendant before Zhangzhou Intermediate Court in Fujian Province. Plaintiff claimed that Defendant Hongning used the trademarks that are identical with or similar to its own registered trademarks "PIEN TZE HUANG" in twenty-seven cosmetics and household chemical goods without PTH's authorization. Also, defendant Hongning used names such as "PIEN TZE HUANG Pearl Cream" on the packaging of its cosmetic products. PTH claimed that Hongning's uses infringed its exclusive trademark rights to "PIEN TZE HUANG."

During the trial, Zhangzhou Intermediate Court found that: the mark "片仔癀" was first used and registered by Zhangzhou Pharmaceuticals Company, the predecessor of PTH. The mark was famous among the consumers and served to identify the source of goods. The registered trademark "片仔癀" under No. 701403, No. 562754, and No. 358318 as well as "PIEN TZE HUANG" under No. 358317 were legally transferred to PTH and thus subject to legal protection. Defendant Hongning featured the disputed trademark on its twenty-seven cosmetic products and other household chemical products, including "Lychee Brand PIEN TZE HUANG Pearl Cream" and "PIEN TZE HUANG Special Effect Toothpaste" without PTH's authorization. The font of the disputed trademark on Hongning's products are nearly identical with that of PTH's trademarks. Because both Hongning and PTH target pharmaceutical companies and pharmacy stores and share a common customer base, the similarity between the two marks will likely confuse and mislead the public, disturb the market order, and infringe PTH's legal rights as holder of the registered trademark. Therefore, the court held that Hongning's actions constituted trademark infringement.

CASE *(continued)*

[During the appeal before the Fujian High Court, the appellate court affirmed the original judgment made by Zhangzhou Intermediate Court. Hongning soon petitioned for a retrial before the Chinese Supreme People's Court based on the following claims:]

(1) Pursuant to Chinese Trademark Law, marks that are generic to the features of the goods should not be allowed for trademark registration. Here, PTH's trademark "PIEN TZE HUANG" is both a generic name and also a natural ingredient to the medicine products, and thus should not be registered in the first place. Hongning already filed a cancellation against PTH's trademarks, which remains pending during the time of the litigation.

(2) Hongning's use of the disputed mark does not constitute trademark uses, but rather is a nominative use, *i.e.* describing the ingredients in its products. When a generic name is registered as a trademark, the trademark owner has no right to prohibit others from using the trademark for nominative purposes. Here, since Hongning's use was merely to describe the raw material of its goods, Hongning did not infringe PTH's trademark rights. Moreover, because Hongning used the disputed trademark in conjunction with its own registered "Lychee Brand," the public would not be confused as to the origin of the goods.

(3) Hongning's shareholder HCC had the prior right to the disputed trademark. Before PTH's trademark was approved for registration, HCC had already used "PIEN TZE HUANG" as part of its household chemical commodities' name for years. HCC's products bearing the aforesaid trademark won many awards and were recognized as well-known commodity, and therefore, HCC enjoyed prior rights for the disputed mark.

[In the counter-claims, PTH responded that: (1) "PIEN TZE HUANG" is the name for a specific medicine, rather than the generic name for the medicine. The TRAB, in its prior rulings, already recognized the disputed trademark as a well-known trademark and and also recognized that it is capable of serving to identify the source of goods. (2) Hongning's unauthorized use of the disputed trademark was not a nominative use, but an effort to free ride on the good reputation of PTH's well-known trademarks. Hongning's use could objectively confuse consumers about the source of goods, and thus infringed PTH's exclusive right to use the registered trademark. (3) HCC did not have any prior right to the disputed trademark. There was insufficient evidence to prove that HCC had been using the disputed trademark in its packaging of commodities before PTH registered it . . .]

The Chinese Supreme Court held that, the issues presented before this court include:

(1) Whether Hongning' use of the disputed trademark was nominative use; (2) Whether Hongning enjoyed prior rights to the disputed trademark . . .

(1) Whether Hongning's use of the disputed trademark was nominative use

Pursuant to Article 49 of *Implementing Regulations of the Trademark Law of the People's Republic of China*, where a registered trademark contains the generic name, shape or model of the goods with respect to which it is used, or directly indicates the quality, main raw material, function, use, weight, quantity and other features of the goods, or contains a place name, the trademark registrant has no right to prohibit others from using such marks for nominative uses.

Here, "PIEN TZE HUANG" is the term referring to a specific medicine. When the

CASE (continued)

medical products include such natural ingredients as "Pien Tze Huang," if the [third-party] manufacturers merely describe the ingredients in such medicine in good faith and do not mislead the consumers as to the origin of such goods, then such uses of the trademark should be deemed as nominative use. In determining whether defendant's use is trademark nominative use based on good faith and whether such uses are necessary and fair, the courts should consider the business customs and other relevant factors.

In this case, defendant Hongning placed the disputed trademark in conspicuous places on the packaging of its goods. The signs are not only similar to PTH's registered trademark in terms of fonts and styles, but are even bigger than Hongning's own trademark "Lychee Brand." As such, Hongning's use exceeded the scope of trademark nominative use, which was to explain or objectively describe the features of the goods. And such uses will cause confusion among the public as to the source of goods because the disputed trademark is relatively more famous. Therefore, Hongning's claim for trademark nominative use cannot be established.

(2) Whether Hongning enjoyed prior rights to the disputed trademark

Hongning claimed that its predecessor HCC started to use the words "PIEN TZE HUANG" on its products before PTH registered the disputed trademarks in China. Therefore, Hongning claimed that it enjoyed prior rights to the disputed mark. However, the evidence submitted by Hongning failed to reveal the exact dates of PCC's uses and could not prove that HCC's uses predated the registration date of the disputed trademark. Therefore, Hongning's claim that HCC enjoyed prior right to its current packaging cannot be established.

In conclusion, Hongning's claims for retrial cannot be established. Pursuant to Article 179 and Article 181(1) of the Chinese Civil Procedure Law, this Court hereby rejects Hongning's petition for a retrial and affirmed the lower courts' decision.

NOTES

1. Trademark nominative use is one of the defenses in trademark infringement cases. As we have heard repeatedly, the primary function of a trademark is to identify the source of its goods and services. When the use of another's registered mark might confuse consumers as to the true origin of the goods or services, such uses will not be allowed and might constitute trademark infringement. However, not all uses of trademarks constitute "uses for trademark purposes." Indeed, trademarks might also be used for other purposes, such as for reference purposes or for comparative advertisement purposes. If the use of trademark by a third party is not for trademark purposes, *i.e.* to identify the source of goods, then such uses might not constitute trademark infringements.

2. In *Shaanxi Maozhi Entertainment Ltd. v. DreamWorks*, (2013) Gaomingzhongzi No. 3027, plaintiff Shaanxi Maozhi is the trademark owner for trademark registration "Kung Fu Panda" in Chinese characters in class 41 (*i.e.* entertainment services) (see Figure 18.1). It alleged that DreamWorks' use of the movie title *Kung Fu Panda 2* constituted trademark infringement against its registered trademark "Kung Fu Panda." During the appeal, Beijing High court considered a number of factors in determining whether DreamWorks' use of "Kung Fu Panda" as a movie title constituted trademark infringement, including whether the alleged infringing use is (1) based on good faith; (2) to identify the source of the goods or services in question;

and (3) to explain or describe the characteristics of the goods or services in question. After the overall evaluation, Beijing High Court rejected Shaanxi Maozhi's trademark claim and held that DreamWorks' use of the movie title *Kung Fu Panda* did not constitute trademark infringement because such a use was not for trademark purposes – to identify the source of the goods or services – but instead was trademark nominative use, "to describe the content and nature of the film, telling a story about a Panda practising Chinese Kung Fu." (See more discussion in Seagull Haiyan Song, *Chinese Entertainment Law Year In Review 2015: Is It Converging with the U.S. Practice?* 49 George Washington Int'l Law Rev. (2016)). Do you agree with the Beijing High Court's reasoning?

Figure 18.1 The "original" Kung Fu Panda brand

18.2.5.1 OEM products and non-trademark use in China

An OEM is an "original equipment manufacturer." This means a company that manufactures products for another company (call it the contracting company) that will be sold by the contracting company, often after export to the contracting company's markets. In many such cases, the OEM's manufactured goods will be made to the specifications of the contracting company and the contracting company's trademark will be affixed to the goods. In the following case, the defendant Yahuan is an OEM, which makes goods (in this case locks) for the contracting company, Truper, which is based in Mexico.

 CASE

Focker v. Yahuan, Chinese Supreme People's Court (2014) Mintizi No. 38

Plaintiff, Focker Security Products International Ltd. ("Focker"), feeling dissatisfied with Zhejiang High People's Court's decision regarding the trademark infringement dispute

CASE (continued)

against defendant Pujiang Yuahuan Locks Co. ("Yahuan"), filed a petition for retrial to this Court. The petition was granted in decision Minzhenzi No. 1644 (2013) on January 2, 2014. On April 11, 2014, this Court formed a panel to hear the case. This case is now closed.

The court of first instance confirmed the following facts:

On May 21, 2003, the Chinese Trademark Office approved the mark "PRETUL (and oval device)" for registration under No. 3071808 filed by XU Hao-Rong ("XU") in Class 6, covering goods "common metals and their alloys, non-electric cables and wires of common metal, ironmongery, small items of metal hardware, etc." On March 27, 2010, the trademark no. 3071808 was assigned from XU to Focker.

Defendant Yahuan was established in September 2000. Its primary business is the manufacturing, processing, and sales of locks, hardware tools, chains, saws and other metal crafts.

Truper Herramientas S.A.D.E. C.V. ("Truper") is a Mexico-based company that owns multiple trademark registrations for marks "PRETUL" and "PRETUL (and oval device)" in Classes 6 and 8 in multiple countries, including Mexico. In this particular case, Truper owns a Mexican trademark registration for "PRETUL" in Class 6 under no. 770611.

On March 24, 2011, Truper issued a trademark authorization letter, stating that Truper is the rightful owner of the registered mark "PRETUL" in Mexico; and that Truper authorizes Yahuan to manufacture padlocks bearing the mark "PRETUL," for the sole purpose of exporting such products to Mexico. Yuhuan acknowledged and agreed that: (1) the authorized products (bearing the trademark "PRETUL") are prohibited for sale in China; (2) all the relevant trademarks and intellectual property rights related to the products belong to Truper; (3) Yahuan shall not register these marks with any trademark offices in the world either directly or indirectly; and (4) Truper has the right to rescind the aforesaid authorization at any time.

Plaintiff Focker alleged that it was the rightful owner of the mark "PRETUL (and oval device)" under no. 3071808 in China. On December 31, 2010 and January 6, 2011, Focker learned from Ningbo Customs Office that two batches of padlocks bearing the trademark "PRETUL" were exported by Yahuan to Mexico. Focker alleged that Yahuan manufactured and sold padlocks with the mark "PRETUL" without its authorization, and therefore, infringed on Focker's trademark right. Accordingly, Focker sought: (1) injunctive relief, (2) confiscation of the two batches of infringing products, and (3) damages.

Yahuan responded that the accused infringing products were authorized by Truper and were intended for export purpose only, without domestic sale or distribution in China. As such, the use of the mark will not cause confusion among the relevant public in China, and therefore, Yahuan did not infringe plaintiff's trademark right.

The court of first instance focused its reasoning on the following issues: (1) whether there was an original equipment manufacturer ("OEM") relationship between Yahuan and Truper; and (2) whether Yahuan's conduct constituted trademark infringement.

On the issue of the OEM relationship between Yahuan and Truper, the court of first

CASE *(continued)*

instance held that, OEM for export generally refers to a trade method that involves processing supplied materials, designs or assemblage. In the OEM relationship, the foreign entrusting party provides the drawings and samples of trademarks, and the domestic entrusted party prints the drawings and samples on the goods being processed. All the processed goods will then be returned to the foreign entrusting party rather than being distributed domestically. Essentially, the OEM relationship is a contractual relationship related to processing goods. Here, no evidence suggested that the alleged infringing goods were sold in mainland China. Instead, based on the evidence provided by Yahuan, which includes Truper's trademark registration certificate in Mexico, the bodies and keys of the padlocks bearing Truper's trademark "PRETUL," and Truper's own confirmation that these products are OEM products for export purpose only, the court affirmed that there is an OEM relationship between Yahuan and Truper.

On the issue of infringement, the court of first instance held that, under Article 3 of *the Implementing Regulations of the Trademark Law* ("Chinese Implementing Regulations"), trademark use refers to "the use of the trademark on goods, packages or containers of the goods or in trading documents, and the use of the trademark in advertising, exhibition or any other business activities." As such, the court concluded that Yahuan's use of the mark "PRETUL" on the body, key and product description of the padlocks, as well as on the packagings, constitute trademark use.

The court of first instance held that, although Truper owns trademark registrations for mark "PRETUL" in Mexico, Truper has not registered this mark in China. Therefore, Truper's trademark "PRETUL" is not protected in China. In contrast, Focker legally obtained the exclusive trademark rights for the mark "PRETUL (and oval device)" under registration no. 3071808 in China, and because this registration is still valid, it is under protection by Chinese Trademark Law. As such, because Yahuan affixed the mark "PRETUL device" on the packaging of its padlocks, an almost identical mark to that of Focker, in terms of similar goods, the court of first instance found Yahuan's action constituted trademark infringement.

[During the appeal, Zhejing High People's Court affirmed the court of first instance, finding Yahuan liable for trademark infringement. Yahuan shortly requested a retrial before the Chinese Supreme People's Court.]

The issues presented before this court include: (1) whether Yahuan's conduct constitutes trademark infringement; and (2) whether Yahuan's use of the mark constitutes trademark use under Chinese Trademark Law.

Under Article 48 of *Chinese Trademark Law* (2013), trademark uses refer to uses such as "using trademarks on goods, goods packaging or containers and goods transaction documents, or using trademarks in advertising, exhibits and other commercial events so as to identify the sources thereof."

Based on the evidence submitted during the trials, Truper is the rightful owner of trademarks "PRETUL" and "PRETUL (and oval device)" in Classes 6 and 8 in Mexico.

CASE (continued)

Yahuan manufactured padlocks bearing the "PRETUL" marks and exported such goods to Mexico, upon the request and authorization from Truper. Since the padlocks manufactured by Yahuan are not for distribution or sale in mainland China, the "PRETUL" marks [that Yahuan affixed on its products] do not fulfill the trademark purpose of "indicating the origin of its commodities" in China. Therefore, the co-existence of the two marks used by Yahuan and that by Focker is unlikely to cause confusion among the relevant public in China.

The essential function of a trademark is to identify the source of its goods or services and to distinguish one manufacturer from the other. As far as China's territory is concerned, Yahuan's use of the mark "PRETUL and device" as authorized by Truper only constitutes "physically affixing a trademark label on its products," an act that makes it possible for Truper to use its mark in Mexico where Truper enjoys exclusive trademark rights. But such uses do not fulfill the trademark function of distinguishing the origin of goods as far as the territory of mainland China is concerned. Therefore, the trademark that Yahuan affixed to the alleged infringing goods could neither identify the source of the processed goods nor indicate the source of the final finished goods. Since the OEM marks do not serve the purpose of trademarks, Yahuan's conduct of affixing mark labels on the alleged infringing goods does not constitute trademark use.

In determining whether the use of identical or similar marks in terms of similar goods is likely to cause confusion among the relevant public, the court should base its findings on whether the trademark fulfills its primary function of indicating the source of its goods and services. Further, in determining whether [defendant's] use constitutes trademark infringement, the court should base its findings on whether the source-identifying function of a trademark is fulfilled. As a general rule, there is no likelihood of confusion if the trademark at stake fails to fulfill its identifying function, and therefore, such a use does not constitute trademark use as stipulated under Trademark Law.

Here, the courts of both instances erred in the application of the law because they based the infringement decisions on the sole fact that the defendant used an identical or similar trademark without authorization, but failed to consider the prerequisite that the litigious conduct must constitute trademark use as stipulated under Trademark Law.

Based on the aforementioned reasoning, Yahuan's act of using the trademark "PRETUL" does not constitute trademark infringement. The courts of both instances erred in the application of the law. This Court overrules both findings. So it is ordered.

NOTES AND QUESTIONS

1. China has been well-known for its "world manufacturing center" during the past few decades. Numerous foreign brand owners have taken advantage of China's low-cost labor and ideal manufacturing environment to outsource their goods, through OEM arrangements. Because most of these OEM products made in China are destined for export purpose only, most brand owners do not bother to file trademark registrations for their brands in China.

2. Before *PRETUL*, there were conflicting opinions as to whether OEM products constitute trademark infringement. In *Nike v. Yin Xing Clothing Ltd.*, (2001) Shenzhongfa zhichanchuzi No. 55, Shenzhen Intermediate Court found the OEM parties, including the Chinese manufacturer Yin Xing Clothing and the Spanish entrusting party CIDE Sport, jointly liable for infringing Nike's trademarks in China, despite the fact that CIDE Sport owned a Spanish trademark registration for mark "Nike" and that the OEM products were destined for export to Spain only. However, in *Shanghai Shenda Sound Equipment Ltd. v. JOLIDA (Shanghai) Ltd.*, (2009) Hugaominsan zhizhongzi No. 65, Shanghai High People's Court found defendant, the OEM subsidiary of the US trademark owner JOLIDA, not liable for trademark infringement. Also see conflicting opinions in *Lacoste v. Jiangyin Hongxin Clothing Ltd.*, (2007) Suminsanzhongzi No. 0034 (finding defendant OEM liable for trademark infringement on the basis that defendant failed to conduct reasonable due diligence before entering the OEM contract); and *YU De-Xin v. SOYODA S.A.*, (2012) Suzhiminzhongzi No. 0297 (finding defendants OEMs not liable for trademark infringement on the grounds that plaintiff registered the mark in China in bad faith).

3. A few months after *PRETUL*, Jiangsu High People's Court was asked to decide on another OEM-related case dealing with the trademark "DONG FENG." See (2015) Suzhiminzhongzi. However, in this case, Jiangsu High Court found the defendant, who had an OEM relationship with its entrusting party in Indonesia, liable for trademark infringement. There follows a brief summary of the *DONG FENG* case. Plaintiff Shanghai Diesel Engine Ltd. (SDE) owned two registered trademarks in China for "DONG FENG & device" (in Chinese characters and *pinyin*) in Class 7 for the designated goods "diesel engines" and "diesel engines and fittings for internal combustion engines." Over the years, plaintiff's marks DONG FENG have been recognized as well-known trademarks in China. Plaintiff has also been exporting its products "diesel engines" bearing the DONG FENG marks since the 1960s to various countries, including Southeast Asia. In 1987, PT ADI PERKASA BUANA (PT ADI), an Indonesian company, registered an almost identical trademark "DONG FENG and device" in Indonesia in Class 7. (See Figure 18.2: PT ADI's trademark on the left, and plaintiff SDE's mark on the right.) SDE shortly thereafter entered into a multi-year court battle with PT ADI in Indonesia, trying to cancel PT ADI's trademark registration in Indonesia, but without success. In 2013, PT ADI entered into an OEM contract with defendant Jinfeng Dynamic Machinery Co., Ltd (Jinfeng) for the manufacture of diesel engines, which bear the trademark "DONG FENG" for exclusive distribution in Indonesia. In the same year, such OEM products bearing the trademark DONG FENG were stopped and confiscated by Changzhou Customs, and plaintiff SDE shortly thereafter sued defendant for trademark infringement. Now you have learned the basic facts and know that Jiangsu High Court ruled in favor of plaintiff SDE and found defendant – the OEM party – liable for trademark infringement. Do you think that this decision conflicts with the Supreme People's court decision in *PRETUL*, and if so, why?

Source: original case decision.

Figure 18.2 Dong Feng diesel engine trademark

18.3 Remedies

18.3.1 United States

18.3.1.1 Injunctions

>
>
> ## New York City Triathlon, LLC v. NYC Triathlon Club, Inc., 704 F. Supp. 2d 305 (S.D.N.Y. 2010)
>
> McMahon, J.
>
> The NYC Triathlon is an Olympic distance triathlon, consisting of a 1500 meter swim in the Hudson River, a 40 kilometer bike ride up the West Side Highway and a ten kilometer run into Central Park. It has been run every summer in New York City since 2001 and Plaintiff has, since that date, exclusively used its name and mark THE NEW YORK CITY TRIATHLON (and its related variations, THE NYC TRIATHLON and THE NYC TRI) in connection with the event. This year over 20,000 people vied for the 5600 entry spots, and they sold out in under seven minutes after registration opened online. It is estimated that 250,000 people come out to watch the race.
>
> Defendant [NYC Trithlon Club, Inc.] [is] a retail outlet selling triathlon equipment. By press release dated January 25, 2010, Defendant announced that effective January 1, 2010, it was changing its name from "SBR Triathlon Club" to "NYC Triathlon Club." Plaintiff sent Defendant a cease and desist letter dated January 8, 2010 seeking a response by January 15, 2010. Defendant did not respond. Plaintiff commenced this action on February 22, 2010, seeking injunctive relief to protect its name mark and goodwill pursuant to Section 43(a) of the Lanham Act.
>
> A plaintiff seeking a preliminary injunction "must establish that he is likely to succeed on the merits, that he is likely to suffer irreparable harm in the absence of preliminary relief, that the balance of equities tips in his favor, and that an injunction is in the public interest." *Winter v. Natural Resources Defense Council, Inc.*, 129 S.Ct. 365, 374 (2008). Irreparable injury must be "likely in the absence of an injunction"; it is not enough for a plaintiff to face some "possibility" of irreparable harm. Id. at 375. This is because a preliminary injunction is an "extraordinary remedy that may only be awarded upon a clear showing that the plaintiff is entitled to such relief." Id. at 376. Notwithstanding the Supreme Court's decision in Winter, the Second Circuit has continued to allow parties to obtain a preliminary injunction either through: (1) "a likelihood of success on the merits"; or (2) "sufficiently serious questions going to the merits to make them a fair ground for litigation and a balance of hardships tipping decidedly in the movant's favor." *Zino Davidoff SA v. CVS Corp.*, 571 F.3d 238, 242 (2d Cir. 2009).
>
> Based upon the application of settled law to the undisputed facts, Plaintiff is likely to succeed on the merits of each of its claims.

CASE (continued)

In the Second Circuit, [the proper standard for awarding injunctive relief is controlled by] *eBay, Inc. v. MercExchange, L.L.C.*, 547 U.S. 388 (2006). [The Second Circuit has] held that a preliminary injunction should issue upon a showing of a plaintiff's likelihood of success on the merits only where the plaintiff has also shown that: (1) "he is likely to suffer irreparable injury in the absence of an injunction"; (2) "remedies at law, such as monetary damages, are inadequate to compensate for that injury"; (3) the balance of hardships tips in his favor; and (4) "the 'public interest would not be disserved' by the issuance of a preliminary injunction." [*Salinger v. Colting*, 607 F.3d 68 (2d Cir. 2010)], at 80 [citing *eBay*, 547 U.S. at 391]. Th[is] Court understands *Salinger* as indicating that the standard for injunctive relief historically applied in this jurisdiction must be abandoned in favor of the one articulated by the Supreme Court (whose mandates we are all bound to follow) in *eBay*. The Court can think of no reason why the standards for injunctive relief articulated by the High Court in a copyright infringement case might not apply in a trademark infringement case. Accordingly, this Court analyzes New York City Triathlon LLC's claims by applying the five-fold test of *eBay*.

[In an earlier portion of its opinion, the *New York City Triathlon* court found that the first two *eBay* factors favored the plaintiff trademark owner. It then turned to the third factor, balance of hardships.]

The issue of relative hardship here tips decidedly toward Plaintiff. If left unremedied, the immediate and irreparable harm to Plaintiff resulting from Defendant's unlawful acts would far exceed any theoretical harm to Defendant from an improvidently granted injunction. Plaintiff lost goodwill and the control of its reputation at the moment Defendant launched its infringing triathlon club name, and Plaintiff continues to face this loss until Defendant's acts are enjoined. No monetary sum can sufficiently remedy Plaintiff for this type of harm to its name and brand. In addition, Plaintiff, which has been the sole operator of the NYC Triathlon since 2001, has already spent ten years, and continues to spend significant time and resources, developing and establishing its brand. Defendant, by contrast, has only just adopted the "NYC Triathlon Club" name, inexplicably changing its name from SBR Triathlon Club, as of January 2010. There seems to be no reason why Defendant could not just as easily select another new non-infringing name for its club. Enjoining Defendant from using Plaintiff's Mark will not preclude Defendant from selling its products or services. Defendant has been using the disputed mark for only a short time and thus has developed little or no goodwill in the mark. The irreparable harm to the Plaintiff clearly outweighs any harm caused to the Defendant by virtue of the entry of a preliminary injunction requiring a defendant to change its name and mark.

[Injunction granted.]

NOTES

Though a patent case, *eBay* has been applied to both copyright and trademark cases, as the opinion above mentions; it has in addition sparked major changes in the area of injunctive relief across many fields of law. *See* Mark P. Gergen et. al., *The Supreme Court's Accidental Revolution? The Test for Permanent Injunctions*, 112 Colum. L. Rev. 203 (2012).

18.3.1.2 Damages: infringer's profits and trademark owner's loss

18.3.1.2.1 Infringer's profits

According to one court: "The defendants' profits . . . are a rough measure of the plaintiff's damages. Indeed, they are probably the best possible measure of damages available" (*Polo Fashions, Inc. v. Craftex, Inc.*, 816 F.2d 145, 149 (4th Cir. 1987)). This makes most sense, of course, when the trademark owner and infringer are direct competitors; only then can it be said that but for the infringer's sales the mark owner would have made all those sales itself. Of course, it is possible that an infringer made sales that a mark owner would not have. This might be due to better marketing, or wider distribution, or the like. Yet the courts have traditionally held that it is best to *presume* that all the defendant's sales would have been made by the mark owner. This removes the burden of proving lost sales from the mark owner, and insures full compensation despite problems of proof. Even when the parties are not direct competitors, courts sometimes award the infringer's profits to the mark owner. They do so in these cases because they feel the infringer has been "unjustly enriched" at the expense of the trademark owner; that the defendant's profits from infringement are "ill-gotten gains" which in fairness must be disgorged. And they also cite another reason in these cases: to deter prospective trademark infringers from selling under the marks of others. See, e.g., *Maier Brewing Co. v. Fleischmann Distilling Corp.*, 390 F.2d 117 (9th Cir. 1968), cert. denied, 391 U.S. 966 (1968) (profits from sale of "Black and White" beer must be paid to owner of mark for Black and White scotch whiskey; citing unjust enrichment and deterrence rationales).

Because an "accounting of profits" (*i.e.*, award of infringing defendant's profits to plaintiff mark holder) is an equitable remedy, trial courts have a good deal of discretion in making these awards. Many, as described in the following case, reserve this remedy for cases of intentional or "willful" infringement. When defendant's profits are awarded, it is important to keep in mind that the award relates to *profits* and not *revenues*. Profits are what is left after expenses are subtracted from revenue. Thus a crucial part of most infringer's profits cases is the proof of gross revenues as well as relevant expenses. Only when the latter are subtracted from the former can an appropriate award be made. The following case illustrates this as well.

Fifty-Six Hope Rd. Music, Ltd. v. A.V.E.L.A., Inc., 778 F.3d 1059 (9th Cir.), cert. denied, 136 S. Ct. 410 (2015)

N.R. Smith, Circuit Judge.

Plaintiff Hope Road is an entity owned by [Bob] Marley's children, formed for the purpose of acquiring and exploiting assets, rights, and commercial interests in the late Bob Marley [, the world-renowned reggae music pioneer]. In 1999, Hope Road granted Zion an exclusive license to design, manufacture, and sell t-shirts and other merchandise bearing Marley's image. Hope Road authorizes Zion to use hundreds of different images of Marley on its products.

Defendants were involved with the sale of competing Marley merchandise. A.V.E.L.A. publishes and licenses photographs, images, movie posters, and other artwork for use in the retail marketplace. Defendant X One X Movie Archive holds the copyrights to these photographs, images, movie posters, and other artwork; and Valencia serves as president and CEO of both companies. In 2004, A.V.E.L.A. acquired some photos of Marley from a photographer named Roberto Rabanne. After acquiring the Marley photographs, A.V.E.L.A. began licensing them to defendants Jem and Freeze (as well as entities not a party to this suit) for the production of Marley t-shirts and other merchandise. These items were sold at Target, Walmart, and other large retailers.

On January 23, 2008, Plaintiffs filed suit against Defendants, alleging [various] claims arising from Defendants' use of Marley's likeness [including]: (1) trademark infringement under 15 U.S.C. §1114, [and] (2) false endorsement under 15 U.S.C. §1125(a).

[A jury found infringement and awarded damages to plaintiff.]

[The court quoted the Lanham Act section on damages in trademark cases.]

> When a violation of any right of the registrant of a mark registered in the Patent and Trademark Office, a violation under section 1125(a) or (d) of this title, or a willful violation under section 1125(c) of this title, shall have been established in any civil action arising under this chapter, the plaintiff shall be entitled, subject to the provisions of sections 1111 and 1114 of this title, and subject to the principles of equity, to recover (1) defendant's profits, (2) any damages sustained by the plaintiff, and (3) the costs of the action. The court shall assess such profits and damages or cause the same to be assessed under its direction. In assessing profits the plaintiff shall be required to prove defendant's sales only; defendant must prove all elements of cost or deduction claimed... If the court shall find that the amount of the recovery based on profits is either inadequate or excessive the court may in its discretion enter judgment for such sum as the court shall find just, according to the circumstances of the case. Such sum... shall constitute compensation and not a penalty.

CASE *(continued)*

Lanham Act §35, 15 U.S.C. §1117(a).

[The court began its analysis of damages by noting that in most cases, disgorgement of defendant's profits is awarded only when the defendant willfully infringed the plaintiff's trademark, *i.e.*, infringed with some level of knowledge or intent concerning the fact of infringement.]

[Defendant] Freeze claims that there was insufficient evidence to support the jury's finding that Freeze violated 15 U.S.C. §1125(a) willfully, requiring reversal of the district court's order disgorging Freeze's profits. Freeze is incorrect. At trial, Kim Cauley, vice president of licensing for Freeze, testified as follows: Before Freeze began selling Marley merchandise, Cauley received a phone call from Doreen Crujeiras, a licensing agent for Hope Road, who notified her that "Hope Road or the Marley family owned the rights in Bob Marley." Crujeiras said that A.V.E.L.A. did not have the right to use Marley's name and likeness. Cauley also knew that Zion had a license to sell Bob Marley merchandise, and this awareness predated Freeze's first sales of Marley merchandise. Thus, viewing the evidence in the light most favorable to Plaintiffs, Cauley's testimony demonstrates Freeze's "awareness of its competitors and its actions at those competitors' expense." Lindy Pen Co., 982 F.2d at 1406 (internal quotation marks omitted); see also *E. & J. Gallo Winery v. Consorzio del Gallo Nero*, 782 F.Supp. 472, 475 (N.D.Cal. 1992) ("Use of an infringing mark, in the face of warnings about potential infringement, is strong evidence of willful infringement.").

"[A]ny decision concerning the awarding of an accounting of profits remedy should remain within the discretion of the trial court." *Playboy Enters., Inc. v. Baccarat Clothing Co.*, 692 F.2d 1272, 1275 (9th Cir. 1982). Accordingly, we will not disturb the district court's decision "unless there is a 'definite and firm conviction that the court below committed a clear error of judgement in the conclusion it reached upon a weighing of the relevant factors.'" Id. The trademark holder has the burden to prove the defendant infringer's gross revenue from the infringement. *Lindy Pen Co.*, 982 F.2d at 1408. Then the burden shifts to the defendant infringer to prove expenses that should be deducted from the gross revenue to arrive at the defendant infringer's lost profits. See *Experience Hendrix v. Hendrixlicensing.com*, 762 F.3d 829, 843 (9th Cir. 2014).

A.V.E.L.A. claims that the district court abused its discretion by not allowing deductions reflecting (1) a 40% royalty fee paid to V. International, which A.V.E.L.A. claimed equaled $222,771.00; and (2) marketing, travel, overhead, and trade show expenses connected with promoting Marley merchandise. Not so. Acting within its discretion, the district court held that A.V.E.L.A. failed to meet its burden to prove these deductions. The royalty fee arrangement was not an arms' length transaction. The sole shareholder and employee of V. International was Valencia's girlfriend, Liza Acuna. Moreover, the documentary evidence leaves uncertainty as to the amount of royalty fees paid. Regarding the other expenses, Plaintiffs argue A.V.E.L.A. did not produce sufficient documentation to prove the specific amounts. A.V.E.L.A. does not attempt to rebut any of these arguments. Given these doubts, the district court was within its discretion to deny these deductions.

[Turning to defendant Jem:] Plaintiffs claim that Jem introduced insufficient supporting

CASE *(continued)*

documentation to sustain its burden to prove that it paid salespersons $130,271.47. The district court did not abuse its discretion by relying on the report by Jem's controller, Linda Lyth. Lyth testified in her declaration as an expert, and in general, experts need not disclose all underlying documents on which they rely. For the same reason, we reject Plaintiffs' objection to Jem's Gross Margin Invoice Summary Register. Plaintiffs [also] challenge the $72,989.64 deduction for discounts given to retailers. The district court considered Jem's agreements with retailers showing their respective discounts. The dollar value of retailer discounts was reached by multiplying these rates by the total sales. Contrary to Plaintiffs' argument, [i]t would be reasonable to infer that the retailers took advantage of wholesale markdowns when they contracted for them, a matter within the district court's discretion. Finally, Plaintiffs argue that Jem did not prove that the $0.80-per-garment processing cost Jem paid its affiliate (Jem Equipment) was competitive. However, the law does not require that an infringer prove its expenses were competitive in addition to proving it actually incurred them.

Plaintiffs also argue that the district court abused its discretion by declining to award increased profits. The district court has discretion to increase the profit award above the net profits proven "[i]f the court shall find . . . the amount of the recovery . . . inadequate." 15 U.S.C. §1117(a). It must apply "principles of equity," id., and ensure that the defendant "may not retain the fruits, if any, of unauthorized trademark use or continue that use [and the] plaintiff is not . . . [given] a windfall," *Bandag, Inc.[v. Al Bolser's Tire Stores, Inc.*, 750 F.2d 903, 918 (Fed. Cir.1984)]. "The Lanham Act allows an award of profits only to the extent the award 'shall constitute compensation and not a penalty.'" *TrafficSchool.com, Inc. v. Edriver Inc.*, 653 F.3d 820, 831 (9th Cir. 2011) (quoting 15 U.S.C. §1117(a)). The district court ought to tread lightly when deciding whether to award increased profits, because granting an increase could easily transfigure an otherwise-acceptable compensatory award into an impermissible punitive measure. Generally, actual, proven profits will adequately compensate the plaintiff. Because the profit disgorgement remedy is measured by the defendant's gain, the district court should award actual, proven profits unless the defendant infringer gained more from the infringement than the defendant's profits reflect.

NOTES AND QUESTIONS

1. Because of the difficulty of proving expenses to be deducted from gross profits, the rule that the defendant/infringer must prove deductible expenses strongly favors trademark owners. Is this fair? Does it matter that willfulness/intent is usually required for an award of infringer's profits to the mark owner?
2. Some courts have sanctioned the use of a "reasonable royalty" analysis when assessing trademark damages. *See Sands, Taylor & Wood v. Quaker Oats Co.*, 34 F.3d 1340 (7th Cir. 1994). In these and other cases, technical experts are often used to make the complex arguments necessary to support various damages approaches. *See* Bruce Abramson, *Making the Best Use of Experts to Evaluate Damages in Intellectual Property Disputes*, 106 Trademark Rep. 1094, 1112 (2016).

18.3.1.3 Mark owner's damages

Lanham Act §35(a), 15 U.S.C. §1117(a) provides that "the plaintiff shall be entitled, . . . subject to the principles of equity, to recover (1) defendant's profits, (2) any damages sustained by the plaintiff, and (3) the costs of the action."

Note the word "and": the statute says that *both* defendant's profits and plaintiff's damages may be recovered. Several cases have reached this result. *See, e.g., Aladdin Mfg. Co. v. Mantle Lamp Co. of America*, 116 F.2d 708, 716 (7th Cir. 1941) ("Courts have, in cases in which the action of the infringer was deliberate, fraudulent and wanton, allowed damages in addition to profits . . ."). Apart from cases where a strong deterrence component is involved, however, it is rare for a plaintiff to recover both. Where a court seeks not to deter, but merely assess compensation for infringement, the defendant's profits and the harm or damage to the plaintiff may be the same. If the mark owner and the infringer are competitors, and assuming their costs and marketing efforts are roughly equivalent, the amount the infringer made in net profit may be a good estimate of how much the plaintiff mark owner was harmed. In such a case, awarding both defendant's profit and plaintiff's damages would give plaintiff a "double recovery." Thus where straight compensation (as opposed to deterrence) is the goal, courts will force a plaintiff to choose between the two measures of recovery. *See, e.g. Victoria Cruises, Inc. v. Changjiang Cruise Overseas Travel Co.*, 630 F. Supp. 2d 255 (E.D. N.Y. 2008) (Denying recovery of plaintiff's own lost profits as damages in addition to defendant-competitor's profits from its infringing sales. "[A]warding plaintiff both defendant's profits and its own lost profits based on the same sales would constitute an impermissible double recovery."). *See generally* 5 J. Thomas McCarthy on Trademarks and Unfair Competition §30:73 (4th ed. & Supp., 2016).

Damages under the Lanham Act are based on principles of tort law. The goal of the remedy is to put the plaintiff back into the position it would have been in had the infringement never occurred. There may be several strands to the plaintiff's harm, as the following case excerpt shows.

CASE

Ramada Inns, Inc. v. Gadsden Motel Co., 804 F.2d 1562 (11th Cir. 1986)

Hatchett, Circuit Judge.
This appeal arises out of an action filed by Ramada Inns, Inc. (Ramada Inns) against

CASE (continued)

Gadsden Motel Company (Gadsden), a partnership, for trademark infringement and breach of contract. The district court awarded Ramada Inns substantial damages on the claims. We affirm.

In August, 1977, the partner[ship] purchased a motel in Attalla, Alabama, and entered into a license agreement with Ramada Inns. In 1982, the motel began receiving poor ratings from Ramada Inns inspectors, and Gadsden fell behind in its monthly franchise fee payments. Despite proddings from Ramada Inns, and the initiation of a refurbishing program to upgrade facilities by Gadsden, the motel never met Ramada Inns' operational standards again. On November 17, 1983, Ramada Inns terminated the license agreement citing quality deficiencies and Gadsden's failure to pay past due license fees. Ramada Inns' termination notice directed Gadsden to remove any materials or signs identifying the motel as a Ramada Inn. Inspections on January 6, 1984, and in March, 1984, revealed that Gadsden continued using Ramada Inns' signage and graphics inside and outside the motel. On September 24, 1984, Ramada Inns brought this action for trademark infringement under the Lanham Trademark Act of 1946, 15 U.S.C. §1051 et seq. (Lanham Act) and for breach of the franchise agreement.

The district court [found in favor of plaintiff and] awarded Ramada Inns $47,165 in trademark infringement damages based on the testimony of Dr. Robert Robicheaux, then associate professor of marketing at the University of Alabama Graduate School of Business. Dr. Robicheaux arrived at his damage calculation by adding the following: (1) $23,610 in lost franchise fees for the six-month "hold over" period when Gadsden Motel Company continued to use Ramada Inns' marks; (2) $3,555 interest on the lost franchise fees; (3) $5,000 needed to develop a new franchise in the area; and (4) $15,000 for advertising to restore Ramada Inns' good reputation.

The partner[ship] contend[s] that the district court should have disregarded Dr. Robicheaux's estimates because they were too speculative. Damages were too uncertain to be awarded, in their view, because [t]he amount was uncertain. Dr. Robicheaux's estimate that it would take $5,000 to attract a new franchise was based solely on a conversation he had with a Ramada Inns official, and because Dr. Robicheaux's estimate that it would take $15,000 in order to restore Ramada Inns' image was based on figures for the entire southeastern area.

The Gadsden Motel Company failed to realize a profit during the period of infringement, thus, the district court's damage award was based on damages sustained by Ramada Inns as a result of the infringement. The partner[ship] stress[es] that a trademark infringement award must be based on proof of actual damages and that some evidence of harm arising from the violation must exist. We agree, but the essence of the question presented remains the same. We must decide whether the district court's assessment of the actual damages or harm suffered by Ramada Inns was speculative. We conclude that it was not.

Lanham Act damages may be awarded even when they are not susceptible to precise calculations:

CASE (continued)

Where the wrong is of such a nature as to preclude exact ascertainment of the amount of damages, plaintiff may recover upon a showing of the extent of damages as a matter of just and reasonable inference, although the result may be only an approximation.

Story Parchment Company v. Paterson Parchment Paper Company, 282 U.S. 555, 563 (1931). The wrongdoer may not complain of inexactness where his actions preclude precise computation of the extent of the injury. Under these teachings, the district court's $47,165 damage award cannot be termed "speculative."

NOTES

1. The *Ramada Inns* case recites a fairly common scenario: After relations sour between a franchisor and franchisee, the franchise is terminated, but the franchisee continues using the franchise trademark. The ex-franchisee here is called a "holdover," and there is a body of law and practice devoted to handling these holdover issues. *See* Christopher P. Bussert & William M. Bryner, *A Practical Approach to Addressing Holdover Ex-Franchisee Trademark Issues*, 27 Franchise L.J. 30 (2007). For more on the structure and incentives of franchising arrangements, *see* Roger D. Blair & Francine Lafontaine, The Economics of Franchising (2005).

   A franchise often involves more than simply trademark rights. Often there is a special product – such as a recipe or a special set of ingredients – that the franchisor provides to its franchisees. When, in the course of a dispute with a franchisee, the franchisor cuts off the supply of a special product, the franchisee may not generally buy a substitute product and continue selling it under the franchise trademark:

   > If [plaintiff] broke the contract when it stopped selling the product to Green River Corporation, the latter's remedy was to sue for breach of contract, not to palm off a different product as the product it could no longer obtain. Having no right to continue using the trademark after losing access to the trademarked product, Green River Corporation also has no right to prevent [plaintiff] from using the trademark on the ground that by doing so it is confusing consumers. Any confusion is due to Green River Corporation's palming off another product as "Green River" (*Green River Bottling Co. v. Green River Corp.*, 997 F.2d 359, 362 (7th Cir. 1993) (Posner, J.)).

2. The award of $15,000 for "corrective advertising" in the *Ramada Inns* case is a fairly common component of damages for an aggrieved trademark owner. These awards are based on the theory that the infringer has harmed the mark owner's reputation, and that investments must be made to rebuild brand awareness and positive consumer associations. Depending on the scope of the infringing activity and the number of consumers that must be reached, these awards can be far in excess of the amount in *Ramada Inns*:

   > [Defendant] U-Haul contends that the $45 million in corrective advertising damages awarded by the jury is excessive, because it is far in excess of [plaintiff, mark owner] PODS' (and U-Haul's) internet advertising spending. Since PODS spent approximately $2 million per year on pay-per-click advertising and under $1 million on internet display advertising, U-Haul contends that corrective advertising damages should be limited to a fraction of those expenditures. [C]onsidering the discretion afforded the trier of fact (here, the jury) in computing damages under the Lanham Act, the verdict will be upheld where, as here, the verdict is supported by the evidence (*PODS Enterprises, LLC v. U-Haul Int'l, Inc.*, 126 F. Supp. 3d 1263, 1284 (M.D. Fla. 2015)).

   Note that the remedy of public apology, which is common in some trademark systems in the world, serves much the same function as corrective advertising. *See* Xuan-Thao Nguyen, *Trademark Apologetic Justice: China's Trademark Jurisprudence on Reputational Harm*, 15 U. Pa. J. Bus. L. 131 (2012).

18.3.2 Europe: damages

The European Community Council Regulation on Trademarks (CTMR), Reg. 207/2009 (26 February 2009) provides in Article 102:

Article 102
Sanctions

1. Where a Community trade mark court finds that the defendant has infringed or threatened to infringe a Community trade mark, it shall, unless there are special reasons for not doing so, issue an order prohibiting the defendant from proceeding with the acts which infringed or would infringe the Community trade mark. It shall also take such measures in accordance with its national law as are aimed at ensuring that this prohibition is complied with.
2. In all other respects the Community trade mark court shall apply the law of the Member State in which the acts of infringement or threatened infringement were committed, including the private international law.

Accordingly, both EU and national law are relevant in determining remedies for violation of Community Trademark (CTM) rights. Except for a claim for "reasonable compensation" after a CTM is published but before it is formally registered (Article 9, CTMR), damages are the province of national law.

The EU Enforcement Directive, Directive 2004/48 of the European Parliament and of the Council of April 29, 2004 on the enforcement of intellectual property rights ("Enforcement Directive"), however, does specify some aspects of damages in European IP cases. Article 13 of the Enforcement Directive, in particular, is relevant:

Article 13
Damages

1. Member States shall ensure that the competent judicial authorities, on application of the injured party, order the infringer who knowingly, or with reasonable grounds to know, engaged in an infringing activity, to pay the rightholder damages appropriate to the actual prejudice suffered by him/her as a result of the infringement.
   When the judicial authorities set the damages:
   (a) they shall take into account all appropriate aspects, such as the negative economic consequences, including lost profits, which the injured party has suffered, any unfair profits made by the infringer and, in appropriate cases, ele-

ments other than economic factors, such as the moral prejudice caused to the rightholder by the infringement;

or

(b) as an alternative to (a), they may, in appropriate cases, set the damages as a lump sum on the basis of elements such as at least the amount of royalties or fees which would have been due if the infringer had requested authorisation to use the intellectual property right in question.

One commentator has noted some of the obvious problems with applying national law on remedies for CTMs which in most cases cover products sold throughout the EU and beyond:

> [I]t may be doubtful, which national law is applicable to a trademark infringement. The provision refers to the national law of the Member State, in which the infringement was committed, including its private international law. If an infringement was committed in several Member States, it is uncertain, whether the laws of all of these Member States shall be applied to the infringement, each with respect to the violating acts committed in its territory. This interpretation might contradict the unitary character of the CTM. Alternatively, the law of the Member State where the seised court or the centre of gravity of the infringement is located could be applied (Frauke Asendorf, *A Piece of (the) Cake – Damages for Proprietor and Licensee Due to Infringements of Community Trade Marks*, 2011 Gruner Verein (GRUR) Int'l 802, 803 (footnotes omitted) (hereafter Asendorf, *Trademark Damages*)).

As with much of IP law, damages may be estimated either from the loss suffered by the plaintiff trademark owner, or from the profits earned by the defendant. This is apparent from Article 13 of the Enforcement Directive, quoted above; but of course as a principle it long predates the Directive, having deep roots in national law. For an instructive German case applying these principles, *see Viosulfal v. Vitasulfal*, BGHZ 34, 320, BGH 24.02.1961, I ZR 83/59 ("*Vitasulfal*"). There the claimant (plaintiff, Viosulfal) was the owner of the word sign (German registration no. 294 418 "Viosulfal") as well as the pictorial sign Registration no. 344 485, which shows the shadows of two kneeling men, between which is a white, standing cross. Both characters were registered, inter alia, for medicaments and pharmaceutical preparations. Defendants, former distributors of plaintiff's product, manufactured a similar drug and sold it under the trademark "Vitasulfal." The German Bundesgerichtshof (Federal Court of Justice) held that the trademark "Viosulfal" was recognized by customers, but that defendants had contributed value also by manufacturing and distributing the pharmaceutical product in markets where it was otherwise unavailable. Thus out of the defendant's total profit of 15,000 German marks (DM) [now roughly

€30,000], the court assigned a value of 1,000 German marks (DM) (€2,000] to the use of the trademark.

Likewise, in *Berechnung des Schadens bei Warenzeichenverletzungen Meßmer-Tee II*, BGH, GRUR 1966, 375, 377 ((LSK 1966, 849369, 12.1.1966), the Bundesgerichtshof established that in a case of trademark infringement damages can be calculated with reference to an established license fee, or other "reasonable royalty"; and in addition, if the infringer attached plaintiff's trademark to an inferior product, which has negatively affected the reputation of the product of the trademark owner, an estimate of the harm to the trademark owner may be added onto the reasonable royalty/license fee. From this case, it appears that under German law there is no election between these damages measures, at least under these facts. In general, German law prohibits "double recovery," that is, recovery of multiple damages for the same harm using different theories (*e.g.*, plaintiff's loss and defendant's gain). *See* Asendorf, *Trademark Damages*, 2011 GRUR 802, 805.

Other national courts may deviate in some particulars, but these are the basic elements of trademark damages across Europe. As one commentator explains:

> The amount of the damages suffered by IPR owners might also be derived from another element, i.e. the royalties or fees which would have been due if the infringer had requested authorisation to use the intellectual property right in question. Let us take the following example. A right holder usually licences to third parties its fancy trademark (for beverages) requesting a royalty equal to seven per cent of the profits made by the said licencees through the sale of licenced products. Let us then imagine that an infringer starts selling beverages bearing an identical trademark and that a court ruling ascertains the trademark infringement. In such a case the trademark holder, as damages, might obtain from the infringer precisely seven per cent of the profits made by the latter by selling the infringing goods. That is why this damages quantification method is called "reasonable royalty rate". Such a damages quantification method may be a successful approach if the right holder can show the royalty the infringer would have paid if the proper licencing procedures had been followed. The exercise will be easy if, as we have seen, the right holder has granted licences to other subjects in the past. If no licencee exists, the right holder will have to demonstrate that the amount claimed for the licence is reasonable or otherwise corresponds to the average royalty rate in the market in question (Enrico Bonadio, *Remedies and Sanctions for the Infringement of Intellectual Property Rights under EC Law*, 30 Euro. I.P. Rev. 320, 325 (2008) (footnotes omitted).

For other types of remedies in Germany, see Detlef von Ahsen et al., *Relief in IP Proceedings other than Injunctions or Damages*, Gruner Verein (GRUR) Int'l 773 (2013). For the situation in France, see Yaniv Benhamou, *Compensation of Damages for Infringements of Intellectual Property Rights in France, Under Directive 2004/48/EC and Its Transposition Law – New Notions?*, 40 Int'l Rev, I.P. & Comp. L. (IIC) 125 (2009).

With these basic principles in mind, consider an actual case on damages in the EU, this one from the UK.

CASE

32Red plc v WHG (International) Ltd, 2013 WL 1563023, [2013] EWHC 815 (Ch) (High Court of Justice Chancery Division, Intellectual Property, sitting as Community Trade Mark Court, 12 April 2013)

The claimant, 32Red plc ("32Red"), has been operating an online casino under the "32Red" brand since 2002. It is not one of the largest operators in its field, but its business is still substantial. In 2009 it had about 25,000 active casino players who placed over 130 million bets with a value of around £170 million, generating gross revenue for 32Red of some £11 million. About 74% of this income was generated by players based in the United Kingdom.

By 2006 32Red was the registered owner of two European Community trade marks: one for the word "32Red" and another for a device consisting of a stylisation of "32Red" in a roulette ball. [Defendant William Hill Group, or WHG, entered the gaming market by acquiring various assets, including an earlier-used but unregistered trademark in the name "32Vegas." Both 32Red and WHG are licensed by the Gibraltar gaming commission and therefore subject to UK (and therefore EU) law. In the lower courts, 32Red succeeded in establishing infringement of its UK mark as well as its Community marks.]

32Red accepts that it is not in a position to prove that it suffered a loss of profits as a result of the defendants' infringement of its trade marks, but it claims to be entitled to a sum equal to a reasonable royalty on the strength of the "user principle".

Nicholls LJ coined the [user principle] term in *Stoke-on-Trent City Council v. W & J Wass Ltd* [1988] 1 WLR 1406 (at 1416) to refer to the principle that a person who has wrongfully used another's property can be liable to pay, as damages, a reasonable sum for such use.

This principle is well-established in relation to patent infringement . . . On occasions, the Courts adopt essentially the same approach when assessing contractual damages.

The defendants' pleaded case was that user principle damages are not available in the present case. By the time of the hearing, however, they had accepted that such damages can

CASE *(continued)*

potentially be appropriate for trade mark infringement. The parties now differ as to how much should be awarded rather than whether there should be any award at all.

The primary basis for the assessment is to consider what sum would have [been] arrived at in negotiations between the parties, had each been making reasonable use of their respective bargaining positions, bearing in mind the information available to the parties and the commercial context at the time that notional negotiation should have taken place. [Citing *Force India Formula One Team Ltd v. 1 Malaysia Racing Team Sdn Bhd* [2012] EWHC 616 (Ch), [2012] RPC 29, at par. 376.]

Two questions call for particular consideration in the present case:

i) How far are the specific characteristics and circumstances of the parties important to the assessment of user principle damages?

ii) How far is it appropriate to have regard to alternative courses of action which would have been available to the parties at the date of the hypothetical negotiation?

There are plainly limits to the extent to which the Courts will have regard to the parties' actual attributes when assessing user principle damages. The parties are taken to have been willing to make a deal even if one or both of them would not in reality have been prepared to do so. It is also assumed that the parties would have acted reasonably regardless of whether that would in fact have been the case.

The defendants maintain that it is of central importance to the assessment of damages that they could have abandoned the name 32Vegas in favour of another brand (say, "21Nova") at relatively little expense. [Indeed, the defendant's business model was to have a large portfolio of gambling sites with different names; whereas the plaintiff's approach was to build up its sole "32Red" brand.] 32Red, on the other hand, argues that this is immaterial. According to 32Red, it is well established that a defendant cannot pay in aid a non-infringing alternative to reduce the damages payable for infringement of a patent, and a non-infringing alternative could be relevant to a hypothetical negotiation about the use of "32Vegas" only if it had all the attributes of that mark.

I do not accept that "the availability of a non-infringing alternative is not a relevant factor in the calculation of a reasonable royalty" in the present context. If the parties can be expected to have taken such an alternative into account in their hypothetical negotiation, it appears to me that I must do so as well. Further, I do not think an alternative need have had all the attributes of the 32Vegas name to be relevant.

32Red's case is that it should be awarded an amount equal to 30% of the NGR for the 32Vegas/21Nova casino in respect of the period of infringement and six months thereafter (*i.e.* a total of about 13 months). That would amount to something of the order of £5 million. The defendants' position is very different. They maintain that an award of between £25,000 and £50,000 would be appropriate. Such a figure would, they claim, represent a reasonable outcome of hypothetical negotiation at the relevant date.

[R]eference to economic benefits provides the best starting point when considering what the parties to the hypothetical negotiation would have agreed. As I have already indicated, the evidence seems to me to be good enough to allow tentative conclusions to

CASE *(continued)*

be drawn as to whether changing the 32Vegas casino's name was damaging to William Hill Online.

32Red, as a hypothetical willing licensor, is to be taken, I think, to have recognised that it could not insist on being paid a sum out of proportion to the financial advantages that the defendants stood to obtain by using the name 32Vegas rather than re-branding at once. That 32Red would have been willing to accept such a sum is further indicated by a number of matters. In the first place, 32Red's profits were relatively modest when the defendants were using the 32Vegas brand: profits for the six months to 30 June 2009 were reported as £233,777. Even the £50,000 that Mr Boulton suggested as a reasonable royalty would therefore have served to increase the company's profitability considerably in percentage terms. Secondly, confusion between the 32Red and 32Vegas brands could, as already mentioned, potentially have resulted in it gaining customers as well as losing them. Thirdly, 32Red was not yet ready to expand its non-UK activities. While Mr Ware explained that it aims to enter new markets in the future, it does not seem to have been inhibited in doing so by the defendants' use of the 32Vegas name during 2009. Fourthly, the contemporary documents do not show 32Red to have seen the 32Vegas casino as acutely damaging to it at the time.

I think it likely that William Hill Online would have been willing to pay somewhat more than the £50,000 suggested by [its representative]. William Hill Online would have needed to factor in, not only the cost and inconvenience attached to re-branding, but the risk that doing so would disrupt the existing carousel [*i.e.*, portfolio of brand names]. While individual brands were not considered important to the carousel model, William Hill Online could still, I think, have been expected to prefer to continue with the 32Vegas name, not least in case changing it had unexpected consequences. The parties to the hypothetical negotiation are also to be assumed to have in mind that William Hill Online (a) stood to derive benefits from using the 32Vegas name for some time after the expiry of the seven-month hypothetical licence, [and] (b) would enjoy de facto exclusivity [due to plaintiff's lack of British operations].

None the less, I do not think that the parties to the hypothetical negotiation would have agreed a figure very substantially in excess of £50,000. Doing the best I can, I have concluded that a licence fee of £150,000 is likely to have been agreed.

£150,000 appears to represent between 1% and 1.5% of the 32Vegas casino's NGR for the period of infringement.

An award of the scale proposed by 32Red would have been out of all proportion to the benefit that the defendants derived from their infringement of 32Red's marks and to any loss that 32Red could realistically be thought to have suffered.

In all the circumstances, I shall award damages of £150,000.

NOTE

The Enforcement Directive provides important additional tools for IP owners, most importantly the right to demand that a suspected infringer present evidence under its control. Thus under Article 6.1: "[I]f a trademark owner is certain that its competitor's goods, leaflets, brochures or commercial catalogues unlawfully bear, or in any way make reference to, its trademark, the said owner may ask the judge to order the defendant to present them in court." See Bonadio, *Remedies, supra*, 30 E.I.P.R. 320, 322. For border enforcement procedures, *see* K. Daele, *Regulation 1383/2003: A New Step in the Fight against Counterfeit and Pirated Goods at the Borders of the European Union*, [2004] Euro. I.P. Rev. 217.

18.3.3 Europe: injunctions

The EU Enforcement Directive covers injunctions at Article 11:

Article 11
Injunctions

Member States shall ensure that, where a judicial decision is taken finding an infringement of an intellectual property right, the judicial authorities may issue against the infringer an injunction aimed at prohibiting the continuation of the infringement. Where provided for by national law, non-compliance with an injunction shall, where appropriate, be subject to a recurring penalty payment, with a view to ensuring compliance. Member States shall also ensure that rightholders are in a position to apply for an injunction against intermediaries whose services are used by a third party to infringe an intellectual property right.

Injunctions are routinely available where a trademark's validity is upheld and the defendant is found to infringe the mark. *See, e.g., Reichweite des Schutzes einer Farbmarke – Gelbe Wörterbücher*, Case I ZR 228/12, (Federal Supreme Court (Bundesgerichtshof) (BGH), 18.9.2014) summarized as "*Langenscheidt Yellow*," 2015 Int'l Rev. I.P. & Comp. L. (IIC) 372 (upholding permanent injunction in case of infringement of trademark for color yellow for bilingual dictionaries, after infringement finding against defendant's language learning software sold in the same color scheme).

Preliminary injunctions are also readily available. The process for obtaining them in Germany, in particular, is said to be quick and relatively inexpensive. This is true even when the only act by the infringer is to register a similar mark. Even in this case, though use by the defendant and harm to the plaintiff have yet to be proven, preliminary relief may be possible due to the *potential* harm signaled by the registration of a competing mark. See *Metrosex*, Case No. I ZR 151/05 Decision Federal Supreme Court (Bundesgerichtshof) (BGH) 13 March 2008, 2008 GRUR 912.

Injunctions are a matter of discretion for the court in most cases. This means that each case must be considered on its own facts. Equity and basic fairness are of paramount importance. So even when an authorized use of a trademark is at issue, facts may intervene which militate against automatic grant of an injunction. *See, e.g., Nikken Kosakusho Works v. Pioneer Trading Company* [2003] EWHC 2006 (Ch), 2003 WL 23508860 (High Court of Justice Chancery Division Patents Court, 5 August 2003) (refusing injunction during period when former distributor is disposing of products acquired prior to termination of distribution agreement).

One important area of controversy in the EU has been the "blocking injunction," meaning injunctions against intermediaries who are seen as somehow facilitating infringement. *See* Martin Husovec & Lisa Van Dongen, Website Blocking, Injunctions and Beyond: View on the Harmonization from the Netherlands (May 12, 2017), available at SSRN: https://ssrn.com/abstract=2967318 or http://dx.doi.org/10.2139/ssrn.2967318. Trademark owners may seek an injunction against intermediaries whose services are used by a third party to infringe an intellectual property right. *See* Article 11 of the EU Enforcement Directive, above. It is important to note that an injunction may be available in this situation regardless of whether the intermediary itself is liable for trademark infringement. It is the assistance to a direct infringer which may, in the right case, be enjoined. *See* Reto Hilty, "The Role of Enforcement in Delineating the Scope of IP Rights" (2015) Max Planck Institute for Innovation & Competition Research Paper No. 15-03 (discussing the argument that Article 11 and the cases under it state a "ceiling" on national enforcement capabilities).

The logic of such an injunction has been explained by a commentator, citing prominent British jurists who have opined on the subject:

> [I]n *Cartier Int'l v. Sky* [(UK High Court, Chancery Div., 17 Oct. 2014), [2014] EWHC 3354 (Ch)] a blocking injunction quite similar to those issued under the copyright regime was issued against five major UK-based ISPs in order to block access to certain identified counterfeit websites that infringed trademark rights. [In the *Richemont* case,] Justice Arnold . . . [adopted] the following principle established in *Norwich Pharmacal Co v. Customs & Excise Commissioners* [[1974] AC pp. 133, 145–46. [1974] A.C. 133; [1973] 3 W.L.R. 164; (House of Lords, 26 June 1973)]:
>
>> If a man has in his possession or control goods the dissemination of which, whether in the way of trade or, possibly, merely by way of gifts . . . will infringe another's patent or trade mark, he becomes, as soon as he is aware of this fact, subject to a duty, an equitable duty, not to allow those goods to pass out of his

possession or control at any rate in circumstances in which the proprietor of the patent or mark might be injured by infringement ensuing. [. . .] This duty is one which will, if necessary, be enforced in equity by way of injunction.

Thus, building on this, Arnold J observed: . . . [I]t is not a long step from this to conclude that, once an ISP becomes aware that its services are being used by third parties to infringe an intellectual property right, then it becomes subject to a duty to take proportionate measures to prevent or reduce such infringements even though it is not itself liable for infringement (Althaf Marsoof, *The Blocking Injunction – A Critical Review of Its Implementation in the United Kingdom in the Context of the European Union*, 46 Int'l Rev. I.P. & Comp. L. 632, 636–37 (2015) (footnotes omitted)).

18.3.4 China

18.3.4.1 Dual enforcement mechanism

With trademarks as with patents, China adopts a "dual-enforcement" mechanism, where the trademark owner can seek either administrative enforcement or judicial enforcement in trademark enforcement scenarios. Each mechanism has its own strengths and limitations.

For example, administrative enforcement is generally known for its simplified procedure, low cost and relatively high efficiency. When a trademark owner finds its trademark being infringed by a third party, he can file an administrative complaint before the local Administration of Industry and Commerce (AIC), presenting his valid trademark registration certificate and evidence regarding the accused infringer. Should the local AIC find the evidence convincing, they will often proceed to a "raid" at the alleged infringer's factory, confiscating the infringing products and tools, and even shutting down the infringer's factory.

Yet the administrative enforcement procedure also has its own limitations. For example, the local AICs might be good at determining a straightforward trademark infringement case, in which the trademark owner has a valid trademark registration certificate and the two marks are identical or confusingly similar in terms of similar goods or services. However, in terms of more complicated trademark infringement cases, such as protection of unregistered trademarks, or conflicts between trademark rights and other prior rights (rights of prior trade names, person's name, copyrights or design patent rights), the local AICs might not be the best authority to deal with such cases. Also, local protectionism might be another concern discouraging right holders to seek local administrative enforcement. Even so AIC actions can be helpful in gathering evidence for full-blown court enforcement efforts, which are the natural alternative choice when simple administrative enforcement might be inadequate. See European Union, China IPR SME [Small and Medium-sized Enterprises] Help Desk, at p. 1, available at http://www.china-iprhelpdesk.eu/sites/all/docs/publications/EN_Enforcement_Aug-2013.pdf.

18.3.4.2 China: monetary damages

Article 63 of the Chinese Trademark Law discusses various types of monetary damages in trademark infringement cases, including compensatory damages that are calculated based on the actual losses of the trademark owner, illegal gains of the infringer or the license royalty rate; statutory damages and also punitive damages. More importantly, this provision also addresses the priority of calculating monetary damages, *i.e.* which calculation method applies first:

> The amount of compensation for infringing the exclusive right of a trademark owner shall be determined based on the right owner's actual losses as a result of the infringement. When the actual losses are difficult to determine, the compensation amount should be determined based on the illegal gains of the infringer. When the actual losses of the trademark owner and illegal gains of the infringer are both difficult to determine, the monetary damage could be determined based on certain times of the royalty rate applied for the use of the registered trademark. With regard to willful infringement under severe conditions, the compensation amount could be between one time and three times of the aforesaid amount as determined in this provision. The amount of compensation shall also include reasonable expenses of the right owner to prevent the infringement.
>
> For the purpose of determining the amount of compensation, where the right owner has done his best to submit evidence but whereas the account books and information regarding the infringement are held by the infringer, the People's Court may order the infringer submit such account books and information. In case the infringer refuses to submit the account books and information or submit a false version thereof, the People's Court may determine the amount of compensation based on the claim and evidence submitted by the right owner.
>
> Where it is difficult to determine the right owner's actual losses, the infringer's illegal gains or the royalties of the registered trademark, the People's Court shall, based on the actual circumstance of infringement, grant a statutory damage no more than 3 million RMB.

Article 63 of the Chinese Trademark Law (2013) includes a few major changes regarding monetary damages. First, the calculation of compensatory damages would be applied in the following priority order, and only when the first calculation method is not available or difficult to determine will the courts move to the next calculation method: (1) actual losses of the right owner; (2) illegal gains of the infringer; and (3) previous license royalty rates. Second, Article 63 raised the amount of statutory damages from one million RMB to three million RMB. Third, treble damages also become available in willful infringement cases, which amount could be as high as three times the reasonable loyalty rate. Lastly, the provision puts the burden of proof on the defendant. Where a defendant fails to prove the appropriate amount for monetary damages, the court will then support the right owner's claim for monetary damage. In summary, Article 63, since its major revision in 2013, has been applauded by trademark owners as an effective measure to deter trademark infringements by raising the monetary damages standard and also shifting the burden of proof to the defendant.

18.4 International enforcement

18.4.1 Extraterritorial application of US law

In the well-known *Bulova Watch* case, the US Supreme Court gave the Lanham Act a broad international reach. But the facts were unusual. The plaintiff placed its mark on high-end watches. Defendant purchased a watch in Mexico, assembled from watch parts purchased in the US. Defendant then brought the watch into the US. Bulova claimed that this had become a common scenario, and that purchasers often brought their foreign-purchased watches into Bulova dealers for repair. There was no issue of personal jurisdiction in this case, because the defendant was a US citizen; thus Bulova had no trouble bringing the defendant before a US court. And there were no competing marks registered in Mexico, so only the US trademark was at issue. On these facts, the Supreme Court found the defendant's acts to be an infringement of Bulova's trademark rights (*Steele v. Bulova Watch Co.*, 344 U.S. 280 (1952)).

Bulova Watch runs up against an important general principle: that US law must not be applied in a way that undermines the sovereignty of foreign nations. See, e.g., *Morrison v. National Australia Bank Ltd.*, 561 U.S. 247, 248 (2010) ("It is a longstanding principle of American law 'that legislation of Congress, unless a contrary intent appears, is meant to apply only within the territorial jurisdiction of the United States.'" (quoting cases)). There is in fact a strong presumption against the application of US law to activities that take place outside the borders of the US. There is a tension here that courts have recognized. On one hand, foreign activities may well affect the rights and interests of US trademark holders; extensive advertising and sales by an unauthorized dealer overseas, for example, may create a substantial likelihood of confusion among those US citizens who travel or are otherwise exposed to the overseas dealer's activities. On the other hand, to purport to enjoin the activities of a citizen of a foreign, sovereign nation would be an extraordinary assertion of national power that would violate the essential respect for national sovereignty that underlies international law.

Courts have resolved this tension in a number of ways. In *Vanity Fair Mills, Inc. v. T. Eaton Co.*, 234 F.2d 633, 643 (2d Cir. 1956), the Second Circuit held that the Lanham Act should not be given extraterritorial application against foreign citizens acting under presumably valid foreign trademarks, even if the actions of those citizens substantially affect US commerce. The *Vanity Fair* Court stated three factors to consider when a plaintiff seeks extraterritorial application of US trademark law: "(1) the defendant's conduct must have a substantial effect on United States commerce; (2) the defendant must be a United States citizen; and (3) there can be no valid trademark registration in the foreign country and no conflict with trademark rights conferred by that foreign country" (*id.*, at 642–43).

Under a similar test, a Ninth Circuit court enjoined a California company and a US citizen, both operating in Mexican–US border towns (such as Tijuana), from selling counterfeit REEBOK athletic shoes. See *Reebok International, Ltd. v. Marnatech Enterprises, Inc.*, 970 F.2d 552 (9th Cir. 1992). The extraterritorial reach of this injunction was justified, the court said, by the substantial impact on US commerce caused by the non-US activities of the defendants. Again, however, it is important to note that the presence of non-US trademarks in a case may well shift the calculus away from a decision to exercise US jurisdiction. See *Juicy Couture, Inc. v. Bella Intern. Ltd.*, 930 F. Supp. 2d 489, 506–07 (S.D. N.Y. 2013) (refusing to extend preliminary injunction to conduct in Hong Kong and to disable a Hong Kong website; parallel litigation over the mark was pending in Hong Kong: "Although this Court is not prevented from applying the Lanham Act extraterritorially before a decision in that [Hong Kong] action is reached, it must proceed with caution in determining whether to do so").

An example of how these factors are applied comes in the next case.

CASE

Tire Engineering & Distribution, LLC v. Shandong Linglong Rubber Co., 682 F.3d 292 (4th Cir. 2012)

Before Shedd, Diaz, and Floyd, Circuit Judges. Per curium.
[Tire Engineering] develops and sells specialized tires for underground mining vehicles. Prior to 2005 and the events giving rise to this suit, [Tire Engineering] flourished in the mining-tire market with its unique and effective designs. To protect its intellectual property and brand, [Tire Engineering] obtained a trademark for its "Mine Mauler" product name. [Tire Engineering accused Shandong Linglong of copying its tire designs and selling tires in China without authorization under the "Mine Mauler" trademark. A jury found for Tire Engineering on several causes of action, including trademark infringement under the Lanham Act. Shandong Linglong appealed.]
Appellants [Shandong Linglong] challenge the jury's finding of liability under the Lanham Act, arguing that the statute's sweep does not extend to the extraterritorial acts alleged by [Tire Engineering]. We agree. Because Appellants' trademark infringement lacks a sufficient effect on U.S. commerce, we find that the Lanham Act does not reach the conduct complained of by [Tire Engineering]. Although the Lanham Act applies extraterritorially in some instances, only foreign acts having a significant effect on U.S. commerce are brought under its compass. *Nintendo [of America, Inc. v. Aeropower Co.,* 34 F.3d 246 (4th Cir.1994)], at 250. Confining the statute's scope thusly ensures that judicial application of the Act will hew closely to its "core purposes ..., which are both to protect the ability of American consumers to avoid confusion and to help assure a trademark's owner that it will reap the financial and reputational rewards associated with having a desirable name or product." *McBee v. Delica Co.,* 417 F.3d 107, 120–21 (1st Cir. 2005). With these aims in mind, we have reasoned that the archetypal injury contemplated by the Act is harm to the plaintiff's "trade reputation in United States markets." See *Nintendo,* 34 F.3d at 250. Other circuits have posited that the Lanham Act's significant-effect requirement may be satisfied by extraterritorial conduct even when that conduct will not cause confusion among U.S. consumers. Under this diversion-of-sales theory, courts find a significant effect on U.S. commerce where sales to foreign consumers would jeopardize the income of an American company. *See, e.g., McBee,* 417 F.3d at 126. The doctrine is narrowly applied, however, because the injury in this context – harm to a U.S. business's income absent confusion among U.S. consumers – "is less tightly tied to the interests that the Lanham Act intends to protect, since there is no United States interest in protecting [foreign] consumers." *Id.* Thus courts invoking the diversion-of-sales theory have required the defendants to be U.S. corporations that conducted operations – including at least some of the infringing activity – within the United States. *Ocean Garden, Inc. v. Marktrade Co.,* 953 F.2d 500, 504 (9th Cir. 1991); *Am. Rice, Inc. v. Ark. Rice Growers Coop. Ass'n,* 701 F.2d 408, 414–15 (5th Cir. 1983). Only in

CASE (continued)

such instances is there a sufficient nexus between U.S. commerce and the infringing activity. Recognizing that it has not alleged confusion among U.S. consumers, [Tire Engineering] grants that its Lanham Act claims can prevail only if we adopt, for the first time, the diversion-of-sales theory. Although we find compelling the reasons underpinning use of the doctrine in other cases, we decline to apply it to the facts before us. Courts upholding liability under the Lanham Act based solely on harm to a U.S. company's income from foreign infringement have stressed that the defendants in those cases were U.S. companies that conducted substantial domestic business activity. *Ocean Garden*, 953 F.2d at 504; *Am. Rice, Inc.*, 701 F.2d at 414–15. Here, in contrast, Appellants are not U.S. corporations and they lack a pervasive system of domestic operations. Thus we cannot conclude that the extraterritorial conduct – exclusively foreign sales of infringing tires – has a significant effect on U.S. commerce as required by the dictates of the Lanham Act, *see Nintendo*, 34 F.3d at 250. We accordingly hold that the Lanham Act does not afford Alpha relief, and we dismiss its claims under that statute.

NOTES

1. Extraterritoriality implies that the infringing act occurs in a foreign jurisdiction. Note that importation occurs in the US, so a suit to block infringing imports does not implicate extraterritoriality concerns. *See McBee v. Delica Co., Ltd.*, 417 F.3d 107, 122 (1st Cir. 2005) ("There can be no doubt of Congress's power to enjoin sales of infringing goods into the United States"; so extraterritoriality tests do not apply where plaintiff seeks a remedy for infringing imported goods sold to American consumers).
2. What if the defendant is infringing the plaintiff's trademark by using it on a website that is hosted (*i.e.*, originates from) a non-US location? Most websites from around the world can be accessed in the US; does this establish enough "U.S. contact" to give the mark holder the right to pursue a trademark infringement claim in the US? Quite possibly. A leading commentator says: "The use of an infringing mark as part of an Internet site available for use in the United States may constitute an infringement of the mark in the United States." 5 J. Thomas McCarthy on Trademarks and Unfair Competition §29:56 (4th ed. & Supp., 2016). *See Euromarket Designs, Inc. v. Crate & Barrel Ltd.*, 96 F. Supp. 2d 824 (N.D. Ill. 2000) (Irish retailer who ran website offering consumer products for sale under the crateandbarrel-ie.com domain name was subject to jurisdiction in a US court); *Stevo Design, Inc. v. SBR Marketing Ltd.*, 919 F. Supp. 2d 1112 (D. Nev. 2013) (court had subject matter jurisdiction over website owner based in Costa Rica whose professional and collegiate sports betting and handicapping website was in English and directed at US consumers). There is, however, the additional matter of *personal jurisdiction* in these cases, which boils down to whether the defendant had enough "minimum contacts" with the US for a US court to assert jurisdiction over that defendant. *See generally Toys "R" Us, Inc. v. Step Two, S.A.*, 318 F.3d 446 (3d Cir. 2003) (no personal jurisdiction found over Spanish company operating website and business in Spain using mark that allegedly infringed plaintiff's U.S. IMAGINARIUM trademark; court noted that website was in Spanish, and goods sold through website were limited to shipment inside Spain; held, not enough contact in forum state in the US to justify personal jurisdiction).

18.4.2 Border enforcement: US

Importation of goods with labels that infringe US trademarks is prohibited under §42 of the Lanham Act. Specifically, no import is allowed if it bears a trademark which "shall copy or simulate" a trademark registered on the Principal Register (*id*). The same is true of a trade name used by a US company: Imports can be excluded if they bear a name "which shall copy or simulate the name of any domestic manufacturer or trader," or of a non-US manufacturer or trader who is owed protection under an international treaty such as the Paris Convention or the TRIPs Agreement. Finally, merchandise can be kept out of the US if it includes a name "calculated to induce the public to believe that the article is manufactured in the United States or that it is manufactured in any foreign country or locality other than the country or locality in which it is in fact manufactured" (*id*).

Policing of imports is handled by the US Customs and Border Protection Service ("Border Service") (the same people who inspect your luggage at a US airport for fruit and vegetables brought from overseas). A federally registered mark will be enforced by the Border Service, *see* 19 C.F.R. §§133.0 et seq., which applies the "copy or simulate" language of §42 in a way consistent with the general "likelihood of confusion" standard under the Lanham Act. *See U.S. v. Able Time, Inc.*, 545 F.3d 824, 830 (9th Cir. 2008), cert. denied, 129 S. Ct. 2864 (2009) ("Th[e] ['copy or simulate' test] is equivalent to the traditional 'likelihood of confusion' test for trademark infringement"). Border Service decisions are reviewable by the federal courts. *See, e.g., B. & R. Choiniere Ltee. v. Art's-Way Mfg. Co.*, 207 U.S.P.Q. 969 (N.D.N.Y. 1979) (issuing preliminary injunction against Border Service, preventing enforcement of US trademark held by defendant Art's-Way, in dispute growing out of defendant's registration of a US trademark and border enforcement of it, where mark originated in and was owned by plaintiff Canadian manufacturing company; court preserved status quo whereby plaintiff could import goods, pending resolution of dispute over US rights to plaintiff's trademark).

Private companies often assist the Border Service by providing information on likely sources of counterfeit goods, in the form of company names, cities or countries of origin, and the like. Anti-counterfeiting intelligence is developed by specialized professionals and companies for this purpose.

An alternative to traditional border enforcement is an action by a mark owner before the International Trade Commission (ITC). ITC actions offer two main advantages: (1) they do not require any proof of personal jurisdiction over an infringing party, because ITC actions are brought "in rem," against the imported *goods* and not a party, *see Sealed Air Corp. v. U.S. International Trade Comm'n*, 645 F.2d 976, 985 (C.C.P.A. 1981) ("An exclusion order operates against goods, not parties"); and (2) they result, if successful, in a remedy known as an "exclusion order," which can in some cases be quite broad, *e.g.*, applying to an entire class of products and not just those made by a particular party or company, *see In re Certain Cube Puzzles*, 219 U.S.P.Q. 322 (Int'l Trade Comm'n 1982). (The color pattern of a "Rubik's Cube" puzzle toy was protectable under Lanham Act §43(a), and a general exclusion order was issued barring importation of puzzles having a defined color pattern associated with the authentic puzzle toy.)

18.4.3 Gray market goods: US

Authorized goods are sold on the legitimate market. Counterfeit goods are sold on the so-called "black market." But what about goods that are authorized for sale in a country outside the US, bought there, and then imported into the US to compete with US-sold goods? This is what is known as the "gray market" (or, sometimes, "parallel imports"). It is gray because the goods in question are not illicit (black market); they are authorized for sale by the mark owner – but *not* for sale in the US.

In general, US trademark law permits the exclusion of gray market goods when the goods purchased overseas are "materially different" from the goods sold in the US. This can happen for a number of reasons. Sometimes non-US tastes and preferences are different; the same product may be formulated differently for non-US sales. (It may be less sweet, for example; or may have a different color, or may be subject to different government standards.) *See, e.g., Hokto Kinoko Co. v. Concord Farms, Inc.*, 738 F.3d 1085, 1094 (9th Cir. 2013) (HOKTO brand mushrooms grown in Japan for the domestic Japanese market, which were imported by defendant into the US, were found to infringe plaintiff's registered US mark for HOKTO; mushrooms grown in Japan were materially different from HOKTO brand mushrooms grown under special supervised conditions in the US so they would meet US standards as certified organic food). The general "likelihood of confusion" standard clearly covers these cases of "materially different" goods.

What about goods that are identical, or at least not "materially different"? The US Tariff Act §526(a), 19 U.S.C.A. §1526, broadly prohibits the importation of a product "that bears a trademark owned by a citizen of... the United States and is registered in the U.S. Patent and Trademark Office." The Supreme Court in 1988 decided that the "extraordinary protection" afforded by Tariff Act §526 is not available when there is a corporate affiliation between the trademark owner and the foreign manufacturer. *See K Mart Corp. v. Cartier, Inc.*, 486 U.S. 281 (1988). Thus a subsidiary of a US company may engage in parallel importation; the parent company cannot invoke the Tariff Act to exclude the goods bearing the company's trademark from entering the US.

On the other hand, even where a trademark owner and a non-US company have a long history of mutual cooperation, lack of ownership or formal corporate control over the non-US company means that the US trademark holder can exclude imports by the non-US firm. *See Vittoria North America, L.L.C. v. Euro-Asia Imports Inc.*, 278 F.3d 1076 (10th Cir. 2001). This applies even when the US company originally acquired its trademark by assignment from a non-US manufacturer – where the US trademark was assigned to the US distributor or importer, for example. In such a case, as long as the US distributor or importer is a separate entity, with no common control shared by the non-US firm, the US distributor or importer can bar gray market goods from being imported without its authorization. *See, e.g., United States v. Eighty-Nine (89) Bottles of "Eau de Joy"*, 797 F.2d 767 (9th Cir. 1986).

Note that Copyright law diverges from trademark law in this respect. This is the result of an important 2013 decision by the US Supreme Court, *Kirtsaeng v. John Wiley & Sons, Inc.*, 133 S. Ct. 1351 (2013) (Copyright law: The "first sale" defense in 17 U.S.C. §109(a), for copies "lawfully made under this title" applies to the importation and sale of copies of a copyrighted work lawfully made and sold outside the US). As a consequence, *Kirtsaeng* effectively ended the use of the Copyright Act to prevent gray market imports into the US.

18.4.4 Choice of law

Trademarks are often global in reach. But business is done differently in different places. And in addition trademark law is stubbornly territorial. As we saw earlier, extraterritorial application of trademark law is often frowned upon.

As a result, in disputes involving parties from different jurisdictions doing business under different national laws, those charged with resolving disputes often must first figure out which nation's laws to apply. This is of course the traditional domain of the legal field known as conflict of laws. In addition, when business partners have signed a contract governing their relationship, they often include provisions relating to which nation's laws will apply to a potential dispute, as well as provisions covering which national courts a dispute may be heard in. This "choice of law" question is a common threshold issue in trademark disputes that grow out of a contractual relationship. We consider this below.

18.4.4.1 *Conflict of laws and activities spanning multiple jurisdictions*

Traditional conflict principles are themselves open-ended. In addition, IP rights such as trademarks involve complex and specialized issues, because it can be difficult to assess the "location" of infringing activity and the "harm" caused by that activity.

The "location of harm" principle has been soundly defended in an important copyright case involving a conflict of laws question. In *Itar-Tass Russian News Agency v. Russian Kurier, Inc.*, 153 F.3d 82 (2d Cir. 1998), the Russian national news service, Tass, sued a New York newspaper catering to Russian immigrants in the US, the *Kurier*. Kurier defended on the ground that, under US law, the individual articles being copied were owned not by the newspaper (*Kurier*) but by the original writers/authors themselves. On this ground, Kurier argued Tass had no standing. (No ownership means no standing under US copyright law, and trademark law as well.) The Second Circuit said:

> On the conflicts issue, we conclude that, with respect to the Russian plaintiffs, Russian law determines the ownership and essential nature of the copyrights alleged to have been infringed and that United States law determines whether those copyrights have been infringed in the United States and, if so, what remedies are available. (*Itar-Tass*, at 84)

This result reached a delicate balance: It recognized that the law of authorship ought to relate closely to the domicile and workplace of the authors (in this case, Russia); while the law of infringement should be based on the ancient legal concept of the *lex loci delicti*, the place where the harm occurred:

> On infringement issues, the governing conflicts principle is usually lex loci delicti, the doctrine generally applicable to torts. Lauritzen v. Larsen, 345 U.S. 571, 583 (1953). We have implicitly adopted that approach to infringement claims, applying United States copyright law to a work that was unprotected in its country of origin. *Hasbro Bradley, Inc. v. Sparkle Toys, Inc.*, 780 F.2d 189, 192–93 (2d Cir. 1985). In the pending case, the place of the tort is plainly the United States. To whatever extent lex loci delicti is to be considered only one part of a broader "interest" approach, *Carbotrade S.p.A. v. Bureau Veritas*, 99 F.3d 86, 9–90 (2d Cir. 1996), United States law would still apply to infringement issues, since not only is this country the place of the tort, but also the defendant is a United States corporation. (*Itar-Tass, supra*, at 91)

As this case shows, the conflicts issue can be quite complex. One solution to the impasse has been to propose general principles. Two noted US IP scholars, Rochelle Dreyfuss and Jane Ginsburg, have done just that. In a project for the American Law Institute, these two professors propounded some basic principles that are designed to provide fairness in litigation transnational IP disputes. For a history of this project, *see* Rochelle Dreyfuss, *The ALI*

Principles on Transnational Intellectual Property Disputes: Why Invite Conflicts? 30 Brook. J. Int'l L. 819 (2005). As the following excerpt makes clear, the authors of the ALI principles tried to find a rational way to state basic rules for resolving these disputes.

> When the defendant has "substantially acted" in the state, the court's jurisdiction over the defendant extends to all claims of harm arising out of the defendant's in-state activity, no matter where the harm is felt. For example, a defendant who is habitually resident in Germany, who operates a server in Angola, where the plaintiff is habitually resident, and who uses that server to distribute infringing content to Portugal, Brazil, and Mozambique will be amenable to suit in Angola for all claims arising out of the activity in Angola, including claims pertaining to harm in Portugal, Brazil, and Mozambique.
>
> When there is less connection to the state, the court's authority is more circumscribed and the ambit of the case is determined by whether the plaintiff is bringing the case in the forum where it is resident. It has, however, proved difficult to draw the line between activity that occurs as a result of the defendant's purposeful availment of the forum's benefits and activity that results from the unilateral actions of others. In the former situation, there is universal sentiment that jurisdiction is justified, whereas in the latter, there is a sense that asserting jurisdiction is inappropriate. In part, the problem is linguistic, for it is hard to describe what the defendant must be doing to be amenable to jurisdiction without involving the court in difficult determinations of intent. Various formulations have been considered, including "directing activity," "targeting the jurisdiction," and "endeavoring to direct."
>
> To a large extent, however, the problem is normative. It revolves around questions of how much responsibility actors should bear to avoid jurisdictions in which they do not wish to be sued and whether it is reasonable to require the same avoidance activities of all intellectual property users, no matter their size, wealth, and degree of technological and legal sophistication. For example, it is fairly clear that a German domiciliary who runs a website in Angola in the Portuguese language, which makes available music that appeals specifically to a Portuguese audience, should be subject to jurisdiction in Brazil for harm occurring there. It is less clear that this defendant should also be subject to jurisdiction in New York where, unknown to the defendant, there is a substantial diaspora of Portuguese speakers who migrated from Madeira and who found the website on its own (Dreyfuss, *supra*, at 830–31 (citing draft of ALI Principles of Intellectual Property, as Adopted and Promulgated by The American Law Institute at Washington, D.C. on May 14, 2007 (2008))).

See also Rochelle C. Dreyfuss and Jane C. Ginsburg, *Draft Convention on Jurisdiction and Recognition of Judgments in Intellectual Property Matters*, 77 Chi.-Kent L. Rev. 1065 (2002).

NOTES

1. For a discussion of the convergences among American, European and Asian Principles in these areas, see Toshiyuki Kono & Paulius Jurcys, Intellectual Property and Private International Law: Comparative Perspectives (Toshiyuki Kono ed., 2012).
2. For other perspectives, see Edouard Treppoz, *International Choice of Law in Trademark Disputes from a Territorial Approach to a Global Approach*, 37 Colum. J.L. & Arts 557, 571 (2014); Graeme Dinwoodie, *Trademarks and Territory: Detaching Trademark Law from the Nation-State*, 41 Hous. L. Rev. 885 (2004) (explaining the need for, and resistance to, a shift from local to international trademark protection); Marketa Trimble, *Advancing National Intellectual Property Policies in A Transnational Context*, 74 Md. L. Rev. 203 (2015) (exploring the relationship between domestic policies and transnational enforcement).

18.4.4.2 Contractual choice of law and forum clauses

There is a strong international consensus that where private parties agree on a choice of forum (*i.e.*, country or place to bring a dispute) and/or a choice of substantive law, these agreements should be respected. See Hague Convention on Exclusive Choice of Court Clauses, June 30, 2005, 64 I.L.M. 1291, 1291–96 (specifically referring to contracts relating to intellectual property); updates and further initiatives described at Hague Conference on Private International Law, http://www.hcch.net.

The cases even prior to the Hague Convention in this area reflect the same basic idea: private choices are to be respected. Beginning with the non-IP case of *M/S Bremen v. Zapata Off-Shore Co.*, 407 U.S. 1, 15 (1972), the Supreme Court said: "In the light of present-day commercial realities and expanding international trade we conclude that the forum clause should control absent a strong showing that it should be set aside." *See also Carnival Cruise Lines, Inc. v. Shute*, 499 U.S. 585, 593–94 (1991) ("[A] clause establishing ex ante the forum for dispute resolution has the salutary effect of dispelling any confusion about where suits arising from the contract must be brought and defended, . . .").

Courts in trademark cases have not been reluctant to apply this general principle. In *Magi XXI, Inc. v. Stato della Citta del Vaticano*, 714 F.3d 714, 723 (2d Cir. 2013), for example, the Vatican Library licensed the right to make and sell reproductions of art in the Vatican collection with the right to sublicense others. Plaintiff Magi, an American sub-licensee, complained about limited access to art works and sued in New York. The court enforced the forum selection clause in the license by which all disputes were to be resolved in the Vatican State, a sovereign nation.

Likewise, in *H-D Michigan, LLC v. Hellenic Duty Free Shops S.A.*, 694 F.3d 827, 841 (7th Cir. 2012), a license from the trademark owner Harley-Davidson permitted defendant Hellenic to sell branded goods in Europe. The licensing agreement vested Wisconsin courts with exclusive jurisdiction over all disputes "arising out of or relating to this Agreement," and Hellenic agreed to personal jurisdiction in Wisconsin as to such disputes. The Seventh Circuit affirmed a district court-granted injunction against use of the mark, and also prohibited the licensee from continuing to prosecute a case concerning the contract in a Greek court. See also *Rosehoff Ltd. v. Cataclean Americas LLC*, 2013 WL 2389725 (W.D.N.Y. 2013) (dismissing patent and trademark infringement claims arising out of license agreement which contained forum section clause designating the UK as the exclusive venue and UK law as the governing law); *Fairchild Semiconductor Corp. v. Third Dimension (3D) Semiconductor, Inc.*, 589 F.Supp.2d 84, 99 (D. Me. 2008) (licensee of both US and Chinese patents filed declaratory action arguing it did not owe royalties for certain of its products under the licenses; court upheld forum selection clause contained in the license agreement, explicitly stating that the District of Maine could be used to resolve all of the parties' license disputes under the agreement, was enforceable; court noted that while the action required interpretation of scope of Chinese patent, its validity was not at issue).

Note that these cases are all based on licensing agreements. When an agreement has long been over, however, the former parties to it are once again mere strangers, so there is no "holdover effect" from the former license (*Altvater Gessler-J.A. Baczewski Intern. (USA) Inc. v. Sobieski Destylarnia S.A.*, 572 F.3d 86, 90 (2d Cir. 2009) ("Gessler's claims do not sound in contract and are not based on rights originating from the licensing agreement")).

NOTES

1. Because private agreements are prevalent in the IP field, some have argued that choice of law provisions are to some extent abrogating the traditional territorial principle in IP law. See Graeme B. Dinwoodie, *Developing A Private International Intellectual Property Law: The Demise of Territoriality?* 51 Wm. & Mary L. Rev. 711, 800 (2009).
2. Another result of the high number of IP transactions based on contracts is that contractual arbitration provisions are common. And so therefore arbitration is a common dispute resolution procedure in IP cases. See *Saucy Susan Products, Inc. v. Allied Old English, Inc.*, 200 F. Supp. 724 (S.D.N.Y. 1961) (enforcing distribution agreement that included a trademark licensing provision). On the general law applicable to arbitration, see Convention on the Recognition and Enforcement of Foreign Arbitral Awards, 21 UST 2517; TIAS 6997; 330 UNTS 3; Inter-American Convention on International Commercial Arbitration, 14 I.L.M. 336 (1975). See also, 9 U.S.C. 201–208 (Federal Arbitration Act).

18.4.5 Enforcing judgments overseas

In the US, courts have often enforced foreign judgments. Both the US Rules of Civil Procedure and many state laws provide for liberal enforcement of overseas judgments. In *Sarl Louis Feraud Int'l v. Viewfinder*, 489 F.3d 474 (2d

Cir. 2007), a New York federal court enforced a judgment from a French court over objections from the defendant that the French ruling was inconsistent with US law. The court, applying a New York statute, held that so long as the judgment was not "repugnant" to the law of New York, it would be enforced.

When it comes to enforcing US judgments in non-US jurisdictions, the key concepts are comity, reciprocity, and *res judicata*. Every nation's courts apply these principles in different combinations and different ways. In general under international law, a foreign state exercises the right to examine foreign judgments for four causes: (1) to determine if the court that issued the judgment had jurisdiction; (2) to determine whether the defendant was properly notified of the action; (3) to determine if the proceedings were vitiated by fraud; and (4) to establish that the judgment is not contrary to the public policy of the foreign country. One issue that frequently arises with respect to US judgments is the perception that US law awards damages at a level considered excessive in many countries.

19

Licensing issues: quality supervision, exclusive territories, termination

Because the basic purpose of trademark law is to protect consumer expectations, there has long been a rule in place in the US that one who assigns or licenses a trademark must take steps to insure that the assignee or licensee makes and sells a product that meets the quality standards associated with the trademarked good:

> The owner of a trademark has a duty to ensure the consistency of the trademarked good or service. If he does not fulfill this duty, he forfeits the trademark... The purpose of a trademark, after all, is to identify a good or service to the consumer, and identity implies consistency and a correlative duty to make sure that the good or service really is of consistent quality, i.e., really is the same good or service (*Gorenstein Enterprises, Inc. v. Quality Care-USA, Inc.*, 874 F.2d 431, 435 (7th Cir. 1989) (Posner, J.)).

In the case of a licensee, quality assurance traditionally takes the form of some sort of contractual duty (often backed by inspections or penalties levied by the licensor) to assure high quality. In the case of an assignment, it takes the form of a requirement that the licensor should not just sell a trademark by itself, but that the transaction should also include manufacturing equipment or some other assets (a formula, for example) designed to assure continued quality in the goods made and sold under the trademark by the trademark assignee. It is often said, in this connection, that a trademark is simply a symbol of goodwill and cannot be sold or assigned apart from the goodwill it symbolizes. *Marshak v. Green*, 746 F.2d 927, 929 (2d Cir. 1984) (citing Lanham Act §10, 15 U.S.C. §1060); *see Haymaker Sports, Inc. v. Turian*, 581 F.2d 257 (C.C.P.A. 1978) (inadequate control in licensing part of assignment and license-back).

An assignment without assets representing goodwill is said to be an assignment "in gross," and it is generally deemed invalid under US law. *See Marshak*, 746

F.2d at 929. It should be noted, however, that the US is somewhat of an outlier in enforcing such a stringent rule. Susan Barbieri Montgomery & Richard J. Taylor, Key Issues in Worldwide Trademark Transfers: Law & Practice 1, 5–6 (2005); Mark A. Greenfield, *Goodwill As a Factor in Trademark Assignments: A Comparative Study*, 60 Trademark Rep. 173, 173–74 (1970). And even in the US, there has been some relaxation of the traditionally strict requirement. *See* Irene Calboli, *Trademark Assignment "With Goodwill": A Concept Whose Time Has Gone*, 57 Fla. L. Rev. 771, 791 (2005) ("[B]y the beginning of the 1970s, most courts... started to declare assignments valid as long as sufficient continuity or substantial similarity, rather than identity, existed between the marked goods"). *See also* Stephen L. Carter, *The Trouble With Trademark*, 99 Yale L.J. 759, 785–87 (1990) (criticizing this liberalizing trend).

19.1 Territorial rights in the US

Franchise agreements (which usually involve licensing a nationally managed trademark to local franchisees) often spell out detailed exclusive territories; profit for an individual franchise location is often closely related to where the nearest competing franchise is located. *See* Josef Windsperger, Gérard Cliquet, George Hendrikse, and Mika Tuunanen, Economics and Management of Franchising Networks (2004). An alleged breach by the franchisor, which locates a competing franchise too close to an existing franchisee location, is handled under state contract law and not federal trademark law. *See, e.g., Shoney's, Inc. v. Schoenbaum*, 686 F. Supp. 554, 564 (E.D. Va. 1988), judgment aff'd, 894 F.2d 92 (4th Cir. 1990) (where restaurant trademark licensee objected that licensor had granted a license in its exclusive territory to another to operate an outlet, the claim was for breach of contract, not for trademark infringement).

Courts will not in general imply an exclusive territory in a franchising or distribution agreement; it must be set out explicitly in the franchise/distribution/trademark licensing agreement. *See Burger King Corp. v. Weaver*, 169 F.3d 1310 (11th Cir. 1999), cert. dismissed, 528 U.S. 948 (1999) (plaintiff franchisee claimed that Burger King violated an implied covenant of good faith and fair dealing by locating a competing franchise nearby, even though the franchise contract did not guarantee him an exclusive territory; held, for defendant, no breach of contract under Florida law). One exception applies: Under California's expansive implied contractual duty of good faith, it has been held that locating a competing franchise very near an existing one violated this implied duty in a franchise agreement. *In re Vylene Enterprises, Inc.*, 90 F.3d 1472, 1477 (9th Cir. 1996) (the franchisee was "entitled to expect that the franchisor would 'not act to destroy the right of the franchisee to enjoy the fruits of the contract'").

CASE

So Good Potato Chip Co. v. Frito-Lay, Inc., 462 F.2d 239 (8th Cir. 1972)

VAN PELT, Senior District Judge [by designation]

Plaintiff, So Good Potato Chip Company, brought this action to permanently enjoin defendant, Frito-Lay, Inc., from manufacturing, selling, and distributing "Doritos," "Fandangos," and "Intermission" corn chips within the licensed territory granted by Frito-Lay to So Good under a franchise agreement dated September 29, 1957. Under that agreement, the plaintiff and defendant agreed that So Good was to be licensed to manufacture and distribute corn chips pursuant to secret formulae and processes and to distribute the corn chips within a prescribed area of Missouri and Illinois under the registered trademark "Fritos." The 1957 agreement is substantially similar to an earlier franchise agreement between the parties, executed November 10, 1945.

Prior to the present litigation, Frito-Lay introduced "Doritos," "Fandangos," and "Intermission" corn chips into the territory licensed to So Good for "Fritos." So Good claims that the three products are so similar to "Fritos" that they too are covered by the franchise agreement.

Chief Judge Meredith, in an opinion reported at 324 F.Supp. 280 (E.D. Mo. 1971), found that the franchise agreement contemplated only the sale of corn chips under the trademark "Fritos," thus leaving the defendant free to sell the other three products within the licensed territory. We affirm.

The trial court, whose findings are not to be set aside unless clearly erroneous, determined that the sales of "Doritos," "Fandangos," or "Intermission" corn chips were not competitive with the sales of "Fritos" as the term "competitive" was intended by the parties in their 1957 agreement. In addition, the court found that the express terms of the agreement precluded any court-imposed "negative covenant" against Frito-Lay. These findings are amply supported by the evidence.

The 1957 agreement is quite long and comprehensive. However, only two or three provisions are material in deciding the question presented here. The only restraint against Frito-Lay distributing other corn chips in the licensed territory is found in Paragraph 23 of the agreement, which states: "The 'territory' referred to in this agreement is the area for which the rights herein specified are conveyed by the Company [Frito-Lay]. During the term of this agreement, the Company will neither authorize nor permit the use of its trademark 'FRITOS' on corn chips in the territory by anyone other than Licensee [So Good]." Paragraph 19(D) allowed Frito-Lay to cancel the agreement, "without liability or recourse," if So Good manufactured or sold "another product so similar to corn chips manufactured pursuant hereto as to be competitive." Paragraph 5 required So Good to "promote and develop, vigorously and consistently, 'FRITOS' in all of the territory hereinafter granted," and prohibited So Good from engaging "directly or indirectly at any time during the term of this agreement in the manufacture and/or sale of corn chips or

CASE (continued)

similar products other than those prepared in accordance with the terms hereof and sold under the trademark 'FRITOS' . . ." Since the contract itself has no similar prohibition against Frito-Lay, So Good argues that paragraphs 5 and 19(D) imply a "negative covenant" that Frito-Lay will also not manufacture or sell within the licensed territory corn chips which might be considered competitive to "Fritos."

We agree with the trial court that paragraph 23 of the 1957 franchise agreement expressly deals with the sale of products by Frito-Lay in the franchised territory, and thus precludes any implied covenant. As the trial court stated: "Consideration of the specific provisions of the agreement precludes the implication that any covenant against sales by Frito-Lay of the products at issue was intended by the parties." 324 F.Supp. at 281. Paragraph 23, quoted above, only prohibits the sales of "Fritos" by Frito-Lay. It does not prohibit the sale of such "similar" products as "Doritos," "Fandangos," and "Intermission."

Even assuming that the contract in question does imply a negative covenant against Frito-Lay, the activities complained of by So Good do not violate any such implied provision. Frito-Lay gave So Good the right to make "Fritos" in the licensed territory. After having given this right, any implied negative covenant would mean that Frito-Lay could not come back into that territory and effectively destroy So Good's use of the franchise. Such a construction of the parties' agreement would be a combination of what the parties intended and of what equity and justice demand. But Frito-Lay's introduction of "Doritos," "Fandangos," and "Intermission" corn chips does not violate such a construction of the contract.

Under such an interpretation of the contract, Frito-Lay was inferentially prohibited from distributing "competitive" corn chip products. A broad construction of the term "competitive" would include any snack item similar to "Fritos." But the evidence shows that the parties intended a more limited definition. At the time the 1957 agreement was made, both parties were distributing a wide variety of "snack food" items, both corn based and otherwise. In addition, the parties have continued to expand their lines of snack food items since 1957. Thus So Good cannot argue that any snack food of a "similar nature" as "Fritos" is prohibited by an implied covenant, since this would include almost all of the products produced by either party and would contradict the parties' clear intent in the 1957 agreement.

There was ample evidence from which the trial judge could find that the sales of "Doritos," "Fandangos," and "Intermission" corn chips were no more "competitive," as the parties used that term, than the sales of the other products, such as cheese flavored corn puffs ("Chee-tos"), onion flavored corn snacks ("Funyuns"), etc., introduced by either party since 1957.

The evidence also establishes that the term "corn chips," of which "Fritos" is an example, has a very distinct meaning in the snack food trade, and that a "corn chip" is clearly distinguishable from a "tortilla chip," such as "Doritos," or a "popped corn chip," such as "Intermission."

Frito-Lay's distribution of "Doritos," "Fandangos," and "Intermission" corn chips was not in violation of the parties' 1957 agreement. The trial court's decision is affirmed.

19.2 Quality supervision and termination in China

Arctic Food v. Arctic Frozen Food, Beijing First Intermediate People's Court (2013) yizhongminzhongzi No. 10822

The Appellants, Beijing Arctic Frozen Food Co. Ltd. ("Frozen Food") and Beijing Shuangdu Food Plant ("Shuangdu"), appealed to this Court after the Beijing Haidian District People's Court ("District Court") ruled in favor of the appellee Beijing Arctic Food Company ("Arctic Food") in a trademark licensing dispute on July 5, 2013. On August 13, 2013, this Court accepted this case and now makes a final ruling.

On September 9, 2000, Pepsi-Arctic Beverages Co. Ltd. registered the trademark "Arctic and Device" under no. 1441636 in Class 30 covering goods "coffee, artificial coffee, tea, cocoa, coffee beverage with milk, cocoa beverage with milk, cocoa beverage, and edible ices." On November 7, 2000, the last item "edible ices" was deleted from the registration. The mark "Arctic and Device" no. 1441636 was shortly assigned to Arctic Food, and was timely renewed with the new valid term until September 6, 2020.

On March 18, 2001, Arctic Food entered into a Joint-Venture Agreement with Shuangdu ("Joint-Venture Contract"). The Joint-Venture Contract confirmed that Arctic Food was the trademark owner for the mark "Arctic and Device" under no. 1441636, and that Arctic Food agreed to grant a trademark license to [the new Arctic Food-Shuangda joint venture entity,] Frozen Food [,] to use this mark.

The three parties, Arctic Food, Shuangdu and Frozen Food [the joint venture entity], shortly entered into an operational agreement ("Operation Agreement"), agreeing that the operation and management of the joint-venture Frozen Food will be dealt with by Shuangdu. Article 10 of the Operation Agreement also provides that, "Arctic Food is the trademark owner of the licensed trademark(s); and that Arctic Food has the right to exploit, the right to supervise and also the right to terminate the use of the licensed trademark(s)."

On March 21, 2001, Arctic Food drafted a trademark license authorization letter ("Trademark Authorization Letter"), stating that the mark "Arctic and Device" under no. 1441636 is a registered trademark owned by Arctic Food, and that Arctic Food agreed to grant a trademark license to Frozen Food to use the mark for 20 years in terms of frozen food.

On July 28, 2004, Arctic Food registered [an additional trademark, and] Arctic Food also granted [a license to the JV entity,] Frozen Food [for this mark. The trademarks are collectively referred as the "Licensed Trademarks."]

In October 2011, Arctic Food created the *Regulations on Brand Strengthening and Quality Safety Management* ("Management Regulations"). The Management Regulations stated that Arctic Food would establish a Brand and Quality Safety Management Committee

CASE *(continued)*

("Committee") to be in charge of brand management and quality safety issues related to all its products under its brand. This Committee enjoys the final approval right determining the quality standard of licensed products, the scope of trademark license, licensing term verification, and also annual evaluation of trademark licenses. Specifically, the Committee is also authorized to conduct an annual inspection on the quality and safety standard of its licencees' products, to order its licensees to rectify any improper practices, and to terminate the trademark license agreement if the licensees fails the inspection and the rectification procedures. The Management Regulations also state that, during the term of the trademark license, the licensee(s) should be fully responsible for the reputation of the licensed trademark(s) as well as the quality and safety of the products bearing the licensed trademarks.

On October 12, 2011, Beijing Municipal Administration of Quality and Technology Supervision found that defendant Frozen Food's ice cream products bearing the Licensed Trademarks exceeded the normal colony-forming level [of bacteria]. As such, Frozen Food was fined a penalty for failing to pass the inspection. This incident was widely covered by the media, which plaintiff Arctic Food claimed to have greatly affected the reputation of its Licensed Trademarks.

A few days after the incident, Arctic Food sent a *Notice to Suspend Business and Rectification* to [the joint venture] Frozen Food, requesting it to suspend its production and to rectify the product quality issue related to the ice cream products. However, neither Frozen Food nor Shuangdu paid much attention to Arctic Food's request, and they continued to produce ice cream products bearing the Licensed Trademarks. On April 24, 2012, Arctic Food sent the ice cream products manufactured by Frozen Food for another inspection, and again, the products failed to pass the quality and safety inspection.

On May 9, 2012, Arctic Food's lawyer sent a letter to Frozen Food and Shuangdu, requesting to terminate the trademark license between the parties so as to protect the goodwill of its Licensed Trademarks. Yet Frozen Food and Shuangdu ignored the lawyer letter and continued to produce and sell frozen food bearing the Licensed Trademarks. A few months later in June 2012, another severe incident occurred, which the news outlets described as "*Arctic Icecream Contained Dead Flies, But the Manufacturer Refused to Comment.*"

Arctic Food shortly filed a law suit before the District Court, claiming that Frozen Food and Shuangdu have materially breached their contracts [because of these quality-control issues.]

Frozen Food and Shuangdu responded that: (1) The authorization to use the Licensed Trademarks was one of the conditions to establish the joint venture between Arctic Food and Shuangdu. Therefore, the trademark license should remain valid as long as the term of the Joint-Venture Contract remains valid; and (2) Arctic Food's trademark registration for the mark "Arctic and Device" does not cover the goods "edible ice." Therefore, Frozen Food and Shuangdu's use of the mark in terms of "edible ice" does not constitute use of the mark for trademark purposes.

CASE *(continued)*

The District Court established that: (1) A trademark owner has rights to grant a trademark license for others to use its trademark; (2) the trademark licensor has an obligation to supervise the quality of the licensee's products bearing the licensed trademark; and (3) the licensee should guarantee the quality of the products bearing the licensed trademark.

Here, Arctic Food granted a trademark license to Frozen Food to use its Licensed Trademarks. Arctic Food, Frozen Food and Shuangdu also agreed that Shuangdu would be the designated party responsible for the management and operation of Frozen Food. Therefore, Shuangdu [and Frozen Food] should use qualified equipment and materials during the production, follow relevant production regulations, and also accept Arctic Food's supervision. However, during the performance of the contract, Frozen Food and Shuangdu both violated the relevant provisions in the Operation Agreement and the Management Regulations. Therefore, Shuangdu and Frozen Food materially breached the contract.

Frozen Food and Shuangdu counterargued that Arctic Food unilaterally created the Management Regulations, which they had no choices but to [agree to]. The District Court found that as the trademark licensor, Arctic Food had the right to make the relevant regulations so as to ensure the quality and safety of its licensed products. The Management Regulations included Frozen Food's official stamp and also the signature of Shuangdu's Legal Representative Degang WANG, and therefore, it is a valid agreement between Arctic Food and Frozen Food and Shuangdu. There was no evidence indicating the invalidity of the Management Regulations, and neither Frozen Food nor Shuangdu sought a revocation or modification of the Management Regulations after it was executed. Therefore, the District Court rejects Frozen Food and Shuangdu's counterargument.

[As such, the District Court held that appellants breached its contract in all of the claimed instances, except for the fourth claim, and thus should bear civil liabilities. The court further held that, from the effective date of this ruling, the trademark license for the Licensed Trademarks shall be terminated, and Frozen Food shall stop using the Licensed Trademarks.]

[Unsatisfied with the initial ruling, the appellants Frozen Food and Shuangdu appealed to the Beijing First Intermediate Court.]

Beijing First Intermediate Court held that, the issues presented before this court include:

(1) the nature of the contractual relationship among three parties; (2) whether there was breach of contract; and (3) whether the contract should be terminated.

(1) The Nature and Validity of the Contractual Relationship Among the Parties

[T]he District Court did not err in finding the Management Regulations to be a binding agreement between Arctic Food and Frozen Food.

(2) Breach of Contract

[This Court affirmed the District Court's findings and held that Shuangdu and Frozen Food had materially breached the contracts in various ways.]

(3) Termination of Contract

[With regard to Arctic Food's request to terminate the license agreement], this Court

CASE (continued)

holds that the contracting parties have discretion to determine the termination conditions of their contract. When the termination condition is satisfied, the non-breaching party has the right to terminate the contract. When the breaching party's breach of contract completely or almost completely undermines the purpose of the contract, the aggrieved party can also request to terminate the contract.

Here, Article 4 and Article 12 in the Management Regulations both specified the conditions for the termination of the trademark license. This court also confirmed the various instances of breach by Shuangdu and Frozen food, so the conditions for terminating the contract have been met. In this case, the appellants first breached the contract by failing to meet the quality standard, and then they also failed to remedy the breach by ignoring the lawyer letter and continuing to produce the goods with inferior quality. As such, the trial court did not err in finding that Frozen Food and Shuangdu's breach of contract already destroyed the purpose of the trademark license. As such, Arctic Food's request to terminate the trademark license should be granted.

This is the final ruling.

NOTES

1. Article 43 of the Chinese Trademark Law provides:

   > The trademark registrant may, by concluding a trademark licensing contract, authorize other persons to use the registered trademark. The licensor shall supervise the quality of the goods on which the licensee uses the licensor's registered trademark, and the licensee shall guarantee the quality of the goods on which the registered trademark is used.

   This is known as the "quality supervision" provision in trademark license arrangements, where the trademark owner (licensor) has an obligation to ensure the consistency of the trademarked goods and services. If the trademark owner fails to fulfill this obligation, the trademark might be vulnerable for cancellation action. Likewise, the licensee is equally responsible for making sure that the licensed products are consistent with the original goods and services provided by the trademark owner. After all, the purpose of a trademark is to identify the (consistent) source of goods and services to the consumers.

2. Often in the US, termination (as in this Chinese case) leads to problems related to the supervision of the quality of former licensees. "Common sense compels the conclusion that a strong risk of consumer confusion arises when a terminated franchisee continues to use the former franchisor's trademarks." *Burger King Corp. v. Mason*, 710 F.2d 1480 (11th Cir. 1983), cert. denied, 465 U.S. 1102 (1984); *S & R Corp. v. Jiffy Lube Int'l, Inc.*, 968 F.2d 371 (3d Cir. 1992) (franchisee stopped paying royalties and alleged that franchisor breached contract by failing to maintain the quality of other franchises; injunction was issued against franchisee's post-termination use of the licensed trademarks).

Part V
Trade secrets

20

Introduction

> **INTRODUCTORY PROBLEM**
>
> Hu Li and Greta Mueller have worked together at RideShare, a very successful ride-sharing company, for three years. Hu is a marketing expert, who specializes in promoting RideShare's service with large group conferences such as the annual meetings of the Medical Association, the Bar Association, and the like. In connection with this work, Hu has developed close contacts with the conference planning staffs at these and other large professional groups that hold annual conferences. Because these conferences can attract as many as 10,000 participants, they are an excellent place to promote RideShare services. So special promotions such as discounts for meeting participants are offered. RideShare also asks for advance notice of large events, such as the annual Doctor of the Year dinner which the Medical Association holds. Knowing when the event begins and ends allows RideShare to have extra cars available in the area, to serve the surge in demand that comes with a large event.
>
> Greta is a programmer who specializes in one type of computer algorithm, called a "Stopping Algorithm." This is an algorithm that determines the optimal amount of time to search for alternatives. Ride sharing is basically a large coordination problem: The computer system must keep track of all ride requests, the current location of all cars in a certain area, and the direction of travel for all cars currently carrying passengers. When a ride request comes in, the system begins considering alternatives regarding which car nearby the requesting rider is heading in the same direction the rider wants to go. There are usually many cars that could be matched with an individual rider, so the computer considers one alternative, calculating the route and estimated arrival time. If multiple riders are on the same trip (a RideShare "PoolShare" trip), the system must calculate the destinations of all riders when considering which car to assign to a request. Greta's expertise is in creating computer code that quickly searches among alternatives, then stops, choosing the best alternative considered so far. The overall goal is to find the closest to optimal match between car and rider without taking too much time to do it.

Hu and Greta are having coffee one day when Hu tells Greta about an idea she has had for a different sort of ride-sharing system. One common complaint with the RideShare service is that it does not allow pets and will not carry heavy parcels or large items (such as furniture, bags of groceries, etc.) after people have purchased them. Hu says she wants to leave RideShare and found a new company that will work on the same principle as RideShare but will also carry anything a passenger needs to transport (as long as it fits in the vehicle requested). The name Hu has chosen is "Carry U," which leads to the slogan "the U is for Unlimited." Hu asks Greta if she would consider leaving RideShare and becoming the Chief Technical Officer at Carry U. Greta is intrigued because she believes that her opportunities to move up in RideShare are limited by the fact that Stopping Algorithm experts like her are rare, and the company cannot afford to move her out of her key position. She agrees to consider Hu's request.

One week later, Hu introduces Greta to Donna Denarius, a venture capital investor with Big Tree Capital. Big Tree has made many early-stage investments in startup companies and has a reputation for aggressive funding and hard charging tactics. Donna tells Greta and Hu that Big Tree wants to be the lead investor in Carry U, but that Hu and Greta must move quickly as several other startup companies have formed recently to compete with RideShare. That evening, Greta and Hu decide to leave RideShare. Before packing up her office, Hu decides to review her contact list of conference organizers, which runs to 40 pages of notes with names, addresses, etc. After she reviews the list she turns off her computer and leaves the office.

The next morning Hu and Greta send a joint email to the human resources (HR) department at RideShare, informing the department that they will be leaving RideShare in 30 days. An official from HR sends an immediate response telling Hu and Greta not to come to the RideShare office from that day forward. The email also includes as an attachment the Employment, IP Assignment, and Confidentiality Agreement that both Hu and Greta signed when they first came to work for RideShare.

Hu and Greta start work on a business plan for Carry U (their new company) immediately. Big Tree Capital makes an initial $10 million investment in Carry U, and Donna Denarius is appointed to the Board of Directors of the newly formed Carry U, Incorporated. After four months of hard work, Carry U introduces the "Beta" (or test) version of its Carry U Ride and Carriage software application for mobile phones. Partly due to a large advertising campaign (funded in part by a second round of financing by a consortium led by Big Tree), the Carry U app is instantly successful, with both riders and drivers signing up at the rate of several thousand a day in the first "test" markets, San Francisco, New York, London, Berlin, Shanghai, and Beijing.

But after only two weeks of successful operation, Carry U receives notice from RideShare, Inc. that Hu, Greta, Carry U, Donna Denarius and Big Tree Capital are being sued for "misappropriation of trade secrets, breach of confidentiality, breach of contract" and other causes of action. RideShare file legal actions in San Francisco (federal court), London, and Beijing, asking for an immediate injunction against the use of RideShare confidential information, and damages for misappropriation. Rideshare alleges specifically that Hu, Greta, and the other defendants have "illicitly taken customer information (particularly with respect to professional conference organizers), proprietary software designs (particularly RideShare-specific 'stopping algorithms' for ride matching), product promotion ideas and other proprietary RideShare trade secrets." The legal actions state that, at the time Hu left RideShare," the company was just about to launch a large ad campaign using the slogan "RideShare: the possibilities are unlimited." But now, with Carry U spending large amounts of advertising dollars on its slogan "the U is for Unlimited!", RideShare has had to delay its ad campaign and replace it with expensive, newly created promotional messages.

Your task is to advise Hu, Greta, and the other Carry U defendants in this matter, across the three major jurisdictions (US, China, and the EU). As you work through this Part, refer back to this problem to see what advice you should give.

20.1 Basic purpose and sources of law

Wherever enacted, and however enforced, trade secret law has several basic features that do not vary. First is some definition of a trade secret. To be protectable, information must be (1) valuable and (2) confidential. And to be actionable, the taking of the information must be somehow "improper" – so that it (3) amounts to misappropriation. This is the core of trade secret protection. Let us take a quick look at the major sources of law that give rise to legal duties and legal actions in this area in the three major jurisdictions we cover.

Trade secret law varies in many ways across countries, despite these core similarities. There is a wide array of different causes of action in different countries that are used to seek redress for misappropriation of trade secrets. It was not until the TRIPs Agreement of 1995 that any attempt was made to harmonize international protection of trade secrets. And it is evident from

Article 39 of TRIPs, which addresses this topic, that a good deal of variation is still permitted. Article 39.1 requires WTO members to protect "undisclosed information," under terms set out in Article 39.2:

> 2. Natural and legal persons shall have the possibility of preventing information lawfully within their control from being disclosed to, acquired by, or used by others without their consent in a manner contrary to honest commercial practices (10) so long as such information:
>
> (a) is secret in the sense that it is not, as a body or in the precise configuration and assembly of its components, generally known among or readily accessible to persons within the circles that normally deal with the kind of information in question;
> (b) has commercial value because it is secret; and
> (c) has been subject to reasonable steps under the circumstances, by the person lawfully in control of the information, to keep it secret (TRIPs Article 39, available at https://www.wto.org/english/docs_e/legal_e/27-trips_04d_e.htm).

To see how different the implementations of this principle are, consider the legal sources of the three major jurisdictions we cover.

20.1.1 United States

Until 2016, US trade secret law was state law; each of the 50 states had its own version, because there was no federal (US-wide) law on the subject. Despite this, a good deal of convergence was achieved by virtue of the Uniform Trade Secrets Act (UTSA), a model state law that was adopted in 47 states. *See* Uniform Law Commission, Legislative Fact Sheet – Trade Secrets, available at http://www.uniformlaws.org/LegislativeFactSheet.aspx?title=Trade%20Secrets%20Act. The UTSA, in §1(4), defines trade secrets to include:

> [I]nformation, including a formula, pattern, compilation, program, device, method, technique, or process, that: (i) derives independent economic value, actual or potential, from not being generally known to, and not being readily ascertainable by proper means by, other persons who can obtain economic value from its disclosure or use.

In 2016, the US adopted the federal Defend Trade Secrets Act (DTSA), which was "modeled on the Uniform Trade Secrets Act," H. Rep. No. 114-529, 114th Cong., 2d Sess. The DTSA adopts the language of the UTSA in defining both trade secret and misappropriation using the language of the UTSA. Now for the first time there is a federal cause of action for misappropriation of trade secrets, which means that these cases may now be brought in federal district courts as well as states courts.

Misappropriation is traditionally defined as the use of improper means to acquire trade secret information. The DTSA defines "improper means" to say that it:

(A) includes theft, bribery, misrepresentation, breach or inducement of a breach of a duty to maintain secrecy, or espionage through electronic or other means; and

(B) does not include reverse engineering, independent derivation, or any other lawful means of acquisition.

20.1.2 China

In China, protection of trade secrets is primarily achieved through the Chinese Anti-Unfair Competition Law (1993). Other laws and regulations, such as contract law, labor law, labor contract law, corporation law, as well as the Chinese Supreme People's Court's Judicial Interpretation on Issues Concerning the Application of Law in the Trial of Civil Cases Involving Unfair Competition (2007), also play an important role in protecting trade secrets. Article 10 of the Chinese Anti-Unfair Competition Law (1993) defines what constitute "trade secrets" and "misappropriation or infringement" of such trade secrets.

The PRC Unfair Competition Law, at Article 10(3), provides this definition:

> "Trade secrets" mentioned in this Article refers to any technology information or business operation information which is unknown to the public, can bring about economic benefits to the obligee, has practical utility and about which the obligee has adopted secret-keeping measures.

See also Interpretation of the Supreme People's Court on Some Matters About the Application of the Law in the Trial of Civil Cases Involving Unfair Competition, at Article 10 (protectable if the "information has practical or potential commercial value, and can be used for enhancing the competitive advantage for the obligee, it shall be ascertained as capable of bringing about benefits to the obligee, and having practical applicability"). As for misappropriation, Article 10 of the Unfair Competition law says:

> A business operator shall not use any of the following means to infringe upon trade secrets:

(1) obtaining trade secret of a right-holder by stealing, luring, intimidating, fraud or any other unfair means;
(2) disclosing, using or allowing another person to use the trade secrets obtained from the right-holder by the means mentioned in the preceding paragraph; or
(3) breaching contract or confidential agreements with the right-holder to disclose, use or allow another person to use the trade secrets he possesses.
The obtaining, using or disclosing another's trade secrets by a third party, who clearly knows or have reasons to know that the case falls under the unlawful acts listed in the preceding paragraphs, shall be deemed as infringement upon trade secrets.
"Trade secrets" mentioned in this Article refers to any technology information or business operation information, which is unknown to the public, can bring about economic benefits to the right-holder, has practical utility and about which the right-holder has adopted security measures to keep its secrecy.

The recent Draft Bill for the Chinese Anti-Unfair Competition Law (2016 Draft) would make this a new Article 9, while also covering (1) misappropriation of trade secrets by former employees; and (2) the obligations of public officials and professionals (*e.g.* attorneys and accountants) to keep trade secrets confidential when they learn of them in the course of their work (Article 10 of 2016 Draft).

20.1.3 The EU

In 2016, the EU adopted a Directive intending to substantially unify the treatment of trade secrets in Member States (Directive (EU) 2016/943 of the European Parliament and of the Council, 8 June 2016 ("On the protection of undisclosed know-how and business information (trade secrets) against their unlawful acquisition, use and disclosure"), available at http://eur-lex.europa.eu/legal-content/EN/TXT/PDF/?uri=CELEX:32016L0943&from=EN). The avowed purpose of the Directive is to provide protection for "investment in generating and applying intellectual capital" (*id.*, at (1)). One motivation behind the Directive was divergence in legal standards in this area of law across Member States. Paragraph (6) points out, for example, that not all Member States have legal provisions defining trade secrets or establishing what acts constitute misappropriation. To harmonize these and other issues (notably the destruction of goods found to infringe trade secrets), was the animating goal for adoption of the Directive (*id.*, at (7)).

Prior to the Directive, trade secrets had been protected in European countries under a variety of different legal theories and sources. One review, prepared in the lead-up to the Directive, summarized the European scene as follows:

Within the EU, Sweden deserves a specific mention as the only country with ad hoc legislation on trade secrets. All the other Member States offer protection to trade secrets through different pieces of civil and criminal legislation. Countries such as Austria, Germany, Poland and Spain strongly rely on unfair competition law, while Italy and Portugal have specific provisions on the protection of trade secrets included in their respective Codes of Industrial Property. France has specific provisions on the protection of manufacturing trade secrets also included in its Code of Industrial Property. Tort law is also widely used to protect trade secrets, and particularly in the Netherlands and Luxemburg represents a preferred option. Tort law principles usually assist for purposes of quantification of damages in the form of damnum emergens [*i.e.*, an emergent wrong] and lucrum cessans [prevention of undue gain]. In common law countries such as the UK and Ireland, lacking any specific legislation, trade secrets are effectively protected by the common law of confidence and by contract law. This is the case also for Malta.

Most Member States – with the exception of Cyprus, the Czech Republic, the Republic of Ireland, Luxemburg, Malta and the UK – have specific provisions on trade secrets in national labour laws or in their Civil Codes. Indeed, misappropriation by disaffected employees is widely recognized as a critical area for trade secrets protection. The minimum common standard is prevention of trade secrets and confidential business information disclosure by employees (at least) during the employment relationship (Baker & McKenzie Law Firm, "Study on Trade Secrets and Confidential Business Information in the Internal Market," April 2013, Prepared for the European Commission Contract number: MARKT/2011/128/D, available at http://ec.europa.eu/internal_market/iprenforcement/docs/trade-secrets/130711_final-study_en.pdf, at p. 4).

See also Natalja Sosnova, *EU Directive Proposal: Trade Secrets*, 20 Marq. Intell. Prop. L. Rev. 53 (2016) (detailed discussion of EU proposal in light of US trade secret case law); Luigi Alberto Franzoni & Arun Kumar Kaushik, *The Optimal Scope of Trade Secrets Law*, 45 Int'l Rev. L. & Econ. 45, 53 (2016).

The European Commission recognized these many divergences, and that is why the EU Trade Secrets Directive was passed. It says in part:

> Notwithstanding the TRIPS Agreement, there are important differences in the Member States' legislation as regards the protection of trade secrets against their unlawful acquisition, use or disclosure by other persons. For example, not all Member States have adopted national definitions of a trade secret or the unlawful acquisition, use or disclosure of a trade secret, therefore knowledge on the scope of protection is not readily accessible and that scope differs across the Member States. Furthermore, there is no consistency as regards the civil law remedies available in the event of unlawful acquisition, use or disclosure of trade secrets, as cease and

desist orders are not always available in all Member States against third parties who are not competitors of the legitimate trade secret holder. Divergences also exist across the Member States with respect to the treatment of a third party who has acquired the trade secret in good faith but subsequently learns, at the time of use, that the acquisition derived from a previous unlawful acquisition by another party.

National rules also differ as to whether legitimate trade secret holders are allowed to seek the destruction of goods produced by third parties who use trade secrets unlawfully, or the return or destruction of any documents . . .

Furthermore, applicable national rules on the calculation of damages do not always take account of the intangible nature of trade secrets, which makes it difficult to demonstrate the actual profits lost or the unjust enrichment of the infringer where no market value can be established for the information in question. Only a few Member States allow for the application of abstract rules on the calculation of damages based on the reasonable royalty or fee which could have been due had a licence for the use of the trade secret existed. Additionally, many national rules do not provide for appropriate protection of the confidentiality of a trade secret where the trade secret holder introduces a claim for alleged unlawful acquisition, use or disclosure of the trade secret by a third party, thereby reducing the attractiveness of the existing measures and remedies and weakening the protection offered.

The differences in the legal protection of trade secrets provided for by the Member States imply that trade secrets do not enjoy an equivalent level of protection throughout the Union, thus leading to fragmentation of the internal market in this area and a weakening of the overall deterrent effect of the relevant rules. The internal market is affected in so far as such differences lower the incentives for businesses to undertake innovation-related cross-border economic activity, including research cooperation or production cooperation with partners, outsourcing or investment in other Member States, which depends on the use of information that enjoys protection as trade secrets. Cross-border network research and development, as well as innovation-related activities, including related production and subsequent cross-border trade, are rendered less attractive and more difficult within the Union, thus also resulting in Union-wide innovation-related inefficiencies (EU Trade Secrets Directive, Recitals 6–8).

This is not to say, however, that trade secret protection in Europe was completely lacking prior to the Directive. In Germany, for example, an important statutory provision, Section 17 of the Act Against Unfair Competition of 1909 (Gesetz gegen unlauteren Wettbewerb, or "UWG") contains a very broad general provision under which all acts in violation of "honest practices" are considered unlawful. Because of its generality, and because a fair number of individual cases have spelled out what these terms mean, it might be said that application of the UWG has a "common law" feel to it, despite being part of the German Civil Code. In Britain, by contrast, trade secret law has developed almost exclusively as a true common law field, based loosely on general principles of unfair competition, restitution, and the like.

Under the Directive, in Article 2, the subject matter of the Directive is defined:

> (1) "[T]rade secret" means information which meets all of the following requirements: (a) it is secret in the sense that it is not, as a body or in the precise configuration and assembly of its components, generally known among or readily accessible to persons within the circles that normally deal with the kind of information in question; (b) it has commercial value because it is secret.

21
What can be protected as a trade secret?

21.1 Defining trade secrets

21.1.1 United States

 CASE

Enterprise Leasing Co. of Phoenix v. Ehmke, 3 P.3d 1064 (Arizona Court of Appeals 1999)

This appeal arises out of the denial of a permanent injunction against a company's former employee from misappropriating trade secrets. We agree with Enterprise Leasing Company of Phoenix ("Enterprise") that the trial court erred in finding that the Enterprise financial records and other documents at issue were no longer trade secrets, if they had been, and, thus, that they are not entitled to protection from disclosure by Rich Ehmke, Enterprise's former employee. We conclude instead that the documents constitute proprietary and confidential information and should be afforded trade-secret protection. As such, Ehmke must be enjoined from the disclosure and use of these documents. We therefore reverse the trial court's denial of a permanent injunction, and we remand the case for entry of appropriate relief.

Ehmke worked for Enterprise in Maricopa County from January 22, 1996, until he was terminated eight months later. As a senior-level manager, Ehmke had access to substantial and proprietary confidential corporate business and financial information concerning Enterprise's market strategy, training methods, and internal financial and operations data. Given his exposure to such information, Ehmke's employment agreement contained a nondisclosure provision, as well as a covenant not to compete. The agreement stated in relevant part that Ehmke: will not at any time . . . take, disclose, misappropriate or misuse any marketing plans, client list, name, file, book, record, or account or other information or confidential data used at or in any of the businesses managed or owned by [Enterprise]. [He] agrees that any . . . trade secrets developed by [him] during the course of [his] employment . . . become the exclusive property of [Enterprise].

CASE *(continued)*

Nonetheless, upon Ehmke's termination, Enterprise discovered that he had absconded with 45 confidential documents comprising Enterprise's strategic plans, programs, methods and approaches. According to Thomas McKinley, Vice President and General Manager of Enterprise, 35 of these documents contained proprietary and confidential information which, if disclosed, would be advantageous to competitors.

Shortly thereafter, Ehmke formed a rental-car consulting firm in Phoenix. In this manner, he blatantly competed with Enterprise, indeed soliciting Enterprise customers and employees with the intent to recruit them for his new business.

On December 17, 1996, the trial court granted Enterprise's motion for a temporary restraining order against Ehmke, prohibiting him from soliciting Enterprise customers and employees, divulging trade secrets and otherwise engaging in direct competition with Enterprise. Not for a year did the trial court conduct a preliminary injunction hearing. Then it found that, not only had Ehmke enjoyed access to confidential business and financial information, but that he had later successfully used this information to compete against Enterprise in Maricopa County. On April 2, 1997, the court granted a preliminary injunction to bar Ehmke from continuing and future breaches of his employment agreement.

In July 1997, undeterred by the preliminary injunction, Ehmke became Vice President of the Western United States for Premier Car Rental ("Premier"), a subsidiary of Budget Rent-A-Car ("Budget") and a direct competitor of Enterprise. In this position, he supervised Premier's Arizona branch offices, including those in the Phoenix area. When it became aware of Ehmke's position, Enterprise subpoenaed those of its documents Ehmke had disclosed to Premier.

In February 1998, Enterprise sought a permanent injunction against Ehmke. During the trial, Ehmke admitted that he knowingly had contravened the preliminary injunction by accepting employment with Premier and disclosing to it confidential documents. He also conceded that he had instituted procedures similar to those at Enterprise, and he further acknowledged that he had prepared and distributed documents similar to ones he had drafted at Enterprise. Ehmke claimed, however, that these documents did not qualify as protectable trade secrets because they were common knowledge and not kept secret by Enterprise. Enterprise countered that the documents did indeed contain trade secrets and other confidential material about its operations and referral sources. McKinley related that, aside from some changes in graphic art, Ehmke's documents bore a strong resemblance to Enterprise's materials to the extent that they were not identical. The trial court concluded simply "that the [Enterprise] forms do not constitute a trade secret" and denied the permanent injunction.

By definition, a trade secret is not simply information as to single or ephemeral business events. See Roger M. Milgrim, *Milgrim on Trade Secrets* §1.01[1] 1-18 (1999). Rather, a trade secret may consist of a compilation of information that is continuously used or has the potential to be used in one's business and that gives one an opportunity to obtain an advantage over competitors who do not know of or use it. See ariz.Rev.Stat. Ann. ("A.R.S")

CASE (continued)

§44-401(4)(a); Restatement of Torts §757 cmt. b (1939). The Arizona Trade Secrets Act defines "trade secret" as follows: (4) "Trade secret" means information, including a formula, pattern, compilation, program, device, method, technique or process, that both:

(a) Derives independent economic value, actual or potential, from not being generally known to, and not being readily ascertainable by proper means by other persons who can obtain economic value from its disclosure or use.
(b) Is the subject of efforts that are reasonable under the circumstances to maintain its secrecy.

A.R.S. §44-401. This rather expansive definition emphasizes the secrecy of the alleged trade secret, as well as the competitive advantage afforded by it. See *Avtec Systems, Inc. v. Peiffer*, 21 F.3d 568, 575 (4th Cir. 1994).

Because the hallmark of a trade secret obviously is its secrecy, not only must the subject-matter of the trade secret be secret, it must be of such a nature that it would not occur to persons in the trade or business. *Wright*, 11 Ariz.App. at 295, 464 P.2d at 366; see A.R.S. §44-401(4)(a). Accordingly, matters that are public knowledge are not safeguarded as trade secrets. Information is considered public knowledge if it is available in trade journals, reference books or published materials, or if it is known to principal trade persons who can obtain an economic benefit from the information and are aware that the information is not a trade secret. unif. Trade Secrets Act §1 cmt. (1985).

In particular, when a process or idea is so common or widely known that it lacks all novelty, uniqueness and originality, it necessarily lacks the element of privacy required to make it legally cognizable as a trade secret. See *Cockerham v. Kerr-McGee Chemical Corp.*, 23 F.3d 101, 105 (5th Cir. 1994), citing *Cataphote Corp. v. Hudson*, 444 F.2d 1313, 1315 (5th Cir. 1971). Although the subject-matter of a trade secret need not rise to the level of novelty to the degree that it does in patent law, the information must be sufficiently novel such that it is not readily ascertainable to the competitors in an industry. Indeed, to allow the protection of material in the public domain would contradict the very purpose of trade-secret law, which is to protect valuable confidential information from discovery.

Although matters of general knowledge cannot be appropriated as secret, a trade secret may consist of a combination of elements even though each individual component may be a matter of common knowledge. See *Kewanee Oil Co.*, 416 U.S. at 481–84, 94 S.Ct. 1879; *Rivendell Forest Products, Ltd. v. Georgia-Pacific Corp.*, 28 F.3d 1042, 1045 (10th Cir. 1994). Specifically, a trade secret may include a grouping in which the components are in the public domain but there has been accomplished an effective, successful and valuable integration of those public elements such that the owner derives a competitive advantage from it. See *Rivendell Forest Products*, 28 F.3d at 1046. Thus, a compilation of general concepts may amount to a trade secret, and the analysis therefore depends on whether the end-product qualifies as a trade secret.

Enterprise's financial documents include sensitive internal economic records concerning its branch offices in Maricopa County, such as profit and loss figures, break-even points and

CASE (continued)

sales revenue. Although Ehmke baldly asserts that this information is so stale as to preclude protection, trade-secret status may continue indefinitely so long as there is no public disclosure. See *Kewanee Oil Co.*, 416 U.S. at 476, 94 S.Ct. 1879; Robert P. Merges et al., *Intellectual Property in the New technological Age* 59 (1997). Thus, secrecy may still attach to proprietary financial information.

Additionally, a document such as the Worksheet reflects a substantial market-research investment by Enterprise delineating several factors helpful to managing a successful branch office. As said above, a compilation need only be a slight advance over common knowledge to receive protection. *Compare Henry Hope X-Ray Products, Inc. v. Marron Carrel, Inc.*, 674 F.2d 1336, 1340 (9th Cir. 1982), with *Buffets*, 73 F.3d at 968. Taken out of context, the information in the Worksheet may, as Ehmke maintains, appear to consist only of the general knowledge of those persons in the car-rental industry. However, the Worksheet as a whole is an original product containing an arrangement of factors that provides Enterprise with a competitive advantage. See *Buffets*, 73 F.3d at 968. Because the compilation of customer-service factors represents originality in managing a car-rental business, the Worksheet is unique to Enterprise.

We recognize that not every commercial secret qualifies as a trade secret. Only those secrets affording a demonstrable competitive advantage may properly be considered a trade secret. *Wright*, 11 Ariz.App. at 295–96, 464 P.2d at 366–67. Value will be inferred if the owner can show that the information confers upon it an economic advantage over others in the industry. *Rivendell Forest Products*, 28 F.3d at 1046.

These documents provide economic value for Enterprise and would allow a competitor to gain an advantage if the documents were discovered in the marketplace. For instance, a competitor would have a detailed account of Enterprise's financial data that might be used to affect the placement of branch offices and/or pricing and sales decisions. The Worksheet could provide a competitor with a blueprint of the Enterprise customer-service principles.

[Reversed and remanded.]

NOTES

1. The standard definition of protectable trade secret information is "capable of having independent economic value." The basic idea is that information has to have some sort of value apart from its value in launching a lawsuit. This is so because almost any plausible legal cause of action has some value: it can be used to extract a settlement from the defendant.

    a. US: DTSA §1839(3):

    (3) the term "trade secret" means all forms and types of financial, business, scientific, technical, economic, or engineering information, including patterns, plans, compilations, program devices, formulas, designs, prototypes, methods, techniques, processes, procedures, programs, or codes, whether tangible or intangible, and whether or how stored, compiled, or memorialized physically, electronically, graphically, photographically, or in writing if–(A) the owner thereof has taken reasonable measures to keep such information secret; and (B) *the information derives independent economic value, actual or potential, from not being generally known to, and not being readily ascertainable through proper means by, another person who can obtain economic value from the disclosure or use of the information* (emphasis added).

Note the close similarity with UTSA: §1(4):

> (4) "Trade secret" means information, including a formula, pattern, compilation, program, device, method, technique, or process, that: (i) derives independent economic value, actual or potential, from not being generally known to, and not being readily ascertainable by proper means by, other persons who can obtain economic value from its disclosure or use.

See also American Law Institute, Restatement (Third) of Unfair Competition §39:

> A trade secret is any information that can be used in the operation of a business or other enterprise and that is sufficiently valuable and secret to afford an actual or potential economic advantage over others.

b. EU: Trade Secrets Directive, Article 2:

> (1) "trade secret" means information which meets all of the following requirements:
> (a) it is secret in the sense that it is not, as a body or in the precise configuration and assembly of its components, generally known among or readily accessible to persons within the circles that normally deal with the kind of information in question;
> (b) it has commercial value because it is secret.

c. China: PRC Unfair Competition Law, at Article 10(3):

> "Trade secrets" mentioned in this Article refers to any technology information or business operation information which is unknown to the public, can bring about economic benefits to the obligee, has practical utility and about which the obligee has adopted secret-keeping measures.

See also Interpretation of the Supreme People's Court on Some Matters About the Application of the Law in the Trial of Civil Cases Involving Unfair Competition, at Article 10 (protectable if the "information has practical or potential commercial value, and can be used for enhancing the competitive advantage for the obligee, it shall be ascertained as capable of bringing about benefits to the obligee, and having practical applicability").

2. The court says this about the originality of the "Worksheet" it found to be a protectable trade secret: "Because the compilation of customer-service factors represents originality in managing a car-rental business, the Worksheet is unique to Enterprise." Note that (1) each element of the Worksheet was in the public domain; and (2) it took some effort to compile the Worksheet into the final usable form. Compare this with the test for originality in copyright law; or novelty in patent law. How is it different? Notice that no matter how hard one works to assemble information, if the same information is available in the same form, it will not be protectable as a trade secret under some legal systems, *even if the version used by the misappropriator was copied from the original compiler and not from the public domain source.* See Restatement (Third), *supra*, §39, Comment f, at 433 ("When the information is readily ascertainable from such [public] sources, however, actual resort to the public domain is a formality that should not determine liability").

21.1.2 China

  CASE

China Tianfu Coke v. Pepsi Tianfu, Chongqing No. 4 Interim Ct. [2009], Yuwuzhongfaminchuzi No. 299

Plaintiff China Tianfu Coke (Chongqing) Group Co. ("China Tianfu") brought a trade secret misappropriation case against Defendants Pepsi Tianfu Beverage Co., Ltd. ("Pepsi Tianfu") and Pepsi Investment (China) Co., Ltd. ("Pepsi Investment").

CASE *(continued)*

In 1981, Chongqing Beverage Factory ("Beverage Factory") and Sichuan Chinese Medicine Center ("Medicine Center") entered into a cooperative Research and Development Agreement ("R&D Agreement") to jointly develop Tianfu Coke. Based on the R&D Agreement, Medicine Center was in charge of developing the syrup; while Beverage Factory and its Beverage Research Institute were in charge of developing the drink formula and flavor formula. The syrup produced by the Medicine Center must be exclusively supplied to Beverage Factory. In the same year, two parties signed a Supplemental Agreement, which designated Medicine Center as the patent owner of the syrup, while Beverage Factory as the owner of the "patent rights (including trademark)" for Tianfu Coke recipe, as well as its production process. Both parties bore the responsibility of maintaining the confidentiality of the relevant documents and should not disclose to any other individual or organization.

In 1985, through expansion, Beverage Factory became Chongqing Tianfu Coke Beverage Industrial Company, which later merged into China Tianfu in 1988. As a result of these merge[r]s, plaintiff China Tianfu became the new owner of the Trade Secret.

On May 23, 1986, Beverage Factory and Medicine Center signed an Amended Tianfu Coke Joint Development and Production Agreement ("Joint-Development Agreement"), which required the parties to share the rights and benefits of Tianfu Coke syrup technology. To ensure the secrecy of the technology, the coke recipe was managed and controlled by the designated staff only.

[O]n April 4, 1988, Chinese Ministry of Health approved the production of Tianfu Coke. China Tianfu then established a team dedicated to ensuring and protecting the confidentiality of Tianfu Coke's ingredients, formula, and production process. These security measures include but are not limited to, stamping of all the relevant documents with visible and obvious "Confidential" watermarks and seals, storing confidential documents in the special filing room, classifying the documents through various categories, and granting access to limited designated employees only.

In 1994, China Tianfu entered a joint-venture agreement ("JV Agreement") with KFC, a subsidiary of Pepsi Co., to co-establish a new joint-venture Pepsi Tianfu. The JV Agreement includes the following key provisions: (1) China Tianfu agrees to invest a total amount of $7,138,000, and KFC agrees to invest a total amount of $10,707,000; (2) China Tianfu's investment in the joint-venture includes its land, factories, and production equipment, which are estimated around $7,138,000; (3) the new joint venture manufactures Tianfu Coke and Pepsi-branded products; (4) the trademark "Tianfu", which is valued at the amount of 3,500,000 RMB, will be transferred to the new joint venture; (5) both parties bear the responsibility of maintaining the confidentiality of the exclusive materials and materials deemed confidential by either party; and (6) an arbitration clause which provides that any unsettled dispute, controversy, or claim shall be arbitrated by CIETAC.

After the joint-venture was established, Pepsi Tianfu has hired majority of its production team from China Tianfu. Pepsi Tianfu has also been using the Tianfu Coke Recipe to manufacture Tianfu Coke.

CASE *(continued)*

Plaintiff claims that, in 2006, it intended to transfer the entirety of its Pepsi Tianfu stocks to Pepsi Investment, thus ending its cooperation with Pepsi Co. and Pepsi Tianfu. However, Pepsi Tianfu continued to possess and use its Tianfu coke technology and other production process (collectively known as "Trade Secrets"), and therefore, violated its trade secret rights.

Accordingly, Plaintiff China Tianfu seeks: (1) declaratory judgment that it is the lawful owner of the Trade Secret; (2) injunctive relief to enjoin Pepsi Tianfu from using the Trade Secret, (3) Pepsi Tianfu to immediately return the confidential material regarding the Trade Secret, and (4) economic compensation of 1,000,000 RMB and attorney's fees from Pepsi Tianfu and Pepsi Investment.

[Defendant's main arguments are summarized as follows]: (1) Jurisdiction: This Court does not have jurisdiction over this case because the dispute arises out of the JV agreement, and therefore shall be subject to the arbitration clause in the JV Agreement, which is to be decided by China International Economic and Trade Arbitration Commission (CIETAC); (2) Defendant does not dispute about the scope of the Trade Secrets, but argued that Plaintiff failed to take reasonable efforts to maintain the confidentiality of such Trade Secrets; and (3) The JV Agreement signed by China Tianfu already transferred the Trade Secrets into the new joint venture (*i.e.* vesting with Pepsi Tianfu now). As such, Pepsi Tianfu, the joint venture, should own the Trade Secrets.

The issues presented before this Court include: (1) Whether this Court has subject matter jurisdiction, (2) whether the Tianfu Coke ingredients, formula, and production process are protectable trade secrets and if so, how to determine its ownership, and (3) whether Pepsi Tianfu and Pepsi Investment are liable for trade secret misappropriation. We address these issues in turn.

A. Subject Matter Jurisdiction

After this Court accepted the case, Pepsi Tianfu objected on grounds of lack of subject matter jurisdiction. The objection was overruled. Because such a ruling is effective, this Court hereby has subject matter jurisdiction. The Contract between the parties states that "any such unsettled dispute, controversy or claim shall be subject to arbitration administered by the China International Economic and Trade Arbitration Commission (CIETAC)." This clause should be interpreted as "any dispute arising out of *this specific contract,* including the breach or validity thereof." (emphasis added) Here, the subject dispute is related to trade secret misappropriation, which was not addressed in this specific contract. Therefore, this Court has subject matter jurisdiction.

B. Protectable Trade Secrets and Determining Ownership

1. *Whether the Ingredients, Formula, and Production Process of Tianfu Coke are Protectable Trade Secrets*

Paragraph 2 of Article 10 of *Anti-Unfair Competition Law of the People's Republic of China* ("Chinese Anti-Unfair Competition Law") provides that "trade secret" means "any technology or business information, which is unknown to the public, can bring about economic benefits to the right holder, and also the right holder has adopted reasonable measures to keep it secret."

CASE *(continued)*

[Further, the Chinese Supreme People's Court *Judicial Interpretation on Issues Concerning the Application of Law in the Trial of Civil Cases Involving Unfair Competition* ("JI on Unfair Competition") provide a detailed explanation on the elements "unknown to the public", "economic benefits" and "reasonable measures to keep it secret" in the trade secrets definition as provided in the Anti-Unfair Competition Law.] For example, Paragraph 1 of Article 9 of the *JI on Unfair Competition* provides that "[i]f the related information may not be known by the related public in the field and is difficult to be obtained, such information shall be deemed as *'unknown to the public'.*" Further, Article 10 of the JI on Unfair Competition continues that "[i]n case the related information has practical or potential commercial value, and can be used for enhancing the competitive advantage for the right holder, such information shall be deemed as capable of bringing about benefits to the right holder." In addition, Article 11 provides, "[i]f the right holder takes commercially reasonable measure to keep the information secret and to prevent it from being known by the public, then such measures shall be deemed as 'measures to keep confidentiality'."

The State Administration of Industry and Commerce (SAIC) also issued regulations addressing trade secrets misappropriation. Article 2 of *Several Provisions on Prohibiting Infringements upon Trade Secrets* provides that, "The term *'trade secret'* refers to practical information about technologies and business operations, which is unknown to the public and is able to bring economic benefits to the owner and for which the owner has taken confidentiality measures. Here, the term *'unknown to the public'* means that the information is not directly available through public channels. The term *'confidentiality measures taken by the owner'* include such measures as signing a confidentiality agreement, setting up a security system, and adopting other reasonable measures. The term *'information about technologies and business operations'* includes designs, procedures, formulae, manufacturing techniques and methods, management secrets, customer lists, information about resources, production and sales strategies, bottom price of a bid, contents of a bidding document, etc. And finally the term *'owner'* refers to citizens, corporate bodies, or other organizations who own trade secrets."

Pursuant to the aforementioned laws and regulations [issued by the Chinese Supreme Court and the SAIC], a trade secret needs to meet the following criteria: (1) the information needs to be unknown to the public, meaning that related personnel in the same industry do not know the subject information and such information is difficult to obtain; (2) the information brings economic benefits to the right holder and has practical utility; and finally (3) the right holder adopts reasonable measures to protect the secrecy of such information.

In this case, the parties agree that the disputed trade secret includes the ingredients, formula, and production process of Tianfu Coke. Because the coke recipe and production process are the core components of Tianfu Coke, [they] as a result, constitute "formula of products and manufacturing techniques and methods." Also, this information is unknown to the public, nor is it made known to related personnel in the industry, and therefore, the first element of trade secret is satisfied.

CASE *(continued)*

China Tianfu and Pepsi Tianfu manufacture beverages. Drink formulas are crucial in the beverage industry because they dictate the quality, reputation, and the popularity of the beverages among consumers. Therefore, the ingredients, formula, and production process have potential or actual commercial value to confer an economic and competitive benefit on the right holder. As a result, the second element of trade secret is met in this case.

To ensure the secrecy of Tianfu coke recipe, [the early founders of the recipe] Beverage Factory and Medical Center included a confidentiality clause in the R&D Agreement. [The successor] China Tianfu also created a team dedicated to ensuring and protecting the confidentiality of its coke recipe and the production process. These measures included stamping the relevant documents with visible and obvious "Confidential" watermarks and seals, storing the documents in the filing room, sorting the documents by categories, and granting limited access to designated employees. The new joint venture Pepsi Tianfu also treated the production technology as a trade secret during its production process. As such, pursuant to Paragraph 3 of Article 11 of the JI on Unfair Competition, the right holder has adopted reasonable measures, such as signing a confidentiality agreement and setting up a confidentiality system, to keep the trade secret confidential. Therefore, the third element is satisfied here.

For the reasons above, the disputed technology satisfies the three elements and therefore, is a trade secret.

2. *How to Determine the Ownership of a Trade Secret*

Medicine Center and Beverage Factory jointly developed the trade secret. The R&D Agreement and later agreements signed by the two parties suggested that the success of the new product is to be shared by both parties jointly, including the trade secret. On July 3, 1995, Medicine Center and China Tianfu agreed to terminate their cooperation, during which China Tianfu paid Medicine Center an amount of 250,000 RMB to "settle all rights." After this payment, China Tianfu has acquired Medicine Center's remaining rights to the trade secret and thus became the sole lawful owner of the jointly-developed trade secret.

Pepsi Tianfu and Pepsi Investment alleged that the disputed trade secret was incorporated into the new joint-venture Pepsi Tianfu as part of China Tianfu's agreed investment capital. However, China Tianfu denied such allegations. Therefore, the defendants bear the burden of proof.

Under the JV Agreement, China Tianfu's investment in the joint venture included "all of its land, factories, production equipment, and supplemental equipment, estimated at the amount of $7,138,000." According to the Registered Investment Capital Report provided by Chongqing Accounting Firm, China Tianfu invested: land use right, equivalent of $682,759; factories and buildings, equivalent of $2,260,710; and equipment, equivalent of $4,194,531, all in total of $7,138,000. The JV Agreement and the Registered Investment Capital Report indicate that China Tianfu did not invest the disputed trade secret into the new joint venture Pepsi Tianfu as registered capital.

The aforementioned findings, and the fact that the trademark transfer for mark "Tianfu" (which is far less important than the formula and production process) required a separate

CASE *(continued)*

contract, supports the conclusion that China Tianfu did not invest its trade secret in the JV Pepsi Tianfu. Therefore, China Tianfu remains the lawful owner of the trade secret.

C. Trade Secret Misappropriation

Pepsi Tianfu was founded to manufacture Tianfu Coke. China Tianfu was fully aware that Pepsi Tianfu was using its trade secret to produce the coke beverages, but did not object to or prevent Pepsi Tianfu from doing it until this litigation was filed. To a certain extent, China Tianfu acknowledged and accepted Pepsi Tianfu's use of the trade secret. The JV Agreement does not have specific provisions addressing trade secret royalties, and therefore, should be interpreted as "China Tianfu has given permission for the joint venture Pepsi Tianfu to use its trade secret for free." Therefore, Pepsi Tianfu's use of the trade secret, before the filing of this litigation, was authorized and did not constitute trade secret misappropriation. China Tianfu's request for economic compensation lacks support, and is therefore denied.

During this litigation, China Tianfu specifically requested Pepsi Tianfu to cease the use of its trade secret and was unwilling to negotiate with Pepsi Tianfu (due to other conflicts between two parties), such contention should be sustained. Therefore, Pepsi Tianfu should cease using the trade secret no later than the time that the Court sets forth.

In summary, this Court grants: (1) the declaratory judgment that the Tianfu Coke recipe and production process trade secret belongs to China Tianfu; (2) the injunctive relief of any further use of the trade secret by Pepsi Tianfu; and (3) the request for Pepsi Tianfu to immediately return the confidential material regarding the trade secret. This Court, however, denies China Tianfu's request for economic damages.

IT IS SO ORDERED.
HU Jin, Chief Judge
CHEN Xiuliang, Judge
PENG Hao, Judge
SUN Xiaoqiao, Clerk
November 23, 2010

NOTES

1. Though it might seem to be associated with the famous US Coca-Cola Company, China Tianfu Coke is an unrelated business. The single name "Coke" has been used by multiple companies in numerous countries. Though Coke is treated as a trademark of the Coca-Cola Company in the US, this trademark does not have foreign counterparts in all countries.
2. The Court refused to award damages for the use of the Tianfu coke formula prior to the initiation of the lawsuit. In effect, it held that the Pepsi Tianfu JV had an implied license from China Tianfu to use the coke formula during this period. However, once China Tianfu challenged the JV's continued use of the formula, this implied license ended. How might the parties have structured their agreement if they had wanted to formally provide a license for the formula to the JV? What protections should Pepsi Tianfu, the JV, have asked for under such an agreement? (Think about the impact of the Court's ruling in the case: a sudden end to the JV's ability to produce its coke product.)
3. If Pepsi Tianfu, the JV, had invested substantial capital to roll out its production and sale of the Tianfu coke

product, could it have argued that a sudden termination of its right to use the coke formula would leave it open to a large and serious economic loss? How might this affect the court's decision regarding an injunction; would it be fair to permit Pepsi Tianfu to continue using the formula until it recouped all or part of its investment in the product?

4. To further clarify the definition of trade secret under the Chinese Anti-Unfair Competition Law (1993), the Chinese Supreme People's Court issued a Judicial Interpretation in 2007 to list specific factors that courts need to consider when determining each element in trade secret, including "unknown to the public," "commercial value," and "measures that right-holder needs to adopt to keep such information confidential."

First of all, with regard to the element "unknown to the public," Article 9 of the 2007 Judicial Interpretation provides a negative list of information that was already made known to the public and thus excluded from trade secret protection, if the information falls under one of the following categories: (1) common sense or industrial practice that is known to people in the related technical or economic field; (2) only involves the simple combination of dimensions, structures, materials and components of products, and can be directly obtained by observing the products by the public concerned after the products enter into the market; (3) has been publicly disclosed on publications or by any other public media; (4) has been publicly displayed at conferences or exhibitions; (5) can be obtained through other public channels; or (6) easily obtained with much difficulty or price.

With regard to the element "measures to keep secrecy," Article 11 of the 2007 Judicial Interpretation deems the following measures, if adopted by right holders, as sufficient to satisfy the element of keeping information secret: (1) limiting the access of trade secrets, and making the trade secrets available only to those who have to know; (2) taking specific preventive measures, such as locking the classified information in a secured location; (3) labeling classified documents "confidential"; (4) adopting passwords or codes on classified information; (5) signing confidential agreements; (6) restricting visits to machinery, factories, workshops or any other places that contain classified information or asking such visitors to sign confidentiality agreements; and (7) any other reasonable measure to keep the secrecy of such information.

21.1.3 EU countries

So far we have seen cases on proprietary financial information and customer worksheets (*Enterprise Rental Car*, from the US), and a secret soft drink formula (*Tianfu Coke*, from China). Next we consider a case about customer lists, this time from Germany in the EU.

 CASE

Federal Supreme Court: Breach of Secrecy of a Representative as Wine Consultant, BGH, Urteil vom 19. 12. 2002 – I ZR 119/00 (Koblenz) Verwertung von Kundenlisten

[Relevant statutes:
Unfair Competition Act §§17 II, 13 IV

1. It is an unlawful use of a list of customers, which is a company's trade secret, when the names of the customers are contained in the personal documents of the representative in the context

CASE *(continued)*

of business activity, and utilized by this representative in the course of their activity outside of that company.
2. The new business owner cannot be made liable (imputed) for the behavior of the person entrusted with confidential information (according to §13 IV). They can, however, be liable for breach of secrecy, independently as a disturber or as an accomplice.

Facts of the case:]
The parties are competitors in the trade of wine and spirits. The wine consultant (W) worked for the plaintiff between October 1, 1986 and October 1, 1988 and was given by the plaintiff a file with at least 1,500 customer addresses for their use. After leaving their position with the plaintiff, W took a job with the defendant, who put them to work on a special wine display from October 29 – November 6 1988. In preparation for this event, the defendant prepared invitations which, next to their own letterhead, included W's picture and the name and these were sent, addressed to "dear customer" to between 200 and 220 customers of the plaintiff, who at the time were not yet customers of the defendant.

The plaintiff alleges that W worked with the defendant to write to ~1000 of their repeat customers to invite them to the defendant's wine display/tasting. The plaintiff allege that W copied down the file of customers before returning it to them.

The defendant countered by alleging that W, with help of a phonebook, recorded the addresses of the customers from memory for the invitations, after returning the complete list obtained from the plaintiff.

The State Court ordered the defendant, under dismissal of the action otherwise, to refrain from the following of importance for the appeal:

1. taking up contact (directly or through representatives) with repeat customers of the plaintiff, of whom the defendant or their representatives are familiar with through previous employees or field representatives of the plaintiff, for the purpose of conducting business regarding wine, sparkling wine, and spirits

Not affected by the ban are:

A. repeat customers of the plaintiff who were recruited for them by the field representative who changed employers
B. customers who were simultaneously customers of the plaintiff before W changed employers
C. customers who had declined to purchase further wine, sparkling wine, or spirits from the plaintiff before the change.

"Repeat customers" are customers who, in the two years before W's change, had made at least two orders with the plaintiff.

The Appellate Court dismissed the defendant's appeal for review. [After Senate

CASE *(continued)*

annulment, the Appellate Court again issued an identical ruling. The case was then appealed to the Supreme Court.]

Reasons:

I. The Appellate Court had supposed that the injunctions were not justified, because the mailing of the invitations to the plaintiff's customers was not objectionable under §1 of the Unfair Competition Act.
The Appellate Court outlined the following on this point:
The representative W, by using the addresses of the plaintiff's customers, did not perform a contractual or legal infringement. An infringement of §90 of the Commercial Code is therefore not the case, because it does not contradict the understanding of a reputable businessman if a representative concerns themselves with the customers of their former employer... The findings of the evidentiary hearing did not confirm that W copied information entrusted to him by the plaintiff and that W used these to prepare the invitations under discussion.

II. The appeal [to the Supreme Court] is successful. This leads to the reversal of the ruling and referral back to the Appellate Court.
1. The Appellate Court rightly assumed that customers' names and addresses, which became known to W during their time working for the plaintiff, constitute trade secrets in accordance with §17 II of the Unfair Competition Act (UWG). It also rightly assumed that the plaintiff needs to prove the presence of the conditions of §17 II of the Unfair Competition Act. In this respect the review raises no objections.
2. The review successfully addresses the assumption of the Appellate Court that the plaintiff did not sufficiently prove an infringement of §17 II UWG by W [*i.e.*, the Appellate Court is reversed for the following reasons].
   a) The Appellate Court determined that W had sent invitations for the wine display to between 200 and 220 customers of the plaintiff who were not yet customers of the defendant... The defendant themselves testified that the addresses came from W, who aided his memory with the telephone book. This was then the source of the addresses. W testified at the hearing of witnesses that after leaving the plaintiff's employ it was possible for them to reconstruct a longer list of customer information with the help of the telephone book. W either had memorized the telephone numbers or they were noted in records W had completed while working for the plaintiff. Therefore it did not have to do with the list compiled by the plaintiff for W but instead W's notes they used while on the road.
   b) Based on W's testimony the Appellate Court could not support a dismissal of the case. It is an unlawful use of the list of customers, itself a trade secret, when the names of the customers are contained in the personal documents of the representative in the context of business activity, and utilized by this representative in the course of their activity outside of the company. It then

CASE *(continued)*

proceeds that the addresses under discussion came from W and it is a fact that W used the addresses for the invitations from notes made by W, so the Appellate Court could not infer that the plaintiff had not brought forward proof of an infringement of §17 II UWG by W.

3. Nevertheless, the Appellate Court would have rightly dismissed the suit with the application for an injunction, had the defendant's liability of competition concerns for W's potential violation of §17 II UWG not come into question. [But the defendant's activities did in fact come into question.]

   a) An attribution of liability as per §13 IV UWG is unsuccessful, however. According to this provision, the owner of a business is liable for violations of their employees or representatives, because the division of labor in the business does not supersede their responsibility for behavior in competition. The owner of the business, who benefits from the competitive practices of their employees and representatives, should not be able to hide behind someone dependent on him (Federal Supreme Court GRUR 1990, 1039 [1040] = NJW 1990, 3204 = WRP 1991, 79).

   W's infringement has to do with their earlier activity for the plaintiff and the defendant cannot be saddled with it because this liability does not originate in the division of labor and organization of the defendant's business.

   b) The defendant's independent liability as a disruptor of competition remains intact, however. In addition, a liability of the defendant, as per §1 with the full power of §17 II UWG, can be considered, if they themselves were to fulfill the prerequisites of §17 II UWG. According to the allegations of the plaintiff, the defendant supported W's anticompetitive violation by offering them (as with others who moved to the employ of the defendant) an extra commission of 15% for customers "brought along" with them. Stemming from this, the defendant's liability as a disturber (or, if in the case that their knowledge of W's behavior is proved) can be established as per §1 with the full power of §17 II UWG.

III. Thereafter the disputed ruling made on the plaintiff's appeal was repealed, and the matter was remanded back to the Appellate Court. This court will also need to consider the plaintiff's petition for an injunction, which obviously goes too far.

NOTES

1. In this case, employee "W" made an invitation list of customers from W's employer. The list was made from notes W took during the employment period with the former company. Although W used a public domain source (a phone book) as a reference to check some addresses, the court said that the notes themselves were confidential trade secrets and thus W was liable under section 17 of the Unfair Competition Act, which prohibits "use of a list of customers, which is a company's trade secret, when the names of the customers are contained in the personal documents of the representative in the context of business activity, and utilized

by this representative in the course of their activity outside of that company." W's new employer is expressly excluded from liability under this section; but it is liable under the subsequent section, 17 II.2, as a "disturber" (or accomplice). This particular provision puts emphasis on the documents themselves; presumably, memorized information, taken from a prior employer, would not be a violation. It could violate other provisions of German law, to the extent they reflect or codify the EU Trade Secrets Directive. Article 4.2.a of the Directive does not require possession of documents, but speaks in broader terms of misappropriation as "unauthorised access to, appropriation of, or copying of any documents, objects, materials, substances or electronic files, lawfully under the control of the trade secret holder, containing the trade secret or from which the trade secret can be deduced." So in this definition, copying from or simply access to trade secrets is required, but not the possession of any documents embodying those secrets. On the other hand, you can appreciate that possession of confidential documents will often be excellent evidence of misappropriation, despite the fact that such possession is not a required element of this cause of action. On memorization as misappropriation, *see, e.g., Rohm & Haas Co. v. Adco Chemical Co.*, 689 F.2d 424 (3d Cir. 1982).

BGH 19.12.1984 I ZR 133/82 "Füllanlage", BGH, Decision dated February 19, 1984 – I ZR 133/82 (OLG Karlsruhe)

[Summary of facts:]
Since 1952, the claimant is manufacturing temperature measuring and controlling devices and belongs to the leading European manufacturers of distance thermometers. Each manufacturer of thermometers constructs a corresponding filling machine which is necessary to manufacture the said product. Defendants 1 to 3 were high ranked employees of the claimant until 1970. One of them was *e.g.* head of the construction division.

[The claimant argued that the defendants 1 to 3 had decided already in Spring of 1969 to incorporate a competing company and that they – for their own benefit – unduly exploited the secret technical and commercial knowledge belonging to the claimant to which they had access or which they had obtained by criminal content or with undue means. In particular, the claimant alleged the defendants had reconstructed and (for their own benefit) used the filling machine which constituted the best preserved know-how of his company.]

[Procedural history:]
The District Court (LG) has sentenced the defendants for omission, disclosure and damages. The Court of Appeal (BerG) has – by dismissing some claims – only partly upheld the verdict of the LG. Most importantly, the BerG dismissed the motion of omission for certain utilizations of the filling machine. It has concluded upon a culpable violation by the defendants of a trade secret of the claimant in using a filling machine until M[ay] 31, 1974 which was to a high extent similar to the machine used by the claimant but, however, did not identify any violation of §17 UWG by using a modification of the described machine from June 1, 1974 onwards. The revision to the Federal High Court of Justice (BGH) was partly successful and led to partial annulment and dismissal, particularly as regards the above described finding of the BerG.

> **CASE** *(continued)*
>
> [Core findings:]
> Claims related to the use of the filling machines: Knowledge of trade secrets that was obtained in violation of §17 UWG can in no way be used by the infringer. Results that are based upon such a violation are therefore from the very beginning and – at least as a general rule – continuously poisoned with this defect of competition law violation. This principle is also applicable to developments which are not wholly based upon unlawfully obtained knowledge but which are concurrently causative, unless they are economically or technically insignificant. The reason is that also in such cases, unduly obtained knowledge is (co-)exploited to the benefit of the infringer because without it (meaning in case of an exclusively independent development) the infringer would either not at all or in any case only later and/or with greater efforts reach the similar development results like with the use of the knowledge which is poisoned with competition law violation. The case at hand meets the above described requirements.

NOTES

1. The 2016 EU Trade Secrets Directive includes an expansive definition of what subject matter is capable of being a trade secret:

   > It is important to establish a homogenous definition of a trade secret without restricting the subject matter to be protected against misappropriation. Such definition should therefore be constructed so as to cover know-how, business information and technological information where there is both a legitimate interest in keeping them confidential and a legitimate expectation that such confidentiality will be preserved. Furthermore, such know-how or information should have a commercial value, whether actual or potential. Such know-how or information should be considered to have a commercial value, for example, where its unlawful acquisition, use or disclosure is likely to harm the interests of the person lawfully controlling it, in that it undermines that person's scientific and technical potential, business or financial interests, strategic positions or ability to compete. The definition of trade secret excludes trivial information and the experience and skills gained by employees in the normal course of their employment, and also excludes information which is generally known among, or is readily accessible to, persons within the circles that normally deal with the kind of information in question (EU Trade Secrets Directive, at Recital 14).

2. Another issue is closely related to the question of what constitutes a trade secret: who has a duty not to disclose or use a trade secret? Often, the answer is clear; the duty to maintain a trade secret usually arises out of a confidential relationship, which may be established either from surrounding facts or through a contractual provision. But even when it is clear that one person has a duty not to disclose or use trade secrets, that person may come to be associated with others. When do these others have a duty not to use or disclose trade secrets? The UK Supreme Court dealt with this issue in a case in which a former employee was found to have misappropriated trade secrets from his former employer. One associate in the former employee's new company was accused of misappropriation, but the Court found she was not aware of the trade secret status of the information and so was not in fact liable:

   > [W]hile a recipient of confidential information may be said to be primarily liable in a case of its misuse, a person who assists her in the misuse can be liable, in a secondary sense. However, as I see it, consistently with the approach of equity in this area, she would normally have to know that the recipient was abusing confidential information. Knowledge in this context would of course not be limited to her actual knowledge, and it would include what is sometimes called "blind-eye knowledge". The best analysis of

what that involves is to be found in *Royal Brunei Airlines Sdn Bhd v. Tan* [1995] 2 AC 378, especially at pp. 390F–391D, where Lord Nicholls approved the notion of "commercially unacceptable conduct in the particular context involved", and suggested that "[a]cting in reckless disregard of others' rights or possible rights can be a tell-tale sign of dishonesty".

Further, even a person who did not know that the information which is being abused is confidential could nonetheless be liable if there were relevant additional facts. Thus, if a person who directly misuses a claimant's trade secret does so in the course of her employment by a third party, then the third party could (at least arguably) be liable to the claimant for the breach of confidence. However, that would simply involve the application of one well established legal principle, vicarious liability, to another, misuse of confidential information (*Vestergaard Frandsen A/S v. Bestnet Europe Ltd.*, 22 May 2013, [2013] UKSC 31, [2013] R.P.C. 33, at pars. 26 and 27).

The notion of "blind eye" knowledge is quite similar to what is called "willful blindness" in US law. *See, e.g., Global-Tech Appliances, Inc. v. SEB S.A.*, 563 U.S. 754 (2011) (finding indirect liability for patent infringement on the part of a company that ordered a review of competitor patents in a field before introducing its own product, but intentionally withholding information about a particular patent it was concerned might be infringed by the product it was about to introduce).

Note that sometimes, a person begins using a trade secret without knowledge that it was obtained lawfully prior to their use. In such cases, the EU Directive permits a remedy but protects the good faith of such a person by providing for a monetary remedy instead of an injunction:

A person could have originally acquired a trade secret in good faith, but only become aware at a later stage, including upon notice served by the original trade secret holder, that that person's knowledge of the trade secret in question derived from sources using or disclosing the relevant trade secret in an unlawful manner. In order to avoid, under those circumstances, the corrective measures or injunctions provided for causing disproportionate harm to that person, Member States should provide for the possibility, in appropriate cases, of pecuniary compensation being awarded to the injured party as an alternative measure (EU Trade Secrets Directive (2016), at Recital 29).

22

Reasonable efforts to protect trade secrets

22.1 United States

CASE

SHI R2 Sols., Inc. v. Pella Corp., 864 N.W.2d 553 (Iowa Ct. App. 2015)

Vaitheswaran, P.J.
SHI R2 Solutions, Inc. (Deimco) designs and manufactures custom finishing equipment. Pella Corporation manufactures windows and doors. Deimco agreed to build custom equipment for Pella. Deimco's president, Kirk Shirar, signed a confidentiality agreement prohibiting the disclosure of Pella's confidential and proprietary information. Pella was not asked to sign a similar agreement prohibiting the disclosure of Deimco's confidential and proprietary information.

In 2004, Pella asked Deimco for a quotation to manufacture an industrial finishing machine with conveyers and ovens. The quotation request form stated, "[a]ny modifications to standard machine configurations shall be the design responsibility of and remain in ownership of the Vendor." The "vendor" was Deimco.

Deimco prepared a quotation and provided Pella with a drawing depicting the equipment, known as an "approval drawing." Deimco's engineering manager testified the drawing was "an overall system drawing that shows the various views of what we are proposing to sell to the customer." The drawing included the following legend: "This drawing contains proprietary information of SHI R2 Solutions, Inc. [Deimco]. Possession thereof does not confer any right to reproduce, use or disclose in whole or in part any such information without written authorization from SHI R2, Inc. [Deimco]." The drawing required the purchaser's endorsement which, according to the engineering manager, was an acknowledgment the purchaser understood what Deimco intended to build. Dan Bartlett, Pella's project manager at the time, endorsed the drawing. Deimco built the equipment and delivered it to Pella.

Pella and Deimco continued to do business with each other. During the negotiations

CASE *(continued)*

for another project, Pella tried to change the ownership language contained in its original request for quotation. Pella replaced the language with, "The original machine design and drawings of custom machine will become property of Pella Corporation." Deimco objected and inserted the following language in its quotation, "The machines designs, sub-assembly, and fabrication drawings are the intellectual property of Deimco finishing equipment." Pella acquiesced in this language by indicating its purchase order was pursuant to Deimco's quotation.

Three years after Deimco and Pella began their business relationship, Pella elected to design and produce its own finishing equipment. Under the auspices of maintaining the Deimco machines in its possession, an engineer assigned to the project asked Deimco to turn over sub-assembly drawings of the spray guns inside the machines. Deimco declined the request. In time, Pella disassembled and replicated a Deimco machine, notwithstanding concern among some within the company as to whether the cited proprietary language allowed it to do so. When Pella informed Deimco the company would not be hired for an upcoming project, Deimco began to suspect Pella was reverse engineering its machines. Deimco filed suit alleging common law and statutory claims of misappropriation of trade secrets and breach of Pella's contractual obligation not to infringe on its intellectual property. Pella moved for summary judgment. The district court granted the motion and this appeal followed.

[Iowa law] defines "trade secret" as:

[I]nformation, including but not limited to a formula, pattern, compilation, program, device, method, technique, or process that is both of the following:

a. Derives independent economic value, actual or potential, from not being generally known to, and not being readily ascertainable by proper means by a person able to obtain economic value from its disclosure or use.
b. Is the subject of efforts that are reasonable under the circumstances to maintain its secrecy.

The parties do not seriously dispute that Deimco's designs for the Pella machines constituted "information" within the meaning of the trade secret definition. They focus on other aspects of their relationship and commercial dealings, which largely implicate the extent to which Deimco made reasonable efforts to maintain the secrecy of the information. On this question, the district court found it "undisputed that Deimco publicly disclosed its equipment through public sales and without confidentiality agreements or patent protection in place, and thus did not take reasonable steps to maintain the secrecy of the device."

[Pella pointed to (1) Deimco equipment exhibited at trade shows; (2) tours of Deimco's factory given to Pella employees; and (3) drawings of Deimco machinery on Deimco's website – all evidence, it said, that Deimco did not make reasonable efforts to maintain its trade secrets. Deimco countered by arguing: (1) the trade show equipment differed in

CASE *(continued)*

important ways from the equipment sold to Pella; (2) the tours did not reveal trade secret information; and (3) the website drawings were too general to disclose trade secrets.]

We are left with Deimco's failure to obtain a confidentiality agreement from Pella. Pella asserts "the lack of a confidentiality agreement . . . means that Deimco did not take reasonable efforts to maintain secrecy."

[I]n construing our [state's] definition [of reasonable efforts], the Iowa Supreme Court has declined to hold the absence of a confidentiality agreement dispositive on the question of whether information constitutes a trade secret. *See Cemen Tech*[*, Inc. v. Three D Indus., L.L.C.*, 753 N.W.2d 1, 7 (Iowa 2008)], at 7–8 (stating a confidentiality agreement "can be an important although not necessarily conclusive factor in determining whether the information qualifies for protection as a trade secret") (quoting Restatement (Third) of Unfair Competition §39 cmt. d)).

As noted, Pella itself included language in its first request for quotation stating the information belonged to Deimco. Pella attempted to alter the language at a later date, but Deimco objected and inserted language in its quotation emphasizing the proprietary nature of the information. Pella proceeded with the purchase, subject to the added language. Additionally, Pella endorsed the approval drawings, which also contained legends stating the machine designs were proprietary.

We conclude Deimco generated a genuine issue of material fact on whether its efforts to maintain the secrecy of its information were reasonable under the circumstances . . . On this summary judgment record, we are unable to find the "reasonable efforts to maintain secrecy" requirement satisfied as a matter of law . . .

The district court found the information readily ascertainable [from public sources, and thus not protectable as a trade secret,] based on the availability of the information at trade shows, tours of the Deimco facility, and Deimco's postings on the internet, all addressed above. Additionally, the court relied on the ability to reverse engineer a machine, a topic we also addressed above. As with the "reasonable efforts to maintain secrecy" prong, we conclude Deimco generated an issue of material fact on the "reasonably ascertainable" requirement precluding summary judgment in favor of Pella. Accordingly, we reverse the grant of summary judgment to Pella on Deimco's common-law and statutory misappropriation-of-trade-secrets claims. [The court also held there was] a genuine issue of material fact on the question of whether the contract language prohibited Pella from reverse engineering the machine. Accordingly, we reverse the grant of summary judgment as to Deimco's breach-of-contract claim [as well].

NOTES

This case well illustrates the interaction of trade secret and contracts law, in two primary ways: First, the obligation of confidentiality arose not from a general duty (such as on the part of an employee to an employer), but from language included in documents exchanged during negotiation of a contract.

When Deimco gave a "quotation" to Pella, Deimco included drawings with this language: "This drawing contains proprietary information of [Deimco]. Possession thereof does not confer any right to reproduce, use or disclose in whole or in part any such information without written authorization from [Deimco]." This was the key language the court used in finding that Pella had agreed to keep Deimco's information confidential.

Second, notice that Deimco's lawsuit against Pella included two causes of action: misappropriation of trade secrets, and breach of contract. By permitting the breach of contract part of the lawsuit to proceed (*i.e.*, by denying summary judgment in favor of Pella on the contracts claim), the court acknowledged that the "quotation" sent by Deimco might also have formed part of the final contract between the parties. US contract law can be somewhat complex on the question of when documents exchanged prior to contract performance can become part of the final contract between the parties. But it is possible that the nondisclosure obligation included on Deimco's drawings might give rise both to a trade secrets cause of action (by putting Pella on notice that Deimco considered the information in the drawing to be a trade secret); and to a breach of contract claim (by making Pella's nondisclosure obligation a provision of the contract between the parties). For comparative analysis of the contractual significance of documents exchanged by parties leading to contract performance, see Kevin C. Stemp, *A Comparative Analysis of the "Battle of the Forms"*, 15 Transnat'l L. & Contemp. Probs. 243 (2005).

 CASE

nClosures Inc. v. Block & Co., 770 F.3d 598 (7th Cir. 2014)

In May 2011, nClosures Inc. and Block and Company, Inc. began a business relationship in which nClosures designed and Block manufactured metal enclosures for electronic tablets, such as iPads. At the outset of the relationship, the parties signed a confidentiality agreement; nClosures then divulged its designs for the enclosure device to Block for manufacture. The first device – known as the Rhino Elite – entered the market for sale in October 2011. By March 2012, however, Block developed its own competing device, known as the Atrio. In November 2012, nClosures brought suit in diversity against Block alleging, among other claims, breach of contract and breach of fiduciary duty. The district court granted summary judgment to Block on both claims. On the breach of contract claim, the district court concluded that no reasonable jury could find that nClosures took reasonable steps to keep its proprietary information confidential, and therefore that the confidentiality agreement was unenforceable. The district court also concluded that no reasonable jury could find that a partnership existed between nClosures and Block that could give rise to a viable breach of fiduciary duty claim. However, the district court denied Block's motion for attorney's fees. nClosures challenges the district court's rulings on summary judgment, and Block – as cross-appellant – challenges its denial of Block's motion for attorney's fees. We affirm in both respects.

CASE *(continued)*

Figure 22.1 Rhino Elite iPad enclosure

nClosures is an industrial design firm co-founded in 2011 by Daniel Gorman, Daniel McKean, and Kemper Barkhurst. After its formation, nClosures developed metal cases for electronic tablets, such as iPads. Designer and independent contractor Ian LeBlanc designed one such device–the Rhino Elite–for nClosures in early 2011. Later that year on May 24th, nClosures co-founders McKean and Gorman attended a trade show in Chicago to display prototypes of the Rhino (a precursor to the Rhino Elite). There, Block CEO Greg Carlson approached them about a potential business relationship. Block previously manufactured and sold metal devices like cash drawers, but had recently identified tablet enclosures as a potential new product line.

At the May 24th meeting between nClosures and Block, the companies signed a confidentiality agreement wherein they agreed to the following:

> The Parties . . . agree that the Confidential Information received from the other Party shall be used solely for the purposes of engaging in the Discussions and evaluating the Objective (the "Permitted Purposes"). Except for such Permitted Purposes, such information shall not be used, either directly or indirectly, by the Receiving Party for any other purpose . . .

The agreement defines "the Objective" as "a potential business relationship with respect to iPad Enclosures." Outside of this initial agreement, nClosures did not require other Block employees or engineers to sign additional agreements in order to access Rhino or Rhino Elite design files. nClosures also did not enter into confidentiality agreements with Rhino Elite designer Ian LeBlanc, or with the manufacturers that produced Rhino Elite predecessors known as the Lab Shield and the Rhino.

After signing the confidentiality agreement, nClosures provided Block with the design

CASE *(continued)*

files for the Rhino products. Subsequently, nClosures and Block attempted to negotiate a written agreement concerning the manufacture and sale of the tablet enclosures. Although the companies never agreed on a written contract, they exchanged at least three draft agreements during negotiations. After these failed attempts, the parties reached an oral agreement on the following terms: Block agreed to manufacture the Rhino Elite and sell the units to nClosures at $19.25 per unit. nClosures was permitted to sell some units to its customers, and some units back to Block at an increased price of $53 per unit. nClosures therefore netted $33.75 on the units it sold back to Block.

To bring a successful breach of contract claim under Illinois law, a party must show "(1) the existence of a valid and enforceable contract; (2) substantial performance by the plaintiff; (3) a breach by the defendant; and (4) resultant damages." *TAS Distrib. Co. v. Cummins Engine Co.*, 491 F.3d 625, 631 (7th Cir. 2007). Additional considerations arise, however, when we assess the enforceability of a confidentiality agreement. *See Tax Track Sys. Corp. v. New Investor World, Inc.*, 478 F.3d 783, 787 (7th Cir. 2007). In *Tax Track*, we held that a federal court applying Illinois law "will enforce [confidentiality] agreements only when the information sought to be protected is actually confidential and reasonable efforts were made to keep it confidential." *Id.* Thus, in order to enforce the confidentiality agreement between nClosures and Block, we must find that nClosures took reasonable steps to keep its proprietary information confidential.

[I]n *Rockwell Graphic Systems Inc. v. DEV Industries, Inc.*, 925 F.2d 174, 180 (7th Cir. 1991) [Posner, J.], we found that the steps taken to protect the proprietary information at issue were substantial enough to preclude summary judgment for the defendants in a trade secrets misappropriation case. In Rockwell, unlike in Tax Track, the engineering drawings at issue were kept in a vault with limited access. *Id.* at 177. The engineers who used the drawings were required to sign agreements not to disseminate the drawings or disclose their contents. Id. Furthermore, vendors permitted to access copies of the drawings also signed confidentiality agreements, and each drawing was marked with an indication that it contained proprietary information. *Id.* While this Court did not determine whether the steps in *Rockwell* were sufficient to protect the trade secrets at issue, we did find that these steps were substantial enough to preclude summary judgment in favor of the defendants. The steps taken in *Rockwell*, however, far exceed the measures employed by nClosures, and more closely resemble the steps taken in *Tax Track*. While nClosures and Block did sign a confidentiality agreement at the outset of their business relationship, no additional confidentiality agreements were required of individuals who accessed the design files for the Rhino or Rhino Elite devices. Additionally, neither the Rhino nor the Rhino Elite drawings were marked with words such as "confidential" or "contains proprietary information." Furthermore, the drawings were not kept under lock and key, nor were they stored on a computer with limited access. While the declaration of Daniel McKean states generally that nClosures had a policy of requiring confidentiality agreements, no such agreements were required of designer Ian LeBlanc or of the manufacturers that produced previous versions of the Rhino Elite. These facts

> **CASE** *(continued)*
>
> show that nClosures did not engage in reasonable steps to protect the confidentiality of its proprietary information, and therefore that the confidentiality agreement with Block is unenforceable. We affirm the district court's ruling that no reasonable jury could find otherwise.

NOTES

1. Recall that in the *China Tianfu* case, Chapter 21, Section 21.1.2, the Chinese court recounted these facts showing reasonable precautions to maintain the secrecy of the soft drink formula at issue there:

   > To ensure the secrecy of Tianfu coke recipe, [the early founders of the recipe] Beverage Factory and Medical Center included a confidentiality clause in the R&D Agreement. [The successor] China Tianfu also created a team dedicated to ensuring and protecting the confidentiality of its coke recipe and the production process. These measures included stamping the relevant documents with visible and obvious "Confidential" watermarks and seals, storing the documents in the filing room, sorting the documents by categories, and granting limited access to designated employees. The new joint venture Pepsi Tianfu also treated the production technology as a trade secret during its production process. As such, pursuant to Paragraph 3 of Article 11 of the JI on Unfair Competition, the right holder has adopted reasonable measures, such as signing a confidentiality agreement and setting up a confidentiality system, to keep the trade secret confidential. Therefore, the third element [required for trade secret protection, *i.e.*, proof of "reasonable efforts to maintain secrecy"] is satisfied here.

   See also PRC Unfair Competition Law, Article 10.3: "'Trade secrets' mentioned in this Article refers to any technology information or business operation information which is unknown to the public, can bring about economic benefits to the obligee, has practical utility and *about which the obligee has adopted secret-keeping measures*" (emphasis added).

3. The EU Trade Secrets Directive likewise requires proof of efforts to maintain secrecy. Article 2.1(c) defines as a trade secret information that "has been subject to reasonable steps under the circumstances, by the person lawfully in control of the information, to keep it secret."
   In some older cases, however, less emphasis is placed on efforts to maintain secret status, and more on the facts and circumstances surrounding the disclosure of information. The key inquiry in cases such as *Coco v. AN Clark (Engineers) Ltd*, [1968] F.S.R. 415 (High Ct. Just., Chanc. Div.) (1968), was whether the "disclosee," the party learning the information, should have been on notice that the information was considered confidential. As the court said in the *Coco* case,

   > It seems to me that if the circumstances are such that any reasonable man standing in the shoes of the recipient of the information would have realised that upon reasonable grounds the information was being given to him in confidence, then this should suffice to impose upon him the equitable obligation of confidence (*Id.*, [1968] F.S.R. 415, 420–21).

   Notice, however, that it is possible to see the "duty" argument and the "reasonable efforts" inquiry as roughly congruent. The party that owns the information, by using effort to impart it under conditions that signify its secret status, tags the information as valuable. Reasonable efforts and acts signifying a duty of confidence can thus be seen to overlap. *See* Deepa Varadarajan, *Trade Secret Precautions, Possession, and Notice*, 68 Hastings L.J. 357 (2017).

23
Misappropriation

23.1 Improper means

23.1.1 United States

The key definitions required to understand misappropriation under US trade secret law are found in section 1 of the Uniform Trade Secrets Act:

> Uniform Trade Secrets Act, with 1985 Amendments
> §1. Definitions
> As used in this [Act], unless the context requires otherwise:
>
> (1) "Improper means" includes theft, bribery, misrepresentation, breach or inducement of a breach of a duty to maintain secrecy, or espionage through electronic or other means;
> (2) "Misappropriation" means:
>   (i) acquisition of a trade secret of another by a person who knows or has reason to know that the trade secret was acquired by improper means; or
>   (ii) disclosure or use of a trade secret of another without express or implied consent by a person who
>   (A) used improper means to acquire knowledge of the trade secret; or
>   (B) at the time of disclosure or use, knew or had reason to know that his knowledge of the trade secret was
>   (I) derived from or through a person who had utilized improper means to acquire it;
>   (II) acquired under circumstances giving rise to a duty to maintain its secrecy or limit its use; or
>   (III) derived from or through a person who owed a duty to the person seeking relief to maintain its secrecy or limit its use; or
>   (C) before a material change of his [or her] position, knew or had

reason to know that it was a trade secret and that knowledge of it had been acquired by accident or mistake. . .

Consider these definitions when reading the following case:

CASE

Schroeder v. Pinterest Inc., 133 A.D.3d 12, 17 N.Y.S.3d 678 (N.Y. App. Div. 2015)

In this action, plaintiff Theodore F. Schroeder and two companies founded by him, plaintiffs Rendezvoo LLC (Rendezvoo) and Skoop Media Associates, Inc. (Skoop Media), allege that defendants Brian S. Cohen, New York Angels, Inc. (N.Y. Angels), and Pinterest Inc. (Pinterest) stole and illegally used Schroeder's confidential ideas, technology and business plans in developing the popular website, Pinterest.com. According to plaintiffs, Schroeder conceived of a novel web application that would allow Internet users to share information about themselves by posting interests, ideas and pictures to their interface boards, a concept very different from then-existing popular social network sites like Facebook, MySpace and Friendster.

Schroeder and two friends embarked on the project and later invited Cohen, an investor and self-proclaimed "entrepreneurial mentor," to join the group. Plaintiffs allege that after learning all about Schroeder's ideas, technology and business plans, Cohen absconded with them, and gave them to Pinterest, which then used the information to develop its own highly-successful website. After subsequently learning that Cohen played a material role in the early stages of the Pinterest website, plaintiffs brought this action for, inter alia, breach of fiduciary duty, misappropriation and unjust enrichment. The facts alleged in the complaint are as follows. In 2005, while attending Columbia Law School, Schroeder and a law school classmate, nonparty Brandon Stroy, developed an idea for a social network bulletin board where users could share their physical locations with their friends over the Internet. According to plaintiffs, no such website existed at the time. Lacking technological expertise, Schroeder taught himself computer programming, and spent more than 2,000 hours learning the necessary programming skills to develop the idea into a web application. Another law school classmate, nonparty William Bocra, came on board to further develop the idea and prepare a business model for the project.

Shortly after the release, Schroeder and his friends decided to redesign the website to allow users to share not only their physical locations but also any interests they had. Rendezvoo's business plan described the website as a place "where people meet to share opinions, views, items and tastes on a variety of subjects – products, services, events, politics, economics – nearly anything of human interest."

Schroeder rebuilt the web application to reflect this expanded scope, and in August 2006, the new concepts were introduced in an "alpha release" to the website's existing user community. This second version of Rendezvoo.com included bulletin boards for users to

CASE *(continued)*

post their interests, and also featured an infinite scroll to make it easier for users to browse large amounts of data. By mid-2006, Schroeder had invested over 5,000 hours developing Rendezvoo's web applications, and delayed his legal career to focus solely on generating additional interest in the website. Excited about their endeavor, Schroeder, Stroy and Bocra began to look for additional capital to further advance the Rendezvoo website. They were eventually introduced to Cohen, an investor affiliated with N.Y. Angels, a not-for-profit corporation that provided capital to entrepreneurs starting new businesses. In January 2007, the three men met with Cohen and shared with him Rendezvoo's concepts, business model and business plan; by this time, the Rendezvoo website had more than 5,000 users.

In May 2007, Schroeder [and his co-founders] asked Cohen to become a partner in Rendezvoo. Despite lacking technical training and skills, Cohen accepted the offer and became Rendezvoo's Chairman and Chief Executive Officer. Cohen agreed to be bound by the restrictive covenants contained in Rendezvoo's operating agreement, including not taking Schroeder's ideas or using Rendezvoo's work product. Cohen's addition to Rendezvoo was never formally memorialized, and plaintiffs allege that the parties routinely ignored corporate formalities at Cohen's direction.

[The website was re-launched as] Skoopwire.com[, which] was a narrower version of Rendezvoo.com; whereas Rendezvoo.com users could post anything of interest to them, Skoopwire.com was focused solely on new product launches. Schroeder developed a technology plan for the Skoopwire website, which included information about the architecture and platform for the site, as well as customer data analysis. Schroeder shared that technology plan with Cohen, and also taught him about the social networking niche in which both the Rendezvoo and Skoopwire websites existed.

In June 2007, the four men formed Skoop Media, with Schroeder named as President, and Cohen serving as Chairman and Chief Executive Officer. Again, corporate formalities were ignored by the parties. [There was a then a falling out over how much one of the co-founders was working on the project.] According to the complaint, Cohen's actions caused significant strains among the four partners and effectively deadlocked the project. By early 2008, the parties began contemplating a liquidation of Skoop Media. Plaintiffs allege that in an effort to conceal his plan to steal Schroeder's ideas, technology and business plans, Cohen stated in an email that he was "saddened that such a marvelous idea and execution is lost forever." In fact, plaintiffs claim that Cohen purposely deadlocked the endeavor "so he could steal the core ideas for himself and freeze out Schroeder from reaping any benefits."

A proposed liquidation agreement circulated among the partners provided that each would not "develop, pursue, or otherwise work on . . . an entity or business reasonably related to the purposes, goals, aims and business models" of Rendezvoo or Skoop Media. Schroeder's requests to have the others sign the liquidation agreement went unanswered. Although the agreement was never executed, Cohen sent a July 1, 2008 email to Schroeder stating: "I have absolutely NO interest in PROFITING from your specific design work on Skoopwire." Plaintiffs allege that in mid-2008, Cohen "abandoned" Rendezvoo and Skoop

CASE (continued)

Media. Although the Skoopwire website was never officially released to the general public, Skoop Media, like Rendezvoo, was never dissolved.

In 2009, Cohen met Pinterest founders Ben Silbermann and Evan Sharp at a business school competition at New York University. Silbermann and another Pinterest founder, Paul Sciarra, had previously formed Cold Brew Labs, Inc., a mobile shopping start-up, [which failed. They then] created Pinterest.com, a social commerce application where "curating and sharing collections of products" was made "dead simple." According to the complaint, this radical change in focus was the result of Cohen's stealing Schroeder's ideas and technology and giving that information to Pinterest's founders. Pinterest.com was launched in March 2010. The website allows users to pull images from elsewhere on the Internet and generate pins which are compiled into various topic boards. Each pin also functions as a link to its original Internet source, such as a blog post, an article, or a shopping site where users can immediately purchase the item pictured. Users have the ability to view both the most popular pins on the site as well as the boards that other users have created. The website also allows users to "like" pins and "re-pin" items "creating a microcosm of image-sharing based solely on user-created content." Upon seeing Pinterest.com, Schroeder noticed that it was nearly identical to the second version of his Rendezvoo website.

[I]t was not until March 2012 that Schroeder became aware of Cohen's scheme to steal his ideas. At that time, Schroeder read an article wherein Cohen "bragged about being Pinterest's 'first investor,'" and described how he met Pinterest's founders in 2009, shortly after he allegedly deadlocked the Rendezvoo and Skoopwire projects. Plaintiffs allege that, in that article, Cohen falsely stated that he did not know where the concept of "pinning on Boards" came from, and claimed that the Pinterest website "came out of nowhere." The complaint further alleges that Pinterest's founders knew that the ideas given to them by Cohen were not his own.

In June 2013, after learning that Cohen played a material role in the early stages of the Pinterest website, plaintiffs commenced this action against Cohen, N.Y. Angels (together, the Cohen defendants) and Pinterest. The complaint asserts causes of action for: (1) unjust enrichment (against all defendants); (2) misappropriation (against all defendants); (3) misappropriation of skills and expenditures [a sub-category of misappropriation unique to New York State law] (against all defendants); (4) promissory estoppel (against Cohen); (5) breach of fiduciary duty (against Cohen); and (6) aiding and abetting breach of fiduciary duty (against Pinterest). The complaint seeks, inter alia, compensatory damages of more than one million dollars and a constructive trust over the earnings derived by defendants from Pinterest.

[Pinterest was dismissed from the law suit after a motion.] The court, however, denied dismissal of the causes of action for misappropriation of skills and expenditures, and promissory estoppel [against defendant Cohen].

[W]e conclude that the lower court erred in dismissing the breach of fiduciary duty claim against Cohen. The complaint alleges that, as Chairman and Chief Executive Officer of both Rendezvoo and Skoop Media, Cohen owed fiduciary duties to both companies

> **CASE** *(continued)*
>
> and to Schroeder, a fellow shareholder and member. Further, the complaint sets forth facts alleging that Cohen breached those duties by intentionally deadlocking the Rendezvoo and Skoopwire projects, stealing confidential and proprietary ideas, technology and business plans related to the projects, and providing that information to Pinterest. These allegations sufficiently state a cause of action for breach of fiduciary duty under Delaware law [which applies because that is the state where the various companies were incorporated]. [But] we conclude that the claim against Pinterest for aiding and abetting Cohen's breach of fiduciary duty was properly dismissed. Plaintiffs failed to assert with the requisite particularity facts alleging that Pinterest had actual knowledge of Cohen's alleged breach and knowingly participated in it. [The unjust enrichment claim against Pinterest was also properly dismissed, as there was never any legal relationship between the plaintiffs and Pinterest.]
>
> The complaint, when read in the light most favorable to plaintiffs, states a claim for trade secret misappropriation against Cohen. Plaintiffs allege that while Cohen was an officer of Rendezvoo and Skoop Media, he was exposed to the companies' confidential and proprietary technology and business plans. Plaintiffs further allege that despite being aware that the information was to be kept confidential, Cohen provided it to Pinterest. According to the complaint, Schroeder devoted nearly four years of his life, and thousands of hours, developing the technology that ultimately led to the Rendezvoo and Skoopwire websites. The complaint alleges that this technology was valuable to plaintiffs, and was not easily acquired or duplicated by others. Further, Schroeder took steps to maintain the secrecy of all of the technology and business information related to the projects. These allegations are sufficient, for pleading purposes, to satisfy the first element of a misappropriation of trade secrets claim, namely, that plaintiffs possessed a trade secret. Plaintiffs have also pleaded facts supporting the second element – that Cohen used the trade secrets in breach of an agreement, confidential relationship or duty, or as a result of discovery by improper means. As noted earlier, plaintiffs allege that Cohen acquired the confidential information while he was a fiduciary of Rendezvoo and Skoop Media, and that he purposely caused the project to deadlock so that he could steal that information. [As for the claim against Pinterest,] [i]n the absence of the requisite legal relationship between plaintiffs and Pinterest, the idea misappropriation claim fails.
>
> Plaintiffs adequately allege that Schroeder invested labor, skill and expenditures, having spent nearly four years of his life, and thousands of working hours, on performing the technical requirements to develop the Rendezvoo and Skoopwire websites. Further, sufficient facts are alleged showing that Cohen misappropriated the fruits of Schroeder's investment by giving the ideas and technology to Pinterest in bad faith. As discussed previously, the complaint asserts that Cohen acquired the confidential information while he was a fiduciary of Rendezvoo and Skoop Media. The complaint also alleges that Cohen knew that the proprietary information he obtained should be kept confidential, and that Cohen agreed to be bound by the restrictive covenants in the Rendezvoo operating agreement, which included not taking Schroeder's ideas or using any of Rendezvoo's work

CASE (continued)

product for his own benefit. [However, the misappropriation of skill and expenditures claim against Pinterest was properly dismissed, because, as stated earlier, there was no legal relationship between the plaintiffs and Pinterest, which is required for this cause of action.]

[Held: Schroeder's complaint states several valid causes of action, and the case may thus proceed.]

NOTES

1. Be aware that this opinion is *not* a final judgment finding Cohen liable for breach of fiduciary duty and misappropriation. It is *only* an opinion rejecting Cohen's attempt to dismiss the suit. The end result is not a victory for Schroeder; it is a holding that Schroeder may pursue his case.
2. Nevertheless, the case is instructive for a number of reasons. First, as is common in "startup company" situations, the dealings of the parties were not particularly formal, nor were detailed records kept. This is quite common during the exciting (and sometimes chaotic) early period of a startup. People come and go; product designs change radically; investors are courted; people become excited, then disillusioned; and so on. As a case study in "startup culture" (and perhaps "startup mania"), the facts here are instructive.

   Second, notice the interaction of two discrete elements of trade secret law: (1) establishing a duty of confidentiality between the parties; and (2) proving misappropriation. Misappropriation hinges on the use of "improper means" in learning of information; and the propriety of the means used is often determined by looking at the relationship between the parties. The same information may, for example, be disclosed to a party under two different circumstances, only one of which results in misappropriation. A presentation or "sales pitch" to the general public would not in general be expected to create a duty of non-disclosure (unless all recipients sign a non-disclosure agreement); thus use of the information presented would not be misappropriation. But the same information, if presented to a specific person under conditions of implied confidentiality (*e.g.*, disclosure to a potential investor, where the information disclosed is accompanied by a legend such as "proprietary trade secrets of Company X"), might well be treated as a trade secret, the use of which constitutes misappropriation. In this way, the conclusion of misappropriation is closely tied to the presence or absence of a duty between the parties.
3. The case also shows the close relationship between the duty a corporate officer has to the corporation (which is the basis for the breach of fiduciary claim in the *Schroeder* case) and the kinds of confidential relationships that may give rise to a misappropriation claim. Even before Cohen joined the various corporations organized by Schroeder, he may have had a duty not to disclose Schroeder's trade secrets. But once a corporation is formed to exploit Schroeder's ideas and technology, Cohen may have an additional duty as an officer of the corporation. This is closely related to another cause of action that sometimes arises when a corporate insider leaves to take advantage of an idea he or she first learned about through the role of officer: the "corporate opportunity" doctrine. On this, see *Broz v. Cellular Info. Sys., Inc.*, 673 A.2d 148, 154–55 (Del. 1996), which says that the corporate opportunity doctrine

   > holds that a corporate officer or director may not take a business opportunity for his own if: (1) the corporation is financially able to exploit the opportunity; (2) the opportunity is within the corporation's line of business; (3) the corporation has an interest or expectancy in the opportunity; and (4) by taking the opportunity for his own, the corporate fiduciary will thereby be placed in a position inimicable to his duties to the corporation.

   The heart of this doctrine is the notion of conflict of interest: the officer's duty to the company versus the officer's self-interest in exploiting an opportunity for personal gain.
4. A keystone case on "improper means" in the US is *E. I. du Pont deNemours & Co. v. Christopher*, 431 F.2d 1012 (5th Cir. 1970). A competitor of plaintiff DuPont wanted to find out how DuPont was constructing a chemical plant, so the competitor commissioned a pilot to fly over the construction site and take pictures.

Overflight in this area, at the relevant altitude, was not illegal; but the court said nonetheless that it was an "improper means" to discover the information about the chemical plant. Authorities have argued about the case ever since, with most attention given to these points: (1) if there was no contract between the parties, and if what the defendant did was not independently illegal (*i.e.*, did not violate any law other than possibly trade secret law), why was it found to be "improper"?; (2) whether the overflight here was a legitimate form of "reverse engineering"; and (3) because it would have been prohibitively expensive to build a shield over the construction site, the fact that photos could be taken did not mean that DuPont failed to take reasonable precautions to keep the plant design secret. Notice that the UTSA in the US covers the *DuPont* case by including "espionage" in the definition of "improper means."

5. There is conflict in the US courts over whether a breach of confidence or other "improper means" leads to liability for misappropriation in cases where the relevant information could have instead been derived from publicly available sources. Compare *Shellmar Products Co. v. Allen-Qualley Co.*, 87 F.2d 104 (7th Cir. 1936) and *Smith v. Dravo*, 203 F.2d 369, 374 (7th Cir. 1953) (the fact that a secret can be lawfully discovered by defendant, whether through reverse engineering or otherwise, does not foreclose action against him where it is proven that he in fact discovered the secret by unlawful means, *i.e.*, in breach of a confidential relationship) with *Den-Tal-Ez, Inc. v. Siemens Capital Corp.*, 389 Pa.Super. 219, 247, 566 A.2d 1214, 1228 (1989) (calling into question the validity of *Smith* in light of other cases that "have shifted the emphasis from whether the conduct of the defendant conformed to its confidential relationship with the plaintiff to a close analysis of whether the information was truly a trade secret"); *Moore v. Kulicke & Soffa Indus., Inc.*, 318 F.3d 561, 571 (3d Cir. 2003) (quoting *Den-Tal-Ez* in its criticism of *Smith*).

23.1.2 China

Wan Lian Internet Company v. ZHOU Huimin, Shanghai High People's Court [2011] (Hugaominsanzhizhongzi No. 100)

Plaintiff Wan Lian Internet Company ("Wan Lian Co.") was founded in May 2001 to specialize in website design, computer programming and other information services. QIU Qi ("QIU") was its legal representative and owned 60 percent of the shares. The other 40% of shares was owned by JIANG (unrelated to this case.)

On June 1, 2001, plaintiff entered into an employment contract ("Contract") with defendant ZHOU Huimin ("ZHOU"). The Contract states: "Party A (Plaintiff) hires Party B (ZHOU) to design webpage and develop software during his spare time;" "The employment lasts for two years, from June 1, 2001 to May 31, 2003;" "Party A pays Party B a fixed salary of 500 RMB in full every month;" "During the contractual period, or after the expiration of the contract, or in the event of mutual termination of the contract, Party B shall not disclose, transfer, or use the software program owned by the company to others without Party A's permission. . ." The parties did not renew the Contract after it expired, but defendant ZHOU continued to work for plaintiff after the expiration of the Contract.

On March 13, 2002, plaintiff registered the domain name www.boxbbs.com and launched a website called "BOX online gaming community."

(continued)

In January 2003, QIU and ZHOU entered into a share transfer agreement, whereby QIU agreed to transfer 30% of his shares to ZHOU. On November 26, 2003, plaintiff held a board meeting, announcing that FENG Hua (FENG, co-defendant), CHEN Yufeng (CHEN YF, co-defendant) and CHEN Yunsheng (CHEN YS, co-defendant) would become its new shareholders.

Towards the end of May and the beginning of June 2005, co-defendants ZHOU, CHEN YF, CHEN Yongping (CHEN YP, co-defendant) decided to leave the plaintiff's company and start a new company. Within this new company, ZHOU would be in charge of technical operations, including designing webpage, downloading databases, and designing computer program. Co-defendants CHEN YF and CHEN YP would be in charge of development of computer programs. Co-defendant CHEN YS would be in charge of webpage design and domain name registration, and FENG would be in charge of marketing.

On June 7, 2004, the five co-defendants released a "Joint Statement regarding Box01 Work Group", which states that, "In view of the uncertainty concerning the shareholding structure in Boxbbs.com (owned by Wan Lian), we the former key members of Wan Lian, including ZHOU, FENG, CHEN YS, CHEN YF and CHEN YP, have decided to leave Wan Lian and start a new company Box01 Work Group. . . . The domain name "box2004.com" will be owned by the new company. The source code and database developed by us will also be owned by the new company. . ."

On June 9, 2004, co-defendant CHEN YS registered a new domain name www.box2004.com (the "Infringing Website No. 1"). Co-defendant ZHOU downloaded the user database from plaintiff's website and also used the same software that was developed for plaintiff's website to launch the Infringing Website No. 1. During this period, ZHOU modified the configuration files of Plaintiff's website such that the website would no longer function. He also directed registered users of plaintiff's website to the Infringing Website No. 1 through public announcements and various online forums.

On August 20, 2004, five co-defendants registered another domain name, www.ibox.com.cn ("Infringing Website No. 2"). The Infringing Website No. 2 was called "ibox entertainment online" and was specialized in online gaming. The defendants stopped operating the Infringing Website No. 1 and replaced it with the Infringing Website No. 2.

On March 4, 2005, co-defendants established a new company, Beijing Century New Oak Network Technology Co. ("New Oak Co."), which hosted online gaming forums. On April 7, 2005, the Infringing Website No. 2's domain name, www.ibox.com.cn, was transferred to New Oak Co.

On December 12, 2005, New Oak Co. entered into a website transfer agreement with Shanghai Yuewei Computer Information Technology Co. Ltd. ("Yuewei") to sell the Infringing Website No. 2 to Yuewei for 200 million RMB. The transfer occurred on February 10, 2006.

During the hearing, plaintiff alleged that the trade secret at issue is the user information obtained and stored on plaintiff's website database between March 13, 2002 to June 8, 2004, which includes the usernames, passwords, and subscribers' registration dates. Defendant

(continued)

ZHOU conceded that, in order to operate the Infringing Website No. 1, he downloaded plaintiff's database remotely with the password he controlled from the plaintiff's website. ZHOU also admitted that he used the aforementioned database when designing the Infringing Website No. 2.

The court of the first instance discussed the four issues presented in the case as follows.

I. Ownership of Database in Plaintiff's website

The court of first instance held that, from March 13, 2002 to June 8, 2004, plaintiff, under the name of Wan Lian Co., registered the domain name www.net.cn, and was the actual operator of the website. Based on the evidence submitted by the parties, from June 2001 to June 2004, co-defendants ZHOU and CHEN YP were former employees of Plaintiff. Co-defendants FENG, CHEN YS and CHEN YF were former shareholders of Plaintiff. As a result, the co-defendants were fully aware that the plaintiff's website was registered and owned by the plaintiff, and that they were working for the plaintiff to perform their job duties involving technology development, website maintenance and business operation as plaintiff's employees. Therefore, between the period March 13, 2002 and June 8, 2004, plaintiff, as the domain name owner and actual operator of the website, had ownership to the database that was developed during the course of the website's operations.

II. Whether the User Information in Plaintiff's Database, Including Usernames, Passwords and Registration Dates, Qualifies as Trade Secrets

The court of first instance held that the trade secrets claimed by plaintiff refer to the user information listed on the client roster, including user names, passwords and registration time. First, the aforementioned user information is business information accumulated from long-term business activities. In an effort to attract online gaming fans, plaintiff has spent significant amount of labor and time to operate its website and interact with its online users. Although the username, password, and registration time log for a single user are relatively easy to obtain, yet the user information for the entire database, which includes over 500,000 entries of usernames, passwords and time entries is neither generally known by persons skilled in the relevant field nor readily ascertainable. Second, the aforementioned user information proves to be valuable to bring a high volume of web traffic to the plaintiff's website. Because the web traffic and advertising revenue are closely related, the aforementioned user information has practical utility value and may bring plaintiff economic benefits. Third, plaintiff set up passwords to protect its database access, which were only known to its chief technical directors, specifically to ZHOU and plaintiff's legal representative QIU. The employment contract that ZHOU signed also contained a confidentiality clause that prevented ZHOU from disclosing the employer's trade secrets without permission. Therefore, plaintiff has adopted sufficient protection measures to keep the secrecy of its trade secret. To summarize, the court of first instance concluded that the user name in plaintiff's database, including usernames, passwords and registration time entries, qualified as trade secret that is entitled to legal protection.

III. Whether Five Defendants' Conduct Constitutes Trade Secret Misappropriation

The court of first instance held, according to the *Anti-Unfair Competition Law of the*

(continued)

People's Republic of China, "stealing, coercing, or using any other unfair method to obtain the other's business secrets; or disclosing, using or permitting others to use the business secrets, constitutes unfair competition practices, specifically misappropriation of trade secrets." Here, plaintiff, as the rightful holder of its database, has ownership to the user information included in the database, and therefore, owns the trade secret. Without plaintiff's permission, co-defendant ZHOU accessed the database with the password he controlled and subsequently copied, downloaded, and used the user information, including usernames, passwords, and registration times, without permission. ZHOU's conduct therefore constituted misappropriation of plaintiff's trade secrets. While although the actual copying of plaintiff's database was done by ZHOU alone, it is clear that the other co-defendants in this case were also aware of ZHOU's misappropriation conduct. The reason that they did not directly copy plaintiff's database was simply because they were assigned with other tasks. The Joint Statement launched by the co-defendants indicated that all these co-defendants should be jointly liable for the legal consequences of their actions. Therefore, the court of first instance held that the five defendants had the joint-intent of trade secrets misappropriation and should be jointly liable.

IV. Remedy

[To prove the economic losses as a result of the trade secret misappropriation], Plaintiff submitted an appraisal report for the estimated value of its entire website. Because there are discrepancies between the value of the user information as a trade secret and the value of the entire database, the appraisal report cannot form the basis for calculating the economic loss in this case. The court of first instance, however, treated the appraisal report as an important factor in consideration of damages. Since plaintiff's actual damages and defendants' actual profits are difficult to determine, the court of first instance, would assess the damage standard based on the following factors: the evidence submitted by both parties, the brand recognition of plaintiff's website, development cost of the trade secret, profit derived from the trade secret, potential profit from the trade secret, how long the trade secret can provide competitive advantages, the appraisal report, the scope of the misappropriation, the degree of faulty behavior, the duration of the misappropriation, and defendant's profits derived from the misappropriation.

In sum, the court of first instance held that co-defendants shall be jointly liable for the monetary damage of one million RMB, including reasonable fees, within ten days after entry of judgment.

This is affirmed by the court of appeal. It is so ordered.

Chief Justice: QIAN Guangwen
Justice: WANG Jing
Justice: WANG Jianfeng
February 24, 2012
Clerk: DONG Erhui

NOTES

1. The employment agreement that Zhou signed with Wan Lian says that "Party B [Zhou] shall not disclose, transfer, or use the software program owned by the company to others without Party A's [Wan Lian's] permission." The court assumes that this agreement covers user registration information obtained when game players visited Wan Lian's gaming website. Could you argue that "software program" might not cover user data? Even if you could, would there be a basis for Wan Lian to protect against misappropriation? A cause of action against Zhou and the other defendants that is not rooted in the employment contract Zhou signed?

2. The name, registration information, and online time logs of an individual user might not be protectable as a trade secret; it is possible that anyone with access to the website could observe a user name, and keep track of how long that user spends online. But when this same information is collected over a long period of time, for many users (such as the 500,000 said to visit the Wan Lian website), it obviously becomes much more valuable. The ability to sell advertising, for example, is closely tied to a website's data on the average age and average site visit times for its various users. The court is surely correct that although the individual user data might be ascertainable by simple observation, the *aggregate* data is very valuable, and thus protectable as a trade secret.

3. Notice the remedy ordered by the trial court, and approved in the opinion set out here from the Court of Appeal: damages of one million RMB (roughly $145,000). There does not appear to be an injunction accompanying this, so the remedy is strictly damages. Does this seem like a reasonable estimate of the value of the trade secrets in this case? Look at the factors the court says were considered in arriving at this figure: "the brand recognition of plaintiff's website, development cost of the trade secret, profit derived from the trade secret, potential profit from the trade secret, how long the trade secret can provide competitive advantages, the appraisal report, the scope of the misappropriation, the degree of faulty behavior, the duration of the misappropriation, and defendant's profits derived from the misappropriation." Notice that the factor "how long the trade secret can provide competitive advantages" might be compared to the "lead time" or "headstart" factor considered in other jurisdictions. Notice too that "the degree of faulty behavior" seems to in effect ask for a weighting of the dollar damages in light of how badly the defendant behaved. Does this leave room for a punitive element in the damages assessment? By the same token, does it permit a court to slightly discount damages when a defendant's misappropriation is wrongful, but not particularly egregious?

23.1.3 Europe

 CASE

Coco v. AN Clark (Engineers) Ltd, [1969] R.P.C. 41, [1968] F.S.R. 415 (High Ct. of Justice – Chancery Div.)

Megarry, J.
[The plaintiff designed a moped engine and sought the co-operation of the defendants in its manufacture. After the plaintiff had disclosed to the defendants all the details of his design and proposals for its manufacture, the parties fell out and the defendants decided to manufacture their own engine. The plaintiff alleged that the defendants had deliberately broken with him with a view to using his design without compensation, and when the defendants brought out their own design which closely resembled the plaintiff's, he brought a motion for an interlocutory injunction to restrain the defendants from misusing

CASE (continued)

information communicated to them in confidence solely for the purposes of the joint venture. The defendants denied that any confidential information had been supplied to them, or used by them in their engine.]

The subject-matter of the dispute is a two-stroke engine for a moped, or motor-assisted cycle. [P]laintiff moves for an interlocutory injunction against the defendant company [ordering defendant not to] make or sell . . . any Scamp moped or any other machine in the design, development or manufacture of which the defendant has used directly or indirectly any confidential information [which is] the property of the plaintiff.

In 1965 [plaintiff Coco] began market research into the possibility of producing and selling a new moped; and, being skilled in such matters, he proceeded to design such a machine. In April 1967 there was the first contact between him and the defendant company about the proposed moped, and the company expressed interest in making it. By a letter dated 24th April 1967 the company suggested to the plaintiff that he should bring the prototype that he had built down to the works of the company with him, and this was done. Over the next three months there were many discussions between the parties, and the plaintiff supplied the company with information, drawings and other aids towards the production of the moped, such as a list of possible suppliers of parts for the machine; and this came to be known by the plaintiff's name as the Coco moped. The company in its turn did work on the plaintiff's ideas, and also put forward for the plaintiff's consideration certain draft documents to regulate the financial and other arrangements between them; but these documents were never signed, nor were terms ever agreed in any other way.

On 20th July 1967 there came the breach between the parties. Mr. A.N. Clark, the managing director of the defendant company, told the plaintiff that . . . the company had decided to make its own moped to a design different from that of the plaintiff . . . In a letter dated 17th April 1968 the defendant company admitted that the piston and carburetter were of the same type, and this confirmed the plaintiff's suspicions. He relies strongly upon the piston being one that he had designed.

[Defendant's] Scamp moped had gone into production, and about 200 a week are now being sold. The Coco moped is not in production and there is no suggestion of any plans for putting it into production. The plaintiff's evidence includes that of a consultant engineer, demonstrating many resemblances between the two engines, but of course at this stage of the proceedings there has been no cross-examination. I should make it clear that there is no issue between the parties on anything save the engine, and that no question of patents arises.

[T]here is no question of any breach of contract, for no contract ever came into existence. Accordingly, what I have to consider is the pure equitable doctrine of confidence, unaffected by contract . . . Thus limited, what are the essentials of the doctrine?

Of the various authorities cited to me, I have found *Saltman Engineering Co. Ltd. v. Campbell Engineering Co. Ltd.* (1948) 65 R.P.C. 203; *Terrapin Ltd. v. Builders' Supply Co. (Hayes) Ltd.* [1960] R.P.C. 128 and *Seager v. Copydex Ltd.* [1967] 1 W.L.R. 923; [1967] R.P.C. 349; of the most assistance. All are decisions of the Court of Appeal. I think it is quite plain from the *Saltman* case that the obligation of confidence may exist where, as in

CASE *(continued)*

this case, there is no contractual relationship between the parties. In cases of contract, the primary question is no doubt that of construing the contract and any terms implied in it. Where there is no contract, however, the question must be one of what it is that suffices to bring the obligation into being; and there is the further question of what amounts to a breach of that obligation. In my judgment, three elements are normally required if, apart from contract, a case of breach of confidence is to succeed. First, the information itself, in the words of Lord Greene, M.R. in the *Saltman* case on page 215, must "have the necessary quality of confidence about it". Secondly, that information must have been imparted in circumstances importing an obligation of confidence. Thirdly, there must be an unauthorised use of that information to the detriment of the party communicating it. I must briefly examine each of these requirements in turn.

First, the information must be of a confidential nature. As Lord Greene said in the *Saltman* case at page 215 "something which is public property and public knowledge" cannot per se provide any foundation for proceedings for breach of confidence . . . But this must not be taken too far. Something that has been constructed solely from materials in the public domain may possess the necessary quality of confidentiality: for something new and confidential may have been brought into being by the application of the skill and ingenuity of the human brain.

The difficulty comes, as Lord Denning, M.R. pointed out in the *Seager* case on page 931, when the information used is partly public and partly private; for then the recipient must somehow segregate the two and, although free to use the former, must take no advantage of the communication of the latter. [Also,] where confidential information is communicated in circumstances of confidence the obligation thus created endures, perhaps in a modified form, even after all the information has been published or is ascertainable by the public; for the recipient must not use the communication as a spring-board.

The second requirement is that the information must have been communicated in circumstances importing an obligation of confidence. However secret and confidential the information, there can be no binding obligation of confidence if that information is blurted out in public or is communicated in other circumstances which negate any duty of holding it confidential. From the authorities cited to me, I have not been able to derive any very precise idea of what test is to be applied . . . It may be that that hard-worked creature, the reasonable man, may be pressed into service once more; for I do not see why he should not labour in equity as well as at law. It seems to me that if the circumstances are such that any reasonable man standing in the shoes of the recipient of the information would have realised that upon reasonable grounds the information was being given to him in confidence, then this should suffice to impose upon him the equitable obligation of confidence. In particular, where information of commercial or industrial value is given on a business-like basis and with some avowed common object in mind, such as a joint venture or the manufacture of articles by one party for the other, I would regard the recipient as carrying a heavy burden if he seeks to repel a contention that he was bound by an obligation of confidence: see the *Saltman* case at page 216.

CASE (continued)

Thirdly, there must be an unauthorised use of the information to the detriment of the person communicating it. Some of the statements of principle in the cases omit any mention of detriment; others include it. At first sight, it seems that detriment ought to be present if equity is to be induced to intervene; but I can conceive of cases where a plaintiff might have substantial motives for seeking the aid of equity and yet suffer nothing which could fairly be called detriment to him, as when the confidential information shows him in a favourable light but gravely injures some relation or friend of his whom he wishes to protect. The point does not arise for decision in this case, for detriment to the plaintiff plainly exists.

I turn to the first and third conditions[:] How far is the information confidential in nature, and how far has the defendant company made an unauthorised use of any information that was confidential in nature? If there has been any such use, it clearly has been an unauthorised use to the detriment of the plaintiff; but the plaintiff's claim must fail if what the defendant company has without authority used to his detriment was not confidential in nature... What matters is how far the Scamp [engine] achieves [its] similarities [to the Coco engine] by drawing on confidential information imparted by the plaintiff in confidence, and how far these factors had produced in the Coco an engine which had any originality or other qualities that could provide information of a confidential nature ... I can only say that, on this motion, [the] evidence [has] in my judgment fallen well short of what is requisite for interlocutory relief. Subject to one matter, I do not think that the plaintiff has shown ... a prima facie case of infringement which is reasonably capable of succeeding. The one matter that I have in mind is the *Terrapin* case; ... [but] in that case there had been cross-examination of witnesses on the hearing of the motion, whereas there has been no such cross-examination here. Where the affidavit evidence is in conflict, as it was in that case and in this, the difference which such cross-examination may produce is indeed significant; for it will often make it possible to resolve many of the conflicts of evidence for the purposes of the motion.

It may be that what I have said presages a simple refusal of interlocutory relief; but I do not think that this would be right. [Defendants have agreed to] keep an account of a royalty of 5/0d. [*i.e.*, £5, 0 pence; worth roughly £51 in 2017 pounds] per Scamp engine manufactured, this being the amount offered by the defendant company when the negotiations broke down. [They will] pay this royalty into a special joint bank account on trusts which would protect the plaintiff in the event of any financial disaster to the defendant company. In addition, the defendant company [will provide] a true account of the total number of Scamp engines made in the previous months. These seem to me to be entirely proper arrangements. [I]t seems to me that this rate of payment is a sensible figure to adopt for the interim period until the trial of the action. Accordingly subject to [the royalty payments and accounting], I dismiss the motion.

NOTES

1. Judge Megarry says that in this case, "no question of patents arises." How might it have changed the case if plaintiff Coco had filed a patent application covering his engine design and/or the combination of his engine and the overall moped? What if Coco had actually obtained an issued patent for one or more aspects of his design? *See generally* Robert P. Merges, *A Transactional View of Property Rights*, 20 Berkeley Tech. L.J. 1477 (2005) (highlighting the benefits of filing a patent application prior to negotiations over a joint venture or licensing agreement).

2. The court says: "[W]here confidential information is communicated in circumstances of confidence the obligation thus created endures, perhaps in a modified form, even after all the information has been published or is ascertainable by the public; for the recipient must not use the communication as a springboard." Courts in various jurisdictions have held that one who is responsible for publicizing a trade secret can continue to be enjoined from using it if it has become public through their own actions. *See, e.g., Conmar Products Co. v. Universal Slide Fastener Co.*, 172 F.2d 150, 156 (2d Cir. 1949) (L. Hand, J.). But is a misappropriator bound not to use a trade secret even after it is made public by a third party? At least one US court has held that in such a situation, the misappropriator should continue to be enjoined for the duration of the "headstart" period, *i.e.*, the full length of time his or her misappropriation saved in developing the product or information lawfully. *See Winston Research Corp. v. Minnesota Mining & Manufacturing Co.*, 350 F.2d 134 (9th Cir. 1965).

In the famous US case of *Warner-Lambert Pharmaceutical Co. v. John J. Reynolds, Inc.*, 178 F. Supp. 655 (S.D.N.Y. 1959), an obligation to pay royalties for use of a trade secret – for a mouthwash formula – was held to survive the eventual disclosure of the trade secret, under the terms of the trade secret licensing agreement between the parties.

On duties created when parties are negotiating a contract – but have not yet agreed to one – see E. Allan Farnsworth, *Precontractual Liability and Preliminary Agreements: Fair Dealing and Failed Negotiations*, 87 Colum. L. Rev. 217 (1987); Juliet P. Kostritsky, *Bargaining with Uncertainty, Moral Hazard, and Sunk Costs: A Default Rule for Precontractual Negotiations*, 44 Hastings L.J. 621 (1993).

BGH, Decision dated May 10, 1995 – 1 StR 764/94 (LG Nürnberg-Fürth)

[This German case deals with the German unfair competition law, called the Gesetz gegen den unlauteren Wettbewerb, or UWG. The particular provision at issue is section 17 par. 2, which is one of the criminal penalty provisions of German unfair competition law. In this case it is used in connection with an allegation of commercial bribery as a means of obtaining information about competitive bids for heating equipment contracts. By bribing the officials who received competing bids, the defendant was able to bid just slightly lower and win the heating equipment contracts. The trade secret question is whether the competing bids were trade secrets of the third-party competitors. Section 17 of the UWG provides:

(2) Whoever for the purposes of competition, for personal gain, for the benefit of a third party, or with the intent of causing damage to the owner of the business, acquires or secures, without authorisation,

1. a trade or industrial secret
   a) by using technical means;

CASE *(continued)*

    b) by creating an embodied communication of the secret; or
    c) by removing an item in which the secret is embodied;
    or
2. without authorisation, uses or communicates to anyone a trade secret which he acquired through one of the communications referred to in subsection (1), or through an act of his own or of a third party pursuant to number 1, or which he has otherwise acquired or secured without authorisation

shall [be liable to imprisonment not exceeding three years or to a fine. UWG §17, available at http://www.gesetze-im-internet.de/englisch_uwg/englisch_uwg.html#p0169.]

[The District Court (LG) held that the defendant was in violation of illegal exploitation of a trade or industrial secret under §17 of the UWG; it announced a sentence of a year and eight months in prison. The court of appeals ruled:]

The offers of the parties to the tender [*i.e.*, bidding] process are to be defined as trade secrets for the tender inviting offices in the meaning of §17 UWG. According to the case law, this definition includes facts that are – to the visible will of the company owner – to be held secret, that are only known to a limited group of people and thereby not public and on which the company owner has a legitimate secrecy interest because the disclosure of the fact would be suitable to pose economic harm to the carrier of the secret.

None too strict requirements shall be attached to the manifestation of the desire for secrecy. In the individual case it shall be sufficient if this desire is apparent from the nature of the fact to be held secret.

These are the facts of the case at hand. It is apparent already from the purpose of the tender procedure that the incoming offers are to be held secret until the award of [contracts] because this is the only way to make sure that the tender inviting office will be able to pick the most favorable offer out of various independently placed offers. An early disclosure of the receiving offers is at risk of leading to price-rigging and similar manipulations and thereby to distort competitive market conditions.

The offers of the competitors of the defendant were not public but only known to a small circle of employees of the relevant [construction] agency.

The defendant has fulfilled the requirements for commercial bribery according to §12 I UWG [the bribery provision of the UWG] and for illegal exploitation of trade secrets according to §17 II No. 2 UWG. §17 II No. 2 UWG is a dual crime, at which the illegal exploitation of a trade or industrial secret must be preceded by the illegal obtaining of the same. The obtaining of secret information was, however, effected by commercial bribery, while unjust enrichment and granting of undue advantage are for their part constituting the crime. Thereby, the manner in which the defendant illegally obtained knowledge of the secret fulfills at the same time the requirements of §§12 I and 17 II No. 2 UWG.

NOTES

1. As mentioned earlier, because there are severe limits on discovery requests in most civil suits, a trade secret action which relies on access to the defendant's records will often be pursued as a criminal matter in Germany. Notice, however, that criminal penalties may follow from a finding of guilt or liability in such a case. When do you believe misappropriation of information warrants a prison sentence? How does a criminal prosecution differ from a civil case in terms of the incentives of the plaintiff (or criminal complainant)? (Recall that criminal fines normally are payable to the state and not to the private party complainant.)

2. A construction company which receives bids surely understands that they are to be kept confidential until all competing bids are received and the contract is awarded (typically to the lowest bidder). The court here extends this duty of confidentiality to other bidders, insofar as bribery to obtain bids is treated as a knowing violation of the trade secret rights of other bidders. Is this duty on the bidders and the recipient of the bids (the construction company) a matter of contract law, or of some other general duty that arises in the situation? Contract formation in the bidding context can be somewhat complex because a bidder does not know whether its bid is the lowest until the contract is awarded; is the bid to be treated as an offer to make a contract? An agreement to contract contingent on a later condition (winning the bidding)? Can a construction company insist on an obligation to respect the trade secret status of other bids even though the individual bidders are not bound to the construction contract at the time they make their bids?

3. The EU Trade Secrets Directive requires Member States to provide "civil redress" for misappropriation claims. *See* Article 6. One can see the significance of this by comparing the German UWG section 17.2, at issue in this case, with Article 4 of the EU Trade Secrets Directive, which covers unlawful acquisition and use of a trade secret.

Article 4.2.

The acquisition of a trade secret without the consent of the trade secret holder shall be considered unlawful, whenever carried out by:

(a) unauthorised access to, appropriation of, or copying of any documents, objects, materials, substances or electronic files, lawfully under the control of the trade secret holder, containing the trade secret or from which the trade secret can be deduced;

(b) any other conduct which, under the circumstances, is considered contrary to honest commercial practices.

3. The use or disclosure of a trade secret shall be considered unlawful whenever carried out, without the consent of the trade secret holder, by a person who is found to meet any of the following conditions:

(a) having acquired the trade secret unlawfully;

(b) being in breach of a confidentiality agreement or any other duty not to disclose the trade secret;

(c) being in breach of a contractual or any other duty to limit the use of the trade secret.

Article 4.4.

The acquisition, use or disclosure of a trade secret shall also be considered unlawful whenever a person, at the time of the acquisition, use or disclosure, knew or ought, under the circumstances, to have known that the trade secret had been obtained directly or indirectly from another person who was using or disclosing the trade secret unlawfully within the meaning of paragraph 3.

The "personal gain" and "intent to damage" provisions of the German UWG (again: a criminal law provision) certainly have their counterpart in the EU Directive; but the emphasis in the Directive is on the acts of the misappropriator and the resulting harm to the trade secret owner, rather than on the intent and motive of the misappropriator. In a more general sense, is the unauthorized use of a trade secret more a harm to the state, the polity; or to a private person or company within the state?

23.2 Departing employees and noncompetition agreements

In addition to contractual restrictions on disclosure and misappropriation causes of action, US companies trying to prevent the use of confidential information by departing employees can rely on noncompetition agreements. These are separate agreements not to compete with a former employer, usually for a fixed number of years after leaving the company. Different states in the US treat these differently. Many "pro-employer" states enforce these agreements whenever they are deemed reasonable. *See, e.g., Comprehensive Technologies Int'l v. Software Artisans, Inc.*, 3 F.3d 730 (4th Cir. 1993). In California, however, a state statute prohibits these agreements entirely, except when a business is being acquired. *See Edwards v. Arthur Andersen LLP*, 81 Cal. Rptr. 3d 282 (Supreme Court of California 2008) (applying Business and Labor Code section 16600 to find a noncompete agreement partially unenforceable).

Noncompetition agreements are enforceable under various scenarios in many jurisdictions worldwide, though there are local variations that must be accounted for. In China, for example, a former employer that enforces a non-compete agreement against a departing employee must continue to pay the salary of the departing employee for the duration of the noncompete period. Under Judicial Interpretation IV of the Supreme People's Court on Several Issues Concerning the Application of Law in Hearing Labor Dispute Cases, if there is an agreement between an employer and an employee regarding post-employment compensation for a noncompete provision, their agreement prevails. If the agreement is silent on the amount of post-employment compensation for the noncompete provision, the employer must pay the employee compensation at 30 percent of the employee's average monthly salary in the 12 months before termination, or the local minimum wage, whichever is higher. This provision is perhaps less restrictive than it looks from the employer's point of view, however, because in general in China noncompetes are limited to senior officers and senior technicians/researchers (*id*).

Note too that the EU Trade Secrets Directive states clearly that there is room in the EU for national variation, and that the Directive is not meant to limit national laws on the question of noncompete agreements. EU Trade Secrets Directive, Recital 13: "This Directive should not be understood as restricting the freedom of establishment, the free movement of workers or the mobility of workers as provided for in Union law. Nor is it intended to affect the possibility of concluding noncompetition agreements between employers and employees, in accordance with applicable law."

For more on the US law relating to departing employees, *see* Section 24.1 below, and the case of *Specialized Technology Resources, Inc. v. JPS Elastomerics Corp.*, 80 Mass. App. Ct. 841, 842, 957 N.E.2d 1116, 1118 (2011).

23.2.1 China

Shanghai Furi Group Ltd. v. HUANG Ziyu, Chinese Supreme People's Court (2011) Minshenzi No. 122

Plaintiff (petitioner) Shanghai Furi Group Co. Ltd. ("Furi Group") was not satisfied with the judgment made by Shanghai High People's Court (appellate court), with regard to the trade secret misappropriation dispute with Defendants (respondents) HUANG Ziyu ("HUANG") and Shanghai Sofia Textile Co. Ltd. ("Sofia Textile"), and thus requested for a retrial before this court.

In 1996, Furi Group was jointly established by HUANG and his business partner GUAN. HUANG contributed 400,000 RMB to the company and held 40% of its equity. Furi Group was engaged in manufacturing and distribution of clothing and textile. HUANG was in charge of the management of the company as the Board supervisor and Vice General Manager.

On April 30, 2002, Furi Group accepted HUANG's resignation letter at a board meeting. During the same month, HUANG founded another company Sofia Textile with his other business partner. Sofia Textile was also engaged in the business of manufacturing and distribution of clothing and textiles.

In the beginning of 2002, Furi Group was in business relationship with Japan Forest Co. ("Forest Co."). After Sofia Textile was founded, Forest Co. began its business dealings with Sofia Textile based on its prior business relationship with HUANG.

[Plaintiff Furi Group claimed that HUANG's business relationship with Forest Co., immediately after his departure from Furi Group, violated Article 37 of Furi Group's by-laws and also Article 11 of the labor contract between Furi Group and HUANG, and also breached his obligation to keep the trade secrets confidential.]

Article 37 of Furi Group's by-laws state that, "Chairman, Board Supervisor and General Managers [of the Company] shall not disclose trade secrets mandated by law or identified by the Board." Article 11 of the labor contract ("Labor Contract") between HUANG and Furi Group states that: "Within five years after Party B (HUANG) terminates the Contract with Party A (Furi Group), Party B shall not establish any kind of business relationship with the existing clients of Party A. Otherwise, Party B shall be liable for Party B's financial damages."

CASE *(continued)*

On appeal, Shanghai High People's Court held that: one of the prerequisites to qualify as trade secret is the security measure adopted by the trade secret owner to maintain its confidentiality. Here, Furi Group alleged that HUANG and Sofia Co. misappropriated its trade secret by exploiting its trade information with Forest Co. through illegal means. To prove [the alleged trade information] as trade secrets, Furi Group must first prove that it has adopted protective measures to maintain the secrecy of such information. To prove this, Furi Group must provide evidence to prove that it has adopted reasonable, specific, and effective protective measures to keep the secrecy of this information. Examples of protective measures might include: limiting the number of employees with access to confidential information, locking up the information in safes, labeling the information as "confidential," and signing confidentiality agreements with employees and others. Here, there is no evidence that supports the finding that Furi Group has adopted such protective measures.

Furi Group argued that Article 11 of the Labor Contract with HUNAG was the protective measures that it adopted to maintain the confidentiality of the alleged trade secrets. Article 11(1) of the Labor Contract states: "Within five years after Party B (HUANG) terminates the Contract with Party A (Furi Group), Party B shall not establish any kind of business relationship with the existing clients of Party A. Otherwise, Party B shall be liable for Party B's financial damages." However, this clause neither spells out what information is categorized as trade secrets, nor specifies what specific information is HUANG obligated to keep confidential. Therefore, this clause should be interpreted as a non-compete clause instead. In addition, this clause only restricts HUANG's freedom in his employment options, but fails to address any compensation package that Furi Group should pay to HUANG for such restrictions. There is also no evidence that suggests that Furi Group paid any such compensation to HUNAG in return for his non-compete agreement. Therefore, Furi Group cannot refer to this clause as proof of its protective measures to keep the information secret.

[As such, Shanghai High People's Court issued a judgment (Hugaominsanzhizhongzi No. 45 (2010)) on August 16, 2010, dismissing the appeal filed by Furi Group and reaffirmed the judgment of the court of first instance.]

[The Supreme People's Court of China accepted the retrial application and rendered its opinion as follows.]

This Court found that, the Labor Contract signed between HUANG and Furi Group included a preamble that: "Pursuant to the Labor Law of the People's Republic of China and Regulations of Shanghai Municipality on Labor Contract, Party A and Party B enter into this contract based on principals of equality, voluntariness, harmony, and uniformity." Article 11 (1) of the Labor Contract states: "Within five years after Party B (HUANG) terminates the Contract with Party A (Furi Group), Party B shall not establish any kind of business relationship with the existing clients of Party A. Otherwise, Party B shall be liable for Party B's financial damages." The Labor Contract does not contain any specific clauses addressing trade secrets.

CASE *(continued)*

This Court held that the issues presented in the case include: (1) whether Article 11 (1) of the Labor Contract constitutes protective measures adopted by Furi Group to maintain the secrecy of its trade secrets . . . (2) . . .

1. Whether Article 11 (1) of the Labor Contract constitutes protective measures adopted by Furi Group to maintain the secrecy of its trade secrets Furi Group claims that the primary purpose of Article 11 (1) in the Labor Contract is to prevent HUANG from using the trade secrets that belonged to Furi Group to engage in competing textile import and export business, and therefore this clause is [a trade secret clause], rather than a non-compete clause. The issue then becomes whether such a clause constitutes "protective measures" required under Article 10 of Chinese Anti-Unfair Competition Law.

Article 10(3) of Chinese Anti-Unfair Competition Law requires that security measures be adopted by the right holder so as to qualify the information as trade secret. Article 11 of the *Judicial Interpretation of the Supreme People's Court on Some Issues Concerning the Application of Law in the Trial of Civil Cases Involving Unfair Competition* ("Judicial Interpretation") further define such "security measures" as "reasonable protective measures adopted by the right holder to prevent public disclosure of the information in accordance with the commercial value of such information should constitute." The following factors should be taken into consideration when courts determine whether the right holder has adopted security measures: the characteristics of the information carrier, the intent of the right holder to maintain confidentiality, the degree to which the confidentiality measures are recognizable, and accessibility of such information by others through legitimate means. Therefore, confidentiality measures, in accordance with Article 10 of Chinese Anti-Unfair Competition Law, should manifest the right holder's intent to maintain confidentiality, specify the scope of the information that is protected as trade secrets, notify the obligors of the right holder's intent and objective to maintain confidentiality, and be sufficient enough to prevent leaking of such confidential information under normal circumstances.

Here, Article 11 (1) of the Labor Contract neither specifies the scope of the information that is protected as trade secrets nor spells out the confidentiality obligations that HUANG needs to comply with. The Clause only restricts HUANG's freedom to do business with Furi Group's existing clients. It clearly does not constitute "security measure" required under Article 10 of Chinese Anti-Unfair Competition Law.

Non-compete agreements refer to the restrictions imposed on certain employees to prevent them from engaging in competing business fields with their employers. There are two types of non-compete scenarios: statutory and contractual non-compete arrangements. Statutory non-compete restrictions apply to board directors and senior officers as required by Chinese Company Law. They are generally in-service non-compete restrictions. Contractual non-compete restrictions, on the other hand, apply to employees through Chinese Contract Law and Chinese Labor Contract Law. They include both in-service non-compete restrictions and also post-employment non-compete restrictions.

In practice, non-compete agreements between employer and employee can be found in local regulations and ministry-level regulations. For instance, Article 23 of Chinese Labor

CASE *(continued)*

Contract Law, effective as of January 1, 2008, specifically mandates that: "*An employer and employee may have such terms stipulated in the labor contract, which require employees to keep confidential the trade secrets of the employer and also matters related to its intellectual property rights. With regard to the employee, who has an obligation to keep such information confidential, the employer may also include a non-compete clause in the labor contract or the confidentiality agreement. During the period when the departing employee is restricted to engage with competing business activities with that of the employer, the employer should make financial arrangements on a monthly basis to compensate for the departing employee. In case of the departing employee's breach of such non-compete agreements, he shall be liable for the financial damages suffered by the employer as agreed upon.*" This provision under Chinese Labor Contract Law was developed based upon Article 22 of Chinese Labor Law (effective as of January 1, 1995), which mandates that the parties to a labor contract may include in the labor contract matters concerning trade secrets. As a matter of fact, Article 23 of Chinese Labor Contract Law was developed and codified based on the recent development of the case law on this subject.

Non-compete agreements are generally enforceable in China. Its purpose is to protect the trade secrets and other legitimate interests of the employer. However, non-compete agreements are different from confidentiality agreements in nature. The former restricts the freedom of certain employees from engaging in competing businesses activities with their employers, while the latter requires employees to maintain the confidentiality of trade secrets owned by their employers. An employer is allowed to enter into a non-compete agreement with its employee, who has an obligation to maintain the confidentiality of the employer's trade secrets. A non-compete agreement therefore becomes a strategy to protect the employer's trade secrets. In other words, by restricting the freedom of certain employees, who have confidentiality obligations, to engage in competing business activities with that of the employer [for a limited period of time], the employer can prevent its departing employees from disclosing and using trade secrets to some extent. However, to be protected as trade secrets, the confidential information must meet all the elements of a trade secret, including the specific security measures adopted by the right holder, as required by Chinese Anti-Unfair Competition Law. Therefore, the mere existence of a non-compete agreement is not enough [to establish trade secrets.] Even if the purpose of the non-compete agreement is to protect the trade secrets owned by the employer, the agreement still does not constitute "security measures" adopted by the right holder, as required under Article 10 of Chinese Anti-Unfair Competition Law because such a agreement neither specified the specific intent of the employer to maintain confidentiality of its trade secrets nor defined the scope of the information that need to be protected as trade secrets.

As a result, we rejected Furi Group's application for retrial.

Chief Justice: JIN Kesheng
Justice: LANG Huimei
Justice: DU Weike
July 27, 2011
Clerk: ZHANG Bo

NOTES

1. In this case the Chinese Supreme Court addressed a very interesting issue related to trade secret protection: noncompetition agreements. The obligation not to compete arises from two scenarios: (1) the fiduciary duties of shareholders, officers, and directors not to compete with their own company, as required by Article 148(5) of the Chinese Company Law (revised in 2013); and (2) the contractual obligations of employees who agree not to compete with their employer in certain trade and/or geographic areas, within a limited time of their departure.
2. For the second type of noncompete arrangement, such agreements will be enforceable in China, if certain conditions are met, including (1) the noncompete agreement only applies to limited employees of a company, who are "senior managers, senior technicians and other persons who are under the confidentiality obligation to the employing unit"; (2) the period of noncompetition is not unreasonably long or burdensome (usually no more than three years); and (3) the employer must make financial compensation to such departing employees when their freedom to work is restricted (Art. 24 Chinese Labor Contract Law (2008) and Chinese Supreme People's Court Judicial Interpretation Regarding Application of Law on Labor Disputes (2013).

23.3 The reverse engineering defense

All trade secret protection schemes give some sort of defense or privilege to reverse engineering. This is generally defined as figuring out the design or operation or content of the trade secret owner's information using public information or by access to the owner's product, acquired in a public manner on the open market. *See, e.g., Kadant, Inc. v. Seeley Machine, Inc.*, 244 F. Supp. 2d 19 (N.D.N.Y. 2003). *See also Hotels Corp. v. Choice Hotels Int'l*, 995 F.2d 1173, 1177 (2nd Cir. 1993) (once a product is put on the market and available to be inspected by those not under a confidentiality agreement, there can be no trade secret).

But when is information fairly acquired for purposes of reverse engineering? Consider one case, *Sasqua Group, Inc. v. Courtney*, No. CV 10-528 ADS AKT, 2010 WL 3613855 (E.D.N.Y. Aug. 2, 2010), report and recommendation adopted, No. 10-CV-528 ADS ETB, 2010 WL 3702468 (E.D.N.Y. Sept. 7, 2010), involving the database information held by the plaintiff Sasqua Group, an executive recruiter (or "headhunter") that was trying to prevent its former employee Courtney from starting a competing executive search firm:

> Plaintiffs assert that their trade secrets encompass "the confidential proprietary and competitively sensitive information about Sasqua's client contacts, their individual profiles, their hiring preferences, their employment backgrounds, and descriptions of previous interactions with client contacts". Sasqua maintained all of this information in a central database. The company had hired a computer technician to maintain the database. According to the Plaintiff,
>
>> The information in the database is the lifeblood of Sasqua's business. The database records reflect the company's ten years of contact-and-relationship-

building, which relationship-building is how Sasqua generates business. Such information is not available from a public source and it is not information that could be easily duplicated.

Plaintiffs have failed to prove that the general contact information for Sasqua clients is not readily ascertainable through outside sources, such as the Internet or telephone books, or directories of firms in the financial services industry, like the ones demonstrated by the Defendants at the hearing. Plaintiffs go on to argue, however, that with respect to specific names of individuals who are key persons in the chain of command for authorizing placements and obtaining business at these firms, such information cannot be so readily ascertained. Although Plaintiffs' counsel argued this point forcefully several times during the hearing, Plaintiffs nevertheless did not produce a single witness to provide sworn testimony supporting this contention or contradicting [defendant] Courtney's testimony in this regard, other than by generalized statements in [a] Declaration. Moreover, since the general contact information is readily ascertainable through other sources, and may therefore readily be used, "follow-up questions to the company in general would reveal the specific names, e-mail addresses, or phone numbers of individuals involved in the [hiring/placement] process for those companies." *Kadant, Inc.*, 244 F.Supp.2d at 36 (citing *Ability Search, Inc. v. Lawson*, 556 F.Supp. 9, 16 (S.D.N.Y. 1981) (executive placement firm not entitled to injunction with respect to information about corporate clients "since it failed to prove that defendants utilize any information about such clients which was not available from public sources or readily ascertainable by defendants in conducting their own business"). If these referenced sources did not directly disclose the appropriate contacts, further inquiry with those firms and further research on the Internet certainly would.

While contact information may be readily ascertainable through other sources, things such as purchasing histories or customer preferences may not. This information, however, is subject to the same logic employed above. The general contact information, at the very least, is readily ascertainable through other sources. Using other sources to obtain the general contact information, he or other agents of defendants may have simply asked the customers about their preferences. Defendants have alleged this, and the burden is on plaintiff to provide sufficient proof that this is not what occurred. Plaintiff has not done so.

If plaintiff had shown that this information was cultivated through great effort, time, and expense . . . the conclusion may not be so easily drawn. In this regard, plaintiff points only to the fact that the prospective customer database costs a great deal to buy/implement and maintain. The fact that the database itself, as a whole, costs a lot of money to maintain, implement, or buy is not enough. Noting the conclusion that the general contact information at this stage of litigation is not entitled to trade secret protection, the concern here is whether the specific contact information and/or purchasing histories are expensive to maintain. Plaintiff does not sufficiently prove that maintaining those specific contact names, together with e-mail addresses and/or phone numbers, cost a great deal of money and, in any event, it is difficult to see how it alone would. Thus, the customer databases, at this stage of the litigation, have not been sufficiently proven to be entitled to trade secret protection.

On the permissibility of reverse engineering in EU Member States after the adoption of the 2016 EU Trade Secrets Directive, see Recital 16 of the Directive:

> In the interest of innovation and to foster competition, the provisions of this Directive should not create any exclusive right to know-how or information protected as trade secrets. Thus, the independent discovery of the same know-how or information should remain possible. Reverse engineering of a lawfully acquired product should be considered as a lawful means of acquiring information, except when otherwise contractually agreed. The freedom to enter into such contractual arrangements can, however, be limited by law.

In the EU, reverse engineering is covered in the Trade Secrets Directive, Article 3:

> 1. The acquisition of a trade secret shall be considered lawful when the trade secret is obtained by any of the following means:
>
> (a) independent discovery or creation;
> (b) observation, study, disassembly or testing of a product or object that has been made available to the public or that is lawfully in the possession of the acquirer of the information who is free from any legally valid duty to limit the acquisition of the trade secret;
> (c) exercise of the right of workers or workers' representatives to information and consultation in accordance with Union law and national laws and practices;
> (d) any other practice which, under the circumstances, is in conformity with honest commercial practices.

Reverse engineering can be prohibited in some cases by contract, though there are limits to this strategy. A "label license" or "shrinkwrap contract" covering a good sold freely in the marketplace (such as an auto part, a kitchen appliance, or a child's toy) might state that "reverse engineering of this product is prohibited"; but there is little chance such a prohibition would be enforced. In a negotiated contract, involving a product or service that is not sold on the open market, or involving information not readily gleaned from the product, contractual restrictions are more generally accepted.

In addition to the rules regarding contracts, it should also be noted that reverse engineering is usually required to be accomplished through "proper means." For a case on this issue, see *Orthoflex, Inc. v. ThermoTek, Inc.*, 983 F. Supp. 2d 866 (N.D. Tex. 2013), where a manufacturer entered into a distributorship agreement with a distributor. The distributor sent the manufacturer's products to third parties that were hired to help the distributor copy the manufacturer's products. When the manufacturer found out it was being "squeezed out" by the distributor, it brought a suit for misappropriation. The manufacturer argued that the distributor's conduct was forbidden by the distributorship agreement, but the court ruled otherwise, holding that the agreement contained no express prohibition against reverse engineering. Even so, the court allowed the manufacturer to proceed in its suit on the theory that the distributor obtained confidential information regarding the function of the manufacturer's products by fraud. (The manufacturer said the distributor represented it had no intention of copying the product.) In its ruling the court pointed out that reverse engineering, to be permissible, must be conducted by proper means.

NOTES

1. In the well-known case of *Warner-Lambert Pharmaceutical Co. v. John J. Reynolds, Inc.*, 178 F. Supp. 655 (S.D.N.Y. 1959), the court dealt with an agreement to pay ongoing royalties for use of a secret formula for making mouthwash. The mouthwash formula eventually became known to the public; but the trade secret licensor argued that the licensee nevertheless had a perpetual obligation to pay royalties under the contract between the parties. The court agreed. The parties agreed on an exchange – early entry into the mouthwash market, in exchange for perpetual royalties – and the court was not unwilling to undo the exchange because the information had eventually become public.

2. To much the same effect is the German case of *Pankreaplex II*, KZR 7/79, GRUR 1980, 750, reported at IIC 1980 695. This case centered on a license agreement for a drug against stomach diseases. The plaintiff terminated the agreement after the death of the licensor, arguing that the drug formula had lost its secrecy when it was printed on the package and the instructions enclosed with the drug product. The German court said that an agreement to pay royalties for the use of secret know-how, not protected by special rights, for an unlimited period of time, does not exceed the scope of the licensed know-how as long as it maintains its secret character. As to the question of whether a formula for a drug has lost its secret character, the court said that the test was not whether a person skilled in the art could manufacture a drug equivalent in medical terms (based on the listed ingredients); but instead whether such a person could copy the process of manufacture using the original materials and following the same procedural steps. Using that test, there was much doubt that the formula for the drug had become public.

3. Is it possible to (a) obtain a valid patent, while (b) keeping some information related to the invention as a trade secret? In general, yes. *See, e.g., Port-a-Pour, Inc. v. Peak Innovations, Inc.*, No. 13-CV-01511-WYD-BNB, 2016 WL 7868828, at *6 (D. Colo. June 7, 2016) (concerning disclosures in US Patents 6,876,904, "Portable Concrete Plant Dispensing System" (to Neil J. Oberg and Jerome J. Daugherty, issued April 5, 2005); and 7,050,886 (to same inventors, issued May 23, 2006). The case dealt with a portable concrete dispenser that could be used to mix and deliver cement at construction sites in the field. Defendant argued that plaintiff's trade secret case must fail because all its trade secrets were disclosed in two patents that it held in the technology. The court said:

   > Thus, Plaintiff asserts that neither patent discloses any of its proprietary designs, software, vendor lists, part lists, specifications, or other data Plaintiff uses to build its own product lines. Further, not a single line of software code is disclosed in the patents. While the idea of an air slide is mentioned in the patents

(although not in the "claims" section), Plaintiff states that the patent does not provide any drawings, specification of material, specification of capacity of the blower, how much pressure to run the system with, or a single line of code controlling the air slide. Further, Plaintiff asserts that the information needed to build, integrate and operate the air slide component of Plaintiff's horizontal silos are trade secrets, and that this information is not disclosed or published in any patent. Plaintiff also notes that many of its proprietary designs, which are its trade secrets, are never mentioned in any patent. For example, Plaintiff's auxiliary bin is not patented, yet is considered to be trade secret per the parties' agreements. Similarly, Plaintiff's design for its low-profile dust filter product is not mentioned in any patent, and no measurements, angles, specifications for filter elements, specifications for pulsing frequency, specifications for materials, wiring diagrams, or any other design detail needed to build and operate the low-profile dust filter appear in any patent. Based on the foregoing, I deny Defendant's motion for summary judgment as to this issue.

24

Remedies

24.1 Injunctions: US

 CASE

Specialized Technology Resources, Inc. v. JPS Elastomerics Corp., 80 Mass. App. Ct. 841, 842, 957 N.E.2d 1116 (2011)

During the 1990s, the plaintiff, Specialized Technology Resources, Inc. (STR), developed an innovative method to produce a specialized encapsulant used in making solar cells. The defendant James P. Galica oversaw the project team within STR that developed the method. Galica left STR in June, 2005, and joined the defendant JPS Elastomerics Corp. (JPS) in September, 2006. Within a year after Galica joined JPS, it began marketing and producing an encapsulant product using a method substantially identical to the one developed by STR. STR commenced this action in the Superior Court, claiming, inter alia, breach of contract, misappropriation of trade secrets, and violation of G.L. c. 93A, §11. The common-law claims were tried to a jury, while the trial judge reserved the G.L. c. 93A claim to herself. In response to special verdict questions, the jury found that the method developed by STR is a trade secret, but that Galica and JPS did not misappropriate it. However, the judge concluded, on the same evidence, that Galica and JPS misappropriated the trade secret and that such misappropriation constituted an unfair and deceptive act or practice within the meaning of c. 93A. She directed entry of judgment awarding $1,075,556 in damages (which she trebled as authorized by the statute) and granting injunctive relief. She also awarded $3,902,595 in attorney's fees and $1,108,731 in costs.

STR manufactures plastic sheeting materials used to encapsulate solar cells, extruded from ethylene vinyl acetate (EVA). STR holds approximately twenty-five percent of the global market for EVA, due in significant measure to its development of "low shrink" EVA,4 which prevents premature deterioration of encapsulated solar cells exposed to the elements. STR developed its method for producing low shrink EVA following an intensive five-year research and design effort that began in late 1990.

[The trial court found the defendants Galica, the STR former employee, and JPS, the

CASE *(continued)*

ex-employee's new employer, liable for a violation of Massachusetts General Law §93, which prohibits deceptive trade practices; this is one of many state statutes that at least partially overlap with common law trade secret causes of action. The court of appeals affirmed the trial court holdings, and moved on to the issue of the remedies awarded by the trial court.]

As originally entered, the injunctive order directed JPS to refrain from use of the particular manufacturing process developed by STR that constituted the trade secret, but allowed it to continue producing EVA by what JPS represented were "conventional means." However, by order entered on January 27, 2011, following an evidentiary hearing directed to the appropriate scope of the injunction, the judge modified the injunction to prohibit production of low shrink EVA by any means for a period of five years (the injunction against use of STR's trade secret method is permanent). JPS contends that the scope of the injunction is overbroad, because it contends that its production of EVA using what it describes as "method 3" does not utilize STR's trade secret but instead relies solely on methods residing in the public domain. JPS separately contends that the evidence did not warrant entry of a permanent injunction against use of STR's trade secret process itself.

In fashioning the duration of an injunction against use of a trade secret manufacturing process, the Supreme Judicial Court has held that the amount of time necessary to reverse engineer the technology without improper use of trade secrets is relevant to determining the scope of any injunctive relief. *See Analogic Corp. v. Data Translation, Inc.*, [371 Mass. 643, 358 N.E.2d 804 (1976),] at 647–49, 358 N.E.2d 804. However, the trial judge in the present case specifically found that the low shrink EVA product is not susceptible of "reverse engineering," and her finding in that regard finds support in the record. The judge likewise found that STR's trade secret has not entered the public domain. We discern no error or abuse of discretion in the imposition of a permanent injunction against use of STR's trade secret.

The trial judge found that, under Galica's supervision, JPS was able to modify its production processes in a manner that utilized [plaintiff STR's] discovery about the causes of shrinkage, but which employed adjustments to the production sequences different from those incorporated in the particular method that constituted STR's trade secret method. Because the method developed by JPS derived from specialized knowledge brought by Galica from STR to JPS, and particularly because the evidence suggested that JPS would not have been able to develop such a method independently, the judge's order enjoining JPS from production of low shrink EVA by any means for a period of five years (a period equivalent to the time STR spent in development of its trade secret method) was justified.

[Injunction affirmed.]

 NOTES

1. The primary theory behind injunctions in US trade secrets cases is they ought to last as long as it would have taken the defendant to duplicate the information that was misappropriated. What does this tell you about the permanent injunction granted in the *Specialized Technology Resources* case? That the court did not

believe the defendant could ever have duplicated the technology, no matter how long it tried? Is this a vote of confidence in the superior inventive skills of the plaintiff? A finding that the specialized knowledge and personnel required for this research were so concentrated in the hands of the plaintiff that the defendant could never have pulled together the team and the background information to do this research?

2. The second part of the injunction that was upheld on appeal in this opinion prevents defendant JPS from using its modified EVA process for five years. This is based on a finding that the modified process differed from the STR (plaintiff) process in significant ways, so was not the same as the misappropriated process; but also, on a finding that the JPS modification was derived from and based on the basic STR process that was misappropriated. Given the permanent injunction granted here (and discussed just above in Note 1), the court must have believed that the JPS modification took less skill and know-how to develop than the basic STR process (which they were permanently enjoined from using); but that it would not be fair to permanently prevent JPS from using its modified process. Is this because the modified process was not derived in toto from STR? Because JPS contributed skill and know-how to making its modification? Or for some other reason?

24.2 China

The court in the *China Tianfu* case granted an injunction in favor of the trade secret holder. Recall the court's holding:

> In summary, this Court grants: (1) the declaratory judgment that the Tianfu Coke recipe and production process trade secret belongs to China Tianfu; (2) the injunctive relief of any further use of the trade secret by Pepsi Tianfu, and (3) the request for Pepsi Tianfu to immediately return the confidential material regarding the trade secret (*China Tianfu, supra*, Chapter 21).

In granting an injunction against "further use" of the formula by defendant Pepsi Tianfu, the court would appear to be duplicating the remedy awarded by the Massachusetts court in the *STR* case. But perhaps not: What if Pepsi Tianfu develops a new version of the China Tianfu Coke formula without having access to the proprietary formula that was misappropriated? The injunction is against further use of the formula – and not against any use of an independently developed substitute for the formula. The order to return the "confidential material" supports this view; if a rival formula is developed without benefit of plaintiff's trade secrets, it would be considered proper "reverse engineering" and not improper misappropriation.

24.3 European Union

The EU now requires a uniform set of remedies, very much along the lines of US and Chinese measures.

Injunctions under the EU Trade Secrets Directive are required under Article 12:

Injunctions and corrective measures

> 1. Member States shall ensure that, where a judicial decision taken on the merits of the case finds that there has been unlawful acquisition, use or disclosure of a trade secret, the competent judicial authorities may, at the request of the applicant, order one or more of the following measures against the infringer:
>
> (a) the cessation of or, as the case may be, the prohibition of the use or disclosure of the trade secret;
> (b) the prohibition of the production, offering, placing on the market or use of infringing goods, or the importation, export or storage of infringing goods for those purposes;
> (c) the adoption of the appropriate corrective measures with regard to the infringing goods;
> (d) the destruction of all or part of any document, object, material, substance or electronic file containing or embodying the trade secret or, where appropriate, the delivery up to the applicant of all or part of those documents, objects, materials, substances or electronic files (EU Trade Secrets Directive, Article 12).

Article 12.2.c says that one "corrective measure" that may be ordered is destruction of infringing goods, or withdrawal of the goods from the market. Article 12.4 requires these measures to be paid for by the infringing party.

In an explanatory note, the Directive includes this concerning duration of injunctions:

> [Regarding] duration, when circumstances require a limitation in time, should be sufficient to eliminate any commercial advantage which the third party could have derived from the unlawful acquisition, use or disclosure of the trade secret. In any event, no measure of this type should be enforceable if the information originally covered by the trade secret is in the public domain for reasons that cannot be attributed to the respondent (EU Trade Secrets Directive, at Recital 27).

Note also the provision calling for prohibition on imports in appropriate cases, paragraph 28: "Considering the global nature of trade, it is also necessary that such measures [*i.e.*, remedies] include the prohibition of the importation of those goods into the Union or their storage for the purposes of offering or placing them on the market."

24.4 Damages

24.4.1 United States

The UTSA includes this provision on damages:

§3 Damages

(a) Except to the extent that a material and prejudicial change of position prior to acquiring knowledge or reason to know of misappropriation renders a monetary recovery inequitable, a complainant is entitled to recover damages for misappropriation. Damages can include both the actual loss caused by misappropriation and the unjust enrichment caused by misappropriation that is not taken into account in computing actual loss. In lieu of damages measured by any other methods, the damages caused by misappropriation may be measured by imposition of liability for a reasonable royalty for a misappropriator's unauthorized disclosure or use of a trade secret.

(b) If willful and malicious misappropriation exists, the court may award exemplary damages in an amount not exceeding twice any award made under subsection (a).

The elements of "actual loss" and "unjust enrichment" are more commonly known as "plaintiff's lost profits" and "defendant's gain from infringing acts." When a plaintiff seeks to recover the defendant's gain, the usual approach is for the plaintiff to establish the defendant's total profits from the infringing product, and then for the defendant to prove the portions of its profits that are not attributable to the misappropriated information. The plaintiff must establish its estimate of the defendant's profits with some precision, however. *See Elcor Chem. Corp. v. Agri-Sul, Inc.*, 494 S.W.2d 204, 214 (Tex.App.-Dallas 1973, writ ref'd n.r.e.); *Carbo Ceramics, Inc. v. Keefe*, 166 F. App'x 714, 722 (5th Cir. 2006) (defendant's profit estimates were based on overly speculative projections, and therefore do not provide an adequate basis for assessing trade secret damages).

In general, a wide variety of expert evidence is permitted to establish each of these elements. *See, e.g., Yeti by Molly, Ltd. v. Deckers Outdoor Corp.*, 259 F.3d 1101 (9th Cir. 2001) (jury's award of almost $2 million in compensatory damages for misappropriation of trade secrets in design elements of boot was supported by testimony of plaintiffs' expert that plaintiffs suffered $8,062,099 in lost opportunities to license their trade secrets to other footwear manufacturers).

A particularly detailed treatment of damages can be found in the American Law Institute's Restatement (3rd) of Unfair Competition Law, at section 45:

> (1) One who is liable to another for an appropriation of the other's trade secret under the rules stated in section 40 is liable for the pecuniary loss to the other caused by the appropriation or for its own pecuniary gain resulting from the appropriation, whichever is greater, unless such relief is inappropriate under the rule stated in subsection (2).
>
> (2) Whether an award of monetary relief is appropriate and the appropriate method of measuring such relief depend upon a comparative appraisal of all of the factors of the case, including the following primary factors:
>
> (a) the degree of certainty with which the plaintiff has established the fact and the extent of its pecuniary loss or the defendant's pecuniary gain resulting from the appropriation;
> (b) the nature and extent of the appropriation;
> (c) the relative adequacy to the plaintiff of other remedies;
> (d) the intent and knowledge of the defendant and the nature and extent of any good faith reliance on the trade secret by the defendant;
> (e) any unreasonable delay by the plaintiff in bringing suit or asserting its rights; and
> (f) any related misconduct on the part of the plaintiff.

Under the case law interpreting the UTSA, damages can be assessed even though the misappropriating party does not incorporate the information into a commercial product. Simply posting the information on the internet is enough to destroy its value, for example, and thus to justify the award of damages under the UTSA. *See Religious Technology Center v. Netcom On-Line Communication Services, Inc.*, 923 F. Supp. 1231 (N.D. Cal. 1995).

24.4.2 China

Article 20 of the PRC Unfair Competition law provides for damages:

> A business operator who violates the provisions of this Law and thus causes damage to the infringed business operators, shall bear the liability of compensation for the damage. If the losses of the infringed business operator are difficult to estimate, the damages shall be the profits derived from the infringement by the infringer during the period of infringement. And the infringer shall also bear the reasonable expense paid by the infringed business operator for investigating the infringer's unfair competition acts violating his lawful rights and interests.

Article 25 also provides for the possibility of administrative penalties, prevention orders and fines to be levied by the government inspection service:

> In case a business operator violates the provisions of Article 10 of this Law and infringes upon trade secrets, the supervision and inspection department shall order the ceasing of the illegal acts and may impose a fine of not less than 10,000 yuan but not more than 200,000 yuan in light of the circumstances.

24.4.3 European Union

As for damages in the EU, the relevant provision is EU Trade Secrets Directive, Article 14:

> 1. Member States shall ensure that the competent judicial authorities, upon the request of the injured party, order an infringer who knew or ought to have known that he, she or it was engaging in unlawful acquisition, use or disclosure of a trade secret, to pay the trade secret holder damages appropriate to the actual prejudice suffered as a result of the unlawful acquisition, use or disclosure of the trade secret.
>
> Member States may limit the liability for damages of employees towards their employers for the unlawful acquisition, use or disclosure of a trade secret of the employer where they act without intent.
>
> 2. When setting the damages referred to in paragraph 1, the competent judicial authorities shall take into account all appropriate factors, such as the negative economic consequences, including lost profits, which the injured party has suffered, any unfair profits made by the infringer and, in appropriate cases, elements other than economic factors, such as the moral prejudice caused to the trade secret holder by the unlawful acquisition, use or disclosure of the trade secret.
>
> Alternatively, the competent judicial authorities may, in appropriate cases, set the damages as a lump sum on the basis of elements such as, at a minimum, the amount of royalties or fees which would have been due had the infringer requested authorisation to use the trade secret in question.

NOTES

1. The EU Trade Secrets Directive provides a coherent rationale, plus suggested measures, for awarding trade secret damages:

    > The amount of damages awarded to the injured trade secret holder should take account of all appropriate factors, such as loss of earnings incurred by the trade secret holder or unfair profits made by the infringer and, where appropriate, any moral prejudice caused to the trade secret holder. As an alternative, for example where, considering the intangible nature of trade secrets, it would be difficult to determine the amount of the actual prejudice suffered, the amount of the damages might be derived from elements such as the royalties or fees which would have been due had the infringer requested authorisation to use the trade secret in question. (EU Trade Secrets Directive, Recital 30)

2. There is some interesting case law in Britain on compensation for a trade secret owner when the trade secret is used as a "springboard" to an improvement or modification that proves profitable for the infringer. A case in point is *Vestergaard Frandsen A/S (now called MVF 3 Aps) v. Bestnet Europe Ltd*, [2017] F.S.R. 5, [2016] EWCA [England and Wales Court of Appeals, Civil Division] Civ 541, [2017] Fleet Street Reports 5, 2–4 March and 13 June 2016.

> It [is] a matter of degree whether the extent and importance of the use of the confidential information was such that continued exploitation of the derived matter should be viewed as continued use of the information. ([86]) *Vercoe v. Rutland Fund Management Ltd* [2010] EWHC 424 (Ch) and *Ocular Sciences Ltd v. Aspect Vision Care Ltd (No.2)* [1997] R.P.C. 289, referred to.
>
> When considering the damages flowing from sales of products which themselves misused confidential information, or which were a camouflaged use of confidential information, it was legitimate to ask whether the defendant's sales caused the claimant to lose sales, and to award lost profits in respect of the claimant's lost sales. Similarly, given that such sales were to be treated as making use of confidential information, it was legitimate to award a reasonable royalty in respect of each such sale. That approach was not automatically legitimate, however, when considering derived products. The act which gave rise to the harm in question was no longer the sale of the defendant's product, because that sale was not itself a wrongful act. In such cases, it was necessary instead to determine what recoverable harm could be traced back to the initial wrongful use of the confidential information in order to develop the product.
>
> Save in rather extreme circumstances, where the misuse of confidential information had been a basis for developing a derived product which did not itself constitute a misuse, the consequences of the activity being wrongful were likely to be the acceleration or facilitation of lawful competition. In such a case the proper measure of damages was the extent to which the claimant had been harmed by having to face such competition sooner, or to a greater extent than it otherwise might.
>
> [Therefore,] [t]here was no basis on which the Court of Appeal could properly interfere with the judge's multifactorial assessment of the six-month delay to the development project.

Part VI

Design protection

25
Introduction

25.1 Design and product appeal

This chapter covers legal protection for product design. Design refers to the appearance and shape of products: everything from shoes to toys to kitchen appliances to tools and beyond.

Compared to technical features, price, and other more measurable aspects of product performance, design seems amorphous and illusive. Yet extensive research establishes that the hard-to-define "look and feel" of a product is often *the essential* feature that makes it attractive to consumers. Critics and skeptics may scoff at it, but by one objective measure, design is an absolutely crucial feature of contemporary consumer products. What measure is that? The market. The simple fact, which has been established over and over, is that in the crowded modern marketplace, design sells. Skeptics may not understand it. But consumers unquestionably appreciate it. Empirical research confirms what design-conscious brand experts have long maintained: Superior design leads to sustained, higher profits. Consider, for example, one study which found a close relationship between superior product design and corporate financial performance:

> This analysis reveals that firms rated as having "good" design were stronger on [almost] all measures [of financial performance]. These results provide strong evidence that good industrial design is related to corporate financial performance and stock market performance even after considering expenditures on industrial design. Further, the patterns of financial performance over the seven-year horizon suggest that these effects are persistent (Julie H. Hertenstein, *The Impact of Industrial Design Effectiveness on Corporate Financial Performance*, 22 J. Prod. Innov. Manag. 3, 3 (2005).

Why does design work to sell products? The answers vary, but enhanced product distinctiveness is the common thread:

> The form or design of a product may contribute to its success in several ways. First, in cluttered markets, product form is one way to gain consumer notice . . . Yoplait

> yogurt successfully entered a competitive market by using a container that was narrower at the top than at the bottom, the opposite of every other yogurt package. Swatch used a variety of unusual product forms to successfully stand out in the mature market for wristwatches. With new product offerings, a distinctive design can render older competitors immediately obsolete and make later competitors appear to be shallow copies. For example, the Ford Taurus, launched in 1986 with a unique rounded shape, soon became one of the nation's best selling passenger cars . . . Product form creates the initial impression and generates inferences regarding other product attributes in the same manner as does price . . . For example, . . . [t]he first Apple Macintosh possessed a compact, simple form to communicate ease of use and an almost anthropomorphic friendliness . . . [P]roduct form also helps to develop corporate and brand identities . . . (Peter H. Bloch, *Seeking the Ideal Form: Product Design and Consumer Response*, 59 Journal of Marketing 16, 6 (1995), at 16).

On the importance of distinctive (re)designs for older, established products, see Jonlee Andrews & Daniel C. Smith, *In Search of the Marketing Imagination: Factors Affecting the Creativity of Marketing Programs for Mature Products*, 33 Journal of Marketing Research 174 (1996).

Another key point is that, from a marketing and design point of view, a product is perceived as the sum of its attributes. As one study said, "When designing new products, the goal is to give the product *physical and psychological attributes* that will lead to success in the market-place" (Darren W. Dahl et al., *The Use of Visual Mental Imagery in New Product Design*, 36 J. Marketing Res. 18, 19 (1999) (emphasis added; citing studies)). Another expert on the branding of product has said that a "genuine brand" is comprised of "an internalized sum of impressions" (Duane E. Knapp, The Brand Mindset, 7 (2000).

The design strategy of leading designers bears this out; they often break the design challenge into smaller parts, focusing first on one attribute, then on a second, and so on, until a holistic design takes shape (Kees Dorst and Nigel Cross, *Creativity in the Design Process: Co-Evolution of Problem-Solution*, 22 Design Studies 434 (2001).

The point is that though consumers perceive products to have a single, comprehensive "design," the design itself is usually composed of a whole series of smaller, more discrete attributes. All the components of a good design combine to create a single (hopefully favorable) impression in the mind of the consumer. As one standard text on product branding puts it, "[p]roducts are built in factories, brands are built in the mind" (Shaun Smith & Joe Wheeler,

Managing the Customer Experience: Turning Customers into Advocates 7 (2002). This has important ramifications for design patent law, where often a single design may be covered by multiple design patents on discrete aspects of a product.

A good example of successful design comes from Apple, Inc., maker of the iPhone, iPad, Apple Watch, etc. These products are often held out as the *paragon* of effective design. One proof of this is that the prestigious trade group Design and Advertising (D&AD) named Apple Computer the best design studio in the world over the past 50 years. *See* http://www.dezeen.com/2012/09/20/apple-named-best-design-studio-of-past-50-years-at-one-off-dad-awards/. The overall look and feel of Apple products is of course what makes them distinctive. But, as the studies referred to here establish so clearly, this overall impression is made up of many, sometimes small, design elements and components.

25.1.1 Is IP protection necessary for innovative designs?

Under some approaches to IP law, the fact that design is important to consumers is enough, by itself, to establish the need for legal protection of design elements. So, for example, in France, where the "unity of art" principle has long been paramount, creativity in consumer design has equal respect as artistic creations such as paintings, sculpture, and novels. *See Design Protection in Domestic and Foreign Copyright Law: From the Berne Revision of 1948 to the Copyright Act of 1976* [1983] Duke Law Journal 1143, 1155–62 (detailed account of origins and implications of French "unity of art" principle). For those who see IP law as more a question of costs and benefits, however, there is more to it. Does design protection lead to a larger number of high-quality designs, or is it better for overall social welfare to leave designs unprotected?

Advocates of the latter view – that IP is best left out of at least some design fields – argue that the evidence shows greater creativity and faster innovation cycles when IP is absent from the scene. *See, e.g.,* Kal Raustiala & Christopher Sprigman, The Knockoff Economy (2012).

Regardless of the ideal solution, in various design-intensive fields such as fashion clothing, designers make use of design protection in jurisdictions where it is available. *See, e.g.,* EUIPO DesignView Database, Locarno Classification 02.02 (Articles of Clothing/Haberdashery; Garments) (showing nearly 3,000 clothing designs registered in the EUIPO that designate the United Kingdom as a country of protection), available at https://www.tmdn.org/tmdsview-web/welcome. And in the US, where there is no specific system of design protection, fashion designers often lament the lack of more effective protection. So, for example, in C. Scott Hemphill & Jeannie Suk, *The Law, Culture, and Economics of Fashion*, 61 Stanford Law Review, 1147–55 (2009), the authors note that the fashion industry is a $200 billion per year field (*id.*, at 1148 n. 1 (citing "The U.S. Apparel Market 2007 Dresses Up . . . Way Up," Bus. Wire, Mar. 18, 2008)).

Among fashion accessories, considering just one category, handbags, adds another $5 billion in sales (Tanya Krim, There's Nothing "Trivial" About the Pursuit of the Perfect Bag, Brandweek, Mar. 29, 2007 (reporting US sales exceeding $5 billion in 2005)). The author argues that the fashion industry itself seems quite motivated to *remedy* the absence of IP protection:

> The adverse effects of copying explain why many [fashion] designers oppose copying, just as they oppose counterfeiting of handbags. ([The negative space] argument, if correct, ought to apply to fashion trade-marks and copyrights as well.) [Raustiala and Sprigman] pitch their paradox as an explanation for the otherwise puzzling equanimity with which designers greet copyists. But that premise is faulty. In fact, many designers are vocal advocates against copying, and . . . make use of the currently limited legal tools available to curb copyists (*id.*, at 1183).

Support for this point can be found in an empirical study of copyright litigation in the US between 2005 and 2008: Christopher A. Cotropia & James Gibson, *Copyright's Topography: An Empirical Study of Copyright Litigation*, 92 Tex. L. Rev. 1981, 1992–93 (2014) (showing that the largest share of copyright litigation, by industry, was in the "Apparel/Fashion/Textile" industry, at 13.58 percent of all litigation in the study). *See generally* Alexandra Mackey, *Made in America: A Comparative Analysis of Copyright Law Protection for Fashion Design in Asia and the United States*, 1 Am. U. Bus. L. Rev. 368 (2012).

In addition to enforcement using the established (though flawed) legal tools available, fashion designers in the US have been active in lobbying for various new forms of design protection. *See, e.g.*, Aya Eguchi, Note, *Curtailing Copycat Couture: The Merits of the Innovative Design Protection And Piracy Prevention Act and A Licensing Scheme for the Fashion Industry*, 97 Cornell Law Review 131, 145 (2011) ("A design protection bill from 2010) garnered support from several well-known designers and the Council of Fashion Designers of America (CFDA) – the creative core of the fashion industry . . ."). This lobbying effort is perhaps the best indicator that innovative firms are indeed not satisfied with the current copying-centric equilibrium in the fashion industry. As a number of scholars have noted, in fact, the speed and ease of copying have created a significant threat to the livelihoods of creative fashion designers, making future lobbying more likely (Susan Scafidi, *F.I.T.: Fashion as Information Technology*, 59 Syracuse Law Review 69–81 (2008)).

As with many other industries, as the value of the creative products increases the calls for strengthened IP protection increases as well. It may not be long until we see greater harmonization in the realm of fashion design protection, and perhaps also protection for designs in all fields.

25.1.2 Practicalities of securing protection

There are two different ways to secure protection for a creative design. The first is through copyright or trademark. Designs for elements of various products are protectable this way, though in each case adjustments are necessary because these traditional forms of protection did not originate as ways to protect product design. So, for example, the visual elements of product design must usually be separated from the underlying functional or useful article for copyright to apply. And trade dress protection, under trademark law, will attach only if it can be shown that the shape or other design features sought to be protected have come to indicate a unique seller or product source.

The second form of protection is specifically aimed at designs. Under many national legal systems, some form of design-specific protection is available. It may take the form of a design registration, "utility model," or "petty patent." Or it may take the form of a design patent, as in the US. Now, within the EU, a Registered Community Design (RCD) may be obtained either by a national filing in an EU country or in the central EUIPO office in Alicante, Spain.

In addition to the RCD, a true international filing is also possible for design protection. The "international layer" for design protection is, however, quite thin. Through an Agreement called the Hague Convention, it is possible to register a design with the World Intellectual Property Organization (WIPO). *See* http://www.wipo.int/hague/en/. A Hague System filing is then available to be used as a design application in any of the 64 countries that belong to the Convention. One positive feature of a Hague System filing is that it may include up to 100 different design variations. However, the volume of filings under this system is quite low. The total number of applications in 2016 was 552, which disclosed a total of 18,716 designs. Usage was dominated by Germany and Switzerland, then the Republic of Korea, the US, and the Netherlands. Under the Hague System, a registrant must choose which national design systems he or she will seek protection in at the time of filing. In 2016, the EU was the most designated system. Thus through a Hague registration, an applicant can initiate design protection in the EU-wide EUIPO office, as well as in other national offices.

The chapters that follow describe in detail the requirements for a valid design under traditional and design-specific protection systems in the US, China, and the EU. Infringement standards, defenses (primarily the defense of functionality) and remedies are also covered.

26
Subject matter and originality requirements

26.1 United States

26.1.1 Design patents

26.1.1.1 Ornamental features and functionality

CASE

Ethicon Endo-Surgery, Inc. v. Covidien, Inc., 796 F.3d 1312 (Fed. Cir. 2015) (Chen, J.)

The patents-in-suit are directed to surgical instruments that use ultrasonic energy created by blades vibrating at high frequencies to cut tissue and blood vessels. These surgical instruments also use the heat generated from the friction of the blade vibrating against the blood vessel to coagulate and seal those blood vessels in order to prevent bleeding. Ethicon develops, manufactures, and sells such ultrasonic surgical instruments. After Covidien launched a competing line of ultrasonic surgical equipment, Ethicon sued Covidien, alleging infringement of the design patents at issue in this appeal. [There were also utility patents at issue but that portion of the opinion is excluded here. The design patent at issue includes an illustration of the surgical instrument (Figure 1[26.1])]

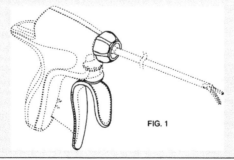

Figure 26.1 Ethicon's Patented Instrument Design

CASE *(continued)*

[T]he district court determined that under each consideration for assessing functionality identified in *PHG Technologies v. St. John Companies*, 469 F.3d 1361, 1366 (Fed. Cir. 2006), Ethicon's claimed designs were dictated by function.

[In this opinion,] [w]e reverse the district court's grant of invalidity [of the design patents] based on functionality. The district court evaluated the claimed designs using too high a level of abstraction, focusing on the unclaimed utilitarian aspects of the underlying article instead of the claimed ornamental designs of that underlying article. We affirm, however, the district court's grant of summary judgment of noninfringement of the Design Patents. After the functional aspects of the claimed designs are properly excluded from the infringement analysis, the claimed ornamental designs are plainly dissimilar from the ornamental design of Covidien's accused products.

Articles of manufacture necessarily serve a utilitarian purpose, but design patents are directed to ornamental designs of such articles. 35 U.S.C. §171. If a particular design is essential to the use of an article, it cannot be the subject of a design patent. [*L.A. Gear, Inc. v. Thom McAn Shoe Co.*, 988 F.2d 1117, 1123 (Fed. Cir. 1993)], at 1123. We have found designs to be essential to the use of an article when the claimed design is "dictated by" the use or purpose of the article. *Id.* Design patents on such primarily functional rather than ornamental designs are invalid. In determining whether a claimed design is primarily functional, "[t]he function of the article itself must not be confused with 'functionality' of the design of the article." *Hupp v. Siroflex of Am., Inc.*, 122 F.3d 1456, 1462 (Fed. Cir. 1997). In *Hupp*, we separated the function inherent in a concrete mold – producing a simulated stone pathway by molding concrete – from the particular pattern of the stone produced by the mold itself – an aesthetic design choice. *Id.* at 1461. Thus, even though the claimed design pattern was embedded within the functional concrete mold, the proper analysis required a determination of whether the design pattern within the mold – and not the concrete mold itself – was "dictated by" its function. Because there was no utilitarian reason the mold had to impress the particular claimed rock walkway pattern into the concrete, we determined that the claimed design was "primarily ornamental," and not invalid as functional. *Id.*

Here, the district court appeared to discount the existence and availability of alternative designs in determining that the claimed Design Patents were "primarily functional" based on its evaluation of the five considerations identified in *PHG*, 469 F.3d at 1366 (quoting [*Berry Sterling Corp. v. Pescor Plastics, Inc.*, 122 F.3d 1452, 1455 (Fed. Cir. 1997)] at 1456). In *Berry Sterling*, we vacated and remanded a district court's grant of summary judgment of invalidity where it had failed to "elicit the appropriate factual underpinnings for a determination of invalidity of a design patent due to functionality." 122 F.3d at 1454. In our instructions on remand, we explained that where the existence of alternative designs is not dispositive of the invalidity inquiry, the district court may look to several other factors for its analysis:

> [W]hether the protected design represents the best design; whether alternative designs would adversely affect the utility of the specified article; whether there are any concomitant utility

CASE *(continued)*

patents; whether the advertising touts particular features of the design as having specific utility; and whether there are any elements in the design or an overall appearance clearly not dictated by function.

Id. at 1456. We explained that evaluating these other considerations "might" be relevant to assessing whether the overall appearance of a claimed design is dictated by functional considerations. *Id.* Thus, while the Berry Sterling factors can provide useful guidance, an inquiry into whether a claimed design is primarily functional should begin with an inquiry into the existence of alternative designs.

Ethicon presented evidence of alternative ornamental designs that could provide the same or similar functionality of the underlying ultrasonic shears. For example, Ethicon's expert testified that "there [we]re many different designs that would function just as well" as the designs claimed in the Design Patents. Ethicon's expert also identified multiple alternative designs for hand-held surgical devices in the prior art.

The foregoing evidence does not support the district court's grant of summary judgment that the claimed designs are primarily functional for two reasons. First, the district court's determination that the designs did not work "equally well" apparently describes the preferences of surgeons for certain basic design concepts, not differences in functionality of the differently designed ultrasonic shears. For example, in supporting its conclusion that alternative designs "would not have worked as well" as the claimed design, the district court pointed to testimony that surgeons preferred ultrasonic shears with certain basic design features like activation buttons on the front, rather than the rear of the device, "open" triggers, rather than closed or loop-style triggers, and forward positions, as opposed to other positions, for placement of the torque knob. Second, to be considered an alternative, the alternative design must simply provide "the same or similar functional capabilities." Here, there is no dispute that the underlying ultrasonic shears could still function in the same manner with a differently-shaped open trigger, activation button, and torque knob, and different relative locations of the trigger, button, and torque knob.

Covidien has not shown by clear and convincing evidence that no designs other than those claimed in the Design Patents allow the underlying ultrasonic shears to perform their intended function. Indeed, the evidence in the record leads to the opposite conclusion. We therefore conclude the district court clearly erred in finding that Ethicon's patented designs are dictated by functional considerations and are therefore invalid as primarily functional. [The court went on to find that although the design patents were not invalid for functionality, they were also not infringed by the surgical instrument sold by defendant Covidien.]

NOTES

In *Best Lock Corp. v. IlcoUnican Corp.*, 94 F.3d 1563 (Fed. Cir. 1996), the plaintiff Best Lock obtained a design patent on a key blade (see Figure 26.2):

Figure 26.2 Patented key blade design

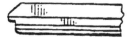

The court affirmed a district court finding that the keyblade was functional, and therefore not protectable with the design patent Best Lock had obtained (design patent number 327,636):

> The design shown in the claim of the '636 patent is limited to a blank key blade. Best Lock did not claim a design for the entire key. The parties do not dispute that the key blade must be designed as shown in order to perform its intended function – to fit into its corresponding lock's keyway. An attempt to create a key blade with a different design would necessarily fail because no alternative blank key blade would fit the corresponding lock. In fact, Best Lock admitted that no other shaped key blade would fit into the corresponding keyway, and it presented no evidence to the contrary. Therefore, we find no clear error in the court's finding that the claimed key blade design was dictated solely by the key blade's function. Any aesthetic appeal of the key blade design shown in the '636 patent is the inevitable result of having a shape that is dictated solely by functional concerns (94 F.3d 1563, at 1566).

CASE

Door-Master Corp. v. Yorktowne, Inc., 256 F.3d 1308 (Fed. Cir. 2001)

[The design in this case is for a cabinet door. It has the appearance of a door that is set within a frame, called in the trade an inset-mounted door; but it is not in fact inset-mounted. It is instead overlay mounted: it covers the cabinet frame. Overlay mounted doors are less appealing visually but easier to install. Thus the purpose of the design: to create the appealing appearance of an inset-mounted door in a door that is in fact an overlay mounted door. Figure 26.3 shows the design, the subject of U.S. Design Patent 338,718.]

Figure 26.3 Patented cabinet door design

[The district court found plaintiff Door-Master's '718 patent both valid and infringed, and awarded damages. Defendant Yorktowne appealed. Conestoga argued on appeal that one of

CASE *(continued)*

its own overlay-mounted but inset-mounted-appearing cabinet door models, the CRP-10 model, was prior art against the '718 design patent.]

As with a utility patent, design patent anticipation requires a showing that a single prior art reference is "identical in all material respects" to the claimed invention. *Hupp v. Siroflex of Am., Inc.,* 122 F.3d 1456, 1461 (Fed. Cir. 1997). Because "[t]hat which infringes, if later, would anticipate, if earlier," *Peters v. Active Mfg. Co.,* 129 U.S. 530, 537 (1889), the design patent infringement test also applies to design patent anticipation. That test requires the court to first construe the claimed design, if appropriate, and then to compare the claimed design to the article. *OddzOn Prods., Inc. v. Just Toys, Inc.,* 122 F.3d 1396, 1404 (Fed. Cir. 1997).

In construing the claimed design, this court first notes that only "the non-functional aspects of an ornamental design as shown in a patent" are proper bases for design patent protection. *KeyStone Retaining Wall Sys., Inc. v. Westrock, Inc.,* 997 F.2d 1444, 1450 (Fed. Cir. 1993). In addition, "generally concealed features are not proper bases for design patent protection because their appearance cannot be a 'matter of concern.'" *Id.* at 1451.

In the second step of the test for infringement or anticipation, the court compares the claim to the accused or allegedly anticipating article. For infringement or anticipation to be found the two designs must be substantially the same. *Gorham Mfg. Co. v. White,* 81 U.S. (14 Wall.) 511, 528 (1871). Two designs are substantially the same if their resemblance is deceptive to the extent that it would induce an ordinary observer, giving such attention as a purchaser usually gives, to purchase an article having one design supposing it to be the other. *Id.* In making this comparison, the court must focus on the protected features of the design, and determine whether those common features would deceive the ordinary observer.

The front of the CRP-10 end panel and the front of the CRP-10 inset door and frame look very similar to the design features shown in the '718 patent. However, the CRP-10 door is mounted on hinges that are visible from the front when the door is closed. The '718 patent shows no such hinges. Moreover, [in] the rear view of the prior art both the end panel and the CRP-10 inset door looks substantially different from the rear features of the '718 patent. On the CRP-10 inset door, the entire outer border is missing. The back of the CRP-10 end panel does not have any visible features similar to the rear features of the '718 patent because it is secured to a substrate that covers the rear of the panel. In light of these differences between the design of the '718 patent and the prior art, a reasonable jury could have concluded that Yorktowne and Conestoga did not meet their burden of showing anticipation by clear and convincing evidence.

[Affirmed.]

NOTES

1. The test for "identicalness" in design patent law melds elements of regular "utility" patent claim interpretation and trademark law's "likelihood of confusion" standard. As the opinion in *Doormaster Corp.* states: "Two designs are substantially the same if their resemblance is deceptive to the extent that it would induce an

ordinary observer, giving such attention as a purchaser usually gives, to purchase an article having one design supposing it to be the other." The visual elements of a design, under this formulation, are analyzed from the point of view of a consumer looking at a product embodying the design. Similarity is judged not by technical or expert criteria, as in patent law, but in terms of the visual impression made on a potential purchaser of the item embodying the design. Note that this same standard is used when comparing a claimed design to the prior art (for validity purposes), and for comparing the design to the accused product (for infringement purposes). For all purposes, it is the drawings in the design patent that serve as the definition of the claimed design. The drawings, in other words, are equivalent to the written, textual claims in a utility patent.

2. Elements of the design which cannot be seen by a purchaser are excluded from the similarity analysis. Likewise, in a design patent drawing, certain features are sometimes represented by "dotted lines" or "broken lines." Under design patent cases, the portions of a drawing so represented are *not* included in the claimed design. They are external to the claimed features. This means that even if an accused product does not look like the part of a design shown in broken lines, it will still infringe if the features of the accused product correspond to the solid line-drawn features of the design. For example, in a case involving "UGG" brand boots (sold by Deckers Outdoor Corp.), the registered design included broken lines as shown in Figure 26.4 (*Deckers Outdoor Corp. v. Romeo & Juliette, Inc.*, No. 215CV02812ODWCWX, 2016 WL 7017219, at *7 (C.D. Cal. Dec. 1, 2016)).

Figure 26.4 Deckers (UGG boot) design

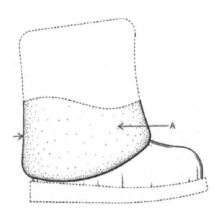

If an accused infringer sells a boot with a thicker sole, it would still infringe if it had the curved, overlap-look two-part appearance of the drawn design. Likewise, an accused infringer selling a boot with that two-part appearance, but having a top that was straight or slanted down toward the front (rather than the back, as shown) might still infringe.

26.1.1.2 Nonobviousness

 CASE

MRC Innovations, Inc. v. Hunter Mfg., LLP, 747 F.3d 1326 (Fed. Cir. 2014)

MRC Innovations, Inc. appeals from a final judgment of the U.S. District Court for the Northern District of Ohio granting summary judgment of invalidity with respect to U.S. Design Patent Nos. D634,488 ("'488 patent"). For the reasons stated below, we affirm.

CASE *(continued)*

MRC is the owner by assignment of both patents-in-suit. The '488 patent claims an ornamental design for a football jersey for a dog. [An example of the '488 patent football jersey is shown in Figure 26.5 on the left. On the right is another dog football jersey, sold prior to the invention date of the '488 patent and cited as prior art against the '488 patent.]

Figure 26.5 Dogwear Designs

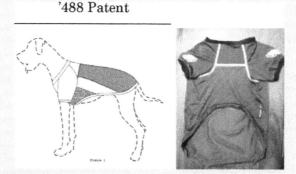

In the context of design patents, "the ultimate inquiry under section 103 is whether the claimed design would have been obvious to a designer of ordinary skill who designs articles of the type involved." *Titan Tire Corp. v. Case New Holland, Inc.*, 566 F.3d 1372, 1380–81 (Fed. Cir. 2009) (quoting *Durling v. Spectrum Furniture Co.*, 101 F.3d 100, 103 (Fed. Cir. 1996)). To answer this question, a court must first determine "whether one of ordinary skill would have combined teachings of the prior art to create the same overall visual appearance as the claimed design." *Durling*, 101 F.3d at 103. That inquiry involves a two-step process. First, the court must identify "a single reference, 'a something in existence, the design characteristics of which are basically the same as the claimed design.'" *Id.* (quoting *In re Rosen*, 673 F.2d 388, 391 (CCPA 1982)). The "basically the same" test requires consideration of the "visual impression created by the patented design as a whole." *Id.* We have noted that "the trial court judge may determine almost instinctively whether the two designs create basically the same visual impression," but "must communicate the reasoning behind that decision." *Id.*

Once the primary reference is found, other "secondary" references "may be used to modify it to create a design that has the same overall visual appearance as the claimed design." *Id.* These secondary references must be "'so related [to the primary reference] that the appearance of certain ornamental features in one would suggest the application of those features to the other.'" *Id.* (quoting *In re Borden*, 90 F.3d 1570, 1575 (Fed.Cir. 1996).

[T]he district court pointed out three key similarities between the claimed design and the Eagles jersey: an opening at the collar portion for the head, two openings and sleeves stitched to the body of the jersey for limbs, and a body portion on which a football logo is applied. [T]he district court went on to point out two additional similarities between the two designs: first, the Eagles jersey is made "primarily of a mesh and interlock fabric"; and

CASE (continued)

second, it contains at least some ornamental serge stitching – both features found in the '488 claimed design.

[As for the minor differences between the primary prior art reference and the design in the '488 patent,] [a]fter concluding that the Eagles jersey could be a "primary reference," the district court determined that the [pictured prior art] jersey and another reference known as the "Sporty K9" jersey were "so related to the primary reference" that they could serve as "secondary references" that would motivate the skilled artisan to make the claimed design. The district court found that both jerseys suggested the use of a V-neck pattern and non-mesh fabric on the side panels [, features that were present in the '488 patented design but absent from the prior art design pictured above]. With respect to the only remaining difference between the Eagles jersey and the '488 claimed design – the presence of additional ornamental serge stitching running down the rear of the jersey – the district court acknowledged that no prior art reference contained exactly that same stitching on the rear of the jersey, but nevertheless concluded that this was not a "substantial" difference that created a patentably distinct design, but rather was a "de minimis change[]" which would be well within the skill of an ordinary designer in the art." [District court opinion,] (citing *In re Carter*, 673 F.2d 1378, 1380 (CCPA 1982)).

[Finding of obviousness affirmed.]

NOTES

1. Notice how similar the analysis in this case is to the general nonobviousness analysis applied to utility (*i.e.*, non-design) patents in *KSR Int'l Co. v. Teleflex Inc.*, 550 U.S. 398 (2007). Perhaps the only difference of note is that for design patents, a court must identify a single "primary reference" from which the nonobviousness analysis must begin. This is not, strictly speaking, necessary, though courts will often focus on one (or at most a few) key references when applying *KSR* to utility patents. The approach in design patents in the US does sound similar to the way "inventive step" analysis is applied in other patent systems, however; in particular, in the European Patent Office, inventive step cases begin by locating the "nearest" prior art, and then examining the differences between that reference and the claimed invention.

2. For critical commentary on the nonobviousness standard as applied to US design patents, *see* Sarah Burstein, Design patent nonobviousness jurisprudence – going to the dogs?, Patently O Blog, April 3, 2014, available at https://patentlyo.com/patent/2014/04/design-nonobviousness-jurisprudence.html.

26.1.2 Copyright: product design as "applied art"

Star Athletica, L.L.C. v. Varsity Brands, Inc., No. 15-866, 2017 WL 1066261, (U.S. Supreme Court Mar. 22, 2017)

[The Copyright Act of 1976 makes "pictorial, graphic, or sculptural features" of the "design of a useful article" eligible for copyright protection as artistic works if those features "can be identified separately from, and are capable of existing independently of, the utilitarian aspects of the article." 17 U.S.C. §101. Respondents have more than 200 copyright registrations for two-dimensional designs – consisting of various lines, chevrons, and colorful shapes – appearing on the surface of the cheerleading uniforms that they design, make, and sell. They sued petitioner, who also markets cheerleading uniforms, for copyright infringement. The District Court granted petitioner summary judgment, holding that the designs could not be conceptually or physically separated from the uniforms and were therefore ineligible for copyright protection. In reversing, the Sixth Circuit concluded that the graphics could be "identified separately" and were "capable of existing independently" of the uniforms under §101.]

Respondents argue that "[s]eparability is only implicated when a [pictorial, graphic, or sculptural] work is the 'design of a useful article.'" Brief for Respondents 25. They contend that the surface decorations in this case are "two-dimensional graphic designs that appear on useful articles," but are not themselves designs *of* useful articles. This argument is inconsistent with the text of §101. The statute requires separability analysis for any "pictorial, graphic, or sculptural features" incorporated into the "design of a useful article." "Design" refers here to "the combination" of "details" or "features" that "go to make up" the useful article. 3 Oxford English Dictionary 244 (def. 7, first listing) (1933) (OED). The statute thus provides that the "design of a useful article" can include two-dimensional "pictorial" and "graphic" features, and separability analysis applies to those features just as it does to three-dimensional "sculptural" features.

The independent-existence requirement is ordinarily more difficult to satisfy. The decisionmaker must determine that the separately identified feature has the capacity to exist apart from the utilitarian aspects of the article. In other words, the feature must be able to exist as its own pictorial, graphic, or sculptural work as defined in §101 once it is imagined apart from the useful article. If the feature is not capable of existing as a pictorial, graphic, or sculptural work once separated from the useful article, then it was not a pictorial, graphic, or sculptural feature of that article, but rather one of its utilitarian aspects. Of course, to qualify as a pictorial, graphic, or sculptural work on its own, the feature cannot itself be a useful article or "[a]n article that is normally a part of a useful article" (which is itself considered a useful article). §101. Nor could someone claim a copyright in a useful article merely by

CASE *(continued)*

creating a replica of that article in some other medium – for example, a cardboard model of a car. Although the replica could itself be copyrightable, it would not give rise to any rights in the useful article that inspired it.

[A] feature of the design of a useful article is eligible for copyright if, when identified and imagined apart from the useful article, it would qualify as a pictorial, graphic, or sculptural work either on its own or when fixed in some other tangible medium. Applying this test to the surface decorations on the cheerleading uniforms is straightforward. First, one can identify the decorations as features having pictorial, graphic, or sculptural qualities. Second, if the arrangement of colors, shapes, stripes, and chevrons on the surface of the cheerleading uniforms were separated from the uniform and applied in another medium – for example, on a painter's canvas – they would qualify as "two-dimensional . . . works of . . . art," §101. And imaginatively removing the surface decorations from the uniforms and applying them in another medium would not replicate the uniform itself. Indeed, respondents have applied the designs in this case to other media of expression – different types of clothing – without replicating the uniform. *see* App. 273–279. The decorations are therefore separable from the uniforms and eligible for copyright protection.

To be clear, the only feature of the cheerleading uniform eligible for a copyright in this case is the two-dimensional work of art fixed in the tangible medium of the uniform fabric. Even if respondents ultimately succeed in establishing a valid copyright in the surface decorations at issue here, respondents have no right to prohibit any person from manufacturing a cheerleading uniform of identical shape, cut, and dimensions to the ones on which the decorations in this case appear. They may prohibit only the reproduction of the surface designs in any tangible medium of expression – a uniform or otherwise.

Because we reject the view that a useful article must remain after the artistic feature has been imaginatively separated from the article, we necessarily abandon the distinction between "physical" and "conceptual" separability, which some courts and commentators have adopted based on the Copyright Act's legislative history. According to this view, a feature is *physically* separable from the underlying useful article if it can "be physically separated from the article by ordinary means while leaving the utilitarian aspects of the article completely intact." *Conceptual* separability applies if the feature physically could not be removed from the useful article by ordinary means. The statutory text indicates that separability is a conceptual undertaking. Because separability does not require the underlying useful article to remain, the physical-conceptual distinction is unnecessary.

[Affirmed.]

 NOTES

1. A concurrence by Justice Ginsburg agrees with the result but would have preserved the distinction between product design and two-dimensional features attached to a product. She points to the copyright registra-

tions for the chevrons and other elements of the uniforms in this case: All were registered as two-dimensional artworks. Thus for Justice Ginsburg, this is not a case about the uniforms themselves, but about separate design elements attached to uniforms. There is no need for any separability analysis at all.

2. Justice Breyer, joined by Justice Kennedy, dissented from the majority conclusion. They point to scholarly literature saying that the fashion design industry has thrived without strong IP protection. From this backdrop, they conclude that there are policy reasons to apply the separability analysis in a way that minimizes protection for fashion designs. Note that the literature they cite has been contested; fashion designers themselves often argue that IP protection for their works in the US is inadequate. *See* Robert P. Merges, "Economics of Intellectual Property Law," in Oxford Handbook of Law and Economics (Francesco Parisi, ed., 2017).

26.1.3. Trademark: product packaging and product configuration design

26.1.3.1 Packaging

 CASE

Two Pesos, Inc. v. Taco Cabana, Inc., 505 U.S. 763 (1992)

[Respondent, the operator of a chain of Mexican restaurants, sued petitioner, a similar chain, for trade dress infringement under §43(a) of the Trademark Act of 1946 (Lanham Act), which provides that "[a]ny person who ... use[s] in connection with any goods or services ... any false description or representation ... shall be liable to ... any person ... damaged by [such] use." The District Court instructed the jury, inter alia, that respondent's trade dress was protected if it either was inherently distinctive – *i.e.*, was not merely descriptive – or had acquired a secondary meaning – *i.e.*, had come through use to be uniquely associated with a specific source. The court entered judgment for respondent after the jury found, among other things, that respondent's trade dress is inherently distinctive but has not acquired a secondary meaning. The Court of Appeals affirmed, and Petitioner Two Pesos lodged this appeal with the Supreme Court.]

A trademark is defined in 15 U.S.C. §1127 as including "any word, name, symbol, or device or any combination thereof" used by any person "to identify and distinguish his or her goods, including a unique product, from those manufactured or sold by others and to indicate the source of the goods, even if that source is unknown." In order to be registered, a mark must be capable of distinguishing the applicant's goods from those of others. §1052. Marks are often classified in categories of generally increasing distinctiveness; following the classic formulation set out by Judge Friendly, they may be (1) generic; (2) descriptive; (3) suggestive; (4) arbitrary; or (5) fanciful. *See Abercrombie & Fitch Co. v. Hunting World, Inc.*, 537 F.2d 4, 9 (CA2 1976).

The latter three categories of marks, because their intrinsic nature serves to identify a particular source of a product, are deemed inherently distinctive and are entitled to protection. Marks which are merely descriptive of a product are not inherently distinctive.

CASE (continued)

When used to describe a product, they do not inherently identify a particular source, and hence cannot be protected. However, descriptive marks may acquire the distinctiveness which will allow them to be protected under the Act. Section 2 of the Lanham Act provides that a descriptive mark that otherwise could not be registered under the Act may be registered if it "has become distinctive of the applicant's goods in commerce." §§2(e), (f), 15 U.S.C. §§1052(e), (f). This acquired distinctiveness is generally called "secondary meaning."

Engrafting onto §43(a) a requirement of secondary meaning for inherently distinctive trade dress also would undermine the purposes of the Lanham Act. Protection of trade dress, no less than of trademarks, serves the Act's purpose to "secure to the owner of the mark the goodwill of his business and to protect the ability of consumers to distinguish among competing producers. National protection of trademarks is desirable, Congress concluded, because trademarks foster competition and the maintenance of quality by securing to the producer the benefits of good reputation." [Park 'N Fly, Inc. v. Dollar Park & Fly, Inc., 469 U.S. 189 (1985)], at 198, citing S.Rep. No. 1333, 79th Cong., 2d Sess., 3–5 (1946) (citations omitted). By making more difficult the identification of a producer with its product, a secondary meaning requirement for a nondescriptive trade dress would hinder improving or maintaining the producer's competitive position.

On the other hand, adding a secondary meaning requirement could have anticompetitive effects, creating particular burdens on the startup of small companies. It would present special difficulties for a business, such as respondent, that seeks to start a new product in a limited area and then expand into new markets. Denying protection for inherently distinctive nonfunctional trade dress until after secondary meaning has been established would allow a competitor, which has not adopted a distinctive trade dress of its own, to appropriate the originator's dress in other markets and to deter the originator from expanding into and competing in these areas.

[Affirmed.]

NOTES

1. The Court's application of the traditional *Abercrombie & Fitch* "spectrum of mark distinctiveness" – arbitrary/fanciful; suggestive; descriptive – to product configurations creates challenges in some cases. How can a product shape be "descriptive," for instance? For examples of courts addressing this issue, see *Herman Miller v. Palazzetti Imports and Exports, Inc.*, 270 F.3d 298 (6th Cir. 2001) (refusing to grant summary judgment motion on issue of whether lounge chair and ottoman had acquired secondary meaning). *But see McNeil Nutrition v. Heartland Sweeteners*, 566 F. Supp. 2d 378 (E.D. Pa. 2008) (finding that the yellow, pillow-shaped packaging of "Splenda" brand sugar substitute was arbitrary and thus inherently distinctive under *Two Pesos*).

2. Note two limitations on trade dress protection mentioned in the opinion: (1) generic trade dress; and (2) functionality. A finding that trade dress is either generic or functional precludes legal protection in the US. What does generic trade dress look like? The esteemed trademark scholar Thomas McCarthy has this to say in his authoritative treatise:

[No company can claim] the shape of a common ice cream cone as its trademark or an Easter rabbit made of chocolate as its trade dress. The federal court in Hawaii dismissed on summary judgment a claim of infringement of alleged trade dress in the design of a shortbread cookie diagonally dipped in chocolate. The court held that this cookie design was not protectable as trade dress because it was "generic," noting that:

> [Defendant] has also submitted evidence that very similar cookies are commonly made and sold, both in Hawaii and elsewhere in the Untied States . . . . One of the reasons that genericness precludes protectability is that producers cannot monopolize basic product designs.

1 J. Thomas McCarthy, McCarthy on Trademarks and Unfair Competition §8:6.50 (4th ed. & Supp. 2017), citing *Big Island Candies, Inc. v. Cookie Corner*, 269 F. Supp. 2d. 1236, 1248-1249 (D. Haw. 2003).

As for functionality, *see* the case of *TrafFix Devices, Inc. v. Marketing Displays, Inc.*, 532 U.S. 23 (2001), *infra* Chapter 28.

26.1.3.2. Configuration

Wal-Mart Stores, Inc. v. Samara Bros., 529 U.S. 205 (2000)

[Respondent Samara Brothers sold children's clothes having distinctive raised features, representing hearts, fruits, and other designs. Petitioner Wal-Mart sold copies of the Samara clothing designs; was sued for trademark infringement under §43(a) of the U.S. Trademark Act (the "Lanham Act"); lost; and appealed to the Supreme Court which took the case.]

The breadth of the definition of marks registrable under §2 [of the Lanham Act], and of the confusion-producing elements recited as actionable by §43(a), has been held to embrace not just word marks, such as "Nike," and symbol marks, such as Nike's "swoosh" symbol, but also "trade dress" – a category that originally included only the packaging, or "dressing," of a product, but in recent years has been expanded by many Courts of Appeals to encompass the design of a product. *See, e.g., Ashley Furniture Industries, Inc. v. Sangiacomo N. A., Ltd.*, 187 F.3d 363 (C.A.4 1999) (bedroom furniture); *Knitwaves, Inc. v. Lollytogs, Ltd.*, 71 F.3d 996 (C.A.2 1995) (sweaters); *Stuart Hall Co., Inc. v. Ampad Corp.*, 51 F.3d 780 (C.A.8 1995) (notebooks). These courts have assumed, often without discussion, that trade dress constitutes a "symbol" or "device" for purposes of the relevant sections, and we conclude likewise. This reading of §2 and §43(a) is buttressed by a recently added subsection of §43(a), which refers specifically to "civil action[s] for trade dress infringement under this chapter for trade dress not registered on the principal register." 15 U.S.C. §1125(a)(3).

In evaluating the distinctiveness of a mark under §2 (and therefore, by analogy, under §43(a)), courts have held that a mark can be distinctive in one of two ways. First, a mark is inherently distinctive if "[its] intrinsic nature serves to identify a particular source." [*Two Pesos, Inc. v. Taco Cabana, Inc.*, 505 U.S. 763, 768 (1992)]. In the context of word

CASE *(continued)*

marks, courts have applied the now-classic test originally formulated by Judge Friendly, in which word marks that are "arbitrary" ("Camel" cigarettes), "fanciful" ("Kodak" film), or "suggestive" ("Tide" laundry detergent) are held to be inherently distinctive. *See Abercrombie & Fitch Co. v. Hunting World, Inc.*, 537 F.2d 4, 10–11 (C.A.2 1976). Second, a mark has acquired distinctiveness, even if it is not inherently distinctive, if it has developed secondary meaning, which occurs when, "in the minds of the public, the primary significance of a [mark] is to identify the source of the product rather than the product itself." *Inwood Laboratories, Inc. v. Ives Laboratories, Inc.*, 456 U.S. 844, 851, n. 11 (1982).

[W]ith respect to at least one category of mark – colors – we have held that no mark can ever be inherently distinctive. *See Qualitex* [*Co. v. Jacobson Products Co.*, 514 U.S. 159, 162 (1995)]. We held that a color could be protected as a trademark, but only upon a showing of secondary meaning. [W]e noted that a product's color is unlike a "fanciful," "arbitrary," or "suggestive" mark, since it does not "almost automatically tell a customer that [it] refer[s] to a brand," 514 U.S., at 162–163, and does not "immediately . . . signal a brand or a product 'source,'" *id.*, at 163. However, we noted that, "over time, customers may come to treat a particular color on a product or its packaging . . . as signifying a brand." *Ibid*. Because a color, like a "descriptive" word mark, could eventually "come to indicate a product's origin," we concluded that it could be protected upon a showing of secondary meaning. *Ibid*.

It seems to us that design, like color, is not inherently distinctive. The attribution of inherent distinctiveness to certain categories of word marks and product packaging derives from the fact that the very purpose of attaching a particular word to a product, or encasing it in a distinctive packaging, is most often to identify the source of the product. Although the words and packaging can serve subsidiary functions – a suggestive word mark (such as "Tide" for laundry detergent), for instance, may invoke positive connotations in the consumer's mind, and a garish form of packaging (such as Tide's squat, brightly decorated plastic bottles for its liquid laundry detergent) may attract an otherwise indifferent consumer's attention on a crowded store shelf – their predominant function remains source identification. Consumers are therefore predisposed to regard those symbols as indication of the producer, which is why such symbols "almost automatically tell a customer that they refer to a brand," [*Qualitex, supra*], at 162–63, and "immediately . . . signal a brand or a product 'source,'" *id.*, at 163. And where it is not reasonable to assume consumer predisposition to take an affixed word or packaging as indication of source – where, for example, the affixed word is descriptive of the product ("Tasty" bread) or of a geographic origin ("Georgia" peaches) – inherent distinctiveness will not be found. That is why the statute generally excludes, from those word marks that can be registered as inherently distinctive, words that are "merely descriptive" of the goods, or "primarily geographically descriptive of them". In the case of product design, as in the case of color, we think consumer predisposition to equate the feature with the source does not exist. Consumers are aware of the reality that, almost invariably, even the most unusual of product designs – such as a cocktail shaker shaped like a penguin – is intended not to identify the source, but to render the product itself more useful or more appealing.

CASE *(continued)*

The fact that product design almost invariably serves purposes other than source identification not only renders inherent distinctiveness problematic; it also renders application of an inherent-distinctiveness principle more harmful to other consumer interests. Consumers should not be deprived of the benefits of competition with regard to the utilitarian and esthetic purposes that product design ordinarily serves by a rule of law that facilitates plausible threats of suit against new entrants based upon alleged inherent distinctiveness. How easy it is to mount a plausible suit depends, of course, upon the clarity of the test for inherent distinctiveness, and where product design is concerned we have little confidence that a reasonably clear test can be devised.

QUESTIONS

1. Are you convinced that consumers rarely or never equate product design with a single source or seller? What about the silhouette of a vintage Porsche car; or the distinctive rounded corners and contrasting color borders of an iPhone? The Burberry tartan pattern? Beats by Dre. Headphones?
2. After *Samara Brothers*, all product designs are presumed to be non-distinctive, *i.e.*, not presumptively identifiable on sight as a certain brand (from a certain source). How difficult will it be under this test to establish secondary meaning for well-known product designs such as those just mentioned?

26.2 China

For an example of how product configuration is protected under Chinese trademark law, *see* Part IV, at section 17.2.7.

("China: Distinctiveness in Three-Dimensional Marks"), and in particular the case of *Coca-Cola v. TRAB*, Beijing High People's Court, Gaoxingzhongzi No. 348 (2011).

26.3 Europe

26.3.1 Background: traditional design protection in European countries

26.3.1.1 Protection under copyright and trademark law

Traditionally, there has been a split of opinion among the countries of Europe on the operation of copyright and trademark law to protect industrial designs. The countries are, to use the common expression, "all over the map." With respect to copyright, for instance, French law permits a wide scope of protection under a sort of "non-discrimination" principles that strives to recognize human creativity however it is expressed. In Germany, copyrighted three-dimensional designs were long held to a higher standard of originality when it came to copyright protection. While only a small degree of originality was required for works in traditional artistic or aesthetic media (written texts, drawings, and sculpture), traditionally an industrial product was required to embody a more creative design to merit protection. This approach was abandoned in 2014, *see* GRUR 2014, 175 – *Geburtstagszug* (the "Birthday Train" copyright case, English version reported in International Intellectual Prop. & Competition Law (Max Planck) 2014, at 831), abandoning cases such as BGH GRUR 1995, 581 – *Silberdistel*; and OLG Nürnberg GRUR 2014, 1199 – *Fußball-Stecktabelle*), partly under the rationale that the old standard was meant to distinguish copyright from design protection, while the new European Directive now awards a separate and distinct design right so German law need not be concerned with the copyright/design interface. (The litigation here involved employee compensation for valuable creations; and the holding permitted a claim to profits by the employee, which can be made under copyright law but not under design protection.) Traditionally, the courts in Italy were also concerned with preventing "double protection" under copyright and design protection. *See* Jerome H. Reichman, *Design Protection in Domestic and Foreign Copyright Law: From the Berne Revision of 1948 to the Copyright Act of 1976*, [1983] Duke L.J. 1143. As with Germany, however, the advent of Europe-wide design protection is leading to changed standards in Italy and elsewhere.

As for trademark protection, there is protection for trade dress under European law. The rule is, however, that it may be more difficult to establish distinctiveness with respect to trade dress than it is for traditional trademarks. *See* Joined Cases C-53/01 to C-55/01, *Linde, Winward and Rado* (ECJ: 8 April 2003), at par. 48:

> [I]t may in practice be more difficult to establish distinctiveness in relation to a shape of product mark than a word or figurative trade mark. But whilst that may explain why such a mark is refused registration, it does not mean that it cannot acquire distinctive character following the use that has been made of it and thus be registered as a trade mark under Article 3(3) of the Directive.

One way this manifests is that in many cases, the shape or design of a product may be said by a trademark office or court to initially lack distinctiveness. So in *Henkel KGaA v. OHIM and Procter & Gamble Co v. OHIM* (Joined Cases T-335/99 to T-337/99; T-30/00; T-117/00 to T-121/00; T-128/00 and T-129/00, 19 September 2001), the court of first instance was presented with applications relating to a dishwashing tablet in several variations including color, speckles, and shapes. The court held that the suggested marks were not distinctive enough to serve as indications of origin. While it may be difficult to register a shape mark, however, it is not impossible. Hence in *Daimler Chrysler Corp v. OHIM* (Case T-128/01, 6 March 2003), a rejection of an attempted registration of a front grille for a car was overturned. The court of first instance said that the grille in question was not conventional or typical, and hence was sufficiently distinctive that it qualified for trademark protection. The matter of proof of distinctiveness remains in some doubt, however, as demonstrated well by the case of *Société des Produits Nestlé SA v. Cadbury UK Ltd*, [2016] EWHC 50 (Ch), at 67, [2016] F.S.R. 19, at 24:

> [I]t is legitimate for the competent authority, when assessing whether the applicant has proved that a significant proportion of the relevant class of persons perceives the relevant goods or services as originating from a particular undertaking [*i.e.*, company] because of the sign in question, to consider whether such persons would rely upon the sign as denoting the origin of the goods if it were used on its own.

There, the shape at issue was the well-known four rectangular bar design of the candy bar known as "Kit-Kat." Though survey evidence (not surprisingly) demonstrated that a majority of consumers associated this shape with Kit-Kat candy, the High Court (after clarification from the CJEU) held that this was not enough to make the shape distinctive under EU trademark law. What *was* required, as the passage shows, is that consumers be shown to "rely upon" the shape itself as a clear indicator of origin. The problem with the proffered evidence, the court said, was that the candy bar was shown to survey respondents in the form in which it is typically sold – viz., in a colored wrapper with the word mark "Kit-Kat" on it. The surveys, then, were not enough to show distinctiveness of the *shape itself*, and hence the registration failed.

Can a distinctive retail store layout be registered as a trademark, in and of itself (without the presence of an accompanying logo or word mark)? Yes, said the CJEU, in a case originating with a rejection of a trademark application in Germany:

CASE

Apple Inc. v. Deutsches Patent-und Markenamt, (C-421/13), [2014] Bus. L.R. 962 (ECJ (3rd Chamber)), available at http://curia.europa.eu/juris/document/document.jsf?text=&docid=154829&pageIndex=0&doclang=EN&mode=lst&dir=&occ=first&part=1&cid=793165

[The registration was for, to quote from the U.S. version of the application: "[A] clear glass storefront surrounded by a panelled, steel gray facade... light brown cantilevered shelves... recessed display spaces along the side walls... light brown rectangular tables arranged in a line in the middle of the store... multi-tiered shelving along the side walls... a light brown oblong table with black stools located at the back of the store."

Here is an illustration of the design sought to be protected as a trademark Figure 26.6: The German Patent and Trademark Office rejected Apple's German trademark application

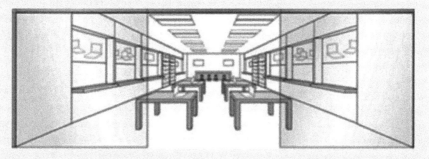

Figure 26.6 Apple's retail store design

on the grounds that consumers would not *see* it as an indication of the origin of Apple goods. Apple appealed to the appropriate German court, the Bundespatentgericht, and that court stayed proceedings pending this referral to the CJEU.]

The questions referred [to the CJEU are:]

(1) Is Article 2 of the Trade Marks Directive to be interpreted as meaning that the possibility of protection for the 'packaging of goods' also extends to the presentation of the establishment in which a service is provided?

(2) Are Articles 2 and 3(1) of the Trade Marks Directive to be interpreted as meaning that a

CASE *(continued)*

sign representing the presentation of the establishment in which a service is provided is capable of being registered as a trade mark?

It is absolutely plain from the wording of Article 2 of Directive 2008/95 [on trademarks] that designs are among the categories of signs capable of graphic representation [and therefore of being registered].

It follows that a representation, such as that at issue in the main proceedings, which depicts the layout of a retail store by means of an integral collection of lines, curves and shapes, may constitute a trade mark provided that it is capable of distinguishing the products or services of one undertaking from those of other undertakings. Consequently, such a representation [may be registered], without it being necessary either, on the one hand, to attribute any relevance to the fact that the design does not contain any indication as to the size and proportions of the retail store that it depicts, or, on the other hand, to examine whether such a design could equally, as a 'presentation of the establishment in which a service is provided', be treated in the same way as 'packaging' within the meaning of Article 2 of Directive 2008/95.

The representation, by a design, of the layout of a retail store is also capable of distinguishing the products or services of one undertaking from those of other undertakings. In that regard, it suffices to observe that it cannot be ruled out that the layout of a retail outlet depicted by such a sign may allow the products or the services for which registration is sought to be identified as originating from a particular undertaking. [T]his could be the case when the depicted layout departs significantly from the norm or customs of the economic sector concerned (see, by analogy, as to signs consisting of the appearance of the product itself, *Storck v. OHIM*, C-25/05 P, EU:C:2006:422, paragraph 28, and *Vuitton Malletier v. OHIM*, C-97/12 P, EU:C:2014:324, paragraph 52).

The fact that a sign is, in general, capable of constituting a trade mark within the meaning of Article 2 of Directive 2008/95 does not mean, however, that the sign necessarily has a distinctive character for the purposes of Article 3(1)(b) of the directive in relation to the products or services for which registration is sought.

The distinctive character of the sign must be assessed *in concreto* by reference to, first, the goods or services in question and, second, the perception of the relevant public, namely the average consumer of the category of goods or services in question, who is reasonably well informed and reasonably observant and circumspect (see, in particular, *Linde and Others*, C-53/01 to C-55/01, EU:C:2003:206, paragraph 41.

It is also by an assessment *in concreto* that the competent authority must determine whether or not the sign is descriptive of the characteristics of the goods or services concerned within the meaning of Article 3(1)(c) of Directive 2008/95 or gives rise to any other ground listed also in Article 3 for the refusal of registration (*Koninklijke KPN Nederland*, EU:C:2004:86, paragraphs 31 and 32).

On those grounds, the Court (Third Chamber) hereby rules:

Articles 2 and 3 of Directive 2008/95 of the European Parliament and of the

CASE *(continued)*

Council of 22 October 2008 to approximate the laws of the Member States relating to trade marks must be interpreted as meaning that the representation, by a design alone, without indicating the size or the proportions, of the layout of a retail store, may be registered as a trade mark for services consisting in services relating to those goods but which do not form an integral part of the offer for sale thereof, provided that the sign is capable of distinguishing the services of the applicant for registration from those of other undertakings; and, that registration is not precluded by any of the grounds for refusal set out in that directive. [Bold type in original.]

NOTES

1. The case is summarized in: *CJEU expands trade mark law to include the design of a store layout: Apple Inc v. Deutsches Patent-und Markenamt (German Patent and Trade Mark Office)*, 36 Euro. Intell. Prop. Rev. 813–17 (2014).
2. The notion that the layout and appearance of a business's space might be distinctive is also reflected in US law; recall that it was a restaurant's décor that was at issue in the US case of *Two Pesos, Inc. v. Taco Cabana, Inc.*, 505 U.S. 763 (1992). *Two Pesos*, as later clarified by the later case of *Wal-Mart Stores, Inc. v. Samara Bros., Inc.*, 529 U.S. 205 (2000), was said to be either product packaging (as opposed to product design) or "some *tertium quid*" [third thing] whose closest equivalent is product packaging:

    > *Two Pesos* unquestionably establishes the legal principle that trade dress can be inherently distinctive, but it does not establish that *product-design* trade dress can be. *Two Pesos* is inapposite to our holding here because the trade dress at issue, the decor of a restaurant, seems to us not to constitute product design. It was either product packaging – which, as we have discussed, normally is taken by the consumer to indicate origin – or else some *tertium quid* that is akin to product packaging and has no bearing on the present case.
    >
    > Respondent replies that this manner of distinguishing *Two Pesos* will force courts to draw difficult lines between product-design and product-packaging trade dress. There will indeed be some hard cases at the margin: a classic glass Coca-Cola bottle, for instance, may constitute packaging for those consumers who drink the Coke and then discard the bottle, but may constitute the product itself for those consumers who are bottle collectors, or part of the product itself for those consumers who buy Coke in the classic glass bottle, rather than a can, because they think it more stylish to drink from the former. We believe, however, that the frequency and the difficulty of having to distinguish between product design and product packaging will be much less than the frequency and the difficulty of having to decide when a product design is inherently distinctive. To the extent there are close cases, we believe that courts should err on the side of caution and classify ambiguous trade dress as product design, thereby requiring secondary meaning. The very closeness will suggest the existence of relatively small utility in adopting an inherent-distinctiveness principle, and relatively great consumer benefit in requiring a demonstration of secondary meaning (*Wal-Mart Stores, Inc. v. Samara Bros.*, 529 U.S. 205, 215–16 (2000)).

    How is this approach different from the CJEU approach in *Apple*? Is there any difference between the labels "product packaging" (*Two Pesos/Samara*) and "the layout of a retail store . . . [as a] service[] relating to . . . goods but [not forming] an integral part of the offer for sale [of the goods]"?

26.3.2. The EU Design Directive (1998) and Design Regulation (2001)

Because of wide differences in the practical details and animating philosophies behind design protection laws in various European countries, a harmonized system was agreed upon in 1998. In Directive 98/71/EC, 13 October 1998, "On the Legal Protection of Designs," available at http://www.wipo.int/wipolex/en/text.jsp?file_id=126961 ("EU Design Directive"), the EU established minimum standards for design protection in its Member Countries. *See generally* Graeme B. Dinwoodie, *Federalized Functionalism: The Future of Design Protection in the European Union*, 24 Am. Intell. Prop. L. Ass'n Q. J. 611 (1996). Shortly after adoption of the Directive, Member States created a Europe-wide registered design system. Joined to the EU-wide trademark regime, the Community Design system is administered from the EU Intellectual Property Office (EUIPO; formerly the Office of Harmonization of the Internal Market, or OHIM).

The EUIPO office is in Alicante, Spain (though applicants may also register in their own national design registration offices as well, or through the Hague System of international design registration described earlier in Section 25.1.2.). Design protection in the EUIPO comes in two varieties: registered and unregistered. The differences are significant: A Registered Community Design (RCD) is initially valid for five years from the date of filing and can be renewed in five-year periods up to a maximum of 25 years of total protection. An Unregistered Community Design (UCD) receives protection for a period of three years from the date on which the design was first made available to the public (via "disclosure") within the EU. A UCD cannot be extended beyond the three-year protection period.

There is no substantive examination of designs. *See* EU Design Regulation, at par. 18 ("This registration system should in principle not be based upon substantive examination as to compliance with requirements for protection prior to registration, thereby keeping to a minimum the registration and other procedural burdens on applicants"). The validity of a design may only be challenged by (1) an administrative action, typically an application for a declaration of invalidity (ADI) in the EUIPO or in a national design office; or (2) as a counterclaim to design infringement litigation initiated by the design owner.

The structure of EU-wide design protection is established in the Directive and the Regulation. Here are some important provisions.

To begin, the Directive defines some basic terms in Article 1:

> For the purpose of this Directive:
>
> (a) 'design' means the appearance of the whole or a part of a product resulting from the features of, in particular, the lines, contours, colours, shape, texture and/or materials of the product itself and/or its ornamentation;
> (b) 'product' means any industrial or handicraft item, including inter alia parts intended to be assembled into a complex product, packaging, get-up, graphic symbols and typographic typefaces, but excluding computer programs;
> (c) 'complex product' means a product which is composed of multiple components which can be replaced permitting disassembly and reassembly of the product.

Among the "protection requirements" in Article 3, the Directive includes these important statements:

> 2. A design shall be protected by a design right to the extent that it is new and has individual character.
> 3. A design applied to or incorporated in a product which constitutes a component part of a complex product shall only be considered to be new and to have individual character:
>
> (a) if the component part, once it has been incorporated into the complex product, remains visible during normal use of the latter, and
> (b) to the extent that those visible features of the component part fulfill in themselves the requirements as to novelty and individual character.

The requirements are spelled out more clearly in Articles 4 and 5, as follows:

> ### Article 4
> **Novelty**
>
> A design shall be considered new if no identical design has been made available to the public before the date of filing of the application for registration or, if priority is claimed, the date of priority. Designs shall be deemed to be identical if their features differ only in immaterial details.
>
> ### Article 5
> **Individual character**
>
> 1. A design shall be considered to have individual character if the overall impression it produces on the informed user differs from the overall impression produced on such a user by any design which has been made available to the public before

the date of filing of the application for registration or, if priority is claimed, the date of priority.

2. In assessing individual character, the degree of freedom of the designer in developing the design shall be taken into consideration.

When does a prior design become available for a lack of novelty defense; in other words, when does a design enter the "prior art" for purposes of RCD law? This is covered in Article 6:

Article 6

Disclosure

1. For the purpose of applying Articles 4 and 5, a design shall be deemed to have been made available to the public if it has been published following registration or otherwise, or exhibited, used in trade or otherwise disclosed, except where these events could not reasonably have become known in the normal course of business to the circles specialised in the sector concerned, operating within the Community, before the date of filing of the application for registration or, if priority is claimed, the date of priority. The design shall not, however, be deemed to have been made available to the public for the sole reason that it has been disclosed to a third person under explicit or implicit conditions of confidentiality.

2. A disclosure shall not be taken into consideration for the purpose of applying Articles 4 and 5 if a design for which protection is claimed under a registered design right of a Member State has been made available to the public:

(a) by the designer, his successor in title, or a third person as a result of information provided or action taken by the designer, or his successor in title; and

(b) during the 12-month period preceding the date of filing of the application or, if priority is claimed, the date of priority.

3. Paragraph 2 shall also apply if the design has been made available to the public as a consequence of an abuse in relation to the designer or his successor in title.

Article 7 provides that purely functional designs ("features of appearance . . . solely dictated by . . . technical function") may not be registered or protected. Article 9 lays out the scope of protection granted by an RCD:

Article 9

Scope of protection

1. The scope of the protection conferred by a design right shall include any design which does not produce on the informed user a different overall impression.

2. In assessing the scope of protection, the degree of freedom of the designer in developing his design shall be taken into consideration.

You will see how the "different overall impression" standard of Article 9.1 is applied in some cases below. They also illustrate what is meant by the constraint of Article 9.2 regarding the designer's "degree of freedom."

A separate defense of prior use is available under Article 22 of the EU Design Directive. It reads:

Article 22
Rights of prior use in respect of a registered Community design

1. A right of prior use shall exist for any third person who can establish that before the date of filing of the application, or, if a priority is claimed, before the date of priority, he has in good faith commenced use within the Community, or has made serious and effective preparations to that end, of a design included within the scope of protection of a registered Community design, which has not been copied from the latter.
2. The right of prior use shall entitle the third person to exploit the design for the purposes for which its use had been effected, or for which serious and effective preparations had been made, before the filing or priority date of the registered Community design.
3. The right of prior use shall not extend to granting a licence to another person to exploit the design.
4. The right of prior use cannot be transferred except [in the transfer of the business].

After a design is registered, its validity can be challenged as described in Article 24:

Article 24
Declaration of invalidity

1. A registered Community design shall be declared invalid on application to the Office in accordance with the procedure in Titles VI and VII or by a Community design court on the basis of a counterclaim in infringement proceedings.
2. A Community design may be declared invalid even after the Community design has lapsed or has been surrendered.
3. An unregistered Community design shall be declared invalid by a Community design court on application to such a court or on the basis of a counterclaim in infringement proceedings.

The various grounds of invalidity are laid out in Article 25:

Article 25
Grounds for invalidity

1. A Community design may be declared invalid only in the following cases:

(a) if the design does not correspond to the definition under Article 3(a);
(b) if it does not fulfil the requirements of Articles 4 to 9;
(c) if, by virtue of a court decision, the right holder is not entitled to the Community design under Article 14;
(d) if the Community design is in conflict with a prior design which has been made available to the public after the date of filing of the application or, if priority is claimed, the date of priority of the Community design, and which is protected from a date prior to the said date

  (i) by a registered Community design or an application for such a design, or
  (ii) by a registered design right of a Member State, or by an application for such a right, or
  (iii) by a design right registered under the Geneva Act of the Hague Agreement . . . or by an application for such a right;

(e) if a distinctive sign is used in a subsequent design, and Community law or the law of the Member State governing that sign confers on the right holder of the sign the right to prohibit such use;
(f) if the design constitutes an unauthorised use of a work protected under the copyright law of a Member State; . . .

2. The ground provided for in paragraph (1)(c) may be invoked solely by the person who is entitled to the Community design under Article 14.
3. The grounds provided for in paragraph (1)(d), (e) and (f) may be invoked solely by the applicant for or holder of the earlier right.
4. The ground provided for in paragraph (1)(g) may be invoked solely by the person or entity concerned by the use . . .

Because the RCD right comes by way of *registration*, there is no detailed administrative examination of the validity of a registered design. Its validity can only be challenged by (1) a request made to the Europe-wide EUIPO (*see* EU Design Regulation, Article 52), or (2) a defendant accused of infringing an RCD. Infringement actions under the RCD regime are brought in national courts that have been designated as Community Design Courts. *See* Design Regulation, at Article 52.

There is a complex jurisdictional regime for these national courts which affects, in particular, the territorial scope of the remedies that may be ordered by a Design Court after a finding of infringement. In particular, if jurisdiction is based on the domicile of the defendant, then the Design Court may order remedies having EU-wide effect. But if jurisdiction is based on the location of infringing activity, the remedies are only effective within the country where the litigation takes place, *i.e.*, the nation where the infringing activity occurred. *See* Article 83 of the Design Regulation:

> 1. A Community design court whose jurisdiction is based on Article 82(1) [domicile] . . . shall have jurisdiction in respect of acts of infringement committed or threatened within the territory of any of the Member States . . . 2. A Community design court whose jurisdiction is based on Article 82(5) [infringing activity] shall have jurisdiction only in respect of acts of infringement committed or threatened within the territory of the Member State in which that court is situated.

In one opinion, however, the EU Advocate General stated that proper jurisdiction under the Design Directive means that remedies (or "sanctions") under Article 89 of the Directive have EU-wide effect even when those remedies go beyond those explicitly listed in Article 89. *See Nintendo Co. Ltd. v. BigBen Interactive GmbH*, 616CC0024, EU Case No. C-24/16 (CJEU – Reference for Preliminary Ruling: March 1, 2017) (citing Article 89 provision: "[A] court shall [render]: . . . (d) any order imposing other sanctions appropriate under the circumstances which are provided by the law of the Member State in which the acts of infringement or threatened infringement are committed").

Article 85.2 of the EU Design Regulation covers the presumption of validity, and invalidity defenses, in Directive- and Regulation-related litigation in the EU:

> 1. In proceedings in respect of an infringement action or an action for threatened infringement of a registered Community design, the Community design court shall treat the Community design as valid. Validity may be challenged only with a counterclaim for a declaration of invalidity.
> 2. In proceedings in respect of an infringement action or an action for threatened infringement of an unregistered Community design, the Community design court shall treat the Community design as valid if the right holder produces proof that the conditions laid down in Article 11 have been met and indicates what constitutes the individual character of his Community design. However, the defendant may contest its validity by way of a plea or with a counterclaim for a declaration of invalidity.

26.3.2.1 Novelty and individual character: EUIPO review of validity

CASE

Julius Samann, Ltd. v. Kubispol., Case no. R1999/2013-3 (OHIM Bd. Appeal, Jan. 20, 2016), available at https://euipo.europa.eu/eSearchCLW/#advanced/community-designs (search: R1999/2013-3)

[In this case, the registrant, Kubi, had registered a design for a car air freshener, typically hung inside a car (*see* Figure 26.7)
Samann filed an application for a declaration of invalidity, stating, among other grounds,

Figure 26.7 Air freshener design

that the design of the registrant (Kubi) lacked novelty (Directive, Article 4). Samann cited a series of its own trademark registrations as evidence of lack of novelty. These registrations cover Samann's well-known car air fresheners, the shape of which is shown in an illustration from one of its registrations (Figure 26.8).

On August 20, 2013, the Invalidity Division issued a decision rejecting Samann's application for a declaration of invalidity. That decision was appealed to this court, the OHIM Board of Appeal within the EUIPO.]

The Invalidity Division found that the contested RCD did not lack novelty and the invalidity applicant does not object to that finding in its statement of appeal grounds. The Board confirms that the RCD is not identical to any of the prior designs and that the many differences concerning the outline, colour scheme and overall aspect of these designs may not be regarded as 'immaterial details' within the meaning of Article 5 CDR. Therefore, the RCD may not be said to lack novelty against the prior art.

The contested RCD must be compared with the earlier designs in order to determine

CASE *(continued)*

Figure 26.8 Fir tree air freshener

if it produces on the informed user the same overall impression. In addition, the degree of freedom of the designer in developing the contested RCD must be considered. Informed users of this kind of product are primarily motor vehicle owners who use the products to deodorise the cabin of the vehicle. They are, according to the case-law, particularly observant and familiar with the products of this kind that the market has to offer, even though they are not professionally involved in the design and marketing thereof. They have become informed by visiting stores selling car accessories, reading specialised magazines and browsing on the internet.

The degree of freedom of the designer is only limited by technical constraints – for example, air fresheners must be conveniently sized and be capable of being hung somewhere – and is, therefore, very broad. In the Board's opinion, the contested RCD does not produce on the informed user the same overall impression as the earlier designs [primarily in the shape of a fir, and, in the case of a third-party registration, not belonging to Samann, the shape of another tree, more rounded than a fir.]

As regards the first category, the Board notes that the contested RCD does not convey, to a particularly observant informed user, the same overall impression conveyed by the earlier designs. The contested RCD appears to outline a tree having a round crown, a short trunk and an essentially round base. The earlier designs, on the contrary, will be immediately perceived by informed users as conventional representations of firs, because of their pyramidal shape and the image of branches tending to stretch downwards. The overall impression produced by the contested RCD, on the one hand, and by the earlier designs on the other, is accordingly different. The contested RCD produces the overall impression of a tree with a round crown whereas the earlier designs convey the impression of a tree belonging to the genus of firs.

As regards the comparison of the contested RCD with the [third-party] designs, the Board notes that the overall impression is completely different. The contested RCD is characterised by an essentially spherical shape whereas the earlier designs are distinctly conical.

CASE *(continued)*

[The Board went on to affirm the findings of the Invalidity Division of the OHIM that Kubi's registered design was not invalid due to conflict with Samann's registered EU trademarks – technically, a different ground of invalidity than simple existence in the prior art. This defense is based on Article 25(1)(e) of the EU Regulation, which provides for invalidity "(e) if a distinctive sign is used in a subsequent design, and Community law or the law of the Member State governing that sign confers on the right holder of the sign the right to prohibit such use." The Board then recounted the relevant legal standard for invalidation under this section; namely, that the applicant for invalidity show a reasonable likelihood of confusion between the prior-registered trademark and the registered community design (here, Kubi's), for the same or similar classes of goods listed in the applicant's trademark registration(s).]

The contested RCD must be compared with the earlier marks as if it were visually perceived as a trade mark and not a design. The earlier marks are all variants of the same sign, namely a monochrome black or white representation of a fir as per CTM [Community Trademarks] No 91 991 and No 3 071 305. [The Board then proceeds to consider three types of similarity: (1) visual; (2) aural (*i.e.*, similarity of sound); and (3) conceptual.]

In the Board's opinion, the contested RCD is not visually similar to the earlier marks, as already mentioned in the preceding paragraphs. Whereas the earlier marks clearly represent a fir tree, the same cannot be said of the contested RCD, which resembles a tree having a round crown with an eyelet and a round base. The contested RCD, therefore, may not be considered as a reproduction of the earlier marks (12/05/2010, T-148/08, *Instruments for writing*, EU:T:2010:190). The signs are, thus, not visually similar. [There is no aural similarity in the names of the products.]

The invalidity applicant argues that the contested RCD and the earlier marks are conceptually identical or at least, similar, because they 'share an identical theme', *i.e.* that of a tree. [After reviewing case law on conflicting designs covering flowers and peacocks (both of which cases found the registered designs novel in spite of prior designs), the Board continued.]

In the case under review, the contested RCD and the earlier marks do not even represent the same tree. The contested RCD represents a tree that cannot be precisely identified whereas the earlier marks clearly represent a fir. These differences do matter, according to the above case-law, in the conceptual comparison. If marks representing the same tree are merely considered conceptually similar, marks representing different trees can thus be considered conceptually dissimilar. The concept and aspect of a fir is very precise in the mind of the average consumer and furthermore, immediately evokes pleasurable notions, namely a characteristic scent, a mountainous or Nordic landscape and the Christmas season. No such pleasurable associations are conveyed by the contested RCD which, as argued by the RCD holder, might at most bring to mind, due to its round shape, an apple-tree. The conflicting signs do not only represent completely different trees, they also call to mind different notions. For these two reasons, they may not be regarded, in accordance with the case-law of the General Court, as conceptually similar, not even to a low degree.

[Invalidity division affirmed; appeal dismissed.]

NOTES

1. This opinion may help give you a better idea of the subject matter of RCD protection. Although the registration document is itself a two-dimensional drawing, the subject matter protected is the three-dimensional object itself – the actual air freshener product, as sold. Note too that there is no discussion here of issues typical in a trademark case, in particular the association (if any) between the product shape and the source or company that sells the product. It is the *design itself* that is the potential subject of protection, as opposed to the consumer association between the shape and the source of the product. While a prior trademark registration may affect the novelty of a design registration (as it did here), be careful to distinguish the legal rights granted by a trademark and a registered design. They are not the same.
2. A key aspect of this case, as with many design-related cases, involves application of the "informed user" test. The next case deals with this important issue in some depth.

26.3.2.2. "Informed user" test

CASE

Pepsico v. GrupoPromer, Case C-281/10 P (CJEU, Oct. 20, 2011)

[Pepsico registered a design in the OHIM for a small disk designed to be distributed with retail products, such as soft drinks or snack items. They are used as collectible items or in contests. Images, messages, or point values can be printed on the disks, which consumers collect as part of retail product promotions and contests. They are sometimes called "pogs," "tazos," or "rappers". The disks look like this (Figure 26.9):

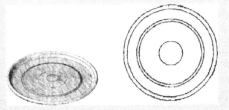

Figure 26.9 Retail contest disks

Pepsico's registration was met with an invalidity request from GroupoPromer ("Promer"), partly on the basis of Promer's own registered design for disks, which it had registered some six months prior to the Pepsico registration. Promer's disks look like this (Figure 26.10):

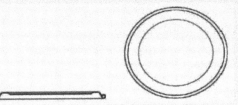

Figure 26.10 Promer disk design

CASE *(continued)*

The Invalidity Division of the OHIM ruled for applicant Promer; this decision was reversed on appeal, primarily on the basis that the registered design was for a very restricted class of goods, viz., "tazos" or "rappers," which severely constrained the designer and therefore made for a different overall impression as compared to the prior registered design. The General Court of the EU reversed the decision of the OHIM Appeals Court and reinstated the decision of the Invalidity Division. The CJEU then took the case.]

It should be noted, first, that [the Design] Regulation does not define the concept of the "informed user". However, that concept must be understood as lying somewhere between that of the average consumer, applicable in trade mark matters, who need not have any specific knowledge and who, as a rule, makes no direct comparison between the trade marks in conflict, and the sectoral expert, who is an expert with detailed technical expertise. Thus, the concept of the informed user may be understood as referring, not to a user of average attention, but to a particularly observant one, either because of his personal experience or his extensive knowledge of the sector in question.

[T]he qualifier "informed" suggests that, without being a designer or a technical expert, the user knows the various designs which exist in the sector concerned, possesses a certain degree of knowledge with regard to the features which those designs normally include, and, as a result of his interest in the products concerned, shows a relatively high degree of attention when he uses them. In the light of the foregoing considerations, the . . . part of the . . . appeal [relating to "the concept of the informed user and his attention level"] must be rejected as unfounded.

Since PepsiCo has been unsuccessful in all the parts of its single ground of appeal [*i.e.,* violation of Article 25], the appeal must be dismissed in its entirety.

NOTES

1. The idea of an "informed user" exerts a good deal of influence on the European design protection system. The fact that this hypothetical person is charged with a good deal of knowledge and attention to detail in the matter of designs means that a rough or glancing similarity between designs will usually not be enough to make out a case of infringement. The degree of similarity must be higher than this. It is close to, but perhaps not quite as stringent as, the notion of "striking similarity" in US copyright law (which sometimes permits an inference of copying even if access to the copyrighted work cannot be proven). Because the attention of the relevant observer is inversely related to the scope of a design right, this means that in effect the "zone of infringement" surrounding a European design is quite constrained or limited. There are good arguments for this result of course: especially that, because designs are registered without examination, granting a broad right might lead to excessive reliance on design protection and ultimately cause a rise in prices for consumer items carrying distinctive designs. *See generally* Uma Suthersanen, "Function, Art and Fashion: Do We Need the EU Designs Law?," in Constructing European IP Law: Achievements and New Perspectives 355–81 (Christophe Geiger, ed., 2013). On the other hand, if the design right is interpreted so narrowly that only direct or "slavish" copies will infringe, this could limit the willingness of private companies to pay for registered designs. As always in IP law, it is a matter of balance. *See* P.G.F.A. Geerts, *The Informed User in Design Law: What Should He Compare and How Should He Make the Comparison?* 36 E.I.P.R. 181–85 (2014).

27
Infringement

27.1 United States

27.1.1 Copyright and trademark

The standards for infringement of a product design covered by a US copyright or trademark are no different than the general infringement standards in those areas of law. In copyright law, substantial similarity is the key test, while in trademark law under the US Lanham Act, "likelihood of confusion" is the reigning test. These are described in some detail earlier in this book, in Chapters 3 and 4, respectively.

27.1.2 Design patents

27.1.2.1 Ordinary observer test

CASE

Egyptian Goddess, Inc. v. Swisa, Inc., 543 F.3d 665 (Fed. Cir. 2008)

[This case was about the alleged infringement of US Design Patent 467,389 (the '389 patent), which was for a rectangular-shaped product with various surfaces on the face of the rectangle, used for shining or buffing fingernails. The design looks like this (Figure 27.1):

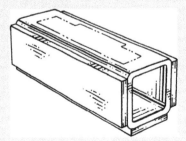

Figure 27.1 Nail buffer design

CASE (continued)

The owner of the '389 patent, Egyptian Goddess, Inc. (EGI) sued defendant Swisa, Inc. for infringement. The district court granted Swisa's summary judgment motion for non-infringement, because Swisa showed that its nail buffer had buffing surfaces on all four sides of the rectangular product, while EGI's, like much of the prior art, had buffers on only three sides. EGI appealed this ruling.]

The starting point for any discussion of the law of design patents is the Supreme Court's decision in *Gorham Co. v. White*, 14 Wall. 511, 81 U.S. 511 (1871). That case involved a design patent for the handles of tablespoons and forks. In its analysis of claim infringement, the Court stated that the test of identity of design "must be sameness of appearance, and mere difference of lines in the drawing or sketch . . . or slight variances in configuration . . . will not destroy the substantial identity." *Id.* at 526–27. Identity of appearance, the Court explained, or "sameness of effect upon the eye, is the main test of substantial identity of design"; the two need not be the same "to the eye of an expert," because if that were the test, "[t]here never could be piracy of a patented design, for human ingenuity has never yet produced a design, in all its details, exactly like another, so like, that an expert could not distinguish them." *Id.* at 527. The Gorham Court then set forth the test that has been cited in many subsequent cases: "[I]f, in the eye of an ordinary observer, giving such attention as a purchaser usually gives, two designs are substantially the same, if the resemblance is such as to deceive such an observer, inducing him to purchase one supposing it to be the other, the first one patented is infringed by the other." 81 U.S. at 528. In the case before it, the Court concluded that "whatever differences there may be between the plaintiffs' design and those of the defendant in details of ornament, they are still the same in general appearance and effect, so much alike that in the market and with purchasers they would pass for the same thing – so much alike that even persons in the trade would be in danger of being deceived." *Id.* at 531.

[T]his court has cited *Litton Systems* [*v. Whirlpool Corp.*, 728 F.2d 1423, 1444 (Fed. Cir. 1984)] for the proposition that the point of novelty test is separate from the ordinary observer test and requires the patentee to point out the point of novelty in the claimed design that has been appropriated by the accused design. We think, however, that Litton and the predecessor cases on which it relied are more properly read as applying a version of the ordinary observer test in which the ordinary observer is deemed to view the differences between the patented design and the accused product in the context of the prior art. When the differences between the claimed and accused design are viewed in light of the prior art, the attention of the hypothetical ordinary observer will be drawn to those aspects of the claimed design that differ from the prior art. And when the claimed design is close to the prior art designs, small differences between the accused design and the claimed design are likely to be important to the eye of the hypothetical ordinary observer. It was for that reason that the Supreme Court in [*Smith v. Whitman Saddle Co.*, 148 U.S. 674 (1893)] focused on the one feature of the patented saddle design that departed from the prior art – the sharp drop at the rear of the pommel. To an observer familiar with the multitude of prior art saddle designs, including the design incorporating the Granger pommel and the

CASE (continued)

Jenifer cantle, "an addition frequently made," 148 U.S. at 682, the sharp drop at the rear of the pommel would be important to the overall appearance of the design and would serve to distinguish the accused design, which did not possess that feature, from the claimed design.

Not only is this approach consistent with the precedents discussed above, but it makes sense as a matter of logic as well. Particularly in close cases, it can be difficult to answer the question whether one thing is like another without being given a frame of reference. The context in which the claimed and accused designs are compared, *i.e.*, the background prior art, provides such a frame of reference and is therefore often useful in the process of comparison. Where the frame of reference consists of numerous similar prior art designs, those designs can highlight the distinctions between the claimed design and the accused design as viewed by the ordinary observer.

The question before this court under the standard we have set forth above is whether an ordinary observer, familiar with the prior art designs, would be deceived into believing the Swisa buffer is the same as the patented buffer. EGI argues that such an observer would notice a difference between the prior art and the '389 patent, consisting of "the hollow tube that is square in cross section and that has raised pads with exposed gaps at the corners."

In light of the similarity of the prior art buffers to the accused buffer, we conclude that no reasonable fact-finder could find that EGI met its burden of showing, by a preponderance of the evidence, that an ordinary observer, taking into account the prior art, would believe the accused design to be the same as the patented design. [The key to this, based on expert testimony, was that the accused design had buffers on all four sides of the rectangular product, while the patented deign had buffer surfaces on only three sides.] In concluding that a reasonable fact-finder could not find infringement in this case, we reach the same conclusion that the district court reached, and for many of the same reasons.

[Affirmed.]

NOTES

1. This case put to rest what had come to be called the "point of novelty" test, which directed the "ordinary observer" to judge the similarity of patented and accused designs in light of the features that distinguish the patented design from the prior art – *i.e.*, the "point of novelty" over the prior art. By subsuming this into the traditional contours of the "ordinary observer" test laid down in the Supreme Court's *Gorham* case, the court dispensed with the explicit two-part test.
2. For more on how design patent "claims" (*i.e.*, drawings) are construed by courts, and how functional elements of design are handled in the analysis, *see Sport Dimension, Inc. v. Coleman Co., Inc.*, 820 F.3d 1316 (Fed. Cir. 2016).

27.2 China

Baili v. Apple, Beijing IP Office Decision, as summarized in Eva Dou & Daisuke *Wakabayashi, Apple's Challenges in China Underlined by Patent Dispute*, Wall Street Journal (June 17, 2016), http://www.wsj.com/articles/beijing-regulator-orders-apple-to-stop-sales-of-two-iphone-models-1466166711 [https://perma.cc/7WGG-EUV7]

In December 2014, Baili, a relatively new Chinese mobile phone maker, filed an administrative complaint in the Beijing Intellectual Property Office. The complaint said that two of Apple, Inc.'s most popular mobile phone models, the iPhone 6 and iPhone 6 Plus, infringed Baili's Chinese Design Patent No. CN20143009113.9 (the "design '113 patent"). Baili requested a permanent injunction, which provoked Apple into filing a petition challenging the validity of the '113 patent before the Patent Re-examination Board ("PRB") of SIPO.

The Baili design looks like this [Figure 27.2]; note the similarity with well-known Apple iPhone design elements (thin cross-section, rounded edges, front screen seamlessly integrated without surrounding border, etc.):

The SIPO Beijing office initially ruled for Baili, saying that, "The iPhone 6 and iPhone 6 Plus infringe on Baili's design patent due to substantial similarities to Baili's 100c [model mobile] [p]hone." The standard the SIPO office applied was that the "average customer" could not "identify the differences" between Baili's patented design and the iPhones. Apple appealed to the Beijing IP Court, and the SIPO office ruling was reversed.

The essence of the IP Court's holding was that the SIPO office improperly applied the "ordinary consumer" or "ordinary observer" test in comparing Baili's patented design to Apple's iPhones. In applying the test, the Court emphasized that according to prior cases from the Supreme People's Court, the test in China is very similar to that applied in the U.S. under the case of *Egyptian Goddess, Inc. v. Swisa, Inc.*, 543 F.3d 665 (Fed. Cir. 2008) [see above, this chapter]. The Court also emphasized that the test is to be applied to remaining design elements after all functional (non-aesthetic) features are removed from the analysis.

In applying the test, the Court noted several key differences between the patented design and the iPhone models at issue: (1) the iPhones have an actual, physical button at the bottom in the middle of their front side; the Baili patented design has no physical button,

> **CASE** *(continued)*
>
> **Figure 27.2** Baili mobile phone design
>
>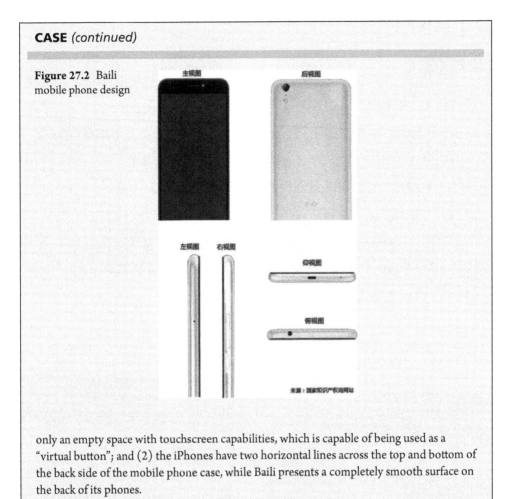
>
> only an empty space with touchscreen capabilities, which is capable of being used as a "virtual button"; and (2) the iPhones have two horizontal lines across the top and bottom of the back side of the mobile phone case, while Baili presents a completely smooth surface on the back of its phones.
>
> Because of these differences, the IP Court said, Apple does not in fact infringe the Baili design patent at issue.

NOTES

1. For more on the *Baili-Apple* case, *see* Xiang Li, Mingji Piao, & Hui Zhang, Determination of Design Patent Infringement in China, Kluwer Patent Blog, July 17, 2017, available at http://patentblog.kluweriplaw.com/2017/07/17/determination-design-patent-infringement-china/.
2. Some commentators describe the standard for determining design patent infringement in China as a variant of the three-step method used for invention (utility) patent infringement. The steps are, first, determine the scope of the design patent by looking at the drawings in the patent document and isolating the aesthetic (non-functional) features; second, establish whether the product accused of infringing the design patent is of the same product type or category, perhaps with reference to the international design classification system (*i.e.*, Locarno Agreement); and third, a careful comparison of the design patent with the product accused of infringement, viewing the key elements of the design from the perspective of an ordinary consumer. *See* Zhipei Jiang & Elizabeth Chien-Hale, "Patent Protection in the People's Republic

of China," Chapter 26 in 1 *Corporate Counsel Guide to Doing Business in China* (3d ed., 2016–17), at §26:16 ("General methods used by Chinese judges in patent infringement cases – Fact finding and application of substantive law").

3. Another important case on design protection in China is *Land Rover v. Land Wind*, reported on by GU Xueni, in "Design patent application strategies to guarantee protection for innovation-driven businesses," Aug. 29, 2016, available at http://www.internationallawoffice.com/Newsletters/Intellectual-Property/China/Wan-Hui-Da-Law-Firm-Intellectual-Property-Agency/Design-patent-application-strategies-to-guarantee-protection-for-innovation-driven-businesses. This case involved an attempt by Land Rover, the well-known British car brand, to prevent a "copycat" car design from being sold in China (the "Land Wind" car). The two designs are shown in Figure 27.3.

Figure 27.3 Land Rover (top) vs. Land Wind (below) designs

Unfortunately for Land Rover, its Chinese design patent was declared invalid for lack of novelty; Land Rover had first exhibited its car at the Guangzhou International Automobile Exhibition in December 2010, but had failed to file a design application until 2014. Because the "grace period" for filing in China is quite limited (*see* Part II for more details), the design patent was invalid and the Land Wind was allowed to blow onto the market, unobstructed.

27.3. European Union

Infringement of RCDs in EU proceedings draws a good deal from the "informed user" standard for testing design validity; *see* above Chapter 26. So, for example, the Court of Appeal in the UK applied the "informed user" standard in an important case, finding, as in the *GrupoPromer* validity case described above in Chapter 26, that the registered design was not infringed because the accused product did not create the same "overall impression" as the registered design. *See Magmatic Ltd v. PMS International Ltd* [2014] EWCA Civ 181; [2014] E.C.D.R. 20. The registered design covered an animal-shaped travelling case for children. It is shown on the left in Figure 27.4; the accused product, made by defendant PMS, is on the right.

Figure 27.4 Animal-shaped children's luggage

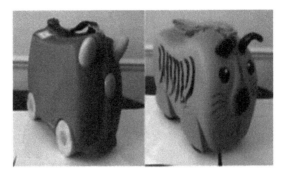

The Court of Appeal, reversing a High Court judgment finding infringement, emphasized that the registered design was "clearly intended to create the impression of a horned animal," in part because it was sold with animal imagery on the surface of the travel case (*Magmatic* [2014] EWCA Civ 181; [2014] E.C.D.R. 20 at [41]). The accused design, however, had different protrusions, which looked more like antennae and were designed to help pull the travel case along as it rolled. This, together with the surface decoration on the accused device (which is absent on Magmatic's registered design), created a different overall impression, according to the Court of Appeal. See Alexander Borthwick, *The Scope of Registered Design Protection Following Magmatic v PMS International*, 37 Euro. Intell. Prop. Rev. 180–85 (2015).

NOTES

1. When you look at the two designs, do they appear closely similar or not? In your view, should the design right protect Magmatic from infringement by the PMS product pictured above?
2. For an interesting comparison of a European-style "informed user" standard with the Chinese "ordinary consumer" test, *see* Justin Davidson, "People's Republic of China: Design Right – Infringement – Comparison with Italian Judgment," 30 Euro. I.P. Rep. 91 (2008) (noting that infringement of a car design was found in Italy, while a patent on the same design was found not infringed by the same accused product in China).
3. Aside from the standard for infringement, it is important to understand what acts constitute infringement of the EU Design Directive. These are described in Article 12, which lists the "Rights conferred by the design right":

> 12.1. The registration of a design shall confer on its holder the exclusive right to use it and to prevent any third party not having his consent from using it. The aforementioned use shall cover, in particular, the making, offering, putting on the market, importing, exporting or using of a product in which the design is incorporated or to which it is applied, or stocking such a product for those purposes.

The sweep is quite broad, including as it does not only "making" and "using," but also importing, exporting, and stocking for sale. This provision confers broad rights to reach acts of infringement affecting virtually every "link" in the distribution chain.

28

Defenses

28.1 United States: functionality

CASE

TrafFix Devices, Inc. v. Mktg. Displays, Inc., 532 U.S. 23 (2001)

Kennedy, J.
[Respondent, Marketing Displays, Inc. (MDI), holds now-expired utility patents for a "dual-spring design" mechanism that keeps temporary road and other outdoor signs upright in adverse wind conditions. An illustration of the MDI road sign is reproduced in Figure 28.1; the twin springs are marked numbers 16 and 18 in the diagram. MDI claims that the shape and outline of its sign stands were recognizable to buyers and users; when petitioner TrafFix Devices, Inc., began marketing sign stands with a dual-spring mechanism copied from MDI's design, MDI brought suit under the Trademark Act of 1946 for trade dress infringement. The District Court ruled for TrafFix. The Sixth Circuit reversed, ordering a trial on the trade dress claim. Other Circuit courts had ruled that an expired utility patent forecloses the possibility of trade dress protection in the product's design, to the Supreme Court granted certiorari to resolve the Circuit split.]

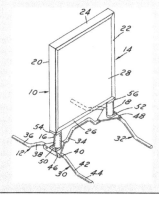

Figure 28.1 Flexible Traffic Sign

CASE *(continued)*

The principal question in this case is the effect of an expired patent on a claim of trade dress infringement. A prior patent, we conclude, has vital significance in resolving the trade dress claim. A utility patent is strong evidence that the features therein claimed are functional. If trade dress protection is sought for those features the strong evidence of functionality based on the previous patent adds great weight to the statutory presumption that features are deemed functional until proved otherwise by the party seeking trade dress protection. Where the expired patent claimed the features in question, one who seeks to establish trade dress protection must carry the heavy burden of showing that the feature is not functional, for instance by showing that it is merely an ornamental, incidental, or arbitrary aspect of the device. In the case before us, the central advance claimed in the expired utility patents is the dual-spring design; and the dual-spring design is the essential feature of the trade dress MDI now seeks to establish and to protect. The rule we have explained bars the trade dress claim, for MDI did not, and cannot, carry the burden of overcoming the strong evidentiary inference of functionality based on the disclosure of the dual-spring design in the claims of the expired patents.

The rationale for the rule that the disclosure of a feature in the claims of a utility patent constitutes strong evidence of functionality is well illustrated in this case. The dual-spring design serves the important purpose of keeping the sign upright even in heavy wind conditions; and, as confirmed by the statements in the expired patents, it does so in a unique and useful manner. The dual-spring design allows sign stands to resist toppling in strong winds. Using a dual-spring design rather than a single spring achieves important operational advantages. In the course of patent prosecution, it was said that "[t]he use of a pair of spring connections as opposed to a single spring connection . . . forms an important part of this combination" because it "forc[es] the sign frame to tip along the longitudinal axis of the elongated ground-engaging members." The dual-spring design affects the cost of the device as well; it was acknowledged that the device "could use three springs but this would unnecessarily increase the cost of the device."

In a case where a manufacturer seeks to protect arbitrary, incidental, or ornamental aspects of features of a product found in the patent claims, such as arbitrary curves in the legs or an ornamental pattern painted on the springs, a different result might obtain. There the manufacturer could perhaps prove that those aspects do not serve a purpose within the terms of the utility patent. The inquiry into whether such features, asserted to be trade dress, are functional by reason of their inclusion in the claims of an expired utility patent could be aided by going beyond the claims and examining the patent and its prosecution history to see if the feature in question is shown as a useful part of the invention. No such claim is made here, however. MDI in essence seeks protection for the dual-spring design alone. The asserted trade dress consists simply of the dual-spring design, four legs, a base, an upright, and a sign. MDI has pointed to nothing arbitrary about the components of its device or the way they are assembled. The Lanham Act does not exist to reward manufacturers for their innovation in creating a particular device; that is the purpose of the patent law and its period of exclusivity. The Lanham Act, furthermore, does not protect trade dress in a functional

CASE (continued)

design simply because an investment has been made to encourage the public to associate a particular functional feature with a single manufacturer or seller. Whether a utility patent has expired or there has been no utility patent at all, a product design which has a particular appearance may be functional because it is "essential to the use or purpose of the article" or "affects the cost or quality of the article." [*Inwood Labs., Inc. v. Ives Labs., Inc.*, 456 U.S. 844, (1982)], at 850, n. 10.

[Reversed.]

NOTES

1. In *Miche Bag, LLC v. Marshall Group*, 818 F. Supp. 2d 1098 (N.D. Ind. 2010), the court distinguished *TrafFix* in a case involving a women's handbag having a removable and interchangeable upper component, shown in Figure 28.2

    The court noted that the removable upper was the subject of a pending utility patent application, but found the handbag trade dress protectable nonetheless:

Figure 28.2 Handbag design

    [Defendant] Marshall Group cites no authority for the proposition that a pending patent application has the same effect as an expired patent, and the court has found none. Perhaps more importantly, Miche Bag's claimed trade dress includes, but extends well beyond, the removability feature. Miche Bag agrees that the shells' removability and interchangeability are functional, but argues that the way the cover itself fits within the trade dress is not. The way in which even functional parts are assembled may be protected as trade dress. *Service Ideas, Inc. v. Traex Corp.*, 846 F.2d 1118, 1123 (7th Cir. 1988). Miche Bag's Classic Bag trade dress consists of a handbag with a two-tone appearance, a rigid and specifically depicted polygonal-shaped body with inset sides, a specifically depicted slightly-curved upper aspect; specifically depicted curved straps, oval chrome buckles, trapezoidal-shaped zipper ends, and removable covers with both full-wrap and side-wrap variations . . . [T]he commonality of the non-functional features indicates the easy availability to The Marshall Group of alternate designs, which may constitute some evidence of non-functionality. *Valu Engineering, Inc. v. Rexnord Corp.*, 278 F.3d 1268, 1276 (Fed.Cir. 2002). When viewed as a whole, [the] claimed trade dress is [not] functional (818 F. Supp. 2d 1098, at 1104–05).

    Note that here, even though each of the named features was, on its own, a common design element, it was the *combination* of the named features that constituted the protected trade dress/design in this case. And none of those features were found to be functional.

2. The functionality test requires courts to ask whether a design element affects the "cost or quality" of an item. This is easy to understand in some cases; for example, imagine a company that sells trailer hitches that attach to the back of a car, and are used for attaching trailers towed behind the car. If such a company

claimed a "metal-colored, spherically-shaped" hitch as its trade dress, this would surely be rejected as functional. A trailer hitch must be sturdy to support the weight of a trailer, so metal is a logical (and traditional) material to use. And almost all trailers come with attachments that are designed to attach to a round trailer hitch on a car, so again the round shape would be functional.

Some cases are closer, however. In one, a company that designed graphics for sporting event broadcasts on television claimed that a yellow line, superimposed on the visual image of a football game and representing the "first down line" (distance needed to reach a first down) should be protected as trade dress. The court in the case disagreed. *See Sportvision v. SportsMedia Tech Corp.*, 2005 WL 1869350 (N.D. Cal. Aug. 4, 2005) (holding that the color yellow was functional for this purpose; although yellow was not the only possible color, it was easier to *see* than other colors).

28.2 Europe

The EU Design Directive provides for a functionality defense which is similar in scope to the defense as applied in the US and China. *See* EU Design Directive (1998), at Article 7.

Article 7
Designs dictated by their technical function and designs of interconnections

1. A design right shall not subsist in features of appearance of a product which are solely dictated by its technical function.
2. A design right shall not subsist in features of appearance of a product which must necessarily be reproduced in their exact form and dimensions in order to permit the product in which the design is incorporated or to which it is applied to be mechanically connected to or placed in, around or against another product so that either product may perform its function.
3. Notwithstanding paragraph 2, a design right shall, under the conditions set out in Articles 4 and 5, subsist in a design serving the purpose of allowing multiple assembly or connection of mutually interchangeable products within a modular system.

A unique feature of this provision is Article 7(3), permitting protection for "a design serving the purpose of allowing multiple assembly or connection of mutually interchangeable products within a modular system." This would appear to cover future versions of products such as Lego brand plastic brick toys, and other toys that use modular parts. (The actual Lego bricks would of course not be novel, as they were created originally in 1958. Furthermore, trademarks for these bricks have been found functional by several European courts. *See* Michaela Huth-Dierig, Germany: Final Revocation of Trademark Protection for Shape of LEGO Bricks, Intn'l Trademark Ass'n (Oct. 1, 2009), available at https://www.inta.org/INTABulletin/Pages/GERMANY FinalRevocationofTrademarkProtectionforShapeofLEGOBricks. asp x.); https://www.lego.com/en-us/aboutus/news-room/2010/septem

ber/eu-court-lego-group-not-allowed-to-register-brick-as-trademark/. *See generally*, Christopher Noyes & Crystal Roberts, *Protecting the Brick: LEGO's Global IP Enforcement Efforts*, N.Y. L. J., Aug. 3 (2015), at p. 1.

The Design Directive goes on, in Article 7(3), to permit design protection for "a design serving the purpose of allowing multiple assembly or connection of mutually interchangeable products within a modular system." This would appear to cover future versions of products such as Lego brand plastic brick toys, and other toys that use modular parts. (The actual Lego bricks would of course not be novel, as they were created originally in 1958. Furthermore, trademarks for these bricks have been found functional by several European courts. *See* Huth-Dierig, *supra*.

28.2.1 Standards under the Directive

28.2.1.1.Effect of registered design on the part of the defendant

 CASE

Case C-488/10, Celaya Emparanza y GaldosInternacional SA v. Proyectos Integrales de Balizamiento SL, (ECJ: 16 Feb. 2012)

Cegasa is the holder of Community registered design No 00421649-0001, consisting of a beacon-like marker used for traffic signalling purposes. The design was lodged with OHIM on 26 October 2005 and published in the Register of Community Designs on 13 December 2005. At the end of 2007, [defendant] PROIN marketed the marker H-75. Cegasa served an extra-judicial cease-and-desist demand upon PROIN in January 2008. The latter denied any infringement but none the less gave an undertaking to make changes to its design. Cegasa repeated its cease-and-desist demand to PROIN in March 2008. On 11 April 2008, PROIN lodged with OHIM an application for registration of a Community design, consisting of a beacon-like marker used for traffic signalling purposes. That design was published in the Register of Community Designs on 7 May 2008 under No 000915426-001.

  The referring court considers that the cylindrical marker marketed by PROIN is a reproduction of Community design No 000421649-0001 registered by Cegasa because an informed user does not receive a different overall impression of that marker from that given by the design registered by Cegasa. It points out that Cegasa has not, however, made any application for a declaration of invalidity of registered Community design No 000915426-001.

CASE *(continued)*

Cegasa has, on the other hand, brought proceedings before the Juzgado de lo Mercantil n° 1 de Alicante y n° 1 de Marca Comunitaria alleging infringement of a registered Community design, claiming that the offering, promoting, advertising, stocking, marketing and distributing of the H-75 signalling device by PROIN constitutes a breach of the rights conferred on it by the Regulation as holder of registered Community design No 000421649-0001.

Article 19 of the [Design] Regulation, entitled "Rights conferred by the Community design", is worded as follows:

> 1. A registered Community design shall confer on its holder the exclusive right to use it and to prevent any third party not having his consent from using it. The aforementioned use shall cover, in particular, the making, offering, putting on the market, importing, exporting or using of a product in which the design is incorporated or to which it is applied, or stocking such a product for those purposes.

[Defendant] PROIN argued that, until such time as the registration of that design is cancelled, its holder enjoys a right of use under the Regulation, so that the exercise of that right cannot be deemed to be an infringement. [This issue was referred to the CJEU.]

[I]t is clear that the wording of Article 19(1) of the Regulation does not make any distinction on the basis of whether the third party is the holder of a registered Community design or not. Thus, that provision states that a registered Community design is to confer on its holder the exclusive right to use it and to prevent "any third party" not having his consent from using it. Similarly, Article 10(1) of the Regulation provides that the scope of the protection conferred by a Community design is to include "any design which does not produce on the informed user a different overall impression". It is apparent from those provisions that the Regulation does not preclude the holder of a registered Community design from bringing infringement proceedings to prevent the use of a later registered Community design which does not produce on the informed user a different overall impression.

It should be noted in that connection that, as submitted by the European Commission in its observations, the provisions of the Regulation must be interpreted in the light of the priority principle, under which the earlier registered Community design takes precedence over later registered Community designs. It follows in particular from Article 4(1) of the Regulation that a design is to be protected by a Community design to the extent that it is new and has individual character. However, where two registered Community designs are in conflict with each other, the design that was registered first is deemed to have met those conditions for obtaining protection before the design that was registered second. Thus, the holder of the later registered Community design may be afforded the protection conferred by the Regulation only if he can demonstrate that the earlier registered Community design fails to meet one of those conditions, by seeking a declaration of invalidity, where appropriate by way of counterclaim.

28.3 Functionality in China

The standards for determining functionality in Chinese design patent cases are the same as those used to determine functionality in trade dress/product configuration cases; *see* Part IV, Section 17.2.7.

29
Remedies

29.1 US: design patents

 CASE

Samsung Elecs. Co. v. Apple Inc., 137 S. Ct. 429 (2016)

[A jury found that various smartphones manufactured by petitioners (collectively, Samsung) infringed design patents owned by respondent Apple Inc. that covered a rectangular front face with rounded edges and a grid of colorful icons on a black screen. Apple was awarded $399 million in damages – Samsung's entire profit from the sale of its infringing smartphones. The Federal Circuit affirmed the damages award.]

Section 289 of the Patent Act provides a damages remedy specific to design patent infringement. A person who manufactures or sells "any article of manufacture to which [a patented] design or colorable imitation has been applied shall be liable to the owner to the extent of his total profit." 35 U.S.C. §289. In the case of a design for a single-component product, such as a dinner plate, the product is the "article of manufacture" to which the design has been applied. In the case of a design for a multicomponent product, such as a kitchen oven, identifying the "article of manufacture" to which the design has been applied is a more difficult task. This case involves the infringement of designs for smartphones. The United States Court of Appeals for the Federal Circuit identified the entire smartphone as the only permissible "article of manufacture" for the purpose of calculating §289 damages because consumers could not separately purchase components of the smartphones.

The text [of the statute] resolves this case. The term "article of manufacture," as used in §289, encompasses both a product sold to a consumer and a component of that product. "Article of manufacture" has a broad meaning. An "article" is just "a particular thing." J. Stormonth, A Dictionary of the English Language 53 (1885) (Stormonth); see also American Heritage Dictionary, at 101 ("[a]n individual thing or element of a class; a particular object or item"). And "manufacture" means "the conversion of raw materials by the hand, or by machinery, into articles suitable for the use of man" and "the articles so made." Stormonth 589; see also American Heritage Dictionary, at 1070 ("[t]he act, craft, or process of manufacturing products, especially on a large scale" or "[a] product

> **CASE** *(continued)*
>
> that is manufactured"). An article of manufacture, then, is simply a thing made by hand or machine. So understood, the term "article of manufacture" is broad enough to encompass both a product sold to a consumer as well as a component of that product. A component of a product, no less than the product itself, is a thing made by hand or machine. That a component may be integrated into a larger product, in other words, does not put it outside the category of articles of manufacture.
>
> This reading of article of manufacture in §289 is consistent with 35 U.S.C. §171(a), which makes "new, original and ornamental design[s] for an article of manufacture" eligible for design patent protection. The Patent Office and the courts have understood §171 to permit a design patent for a design extending to only a component of a multicomponent product.
>
> The parties ask us to go further and resolve whether, for each of the design patents at issue here, the relevant article of manufacture is the smartphone, or a particular smartphone component. Doing so would require us to set out a test for identifying the relevant article of manufacture at the first step of the §289 damages inquiry and to parse the record to apply that test in this case. We decline to lay out a test for the first step of the §289 damages inquiry in the absence of adequate briefing by the parties. [Reversed and remanded.]

29.2 Europe/EU

The EU Design Regulation, at Article 89, describes "Sanctions in actions for infringement." It reads as follows:

> 1. Where in an action for infringement or for threatened infringement a Community design court finds that the defendant has infringed or threatened to infringe a Community design, it shall, unless there are special reasons for not doing so, order the following measures:
>
> (a) an order prohibiting the defendant from proceeding with the acts which have infringed or would infringe the Community design;
>
> (b) an order to seize the infringing products;
>
> (c) an order to seize materials and implements predominantly used in order to manufacture the infringing goods, if their owner knew the effect for which such use was intended or if such effect would have been obvious in the circumstances;
>
> (d) any order imposing other sanctions appropriate under the circumstances which are provided by the law of the Member State in which the acts of infringement or threatened infringement are committed, including its private international law.

2. The Community design court shall take such measures in accordance with its national law as are aimed at ensuring that the orders referred to in paragraph 1 are complied with.

There have been several relevant amendments that affect the availability of remedies. One set of changes makes RCD remedies cumulative with those available under national law. This resolves, in the RCD context, a longstanding argument over the cumulation of various forms of IP protection for designs in Europe. *See* J. H. Reichman, *Of Green Tulips and Legal Kudzu: Repackaging Rights in Subpatentable Innovation*, 53 Vand. L. Rev. 1743 (2000).

Another change excuses innocent infringers (those who "were not aware, and had no reasonable ground for supposing, that the design was registered") of the obligation to pay damages. This amendment makes clear that products must be marked with the specific *number* of the design registration in order to put potential infringers on notice. See Community Design Regulations 2005, SI 2005 No. 2339 (Oct. 1, 2005), available at http://www.wipo.int/edocs/lexdocs/laws/en/gb/gb157en.pdf.

Finally, in the UK, registered designs have been incorporated into the system if "Crown Use," *i.e.*, permitted governmental use, with requirement of compensation. This is covered in section 14.2A of the UK Registered Designs Act of 1949, as amended through 2015, available at https://www.gov.uk/government/uploads/system/uploads/attachment_data/file/498821/Registered_Designs_Act_1949.pdf. Section 2A reads:

2A. Compensation for loss of profit

(1) to the registered proprietor, or

    (a) If there is an exclusive licence in force in respect of the design, to the exclusive licensee,

    (b) If there is an exclusive licence in force in respect of the design, to the exclusive licensee,

compensation for any loss resulting from his not being awarded a contract to supply the products to which the design is applied or in which it is incorporated.

(2) Compensation is payable only to the extent that such a contract could have been fulfilled from his existing manufacturing capacity; but is payable notwithstanding the existence of circumstances rendering him ineligible for the award of such a contract.

(3) In determining the loss, regard shall be had to the profit which would have been made on such a contract and to the extent to which any manufacturing capacity was underused.

One final note: A design infringement case was the basis for a ruling relating to the payment of litigation costs (attorney fees, etc.) in the specialized Patents County Court (PCC) in the UK. Under the PCC cost-capping regulations, losing parties in PCC cases are generally shielded from having to pay costs greater than £50,000. In a case involving two sets of defendants, and slightly different facts regarding each, the winning design owner/plaintiff in the case sought cumulative costs greater than the £50,000 cap. The PCC rejected this argument, emphasizing the risk-reducing rationale behind the cap:

> I think the terms of [the costs cap] were drafted with a clear intention behind them. The words are clear. The court will not order a party to pay total costs of more than the capped sum. That means a litigant in the PCC has the security of knowing that, subject to certain exceptions, the costs cap will protect their exposure to the other party's costs. This interpretation of . . . [the cap] facilitates access to justice for smaller and medium sized enterprises. This interpretation cuts against a fully compensatory approach to costs but it does so in a context in which another forum is available with a more compensatory costs regime (the High Court) (*Gimex International Groupe Import Export v. Chill Bag Co Ltd*, 2012 WL 3963576, at par. 22).

Index

3-D shape trademarks 535–8, 549, 552
007 (TM) 580–83
24 Hour Fitness (TM) 521
32 Red (TM) 639–42
32 Vegas (TM) 639–42

Abie's Irish Rose (play) 338–41
abstract ideas, patents 42–53
abstracts, copyright 360–65
accounting systems, copyright 282–5
Acid Lover (book) 452–6
advertising 590–91, 633–5
air freshener, product design 771–4
Amazon.com 5, 539, 616
antenna control system, patents 169–71
Anti-Unfair Competition Law 1993 (China) 673–4, 682, 684–8, 701, 722–3, 734–5
antibodies, patents 110–111
Apple 513, 521, 741
applied art, copyright 295–7, 320–21
  product design, and 753–5
arbitrary marks 513, 521, 524–5, 758
arbitration awards, international recognition 256
architecture, copyright 274, 282, 320, 388–9, 414
Arctic and Device (TM) 662–5
artistic works
  applied art 295–7, 320–21
  copyright protection 295–7, 319–21, 450–51
  landscaping 391–9
  moral rights 391–9
  neighboring rights 413–14
  sculpture 274, 278, 285–8, 330, 396, 414
  visual art 391–9
Aspirin 538
authors' rights
  civil law systems, in 331
  moral rights 331–2, 383–4
    alienability 384, 391
    attribution 383, 394, 399

Berne Convention 383, 391, 393
China, in 389–90
duration 384–9, 391
economic rights, compared 383, 389
Europe, in 384–9
exceptions 395–6
France, in 384–8
Germany, in 364–5, 385, 388–9
integrity, rights of 331, 383, 387–8, 390–99
UK, in 385
US, in 332, 391–9
visual art 391–9
neighboring rights 266, 331–2
  artistic works 413–14
  audiovisual works 411–13
  Berne Convention 266–7
  China, in 264–5, 407–13
  copyright, differences from 399–400
  databases 404–7
  digital performances 371–2, 415–16
  duration 400
  Europe, in 400
  France, in 400
  Germany, in 400–3
  music 401–3, 414
  performers' rights 410–411, 413–16
  publishers' rights 408–10
  rental and lending rights 400
  US, in 332, 413–16
paternity right 331
right of integrity 331, 383, 387–8, 390–99
similar works 338–41
visual art 391–9
authorship 305–7
  China, in 302–7
  co-authorship 289–91, 302–5, 329–30
  ghost writers 305–7
  speeches 304–5
  US, in 285–91, 330, 395
  work for hire 268, 285–8, 305–7, 328–9
AutoZone (TM) 597

Baidu (TM) 569–72
Barbie (TM) 597
bathtubs, patents 96–9
Beebe, Barton 418–19
Bell Telephone (TM) 493
Berne Convention 1886
  applied art 296
  architecture 282
  background 266
  cinematographic works 266
  minimum standards of protection 267
  moral rights 383, 391, 393
  neighboring rights 266–7
Best Buy (TM) 532–5
bicycles/bicycle parts 150–52, 231–4, 595
bilateral contracts 5
biotechnology, patentability
  biological mechanisms 156
  BRCA1 and BRCA2 genes 65–8
  cell free fetal DNA 67
  cell growth enzymes 87–90
  China, in 68
  Europe, in 69–74
  Oncomouse 70–74
  stem cells 74
  synthetic erythropoietin (EPO) 180–86
  US, in 63–8, 156
Birthday Train, copyright 320–21, 760
Bliss (TM) 521–2
Bond, James 580–83
Bonpie (TM) 547–8
book review extracting, copyright 433–8
Boomerang (TM) 564–5
bottles, shape 535–8, 549, 552–7
BRCA1 and BRCA2 genes 65–8
broadcasting
  copyright infringement 331
    China, in 263–367, 449–50
    errors and omissions insurance 273
    Europe, in 268–70
    generally 272–3
    public broadcasting responsibility 449–50
    US, in 271–2
  distribution rights
    communication to public 377–8, 381–2
    internet television services 376–9
    public broadcasting responsibility 449–50
    sound recordings 371–2

  transmit clauses 365–72
    US, in 365–72
  neighboring rights 410–411
Bud (TM) 576–80
Budweiser (TM) 596
bullshit (TM) 545

Camel (TM) 524, 758
Castaway (movie) 351–4
Cellophane (TM) 605–6
chairs, copyright 308–11, 467–72
Charging Out Amazon (movie) 449–50
China
  civil courts 39–40
  copyright
    apology 466–7
    applied art 295–7
    artistic features 295–7
    artistic works 450–51
    audio-visual works 411–13
    authors' rights 407
    authorship 302–7
    Berne Convention, and 267
    broadcasting rights 265, 449–50
    co-authorship 302–5
    compilation works 297–8
    creativity requirement 291
    damages 265–6, 465–6, 465–7
    databases 297–8
    derivative works 306–7, 356–60
    digital copyright 476
    digital publishing 452–6
    direct infringement 462
    exclusions 448–56
    fair dealing 448–56
    indirect infringement 462–3
    injunctions 265, 463–5
    internet service provider liability 476
    joint liability 464–5, 476
    limitations 292–4
    moral rights 389–90
    music 294
    neighboring rights 264–5, 407–13
    originality 291–2
    orphan works 263–6
    protectable subject matter 294–5, 297–302
    remedies 265, 463–7
    reproduction requirement 292
    reproduction rights 342–5, 455–6

service works 306–7
substantial similarity test 344
term of protection 267
typefaces 298–302
utilitarian features 295–7
work for hire 305–7
written works 294
patents 169–79
  absolute novelty 91
  amendments 146, 150–53
  animals and plants 54
  applications trends 37–8
  biotechnology 68
  burden of proof 229–30
  clear requirement 169–71
  compensation trends 229
  computer programs 54–8
  cultural influences on 225–6
  damages 224–30
  design patents 37–8
  direct and explicit derivation standard 146–50
  disclosure 91–2, 146–53
  disease, diagnosis or treatment methods 54
  enforcement mechanisms 38–9
  enhanced damages, proposal for 229–30
  Examination Guidelines 54
  functional limitations 171–9
  General Administration of Customs (GAC) 39
  genetic resources 55
  grace period 92–5
  Guidelines for Patent Examination 54
  historical development 33–4
  identity requirement 102–6
  injunctions 199–206
  international priority 92–5
  intrinsic *vs.* extrinsic evidence 171
  invalidity defense 99
  inventions as technical solutions 53, 57
  inventive step 129–35
  loss interpretation 204–5
  mental activities exception 53–8
  notable progress standard 129
  novelty 91–106
  nuclear transformation, products of 54
  ordinary skill 171
  Patent Review Board 240
  patentable subject matter 53–8
  permanent injunctions 205–6
  preliminary injunctions 199–205
  prior art defense 95–9, 104
  prior art, definition 90–92
  prior art disclosure 99–102
  public interest exception 55
  public use 90–91
  relative novelty 90–91
  remedies 199–206, 225–30
  scientific discoveries 54
  separate comparison 105–6
  simple 2-D designs 54
  State Intellectual Property Office (SIPO) 37–8
  technical problem recognition 130–35
  technical processes 54–5
  three-step approach 129–31
  types and strategies 37–8
  utility models 37–8, 91
  willful infringement, for 229
  written description requirement 157–8
product design
  infringement 779–81
  infringement defenses 789
  ordinary consumer test 782
  product configuration/protection 759
trade secrets
  damages 734–5
  definition 682–8
  improper means 708–12
  injunctions 731–2
  non-competition agreements 719–24
  protection 673–4
  remedies 731–2, 734–5
  unfair competition 673–4, 682, 684–8, 701, 722–4, 734–5
trademarks
  3-D shapes 535–8, 552
  acquired distinctiveness 532–5, 555
  applications 506, 510
  confusing similarity 591–4
  damages 644–5, 645–6
  distinctiveness 510, 514, 517–21, 532–8
  dual enforcement 644–5
  exclusions 511–12
  first to file principle 510
  functionality 552–7
  geographic terms/indications 543–4
  infringement defenses 618–26
  infringement remedies 644–6
  licensing 662–5
  nominative use 601–2, 605, 618–22

non-trademark use 622–6
non-well-known marks 580–83
original equipment manufacture (OEM)
    products 622–6
protection without registration 566–72, 580–83
quality supervision 662–5
refusal, grounds for 510
registration 504, 510–512
reviews and appeals 510
scandalous marks 547–8
similar marks 591–4
well-known marks 566–72, 597–600
unfair competition 673–4, 682, 684–8, 701, 734–5
utility models 37–8, 91
China Jing Wine (TM) 518–21, 548
Chiung Yao 263–4
choreographic works see dance
Christmas tree spigots, patents 250–55
cinematographic works
    co-authorship 330
    copyright 266–7, 330
    digital downloading 476
Coach (TM) 596
coal gasification, patents 111–13
Coca-Cola 535–8, 549, 687
Code of Chinese Character: Story of the Invention of Chinese Character, The (book) 408–10
colors, trademarks 516–17, 525, 543–4, 550–51, 758
combination locks, patents 219–22
Community Patent Convention 35–6
Company Law 2013 (China) 724
competition
    copyright conflicts with 438–42
    non-competition agreements 719–24
    unfair competition 673–4, 682, 684–8, 701, 722–4, 734–5
compilations, copyright 277, 297–8, 329, 355
compulsory licensing 10–11, 16
compulsory working 10–11
computer algorithms
    patentability 45–53
    trade secrets 669–71
computer programs
    copyright
        client-server-software 441–8
        Europe, in 315–19, 441–8
        TRIPS Agreement 317
        updates and patches 441–8
        US, in 274, 281–2, 319

licensing
    exhaustion of rights 441–8
    maintenance agreements 441–2
patentability
    binary-coded decimals 49–50
    China, in 54–8
    Europe, in 59–63
    facial and speech animation 51–2, 57–8
    technical character requirement 60–62
    US, in 44–52, 59
Convention for the Recognition and Enforcement of Foreign Arbitral Awards 1958 256
Convention on Jurisdiction and the Enforcement of Judgments in Civil and Commercial Matters 1968 269
Coppertone (TM) 513–14
copyright
    applied art 295–7, 320–21
        product design, and 753–5
    architecture 274, 282, 320, 388–9, 414
    artistic works 319–20, 450–51
    authors' rights model 331
    authorship 305–7
        China, in 302–7
        co-authorship 289–91, 302–5, 329–30
        Europe, in 327–30
        ghost writers 305–7
        speeches 304–5
        US, in 285–91, 330, 395
        work for hire 268, 285–8, 305–7, 328–9
    broadcasting, and
        China, in 263–367, 449–50
        communication to public 377–8, 381–2
        digital performance 371–2, 415–16
        errors and omissions insurance 273
        Europe, in 376–9
        internet television services 376–9
        rights 267, 331
        sound recordings 371–2
        transmit clauses 365–72
        US, in 365–72
    broadcasts 319
    China, in
        apology 466–7
        applied art 295–7
        artistic works 450–51
        audio-visual works 411–13
        authors' rights 407
        authorship 302–7

broadcasting 263–367, 449–50
calligraphy 298–302
co-authorship 302–5
compilation works 297–8
creativity requirement 291
damages 465–6
databases 297–8
derivative works 306–7, 356–60
direct infringement 462
ideas/expression dichotomy 292–4, 343
indirect infringement 462–3
injunctions 265, 463–5
limitations 292–4
originality 291–2
orphan works 263–6
protected works, categories 294
remedies 265, 463–7
reproduction/duplicability requirement 292
reproduction rights 342–5, 455–6
service works 306–7
substantial similarity test 344
typefaces 298–302
work for hire 305–7
cinematographic works 266–7, 330
compilations 277, 297–8, 329, 355
computer programs 274, 281–2, 315–19
   exhaustion of rights 441–8
   maintenance agreements 441–2
creativity requirement 274, 291
damages 265–6, 270–72, 465–7
dance/choreographic works 274, 294, 320, 371, 414
databases 297–8, 321–8, 346–51
   China, in 297–8
   Europe, in 321–8, 346–51, 404–7
   neighboring rights 404–7
   protectable subject matter, whether 297–8
   reproduction right 346–51
derivative works 268
   abstracts 360–65
   China, in 306–7, 356–60
   compilation 355
   divisible works 359–60
   Europe, in 360–65
   fair use/fair dealing 355
   free vs. dependent uses 364
   TV series episodes 271–4
   US, in 351–5
distribution rights 308–11, 331
   communication to public 377–8, 381–2

Europe, in 308–11, 376–9, 438–42
exclusions 371
exhaustion 438–48
France, in 375
Germany, in 372–5
internet publishing 380–83
internet television services 376–9
material vs. non-material form, goods in 375
resale rights 375
sound recordings 371–2
transmit clauses 365–72
UK, in 375
US, in 365–72
economic rights
   derivative rights 351–65
   fair use/fair dealing 355
   moral rights, compared 383, 389
   reproduction rights 332–51
   US, in 332–41
efficient infringement 461–2
enforcement
   alternative measures 269–70
   proportionality 270
Europe, in
   applied art 320–21
   authors' rights model 331
   competition, conflicts with 438–42
   computer programs 315–19, 441–8
   databases 321–8, 346–51, 404–7
   derivative works 360–65
   distribution rights 308–11, 372–83, 438–42
   exhaustion 438–48
   fixation requirement 327
   harmonization 307–8, 311–12, 315, 319, 346, 375, 467
   limitations 315–19, 432–3
   originality 307–15
   orphan works 268–70
   photographic works 312–15, 320
   reproduction rights 344–438, 345–51
   work for hire 328–9
exhaustion 438–48
fair use/fair dealing 355, 417–27, 455–6
fixation requirement
   China, in 292
   Europe, in 327
   US, in 278
France, in 320, 329–30
furniture 308–11, 372–5

Germany, in
  co-authorship 329–30
  damages 467–72
  fixation requirement 327
  protected works 320
  work for hire 328–9
grey market goods 652
illustrations 320
injunctions 265, 269–72, 463–5, 467
integrity, right of 331, 383, 387–8, 390–99
literary adaptations 319, 331
literary works 294, 319–20
moral rights 331–2
  alienability 384, 391
  attribution 383, 394, 399
  Berne Convention 383, 391, 393
  China, in 389–90
  duration 384–9, 391
  economic rights, compared 383, 389
  Europe, in 384–9
  exceptions 395–6
  France, in 384–8
  Germany, in 364–5, 385, 388–9
  integrity, rights of 331, 383, 387–8, 390–99
  UK, in 385
  US, in 332, 391–9
  visual art 391–9
music 282, 294, 319
  neighboring rights 414
  reproduction rights 332–41
neighboring rights 266, 331–2
  artistic works 413–14
  Berne Convention 266–7
  China, in 264–5, 407–13
  copyright, differences from 399–400
  databases 404–7
  digital performances 371–2, 415–16
  duration 400
  Europe, in 400
  France, in 400
  Germany, in 400–3
  music 414
  performers' rights 410–411, 413–16
  publishers' rights 408–10
  rental and lending rights 400
  US, in 332
originality requirement
  China, in 291–2
  Europe, in 307–15

factual information 277
  sweat of the brow theory 277, 297–8, 308
  UK law, in 308
  US, in 274–7, 297–8
orphan works 270–72
  China, in 263–6, 263–7
  Europe, in 268–70
  US, in 270–72
  work for hire 268
ownership
  fixation 278
  transfer 278
paternity rights 331
performances 278, 331
performers' rights 266–7
photographic works 312–15, 320
pictorial works 274
product design, and 753–5
  Europe, in 759–60
product design, overlap with 742–3
remedies 269
  alternative measures 269–70
  apology 466–7
  apportionment 272, 459–62
  China, in 265–6, 463–7, 465–7
  damages 265–6, 270–72, 458–62, 465–7
  Europe, in 270, 467–72
  Germany, in 269, 467–72
  injunctions 265, 269–70, 269–72, 463–5, 467
  statutory damages 462, 465–6
  US, in 271–2, 458–62
reproduction/duplicability requirement 292
reproduction rights
  accompilation 355
  China, in 342–5, 455–6
  credibility test 334
  derivative works 268, 306–7, 351–65
  Europe, in 345–51, 433–8
  fair use/fair dealing 355, 455–6
  improper appropriation 333
  independent economic significance 436
  legitimate interests of rights holder, conflicts
    with 436–7
  limitations 433–8
  sole purpose 435–6
  special experience test 343
  technological process, integral part of 433–8
  US, in 332–41
sculptural works 274, 278, 285–8, 330, 396, 414

similar works 338–41
sound recordings 319, 336–8
   exhaustion of rights 438–42
   neighboring rights 415–16
   performance/distribution rights 371–2, 438–42
special experience test 343
subject matter
   accounting systems 282–5
   applied art 295–7, 320–21
   architecture 274, 282, 320, 414
   artistic works 319–20
   broadcasts 319
   China, in 294–5, 297–302
   cinematographic works 266–7
   collective works 329
   compilations 277, 329
   computer programs 274, 281–2, 319
   creativity 274
   dance/choreographic works 294, 320
   databases 297–8
   dramatic works 294, 338–41
   exclusions 282–5
   fixation requirement 278
   graphic works 294
   ideas and concepts 282–5, 343
   illustrations 320
   literary/written works 294, 319–20
   literary works 294
   music 282, 294, 319
   no copyright for facts rule 277
   originality 274–7
   orphan works 270–72
   photographic works 279–82, 320
   pictorial works 274, 294
   recorded music 278
   sculptural works 274, 278, 285–8, 330, 396, 414
   separability test 297
   sound recordings 319
   telephone directories 275–7
   titles 282
   typefaces 298–302
   typographical arrangements 319
   US, in 270–72, 274–8, 281–8, 294, 297, 319, 396, 414
   utilitarian works 282
telephone directories 275–7
titles 282
translations 332
typefaces 298–302

typographical arrangements 319
UK, in
   abstraction test 345
   co-authorship 330
   derivative works 268
   fixation requirement 327
   ideas/expressions dichotomy 345
   limitations 319
   originality 308
   orphan works 268
   protected works 319–20
   work for hire 329
US, in
   accounting systems 282–5
   applied art 297
   architecture 274, 282, 414
   authorship 285–91
   co-authorship 289–91, 330
   common law model 332
   computer programs 274, 281–2, 319
   creativity 274
   damages 271–2, 458–62
   derivative works 351–5
   distribution rights 365–72
   economic rights 232–341, 332–41
   exclusions 282–5
   fair use 355, 417–27
   fixation requirement 278
   ideas and concepts 282–5
   integrity, rights to 391–9
   music 282
   no copyright for facts rule 277
   originality 274–7
   orphan works 270–72
   photographic works 279–82
   pictorial works 274
   proof of infringement 457–8
   remedies 271–2, 458–62
   reproduction rights 332–41
   sculptural works 274, 278, 285–8, 396, 414
   separability test 297
   statutory damages 462
   sweat of the brow theory 277, 297–8
   telephone directories 275–7
   titles 282
   typefaces 302
   utilitarian works 282
   visual art 391–9
   work for hire 285–8

utilitarian works 282
wrongful gain 461
Copyright Act 1965 (Germany)
  authors' rights 361–5, 375
  co-authorship 329–30
  fixation 327
  moral rights 385
  neighboring rights 400–403
  protected works 320–21
  work for hire 328–9
Copyright Act 1976 (US)
  applied art 753–5
  computer programs 285
  damages 271, 458, 469
  derivative works 352–3, 359
  distribution and performance rights 15, 362–72, 415
  efficient infringement 460–61
  exclusions 282–3
  fair use 418–23
  fixation 278
  import restrictions 652
  joint works 290
  limitations 428–32
  literary works 294
  moral rights 385, 391
  movies 281
  originality 274, 302
  product design 753–5
  sound recordings 282
  TRIPS, compliance with 15
  visual artists rights 391–9
  work for hire 286–7
Copyright, Designs and Patents Act 1988 (UK) 267, 319, 329, 376
Copyright Law 2010 (China)
  adaptations 264–5, 267, 359, 390
  audio-visual works 413
  digital copyright 448–56
  exclusions 448–52
  fair use 450–56
  neighboring rights 407, 411–13
  protected subject matter 294–5, 297–302
  work for hire 306–7
counterfeit goods
  design protection, and 741–2
culpa in contrahendo 244–9
curve charts, copyright 293–4

damages
  copyright 265–6, 270–72, 465–7
    apportionment 459–62
    China, in 265–6, 465–6
    Europe, in 270
    statutory damages 462, 465–6
    US, in 271–2, 458–62
  patents
    apportionment tests 236–7
    causality 233
    China, in 224–30
    disgorgement remedy 233–4
    enhanced damages 229–30
    Germany, in 230–34
    loss of profits, for 218–22, 231–4
    reasonable royalty 222–4
    standard essential patents, and 226–9
    UK, in 230–31, 234–9
    unjust enrichment 235–6
    US, in 217–24
    willful infringement, for 229
  product design
    US, in 790–91
  trademarks
    China, in 645–6
    Europe, in 636–42
    US, in 629–35
dance and choreographic works/performances 274, 294, 320, 371, 414
Darjeeling (TM) 531–2
data transfer mechanisms, patents 172–6
databases, copyright
  authorship 328
  China, in 297–8
  Europe, in 321–8, 346–51, 404–7
  neighboring rights 404–7
  reproduction right 346–51
Defend Trade Secrets Act 2016 (US) 672–3, 681–2
dental floss, patents 153–6
diagnosis or treatment methods, patentability 54, 59
dictionaries, trademarks in 611
Dietz, Adolf 384
digital commerce
  trademarks, extraterritorial jurisdiction 649
digital copyright
  anti-circumvention provisions 473
  cinematographic works 476
  internet service providers liability
    China, in 476

Europe, in 475–6
  generally 473–4
  Graduated Response program 476–7
  internet content providers 474
  US, in 474–5
 music
  China digital performances 371–2, 415–16
  downloading 415, 462, 475
  sampling 400–403
  videos 411–13
Digital Millennium Copyright Act 1998 (US) 415, 473, 474–5
Digital Performance Right in Sound Recordings Act 1995 (US) 415
digital publishing
 distribution rights 380–83
 fair use/fair dealing doctrine 433–8
  China, in 452–6
  free riding, and 602–5
  keywords, use as 602–5, 613–15
  snippets 426–7
  sponsored adverts 603, 613–15
  tort, place of 453–4
  US, in 413–16, 426–7
 graduated response program 476–7
 neighboring rights 371–2, 415–16
 trademarks
  keywords, use as 602–5, 613–15
Digital Rights Management (DRM) systems 473
digital sampling
 copyright 400–403
 patent infringement 200–202
dilution, trademarks
 anti-dilution protection 594–7, 605
Directive 84/450 on misleading and comparative advertising 590
Directive 89/104 on trademarks
 genuine use 489
 likelihood of confusion 589
 similar or identical marks 613–15
Directive 93/98 on copyright duration
 intellectual creation 313–14, 348
 photographs 313–14
Directive 96/9 on database protection 406–7
 intellectual creation 308, 323–5, 348
 national law, priority of 326
Directive 97/55 on misleading and comparative advertising 590–91

Directive 98/71 on product design
 definitions 766
 disclosure 767
 functionality test 786–7
 general principles 765–6
 novelty and individual character 741–4, 766–7
 registered designs, role of 787–8
 registration 765–6
 scope of protection 767–8
 validity challenges 765
Directive 2000/31 on E-Commerce 475
Directive 2001/29 on Information Society 346–50
 distribution rights 309–10, 373–4, 376–83
 exhaustion of rights 310
 intellectual creation 318, 348–50
 reproduction rights 313–14, 348–9, 364, 433–8
Directive 2004/48 on IPR enforcement 269
 damages 636–7
 injunctions 642–3
Directive 2006/114 on misleading and comparative advertising 590–91
Directive 2006/116 on copyright term
 computer programs 308, 348
 photographs 308, 313
Directive 2008/95 on trademarks
 descriptiveness 762–4
 packaging, design protection 763–4
 trademark inactivity 612
Directive 2009/24 on protection of computer programs 308
 exhaustion of rights 441–8
Directive 2015/2436 on trademarks
 acquired distinctiveness 527–32
 applications, refusal grounds 506–9
 dictionaries, trademark reproduction in 611
 foreign language, distinctiveness 560–61
 functionality 551–2
 genuine use requirement 488
 graphic representability 515–17
 invalidity, grounds for 573–4
 non-well-known marks 573–4
 refusal of registration, grounds for 506–9
Directive 2016/943 on trade secrets protection
 access, unauthorized or unlawful 692–4, 718
 background 674–7
 damages 735–6
 definitions 677, 682
 injunctions 731–2
 non-competition agreements 719

protection efforts, proof of 701
purpose 674
remedies 731–2, 735–6
reverse engineering 726
disease, diagnosis or treatment methods, patentability 54, 59
Dishonored Lady (play) 459–61
dispute resolution 6
  arbitration awards, international recognition 256
  choice of law/forum clauses 652, 655–6
  conflict of laws 652–5
  Dispute Settlement Board (DSB) 14
  enforcement of foreign judgments 269, 656–7
  location of harm principle 653
  patent licensing 256–60
distribution rights
  broadcasting
    communication to public 377–8, 381–2
    digital performances 371–2, 415–16
    Europe, in 376–9
    internet television services 376–9
    sound recordings 371–2
    transmit clauses 365–72
    US, in 365–72
  copyright 331
    communication to public 377–8, 381–2
    Europe, in 308–11, 372–83, 376–9, 438–42
    exclusions 371
    exhaustion 438–48
    France, in 375
    free movement of goods, and 308–11, 372–83, 438–42
    Germany, in 372–5
    internet publishing 380–83
    internet television services 376–9
    material *vs.* non-material form, goods in 375
    resale rights 375
    sound recordings 371–2
    transmit clauses 365–72
    UK, in 375
    US, in 365–72
DNA, patentability 65–8, 74
dog jersey, product design 750–52
Dong Feng (TM) 626
doors, overlay mounted, design patents 748–9
dramatic works, copyright 388–9, 459–62
Dreyfuss, Rochelle 653–4
Durango, Kwami 481–2

eBay.com 196–9, 603
electric light bulbs, patents 142–6
employees
  non-competition agreements 719–24
  patent service rights 307
  work for hire 268, 285–8, 305–7, 328–9
errors and omissions insurance 273
erythropoietin, synthetic (EPO), patent 180–86
estoppel 243
EU Intellectual Property Office 503–4, 743–4, 765–6
Europe
  copyright
    applied art 320–21
    authorship 327–30
    competition, conflicts with 438–42
    computer programs 315–19, 441–8
    damages 270
    derivative works 365
    digital copyright protections 475–6
    distribution rights 308–11, 372–83, 438–42
    exhaustion 438–48
    fixation requirement 327
    free movement of goods, and 438–42
    harmonization 307–8, 311–12, 315, 319, 346, 375, 467
    injunctions 269–70, 467
    internet service providers liability 475–6
    limitations 315–19
    moral rights 384–9
    originality 307–15
    orphan works 7, 268–9
    photographic works 312–15, 320
    proportionality 270
    remedies 467–72
    reproduction rights 345–51, 433–8
    resale rights 375
  free movement of goods 373–4
  Information Society
    digital copyright protection 473, 475–6
    distribution rights 375, 383
    neighboring rights 400
    reproduction rights 346, 432–3, 437–8
  patents
    aesthetic creations 58
    amendments 161–2
    animal and plant varieties 59, 70–74
    application trends 36
    biotechnology 69–74
    Brexit implications 36

business methods 58
claims 179–86
closest prior art reference 135–41
Community Patent Convention 35–6
computer programs 58–63
disclosure 36, 106–7, 113–15, 158–62
disease, diagnosis or treatment methods 59
dispute settlement 15
equivalent elements 179–86
European Patent Convention 12–13, 35
European Patent Office 35
grace period 117–19
industrial application 36, 58
information, presentation methods 58
internet disclosure 107–9
interpretation challenges 179–86
invalidity/opposition proceedings 240
inventive step 135–41
mathematical formulae 58
mental activities exception 58
microbiological processes 59
national court challenges 36–7
novelty 106–21
opposition, grounds for 36–7
partial priority 119–21
prior art 107–15
prior-filed applications 115–17
problem-solution approach 135–41
prosecution procedures 12–13
public disclosure 110–111
public interest exception 36, 59, 70, 73
publication date 109–11
scientific discoveries 58
single disclosure 111–15
skilled person, ability to understand 158–62
state of the art rule 115–17
subject matter 58–63
technical character requirement 60–62, 72
textual infringement 184–6
two-step test 71–3
Unified Patent Court 13, 35–6
Unified Patents 13, 35–6
product design
 copyright law, and 759–60
 definitions 766
 Design Court jurisdiction 770
 disclosure 767
 duration of protection 765
 European Design Regulation 765, 769–70
 functionality test 786–7
 informed user test 774–5
 infringement 781–2, 792
 infringement defenses 786–8
 innocent infringement 792
 invalidity 768–9, 771–4
 novelty and individual character 766–7, 771–4
 prior art 766–7
 prior use rights 768
 protectable subject matter 759–75
 Registered Community Design 743–4, 765–7, 769
 remedies 770, 791–2
 scope of protection 766–8
 trademark law, and 760–64
 Unregistered Community Design 765
trade secrets
 damages 735–6
 definition 688–94
 injunctions 731–2
 non-competition agreements 719
 protections 674–7
 remedies 731–2, 735–6
 reverse engineering 726–7
trademarks
 acquired distinctiveness 527–32
 blocking injunctions 643–4
 Community trademarks 503, 636
 damages 636–42
 distinctiveness 514–17, 527–32, 560–61
 exclusions 506–9
 exclusively descriptive doctrine 560–61
 foreign language, in 560–61
 functionality 551–2
 genuine use requirement 488–90
 geographic terms/indications 543, 574
 infringement 611–16
 infringement defenses 611–15
 infringement remedies 636–44
 injunctions 642–4
 likelihood of confusion 588–91
 more than local significance 543, 574–80
 non-well-known marks 573–80
 preliminary injunctions 642
 protection without registration 564–5, 573–80
 refusal, grounds for 506–9
 scandalous marks 546
 well-known marks 564–5

European Patent Convention 1973
   applications procedures 12–13
   background 11–12, 35
   limitations 13
   patentable subject matter 58–9
      biotechnology 69–74
      computer programs 59–63
      technical character 60–62, 72
      two-stage test 71–3
European Patent Office 35
expositions, international 9–10
Exxon 521

fair use/fair dealing, copyright
   China, in 448–56
      digital publishing 452–6
      public broadcasting 449–50
      tort, place of 453–4
   codification 417–18
   copyright 355
   criticism 418–19
   Europe, in 418
      harmonization 432
      limitations 432–3
   models, generally 417
   UK law 417–18
   US, in 355, 417–23
      amount and substantiality 426
      digital sampling 419–23
      effect on use 421–3
      first sale doctrine 428–32, 457, 652
      four-part test 419–27
      parodies 420–22, 616–18
      reverse engineering 423
      snippets 426–7
      time-shifting 422
      transformative uses 422–7
      unpublished works 420
fair use/fair dealing, trademarks
   descriptive marks 600–601
   generic marks 562–4
   US, in 600–601
famous trademarks *see* well-known trademarks
fanciful marks 513, 521, 524–5, 758
Farewell, My concubine (opera) 410
fashion accessories, product design 741–3
First Half of My Life, The (book) 303–5
first sale doctrine 428–32, 457, 652
flags, trademarks 511

flanged pipes, patents 99–102
football fixture lists, copyright 322–7
France
   copyright
      co-authorship 330
      collective works 329
      digital copyright, graduated response program 477
      distribution rights 375
      moral rights 384–8, 385
      neighboring rights 400
      protected works 320
      work for hire 329
   product design
      copyright and trademark protection 759–60
      unity of art principle 741
franchises
   trademark agreements 659–61, 665
   trademark holdover conflicts 633–5
   US, in 659–61, 665
FRAND terms 228–9
free movement of goods 438–42
free-trade liberalism 9
freedom of expression 616–18
Fritos (TM) 660–61
furniture, copyright 308–11, 372–5, 467–72

Gap 513
GATT 14
gemstone etching, patents 159–61
gene enhancers, patents 256–9
genericide, trademarks 605–11
Germany
   copyright
      co-authorship 329–30
      damages 467–72
      derivative works 360–65
      distribution rights 372–5
      fixation requirement 327
      injunctions 269
      material *vs.* non material form, goods in 375
      moral rights 364–5, 385, 388–9
      neighboring rights 400–403
      protected works 320
      work for hire 328–9
   patent infringement
      claims, interpretation 185–92
      damages 230–34
      disgorgement remedy 233–4
      equivalence, doctrine of 187–92

fault liability, and 249
injunctions 206–13
patents
  applications trends 36
  courts 180
  licensing dispute enforcement 256–60
  national law challenges 37
product designs 760
trade secrets 688–92
  reverse engineering 726–7
trademarks
  applications 506
  damages 637–8
  Freihaltebedurfnis (need to keep free) 531
  injunctions 642
unfair competition 676, 688–94, 716–18
ghost writers 305–7
Ginsburg, Jane 653–4
globalization 8–9
glutamic acid derivatives, patents 131–5
Goddess in Exile (book) 356–9
goodwill 658–9
Google AdWords 613–15
Google Library Project 418, 423–7
Google.com 452–6, 513, 602–5, 610–611
GPS transmission to cell phone, patent 157–8
Graduated Response program, ISP liability 476–7
grey market goods 651–2
Guantanamera (TM) 539–43

Hague Conference on Private International Law 655
Hague Convention on the International Registration of
    Industrial Designs (2012) 743–4
Half Moon Bay beer 18–21
Hamilton, Alexander 33
hard disk drives, patents 222–4
Harrison, George 336–8
hedging, patents 45–50
Hegel, G.W.F. 385
Herbrozac (TM) 585–8

ideas and concepts
  computer algorithms 45–53
  copyright exclusions
    China, in 292–4, 343
    ideas/expression dichotomy 292–4, 343
    merger doctrine 292–4, 343–4
    scènes à faire doctrine 343–4
    US, in 282–5

patentable, whether 42–53
  mathematical formulae 42–5, 50, 58
  scientific ideas 42–5, 50, 54, 58
illustrations, copyright 320
import restrictions
  trade secrets infringement, and 732
  trademarks 651–2
initials, trademarks 513
injunctions
  copyright
    China, in 265, 463–5
    Europe, in 269–70, 467
    US, in 271–2
  patents 196–217
    China, in 199–206
    FRAND term injunctions 211–17
    Germany, in 209–13
    permanent injunctions 205–6
    preliminary injunctions 199–205
    standard essential patents, and 209–17
    UK, in 214–17
    US, in 196–9
  trade secrets 729–32
    China, in 731
    Europe, in 731–2
    US, in 729–31
  trademarks
    blocking injunctions 643–4
    Europe, in 642–4
    US, in 627–8
ink cartridges, patents 147–9
integrity, right of 331, 383, 387–8, 390–99
Intellectual Property Code (France) 320, 329–30
international criminal court 4
international IP treaties 5, 7–8
international law, principles of 4–5
international trade
  expositions 9–10
  trends 8–9
International Trade Commission 650–51
internet publishing *see* digital publishing
internet service providers
  copyright liabilities
    China, in 476
    Europe, in 475–6
    exclusions 475
    generally 473–4
    Graduated Response program 476–7
    US, in 474–5

TV distribution rights 376–9
inventive step, patents
   China, in
      notable progress standard 129
      technical problem recognition 130–35
      three-step approach 129–31
   Europe, in
      closest prior art reference 135–41
      problem-solution approach 135–41
      two-step approach 135–41
   TRIPS Agreement 16
   US, in
      beyond novelty requirement 122
      double patenting doctrine 126
      historical development 122–3
      secondary considerations 123–4, 126
      terminal disclaimers 126
      TSM test 126–9
inventive step, product design 750–52
IP address protection mechanisms 176–9

Jackhead ball (TV advert) 351–4
Jello (TM) 611
Journey of New Year Paintings from the YANG Family, A (book) 450–52
jurisdiction
   European Design Court 770
   extraterritoriality, trademark law 646–9
   national jurisdiction 4–5

Kant, Immanuel 384–5
Kaufman, Debra 51
KayDee Cosmetics (KDC) 481
Kelley, Chapman 391–9
Kit-Kat (packaging design) 761
Kodak 513, 524, 595, 758
Koln-Dusseldorfer Steamship Lines 481
Kornspitz (TM) 612
Kung Fu Panda (TM) 582, 621–2

Labor Contract Law 2007 (China) 722–3
Land Rover 566–9, 781
landscaping, copyright 391–9
Lanham Act 1946 *see* Trademarks Act 1946 (US)
Last Aristocrats, The (movie) 356–9
Leahy-Smith America Invents Act 2011 78, 240–43
legal authority, in private international law 5–6
Lego 786–7
Les Misérables (book) 386–7

letters, trademarks 516
Letty Lynton (movie) 459–61
Lexus (TM) 602
licensing
   compulsory 10–11, 16
   computer programs 441–8
   patents
      arbitration awards, recognition 256
      dispute resolution 256–60
      enforcement 256–60
      FRAND terms calculation 228–9
      generally 244
      most favored nation clauses 250–56
      no challenge clauses 256
      non-disclosure agreements 244, 246–7
      pharmaceuticals 256–60
      pre-contractual liability 244–9
      substantive terms 250–56
      trade secrets, misappropriation 244–9
      US, in 244–56
   trade secrets
      label licenses/shrinkwrap contracts 726
   trademarks 655–6
      assignment in gross 658–9
      China, in 662–5
      franchise agreements 659–61, 665
      goodwill, and 658–9
      purpose 658
      quality assurance requirement 658
      territorial rights 659–61
      US, in 659–61, 665
likelihood of confusion
   product design 748–9
      informed user test 775–6, 781–2
      ordinary observer test 776–8
      point of novelty 778
   trademarks
      China, in 591–4
      comparative advertising 590–91
      Europe, in 588–91
      generally 584–5
      grey market goods 651–2
      identical marks 491, 575, 585, 588, 591
      similar goods and services 591, 651–2
      similar marks 491, 575, 585–94
      US, in 585–8, 651–2
loaned servant doctrine 288
Locke, John 277
London Exhibiton 1851 9

long path gas cells, patents 245–9
Louis Vuitton 613–18
Lychee Brand (TM) 618–22

Madrid Agreement Concerning the International Registration of Marks 1891 502
Madrid Protocol 501–3
Malcolm X (movie) 289–91
Marley, Bob 630–32
mercantilism 31–2
merger doctrine, copyright 292–4, 343–4
Miche Bag (product design) 785
microcolor (TM) 601
milk powder containers, patents 203–5
Mine Mauler (TM) 648–9
Minimax (TM) 488–90
moral rights 331–2
  alienability 384, 391
  attribution 383, 394, 399
  Berne Convention 383, 391, 393
  China, in 389–90
  duration 384–9, 391
  economic rights, compared 383, 389
  Europe, in 384–9
  exceptions 395–6
  France, in 384–8
  Germany, in 364–5, 385, 388–9
  integrity, rights of 331, 383, 387–8, 390–99
  UK, in 385
  US, in 332, 391–9
  visual art 391–9
Moskovskaya (TM) 541–2
most favored nation clauses 244–9
music, copyright
  digital performances 371–2, 415–16
  digital sampling 400–403
  distribution/performance rights 371
  fair use 419–23
  music downloading 415, 462, 475
  music videos 411–13
  neighboring rights 401–3, 414
  phonographic recording, fixation 278
  sheet music 371

national treatment principle 10
nationalism 9
nature, patentability
  animals and plants 44, 54, 59, 70–74
  laws of 44

Needham, Joseph 33
neighboring rights 266, 331–2
  artistic works 413–14
  audio-visual works 411–13
  Berne Convention 266–7
  China, in 264–5, 407–13
  copyright, differences from 399–400
  databases 404–7
  digital performances 371–2, 415–16
  duration 400
  France, in 400
  Germany, in 400–3
  music 401–3, 414
  performers' rights 410–411, 413–16
  publishers' rights 408–10
  rental and lending rights 400
  US, in 332, 413–16
New Kids on the Block, The (rock band) 602
newspaper article services, copyright 346–51, 360–65, 380–83
Nike 524, 626, 757
Nimmer, David 418–19
no challenge clauses 256
non-obviousness *see* inventive step
novelty, patents
  China, in
    absolute novelty 91
    disclosure 91–2
    grace period 92–5
    identity requirement 102–6
    international priority 92–5
    invalidity defense 99
    prior art defense 95–9, 104
    prior art, definition 90–92
    prior art disclosure 99–102
    public use 90–91
    relative novelty 90–91
    separate comparison 105–6
  Europe, in
    disclosure, adequacy of 113–15
    disclosures, non-prejudicial 106–7
    general principles 106–9
    grace period 117–19
    internet disclosure 107–9
    partial priority 119–21
    prior art 107–15
    prior art reference 113–15
    prior-filed applications 115–17
    public disclosure 110–111

publication date 109–11
single disclosure 111–15
state of the art rule 115–17
US, in
  conception date 85–6
  critical date 78–9, 82, 85
  date of invention 85
  date of working 85
  definition 75
  diligence rule 85–90
  first to file rule 75–9, 81–5
  first to file rule exceptions 82–5
  first to invent rule 78–9, 81–2, 85–90
  grace period 83–4
  identity standard 75–9
  joint/team inventors 84–5
  post-AIA patents 75–9, 81–5
  pre-AIA patents 78–9, 81–2, 85–90
  prior art 80–82
  prior knowledge 84–5
  priority rule 86–90
  public disclosure 83–4
  rule of diligence 85–6
NYC Triathlon (TM) 627–8

Office for Harmonization in the Internal Market (OHIM)(EU) 503
olfactory marks 515–17
Olympia (TM) 538
Oncomouse (patent) 70–74
Online Copyright Infringement Liability Limitation Act 1998 (US) 474
Orbison, Roy 419–22
Oriental Daily News 557–9
original equipment manufacture (OEM)
  products 622–6
orphan works
  China, in 263–7
  Europe, in 7, 268–70
  US 270–72

paintings *see* artistic works
Palace III, The: The Lost Daughter (TV series) 263, 342–5, 464–5
paper sizing process, patent 135–40
parallel imports 651–2
Paris Convention 1883
  background 7, 9–10, 33
  benefits 34–5

patents
  compulsory licensing 10–11
  compulsory working 10–11
  enforcement 14
  filing procedures 34–5
  international priority 10, 34–5
  national treatment principle 10, 35
  sovereignty, impacts on 8, 10–11
  trademarks
    exclusions 507–8
    foreign trademarks, equal treatment 495
    Madrid System registration procedures 501–3
    well-known marks 500
Paris Exposition 1878 9–10
Park 'n Fly (TM) 562–4, 609
parodies
  copyright 420–22
  trademarks 597, 616–18
passing off 602
Patent Act 1790 (US) 42
Patent Act 1952 (US)
  damages 221–2
  disclosure 84
  exceptions 83, 90
  identity standard 75–9
  indirect infringement 192–3
  injunctions 198
  nonobviousness 122–9
  novelty 75–9, 84
  patentable subject matter 42–6, 62–4
  prior art 79–80, 84–5
  technical character test 62
Patent Act 1980 (Germany) 190, 206, 230
Patent Cooperation Treaty 1970 11–13
Patent Law 2008 (China) 53–4, 57
patent law development
  background 7–10, 31–3
  China, in 33
  Europe, in 11–13, 32
  harmonization 13–17
  Industrial Revolution 32
  international expositions, and 9–10
  IP as trade 14
  mercantilism 31–2
  Paris Convention 9–11, 33
  Patent Cooperation Treaty 11–13
  TRIPS Agreement 7–8, 14–17, 34
  UK, in 32
  US, in 32–3

Venetian guilds 32
WIPO role 13–14
patent trolls 198–9
patents
　disclosure 40, 142–62
　　adequacy of 142–62
　　amendments 150–53, 161–2
　　China, in 146–53, 157–8
　　direct and explicit derivation standard 146–50
　　Europe, in 158–62
　　non-disclosure agreements 244
　　pre-contractual protection 244–9
　　skilled person, ability to understand 158–62
　　undue experimentation test 142–6, 157
　　US, in 142–6, 153–7
　　written descriptions 153–8
　infringement claims
　　China in 169–79, 240
　　clear requirement 169–71
　　contributory infringement 192–5
　　disavowal 168–9
　　equivalent elements 179–86
　　Europe, in 179–86, 240
　　functional limitations 171–9
　　Germany, in 186–92
　　indirect infringement 192–5
　　inducement 192–4
　　intention 193–4
　　interpretation challenges 163–9, 179–86
　　intrinsic *vs.* extrinsic evidence 171
　　invalidity proceedings 240–43
　　inventive essence 186–92
　　knowledge requirement 194–5
　　textual infringement 184–6
　inventive step 40
　　beyond novelty requirement 122
　　China, in 129–35
　　closest prior art reference 135–41
　　double patenting doctrine 126
　　Europe, in 135–41
　　historical development 122–3
　　notable progress standard 129
　　problem-solution approach 135–41
　　product design 750–52
　　secondary considerations 123–4, 126
　　technical problem recognition 130–35
　　terminal disclaimers 126
　　three-step approach 129–31
　　TRIPS Agreement 16

　　TSM test 126–9
　　US, in 122–4, 126–9
　licensing
　　arbitration awards, recognition 256
　　dispute resolution 256–60
　　enforcement 256–60
　　FRAND terms calculation 228–9
　　generally 244
　　most favored nation clauses 250–56
　　no challenge clauses 256
　　non-disclosure agreements 244, 246–7
　　pharmaceuticals 256–60
　　pre-contractual liability 244–9
　　substantive terms 250–56
　　trade secrets, misappropriation 244–9
　　US, in 244–56
　novelty 40
　　absolute novelty 91
　　China, in 91–106
　　conception date 85–6
　　critical date 78–9, 82, 85
　　date of invention 85
　　date of working 85
　　definition 75
　　diligence rule 85–90
　　disclosure 91–2, 106–15
　　Europe, in 106–19
　　first to file rule 75–9, 81–5
　　first to invent rule 78–9, 81–2, 85–90
　　general principles 106–9
　　grace period 83–4, 92–5, 117–19
　　identity requirement 102–6
　　identity standard 75–9
　　international priority 92–5
　　internet disclosure 107–9
　　invalidity defense 99
　　joint/team inventors 84–5
　　partial priority 119–21
　　post-AIA patents 75–9, 81–5
　　pre-AIA patents 78–9, 81–2, 85–90
　　prior art 80–82, 90–92, 107–15
　　prior art defense 95–9, 104
　　prior art disclosure 99–102
　　prior art reference 113–15
　　prior-filed applications 115–17
　　prior knowledge 84–5
　　priority rule 86–90
　　public disclosure 83–4, 110–111
　　public use 90–91

publication date 109–11
relative novelty 90–91
separate comparison 105–6
single disclosure 111–15
state of the art rule 115–17
US, in 75–9, 81–90
ordinary and customary meaning 164–9
ordinary skill 171
patentable subject matter 40
   abstract ideas 42–53
   aesthetic creations 58
   animal and plant varieties 54, 59, 70–74
   biotechnology 63–8, 69–74, 156
   business methods 50–51, 58
   China, in 53–8
   computer programs 44–53, 54–8, 58–63, 59
   diagnosis or treatment methods 54, 59
   DNA 65–8
   Europe, in 58–63
   facial and speech animation 51–2, 57–8
   genetic resources 55, 65–8
   Guidelines for Patent Examination 54
   industrial application 58
   information, presentation methods 58
   inventions as technical solutions 53, 57
   inventive step 16, 47
   limitations, historical development 42–5
   mathematical formulae 42–5, 50, 58
   mental activities exception 53–8
   microbiological processes 59
   nature, laws of 44
   nuclear transformation, products of 54
   pharmaceutical patents 16
   physical phenomena 42–5
   processes 42–5, 50–51
   public interest exception 55, 59, 70, 73
   requirement, importance of 40–41
   scientific ideas/discoveries 42–5, 50
   simple 2-D designs 54
   technical character 54, 60–62, 72
   technical processes 54–5
   TRIPS Agreement 16, 67–8, 74
   two-step test 51, 64–5, 71–3
   UK, in 63–4
   US, in 16, 40–53, 57–8, 63–8, 156
   utility requirement 59
remedies
   apportionment tests 236–7
   causality 233
   China, in 199–205, 224–30
   damages 217–37
   disgorgement remedy 233–4
   enhanced damages 229–30
   FRAND term injunctions 211–17
   Germany, in 209–13, 230–34
   injunctions 196–217
   loss of profits, for 218–22, 231–4
   permanent injunctions 205–6
   preliminary injunctions 199–205
   reasonable royalty 222–4
   standard essential patents, and 209–17, 226–9
   UK, in 214–17, 230–31, 234–9
   unjust enrichment 235–6
   US, in 196–9, 217–24
   willful infringement, for 229
Patents Act 1977 (UK) 182–3, 230–31, 235–6
paternity rights 331
Patient Bride, The (TV series) 263–4, 270
Pearl Driver, The (newspaper article summary service) 360–65
Pepsi 681–8
performance, definition 414–15
performances, copyright 278, 331
   dance and choreographic works 274, 294, 320, 371, 414
   digital performances 371–2, 415–16
   distribution rights 371
   music downloading 415, 462, 475
   music videos 411–13
performers' rights *see also* neighboring rights
   copyright 266–7
   digital performances 371–2, 415–16
perfumes, trademarks 485–7, 589–91
petty patents 743, 750, 752
pharmaceutical patents
   licensing 256–60
   loss of profits, damages for 218
Phase Change Material membranes, patent 103–4
phone cases, product design 779–81
phonographic recordings, copyright
   authors' rights 331
   fixation 278
   neighboring rights 410–11
photographs, copyright 279–82
   Europe, in 312–15, 320
   US, in 274
pictorial works, copyright 274, 753
Pien Tze Huang (TM) 618–22

plants, patentability 54, 59, 70–74
plow shanks, patents 123–6
Plum Blossom Scar (book) 263, 342–5, 464–5
pogs (product design) 774–5
Polo (TM) 563–4
porous inorganic oxide particles (patent) 113–15
Porter, Cole 332–5
PowerZone (TM) 597
Preston, Billy 235–8
Pretty Woman (song) 419–22
Pretul (TM) 622–6
prior art/invention
  China, in
    absolute novelty 91
    definition 90–92
    disclosure 99–102
    international priority exceptions 92–5
    invalidity defense 99
    printed publications 90–91
    prior art defense 95–9, 104
    public use 90
    separate comparison 105–6
  Europe, in
    disclosure, adequacy of 113–15
    disclosures, non-prejudicial 106–7
    general principles 106–9
    grace period 117–19
    internet disclosure 107–9
    partial priority 119–21
    prior art 107–15
    prior art reference 113–15
    prior-filed applications 115–17
    product designs 766–7
    public disclosure 110–111
    publication date 109–11
    single disclosure 111–15
    state of the art rule 115–17
  US, in 79, 82
    categories 79–80
    filing date, implications of 82
    information available to the public 79, 81–2
    judicial interpretation 80–82
    printed publications 79–81
    things in public use 79
    things on sale 79–81
producers' rights *see* neighboring rights
product design
  characteristics of 740–41
  definitions 739, 766

  importance 739–41
  infringement
    China, in 779–82, 789
    copyright and trademark law 776
    damages 790–91, 793
    defenses 783–9
    design patents 776–8, 790–91
    Europe, in 781–2, 786–8, 791–2
    functionality test 783–7, 789
    innocent infringement 792
    ordinary observer test 776–8
    point of novelty 778
    registered designs, role of 787–8
    remedies 790–93
    US, in 776–8, 783–6
  protectable subject matter
    applied art 753–5
    China, in 759
    conceptual separability, and 753–5
    design patents 745–50
    Europe, in 759–75
    likelihood of confusion 748–9
    nonobviousness/inventive step 750–52
    novelty and individual character 766–7, 771–4
    ornamental features and functionality 745–50
    US, in 745–59
  protection
    copyright, overlap 742–3
    court jurisdiction 770
    Crown use 792–3
    Europe, in 743–4, 765–70
    European Design Regulation 765, 769–70, 791–2
    fashion accessories 741–3
    informed user test 774–5, 781–2
    invalidity 768–9, 771–4
    mechanisms for 743–4
    need for 741–3
    prior use rights 768
    Registered Community Design 743–4, 765–7, 769
    remedies 770
    unity of art principle 741
    Unregistered Community Design 765
    US, in 743
    use trends 741–2
    utility models/petty patents 743, 750
  trade dress/packaging 755–7, 785–6
    secondary meaning requirement 756

trademarks, and
  packaging 755–7
  symbol/device configuration 757–9
property, theory of 277, 384
Prozac (TM) 585–8
public policy
  trademark exclusions 507, 511, 544–8

racial discrimination, trademarks 511
radio communication systems, patents 209–13
railway car connection mechanisms, patents 187–92
Ramada Inns (TM) 633–5
Red Cross/Red Crescent 511, 548
Red Dragon Software, Inc 25–31
Red River (TM) check 543–4
Registered Community Design (RCD) 743–4, 765–7, 769
Registered Designs Act 1949 (UK) 792–3
remedies
  copyright 269
    alternative measures 269–70
    apology 466–7
    apportionment 272, 459–62
    China, in 265–6, 463–7, 465–7
    damages 265–6, 270–72, 458–62, 465–7
    Europe, in 270, 467–72
    Germany, in 269, 467–72
    injunctions 265, 269–70, 269–72, 463–5, 467
    statutory damages 462, 465–6
    US, in 271–2, 458–62
  patents
    apportionment tests 236–7
    causality 233
    China, in 199–205, 224–30
    damages 217–37
    disgorgement remedy 233–4
    enhanced damages 229–30
    FRAND term injunctions 211–17
    Germany, in 209–13, 230–34
    injunctions 196–217
    loss of profits, for 218–22, 231–4
    permanent injunctions 205–6
    preliminary injunctions 199–205
    reasonable royalty 222–4
    standard essential patents, and 209–17, 226–9
    UK, in 214–17, 230–31, 234–9
    unjust enrichment 235–6
    US, in 196–9, 217–24
    willful infringement, for 229

trade secrets 694
  China, in 731
  damages 732–6
  Europe, in 731–2, 735–6
  injunctions 731–2
  US, in 729–31, 733–4
trademarks
  blocking injunctions 643–4
  China, in 644–6
  corrective advertising costs 633–5
  costs, recovery 633
  damages 629–44, 629–46
  dual enforcement 644–5
  Europe, in 636–9, 636–44
  extraterritorial jurisdiction, US law 646–9
  grey market goods restrictions 651–2
  holdover effects 633–5, 656
  import restrictions 650–51
  infringer's profits 629–32
  injunctions 627–8, 642–4
  international enforcement 646–9
  mark owner's damages 633–5
  unjust enrichment 629–32
  US, in 627–35, 646–9
Renoir, Pierre-August 330
Restatement (Third) of Unfair Competition (US) 682, 697, 734
RideShare (trade secrets) 669–71
Rome Convention 1961 266–7

scandalous marks
  China, in 547–8
  Europe, in 546
  US, in 544–6
scènes à faire doctrine, copyright 343–4
Schöttler (TM) 542–3
scientific principles, patentability 44
Screw You (TM) 546
sculptural works, copyright 274, 278, 285–8, 396, 414
sheet music 371
shop displays/layouts, product design 234–9, 552, 762–4
signs, trademarks 507, 511, 515
similar goods and services
  informed user test 774–5, 781–2
  likelihood of confusion 591, 651–2
  product design protection 774–5, 781–2
similar marks 508–9, 511, 518–21, 573–4
  grey market goods 651–2

likelihood of confusion 491, 575, 585–94, 651–2
  registration 491, 575
Slants, The (rock band) 545–6
Sleekskin (TM) 601
smells, trademarks 515–17
Sotheby's (TM) 597–600
sound recordings, copyright 319, 336–8
  digital performances 371–2, 415–16
  distribution rights 371–2
  exhaustion 438–41
  neighboring rights 415–16
SoundExchange 371, 416
South Korea 417, 477
sovereignty 6
  international treaties, impacts on 7–8
  limitations on 10
  TRIPS Agreement, and 14, 16–17
sportswear/shoes, trademarks 481, 596, 626, 647
standard essential patents 214–17
  patent infringement remedies
    damages 226–9
    injunctions 209–17
Starhave (promotional campaign) 389–90
Statute of Monopolies 1624 32
stem cells, patentability 74
suggestive marks 513–14, 521–2, 524–5, 758
surgical instruments, design patents 745–8
Sweden 675
symbols, trademarks 524–7

Taiwan 417, 477
Teleflex pedal assembly, patents 126–9
telephone directories 275–7, 606–11
Thermos (TM) 605–6
Tide (TM) 521–2, 524, 758
tort law 602, 675
toys 295–7, 606–11
trade names, copyright 305–6
trade packaging
  product design 755–7
    distinctiveness 760–64
    Europe, in 760–61
    functionality test 785–6
    generic nature 756–7
    shop design/layout 762–4
  trademarks
    distinctiveness 523–7, 548–50
    functionality 549–50
    generic nature 610, 756–7

trade secrets
  definition 671, 673–4, 682, 696
  blind-eye knowledge 693–4
  China, in 682–8
  commercial value 693
  Europe, in 688–94
  trivial information exclusion 693
  US, in 678–82
  willful blindness 694
  disclosure
    duties, for/against 693–4, 701–7
    reasonable efforts to prevent 695–701
  dishonesty, and 693–4
  good faith, and 694
  improper means 671, 673
    China, in 708–12
    civil *vs.* criminal actions 718
    contractual relationships 703–16
    definition 702–3, 707–8
    Europe, in 712–18
    startup companies 707
    unfair competition 716–18
    US, in 702–8
  label licenses 726
  misappropriation
    civil *vs.* criminal actions 718
    confidential relationships 702–7
    definition 671–4, 692, 702–3
    headstart periods 716
    improper means 671, 673, 702–16
    memorization as 692
    proof, difficulties with 244–9, 701, 707
  non-competition agreements 719–20
    China, in 719–24
    Europe, in 719
    US, in 719–20
  protectable information 671, 693
  protection, reasonable efforts 695–701
  protection, sources of 671–2
    China, in 673–4
    Europe, in 674–7
    TRIPS Agreement 671–2
    US, in 672–3
  remedies 694
    China, in 731
    damages 732–6
    Europe, in 731–2, 735–6
    injunctions 731–2
    US, in 729–31, 733–4

reverse engineering defense 724–8
    Europe, in 726–7
    label license/shrinkwrap contracts 726
    patent disclosures, and 726–8
    proper means requirement 727
    US, in 724–8
Rideshare case study 669–71
shrinkwrap contracts 726
unjust enrichment 733
vicarious liability, and 694
Trademark Dilution Reform Act 2006 (US) 596, 605
Trademark Law 1982 (China) 600, 624–5, 644–5, 665
Trademark Law Revision Act 1989 (US) 487
trademarks
    3-D shapes 535–8, 549, 552
    antidilution protection 594–7, 605
    arbitrary marks 513, 521, 524–5, 758
    China, in
        acquired distinctiveness 532–5, 555
        applications 506, 510
        confusing similarity 591–4
        damages 644–5
        distinctiveness 510, 514, 517–21, 532–8
        exclusions 511–12
        first to file principle 510
        functionality 552–7
        geographic terms/indications 543–4
        infringement defenses 618–26
        infringement remedies 644–6
        licensing 662–5
        non-trademark use 622–6
        non-well-known marks 580–83
        original equipment manufacture (OEM) products 622–6
        protection without registration 566–72, 580–83
        quality supervision 662–5
        refusal, grounds for 510
        registration 504, 510–512
        reviews and appeals 510
        scandalous marks 547–8
        well-known marks 566–72, 597–600
    choice of law/forum 652, 655–6
    claims
        dilution 594–7, 605
        enforcement of foreign judgments 269, 656–7
        Europe, in 611–16
        grey market goods 651–2
        likelihood of confusion 491, 508, 575, 584–94, 651–2

        tarnishment 596–59700
        well-known marks 594–600
    colors 516–17, 525, 543–4, 550–51, 758
    conflict of laws 652–5
    damages
        Europe, in 636–44
        US, in 629–35
    descriptive marks
        fair use defense 600–601
        incontestability 562–4
        secondary meaning 522–3
        US, in 521–3, 562–4, 600–601
    devices 524–7
    dilution 594–7, 605
    dispute resolution 652–6
        enforcement of foreign judgments 269, 656–7
        location of harm principle 653
    distinctiveness
        3-D shapes 535–8, 549, 552
        acquired distinctiveness 527–35, 555
        arbitrary marks 513, 521, 524–5, 758
        capability of distinguishing 514
        categories of marks 512
        China, in 510, 514, 517–21, 532–8
        dilution, protection from 595–7, 605
        Europe, in 514–17, 527–32, 560–61
        fanciful marks 513, 521, 524–5, 758
        foreign language, in 557–61
        inactivity, loss due to 611–12
        inherent distinctiveness 514, 517–21, 554–5
        suggestive marks 513–14, 521–2, 524–5, 758
        trade dress/packaging 523–7, 548–50
        US, in 507, 509, 512–14, 516–17, 521–7, 557–9
    earlier marks, priority 508–9, 573, 575
    Europe, in
        acquired distinctiveness 527–32
        Community trademarks 503, 636–7
        damages 636–44
        distinctiveness 514–17, 527–32, 560–61
        EU Intellectual Property Office 503–4
        exclusions 506–9
        exclusively descriptive doctrine 560–61
        foreign language, in 560–61
        functionality 551–2
        genuine use requirement 487–90, 488–90
        geographic terms/indications 543, 574
        infringement 611–16
        infringement defenses 611–15
        infringement remedies 636–44

Index · 817

injunctions 642–4
likelihood of confusion 588–91
more than local significance 543, 574–80
non-well-known marks 573–80
Office for Harmonization in the Internal Market (OHIM) 503
protection without registration 564–5, 573–80
refusal, grounds for 506–9
scandalous marks 546
well-known marks 564–5
fair use defense 564, 600–602
fanciful marks 513, 521, 524–5, 758
flags 511
foreign applications
bad faith 509
equal treatment 494–7, 505
foreign judgments, enforcement of 269, 656–7
foreign language, in
Europe, in 560–61
exclusively descriptive doctrine 560–61
foreign equivalents doctrine 557–9
US, in 557–9
functionality
aesthetic functionality 550–51
China, in 552–7
Europe, in 551–2
trade dress/packaging, and 549–50
US, in 548–51
generally 481–3
generic marks 507, 512, 521–2, 538
fair use/fair dealing 562–4
genericide 605–11
geographic terms/indications 507, 511, 531–2
China, in 543–4
deceptive misdescription 539–43
designation of origin 574
Europe, in 543, 574
geographic location 540
goods-place association 540
materiality 541
more than local significance 543, 574–80
US, in 538–43
graphic representability 515–17
identical marks 508–9, 511, 518–21, 573–5, 585, 588
incontestability 562–4
infringement defenses
China, in 618–26
descriptive marks 600–601
dictionaries, use in 611
Europe, in 611–15
fair use 564, 600–602
free riding, and 602–5
genericide 605–11
inactivity 611–12
keywords, use as 602–605, 613–15
nominative use 601–2, 605, 618–22
non-trademark use 602–5, 622–6
original equipment manufacture (OEM) products 622–6
parodies 597, 616–18
passing off, and 602
sponsored adverts 603, 613–15
US, in 600–611
initials 513
injunctions
Europe, in 642–4
US, in 627–8
invalidity 506–9
letters 516
licensing 655–6
assignment in gross 658–9
China, in 662–5
franchise agreements 659–61, 665
goodwill, association with 658–9
purpose 658
quality assurance requirement 658
territorial rights 659–61
US, in 658–61, 659–61, 665
likelihood of confusion 508, 575
China, in 591–4
comparative advertising 590–91
Europe, in 588–91
generally 584–5
grey market goods 651–2
identical marks 491, 575, 585, 588, 591
similar marks 491, 575, 585–94
US, in 585–8, 651–2
names 509, 511–12, 548, 574
non-profit entities, by 489–90
non-well-known marks
China, in 580–83
Europe, in 573–80
US, in 572–3
olfactory marks 515–17
parodies 597, 616–18
priority
concurrent use 573

earlier marks 508–9, 573, 575
non-well-known marks 572–83
protection without registration 564–83
token use 572–3
use in commerce 572–3
well-known marks 564–72
product design, and
configuration 757–9
distinctiveness 760–64
Europe, in 760–64
packaging 755–7
protection without registration
China, in 566–72, 580–83
Europe, in 564–5, 573–80
non-well-known marks 572–83
US, in 497–501, 564, 572–3
well-known marks 564–72
public policy/morality exclusions 507, 511, 544–8
racial discrimination 511
Red Cross/Red Crescent 511, 548
registration
civil law *vs.* common law regimes 490–94
international treaties, and 501–3
Madrid Protocol regime 502–3, 505–6
national regimes 490–91
Paris Convention, and 501–2
priority conflicts 491, 493–4
protection without 564–83
similar marks, confusion 491, 575
US, in 503–5
remedies
blocking injunctions 643–4
China, in 644–6
corrective advertising costs 633–5
costs, recovery 633
damages 629–44
Europe, in 636–44
extraterritorial jurisdiction, US law 646–9
grey market goods restrictions 651–2
holdover effects 633–5, 656
import restrictions 650–51
infringer's profits 629–32
injunctions 627–8, 642–4
international enforcement 646–9
mark owner's damages 633–5
unjust enrichment 629–32
US, in 627–35, 646–9
scandalous marks
China, in 547–8

Europe, in 546
US, in 544–6
shapes 535–8, 549, 551–2, 761
signs 507, 511, 515
similar marks 508–9, 511, 518–21, 573–4
likelihood of confusion 491, 575, 585–94, 651–2
registration 491, 575
smells 515–17
suggestive marks 513–14, 521–2, 524–5, 758
symbols 524–7
US, in
analogous use 487
antidilution protection 594–7, 605
applications 505–6
constructive use 487
continuous use 493
damages 629–35
descriptive marks 521–3, 562–4, 600–601
distinctiveness 507, 509, 512–14, 516–17, 521–7, 557–9
electronic applications 506
foreign applicants, equal treatment 494–7, 505
foreign equivalents doctrine 557–9
functionality 548–51
geographic terms/indications 538–43
grey market goods restrictions 651–2
import restrictions 649–51
incontestability 562–4
infringement defenses 600–611
infringement remedies 627–35, 651–2
injunctions 627–8
jurisdiction, extraterritoriality 646–9
licensing 658–61
likelihood of confusion 585–8, 651–2
non-well-known marks 572–3
notice of allowance 487, 504
Patent and Trademark Office (PTO) 503–4
Principal Register 504
priority conflicts 491, 493–4
protection without registration 497–501, 564, 572–3
registration 503–5
scandalous marks 544–6
scrutiny of applications 504
secondary meaning 522–3
Statement of Use 504
Supplemental Register 504–5
trade dress/packaging 523–7, 548–50

Trademark Manual of Examining Procedure
  (TMEP) 487, 504
  use in commerce requirement 485–7, 494–7
  use *vs.* registration conflicts 487
  well-known marks 497–501, 564
use *vs.* registration
  analogous use 487
  common law *vs.* civil law regimes 484
  constructive use 487
  Europe, in 488–90
  generally 484
  genuine use requirement 488–90
  US, in 485–7
  use in commerce requirement 485–7
well-known marks
  antidilution protection 594–7, 605
  China, in 566–72, 597–600
  Europe, in 564–5
  exclusions 509
  fame, proof of 596–7
  Paris Convention 500
  tarnishment 596–7
  TRIPS Agreement 500–501
  US, in 497–501, 564
Trademarks Act 1946 (US)
  antidilution protection 594–7, 605
  applications 505–6
  damages, apportionment 630–33
  distinctiveness 512, 523–7
  extraterritorial jurisdiction 646–9
  foreign applicants, protection 493–7
  foreign equivalence doctrine 557–9
  generic descriptors 562–4
  geographical misdescriptions 539–43
  import restrictions 649–51
  likelihood of confusion 523–7, 563, 588, 757, 776
  registration 504–5
  remedies 627, 630–35
  scandalous marks 544–6, 548
  trade dress/packaging 523–7, 550, 755–7
  well-known marks 497–501, 564, 585–8, 594–7, 605
translations, copyright 332
transnational, definition 4
transnational law
  characteristics 17–18
  convergence v. divergence 22
  definition 4–5
  strategies 17–21
Tripp-Trapp chair 467–72

TRIPS Agreement
  administrative procedures 16–17
  background 7–8, 14, 34
  biotechnology 74
  compulsory licensing 16
  computer programs 317
  enforcement 14–15
  exclusions 67–8
  inventive step 16
  limitations 15
  obligations 15–17
  patentable subject matter 16, 67–8, 74
  pharmaceutical patents 16
  sovereignty, impacts on 8, 14, 16–17
  trade secrets 671–2
  well-known marks 500–501
Trunki (product design) 781–2
Two Men and A Truck (TM) 514
typefaces, copyright 298–302

U drive (TM) 538
UGG 750
UK
  copyright
    abstraction test 345
    co-authorship 330
    derivative works 268
    distribution rights 375
    exceptions 417–18
    fair dealing 417–18
    fixation requirement 327
    ideas/expression dichotomy 345
    limitations 319
    moral rights 385
    neighboring rights 400
    originality 308
    orphan works 268
    protected works 319–20
    work for hire 329
  Crown use 792–3
  patents
    applications trends 36
    Brexit implications 36
    claims interpretation 180–86
    courts 180
    damages 230–31, 234–9
    injunctions 214–17
    patentable subject matter 63–4
    unjust enrichment 223–36

product design 792–3
trade secrets 676–7
  damages 736
  improper means 712–16
trademarks
  damages 639–42
unfair competition 676–7
Ultra-Pure (TM) 531
UltraPlus (TM) 531
undue experimentation test 142–6, 157
unfair competition 673–4, 682, 734–5
  China, in 673–4, 682, 684–8, 701, 722–4, 734–5
  Germany, in 676, 688–94, 716–18
  trade secrets protection, and 673–7
    improper means 716–18
  UK, in 676–7
  US, in 682, 697, 734
Unfair Competition Act 1909 (Germany) 676, 688–94, 716–18
Unified Patent Court (EU, proposed) 13, 35–6
Unified Patents (EU, proposed) 13, 35–6
Uniform Trade Secrets Act 1979 (US) 672, 702–3, 734
United International Bureaux for the Protection of Intellectual Property 13
unjust enrichment 223–36, 629–32, 733
Unregistered Community Designs (UCD) 765
USA
  copyright
    accounting systems 282–5
    applied art 297
    apportionment of damages 272
    architecture 274, 282, 414
    artistic works 413–14
    authors' rights 332
    authorship 285–91, 330, 395
    broadcasting 271–2
    co-authorship 285–91
    computer programs 274, 281–2, 319
    conception of 332
    creativity 274
    damages 271–2, 458–62, 469
    derivative works 271, 351–5
    digital copyright 473, 474–5
    digital performances 415–16
    distribution rights 365–72
    divisible works 359–60
    exclusions 282–5
    fair use doctrine 355, 417–23, 417–27
    fixation requirement 278

ideas and concepts 282–5
injunctions 271
integrity, right to 391–9
internet service providers liability 474–5
literary works 294
moral rights 332, 391–9
music 282, 401–3, 414
neighboring rights 332, 401–3, 410–411, 413–16
no copyright for facts rule 277
originality 274–7
orphan works 270–72
performers' rights 410–411, 413–16
pictorial works 274, 753
recorded music 278
remedies 271–2, 458–62
sculptural works 274, 278, 285–8, 396, 414
separability test 297
statutory damages 462
subject matter 270–72, 274–8, 281–5, 294, 297, 319, 396, 414
sweat of the brow theory 277, 297–8
telephone directories 275–7
titles 282
typefaces 302
utilitarian works 282
visual art 391–9
work for hire 285–8
fair use doctrine 355, 417–23
  amount and substantiality 426
  descriptive marks 600–601
  digital sampling 419–23
  effect on use 421–3
  first sale doctrine 428–32, 457, 652
  four-part test 419–27
  parodies 420–22, 616–18
  reverse engineering 423
  snippets 426–7
  time-shifting 422
  transformative uses 422–7
  unpublished works 420
licensing
  most favored nation clauses 250–56
  no challenge clauses 256
  non-disclosure agreements 244, 246–7
  patents, generally 244
  pre-contractual liability 244–9
  substantive terms 250–56
  trade secrets, misappropriation 244–9
  trademarks 659–61, 665

patents
- abstract ideas 42–53
- beyond novelty requirement 122
- biotechnology 63–8, 156
- business methods 50–51
- claims 163–9, 192–5
- computer programs 44–53
- conception date 85–6
- contributory infringement 192–5
- Covered Business Method review 242–3
- critical date 78–9, 82, 85
- damages 217–24
- date of invention 85
- date of working 85
- definition 75
- diligence rule 85–6, 85–90
- disavowal 168–9
- disclosure 142–6, 153–7
- dispute resolution 15
- double patenting doctrine 126
- estoppel 243
- Federal Circuit, creation 13
- first to file rule 75–9, 81–5
- first to file rule exceptions 82–5
- first to invent rule 78–9, 81–2, 85–90
- grace period 83–4
- historical development 32–3, 122–3
- identity standard 75–9
- indirect infringement 192–5
- inducement 192–4
- injunctions 196–9
- inter partes review 240–43
- interpretation challenges 163–9
- invalidity claims 240–43
- inventive step 16, 47, 122–4, 126–9
- joint/team inventors 84–5
- knowledge requirement, infringement 194–5
- licensing 244–56
- limitations, historical development 42–5
- loss of profits, for 218–22
- mathematical formulae 42–5, 50
- nature, laws of 44
- novelty 75–90
- ordinary and customary meaning 164–9
- pharmaceutical patents 16
- physical phenomena 42–5
- post-AIA patents 75–9, 81–5
- post grant review 242–3
- post-TRIPS domestic law amendments 15–16
- pre-AIA patents 78–9, 81–2, 85–90
- prior art 80–82
- prior knowledge 84–5
- priority rule 86–90
- processes 42–5, 50–51
- public disclosure 83–4
- reasonable royalty, and 222–4
- remedies 196–9, 217–24
- scientific ideas 42–5, 50
- secondary considerations 123–4, 126
- shop rights 307
- stay proceedings 243
- subject matter 16, 42–53, 59, 62, 63–8, 64–5, 156
- technical character test 62
- terminal disclaimers 126
- trade secrets, misappropriation 244–9
- TRIPS Agreement 16
- TSM test 126–9
- two-step test 51, 64–5
- undue experimentation test 142–6, 157
- utility requirement 59
- written description requirement 153–7

product design
- copyright infringement 776
- design patent infringement 776–8, 790–91
- functionality test 783–6
- infringement defenses 783–6
- likelihood of confusion 757, 776–8
- ordinary observer test 776–8
- petty patents 743, 750, 752
- point of novelty 778
- protectable subject matter 745–59
- remedies 790–91
- trade dress/packaging 755–7, 785–6
- trademark infringement 776
- utility models 743, 750, 752

sovereignty of foreign nations 646–7

trade secrets
- damages 733–4
- definition 678–82
- improper means 702–8
- injunctions 729–31
- misappropriation 244–9
- non-competition agreements 719–20
- protection, reasonable efforts 695–701
- protection, sources of 672–3
- remedies 729–31, 733–4
- reverse engineering defense 724–8
- willful knowledge 694

trademarks
  analogous use 487
  antidilution protection 594–7, 605
  applications 505–6
  constructive use 487
  continuous use 493
  corrective advertising 633–5
  costs, recovery 633–5
  damages 629–35
  descriptive marks 521–3, 562–4, 600–601
  distinctiveness 507, 509, 512–14, 516–17, 521–7, 557–9
  electronic applications 506
  foreign applicants (equal treatment) 494–7, 505
  foreign equivalents doctrine 557–9
  franchise agreements 659–61, 665
  functionality 548–51
  geographic terms/indications 538–43
  good faith contractual duties 659
  goodwill, and 658–9
  grey market goods restrictions 651–2
  holdover effects 633–5, 656
  import restrictions 649–51
  incontestability 562–4
  infringement defenses 600–611
  infringer's profits 629–32
  injunctions 627–8
  jurisdiction, extraterritoriality 646–9
  licensing 658–61
  likelihood of confusion 585–8, 651–2
  mark owner's damages 633–5
  non-well-known marks 572–3
  notice of allowance 487, 504
  Principal Register 504
  priority conflicts 491, 493–4
  protection without registration 497–501, 564, 572–3
  registration 503–5
  remedies 629–35
  scandalous marks 544–6
  scrutiny of applications 504
  secondary meaning 522–3
  Statement of Use 504
  Supplemental Register 504–5
  territorial rights 659–61
  trade dress/packaging 523–7, 548–50
  Trademark Manual of Examining Procedure (TMEP) 487, 504
  unjust enrichment 629–32
  use in commerce requirement 485–7, 494–7
  use *vs.* registration conflicts 487
  well-known marks 497–501, 564
user manuals 80–82
utility models/patents
  China 37–8, 91
  US, in 743, 750, 752

vandalism resistant walls, patent 164–9
Venetian guild patents 32m
vicarious liability 458, 694
Vienna Exposition 1873 9–10
Village Healer, The (story) 263–7
Visual Artists Rights Act 1990 (US) 391–9
von Gierke, Otto F. 385

Waiting for Godot (play) 388–9
Washington Redskins (TM) 545
water guns, patents 163
well-known trademarks *see under* trademarks
Wilde, Oscar 279–81
Wildflower Works (landscape art installation) 391–9
World Intellectual Property Organization
  design protection 743–4
  establishment 13–14
  trademarks 502, 506
World Trade Organization 14–16

Xerox 513, 606

Yellow Pages (TM) 606–11
Yellowstone (TM) 538–9
YKK (TM) 513
Yosemite (TM) 538

Zyrtec (TM) 513